The Oxford Handbook of Evolutionary Psychology and Romantic Relationships

OXFORD LIBRARY OF PSYCHOLOGY

The Oxford Handbook of Evolutionary Psychology and Romantic Relationships

Edited by

Justin K. Mogilski and Todd K. Shackelford

OXFORD
UNIVERSITY PRESS

OXFORD
UNIVERSITY PRESS

Oxford University Press is a department of the University of Oxford. It furthers the University's objective of excellence in research, scholarship, and education by publishing worldwide. Oxford is a registered trade mark of Oxford University Press in the UK and certain other countries.

Published in the United States of America by Oxford University Press
198 Madison Avenue, New York, NY 10016, United States of America.

Library of Congress Cataloging-in-Publication Data
Names: Mogilski, Justin K., author. | Shackelford, Todd K. (Todd Kennedy), 1971- author.
Title: The Oxford handbook of evolutionary psychology and romantic relationships / Justin K. Mogilski & Todd K. Shackelford.
Description: 1 Edition. | New York, NY : Oxford University Press, [2023] |
Series: Oxford library of psychology series |
Includes bibliographical references and index.
Identifiers: LCCN 2022031994 (print) | LCCN 2022031995 (ebook) |
ISBN 9780197524718 (hardback) | ISBN 9780197524749 | ISBN 9780197524732 (epub)
Subjects: LCSH: Evolutionary psychology. | Intimacy (Psychology) |
Interpersonal relations—Psychological aspects.
Classification: LCC BF698.95 .M64 2022 (print) | LCC BF698.95 (ebook) |
DDC 155.7—dc23/eng/20220729
LC record available at https://lccn.loc.gov/2022031994
LC ebook record available at https://lccn.loc.gov/2022031995

DOI: 10.1093/oxfordhb/9780197524718.001.0001

9 8 7 6 5 4 3 2 1

Printed by Marquis, Canada

ABOUT THE EDITORS

Justin K. Mogilski I research how evolution has shaped brain computation to adaptively guide the decisions that people make to initiate, maintain, and dissolve intimate relationships. I have published original research within peer-reviewed evolutionary, social, personality, and sexual psychology journals on topics spanning mate poaching, infidelity, cross-gender friendship, intimate partner conflict, moral decision-making, morphometric cues of partner attractiveness, and multivariate statistical analyses of human mate preference. My current program of research examines (a) conflict resolution within consensually nonmonogamous (CNM; e.g., polyamorous, swinging, and open) relationships, (b) how sexual conflict shapes moral decision-making, and (c) individual differences in predatory relationship behaviors.

Todd K. Shackelford received his Ph.D. in evolutionary psychology in 1997 from the University of Texas at Austin. Since 2010, he has been Professor and Chair of the Department of Psychology at Oakland University in Rochester, Michigan. Shackelford has published around 400 journal articles and his work has been cited around 28,000 times. Much of Shackelford's research addresses sexual conflict between men and women, with a focus on men's physical, emotional, and sexual violence against their intimate partners.

TABLE OF CONTENTS

Part II: Relationship Maintenance

Part III: Relationship Dissolution

CONTRIBUTORS

Lora Adair
Department of Life Sciences, Brunel University London

Christopher R. Agnew
Department of Psychological Sciences, Purdue University

Jenna Alley
Department of Psychology, University of Utah

Laith Al-Shawaf
Psychology Department, University of Colorado

Bruno Henrique Amaral
Department of Experimental Psychology, University of São Paulo

Liat Ayalon
Louis and Gabi Weisfeld School of Social Work, Bar Ilan University

Rhonda N. Balzarini
Department of Psychology, Texas State University

Mons Bendixen
Department of Psychology, Norwegian University of Science and Technology

Clair Bennett
Columbia University Department of Psychiatry, Columbia University Irving Medical Center, New York State Psychiatric Institute, La Trobe University

Michelle Benstead
School of Psychology, The Centre for Social and Early Emotional Development, Deakin University

Hannah K. Bradshaw
Department of Psychology, Washington & Jefferson College

Jeannette Brodbeck
Department of Psychology University of Bern, University for Applied Sciences and Arts Northwestern Switzerland

Rebecca L. Burch
Department of Human Development, SUNY Oswego

David M. Buss
Department of Psychology, University of Texas, Austin

Abraham P. Buunk
University of Groningen, The Netherlands

Neil R. Caton
School of Psychology, The University of Queensland

Bryan K. C. Choy
School of Social Sciences, Singapore Management University

John P. Crowley
Department of Communication, University of Delaware

Amanda Denes
Department of Communication, University of Connecticut

Anuraj Dhillon
Communication Studies Department, California Polytechnic State University, San Luis Obispo

Lisa M. Diamond
Department of Psychology, University of Utah

Kortnee C. Evans
Psychology Department, Murdoch University

Nelli Ferenczi
Department of Life Sciences, Brunel University London

Maryanne L. Fisher
Department of Psychology, The Kinsey Institute, Saint Mary's University

Gordon G. Gallup, Jr.
Department of Psychology, University at Albany

Trond Viggo Grøntvedt
Department of Psychology, Norwegian University of Science and Technology

Jan Havlíček
Department of Zoology, Charles University

Madeleine Redlick Holland
Department of Communication Studies, The University of Texas at Austin

Ledina Imami
Department of Psychological Sciences, Purdue University

Peter K. Jonason
Department of General Psychology, University of Padua and University of Cardinal Stefan Wyszyński

Victor Karandashev
Department of Psychology, Aquinas College

Gery C. Karantzas
School of Psychology, The Centre for Social and Early Emotional Development, Deakin University

Leif Edward Ottesen Kennair
Department of Psychology, Norwegian University of Science and Technology

Andrea Melanie Kessler
Department of Psychology, Norwegian University of Science and Technology

Gabriella King
School of Psychology, Deakin University

Chaya Koren
School of Social Work and the Center for the Study of Society, University of Haifa

Jaimie Arona Krems
Department of Psychology, Oklahoma Center for Evolutionary Analysis (OCEAN), Oklahoma State University

Michael R. Langlais
Department of Educational Psychology, Florida State University

Pamela J. Lannutti
Center for Human Sexuality Studies, Widener University

Leah E. LeFebvre
Department of Communication Studies, University of Alabama

Justin J. Lehmiller
Kinsey Institute, Indiana University

Edward P. Lemay, Jr.
Department of Psychology, University of Maryland, College Park

David M. G. Lewis
Discipline of Psychology, Murdoch University
Centre for Healthy Ageing, Health Futures Institute, Murdoch University

Norman P. Li
School of Social Sciences, Singapore Management University
Severi Luoto
School of Population Health, University of Auckland
Anastasia Makhanova
Psychological Science, University of Arkansas
Evita March
Department of Psychology, Federation University Australia
Emma M. Marshall
School of Psychology Deakin University
Karlijn Massar
Work and Social Psychology, Maastricht University
Laureon A. Merrie
Department of Psychology, Oklahoma Center for Evolutionary Analysis (OCEAN), Oklahoma State University
Justin K. Mogilski
Department of Psychology, University of South Carolina Salkehatchie
Lawrence J. Moloney
School of Psychology and Public Health, La Trobe University
James B. Moran
Department of Psychology, Tulane University
Dimitri Mortelmans
Department of Sociology, Antwerp University
Giuseppe Pantaleo
UniSR-Social.Lab, Faculty of Psychology, Vita-Salute San Raffaele University
Ryan D. Rasner
Department of Communication Studies, Louisiana State University
S. Craig Roberts
Division of Psychology, University of Stirling
David L. Rodrigues
Centre for Social Research and Intervention, Iscte-Instituto Universitário de Lisboa
Joshua Everett Ryan
Department of Psychology University of Maryland, College Park
Simona Sciara
UniSR-Social.Lab, Faculty of Psychology, Vita-Salute San Raffaele University
Bruce M. Smyth
Centre for Social Research and Methods, Australian National University
Valerie G. Starratt
Department of Psychology and Neuroscience, Nova Southeastern University
Ian D. Stephen
NTU Psychology, Nottingham Trent University
Jaroslava Varella Valentova
Department of Experimental Psychology, University of Sao Paulo
Marco Antonio Correa Varella
Department of Experimental Psychology, University of São Paulo
T. Joel Wade
Department of Psychology, Psychological Adaptations Research Consortium, Bucknell University
Elizabeth M. Westrupp
School of Psychology, The Centre for Social and Early Emotional Development, Deakin University

He Xiao
Department of Educational Psychology, University of North Texas

Hans Joerg Znoj
Department of Psychology, University of Bern

Introduction

Justin K. Mogilski *and* Todd K. Shackelford

Abstract

Evolutionary social science is having a renaissance. What started with a collection of estimates by Charles Darwin and colleagues about biological change and diversity has manifested a theoretical powerhouse incorporating varied disciplinary perspectives and methodologies. In this chapter, we introduce these advancements and provide an overview of how evolutionary perspectives have enriched the scientific study of intimate relationship initiation, maintenance, and dissolution. We highlight several areas of research that feature prominently throughout this handbook, including studies of gender and sexual diversity, social neuroendocrinology, personality science, and international trends in human mating. We conclude with a brief editorial note to current and future relationship scientists, to whom this volume is dedicated.

Key Words: Evolutionary science, intimate relationships, romantic relationships, gender and sexual diversity, social neuroendocrinology, personality science, international

Psychologists who adopt the evolutionary paradigm (see Nettle & Scott-Phillips, 2021) seek to document how information processing of the mind has been engineered to address the unremitting challenges of survival and reproduction. Its predictive framework has been broadly adopted within the social sciences, including anthropology (Fessler et al., 2015; Gibson & Lawson, 2015), sociology (Tanskanen & Danielsbacka, 2018), consumer research (Otterbring, 2021; Saad, 2017), decision science (Morris et al., 2021), animal behavior and cognition (Vonk, 2021), political science (McDermott & Hatemi, 2018; Petersen, 2020), and law and social policy (James et al., 2020; Palomo-Vélez & van Vugt, 2021). Natural selection of genes is a popular level of analysis at which to propose and test evolutionary hypotheses because DNA is the fundamental unit of inheritance in sexually reproducing organisms (see Williams, 1966). Biological evolution occurs when populations undergo cross-generational change in heritable trait frequency. These traits are pitted against the reproductive and survival demands of life, and those which better promote self-replication compared to competing alternatives become more prevalent. However, evolutionary change occurs in any cyclic system where modification by competitive replacement occurs over time, such as in neural network modeling (Badcock et al., 2019; Hasson et al., 2020; Stanley et al., 2019), cellular growth (Aktipis, 2020), decision-making (Morris et al., 2021), or multilevel selection (Hertler et al., 2020; Wilson

& Coan, 2021). Each application shares the common premise that if you study how evolution has engineered a system, you will discover that system's functional design.

The evolutionary study of romantic relationships has accordingly uncovered the adapted psychology underlying intimate relationships (Bode & Kushnick, 2021; Buss & Schmitt, 2019; Durante et al., 2016). For example, it is well documented that reproduction entails unique adaptive challenges for men and women (e.g., paternal uncertainty and minimum investment in gestation), which create unique mating optima for each sex (Trivers, 1972; see Mogilski et al., 2021). These optima can conflict (see Kennair et al., this volume) causing sexual selection for different ideal mating strategies for men and women (Buss & Schmitt, 1993; Luoto 2019; Puts, 2016). Understanding how attraction and competition occurs between the sexes thus becomes a useful framework for predicting how people initiate, maintain, and dissolve their relationships. That is, the collaboration and conflict that people experience within their relationship(s) may follow computationally adaptive scripts that—at least across deep evolutionary time—alleviated the exigencies of men's and women's unique reproductive challenges. These foundations and their empirical support are reviewed in Chapter 1 and referenced throughout this volume.

Of course, good theory reliably and expansively predicts the phenomena that it explains. Relationship researchers who use the evolutionary paradigm have rapidly integrated it with gender and women's studies (Fisher et al., 2020; van Anders, 2013), sexuality (Diamond, 2021; Sommer & Vasey, 2006), marriage and family studies (Aspara et al., 2018), neuroendocrinology (Welling & Shackelford, 2019), mating cognition (Joel & MacDonald, 2021; Lenton & Stewart, 2008; Miller & Todd, 1998), intelligence (Baur et al., 2019; Miller, 2000), and comparative psychology (Fraley et al., 2005). This wellspring of novelty has matured to create robust, replicable models of mate choice (Conroy-Beam et al., 2019, 2021; Walter et al., 2020), same-sex competition (see Krems et al., in this volume; also Ayers, 2021; Bradshaw & DelPriore, 2022; Reynolds et al., 2018), friendship (Seyfarth & Cheney, 2012; Williams et al., 2022), jealousy (Buss, 2018; Edlund et al., 2018), face and body perception (Antar & Stephen, 2021; Brown et al., 2021; Fink et al., 2018), and interpersonal deception (Desrochers et al., 2021; Redlick & Vangelisti, 2018; Trivers, 1991). Research once dominated by self-report and forced-choice paradigms has developed multivariate solutions for describing the logic of partner choice (Brandner et al., 2020; Csajbók and Berkics, 2022 Li et al., 2002; Mogilski et al. 2014, 2017, 2018; Jones, 2018; Stephen et al., 2017), relationship maintenance (Vowels et al., 2021). Behavioral genetics (e.g., twin studies) have disentangled the contributions of genes and environment to variation in human development (Kupfer et al., 2022), and applied sciences, such as medicine and mental health (Nesse, 2019; Giosan et al., 2020; Hollon et al., 2021) have advanced how knowledge of evolutionary design can improve personal and relational outcomes.

This diaspora has developed alongside larger trends within relationship science, such as the rising utility and rigor of personality measurement (Del Giudice, 2017; Durkee et al., 2022; Lukaszewski et al., 2020). Personality science has become central to relationship science because it models how natural variation between individuals impacts interpersonal functioning across time and ecology. Life history theory, for example, meaningfully explains how human cognition is altered by environmental unpredictability and harshness (Simpson et al., 2017). When environments are less predictable, planned investments are unsteady and cost prone. This favors immediate over delayed reward and thereby disposes individuals to present-oriented decisions (Frankenhuis et al., 2016; also see Fenneman & Frankenhuis, 2020; Fennis et al., 2022), less deliberation (Wang et al., 2022), more unrestricted sociosexuality (Szepsenwol et al., 2017), greater interpersonal antagonism and detachment (Jonason et al., 2017), and poor emotional control (see Szepsenwol et al., 2021)—traits which may aid lone survival amid environmental irregularity. As an exemplar of evolutionary theorizing, life history has been successful in integrating findings from varied disciplines (Nettle & Frankenhuis, 2019) and across cultures (Pelham, 2021), but it has accordingly inspired controversy and revision (see Dinh et al., 2022; Woodley et al., 2021; Zeitsch & Sidari, 2020).

Neuroendocrinological research has complemented evolutionary relationship science's focus on individual differences (Baugh et al., 2017; Trillmich et al., 2018) because hormones mediate sex/gender differences and the intimate processes that develop within and between people (Edelstein & Chin, 2018; Roney & Simmons, 2018; also see Welling & Shackelford, 2019). Corticosteroids guide responsivity to relationship stressors (Mogilski et al., 2019b), oxytocin promotes pair-bonding formation (Walum et al., 2012), and sex hormones shape the morphological and psychological characteristics that systematically differ between men and women (Gurvich et al., 2018; Rehbein et al., 2021)—traits to which people are sensitive when assessing a potential intimate partner (Jones & Jaeger, 2019; Marcinkowska et al., 2014). Indeed, morphometric analyses have allowed researchers to quantify developmental change in sex/gender to study how its fluctuation impacts relationship process (e.g., Stephen et al., 2017). Others have documented how sexual behavior and preferences shift with hormone deficiency (Shirazi et al., 2021), hormonal contraception use (Hill, 2019), and temporal fluctuations in hormone levels, such as across the menstrual cycle (see Havlicek & Roberts, this volume). Endocrinology has thus become a fundamental level of analysis for the evolutionary study of romantic processes (Denes et al., this volume; Makhanova, this volume).

International differences are a substantial source of natural variation in relationship behavior (Kline et al., 2018; Segall et al., 1990; Silan et al., 2021). Evolutionary theorizing has revealed pervasive, culture-sensitive psychological effects related to gender (Lippa, 2010), kin favoritism (Schulz et al., 2019), game theory (Pan, Gelfand, & Nau, 2021), and social organization (see Henrich & Muthukrishna, 2021). Broadly, relationship behaviors are expected to adaptively shift to address local and historical demands on individuals' survival and well-being. This thereby influences how people initiate (see Karandashev, this volume) and maintain (Adair & Ferenczi, this volume) relationships across cultures.

Studies of sexually and gender diverse people (e.g., those who are lesbian, gay, bisexual, transgender, queer, etc.; i.e., LGBTQ+) have revealed unique variation in human bonding and competition (see Holland & Lannuti, this volume; Pachankis et al., 2020; Semenyna et al., 2021; Valentova et al., this volume). For example, Diamond and Alley (this volume) argue that safety concerns are salient among LGBTQ+ relationships because same-sex attraction and gender nonconformity are targeted more often for condemnation and violence. Eliminating prejudice and wrongful discrimination against LGBTQ individuals (Blair & Hoskin, 2019) may be aided by a technical knowledge of which adaptive concerns these beliefs and attitudes have historically addressed—and whether they still do. Computation that ancestrally enhanced reproduction may be mismatched to modern circumstances (Li et al., 2020). Similarly, studying how people form and maintain multiple, concurrent intimate relationships (i.e., consensual nonmonogamy) (Mogilski et al., this volume) may reveal novel strategies for managing extra-pair romance (also see Brady & Baker, 2022; Hunter & Stockwell, 2022).

By harnessing the insights of interdisciplinary collaboration, evolutionary relationship scientists have identified novel features of human mating, have expanded durable theories and perspectives of human development, and strengthened the methodological robustness of its core predictions. The editors assembled this handbook to showcase the empirical and theoretical progress of the evolutionary study of intimate relationships. We dedicate this volume to future generations of relationship scientists. It is our intent that this collection will be a primer for those seeking to incorporate contemporary evolutionary reasoning and methodology into their research program. Many of its contributors self-identify as evolutionary psychologists. Others do not but are familiar with the evolutionary sciences and have successfully incorporated its reasoning into their work. All have challenged orthodoxy to improve how evolutionary psychology studies intimacy. The authors' words are their own, but the editors offered feedback for improving the interdisciplinary scope of their writing. Our reflections on each chapter precede each of the three major sections of this handbook: relationship initiation, maintenance, and dissolution.

We hope that readers of this volume walk away feeling that their views on intimacy and interpersonal relationships have been enriched.

References

Aktipis, A. (2020). *The cheating cell.* Princeton University Press.

Antar, J. C., & Stephen, I. D. (2021). Facial shape provides a valid cue to sociosexuality in men but not women. *Evolution and Human Behavior, 42*(4), 361–370.

Aspara, J., Wittkowski, K., & Luo, X. (2018). Types of intelligence predict likelihood to get married and stay married: Large-scale empirical evidence for evolutionary theory. *Personality and Individual Differences, 122*, 1–6.

Ayers, J. D. (2021). Competitive scenarios increase competition in women: A meta-analysis. *Evolutionary Behavioral Sciences.* Advance online publication. https://doi.org/10.1037/ebs0000278

Badcock, P. B., Friston, K. J., Ramstead, M. J., Ploeger, A., & Hohwy, J. (2019). The hierarchically mechanistic mind: an evolutionary systems theory of the human brain, cognition, and behavior. *Cognitive, Affective, & Behavioral Neuroscience, 19*(6), 1319–1351.

Baugh, A. T., Senft, R. A., Firke, M., Lauder, A., Schroeder, J., Meddle, S. L., Meddle, S. L. Meddle; van Oers, K., & Hau, M. (2017). Risk-averse personalities have a systemically potentiated neuroendocrine stress axis: A multilevel experiment in Parus major. *Hormones and Behavior, 93*, 99–108.

Baur, J., Nsanzimana, J. D. A., & Berger, D. (2019). Sexual selection and the evolution of male and female cognition: A test using experimental evolution in seed beetles. *Evolution, 73*(12), 2390–2400.

Blair, K. L., & Hoskin, R. A. (2019). Transgender exclusion from the world of dating: Patterns of acceptance and rejection of hypothetical trans dating partners as a function of sexual and gender identity. *Journal of Social and Personal Relationships, 36*(7), 2074–2095.

Bode, A., & Kushnick, G. (2021). Proximate and ultimate perspectives on romantic love. *Frontiers in Psychology, 12*, 1088.

Bradshaw, H. K., & DelPriore, D. J. (2022). Beautification is more than mere mate attraction: extending evolutionary perspectives on female appearance enhancement. *Archives of Sexual Behavior, 51*, 43–47.

Brady, A., & Baker, L. R. (2022). The changing tides of attractive alternatives in romantic relationships: Recent societal changes compel new directions for future research. *Social and Personality Psychology Compass, 16*(1), e12650.

Brandner, J. L., Brase, G. L., & Huxman, S. A. (2020). "Weighting" to find the right person: compensatory trait integrating versus alternative models to assess mate value. *Evolution and Human Behavior, 41*(4), 284–292.

Brown, M., Sacco, D. F., Boykin, K., Drea, K., & Macchione, A. (2021). Inferences of parental abilities through facial and bodily features. In V. A. Weekes-Shackelford & T. K. Shackelford (Eds.), The Oxford *handbook of evolutionary psychology and parenting* (pp. 453–467). Oxford University Press.

Buss, D. M. (2018). Sexual and emotional infidelity: Evolved gender differences in jealousy prove robust and replicable. *Perspectives on Psychological Science, 13*(2), 155–160.

Buss, D. M., & Schmitt, D. P. (1993). Sexual Strategies Theory: An evolutionary perspective on human mating. *Psychological Review, 100*(2), 204–232. https://doi.org/10.1037/0033-295X.100.2.204

Buss, D. M., & Schmitt, D.P. (2019). Mate preferences and their behavioral manifestations. *Annual Review of Psychology, 70*, 77–110.

Conroy-Beam, D. (2021). Couple simulation: A novel approach for evaluating models of human mate choice. *Personality and Social Psychology Review, 25*(3), 198–228.

Conroy-Beam, D., Buss, D. M., Asao, K., Sorokowska, A., Sorokowski, P., Aavik, T., Akello, G., Alhabahba, M. M., Alm, C., Amjad, N., Anjum, A., Atama, C. S., Duyar, D. A., Ayebare, R., Batres, C., Bendixen, M., Bensafia, A., Bizumic, B., Boussena, M. . . . Zupančič, M. (2019). Contrasting computational models of mate preference integration across 45 countries. *Scientific Reports, 9*(1), 1–13.

Csajbók, Z., & Berkics, M. (2022). Seven deadly sins of potential romantic partners: The dealbreakers of mate choice. *Personality and Individual Differences, 186*, 111334.

Del Giudice, M. (2017). Integration in personality research: Evolution is the missing catalyst. *European. Journal of Personality, 31*, 529–595.

Desrochers, J., MacKinnon, M., Kelly, B., Masse, B., & Arnocky, S. (2021). Sex differences in response to deception across mate-value traits of attractiveness, job status, and altruism in online dating. *Archives of Sexual Behavior, 50*, 3675–3685.

Diamond, L. M. (2021). The new genetic evidence on same-gender sexuality: Implications for sexual fluidity and multiple forms of sexual diversity. *The Journal of Sex Research, 58*(7), 818–837.

Dinh, T., Haselton, M. G., & Gangestad, S. W. (2022). "Fast" women? The effects of childhood environments on women's developmental timing, mating strategies, and reproductive outcomes. *Evolution and Human Behavior, 43*(2), 133–146.

Durante, K. M., Eastwick, P. W., Finkel, E. J., Gangestad, S. W., & Simpson, J. A. (2016). Pair-bonded relationships and romantic alternatives: Toward an integration of evolutionary and relationship science perspectives. *Advances in Experimental Social Psychology, 53*, 1–74.

Durkee, P., Lukaszewski, A., von Rueden, C., Gurven, M., Buss, D. M., & Tucker-Drob, E. (2022). Niche diversity predicts personality structure across 115 nations. *Psychological Science, 33*(2), 285–298. https://doi.org/10.1177/09567976211031571

Edelstein, R. S., & Chin, K. (2018). Hormones and close relationship processes: neuroendocrine bases of partnering and parenting. In O. C. Schultheiss & P. H. Mehta (Eds.), *Routledge international handbook of social neuroendocrinology* (pp. 281–297). Routledge.

Edlund, J. E., Heider, J. D., Nichols, A. L., McCarthy, R. J., Wood, S. E., Scherer, C. R., Hartnett, J. L., & Walker, R. (2018). Sex differences in jealousy: The (lack of) influence of researcher theoretical perspective. *The Journal of Social Psychology, 158*(5), 515–520.

Fenneman, J., & Frankenhuis, W. E. (2020). Is impulsive behavior adaptive in harsh and unpredictable environments? A formal model. *Evolution and Human Behavior, 41*(4), 261–273.

Fennis, B. M., Gineikiene, J., Barauskaite, D., & van Koningsbruggen, G. M. (2022). Acute stress can boost and buffer hedonic consumption: The role of individual differences in consumer life history strategies. *Personality and Individual Differences, 185*, Article 111261.

Fessler, D. M. T., Clark, J. A., & Clint, E. K. (2015). Evolutionary psychology and evolutionary anthropology. In D. M. Buss (Ed.), *the handbook of evolutionary psychology, volume 2: integrations* (pp. 1029–1046). John Wiley & Sons.

Fink, B., Liebner, K., Müller, A. K., Hirn, T., McKelvey, G., & Lankhof, J. (2018). Hair colour and skin colour together influence perceptions of age, health and attractiveness in lightly pigmented young women. *International Journal of Cosmetic Science, 40*(3), 303–312.

Fisher, M. L., Garcia, J. R., & Burch, R. L. (2020). Evolutionary psychology: Thoughts on integrating feminist perspectives. In L. Workman, W. Reader, & J. H. Barkow (Eds.), *The Cambridge handbook of evolutionary perspectives on human behavior* (pp. 378–391). Cambridge University Press. https://doi.org/10.1017/9781108131797.032

Fraley, R. C., Brumbaugh, C. C., & Marks, M. J. (2005). The evolution and function of adult attachment: a comparative and phylogenetic analysis. *Journal of Personality and Social Psychology, 89*(5), 731.

Frankenhuis, W. E., Panchanathan, K., & Nettle, D. (2016). Cognition in harsh and unpredictable environments. *Current Opinion in Psychology, 7*, 76–80.

Gibson, M. A., & Lawson, D. W. (2015). Applying evolutionary anthropology. *Evolutionary Anthropology: Issues, News, and Reviews, 24*(1), 3–14.

Giosan, C., Cobeanu, O., Wyka, K., Muresan, V., Mogoase, C., Szentagotai, A., Malta, L. S., & Moldovan, R. (2020). Cognitive evolutionary therapy versus standard cognitive therapy for depression: A single-blinded randomized clinical trial. *Journal of Clinical Psychology, 76*(10), 1818–1831.

Gurvich, C., Hoy, K., Thomas, N., & Kulkarni, J. (2018). Sex differences and the influence of sex hormones on cognition through adulthood and the aging process. *Brain Sciences, 8*(9), 163.

Hasson, U., Nastase, S. A., & Goldstein, A. (2020). Direct fit to nature: An evolutionary perspective on biological and artificial neural networks. *Neuron, 105*(3), 416–434.

Henrich, J., & Muthukrishna, M. (2021). The origins and psychology of human cooperation. *Annual Review of Psychology, 72*, 207–240.

Hertler, S. C., Figueredo, A. J., & Peñaherrera-Aguirre, M. (2020). *Multilevel selection: theoretical foundations, historical examples, and empirical evidence*. Springer Nature.

Hill, S. (2019). This is your brain on birth control: *The surprising science of women, hormones, and the law of unintended consequences*. Penguin.

Hollon, S. D., Andrews, P. W., & Thomson Jr, J. A. (2021). Cognitive behavior therapy for depression from an evolutionary perspective. *Frontiers in Psychiatry, 12*, Article 667592.

Hunter, G., & Stockwell, A. (2022). Toward a behavior-analytic understanding of jealousy and compersion in romantic and sexual relationships. *European Journal of Behavior Analysis, 23*(1), 78–108.

James, L., Todak, N., & Savage, J. (2020). Unnecessary force by police: Insights from evolutionary psychology. *Policing: A Journal of Policy and Practice, 14*(1), 278–291.

Joel, S., & MacDonald, G. (2021). We're not that choosy: Emerging evidence of a progression bias in romantic relationships. *Personality and Social Psychology Review, 25*, 317–343.

Jonason, P. K., Zeigler-Hill, V., & Baldacchino, J. (2017). Before and after: Personality pathology, childhood conditions, and life history outcomes. *Personality and Individual Differences, 116*, 38–43.

Jones, A. L. (2018). The influence of shape and colour cue classes on facial health perception. *Evolution and Human Behavior, 39*(1), 19–29.

Jones, A. L., & Jaeger, B. (2019). Biological bases of beauty revisited: The effect of symmetry, averageness, and sexual dimorphism on female facial attractiveness. *Symmetry, 11*(2), 279.

Kline, M. A., Shamsudheen, R., & Broesch, T. (2018). Variation is the universal: Making cultural evolution work in developmental psychology. *Philosophical Transactions of the Royal Society B: Biological Sciences, 373*(1743), 20170059.

Kupfer, T. R., Sidari, M. J., Zietsch, B. P., Jern, P., Tybur, J. M., & Wesseldijk, L. W. (2022). Why are some people more jealous than others? Genetic and environmental factors. *Evolution and Human Behavior, 43*(1), 26–33.

Lenton, A. P., & Stewart, A. (2008). Changing her ways: The number of options and mate-standard strength impact mate choice strategy and satisfaction. *Judgment and Decision Making, 3*(7), 501.

Li, N. P., Bailey, J. M., Kenrick, D. T., & Linsenmeier, J. A. (2002). The necessities and luxuries of mate preferences: testing the tradeoffs. *Journal of Personality and Social Psychology, 82*(6), 947.

Li, N. P., Yong, J. C., & Van Vugt, M. (2020). Evolutionary psychology's next challenge: Solving modern problems using a mismatch perspective. *Evolutionary Behavioral Sciences, 14*(4), 362.

Lippa, R. A. (2010). Gender differences in personality and interests: When, where, and why? *Social and Personality Psychology compass, 4*(11), 1098–1110.

Lukaszewski, A. W., Lewis, D. M., Durkee, P. K., Sell, A. N., Sznycer, D., & Buss, D. M. (2020). An adaptationist framework for personality science. *European Journal of Personality, 34*(6), 1151–1174.

Luoto, S. (2019). An updated theoretical framework for human sexual selection: From ecology, genetics, and life history to extended phenotypes. *Adaptive Human Behavior and Physiology, 5*(1), 48–102.

Marcinkowska, U. M., Kozlov, M. V., Cai, H., Contreras-Garduño, J., Dixson, B. J., Oana, G. A., ... & Rantala, M. J. (2014). Cross-cultural variation in men's preference for sexual dimorphism in women's faces. *Biology Letters, 10*(4), 20130850.

McDermott, R., & Hatemi, P. K. (2018). To go forward, we must look back: The importance of evolutionary psychology for understanding modern politics. *Evolutionary Psychology, 16*(2), 1474704918764506.

Miller, G. (2000). Sexual selection for indicators of intelligence. In G. R. Bock, J. A. Goode, and K. Webb (Eds.), *Novartis foundation symposium* (pp. 260–270). John Wiley & Sons.

Miller, G. F., & Todd, P. M. (1998). Mate choice turns cognitive. *Trends in Cognitive Sciences, 2*(5), 190–198.

Mogilski, J. K. (2021). Parental investment theory. In T. K. Shackelford (Ed.), *The SAGE handbook of evolutionary psychology* (pp. 137-154). SAGE.

Mogilski, J. K., Mitchell, V. E., Reeve, S. D., Donaldson, S. H., Nicolas, S. C., & Welling, L. L. (2020). Life history and multi-partner mating: A novel explanation for moral stigma against consensual non-monogamy. *Frontiers in Psychology, 10*, Article 3033.

Mogilski, J. K., Wade, T. J., & Welling, L. L. M. (2014). Prioritization of potential mates' history of sexual fidelity during a conjoint ranking task. *Personality and Social Psychology Bulletin, 40*, 884–897.

Mogilski, J. K., & Welling, L. L. M. (2017). The relative importance of sexual dimorphism, fluctuating asymmetry, and color cues to health during evaluation of potential partners' facial photographs: A conjoint analysis study. *Human Nature, 28*, 53–75.

Mogilski, J. K., & Welling, L. L. M. (2018). The relative contribution of jawbone and cheekbone prominence, eyebrow thickness, eye size, and face length to evaluations of facial masculinity and attractiveness: A conjoint data-driven approach. *Frontiers in Psychology: Section Evolutionary Psychology, 9*, Article 2428.

Mogilski, J. K., Wysocki, A., Reeve, S. D., Mitchell, V. E., Lunge, J., & Welling, L. L. (2019b). Stress hormones, physiology, and behavior. In L. M. Welling & T. K. Shackelford (Eds.), The *Oxford handbook of evolutionary psychology and behavioral endocrinology* (p. 351). Oxford University Press.

Morris, A., Phillips, J., Huang, K., & Cushman, F. (2021). Generating options and choosing between them depend on distinct forms of value representation. *Psychological Science, 32*(11), 1731–1746.

Nesse, R. M. (2019). Core principles for evolutionary medicine. In M. Brüne & W. Schiefenhövel (Eds.), *Oxford handbook of evolution and medicine* (pp. 3–43). Oxford University Press.

Nettle, D., & Frankenhuis, W. E. (2019). The evolution of life-history theory: a bibliometric analysis of an interdisciplinary research area. *Proceedings of the Royal Society B, 286*(1899), 20190040.

Nettle, D., & Scott-Phillips, T. (2021). Is a non-evolutionary psychology possible? https://doi.org/10.31234/osf.io/wky9h

Otterbring, T. (2021). Evolutionary psychology in marketing: Deep, debated, but fancier with fieldwork. *Psychology & Marketing, 38*, 229–238.

Pachankis, J. E., Clark, K. A., Burton, C. L., Hughto, J. M. W., Bränström, R., & Keene, D. E. (2020). Sex, status, competition, and exclusion: Intraminority stress from within the gay community and gay and bisexual men's mental health. *Journal of Personality and Social Psychology, 119*(3), 713.

Palomo-Vélez, G., & van Vugt, M. (2021). The evolutionary psychology of climate change behaviors: Insights and applications. *Current Opinion in Psychology, 42*, 54–59.

Pan, X., Gelfand, M., & Nau, D. (2021). Integrating evolutionary game theory and cross-cultural psychology to understand cultural dynamics. *American Psychologist, 76*(6), 1054.

Pelham, B. W. (2021). The husband-older age gap in marriage is associated with selective fitness. *Journal of Personality and Social Psychology, 121*(3), 601.

Petersen, M. B. (2020). The evolutionary psychology of mass mobilization: How disinformation and demagogues coordinate rather than manipulate. *Current Opinion in Psychology, 35*, 71–75.

Puts, D. (2016). Human sexual selection. *Current Opinion in Psychology, 7*, 28–32.

Redlick, M. H., & Vangelisti, A. L. (2018). Affection, deception, and evolution: Deceptive affectionate messages as mate retention behaviors. *Evolutionary Psychology, 16*(1), Article 1474704917753857.

Rehbein, E., Hornung, J., Poromaa, I. S., & Derntl, B. (2021). Shaping of the female human brain by sex hormones: A review. *Neuroendocrinology, 111*(3), 183–206.

Reynolds, T., Baumeister, R. F., & Maner, J. K. (2018). Competitive reputation manipulation: Women strategically transmit social information about romantic rivals. *Journal of Experimental Social Psychology, 78*, 195–209.

Roney, J. R., & Simmons, Z. L. (2018). Ovarian hormone fluctuations predict within-cycle shifts in women's food intake. *Hormones and Behavior, 90*, 8–14.

Saad, G. (2017). On the method of evolutionary psychology and its applicability to consumer research. *Journal of Marketing Research, 54*(3), 464–477.

Schulz, J. F., Bahrami-Rad, D., Beauchamp, J. P., & Henrich, J. (2019). The church, intensive kinship, and global psychological variation. *Science, 366*(6466), Article eaau5141.

Segall, M. H., Dasen, P. R., Berry, J. W., & Poortinga, Y. H. (1990). *Human behavior in global perspective: An introduction to cross-cultural psychology*. Pergamon Press.

Semenyna, S. W., Gómez Jiménez, F. R., & Vasey, P. L. (2021). Women's reaction to opposite-and same-sex infidelity in three cultures. *Human Nature, 32*(2), 450–469.

Seyfarth, R. M., & Cheney, D. L. (2012). The evolutionary origins of friendship. *Annual Review of Psychology, 63*(1), 153–177.

Shirazi, T. N., Self, H., Dawood, K., Welling, L. L., Cárdenas, R., Rosenfield, K. A., Bailey, J. M., Balasubramanian, R., Delaney, A., Breedlove, S. M., & Puts, D. A. (2021). Evidence that perinatal ovarian hormones promote women's sexual attraction to men. *Psychoneuroendocrinology, 134*, 105431.

Silan, M., Adetula, A., Basnight-Brown, D. M., Forscher, P. S., Dutra, N., & IJzerman, H. (2021). Psychological science needs the entire globe, part 2. *APS Observer, 34*(6).

Simpson, J. A., Griskevicius, V., Szepsenwol, O., & Young, E. (2017). *An evolutionary life history perspective on personality and mating strategies*. Praeger/ABC-CLIO.

Sommer, V., & Vasey, P. L. (Eds.). (2006). *Homosexual behaviour in animals: An evolutionary perspective*. Cambridge University Press.

Stanley, K. O., Clune, J., Lehman, J., & Miikkulainen, R. (2019). Designing neural networks through neuroevolution. *Nature Machine Intelligence, 1*(1), 24–35.

Stephen, I. D., Hiew, V., Coetzee, V., Tiddeman, B. P., & Perrett, D. I. (2017). Facial shape analysis identifies valid cues to aspects of physiological health in Caucasian, Asian, and African populations. *Frontiers in Psychology, 8*, 1883.

Szepsenwol, O., Griskevicius, V., Simpson, J. A., Young, E. S., Fleck, C., & Jones, R. E. (2017). The effect of predictable early childhood environments on sociosexuality in early adulthood. *Evolutionary Behavioral Sciences, 11*(2), 131.

Szepsenwol, O., Simpson, J., Griskevicius, V., Zamir, O., Young, E. S., Shoshani, A., & Doron, G. (2021). The effects of childhood unpredictability and harshness on emotional control and relationship quality: A life history perspective. *Development and Psychopathology*. Advance online publication. https://doi.org/10.1017/S0954579421001371

Tanskanen, A. O., & Danielsbacka, M. (2018). *Intergenerational family relations: An evolutionary social science approach*. Taylor & Francis.

Trillmich, F., Müller, T., & Müller, C. (2018). Understanding the evolution of personality requires the study of mechanisms behind the development and life history of personality traits. *Biology Letters, 14*(2), Article 20170740.

Trivers, R. L. (1972). Parental investment and sexual selection. In B. Campbell (Ed.), *Sexual selection and the descent of man* (pp. 136–179). Aldine.

Trivers, R. (1991). Deceit and self-deception: The relationship between communication and consciousness. *Man and Beast Revisited, 907*, 175–191.

van Anders, S. M. (2013). Beyond masculinity: Testosterone, gender/sex, and human social behavior in a comparative context. *Frontiers in Neuroendocrinology, 34*(3), 198–210.

Vonk, J. (2021). The journey in comparative psychology matters more than the destination. *Journal of Comparative Psychology, 135*(2), 156–167.

Vowels, L. M., Vowels, M. J., & Mark, K. P. (2021). Uncovering the most important factors for predicting sexual desire using explainable machine learning. *The Journal of Sexual Medicine, 18*(7), 1198–1216.

Walter, K. V., Conroy-Beam, D., Buss, D. M., Asao, K., Sorokowska, A., Sorokowski, P., Aavik, T., Akello, G., Alhababhba, M. M., Alm, C., Amjad, N., Anjum, A., Atama, C. S., Duyar, D. A., Ayebare, R., Batres, C., Bendixen, M., Bensafia, A., Bizumic, B. ... Zupančič, M. (2020). Sex differences in mate preferences across 45 countries: A large-scale replication. *Psychological Science, 31*(4), 408–423.

Walum, H., Lichtenstein, P., Neiderhiser, J. M., Reiss, D., Ganiban, J. M., Spotts, E. L., Pedersen, N. L., Anckarster, H., Larsson, L., & Westberg, L. (2012). Variation in the oxytocin receptor gene is associated with pair-bonding and social behavior. *Biological Psychiatry, 71*(5), 419–426.

Wang, X., Zhu, N., & Chang, L. (2022). Childhood unpredictability, life history, and intuitive versus deliberate cognitive styles. *Personality and Individual Differences, 184*, 111225.

Welling L. L., M., & Shackelford, T. K. (2019). *The Oxford handbook of evolutionary psychology and behavioral endocrinology*. Oxford University Press.

Williams, G. C. (1966). *Adaptation and natural selection*. Princeton University Press.

Williams, K. E. G., Krems, J. A., Ayers, J. D., & Rankin, A. M. (2022). Sex differences in friendship preferences. *Evolution and Human Behavior, 43*(1), 44–52.

Wilson, D. S., & Coan, J. A. (2021). Groups as organisms: Implications for therapy and training. *Clinical Psychology Review, 85*, Article 101987.

Woodley, M. A., Luoto, S., Peñaherrera-Aguirre, M., & Sarraf, M. A. (2021). Life history is a major source of adaptive individual and species differences: A critical commentary on Zietsch and Sidari (2020). *Evolutionary Psychological Science, 7*(3), 213–231.

Zietsch, B. P., & Sidari, M. J. (2020). A critique of life history approaches to human trait covariation. *Evolution and Human Behavior, 41*(6), 527–535.

PART I

Relationship Initiation

Relationship initiation refers to how people find and choose a relationship partner. In chapter 1, Buss reviews the foundations of evolutionary science and its application to the study of human mating. He focuses on the processes of sexual selection and how it has shaped men's and women's partner preferences and selection criteria. He highlights the fundamentals and premises of sexual strategies theory, including the sex-specific challenges recurrently faced by those seeking long- and short-term partners and the adaptations that men and women have evolved to heuristically address these challenges. He considers alternative explanations for variation in men's and women's mate preferences (e.g., the good genes hypothesis and the mate-switching hypothesis) and strategies of contest competition. Moreover, he integrates recent evidence for how individual and environmental variations (e.g., mate value discrepancies, operational sex ratio, and parasite load) shape expression of these adaptations. He concludes with a discussion of future directions in the study of sexual coercion (i.e., behavior aimed at securing reproduction by bypassing mate choice) and men's and women's adaptations and counter-adaptations for enacting and resisting this type of mating.

In chapter 2, Stephen and Luoto review how humans and other animals use morphological cues (e.g., face and body condition) to assess partner qualities that are of consequence to successful mating and reproduction. Their review includes a balanced discussion of traits associated with immune functioning, health status, and desirable personality traits, including cues of developmental health (e.g., symmetry and sexual dimorphism), current health (e.g., adiposity and skin color and texture), genetic quality (e.g., major histocompatibility, height, and muscularity), and personality. They discuss the myriad strategies for augmenting these cues with nonbodily ornamentation, such as luxury items, cosmetics, and other conspicuous superstimuli that exaggerate cues of phenotypic quality. They conclude by discussing how modern technology, such as social media and online dating, has decoupled the evolved psychology underlying partner evaluation from the adaptive behavior that it has historically produced, thereby creating evolutionary mismatches.

In chapter 3, Jonason and March review the psychological traits that people assess in potential mates and argue that these qualities can be organized into three superordinate traits: competence, compassion, and compatibility. Competence includes traits that assist in goal pursuit and attainment (e.g., intelligence, education, and income), compassion reflects traits that signal a partner's willingness to invest in a partner or shared offspring, and compatibility refers to similarity in interests and belief. They outline differences and similarities among men's and women's preferences for these traits and draw on sociocultural (i.e., social role theory, structural powerlessness, and social learning theory) and evolutionary models (i.e., sexual strategies theory and life history theory) to explain how and when people vary in these preferences. They conclude with the importance of studying how these preferences generalize to non-Western and sexual/gender minority populations and how researchers might begin to appraise their "three Cs" model of psychological preferences.

In chapter 4, Li and Choy review the mechanisms of mate choice, including the evolved algorithms that humans employ to weigh and prioritize competing partner traits. They assess these mechanisms within the context of sexual strategies theory, agent-based simulation models (e.g., Euclidean algorithmic mate value integration), modern platforms for courting partners (e.g., social media and online dating), and speed-dating experimental paradigms. They conclude by discussing sources of evolutionary mismatch caused by the emergence of supernormal stimuli, such as sexual technology and pornography, potential partner abundance, and anonymity, that which be altering how mate choice mechanisms guide peoples' relationship decisions.

In chapter 5, Makhanova synthesizes the experimental and cross-species evidence for how hormones mediate sexual behavior and partnership formation. She reviews the general functional design of gonadal hormones, including testosterone, estrogen, and progesterone, and the physiological systems through which these hormones influence the development and expression of male- and female-typical mating behavior. Throughout, she emphasizes how these hormonal effects are sensitive to context (e.g., social status, ovulatory fluctuation, and presence of rivals) to produce situationally malleable adaptive responses. She concludes by discussing sources of individual difference in hormone-mediated relationship formation and identifies methodological advancements that are yet needed within this field of study.

In chapter 6, Caton, Lewis, Al-Shawaf, and Evans catalogue the diverse courtship signals and behaviors that humans and other animals employ to attract partners and promote their reproductive success. Discussion is organized around the five senses to showcase how courtship is guided by sensory input and the adapted cognition that processes each sensory mode (i.e., visual, auditory, tactile, olfactory, and gustatory). Throughout, they maintain focus on cutting-edge research on psychophysical cues of mate quality, including neck musculature, lumbar curvature, and sebum detection. They conclude by discussing future directions for studying how humans use each sensory modality to assess potential partners.

In chapter 7, Krems, Bradshaw, and Merrie provide an overview of the major theories and evidence underlying research on intrasexual competition in humans. They discuss the contributions of parental investment theory and sexual strategies theory as well as the influence of biological markets and ecological factors (e.g., sex ratios and income inequality) that shape same-sex competition within men and women. They bridge historical and recent work to identify unresolved gaps in the empirical study of contest competition and spend considerable time identifying future directions in the study competition among women, sexual and gender minorities, and parents and older adults.

In chapter 8, Valentova, Amaral, and Varella give an authoritative summary of mate preference, mate choice, and relationship initiation research among hetero- and nonheterosexuals and evaluates how evolutionary scientists have approached the study of relationship initiation among LGBTQ+ individuals. They note which sex differences appear to be robust with LGBTQ+ samples and which features of attraction and courtship diverge from findings among heterosexual individuals. They identify several current limitations, including a largely restrictive focus on Western samples, insufficiently nuanced measures of sexual orientation, and interactions between sexual attraction and gender (a) typical developmental process.

In chapter 9, Koren and Ayalon consider how relationship initiation varies across age and the unique challenges that individuals must resolve to form partnerships later in life. They consider the roles of individualistic versus collectivistic cultural values, the influence that children and grandchildren exert on mate choice and repartnering, and the barriers that later-life health and living conditions can introduce. Throughout, they reference prominent models of socioemotional functioning and successful aging to highlight the importance of studying the diversity of relationships among older adults, the intersecting effects of culture and parent–offspring interactions and expectations, and the roles of physical and emotional togetherness/apartness. They conclude with research on LGBTQ+ populations, extreme old age, and emerging technologies for helping older individuals find and achieve relational satisfaction.

In chapter 10, Karandashev concludes the first section by describing the influence of biological, ecological, and cultural selection processes on cross-cultural variation in relationship initiation. Throughout, he focuses on distinctions between traditional and modern societies' courtship customs. In doing so, he highlights international differences in beauty standards and their relation to socioeconomic status, infant mortality rates, sex ratio, and individualism/collectivism, the importance of physical appearance versus expressive behavior, survival and self-expression values, education and reproductive rate, wealth concentration and women's access to financial resources, social rituals and symbolic gestures of love and commitment, dating customs, and the role of parental oversight (e.g., arranged marriages). He concludes by critiquing methodological customs in cross-cultural research and provides several fruitful avenues for future directions.

CHAPTER

1

The Sexual Selection of Human Mating Strategies: Mate Preferences and Competition Tactics

David M. Buss

Abstract

Darwin's theory of sexual selection provided a cogent theoretical framework for understanding the major causal processes of the mating strategies of sexually reproducing species—intrasexual competition and preferential mate choice. This framework, along with important theoretical elaborations, has proven extraordinarily useful in scientific theories and empirical discoveries about human mating strategies. Darwin described intrasexual competition as the primary province of males and preferential mate choice as the primary province of females. Unlike many species, however, humans display mutual mate choice and both sexes compete intensely for desirable mates. Moreover, humans are at least somewhat unique in using complex language to deploy courtship tactics to attract mates and to impugn the qualities of mating rivals. This chapter reviews the impact of sexual selection theory on scientific discoveries about human mating strategies, focusing on mate selection criteria and tactics of intrasexual competition.

Key Words: sexual selection, mating strategies, mate preferences, intrasexual competition, sex differences

Darwin was rightly hailed for his discovery of *natural selection*, which is a form of selection that favors traits that lead to greater survival (Darwin, 1859). These traits subsumed those that helped organisms combat three classes of "hostile forces of nature." These include threats from the physical environment (e.g., extreme temperature, falls from cliffs, and drowning), other species (e.g., predators and parasites), and conspecifics (e.g., in *Homo sapiens*, homicide at the hands of other humans). Organisms with traits that favored surviving these hostile forces lived to reproductive age and produced more offspring than those felled by these forces.

Sexual Selection Theory

Some traits, Darwin observed, did not readily lend themselves to explanation via natural selection. The elaborate plumage of peacocks and loud songs sung by some birds are prime examples. Many of these traits seemed detrimental to survival, being both metabolically costly and conspicuous to predators. So troubled was Darwin by these contrasurvival traits that he noted in one of his correspondences: "the sight of a feather in a peacock's tail, whenever I gaze at it, makes me sick!" (Darwin, 1860). Grappling with these explanatory puzzles ultimately led Darwin to formulate his theory of sexual selection. *Sexual selection* favors traits that lead to mating success and can be favored even if those traits carry some cost to an organism's survival (Darwin, 1871).

Darwin identified two distinct causal processes by which sexual selection for mating success could be achieved. The first was *intrasexual selection*, a process by which members of one sex compete with one another, the outcome of which is greater sexual access to members of the opposite sex. The greater size and strength of males of many species, as well as sexually dimorphic animal weapons of combat such as horns, antlers, and claws, presumably evolved via the process of intrasexual selection. These armaments gave their bearers an advantage in physical battles, or what has been termed "contest competition," and Darwin believed this process applied primarily to males of different species. As we will see, however, contest competition is only one form of intrasexual selection, and when it comes to humans, both sexes engage in vigorous same-sex competition.

The second causal process of sexual selection is *intersexual selection*, or preferential mate choice. The logic is that if members of one sex prefer certain qualities in potential mates, then potential mates who possess those qualities have a mating advantage. Heritable traits can evolve over time simply because they are consensually valued by those doing the choosing. Darwin believed that preferential mate choice was primarily the province of females, based in part on his observation that males were less discriminating and had lower thresholds for mating. When it comes to humans, however, both sexes exert strong preferential mate choice, so this causal process applies to both women and men. In short, mating success can be achieved by besting same-sex rivals or by displaying or possessing qualities desired by the other sex. Evolution occurs if these causal processes are iterated over time. Although the intrasexual component of Darwin's sexual selection theory was largely embraced by his contemporaries, the preferential mate choice component was not. And although the theory of natural selection in its survival selection form came to dominate the field of biology after Darwin, his theory of sexual selection was largely ignored for a century (with some notable exceptions, such as Fisher, 1958).

In 1972, an edited book celebrated Darwin's theory of mating success (Campbell, 1972). The most influential chapter was written by Robert Trivers (1972), who proposed a theory centering on which sex does the choosing and which sex does the competing—*the theory of parental investment and sexual selection*. The sex that invests more than the other, he argued, does the choosing, so the intersexual selection component applies mainly to that sex. The sex that invests less, in contrast, is more competitive with members of their own sex for mating access to the higher investing sex. Trivers's theory was based on the work of Bateman (1948), and the key principle is termed the "Bateman gradient," the steepness of the slope between mating success and reproductive success. Sexual access to additional mates (one form of mating success), according to Bateman and Trivers, pays more reproductive dividends for the low-investing sex than for the high-investing sex.

Trivers's elaboration of sexual selection theory has largely been supported empirically (see Mogilski, 2020, for a recent review), including in "sex-role reversed" species such as the pipefish seahorse and the Mormon cricket. In species in which males invest more than females, it is the females who are more aggressively competitive with each other for access to the high-investing males. Although the Bateman gradient and Trivers's theory of parental investment on which it is based have been challenged by some (e.g., Gowaty et al., 2012; Tang-Martínez, 2016), meta-analyses across many species and mating systems have largely supported their derived predictions about sex differences (e.g., Janicke et al., 2016).

Sexual Strategies Theory Fundamentals

Sexual strategies theory (SST) is anchored in sexual selection theory, but in the human case there are additional complexities that require conceptual and empirical examination (Buss & Schmitt, 1993, 2019). SST suggests that humans have faced two fundamental classes of adaptive problems of mating: (a) exerting fitness-enhancing preferential mate choice, and (b) out-competing rivals for desirable mates. Although sometimes conceptualized as distinct, they can be causally linked in at least two ways (Buss, 1988a). First, if men compete with each other in physical contests such as wrestling or chest-pounding duals, the informative variance produced can create or amplify women's preferences for athletic prowess of physical formidability. Second, the mate preferences of one sex can dictate the domains of intrasexual competition in the other sex. If women value bravery in the face of danger, generosity in food sharing, or signs of social status, these mate preferences can create selection pressure on men to compete with other men to display honest indicators of bravery and generosity and to place a high motivational priority on achieving social rank. This conceptualization expands the domain of intrasexual competition beyond physical contest competition as conceptualized by Darwin—a topic covered in greater detail below in the section on Sexual Selection and Mate Competition.

When applied to humans, the role of sexual selection becomes even more complex due in part to the facultatively variable nature of male and female investment and the multiplicity of mating strategies of both sexes. Men's mating strategies vary from low investment (e.g., one-night stand and casual sex) to high investment (e.g., many years of provisioning and protecting offspring). Women's mating strategies also vary from low to high investment, although for offspring production per se, an undoubtedly important component of investment, human reproductive biology dictates that women have a higher level of *minimum obligatory* parental investment than men (nine months of pregancy vs. one act of sex). High-investment mating strategies include attachment, pair-bonding, and prolonged resource commitment. Low-investment strategies can be as minimal as a brief sexual encounter or casual hookup. As a shorthand, SST has labeled the ends of the investment continuum as short-term and long-term mating strategies, with the recognition that the temporal dimension captures only one form of investment (Buss & Schmitt, 1993, 2019).

Important premises of SST include:

(a) *Humans have evolved distinct mating-specific adaptations.* Humans have evolved distinct adaptations for specific problems that must be solved to reap the fitness benefits and avoid the fitness costs of pursuing each sexual strategy.

(b) *Sex similarity in mating psychology.* In domains in which the sexes confront similar adaptive challenges, such as solving the commitment problem in long-term mating, they have evolved a similar sexual psychology.

(c) *Sex differences in mating psychology.* In domains in which the sexes have confronted somewhat different adaptive challenges, such as assessing the fertility or social status of a potential mate, they have evolved somewhat distinct features of their sexual psychology (see Buss, 1995, for the evolutionary meta-theory of sex differences).

(d) *Common long-term mating challenges faced by both sexes.* In long-term mating, common challenges faced by both sexes include identifying a partner able and willing to commit, assessing long-term mate attributes such as an altruistically skewed welfare trade-off ratio (i.e., one in which the partner makes decisions that reflect valuing your welfare more than their own) (Tooby et al., 2008), identifying mates with similar mate value trajectories over time, and identifying mates who are not overly encumbered with costly commitments such as children from prior mateships or in the modern environment great financial debt.

(e) *Male-specific long-term mating challenges.* Male-specific problems of long-term mating include identifying potential partners high in reproductive value and solving the paternity uncertainty problem.

(f) *Female-specific long-term mating challenges.* Female-specific challenges of long-term mating include identifying men who are able to acquire resources consistently over time, who are willing to invest those resources in her and her children without diverting them to other women and their children, and who are able and willing to protect her and her children from harm and exploitation by conspecifics.

(g) *Male-specific short-term mating challenges.* Because of asymmetries of obligatory parental investment, combined with differences in the fitness benefits reaped from short-term mating, the sexes have evolved somewhat distinct motivational priorities, mate preferences, and mate attraction strategies for short-term mating; in men, these include desiring a larger number of sex partners, letting less time and commitment elapse before initiating sexual intercourse, and tactics for minimizing entangling commitments that would interfere with a short-term mating strategy (e.g., Jonason & Buss, 2012).

(h) *Female-specific short-term mating challenges.* In short-term mating, women have evolved to reap several potential fitness benefits, including immediate access to resources, obtaining high-quality genes, and mate switching to divest themselves of a cost-inflicting partner or to trade up to a superior partner (Buss et al., 2017).

(i) *Context-specificity of sexual strategies.* Humans have evolved mating adaptations to implement different sexual strategies depending on features of condition and context such as operational sex ratio, mate value, social norms surrounding sexuality, culture-specific mating system, and ecological variables such as parasite prevalence, sex-specific mortality, food scarcity or abundance, and individual resource demands driven by the number of dependent children (e.g., Gangestad & Buss, 1993; Prall & Scelza, 2020; Schmitt, this volume).

(j) *Sexual strategies are evolved psychological solutions and their behavioral manifestations.* Sexual strategies are evolved solutions to common and sex-differentiated mating problems. They include psychological design features sensitive to multiple features of context that activate or suppress them, information-processing procedures and decision rules, and manifest emotional, cognitive, and behavioral outputs that include attraction, sexual arousal, tactics of attraction, derogation of competitors, mate guarding, and many others.

(k) *Humans have little conscious awareness of their mating psychology.* No conscious awareness about origins, nature, or evolved functions of sexual strategies is implied by SST. Nonetheless, humans may possess partial insight into some aspects of sexual strategies either through observation of others or through introspection about the self, partially driven by the degree to which this awareness facilitates navigating the complex maze of mating challenges posed by the processes of sexual selection.

With these core premises in mind, we review the substantial bodies of empirical findings that have tested different aspects of SST.

Preferential Mate Choice

Evolved mate preferences create deviations from panmixia, or random mating. There exists no known species in which mating is truly panmictic. Although Darwin envisioned females to have evolved mate preferences, it is now clear that males of many species do as well, and in humans both sexes have evolved clear and distinct mate preferences. These become especially important in long-term high-investment mating. Indeed, as predicted by Trivers's theory of parental investment and sexual selection, it is relative investment, not biological sex per se, that influences who does the choosing. Because both sexes invest heavily in long-term mating contexts, we expect both sexes to be extremely choosy. Although women have greater obligatory minimum investment than men, men typically invest much beyond the minimum, and in some cases a man's investment can exceed a woman's, as in cases in which upon divorce the man becomes the primary parent responsible for rearing the child.

Consensually Desired Mate Preferences

Cross-cultural studies bear out the prediction that men and women both have evolved specialized mate preferences. In studies of expressed preferences, both sexes place a priority on qualities such as *good health*, *dependability*, *kindness*, *intelligence*, and *honesty* (Buss, 1989; Lippa, 2007; Walter et al., 2020). Although these universal preferences were not predicted in advance of their discovery, a few evolutionarily informed speculations seem reasonable. Good health likely conveys a robust phenotype, a lack of debilitating diseases, and low parasite and virus loads. High parasite or virus loads could be transmitted to the mate choosers or their children. Moreover, to the degree that good health is heritable, genes for good health can be transmitted to offspring (Buss, 2016). Dependability as a personality trait may convey reliability through adversity and durability of commitment to the pair-bond over time. Kindness may signal a cooperative disposition and an altruistically skewed welfare trade-off ratio. An intelligent mate may aid in solving the many complicated problems a couple and their family face. And an honest mate may signal sexual and emotional fidelity to a partner and a nondeceptive or nonexploitative social strategy. Whether these speculations turn out to be supported or not, they lead to testable predictions that are amenable to empirical testing and potential falsification.

Love as an Evolved Emotion Signaling Willingness to Commit

The emotion of love has been hypothesized to be an evolved mate commitment device (Buss, 1988c, 2018; Frank, 1988). Love is a human universal (Jankowiak, 1997). Across cultures, people sing love songs, elope with a loved one against the wishes of their parents, and report personal anguish and longing when separated from a loved one. Committing reproductively relevant resources to a partner tops the list of most prototypical love acts (Buss, 1988c). This includes giving up romantic relations with others, talking of marriage, and expressing a desire to have children. Reports of experiencing love powerfully predict feelings of subjective commitment, far more than feelings of sexual desire (Gonzaga et al., 2008). Despite widespread views in the social sciences over the past century that love is a European phenomenon of recent origin (e.g., Bloch, 2009), love is prioritized as a key preference in long-term mating in countries ranging from Brazil to Zambia (Buss et al., 1990).

Male-Specific Long-Term Mate Preferences

Several evolution-based predictions were generated in advance of large cross-cultural tests of them. Two centered on men solving the problem of choosing fertile or reproductively valuable women—a preference for *youth* and a preference for *physical attractiveness.* Fertility (immediate chances of conception per act of sex) and reproductive value (age and sex specific future reproductive potential) show pronounced age gradients in women. Female reproductive value peaks in the late teens and fertility peaks in the mid-20s, and both show steep drops after those ages. For most women in most cultures, fertility is low by age 40 and close to zero by age 50 with the onset of menopause. In contrast, men's fertility is more gradually age-graded, and men in their 50s, 60s, and 70s can and sometimes do reproduce.

Empirical studies from well over 50 different cultures, from Brazil to Zambia, show that men strongly prefer youth in long-term mates (Buss, 1989; Conroy-Beam & Buss, 2019; Kenrick & Keefe, 1992). This universal sex difference in age preference holds in cultures that are presumptively monogamous such as Poland, as well as those that permit polygyny such as Zambia (Buss, 1989). The findings remain robust across cultures that vary in religion, ethnicity, political system, and distance from the equator.

As men get older, they prefer women who are increasingly younger than they are. Upon divorce and remarriage, men marry women who are increasingly younger than they are—three years younger at first marriage, five years younger at second marriage, and eight at third marriage (Guttentag & Secord, 1983). Moreover, men who are higher in mate value, such as those of higher status and resources, are more likely than men lacking these qualities to fulfill their mate preferences. A study of Swedes analyzing meticulous records from hundreds of years ago found that men with greater land holdings married women substantially younger than men lacking these resources (Low, 1991). And among the Kipsigis of Kenya, younger brides command a higher bride price than older brides in cows, sheep, and shillings, so only men with large resource holdings can afford to marry them (Borgerhoff Mulder, 1988). A study of men in Korea who purchased foreign brides (n = 45,528) found that men married younger brides, with the age gap reaching 20 years for the older sample of men (Sohn, 2017). In sum, men across cultures and over time have preferences for women who are young and hence fertile, and men who are in positions to implement their preferences do so.

Beauty Is in the Adaptations of the Beholder

According to Symons (1995), appearance conveys a wealth of information about age, developmental history, parasite load, disease history, and health. Because of its strong link to youth, evolutionists have long predicted that men have evolved a preference for physical attractiveness in mates (Symons, 1979; Williams, 1975). Observable cues reliably linked to youth have become part of our evolved standards of female beauty.

A large body of empirical evidence supports this evolutionary theory of female attractiveness, although each discrete element can be empirically tested and new features continue to be discovered (see Stephen & Luoto, this volume). For example, there is substantial evidence that facial femininity, likely caused by high levels of circulating estrogen (a hormone linked to fertility that declines with female age), is a strong predictor of the attractiveness of female faces (Rhodes, 2006). A low waist-to-hip ratio (WHR), another characteristic of youth and fertility, is judged to be more attractiveness than a high WHR (Bovet, 2019; Singh et al., 2010). More recent discoveries include lumbar curvature and limbal ring thickness and darkness, which studies have linked to attractiveness and fertility (e.g., Lewis et al., 2015; Peshek et al., 2011). In short, the evolutionary theory of female attractiveness and its importance in men's mate preferences have received substantial empirical support.

All observable cues are only probabilistically linked to fertility and reproductive value. Most cues, such as symmetry, WHR, and facial femininity have been studied singly (though notable exceptions exist; see Jones, 2018; Mogilski & Welling, 2017, 2018; Perilloux & Cloud, 2019). Much empirical work remains to be conducted to obtain more precise probabilistic estimates about cue validity for each hypothesized attribute and cue combination. Future studies should examine multiple cues simultaneously to evaluate (a) cue validity, that is the strength of each cue's relationship to reproductive value; (b) predictive validity, that is the strength of each cue's correlation with judgments of attractiveness; and (c) whether particular combinations or configurations of cues prove more valid and predictive above and beyond those captured by the sum of individual cues.

Darwin's theory of mate choice sexual selection included both preferences based on functional attributes such as vigor and health that provide direct benefits to the mate chooser as well as aesthetic preferences that may be arbitrary, lacking any direct benefit to the mate chooser (e.g., Prum, 2012). In the case of human judgments of female beauty, the cumulative body of evidence points to the functional rather than arbitrarily aesthetic explanation—preferences are functional when attraction occurs toward cues to fertility and reproductive value.

In addition to choosing a fertile mate, men over evolutionary history repeatedly confronted another adaptive challenge—solving *the problem of paternity uncertainty*. Because fertilization occurs internally within women, men cannot be certain that they are the genetic father of a woman's child. Men who failed to solve this problem would have risked investing valuable resources in the offspring of intrasexual rivals. To compound these costs, the mates of those men would have also devoted their investments into offspring of their rivals. Unless ancestral men were able to solve this problem, it is unlikely that men would have evolved a long-term high-investment mating strategy. Perhaps the difficulty of solving the problem of paternity uncertainty explains why long-term, high-investment mating strategies are so rare in the mammalian world, characterizing only 3–5% of mammals.

In principle, men could have evolved to solve this adaptive problem in a variety of ways. One is through mate guarding (e.g., Buss, 2002; Kaighobadi et al., 2010). Another is through adaptations that displace the sperm of rival males (Starrett & Shackelford, this volume). A third is by selecting a mate likely to remain sexually faithful. An early test of the mate preference solution posited a desire for *chastity* in a potential mate as a solution, defined as someone who has not had sexual intercourse. An empirical test of this hypothesis across 37 cultures failed to provide universal support for it (Buss, 1989). Indeed, a preference for virginity in potential spouses was the most culturally variable preference in the 37-culture study. In mainland China, virginity was viewed as "indispensable" in a mate by both sexes. In Sweden, in contrast, virginity was viewed as "irrelevant" in selecting a spouse. Across cultures, 62% indicated a sex difference, with men valuing virginity in mates more than women in each instance. In 38% of the cultures, no sex difference emerged. These findings were in sharp contrast to the universal sex differences found for youth and physical attractiveness.

Some researchers then hypothesized that virginity before marriage may be less important than likelihood of future fidelity postmarriage (Buss, 2016). Subsequent studies of limited scope found that *sexual fidelity* was indeed highly valued by men, in one study emerging as the top mate preference from among a list of several dozen (Buss & Schmitt, 1993). Other studies discovered that both men and women are attentive to the sexual history of potential spouses, attempting to obtain information about their sexual reputation and number of prior sex partners (Buss, 2016; Mogilski et al., 2014). Because a good predictor of future behavior is past behavior, and number of prior sex partners is a predictor of infidelity likelihood, it's possible that men's inquiries into this information is part of how they deal with the challenge of paternity uncertainty. Nonetheless, at the current time, there is no compelling evidence that men have evolved a universal solution to this problem in the form of a specific mate preference, although it is equally clear that the emotion of sexual jealousy and the intensity with which men guard their mates and prevent them from having sexual contact with rivals are robust phenomena (e.g., Buss, 2000; Buss et al., 1992; Daly et al., 1982; Edlund & Sagarin, 2017; Symons, 1979).

In summary, there is good evidence that men have evolved long-term mate preferences, some of which they have in common with women (e.g., good health and kindness) and some of which are more characteristic of men than women (e.g., prioritizing youth and physical attractiveness). Hypotheses about mate preferences as solutions to the paternity uncertainty problem have not been investigated with sufficient rigor cross-culturally to draw definitive conclusions.

Female-Specific Long-Term Mate Preferences

Due to the heavy demands of prolonged pregnancy and an extremely long childhood characteristic of humans, ancestral women faced the challenge of providing resources for herself and her offspring. Based on studies of traditional cultures, women do much of the provisioning work themselves, contributing as much as 60% of the calories to their families (Hill & Hurtado, 1996). Nonetheless, the later stages of pregnancy limit a woman's resource acquisition abilities, and may impede tasks such as foraging and small-game hunting. The metabolic demands of pregnancy and lactation create greater needs. And during harsh winters and droughts in which gatherable foods are scarce and humans risked starvation, as evidenced by periods of dramatic population shrinkage, having a mate able and willing to provide resources to a woman and her children would have been extremely valuable. Moreover, the key selective force would not have been whether a woman could, in principle, forage for all the resources she and her children need but rather whether having a mate who was willing and able to provide resources would have given her an advantage in survival and reproductive success compared to women who lacked a provisioning mate. Humans, moreover, evolved as omnivores, and meat was a key part of human diet as convergent evidence suggests, such as our massive small intestines and the importance of large-game hunting, which was almost exclusively a male resource acquisition endeavor (Wrangham, 2009).

For these reasons, evolutionists have long hypothesized that women have evolved a specialized mate preference for men who have both the *ability and the willingness to provide resources*. The first large-scale test of this hypothesis received support in the 37-culture study (Buss, 1989), and the findings have been replicated in dozens of other cultures (see Buss & Schmitt, 2019, for summaries). Women also value qualities that are linked to resource acquisition, such as ambition-industriousness and social status, although the sex differences in valuation of these qualities are not as strong or as universal as the preference for good financial prospects.

Wang et al. (2018) asked men and women from China, the United States, and Europe to rate the attractiveness of opposite-sex individuals, experimentally manipulating the physical and economic (i.e., salary) information about the targets. Across all cultures, women were roughly 1,000 times more sensitive to salary when rating men than men were when rating women. An in-depth study of the Hadza, a traditional hunter–gatherer group in Tanzania, found that women placed great importance on a man's foraging abilities, centrally his ability to hunt and provide meat (Marlowe, 2004).

Women face another adaptive challenge in long-term mating which entails solving *the problem of protection*—securing a "bodyguard" who can safeguard them and their children from aggression, including sexual aggression, at the hands of other men. Women's expressed mate preferences for men who are *taller than average, athletic, physically fit*, and *physically formidable* appear designed to help deal with this challenge (see Buss, 2016, for a summary of the evidence). Women also value the psychological quality of *bravery* in the face of danger in long-term mates, which indicates a willingness to offer protection against aggressive conspecifics.

Condition-Dependent Shifts in Mating Strategies

Mate preferences and strategies shift according to personal, social, ecological, and cultural contexts. One context is *personal mate value*. Those who are high in desirability appear to increase their standards, particularly on sex-linked mate preferences. Women high in mate value, for example, become more exacting on many mate preferences (Buss & Shackelford, 2008). They impose higher minimum standards and provide a longer list of desired traits in studies conducted in Croatia, Poland, Canada, and the United States (Pawlowski & Dunbar, 1999; Regan, 1998).

Sex ratio. A key social context affecting mating is *operational sex ratio*—the ratio of men to women in the extant mating pool (Moss & Maner, 2016). Many factors affect this sex ratio, including wars, which kill larger numbers of men than women; risk-taking activities such as physical fights, which more frequently affect men; homicides, in which roughly seven times more men than women die; and different remarriage rates by age, whereby with increasing age women remarry less often than men. Men shift to brief sexual encounters when many women are sexually available because the sex ratio is in their favor and they are therefore better able to satisfy their desire for variety (Pedersen, 1991). Ache men of Paraguay, for example, appear to be highly promiscuous because there are 50% more women than men (Hill & Hurtado, 1997). In the most comprehensive cross-cultural study of sex ratio and sexual strategies, involving 14,059 individuals in 48 nations, people in cultures with a surplus of women were more likely to endorse attitudes and behaviors associated with a short-term mating strategy (Schmitt, 2005). When there is a surplus of men, in contrast, both sexes appear to shift to a long-term mating strategy marked by stable marriages and fewer divorces (Pedersen, 1991). A surplus of males also predicts polyandry—a form of mating in which one woman marries more than one man, often brothers (Starkweather & Hames, 2012).

Ecological parasite prevalence. Because parasites are known to degrade physical appearance, people living in ecologies with a high prevalence of parasites should place a greater value on physical attractiveness in a mate than people living in ecologies with a low prevalence of parasites (Gangestad & Buss, 1993). To test this hypothesis, the prevalence of parasites in 29 cultures was correlated with the importance that the people in those cultures attached to physical attractiveness in a marriage partner. The results confirmed the hypothesis: The greater the parasite prevalence, the more important was physical attractiveness (see also Gangestad et al., 2006). A more recent study of 45 countries, however, failed to replicate this finding (Walter et al., 2020), while simultaneously successfully replicating the above sex differences in mate preferences, so the importance of this ecological variable is currently in question, awaiting further research.

Short-Term Mate Preferences

Because of the large sexual asymmetry in obligatory parental investment, a straightforward set of predictions follows from SST about sex differences in short-term mating. Buss and Schmitt (1993) originally specified four that directly pertain to sex differences in desires for *sexual variety*: (a) men will express greater desire for, or interest in, short-term mates than will women, (b) men will desire larger numbers of sex partners than will women, (c) men will be willing to engage in sexual intercourse after less time has elapsed than will women, and (d) men will relax their mate preference standards in short-term mating contexts more than women. The cross-cultural empirical tests of this body of predictions have provided powerful support for them (e.g., Buss & Schmitt, 2011, table 1; Lippa, 2009; Schmitt, et al., 2017).

Sex differences in desires for sexual variety are among the most robust and well-replicated of all effects in the psychological sciences, with effect sizes often reaching *ds* of +.74. Men more than women desire a larger number of sex partners across time intervals ranging from a month to a lifetime. If married, they are more likely to desire extradyadic sex. Men are more likely to have sexual fantasies that involve short-term sex, multiple sex partners, and sex with strangers. They are more likely to consume pornography depicting short-term sex devoid of context, emotion, and relationships. Men have more permissive attitudes toward casual sex (Petersen & Hyde, 2010) and express a more unrestricted sociosexuality than do women. These findings have been supported by two independent cross-cultural studies, with not a single cultural exception (Lippa, 2009; Schmitt, 2005). Men more than women relax their standards for low-cost short-term matings across an array of mate qualities, including personality, intelligence, and even attractiveness.

Not only are these sex differences robust across cultures, on some measures, the magnitude *increases* in more gender-egalitarian cultures. For example, sex differences in expressed comfort with multiple casual sex partners are higher in Denmark, Norway, Finland, and Iceland than they are in less gender-egalitarian cultures such as Ethiopia, Nigeria, and Swaziland (Schmitt, 2005).

In short, voluminous empirical evidence supports key predictions from SST regarding predicted design features of men's short-term sexual psychology. SST, from its inception, has emphasized that women as well as men have evolved short-term mating strategies. Mathematically, the number of heterosexual short-term matings must be identical for the sexes, given an equal sex ratio in the mating pool. Each time a man has a casual sexual encounter with a woman, a woman is simultaneously having a casual sexual encounter with a man, although they may construe the encounter differently. One person's one-night stand may be another person's failure to pair-bond. Still, the fact is that some women in some circumstances initiate and willingly engage in short-term mating—whether in the form of hooking up, friends with benefits, one-night stands, or extra-pair sexual encounters. And they do so strategically.

Because ancestral women typically could not have dramatically increased their reproductive output from adding more sex partners (unless their regular partners were infertile), a key scientific puzzle has been whether adaptations for short-term mating exist in women, and if so, what their evolved function might be. Buss and Schmitt (1993) proposed four possible adaptive functions of women's short-term mating: immediate resources, good genes, evaluating short-term mates for long-term possibilities, and mate switching.

Although these are qualitatively distinct hypotheses, they are not in competition with each other in a zero-sum scientific contest. Women in circumstances of harsh winters or severe food shortages, for example, might use short-term mating as a desperate measure to obtain calories that might make the difference between survival and starvation for herself and her children. Women in other circumstances, such as those in long-term mateships with men of low genetic quality, might use short-term mating to obtain better genes for her offspring—the hypothesis most vigorously advocated by many evolutionary scientists (e.g., Thornhill &Gangestad, 2008; Gildersleeve et al., 2014). And some women, finding themselves in a cost-inflicting mateship that has not lived up to its initial promise, or when an incrementally better option comes along, might use short-term mating as a mate-switching tactic—a hypothesis advocated by Buss and colleagues (Buss et al., 2017).

What do the empirical tests show? One of the first tests was conducted by Greiling and Buss (2000) who examined predictions from all except the good genes hypothesis in four studies. They examined women's perceptions of an array of benefits from short-term mating, the likelihood of receiving those benefits, the contexts in which short-term mating occurred, and benefit perceptions by women who actively pursued short-term mating. They found some support consistent with the resource acquisition and mate-switching hypotheses, although these findings cannot be viewed as decisive or definitive.

The Good Genes Hypothesis

Most research on the possible functions of women's short-term mating has focused on the good genes hypothesis. The primary source of evidence has been shifts in women's mate preferences at ovulation (Gangestad et al., this volume). The logic of the hypothesis is that some women pursue a dual mating strategy—obtaining investment and resources from one regular committed partner and obtaining superior genes from an affair partner. This hypothesis predicts that women will experience a mate preference shift around the brief window of ovulation, the only time in which a woman can conceive, to prioritize hypothesized "good genes" qualities (e.g., symmetry, masculine features, and physical attractiveness); that these preference shifts will center on short-term rather than long-term mating; and that sexual desire will peak for men other than women's regular partners.

The empirical evidence for these mate preference shifts is mixed. One large meta-analysis reviewed 134 effects from 50 different studies and found some support for the predicted preference shifts, although the effect sizes were small (Gildersleeve et al., 2014).

A subsequent large-scale longitudinal study of 584 women, however, found no correlation between hormonally assessed ovulation status and preference for masculinity in male faces, although it did find that the preference for masculine faces was more pronounced for short-term rather than long-term mateships (Jones et al., 2018). A preregistered study of 157 women did not find women's preferences for masculine bodies increased at ovulation, as predicted by the good genes hypothesis (Junger et al., in press). Based on the studies conducted thus far, empirical support for the hypothesized good genes function of women's short-term mating is weak or mixed (Jones et al., 2019).

The good genes hypothesis has also been questioned on theoretical grounds (Buss & Shackelford, 2008; Buss et al., 2017). First, to the degree that women do elevate their preferences for certain features such as masculinity at ovulation, these finding could be conceptually interpreted as a shift in women's self-perceived mate value rather than a switch to a preference for good genes (Buss & Shackelford, 2008). It is known that women higher in mate value elevate their standards, desiring higher levels for many characteristics in a mate, including hypothesized good genes indicators, good partner qualities, and resources (Buss & Shackelford, 2008). Conceptually, women are higher in mate value when they are ovulating compared to when they are not ovulating, since they are maximally fecund at precisely this time in their cycle. Indirect evidence for ovulation shifts in women's mate value comes from a study of 26,000 online self-reports that tracked ovulation cycles, which found reliable increases in self-perceived desirability around ovulation—possibly a psychological tracking adaptation (Arslan et al., 2018).

Second, because all traits highly valued by women in long-term mating show moderate heritability, including intelligence, emotional stability, dependability, ambition, and industriousness, it is not clear conceptually why masculine and symmetrical features should be singled out as special cases of "good genes" indicators. To take one example, intelligence shows somewhat higher heritability than most other traits, has been hypothesized to be a cardinal good-genes indicator (e.g., Miller, 2001), yet there is no evidence that women elevate the importance they attach to intelligence at ovulation. In short, on both theoretical and empirical grounds, the good genes hypothesis of women's short-term mating, although potentially applicable to a small subset of women pending future tests, can be regarded as questionable theoretically and not well supported empirically. In contrast, an alternative function of women's short-term mating may be more promising—the mate-switching hypothesis.

The Mate-Switching Hypothesis

There are several variants of the mate-switching hypothesis of women's short-term mating. One involves cultivating a *backup mate* should something befall a woman's regular mateship, such as a partner becoming injured, dying in a war, or in probabilistic anticipation of a potential breakup. This has been called the "mate insurance" function of short-term mating (Buss, 2016). Another variant involves having a short-term sexual encounter to make it easier to divest herself of an existing mate. A third variant involves trading up to a partner of higher mate value, or one who offers more benefits and fewer costs than her current partner. A fourth variant involves using short-term mating as a means of assaying her mate value to evaluate whether there might be more desirable and accessible potential partners on the mating market.

Few empirical studies have tested the mate-switching hypothesis directly, but several independent findings converge on its plausibility. First, *relationship dissatisfaction* is one of the most powerful predictors of women's infidelity but not men's infidelity (Glass & Wright, 1992). Second, relationship dissatisfaction predicts women's sexual interest in other men both during the fertile *and* luteal phases of the ovulation cycle (Gangestad et al., 2005). This finding is consistent with infidelity functioning for mate switching, but it cannot be explained by the good genes hypothesis, which predicts interest in other men only during the ovulation phase. Third, *women's reported benefits* of extra-pair mating include (a) finding a partner more desirable than their current partner, (b) making it easier to break up with their current partner, (c) being able to replace their current partner, and (d) discovering other potential partners who might be interested in a relationship (Greiling & Buss, 2000). Fourth, the *contexts* that women report would incline them to infidelity include a partner who cannot hold down a job, meeting someone more successful than their current partner who seems interested in them, and meeting someone who is willing to spend a lot of time with them (Greiling & Buss, 2000).

Fifth, 79% of women who have affairs report *falling in love* with their affair partner, in contrast to only a third of men who have affairs (Glass & Wright, 1992)—and love is an emotion hypothesized to come online in long-term mating contexts (Buss, 1988c, 2018). If the primary function of female infidelity were to secure superior genes from an affair partner, falling in love would be both superfluous and costly because it might interfere with securing continued investment from a woman's regular partner.

Sixth, the *qualities women want in an affair partner* are similar to those they want in a long-term committed mate (Greiling & Buss, 2000; Kenrick et al., 1990). These include a minimum 70th percentile rank on being dependable, emotionally stable, successful, honest, intelligent, mature, and unselfish. These six clusters of empirical findings are consistent with the mate-switching explanation for female infidelity but appear difficult to explain with the good genes hypothesis.

Moreover, one meta-analysis of misattributed paternity reported a rate of only 1.7% (Anderson, 2006). A second meta-analysis reported a rate between 3.1% and 3.7% (Voracek et al., 2008). And a large-scale study in Germany found a lower nonpaternity rate of 0.94% (Wolf et al., 2012). It is possible, of course, that misattributed paternity rates were higher in ancestral environments, and studies of more traditional cultures may shed light on this issue. For instance, among the semi-nomadic Himba of Namibia, 23% of children from arranged marriages, but none from "love" marriages, were cases of misattributed paternity (Scelza, 2011). The majority of women appear to be securing both genes and investment from the same partner, which poses an empirical problem for the dual mating strategy hypothesis.

The good genes and mate-switching hypotheses are not mutually exclusive. A small minority of women in some contexts could successfully implement a dual mating strategy and secure good genes from an affair partner, while other women who have affairs are implementing one or another variant of mate switching. I suggest that the mate-switching hypothesis provides a more parsimonious explanation for the function of infidelity for most women (for a fuller elaboration of hypotheses about mate-switching adaptations, including its inputs, decision rules, and outputs, see Buss et al., 2017).

Additional Functions of Short-Term Mating for Women

The mate-switching and good genes hypotheses do not exclude other possible functions of female short-term mating. Other candidates include securing immediate resources or protection from affair partners (Greiling & Buss, 2000; Symons, 1979), instilling confusion about paternity to prevent infanticide or to elicit resources from multiple mates (Hrdy, 1979), securing a fertility backup in the event that the regular mate is infertile, seeking revenge on a current mate as a means of deterring his future infidelity, and screening men for qualities desired in a potential long-term mate (Greiling & Buss, 2000). Although these alternative hypotheses for female short-term mating have some supporting evidence in delimited circumstances (Buss, 2016; Scelza & Prall, 2018), they cannot explain the panoply of findings that support the mate-switching hypothesis regarding female infidelity. The key point is that mate switching may be the most frequent or primary function of female infidelity, in contrast to the common assumption among evolutionary scientists that securing good genes is the primary function.

Sexual Selection Through Mate Competition

Although human mating research guided by Darwin's sexual selection theory has focused on mate preferences, much research has also focused on the second causal process of sexual selection—intrasexual competition.

Contest Competition

Darwin's initial theory focused on contest competition (i.e., physical battles, typically among males, the outcomes of which led to mating success for the victors). As Darwin described, "the greater size, strength, courage, pugnacity, and energy of man, in comparison with woman, were acquired during primeval times, and have subsequently been augmented, chiefly through the contests of rival males for the possession of the females" (Darwin, 1871, p. 605). Some evolutionary scholars, in contrast, have suggested that contest competition has played little role in humans (e.g., Schacht & Kramer, 2019). They point to lower levels of sexual dimorphism in humans compared to many other primate species on attributes such as size, height, and weight. More recently, the study of contest competition among humans has seen a resurgence that may overturn conventional wisdom among evolutionary scholars (Puts et al., this volume).

One source of evidence centers on sexual dimorphism—sex differences in features of body morphology. Sexual dimorphism can be caused by several evolutionary forces, including sex differences in mate preferences and division of labor between the sexes. If women prefer to mate with tall men, for example, and men do not impose an analogous selection pressure on women, the sexes will diverge in height over evolutionary time. If men specialize in large-game hunting and women in gathering and small-game hunting, then qualities that lead to success in these sex-differentiated endeavors can create sexual dimorphism as well. Contest competition also creates sexual dimorphism, and species in which contest competition is intense, from elephant seals to chimpanzees, show marked sexual dimorphism. Elephant seal males, for example, weigh four times as much as females—a species marked by harem polygyny and markedly higher reproductive variance among males than among females (Le Boeuf, 1974).

Puts and his colleagues argue that convergent findings from multiple sources support the hypothesis that humans have experienced a long and intense evolutionary history of sexual selection via contest competition (Puts, 2010; Puts et al., this volume). They examined more than a dozen traits using multiple criteria for evaluation: (a) Does the trait show sexual dimorphism? (b) Does the trait emerge at puberty when the sexes enter reproductive competition? (c) Is the trait linked with mating success?

It is true that humans show comparatively low levels of sexual dimorphism on overall body mass—males exceed females by only 15–20%. This global index, however, overlooks specific components of sexual dimorphism such as muscle mass. Men have 61% more muscle mass than women, and 75% more upper-body muscle mass (Puts et al., this volume). This translates into the average young man having more upper-body muscle mass than 99.9% of same-age young women. The male bias in upper-body muscle mass is especially pronounced in elements conducive to punching, such as forward arm thrusting, shoulder flexion, and power generated by elbow extension (Puts et al., this volume).

Other large sex differences include proclivity to physical aggression, same-sex homicides of which 95% are male-on-male, coalitional aggression (e.g., gangs and intergroup warfare), throwing velocity, craniofacial structure in which men's greater robustness appears to function as a defense against punches, displays of physical prowess, sports that involve direct one-on-one combat such as boxing or mixed martial arts, and many others. Men more than women appear to spontaneously assess whether they are more physically formidable compared to same-sex others. Although no single element of this sexually dimorphic evidence provides definitive confirmation of the importance of human contest competition as a force of sexual selection, Puts et al. (this volume) argue that a history of contest competition is the most parsimonious explanation of the entire array. Over the next decade, the field can anticipate more empirical research devoted to this neglected aspect of Darwin's theory of sexual selection.

Tactics of Attraction and Derogation of Competitors

The mate preferences of one sex should determine the dimensions along which members of the opposite sex compete. If men and women strongly prefer kind and dependable mates, both sexes are predicted to display acts of kindness and dependability in their attraction tactics. If there are sex-differentiated mate preferences, theory predicts sex-differentiated attraction tactics. These predictions have been supported. Studies of undergraduate and newlywed couples support the predictions that display of kindness, helping, and altruism figure heavily in the early stages of tactics of attraction (Buss, 1988a; Bleske-Rechek & Buss, 2006; Schmitt & Buss, 1996). For example, both sexes show sympathy for the potential partner's troubles and make offers to help. Both sexes derogate their mating competitors by implying that they are unkind, mean, selfish, and enjoy "using" members of the opposite sex (Buss & Dedden, 1990; Schmitt & Buss, 1996). Both sexes impugn their rival's intelligence, mentioning that the rival is stupid or an "airhead," or arranging to make the rival seem dumb. Both sexes prioritize "good health" in potential mates, so both display tactics of attraction such as showing good hygiene and derogate their rivals by mentioning that they have a sexually transmitted disease (Buss & Dedden, 1990). Sense of humor is highly valued by both sexes, and both sexes display humor roughly equally as tactics of attraction (Schmitt & Buss, 1996).

Predictions about sex-differentiated tactics of attraction are also strongly supported. Men more than women display resources, boast about their resources, and showcase their ambition as tactics of attraction (Schmitt & Buss, 1996). They also belittle their mating rivals on these dimensions, telling a prospective mate the rival has no money, lacks drive or ambition, or drives a cheap old car. Women more than men value signs that a prospective mate will offer protection, and men's tactics of attraction follow suit. While showing off their own strength, men also impugn a rival's strength, attempt to outshine him in athletic contests, physically dominate him in front of the prospective mate, and call him cowardly.

Men more than women prioritize physical attractiveness in mate preferences, and women's tactics of attraction and competitor derogation follow suit. Women more than men wear facial makeup, report spending more than an hour making their appearance attractive, diet to improve their figures, and groom and style their hair carefully (Buss, 1988a). More than men, women derogate their mating rivals by making fun of their appearance, laughing at their hair, mentioning that the rival is fat or ugly, making fun of the size or shape of the rival's body, and mentioning that the rival's thighs are unusually heavy (Buss & Dedden, 1990; Krems, 2021; Schmitt & Buss, 1996).

Men more than women prefer sexual fidelity in a long-term mate, and women's tactics of attraction and competitor derogation appear to embody these preferences. In long-term mating, women are especially likely to show signs of sexual exclusiveness and are more likely than men to call rivals a slut, promiscuous, or "loose" (i.e., having had many previous sex partners), and mention that their rival cannot remain loyal to one man (Buss & Dedden, 1990; Krems, 2021; Schmitt & Buss, 1996).

In summary, tactics of attraction and competitor derogation are well-predicted by mate preferences. Both sexes compete to embody the qualities consensually desired in mates, and show sex-differentiated competition tactics precisely in the domains in which there exist sex-differentiated mate preferences. Confirmation of the hypothesis that patterns of mate competition can be well predicted by expressed mate preferences supports the close causal connection between the two major components of Darwin's sexual selection theory.

Mate Poaching and Mate Guarding

The causal processes of sexual selection do not end once a mateship has formed. Intrasexual competition continues in the form of mate poachers who vie to lure a mate away, either for a temporary liaison or for a more permanent mateship (Schmitt & Buss, 2001). Existing partners engage in mate retention or mate guarding efforts to combat mate poachers and deter defection from their regular mate (Buss, 1988b; Buss & Shackelford, 1997; Kaighobadi et al., 2010). Mate poachers attempt to embody the mate preferences of their targets more fully than the target's existing partner. For both sexes, this includes displaying higher mate value on both consensually desired and sex-differentiated mate preferences. Mate guarders attempt to fend off mate poachers. For men, these involve tactics as diverse as vigilance, physically assaulting a mate poacher, displaying more extravagant kindnesses and resources toward their mate, or sequestering her. For women, these involve tactics such as escalating her vigilance, displaying renewed kindnesses, doubling her efforts to enhance her physical appearance, and performing sexual favors. The two causal processes of sexual selection, in short, begin with the initial stages of mate attraction and mate competition, continue after a mateship has been initiated in forms such as mate poaching, mate guarding, and mate switching, and even continue in the aftermath of a breakup in forms such as stalking and efforts to entice a former mate back for sexual encounters or a more permanent mateship (Buss, 2021).

Sexual Coercion and Sexual Selection: Unresolved Issues

The nonhuman animal scientific literature is replete with studies of sexual coercion—instances in which males use tactics that appear to bypass female choice (Arnqvist & Rowe, 2005). Examples of these tactics include both indirect and direct methods (Thompson & Alvarado, 2012). Two indirect tactics are *sequestration* (i.e., the male enforces a separation of the female from other males) and *punishment* of the female for interacting with other males. Three direct tactics are *intimidation* (i.e., aggression toward the female for resisting mating), *harassment* (i.e., repeated efforts to mate with a reluctant or resisting female, creating a war of attrition that is sometimes asymmetric), and *forced copulation* (i.e., the use of physical restraint or violence to obtain sexual intercourse).

Smuts and Smuts (1993) proposed that sexual coercion should be regarded as a third form of sexual selection, supplementing the two traditional Darwinian processes of preferential mate choice and intrasexual competition. Among evolutionary biologists, Thornhill and Palmer (2000) endorsed this view. Some evolutionary theoreticians argued that all sexual selection ultimately stems from preferential mate choice creating mating biases, directly and sometimes indirectly (Cunningham & Birkhead, 1998). According to this view, females preferring to mate with some males while rejecting others could select for male tactics to overcome female resistance. So male sexual coercion, according this view, would be a tactic evolving due to female mate choice for resisting sex with a subset of males. Other evolutionary biologists argued that all forms of sexual selection ultimately stemmed from competition among members of one sex for matings with the opposite sex (e.g., Andersson & Iwasa, 1996). In this framing, sexual coercion would be one form of intrasexual competition, along with other forms such as contest competition, scramble competition, and sperm competition. Both views may be correct, and may be somewhat different framings of the same issues.

Watson-Capps (2009) suggested that the key issue is *mating bias*. In traditional female mate choice, mating bias occurs when females select one or a subset of mates possessing desirable traits, and in consequence, that subset of males experiences increased mating success. In sexual coercion, mating bias occurs when a subset of males increases their mating success by overcoming female resistance to their mating advances. If females experience harm from sexual coercion, either through bodily injury, reputational damage, or siring suboptimal offspring as a consequence of being inseminated by suboptimal males, then sexual coercion could be regarded as a form of male–male competition, but one that differs in kind from other forms of intrasexual competition such as contest competition, scramble competition, resource acquisition competition, or sperm competition.

In short, sexual coercion is often intimately intertwined with the Darwinian processes of preferential mate choice and intrasexual competition. The particular ways in which it is intertwined vary according to different contexts, such as whether the act of coercion harms the female (or even creates a fitness benefit in the form of successfully coercive sons).

A key issue is whether evolution by selection favored distinct male strategies of sexual coercion in humans, regardless of how it is framed vis-à-vis sexual selection theory. This issue is highly contentious. On one side, some hypothesize that human males have evolved specific adaptations to rape females (Thornhill & Palmer, 2000). On the other side, some hypothesize that human males have not evolved rape-specific adaptations but rather that rape is a nonadaptive or even maladaptive by-product of other male adaptations, such as a desire for sexual variety, a willingness to have impersonal sex, and the use of aggression to obtain a variety of ends (Symons, 1979; Thornhill & Palmer, 2000).

Unfortunately, little research has been devoted directly to adjudicating between these competing hypotheses. Extant studies refute one version of the rape adaptation view, the so-called *mate deprivation hypothesis* (Buss, 2021). According to this hypothesis, men who lack sexual opportunity as a consequence of being disfavored by women (or failing to embody women's mate preferences) use force as a last-ditch tactic to avoid total matelessness. Studies of convicted rapists show that they are disproportionately men of low socioeconomic status, which would seem to favor the mate deprivation hypothesis. This support, however, is illusory (Buss, 2021). Convicted rapists are not representative of all rapists, and men with money and means are less likely to be accused when they have committed acts of sexual coercion, and when accused, often use their resources to hire high-priced lawyers to escape conviction. They silence victims with monetary settlements that require nondisclosure, so many instances of sexual coercion are never revealed. Moreover, several studies suggest that men who are high in status and successful in consensual mating contexts are more, not less, likely to also use sexual coercion (e.g., Lalumiere et al., 1996). Although some mate-deprived men undoubtedly sometimes rape, the weight of the evidence falsifies a strict version of the mate deprivation component of the rape-adaptation hypothesis.

The evidence for other versions of the rape adaptation hypothesis, such as marital rape in the context of sperm competition (e.g., Thornhill & Palmer, 2000), has received some empirical support, but the evidence is largely equivocal or inconclusive (Buss, 2021). Most predictions from the rape adaptation hypothesis have yet to be tested. Moreover, it is proving difficult to identify critical tests that can distinguish between the adaptation versus by-product hypotheses. Some have argued, for example, that the finding that rape victims are disproportionately concentrated among young, and hence fertile, women is evidence consistent with the rape adaptation hypothesis (Thornhill & Palmer, 2000). However, the fact that men are attracted to such women in regular consensual mating contexts means that this finding is equally consistent with the by-product hypothesis (Thornhill & Palmer, 2000). No specialized rape adaptation needs be invoked to explain the finding. Future empirical research may be better able to adjudicate between the competing hypotheses about sexual coercion.

Regardless of the origins of sexual coercion, there is consensus that sexual coercion has recurred throughout human history, and likely has been a harm inflicted on women over deep time. Biblical writings from thousands of years ago, ancient paintings depicting rape, ethnographies of traditional societies descripting episodes of rape, and even circumstantial molecular evidence of genetic sweeps occurring in Mongolia, Ireland, and Norway all converge on the deep-time history of human rape (Buss, 2021). Consequently, it is reasonable to hypothesize that women have evolved defenses to prevent becoming a victim of male sexual coercion (e.g., Buss, 2021; Smuts & Smuts, 1993; Thornhill & Palmer, 2000; Wilson & Mesnick, 1997). If sexual coercion has inflicted fitness costs on women over deep time, as seems likely, it would be astonishing if women had not evolved defenses against it.

Hypotheses about women's evolved defenses are many in number and diverse in nature (Buss, 2021). They include adaptations to form social alliances with kin, female friends, male friends, or male mates who function as "bodyguards"; specialized rape fears that motivate avoidance of sexually vulnerable situations and sexually aggressive men; fighting, appeasing, fleeing, and refuging when confronted with an attacker; tonic immobility when entrapped with no escape possible; and concealment in the aftermath to avoid reputational damage (Buss, 2021). Women's defenses presumably have evolved through the mate choice component of sexual selection, function to resist mating with nonpreferred men, and have the effect of creating a mating bias in the reproductive success of males.

Sexual Selection is the Key to Human Mating Strategies

Darwin's theory of sexual selection, with modern elaborations unknown in Darwin's day, is the most important overarching framework for understanding human mating strategies. There exist no alternative theoretical frameworks that better explain observed patterns of human mating. Although preferential mate choice was initially proposed to operate primarily within females and intrasexual competition primarily within males, both causal processes operate strongly within both sexes in the human case. In long-term mating, both sexes typically invest heavily in offspring, so both sexes are predicted to be choosy or discriminating. And both sexes compete with members of their own sex for desirable members of the other sex.

The forms of intrasexual competition are more variable and complex than Darwin envisioned. In addition to physical battles of *contest competition*, other forms include *scramble competition for locating mates*; *competition to satisfy the mate preferences of the opposite sex*, such as resources, social status, beauty, and dependability that are attractive to mates (Buss, 1988a); *endurance rivalry*, which involves the ability to sustain mating effort over long periods of time (Andersson & Iwasa, 1996); *sperm competition*, in which the sperm from two or more males compete within the female reproductive tract for access to the valuable egg (Parker, 1970; Shackelford & Goetz, 2007); and possibly *sexual coercion*, in which nonpreferred males displace preferred males, leading to sexually selected defenses in women to prevent males from bypassing their mate choice (Andersson & Iwasa, 1996; Arnqvist & Rowe, 2005; Parker, 1979).

Intrasexual competition also takes on a unique form in the human case as a consequence of the evolution of language. Both sexes use language to attract mates, including displays of humor, charm, or verbal prowess. Humans also use language to derogate their rivals, rendering them less attractive to target mates through slings and arrows of insults and character-impugning reputational damage (Buss & Dedden, 1990; Krems, 2021).

In a scientific era of replication crisis, sex differences in the components of human mating strategies are among the most robust and replicable of all findings in the social sciences. Sex differences in mate preferences, for example, remain replicable through multiple data sources that include self-reported preferences, studies of online dating searches, studies of sex differences in response rates to preferred qualities of online dates, attraction tactics used by the opposite sex, derogation tactics used to lower the desirability of mating competitors, patterns of dating deception, tactics of mate poaching, predictors of mate guarding, causes of divorce, and many others (Buss & Schmitt, 2019). Research on the evolution of human mating is theoretically robust and empirically cumulative.

Sexual selection theory, initially advanced by Darwin more than 150 years ago, continues to bear scientific fruit in human mating research. It leads to novel discoveries, such as the use of language in intrasexual mate competition. It illuminates areas not envisioned by Darwin, such as sexual coercion and women's defenses against male attempts to bypass female mate choice. And it provides heuristic value, guiding scientists to important domains of hypothesis generation and empirical study. Sexual selection theory, so important in understanding the mating of all sexually reproducing species, is no less important in understanding the mating strategies of our own species.

References

Anderson, K. (2006). How well does paternity confidence match actual paternity? Evidence from worldwide nonpaternity rates. *Current Anthropology, 47*(3), 513–520.

Andersson, M., & Iwasa, Y. (1996). Sexual selection. *Trends in Ecology & Evolution, 11*(2), 53–58.

Arnqvist, G., & Rowe, L. (2005). *Sexual conflict*. Princeton University Press.

Bateman, A.J. (1948). Intrasexual selection in Drosophila. *Heredity, 2*, 349–368.

Arslan, R. C., Schilling, K. M., Gerlach, T. M., & Penke, L. (2018). Using 26,000 diary entries to show ovulatory changes in sexual desire and behavior. *Journal of Personality and Social Psychology.*

Bleske-Rechek, A., & Buss, D. M. (2006). Sexual strategies pursued and mate attraction tactics deployed. *Personality and Individual Differences, 40*(6), 1299–1311.

Bloch, R. H. (2009). *Medieval misogyny and the invention of western romantic love*. University of Chicago Press.

Borgerhoff Mulder, M., & Turke, P. (1988). Kipsigis bridewealth payments. *Human Reproductive Behaviour: A Darwinian Perspective, 7*(3), 65–82.

Bovet, J. (2019). Evolutionary theories and men's preferences for women's waist-to-hip ratio: Which hypotheses remain? A systematic review. *Frontiers in Psychology, 10*, Article 1221.

Buss, D. M. (1988a). The evolution of human intrasexual competition: Tactics of mate attraction. *Journal of Personality and Social Psychology, 54*(4), 616–628.

Buss, D. M. (1988b). From vigilance to violence: Tactics of mate retention in American undergraduates. *Ethology and Sociobiology, 9*(5), 291–317.

Buss, D. M. (1988c). Love acts. *The evolutionary biology of love*. In R. J. Sternberg & M. L. Barnes (Eds.), *Psychology of love* (pp. 100–118). Yale University Press.

Buss, D. M. (1989). Sex differences in human mate preferences: Evolutionary hypotheses tested in 37 cultures. *Behavioral and Brain Sciences, 12*(1), 1–14.

Buss D. M. (1995). Psychological sex differences: Origins through sexual selection. *American Psychologist,* 50, 164–168.

Buss, D. M. (2002). Human mate guarding. *Neuroendocrinology Letters, 23*(4), 23–29.

Buss, D. M. (2000. *The dangerous passion: Why jealousy is a necessary as love and sex*. Free Press.

Buss, D.M. (2016). *The evolution of desire: Strategies of human mating*. New York: Basic Books

Buss, D. M. (2018). The evolution of love in humans. In R. J. Sternberg & K. Sternberg (Eds.), *The new psychology of love (pp. 42-63)*. Cambridge University Press.

Buss, D. M. (2021). *When men behave badly: The hidden roots of sexual deception, harassment, and assault*. Little, Brown Sparks.

Buss, D. M., Abbott, M., Angleitner, A., Asherian, A., Biaggio, A., Blanco-Villasenor, A., Bruchon-Schweitzer, M., Ch'U, H-Y., Czapinski, J., Deraad, B., Ekehammar, B., El Lohamy, N., Fioravanti, M., Georgas, J., Gjerde, P., Guttman, R., Hazan, F., Iwawaki, S., Janakiramaiah, N. . . . Yang, K-S. (1990). International preferences in selecting mates: A study of 37 cultures. *Journal of Cross-Cultural Psychology, 21*, 5–47.

Buss, D. M., & Dedden, L. A. (1990). Derogation of competitors. *Journal of Social and Personal Relationships, 7*(3), 395–422.

Buss, D. M., Goetz, C., Duntley, J. D., Asao, K., & Conroy-Beam, D. (2017). The mate switching hypothesis. *Personality and Individual Differences, 104*, 143–149.

Buss, D. M., Larsen, R. J., Westen, D., & Semmelroth, J. (1992). Sex differences in jealousy: Evolution, physiology, and psychology. *Psychological Science, 3*(4), 251–256.

Buss, D. M., & Schmitt, D. P. (1993). Sexual strategies theory: An evolutionary perspective on human mating. *Psychological Review, 100*(2), 204–232.

Buss, D. M., & Schmitt, D. P. (2011). Evolutionary psychology and feminism. *Sex Roles, 64*(9–10), 768–787.

Buss, D. M., & Schmitt, D. P. (2019). Mate preferences and their behavioral manifestations. *Annual Review of Psychology, 70*, 77–110.

Buss, D. M., & Shackelford, T. K. (1997). From vigilance to violence: Mate retention tactics in married couples. *Journal of Personality and Social Psychology, 72*(2), 346.

Buss, D. M., & Shackelford, T. K. (2008). Attractive women want it all: Good genes, economic investment, parenting proclivities, and emotional commitment. *Evolutionary Psychology, 6*(1), 134–146.

Campbell, B. G. (Ed.). (1972). *Sexual selection and the descent of man, 1871-1971*. Aldine.

Conroy-Beam, D., & Buss, D. M. (2019). Why is age so important in human mating? Evolved age preferences and their influences on multiple mating behaviors. *Evolutionary Behavioral Sciences, 13*(2), 127–157.

Cunningham, E. J. A., & Birkhead, T. R. (1998). Sex roles and sexual selection. *Animal Behaviour, 56*(6), 1311–1321.

Daly, M., Wilson, M., & Weghorst, S. J. (1982). Male sexual jealousy. *Ethology and sociobiology, 3*(1), 11–27.

Darwin, C. (1859). *On the origin of species by means of natural selection*. London: Murray.

Darwin, C. (1860). Letter 2743 of Darwin Correspondence Project. Cambridge University. http://www.darwinproject.ac.uk/entry 2743

Darwin, C. (1871). *The descent of man and selection in relation to sex*. Murray.

Darwin, C. (1872). *The expression of the emotions in man and animals*. Murray.

Edlund, J. E., & Sagarin, B. J. (2017). Sex differences in jealousy: A 25-year retrospective. In J. M. Olson (Ed.), *Advances in experimental social psychology* (Vol. 55, pp. 259–302). Academic Press.

Fisher, R. A. (1958). *The genetical theory of natural selection*. Clarendon Press. (Original work published 1930)

Frank, R. H. (1988). *Passions within reason: The strategic role of the emotions*. W.W. Norton.

Gangestad, S. W., & Buss, D. M. (1993). Pathogen prevalence and human mate preferences. *Ethology and Sociobiology, 14*(2), 89–96.

Gangestad, S. W., Haselton, M. G., & Buss, D. M. (2006). Evolutionary foundations of cultural variation: Evoked culture and mate preferences. *Psychological Inquiry, 17*(2), 75–95.

Gildersleeve, K., Haselton, M. G., & Fales, M. R. (2014). Do women's mate preferences change across the ovulatory cycle? A meta-analytic review. *Psychological Bulletin, 140*(5), 1205.

Glass, S. P., & Wright, T. L. (1992). Justifications for extramarital relationships: The association between attitudes, behaviors, and gender. *Journal of Sex Research, 29*(3), 361–387.

Gonzaga, G. C., Haselton, M. G., Smurda, J., Davies, M., & Poore, J. C. (2008). Love, desire, and the suppression of thoughts of romantic alternatives. *Evolution and Human Behavior, 29*(2), 119–126.

Gowaty, P. A., Kim, Y.-K., & Anderson, W. W. (2012). No evidence of sexual selection in a repetition of Bateman's classic study of Drosophila melanogaster. *Proceedings of the National Academy of Sciences, 109*(29), 11740–11745.

Greiling, H., & Buss, D. M. (2000). Women's sexual strategies: The hidden dimension of extra-pair mating. *Personality and Individual Differences, 28*(5), 929–963.

Guttentag, M., & Secord, P. F. (1983). *Too many women?: The sex ratio question*. SAGE Publications, Incorporated.

Hill, K., & Hurtado, A. M. (1996). *Ache life history: The ecology and demography of a foraging people*. Routledge.

Hrdy, S. B. (1979). Infanticide among animals: A review, classification, and examination of the implications for the reproductive strategies of females. *Ethology and Sociobiology, 1*(1), 13–40.

Janicke, T., Häderer, I. K., Lajeunesse, M. J., & Anthes, N. (2016). Darwinian sex roles confirmed across the animal kingdom. *Science Advances, 2*(2), Article e1500983.

Jankowiak, W. (Ed.). (1997). *Romantic passion: A universal experience?* Columbia University Press.

Jonason, P. K., & Buss, D. M. (2012). Avoiding entangling commitments: Tactics for implementing a short-term mating strategy. *Personality and Individual Differences, 52*(5), 606–610.

Jones, A. L. (2018). The influence of shape and colour cue classes on facial health perception. *Evolution and Human Behavior, 39*(1), 19–29.

Jones, B. C., Hahn, A. C., Fisher, C. I., Wang, H., Kandrik, M., Han, C., Fasolt, V., Morrison, D., Lee, A. J., Holzleitner, I. J., O'Shea, K. J., Roberts, S. C., Little, A. C., & DeBruine, L. M. (2018). No compelling evidence that preferences for facial masculinity track changes in women's hormonal status. *Psychological Science, 29*(6), 996–1005.

Jones, B. C., Hahn, A. C., & DeBruine, L. M. (2019). Ovulation, sex hormones, and women's mating psychology. *Trends in Cognitive Sciences, 23*(1), 51–62.

Kaighobadi, F., Shackelford, T. K., & Buss, D. M. (2010). Spousal mate retention in the newlywed year and three years later. *Personality and Individual Differences, 48*(4), 414–418.

Kenrick, D. T., & Keefe, R. C. (1992). Age preferences in mates reflect sex differences in human reproductive strategies. *Behavioral and Brain Sciences, 15*(1), 75–91.

Kenrick, D. T., Sadalla, E. K., Groth, G., & Trost, M. R. (1990). Evolution, traits, and the stages of human courtship: Qualifying the parental investment model. *Journal of Personality, 58*(1), 97–116.

Krems, J. A. (2021). Verbal derogation among women. In T. K. Shackelford & V. A. Shackelford (Eds.), *Encyclopedia of evolutionary psychological science* (pp. 8358–8359) Cham Springer.

Lalumière, M. L., Chalmers, L. J., Quinsey, V. L., & Seto, M. C. (1996). A test of the mate deprivation hypothesis of sexual coercion. *Ethology and Sociobiology, 17*(5), 299–318.

Le Boeuf, B. J. (1974). Male-male competition and reproductive success in elephant seals. *American Zoologist, 14*(1), 163–176.

Lewis, D. M., Russell, E. M., Al-Shawaf, L., & Buss, D. M. (2015). Lumbar curvature: A previously undiscovered standard of attractiveness. *Evolution and Human Behavior, 36*(5), 345–350.

Lippa, R. A. (2007). The preferred traits of mates in a cross-national study of heterosexual and homosexual men and women: An examination of biological and cultural influences. *Archives of Sexual Behavior, 36*(2), 193–208.

Lippa, R. A. (2009). Sex differences in sex drive, sociosexuality, and height across 53 nations: Testing evolutionary and social structural theories. *Archives of Sexual Behavior, 38*(5), 631–651.

Low, B. S. (1991). Reproductive life in nineteenth century Sweden: an evolutionary perspective on demographic phenomena. *Ethology and Sociobiology, 12*(6), 411–448.

Marlowe, F. W. (2004). Mate preferences among Hadza hunter-gatherers. *Human Nature, 15*(4), 365–376.

Miller, G. (2001). *The mating mind: How sexual choice shaped the evolution of human nature*. Anchor.

Mogilski, J. K. (2020). Parental investment theory. In T. K. Shackelford (Ed.), *The SAGE handbook of evolutionary psychology*. SAGE.

Mogilski, J. K., Wade, T. J., & Welling, L. L. (2014). Prioritization of potential mates' history of sexual fidelity during a conjoint ranking task. *Personality and Social Psychology Bulletin, 40*(7), 884–897.

Mogilski, J. K., & Welling, L. L. (2017). The relative importance of sexual dimorphism, fluctuating asymmetry, and color cues to health during evaluation of potential partners' facial photographs. *Human Nature, 28*(1), 53–75.

Mogilski, J. K., & Welling, L. L. (2018). The relative contribution of jawbone and cheekbone prominence, eyebrow thickness, eye size, and face length to evaluations of facial masculinity and attractiveness: A conjoint data-driven approach. *Frontiers in Psychology, 9*, Article 2428.

Moss, J. H., & Maner, J. K. (2016). Biased sex ratios influence fundamental aspects of human mating. *Personality and Social Psychology Bulletin, 42*(1), 72–80.

Parker, G. A. (1970). Sperm competition and its evolutionary consequences in the insects. *Biological Reviews, 45*(4), 525–567.

Parker, G. A. (1979). Sexual selection and sexual conflict. *Sexual selection and reproductive competition in insects, 123*, 166.

Pawłowski, B., & Dunbar, R. I. (1999). Impact of market value on human mate choice decisions. *Proceedings of the Royal Society of London. Series B: Biological Sciences, 266*(1416), 281–285.

Pedersen, F. A. (1991). Secular trends in human sex ratios. *Human Nature, 2*(3), 271–291.

Perilloux, C., & Cloud, J. M. (2019). Mate-by-numbers: Budget, mating context, and sex predict preferences for facial and bodily traits. *Evolutionary Psychological Science, 5*(3), 294–299.

Petersen, J. L., & Hyde, J. S. (2010). A meta-analytic review of research on gender differences in sexuality, 1993–2007. *Psychological Bulletin, 136*(1), 21–38.

Peshek, D., Semmaknejad, N., Hoffman, D., & Foley, P. (2011). Preliminary evidence that the limbal ring influences facial attractiveness. *Evolutionary Psychology, 9*(2), 147470491100900201.

Prall, S. P., & Scelza, B. A. (2020). Resource demands reduce partner discrimination in Himba women. *Evolutionary Human Sciences, 2*, Article E45. https://doi.org/10.1017/ehs.2020.43

Prum, R. O. (2012). Aesthetic evolution by mate choice: Darwin's really dangerous idea. *Philosophical Transactions of the Royal Society B: Biological Sciences, 367*(1600), 2253–2265.

Puts, D. A. (2010). Beauty and the beast: Mechanisms of sexual selection in humans. *Evolution and Human Behavior, 31*(3), 157–175. https://doi.org/10.1016/j.evolhumbehav.2010.02.005

Scelza, B. A. (2011). Female choice and extra-pair paternity in a traditional human population. *Biology Letters, 7*, 889–891. 788–991. https://doi.org/10.1098/rsbl.2011.0478

Scelza, B. A., & Prall, S. P. (2018). Partner preferences in the context of concurrency: what Himba want in formal and informal partners. *Evolution and Human Behavior, 39*(2), 212–219.

Schacht, R., & Kramer, K. L. (2019). Are we monogamous? A review of the evolution of pair-bonding in humans and its contemporary variation cross-culturally. *Frontiers in Ecology and Evolution, 7*(230). https://doi.org/10.3389/fevo.2019.00230

Schmitt, D. P. (2005). Sociosexuality from Argentina to Zimbabwe: A 48-nation study of sex, culture, and strategies of human mating. *Behavioral and Brain Sciences, 28*(2), 247–275.

Schmitt, D. P., & Buss, D. M. (1996). Strategic self-promotion and competitor derogation: Sex and context effects on the perceived effectiveness of mate attraction tactics. *Journal of Personality and Social Psychology, 70*(6), 1185–1204.

Schmitt, D. P., & Buss, D. M. (2001). Human mate poaching: Tactics and temptations for infiltrating existing mateships. *Journal of Personality and Social Psychology, 80*(6), 894–917

Schmitt, D. P., Long, A. E., McPhearson, A., O'Brien, K., Remmert, B., & Shah, S. H. (2017). Personality and gender differences in global perspective. *International Journal of Psychology, 52*, 45–56.

Shackelford, T. K., & Goetz, A. T. (2007). Adaptation to sperm competition in humans. *Current Directions in Psychological Science, 16*(1), 47–50.

Singh, D., Dixson, B. J., Jessop, T. S., Morgan, B., & Dixson, A. F. (2010). Cross-cultural consensus for waist–hip ratio and women's attractiveness. *Evolution and Human Behavior, 31*(3), 176–181.

Smuts, B. B., & Smuts, R. W. (1993). Male aggression and sexual coercion of females in nonhuman primates and other mammals: evidence and theoretical implications. *Advances in the Study of Behavior, 22*(22), 1–63.

Sohn, K. (2017). Men's revealed preference for their mates' ages. *Evolution and Human Behavior, 38*, 58–62. https://doi.org/10.1016/j.evolhumbehav.2016.06.007

Symons, D. (1979). *The evolution of human sexuality.* Oxford University Press.

Symons, D. (1995). Beauty is in the adaptations of the beholder: The evolutionary psychology of human female sexual attractiveness. In P. R. Abramson & S. D. Pinkerton (Eds.), *Sexual nature/sexual culture* (pp. 80–118). University of Chicago Press.

Regan, P. C. (1998). What if you can't get what you want? Willingness to compromise ideal mate selection standards as a function of sex, mate value, and relationship context. *Personality and Social Psychology Bulletin, 24*(12), 1294–1303.

Rhodes, G. (2006). The evolutionary psychology of facial beauty. *Annual Review of Psychology, 57*, 199–226.

Starkweather, K. E., & Hames, R. (2012). A survey of non-classical polyandry. *Human Nature, 23*(2), 149–172.

Tang-Martínez, Z. (2016). Rethinking Bateman's principles: Challenging persistent myths of sexually reluctant females and promiscuous males. *The Journal of Sex Research, 53*(4–5), 532–559.

Thompson, M. E., & Alvarado, L. C. (2012). Sexual conflict and sexual coercion in comparative evolutionary perspective. In T.K. Shackelford & A.T. Goetz (Eds.), *The Oxford Handbook of Sexual Conflict in Humans.* NY: Oxford University Press.

Thornhill, R., & Gangestad, S. W. (2008). *The evolutionary biology of human female sexuality.* Oxford University Press.

Thornhill, R., & Palmer, C. T. (2000). Why men rape. *SCIENCES-NEW YORK-, 40*(1), 30–36.

Tooby, J., Cosmides, L., Sell, A., Lieberman, D., & Sznycer, D. (2008). Internal regulatory variables and the design of human motivation: A computational and evolutionary approach. In A. J. Elliott (Ed.), Handbook of *approach and avoidance motivation* (pp. 251–271). Psychology Press.

Trivers, R. L. (1972). Parental investment and sexual selection. In B. Campbell (Ed.), *Sexual selection and the descent of man* (pp. 136–179). Aldine.

Voracek, M., Haubner, T., & Fisher, M. L. (2008). Recent decline in nonpaternity rates: A cross-temporal meta-analysis. *Psychological Reports, 103*(3), 799–811.

Walter, K. V., Conroy-Beam, D., Buss, D. M., Asao, K., Sorokowska, A., Sorokowski, P., Aavik, T., Akello, G., Alhabahba, M. M., Alm, C., Amjad, N., Anjum, A., Atama, C. S., Duyar, D. A., Ayebare, R., Batres, C., Bendixen, M., Bensafia, A., Bizumic, B. . . . Zupančič, M. (2020). Sex differences in mate preferences across 45 countries: A large-scale replication. *Psychological Science, 31*(4), 408–423.

Wang, G., Cao, M., Sauciuvenaite, J., Bissland, R., Hacker, M., Hambly, C., Vaanholt, L. M., Niu, C., Faries, M. D., & Speakman, J. R. (2018). Different impacts of resources on opposite sex ratings of physical attractiveness by males and females. *Evolution and Human Behavior*, 39, 220–225.

Watson-Capps, J. J. (2009). Evolution of sexual coercion with respect to sexual selection and sexual conflict theory. In M. N. Muller & R. W. Wrangham (Eds.), *Sexual coercion in primates and humans* (pp. 23–41). Harvard University Press.

Williams, G. C. (1975). *Sex and evolution.* Princeton University Press.

Wilson, M., & Mesnick, S. L. (1997). An empirical test of the bodyguard hypothesis. In P. A. Gowaty (Ed.), *Feminism and evolutionary biology: Boundaries, intersections, and frontiers (505-511).* Chapman & Hall.

Wolf, M., Musch, J., Enczmann, J., & Fischer, J. (2012). Estimating the prevalence of nonpaternity in Germany. *Human Nature, 23*(2), 208–217.

Wrangham, R. (2009). *Catching fire: How cooking made us human.* Basic Books.

CHAPTER

2

Physical Cues of Partner Quality

Ian D. Stephen *and* Severi Luoto

Abstract

The dominant evolutionary theory of sexual attraction posits that attraction serves as a psychobehavioral and motivational mechanism for identifying healthy, fertile, and appropriate mates. According to this theory, humans and animals display cues that reflect their mate quality and, if successful, are perceived as attractive by potential mates. There is evidence for such valid cues in human faces, bodies, and non-bodily traits, which include adornments and items that signal provisioning ability, creativity, artistic skills, or conspicuous consumption. In this chapter, we discuss the evidence for the existence of these facial, bodily, and non-bodily cues and for their role in communicating aspects of partner quality, including health, fertility, developmental stability, genetic quality, and potential for parental investment. We further discuss sex differences in the physical cues that men and women rely on in mate choice. We conclude by highlighting the centrality and evolutionary importance of physical cues in contemporary sexual selection, and how they manifest in evolutionarily novel inventions such as physical self-enhancements, "sexy selfies," social media, and online dating.

Key Words: sexual selection, evolution, attraction, beauty, physical attractiveness, mate choice, non-bodily ornaments, creativity, health cues

"Beauty, n: the power by which a woman charms a lover and terrifies a husband."
—Ambrose Bierce

"Since brass, nor stone, nor earth, nor boundless sea,
But sad mortality o'ersways their power,
How with this rage shall beauty hold a plea,
Whose action is no stronger than a flower?
O, how shall summer's honey breath hold out
Against the wrackful siege of battering days,
When rocks impregnable are not so stout,
Nor gates of steel so strong, but Time decays?

O fearful meditation! where, alack,
Shall time's best jewel from time's chest lie hid?"
—William Shakespeare, Sonnet 65

It has long been recognized that individuals of many species prefer to mate with individuals with certain physical traits (Darwin, 1871). Since this initial observation, debate has focused on whether physical trait preferences are arbitrary (i.e., a result of cultural biases (Wolf, 1990) or biases in the visual system (Fisher, 1930)), or whether they act as cues to some aspect of underlying partner quality, such as a strong immune system, good state of health, or positive personality traits (Thornhill & Gangestad, 1999). This latter hypothesis has come to dominate evolutionary thinking about mate selection, with attraction being understood as an evolved psychobehavioral mechanism for identifying and pursuing healthy, fertile, high-quality mates (Lee et al., 2008), and attractive cues understood as valid cues to underlying physiological or psychological quality (Coetzee et al., 2009; Stephen & Tan, 2015). A wide range of physical traits in the human face and body, and indeed beyond the body, have been proposed as valid cues to aspects of partner quality. To be considered a valid cue to partner quality, the cue must both be perceived as healthy or attractive *and* reflect some aspect of underlying quality (Coetzee et al., 2009; Stephen & Tan, 2015). In this chapter, we consider the evidence for the quality-cueing properties of facial, bodily, and non-bodily cues (see fig. 2.1).

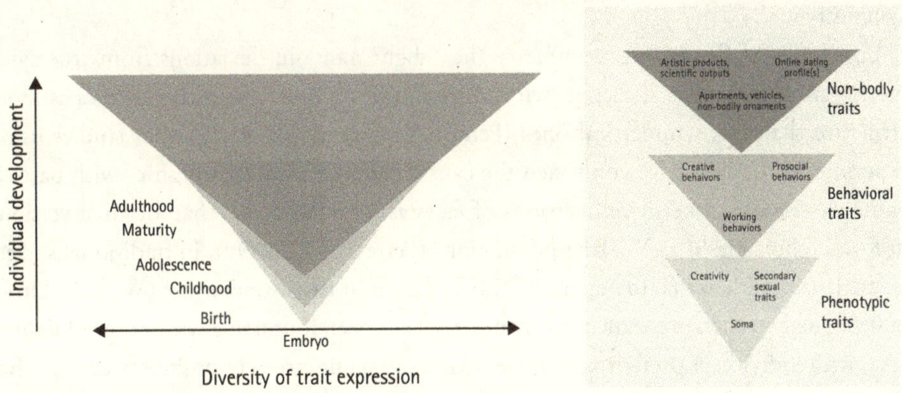

Figure 2.1 *Three Categories of Sexual Traits Projected as a Function of Individual Development*

Note. The lowest triangle (light gray) represents phenotypic traits (e.g., physical attractiveness, facial symmetry, and secondary sexual signals). The second triangle (gray) represents behavioural traits (e.g., artistic, prosocial, construction, and working behaviours). The third triangle (dark gray) represents non-bodily traits (e.g., artistic products, vehicles, online dating profiles, apartments, and pets). The examples in these categories are not exhaustive. The triangles overlap vertically because each successive category starts to develop in ontogeny before the earlier stage ceases to develop. Each successive category occupies more space on the x-axis because the quantity of sexual traits grows with each successive trait category: that is, behavioral traits are hypothetically more diverse than phenotypic traits, and non-bodily traits are hypothetically more diverse than behavioral traits. From "An Updated Theoretical Framework for Human Sexual Selection: From Ecology, Genetics, and Life History to Extended Phenotypes," by S. Luoto, 2019a, *Adaptive Human Behavior and Physiology*, *5*(1), p. 13. (https://doi.org/10.1007/s40750-018-0103-6). Adapted with permission from Springer. Copyright © 2019.

The benefits of having evolved mechanisms for identifying high-quality mates may be twofold: a high-quality partner may be better able or willing to provide direct benefits (benefits that accrue to the chooser), such as protection from violence; gifts such as money, food, or access to high-quality territory; or investment in offspring (Luoto, 2019a; Trivers, 1972). A high-quality partner may also provide indirect benefits (benefits that accrue to the offspring) such as good genes (Fisher, 1930; Jones & Ratterman, 2009). Individuals who are able to identify cues to mate quality may therefore secure better access to both direct and indirect fitness benefits, thus enhancing their reproductive success and providing a selection pressure which favors genes that enhance successful identification of a partner's quality.

A range of potential cues to mate quality have been proposed, with different facial, bodily, and non-bodily cues hypothesized to provide information about different aspects of mate quality (Luoto, 2019a; Stephen & Tan, 2015). From an evolutionary point of view, these can be divided into four categories: cues to health during development, cues to current condition, cues to genetic quality, and cues to psychological traits. We discuss each in turn, and conclude this chapter by focusing on non-bodily traits in human sexual selection.

Cues to Developmental Health

A number of facial cues have been proposed as valid cues to an individual's health status during development.

Symmetry

Low levels of fluctuating asymmetry (i.e., slight, random deviations from true symmetry) are perceived as attractive, with observers rating more symmetrical faces as more attractive than less symmetrical ones (Penton-Voak et al., 2001). Further studies using experimental designs have confirmed the causal nature of this relationship, with participants choosing symmetricized versions of faces as more attractive than original versions in forced choice tasks in Western populations (Perrett et al., 1999), in traditional societies such as the Hadza (Little et al., 2007), and even in rhesus macaques (Waitt & Little, 2006). Further, such preferences for symmetry have been found in a wide range of animal taxa, with individuals preferring to mate with more symmetrical opposite-sex conspecifics (Møller & Thornhill, 1998). A relationship between the cue of symmetry and perceived attractiveness has therefore been relatively well established (though for recent null findings, see Borráz-León et al., 2021; Luoto et al., 2021). However, the relationship between symmetry and physiological or psychological health during development, which is also required to conclude that symmetry is a valid cue to developmental health, is less well established.

Researchers have theorized that increased deviations from true symmetry reflect developmental instability (Gangestad et al., 1994). The hypothesis is that during gestation, childhood, and adolescence, interruptions to development—which may include challenges such as malnutrition, injury, or invasion by pathogens—result in deviations from symmetry, and these deviations accumulate until adulthood is reached (Gangestad et al., 1994). A number of studies have attempted to establish a relationship between health during development and levels of facial asymmetry, with little success. Rhodes et al. (2001) found that the measured symmetry of a sample of 316 17-year-olds was not associated with health scores obtained from physicians' examination of the participants' medical records from childhood and adolescence (Rhodes et al., 2001). A study of 4732 British 15-year-olds from the ALSCAP (Avon Longitudinal Study of Parents and Children) found that symmetry, as measured from 3D facial scans, was not predictive of a range of measures of childhood health collected during development (Pound et al., 2014). Likewise, facial asymmetry was not associated with the occurrence of minor ailments (as an indicator of general health) in young adults in Mexico (Borráz-León et al., 2021). A study on Latvian young men found a positive correlation between family income during ontogeny and immune function, and a negative correlation between immune function and facial asymmetry. The results indicate that facial asymmetry may be a reliable cue of the robustness of immune function (Luoto et al., 2021), although other studies in African and Polish populations have not found such a relationship when measuring facial (Phalane et al., 2017) or bodily symmetry (Pawłowski et al., 2018) and the robustness of immune function. While symmetry, then, is perceived as healthy and attractive, there is limited evidence that it reflects aspects of health during development or in adulthood (cf. Borráz-León et al., 2021).

Sexual Dimorphism

Sexual dimorphism (also referred to as "sex typicality" or "masculinity/femininity") has also been proposed to act as a valid cue to health during development (Fink & Penton-Voak, 2002; Thornhill & Gangestad, 1999). Sex-typical traits develop under the influence of sex hormones, with testosterone driving the development of taller stature; increased muscularity; increased body and facial hair; and growth of the jaw, nose, and brow ridges in men (Penton-Voak & Chen, 2004). Conversely, estrogen is associated with the development of larger breasts, buttocks, and lips and the inhibition of the growth of body and facial hair, nose, jaw, and brow ridges (Javed & Lteif, 2013; Law Smith et al., 2006). The degree of sexual dimorphism is thought to be largely fixed by the end of puberty, so it is hypothesized that sexual dimorphism may act as a valid cue to hormone levels during development (Luoto et al., 2019; Swift-Gallant et al., 2020).

FEMININITY

It is well-established that increased femininity of women's faces is perceived as more attractive. When presented with a series of women's faces that had been transformed to appear more feminine (i.e., more typically female) or masculine (i.e., more typically male), participants chose feminized versions of the faces as appearing more attractive (Perrett et al., 1998). This effect has been replicated in Western, Asian (Perrett et al., 1998), and African (Coetzee et al., 2014) human populations, though men from countries with a higher national health index have greater preference for femininity in women's faces than men from countries with a lower national health index (Marcinkowska et al., 2014). Estrogen is critical to the functioning of the female reproductive system, with evidence suggesting that women with higher levels of estrogen are more likely to conceive both naturally and when undergoing in vitro fertilization (IVF; Baird et al., 1997, 1999; Lipson & Ellison, 1996). Further, women with higher levels of circulating estrogen and progesterone are perceived as healthier, more attractive, and more feminine (Law Smith et al., 2006), suggesting that facial femininity may act as a valid cue to fecundity.

There is further evidence that a feminine body shape (associated with higher estrogen levels in women) is perceived as attractive. Women with a lower waist-to-hip ratio (WHR) have been shown to be perceived as more attractive than women with a higher WHR; specifically, waist circumference that is approximately 0.7x hip circumference is rated highest on attractiveness by male observers (Cornelissen et al., 2009; Singh, 1993a, 1993b; Tovée & Cornelissen, 2001). Studies have also shown that low WHR is associated with a more fecund hormonal profile (Jasieńska et al., 2004; but see Grillot et al., 2014, Bovet, 2019). Indeed, a study of 500 women at a fertility clinic suggests that each 0.1 increase in WHR is associated with a 30% reduction in the probability of conception each cycle (Zaadstra et al., 1993). There is also evidence that a low WHR is associated with improved cognitive abilities in women and their offspring (Lassek & Gaulin, 2008), possibly because of a more favorable hormonal profile during development, or because gluteofemoral fat deposits are used as developmental resources for the human brain (Lassek & Gaulin, 2008). This suggests that low WHR may act as a valid cue to women's current and developmental sex hormone profile and nubility (Lassek & Gaulin, 2019). However, Cashdan (2008) argued that women face a trade-off between a more fecund hormonal profile (low androgen, low cortisol, high estrogen; associated with low WHR) and a more robust hormonal profile (higher androgen, higher cortisol, lower estrogen; associated with high WHR), demonstrating that few women, particularly older women and women living in more challenging environments, exhibit a WHR as low as 0.7. Although this may be the case, it appears that men living in more challenging environments show a preference for even lower WHR than men living in less challenging environments (Swami et al., 2009). The mechanisms controlling the perception of attractive body shape in men's brains may thus prioritize fecundity above other aspects of health.

Women's enlarged breasts are a sexually dimorphic exaggerated secondary sexual trait that is not found in other primate species (except during lactation). They are thought to have evolved as a sexually selected ornament via intersexual choice (Puts, 2010). A number of studies using a variety of stimuli, such as line drawings (Furnham et al., 1998; Singh & Young, 1995; Swami et al., 2009), 3D avatars (Pazhoohi et al., 2020; Swami & Tovée,

2013; Valentova et al., 2017), and photographs (Dixson et al., 2011, 2015; Havlíček et al., 2017), have shown that breast size, shape, symmetry, and firmness influence the perceived attractiveness of women's breasts, typically indicating that women with medium and large breasts are perceived as more attractive, healthy, young, and fertile than women with small or very large breasts (Furnham et al., 1998; Havlíček et al., 2017; Pazhoohi et al., 2020; Singh & Young, 1995; Swami et al., 2009; Valentova et al., 2017). Larger breasts are associated with higher levels of circulating estradiol (Jasieńska et al., 2004), a correlate of fecundity, suggesting that men who prefer mating with women with larger breasts may have acquired a reproductive advantage over men without such a preference. However, there is also evidence that women with larger breasts are at higher risk of developing breast cancer (Scutt et al., 1997). Increased breast cancer risk may provide a balancing selection pressure that prevents the evolution of men's preferences for very large breasts. However, this selection pressure is relatively novel, as breast cancer risk has seen a sharp increase only with the advent of agriculture and the resulting dietary, energetic, and life history changes (Crespi & Summers, 2005). Another study reported that women's breast size was positively correlated with the number of respiratory infections but not with digestive infections (Kościński et al., 2020). As breast size is positively correlated with body symmetry, and as symmetry is associated with developmental stability, the development of large, sexually attractive breasts is optimized in stable developmental environments (Kościński et al., 2020).

There is also evidence that firmer breasts and breasts with less ptosis (i.e., sagging), are perceived as more attractive (Havlíček et al., 2017; Pazhoohi et al., 2020), particularly breasts with a 45:55 upper-pole (i.e., distance from the nipple to the top of the breast) to lower-pole (i.e., distance from the nipple to the bottom of the breast) ratio (Mallucci & Branford, 2012, 2014). Since women's breasts become less firm and more ptotic with increasing age and increasing parity (i.e., number of children), it has been argued that breast firmness and ptosis represent valid cues to remaining reproductive value (Pazhoohi et al., 2020). Finally, more symmetrical breasts are perceived as more attractive (Møller et al., 1995; Singh, 1995), and women with more symmetrical breasts are more fecund (Møller et al., 1995) and at lower risk of breast cancer (Scutt et al., 1997), again suggesting that breast symmetry may act as a valid cue to health.

MASCULINITY

Evidence that masculinity is a valid cue to men's health is more mixed. The immunocompetence handicap hypothesis (IHH; Folstad & Karter, 1992) suggests that because testosterone has a suppressant effect on the immune system (Foo et al., 2017), and masculine traits develop under the influence of testosterone (Penton-Voak & Chen, 2004), only high-quality males are able to bear the immunosuppressive effect of the high testosterone levels required to develop strongly masculinized faces and bodies. Women are therefore expected to show a preference for masculine facial appearance and muscular bodies in men. However, studies asking participants to choose between masculinized and feminized versions of men's faces typically find either no preference for masculinity (Scott et al., 2010; Stephen et al., 2012; Swaddle & Reierson, 2002) or a preference for feminized faces (Mogilski & Welling, 2017; Perrett et al., 1998; Stephen et al., 2018), possibly because high testosterone levels and masculine facial shapes are associated with personality traits that are detrimental in long-term partnerships (e.g., aggression and infidelity; Lee et al., 2017; Mazur & Booth, 1998; Perrett et al., 1998). This hypothesis suggests that women's mate selection mechanisms may be performing a trade-off between masculine men who may have "good genes" but personality traits that are undesirable in a long-term partner and father, and feminine men who may be less prone to aggressive behavior and are more suitable as husbands and fathers. Further evidence for this hypothesis comes from studies showing that women's preferences for men's facial masculinity changes depending on the (internal and external) environment. For example, women living in societies with high levels of income inequality, pathogen prevalence, and poor health outcomes show stronger preferences for masculinity in men's faces compared to women in countries with low levels of inequality and good health outcomes (Brooks et al., 2011; DeBruine et al., 2010; Moore et al., 2013). However, the opposite results were found in a more recent study: women had stronger preferences for facial masculinity in countries with higher health indices, lower pathogen prevalence, and greater indices of economic and social development (Marcinkowska et al., 2019), which indicates that earlier assumptions about the link between women's facial masculinity preferences in socioecologically harsh conditions may need to be revised.

Similarly, there is evidence that women's preferences for men's facial masculinity fluctuates according to phase of the menstrual cycle, with women preferring more masculine men's faces (and therefore good genes) in the fertile phase and more feminine men's faces (and therefore more paternal personality traits) in the nonfertile phase (Penton-Voak et al., 1999). However, the reliability of these effects has been debated, with competing meta-analyses finding that menstrual cycle effects on mate choice are well supported (Gildersleeve et al., 2014) and unsupported (Wood et al., 2014). More recent studies have also failed to find significant cycle shifts in women's preferences for men's facial masculinity (Dixson et al., 2018; Jones et al., 2018), masculine voices (Jünger, Motta-Mena, et al., 2018), muscular bodies (Jünger, Kordsmeyer, et al., 2018; but see Gangestad et al., 2019), or beardedness (Dixson et al., 2018). The evidence that male facial masculinity is a valid cue to partner quality is therefore mixed or, at minimum, complex.

Cues to Current Health

Some facial and bodily traits have been proposed to represent valid cues to aspects of potential partners' current health status, such as nutritional status, parasite and pathogen load, or cardiovascular health.

Adiposity

One trait proposed as a valid cue to current health is adiposity (i.e., amount of body fat; Coetzee et al., 2009). Coetzee et al. (2009) found that observers showed above-chance accuracy when asked to judge the body mass index (BMI) of people from photographs of their faces. There was also a relationship between the apparent adiposity of the faces and how healthy and attractive they appeared: faces near the average level of apparent facial adiposity were perceived as healthiest and most attractive, with faces near the high and low ends of the apparent adiposity scale perceived as less healthy and attractive. Participants with higher BMIs also self-reported more frequent and severe cold and flu bouts, and higher blood pressure, suggesting that facial adiposity may act as a valid cue to health (Coetzee et al., 2009). This hypothesis is supported by another study which reported that facial and bodily adiposity (negatively) and facial attractiveness (positively) were linked to more robust immune function in men (Rantala et al., 2013a). In women, however, facial attractiveness did not predict robustness of immune function (Rantala et al., 2013b) or current metabolic health (i.e., glucose metabolism, liver functioning, and inflammatory markers), although facial attractiveness was negatively associated with lipid profile components detrimental to health (i.e., total cholesterol, LDL, and triglycerides) (Żelaźniewicz et al., 2020).

There have also been efforts to identify aspects of facial shape that may act as valid cues to aspects of cardiovascular health. Coetzee et al. (2010) found that facial width-to-height ratio (in men and women), cheek-to-jaw-width ratio (in men and women), and perimeter-to-area ratio (in men only), as measured from 2D facial photographs of African and Caucasian people, predicted BMI.

More recently, researchers have begun to take a data-driven approach to identifying cues to cardiovascular health (Stephen et al., 2017; Tan et al., 2018; Wolffhechel et al., 2015). This has become possible by the application of statistical techniques for analyzing the shape, color, and texture of facial photographs. Geometric morphometric methods (GMM) allow researchers to first standardize the orientation, size, and location of faces and then to use principal components analysis (PCA) to identify underlying components that explain the variance in the shape of a sample of faces. This allows the data to inform the researchers of which facial metrics may be most important, rather than requiring the researchers to make educated guesses in advance. These components can then be used to predict aspects of underlying health, such as BMI. Wolffhechel et al. (2015) found that the GMM approach is significantly more accurate at predicting underlying BMI than Coetzee et al.'s (2010) three metrics. This approach can be applied to other aspects of underlying health, and Stephen et al. (2017) found that GMM techniques can also successfully predict blood pressure and body adiposity from photographs of African, Asian, and Caucasian faces. The models that are produced to predict these aspects of cardiovascular health can also be "reverse-engineered" to manipulate faces to look either higher or lower in body adiposity, BMI, and blood pressure. When presented with a series of such faces and asked to manipulate them to appear as healthy as possible, participants chose faces corresponding to lower BMI and lower adiposity. These shape components may therefore act as valid facial cues to health (Stephen et al., 2017).

Skin Color and Texture

Facial skin quality, particularly color and texture, have also been proposed to represent valid cues to aspects of current health. Skin color is determined by the amounts of colored pigments in the skin—particularly oxyhaemoglobin (bright red), deoxyhaemoglobin (dark, purplish red), melanin (dark yellowy brown), and carotenoids (bright yellow; Edwards & Duntley, 1939).

When asked to manipulate the color of the skin portions of facial photographs to make the faces look as healthy as possible, participants chose to increase the skin lightness (CIELab L*), redness (a*), and yellowness (b*) (Stephen, Law-Smith, et al., 2009). These preferences have been argued to reflect a preference for oxygenated over deoxygenated blood coloration (Stephen, Coetzee, et al., 2009), which is associated with improved cardiovascular health (Armstrong & Welsman, 2001; Charkoudian et al., 1999; Panza et al., 1990); and with carotenoid coloration (Stephen et al., 2011), reflective of levels of antioxidant carotenoid pigments obtained from fruit and vegetables in the diet (Alaluf et al., 2002; Stahl et al., 1998). These findings indicate that skin coloration may act as a valid cue to aspects of underlying health. The role of skin color in predicting the perceived health and attractiveness of faces appears to be replicable across racial groups (Coetzee et al., 2012; Pezdirc et al., 2018; Stephen et al., 2011, 2012; Tan et al., 2017; Tan & Stephen, 2019; Whitehead et al., 2012, but see Han et al., 2018). Indeed, there is evidence that the human visual system may be particularly sensitive to small differences in the coloration of facial skin, as compared to color patches or non-face objects (Re et al., 2011; Tan & Stephen, 2013), suggesting that specialized health-detection mechanisms may be present in the brain.

Cues to Genetic Quality

Identifying mates with high genetic quality (i.e., genes for good health, immune function, and attractiveness, and other genes that are advantageous for survival and reproduction) is a valuable ability, allowing increased chances for offspring to inherit these "good genes." Selecting a mate with good genes increases the likelihood of survival and reproductive success of offspring, thereby increasing the probability that one's own genes will be passed on to subsequent generations (Fisher, 1930). Whereas "good genes" can refer to any area of the genome that impacts health or other traits, research in this area has typically focused on the major histocompatibility complex (MHC) (also known as the human leukocyte antigen, HLA, in humans), a part of the genome that determines our ability to distinguish pathogens from our own body's cells. Male height and muscularity may constitute other relevant cues of genetic quality. We discuss the evidence for MHC, height, and muscularity in turn below.

Major Histocompatibility Complex

MHC diversity can act as a cue to mate quality in two ways. First, individuals who are heterozygous at a greater number of alleles in the MHC are thought to be better able to fight off pathogens either because they can detect a broader range of pathogens by producing a broader array of antibodies (Brown, 1997, 1999) or because they are better able to detect new pathogen forms as they mutate (Van Valen, 1973). These individuals may therefore be healthier (Lie et al., 2009) and thus appear more attractive because healthier individuals may be better able to provide direct benefits such as help with parenting, protection, or resources, and indirect benefits by passing on genes for a strong immune system to offspring. MHC heterozygosity is thought to be detectable via (largely unknown) cues in individuals' odor and facial appearance (Lie et al., 2009), though recent evidence suggests that facial masculinity is not a valid cue of MHC heterozygosity (Zaidi et al., 2019). Studies examining men's and women's preferences for the bodily odor of MHC heterozygous versus homozygous individuals tend to involve asking participants to wear a t-shirt for a period of time to collect sweat, measuring participant heterozygosity at a number of loci in the MHC, and then asking a second group of participants to smell the sweaty t-shirts and rate them on traits such as attractiveness or pleasantness. Studies on preferences for MHC heterozygosity are relatively rare, but there is some support for the idea, particularly for women's preferences for men's body odor, possibly because MHC-heterozygotes' body odor smells less intense (Thornhill et al., 2003; Wedekind et al., 2006). Studies of preferences for the faces of individuals with greater MHC heterozygosity tend to involve genotyping a group of participants who are then photographed. A second group of participants then rates the attractiveness of the photographs of the first group's faces. While results for these studies are mixed, a recent meta-analysis suggested that the evidence favors a small preference for faces of potential partners with greater MHC heterozygosity (Winternitz et al., 2017), possibly because the faces of MHC-heterozygous individuals are more average (closer to the population average shape; Lie et al., 2008).

Second, individuals may be expected to be more attracted to potential partners who are dissimilar to themselves in their MHC. By choosing to mate with genetically dissimilar potential partners, individuals can increase the likelihood of their offspring receiving the indirect benefits of being heterozygous at MHC loci, and thus having stronger immune systems (Havlíček & Roberts, 2009). Evidence that people find the body odor and faces of MHC-dissimilar partners more attractive is mixed, with studies finding both preferences for more MHC-dissimilar (Sorokowska et al., 2018) and preferences for more MHC-*similar* (Coetzee et al., 2007; Roberts et al., 2005) potential partners. Recent meta-analyses suggest that the evidence is either currently marginally in favor of preferences for

MHC-dissimilar potential partners' odors and faces (Winternitz et al., 2017) or supporting no effect in either direction (Havlíček et al., 2020).

Height

The role of height in human mate choice is important—but in ways that are sex-specific. It is becoming clear that height is a highly polygenic trait (Rotwein, 2020; Stulp & Barrett, 2016), meaning that its expression is influenced by a large number of genes, besides a number of environmental factors. Estimates of the heritability of height have consistently indicated that 80% of the variability seen between people is potentially controlled by genes (McEvoy & Visscher, 2009). But height appears to be more heritable in men than in women. In men, the heritability estimates of height range around 0.87–0.93, while in women they are lower, between 0.68 and 0.84 (Silventoinen et al., 2003). The remaining variation is caused by environmental factors such as nutrition and disease exposure (Krams et al., 2019; McEvoy & Visscher, 2009).

In contemporary populations, women's height does not appear to strongly affect men's perceptions of women's attractiveness. However, in men, taller stature is sometimes associated with greater reproductive success, and there is some evidence suggesting that this link is driven by female preferences for taller men (Stulp & Barrett, 2016). For example, a study on speed-dating reported that women were choosier than men about potential partners' height, and were most likely to choose men 25 cm taller than themselves. Men, however, were most likely to choose women only 7 cm shorter than themselves (Stulp et al., 2013). Taller men were choosier than shorter men yet still had a higher likelihood of ending up with a match than shorter men; this is because taller men were more frequently given a "Yes" response by women and had to compete with fewer rivals than shorter men (Stulp et al., 2013). Women had a narrower preferred height range than men, and women were less likely than men to choose individuals who fell outside this preference range. Women therefore had a higher strength of preference for male height than vice versa (Stulp et al., 2013). Taller-than-average men have more attractive mates, are more likely to be married, and are favored as sperm donors (reviewed in Sugiyama, 2015). Overall, the evidence indicates that female mate choice is a likely contributor to the evolution of human sexual dimorphism in size, favoring taller stature in men (Stulp et al., 2013; Stulp & Barrett, 2016).

Taller men have been shown to be healthier and have lower mortality rates than shorter men (Stulp & Barrett, 2016). Men's height is positively associated with status, strength, reach, frequency of aggressive acts, and perceived fighting ability (Stulp et al., 2015; Sugiyama, 2015). Height is moderately correlated with intelligence in children and in adults (Marioni et al., 2014; Sundet et al., 2005), and estimates suggest that between 35% and 71% of this correlation may be explained by genetic factors (Marioni et al., 2014; Sundet et al., 2005). Better cognitive ability in taller men may explain why taller men have higher wages (Böckerman & Vainiomäki, 2013) than shorter men (up to about

191 cm, above which the effect decreases; reviewed in Krams et al., 2019; McEvoy & Visscher, 2009).

The relationship between male height and reproductive success may be curvilinear, decreasing after an optimal height has been reached (Sugiyama, 2015). Even though taller men are favored by women, taller men have lower reproductive success than average-height men in some populations (Stulp & Barrett, 2016). Increased reproductive success of average-height men in such populations can be driven by their early age at birth of first offspring, which can, in turn, be associated with an elevated likelihood of pairing with shorter women, who have higher reproductive success themselves (Stulp & Barrett, 2016). This explanation would support assortative mating for height (Stulp et al., 2017), as well as life history hypotheses whereby height is an important somatic trait that requires bioenergetic investment to develop, meaning that taller men have slower life history strategies than shorter men (Krams et al., 2019; Stulp & Barrett, 2016), spending longer to develop and reproducing later than shorter men. Higher family socioeconomic status during development predicts both greater height and improved immune function in adult men, suggesting that these traits cluster toward the slow end of the life history spectrum (Krams et al., 2019). A study on a similar population of women as the Latvian male sample of Krams et al. (2019), however, found that women's height was not predicted by their family income during development, even though immune function was (Rubika et al., 2020). It is thus possible that the development and expression of male height are condition-dependent in a similar way to many other sexually selected traits, therefore being more sensitive to resource availability than female height (Krams et al., 2019; Rubika et al., 2020). Overall, height can be useful as a cue of good genes, better immunity, higher intelligence, and more resource-rich developmental environments in men (Krams et al., 2019; Marioni et al., 2014), making male height an important cue for women for a number of different reasons.

Overall, the female preference for taller-than-average men may result in a range of direct and indirect genotypic and phenotypic advantages accruing to the women and their offspring, though there may also be disadvantages such as increased risk of birth complications in women who are partnered with much taller men (Stulp & Barrett, 2016).

While men show a much weaker preference for tall partners, women's height is positively associated with improved educational and economic outcomes (Čvorović, 2020), partner's education and occupation status (Murasko, 2020), better health and offspring survival, and reduced mortality and obstetric problems (Stulp & Barrett, 2016).

Muscularity

Male muscularity has also been studied as a potential cue to mate quality in humans. While men are approximately 10% taller than women on average (Gaulin & Boster, 1985), they are 33% heavier, have 61% more total lean muscle mass, 75% more arm muscle mass, and 90% higher upper- body strength, on average (Lassek & Gaulin, 2009).

The difference in upper-body strength is large enough that the median man has greater upper-body strength than 99.9% of women (Lassek & Gaulin, 2009). When such large sexual dimorphism of a trait is observed, it typically means that there has been sexual selection driving the exaggeration of the trait (in contrast, viability selection, which is concerned with survival, tends to act more equally on the two sexes than sexual selection, since a trait useful for survival in one sex is typically also useful for survival in the other).

There is currently debate in the literature over the role of intersexual choice (women preferring to mate with more muscular men) versus intrasexual competition (men fighting each other over access to women) in the evolution of male muscularity (Kordsmeyer et al., 2018; Puts, 2010). Puts (2010) argued that men's muscularity and the ancestral human environment were more suited for intrasexual contest competition (fighting) than for intersexual choice, since contest competition could facilitate men's monopolization of women's reproductive output, potentially overriding intersexual choice. Further, observers are able to accurately judge men's upper-body strength and fighting ability from photographs of their bodies and even from photographs of faces, suggesting that we may have evolved the ability to detect these traits because of their importance in our evolutionary history (Sell et al., 2009). Men's physical dominance—as rated by other men—predicts men's quantitative mating success (measured via sociosexual behavior), whereas female-judged sexual attractiveness doesn't (Kordsmeyer et al., 2018). These findings provide tentative evidence for a stronger influence of male–male competition than female mate choice on the evolution of men's physical formidability.

Others argue, however, that women's preferences for mating with more muscular men may have also played a significant role in the evolution of men's muscularity, though evidence about the preferred level of muscularity is mixed. Frederick and Haselton (2007) found, using line drawings and computer-generated avatars as stimuli, that moderate muscularity in men was perceived as most attractive by women. Similarly, using empirically derived transformations of body photographs along fat mass and muscularity dimensions, Brierley et al. (2016) found that levels of fat and muscularity that were in line with health guidelines were perceived as most attractive and healthy in men's bodies. Others have found, using regression models of ratings of photographs, that perceived physical strength strongly predicts men's attractiveness: the stronger the men appear, the more attractive they are rated (Lassek & Gaulin, 2009; Sell et al., 2017).

The aspects of physiological health that muscularity is thought to communicate is also a matter of debate. While some argue that the preference for moderate levels of lean muscularity is indicative of muscularity being a valid cue to good current cardiovascular health (Brierley et al., 2016), others argue that the preference for high levels of muscularity indicates that muscularity acts as a handicapping sexual signal (Folstad & Karter, 1992). According to this hypothesis, muscularity conveys information about the man's genes which provide him with the ability to maintain a high level of circulating testosterone while maintaining good immune function and the calorific costs of increased muscularity, all the while maintaining other bodily functions (Frederick & Haselton, 2007; Lassek & Gaulin, 2009; Sell et al., 2017). So, although it is clear that muscularity does influence the apparent strength and attractiveness of men, the details are less clear, and more research is required to determine its link with underlying health.

Cues to Personality

There have been a number of attempts to identify the aspects of facial appearance that are associated with different personality traits. For example, there is some evidence that individuals who express a preference for certain personality traits in a romantic partner find the faces of opposite-sex people who report that personality trait more attractive (Little et al., 2006). There is also evidence that intelligence (Zebrowitz et al., 2002) may be visible in the face, though the facial traits that convey the information are unknown. Sociosexuality (openness to casual sex) is thought to be accurately perceived from facial appearance (Boothroyd et al., 2008, 2011), at least in men's faces (Antar & Stephen, 2021), with statistical analysis of facial shape recently finding that longer men's faces may be predictive of more unrestricted sociosexuality (Antar & Stephen, 2021). Further studies examining the relationship between self-reported personality traits, measured using questionnaires, and perceived personality traits, as rated from facial photographs, have found that observers can accurately perceive extroversion, agreeableness, emotional stability (Penton-Voak et al., 2006), openness, and neuroticism (Kramer & Ward, 2010). Likewise, personality traits that observers associated with babyfacedness (i.e., weakness and approachability) were also reported by individuals with higher levels of babyfacedness (Berry & Brownlow, 1989; Paunonen et al., 1999). Recently, analyses of 3D facial scans have shown that some aspects of facial shape are predictive of personality traits (Hu et al., 2017; Jones et al., 2012). Conversely, although large breasts are perceived by observers as cues of increased willingness to engage in casual sex, larger breasts are not actually associated with women's sociosexuality (Kościński et al., 2020). Overall, however, behavioral traits convey personality-related information more reliably than physical ones (e.g., Buss & Penke, 2015; Miller & Todd, 1998).

The Role of Non-Bodily Traits in Sexual Selection

As seen in the previous sections, the role of facial and bodily traits in human mate choice has been extensively studied. But partner quality can be communicated also by traits that are not limited to the human body. These *non*-bodily traits may range from luxurious apartments and cars to other culturally salient products like paintings, novels, musical recordings, and other creative artifacts. Think, for example, how limited the signaling capacity of William Shakespeare, Jimi Hendrix, or Hugh Hefner would have been if they only had their bodily traits with which to signal their mate quality. By using their instruments, creative tools, and surrounding social organizations in new ways, such men have succeeded in amplifying their signaling capacity far beyond what would be possible merely with bodily traits (Luoto, 2019a). Even in contemporary mate choice in humans, physical traits that occur outside the body boundary influence some people's decisions about whom to pursue romantically and with whom to establish a family. It is therefore important to understand how and why such traits influence assessments of partner quality, and an evolutionary approach to the role of non-bodily traits in sexual selection (Luoto, 2019a; Schaedelin & Taborsky, 2009) is uniquely positioned to explain this fascinating dimension of mate choice.

The key point to note with most non-bodily traits in human mate choice is that they tend to be difficult to produce, acquire, and fake—and it is also likely that a genetic component explains individual differences in non-bodily ornaments (Luoto, 2019a, 2019b). Hence, showcasing such bioenergetically costly non-bodily traits can signal a number of important qualities about potential mates. In the following sections, we review the existing evidence for the role of non-bodily traits in human sexual selection and discuss sex differences in how such traits are evaluated.

Clothing as an Example of Non-Bodily Traits

"Clothes make the man. Naked people have little or no influence in society."

—*Mark Twain*

"She wore far too much rouge last night and not quite enough clothes. That is always a sign of despair in a woman."

—*Oscar Wilde, "An Ideal Husband"*

As central as physical attractiveness is for evaluating partner quality, it is uncommon in most modern societies, as Mark Twain notes (Vizental, 2010), to flaunt physical attractiveness unveiled by clothing. While clothing has the obvious physiological function of enabling humans to occupy ecological niches characterized by cold temperature, clothing has also been exapted for signaling purposes—to convey information about aspects of the bearer's potential as a romantic or social partner (Luoto, 2019a). Clothing can be used strategically to signal important characteristics about one's partner quality and mating motives.

From flamboyant to plain, luxurious to inexpensive, *à la mode* to dowdy, formal to informal, revealing to concealing, and high-end brands to everyday apparel, clothing can be manipulated on a number of dimensions to send myriad signals to would-be mates. When close to ovulation, for instance, some women tend to prefer clothing that is more revealing and more appealing to men (Durante et al., 2008; Eisenbruch et al., 2015). Unsurprisingly, more revealing clothing increases women's attractiveness as a short-term partner (Hendrie et al., 2009; Hill et al., 1987). One possible function of clothing in human mate choice, therefore, is that it is a malleable non-bodily ornament that signals its displayer's mating motives or even mate quality (Elliot et al., 2013). Women may strategically use clothing in this way; for example, women consciously use clothing to signal their sexual desire and to attract sexual attention from men, wearing more revealing clothing when clubbing, and men perceive sexual intent in women who do so (Hendrie et al., 2020; Lennon et al., 2017). Women are more likely to wear high heels if they anticipate interacting with an attractive male, and are less likely to do so if they anticipate interacting with an unattractive male (Prokop & Švancárová, 2020). Women's dyadic sexual desire (i.e., an interest in, or a wish to engage in, sexual activity with another person, and desire for sharing and intimacy with that person) predicts their inclination to buy high-heeled rather than low-heeled shoes (Watkins & Leitch, 2020). Using high-heeled footwear modifies women's lumbar curvature and gait to be more appealing to men (Lewis et al., 2017; Morris et al., 2013). Clothing items such as high heels or a push-up bra, above and beyond their own signaling value, can thus be used to *augment evolved physiological features* in such a way as to appear more attractive to the opposite sex.

On the other hand, clothing can also be used to *suppress* sexuality, as is the case in the cultural practice of Islamic veiling, which decreases women's rated attractiveness (Pazhoohi & Kingstone, 2020). Both men and women can advocate veiling as a facultative strategy that suppresses female sexuality and serves the Darwinian fitness interests of those who support the practice (Blake et al., 2018). A cross-cultural study on veiling reported that in all of the 25 countries included in the analysis, men supported veiling more than women. Veiling may thus serve men's fitness interests more than those of women (Pazhoohi & Kingstone, 2020), for example by reducing women's attractiveness to men who are not their husband.

Another potential function of clothing is that it signals status, which can be highly important in mate choice contexts. Nevertheless, current evidence on the relationship between clothing-related status and attractiveness is still mixed. Perhaps surprisingly, Gouda-Vossos et al. (2019) found that business attire (as opposed to casual attire) had no effect on how attractive females rated males. Business attire only influenced women's ratings of men's economic status, but not men's attractiveness (Gouda-Vossos et al., 2019). It should be noted that this null finding may have partially been influenced by the fact that some of the business attire stimuli used by Gouda-Vossos et al. (2019, fig. 3) included a man in a rather ill-fitting business suit, which may have negatively influenced the men's rated attractiveness. Business attire slightly increased ratings of women's attractiveness when compared with women in casual attire in Study 1, whereas Study 2 provided the opposite results: men rated women in business suits as lower on attractiveness than women in casual attire (Gouda-Vossos et al., 2019). These mixed results indicate that business as opposed to casual attire may not have a major influence on women's attractiveness. Unsurprisingly, however, business attire slightly increased ratings of women's economic status (Gouda-Vossos et al., 2019). These studies manipulated attire mainly on one or two dimensions (formal vs. informal, and high status vs. normal status). Manipulating attire on more dimensions, such as flamboyant/plain, or revealing/concealing, or trendy/dowdy, could have a stronger influence on perceived attractiveness and partner quality. Other research has shown that women who emphasize their sexiness via clothing in the workplace may be judged to be less competent and less intelligent; outside the workplace, such women may be perceived more negatively by other women, to the extent that women are less likely to befriend or introduce their boyfriends to them (Lennon et al., 2017). Although there is some research on the role of clothing in human sexual selection, this is an area that is underresearched in comparison with many other areas of human mate choice (Luoto, 2019a).

Other Non-Bodily Traits, and Sex Differences in the Importance of Non-Bodily vs. Bodily Traits

It is a basic fact of human biology that reproduction is costlier for females than it is for males. This fundamental biological asymmetry can cause various downstream effects on human psychology and behavior (Archer, 2019; Buss & Schmitt, 2019). One such widely reported effect is the sex difference in how selective one is about with whom and when to have sex: women, on average, tend to be choosier about their sexual partners, while men, on average, are less restricted with their sexual behavior (Hughes et al., 2021; Luoto et al., 2019). Men, therefore, face ruthless though often tacit competition with one another to be desirable as partners and to acquire sexual access to women—though women also have to compete with one another to secure the best males (Baumeister et al., 2017; Rantala et al., 2019).

Much research in evolutionary psychology has focused on these reproductive dynamics, and an oft-cited finding is the sex difference in the importance of a partner's status and resources on mate choice (Archer, 2019; Buss & Schmitt, 2019; Luoto, 2019a; Scelza & Prall, 2018). Resource acquisition and provisioning have enhanced male reproductive success throughout human evolution, and sexual selection may have favored status-seeking behaviors in men (reviewed in Gouda-Vossos et al., 2019; Luoto, 2019a; Scelza & Prall, 2018). Men's status is associated with reproductive success across many small-scale and industrialized societies (reviewed in Gouda-Vossos et al., 2019; see also Luoto & Varella, 2021; Scelza & Prall, 2018). Resources and status, therefore, offer ways in which men are able to bridge the biological asymmetry between the sexes in minimal parental investment (Trivers, 1972): raising human infants is costly, and men's paternal investment has a clear evolutionary role in increasing the likelihood of raising viable offspring by provisioning resources and by providing a more stable and secure developmental environment for offspring (Kuzawa, 2007; Luoto, 2019a). But which cues do women use in mate choice to acquire information about the potential resource-provisioning ability of a male? And are women's status and resources similarly salient to men?

Although the original function of housing was to provide shelter from the harsh elements of nature and a stable workspace for routine labor such as tool and clothing manufacture, human housing has also taken on a signaling component: the kind of house one occupies may act as a cue of one's status and resource-provisioning capacity (Dunn

& Hill, 2014; Luoto, 2019a). Men presented in a luxury apartment are rated as more attractive by women than men presented in a standard apartment (Dunn & Hill, 2014). The evolutionarily exapted signaling function of housing may not be limited to contemporary societies or to humans (Luoto, 2019a; Schaedelin & Taborsky, 2009). In Jane Austen's classic novel *Pride and Prejudice*, for instance, the heroine's resistance to a prominent male's otherwise unsuccessful courtship efforts undergoes a gradual transformation when she is exposed to the grandeur and style of his territory. While visiting Mr. Darcy's estate, Elizabeth suddenly gets the revelation "that to be mistress of [that territory] might be something!" (Austen, 2007, p. 207). Mr. Darcy's physical and behavioral cues were insufficiently appealing to the heroine, and Mr. Darcy's courtship efforts were, perhaps paradoxically, boosted only when Elizabeth visited his estate *in his absence*. Though based "merely" on classic fiction, many of us may be able to conjure up similar examples of mate choice from anecdotal evidence or lived experience. The signaling function of housing is just one example of the evolutionarily important effects that non-bodily traits may have in mate choice (Luoto, 2019a).

Another such example is cars. Besides the obvious function of transportation, cars have acquired important signaling characteristics in the course of human cultural evolution, which has seen cars arise as one of the most prototypical examples of conspicuous consumption and wealth signaling. Men who were seated in a luxurious Silver Bentley Continental GT were rated as significantly more attractive by women than when seated in a Red Ford Fiesta ST (Dunn & Searle, 2010). This finding about the effects of a luxury versus a standard car in mate choice has been replicated using other car models in other studies (Shuler & McCord, 2010; Sundie et al., 2011).

But are men swayed by these non-bodily traits to the same extent as women are? That does not appear to be the case. Women presented in a luxury apartment are rated equally attractive by men as when presented in a standard apartment (Dunn & Hill, 2014). Likewise, women presented in a luxury versus standard car are not rated as more attractive by men (Dunn & Searle, 2010). Men are more likely than women to use their car as a cue of their wealth and their phenotypic quality (Belk, 2004), while some men believe that owning the right kind of car is similar to possessing a powerful sexual charm that can render them irresistible to women (Saad & Vongas, 2009). Why should there be such a sex difference in the importance of non-bodily versus bodily traits in sexual selection?

The "traditional dating arrangement" where men are expected to court women with gifts and dinners is by no means strictly a human occurrence: it is a broader evolutionary trend that has evolved to counter the sexual asymmetry in parental investment (Lewis & South, 2012). For instance, the transfer of important material gifts from males to females is common in many arthropod species. In some species, females do not hunt at all, relying instead on food gifts from males (Gwynne, 2008). In wild chimpanzees, food sharing is associated with increased copulation in males who share meat with females over an extended period of time. Male chimpanzees are also more likely to share meat with estrous than anestrous females, suggesting that male chimpanzees exchange meat for reproductive opportunities (Gomes & Boesch, 2009). Anthropological evidence in humans has shown that Siriono men in Bolivia obtain extramarital sex with meat gifts (Holmberg, 1969), Mehinaku women in the Amazon use their sexuality to obtain food from men (Gregor, 1985, pp. 36–37), and the Kulina in South America have a ritual practice in which women have sexual intercourse with successful hunters (Pollock, 2002, p. 53). Some contemporary women engage in *foodie calls*, that is, going on a date in order to get a free meal. A study on foodie calls found that 33% of women had engaged in a foodie call, and some women engaged in them frequently or very frequently (Collisson et al., 2020). We are not aware of any studies on foodie calls in men, and suspect that few men would go on dates in hopes of a free meal. In a large contemporary German sample of heterosexual individuals, most men (75.3%) could imagine marrying someone who does not have regular employment, but relatively few women (28.0%) had marriage interest in such a mate. However, more women (47.7%) than men (35.2%) could imagine marrying someone who is not good-looking (Schwarz & Hassebrauck, 2012). These findings exemplify the sex difference placed on bodily versus non-bodily traits, possibly highlighting the greater somatic investment that women make in producing offspring in humans. In the aggregate, men tend to place a higher premium than women on bodily rather than non-bodily traits, whereas women may value men's ability to bridge the sexual asymmetry in parental investment by providing resources (Janicke et al., 2016; Kuzawa, 2007; Luoto, 2019a). Food provisioning is a simple example of resource sharing that can indicate the evolutionarily valuable ability to provide for offspring.

Creativity is another important trait in mate choice, at least once a baseline level of other traits has been satisfied (Li et al., 2002). In a cross-cultural mate preference study, creativity was ranked the sixth most desirable trait by women and seventh by men (Buss et al., 1990; cf. Zietsch et al., 2012). Creativity takes several different forms, and these forms are not necessarily rated equally desirable by the opposite sex (Kaufman et al., 2014). Sculptures, paintings, musical recordings, and literature can comprise physical cues of their producer's phenotypic and/or genetic quality, and as such, they may influence the sexual attractiveness of the artist (Clegg et al., 2011; Madison et al., 2018; Miller, 2001; Winegard et al., 2018). Although there are few studies of how works of art as non-bodily ornaments influence artists' mate value, one study found that written records of men's compliments to women increased a man's attractiveness when the compliments were creative rather than trite (Gao, Gao, et al., 2017). A correlational study found that men's success with visual art was a significant predictor of their number of self-reported mating partners—while in female artists such a pattern was not found (Clegg et al., 2011) (see also Varella et al., 2017 for a broader discussion). Corresponding findings have been reported with literary art and other creative products. Men comprise an overwhelming majority of producers of creative products for public consumption (Kanazawa, 2000; Lange & Euler, 2014; Miller, 1999). Men are also more motivated to write books than women (Lange, 2011), whereas women are more avid readers of fiction than men and also tend to consume more high-brow culture than men (reviewed in Christin, 2012). These findings support the hypothesis of male supply and female evaluation of creative products (i.e., the "art as sexual display" hypothesis) that arises from the theory of sexual selection (Crocchiola, 2014; Gao, Yang, et al., 2017; Lange & Euler, 2014) (for a broader discussion, readers may refer to Varella et al., 2017, 2022; Winegard et al., 2018). We note that more research is needed in this area to provide more robust evidence of sex differences in how art is evaluated within a mate choice context.

Evolutionary Mismatches in Mating

It is intriguing that such sex differences as reported above exist even in contemporary societies that have undergone millennia of cultural evolution since our ancestral hunter–gatherer past. Wouldn't it be preferable for men to partner up with a wealthier female, all other things being equal, since material wealth will likely increase the likelihood of raising viable offspring in contemporary humans? The findings reviewed above indicate that this may not necessarily be an important consideration for most contemporary males, suggesting that men have not overridden their evolved mate preferences (Buss & Schmitt, 2019) even if rationally it might in some contexts be beneficial for them to do so. What is more, that many women still emphasize the importance of resource-provisioning ability in males (Buss & Schmitt, 2019; Hughes & Aung, 2017), either consciously or subconsciously, suggests that sex differences in partner preferences, which are reminiscent of traditional Darwinian gender roles (Archer, 2019; Janicke et al., 2016), still persist despite environmental and cultural novelties, such as some branches of modern feminism and gender equity movement. This highlights the oft-repeated insight from evolutionary psychology: when there has been a rapid change in environmental conditions, individuals may still be genetically, psychologically, and behaviorally adapted to the past and therefore maladapted to the present, engaging in goal-directed behaviors that end up decreasing their fitness (Crespi, 2020; Goetz,et al., 2019; Li et al., 2018). This outcome may be highly prevalent in contemporary humans, since rapid change in our environments can create cascades of "mismatches" between evolved psychological mechanisms and the current environment, decoupling behavior from its formerly adaptive contexts and outcomes (Crespi, 2020; Rantala et al., 2019; Rantala et al., 2018).

Many such mismatches also occur in mating. From an evolutionary point of view, it is important to recognize that our mate choice mechanisms were calibrated in environments where potential mates were evaluated in person by using the full array of cues available to us from in vivo observations of a person's characteristics (Goetz et al., 2019). However, the proliferation of online dating technologies and social networking platforms has generated a new kind of mismatch with interpersonal evaluation and courtship. Physical cues conveyed by a person's online dating profile or in social media may imperfectly (or deceptively) represent the actual underlying mate quality of that person (Goetz et al.,

2019; Luoto, 2019a). The ubiquity of contemporary interactions in social media, both with regard to finding *and* keeping a mate, may mismatch our evolved psychological mechanisms—geared as they are toward in vivo interactions and observing physical cues of potential mates in person. Thus, in contemporary technologically advanced environments, evolved psychological mechanisms that guide human mate choice may be suboptimally adapted to such scenarios in which a handheld mobile device smaller than a stone-age handaxe contains the potentially deceptive virtual representation of physical cues of thousands more potential mates than any ancestral human being would encounter in their lifetimes (Goetz et al., 2019; Luoto, 2019a). This mismatch highlights the importance of an evolutionary understanding of how mate quality is signaled via physical cues, as well as the modern proliferation and potential deceptive modification of such cues in social media. Understanding the evolutionary underpinnings of sexual signaling via physical cues may help people navigate the contemporary complexity of sexual selection and avoid making suboptimal or poorly informed mate choice decisions.

Conclusions

The human face and body convey a large amount of information, from salient traits such as age, sex, and ancestry to less obvious information such as nutritional status, hormonal status, and personality. The human body also conveys information about sex via sexually dimorphic and gendered traits, body composition, hormonal status, age, and other traits. In this chapter, we have shown how these physical cues of partner quality can convey information essential to successful reproduction, such as a partner's genetic quality, health during development, and current condition. But partner quality can also be inferred from non-bodily objects, including clothes, jewelery, cars, and houses. Given the evolutionary importance of physical cues on sexual selection, it is unsurprising that physical cues of partner quality remain central to the human experience, from Shakespeare's sonnets to visual art and from the multi-billion-dollar industries of fashion, cosmetics, and physical self-enhancement to the "sexy selfies" that have proliferated in recent cultural evolution via internet, social media, and online dating. Mary Wollstonecraft (1992) made the following remark in 1792, which still resonates in contemporary sexual selection: "Taught from infancy that beauty is woman's sceptre, the mind shapes itself to the body, and roaming round its gilt cage, only seeks to adorn its prison." As evolved mate preferences continue to fixate on evolutionarily and reproductively relevant traits, various bodily and non-bodily physical cues of partner quality will remain highly relevant to human sexual selection, shaping the choices of whom we pursue romantically and with whom we choose to enter committed long-term relationships.

Acknowledgements

The authors wish to thank Markus J. Rantala for his comments on this chapter.

References

Alaluf, S., Heinrich, U., Stahl, W., Tronnier, H., & Wiseman, S. (2002). Human nutrition and metabolism: Dietary carotenoids contribute to normal human skin color and UV photosensitivity. *Journal of Nutrition, 132*, 399–403.

Antar, J., & Stephen, I. D. (2021). Facial shape provides a valid cue to sociosexuality in men but not women. *Evolution and Human Behavior, 42*, 361–370.

Archer, J. (2019). The reality and evolutionary significance of human psychological sex differences. *Biological Reviews, 94*(4), 1381–1415. https://doi.org/10.1111/brv.12507

Armstrong, N., & Welsman, J. (2001). Peak oxygen uptake in relation to growth and maturation in 11- to 17–year-old humans. *European Journal of Applied Physiology, 85*(6), 546–551. https://doi.org/10.1007/s004210100485

Austen, J. (2000). *Pride and prejudice*. Global Media. (Original work published 1813)

Baird, D. D., Weinberg, C. R., Zhou, H., Kamel, F., McConnaughey, D. R., Kesner, J. S., & Wilcox, A. J. (1999). Preimplantation urinary hormone profiles the probability of conception in healthy women. *Fertility and Sterility, 71*(1), 40–49. https://doi.org/10.1016/S0015-0282(98)00419-1

Baird, D. D., Wilcox, A. J., Weinberg, C. R., Kamel, F., McConnaughey, D. R., Musey, P. I., & Collins, D. C. (1997). Preimplantation hormonal differences between the conception and non-conception menstrual cycles of 32 normal women. *Human Reproduction, 12*(12), 2607–2613. http://www.ncbi.nlm.nih.gov/pubmed/9455822

Baumeister, R. F., Reynolds, T., Winegard, B., & Vohs, K. D. (2017). Competing for love: Applying sexual economics theory to mating contests. *Journal of Economic Psychology, 63*, 230–241. https://doi.org/10.1016/j.joep.2017.07.009

Belk, R. W. (2004). Men and their machines. *Advances in Consumer Research, 31*, 273–278.

Berry, D. S., & Brownlow, S. (1989). Were the physiognomists right? *Personality and Social Psychology Bulletin, 15*(2), 266–279. https://doi.org/10.1177/0146167289152013

Blake, K. R., Fourati, M., & Brooks, R. C. (2018). Who suppresses female sexuality? An examination of support for Islamic veiling in a secular Muslim democracy as a function of sex and offspring sex. *Evolution and Human Behavior, 39*(6), 632–638.

Böckerman, P., & Vainiomäki, J. (2013). Stature and life-time labor market outcomes: Accounting for unobserved differences. *Labour Economics, 24*, 86–96.

Boothroyd, L. G., Cross, C. P., Gray, A. W., Coombes, C., & Gregson-Curtis, K. (2011). Perceiving the facial correlates of sociosexuality: Further evidence. *Personality and Individual Differences, 50*(3), 422–425. https://doi.org/10.1016/j.paid.2010.10.017

Boothroyd, L. G., Jones, B. C., Burt, D. M., DeBruine, L. M., & Perrett, D. I. (2008). Facial correlates of sociosexuality. *Evolution and Human Behavior, 29*(3), 211–218. https://doi.org/10.1016/j.evolhumbehav.2007.12.009

Borráz-León, J. I., Rantala, M. J., Luoto, S., Krams, I., Contreras-Garduño, J. Krama, T., & Cerda-Molina, A. L. (2021). Self-perceived facial attractiveness, fluctuating asymmetry, and minor ailments predict mental health outcomes. *Adaptive Human Behavior and Physiology, 7*, 363–381. https://doi.org/10.1007/s40750-021-00172-6

Bovet, J. (2019). Evolutionary theories and men's preferences for women's waist-to-hip ratio: Which hypotheses remain? A systematic review. *Frontiers in Psychology, 10*, Article 1221. https://doi.org/10.3389/fpsyg.2019.01221

Brierley, M.-E., Brooks, K. R., Mond, J., Stevenson, R. J., & Stephen, I. D. (2016). The body and the beautiful: Health, attractiveness and body composition in men's and women's bodies. *PLoS ONE, 11*(6). https://doi.org/10.1371/journal.pone.0156722

Brooks, R., Scott, I. M., Maklakov, A. A., Kasumovic, M. M., Clark, A. P., & Penton-Voak, I. S. (2011). National income inequality predicts women's preferences for masculinized faces better than health does. *Proceedings of the Royal Society B: Biological Sciences, 278*(1707), 810–814. https://doi.org/10.1098/rspb.2010.0964

Brown, J. L. (1997). A theory of mate choice based on heterozygosity. *Behavioral Ecology, 8*(1), 60–65. https://doi.org/10.1093/beheco/8.1.60

Brown, J. L. (1999). The new heterozygosity theory of mate choice and the MHC. *Genetica, 104*(3), 215–221. http://www.ncbi.nlm.nih.gov/pubmed/10386385

Buss, D. M., Abbott, M., Angleitner, A., Asherian, A., Biaggio, A., Blanco-Villasenor, A., Bruchon-Schweitzer, M., Ch'U, H-Y., Czapinski, J., Deraad, B., Ekehammar, B. El Lohamy, N., Fioravanti, M., Georgas, J., Gjerde, P, Guttman, R., Hazan, F., Iwawaki, S., Janakiramaiah, N. . . . Yang, K-S. (1990). International preferences in selecting mates: A study of 37 cultures. *Journal of Cross-Cultural Psychology, 21*(1), 5–47.

Buss, D. M., & Penke, L. (2015). Evolutionary personality psychology. In M. Mikulincer, P. R. Shaver, M. L. Cooper, & R. J. Larsen (Eds.), *APA handbooks in psychology®. APA handbook of personality and social psychology, Vol. 4. Personality processes and individual differences* (pp. 3–29). American Psychological Association Press. https://doi.org/10.1037/14343-001

Buss, D. M., & Schmitt, D. P. (2019). Mate preferences and their behavioral manifestations. *Annual Review of Psychology, 70,* 77–110. https://doi.org/10.1146/annurev-psych-010418-103408

Cashdan, E. (2008). Waist-to-hip ratio across cultures: Trade-offs between androgen- and estrogen-dependent traits. *Current Anthropology, 49*(6), 1099–1107. https://doi.org/10.1086/593036

Charkoudian, N., Stephens, D. P., Pirkle, K. C., Kosiba, W. A., & Johnson, J. M. (1999). Influence of female reproductive hormones on local thermal control of skin blood flow. *Journal of Applied Physiologyy, 87*(5), 1719–1723. https://doi.org/10.1152/jappl.1999.87.5.1719

Christin, A. (2012). Gender and highbrow cultural participation in the United States. *Poetics, 40*(5), 423–443. https://doi.org/10.1016/j.poetic.2012.07.003

Clegg, H., Nettle, D., & Miell, D. (2011). Status and mating success amongst visual artists. *Frontiers in Psychology, 2,* 310. https://doi.org/10.3389/fpsyg.2011.00310

Coetzee, V., Barrett, L., Greeff, J. M., Henzi, S. P., Perrett, D. I., & Wadee, A. A. (2007). Common HLA alleles associated with health, but not with facial attractiveness. *PLoS ONE, 2*(7), 1–8. https://doi.org/10.1371/journal.pone.0000640

Coetzee, V., Chen, J., Perrett, D. I., & Stephen, I. D. (2010). Deciphering faces: Quantifiable visual cues to weight. *Perception, 39*(1), 51–61. https://doi.org/10.1068/p6560

Coetzee, V., Faerber, S. J., Greeff, J. M., Lefevre, C. E., Re, D. E., & Perrett, D. I. (2012). African perceptions of female attractiveness. *PLoS ONE, 7*(10), Article e48116. https://doi.org/10.1371/journal.pone.0048116

Coetzee, V., Greeff, J. M. J. M., Stephen, I. D., & Perrett, D. I. (2014). Cross-cultural agreement in facial attractiveness preferences: The role of ethnicity and gender. *PLoS ONE, 9*(7). https://doi.org/10.1371/journal.pone.0099629

Coetzee, V., Perrett, D. I., & Stephen, I. D. (2009). Facial adiposity: A cue to health? *Perception, 38*(11), 1700–1711. https://doi.org/10.1068/p6423

Collisson, B., Howell, J. L., & Harig, T. (2020). Foodie calls: When women date men for a free meal (rather than a relationship). *Social Psychological and Personality Science, 11*(3), 425–432. https://doi.org/10.1177/1948550619856308

Cornelissen, P. L., Toveé, M. J., & Bateson, M. (2009). Patterns of subcutaneous fat deposition and the relationship between body mass index and waist-to-hip ratio: Implications for models of physical attractiveness. *Journal of Theoretical Biology, 256*(3), 343–350. https://doi.org/10.1016/j.jtbi.2008.09.041

Crespi, B. (2020). Evolutionary and genetic insights for clinical psychology. *Clinical Psychology Review, 78,* Article 01857.https://doi.org/10.1016/j.cpr.2020.101857

Crespi, B., & Summers, K. (2005). Evolutionary biology of cancer. *Trends in Ecology & Evolution, 20*(10), 545–552.

Crocchiola, D. (2014). Art as an indicator of male fitness: Does prenatal testosterone influence artistic ability? *Evolutionary Psychology, 12*(3), 521–533. https://doi.org/10.1177/147470491401200303

Čvorović, J. (2020). Stature and education among Roma women: Taller stature is associated with better educational and economic outcomes. *Journal of Biosocial Science, 52*(2), 260–271.

Darwin, C. (1871). *The descent of man and selection in relation to sex.* Murray.

DeBruine, L. M., Jones, B. C., Crawford, J. R., Welling, L. L. M., & Little, A. C. (2010). The health of a nation predicts their mate preferences: Cross-cultural variation in women's preferences for masculinized male faces. *Proceedings of the Royal Society of London B: Biological Sciences, 277*(1692), 2405–2410. https://doi.org/10.1098/rspb.2009.2184

Dixson, B. J. W., Blake, K. R., Denson, T. F., Gooda-Vossos, A., O'Dean, S. M., Sulikowski, D., Rantala, M. J., & Brooks, R. C. (2018). The role of mating context and fecundability in women's preferences for men's facial masculinity and beardedness. *Psychoneuroendocrinology, 93,* 90–102. https://doi.org/10.1016/j.psyneuen.2018.04.007

Dixson, B. J. W., Duncan, M., & Dixson, A. F. (2015). The role of breast size and areolar pigmentation in perceptions of women's sexual attractiveness, reproductive health, sexual maturity, maternal nurturing abilities, and age. *Archives of Sexual Behavior, 44*(6), 1685–1695. https://doi.org/10.1007/s10508-015-0516-2

Dixson, B. J. W., Grimshaw, G. M., Linklater, W. L., & Dixson, A. F. (2011). Eye-tracking of men's preferences for waist-to-hip ratio and breast size of women. *Archives of Sexual Behavior, 40*(1), 43–50. https://doi.org/10.1007/s10508-009-9523-5

Dunn, M. J., & Hill, A. (2014). Manipulated luxury-apartment ownership enhances opposite-sex attraction in females but not males. *Journal of Evolutionary Psychology, 12*(1), 1–17.

Dunn, M. J., & Searle, R. (2010). Effect of manipulated prestige-car ownership on both sex attractiveness ratings. *British Journal of Psychology, 101*(1), 69–80.

Durante, K. M., Li, N. P., & Haselton, M. G. (2008). Changes in women's choice of dress across the ovulatory cycle: Naturalistic and laboratory task-based evidence. *Personality & Social Psychology Bulletin, 34*(11), 1451–1460. https://doi.org/10.1177/0146167208323103

Edwards, E. A., & Duntley, S. Q. (1939). The pigments and color of living human skin. *American Journal of Anatomy, 65*, 1–33.

Eisenbruch, A. B., Simmons, Z. L., & Roney, J. R. (2015). Lady in red: Hormonal predictors of women's clothing choices. *Psychological Science, 26*(8), 1332–1338. https://doi.org/10.1177/0956797615586403

Elliot, A. J., Greitemeyer, T., & Pazda, A. D. (2013). Women's use of red clothing as a sexual signal in intersexual interaction. *Journal of Experimental Social Psychology, 49*(3), 599–602.

Fink, B., & Penton-Voak, I. S. (2002). Evolutionary psychology of facial attractiveness. *Current Directions in Psychological Science, 11*(5), 154–158. https://doi.org/10.1111/1467-8721.00190

Fisher, R. (1930). *The genetical theory of natural selection*. Clarendon Press.

Folstad, I., & Karter, A. (1992). Parasites, bright males, and the immunocompetence handicap. *The American Naturalist, 139*(3), 603–622.

Foo, Y. Z., Nakagawa, S., Rhodes, G., & Simmons, L. W. (2017). The effects of sex hormones on immune function: A meta-analysis. *Biological Reviews, 92*(1), 551–571. https://doi.org/10.1111/brv.12243

Frederick, D. A., & Haselton, M. G. (2007). Why is muscularity sexy? Tests of the fitness indicator hypothesis. *Personality and Social Psychology Bulletin, 33*(8), 1167–1183. https://doi.org/10.1177/0146167207303022

Furnham, A., Dias, M., & McClelland, A. (1998). The role of body weight, waist-to-hip ratio, and breast size in judgments of female attractiveness. *Sex Roles, 39*, 311–326. https://doi.org/10.1023/A:1018810723493

Gangestad, S. W., Dinh, T., Grebe, N. M., Del Giudice, M., & Thompson, M. E. (2019). Psychological cycle shifts redux: Revisiting a preregistered study examining preferences for muscularity. *Evolution and Human Behavior, 40*, 501–516. https://doi.org/10.1016/j.evolhumbehav.2019.05.005

Gangestad, S. W., Thornhill, R., & Yeo, R. A. (1994). Facial attractiveness, developmental stability, and fluctuating asymmetry. *Science, 15*(2), 73–85. https://doi.org/10.1016/0162-3095(94)90018-3

Gao, Z., Gao, S., Xu, L., Zheng, X., Ma, X., Luo, L., & Kendrick, K. M. (2017). Women prefer men who use metaphorical language when paying compliments in a romantic context. *Scientific Reports, 7*, 40871. https://doi.org/10.1038/srep40871

Gao, Z., Yang, Q., Ma, X., Becker, B., Li, K., Zhou, F., & Kendrick, K. M. (2017). Men who compliment a woman's appearance using metaphorical language: Associations with creativity, masculinity, intelligence and attractiveness. *Frontiers in Psychology, 8*, 2185. https://doi.org/10.3389/fpsyg.2017.02185

Gaulin, S., & Boster, J. (1985). Cross-cultural differences in sexual dimorphism. Is there any variance to be explained? *Ethology and Sociobiology, 6*(4), 219–225. https://doi.org/10.1016/0162-3095(85)90014-7

Gildersleeve, K., Haselton, M. G., & Fales, M. R. (2014). Meta-analyses and p-curves support robust cycle shifts in women's mate preferences: Reply to Wood and Carden (2014). *Psychological Bulletin, 140*(5), 1272–1280. https://doi.org/10.1037/a0037714

Goetz, C. D., Pillsworth, E. G., Buss, D. M., & Conroy-Beam, D. (2019). Evolutionary mismatch in mating. *Frontiers in Psychology, 10*, 2709. https://doi.org/10.3389/fpsyg.2019.02709

Gomes, C. M., & Boesch, C. (2009). Wild chimpanzees exchange meat for sex on a long-term basis. *PLoS ONE, 4*(4), Article e5116. https://doi.org/10.1371/journal.pone.0005116

Gouda-Vossos, A., Brooks, R. C., & Dixson, B. J. W. (2019). The interplay between economic status and attractiveness, and the importance of attire in mate choice judgments. *Frontiers in Psychology, 10*, 462. https://doi.org/10.3389/fpsyg.2019.00462

Gregor, T. (1985). *Anxious pleasures: The sexual lives of an Amazonian people*. University of Chicago Press.

Grillot, R. L., Simmons, Z. L., Lukaszewski, A. W., & Roney, J. R. (2014). Hormonal and morphological predictors of women's body attractiveness. *Evolution and Human Behavior, 35*(3), 176–183. https://doi.org/10.1016/j.evolhumbehav.2014.01.001

Gwynne, D. T. (2008). Sexual conflict over nuptial gifts in insects. *Annual Review of Entomology, 53,* 83–101. https://doi.org/10.1146/annurev.ento.53.103106.093423

Han, C., Wang, H., Hahn, A. C., Fisher, C. I., Kandrik, M., Fasolt, V., Morrison, D. K., Lee, A. J., Holzleitner, I. J., DeBruine, L. M., & Jones, B. C. (2018). Cultural differences in preferences for facial coloration. *Evolution and Human Behavior, 39*(2), 154–159. https://doi.org/10.1016/j.evolhumbehav.2017.11.005

Havlíček, J., & Roberts, S. C. (2009). MHC-correlated mate choice in humans: A review. *Psychoneuroendocrinology, 34*(4), 497–512. https://doi.org/10.1016/j.psyneuen.2008.10.007

Havlíček, J., Třebický, V., Valentova, J. V., Kleisner, K., Akoko, R. M., Fialová, J., Jash, R., Kočnar, T., Pereira, K. J., Štěrbová, Z., Varella, M. A. C., Vokurková, J., Vunan, E., & Roberts, S. C. (2017). Men's preferences for women's breast size and shape in four cultures. *Evolution and Human Behavior, 38*(2), 217–226. https://doi.org/10.1016/j.evolhumbehav.2016.10.002

Havlíček, J., Winternitz, J., & Roberts, S. C. (2020). MHC-associated odour preferences and human mate choice: Near and far horizons. *Philosophical Transactions of the Royal Society B: Biological Sciences, 375*(1800), Article 20190260. https://doi.org/10.1098/rstb.2019.0260

Hendrie, C., Chapman, R., & Gill, C. (2020). Women's strategic use of clothing and make-up. *Human Ethology, 35,* 16–26. https://doi.org/10.22330/he/35/016-026

Hendrie, C. A., Mannion, H. D., & Godfrey, G. K. (2009). Evidence to suggest that nightclubs function as human sexual display grounds. *Behaviour, 146*(10), 1331–1348.

Hill, E. M., Nocks, E. S., & Gardner, L. (1987). Physical attractiveness: Manipulation by physique and status displays. *Ethology and Sociobiology, 8*(2), 143–154.

Holmberg, A. R. (1969). *Nomads of the long bow: The Siriono of eastern Bolivia.* Natural History Press.

Hu, S., Xiong, J., Fu, P., Qiao, L., Tan, J., Jin, L., & Tang, K. (2017). Signatures of personality on dense 3D facial images. *Scientific Reports, 7*(1), 1–10. https://doi.org/10.1038/s41598-017-00071-5

Hughes, S. M., & Aung, T. (2017). Modern-day female preferences for resources and provisioning by long-term mates. *Evolutionary Behavioral Sciences, 11*(3), 242–261.

Hughes, S. M., Aung, T., Harrison, M. A., Lafayette, J. N., & Gallup, G. G. (2021). Experimental evidence for sex differences in sexual variety preferences: Support for the Coolidge Effect in humans. *Archives of Sexual Behavior, 50*(2), 495–509.

Janicke, T., Häderer, I. K., Lajeunesse, M. J., & Anthes, N. (2016). Darwinian sex roles confirmed across the animal kingdom. *Science Advances, 2*(2), Article e1500983. https://doi.org/10.1126/sciadv.1500983

Jasieńska, G., Ziomkiewicz, A., Ellison, P. T., Lipson, S. F., & Thune, I. (2004). Large breasts and narrow waists indicate high reproductive potential in women. *Proceedings of the Royal Society B: Biological Sciences, 271*(1545), 1213–1217. https://doi.org/10.1098/rspb.2004.2712

Javed, A., & Lteif, A. (2013). Development of the human breast. *Seminars in Plastic Surgery, 27*(1), 5–12. https://doi.org/10.1055/s-0033-1343989

Jones, A. G., & Ratterman, N. L. (2009). Mate choice and sexual selection: What have we learned since Darwin? *Proceedings of the National Academy of Sciences of the United States of America, 106*(Suppl. 1), 10001–10008. https://doi.org/10.1073/pnas.0901129106

Jones, A. L., Kramer, R. S. S., & Ward, R. (2012). Signals of personality and health: The contributions of facial shape, skin texture and viewing angle. *Journal of Experimental Psychology: Human Perception and Performance, 38*(6), 1353–1361. https://doi.org/10.1037/a0027078

Jones, B. C., Hahn, A. C., Fisher, C. I., Wang, H., Kandrik, M., Han, C., Fasolt, V., Morrison, D., Lee, A. J., Holzleitner, I. J., O'Shea, K. J., Roberts, S. C., Little, A. C., & DeBruine, L. M. (2018). No compelling evidence that preferences for facial masculinity track changes in women's hormonal status. *Psychological Science, 29*(6), 996–1005. https://doi.org/10.1177/0956797618760197

Jünger, J., Kordsmeyer, T. L., Gerlach, T. M., & Penke, L. (2018). Fertile women evaluate male bodies as more attractive, regardless of masculinity. *Evolution and Human Behavior, 39*(4), 412–423. https://doi.org/10.1016/j.evolhumbehav.2018.03.007

Jünger, J., Motta-Mena, N. V., Cardenas, R., Bailey, D., Rosenfield, K. A., Schild, C., Penke, L., & Puts, D. A. (2018). Do women's preferences for masculine voices shift across the ovulatory cycle? *Hormones and Behavior, 106,* 122–134. https://doi.org/10.1016/j.yhbeh.2018.10.008

Kanazawa, S. (2000). Scientific discoveries as cultural displays: A further test of Miller's courtship model. *Evolution and Human Behavior, 21*(5), 317–321. https://doi.org/10.1016/S1090-5138(00)00051-9

Kaufman, S. B., Kozbelt, A., Silvia, P., Kaufman, J. C., Ramesh, S., & Feist, G. J. (2014). Who finds Bill Gates sexy? Creative mate preferences as a function of cognitive ability, personality, and creative achievement. *The Journal of Creative Behavior, 50*(4), 294–307.

Kordsmeyer, T. L., Hunt, J., Puts, D. A., Ostner, J., & Penke, L. (2018). The relative importance of intra- and intersexual selection on human male sexually dimorphic traits. *Evolution and Human Behavior, 39*(4), 424–436. https://doi.org/10.1016/j.evolhumbehav.2018.03.008

Kościński, K., Makarewicz, R., & Bartoszewicz, Z. (2020). Stereotypical and actual associations of breast size with mating-relevant traits. *Archives of Sexual Behavior, 49*(3), 821–836. https://doi.org/10.1007/s10508-019-1464-z

Kramer, R. S. S., & Ward, R. (2010). Internal facial features are signals of personality and health. *Quarterly Journal of Experimental Psychology, 63*(11), 2273–2287. https://doi.org/10.1080/17470211003770912

Krams, I., Luoto, S., Rubika, A., Krama, T., Elferts, D., Kecko, S., Skrinda, I., Moore, F., Krams, R., & Rantala, M. J. (2019). A head start for life history development? Family income mediates associations between body height and immune response in men. *American Journal of Physical Anthropology, 168*(3), 421–427. https://doi.org/10.1002/ajpa.23754

Kuzawa, C. W. (2007). Developmental origins of life history: Growth, productivity, and reproduction. *American Journal of Human Biology, 19*(5), 654–661.

Lange, B. P. (2011). Male proneness to verbal display production. *Acta Linguistica, 5*, 97–104.

Lange, B. P., & Euler, H. A. (2014). Writers have groupies, too: High quality literature production and mating success. *Evolutionary Behavioral Sciences, 8*(1), 20–30. https://doi.org/10.1037/h0097246

Lassek, W. D., & Gaulin, S. J. C. (2008). Waist-hip ratio and cognitive ability: Is gluteofemoral fat a privileged store of neurodevelopmental resources? *Evolution and Human Behavior, 29*(1), 26–34. https://doi.org/10.1016/j.evolhumbehav.2007.07.005

Lassek, W. D., & Gaulin, S. J. C. (2009). Costs and benefits of fat-free muscle mass in men: Relationship to mating success, dietary requirements, and native immunity. *Evolution and Human Behavior, 30*(5), 322–328. https://doi.org/10.1016/j.evolhumbehav.2009.04.002

Lassek, W. D., & Gaulin, S. J. (2019). Evidence supporting nubility and reproductive value as the key to human female physical attractiveness. *Evolution and Human Behavior, 40*(5), 408–419.

Law Smith, M. J., Perrett, D. I., Jones, B. C., Cornwell, R. E., Moore, F. R., Feinberg, D. R., Boothroyd, L. G., Durrani, S. J., Stirrat, M. R., Whiten, S., Pitman, R. M., & Hillier, S. G. (2006). Facial appearance is a cue to oestrogen levels in women. *Proceedings of the the Royal Society: Biological Sciences, 273*(1583), 135–140. https://doi.org/10.1098/rspb.2005.3296

Lee, A. J., Wright, M. J., Martin, N. G., Keller, M. C., & Zietsch, B. P. (2017). Facial trustworthiness is associated with heritable aspects of face shape. *Adaptive Human Behavior and Physiology, 3*(4), 351–364. https://doi.org/10.1007/s40750-017-0073-0

Lee, L., Loewenstein, G., Ariely, D., Hong, J., & Young, J. (2008). If I'm not hot, are you hot or not? *Psychological Science, 19*(7), 669. https://doi.org/10.1111/j.1467-9280.2008.02141.x

Lennon, S. J., Adomaitis, A. D., Koo, J., & Johnson, K. K. (2017). Dress and sex: A review of empirical research involving human participants and published in refereed journals. *Fashion and Textiles, 4*(1), 14.

Lewis, D. M. G., Russell, E. M., Al-Shawaf, L., Ta, V., Senveli, Z., Ickes, W., Buss, D. (2017). Why women wear high heels: Evolution, lumbar curvature, and attractiveness. *Frontiers in Psychology, 8*, Article 1875. https://doi.org/10.3389/fpsyg.2017.01875

Lewis, S., & South, A. (2012). The evolution of animal nuptial gifts. *Advances in the Study of Behavior, 44*, 53–97. https://doi.org/10.1016/B978-0-12-394288-3.00002-2

Li, N. P., Bailey, J. M., Kenrick, D. T., & Linsenmeier, J. A. W. (2002). The necessities and luxuries of mate preferences: Testing the tradeoffs. *Journal of Personality and Social Psychology, 82*(6), 947–955.

Li, N. P., van Vugt, M., & Colarelli, S. M. (2018). The evolutionary mismatch hypothesis: Implications for psychological science. *Current Directions in Psychological Science, 27*(1), 38–44.

Lie, H. C., Rhodes, G., & Simmons, L. W. (2008). Genetic diversity revealed in human faces. *Evolution; International Journal of Organic Evolution, 62*(10), 2473–2486. https://doi.org/10.1111/j.1558-5646.2008.00478.x

Lie, H. C., Simmons, L. W., & Rhodes, G. (2009). Does genetic diversity predict health in humans? *PLoS ONE, 4*(7), Article e6391. https://doi.org/10.1371/journal.pone.0006391

Lipson, S. F., & Ellison, P. T. (1996). Comparison of salivary steroid profiles in naturally occurring conception and non-conception cycles. *Human Reproduction, 11*(10), 2090–2096. https://doi.org/10.1093/oxfordjournals.humrep.a019055.

Little, A. C., Apicella, C. L., & Marlowe, F. W. (2007). Preferences for symmetry in human faces in two cultures: Data from the UK and the Hadza, an isolated group of hunter-gatherers. *Proceedings of the Royal Society: Biological Sciences, 274*(1629), 3113–3117. https://doi.org/10.1098/rspb.2007.0895

Little, A. C., Burt, D. M., & Perrett, D. I. (2006). Assortative mating for perceived facial personality traits. *Personality and Individual Differences, 40*(5), 973–984. https://doi.org/10.1016/j.paid.2005.09.016

Luoto, S. (2019a). An updated theoretical framework for human sexual selection: From ecology, genetics, and life history to extended phenotypes. *Adaptive Human Behavior and Physiology, 5*(1), 48–102. https://doi.org/10.1007/s40750-018-0103-6

Luoto, S. (2019b). Response to Commentaries: Life history genetics, fluid intelligence, and extended phenotypes. *Adaptive Human Behavior and Physiology, 5*(1), 112–115. https://doi.org/10.1007/s40750-019-0109-8

Luoto, S., Krama, T., Rubika, A., Borráz-León, J. I., Trakimas, G., Elferts, D., Skrinda, I., Krams, R., Rantala, M. J., & Krams, I. (2021). Socioeconomic position, immune function, and its physiological markers, *Psychoneuroendocrinology, 127*, 105202. https://doi.org/10.1016/j.psyneuen.2021.105202

Luoto, S., Krams, I., & Rantala, M. J. (2019). A life history approach to the female sexual orientation spectrum: Evolution, development, causal mechanisms, and health. *Archives of Sexual Behavior, 48*(5), 1273–1308. https://doi.org/10.1007/s10508-018-1261-0

Luoto, S., & Varella, M. A. C. (2021). Pandemic leadership: Sex differences and their evolutionary–developmental origins. *Frontiers in Psychology, 12*, 618. https://doi.org/10.3389/fpsyg.2021.633862

Madison, G., Holmquist, J., & Vestin, M. (2018). Musical improvisation skill in a prospective partner is associated with mate value and preferences, consistent with sexual selection and parental investment theory: Implications for the origin of music. *Evolution and Human Behavior, 39*(1), 120–129. https://doi.org/10.1016/j.evolhumbehav.2017.10.005

Mallucci, P., & Branford, O. A. (2012). Concepts in aesthetic breast dimensions: Analysis of the ideal breast. *Journal of Plastic, Reconstructive and Aesthetic Surgery, 65*(1), 8–16. https://doi.org/10.1016/j.bjps.2011.08.006

Mallucci, P., & Branford, O. A. (2014). Population analysis of the perfect breast: A morphometric analysis. *Plastic and Reconstructive Surgery, 134*(3), 436–447. https://doi.org/10.1097/PRS.0000000000000485

Marcinkowska, U. M., Kozlov, M. V., Cai, H., Contreras-Garduño, J., Dixson, B. J., Oana, G. A., Kaminski, G., Li, N. P., Lyons, M. T., Onyishi, I. E., Prasai, K., Pazhoohi, F., Prokop, P., Rosales Cardozo, S. L., Sydney, N., Yong, J. C., & Rantala, M. J. (2014). Cross-cultural variation in men's preference for sexual dimorphism in women's faces. *Biology Letters, 10*(4), Article 20130850.

Marcinkowska, U. M., Rantala, M. J., Lee, A. J., Kozlov, M. V., Aavik, T., Cai, H., Contreras-Garduño, J., David, O. A., Kaminski, G., Li, N. P., Onyishi, I. E., Prasai, K., Pazhoohi, F., Prokop, P., Cardozo, S. L. R., Sydney, N., Taniguchi, H., Krams, I., & Dixson, B. J. W. (2019). Women's preferences for men's facial masculinity are strongest under favorable ecological conditions. *Scientific Reports, 9*(1), 1–10.

Marioni, R. E., Batty, G. D., Hayward, C., Kerr, S. M., Campbell, A., Hocking, L. J., Generation Scotland, Porteous, D. J., Visscher, P. M., & Deary, I. J. (2014). Common genetic variants explain the majority of the correlation between height and intelligence: The generation Scotland study. *Behavior Genetics, 44*(2), 91–96.

Mazur, A., & Booth, A. (1998). Testosterone and dominance in men. *The Behavioral and Brain Sciences, 21*(3), 353–397. http://www.ncbi.nlm.nih.gov/pubmed/10097017

McEvoy, B. P., & Visscher, P. M. (2009). Genetics of human height. *Economics and Human Biology, 7*, 294–306.

Miller, G. F. (1999). Sexual selection for cultural displays. In R. Dunbar, C. Knight, & C. Power (Eds.), *The evolution of culture* (pp. 71–91). Rutgers University Press.

Miller, G. F. (2001). Aesthetic fitness: How sexual selection shaped artistic virtuosity as a fitness indicator and aesthetic preferences as mate choice criteria. *Bulletin of Psychology and the Arts, 2*(1), 20–25.

Miller, G. F., & Todd, P. M. (1998). Mate choice turns cognitive. *Trends in Cognitive Sciences, 2*(5), 190–198.

Mogilski, J. K., & Welling, L. L. (2017). The relative importance of sexual dimorphism, fluctuating asymmetry, and color cues to health during evaluation of potential partners' facial photographs. *Human Nature, 28*, 53–75.

Møller, A. P., Soler, M., & Thornhill, R. (1995). Breast asymmetry, sexual selection, and human reproductive success. *Ethology and Sociobiology, 16*, 207–219.

Møller, A. P., & Thornhill, R. (1998). Bilateral symmetry and sexual selection: A meta-analysis. *American Naturalist, 151*(2), 174–192. https://doi.org/10.1086/286110

Moore, F. R., Coetzee, V., Contreras-Garduno, J., Debruine, L. M., Kleisner, K., Krams, I., Marcinkowska, U., Nord, A., Perrett, D. I., Rantala, M. J., Schaum, N., & Suzuki, T. N. (2013). Cross-cultural variation in women's preferences for cues to sex- and stress-hormones in the male face. *Biology Letters, 9*(3), Article 20130050. https://doi.org/10.1098/rsbl.2013.0050

Morris, P. H., White, J., Morrison, E. R., & Fisher, K. (2013). High heels as supernormal stimuli: How wearing high heels affects judgements of female attractiveness. *Evolution and Human Behavior, 34*(3), 176–181. https://doi.org/10.1016/j.evolhumbehav.2012.11.006

Murasko, J. E. (2020). Height, marriage, and partner characteristics for women in low-and middle-income countries. *Economics & Human Biology, 38*, Article 100876.

Panza, J., Quyyumi, A., Brush, J., & Epstein, S. (1990). Abnormal endothelium-dependent vascular relaxation in patients with essential hypertension. *New England Journal of Medicine, 323*(1), 22–27. https://doi.org/10.1056/NEJM199007053230105

Paunonen, S. V., Ewan, K., Earthy, J., Lefave, S., & Goldberg, H. (1999). Facial features as personality cues. *Journal of Personality, 67*(3), 555–583. https://doi.org/10.1111/1467-6494.00065

Pawłowski, B., Borkowska, B., Nowak, J., Augustyniak, D., & Drulis-Kawa, Z. (2018). Human body symmetry and immune efficacy in healthy adults. *American Journal of Physical Anthropology 167*, 207–216.

Pazhoohi, F., Garza, R., & Kingstone, A. (2020). Effects of breast size, intermammary cleft distance (cleavage) and ptosis on perceived attractiveness, health, fertility and age: Do life history, self-perceived mate value and sexism attitude play a role? *Adaptive Human Behavior and Physiology, 6*, 75–92. https://doi.org/10.1007/s40750-020-00129-1

Pazhoohi, F., & Kingstone, A. (2020). Sex difference on the importance of veiling: A cross-cultural investigation. *Cross-Cultural Research, 54*(5), 486–501.

Penton-Voak, I. S., & Chen, J. Y. (2004). High salivary testosterone is linked to masculine male facial appearance in humans. *Evolution and Human Behavior, 25*(4), 229–241. https://doi.org/10.1016/j.evolhumbehav.2004.04.003

Penton-Voak, I. S., Jones, B. C., Little, A. C., Baker, S., Tiddeman, B., Burt, D. M., & Perrett, D. I. (2001). Symmetry, sexual dimorphism in facial proportions and male facial attractiveness. *Proceedings of the Royal Society of London B: Biological Sciences, 268*(1476), 1617–1623. https://doi.org/10.1098/rspb.2001.1703

Penton-Voak, I. S., Perrett, D. I., Castles, D. L., Kobayashi, T., Burt, D. M., Murray, L. K., & Minamisawa, R. (1999). Menstrual cycle alters face preference. *Nature, 399*(6738), 741–742. https://doi.org/10.1038/21557

Penton-Voak, I. S., Pound, N., Little, A. C., & Perrett, D. I. (2006). Personality judgments from natural and composite facial images: More evidence for a "kernel of truth" in social perception. *Social Cognition, 24*(5), 607–640. https://doi.org/10.1521/soco.2006.24.5.607

Perrett, D. I., Burt, D. M., Penton-Voak, I. S., Lee, K. J., Rowland, D. A., & Edwards, R. (1999). Symmetry and human facial attractiveness. *Perception, 307*, 295–307.

Perrett, D. I., Lee, K. J., Penton-Voak, I. S., Rowland, D., Yoshikawa, S., & Burt, D. M. (1998). Effects of sexual dimorphism on facialattractiveness. *Nature, 394*(August), 884–887.

Pezdirc, K., Rollo, M. E., Whitehead, R., Hutchesson, M. J., Ozakinci, G., Perrett, D. I., & Collins, C. E. (2018). Perceptions of carotenoid and melanin colouration in faces among young Australian adults. *Australian Journal of Psychology, 70*(1), 85–90. https://doi.org/10.1111/ajpy.12163

Phalane, K. G., Tribe, C., Steel, H. C., Cholo, M. C., & Coetzee, V. (2017). Facial appearance reveals immunity in African men. *Scientific Reports, 7*(1), 7443.

Pollock, D. (2002). Partible paternity and multiple maternity among the Kulina. In S. Beckerman & P. Valentine (Eds.), *Cultures of multiple fathers: The theory of practice of partible paternity in lowland South America* (pp. 42–61). University Press of Florida.

Pound, N., Lawson, D. W., Toma, A. M., Richmond, S., Zhurov, A. I., & Penton-voak, I. S. (2014). Facial fluctuating asymmetry is not associated with childhood ill-health in a large British cohort study. *Proceedings of the Royal Society of London B, 281*, Article 20141639. https://doi.org/10.1098/rspb.2014.1639

Prokop, P., & Švancárová, J. (2020). Wearing high heels as female mating strategy. *Personality and Individual Differences, 152*, Article 109558. https://doi.org/10.1016/j.paid.2019.109558

Puts, D. A. (2010). Beauty and the beast: Mechanisms of sexual selection in humans. *Evolution and Human Behavior, 31*(3), 157–175. https://doi.org/10.1016/j.evolhumbehav.2010.02.005

Rantala, M. J., Coetzee, V., Moore, F. R., Skrinda, I., Kecko, S., Krama, T., Kivleniece, I., & Krams, I. (2013a). Adiposity, compared with masculinity, serves as a more valid cue to immunocompetence in human mate choice. *Proceedings of the Royal Society B: Biological Sciences, 280*(1751), Article 20122495.

Rantala, M. J., Coetzee, V., Moore, F. R., Skrinda, I., Kecko, S., Krama, T., Kivleniece, I., & Krams, I. (2013b). Facial attractiveness is related to women's cortisol and body fat, but not with immune responsiveness. *Biology Letters, 9*(4), Article 20130255.

Rantala, M. J., Luoto, S., Krama, T., & Krams, I. (2019). Eating disorders: An evolutionary psychoneuroimmunological approach. *Frontiers in Psychology, 10*. https://doi.org/10.3389/fpsyg.2019.02200

Rantala, M. J., Luoto, S., Krams, I., & Karlsson, H. (2018). Depression subtyping based on evolutionary psychiatry: Proximate mechanisms and ultimate functions. *Brain, Behavior, and Immunity*, 69, 603–617. https://doi.org/10.1016/j.bbi.2017.10.012

Re, D. E., Whitehead, R. D., Xiao, D., & Perrett, D. I. (2011). Oxygenated-blood colour change thresholds for perceived facial redness, health, and attractiveness. *PLoS ONE, 6*(3), Article e17859. https://doi.org/10.1371/journal.pone.0017859

Rhodes, G., Zebrowitz, L. A., Clark, A., Kalick, S. M., Hightower, A., & McKay, R. (2001). Do facial averageness and symmetry signal health? *Evolution and Human Behavior, 22*(1), 31–46. https://doi.org/10.1016/S1090-5138(00)00060-X

Roberts, S. C., Little, A. C., Gosling, L. M., Jones, B. C., Perrett, D. I., Carter, V., & Petrie, M. (2005). MHC-assortative facial preferences in humans. *Biology Letters, 1*, 400–403.

Rotwein, P. (2020). Revisiting the population genetics of human height. *Journal of the Endocrine Society, 4*(4), Article bvaa025.

Rubika, A., Luoto, S., Krama, T., Trakimas, G., Rantala, M. J., Moore, F., Skrinda, I., Elferts, D., Krams, R., Contreras-Garduño, J., & Krams, I. (2020). Women's socioeconomic position in ontogeny is associated with improved immune function and lower stress, but not with height. *Scientific Reports, 10*, Article 11517. https://doi.org/10.1038/s41598-020-68217-6

Scelza, B. A., & Prall, S. P. (2018). Partner preferences in the context of concurrency: What Himba want in formal and informal partners. *Evolution and Human Behavior, 39*(2), 212–219. https://doi.org/10.1016/j.evolhumbehav.2017.12.005

Schaedelin, F. C., & Taborsky, M. (2009). Extended phenotypes as signals. *Biological Reviews, 84*(2), 293–313. https://doi.org/10.1111/j.1469-185X.2008.00075.x

Schwarz, S., & Hassebrauck, M. (2012). Sex and age differences in mate-selection preferences. *Human Nature, 23*(4), 447–466.

Scott, I. M. L., Pound, N., Stephen, I. D., Clark, A. P., & Penton-Voak, I. S. (2010) Does masculinity matter? The contribution of masculine face shape to male attractiveness in humans. *PLoS ONE 5*(10), Article e13585. https://doi.org/10.1371/journal.pone.0013585

Scutt, D., Manning, J. T., Whitehouse, G. H., Leinster, S. J., & Massey, C. P. (1997). The relationship between breast asymmetry, breast size and the occurrence of breast cancer. *The British Journal of Radiology, 70*(838), 1017–1021. http://www.ncbi.nlm.nih.gov/pubmed/9404205

Sell, A., Cosmides, L., Tooby, J., Sznycer, D., Rueden, C. Von, Sell, A., Cosmides, L., Tooby, J., Sznycer, D., Rueden, C. Von, & Gurven, M. (2009). Human adaptations for the visual assessment of strength and fighting ability from the body and face. *Proceedings of the Royal Society B: Biological Sciences, 276*, 575–584. https://doi.org/10.1098/rspb.2008.1177

Sell, A., Lukazsweski, A. W., & Townsley, M. (2017). Cues of upper body strength account for most of the variance in men's bodily attractiveness. *Proceedings of the Royal Society B: Biological Sciences, 284*(1869), Article 20171819. https://doi.org/10.1098/rspb.2017.1819

Shuler, G. A., & McCord, D. M. (2010). Determinants of male attractiveness: "Hotness" ratings as a function of perceived resources. *American Journal of Psychological Research, 6*(1), 10–23.

Silventoinen, K., Sammalisto, S., Perola, M., Boomsma, D. I., Cornes, B. K., Davis, C., Dunkel, L., de Lange, M., Harris, J. R., Hjelmborg, J. V. B., Luciano, M., Martin, N. G., Mortensen, J., Nistico, L., Pedersen, N. L., Skytthe, A., Spector, T. D., Stazi, M. A., Willemsen, G., & Kaprio, J. (2003). Heritability of adult body height: A comparative study of twin cohorts in eight countries. *Twin Research, 6*, 399–408.

Singh, D. (1993a). Body shape and women's attractiveness—The critical role of waist-to-hip ratio. *Human Nature, 4*(3), 297–321. https://doi.org/10.1007/BF02692203

Singh, D. (1993b). Adaptive significance of female physical attractiveness: Role of waist-to-hip ratio. *Journal of Personality and Social Psychology, 65*(2), 293–307. http://www.ncbi.nlm.nih.gov/pubmed/8366421

Singh, D. (1995). Female health, attractiveness, and desirability for relationships: Role of breast asymmetry and waist-to-hip ratio. *Ethology and Sociobiology, 16*(6), 465–481. https://doi.org/10.1016/0162-3095(95)00073-9

Singh, D., & Young, R. K. (1995). Body weight, waist-to-hip ratio, breasts, and hips: Role in judgments of female attractiveness and desirability for relationships. *Ethology and Sociobiology, 16*(6), 483–507. https://doi.org/10.1016/0162-3095(95)00074-7

Sorokowska, A., Pietrowski, D., Schäfer, L., Kromer, J., Schmidt, A. H., Sauter, J., Hummel, T., & Croy, I. (2018). Human leukocyte antigen similarity decreases partners' and strangers' body odor attractiveness for women not using hormonal contraception. *Hormones and Behavior, 106*, 144–149. https://doi.org/10.1016/j.yhbeh.2018.10.007

Stahl, W., Heinrich, U., Jungmann, H., Laar, J. Von, Schietzel, M., Sies, H., Tronnier, H., von Laar, J., Schietzel, M., Sies, H., & Tronnier, H. (1998). Increased dermal carotenoid levels assessed by noninvasive reflection spectrophotometry correlate with serum levels in women ingesting Betatene. *The Journal of Nutrition, 128*(January), 903–907. https://doi.org/10.1093/jn/128.5.903

Stephen, I. D., Coetzee, V., Law Smith, M., & Perrett, D. I. (2009). Skin blood perfusion and oxygenation colour affect perceived human health. *PLoS ONE, 4*(4), Article e5083. https://doi.org/10.1371/journal.pone.0005083

Stephen, I. D., Coetzee, V., & Perrett, D. I. (2011). Carotenoid and melanin pigment coloration affect perceived human health. *Evolution and Human Behavior, 32*(3), 216–227. https://doi.org/10.1016/j.evolhumbehav.2010.09.003

Stephen, I. D., Hiew, V., Coetzee, V., Tiddeman, B. P., & Perrett, D. I. (2017). Facial shape analysis identifies valid cues to aspects of physiological health in Caucasian, Asian, and African populations. *Frontiers in Psychology, 8*, Article 1883. https://doi.org/10.3389/fpsyg.2017.01883

Stephen, I. D., Law Smith, M. J., Stirrat, M. R., & Perrett, D. I. (2009). Facial skin coloration affects perceived health of human faces. *International Journal of Primatology, 30*(6), 845–857. https://doi.org/10.1007/s10764-009-9380-z

Stephen, I. D., Scott, I. M. L. I. M. L., Coetzee, V., Pound, N., Perrett, D. I., & Penton-Voak, I. S. (2012). Cross-cultural effects of color, but not morphological masculinity, on perceived attractiveness of men's faces. *Evolution and Human Behavior, 33*(4), 260–267. https://doi.org/10.1016/j.evolhumbehav.2011.10.003

Stephen, I. D., & Tan, K. W. (2015). Healthy body, healthy face? Evolutionary approaches to attractiveness perception. In S. Haque & E. Sheppard (Eds.), *Culture and cognition: A collection of critical essays* (pp. 45–66). Peter Lang International. https://doi.org/10.3726/978-3-0351-0826-2

Stephen, I. D., Salter, D. L. H., Tan, K. W., Tan, C. B. Y., & Stevenson, R. J. (2018). Sexual dimorphism and attractiveness in Asian and White faces. *Visual Cognition, 26*(6), 442–449. https://doi.org/10.1080/13506285.2018.1475437

Stulp, G., & Barrett, L. (2016). Evolutionary perspectives on human height variation. *Biological Reviews, 91*(1), 206–234.

Stulp, G., Buunk, A. P., Kurzban, R., & Verhulst, S. (2013). The height of choosiness: Mutual mate choice for stature results in suboptimal pair formation for both sexes. *Animal Behaviour, 86*(1), 37–46.

Stulp, G., Buunk, A. P., Verhulst, S., & Pollet, T. V. (2015). Human height is positively related to interpersonal dominance in dyadic interactions. *PLoS ONE, 10*(2), Article e0117860.

Stulp, G., Simons, M. J., Grasman, S., & Pollet, T. V. (2017). Assortative mating for human height: A meta-analysis. *American Journal of Human Biology, 29*(1), Article e22917.

Sugiyama, L. S. (2015). Physical attractiveness: An adaptationist perspective. In D. M. Buss (Ed.), *The handbook of evolutionary psychology* (2nd ed., pp. 317–384). Wiley Online Library. https://doi.org/10.1002/9781119125563.evpsych112.

Sundet, J. M., Tambs, K., Harris, J. R., Magnus, P., & Torjussen, T. M. (2005). Resolving the genetic and environmental sources of the correlation between height and intelligence: A study of nearly 2600 Norwegian male twin pairs. *Twin Research and Human Genetics, 8*(4), 307–311.

Sundie, J. M., Kenrick, D. T., Griskevicius, V., Tybur, J. M., Vohs, K. D., & Beal, D. J. (2011). Peacocks, porsches, and Thorstein Veblen: Conspicuous consumption as a sexual signaling system. *Journal of Personality and Social Psychology, 100*(4), 664–680.

Swaddle, J. P., & Reierson, G. W. (2002). Testosterone increases perceived dominance but not attractiveness in human males. *Proceedings of the Royal Society B: Biological Sciences, 269*(1507), 2285–2289. https://doi.org/10.1098/rspb.2002.2165

Swami, V., Jones, J., Einon, D., & Furnham, A. (2009). Men's preferences for women's profile waist-to-hip ratio, breast size, and ethnic group in Britain and South Africa. *British Journal of Psychology, 100*(Pt. 2), 313–325. https://doi.org/10.1348/000712608X329525

Swami, V., & Tovée, M. J. (2013). Resource security impacts men's female breast size preferences. *PLoS ONE, 8*(3), Article e57623. https://doi.org/10.1371/journal.pone.0057623

Swift-Gallant, A., Johnson, B. A., Di Rita, V., & Breedlove, S. M. (2020). Through a glass, darkly: Human digit ratios reflect prenatal androgens, imperfectly. *Hormones and Behavior, 120,* Article 104686.

Tan, K. W., Graf, B. A., Mitra, S. R., & Stephen, I. D. (2017). Impact of fresh fruit smoothie consumption on apparent health of Asian faces. *Evolution and Human Behavior, 38*(4), 522–529. https://doi.org/10.1016/j.evolhumbehav.2017.02.004

Tan, K. W., & Stephen, I. D. (2013). Colour detection thresholds in faces and colour patches. *Perception, 42*(7), 733–741. https://doi.org/10.1068/p7499

Tan, K. W., & Stephen, I. D. (2019). Skin color preferences in a Malaysian Chinese population. *Frontiers in Psychology, 10*(June). https://doi.org/10.3389/fpsyg.2019.01352

Tan, K. W., Tiddeman, B., & Stephen, I. D. (2018). Skin texture and colour predict perceived health in Asian faces. *Evolution and Human Behavior, 39*(3), 320–335. https://doi.org/10.1016/j.evolhumbehav.2018.02.003

Thornhill, R., & Gangestad, S. W. (1999). Facial attractiveness. *Trends in Cognitive Sciences, 3*(12), 452–460. http://www.ncbi.nlm.nih.gov/pubmed/10562724

Thornhill, R., Gangestad, S. W., Miller, R., Scheyd, G., McCollough, J. K., & Franklin, M. (2003). Major histocompatibility complex genes, symmetry, and body scent attractiveness in men and women. *Behavioral Ecology, 14*(5), 668–678. https://doi.org/10.1093/beheco/arg043

Tovée, M. J., & Cornelissen, P. L. (2001). Female and male perceptions of female physical attractiveness in front-view and profile. *British Journal of Psychology, 92*(Pt 2), 391–402. https://doi.org/10.1348/000712601162257

Trivers, R. (1972). Parental investment and sexual selection. In B. Campbell (Ed.), *Sexual selection and the descent of man: 1871–1971* (pp. 136–179). Aldine.

Valentova, J. V., Bártová, K., Štěrbová, Z., & Corrêa Varella, M. A. (2017). Influence of sexual orientation, population, homogamy, and imprinting-like effect on preferences and choices for female buttock size, breast size and shape, and WHR. *Personality and Individual Differences, 104*, 313–319. https://doi.org/10.1016/j.paid.2016.08.005

Van Valen, L. (1973). A new evolutionary law. *Evolutionary Theory, 1*, 1–30.

Varella, M. A. C., Valentova, J. V., & Fernández, A. M. (2017). Evolution of artistic and aesthetic propensities through female competitive ornamentation. In M. L. Fisher (Ed.), *The Oxford handbook of women and competition* (pp. 757–783). Oxford University Press. https://doi.org/10.1093/oxfordhb/9780199376377.013.46

Varella, M. A. C., Štěrbová, Z., Bártová, K., Fisher, M. L., & Valentova, J. V. (2022). Evolution of artistic and athletic propensities: Testing of intersexual selection and intrasexual competition. *Frontiers in Psychology, 13*, 925862. doi: 10.3389/fpsyg.2022.925862

Vizental, A. (2010). Meaning, image and attitude (I). *Journal of Humanistic and Social Studies, 1*(2), 77–88.

Waitt, C., & Little, A. C. (2006). Preferences for symmetry in conspecific facial shape among Macaca mulatta. *International Journal of Primatology, 27*(1), 133–145. https://doi.org/10.1007/s10764-005-9015-y

Watkins, C., & Leitch, A. (2020). Using sexual selection theories to examine contextual variation in heterosexual women's orientation toward high heels. *Archives of Sexual Behavior, 49*, 849–860. https://doi.org/10.1007/s10508-019-01539-3

Wedekind, C., Seebeck, T., Bettens, F., & Paepke, A. J. (2006). The intensity of human body odors and the MHC: Should we expect a link? *Evolutionary Psychology, 4*(1), Article 147470490600400. https://doi.org/10.1177/147470490600400106

Whitehead, R. D., Coetzee, V., Ozakinci, G., & Perrett, D. I. (2012). Cross-cultural effects of fruit and vegetable consumption on skin color. *American Journal of Public Health, 102*(2), 212–213. https://doi.org/10.2105/AJPH.2011.300495

Winegard, B., Winegard, B., & Geary, D. C. (2018). The status competition model of cultural production. *Evolutionary Psychological Science, 4*(4), 351–371.

Winternitz, J., Abbate, J. L., Huchard, E., Havlíček, J., & Garamszegi, L. Z. (2017). Patterns of MHC-dependent mate selection in humans and nonhuman primates: A meta-analysis. *Molecular Ecology, 26*(2), 668–688. https://doi.org/10.1111/mec.13920

Wolf, N. (1990). *The beauty myth: How images of beauty are used against women.* Chato & Windus.

Wolffhechel, K., Hahn, A. C., Jarmer, H., Fisher, C. I., Jones, B. C., & DeBruine, L. M. (2015). Testing the utility of a data-driven approach for assessing BMI from face images. *PLoS ONE, 10*(10), e0140347. https://doi.org/10.1371/journal.pone.0140347

Wollstonecraft, M. (1992). *A vindication of the rights of woman.* Peter Edes. (Original work published 1792) Retrieved September 4, 2020, from https://www.bartleby.com/144/3.html

Wood, W., Kressel, L., Joshi, P. D., & Louie, B. (2014). Meta-analysis of menstrual cycle effects on women's mate preferences. *Emotion Review, 6*(3), 229–249. https://doi.org/10.1177/1754073914523073

Zaadstra, B. M., Seidell, J. C., Van Noord, P. A. H., Te Velde, E. R., Habbema, J. D. F., Vrieswijk, B., & Karbaat, J. (1993). Fat and female fecundity: Prospective study of effect of body fat distribution on conception rates. *Obstetrical and Gynecological Survey, 48*(7), 484–486. https://doi.org/10.1097/00006254-199307000-00022

Zaidi, A. A., White, J. D., Mattern, B. C., Liebowitz, C. R., Puts, D. A., Claes, P., & Shriver, M. D. (2019). Facial masculinity does not appear to be a condition-dependent male ornament and does not reflect MHC heterozygosity in humans. *Proceedings of the National Academy of Sciences, 116*(5), 1633–1638.

Zebrowitz, L. A., Hall, J. A., Murphy, N. A., & Rhodes, G. (2002). Looking smart and looking good: Facial cues to intelligence and their origins. *Personality and Social Psychology Bulletin, 28*(2), 238–249. https://doi.org/10.1177/0146167202282009

Żelaźniewicz, A., Nowak, J., Łącka, P., & Pawłowski, B. (2020). Facial appearance and metabolic health biomarkers in women. *Scientific Reports, 10*(1), 1–8.

Zietsch, B. P., Verweij, K. J. H., & Burri, A. V. (2012). Heritability of preferences for multiple cues of mate quality in humans. *Evolution, 66*(6), 1762–1772.

CHAPTER 3

The Three Cs of Psychological Mate Preferences: The Psychological Traits People Want in Their Romantic and Sexual Partners

Peter K. Jonason *and* Evita March

Abstract

In this chapter, we discuss the psychological traits desired in modern romantic and sexual relationships. We begin by distinguishing and providing a brief overview of modern relationships, including long-term, committed, monogamous relationships, casual, primarily sexual relationships, and hybrid relationships such as booty-call and friends-with-benefits relationships. Following this, we explore the psychological traits desired in these relationships. These psychological traits are thematically organized into three higher-order psychological preferences: competence, compassion, and compatibility. For each of these higher-order preferences, we outline the traits captured by the theme (e.g., compassion includes kindness and agreeableness), and explore the research on preferences for these traits across the different types of modern relationships. We then explore the "why" of these trait preferences by appealing to sociocultural and evolutionary psychological models. Lastly, we consider limitations of previous research and provide suggestions for future research exploring psychological mate preferences in modern relationships.

Key Words: mate preferences, mate choice, sex differences, relationships, evolutionary psychology

The choices people make when selecting romantic/sexual partners have fundamental consequences for their psychosocial health and evolutionary-related success. Unsurprisingly, these choices have been a major source of scientific inquiry. In this chapter, we describe how mate preferences manifest in modern relationships. First, we review several modern relationships styles (e.g., booty-call relationships and committed relationships). Next, we discuss the history of mate preference research and provide a thematic overview of the psychological features that are desired in potential mates. Third, we attempt to frame these mate preferences in the two major traditions of sociocultural psychology and evolutionary psychology. And, last, we provide some critical thoughts and future directions for research in this area.

Modern Relationships

A classic distinction in sexuality and relationship research is that relationships can be long-term and committed in nature or casual and primarily sexual in nature (Buss & Schmitt, 1993). The former is characterized by two people engaging in a relationship with relatively clear expectations of sexual and social monogamy, relationship longevity, trust, and interdependence. But not all relationships are so "serious" in nature. The most well-researched manifestation of casual sex is the one-night stand (Tappé et al., 2013). In this kind of relationship, two people meet and, over an accelerated period, go from zero-acquaintance to sexual activity by engaging in various "emotional" and "sexual" acts (Jonason et al., 2010). Individuals engaged in these relationships have limited expectations of monogamy or commitment and indeed may not know more than the person's name (and sometimes not even that) when the relationship concludes.

Researchers often use "one-night stand" as a representative term to define a range of casual relationships (Greitemeyer, 2007). Although a useful distinction for theoretical models and a simple way to understand sexual relationships, seeing relationships as serious or not obscures the more complicated nature of sexual relationships and likely commits the either-or fallacy (i.e., false dichotomy or the black-or-white fallacy). Unlike monogamous relationships where both sexes have interests that converge more in regard to investment in the partnership and offspring, casual sex relationships are characterized by a greater degree of conflict over obligations and investment to offspring. Given this greater conflict, there are many more solutions to the problems of investment.

These solutions have received limited investigation, but what has been revealed is that there are hybrid relationships that serve as compromises between what each partner wants (Jonason & Balzarini, 2016). There are at least two relevant hybrid relationships. First, booty-call relationships are characterized by two people who engage in regular and repeated bouts of sex who attempt to keep their relationship sexual in nature by minimizing emotional acts (e.g., kissing), and do so often for pleasure (Jonason, 2013; Jonason et al., 2010). In this kind of relationship, women may forgo their relatively greater apprehension toward casual sex (compared to men) in hopes of gaining access to a particular man who they might not otherwise secure if they were more sexually reserved. These relationships may deteriorate because men (more than women) want the relationship to stay sexual whereas women (more than men) want something more to come of it (Jonason et al., 2009). Second, friends-with-benefits describes a kind of relationship where two people who have an existing friendship opt into having sex with one another to satisfy their sexual needs but also to test the partner for a more serious relationship (Jonason, 2013). These people maintain a relatively independent friendship with sex being something of a hobby the people jointly enjoy. Despite the nascent state of research on these relationships, we cover the little research there is and conjecture further to integrate them in our understanding of the psychological characteristics people want in their sexual and romantic partners.

Psychological Mate Preferences

There can be no doubt that physical attractiveness is extremely important in mate choice (Regan et al., 2000). This is not to say that men only want to date Victoria's Secret fashion models (e.g., Adriana Lima) or that women only want to date the cast of the movie Magic Mike (e.g., Matthew Boomer). Men and women need their minimum standards of attractiveness fulfilled to engage in a relationship with anyone (Jonason & Antoon, 2019; Jonason et al., 2019; Li & Kenrick, 2006); without that, people will lack minimum sexual attraction and may go their separate ways or just be friends. Once these minimum standards—these necessities—have been reached, there appears to be a proliferation of potential psychological features people find appealing (e.g., IQ, status and religiousness). Specifically, despite psychological features (e.g., humor, friendliness, and personality) appearing to receive preference over physical appearance (Regan et al., 2000), we posit that attention is only turned toward these psychological traits once the minimum threshold of physical attraction is met. In other words, minimum standards for external characteristics must initially be met before consideration of these psychological characteristics (Li et al., 2002).

Indeed, a quick perusal of the research in this area reveals dozens of psychological traits that appear to be interesting to people. Take, for instance, the seminal work on long-term mate preferences around the world. Buss (1989) relied on approximately 20 indicators of mate preferences (and see Bech-Sørensen & Pollet, 2016; Souza et al., 2016). Subsequent attempts to factor analyze these and other indicators has reliably revealed a three-factor solution (Campbell et al., 2001; Jonason et al., 2013) but these attempts have (a) taken a narrow view of psychological features, (b) only included personality features and not psychological features (e.g., values), and (c) always included physical features which may overwhelm the factor analysis, acting like a gravity well where other features are obscured in relation to this "super factor." Although we do not collect and analyze new data here, we put physical features aside and attempt to organize these traits (like indicators) into three themes (like latent factors) that we think summarize the psychological features people desire in modern relationships. Later we consider the potential reasons why these are important features. We consider three levels of mate preferences. The first level are those traits that are consensually sought by men and women (and likely homosexual and heterosexuals alike). The second level are those traits that are differentiated in the sexes. And the third level are those traits that are more idiosyncratic.

Competence

Dating and childrearing are expensive endeavors for both sexes. According to UNICEF, raising a child from birth to 17 years of age costs between $900/year in developing countries and $16,200/year in developed countries. Just 100 years ago, around 90% of children died before the age of five,[1] suggesting a recurrent and modern challenge created

[1] https://data.unicef.org/topic/child-survival/under-five-mortality/

by childrearing that may have driven preferences of mates who could acquire sufficient resources to raise offspring. The first theme of these higher-order psychological preferences, competence, serves to deal with this recurrent challenge. It reflects something akin to one's ability to invest in a partner and potential offspring. This ability to invest is evidenced in several characteristics (e.g., intelligence, education, income, creativity, and sense of humor) that we discuss below and these may operate in additive or multiplicative fashions to both enable and signal one's ability to engage in a relationship and to rear offspring. Those who could signal their ability and attraction for these features will have evolved hand in hand; increasing the reproductive fitness of the adept over the less so.

For both men and women, intelligence is a highly sought after characteristics in a long-term mate (Buss, 1989; Jonason & Antoon, 2019). In our ancestors, intelligence likely played a role in hunting, gathering, wayfinding, and tool making. In addition to addressing adaptive problems, a mate's intelligence also offers distinct advantages for navigating modern life. While intelligence might be an important trait (i.e., the most general indicator of competence), people's mate preferences are not necessarily indexed only on intelligence. Intelligence is obscured to observers, mate selection may also operate on more apparent cues to intelligence, such as education, income (or earning capacity), social status, creativity, and a sense of humor (Miller, 2001). Indeed, intelligence (the primary trait) is closely related to these secondary competence traits, positively correlating with education (Ganzach et al., 2013), occupation and income (Strenze, 2007), creativity (Silva, 2008), and humor production (Howrigan & MacDonald, 2008). This suggests to us that all these traits may be concurrent but not collinear indicators of competence, with the possibility that intelligence might be the most central trait in the group. It would be natural to expect an individual with higher intelligence to attain and complete higher levels of education (on average), thus resulting in increased social status and income (on average). Indeed, studies of mate preference for intelligence and level of education converge on similar conclusions (Jonason & Antoon, 2019; Jonason et al., 2019), with some researchers even combining education/intelligence as one dimension (Fletcher et al., 1999) and status/resources as another (Shackelford et al., 2005). Still, despite the overlap, an intelligent person may not have had access to education opportunities, he or she may be unemployed, and intelligence does not mean someone will have a sense of humor. Thus, the term "competence" is more appropriate than "intelligence" because it captures a wider and more realistic description of the multiple cues people use to detect whether a mate is able to invest in a relationship and any offspring that might result.

The competence traits of intelligence, education, income, social status, creativity, and sense of humor are all considered desirable traits for a mate to possess (Buunk et al., 2002; Jonason et al., 2019; Li et al., 2013; McGee & Shevlin, 2009; Shackelford et al., 2005), and yet results regarding preferences for a mate's education are mixed. Both men and women desire a mate with education similar to their own (Jonason & Antoon, 2019); other research has reported that women desire a mate with higher education than their own (Buunk et al., 2002). Preferences for a mate's education also fluctuates with educational equality; in cultures where educational equality between the sexes is low, women's preference for a mate's education increases (Kasser & Sharma, 1999). Still, despite the inconsistency regarding preferences for similar or higher education, men and women do not appear to desire a mate with lower levels of education. One possibility is that men and women do not necessarily seek to attain high intelligence, income, and education but rather to avoid low intelligence, income, and education: ostensible dealbreakers.

Like intelligence, creativity may also convey important information regarding genetic quality and fitness benefits (Prokosch et al., 2009). Creativity may be a sexually appealing characteristic for both sexes, correlating positively with number of sexual partners (Nettle & Clegg, 2006). Testament to this sexual appeal, a young man carrying a guitar (i.e., indicative of creativity) can solicit more phone numbers from young women compared to a young man carrying a sports bag or nothing (Guéguen et al., 2014). Sense of humor, conceptualized as a manifestation of creativity and intelligence (Kaufman et al., 2008), is also a desirable trait in a mate and can predict mating success (Greengross & Miller, 2011), with both men and women preferring a mate with a good sense of humor (Cowan & Little, 2013).

Although both sexes would consider any of these competence traits desirable for a mate to possess, differences exist in the importance that men and women place on these traits. Both sexes desire an intelligent mate; however, women ascribe more importance to a mate's intelligence than men do (Buss et al., 2001). One possibility for this sex difference is that women's preference for a mate's high intelligence may be adaptive. A mate's intelligence may operate as a reliable indicator of both provisioning ability and genetic fitness; in fact, such reproductive advantages of intelligence may have resulted in women being skilled at detecting a mate's intelligence, even assessing men's intelligence via behavioral cues at a level above chance (Prokosch et al., 2009).

Sex differences are also found in preferences for a mate's income, educational attainment, and social status. Although men and women both desire mates with higher income compared to low, this preference is more pronounced for women (Jonason et al., 2019; Souza et al., 2016), especially in the case of long-term, committed relationships (Jonason et al., 2012). Further, although both sexes desire similar education in a long-term mate (Jonason & Antoon, 2019), some research has found that compared to men, women place more importance on a similar educational background with a mate (Buss et al., 2001). Lastly, compared to men, women demonstrate greater preference for social status and dominance in a long-term mate (Li, 2007; Li et al., 2013).

In addition to these sex differences, desire for some competence traits can also fluctuate with relationship involvement. For both sexes, the desire for creativity and income appears mostly stable across all levels of relationship involvement. Although this preference for high income does not abate over relationship involvement, it does appear that how a potential mate acquired their riches is important. Both men and women show preference for a long-term mate who "earned" their resources over other potential means (i.e., inheritance and embezzlement); men (vs. woman) relax this preference in the short-term (Jonason et al., 2012). Compared to creativity and income, preference for a mate's intelligence, sense of humor, and social level may fluctuate. Preferences for a mate's intelligence was assessed across five levels of relationship involvement including sexual fantasy (least involvement), casual affair, falling in love, serious relationship, and marriage (most involvement; Buunk et al., 2002). For all relationships, women preferred a mate more intelligent than themselves, and men only desired a mate more intelligent than themselves for marriage, a serious relationship, and falling in love. For women, a mate's intelligence appears to be a nonnegotiable psychological characteristic in any relationship, regardless of involvement (Jonason & Antoon, 2019; Jonason et al., 2019). Men, however, seem to lower their standards for a mate's intelligence when considering relationships with less involvement and commitment. Women may also consider the social level of a long-term mate but not a short-term mate (Li & Kenrick, 2006). Lastly, compared to short-term mates, men (but not women) place more importance on the sense of humor of a long-term mate (Cowan & Little, 2013).

In sum, the relationship between sex and level of relationship involvement interacts with competence traits to form consistent, predictable patterns of mate preferences. However, a particular shortcoming of the research exploring mate preferences is that these preferences have largely been considered in the context of a dichotomy of relationships: Short-term (i.e., one-night stand) compared to long-term (i.e., marriage). Not all relationships fall into this dichotomy, and although some researchers have sought to explore mate preferences outside of the relationship dichotomy, this research is limited. For example, Buunk et al. (2002) explored mate preferences in sexual fantasies, casual affairs, falling in love, a serious relationship, and marriage, and March et al. (2018) explored mate preferences in booty-call relationships. Regarding competence traits, women considered the social level of a long-term mate, but not a booty-call or short-term mate, a necessity. However, there is a shortage of research on mate preferences in relationships other than one-night stands and serious romantic relationship partners. Therefore, we must extrapolate and theorize about competence in relationships like booty-call relationships and friends-with-benefits.

Based on the definitions of booty-call and friends-with-benefits relationships, we might conclude friends-with-benefits relationships to have more involvement (based on existing friendship) than booty-call relationships. Thus, competence traits that are more desired in longer-term relationships should be more important in a friends-with-benefits relationship compared to a booty-call relationship. Although speculative, men and women should desire the intelligence of a friend-with-benefits more than a booty-call mate. Further, women should desire the social level of a friend-with-benefits more than a booty-call mate, and men should desire the sense of humor of a friend-with-benefits more than a booty-call mate. Further, we would also expect to see a pattern of sex differences; specifically, given that men's preference for a mate's intelligence relaxes with less relationship involvement, in both of these "less involved" relationships, women's desire for intelligence should be greater than men's.

Another more modern relationship not yet explored in the mate preferences literature is "sex with an ex," where two former partners have (in some cases repeated) sexual intercourse (Spielmann et al., 2019). Extrapolating preference for competence traits to the "sex with an ex" relationship is more challenging. In this relationship, intimate encounters lack commitment but are based on a prior relationship where longer-term traits may have been more valued. In this relationship, it is possible that the mate falls short of traits desired in a long-term relationship (i.e., intelligence, income (for women)), but possesses traits that render them a desirable short-term mate (i.e., creativity and sense of humor).

Compassion

The second theme of these higher-order mate preferences we call compassion. As a higher-order factor, it reflects a person's willingness to invest in a partner and potential offspring. Ability to invest is necessary but insufficient on its own. Without a willingness to invest, access to lots of resources is of limited utility to a romantic or sexual partner. One's willingness to invest may be manifested in various ways (i.e., considerate, honest, dependable, kind, understanding, and loyal; Buss & Barnes, 1986), but the willingness to do so will have had reproductive consequences for the same reasons as one's ability to invest and may also have modern consequences in modern legal systems (e.g., child-support payments mandated by a court). These consequences will serve as selection (and social) pressures shaping the mate selection mechanisms of the sexes; those who cared more and could better signal this ability will have made more offspring than those who were less adept at this. We operationalize the higher-order trait of compassion to include kindness, agreeableness, generosity, altruism, and even owning a dog, which we will discuss in turn. The selection of these traits as representative of a mate's compassion are further reinforced by mate "dealbreakers," which include aggression, inattentiveness, and untrustworthiness (Jonason et al., 2020).

Like intelligence, a mate's kindness may be a particularly reliable indicator of the presence of other desired compassion traits. This trait of kindness is quite central in this literature and is related to other compassion traits such as "affectionate, considerate, generous, gentle, helpful, kind, sensitive, supportive, sympathetic, and thoughtful" (Lukaszweski & Roney, 2009, pp. 192–193). Men and women may seek a kind mate as this trait indicates the tendency to support, commit to, and cooperate with a mate; characteristics considered especially important in a long-term mate (Buss, 1989). However, we considered the term "compassion" as the higher-order trait more appropriate than kindness, as compassion encompasses a broader spectrum of traits and states that focus on concern and care for others. Further, compassion implies an established capacity for a number of reproductive benefits, such as sensitivity to the needs of others and decreased infidelity (Goetz et al., 2010).

Both sexes appear to desire a mate who is kind (Buss, 1989), agreeable (Botwin et al., 1997), generous (Griskevicius et al., 2007), and altruistic (Farrelly, 2013), and one who perhaps even owns a puppy (Tifferet et al., 2013). In modern relationships, a mate's kindness is considered especially important by both sexes (Buss, 1989), with 30 years of research across both collectivistic and individualistic cultures demonstrating both men and women desire a kind mate (Atari & Jamali, 2016). Trait agreeableness is one of the most valued personality traits of a long-term mate, and predicts marital stability in both sexes (Botwin et al., 1997); further, trait agreeableness tends to be assortative, with more agreeable individuals exhibiting stronger preference for more communal mates (i.e., sensitive and soft-hearted; Wood & Brumbaugh, 2009).

A mate's generosity and altruism are also appealing compassionate traits to both sexes. Although the terms generosity and altruism are often used interchangeably in the literature, they are different constructs. Generosity refers to the act of giving, whereas altruism reflects selflessness (Wright, 2001). Acts of generosity may signal important information about mate quality, specifically, information about their resources and their willingness to contribute these resources. Evidence indicates that men are keenly aware that generosity is an attractive mate quality; when being observed by attractive women, men "show off" by donating more to charity (Iredale et al., 2008). A competitive mating market (i.e., having more rivals to compete with for a mate) may even increase men's generosity (Barclay & Willer, 2007), particularly if they consider themselves less attractive (Iredale et al., 2008). Both men and women also desire an altruistic mate (Arnocky et al., 2017; Farrelly, 2013). Acts of altruism may signal both genetic and nongenetic benefits, such as important phenotypic information relating to being a good partner and parent (Moore et al., 2013). Lastly, a particularly effective way to demonstrate one's generous and altruistic nature might be via the act of owning a dog. Dog ownership is a particularly attractive mate characteristic to women seeking a long-term mate (Tifferet et al., 2013), and owning a dog may signal that the potential mate has the material resources to take care of the dog and the emotional resources to bond and commit to the animal (Guéguen & Ciccotti, 2008).

Like the competence traits, men and women's desire for a mate with compassion traits also tend to fluctuate with relationship involvement. Both sexes consider a long-term mate's kindness a necessity; in fact, both sexes may "desire a mate as kind as possible" (Li et al., 2002, p. 953). However, for short-term mates (i.e., casual sex), both sexes express less desire for a mate's kindness (Li, 2007) and consider kindness less of a necessity (Li & Kenrick, 2006). Still, despite the desire for a mate's kindness decreasing with relationship involvement, both men and women still trade off a short-term mate's status/and resources of short-term mates to obtain warmth/trustworthiness (Fletcher et al., 2004). However, it should be noted they also trade off a short-term mate's warmth/trustworthiness for physical attractiveness/vitality. Both men and women also desire an altruistic long-term mate compared to an altruistic short-term mate (Phillips et al., 2008).

Sex differences are also present in the desire for a mate's compassion traits. Compared to men, women express greater desire for altruistic short-term (Moore et al., 2013) and long-term mates (Barclay, 2010). The tendency for women to express stronger preferences for an altruistic mate could be attributed to the resource/provisions propensity this characteristic signals (Moore et al., 2013; Phillips et al., 2008), overlapping as a potential competence trait. When physical attractiveness was paired with altruism (i.e., high physical attractiveness/low altruism in one condition and high altruism/low physical attractiveness in another condition), women desired a long-term mate with high altruism/low physical attractiveness condition. No preference was present for short-term relationships (Farrelly et al., 2016).

Based on the above, both sexes express greater desire for compassion traits in a long- than short-term mate, and women may indicate greater desire for some compassion traits compared to men. Like the competence traits, we can also extrapolate these trends to relationships that fall outside the short- and long-term dichotomy (e.g., booty-call relationship and friends-with-benefits). To date, one study explored sex differences and mate preferences in a booty-call relationship, finding that only women, not men, consider the kindness of a booty-call partner a necessity (March et al., 2018). The authors concluded this result supported the supposition that the booty-call relationship could be conceptualized as a compromise relationship (Jonason et al., 2009).

Given that both sexes ascribe greater importance to compassion traits of a long-term mate, and that a friends-with-benefits relationship may have greater longevity compared to booty-call relationships, we speculate that both sexes will desire more compassion traits in a friends-with-benefits. As relationship involvement decreases, men's desire for compassion traits will decrease (e.g., men considered the kindness of a booty call mate a luxury; March et al., 2018). Comparatively, women may still desire a short-term mate's kindness and altruism, though other characteristics (such as physical attractiveness) increase in importance.

Compatibility

The third and final theme we see in psychological features that people desire in their partners is compatibility, reflecting preferences for a mate one is likely to get along with interpersonally. People are complex beings and reducing mate preferences to just the prior two higher-order personality traits and physical attractiveness fails to capture a rather important aspect of relationships. There are many other apparently idiosyncratic features that need to be considered, however, they may have, thus, far been understudied because researchers have trouble pinning them down. That is, when people are interested in the same/similar things (e.g., travel) or hold similar beliefs (e.g., dogs are better than cats), they are more likely to meet, choose one another, and have a satisfactory relationship (Buss, 1985). Rearing offspring and having anything more than a passing relationship requires partners to get along with one another. Getting along will result in the coordination of efforts and solidify pair-bonding (i.e., assortative mating) and finding partners who one gets along with may have improved reproductive fitness of our ancestors. Take for instance, shared religious beliefs. These beliefs have implications for not only partnering but also how a child is raised and subsequently that child's mating behavior. We operationalize the higher-order trait of compatibility to include similarity regarding interests, affection, sexual desire, and religiousness, which we will discuss in turn.

Both sexes are likely to be attracted to mates who share similar interests (Vandenberg, 1972). When creating online dating profiles, both men and women include descriptions of interests (e.g., movies, video games, and television) in an effort to attract a mate with similar interests (Lee et al., 2019). Similar interests predict relationship quality and maintenance (Castro et al., 2012), and may even reflect underlying similar values—for example, "love of travel" may reflect a value of curiosity and freedom, and "political views" may reflect values of conservatism and traditionalism.

In addition to compatibility of interests, other compatible traits that are desired include affection (Buss & Barnes, 1986), sex drive (Regan, 1998), and religiousness (Sherkat, 2003). What is key is the element of compatibility—men and women do not necessarily desire an affectionate mate with a high sex drive; rather, they desire a mate whose affection tendencies and sex drive is compatible with their own. An overly affectionate mate in public is not going to appeal to someone who wishes to avoid public displays of affection at all costs, and someone who desires an exceptionally affectionate mate may feel disappointed with and rejected by a mate who characteristically is unaffectionate. Similar to the overly affectionate mate, a mate with high sexual ambitions may find themselves disappointed with a mate who only enjoys sporadic coitus, and the mate with less interest in sex may find themselves frustrated with an overly enthusiastic sexual mate. Similarly, there is evidence that both sexes show preference for similar erotic talk (Jonason et al., 2016). Lastly, compatibility of religious affiliations of a mate is also desirable (Sherkat, 2003), with American couples reporting a high degree of religious similarity (Botwin et al., 1997). In addition to compatible values, practices, and traditions, a mate's religiousness may signal adaptive strengths including resource charity and restrictions on sexual activity (e.g., infidelity is discouraged; Buss, 2002).

Like the competence and compassion traits, preference for compatibility fluctuates with participant's sex and relationship involvement. Compared to other relationships, such as friendships and casual short-term relationships, men and women place greater importance on compatibility of interests with a long-term mate (Treger & Masciale, 2018). Both sexes desire short- and long-term mates to have above-average sexual passion and drive (Regan, 1998), though men express greater desire than women do. This desire for sex may also change with relationship involvement, as women attribute less importance to this in a long-term mate (Regan et al., 2000), though men's desire for a mate's sexual passion and drive does not abate with relationship involvement (Regan, 1998). In research on dealbreakers in the long-term mating context, women (more than men) selected "bad sex" as a dealbreaker whereas men (compared to women) selected "low sex drive" as a dealbreaker (Jonason et al., 2015). Sexual acts also change depending on relationship involvement and commitment; compared to one-night stands, kissing, manual, and anal sex were more likely to occur in booty-call relationships (Jonason et al., 2010). It is important to note though that this research on sexual desire may not necessarily be explicitly exploring similarity. Put simply, research is yet to consider how preference for a mate with a similar sexual drive changes across relationship involvement.

Despite this, based on the research above some preliminary conclusions can be made about the desire for compatibility traits in relationships outside the short- and long-term dichotomy. Both sexes prefer a long-term relationship with similar interests but relax this preference with shorter-term relationships, including friendships (Treger & Masciale, 2018). As such, it is possible that men and women may not necessarily care about similar interests when considering friends-with-benefits and booty-call relationships. Both men and women desire a short- and long-term mate who has the "appropriate" amount of sexual passion and drive, though women relax this preference for longer-term mates. As such, we would expect both sexes to desire more sexual drive and passion in a booty-call relationship compared to a friend-with-benefits. However, as noted above, this desire does not necessarily reflect a desire for similarity. Overall, the interaction of sex and relationship involvement and subsequent impact on desire for compatibility traits of a mate are, simply, understudied.

The "Why" of Mate Preferences

Only the staunchest science denialist would contest the patterns we have reported above at the level of the specific traits desired. For instance, someone who took Plato's allegory of the cave or the movie *The Matrix* too seriously and contested the nature of reality might say that we cannot trust the aforementioned observations because we cannot trust our ability to access information about reality (i.e., anti naive realism). Thankfully, this is a rather fringe element of scientific psychology. Where researchers disagree typically is about why effects exist. In the following sections we detail two classes of explanations for mate preferences: sociocultural models and evolutionary models. Where possible, we highlight assumptions in these models that influence the research that are rarely made explicit.

Sociocultural Models

Traditional social psychology emphasizes the role of mechanistic and immediate contextual factors that predict behavior. These models are based—implicitly usually—on assumptions from behaviorism. Behaviorism, strictly speaking, tends to minimize the importance of innate cognitive systems with the exceptions of basic learning mechanisms (i.e., the tabula rasa or the blank slate; Pinker, 2002). In the context of mate preferences, researchers from this tradition might suggest that mate preferences are created within the lifetime of the person by interactions with others (e.g., learning), cultural programming (e.g., media effects), or imposed inequalities in one's life (e.g., pay inequalities). There is a strong appeal of these models because they require no deep understanding of human nature or biology (traditional social psychology is more concerned with thoughts, feelings and behaviors as a function of the actual, imagined, and real presence of others; Allport, 1985), are environmentally deterministic (which is implicitly viewed as the more acceptable kind of determinism), and focus on manageable and immediate mechanisms (i.e., stimulus and response) to predict behavior with the implicit/explicit agenda of "fixing" the world as they see it damaged (Thrift & Sugarman, 2019).

There are at least three theories worth mentioning here. The first such theory is social role theory (Eagly & Wood, 1999). As the name of the theory hints, this theory argues that mate preferences are artifacts of cultural progamming around sex roles. For example, men are taught to be "success objects" and women are taught to be "sex objects" (Davis, 1990). Individuals internalize these roles for themselves and build expectations about the opposite sex. The degree to which people conform to their "appropriate" sex role then predicts what they want not only in their mates but also in their relationship satisfaction (Burn & Ward, 2005). People who conform more to their prescribed sex roles are more attractive to others because people do not like to have their expectations violated. This model holds, at its core, a set of assumptions of the learned nature of these "arbitrary" sex roles and how these roles are imposed on people. This theory is a mediation hypothesis for sex differences suggesting, for instance, that women who adopt a strong feminine sex role are likely to be more attractive to men. The model says nothing about the origins of these or any specific sex role differences beyond the simple explanation of they were learned and internalized.

The second theory worth mentioning here is called structural powerlessness (Buss & Barnes, 1986). In this theory, mate preferences reflect differences in access to work and financial security. It is incontestable that women, in the immediate cultural past (e.g., last 500 years), have been discriminated against, and in many developing nations major discrimination still occurs. This pattern has led some to adopt this theory to make claims about mate preferences. These researchers contend that the reason women value competence traits more than men do is because the former have been traditionally excluded from access to resources (Kümmerling & Hassebrauck, 2001). Therefore, to survive, they need to be pragmatic, adjusting their mate preferences to secure financial security. In contrast, men who tend to have access to resources more than women do, are free to seek mates who are characterized by physical attractiveness. This theory implies that preferences for physical attractiveness are superficial and that men's mating priority are artifacts of immaturity (e.g., in a quasi-Freudian way) and sexism (e.g., only valuing women for their looks). The theory implies that if the sexes had equal access to resources, then sex differences in mate preferences would disappear or at least shrink. Cues to competence may be evaluated as morally less problematic—because they are pragmatic solutions to economic inequalities and issues of survival rather than preferences for physical attractiveness, which are often viewed as trivial.

The final theory we discuss here is social learning theory (Bandura, 1977). This theory places the emphasis on the implicit and explicit power of learning cultural norms. Children are exposed to "models" who teach them how to behave and what to think. These models can be parents, siblings, conspecifics, and even media content. For example, researchers from this tradition would contend that there is heavy variability in the physical shape individuals desire in their romantic partners, and this variability can be seen in the media (El Jurdi & Smith, 2018). They would point to the fact that there is cultural variability in mate preferences (Yu & Shepard, 1998). They would point to cultures where a man is judged not by his watches and suits but by the number of cows he owns. They would contend that these apparent differences are prima facie evidence that mate preferences are learned because they are apparently culturally bound (Yu & Shepard, 1998). Researchers insisting that mate preferences are learned assert that there are no/minimal innate tendencies or preferences in mate preferences and that any apparent patterns are artifacts of learning models imposed from above by similar cultural systems across groups (e.g., American media hegemony; Rich & Cash, 1993). These researchers further imply that if we could just change the messages children and people receive, mate preferences could be adjusted to any arbitrary preference (Sypeck et al., 2006).

Evolutionary Psychology Models

Sociocultural models have considerable appeal and have characterized social psychology for several decades. However, these models may be inadequate at dealing with the fact that (a) preferences are remarkably similar around the world (Buss, 1989; Thomas et al., 2020), (b) preferences often look the same in different species (Wroblewski et al., 2009), and (c) preferences are consistent across age groups and time (Kenrick & Keefe, 1997). From an evolutionary perspective, the primary features people want in their mates are ones that would have facilitated the reproductive success of their ancestors (they may or may not facilitate success in people alive today). Unlike sociocultural models, evolutionary models of mate preferences assume that some traits have intrinsic value. They do not assert that a given trait had some a priori significance, but instead, those who valued certain traits—those that we see people wanting today—over generations will have made more offspring leading to selection for psychological systems that underlie mate preferences. Therefore, today's mate preferences are the phylogenetic inertia from generations of systematic patterns in mate choice over generations. The models do not assume that mate preferences are primarily created by immediate, local circumstances but, instead, are part of deep wiring from generations of selection. However, unlike sociocultural models which often struggle to deal with, for example, genetics, evolutionary models are able to incorporate local, learning effects because organisms are expected to fine-tune their adaptive systems to local conditions through learning mechanisms. People calibrate their preferences to local contingencies. For instance, in the Maasai, the number of cattle a man has may be a more relevant competence marker than having a college degree.[2]

A fundamental advantage of evolutionary models of mate preferences is that they hold as their assumptions well-tested observations regarding asymmetries in obligation to offspring. Men and women have different obligations to their offspring, reproductively, metabolically, and economically (at least in the past). This is not an emergent reality created by patriarchal power systems but, instead, a deep evolutionary pattern that traverses all sexually reproducing genera. This theory of parental investment (Trivers, 1972) asserts that the sex that invests more will act as the chooser whereas the sex being chosen will engage in competition. The sex that invests less has more expensive, larger, and fewer sex cells whereas the sex that invests less tends to have cheaper, smaller, and more numerous sex cells. In mammals—of which humans are a member—males tend to have the former whereas females have the latter. Given this biological constraint imposed on humans, there is good reason to expect sex differences in mate preferences. In contrast, sex differences in sociocultural models tend to be explained away as trivial or with post hoc hand-waving and victimhood (e.g., people are the "victims" of cultural forces).

One theory that addresses this is sexual strategies theory (Buss & Schmitt, 1993). This theory explains why, in the long-term context, both sexes want an equally educated/intelligent partner (i.e., competent), but in the short-term context, women increase their emphasis on this aspect of their partners whereas men devalue it (Jonason & Antoon, 2019; Jonason et al., 2019). Similarly, it can be used to explain why, when considering long-term partners, both sexes want partners characterized by access to resources, but in the short-term, men appear to devalue this trait (Jonason et al., 2012). Because women's investment in their offspring is constant across this contextual factor they should maintain interest in having a relatively high quality partner. Men's mate preferences are sensitive to the fact that they are obligated less to a partner and her offspring in the short-term mating context and change (with limited conscious awareness) in accordance. Whether a casual sex partner is smart or educated may be a tangential concern for men; physical attractiveness becomes more important to men in this context because it serves as an insurance policy for any offspring where the men will invest little in their partners (Li & Kenrick, 2006). This may seem like a just-so story, but sociocultural models would make a different prediction. Instead, such models would predict that given that it is a casual sex encounter, both sexes should devalue competence markers relative to physical attractiveness in a pragmatic fashion or motivated by hedonism only.

One of the most powerful interactionist paradigms for evolutionists is called life history theory (Wilson, 1975). Life history theory was originally proposed to account for species-level differences in how organisms allocate time and effort (finite commodities)

---

[2] http://www.siyabona.com/maasai-tribe-east-africa.html

to somatic effort (e.g., staying alive and building a body) and mating effort (e.g., mate attraction). As far as we know, the theory has not commonly been applied to mate preferences, but it does lend itself to explaining mate preferences. Organisms that tend to focus on somatic effort (e.g., chimpanzees, elephants, and humans) and, thus, invest heavily in offspring should have mate preferences that reflect traits like competence and compassion. Kind chimpanzees (e.g., Freud from Gombe) have reproductive success (Wroblewski et al., 2009) and competence markers are universal mate preferences in people (Buss, 1989). Traits like competence and compassion will serve species that are longer lived and those who live in social groups like humans. In contrast, species that invest little in their offspring are likely to focus only on physical traits; physical traits act as an insurance policy to offset limited investment in offspring (Gangestad & Simpson, 2000).

In addition, thanks to observations regarding parental investment, this theory can also accommodate sex differences in mate preferences. While both sexes value somatic effort the most, men value mating effort more than women do (Jonason & Tome, 2019). This means when both sexes are investing, both are likely to converge on investment-oriented traits like competence and compassion. In contrast, when only one sex is investing (typically women), women will continue to prioritize investment-oriented traits whereas men may place their emphasis on physical attractiveness to offset the limited investment they may afford any subsequent offspring. While life history theory has not yet been applied to mate preferences, it seems to explain available evidence and provide further clarification for why some traits (and not others) are emphasized in the long-term and short-term contexts.

Limitations, Future Research, and Conclusions

Despite the large body of research on mate preferences there are some limitations worth noting. As has become abundantly clear over the last decade, there are sample problems in social and personality psychology. The reliance on Western, educated, industrialized, rich, and democratic (i.e., WEIRD) samples (Henrich et al., 2010) may undermine the generalizability of some of the findings in this area. While descriptive work often relies on cross-cultural samples—especially by evolutionary psychologists—experimental work in most research traditions fails to include data from different countries and rarely examines mechanisms for cultural differences in mate preferences (Hatfield & Rapson, 2005). Modern research traditions might be useful here and we encourage large-scale, multisite studies like those advanced by the Psychological Science Accelerator project. Such work will improve sample sizes and allow for the integration of mechanisms of cultural shifts in mate preferences that have evaded researchers thus far (e.g., Thomas et al., 2020).

While we focused on a handful of relationship types, one should not take that as an indication that these are the only relationship types available (Jonason & Balzarini, 2016). For instance, an increasing interest in academic and interpersonal circles for polyamory or consensual nonmonogamy has grown (Rubel & Bogaert, 2014). We did not address this kind of relationship here because there is limited research on mate preferences in these groups and we expect that as a combination of their short- and long-term mating aspects, mate preferences for those in these relationships should mirror those of others engaged in either of these other two kinds of relationships. That being said, there may be some traits in consensual nonmonogamy that are particularly important, more so than in monogamous relationships, like high rates of trait openness, agreeableness, and honesty along with limited jealousy, but these are questions for future research.

And, lastly, although there is copious amounts of research on personality indicators or psychological mate preferences, there is (a) much less research on value/interest/belief convergence and (b) no real research validating our ad hoc "thematic" analysis. The three Cs we identified are based on our appraisal of the body of research and not only warrant investigation but are a matter of debate and may be biased by our epistemological approach as two personality psychologists who regularly appeal to evolutionary approaches of human behavior. Future work should engage in large-scale factor analyses and to simply test the appeal of these classes of mate preferences overtly.

In closing, we have offered here a reductionist account of mate preferences in psychological features, where we identified three higher-order traits: competence, compassion, and compatibility. These traits play an important role in mate preferences, primarily after minimum standards of physical attractiveness are satisfied. We detailed sex differences and relationship types of variance in these mate preferences and summarized and critiqued sociocultural and evolutionary accounts of mate preferences. While up for debate, we think these three categories will help people better organize their knowledge of mate preferences and may be generative for future research.

Acknowledgments

The first author was partially funded by the Polish National Agency for Academic Exchange (PPN/ULM/2019/1/00019/U/00001).

References

Allport, G. W. (1985). The historical background of social psychology. In G. Lindzey & E. Aronson (Eds.), *The handbook of social psychology*. McGraw-Hill.

Arnocky, S., Piché, T., Albert, G., Ouellette, D., & Barclay, P. (2017). Altruism predicts mating success in humans. *British Journal of Psychology*, *108*, 416–435.

Atari, M., & Jamali, R. (2016) Mate preferences in young Iranian women: Cultural and individual difference correlates. *Evolutionary Psychological Science*, *2*, 1–7.

Bandura, A. (1977). *Social learning theory*. Prentice-Hall.

Barclay, P. (2010). Altruism as a courtship display: Some effects of third-party generosity on audience perceptions. *British Journal of Psychology*, *101*, 123–135.

Barclay, P., & Willer, R. (2007). Partner choice creates competitive altruism in humans. *Proceedings of the Royal Society B: Biological Sciences*, *274*, 749–753.

Bech-Sørensen, J., & Pollet, T. V. (2016). Sex differences in mate preferences: A replication study, 20 years later. *Evolutionary Psychological Science*, *2*, 171–176.

Botwin, M. D., Buss, D. M., & Shackelford, T. K. (1997). Personality and mate preferences: Five factors in mate selection and marital satisfaction. *Journal of Personality*, *65*, 107–136.

Burn, S. M., & Ward, A. Z. (2005). Men's conformity to traditional masculinity and relationship satisfaction. *Psychology of Men & Masculinity, 6*, 254–263.

Buss, D. M. (1985). Human mate selection: Opposites are sometimes said to attract, but in fact we are likely to marry someone who is similar to us in almost every variable. *American Scientist, 73*, 47–51.

Buss, D. M. (1989). Sex differences in human mate preferences: Evolutionary hypotheses tested in 37 cultures. *Behavioral and Brain Sciences, 12*, 1–49.

Buss, D. M. (2002). Sex, marriage, and religion: What adaptive problems do religious phenomena solve? *Psychological Inquiry, 13*, 201–238.

Buss, D. M., & Barnes, M. (1986). Preferences in human mate selection. *Journal of Personality and Social Psychology, 50*, 559–570.

Buss, D. M., & Schmitt, D. P. (1993). Sexual strategies theory: An evolutionary perspective on human mating. *Psychological Review, 100*, 204–232.

Buss, D. M., Shackelford, T. K., Kirkpatrick, L. A., & Larsen, R. J. (2001). A half century of mate preferences: The cultural evolution of values. *Journal of Marriage and Family, 63*, 491–503.

Buunk, B. P., Dijkstra, P., Fetchenhauer, D., & Kenrick, D. T. (2002). Age and gender differences in mate selection criteria for various involvement levels. *Personal Relationships, 9*, 271–278.

Campbell, L., Simpson, J., Kashy, D., & Fletcher, G. (2001). Ideal standards, the self, and flexibility of ideals in close relationships. *Personality and Social Psychology Bulletin, 27*, 447–462.

Castro, F. N., Hattori, W. T., & de Araújo Lopes, F. (2012). Relationship maintenance or preference satisfaction? Male and female strategies in romantic partner choice. *Journal of Social, Evolutionary, and Cultural Psychology, 6*, 217–226.

Cowan, M. L., & Little, A. C. (2013). The attractiveness of humour types in personal advertisements: Affiliative and aggressive humour are differentially preferred in long-term versus short-term partners. *Journal of Evolutionary Psychology, 11*, 159–170.

Davis, S. (1990). Men as success objects and women as sex objects: A study of personal advertisements. *Sex Roles, 23*, 43–50.

Eagly, A. H., & Wood, W. (1999). The origins of sex differences in human behavior: Evolved dispositions versus social roles. *American Psychologist, 54*, 408–423.

El Jurdi, H., & Smith, S. (2018), Mirror, mirror: National identity and the pursuit of beauty. *Journal of Consumer Marketing, 35*, 40–50.

Farrelly, D. (2013). Altruism as an indicator of good parenting quality in long-term relationships: Further investigations using the mate preferences towards altruistic traits scale. *The Journal of Social Psychology, 153*, 395–398.

Farrelly, D., Clemson, P., & Guthrie, M. (2016). Are women's mate preferences for altruism also influenced by physical attractiveness? *Evolutionary Psychology, 14*, Article 1474704915623698.

Fletcher, G. J., Simpson, J. A., Thomas, G., & Giles, L. (1999). Ideals in intimate relationships. *Journal of Personality and Social Psychology, 76*, 72–89.

Fletcher, G. J., Tither, J. M., O'Loughlin, C., Friesen, M., & Overall, N. (2004). Warm and homely or cold and beautiful? Sex differences in trading off traits in mate selection. *Personality and Social Psychology Bulletin, 30*, 659–672.

Gangestad, S., & Simpson, J. (2000). The evolution of human mating: Trade-offs and strategic pluralism. *Behavioral and Brain Sciences, 23*, 573–644.

Ganzach, Y., Ellis, S., & Gotlibovski, C. (2013). On intelligence education and religious beliefs. *Intelligence, 41*, 121–128.

Goetz, J. L., Keltner, D., & Simon-Thomas, E. (2010). Compassion: An evolutionary analysis and empirical review. *Psychological Bulletin, 136*, 351.

Greengross, G., & Miller, G. (2011). Humor ability reveals intelligence, predicts mating success, and is higher in males. *Intelligence, 39*, 188–192.

Greitemeyer, T. (2007). What do men and women want in a partner? Are educated partners always more desirable? *Journal of Experimental Social Psychology, 43*, 180–194.

Griskevicius, V., Tybur, J. M., Sundie, J. M., Cialdini, R. B., Miller, G. F., & Kenrick, D. T. (2007). Blatant benevolence and conspicuous consumption: When romantic motives elicit strategic costly signals. *Journal of Personality and Social Psychology, 93*, 85–102.

Guéguen, N., & Ciccotti, S. (2008). Domestic dogs as facilitators in social interaction: An evaluation of helping and courtship behaviors. *Anthrozoös, 21*, 339–349.

Guéguen, N., Meineri, S., & Fischer-Lokou, J. (2014). Men's music ability and attractiveness to women in a real-life courtship context. *Psychology of Music, 42*, 545–549.

Hatfield, E., & Rapson, R. L. (2005). *Love and sex: Cross-cultural perspectives*. Allyn & Bacon.

Henrich, J., Heine, S. J., & Norenzayan, A. (2010). The weirdest people in the world? *Behavioral and Brain Sciences, 33*, 61–83.

Howrigan, D. P., & MacDonald, K. B. (2008). Humor as a mental fitness indicator. *Evolutionary Psychology, 6*, 652–666.

Iredale, W., Van Vugt, M., & Dunbar, R. I. M. (2008). Showing off in humans: Male generosity as a mating signal. *Evolutionary Psychology, 6*, 386–392.

Jonason, P. K. (2013). Four functions for four relationships: Consensus definitions in university students. *Archives of Sexual Behavior, 42*, 1407–1414.

Jonason, P. K., & Antoon, C. N. (2019). Mate preferences for educated partners: Similarities and differences in the sexes depend on mating context. *Personality and Individual Differences, 148*, 57–61.

Jonason, P. K., & Balzarini, R. (2016). Unweaving the rainbow of human sexuality. In K. Aumer (Ed.), *The psychology of love and hate in intimate relationships* (pp. 13–28). Springer.

Jonason, P. K., Betteridge, G. L., & Kneebone, I. I. (2016). An examination of the nature of erotic talk. *Archives of Sexual Behavior, 45*, 21–31.

Jonason, P. K., Garcia, J., Webster, G. D., Li, N. P., & Fisher, H. (2015). Relationship dealbreakers: What individuals do not want in a mate. *Personality and Social Psychological Bulletin, 41*, 1697–1711.

Jonason, P. K., Li, N. P., & Cason, M. J. (2009). The "booty call": A compromise between men and women's ideal mating strategies. *The Journal of Sex Research, 46*, 1–11.

Jonason, P. K., Li, N. P., & Madson, L. (2012). It's not all about the *Benjamins*: Understanding preferences for mates with resources. *Personality and Individual Differences, 52*, 306–310.

Jonason, P. K., Li, N. P., & Richardson, J. (2010). Positioning the booty-call on the spectrum of relationships: Sexual but more emotional than one-night stands. *The Journal of Sex Research, 47*, 1–10.

Jonason, P. K., Marsh, K., Dib, O., Plush, D., Doszpot, M., Fung. E., Crimmins, K., Drapski, M., & Di Pietro, K. (2019). Is smart sexy? Examining the role of relative intelligence in mate preferences. *Personality and Individual Differences, 139*, 53–59.

Jonason, P. K., & Tome, J. (2019). How happiness expectations relate to the Dark Triad traits. *The Journal of Social Psychology, 159*, 371–382.

Jonason, P. K., Webster, G. D., & Gesselman, A. N. (2013). The structure and content of long-term and short-term mate preferences. *Interpersona, 7*, 167–179.

Jonason, P. K., White, K. P., & Al-Shawaf, L. (2020). Should I stay or should I go: Individual differences in response to romantic dealmakers and dealbreakers. *Personality and Individual Differences, 164*, Article 110120.

Kasser, T., & Sharma, Y. S. (1999). Reproductive freedom, educational equality, and females' preference for resource-acquisition characteristics in mates. *Psychological Science, 10*, 374–377.

Kaufman, S.B., Kozbelt, A., Bromley, M.L., Miller, G.F. (2008). The role of creativity and humor in human mate selection. Mating intelligence: Sex, relationships, and the mind's reproductive system. In G. Geher & G. Miller (Eds.), *Mating intelligence; Sex, relationships, and the mind's reproductive system* (pp. 227–262). Erlbaum.

Kenrick, D. T., & Keefe, R. C. (1997). Age preferences in mates: An even closer look without the distorted lenses. *Behavioral and Brain Sciences, 20*, 140–143.

Kümmerling, A., & Hassebrauck, M. (2001). Schöner mann und reiche frau? [Handsome and rich woman?] *Zeitschrift für Sozialpsychologie* [*Journal of Social Psychology*], *32*, 81–94.

Lee, A. J., Jones, B. C., & DeBruine, L. M. (2019). Investigating the association between mating-relevant self-concepts and mate preferences through a data-driven analysis of online personal descriptions. *Evolution and Human Behavior, 40*, 325–335.

Li, N. P. (2007). Mate preference necessities in long-and short-term mating: People prioritize in themselves what their mates prioritize in them. *Acta Psychologica Sinica, 39*, 528–535.

Li, N. P., Bailey, J. M., Kenrick, D. T., & Linsenmeier, J. A. W. (2002). The necessities and luxuries of mate preferences: Testing the tradeoffs. *Journal of Personality and Social Psychology, 82*, 947–955.

Li, N. P., & Kenrick, D. T. (2006). Sex similarities and differences in preferences for short-term mates: What, whether, and why. *Journal of Personality and Social Psychology, 90*, 468–489.

Li, N. P., Yong, J. C., Tov, W., Sng, O., Fletcher, G. J., Valentine, K. A., Jiang, Y. F., & Balliet, D. (2013). Mate preferences do predict attraction and choices in the early stages of mate selection. *Journal of Personality and Social Psychology, 105*, 757–776.

Lukaszewski, A. W., & Roney, J. R. (2009). Estimated hormones predict women's mate preferences for dominant personality traits. *Personality and Individual Differences, 47*, 191–196.

March, E., Van Doorn, G., & Grieve, R. (2018). Netflix and chill? What sex differences can tell us about mate preferences in (hypothetical) booty-call relationships. *Evolutionary Psychology, 16*, 1–10

McGee, E., & Shevlin, M. (2009). Effect of humor on interpersonal attraction and mate selection. *The Journal of Psychology, 143*, 67–77.

Miller, G. (2001). *The mating mind: How sexual choice shaped the evolution of human nature*. Anchor Books.

Moore, D., Wigby, S., English, S., Wong, S., Székely, T., & Harrison, F. (2013). Selflessness is sexy: Reported helping behaviour increases desirability of men and women as long-term sexual partners. *BMC Evolutionary Biology, 13*, 182–189.

Nettle, D., & Clegg, H. (2006). Schizotypy, creativity and mating success in humans. *Proceedings of the Royal Society B: Biological Sciences, 273*, 611–615.

Phillips, T., Barnard, C., Ferguson, E., & Reader, T. (2008). Do humans prefer altruistic mates? Testing a link between sexual selection and altruism towards non-relatives. *British Journal of Psychology, 99*, 555–572.

Pinker, S. (2002). *The blank slate: The modern denial of human nature*. Penguin Books.

Prokosch, M. D., Coss, R. G., Scheib, J. E., & Blozis, S. A. (2009). Intelligence and mate choice: Intelligent men are always appealing. *Evolution and Human Behavior, 30*, 11–20.

Regan, P. C. (1998). Of lust and love: Beliefs about the role of sexual desire in romantic relationships. *Personal Relationships, 5*, 139–157.

Regan, P. C., Levin, L., Sprecher, S., Christopher, F. S., & Gate, R. (2000). Partner preferences: What characteristics do men and women desire in their short-term sexual and long-term romantic partners? *Journal of Psychology and Human Sexuality, 12*, 1–21.

Rich, M. K., & Cash, T. F. (1993). The American image of beauty: Media representations of hair color for four decades. *Sex Roles*, 29, 113–124.

Rubel, A. N., & Bogaert, A. F. (2014). Consensual nonmonogamy: Psychological well-being and relationship quality correlates. *The Journal of Sex Research, 4*, 1–22.

Shackelford, T. K., Schmitt, D. P., & Buss, D. M. (2005). Universal dimensions of human mate preferences. *Personality and Individual Differences, 39*, 447–458.

Sherkat, D. E. (2003). Religious socialization: Sources of influence and influences of agency. In M. Dillon (Ed.), *Handbook of the sociology of religion* (pp. 151–163). Cambridge University Press.

Silvia, P. (2008). Another look at creativity and intelligence: Exploring higher-order models and probable confounds. *Personality and Individual Differences, 44*, 1012–1021.

Spielmann, S.S., Joel, S., & Impett, E.A. (2019). Pursuing sex with an ex: Does it hinder breakup recovery? *Archives of Sexual Behavior, 48*, 691–702.

Souza, A. L., Conroy-Beam, D., & Buss, D. M. (2016). Mate preferences in Brazil: Evolved desires and cultural evolution over three decades. *Personality and Individual Differences, 95*, 45–49.

Strenze, T. (2007). Intelligence and socioeconomic success: A meta-analytic review of longitudinal research. *Intelligence, 35*, 401–426.

Sypeck, M. F., Gray, J. J., Etu, S. F., Ahrens, A. H., Mosimann, J. E., & Wiseman, C. V. (2006). Cultural representations of thinness in women, redux: *Playboy* magazine's depiction of beauty from 1979 to 1999. *Body Image, 3*, 229–235.

Tappé, M., Bensman, L., Hayashi, K., & Hatfield, E. (2013). Gender differences in receptivity to sexual offers: A new research prototype. *Interpersona, 7*, 323–334.

Thomas, A. G., Jonason, P. K., Blackburn, J. D., Kennair, L. E. O., Lowe, R., Malouff, J., Stewart-Williams, S., Sulikowski, D., & Li, N. P. (2020). Mate preference priorities in the East and West: A cross-cultural test of the mate preference priority model. *Journal of Personality, 88*, 606–620.

Thrift, E., & Sugarman, J. (2019). What is social justice? Implications for psychology. *Journal of Theoretical and Philosophical Psychology, 39*, 1–17

Tifferet, S., Kruger, D. J., Bar-Lev, O., & Zeller, S. (2013). Dog ownership increases attractiveness and attenuates perceptions of short-term mating strategy in cad-like men. *Journal of Evolutionary Psychology, 11*, 121–129.

Treger, S., & Masciale, J. (2018). Domains of similarity and attraction in three types of relationships. *Interpersona, 12*, 254–266

Trivers, R. (1972). Parental investment and sexual selection. In B. Campbell (Ed.), *Sexual selection and the descent of man, 1871–1971* (pp. 136–179). Aldine.

Vandenberg, S. G. (1972). Assortative mating, or who marries whom? *Behavior Genetics, 2*, 127–157.

Wilson, E. O. (1975). *Sociobiology: The new synthesis.* Harvard University Press.

Wood, D., & Brumbaugh, C.C. (2009). Using revealed mate preferences to evaluate market force and differential preference explanations for mate selection. *Journal of Personality and Social Psychology, 96*, 1226–1244.

Wright, K. (2001). Generosity vs. altruism: Philanthropy and charity in the United States and United Kingdom. *Voluntas, 12*, 399–416.

Wroblewski, E. E., Murray, C. M., Keele, B. F., Schumacher-Stankey, J. C., Hahn, B. H., & Pusey, A. E. (2009). Male dominance rank and reproductive success in chimpanzees, *Pan troglodytes schweinfurthii. Animal Behaviour, 77*, 873–885.

Yu, D., & Shepard, G. (1998). Is beauty in the eye of the beholder? *Nature, 396*, 321–322.

CHAPTER

4

Partner Evaluation and Selection

Norman P. Li *and* Bryan K. C. Choy

Abstract

Not all mates are equally reproductively fit. As such, it makes sense that humans have evolved mate preferences to guide the evaluation and selection of partners who offer more versus less reproductive value. This chapter examines theory and empirical work on evolved preferences for long- and short-term mates and considers the emergence of new forms of casual, hybrid relationships. It examines basic sex-differentiated preferences for physical attractiveness and resources, as well as the prioritization of these traits, and developments in uncovering the processes that underlie the holistic valuation of a potential mate's value. The chapter then discusses the criticisms and debates on the validity of mate preferences and research on mate preferences fluctuating adaptively with women's menstrual cycle. Finally, the chapter closes with a consideration of principles of evolutionary mismatch, which may explain why there is a disconnect between theory and findings and why humans and other species are mating with human-made objects rather than their conspecifics.

Key Words: evolutionary psychology, mate preferences, mate selection, ovulation, evolutionary mismatch

Kazakh actor and bodybuilder Yuri Tolochko met his true love and fiancée Margo at a bar one night, where Margo was not being treated well by another man. Starting from that fateful evening, their romance grew stronger with each passing day. After eight months of intense dating, Yuri announced that he recently paid for Margo to undergo extensive cosmetic surgery and that he proposed marriage to her. On *Instagram*, Yuri regularly posts updates on the couple's evenings out on the town. Recently, the couple was seen vacationing in Thailand, relaxing by the beach and enjoying a traditional Thai couples massage.

In a small, picturesque French village, cheese, crackers, and champagne are served at an engagement party for Lilly and her fiancée. The room is adorned with pictures of the couple and guests can feel love in the air. Lilly admits she is attracted to her partner and she is certain that he will not be an alcoholic, wife beater, or liar—traits that she could never be sure about in the guys she met in her earlier days. Meanwhile in Japan, Akihiko Kondo recently tied the knot with Miku, spending two million yen on a ceremony held at a Tokyo hall and attended by forty guests. As the thirty-five-year-old school administrator explains, his wife wakes him up every morning to send him off to work. She prepares the house for his arrival home and lets him know each night that it is time to go to sleep. Mr. Kondo has been nothing but in love with Miku, who he refers to as his savior, and has been faithful to her from day one.

The romance and courtship of these couples from around the world sound fairly typical of many modern-day couples, yet, their stories could fit nicely into a Ray Bradbury novel or be narrated by Rod Serling for an episode of *The Twilight Zone*. Indeed, Yuri, Lilly, and Akihiko can be said to all be on the leading edge of modernity because none of the targets of their affection and lifelong commitment are human: Margo is a silicone sex doll (P. Ellis, 2019), Lilly's fiancé is a robot that she designed (Rawlins, 2017), and Miku is a hologram (Hegarty, 2019). Yet, as we shall see in this chapter, these mate choices may reflect evolved mechanisms for mate evaluation and selection that are now operating in modern, evolutionarily novel environments.

The rest of the chapter is organized as follows. First, we review the evolutionary psychological literature on mate preferences—both the basics and some important developments that extend beyond the basics. We then discuss modern mate selection platforms and venues and critiques on the validity of mate preferences, as well as research on mate preferences as an adaptive function of women's menstrual cycle. Finally, we discuss how evolved mechanisms are now operating in evolutionarily novel environments and how an understanding of this phenomenon may explain the opening examples and provide insights into the disconnect between mate preferences and mate selection.

Evolved Mate Preferences: The Basics

People vary in their mate value, or the degree to which they would promote the reproductive success of those who mate with them (Buss & Schmitt, 1993; Symons, 1979, 1995). Given that reproduction is at the heart of evolution, it makes sense that humans have evolved not to mate indiscriminately but have evolved psychological mechanisms to evaluate and prefer mates who possess greater, as opposed to lesser, reproductive value. Indeed, intersexual selection processes have been extensively studied in numerous nonhuman species, with the emergence of theoretical models starting with Darwin (1871) and progressing through Fisher (1915) and other notable researchers (e.g., Andersson, 1994; Kirkpatrick, 1982; Zahavi, 1975).

Take, for example, the blue-footed booby, a marine bird living in tropical and subtropical lands in the eastern Pacific Ocean, including the Galapagos Islands. The males perform an elaborate mating dance—a sort of strutting—that involves slowly moving their feet up and down while regularly taking a bow with wings fully fanned out. During this time, females evaluate and select mates based largely on the brightness of their light blue-colored feet. The bright color of the males' feet serves as an honest signal that varies with the male's condition (Torres & Velando, 2005; Velando et al., 2006). Hence, the preference for that trait confers an adaptive advantage to the chooser.

In many species, females, but not males, exhibit choosiness. This difference is due in part to females of most species being physiologically obligated to make a greater investment in offspring than males. Where this occurs, females have evolved to be more discriminating, in order to avoid the greater costs associated with mating with those who have low reproductive value (Haselton & Buss, 2000). As such, males in most species have evolved to compete with each other for access to or to be chosen by the more valuable females (Trivers, 1972). In species such as the pipefish seahorse where males make a larger parental investment than females by carrying fertilized eggs in their brood pouch, males are the choosier sex. For the blue-footed booby, males help out by incubating the eggs, keeping watch over them, and plunge-diving—an impressive ordeal where males flying high above the ocean dive-bomb toward the water, hitting it hard and torpedoing down to a range of 25 meters below the water surface—for fish in the earlier part of their offspring's life. Although male boobies do not appear to exercise mate choice per se (they seem perfectly content to let the females do the choosing), they have nonetheless evolved to adjust their parental investment based on the brightness of female feet and the size and brightness of her eggs (Morales et al., 2012).

Long-Term and Short-Term Mating

For humans, the relative levels of investment and, hence, degree of choice, depends on the mating context. For short-term, casual sexual relationships, sex differences in minimum obligatory parental investment are large. That is, if a pregnancy occurs, females will necessarily invest significant resources for nine months and then continue to provide nourishment via lactation and breastfeeding for up to several years later. In contrast, males are physiologically required to contribute only a few minutes of time and a teaspoon's worth of seminal fluid to make offspring. Reflecting these stark differences, human females have evolved to be choosier when evaluating or considering sexual partners (Buss, 1989; Kenrick et al., 1990; Trivers, 1972).

Evidence from various sources supports this hypothesis (see Buss & Schmitt, 2019). For instance, in a classic study (one that this chapter's authors would replicate if it were easier to get ethical review board approval at their institution), male and female experimenters approached opposite-sex individuals on the Florida State University campus and asked them to go out on a date, go back to their apartment, or have sex (Clark & Hatfield, 1989). Half of the men and women agreed to a date, but they significantly diverged as the possibility of sex became apparent. About 65% of men agreed to the apartment invitation whereas only 5% of women agreed. When sex was directly requested, around 75% of men agreed (notably, many who declined gave excuses or tried to reschedule) but not one woman consented (and several threatened to call the campus police). Likewise, studies of sociosexuality—a person's behavioral tendencies and openness toward having casual sex—have indicated that men tend to have a significantly less restricted sociosexual orientation than women (Oliver & Hyde, 1993; Simpson & Gangestad, 1991) and that this is a cross-cultural universality (Schmitt, 2005).

In essence, men have evolved to have as many casual sexual partners as possible, whereas women's evolved mechanisms tend to orient them away from casual sex. Given these opposing evolved desires, men's preference for short-term mating is limited (and, importantly, doesn't show up in the behavior of most heterosexual men) unless men have the traits that women who engage in short-term mating seek in such a partner (Gangestad & Simpson, 2000). Given this constraint and the need for biparental investment to ensure offspring survival (Geary, 2000), men and women have evolved to enter long-term relationships with each other, with short-term relationships also occurring from time to time (see Kenrick et al., 2003, for a simulation on how this pattern emerges in a society from simple, evolved decision rules at the individual level). In the next section, we review the literature on mate preferences for both long-term and short-term relationships.

KEY LONG-TERM MATE PREFERENCES

Humans are one of 3-9% of mammalian species that form long-term pair bonds (Kleiman, 1977; also see Lukas & Clutton-Brock, 2013, for a recent review). Long-term relationships, including marriages, are found throughout the world, and represent the dominant mating arrangement among humans (Schact & Kramer, 2019). According to recent statistics from the General Social Survey, 65% of Americans had a current steady romantic partner (Smith et al., 2020).

Theory

For long-term relationships, both men and women invest significantly in the relationship (Kenrick et al., 1990). Although men are not physiologically bound to invest in offspring via gestation and lactation, they have evolved to provide resources given that ancestral environments were often harsh and that men's resources and protective presence likely contributed to offspring survival (Buss, 1989; Buss & Schmitt, 1993; Geary, 2000, 2015). Thus, men also evolved to be selective and cautious when considering long-term relationships (Kenrick et al., 1990; Li & Kenrick, 2006).

Evolutionary theorists have proposed preferences that would be beneficial to have in a long-term partner. In particular, two key sex differences have been identified regarding women's versus men's long-term reproductive value. First, women are constrained by their reproductive capacity or fertility. That is, women's fertility across the lifespan peaks by the mid-20s and then begins to decline after age 30; by age 45 to 50, a woman's fertility drops to zero (Hawkes & Smith, 2010). As such, men have evolved to value perceptible cues to women's fertility (Buss, 1989; Buss & Schmitt, 1993; Symons, 1995), such as youth (Conroy-Beam & Buss, 2019; Kenrick & Keefe, 1992; Sohn, 2016), a low waist-to-hip ratio (Bovet, 2019; Singh, 1993), smooth skin and hair (Jaeger et al., 2018; Sugiyama,

2015; Symons, 1979), firm breasts and buttocks (Cant, 1981; Dagnino et al., 2012; Havlíček et al, 2017; Manning et al., 1997), facial and vocal femininity (Fraccaro et al., 2010; Jones et al., 2007; Jones & Jaeger, 2019; Marcinkowska et al., 2014), lumbar curvature (Lewis et al., 2015), and other characteristics that tend to track women's fertility.

Men's fertility, in contrast, tends to decrease more slowly across the lifespan (e.g., Anderson, 1975); thus, men's age is not as much of a determinant of their reproductive value as it is for women. Accordingly, women's preference for a young, fertile-looking partner has been theorized and found to be weaker than that of men (Antfolk, 2017; Buss, 1989; Conroy-Beam & Buss, 2019; Kenrick & Keefe, 1992). However, more than women, men display significant variation in their ability to access and provide resources—on traits such as aggression, risk-taking, and hunting abilities—that, at least in ancestral times, were critical to offspring survival (Conoy-Beam & Buss, 2019; Copping & Richardson, 2020; also see Buss et al., 2020). Hence, women are theorized to place greater emphasis on a potential long-term partner's social status, ambition, and industriousness—traits that indicate long-term access to resources—than men do (Buss, 1989).

Evidence

In Buss's (1989) landmark mate preference study, men's greater preference for physical attractiveness and youth in a marriage partner and women's greater preference for social status-related traits (including older partners) were observed across the 37 cultures (in 33 countries) that were surveyed. This work has recently been replicated in 45 countries (Walter et al., 2020), adding to the list of numerous other studies that have also confirmed these sex-differentiated preferences (e.g., Atari et al., 2020; Chang et al., 2011; Fales et al., 2016; Kamble et al., 2014; Shackelford et al., 2005b; Souza et al., 2016; Zhang et al., 2019), including one that relied on a large, nationally representative U.S. sample (Sprecher et al., 1994) and an online replication (Bech-Sørensen & Pollet, 2016) of that study. The strength of these sex-differentiated preferences remains stable across time (Shackelford et al., 2005a). Further, the same relative preferences have also been found in American (Perilloux et al., 2011), Chinese (Guo et al., 2017), and preindustrial (Apostolou, 2010) parents' preferences for their children's mates.

Various studies have also confirmed that men and women diverge in their ideal age preferences for a mate, finding that on average, women generally prefer a slightly older mate, whereas men prefer substantially younger mates (Buss 1989; Conroy-Beam & Buss, 2019). Beyond the use of surveys (Antfolk, 2017; Antfolk et al., 2015; Buss 1989), these findings have been documented via speed-dating (Kurzban & Weeden, 2007), online dating, and personal advertisements (Dunn et al., 2010; Hitsch et al., 2010; Phua et al., 2018); marriage data (Grøntvedt & Kennair, 2013; Kenrick & Keefe, 1992; Sohn, 2017); and sexual services (Griffith et al., 2016; Prokop et al., 2020; Sohn, 2016).

Kenrick and Keefe (1992) found a more nuanced pattern when examining age preferences for mates in people of different ages. Whereas women in their 20s all the way to their 60s consistently preferred a mate roughly their own age or up to 10 years older, men showed a different pattern. Men in their 20s preferred a mate around their own age, but as men aged, they preferred a mate who was increasingly younger relative to their own age. By age 40, men's acceptable age range no longer included women of their own age. These findings have been largely replicated in various studies, with similar patterns found around the world (Antfolk et al., 2015; Buunk et al., 2001; de Sousa et al., 2002; Dunn et al., 2010). Kenrick et al. (1996) also found that teenage boys showed a preference for older women who are in their early 20s, despite these women having no interest in dating teenagers. Taken together, this pattern of findings provides strong support for the view that whereas women have evolved preferences for older men who can better provide resources, men have evolved to be attracted to cues to fertile and reproductively viable mates.

Although most mate preference studies have employed traditional self-report survey methods where traits are rated on or ranked by their importance, other studies have ventured outside this traditional format, finding the same sex-differentiated preferences in other methodologies including budget allocation paradigms (Li et al., 2002; Li & Kenrick, 2006), tasks that are examined with conjoint analysis (Mogilski et al., 2014), and photographic stimuli that convey different levels of physical attractiveness and social status (Townsend, 1993; Townsend & Levy, 1990; Townsend & Roberts, 1993; Yong et al., 2022), as well as by analyzing personal advertisements (e.g., Greenlees & McGrew, 1994; Kenrick & Keefe, 1992; Thiessen et al., 1993; Wiederman, 1993), folktales (Gottschall et al., 2004), romance novels (Cox & Fisher, 2009), and erotica (Salmon, 2012).

Studies of mate preferences in non-heterosexual individuals tend also to confirm these patterns, and find sex differences consistent with evolutionary predictions (e.g., Regan et al., 2001). Gay men tend to be sociosexually unrestricted (Bailey et al., 1994; Schmitt, 2007), and they tend to engage in much more short-term sex than heterosexual men (Jackson et al., 2019; Schmitt, 2007; Symons, 1979). Although it has been proposed that this proclivity toward having large numbers of casual sexual partners is unique to the sex drive or sexual norms of gay men, it is more likely the simple outcome of individuals with a preference for short-term relationships dealing with mates who are similarly minded (Bailey, 2003; Kenrick et al., 2003; Symons, 1979). Heterosexual men's mating behavior is, in contrast, confined by women's mating preferences. Consistent with this reasoning, both heterosexual and non-heterosexual women display greater selectivity in their mates (Valentova et al., 2016); lesbian women, in particular, tend to have committed, long-term relationships in similar or greater proportion to casual sexual encounters as heterosexual women. Similar to heterosexual men, homosexual men value physical attractiveness in their partners—though unlike heterosexual men, homosexual men prioritize femininity in a partner less (Welling et al, 2013; Zhang et al., 2018)—suggesting that the mechanisms determining male sexual orientation function somewhat independently of those that govern mate preferences (Bailey et al., 1994; Howard & Perilloux, 2017; Kenrick

& Keefe, 1992). Lesbian women's mating psychology somewhat resembles that of heterosexual women (Howard & Perilloux, 2017), though there is a divide between more masculine "butch" lesbians and more feminine "femme" lesbians. Femme lesbians place greater emphasis on a romantic partner's financial resources than butch lesbians do and report greater jealousy toward a physically attractive competitor, whereas butch lesbians are less sensitive to a mate's financial resources but report greater jealousy to a wealthy competitor (Bassett et al., 2001).

Other sex-differentiated preferences include women's greater preference for taller partners (e.g., Shepperd & Strathman, 1989; Stulp et al., 2013). However, men and women have also likely evolved to equally value traits that are conducive to reproductively successful long-term relationships. Such traits include intelligence (e.g., Li et al., 2002), warmth-trustworthiness (Buss et al., 2001; Fletcher et al., 1999, 2004; Valentine et al., 2020), good parenting (Lu et al., 2015), agreeableness (Botwin et al., 1997), and kindness and honesty (Barclay, 2010; Buss, 1989; Li et al., 2011; Mogilski, Reeve, et al., 2019)—all of which have been shown to be consensually desired by men and women. Such traits allow individuals to not only successfully cooperate and solve various problems that inevitably come their way (e.g., Barkow, 1989) but to also maintain a satisfying pair bond (e.g., Shackelford et al., 2008).

KEY SHORT-TERM MATE PREFERENCES

Despite women's tendency to prefer long-term relationships, casual short-term relationships do occur. A large, recent study indicated that just over half of all respondents have had a one-night stand (Match.com, 2019).

Theory

When the intended mating duration is brief, a male partner's investment of resources is no longer a major consideration (Li & Kenrick, 2006). However, a woman is able to gain from a short-term partner's genetic quality, which can be passed on to her offspring (Gangestad, 1993; Gangestad & Simpson, 2000). As such, women have evolved to more highly value physical attractiveness in a short-term partner than a long-term partner (Buss & Schmitt, 1993). For men, the brevity of a short-term sexual relationship reduces the importance of various traits that may confer long-term benefits and increases the relative importance of obtaining a fertile partner (Li & Kenrick, 2006). Hence, physical attractiveness is hypothesized to be valued even more highly by men in a short-term context than long-term context (Buss & Schmitt, 1993; Gangestad & Simpson, 2000; Li & Kenrick, 2006; Symons, 1979).

Evidence

Various studies confirm the hypothesis that physical attractiveness is more highly valued by both sexes for short-term relationships than for long-term relationships, in samples of college students (e.g., Buss & Schmitt, 1993; Fletcher et al., 2004; Li & Kenrick, 2006; Regan, 1998; Regan & Berscheid, 1997; Simpson & Gangestad, 1992), adolescents (Regan & Joshi, 2003), and adults of various ages (Buunk et al., 2002), as well as homosexual men and women (Regan et al., 2001). Also in line with a good genes argument, men who are considered physically attractive by women tend to be more bilaterally symmetrical (Scheib et al., 1999; Thornhill & Gangestad, 1994) and have more masculine faces (e.g., Johnston et al., 2001; Penton-Voak et al., 1999) than men who are not considered physically attractive. Women, more than men, have also been shown to be sexually attracted to behavioral cues of male social dominance (Gangestad et al., 2004; Sadalla et al., 1987) and social confidence (Li, Yong, Tsai, et al., 2020). The simultaneous presence of symmetry, masculinity, and masculine behaviors is theorized to signal genes that are strong enough to withstand the immunosuppressive effects of high underlying testosterone and, thus, have been resistant to the deleterious effects of pathogens encountered in development (Gangestad & Thornhill, 1997a; Møller & Thornhill, 1998). Consistent with this theorizing, symmetrical men tend to have more sexual partners than asymmetrical men and are chosen more often as affair partners (Gangestad & Thornhill, 1997b; Thornhill & Gangestad, 1994).

Studies on the mate preferences of nonhuman animal species converge with the findings above. The preference for symmetrical (compared to asymmetrical) conspecifics has been shown in mate choice decisions of animal species such as zebra finches (Swaddle, 1996), bluethroats (Fiske & Amundsen, 1997), swordtail fish (Morris & Casey, 1998), and Iberian rock lizards, (López et al., 2002). Studies of rhesus macaques (*Macaca Mulatta*), an Old World monkey species that shares 93% of the human DNA, are also instructive. As in humans, symmetry has been theorized to signal an organism's ability to withstand environmental stress, which, in turn, facilitates the development of costly sexual characteristics (Møller & Höglund, 1991). Accordingly, symmetry may be displayed only among organisms of high genetic quality. Consistent with such theorizing, among rhesus macaques, symmetry is positively associated with greater sexual dimorphism and health (Little et al., 2008, 2012) and is preferred by opposite-sex conspecifics (Waitt & Little, 2006).

Ovulatory Effects on Mate Selection

Like many other mammals, women are fertile for only several days each month, with the chances of conception being highest if copulation occurs just before ovulation; Although women do not advertise their fertility through pronounced physiological cues (e.g., reddening and swelling of genitals) like many other primates do when experiencing estrus, substantive changes have been documented in the mating behaviors of women during peak fertility. For instance, women experience similarly large increases in sexual desire and arousal when nearing their ovulation period (e.g., Dawson et al., 2012; Roney & Simmons, 2013; see Gangestad et al., 2015, for a review).

Women are motivated to engage in mate-seeking behaviors during peak fertility, such as displaying a preference for social gatherings (Haselton & Gangestad, 2006). Around ovulation, women have been shown to reveal more skin and wear tighter clothing at a nightclub (Grammer et al., 2004) and report greater desires to purchase and wear sexier clothing, especially in response to attractive same-sex rivals (Durante et al., 2008, 2011). Importantly, though, ovulating women do not have an increased desire to mate indiscriminately. Rather, theory and evidence suggests that they gravitate toward short-term mating with men who have good genes (Gangestad et al., 2015). For instance, women nearing ovulation prefer masculine versus feminine faces (Penton-Voak et al., 1999) and cues to more physically attractive men (Durante et al., 2012; Gangestad et al., 2007; Havlíček et al., 2005; Puts, 2005), including scents of men who are more symmetrical (Gangestad & Thornhill, 1998).

The validity of ovulation-induced shifts in mating behaviors has come under question as recent meta-analyses have documented both a presence (Gildersleeve et al., 2014a) and absence (Wood et al., 2014) of support for ovulation-related effects on mate choice. Additionally, some studies have failed to replicate previously demonstrated shifts in women's preferences for masculinity. In one recent preregistered study, although women in their fertile phase (vs. those in the luteal phase) increased their preference for male bodies in general, they did not show any shifts in preferences for six cues to masculinity as would be expected by an ovulatory shift perspective (Jünger et al., 2018; Stern et al., 2019). Similarly, others showed evidence that average hormonal levels (as opposed to fluctuating shifts) were better predictors of preferences for masculinity (Marcinkowska, Jasienska, et al., 2018; Marcinkowska, Kaminski, et al., 2018). In response, some scholars have critiqued these interpretations and conclusions on the basis of methodological and analytical concerns (Gangestad, 2016; Gangestad et al., 2016, 2019a, 2019b; Gildersleeve et al., 2014b), which may have led to unwarranted conclusions about the (limited) validity of ovulationary shifts in preferences (Gangestad et al., 2019b, 2019a). Nonetheless, it is also likely that findings may reflect the widely varying methods used to study behaviors associated with the ovulatory shift; greater clarity may potentially be obtained with more consistent and robust study designs (Gangestad et al., 2016; Jones et al., 2019).

Preferences in Relationships That Are Neither Long Term Nor Short Term

Although much of the evolutionary theory and associated empirical evidence centers around long- and short-term relationships, not all relationships neatly fit into these two categories (Choy et al., 2022; Jonason & Balzarini, 2016; Schmitt, 2015). Various types of modern relationships may fall somewhere in between, especially when the two anchors are framed as marriage and one-night stands—opposite extremes of the spectrum (Li & Kenrick, 2006). Two such relationships are friends-with-benefits (Afifi & Faulkner, 2000) and booty-call relationships (Jonason et al., 2009, 2010). Friends with benefits refers to casual sex occurring between friends, often repeatedly. In one study, it was revealed that about two thirds of the casual sex that young adults were having was with their friends (Grello et al., 2006). Likewise, another study indicated that around 60% of college students have engaged in arrangements such as booty calls or friends with benefits (Claxton & van Dulmen, 2013). Whereas men seem to be in it for sex, women are more interested in emotional connection (Lehmiller et al., 2011). Recent longitudinal evidence suggests that most friends-with-benefits relationships do not actually transition into long-term relationships (Machia et al., 2020).

Booty calls involve sex that is initiated through solicitation among acquaintances, also often occurring between friends. Studies indicate that both physical attractiveness and kindness are highly valued in booty-call partners (March et al., 2018), consistent with preferences for both a short-term relationship and a long-term relationship, respectively (Buss, 1989; Buss & Barnes, 1986; Li et al., 2002). Whereas partners in booty calls are likely to depart the scene after sex and not engage in handholding as in purely sexual relationships or one-night stands, they do, however, frequently engage in romantic acts like kissing in which long-term partners typically engage (Jonason et al., 2010). A key draw for women to take part in booty calls may be intimacy and the potential for a more long-term relationship (Jonason et al., 2009). As such, friends with benefits and booty calls, both of which are prevalent in the modern day, may represent compromises between men's ideal desire for casual sex and women's ideal desire for committed, long-term relationships with partners who invest significantly, the emergence of which is fueled by technological advances in interpersonal communication (Jonason et al., 2009, 2010).

An additional form of hybrid relationship that seems to incorporate both short- and long-term aspects is consensual nonmonogamy (CNM; e.g., polyamory, open relationships, and swinging), which involves having multiple simultaneous romantic relationships (Jonason & Balzarini, 2016). A key component that separates such relationships from people simply having both a primary partner and extra-pair affairs is that for CNM, all the involved partners consent to the relationship. Such relationships commonly have a two-tiered structure involving a primary partner and one or more secondary partners, though increasing efforts are being made by researchers to study CNM relationships with different structures (e.g., co-primary partners; Balzarini et al., 2019). Primary relationships seem to more closely reflect long-term relationships. For instance, individuals who participate in CNM tend to report more investment in, satisfaction with, and commitment to their primary partner, and a greater proportion of sexual activity with their secondary partner(s) (Balzarini et al., 2017). Primary partners are also rated as more desirable long-term mates than secondary partners (Mogilski et al., 2017) and are mate guarded more than secondary partners (Mogilski et al., 2017; Mogilski, Reeve, et al., 2019).

Beyond the Basics

Despite the sound theorizing and empirical grounding for the sexes' relative preferences for physical attractiveness and social status described above, early evolutionary models and empirical studies captured only a portion of the mate selection process. Here, we review two developments that extend beyond the basic mate preferences discussed above.

Mate Preference Priorities

The initial focus on sex differences in basic preferences left the evolutionary mate preference literature with a paradox. That is, although between-sex differences in preferences had been theorized and empirical work indicated that men value physical attractiveness more than women do and women value social status and resources more than men do, an examination of the between-trait preferences showed that compared to other traits, physical attractiveness was not all that highly valued by men and social status was even less highly valued by women (Li et al., 2002).

To address this paradox, Li et al. (2002) suggested that important insights into mate preferences could be gained by understanding basic microeconomic principles. That is, consumers tend to allocate their budgets according to how much they have to spend and what they already have of different goods that provide different levels of utility (a unit of measurement for usefulness, happiness, etc.) depending on how much of the good is already in possession. When people have a small, limited budget, they tend to spend a significant amount of that budget on necessities—things that offer the greatest utility up front when a person has nothing. Classic necessities might include basic food and water, a place to sleep, and access to electricity. In today's world, a mobile phone and internet access arguably also constitute necessities. As people gain more income, diminishing marginal utility sets in and the incremental value of obtaining more of these necessity goods diminishes. As such, after buying these necessities, if people are given more money, they are less likely to keep buying such goods in the same high proportion. Rather, they will start allocating their money toward other things—luxuries—that provide higher utility at that point. Classic luxuries include television sets, vacations, and private education.

Using this framework, if we define utility as reproductive fitness (Kenrick et al., 2009) and goods as partner traits, we then have an evolutionary model for the prioritization of mate preferences (Li, 2007a; Li et al., 2002, 2011, 2013). That is, because infertile women cannot reproduce, but women who lack traits other than fertility still can reproduce, a mate's fertility is a necessity for men considering either a long- or short-term relationship (Li et al., 2002; Li & Kenrick, 2006). As such, it would be adaptive for men to prioritize physical attractiveness (i.e., fertility) above other traits. However, as some physical attractiveness is obtained (and a corresponding level of fertility is ensured), the incremental contribution to reproductive fitness of obtaining more physical attractiveness begins to decrease, such that obtaining other traits begins to provide greater value. Thus, when choices are less constrained and mates are reasonably physically attractive, men are hypothesized to focus more on obtaining other traits versus continuing to desire physical attractiveness.

A similar process may be true of social status for women considering long-term partners. That is, because a destitute man contributes little to nothing to offspring survival—no matter how artistic, nice, or attractive he is—women may have evolved to prioritize having some social status in a long-term mate but to favor other traits once an average level of social status has been obtained (and hence, a corresponding level of access to resources has been verified). Li and colleagues confirmed the priority model using a budget allocation paradigm, where budgets of low, medium, and high "mate dollars" constitute disposable income for purposes of purchasing traits for an ideal mate (Li et al., 2002; Li & Kenrick, 2006). For long-term mates, men tend to allocate a significant portion of their low budgets on physical attractiveness, whereas women allocate a significant portion to social status traits. As budgets increase, however, significantly less is spent on these necessities, and more is spent on other traits—so-called luxuries (Li et al., 2002). For short-term mates, men exhibit the same pattern, initially weighting physical attractiveness even more strongly. Women considering short-term mates also prioritize physical attractiveness, about as strongly as men do for long-term mates, but spend increasingly more on other traits as budgets increase (Li & Kenrick, 2006).

Using another method, participants were asked to screen a list of opposite-sex individuals for potential long-term and short-term relationships (Li et al., 2002, Study 3; Li & Kenrick, 2006, Study 3). Information could be obtained on five different traits for each potential mate. When asked to use as little information as possible to make a reasonable decision on each mate's acceptability, the first thing that men wanted to know about both their long-term and short-term mates is their physical attractiveness. Women inquired first about physical attractiveness for short-term mates but social level for long-term mates. Moreover, regression analyses indicated that for these traits in these contexts, being below average hurt a potential mate's chances of being accepted more than being above average helped—a curvilinear pattern indicating a necessity's diminishing marginal returns. This method highlights another way to look at how people evolved to choose mates: people prioritize avoiding those who are on the low end of key traits, lest they end up with no offspring or offspring with no resources. Beyond ensuring these priorities, people tend to desire a well-rounded mate who is high on every trait. Parts of the mate preference priority model have been replicated in various studies, including those that span different cultures (Li et al., 2011; Thomas et al., 2020).

The mate preference priority model is consistent with the marginal value model of animal foraging (Charnov, 1976) and extends mate preference models built around concepts of sequential satisficing, where traits are sought after one at a time, in order of their accessibility (Grammer et al., 2001; Miller & Todd, 1998; Todd & Miller, 1999); studies using ecologically valid stimuli to convey low, medium, and high levels of physical attractiveness and social status (Townsend, 1993; Townsend & Levy, 1990; Townsend & Roberts, 1993); and studies investigating trade-offs (Fletcher et al., 2004) and those using other methods to assess priorities (Mogilski et al., 2014; Mogilski & Welling, 2017, 2018;

Mogilski, Vrabel, et al., 2019). Mate preference priorities are also reflected in people's (potentially evolved) views of their ideal selves as long-term and short-term partners (Li, 2007b).

Emerging Models for Assessing Overall Mate Value

While voluminous research has been dedicated to understanding the contents of mate preferences and which particular traits receive more weight or priority, a recent development has taken a more general approach by proposing algorithms that account for the simultaneous assessment of all of a potential mate's traits (i.e., mate value). For instance, Conroy-Beam and Buss (2016b) proposed that humans may have evolved to compute a mate's desirability by integrating and evaluating multiple mate cues using a Euclidean algorithm. A Euclidean view represents potential mates or one's ideal preferences as points within a multidimensional space, with every point in this space representing a possible set of traits or preferences. The extent to which a potential partner's traits deviate in total from one's ideals can be represented by the Euclidean distance, calculated as the sum of squared deviations between the actual or assessed value of each trait and the value of one's ideal preferences for the corresponding trait. In turn, attraction to a potential partner can be computed as the inverse of the Euclidean distance; the more a potential partner fulfills one's ideal preferences, the shorter the Euclidean distance, and the higher the attraction.

In a study using agent-based simulation models, agents employing a Euclidean algorithm to make their mate choice decisions reproduced most successfully, outperforming models where agents employed alternative mate choice algorithms (e.g., regression and polynomial) (Conroy-Beam & Buss, 2016b). Further tests have examined the model's validity in predicting actual mate choice. In one study, participants rating their short-term and long-term attraction to profiles that varied in their Euclidean distance reported greater long-term attraction to profiles that were of closer Euclidean distance (and hence, of greater Euclidean mate value) to oneself (Conroy-Beam, 2018; Conroy-Beam & Buss, 2017). Among newlyweds and long-term couples, Euclidean distances between partners were also found to be most comparable to those derived of agent-based models that employed Euclidean (but not alternative) algorithms (Conroy-Beam & Buss, 2016b). Finally, opposite-sex individuals with a shorter Euclidean distance to people's ideal preferences were found to be more desirable (Conroy-Beam et al., 2019; Conroy-Beam & Buss, 2016b).

Even more recently, researchers demonstrated that a compensatory decision-making strategy (where traits that are high in value can offset those that are low in value) using weighted-sum calculations outperformed the Euclidean distance model and noncompensatory models such as take-the-best, threshold, and aspiration (Brandner et al., 2020). As such, future research is needed to further test the different models and to reconcile such models with previous research. The performance of one model over another likely depends on what assumptions are being made, including those that concern the number of traits being considered, the availability and cost of obtaining information for each trait, the uncertainty associated with trait information, the distribution of trait levels in the population, the differential strength of trait preferences, and how reproductive fitness varies as a function of each trait. The last point may be particularly complex in reality, because traits may interact such that a trait's contribution to fitness may depend on the levels of the other traits.

Modern Platforms and Venues for Evaluating and Selecting Mates

In the last decade or two, the dating landscape has greatly changed. More and more people are using electronic means to evaluate, select, and meet prospective mates. Starting with the ability to send text messages to prospective mates, technology has advanced to the point where websites like *match.com* and *eharmony.com* have been set up to allow people to create profiles, investigate other people's profiles, and communicate with each other. More recently, social media platforms such as *Myspace, Facebook, WeChat, QQ, Tik Tok, Twitter, Instagram, Viber, Messenger, Whatsapp, Telegram,* and *Line* have come into play, where people can set up profiles, post pictures and comments, and communicate with one another. Moreover, apps specifically geared toward dating such as *Tinder* and *OKCupid* have become quite commonplace. In a recent survey, 30% of American adults report that they have used a dating site or application. Of those who have used a dating app, 23% have gone on a date with, while 12% have married or been in a committed relationship with someone they met through an app (Pew Research Center, 2020).

Although technology has advanced in recent years, studies of online dating preferences indicate that basic preferences are largely the same. Sociosexually unrestricted individuals are more likely to report using online dating services for casual sex (Sevi et al., 2018), while restricted individuals report being more likely to use online dating services for love (Hallam et al., 2018). Whereas men tend to seek younger partners online, women seek older partners (Alterovitz & Mendelsohn, 2009; Burrows, 2013; Conway et al., 2015; Kreager et al., 2014; Phua et al., 2018). In line with these preferences, women reported being more likely than men to focus on curating a more physically attractive profile (McWilliams & Barrett, 2014). More than men, women misrepresent their attractiveness (Lo et al., 2013) and weight (Hall et al., 2010).

In contrast, men offer more status-related information (e.g., education) on their advertisements than women do (Lee et al., 2019), while women are more likely to seek status-related information in profiles than men do (Alterovitz & Mendelsohn, 2009). Whereas women display a preference for highly educated men, men show no such preferences for women (Neyt et al., 2019; Ong, 2016). In one study, 360 fake male and female profiles varying in reported income levels were posted on a Chinese online dating website. Whereas men's visits to women's profiles were not associated with women's income, women's visits to men's profiles was positively associated with the income that men's profiles reported (Ong & Wang, 2015). Likewise, in a large study of more than 40,000 dating profiles, women stated a higher minimum educational preference than men did and were more explicit in specifying the educational preferences of a partner (i.e., women were more likely to state a specific level of education they wanted potential dates to have) than men were (Whyte et al., 2018). Not surprisingly, men, more than women, tend to misrepresent their income and education (Hall et al., 2010).

Speed-Dating and the Debate Concerning the Validity of Mate Preferences

One particular modern mating-market venue that involves live, face-to-face interactions as the first point of contact is speed-dating. In this venue, men and women chat sequentially with each other for typically up to five minutes each, and at the end of each chat, each person indicates whether he or she would like to exchange contact information or otherwise pursue further contact. Speed-dating offers an opportunity to examine both members of dyads as they simultaneously display their own romantic potential and assess that of the other person (Finkel et al., 2007). Importantly, by combining pre-event survey methods and measures of the outcomes of numerous interactions, the speed-dating paradigm allows researchers to test which mate preferences match up with the criteria actually used to select or reject (by indicating "yes" or "no") potential mates. Various studies have been conducted on speed-dating in recent years, with varying findings.

As reviewed in Li et al. (2013), an early study examined speed-dating events held by the now-defunct company HurryDate (Kurzban & Weeden, 2005). In contrast to predictions made by an evolutionary perspective, the researchers did not find sex differences in the extent to which individuals' physical attractiveness and social status predicted their speed-dating success. Physical attributes such as body size or an attractive face or body predicted the extent to which speed-dates were chosen by both sexes. In contrast, education and income made no difference to either men or women. Furthermore, people's mate preferences had limited predictive power over which speed-dates they accepted. On the other hand, a study of speed-dating events involving graduate and professional school students at Columbia University found different results. Men's decision to "yes" their speed-dates was influenced by the speed-dates' physical attractiveness more than women's decisions were. Women's yessing decisions depended more than men's on intelligence (Fisman et al., 2006). People's mate preferences for physical attractiveness, status, and other traits were also found to be uncorrelated with the choices they made in a speed-dating study in Germany (Todd et al., 2007). Likewise, the sexes did not differ in the impact of partner physical attractiveness on choices in other studies (Asendorpf et al., 2011; Luo & Zhang, 2009), though one study did find for women, but not men, that partners' income influenced their being accepted (Asendorpf et al., 2011).

As these studies illustrate, findings from speed-dating research are at best mixed regarding basic hypotheses and predictions that follow from evolutionary psychology. As such, some researchers have challenged the idea that mate preferences have evolved to guide mate selection processes for humans. In a comprehensive campus speed-dating study,

Eastwick and Finkel (2008) found no link between people's stated mate preferences and their evaluation of speed-dates at and beyond the event. Men yessed their speed-dates more than women on the basis of physical attractiveness, but the sexes did not differ in the extent to which their speed-dates' physical attractiveness or earning prospects influenced evaluations of romantic desire or chemistry. These researchers proposed that people inherently lack awareness of their ideal preferences, which are based on flawed, internalized ideas. These initial arguments were bolstered and fine-tuned as they found similar null results in other studies (Eastwick et al., 2011) and in a meta-analysis (Eastwick et al., 2014b).

The findings and conclusions put forth by the opposing camp have been directly critiqued by various mate preferences scholars on both theoretical and methodological grounds (Campbell & Stanton, 2014; Fletcher et al., 2014; Li & Meltzer, 2015; Li et al., 2013; Meltzer et al., 2014a, 2014b; Schmitt, 2014). In one response to the criticisms, Li et al. (2013) pointed out that the lack of sex differentiation in mate choices and the disconnect between ideal preferences and actual choices may be an artifact of not having enough representation from potential partners at the low end of earning prospects and physical attractiveness. That is, people who can afford to attend private universities and speed-dating events marketed to working professionals are not likely to include too many individuals that attendees consider to be unacceptably poor. Similarly, people who are particularly physically unattractive may stay clear of such events. As such, the influence of these key traits may not be as pronounced as they could be if the full range of these traits were represented. This is especially the case in light of the mate preference priority model, which, as suggested above, indicates that the interesting action happens—and where sex differences most likely lie—at the low- to mid-range of traits as people prioritize avoiding people who are too low on key traits.

A series of experiments supported these ideas. Participants speed-dated individuals who were prerated as low or moderate on physical attractiveness and who had low or moderate social status. With the key traits experimentally manipulated, the predicted sex differences surfaced—men based their evaluations and decisions more on physical attractiveness than women, and women based their evaluations and decision more on social status. People's mate preferences also predicted how they evaluated and chose their partners. For those who rated physical attractiveness as more important versus those who rated it as less important, a chat partner's physical attractiveness was more likely to influence evaluations of the partner's desirability and acceptability. The same held true for social status. When mating context was introduced, mate choices were sex-differentiated when considering long-term relationships but not short-term ones, where both sexes rejected partners with low physical attractiveness. Moreover, results were consistently significant in the predicted directions when analyses were based on manipulated trait levels, less consistently significant when analyses were based on participant-perceived levels of a manipulated trait, and even less so when analyses used participant-perceived levels of a trait that was not manipulated (Li et al., 2013).

Meltzer et al. (2014a) noted various methodological standards for designing valid tests of sex differences in mate preferences that Eastwick and colleagues failed to meet in their 2014 meta-analysis. They then presented a set of four longitudinal studies where these limitations were addressed. Whereas husbands' marital satisfaction was associated with their wife's attractiveness throughout the marriage, wives' satisfaction was not associated with their husband's attractiveness (Meltzer et al., 2014a). In turn, Eastwick et al. (2014c) criticized the theoretical and statistical validity of several of the standards forwarded by Meltzer et al. (2014a); they further offered new evidence that purportedly included these standards and a reanalysis of their original data that met these standards and that also included data from Meltzer et al. (2014a) yet did not produce the predicted sex differences. In a rejoinder, Meltzer et al. (2014b) highlighted several deficiencies in the critique and evidence from commentary by Eastwick et al. (2014c).

Similarly, Schmitt (2014) raised several conceptual and methodological issues with meta-analysis by Eastwick et al. (2014b). Li and Meltzer (2015) reviewed the debate and, as with Li et al. (2013), described various reasons why mate preferences might be disconnected from actual mate choice (e.g., trait information asymmetry, mating context ambiguity, and trait measurement). In line with these reasons, Conroy-Beam and Buss (2016a) also argued that correlations between stated preferences and actual mate choice may be low given the inherent complexity and constraints of mating markets. They then used an agent-based model to show a link between mate preferences and mate choices in newlywed couples. Subsequently, Eastwick and colleagues have come back with various other arguments and studies to refute the arguments and evidence put forth by evolutionary psychologists and support their own arguments (e.g., Eastwick et al., 2014a; Eastwick & Smith, 2018). These arguments and studies, however, are not likely to be the last word on this important topic. As suggested in the next section, an understanding of the disconnect between preferences and choices may strongly benefit from a consideration of how evolved mate preferences are now operating amidst evolutionary novel contexts and novel cultures.

Mismatched Mate Preferences

The failure to consistently find hypothesized sex-differentiated links between evolved mate preferences and actual mate choices in speed-dating (and some other contexts) and the failure of the individuals in the opening examples to mate with humans may have a common factor: evolutionary mismatch (Crawford & Anderson, 1989; Li et al., 2018; Tooby & Cosmides, 1990). That is, psychological mechanisms, including those for guiding the evaluation and selection of mates, evolved over a period of two or so million years (Hagen, 2015; Jobling et al., 2014; Starratt & Shackelford, 2009, p. 232). However, due to rapid human-driven technological change, especially in the last few decades, modern environments vastly differ in many ways from ancestral environments. Hence, there is now a mismatch between the evolved mechanisms, many of which (though not all; see Hagen, 2015, p. 152; Stearns et al., 2010) have likely remained unchanged since the agricultural revolution, and the novel environment in which they now operate (Giphart & van Vugt, 2016). As such, many psychological (and physiological) mechanisms are now processing inputs that they did not evolve to handle, thereby leading to maladaptive cognitive, affective, and behavioral outputs (Li et al., 2018; Li, Yong, van Vugt, 2020; Maner & Kenrick, 2010), including those related to mating (Sbarra et al., 2019; Yong et al., 2017).

Mating With Nonhuman Objects

Consider the Australian male jewel beetles that were discovered on the western side of the country/continent to be choosing "stubby" beer bottles as mates. The beetles took a liking to these beer bottles for their brown color and size because female beetles are brown and larger females carry more fertilizable eggs than smaller females. The stubbies also had numerous small, dimpled tubercles around the bottom, which probably resemble the small bumps on female forewings and reflect sunlight in a way that the female wing covers do (Gwynne & Rentz, 1983). The male beetles took such a liking that they would continue attempting to copulate with a bottle despite being attacked and having their genitalia dismantled by predatory ants. This phenomena indicates that the beetle's mechanisms for mate evaluation and selection, like those of other species, evolved to place weight on features closely linked to the identification of suitable conspecifics of higher versus lower mate value. However, due to the evolutionarily novel presence of objects that resemble—but are not actually—supermates of extraordinary reproductive value, the male beetles' preference mechanisms have been hijacked by evolutionarily novel, supernormal stimuli (Barrett, 2010), inducing the mechanisms to maladaptively prefer mating with these objects over actual conspecifics.

In similar fashion, mismatch processes may be affecting human mate choice in the modern day. The opening examples demonstrate this idea rather clearly. Nonhuman objects with particular features that resemble cues to reproductive value in greater quantity than humans normally have are evaluated as highly desirable by evolved mechanisms. This may be especially the case for individuals whose mechanisms are particularly attuned to processing those cues and whose real mating options fall short of their high standards.

For men, this means that technology-driven nonhuman objects that are chosen as mates are likely to be particularly physically attractive. Indeed, sex dolls can offer supernormal versions of secondary sexual characteristics and provide unlimited sexual access—key features to which men's mate selection mechanisms have evolved to respond positively. Holograms do not offer tactile sensation but can be made to present a realistic image of a woman with attractive, youthful features, a sweet voice, and a caring personality. In the case above, Akihiko Kondo was bullied at work by female colleagues to the point of contemplating suicide. During a two-year respite from work, he came across Hatsune Miku, a "moe anthropomorph" in the form of a long-haired teenage girl with a Yamaha voice synthesizer. Kondo was soothed to sleep each night by her songs and eventually was able to return to work. Upon finding out that Gatebox made Miku available in an encapsulated hologram, Kondo bought one and immediately proposed marriage. The hologram responded, "I hope you'll cherish me" (Miyazaki, 2020).

In the example of the woman getting engaged to the robot, it appears that the robot offers companionship without the costs of undesirable personality traits or behaviors that were typically found in the men that she knew before. More generally, mismatch cases where nonhuman objects or images are selected over actual humans likely reflect evolved, sex-differentiated trait preferences, perhaps even more so than in natural settings. Pornography and romance novels reflect this idea. Males but not females are drawn to pornography's visual focus on secondary sexual characteristics and visceral sex with strangers (Ellis & Symons, 1990; Symons, 1979). In contrast, women but not men, consume romance novels and fall for its main characters, who have numerous strengths and qualities and engage in emotionally satisfying romantic love (Cox & Fisher, 2009; Salmon, 2012).

Other Misrepresentations of Desirable Mates

Another mate choice mismatch is illustrated by studies on contrast effects, which found that when exposed to 10 printed photos of attractive women, men reported having lower commitment to their current partners, and women felt worse about themselves as a potential mate. Similarly in line with evolved, sex-differentiated preferences, when exposed to 10 written profiles of socially dominant men, women reported having lower commitment to their current partners, whereas men felt worse about their own mate value (Gutierres et al., 1999; Kenrick et al., 1994). Such findings indicate that evolved mechanisms for evaluating potential mates cannot distinguish between actual potential mates and images of such people. This is understandable considering that in the ancestral world when mate choice mechanisms were evolving, anything resembling a person was actually a person (Kanazawa, 2002). Given that in today's world people can be exposed to hundreds of images of attractive and successful people in a day, this form of mismatch may very well lead to lower relationship commitment and stability.

Consequently, such mismatch may be leading to a narrowing of sex-differentiated preferences when humans interact with each other as people's mating context mechanisms adjust away from the stability of long-term mating and become more short-term oriented, where the sexes both tend to value (Buss & Schmitt, 1993) and prioritize physical attractiveness (Li & Kenrick, 2006). This may also apply to speed-dating events, where people are surrounded by various potential mates who appear interested in getting to know them. Moreover, having to evaluate mating suitability in a few minutes may not be enough time to assess various personal characteristics. Accordingly, both sexes' decisions may rely more on physical attractiveness, which is readily assessable. For apps like *Tinder*, this is even more the case, as people can meet and swipe through 100 potential mates in a matter of minutes based only on the most salient feature: the photo.

Anonymity and Sex Ratio

Another key feature of modern urbanized societies is the significantly higher levels of anonymity than that of ancestral societies. Being able to engage in casual sexual relations anonymously, or without having to further interact with a partner ever again if one chooses, significantly reduces the costs associated with short-term mating. For men, the greater ease of withholding investment (coupled with an abundance of options) may function as a supernormal stimulus that facilitates short-term mating strategies (Goetz et al., 2019). For women, increased anonymity may buffer against any potential reputational damage, thereby lowering a key barrier to short-term mating. Moreover, in some places such as college populations, there are increasingly more women than men. A surplus of women in the local mating market has been found to shift women toward short-term mating behaviors (Baumeister & Vohs, 2004; Schmitt, 2005) and societal norms toward delayed marriage and greater acceptance of promiscuity (Guttentag & Secord, 1983; Maner & Ackerman, 2020).

Thus, such factors may be inducing women (and hence, men) toward more short-term mating, accompanied by a greater emphasis on physical attractiveness in their mates. However, due to the heavy reproductive costs associated with pure, short-term mating in the evolutionary past, this novel tendency may be inducing women to enter hybrid relationships (e.g., booty calls, friends with benefits, or CNM) that retain some features of long-term mating. In this way, variation in the sex ratio of local mating pools and other novel factors may explain the increasing occurrence of hybrid relationships (Goetz et al., 2019).

Finally, there is the evolutionarily novel social climate where gender equality and androgyny increasingly constitute both descriptive and injunctive norms in many aspects of life. How this movement and other emerging trends not only influence mate choice but also arise from evolved mating mechanisms interacting in novel environments is an interesting question and likely to be an important question for the field to address.

In closing: exciting times lie ahead for mating research

To summarize, partner evaluation and selection comprise a central part of human mating and, hence, the evolutionary process itself. As discussed in this chapter, men and women have evolved preferences for different types of relationships that serve to increase the reproductive fitness of individuals who evaluate and select mates on the basis of those preferences. Preferences for some key traits are sex-differentiated, reflecting the different constraints men versus women faced throughout evolutionary history. As indicated in this chapter, important parts of mate evaluation and selection have been debated and expanded upon in recent years. For evolutionary psychologists, future research in this area will likely engage further work in these areas—substantiating the validity of mate preferences and the robustness of mate preferences within ovulatory cycles, as well as unpacking the processes that underlie evaluation mechanisms. Given how fast the mating landscape has changed in recent years, it will also be increasingly important to investigate how evolved mechanisms are now functioning in evolutionarily novel environments and the impact of evolutionary mismatch not only on mate choice but also on reproductive outcomes.

References

Afifi, W. A., & Faulkner, S. L. (2000). On being "just friends": The frequency and impact of sexual activity in cross-sex friendships. *Journal of Social and Personal Relationships, 17*, 205–222. https://doi.org/10.1177/0265407500172003

Alterovitz, S. S.-R., & Mendelsohn, G. A. (2009). Partner preferences across the life span: Online dating by older adults. *Psychology and Aging, 24*, 513–517. https://doi.org/10.1037/a0015897

Anderson, B. A. (1975). Male age and fertility results from Ireland prior to 1911. *Population Index, 41*, 561–567. https://doi.org/10.2307/2734844

Andersson, M. (1994). *Sexual selection*. Princeton University Press.

Antfolk, J. (2017). Age limits: Men's and women's youngest and oldest considered and actual sex partners. *Evolutionary Psychology, 15*, 1-9. https://doi.org/10.1177/1474704917690401

Antfolk, J., Salo, B., Alanko, K., Bergen, E., Corander, J., Sandnabba, N. K., & Santtila, P. (2015). Women's and men's sexual preferences and activities with respect to the partner's age: Evidence for female choice. *Evolution and Human Behavior, 36*, 73–79. https://doi.org/10.1016/j.evolhumbehav.2014.09.003

Apostolou, M. (2010). Parental choice: What parents want in a son-in-law and a daughter-in-law across 67 pre-industrial societies. *British Journal of Psychology, 101*, 695–704. https://doi.org/10.1348/000712609X480634

Asendorpf, J. B., Penke, L., & Back, M. D. (2011). From dating to mating and relating: Predictors of initial and long-term outcomes of speed-dating in a community sample. *European Journal of Personality, 25*, 16–30. https://doi.org/10.1002/per.768

Atari, M., Chaudhary, N., & Al-Shawaf, L. (2020). Mate preferences in three Muslim-majority countries: Sex differences and personality correlates. *Social Psychological and Personality Science, 11*, 533–545. https://doi.org/10.1177/1948550619866187

Bailey, J. M. (2003). *The man who would be queen: The science of gender-bending and transsexualism*. Joseph Henry.

Bailey, J. M., Gaulin, S., Agyei, Y., & Gladue, B. A. (1994). Effects of gender and sexual orientation on evolutionarily relevant aspects of human mating psychology. *Journal of Personality and Social Psychology, 66*, 1081–1093. https://doi.org/10.1037/0022-3514.66.6.1081

Balzarini, R. N., Campbell, L., Kohut, T., Holmes, B. M., Lehmiller, J. J., Harman, J. J., & Atkins, N. (2017). Perceptions of primary and secondary relationships in polyamory. *PLOS ONE, 12*, Article e0177841. https://doi.org/10.1371/journal.pone.0177841

Balzarini, R. N., Dharma, C., Kohut, T., Campbell, L., Lehmiller, J. J., Harman, J. J., & Holmes, B. M. (2019). Comparing relationship quality across different types of romantic partners in polyamorous and monogamous relationships. *Archives of Sexual Behavior, 48*, 1749–1767. https://doi.org/10.1007/s10508-019-1416-7

Barclay, P. (2010). Altruism as a courtship display: Some effects of third-party generosity on audience perceptions. *British Journal of Psychology, 101*, 123–135. https://doi.org/10.1348/000712609X435733

Barkow, J. H. (1989). *Darwin, sex, and status: Biological approaches to mind and culture* (pp. xx, 453). University of Toronto Press.

Barrett, D. (2010). *Supernormal stimuli: How primal urges overran their evolutionary purpose*. W. W. Norton.

Bassett, J., Pearcey, S., & Dabbs, J. M. (2001). Jealousy and partner preference among butch and femme lesbians. *Psychology, Evolution & Gender, 3*, 155–165. https://doi.org/10.1080/14616660110067375

Baumeister, R. F., & Vohs, K. D. (2004). Sexual economics: Sex as female resource for social exchange in heterosexual interactions. *Personality and Social Psychology Review, 8*, 339–363. https://doi.org/10.1207/s15327957pspr0804_2

Bech-Sørensen, J., & Pollet, T. V. (2016). Sex differences in mate preferences: A replication study, 20 years later. *Evolutionary Psychological Science, 2*, 171–176. https://doi.org/10.1007/s40806-016-0048-6

Botwin, M. D., Buss, D. M., & Shackelford, T. K. (1997). Personality and mate preferences: Five factors in mate selection and marital satisfaction. *Journal of Personality, 65*, 107–136.

Bovet, J. (2019). Evolutionary theories and men's preferences for women's waist-to-hip ratio: Which hypotheses remain? A systematic review. *Frontiers in Psychology, 10*, 1221. https://doi.org/10.3389/fpsyg.2019.01221

Brandner, J. L., Brase, G. L., & Huxman, S. A. J. (2020). "Weighting" to find the right person: Compensatory trait integrating versus alternative models to assess mate value. *Evolution and Human Behavior, 41*, 284–292. https://doi.org/10.1016/j.evolhumbehav.2020.05.001

Burrows, K. (2013). Age preferences in dating advertisements by homosexuals and heterosexuals: From sociobiological to sociological explanations. *Archives of Sexual Behavior, 42*, 203–211. https://doi.org/10.1007/s10508-012-0031-7

Buss, D. M. (1989). Sex differences in human mate preferences: Evolutionary hypotheses tested in 37 cultures. *Behavioral and Brain Sciences, 12*, 1–14. https://doi.org/10.1017/S0140525X00023992

Buss, D. M., & Barnes, M. (1986). Preferences in human mate selection. *Journal of Personality and Social Psychology, 50*, 559–570. https://doi.org/10.1037/0022-3514.50.3.559

Buss, D. M., Durkee, P. K., Shackelford, T. K., Bowdle, B. F., Schmitt, D. P., Brase, G. L., Choe, J. C., & Trofimova, I. (2020). Human status criteria: Sex differences and similarities across 14 nations. *Journal of Personality and Social Psychology, 119*, 979–998. https://doi.org/10.1037/pspa0000206

Buss, D. M., & Schmitt, D. P. (1993). Sexual strategies theory: An evolutionary perspective on human mating. *Psychological Review, 100*, 204–232. https://doi.org/10.1037/0033-295X.100.2.204

Buss, D. M., & Schmitt, D. P. (2019). Mate preferences and their behavioral manifestations. *Annual Review of Psychology, 70*, 77–110. https://doi.org/10.1146/annurev-psych-010418-103408

Buss, D. M., Shackelford, T. K., Kirkpatrick, L. A., & Larsen, R. J. (2001). A half century of mate preferences: The cultural evolution of values. *Journal of Marriage and Family, 63*, 491–503.

Buunk, B. P., Dijkstra, P., Fetchenhauer, D., & Kenrick, D. T. (2002). Age and gender differences in mate selection criteria for various involvement levels. *Personal Relationships, 9*, 271–278. https://doi.org/10.1111/1475-6811.00018

Buunk, B. P., Dijkstra, P., Kenrick, D. T., & Warntjes, A. (2001). Age preferences for mates as related to gender, own age, and involvement level. *Evolution and Human Behavior*, 22(4), 241–250. https://doi.org/10.1016/S1090-5138(01)00065-4

Campbell, L., & Stanton, S. C. E. (2014). The predictive validity of ideal partner preferences in relationship formation: What we know, what we don't know, and why it matters: Ideal preferences and relationship initiation. *Social and Personality Psychology Compass, 8*, 485–494. https://doi.org/10.1111/spc3.12126

Cant, J. G. H. (1981). Hypothesis for the evolution of human breasts and buttocks. *American Naturalist, 117*, 199–204. https://doi.org/10.1086/283699

Chang, L., Wang, Y., Shackelford, T. K., & Buss, D. M. (2011). Chinese mate preferences: Cultural evolution and continuity across a quarter of a century. *Personality and Individual Differences, 50*, 678–683. https://doi.org/10.1016/j.paid.2010.12.016

Charnov, E. L. (1976). Optimal foraging, the marginal value theorem. *Theoretical Population Biology, 9*, 129–136. https://doi.org/10.1016/0040-5809(76)90040-X

Choy, B. K. C., Li, N. P., & Tan, K. (2022). The long and short of mistress relationships: Sex-differentiated mate preferences reflect a compromise of mating ideals. *Journal of Personality,* Advanced Online Publication. https://doi.org/10.1111/jopy.12734

Clark, R. D. I., & Hatfield, E. (1989). Gender differences in receptivity to sexual offers. *Journal of Psychology & Human Sexuality, 2*, 39–55. https://doi.org/10.1300/J056v02n01_04

Claxton, S. E., & van Dulmen, M. H. M. (2013). Casual sexual relationships and experiences in emerging adulthood. *Emerging Adulthood, 1*, 138–150. https://doi.org/10.1177/2167696813487181

Conroy-Beam, D. (2018). Euclidean mate value and power of choice on the mating market. *Personality and Social Psychology Bulletin, 44*, 252–264. https://doi.org/10.1177/0146167217739262

Conroy-Beam, D., & Buss, D. M. (2016a). Do mate preferences influence actual mating decisions? Evidence from computer simulations and three studies of mated couples. *Journal of Personality and Social Psychology, 111*, 53–66. https://doi.org/10.1037/pspi0000054

Conroy-Beam, D., & Buss, D. M. (2016b). How are mate preferences linked with actual mate selection? Tests of mate preference integration algorithms using computer simulations and actual mating couples. *PLoS ONE, 11*, Article e0156078. https://doi.org/10.1371/journal.pone.0156078

Conroy-Beam, D., & Buss, D. M. (2017). Euclidean distances discriminatively predict short-term and long-term attraction to potential mates. *Evolution and Human Behavior, 38*, 442–450. https://doi.org/10.1016/j.evolhumbehav.2017.04.004

Conroy-Beam, D., & Buss, D. M. (2019). Why is age so important in human mating? Evolved age preferences and their influences on multiple mating behaviors. *Evolutionary Behavioral Sciences, 13*, 127–157. https://doi.org/10.1037/ebs0000127

Conroy-Beam, D., Buss, D. M., Asao, K., Sorokowska, A., Sorokowski, P., Aavik, T., Akello, G., Alhabahba, M. M., Alm, C., Amjad, N., Anjum, A., Atama, C. S., Duyar, D. A., Ayebare, R., Batres, C., Bendixen, M., Bensafia, A'., Bizumic, B., Boussena, M., . . . Zupančič, M. (2019). Contrasting computational models of mate preference integration across 45 countries. *Scientific Reports, 9*, Article 16885. https://doi.org/10.1038/s41598-019-52748-8

Copping, L. T., & Richardson, G. B. (2020). Studying sex differences in psychosocial life history indicators. *Evolutionary Psychological Science, 6*, 47–59. https://doi.org/10.1007/s40806-019-00211-2

Conway, J. R., Noë, N., Stulp, G., & Pollet, T. V. (2015). Finding your soulmate: Homosexual and heterosexual age preferences in online dating. *Personal Relationships, 22*, 666–678. https://doi.org/10.1111/pere.12102

Cox, A., & Fisher, M. (2009). The Texas billionaire's pregnant bride: An evolutionary interpretation of romance fiction titles. *Journal of Social, Evolutionary, and Cultural Psychology, 3*, 386–401. https://doi.org/10.1037/h0099308

Crawford, C. B., & Anderson, J. L. (1989). Sociobiology: An environmentalist discipline? *American Psychologist, 44*, 1449–1459. https://doi.org/10.1037/0003-066X.44.12.1449

Dagnino, B., Navajas, J., & Sigman, M. (2012). Eye fixations indicate men's preference for female breasts or buttocks. *Archives of Sexual Behavior, 41*, 929–937. https://doi.org/10.1007/s10508-012-9945-3

Darwin, C. (1871). *The descent of man, and selection in relation to sex.* Murray.

Dawson, S. J., Suschinsky, K. D., & Lalumière, M. L. (2012). Sexual fantasies and viewing times across the menstrual cycle: A diary study. *Archives of Sexual Behavior, 41*, 173–183. https://doi.org/10.1007/s10508-012-9939-1

de Sousa Campos, L., Otta, E., & de Oliveira Siqueira, J. (2002). Sex differences in mate selection strategies: Content analyses and responses to personal advertisements in Brazil. *Evolution and Human Behavior, 23*, 395–406. https://doi.org/10.1016/S1090-5138(02)00099-5

Dunn, M. J., Brinton, S., & Clark, L. (2010). Universal sex differences in online advertisers age preferences: Comparing data from 14 cultures and 2 religious groups. *Evolution and Human Behavior, 31*, 383–393. https://doi.org/10.1016/j.evolhumbehav.2010.05.001

Durante, K. M., Griskevicius, V., Hill, S. E., Perilloux, C., & Li, N. P. (2011). Ovulation, female competition, and product choice: Hormonal influences on consumer behavior. *Journal of Consumer Research, 37*, 921–934. https://doi.org/10.1086/656575

Durante, K. M., Griskevicius, V., Simpson, J. A., Cantú, S. M., & Tybur, J. M. (2012). Sex ratio and women's career choice: Does a scarcity of men lead women to choose briefcase over baby? *Journal of Personality and Social Psychology, 103*, 121–134. https://doi.org/10.1037/a0027949

Durante, K. M., Li, N. P., & Haselton, M. G. (2008). Changes in women's choice of dress across the ovulatory cycle: Naturalistic and laboratory task-based evidence. *Personality and Social Psychology Bulletin, 34*, 1451–1460. https://doi.org/10.1177/0146167208323103

Eastwick, P. W., & Finkel, E. J. (2008). Sex differences in mate preferences revisited: Do people know what they initially desire in a romantic partner? *Journal of Personality and Social Psychology, 94*, 245–264. https://doi.org/10.1037/0022-3514.94.2.245

Eastwick, P. W., Finkel, E. J., & Eagly, A. H. (2011). When and why do ideal partner preferences affect the process of initiating and maintaining romantic relationships? *Journal of Personality and Social Psychology, 101*, 1012–1032. https://doi.org/10.1037/a0024062

Eastwick, P. W., Luchies, L. B., Finkel, E. J., & Hunt, L. L. (2014a). The many voices of Darwin's descendants: Reply to Schmitt (2014). *Psychological Bulletin, 140*, 673–681. https://doi.org/10.1037/a0036111

Eastwick, P. W., Luchies, L. B., Finkel, E. J., & Hunt, L. L. (2014b). The predictive validity of ideal partner preferences: A review and meta-analysis. *Psychological Bulletin, 140*, 623–665. https://doi.org/10.1037/a0032432

Eastwick, P. W., Neff, L. A., Finkel, E. J., Luchies, L. B., & Hunt, L. L. (2014c). Is a meta-analysis a foundation, or just another brick? Comment on Meltzer, McNulty, Jackson, and Karney (2014). *Journal of Personality and Social Psychology, 106*, 429–434. https://doi.org/10.1037/a0034767

Eastwick, P. W., & Smith, L. K. (2018). Sex-differentiated effects of physical attractiveness on romantic desire: A highly powered, preregistered study in a photograph evaluation context. *Comprehensive Results in Social Psychology, 3*, 1–27. https://doi.org/10.1080/23743603.2018.1425089

Ellis, B., & Symons, D. (1990). Sex differences in sexual fantasy: An evolutionary psychological approach. *Journal of Sex Research, 27*, 527–555. https://doi.org/10.1080/00224499009551579

Ellis, P. (2019, December 11). A bodybuilder is marrying his sex doll girlfriend, Margo. *Men's Health*. https://www.menshealth.com/sex-women/a30195385/bodybuilder-yuri-tolochko-engaged-sex-doll-girlfriend/

Fales, M. R., Frederick, D. A., Garcia, J. R., Gildersleeve, K. A., Haselton, M. G., & Fisher, H. E. (2016). Mating markets and bargaining hands: Mate preferences for attractiveness and resources in two national U.S. studies. *Personality and Individual Differences, 88*, 78–87. https://doi.org/10.1016/j.paid.2015.08.041

Finkel, E. J., Eastwick, P. W., & Matthews, J. (2007). Speed-dating as an invaluable tool for studying romantic attraction: A methodological primer. *Personal Relationships, 14*, 149–166. https://doi.org/10.1111/j.1475-6811.2006.00146.x

Fisher, R. A. (1915). The evolution of sexual preference. *The Eugenics Review, 7*, 184–192.

Fiske, P., & Amundsen, T. (1997). Female bluethroats prefer males with symmetric colour bands. *Animal Behaviour, 54*, 81–87. https://doi.org/10.1006/anbe.1996.0436

Fisman, R., Iyengar, S. S., Kamenica, E., & Simonson, I. (2006). Gender differences in mate selection: Evidence from a speed-dating experiment. *The Quarterly Journal of Economics, 121*, 673–697. https://doi.org/10.1162/qjec.2006.121.2.673

Fletcher, G. J. O., Kerr, P. S. G., Li, N. P., & Valentine, K. A. (2014). Predicting romantic interest and decisions in the very early stages of mate selection: Standards, accuracy, and sex differences. *Personality and Social Psychology Bulletin, 40*, 540–550. https://doi.org/10.1177/0146167213519481

Fletcher, G. J. O., Simpson, J. A., Thomas, G., & Giles, L. (1999). Ideals in intimate relationships. *Journal of Personality and Social Psychology, 76*, 72–89.

Fletcher, G. J. O., Tither, J. M., O'Loughlin, C., Friesen, M., & Overall, N. (2004). Warm and homely or cold and beautiful? Sex differences in trading off traits in mate selection. *Personality and Social Psychology Bulletin, 30*, 659–672. https://doi.org/10.1177/014616720326284

Fraccaro, P. J., Feinberg, D. R., DeBruine, L. M., Little, A. C., Watkins, C. D., & Jones, B. C. (2010). Correlated male preferences for femininity in female faces and voices. *Evolutionary Psychology, 8*, 447-461. https://doi.org/10.1177/147470491000800311

Gangestad, S. W. (1993). Sexual selection and physical attractiveness. *Human Nature, 4*, 205–235. https://doi.org/10.1007/BF02692200

Gangestad, S. W. (2016). Comment: Wood et al.'s (2014) Speculations of inappropriate research practices in ovulatory cycle studies. *Emotion Review, 8*, 87–90. https://doi.org/10.1177/1754073915580400

Gangestad, S. W., Dinh, T., Grebe, N. M., Del Giudice, M., & Emery Thompson, M. (2019a). Psychological cycle shifts redux, once again: Response to Stern et al., Roney, Jones et al., and Higham. *Evolution and Human Behavior, 40*, 537–542. https://doi.org/10.1016/j.evolhumbehav.2019.08.008

Gangestad, S. W., Dinh, T., Grebe, N. M., Del Giudice, M., & Emery Thompson, M. (2019b). Psychological cycle shifts redux: Revisiting a preregistered study examining preferences for muscularity. *Evolution and Human Behavior, 40*, 501–516. https://doi.org/10.1016/j.evolhumbehav.2019.05.005

Gangestad, S. W., Garver-Apgar, C. E., Simpson, J. A., & Cousins, A. J. (2007). Changes in women's mate preferences across the ovulatory cycle. *Journal of Personality and Social Psychology, 92*, 151–163. https://doi.org/10.1037/0022-3514.92.1.151

Gangestad, S. W., Haselton, M. G., Welling, L. L. M., Gildersleeve, K., Pillsworth, E. G., Burriss, R. P., Larson, C. M., & Puts, D. A. (2016). How valid are assessments of conception probability in ovulatory cycle research? Evaluations, recommendations, and theoretical implications. *Evolution and Human Behavior, 37*, 85–96. https://doi.org/10.1016/j.evolhumbehav.2015.09.001

Gangestad, S. W., & Simpson, J. A. (2000). The evolution of human mating: Trade-offs and strategic pluralism. *Behavioral and Brain Sciences*, *23*, 573–587. https://doi.org/10.1017/s0140525x0000337x

Gangestad, S. W., Simpson, J. A., Cousins, A. J., Garver-Apgar, C. E., & Christensen, P. N. (2004). Women's preferences for male behavioral displays change across the menstrual cycle. *Psychological Science*, *15*, 203–207. https://doi.org/10.1111/j.0956-7976.2004.01503010.x

Gangestad, S. W., & Thornhill, R. (1997a). Human sexual selection and developmental stability. In J. A. Simpson & D. T. Kenrick (Eds.), *Evolutionary social psychology* (pp. 169–196). Erlbaum.

Gangestad, S. W., & Thornhill, R. (1997b). The evolutionary psychology of extrapair sex: The role of fluctuating asymmetry. *Evolution and Human Behavior*, *18*, 69–88. https://doi.org/10.1016/S1090-5138(97)00003-2

Gangestad, S. W., & Thornhill, R. (1998). Menstrual cycle variation in women's preferences for the scent of symmetrical men. *Proceedings of the Royal Society B: Biological Sciences*, *265*, 927–933.

Gangestad, S. W., Thornhill, R., & Garver-Apgar, C. E. (2015). Women's sexual interests across the ovulatory cycle. In D. M. Buss (Ed.), *The handbook of evolutionary psychology: Foundations* (pp. 403–426). John Wiley & Sons.

Geary, D. C. (2000). Evolution and proximate expression of human paternal investment. *Psychological Bulletin*, *126*, 55–77. https://doi.org/10.1037/0033-2909.126.1.55

Geary, D. C. (2015). Evolution of paternal investment. In D. M. Buss (Ed.), *The handbook of evolutionary psychology: Foundations* (pp. 524–541). John Wiley & Sons.

Gildersleeve, K., Haselton, M. G., & Fales, M. R. (2014a). Do women's mate preferences change across the ovulatory cycle? A meta-analytic review. *Psychological Bulletin*, *140*, 1205–1259. https://doi.org/10.1037/a0035438

Gildersleeve, K., Haselton, M. G., & Fales, M. R. (2014b). Meta-analyses and p-curves support robust cycle shifts in women's mate preferences: Reply to Wood and Carden (2014) and Harris, Pashler, and Mickes (2014). *Psychological Bulletin*, *140*, 1272–1280. https://doi.org/10.1037/a0037714

Giphart, R., & van Vugt, M. (2016). Mismatch: How our ancestral mind deceives us daily. Podium.

Goetz, C. D., Pillsworth, E. G., Buss, D. M., & Conroy-Beam, D. (2019). Evolutionary mismatch in mating. *Frontiers in Psychology*, *10*. https://doi.org/10.3389/fpsyg.2019.02709

Gottschall, J., Martin, J., Quish, H., & Rea, J. (2004). Sex differences in mate choice criteria are reflected in folktales from around the world and in historical European literature. *Evolution and Human Behavior*, *25*, 102–112. https://doi.org/10.1016/S1090-5138(04)00007-8

Grammer, K., Fink, B., Juette, A., Ronzal, G., & Thornhill, R. (2001). Female faces and bodies: N-dimensional feature space and attractiveness. In G. Rhodes & L. A. Zebrowitz (Eds.), *Advances in visual cognition. Volume I: Facial attractiveness* (pp. 91–125). Ablex.

Grammer, K., Renninger, L., & Fischer, B. (2004). Disco clothing, female sexual motivation, and relationship status: Is she dressed to impress? *Journal of Sex Research*, *41*, 66–74. https://doi.org/10.1080/00224490409552214

Greenlees, I. A., & McGrew, W. C. (1994). Sex and age differences in preferences and tactics of mate attraction: Analysis of published advertisements. *Ethology and Sociobiology*, *15*, 59–72. https://doi.org/10.1016/0162-3095(94)90017-5

Grello, C. M., Welsh, D. P., & Harper, M. S. (2006). No strings attached: The nature of casual sex in college students. *Journal of Sex Research*, *43*, 255–267. https://doi.org/10.1080/00224490609552324

Griffith, J. D., Capiola, A., Balotti, B., Hart, C. L., & Turner, R. (2016). Online female escort advertisements: The cost of sex. *Evolutionary Psychology*, *14*, 1-9. https://doi.org/10.1177/1474704916651270

Grøntvedt, T. V., & Kennair, L. E. O. (2013). Age preferences in a gender egalitarian society. *Journal of Social, Evolutionary, and Cultural Psychology*, *7*, 239–249. https://doi.org/10.1037/h0099199

Guo, Q., Li, Y., & Yu, S. (2017). In-law and mate preferences in Chinese society and the role of traditional cultural values. *Evolutionary Psychology*, *15*, Article 1474704917730518. https://doi.org/10.1177/1474704917730518

Gutierres, S. E., Kenrick, D. T., & Partch, J. J. (1999). Beauty, dominance, and the mating game: Contrast effects in self-assessment reflect gender differences in mate selection. *Personality and Social Psychology Bulletin*, *25*, 1126–1134.

Guttentag, M., & Secord, P. F. (1983). *Too many women? The sex ratio question*. SAGE.

Gwynne, D. T., & Rentz, D. C. F. (1983). Beetles on the bottle: Male buprestids mistake stubbies for females (coleoptera). *Australian Journal of Entomology*, *22*, 79–80. https://doi.org/10.1111/j.1440-6055.1983.tb01846.x

Hagen, E. H. (2015). Evolutionary psychology and Its critics. In D. M. Buss (Ed.), *The handbook of evolutionary psychology: Foundations* (pp. 136–160). John Wiley & Sons. https://doi.org/10.1002/9781119125563.evpsych104

Hall, J. A., Park, N., Song, H., & Cody, M. J. (2010). Strategic misrepresentation in online dating: The effects of gender, self-monitoring, and personality traits. *Journal of Social and Personal Relationships, 27*, 117–135. https://doi.org/10.1177/0265407509349633

Hallam, L., De Backer, C. J. S., Fisher, M. L., & Walrave, M. (2018). Are sex differences in mating strategies overrated? Sociosexual orientation as a dominant predictor in online dating strategies. *Evolutionary Psychological Science, 4*, 456–465. https://doi.org/10.1007/s40806-018-0150-z

Haselton, M. G., & Buss, D. M. (2000). Error management theory: A new perspective on biases in cross-sex mind reading. *Journal of Personality and Social Psychology, 78*, 81–91.

Haselton, M. G., & Gangestad, S. W. (2006). Conditional expression of women's desires and men's mate guarding across the ovulatory cycle. *Hormones and Behavior, 49*, 509–518. https://doi.org/10.1016/j.yhbeh.2005.10.006

Havliček, J., Roberts, S. C., & Flegr, J. (2005). Women's preference for dominant male odour: Effects of menstrual cycle and relationship status. *Biology Letters, 1*, 256–259. https://doi.org/10.1098/rsbl.2005.0332

Havlíček, J., Třebický, V., Valentova, J. V., Kleisner, K., Akoko, R. M., Fialová, J., Jash, R., Kočnar, T., Pereira, K. J., Štěrbová, Z., Varella, M. A. C., Vokurková, J., Vunan, E., & Roberts, S. C. (2017). Men's preferences for women's breast size and shape in four cultures. *Evolution and Human Behavior, 38*, 217–226. https://doi.org/10.1016/j.evolhumbehav.2016.10.002

Hawkes, K., & Smith, K. R. (2010). Do women stop early? Similarities in fertility decline in humans and chimpanzees. *Annals of the New York Academy of Sciences, 1204*, 43–53. https://doi.org/10.1111/j.1749-6632.2010.05527.x

Hegarty, S. (2019, August 17). Why I "married" a cartoon character. *BBC News*. https://www.bbc.com/news/stories-49343280

Hitsch, G. J., Hortaçsu, A., & Ariely, D. (2010). What makes you click?—Mate preferences in online dating. *Quantitative Marketing and Economics, 8*, 393–427. https://doi.org/10.1007/s11129-010-9088-6

Howard, R. M., & Perilloux, C. (2017). Is mating psychology most closely tied to biological sex or preferred partner's sex? *Personality and Individual Differences, 115*, 83–89. https://doi.org/10.1016/j.paid.2016.05.009

Jackson, S. E., Yang, L., Veronese, N., Koyanagi, A., López Sánchez, G. F., Grabovac, I., Soysal, P., & Smith, L. (2019). Sociodemographic and behavioural correlates of lifetime number of sexual partners: Findings from the English Longitudinal Study of Ageing. *BMJ Sexual & Reproductive Health, 45*, 138–146. https://doi.org/10.1136/bmjsrh-2018-200230

Jaeger, B., Wagemans, F. M. A., Evans, A. M., & van Beest, I. (2018). Effects of facial skin smoothness and blemishes on trait impressions. *Perception, 47*, 608–625. https://doi.org/10.1177/0301006618767258

Jobling, M., Hollox, E., Hurles, M., Kivisild, T., & Tyler-Smith, C. (2014). Human evolutionary genetics (3rd ed.). Garland Science.

Johnston, V. S., Hagel, R., Franklin, M., Fink, B., & Grammer, K. (2001). Male facial attractiveness: Evidence for hormone-mediated adaptive design. *Evolution and Human Behavior, 22*, 251–267. https://doi.org/10.1016/S1090-5138(01)00066-6

Jonason, P. K., & Balzarini, R. N. (2016). Unweaving the rainbow of human sexuality: A review of one-night stands, serious romantic relationships, and the relationship space in between. In K. Aumer (Ed.), *The psychology of love and hate in intimate relationships* (pp. 13–28). Springer.

Jonason, P. K., Li, N. P., & Cason, M. J. (2009). The "Booty Call": A compromise between men's and women's ideal mating strategies. *Journal of Sex Research, 46*, 460–470.

Jonason, P. K., Li, N. P., & Richardson, J. (2010). Positioning the booty-call relationship on the spectrum of relationships: Sexual but more emotional than one-night stands. *Journal of Sex Research, 48*, 486–495. https://doi.org/10.1080/00224499.2010.497984

Jones, A. L., & Jaeger, B. (2019). Biological bases of beauty revisited: The effect of symmetry, averageness, and sexual dimorphism on female facial attractiveness. *Symmetry, 11*, 279. https://doi.org/10.3390/sym11020279

Jones, B. C., DeBruine, L. M., Little, A. C., Conway, C. A., Welling, L. L. M., & Smith, F. (2007). Sensation seeking and men's face preferences. *Evolution and Human Behavior, 28*, 439–446. https://doi.org/10.1016/j.evolhumbehav.2007.07.006

Jones, B. C., Hahn, A. C., & DeBruine, L. M. (2019). Ovulation, sex hormones, and women's mating psychology. *Trends in Cognitive Sciences, 23*, 51–62. https://doi.org/10.1016/j.tics.2018.10.008

Jünger, J., Kordsmeyer, T. L., Gerlach, T. M., & Penke, L. (2018). Fertile women evaluate male bodies as more attractive, regardless of masculinity. *Evolution and Human Behavior, 39*, 412–423. https://doi.org/10.1016/j.evolhumbehav.2018.03.007

Kamble, S., Shackelford, T. K., Pham, M., & Buss, D. M. (2014). Indian mate preferences: Continuity, sex differences, and cultural change across a quarter of a century. *Personality and Individual Differences, 70*, 150–155.

Kanazawa, S. (2002). Bowling with our imaginary friends. *Evolution and Human Behavior, 23*, 167–171. https://doi.org/10.1016/S1090-5138(01)00098-8

Kenrick, D. T., Griskevicius, V., Sundie, J. M., Li, N. P., Li, Y. J., & Neuberg, S. L. (2009). Deep rationality: The evolutionary economics of decision making. *Social Cognition, 27*, 764–785. https://doi.org/10.1521/soco.2009.27.5.764

Kenrick, D. T., & Keefe, R. C. (1992). Age preferences in mates reflect sex differences in human reproductive strategies. *Behavioral and Brain Sciences, 15*, 75–91. https://doi.org/10.1017/S0140525X00067595

Kenrick, D. T., Keefe, R. C., Gabrieldis, C., & Cornelius, J. S. (1996). Adolescents' age preferences for dating partners: Support for an evolutionary model of life-history strategies. *Child Development, 67*, 1499–1511. https://doi.org/10.1111/j.1467-8624.1996.tb01810.x

Kenrick, D. T., Li, N. P., & Butner, J. (2003). Dynamical evolutionary psychology: Individual decision rules and emergent social norms. *Psychological Review, 110*, 3–28. https://doi.org/10.1037/0033-295X.110.1.3

Kenrick, D. T., Neuberg, S. L., Zierk, K. L., & Krones, J. M. (1994). Evolution and social cognition: Contrast effects as a function of sex, dominance, and physical attractiveness. *Personality and Social Psychology Bulletin, 20*, 210–217. https://doi.org/10.1177%2F0146167294202008

Kenrick, D. T., Sadalla, E. K., Groth, G., & Trost, M. R. (1990). Evolution, traits, and the stages of human courtship: Qualifying the parental investment model. *Journal of Personality, 58*, 97–116. https://doi.org/10.1111/j.1467-6494.1990.tb00909.x

Kirkpatrick, M. (1982). Sexual selection and the evolution of female choice. *Evolution, 36*, 1–12. https://doi.org/10.1111/j.1558-5646.1982.tb05003.x

Kleiman, D. G. (1977). Monogamy in mammals. *The Quarterly Review of Biology, 52*, 39–69. https://doi.org/10.1086/409721

Kreager, D. A., Cavanagh, S. E., Yen, J., & Yu, M. (2014). "Where have all the good men gone?" gendered interactions in online dating. *Journal of Marriage and the Family, 76*, 387–410. https://doi.org/10.1111/jomf.12072

Kurzban, R., & Weeden, J. (2005). HurryDate: Mate preferences in action. *Evolution and Human Behavior, 26*, 227–244. https://doi.org/10.1016/j.evolhumbehav.2004.08.012

Kurzban, R., & Weeden, J. (2007). Do advertised preferences predict the behavior of speed daters? *Personal Relationships, 14*, 623–632. https://doi.org/10.1111/j.1475-6811.2007.00175.x

Lee, A. J., Jones, B. C., & DeBruine, L. M. (2019). Investigating the association between mating-relevant self-concepts and mate preferences through a data-driven analysis of online personal descriptions. *Evolution and Human Behavior, 40*, 325–335. https://doi.org/10.1016/j.evolhumbehav.2019.01.005

Lehmiller, J. J., VanderDrift, L. E., & Kelly, J. R. (2011). Sex differences in approaching friends with benefits relationships. *Journal of Sex Research, 48*, 275–284. https://doi.org/10.1080/00224491003721694

Lewis, D. M. G., Russell, E. M., Al-Shawaf, L., & Buss, D. M. (2015). Lumbar curvature: A previously undiscovered standard of attractiveness. *Evolution and Human Behavior, 36*, 345–350. https://doi.org/10.1016/j.evolhumbehav.2015.01.007

Li, N. P. (2007a). Intelligent priorities: Adaptive long- and short-term mate preferences. In G. Geher & G. Miller (Eds.), *Mating intelligence: Sex, relationships, and the mind's reproductive system* (pp. 105–119). Erlbaum.

Li, N. P. (2007b). Mate preference necessities in long- and short-term mating: People prioritize in themselves what their mates prioritize in them. *Acta Psychologica Sinica, 39*, 528–535.

Li, N. P., Bailey, J. M., Kenrick, D. T., & Linsenmeier, J. A. W. (2002). The necessities and luxuries of mate preferences: Testing the tradeoffs. *Journal of Personality and Social Psychology, 82*, 947–955. https://doi.org/10.1037/0022-3514.82.6.947

Li, N. P., & Kenrick, D. T. (2006). Sex similarities and differences in preferences for short-term mates: What, whether, and why. *Journal of Personality and Social Psychology, 90*, 468–489. https://doi.org/10.1037/0022-3514.90.3.468

Li, N. P., & Meltzer, A. L. (2015). The validity of sex-differentiated mate preferences: Reconciling the seemingly conflicting evidence. *Evolutionary Behavioral Sciences, 9*, 89–106. https://doi.org/10.1037/ebs0000036

Li, N. P., Valentine, K. A., & Patel, L. (2011). Mate preferences in the US and Singapore: A cross-cultural test of the mate preference priority model. *Personality and Individual Differences, 50*, 291–294. https://doi.org/10.1016/j.paid.2010.10.005

Li, N. P., van Vugt, M., & Colarelli, S. M. (2018). The evolutionary mismatch hypothesis: Implications for psychological science. *Current Directions in Psychological Science, 27*, 38–44. https://doi.org/10.1177/0963721419885877

Li, N. P., Yong, J. C., Tov, W., Sng, O., Fletcher, G. J. O., Valentine, K. A., Jiang, Y. F., & Balliet, D. (2013). Mate preferences do predict attraction and choices in the early stages of mate selection. *Journal of Personality and Social Psychology, 105*, 757–776. https://doi.org/10.1037/a0033777

Li, N. P., Yong, J. C., Tsai, M.-H., Lai, M. H. C., Lim, A. J. Y., & Ackerman, J. M. (2020). Confidence is sexy and it can be trained: Examining male social confidence in initial, opposite-sex interactions. *Journal of Personality, 88*, 1235-1251. https://doi.org/10.1111/jopy.12568

Li, N. P., Yong, J. C., & van Vugt, M. (2020). Evolutionary psychology's next challenge: Solving modern problems using a mismatch perspective. *Evolutionary Behavioral Sciences, 14*, 362-367. https://doi.org/10.1037/ebs0000207

Little, A. C., Jones, B. C., Waitt, C., Tiddeman, B. P., Feinberg, D. R., Perrett, D. I., Apicella, C. L., & Marlowe, F. W. (2008). Symmetry is related to sexual dimorphism in faces: Data across culture and species. *PLoS ONE, 3*, Article e2106. https://doi.org/10.1371/journal.pone.0002106

Little, A. C., Paukner, A., Woodward, R. A., & Suomi, S. J. (2012). Facial asymmetry is negatively related to condition in female macaque monkeys. *Behavioral Ecology and Sociobiology, 66*(9), 1311–1318. https://doi.org/10.1007/s00265-012-1386-4

Lo, S.-K., Hsieh, A.-Y., & Chiu, Y.-P. (2013). Contradictory deceptive behavior in online dating. *Computers in Human Behavior, 29*, 1755–1762. https://doi.org/10.1016/j.chb.2013.02.010

López, P., Muñoz, A., & Martín, J. (2002). Symmetry, male dominance and female mate preferences in the Iberian rock lizard, Lacerta monticola. *Behavioral Ecology and Sociobiology, 52*, 342–347. https://doi.org/10.1007/s00265-002-0514-y

Lu, H. J., Zhu, X. Q., & Chang, L. (2015). Good genes, good providers, and good fathers: Economic development involved in how women select a mate. *Evolutionary Behavioral Sciences, 9*, 215–228. https://doi.org/10.1037/ebs0000048

Lukas, D., & Clutton-Brock, T. H. (2013). The evolution of social monogamy in mammals. *Science, 341*, 526–530. https://doi.org/10.1126/science.1238677

Luo, S., & Zhang, G. (2009). What leads to romantic attraction: Similarity, reciprocity, security, or beauty? Evidence from a speed-dating study. *Journal of Personality, 77*, 933–964. https://doi.org/10.1111/j.1467-6494.2009.00570.x

Machia, L. V., Proulx, M. L., Ioerger, M., & Lehmiller, J. J. (2020). A longitudinal study of friends with benefits relationships. *Personal Relationships, 27*, 47–60. https://doi.org/10.1111/pere.12307

Maner, J. K., & Ackerman, J. M. (2020). Ecological sex ratios and human mating. *Trends in Cognitive Sciences, 24*, 98–100. https://doi.org/10.1016/j.tics.2019.11.008

Maner, J., & Kenrick, D. T. (2010). When adaptations go awry: Functional and dysfunctional aspects of social anxiety. *Social Issues and Policy Review, 4*, 111–142.

Manning, J. T., Scutt, D., Whitehouse, G. H., & Leinster, S. J. (1997). Breast asymmetry and phenotypic quality in women. *Evolution and Human Behavior, 18*, 223–236. https://doi.org/10.1259/bjr.70.838.9404205

March, E., Van Doorn, G., & Grieve, R. (2018). Netflix and chill? What sex differences can tell us about mate preferences in (hypothetical) booty-call relationships. *Evolutionary Psychology, 16*, 1–10.

Marcinkowska, U. M., Jasienska, G., & Prokop, P. (2018). A comparison of masculinity facial preference among naturally cycling, pregnant, lactating, and post-menopausal women. *Archives of Sexual Behavior, 47*, 1367–1374. https://doi.org/10.1007/s10508-017-1093-3

Marcinkowska, U. M., Kaminski, G., Little, A. C., & Jasienska, G. (2018). Average ovarian hormone levels, rather than daily values and their fluctuations, are related to facial preferences among women. *Hormones and Behavior, 102*, 114–119. https://doi.org/10.1016/j.yhbeh.2018.05.013

Marcinkowska, U. M., Kozlov, M. V., Cai, H., Contreras-Garduno, J., Dixson, B. J., Oana, G. A., Kaminski, G., Li, N. P., Lyons, M. T., Onyishi, I. E., Prasai, K., Pazhoohi, F., Prokop, P., Rosales Cardozo, S. L., Sydney, N., Yong, J. C., & Rantala, M. J. (2014). Cross-cultural variation in men's preference for sexual dimorphism in women's faces. *Biology Letters*, *10*, 20130850. https://doi.org/10.1098/rsbl.2013.0850

Match.com. (2019). *Singles in America tell all.* Singles in America. https://www.singlesinamerica.com/

McWilliams, S., & Barrett, A. E. (2014). Online dating in middle and later life: Gendered expectations and experiences. *Journal of Family Issues*, *35*, 411–436. https://doi.org/10.1177/0192513X12468437

Meltzer, A. L., McNulty, J. K., Jackson, G., & Karney, B. R. (2014a). Sex differences in the implications of partner physical attractiveness for the trajectory of marital satisfaction. *Journal of Personality and Social Psychology*, *106*, 418–428. https://doi.org/10.1037/a0034424

Meltzer, A. L., McNulty, J. K., Jackson, G. L., & Karney, B. R. (2014b). Men still value physical attractiveness in a long-term mate more than women: Rejoinder to Eastwick, Neff, Finkel, Luchies, and Hunt (2014). *Journal of Personality and Social Psychology*, *106*, 435–440. https://doi.org/10.1037/a0035342

Miller, G. F., & Todd, P. M. (1998). Mate choice turns cognitive. *Trends in Cognitive Sciences*, *2*, 190–198. https://doi.org/10.1016/S1364-6613(98)01169-3

Miyazaki, T. (2020, April 17). AI love you: Japanese man not alone in "marriage" to virtual character. *Mainichi Daily News*. https://mainichi.jp/english/articles/20200417/p2a/00m/0na/027000c

Mogilski, J. K., Memering, S. L., Welling, L. L. M., & Shackelford, T. K. (2017). Monogamy versus consensual non-monogamy: Alternative approaches to pursuing a strategically pluralistic mating strategy. *Archives of Sexual Behavior*, *46*, 407–417. https://doi.org/10.1007/s10508-015-0658-2

Mogilski, J. K., Reeve, S. D., Nicolas, S. C. A., Donaldson, S. H., Mitchell, V. E., & Welling, L. L. M. (2019). Jealousy, consent, and compersion within monogamous and consensually non-monogamous romantic relationships. *Archives of Sexual Behavior*, *48*, 1811–1828. https://doi.org/10.1007/s10508-018-1286-4

Mogilski, J. K., Vrabel, J., Mitchell, V. E., & Welling, L. L. M. (2019). The primacy of trust within romantic relationships: Evidence from conjoint analysis of HEXACO-derived personality profiles. *Evolution and Human Behavior*, *40*, 365–374. https://doi.org/10.1016/j.evolhumbehav.2019.04.001

Mogilski, J. K., Wade, T. J., & Welling, L. L. M. (2014). Prioritization of potential mates' history of sexual fidelity during a conjoint ranking task. *Personality and Social Psychology Bulletin*, *40*, 884–897. https://doi.org/10.1177/0146167214529798

Mogilski, J. K., & Welling, L. L. M. (2017). The relative importance of sexual dimorphism, fluctuating asymmetry, and color cues to health during evaluation of potential partners' facial photographs: A conjoint analysis study. *Human Nature*, *28*, 53–75. https://doi.org/10.1007/s12110-016-9277-4

Mogilski, J. K., & Welling, L. L. M. (2018). The relative contribution of jawbone and cheekbone prominence, eyebrow thickness, eye size, and face length to evaluations of facial masculinity and attractiveness: A conjoint data-driven approach. *Frontiers in Psychology*, *9*, 2428. https://doi.org/10.3389/fpsyg.2018.02428

Møller, A. P., & Höglund, J. (1991). Patterns of fluctuating asymmetry in avian feather ornaments: Implications for models of sexual selection. *Proceedings of the Royal Society of London. Series B*, *245*, 1–5. https://doi.org/10.1098/rspb.1991.0080

Møller, A. P., & Thornhill, R. (1998). Bilateral symmetry and sexual selection: A meta-analysis. *American Naturalist*, *151*, 174–192. https://doi.org/10.1086/286110

Morales, J., Torres, R., & Velando, A. (2012). Safe betting: Males help dull females only when they raise high-quality offspring. *Behavioral Ecology and Sociobiology*, *66*, 135–143. https://doi.org/10.1007/s00265-011-1261-8

Morris, M. R., & Casey, K. (1998). Female swordtail fish prefer symmetrical sexual signal. *Animal Behaviour*, *55*, 33–39. https://doi.org/10.1006/anbe.1997.0580

Neyt, B., Vandenbulcke, S., & Baert, S. (2019). Are men intimidated by highly educated women? Undercover on Tinder. *Economics of Education Review*, *73*, 101914. https://doi.org/10.1016/j.econedurev.2019.101914

Oliver, M. B., & Hyde, J. S. (1993). Gender differences in sexuality: A meta-analysis. *Psychological Bulletin*, *114*, 29–51. https://doi.org/10.1037/0033-2909.114.1.29

Ong, D. (2016). Education and income attraction: An online dating field experiment. *Applied Economics*, *48*, 1816–1830. https://doi.org/10.1080/00036846.2015.1109039

Ong, D., & Wang, J. (2015). Income attraction: An online dating field experiment. *Journal of Economic Behavior & Organization*, *111*, 13–22. https://doi.org/10.1016/j.jebo.2014.12.011

Penton-Voak, I. S., Perrett, D. I., Castles, D. L., Kobayashi, T., Burt, D. M., Murray, L. K., & Minamisawa, R. (1999). Menstrual cycle alters face preference. *Nature*, *399*, 741–742. https://doi.org/10.1038/21557

Perilloux, C., Fleischman, D. S., & Buss, D. M. (2011). Meet the parents: Parent-offspring convergence and divergence in mate preferences. *Personality and Individual Differences, 50*, 253–258. https://doi.org/10.1016/j.paid.2010.09.039

Pew Research Center. (2020, February 6). *The virtues and downsides of online dating*. Pew Research Center: Internet, Science & Tech. https://www.pewresearch.org/internet/2020/02/06/the-virtues-and-downsides-of-online-dating/

Phua, V. C., Sosa, C. J., & Aloisi, K. (2018). Males prefer younger females: Age preference among online daters in the Dominican Republic. *Sexuality & Culture, 22*, 39–47. https://doi.org/10.1007/s12119-017-9451-9

Prokop, P., Dylewski, Ł., Woźna, J. T., & Tryjanowski, P. (2020). Cues of woman's fertility predict prices for sex with prostitutes. *Current Psychology, 39*, 919–926. https://doi.org/10.1007/s12144-018-9807-9

Puts, D. A. (2005). Mating context and menstrual phase affect women's preferences for male voice pitch. *Evolution and Human Behavior, 26*, 388–397. https://doi.org/10.1016/j.evolhumbehav.2005.03.001

Rawlins, A. (2017, March 17). Mostly human: I love you, bot. *CNNgo*. https://www.money.cnn.com/mostly-human/i-love-you-bot/

Regan, P. C. (1998). What if you can't get what you want? Willingness to compromise ideal mate selection standards as a function of sex, mate value, and relationship context. *Personality and Social Psychology Bulletin, 24*, 1294–1303. https://doi.org/10.1177/01461672982412004

Regan, P. C., & Berscheid, E. (1997). Gender differences in characteristics desired in a potential sexual and marriage partner. *Journal of Psychology & Human Sexuality, 9*, 25–37. https://doi.org/10.1300/J056v09n01_02

Regan, P. C., & Joshi, A. (2003). Ideal partner preferences among adolescents. *Social Behavior and Personality, 31*, 13–20. https://doi.org/10.2224/sbp.2003.31.1.13

Regan, P. C., Medina, R., & Joshi, A. (2001). Partner preferences among homosexual men and women: What is desirable in a sex partner is not necessarily desirable in a romantic partner. *Social Behavior and Personality, 29*, 625–633. https://doi.org/10.2224/sbp.2001.29.7.625

Roney, J. R., & Simmons, Z. L. (2013). Hormonal predictors of sexual motivation in natural menstrual cycles. *Hormones and Behavior, 63*, 636–645. https://doi.org/10.1016/j.yhbeh.2013.02.013

Sadalla, E. K., Kenrick, D. T., & Vershure, B. (1987). Dominance and heterosexual attraction. *Journal of Personality and Social Psychology, 52*, 730–738. https://doi.org/10.1037/0022-3514.52.4.730

Salmon, C. (2012). The pop culture of sex: An evolutionary window on the worlds of pornography and romance. *Review of General Psychology, 16*, 152–160. https://doi.org/10.1037/a0027910

Sbarra, D. A., Briskin, J. L., & Slatcher, R. B. (2019). Smartphones and close relationships: The case for an evolutionary mismatch. *Perspectives on Psychological Science, 14*, 596–618. https://doi.org/10.1177/1745691619826535

Schacht, R., & Kramer, K. L. (2019). Are we monogamous? A review of the evolution of pair-bonding in humans and its contemporary variation cross-culturally. *Frontiers in Ecology and Evolution, 7*, 230. https://doi.org/10.3389/fevo.2019.00230

Scheib, J. E., Gangestad, S. W., & Thornhill, R. (1999). Facial attractiveness, symmetry and cues of good genes. *Proceedings of the Royal Society B, 266*, 1913–1917. https://doi.org/10.1098/rspb.1999.0866

Schmitt, D. P. (2005). Sociosexuality from Argentina to Zimbabwe: A 48-nation study of sex, culture, and strategies of human mating. *Behavioral and Brain Sciences, 28*, 247–275. https://doi.org/10.1017/s0140525x05000051

Schmitt, D. P. (2007). Sexual strategies across sexual orientations: How personality traits and culture relate to sociosexuality among gays, lesbians, bisexuals, and heterosexuals. *Journal of Psychology & Human Sexuality, 18*, 183–214. https://doi.org/10.1300/J056v18n02_06

Schmitt, D. P. (2014). On the proper functions of human mate preference adaptations: Comment on Eastwick, Luchies, Finkel, and Hunt (2014). *Psychological Bulletin, 140*, 666–672. https://doi.org/10.1037/a0036225

Schmitt, D. P. (2015). Fundamentals of human mating strategies. In D. M. Buss (Ed.), *The handbook of evolutionary psychology: Foundations* (pp. 294–316). John Wiley & Sons.

Sevi, B., Aral, T., & Eskenazi, T. (2018). Exploring the hook-up app: Low sexual disgust and high sociosexuality predict motivation to use Tinder for casual sex. *Personality and Individual Differences, 133*, 17–20. https://doi.org/10.1016/j.paid.2017.04.053

Shackelford, T. K., Besser, A., & Goetz, A. T. (2008). Personality, marital satisfaction, and probability of marital infidelity. *Individual Differences Research, 6*, 13–25.

Shackelford, T. K., Schmitt, D. P., & Buss, D. (2005a). Mate preferences of married persons in the newlywed year and three years later. *Cognition & Emotion, 19*, 1262–1270. https://doi.org/10.1080/02699930500215249

Shackelford, T. K., Schmitt, D. P., & Buss, D. M. (2005b). Universal dimensions of human mate preferences. *Personality and Individual Differences, 39*, 447–458. https://doi.org/10.1016/j.paid.2005.01.023

Shepperd, J. A., & Strathman, A. J. (1989). Attractiveness and height: The role of stature in dating preference, frequency of dating, and perceptions of attractiveness. *Personality and Social Psychology Bulletin, 15*, 617–627. https://doi.org/10.1177/0146167289154014

Simpson, J. A., & Gangestad, S. W. (1991). Individual differences in sociosexuality: Evidence for convergent and discriminant validity. *Journal of Personality and Social Psychology, 60*, 870–883. https://doi.org/10.1037/0022-3514.60.6.870

Simpson, J. A., & Gangestad, S. W. (1992). Sociosexuality and romantic partner choice. *Journal of Personality, 60*(1), 31–51. https://doi.org/10.1111/j.1467-6494.1992.tb00264.x

Singh, D. (1993). Adaptive significance of female physical attractiveness: Role of waist-to-hip ratio. *Journal of Personality and Social Psychology, 65*, 293–307. https://doi.org/10.1037/0022-3514.65.2.293

Smith, T. W., Davern, M., Freese, J, & Morgan, S. (2020). General Social Surveys, 1972-2018 [machine-readable data file]. https://gssdataexplorer.norc.org/trends/Gender%20&%20Marriage?measure=posslq

Sohn, K. (2016). Men's revealed preferences regarding women's ages: Evidence from prostitution. *Evolution and Human Behavior, 37*, 272–280. https://doi.org/10.1016/j.evolhumbehav.2016.01.002

Sohn, K. (2017). Men's revealed preference for their mates' ages. *Evolution and Human Behavior, 38*, 58–62. https://doi.org/10.1016/j.evolhumbehav.2016.06.007

Souza, A. L., Conroy-Beam, D., & Buss, D. M. (2016). Mate preferences in Brazil: Evolved desires and cultural evolution over three decades. *Personality and Individual Differences, 95*, 45–49. https://doi.org/10.1016/j.paid.2016.01.053

Sprecher, S., Sullivan, Q., & Hatfield, E. (1994). Mate selection preferences: Gender differences examined in a national sample. *Journal of Personality and Social Psychology, 66*, 1074–1080. https://doi.org/10.1037//0022-3514.66.6.1074

Stearns, S. C., Byars, S. G., Govindaraju, D. R., & Ewbank, D. (2010). Measuring selection in contemporary human populations. *Nature Reviews Genetics, 11*, 611–622. https://doi.org/10.1038/nrg2831

Stern, J., Arslan, R. C., Gerlach, T. M., & Penke, L. (2019). No robust evidence for cycle shifts in preferences for men's bodies in a multiverse analysis: A response to Gangestad, Dinh, Del Giudice, and Emery Thompson (2019). *Evolution and Human Behavior, 40*, 517–525. https://doi.org/10.1016/j.evolhumbehav.2019.08.005

Stulp, G., Buunk, A. P., & Pollet, T. V. (2013). Women want taller men more than men want shorter women. *Personality and Individual Differences, 54*, 877–883. https://doi.org/10.1016/j.paid.2012.12.019

Sugiyama, L. S. (2015). Physical attractiveness: An adaptationist perspective. In D. M. Buss (Ed.), *The handbook of evolutionary psychology: Foundations* (pp. 317–384). John Wiley & Sons.

Swaddle, J. P. (1996). Reproductive success and symmetry in zebra finches. *Animal Behaviour, 51*, 203–210. https://doi.org/10.1006/anbe.1996.0017

Symons, D. (1979). *The evolution of human sexuality*. Oxford University Press.

Symons, D. (1995). Beauty is in the adaptations of the beholder: The evolutionary psychology of human female sexual attractiveness. In P. R. Abramson, & S. D. Pinkerton (Eds.), *Sexual nature, sexual culture* (pp. 80–119). University of Chicago Press.

Thiessen, D., Young, R. K., & Burroughs, R. (1993). Lonely hearts advertisements reflect sexually dimorphic mating strategies. *Ethology and Sociobiology, 14*, 209–229. https://doi.org/10.1016/0162-3095(93)90007-5

Thomas, A. G., Jonason, P. K., Blackburn, J. D., Kennair, L. E. O., Lowe, R., Malouff, J., Stewart-Williams, S., Sulikowski, D., & Li, N. P. (2020). Mate preference priorities in the East and West: A cross-cultural test of the mate preference priority model. *Journal of Personality, 88*, 606–620. https://doi.org/10.1111/jopy.12514

Thornhill, R., & Gangestad, S. W. (1994). Human fluctuating asymmetry and sexual behavior. *Psychological Science, 5*, 297–302. https://doi.org/10.1111/j.1467-9280.1994.tb00629.x

Todd, P. M., & Miller, G. F. (1999). From pride and prejudice to persuasion: Satisficing in mate search. In G. Gigerenzer, P. M. Todd, & ABC Research Group (Eds.), *Simple heuristics that make us smart* (pp. 287-308). Oxford University Press.

Todd, P. M., Penke, L., Fasolo, B., & Lenton, A. P. (2007). Different cognitive processes underlie human mate choices and mate preferences. *Proceedings of the National Academy of Sciences, USA, 104*, 15011–15016. https://doi.org/10.1073/pnas.0705290104

Tooby, J., & Cosmides, L. (1990). The past explains the present. *Ethology and Sociobiology, 11*, 375–424. https://doi.org/10.1016/0162-3095(90)90017-Z

Torres, R., & Velando, A. (2005). Male preference for female foot colour in the socially monogamous blue-footed booby, Sula nebouxii. *Animal Behaviour, 69*, 59–65. https://doi.org/10.1016/j.anbehav.2004.03.008

Townsend, J. M. (1993). Sexuality and partner selection: Sex differences among college students. *Ethology and Sociobiology, 14*, 305–330. https://doi.org/10.1016/0162-3095(93)90002-Y

Townsend, J. M., & Levy, G. D. (1990). Effects of potential partners' costume and physical attractiveness on sexuality and partner selection. *The Journal of Psychology, 124*, 371–389. https://doi.org/10.1080/00223980.1990.10543232

Townsend, J. M., & Roberts, L. W. (1993). Gender differences in mate preference among law students: Divergence and convergence of criteria. *The Journal of Psychology, 127*, 507–528. https://doi.org/10.1080/00223980.1993.9914888

Trivers, R. (1972). Parental investment and sexual selection. In B. Campbell (Ed.), *Sexual selection and the descent of man* (pp. 136–179). Aldine.

Valentine, K. A., Li, N. P., Meltzer, A. L., & Tsai, M.-H. (2020). Mate preferences for warmth-trustworthiness predict romantic attraction in the early stages of mate selection and satisfaction in ongoing relationships. *Personality and Social Psychology Bulletin, 46*, 1–14. https://doi.org/10.1177/0146167219855048

Valentova, J. V., Štěrbová, Z., Bártová, K., & Varella, M. A. C. (2016). Personality of ideal and actual romantic partners among heterosexual and non-heterosexual men and women: A cross-cultural study. *Personality and Individual Differences, 101*, 160–166. https://doi.org/10.1016/j.paid.2016.05.048

Velando, A., Beamonte-Barrientos, R., & Torres, R. (2006). Pigment-based skin colour in the blue-footed booby: An honest signal of current condition used by females to adjust reproductive investment. *Oecologia, 149*, 535–542. https://doi.org/10.1007/s00442-006-0457-5

Waitt, C., & Little, A. C. (2006). Preferences for symmetry in conspecific facial shape among Macaca mulatta. *International Journal of Primatology, 27*, 133–145. https://doi.org/10.1007/s10764-005-9015-y

Walter, K. V., Conroy-Beam, D., Buss, D. M., Asao, K., Sorokowska, A., Sorokowski, P., Aavik, T., Akello, G., Alhabahba, M. M., Alm, C., Amjad, N., Anjum, A., Atama, C. S., Atamtürk Duyar, D., Ayebare, R., Batres, C., Bendixen, M., Bensafia, A., Bizumic, B. . . . Zupančič, M. (2020). Sex differences in mate preferences across 45 countries: A large-scale replication. *Psychological Science, 31*, 408–423. https://doi.org/10.1177/0956797620904154

Welling, L. L. M., Singh, K., Puts, D. A., Jones, B. C., & Burriss, R. P. (2013). Self-reported sexual desire in homosexual men and women predicts preferences for sexually dimorphic facial cues. *Archives of Sexual Behavior, 42*, 785–791. https://doi.org/10.1007/s10508-012-0059-8

Whyte, S., Chan, H. F., & Torgler, B. (2018). Do men and women know what they want? Sex differences in online daters' educational preferences. *Psychological Science, 29*, 1370–1375. https://doi.org/10.1177/0956797618771081

Wiederman, M. W. (1993). Evolved gender differences in mate preferences: Evidence from personal advertisements. *Ethology and Sociobiology, 14*, 331–351. https://doi.org/10.1016/0162-3095(93)90003-Z

Wood, W., Kressel, L., Joshi, P. D., & Louie, B. (2014). Meta-analysis of menstrual cycle effects on women's mate preferences. *Emotion Review, 6*, 229–249. https://doi.org/10.1177/1754073914523073

Yong, J. C., Li, N. P., Valentine, K. A., & Smith, A. R. (2017). Female virtual intrasexual competition and its consequences. In M. L. Fisher (Ed.), *The Oxford handbook of women and competition* (pp. 657–680). Oxford University Press. https://doi.org/10.1093/oxfordhb/9780199376377.013.38

Yong, J. C., Tan, Y. W., Li, N. P., & Meltzer, A. L. (2022). Looks and status are still essential: Testing the mate preference priority model with the profile-based experimental paradigm. *Journal of Personality*, Advanced Online Publication. https://doi.org/10.1111/jopy.12699

Zahavi, A. (1975). Mate selection—A selection for a handicap. *Journal of Theoretical Biology*, *53*, 205–214. https://doi.org/10.1016/0022-5193(75)90111-3
Zhang, L., Wang, H., Lee, A. J., DeBruine, L. M., & Jones, B. C. (2019). Chinese and UK participants' preferences for physical attractiveness and social status in potential mates. *Royal Society Open Science*, *6*, Article 181243. https://doi.org/10.1098/rsos.181243
Zhang, J., Zheng, L., & Zheng, Y. (2018). Consistency in preferences for masculinity in faces, bodies, voices, and personality characteristics among homosexual men in China. *Personality and Individual Differences*, *134*, 137–142. https://doi.org/10.1016/j.paid.2018.06.009

CHAPTER

5 Hormonal Mechanisms of Partnership Formation

Anastasia Makhanova

Abstract

People are motivated to form romantic partnerships, and this motivation is underpinned by biological processes that facilitate sexual drive and mating motives. Gonadal steroid hormones—testosterone, estrogen, and progesterone—regulate many sexual behaviors in humans and nonhuman animals. Testosterone, for example, is positively associated with sexual desire, mate seeking, sexual behavior, and intrasexual competition. Although testosterone seems to be important for sexual processes in men and other male animals, some evidence suggests that testosterone is also important for women. Estrogen and progesterone, on the other hand, seem to be especially important for regulating sexual processes in women and other female animals. These hormones promote cyclical fluctuations in sexual desire and mating-relevant behavior across the menstrual or estrus cycle. Contrary to lay beliefs that female animals are passive in their sexual encounters, research in psychoneuroendocrinology demonstrates the active role of female animals in pursuing and regulating sexual interactions to increase their reproductive success. This chapter thus highlights the hormonal mechanisms that promote partnership formation, clarifies appropriate methodological practices for assessing these mechanisms in humans, and outlines current and future directions for research on contemporary romantic partnerships.

Key Words: mating, sex differences, testosterone, estradiol, comparative psychology

Natural selection operates on the principle of differential survival and reproduction. For sexually reproducing organisms, finding mating partners is important for passing genes to the next generation. Consequently, many biological processes promote mating and reproduction. This chapter focuses on the endocrinological processes that motivate people and nonhuman animals to seek mates, compete for reproductive opportunities, and engage in sexual behavior—behaviors largely underpinned by gonadal hormones. The first two sections cover the role of sex steroid hormones (e.g., testosterone, estradiol, and progesterone) in male and female mating behaviors separately. The third section covers research examining how cortisol may be associated with partnership formation for both men and women. In addition to covering the hormonal mechanisms underlying human partnership formation, each section provides historical context for the understanding of hormonal influences on mating behavior and highlights research from nonhuman animals (e.g., birds, rats, and nonhuman primates). These animal models serve as frameworks for interpreting and organizing the human research on hormones and mating.

Hormones

In service of the ultimate function of reproduction, hormones regulate the proximate mechanisms that make reproduction possible. Not only are hormones critical for the maturation of gametes, but they also regulate mating behaviors. Before delving into how hormones affect mating behavior, it is important to clarify what hormones are and what they do. Hormones are chemical messengers, which are released into the bloodstream from endocrine glands. These messengers circulate throughout the body—including the brain—to affect different types of cells that have hormone receptors. Regardless of where hormones are produced (e.g., in the gonads or in the adrenal glands), their effects are not localized. Indeed, hormone effects are widespread, modulating many physiological and behavioral processes.

Hormones regulate behavior by increasing the probability that a stimulus or situation will produce a given response (which can result in either approach or avoidance of the stimulus), but hormone changes are not deterministic. Factors of the situation, the individual, and the stimulus interact with hormone levels to influence behavior. When mating-relevant hormones increase, it is more likely that an animal or person will exhibit mating behavior, especially if the potential mate is attractive (Beach, 1976). This ability, interest, or lower threshold for engaging in mating behavior is due to changes in a variety of systems. Indeed, hormones influence various processes in the sensory system to directly affect sensitivity toward and discrimination between relevant cues. For example, greater estradiol levels (a hormone associated with increased mating motivation for women) are associated with increased neural activity linked to positive evaluation of a stimulus in response to men's photographs (Rupp et al., 2009). Moreover, removal of gonadal hormones in rats disrupts males' and females' ability to discriminate between same-sex versus opposite-sex conspecifics (Xiao et al., 2004). To the extent that a conspecific may be seen as a threat, as a potential mate, or a neutral target unrelated to one's current goals, hormones affect perceptions of a stimulus. Overall, hormones regulate myriad processes throughout the body and within the central nervous system to promote motive-relevant behavior.

Hormones and Male Mating Behaviors

When people think about hormones and male mating behaviors, testosterone undoubtedly first comes to mind. Testosterone is a steroid hormone produced by the Leydig cells in the testes and, to a lesser extent, in the adrenal glands. Testosterone has widespread effects throughout the body including the development of male genitalia during embryogenesis and the masculinization of the body during puberty. As part of sexual maturation, testosterone modulates the development of secondary sexual characteristics (e.g., axillary hair and broadening of the shoulders) and increases in muscle mass. Testosterone produces these effects through its conversion to the androgen dihydrotestosterone (DHT). Masculinizing effects of testosterone in the brain, however, including those relevant to the development of male sexual behavior, occur through the aromatization of testosterone into estradiol (a type of estrogen) (McCarthy, 2008). Thus, testosterone can have effects on male mating behavior through either estrogen or androgen receptors.

Testosterone has been linked to consummatory and appetitive male sexual behaviors. Consummatory behaviors are the mechanics that make copulation possible (e.g., mounting, intromissions, and ejaculation). Appetitive behaviors include sex drive and libido, intersexual attraction (e.g., courtship displays), and intrasexual competition. Intrasexual competition and aggression are often a major part of male mating behavior, with dominance contests having tremendous consequences for males' reproductive opportunities (Trivers, 1972). In many animal species, males have more variable reproductive success (i.e., some males have many offspring and others have none) because males at the top of the dominance hierarchy monopolize mating opportunities (Trivers, 1972). Thus, male mating behaviors include competition for resources and status, pursuit of mating opportunities, and the ability to successfully copulate. The next sections outline the links between testosterone and male mating behaviors in nonhuman animals and men.

Insights From Birds

Although some early observations linking testes to sexual behavior come from historical observations of human eunuchs (men who were castrated before puberty; Nelson & Kriegsfeld, 2017), much of the behavioral endocrinological knowledge linking testosterone and male mating behavior comes from research on avian species. Arnold Berthold conducted a seminal experiment (pun intended) that linked testes to sexual behavior in roosters (Nelson & Kriegsfeld, 2017). He examined whether experimentally manipulated presence or absence of testes affected the normal sexual development of young roosters (e.g., change in plumage, interest in mating with hens, and crowing). Young roosters were castrated and divided into three groups. One group received no other interventions and, as predicted, did not develop the plumage or behavior (crowing or mating) observed in intact roosters. The other two groups were reimplanted with either their own testis or another bird's testis. Both groups developed indistinguishably from intact roosters, suggesting that the implanted testis that reconnected to the blood supply affected these observed mating behaviors. Berthold further concluded that some blood-borne product of the testes was essential to sexual development. This experiment is retrospectively credited with founding the field of behavioral endocrinology by demonstrating how a hormone is necessary and sufficient for behavior.

Also vital to understanding the relationship between testosterone and male sexual development were field studies conducted by James Wingfield and colleagues in the 1970s and 1980s. Wingfield synthesized previous findings to propose the challenge hypothesis (Wingfield et al., 1990), which outlined the relationships between testosterone and territoriality as well as parental behavior in male birds. First, male birds displayed increases in testosterone at the onset of the breeding season. At these breeding levels of testosterone, male birds produced sperm and engaged in sexual behavior when observed with a female. Thus, this rise in testosterone seems to prompt mating motivation, development of secondary sex characteristics, and the ability to reproduce. Consequently, Wingfield concluded that any subsequent rise in testosterone prompts other aspects of mating behavior such as territoriality and mate guarding. Indeed, increases in testosterone are associated with social challenges such as when males must compete for territory, rank, or reproductive partners. Furthermore, at levels above the breeding season baseline, testosterone is inversely related to parenting behavior, such that increases in testosterone in response to social challenges block parenting behavior and parenting behavior is restored when testosterone decreases in times of relative peace. This theoretical perspective demonstrates how environmental factors influence testosterone levels and provides a functional understanding of how increased testosterone affects male mating behavior.

Overall, research on male birds' mating behavior highlights the importance of testosterone for behaviors from courtship to copulation to parenting (Ball & Balthazart, 2002). Indeed, castrating male birds quickly eliminates mating behaviors (appetitive and consummatory), and these effects are reversed through testosterone administration.

Insights From Rats

Male rats are motivated to mate with receptive females and will even cross obstacles (e.g., electrical shocks) to copulate (Stone et al., 1935). To examine how testosterone affects male rats' mating behavior, early research investigated how castration changes male behavior in response to a female rat in estrus (see section "Hormones and Female Mating Behaviors" for the importance of this distinction). Indeed, both motivation and ability to copulate are affected when males are castrated, although these changes are not immediate (Hull & Dominguez, 2007). Within a few days of castration, males demonstrate decreased appetitive behaviors: castrated males take longer following initial contact to mount the female. The consummatory phase of mating behavior is also affected: castrated males engage in fewer intromissions (i.e., a mount during which the penis is inserted into the vagina) prior to ejaculation which may not provide enough stimulation for the female to become pregnant and may result in lower sperm concentrations in the ejaculate. This sequence is followed by the disappearance of ejaculation, then intromission, and finally the males will not mount females (even if they are in estrus). After a few days of testosterone treatment, the male mating behaviors return in reverse-order.

An interesting social moderator of this general pattern is male rats' prior sexual experience (Hull et al., 2006; Larsson, 2003). The sequential decline of mating behavior following castration tends to be relatively stable for males who are sexually inexperienced.

Inexperienced males still demonstrate mating behavior if they encounter a female soon after the castration but will then show the predictable decline over the next two weeks. Males who have mated in the past, however, show tremendous variability in the length of time their mating behaviors persist following castration. Thus, individuals vary in the extent to which social learning and environment influence how testosterone modulates mating behavior.

The effects of testosterone on male rodent sexual motivation occur through the aromatization of testosterone into estradiol (Brooks et al., 2020), and treatment with estradiol is effective in restoring male sexual behavior after castration (Hull & Dominguez, 2007). Estradiol treatment is particularly effective if paired with DHT which binds to androgen receptors in the periphery, including in the penis. Treatment with the steroid hormones (i.e., testosterone and estrogen) has immediate effects in the brain but takes several days to fully restore mating behaviors.

To examine appetitive behavior in male rats, researchers have developed behavioral assessments to measure sexual motivation (Hull et al., 2006). One method is a place preference test which examines whether a male will spend time in a cage location that has previously been associated with copulation even when there is no female in the cage. The male returning to the location indicates mating interest. Sexual motivation can also be assessed by examining whether a male will cross an obstacle (a barrier or an electric grid) or press a lever to gain access to a female.

One study examined the effect of a female rat in estrus on male rats' behavior and testosterone levels (Amstislavskaya & Popova, 2004). Male rats were placed in a cage that was separated from another cage by a plexiglass pane. In one condition, a female rat in estrus was placed on the other side of the plexiglass. Male sexual motivation was operationalized as the amount of time males spent touching the plexiglass. Sexual motivation and testosterone were compared between this condition and two control conditions (with a male rate in the compartment or an empty compartment). Males approached the partition more frequently in the estrus female condition and spent more time at the partition. Twenty minutes into the experimental session, males had elevated testosterone in the estrus female condition. These effects did not emerge for a female that was not in estrus. Together, this evidence suggests that testosterone is associated with both consummatory and appetitive behaviors in male rats.

Insights From Nonhuman Primates

Male consummatory behavior in primates also involves mounting, intromissions, and ejaculation. To some extent, testosterone underlies these behaviors in primates because they are reduced or eliminated by castration and testosterone treatment restores copulatory behaviors. However, some primates maintain the ability to engage in consummatory mating behaviors, including ejaculation (albeit without seminal fluid), after castration. One study found that most male rhesus monkeys demonstrated intromissions when tested with a female a full year after castration and nearly a third demonstrated ejaculation behavior (Phoenix et al., 1973). Although one year after castration males had detectable testosterone levels (likely produced by the adrenals), these circulating testosterone levels did not correlate with the maintained mounting, intromission, or ejaculation ability (Resko & Phoenix, 1972). Similarly, in a study of captive chimpanzees, testosterone was not related to the frequency of male copulations and increased frequency of copulation was not associated with increases in testosterone (Klinkova et al., 2004). Examining rhesus monkeys one year after castration, the researchers noted that "if castrated males mounted once in a test, their average mounting rate did not differ from the precastration mounting rate and the same was true for intromission rate" (Phoenix et al., 1973, p. 481), which led them to conclude that perhaps testosterone has a stronger effect on appetitive, motivational aspects of male sexual behavior than on consummatory behavior.

The challenge hypothesis has also been applied to the examination of mating behavior in primates such as chimpanzees (Muller & Wrangham, 2004; Sobolewski et al., 2013). These studies examined the links between intrasexual aggression and testosterone in wild chimpanzees for whom intrasexual aggression is an adaptive strategy because dominant males secure access to more reproductive opportunities. Notably, chimpanzee intrasexual aggression is particularly intense when males are around a parous female in estrus (i.e., a female who has had offspring previously and is currently fertile) compared to when males are around a nulliparous female in estrus (i.e., a female who has never had an offspring but is currently fertile). When parous females are in estrus, males exhibit increased charging, chasing, and attacking behaviors compared to when females are not in estrus. This increase in aggression corresponded with greater urinary testosterone concentrations when males were around parous females in estrus, compared to when males were around females not in estrus or nulliparous females in estrus. These findings suggest that testosterone is specifically associated with intrasexual competition and not copulation. Although males copulated with both parous and nulliparous females, testosterone only increased when males were around parous females and intrasexual competition was high. Muller and Wrangham (2004) found that high-ranking males were more aggressive than lower-ranking males, with the highest status male demonstrating the most aggression. This male also had the highest testosterone level, and afternoon (but not morning) testosterone was positively correlated with dominance rank for the other males. Sobolewski et al. (2013), however, did not replicate this association between testosterone and dominance. Overall, this field research shows that the link between testosterone and male intrasexual competition in chimpanzees is consistent with the challenge hypothesis.

Applications of the challenge hypothesis to male primate behavior need to be couched in the mating systems of each species (Muller, 2017). For example, chimpanzees differ from birds because they do not breed seasonally, and neither do males engage in direct parental behavior the way that males of monogamous bird species do. Other primate species have different social and mating systems, so what constitutes a challenge differs between species. Increases in testosterone coincide with mating in species where males have to compete for dominance rank or access to fertile females. In primate species without much intrasexual competition, testosterone has been shown to rise during times of peak female fertility (Lynch et al., 2002).

Research on chacma baboons also demonstrates important connections between testosterone, dominance, and mating success (Beehner et al., 2006). In baboons, higher dominance rank directly corresponds with more mating opportunities, and high dominance rank correlates positively with testosterone levels. More specifically, this study demonstrated that testosterone was positively correlated with *changes* in dominance rank. That is, higher testosterone levels corresponded with ascent in the hierarchy and lower testosterone levels corresponded with males losing their status. Moving from one group to another was likewise associated with higher testosterone, presumably because dominance competitions were likely to follow. When females are fertile, dominant baboons form consortships with females which are characterized by mating and mate guarding. Between-male analyses revealed that male baboons engaging in consortship had higher testosterone levels than males not engaging in consortship; though within-male analyses did not find a link between testosterone and consortship. Bolstering the hypothesis that testosterone predicts ascent in dominance and mating access, an individual's testosterone levels during an observed month positively predicted their future dominance rank for up to 11 months and future consortships for up to 9 months. Collectively, this suggests that testosterone is important for male primate intrasexual competition, but that sexual behavior is less dependent on testosterone in primates compared to rodents.

Testosterone and Human Male Mating

Although testosterone is necessary for the development and functionality of male genital organs, the link between testosterone and men's consummatory behavior is tenuous (Schmidt et al., 2009). Men with low testosterone tend to report lower sexual functioning. However, some evidence suggests that, although more spontaneous function is lowered, men with low testosterone levels still experience normal erections in response to sexual stimuli (LaFerla et al., 1978). For men who have atypically low testosterone levels, but not for men with normal levels, testosterone administration appears to benefit sexual function and libido (Isidori et al., 2005). Research examining the effect of castration on men's ability to engage in sexual behavior is largely informed by studies of sexual offenders (Heim & Hursch, 1979). Although some men experienced rapid declines in sexual behavior, other men experienced slower declines over several years, and yet other men experienced no decline at all. Average young men who went through temporary, chemically induced hypogonadism (i.e., men who took a medication that prevented their testes from producing hormones) demonstrated reduced sexual interest, but testosterone administration returned sexual interest to baseline (Schmidt et al., 2004). The authors found that effects were pronounced for men with higher baseline sexual interest, but these higher levels of sexual interest were unrelated to testosterone levels (Schmidt et al., 2004). A similar pattern was observed in another study using a similar design: men with higher baseline sexual functioning were most affected by the chemical hypogonadism manipulation (Schmidt et al., 2009). In this study, chemical hypogonadism lowered sexual functioning across five domains: sexual cognition and fantasy, sexual arousal, sexual behavior, quality of orgasm, and sexual drive, but the majority of men did not report *substantial* declines. Moreover, it remains unclear which metabolite of testosterone (DHT, estradiol, etc.) was responsible for these changes. Overall, the sensitivity of men's sexual function to testosterone loss and testosterone administration seems to depend on the individual.

Although some research has linked testosterone to frequency in sexual behavior, the findings are not conclusive. On the one hand, longitudinal within-subjects studies tracking men's testosterone levels and sexual activity have demonstrated a positive association (Knussmann et al., 1986; Kraemer et al., 1976). Similarly, a study of couples found that testosterone levels were higher on evenings when the couple engaged in sexual activity compared to evenings without sexual activity (Dabbs & Mohammed, 1992). On the other hand, in one study testosterone was higher in men who had not had sex in a month or more, relative to men who had more recent sexual encounters (van der Meij et al., 2008), and in another sample, testosterone and sexual behavior were not correlated (Brown et al., 1978). These inconsistencies may be due to the fact that testosterone levels and sexual behavior are not correlated for men, or that future research is needed to examine moderating variables such as life history trade-offs or intrasexual competition.

More consistently, testosterone seems to be associated with mate-seeking behavior. Similar to the trade-off between mating and parenting effort in birds (Wingfield et al., 1990), men's testosterone levels are higher when they are single compared to when they are partnered, with men who have children having even lower levels of testosterone (Gray et al., 2002). The higher testosterone levels of single men may reflect a motivation to seek out potential romantic partners and competing with rivals for the attention of those potential partners. Men who are partnered but are not monogamous (i.e., men who do not experience a reduction in mate-seeking motivations) have even higher testosterone levels than single men (van Anders, Hamilton, & Watson, 2007). Similarly, men who are in monogamous relationships but maintain interests in alternative partners (e.g., higher sociosexual orientation, greater willingness to have an affair, and having a history of affairs) have higher levels of testosterone than men who are monogamous and do not report interest in alternative partners (Edelstein et al., 2011; McIntyre et al., 2006; van Anders & Goldey, 2010). Thus, men who are seeking mates have higher testosterone than men who are not seeking mates.

If testosterone is linked to mate seeking, it may also be linked with mating success. Indeed, one longitudinal study found that single men with higher testosterone levels at one time point were more likely to become partnered by the next time point compared to single men with lower testosterone levels (Gettler et al., 2011). Men's self-reported number of partners has been positively linked to testosterone levels (Peters et al., 2008; Pollet et al., 2011), particularly for dominant men (Slatcher et al., 2011). Consistent evidence comes from more traditional societies. In a Senegalese village, higher testosterone levels were linked with traits and behaviors associated with greater reproductive effort and success (Alvergne et al., 2009, 2010). Similarly, Hadza hunter–gatherers with lower vocal pitch (a trait linked to high testosterone) demonstrated greater reproductive success (Apicella et al., 2007; Dabbs & Mallinger, 1999). Overall, it appears that men with higher testosterone have higher mating and reproductive success.

The challenge hypothesis has been extended to human behavior, with some adjustments because human mating systems are different from those of birds and chimpanzees (Archer, 2006). Developmentally, testosterone increases during puberty (akin to the breeding season baseline increase for birds) and corresponds with higher mating motives but not higher aggression. After sexual maturity is reached, however, further increases in testosterone are expected to coincide with situations that increase the salience of mating opportunities or intrasexual competition. A substantial literature provides support for this hypothesis. Men demonstrate increased testosterone when mating is salient, such as when watching an erotic movie (Hellhammer et al., 1985; Stoleru et al., 1999) or interacting with a female confederate (Roney et al., 2003, 2007; van der Meij et al., 2008). However, testosterone increases when interacting with women appear to be context-dependent: although men's testosterone increases around women who may be potential mates, men interacting with women who are their friends' romantic partners did not show the same increase (Flinn et al., 2012).

Men also demonstrate increased testosterone when competing against other men in various domains including chess (Mazur et al., 1992), tennis (Mazur & Lamb, 1980), and wrestling (Fry et al., 2011). Combining the mating and competitive motives, men competing in an ultimate frisbee game had higher testosterone increases when the audience was predominantly female compared to when the audience was predominantly male (Miller et al., 2012). In another naturalistic setting (i.e., a skateboard park) men's risk-taking and testosterone levels were higher when they were video recorded by an attractive female confederate than when they were recorded by a male confederate (Ronay & Hippel, 2010). Furthermore, in men who engaged in a competitive lab interaction, higher testosterone increases were positively associated with flirtation behavior directed toward a female interaction partner in a later part of the laboratory study (van der Meij et al., 2012).

One aspect of the challenge hypothesis missing from Archer's expansion is specific competition over women high in reproductive value. Recall that chimpanzee males specifically demonstrated increases in testosterone and intrasexual competition around parous females in estrus—who in the chimpanzee social sphere have higher reproductive value. Archer dismissed this parallel from the human application of the theory saying that "humans show neither breeding seasons nor estrus" (Archer, 2006, p. 321). The fact that the manuscript contains no mention of the word "ovulation" is likely a reflection of the fact that, at this time, the evidence for changes in women's behavior—and men's behavior—as a function of fertility was only starting to emerge (Gangestad et al., 2002, 2005; Gangestad & Thornhill, 1998; Pillsworth et al., 2004). More recently, research has directly examined the links between testosterone and women's fertility. Men exposed to the scent of a woman who was ovulating demonstrated increases in testosterone (Miller & Maner, 2010a; cf. Roney & Simmons, 2012). Partnered men were more likely to demonstrate increases in testosterone when interacting with a competitive rival when their partner was ovulating compared to when their partner was not ovulating (Fales et al., 2014). One rigorous study examined men's testosterone fluctuations across their partners' menstrual cycle and did not find evidence for an association (Strom et al., 2012). However, in this study samples were collected in the morning, which may be more reflective of sleep and circadian patterns of testosterone release compared to evening samples which correlate with social environments and behaviors (Gray et al., 2002; Saxbe et al., 2017). Future research should continue to examine how signs of women's cyclic changes in fertility may be associated with men's testosterone—both in single and partnered men. To the extent that partnered men demonstrate more self- and relationship-protective responses when faced with an attractive or ovulating woman (Miller & Maner, 2010b; Plant et al., 2010), men's testosterone responses to these women may be moderated by their relationship status. Finally, unlike chimpanzee males who compete over parous females, it appears that women's attractiveness is linked to signs of being *nulli*parous (Lassek & Gaulin, 2019). Thus, men may engage in more intrasexual competition and experience greater increases in testosterone when they are around nulliparous women compared to parous women.

Future research examining the links between testosterone and intrasexual competition in men should examine the moderating role of individual differences. For example, testosterone increases may be moderated by individual differences in dominance. Social dominance is positively linked to testosterone (van der Meij et al., 2008). Social anxiety, on the other hand, may be negatively linked to testosterone change during intrasexual competition, given that socially anxious men have significantly lower testosterone after being defeated in a competition compared to men low in social anxiety (Maner et al., 2008).

Overall, men are powerfully motivated to seek sexual opportunities and these motives positively correspond with testosterone. After partnerships are formed and men's motives shift toward intimacy and parenting, testosterone declines (van Anders et al., 2011). Finally, the most robust effect of testosterone on mating-related behavior comes from studies on intrasexual competition and aggression, which show that men's testosterone increases when their social status is challenged and these increases facilitate competitive responses.

Hormones and Female Mating Behaviors

Whereas testosterone is the primary hormone underlying male mating, female mating behavior is closely connected to ovarian hormones (i.e., estrogen and progesterone).

Female mammals experience cyclical hormone fluctuations that regulate their fertility. Most female mammals have a version of an estrus cycle whereas women, as well as some nonhuman primates, have a menstrual cycle. There are two key differences between these two types of cycles. First, in females with menstrual cycles, the endometrial lining is shed if embryo implantation does not occur (e.g., women's periods), but in females with estrus cycles the uterine lining is reabsorbed. Second, and more relevant to this chapter, females with menstrual cycles engage in sexual behavior across the entire cycle whereas females with estrus cycles only engage in sexual behavior during the fertile phase. Consequently, sexual behavior is coupled with ovarian hormones to a greater extent in species with estrus rather than menstrual cycles. Nonetheless, aspects of female sexual behavior are still linked with ovarian hormone levels for females with menstrual cycles.

Estrus and menstrual cycles are comprised of phases that modulate processes relevant to fertility and reproduction. Although the nomenclature and hormone profiles differ somewhat between species, phases are largely classified by whether the egg-containing follicles are developing (i.e., follicular phase), whether these follicles release an egg (i.e., ovulatory phase), and whether the body is preparing for possible pregnancy (i.e., luteal phase). These cycle phases are characterized by different levels of estrogen and progesterone. In women, for example, estrogen peaks before ovulation and progesterone peaks during the luteal phase (during which a smaller rise in estrogen is also observed). Hormonal processes during the high fertility phases (i.e., late follicular and ovulatory)—when conception is possible and when females experience the most reproductive risks and opportunities—are particularly important for partnership formation, mating, and sexual behavior.

Lengths and types of ovarian hormone cycles vary between species (Nelson & Kriegsfeld, 2017). Some theoretical perspectives argue that between-species patterns reflect adaptations to species' ecologies. It may be evolutionarily adaptive, for example, for small prey animals to reproduce as quickly and as often as possible because of their shorter life spans. Thus, estrus cycles may be shorter in length, and some phases may only occur if they are induced, thereby constraining cyclic change to when that phase is relevant. For example, in some species (e.g., prairie voles) ovulation only occurs if there is a chemosensory cue that males are around. Conversely, in other species (e.g., rats) it is the luteal phase (also termed "pseudopregnancy") that only occurs if the female copulated during ovulation. If copulation did not take place, then the two-week pseudopregnancy does not occur, and the next conception opportunity comes quicker.

Although a given cycle type may be shaped by a species' ecology, females of different species share an evolutionary pressure to maximize reproduction when they are able to conceive. Because females can only conceive during a particular phase of the cycle, it would be adaptive to maximize energy toward reproductive goals at this time. Specifically, females may shift energy away from other goals, such as eating (Asarian & Geary, 2006), to focus on pursuing reproductive opportunities, avoiding reproductive risks, and engaging in intrasexual competition. Consequently, female animals display sexual drive or motivation in discrete situations when reproduction goals are most relevant.[1] The next sections outline the links between females' reproductive cycles (as well as changes in reproductive hormones) and female mating behaviors in nonhuman animals and women.

Insights from Rats

Much of the knowledge on the behavioral endocrinology of female sexual behavior comes from research on rats. Female rats have four-day estrus cycles (Long & Evans, 1922) and cycle phase is typically assessed by examining vaginal cells through a microscope because they appear visually different across the phases. During the vaginal proestrus phase (also termed the behavioral estrus phase), females will mate with males they encounter and will demonstrate behavior indicative of sexual interest. As is typical for female mammals with estrus cycles, outside the behavioral estrus phase, female rats do not engage in sexual behavior and often respond aggressively to males that approach and try to mount them. Thus, ovarian hormones that vary across the cycle phases may also modulate sexual behaviors. However, in order to study the effects of ovarian hormones such as estradiol and progesterone on female sexual behavior, female sexual behavior must first be operationalized.

DESCRIBING AND UNDERSTANDING FEMALE SEXUAL BEHAVIOR

The full range of behaviors that female rats engage in prior to, during, and following sexual interactions (i.e., behaviors that promote successful fertilization termed "progestative" behaviors; Blaustein & Erskine, 2002) was initially obscured by typical research paradigms used to examine sexual behavior (McClintock & Adler, 1978). These typical paradigms used a single chamber and lacked ecological validity—in the wild, rats do not live in a small box, with only one male, and with no other females. Martha McClintock and her colleagues conducted important studies addressing this limitation by creating a semi-natural environment within a large cage (McClintock, Toner, et al., 1982). This environment had open space, nest boxes, and burrows, and the cage was embellished with natural elements such as sticks and stones. Animals were thus able either to be near others or to hide. Instead of limiting the interaction to a single pair, several sexually mature animals of each sex were tested together; as in past research, female rats were tested during behavioral estrus. This paradigm provided crucial insight into female sexual behavior. For example, rather than being passive, females competed against other females for mating opportunities with the males (McClintock, Anisko, et al., 1982). Moreover, female rats were more likely than males to initiate sexual encounters following the postcopulatory rest intervals. Thus, the seminatural environment highlighted previously unknown aspects of females' *active* behavior during sexual interactions.

---

[1] For humans and some nonhuman primates, extended sexuality suggests that goals relevant to reproduction may promote sexual motivation outside of the ovulatory phase as well (see Grebe et al., 2016).

Other creative alterations of the cage environment also highlighted females' sexual interest and active behavior. One involved placing an obstacle between a female and a male that the male was unable to cross (Meyerson & Lindström, 1973; Warner, 1927). Therefore, to engage in sexual interactions, the female had to cross the obstacle herself. The obstacle was an electrical grid that shocked the female when she crossed it. It may be of surprise to some readers, but female rats were willing to get shocked in order to gain access to the male. Notably, this willingness to cross the electrical grid is significantly higher during estrus, exemplifying the cyclical changes in females' sexual behavior. Female rats can also be readily trained to press a lever in order to gain access to a male, and lever-pressing is affected by the estrus cycle (Bermant, 1961). Thus, estrus seems to motivate females to actively seek mating opportunities.

Empirical studies have also demonstrated that females actively regulate contact with a male following a sexual encounter in ways that promote pregnancy (Bermant, 1961; Blaustein & Erskine, 2002). Female pacing leads to reproductive benefits via increased likelihood of pregnancy or pseudopregnancy following copulation (Erskine, 1989). The pacing of intromissions is critical because for rats the luteal phrase or pseudopregnancy occurs only if a particular level of vaginal stimulation, termed "vaginal code," has been reached during copulation. If female rats do not receive the necessary level of stimulation, they will begin a new estrus cycle.

Frank Beach (1976) grouped female rats' sexual behaviors into three categories: attractivity, proceptivity, and receptivity. *Attractivity* focuses on behavioral changes that make females more attractive to males. This category, however, arguably focuses on male rats because attractivity is measured by the males' behavioral choice to preferentially spend time with a female in estrus. *Proceptivity* focuses on behaviors that females engage in when initiating or soliciting sexual interactions. These are the behaviors like darting, hopping, and ear-quivering that occur directly prior to a sexual interaction. Finally, *receptivity* refers to behaviors that occur during a sexual interaction, such as a female assuming the lordosis posture in response to being mounted by a male. Prior to Beach's detailed description and nomenclature of female sexual behavior, the understanding of both the range of behaviors and the endocrinological processes underlying these behaviors was severely lacking.

OVARIAN HORMONES AND FEMALE SEXUAL BEHAVIOR

Early research confirmed the importance of ovaries for general sexual behavior in female rats by demonstrating that ovariectomized rats do not engage in these behaviors (Davidson et al., 1968). Moreover, injecting ovariectomized rats with estradiol restored sexual behavior, thus suggesting that estradiol underpins these behaviors. Subsequent research additionally demonstrated that treatment with estradiol followed by treatment with progesterone was particularly effective for reinstantiating female rats' sexual behavior

(Blaustein & Erskine, 2002). To fully understand how estradiol and progesterone affect female sexual behavior, attractivity, proceprivity, and receptivity must be considered independently.

Attractivity is typically assessed using paradigms where three chambers are connected together by small pipes. The male is placed into the middle chamber and can move around freely. Two females—one that is ovariectomized and one that is ovariectomized and estrogen-treated—are tethered in the outer chambers. Attractivity is assessed by the proportion of time the male spends near each female. Males typically spend more time with the estrogen-treated female, demonstrating a link between estrogen and female attractivity (Beach, 1976). Proceptivity is typically assessed by examining darting, hopping, and ear-wiggling behaviors demonstrated by females when they are near a male. Ovariectomized rats do not display proceptive behaviors, but subsequent treatment with estrogen followed by progesterone restores proceptive behaviors (Tennent et al., 1980). Notably, the rat estrus cycle is different from that of nonhuman primates and women to the extent that the behavioral estrus phase is characterized by sequential increases in estradiol and progesterone (whereas nonhuman primates and women do not experience a progesterone surge until postovulation). Receptivity is typically assessed by examining a female's lordosis posture in response to a male. Ovariectomized rats do not display lordosis. However, injecting ovariectomized rats with estradiol restores lordosis (Beach, 1976) and it appears that progesterone is not necessary (Davidson et al., 1968; Tennent et al., 1980). Thus, the estrogen surge that occurs naturally during behavioral estrus modulates female receptivity. Overall, females' attractivity, proceptivity, and receptivity increase during estrus, and estrogen is necessary for each of these aspects of female sexual behavior.

Insights From Primates

Many nonhuman primates such as rhesus monkeys, chimpanzees, bonobos, orangutans, and gorillas have menstrual cycles; females engage in sexual behavior throughout the hormone cycle, not just at peak fertility. Similar to traditional paradigms examining rat sexual behavior, early research focusing on primate sexual behavior examined pairs in small enclosures. In these studies, overall mating was unrelated to female hormones. However, research examining primate mating in more natural enclosures demonstrates that female primates' sexual behavior is indeed linked to estrus, especially when examining female sexual motivation and female-initiated sexual interactions rather than all sexual interactions (Wallen, 1990; Wallen & Zehr, 2004).

It may surprise some readers that female primates are highly proceptive during estrus. Females' active role in sexual encounters tends to be overlooked in narratives that emphasize high-status males monopolizing access to females, which promote inferences that males initiate and dictate mating interactions. However, females initiate nearly all sexual interactions between gorillas (Nelson & Kriegsfeld, 2017), chimpanzees (Yerkes & Elder,

1936), and rhesus monkey (Wallen et al., 1984). Of all great apes, sexual coercion appears to be relatively common only in orangutans (Knott & Kahlenberg, 2007).

In order to examine the full range of sexual behaviors of female primates, investigations must take into account the social context and ecology of the species. Chimpanzees live in large multimale–multifemale social groups. Observations of females' sexual behavior in these group situations demonstrate the social risk females are willing to take when they are in estrus (Yerkes & Elder, 1936). Approaching a male for copulation puts a female at increased risk of aggression from other males and females, and females in estrus will take this risk in order to initiate a sexual interaction. Similar social dynamics exist for rhesus monkeys: females risk aggressive behaviors from other females to interact with males (Wallen & Tannenbaum, 1997). Thus, only in estrus do females overcome these inhibitory social dynamics to initiate copulation. Again, it appears that female proceptivity is increased during estrus. Moreover, females with higher social rank demonstrated longer periods of proceptivity and initiated more interactions compared to females with lower rank (Wallen, 1990). In orangutans, female sexual behavior is more nuanced due to two distinct physical morphs of the males; at estrus, female orangutans preferentially demonstrate proceptivity toward higher status males of the flanged morph relative to lower status males of the flanged morph, and sometimes violent resistance males of the unflanged morph (Knott & Kahlenberg, 2007).

In primates, the fertile phase of the menstrual cycle is linked to rising levels of estradiol. Attractivity, proceptivity, and receptivity are all positively associated with estradiol (Bonsall et al., 1978; Wallen et al., 1984). Female primates have higher attractivity if injected with estradiol after ovariectomy (Wallen, 1990) and estradiol treatment after ovariectomy promotes proceptivity in primate females (Zehr et al., 1998). For example, in paradigms that require monkeys to press a lever for access to a mate, ovariectomized rhesus monkeys demonstrate quicker lever presses when injected with estradiol (Bonsall et al., 1978). Notably, unlike rats, primates' estradiol-induced attractivity is ended by progesterone treatment (Zehr et al., 1998), because in primates progesterone is associated with pregnancy and nonfertile phases (e.g., luteal).

Endocrinology of Women's Sexual Behavior

Women have menstrual cycles and engage in sexual behavior throughout their cycle. When ovulating, however, women do not assume the lordosis position like rats, nor do women have visible sexual swellings like chimpanzees. Because of the lack of overt signals that alert potential sexual partners and women themselves to women's fertility status, until recently many thought that women's ovulation was concealed and that women "lost" the estrus phase (Gangestad & Thornhill, 2008; Haselton & Gildersleeve, 2016). Indeed, most researchers focused on explaining the evolutionary function of concealed ovulation (e.g., Alexander & Noonan, 1979; Burley, 1979; Symons, 1979). Nevertheless, it would be adaptive if women's psychology and behavior varied alongside fertility because ovulation is a time of drastically different reproductive risks and opportunities; more recent research has documented this association (Gangestad & Thornhill, 2008; Haselton & Gildersleeve, 2016).

Typical menstrual cycles last approximately 28 days (normal range: 25 to 35; Blake et al., 2016) and can be broken down into three phases: follicular, ovulatory, and luteal. Estrogen peaks toward the end of the follicular phase, followed by a surge of luteinizing hormone (LH); ovulation occurs approximately 30 hours after this surge (Bullivant et al., 2004). Women's fertile window includes the day of ovulation and up to five days prior (Wilcox et al., 1995). The luteal phase occurs spontaneously after ovulation and is characterized by high progesterone levels.

Women's menstrual cycle phases can be determined using several different methods (reviewed in Gangestad et al., 2016). The backward-counting method is considered more accurate than the forward-counting method because the luteal phase varies in length considerably less than the follicular phase. Researchers count backward from the onset of the next *estimated* menstruation which is determined from the previous menstruation start date and the average menstrual cycle length. In this method, the 14 days preceding the next estimated menstruation are labeled as the luteal phase and the preceding 5 days are considered to be the ovulatory phase (i.e., days 15 through 20 when reverse counting). For best practices, researchers using the backward-counting method should follow up with participants to confirm the accuracy of their next estimated menstruation. Using over-the-counter LH tests to confirm an LH surge leads to the most accurate assessment of ovulation. Several research teams (Blake et al., 2016; Gangestad et al., 2016) have put forth detailed guidelines for estimating the fertile window and conducting well-powered research on menstrual cycles.

MATING BEHAVIORS ACROSS THE MENSTRUAL CYCLE

Although the research on women's mating behavior has not always used this nomenclature, using Frank Beach's terminology of attractivity, proceptivity, and receptivity helps draw parallels to the nonhuman animal literature.

Attractivity

One of the most well-known studies examining the effect of menstrual cycle phase on women's attractivity assessed real-world implications of hormone fluctuations (Miller et al., 2007). Women who worked as exotic dancers reported their tip earnings in a diary study that tracked their menstrual cycles and fertile window. Women who were naturally cycling (i.e., did not use hormonal contraceptives) received the highest number of tips during dance shifts occurring during the ovulatory phase compared to shifts occurring during other phases. Although it is unclear which processes mediate this effect (e.g., aspects of women's appearance or women's behavior), this study showed that menstrual cycle phases influence women's real-world sexual behavior.

Since then, researchers have brought interactions between men and women into a more controlled lab setting to examine whether ovulation affects men's behavior (and thus women's attractivity). When men interacted with a confederate woman during her ovulatory phase, compared to other phases, men displayed greater behavioral mimicry of the woman's nonverbal behavior (Miller & Maner, 2011), which is an often-unconscious strategy of ingratiation. Because of the effect on men's impression management, these findings suggest that women's attractivity is heightened around ovulation.

Other experiments began to isolate specific cues (e.g., scent) that may convey women's fertility status to examine whether exposure to that cue affected men's physiology and cognition. In one study, men's testosterone levels were relatively higher after smelling t-shirts worn by women during the ovulatory phase than after smelling t-shirts worn by the same women during the luteal phase (Miller & Maner, 2010; cf. Roney & Simmons, 2012). Scent cues of ovulation also heighten mating-relevant cognitions (Miller & Maner, 2011): men who smelled t-shirts worn by ovulating women were more likely to complete the word stem "S_X" as *sex* (vs. *six*) compared to men who smelled t-shirts worn by nonovulating women. Overall, men can discriminate between scents from different cycle phases and find shirts that women wear around ovulation to smell more pleasant (Gildersleeve et al., 2012). Research examining vaginal odors likewise demonstrate that scent preferences track ovulation (Doty et al., 1975). Thus, scent appears to be one cue that conveys women's fertility status and increases women's attractivity during ovulation.

Research has also identified other important fertility cues affecting women's attractivity. Women's vocal pitch, for example, varies across the menstrual cycle (Bryant & Haselton, 2009; Pipitone & Gallup, 2008). Women have higher vocal pitches near ovulation and these higher pitches are rated as more attractive than the lower pitches observed in the luteal phase. Visual cues have also been linked to fertility and attractivity: women may choose to wear different clothing when they are in the ovulatory phase compared to the luteal phase (Durante et al., 2008; Haselton et al., 2007; Schwarz & Hassebrauck, 2008) and may move in a more attractive manner during the ovulatory phase (Fink et al., 2012). One study even followed couples longitudinally and verified fertility using transvaginal ultrasounds; men perceived their partner to be more attractive when conception was more likely (Cobey et al., 2013). Overall, research supports the hypothesis that men perceive women to be more attractive when they are ovulating.

Some research has specifically examined whether ovarian hormones underpin these increases in attractivity. Puts et al. (2013) examined whether the attractiveness of two cues—vocal pitch and facial attractiveness—was affected by estradiol, progesterone, and the interaction of the two hormones. Women attended two lab sessions (during ovulatory and luteal phases) during which they were photographed, recorded reading a paragraph, and provided saliva samples. Later, raters judged the attractiveness of those stimuli. In terms of cycle phase, men rated photographs and voices of women with a hormone profile corresponding to high fertility (i.e., ovulatory phase) as more attractive. In terms of hormones, a negative association between perceived attractiveness and progesterone emerged. Although estradiol did not have its own effect, estradiol levels did interact with progesterone, particularly for vocal attractiveness. In this case, in addition to the within-woman progesterone effect, women who had lower progesterone overall (across both sessions; between-woman effect) were rated as more attractive when they had higher estradiol levels (i.e., during the ovulatory phase compared to the luteal phase). Several other studies have connected estradiol to women's attractivity in terms of their waist-to-hip ratio (Jasieńska et al., 2004; Mondragón-Ceballos et al., 2015), as well as the women's health and femininity (Law Smith et al., 2006). Although effects are small and somewhat inconsistent, research has begun to examine whether women's attractivity is positively associated with estrogen and negatively associated with progesterone.

Proceptivity

To understand hormonal influences on women's mating behaviors, researchers must measure women's sexual motivation. It would be adaptive for women's reproductive hormones to modulate their *own* behavior because of the increased opportunities to reproduce; natural selection is unlikely to select for passive behaviors (i.e., stand and look pretty). Indeed, failure of early research to document midcycle peaks in sexual motivation may have been because research did not separately examine male- and female-initiated sexual interactions. In a longitudinal study, women who were naturally cycling demonstrated increases in both autosexual (e.g., fantasies and masturbation) and female-initiated dyadic sexual behavior around ovulation (Adams et al., 1978). Likewise, women reported greater sexual activity, sexual desire, and sexual fantasies around the LH surge and female-initiated sexual activity was highest in the three days leading up to the LH surge (Bullivant et al., 2004). The increase in sexual desire in the ovulatory phase appears to be stronger for partnered women (Bullivant et al., 2004). Single women, on the other hand, reported stronger feelings of loneliness in the early follicular phase, which may have motivated women to seek out potential partners around ovulation. Notably, women who are sexually attracted to women also report increased sexual motivation around ovulation (Diamond & Wallen, 2011; Matteo & Rissman, 1984).

More recently, studies have examined whether these shifts in women's sexual desire are underpinned by estradiol and progesterone levels (Grebe et al., 2016; Jones et al., 2018; Roney & Simmons, 2013). A pivotal study examined daily fluctuations in ovarian hormones and women's sexual desire (Roney & Simmons, 2013). Women's sexual motivation was positively linked with within-woman changes in estradiol[2] and negatively linked

---

[2] The estradiol effect was time-lagged such that current day estradiol did not predict sexual desire but estradiol two days previously did.

with within-woman changes in progesterone. That is, sexual desire was highest during the ovulatory phase when estradiol was high and progesterone was low, and sexual desire was markedly lower during the luteal phase when estradiol was low and progesterone was high. Sexual behavior initiated by the women was similarly positively associated with estradiol and negatively associated with progesterone.

Shirazi et al. (2019) conducted a high-powered study to investigate the targets of women's increased sexual desire around ovulation. A main effect of estradiol emerged such that within-woman changes were positively associated with sociosexual desire (i.e., desire for either casual or extra-pair partners) but this main effect was qualified by a significant interaction between changes in estradiol and progesterone. Specifically, sociosexual desire increased the most when estradiol was increasing and progesterone was decreasing. However, estradiol was not associated with increased general desire. Notably, another study found the opposite pattern: progesterone negatively predicted general desire but not sociosexual desire (Jones et al., 2018).

Blake et al. (2017) broadened the methodological assessment of women's sexual behavior to examine assertiveness and implicit measures of sexual availability. Implicit measures allow researchers to bypass some of the sociocultural constraints of explicit measures (for an overview, see Gawronski & De Houwer, 2014) that, for example, may make women answer questions about their sexual motivation in a biased way due to cultural pressures and social desirability. In the ovulatory (vs. nonovulatory) phase, women reported behaving more assertively, having higher mate value, and women were more likely to implicitly associate themselves with words representing sexual availability (e.g., seductive and sexy). Estradiol significantly positively predicted self-reported and implicitly measured assertiveness; progesterone significantly negatively predicted self-reported assertiveness. Neither hormone was associated with implicit sexual availability. Overall, this rigorous study shows that higher estradiol and lower progesterone are important for women's mating goal pursuit. Results provide support for the fertility-assertiveness hypothesis, suggesting that women exhibit greater desire to control their environment when conception risk is high (i.e., when reproductive opportunities and threats are more pronounced).

An interesting future direction would be to examine the specific behaviors women engage in when they initiate sexual behavior and whether these behaviors are associated with ovarian hormone fluctuations. Flirting may be one such behavior. Women are more verbally and nonverbally flirtatious during the ovulatory versus luteal phase of their cycle, in particular when interacting with a confident and socially dominant male target (Cantú et al., 2014). The specificity of female proceptivity toward socially dominant males parallels patterns observed in primates.

Receptivity

Because women engage in sexual behavior throughout their menstrual cycle, receptivity may be decoupled from ovarian hormone influence. Nevertheless, women's receptivity may be upregulated during the ovulatory phase. Women, for example, are responsive to sexual stimuli during ovulation; women's neural activity in response to erotic images appears to be positively associated with estradiol (Munk et al., 2018). Notably, this association was moderated by cycle phase: estradiol was only associated with neural activity in the early follicular and ovulatory phases but not in the luteal phase. Neural activity in response to erotic stimuli was not associated with progesterone. Other research found that exposure to audiovisual sexual stimuli appears to increase women's estradiol (but not progesterone) levels (Shirazi et al., 2018). Overall, these studies suggest that estradiol may be associated with receptivity to sexual stimuli.

Another aspect of receptivity that may be upregulated during the ovulatory phase is selectivity. Similar to primate females, women may be receptive only to certain types of sexual experiences (or certain partners) and may be unreceptive to others. Specifically, due to heightened conception risk, women may avoid threatening situations when they are ovulating. Indeed, women who were ovulating reported a significant decrease in their total number of risk-taking behaviors such as going to a bar or walking in a dimly lit area compared to women who were not ovulating (Chavanne & Gallup, 1998). These findings were replicated and extended using a within-subject design (Bröder & Hohmann, 2003). Furthermore, women who were ovulating (compared to women who were not ovulating) were also more likely to sit far away from a suspicious man in the study waiting room (Guéguen, 2012) and were more likely to judge men as more sexually coercive (Garver-Apgar et al., 2007). Thus, these studies suggest that women's receptivity toward unwanted advances may be lower when they are ovulating, but no study assessed whether estradiol or progesterone underpins these effects.

MODERATING ROLE OF INDIVIDUAL DIFFERENCES

Much like primates who live in social groups, humans do not experience their mating and partnership formation in a vacuum. In rhesus monkeys, for example, individual differences in females' dominance affect their mating profiles over the course of the menstrual cycle (Wallen & Zehr, 2004). Perhaps similar processes emerge for women such that women who face fewer social repercussions (e.g., aggressive responses from social partners that may be linked to sociocultural background or social status) may demonstrate stronger links between ovarian hormone fluctuations and sexual motivation. This may be especially important to examine developmentally, as younger females and women may have less established social hierarchies (Wallen & Zehr, 2004). Situational factors such as stress may also affect the link between ovarian hormones and sexual motivation (Bodenmann et al., 2010). Contextual information is important to integrate into future research.

Other individual differences may also moderate associations between ovulation and women's sexual motives. For example, a recent study examined whether life history strategy affected the link between conception risk and women's sexual motivation (Dinh et al., 2017). Life history theory argues that early life experiences can calibrate future behaviors to prioritize investment in reproductive versus somatic efforts (see Del Giudice et al., 2015, for an overview). People who faced greater childhood adversity are more likely to develop faster life history strategies, which are associated with earlier sexual maturity and greater sexual motivation relative to people with slower life history strategies. Dinh et al. (2017) found that women with faster life history strategies demonstrated a robust, positive association between conception risk and sexual motivation. Or perhaps said differently, when there was an *opportunity* for conception, women with faster life history strategies experienced upregulation in sexual motivation. Women with slower life history strategies, however, demonstrated a negative association between conception risk and sexual motivation. Thus, women who experienced unstable and harsh early environments were more likely to maximize reproductive opportunities, and this resulted in a closer coupling of ovarian hormones with sexual motivation compared to women who experienced more stable and plentiful early environments. A potentially fruitful avenue for future research would be to examine other aspects of women's ecologies and individual differences that may affect the link between hormones and sexual behavior.

Finally, an important aspect of modern women's lives that helps them control their reproductive processes—hormonal contraceptives—also affects the link between ovarian hormones and women's sexual motivation (for a review of hormonal contraceptive effects on social behavior, see Welling, 2013). Several studies reviewed earlier in the chapter (e.g., Adams et al., 1989; Bröder & Hohmann, 2003; Miller et al., 2007) have demonstrated that women taking hormonal contraceptives do not show the same positive association between the ovulatory phase (and estrogen levels) and attractivity and proceptivity that have been documented in naturally cycling women. Exotic dancers received a consistent rate of tips across their menstrual cycles if they were on hormonal contraceptives, a rate lower than naturally cycling women around ovulation (Miller et al., 2007). Women taking hormonal contraceptives also did not demonstrate increases in autosexual and female-initiated couple behavior around ovulation or the middle of their cycles (Adams et al., 1978). Even in terms of receptivity and risk vigilance to unwanted advances, women taking hormonal contraceptives did not demonstrate fluctuations in risky behaviors (Bröder & Hohmann, 2003). Future research should continue to attend to this important effect of women's modern environments.

METHODOLOGICAL COMMENTS

Although research on women's menstrual cycles has adopted a more uniform methodological approach, several issues remain. First, many studies, in particular, those that do not measure hormone levels, compare the ovulatory phase to the luteal phase. The luteal phase is not an ideal comparison for effects of ovulation on women's sexual behavior. The nonhuman animal literature has linked increasing estrogen in the follicular phase with increases in attractivity, proceptivity, and receptivity. Comparing the ovulatory phase (the peak of estrogen) to the luteal phase (what happens *after* the peak), is missing any change from the early follicular phase (what happens *before* the peak). Furthermore, the luteal phase is characterized by high progesterone levels. Thus, it is unclear from comparing two cycle points whether the ovulatory phase is linked to greater sexual motivation because of higher estrogen or if the luteal phase is lower in sexual motivation because of higher progesterone. A more nuanced approach would be to assess three or more points in distinct cycle phases, for example, early follicular, late follicular/ovulatory, and luteal. Over and above hormone assessments, ascertaining the phases during which the sessions occurred is beneficial. Recall that some aspects of women's sexual behavior were associated with estradiol only in the follicular and ovulatory (but not luteal) phases (e.g., Munk et al., 2018). If researchers just have estradiol levels but no phase information, they may fail to accurately detect effects of estradiol around ovulation. Future research should assess both hormones and cycle phases in order to clarify the links between ovarian hormones and women's sexual behavior.

Another important consideration revolves around the statistical analyses of data from within-subject studies. Research designs that assess women several times within one or more menstrual cycles necessitate the use of multilevel modeling to account for the nested nature of the data and the fact that each woman's answers across sessions are inextricably linked. A lot of research does take this approach, but not always in the most statistically appropriate manner. Many researchers are interested in whether women's deviations from their own average hormone levels are associated with changes in behavior. To answer this question, women's scores are centered on their own means. That is, Woman A may have estrogen levels of 120, 135, 126 across three sessions, after subtracting the mean (127), the values -7, 8, and -1 are used as the predictors of behavior. Woman B, however, may end up with the same values -7, 8, and -1 if she has a completely different mean (e.g., 247 with raw values of 240, 255, and 246). Only including the within-person fluctuations fails to control for the fact that Woman B had higher estrogen levels overall than Woman A. Proper modeling of within-person effects must include the mean (i.e., between-person effect) as a covariate (Raudenbush & Bryk, 2002). Furthermore, these calculations should be done within each menstrual cycle separately, because cycle hormone profiles are not a stable individual trait (Jasienska & Jasienski, 2008). Roney and Simmons (2013) used this analytic strategy and found evidence for within-woman effects, not between-woman effects (Roney & Simmons, 2013); however, this approach is not common. Not only would these methods be most appropriate, but they provide opportunities to test other hypotheses such as whether the likelihood of conception in a given cycle (higher estrogen and progesterone) moderates the link between ovarian hormones and women's sexual behavior.

Testosterone and Women's Sexual Behavior

In focusing on the specific role of ovarian hormones, this section has thus far avoided the discussion of testosterone and women's sexual behavior. However, research suggests that for women (unlike nonhuman animals), testosterone may play an important role for some aspects of sexual behavior. When women watched romantic scenes from *The Notebook,* their testosterone levels increased (Lopez et al., 2009). A similar effect has been demonstrated when women viewed photographs of men's faces (Zilioli et al., 2014) and imagined engaging in a sexual interaction with an attractive partner (Goldey & van Anders, 2011). Women also experienced increased testosterone during a speed-dating event during which they interacted with potential mates compared to a meet-and-greet with potential female friends (van der Meij et al., 2019). In real-life activities with a partner, women's testosterone has been shown to increase following romantic contact and sexual intercourse (van Anders, Hamilton, Schmidt, et al., 2007). Although testosterone is lower for women who are in committed and satisfying relationships (Edelstein et al., 2014), women experience increases in testosterone during the early stages of a relationship (Marazziti & Canale, 2004). Thus, state fluctuations in testosterone are associated with women's sexual behavior, although fluctuations in testosterone across the menstrual cycle do not predict women's sexual motivation (Roney & Simmons, 2013).

Testosterone and estradiol may be linked to different aspects of women's sexual behavior. For example, testosterone appears to be positively associated with women's psychological orgasm experiences whereas estradiol appears to be linked to more pronounced physical sensations during an orgasm (e.g., flooding and flushing) (van Anders & Dunn, 2009). Moreover, testosterone may also interact with ovarian hormones to exert some effects on women's sexual behavior. In research reviewed earlier, when estradiol was high in the follicular phase (but not in the luteal phase), women experienced increases in testosterone in response to audiovisual sexual stimuli (Shirazi et al., 2018). More research is necessary to examine how testosterone may facilitate aspects of women's sexual behavior and how testosterone may interact with ovarian hormone fluctuations. Future research, however, should consider assessing women's testosterone levels using liquid chromatography tandem mass spectrometry (LC-MS/MS) rather than the commonly-used salivary enzyme-linked immunosorbent assays (EIA) (Welker et al., 2016). Although EIAs provide easier and less expensive protocols, LC-MS/MS offers a more precise quantification of testosterone concentrations that is less prone to overestimation, which are especially problematic at low levels of testosterone more frequently seen in women (Welker et al., 2016).

Cortisol and Partnership Formation

Some recent research has begun to examine a non-gonadal hormone that may facilitate partnership formation in humans—cortisol. Cortisol is regulated by the activation of the hypothalamic-pituitary-adrenal (HPA) axis such that levels increase in response to negative and stressful events (Dickerson & Kemeny, 2004). Although the link between cortisol and human partnership formation is recent, perhaps it should not be surprising given the classic research on misattribution of arousal (Dutton & Aron, 1974). Crossing a river over a suspension bridge increased men's physiological arousal, which led to increased perceptions of a confederate woman's attractiveness. Although cortisol is not mentioned in the original paper, suffice to say that crossing a suspension bridge would activate the HPA axis and elevate cortisol levels.

Indirect evidence for the link between attraction and cortisol comes from research showing that men and women who had recently fallen in love had higher cortisol levels compared to men and women who had not recently fallen in love (Marazziti & Canale, 2004).

More directly, men's cortisol increased when they interacted with women (regardless of whether she was actively flirtatious or friendly) but not when they were alone or when they interacted with men (Roney et al., 2003). This association appears to be moderated by variation in androgen receptor genes (Roney et al., 2010), suggesting that some men may be genetically predisposed to be more sensitive to mating-relevant stimuli. Taken together, these findings suggest that interacting with a member of the opposite sex leads to increased cortisol for men.

A pair of studies examined men's and women's cortisol responses to imagined sexual interactions (Goldey & van Anders, 2011, 2012). Participants were asked to imagine a sexual interaction with an attractive member of the opposite sex. Women's cortisol was not affected by the manipulation or associated with self-reported arousal (though, as mentioned earlier, women's testosterone did increase). Although men's cortisol did not increase with the manipulation, cortisol levels were positively associated with men's perceptions of their sexual and autonomic arousal. Thus, it may be that cortisol primes sexual thoughts and behaviors in men. Although imagining an interaction did not affect women's cortisol, another study found that alongside increases in testosterone reviewed earlier, women experienced increased cortisol when watching a romantic scene from *The Notebook* (Lopez et al., 2009).

Perhaps the best test to date of links between cortisol and partnership formation comes from a speed-dating study where both men and women went on speed-dates (or meet-and-greets with people of the same sex; within-subject design) and provided saliva samples that were assayed for cortisol (van der Meij et al., 2019). The findings suggested that both events cause anticipatory increases in cortisol (because cortisol was higher presession than postsession). However, whereas cortisol levels declined sharply for same-sex meet-and-greets, this effect was blunted for romantic interactions; cortisol levels postsession were higher for the speed-dating sessions than for the same individuals' meet-and-greet sessions. Thus, contexts that make relationship formation salient may be relevant for cortisol fluctuations in both men and women.

The most comprehensive theory that outlines the role of not just cortisol but the entire stress response system in pair-bond processes is the physiology of romantic pair-bond initiation and maintenance model (Mercado & Hibel, 2017). This model argues it is adaptive for the pair-bond system to co-opt the stress response system to manage approach-avoidance responses. The role of the stress response system is likely nuanced and context-dependent. To the extent that increases in cortisol may prompt affiliative motives, increased cortisol during interactions with potential mates may be a catalyst for mating and pair-bond formation. After pair-bond formation, cortisol may be associated (sometimes positively and sometimes negatively) with different relationship maintenance processes relating to the co-regulation of individuals' stress physiology, the navigation of conflict in the relationship, and the ability to perceive and understand partners' emotions. Testing facets of this physiology of pair-bonds model, as well as answering important questions posed by initial studies examining the link between cortisol and attraction (Roney et al., 2007; van der Meij et al., 2019), are fruitful avenues for future research on the endocrinology of partnership formation.

Conclusion

A burgeoning literature in evolutionary psychology and psychoneuroendocrinology has begun to clarify the links between hormonal fluctuations and human mating behaviors. Gonadal hormones promote the drive to reproduce for men and women in patterns that largely parallel those of nonhuman animals such as birds, rats, and nonhuman primates. Nevertheless, research examining effects of hormones on mating behavior must take the social ecology of a given species into account because such features impact the manifestation of hormonal effects. Furthermore, in humans and nonhuman animals, the associations between hormones and mating are moderated by various individual differences such as social status, presence of same-sex and opposite-sex conspecifics, and females' fertility. Gonadal hormones such as testosterone, estrogen, and progesterone affect males' and females' propensity to respond to environmental stimuli with mating-relevant behaviors, and this link between hormones and the *active* pursuit of mating relevant goals has been shaped by natural selection for males *and females.*

References

Adams, D. B., Gold, A. R., & Burt, A. D. (1978). Rise in female-initiated sexual activity at ovulation and its suppression by oral contraceptives. *New England Journal of Medicine, 299*(21), 1145–1150.

Alexander R. D., & Noonan, K. M. (1979). Concealment of ovulation, parental care, and human social evolution. In N. A. Chagnon & W. Irons (Eds.)., Evolutionary *biology and human social behavior: an anthropological perspective* (pp. 436–453). Duxbury Press.

Alvergne, A., Faurie, C., & Raymond, M. (2009). Variation in testosterone levels and male reproductive effort: Insight from a polygynous human population. *Hormones and Behavior, 56*(5), 491–497.

Alvergne, A., Jokela, M., Faurie, C., & Lummaa, V. (2010). Personality and testosterone in men from a high-fertility population. *Personality and Individual Differences, 49*(8), 840–844.

Amstislavskaya, T. G., & Popova, N. K. (2004). Female-induced sexual arousal in male mice and rats: Behavioral and testosterone response. *Hormones and Behavior, 46*(5), 544–550.

Apicella, C. L, Feinberg, D. R, & Marlowe, F. W. (2007). Voice pitch predicts reproductive success in male hunter-gatherers. *Biology Letters, 3*(6), 682–684.

Archer, J. (2006). Testosterone and human aggression: An evaluation of the challenge hypothesis. *Neuroscience & Biobehavioral Reviews, 30*(3), 319–345.

Asarian, L., & Geary, N. (2006). Modulation of appetite by gonadal steroid hormones. *Philosophical Transactions of the Royal Society B: Biological Sciences, 361*(1471), 1251–1263.

Ball, G. F., & Balthazart, J. (2002). Neuroendocrine mechanisms regulating reproductive cycles and reproductive behavior in birds. In D. W. Pfaff, A. P. Arnold, S. E. Fahrbach, A. M. Etgen, & R. T. Rubin (Eds.), *Hormones, brain and behavior* (pp. 649–798). Academic Press.

Beach, F. A. (1976). Sexual attractivity, proceptivity, and receptivity in female mammals. *Hormones and Behavior, 7*(1), 105–138.

Beehner, J. C., Bergman, T. J., Cheney, D. L., Seyfarth, R. M., & Whitten, P. L. (2006). Testosterone predicts future dominance rank and mating activity among male chacma baboons. *Behavioral Ecology and Sociobiology, 59*(4), 469–479.

Bermant, G. (1961). Response latencies of female rats during sexual intercourse. *Science, 133*(3466), 1771–1773.

Blake, K. R., Bastian, B., O'Dean, S. M., & Denson, T. F. (2017). High estradiol and low progesterone are associated with high assertiveness in women. *Psychoneuroendocrinology, 75*, 91–99.

Blake, K. R., Dixson, B. J. W., O'Dean, S. M., & Denson, T. F. (2016). Standardized protocols for characterizing women's fertility: A data-driven approach. *Hormones and Behavior, 81*, 74–83.

Blaustein, J. D., & Erskine, M. S. (2002). Feminine sexual behavior: Cellular integration of hormonal and afferent information in the rodent forebrain. In D. W. Pfaff, A. P. Arnold, S. E. Fahrbach, A. M. Etgen, & R. T. Rubin (Eds.), *Hormones, brain and behavior* (pp. 139–214). Academic Press.

Bodenmann, G., Atkins, D., Schär Gmelch, M., & Poffet, V. (2010). The association between daily stress and sexual activity. *Journal of Family Psychology, 24*(3), 271–279.

Bonsall, R. W., Zumpe, D., & Michael, R. P. (1978). Menstrual cycle influences on operant behavior of female rhesus monkeys. *Journal of Comparative and Physiological Psychology, 92*(5), 846–855.

Bröder, A., & Hohmann, N. (2003). Variations in risk taking behavior over the menstrual cycle: An improved replication. *Evolution and Human Behavior, 24*(6), 391–398.

Brooks, D. C., Coon V, J. S., Ercan, C. M., Xu, X., Dong, H., Levine, J. E., Bulun, S. E., & Zhao, H. (2020). Brain aromatase and the regulation of sexual Activity in male mice. *Endocrinology, 161*(10), Article bqaa137.

Brown, W. A., Monti, P. M., & Corriveau, D. P. (1978). Serum testosterone and sexual activity and interest in men. *Archives of Sexual Behavior, 7*(2), 97–103.

Bullivant, S. B., Sellergren, S. A., Stern, K., Spencer, N. A., Jacob, S., Mennella, J. A., & McClintock, M. K. (2004). Women's sexual experience during the menstrual cycle: Identification of the sexual phase by noninvasive measurement of luteinizing hormone. *The Journal of Sex Research, 41*(1), 82–93.

Burley, N. (1979). The evolution of concealed ovulation. *American Naturalist, 114*, 835–858.

Cantú, S. M., Simpson, J. A., Griskevicius, V., Weisberg, Y. J., Durante, K. M., & Beal, D. J. (2014). Fertile and selectively flirty: Women's behavior toward men changes across the ovulatory cycle. *Psychological Science, 25*(2), 431–438.

Chavanne, T. J., & Gallup, G. G. (1998). Variation in risk taking behavior among female college students as a function of the menstrual cycle. *Evolution and Human Behavior, 19*(1), 27–32.

Dabbs, J. M., & Mallinger, A. (1999). High testosterone levels predict low voice pitch among men. *Personality and Individual Differences, 27*(4), 801–804.

Dabbs, J. M., & Mohammed, S. (1992). Male and female salivary testosterone concentrations before and after sexual activity. *Physiology & Behavior, 52*(1), 195–197.

Davidson, J. M., Rodgers, C. H., Smith, E. R., & Bloch, G. J. B. (1968). Stimulation of female sex behavior in adrenalectomized rats with estrogen alone. *Endocrinology, 82*(1), 193–195.

Del Giudice, M., Gangestad, S. W., & Kaplan, H. S. (2015). Life history theory and evolutionary psychology. In D. M. Buss (Ed.), *The handbook of evolutionary psychology* (pp. 1–27). American Cancer Society.

Diamond, L. M., & Wallen, K. (2011). Sexual minority women's sexual motivation around the time of ovulation. *Archives of Sexual Behavior, 40*(2), 237–246.

Dickerson, S. S., & Kemeny, M. E. (2004). Acute stressors and cortisol responses: A theoretical integration and synthesis of laboratory research. *Psychological Bulletin, 130*(3), 355–391.

Dinh, T., Pinsof, D., Gangestad, S. W., & Haselton, M. G. (2017). Cycling on the fast track: Ovulatory shifts in sexual motivation as a proximate mechanism for regulating life history strategies. *Evolution and Human Behavior, 38*(6), 685–694.

Durante, K. M., Li, N. P., & Haselton, M. G. (2008). Changes in women's choice of dress across the ovulatory cycle: Naturalistic and laboratory task-based evidence. *Personality and Social Psychology Bulletin, 34*(11), 1451–1460.

Dutton, D. G., & Aron, A. P. (1974). Some evidence for heightened sexual attraction under conditions of high anxiety. *Journal of Personality and Social Psychology, 30*(4), 510–517.

Edelstein, R. S., Chopik, W. J., & Kean, E. L. (2011). Sociosexuality moderates the association between testosterone and relationship status in men and women. *Hormones and Behavior, 60*(3), 248–255.

Edelstein, R. S., van Anders, S. M., Chopik, W. J., Goldey, K. L., & Wardecker, B. M. (2014). Dyadic associations between testosterone and relationship quality in couples. *Hormones and Behavior, 65*(4), 401–407.

Erskine, M. S. (1989). Solicitation behavior in the estrous female rat: A review. *Hormones and Behavior, 23*(4), 473–502.

Fales, M. R., Gildersleeve, K. A., & Haselton, M. G. (2014). Exposure to perceived male rivals raises men's testosterone on fertile relative to nonfertile days of their partner's ovulatory cycle. *Hormones and Behavior, 65*(5), 454–460.

Fink, B., Hugill, N., & Lange, B. P. (2012). Women's body movements are a potential cue to ovulation. *Personality and Individual Differences, 53*(6), 759–763.

Flinn, M. V., Ponzi, D., & Muehlenbein, M. P. (2012). Hormonal mechanisms for regulation of aggression in human coalitions. *Human Nature, 23*(1), 68–88.

Fry, A. C., Schilling, B. K., Fleck, S. J., & Kraemer, W. J. (2011). Relationships between competitive wrestling success and neuroendocrine responses. *The Journal of Strength & Conditioning Research, 25*(1), 40–45.

Gangestad, S. W., Haselton, M. G., Welling, L. L. M., Gildersleeve, K., Pillsworth, E. G., Burriss, R. P., Larson, C. M., & Puts, D. A. (2016). How valid are assessments of conception probability in ovulatory cycle research? Evaluations, recommendations, and theoretical implications. *Evolution and Human Behavior, 37*(2), 85–96.

Gangestad, S. W., & Thornhill, R. (1998). Menstrual cycle variation in women's preferences for the scent of symmetrical men. *Proceedings of the Royal Society of London. Series B: Biological Sciences, 265*(1399), 927–933.

Gangestad, S. W., & Thornhill, R. (2008). Human oestrus. *Proceedings of the Royal Society of London. Series B: Biological Sciences, 275*(1638), 991–1000.

Gangestad, S. W., Thornhill, R., & Garver, C. E. (2002). Changes in women's sexual interests and their partner's mate–retention tactics across the menstrual cycle: Evidence for shifting conflicts of interest. *Proceedings of the Royal Society of London. Series B: Biological Sciences, 269*(1494), 975–982.

Gangestad, S. W., Thornhill, R., & Garver-Apgar, C. E. (2005). Adaptations to ovulation: Implications for sexual and social behavior. *Current Directions in Psychological Science, 14*(6), 312–316.

Garver-Apgar, C. E., Gangestad, S. W., & Simpson, J. A. (2007). Women's perceptions of men's sexual coerciveness change across the menstrual cycle. *Acta Psychologica Sinica, 39*(3), 536–540.

Gawronski, B., & De Houwer, J. (2014). Implicit measures in social and personality psychology. In H. T. Reis & C. M. Judd (Eds.), *Handbook of research methods in social and personality psychology* (Vol. 2, pp. 283–310). Cambridge University Press.

Gettler, L. T., McDade, T. W., Feranil, A. B., & Kuzawa, C. W. (2011). Longitudinal evidence that fatherhood decreases testosterone in human males. *Proceedings of the National Academy of Sciences, 108*(39), 16194–16199.

Gildersleeve, K. A., Haselton, M. G., Larson, C. M., & Pillsworth, E. G. (2012). Body odor attractiveness as a cue of impending ovulation in women: Evidence from a study using hormone-confirmed ovulation. *Hormones and Behavior, 61*(2), 157–166.

Goldey, K. L., & van Anders, S. M. (2011). Sexy thoughts: Effects of sexual cognitions on testosterone, cortisol, and arousal in women. *Hormones and Behavior, 59*(5), 754–764.

Goldey, K. L., & van Anders, S. M. (2012). Sexual thoughts: Links to testosterone and cortisol in men. *Archives of Sexual Behavior, 41*(6), 1461–1470.

Gray, P. B., Kahlenberg, S. M., Barrett, E. S., Lipson, S. F., & Ellison, P. T. (2002). Marriage and fatherhood are associated with lower testosterone in males. *Evolution and Human Behavior, 23*(3), 193–201.

Grebe, N. M., Emery Thompson, M., & Gangestad, S. W. (2016). Hormonal predictors of women's extra-pair vs. in-pair sexual attraction in natural cycles: Implications for extended sexuality. *Hormones and Behavior, 78*, 211–219.

Guéguen, N. (2012). Risk taking and women's menstrual cycle: Near ovulation, women avoid a doubtful man. *Letters on Evolutionary Behavioral Science, 3*(1), 1–3.

Haselton, M. G., & Gildersleeve, K. (2016). Human ovulation cues. *Current Opinion in Psychology, 7*, 120–125.

Haselton, M. G., Mortezaie, M., Pillsworth, E. G., Bleske-Rechek, A., & Frederick, D. A. (2007). Ovulatory shifts in human female ornamentation: Near ovulation, women dress to impress. *Hormones and Behavior, 51*(1), 40–45.

Heim, N., & Hursch, C. J. (1979). Castration for sex offenders: Treatment or punishment? A review and critique of recent European literature. *Archives of Sexual Behavior, 8*(3), 281–304.

Hellhammer, D. H., Hubert, W., & Schürmeyer, T. (1985). Changes in saliva testosterone after psychological stimulation in men. *Psychoneuroendocrinology, 10*(1), 77–81.

Hull, E. M., & Dominguez, J. M. (2007). Sexual behavior in male rodents. *Hormones and Behavior, 52*(1), 45–55.

Hull, E. M., Wood, R. I., & Mckenna, K. E. (2006). Neurobiology of male sexual behavior. In T. M. Neill (Ed.), *Knobil and Neill's physiology of reproduction* (3rd ed., pp. 1729–1824). Academic Press.

Isidori, A. M., Giannetta, E., Gianfrilli, D., Greco, E. A., Bonifacio, V., Aversa, A., Isidori, A., Fabbri, A., & Lenzi, A. (2005). Effects of testosterone on sexual function in men: Results of a meta-analysis. *Clinical Endocrinology, 63*(4), 381–394.

Jasienska, G., & Jasienski, M. (2008). Interpopulation, interindividual, intercycle, and intracycle natural variation in progesterone levels: A quantitative assessment and implications for population studies. *American Journal of Human Biology, 20*(1), 35–42.

Jasieńska, G., Ziomkiewicz, A., Ellison, P. T., Lipson, S. F., & Thune, I. (2004). Large breasts and narrow waists indicate high reproductive potential in women. *Proceedings of the Royal Society of London. Series B: Biological Sciences, 271*(1545), 1213–1217.

Jones, B. C., Hahn, A. C., Fisher, C. I., Wang, H., Kandrik, M., & DeBruine, L. M. (2018). General sexual desire, but not desire for uncommitted sexual relationships, tracks changes in women's hormonal status. *Psychoneuroendocrinology, 88*, 153–157.

Klinkova, E., Heistermann, M., & Hodges, J. K. (2004). Social parameters and urinary testosterone level in male chimpanzees (*Pan troglodytes*). *Hormones and Behavior, 46*(4), 474–481.

Knott, C. D., & Kahlenberg, S. M. (2007). Orangutans in perspective: Forced copulations and female mating resistance. In S. Bearder. C. J. Campbell, A. Fuentes, K. C. MacKinnon, & M. Panger (Eds.), *Primates in perspective* (pp. 209–305). Oxford University Press.

Knussmann, R., Christiansen, K., & Couwenbergs, C. (1986). Relations between sex hormone levels and sexual behavior in men. *Archives of Sexual Behavior, 15*(5), 429–445.

Kraemer, H. C., Becker, H. B., Brodie, H. K. H., Doering, C. H., Moos, R. H., & Hamburg, D. A. (1976). Orgasmic frequency and plasma testosterone levels in normal human males. *Archives of Sexual Behavior, 5*(2), 125–132.

LaFerla, J. J., Anderson, D. L., & Schalch, D. S. (1978). Psychoendocrine response to sexual arousal in human males. *Psychosomatic Medicine, 40*(2), 166–172.

Larsson, K. (2003). My way to biological psychology. *Scandinavian Journal of Psychology, 44*(3), 173–187.

Lassek, W. D., & Gaulin, S. J. C. (2019). Evidence supporting nubility and reproductive value as the key to human female physical attractiveness. *Evolution and Human Behavior, 40*(5), 408–419.

Law Smith, M. J., Perrett, D. I, Jones, B. C., Cornwell, R. E., Moore, F. R., Feinberg, D. R., Boothroyd, L. G., Durrani, S. J., Stirrat, M. R., Whiten, S., Pitman, R. M., & Hillier, S. G. (2006). Facial appearance is a cue to oestrogen levels in women. *Proceedings of the Royal Society B: Biological Sciences, 273*(1583), 135–140.

Long, J. A., & Evans, H. M. (1922). *The oestrous cycle in the rat and its associated phenomena* (Vol. 6). University of California Press.

Lopez, H. H., Hay, A. C., & Conklin, P. H. (2009). Attractive men induce testosterone and cortisol release in women. *Hormones and Behavior, 56*(1), 84–92.

Lynch, J. W., Ziegler, T. E., & Strier, K. B. (2002). Individual and seasonal variation in fecal testosterone and cortisol levels of wild male tufted capuchin monkeys, *Cebus apella nigritus. Hormones and Behavior, 41*(3), 275–287.

Maner, J. K., Miller, S. L., Schmidt, N. B., & Eckel, L. A. (2008). Submitting to defeat: Social anxiety, dominance threat, and decrements in testosterone. *Psychological Science, 19*(8), 764–768.

Marazziti, D., & Canale, D. (2004). Hormonal changes when falling in love. *Psychoneuroendocrinology, 29*(7), 931–936.

Matteo, S., & Rissman, E. F. (1984). Increased sexual activity during the midcycle portion of the human menstrual cycle. *Hormones and Behavior, 18*(3), 249–255.

Mazur, A., Booth, A., & Dabbs, J. M. (1992). Testosterone and chess competition. *Social Psychology Quarterly, 55*(1), 70–77.

Mazur, A., & Lamb, T. A. (1980). Testosterone, status, and mood in human males. *Hormones and Behavior, 14*(3), 236–246.

McCarthy, M. M. (2008). Estradiol and the developing brain. *Physiological Reviews, 88*(1), 91–134.

McClintock, M. K., & Adler, N. T. (1978). The role of the female during copulation in wild and domestic Norway rats (*Rattus Norvegicus*). *Behaviour, 67*(1–2), 67–95.

McClintock, M. K., Anisko, J. J., & Adler, N. T. (1982). Group mating among Norway rats II. The social dynamics of copulation: Competition, cooperation, and mate choice. *Animal Behaviour, 30*(2), 410–425.

McClintock, M. K., Toner, J. P., Adler, N. T., & Anisko, J. J. (1982). Postejaculatory quiescence in female and male rats: Consequences for sperm transport during group mating. *Journal of Comparative and Physiological Psychology, 96*(2), 268–277.

McIntyre, M., Gangestad, S. W., Gray, P. B., Chapman, J. F., Burnham, T. C., O'Rourke, M. T., & Thornhill, R. (2006). Romantic involvement often reduces men's testosterone levels—but not always: The moderating role of extrapair sexual interest. *Journal of Personality and Social Psychology, 91*(4), 642–651.

Mercado, E., & Hibel, L. C. (2017). I love you from the bottom of my hypothalamus: The role of stress physiology in romantic pair bond formation and maintenance. *Social and Personality Psychology Compass, 11*(2), e12298.

Meyerson, B. J., & Lindström, L. (1973). Sexual motivation in the neonatally androgen-treated female rat. In K. Lissák (Ed.), *Hormones and brain function* (pp. 443–448). Springer.

Miller, G., Tybur, J. M., & Jordan, B. D. (2007). Ovulatory cycle effects on tip earnings by lap dancers: Economic evidence for human estrus? *Evolution and Human Behavior, 28*(6), 375–381.

Miller, S. L., & Maner, J. K. (2010a). Scent of a woman: Men's testosterone responses to olfactory ovulation cues. *Psychological Science, 21*(2), 276–283.

Miller, S. L., & Maner, J. K. (2010b). Evolution and relationship maintenance: Fertility cues lead committed men to devalue relationship alternatives. *Journal of Experimental Social Psychology, 46*(6), 1081–1084.

Miller, S. L., Maner, J. K., & McNulty, J. K. (2012). Adaptive attunement to the sex of individuals at a competition: The ratio of opposite- to same-sex individuals correlates with changes in competitors' testosterone levels. *Evolution and Human Behavior, 33*(1), 57–63.

Mondragón-Ceballos, R., García Granados, M. D., Cerda-Molina, A. L., Chavira-Ramírez, R., & Hernández-López, L. E. (2015). Waist-to-hip ratio, but not body mass index, is associated with testosterone and estradiol concentrations in young women. *International Journal of Endocrinology*, 2015, Article 654046.

Muller, M. N. (2017). Testosterone and reproductive effort in male primates. *Hormones and Behavior, 91*, 36–51.

Muller, M. N., & Wrangham, R. W. (2004). Dominance, aggression and testosterone in wild chimpanzees: A test of the "challenge hypothesis." *Animal Behaviour, 67*(1), 113–123.

Munk, A. J. L., Zoeller, A. C., & Hennig, J. (2018). Fluctuations of estradiol during women's menstrual cycle: Influences on reactivity towards erotic stimuli in the late positive potential. *Psychoneuroendocrinology, 91*, 11–19.

Nelson, R. J., & Kriegsfeld, L. J. (2017). *An introduction to behavioral endocrinology* (5th ed.). Sinauer.

Peters, M., Simmons, L. W., & Rhodes, G. (2008). Testosterone is associated with mating success but not attractiveness or masculinity in human males. *Animal Behaviour, 76*(2), 297–303.

Phoenix, C. H., Slob, A. K., & Goy, R. W. (1973). Effects of castration and replacement therapy on sexual behavior of adult male rhesuses. *Journal of Comparative and Physiological Psychology, 84*(3), 472–481.

Pillsworth, E. G., Haselton, M. G., & Buss, D. M. (2004). Ovulatory shifts in female sexual desire. *The Journal of Sex Research, 41*(1), 55–65.

Plant, E. A., Kunstman, J. W., & Maner, J. K. (2010). You do not only hurt the one you love: Self-protective responses to attractive relationship alternatives. *Journal of Experimental Social Psychology, 46*(2), 474–477.

Pollet, T. V., der Meij, L. van, Cobey, K. D., & Buunk, A. P. (2011). Testosterone levels and their associations with lifetime number of opposite sex partners and remarriage in a large sample of American elderly men and women. *Hormones and Behavior, 60*(1), 72–77.

Puts, D. A., Bailey, D. H., Cárdenas, R. A., Burriss, R. P., Welling, L. L. M., Wheatley, J. R., & Dawood, K. (2013). Women's attractiveness changes with estradiol and progesterone across the ovulatory cycle. *Hormones and Behavior, 63*(1), 13–19.

Raudenbush, S. W., & Bryk, A. S. (2002). *Hierarchical linear models: Applications and data analysis methods*. SAGE.

Resko, J. A., & Phoenix, C. H. (1972). Sexual behavior and testosterone concentrations in the plasma of the rhesus monkey before and after castration. *Endocrinology, 91*(2), 499–503.

Ronay, R., & Hippel, W. von. (2010). The presence of an attractive woman elevates testosterone and physical risk taking in young men. *Social Psychological and Personality Science, 1*(1), 57–64.

Roney, J. R., Lukaszewski, A. W., & Simmons, Z. L. (2007). Rapid endocrine responses of young men to social interactions with young women. *Hormones and Behavior, 52*(3), 326–333.

Roney, J. R., Mahler, S. V., & Maestripieri, D. (2003). Behavioral and hormonal responses of men to brief interactions with women. *Evolution and Human Behavior, 24*(6), 365–375.

Roney, J. R., & Simmons, Z. L. (2012). Men smelling women: Null effects of exposure to ovulatory sweat on men's testosterone. *Evolutionary Psychology, 10*(4), Article 147470491201000.

Roney, J. R., & Simmons, Z. L. (2013). Hormonal predictors of sexual motivation in natural menstrual cycles. *Hormones and Behavior, 63*(4), 636–645.

Roney, J. R., Simmons, Z. L., & Lukaszewski, A. W. (2010). Androgen receptor gene sequence and basal cortisol concentrations predict men's hormonal responses to potential mates. *Proceedings of the Royal Society B: Biological Sciences, 277*(1678), 57–63.

Rupp, H. A., James, T. W., Ketterson, E. D., Sengelaub, D. R. Janssen, E., & Heiman, J. R. (2009). Neural activation in the orbitofrontal cortex in response to male faces increases during the follicular phase. *Hormones and Behavior, 56*(1), 66-72.

Saxbe, D. E., Schetter, C. D., Simon, C. D., Adam, E. K., & Shalowitz, M. U. (2017). High paternal testosterone may protect against postpartum depressive symptoms in fathers, but confer risk to mothers and children. *Hormones and Behavior, 95*, 103–112.

Schmidt, P. J., Berlin, K. L., Danaceau, M. A., Neeren, A., Haq, N. A., Roca, C. A., & Rubinow, D. R. (2004). The effects of pharmacologically induced hypogonadism on mood in healthy men. *Archives of General Psychiatry, 61*(10), 997.

Schmidt, P. J., Steinberg, E. M., Negro, P. P., Haq, N., Gibson, C., & Rubinow, D. R. (2009). Pharmacologically induced hypogonadism and sexual function in healthy young women and men. *Neuropsychopharmacology, 34*(3), 565–576.

Schwarz, S., & Hassebrauck, M. (2008). Self-perceived and observed variations in women's attractiveness throughout the menstrual cycle—A diary study. *Evolution and Human Behavior, 29*(4), 282–288.

Shirazi, T. N., Bossio, J. A., Puts, D. A., & Chivers, M. L. (2018). Menstrual cycle phase predicts women's hormonal responses to sexual stimuli. *Hormones and Behavior, 103*, 45–53.

Shirazi, T. N., Self, H., Dawood, K., Rosenfield, K. A., Penke, L., Carré, J. M., Ortiz, T., & Puts, D. A. (2019). Hormonal predictors of women's sexual motivation. *Evolution and Human Behavior, 40*(3), 336–344.

Slatcher, R. B., Mehta, P. H., & Josephs, R. A. (2011). Testosterone and self-reported dominance interact to influence human mating behavior. *Social Psychological and Personality Science, 2*(5), 531–539.

Sobolewski, M. E., Brown, J. L., & Mitani, J. C. (2013). Female parity, male aggression, and the Challenge Hypothesis in wild chimpanzees. *Primates; Tokyo, 54*(1), 81–88.

Stoleru, S., Gregoire, M.-C., Gerard, D., Decety, J., Lafarge, E., Cinotti, L., Lavenne, F., Bars, D. L., Vernet-Maury, E., Rada, H., Collet, C., Mazoyer, B., Forest, M. G., Magnin, F., Spira, A., & Comar, D. (1999). Neuroanatomical correlates of visually evoked sexual arousal in human males. *Archives of Sexual Behavior, 28*(1), 1–21.

Stone, C. P., Tomilin, M. I., & Barker, R. G. (1935). A comparative study of sexual drive in adult male rats as measured by direct copulatory tests and by the Columbia obstruction apparatus. *Journal of Comparative Psychology, 19*(2), 215–241.

Strom, J. O., Ingberg, E., Druvefors, E., Theodorsson, A., & Theodorsson, E. (2012). The female menstrual cycle does not influence testosterone concentrations in male partners. *Journal of Negative Results in BioMedicine, 11*(1), 1.

Symons, D. (1979). *The evolution of human sexuality*. Oxford University Press.

Tennent, B. J., Smith, E. R., & Davidson, J. M. (1980). The effects of estrogen and progesterone on female rat proceptive behavior. *Hormones and Behavior, 14*(1), 65–75.

Trivers, R. L. (1972). Parental investment and sexual selection. In B. Campbell (Ed.), *Sexual selection and the descent of man* (pp. 136–179). Aldine.

van Anders, S. M., & Dunn, E. J. (2009). Are gonadal steroids linked with orgasm perceptions and sexual assertiveness in women and men? *Hormones and Behavior, 56*(2), 206–213.

van Anders, S. M., & Goldey, K. L. (2010). Testosterone and partnering are linked via relationship status for women and "relationship orientation" for men. *Hormones and Behavior, 58*(5), 820–826.
van Anders, S. M., Goldey, K. L., & Kuo, P. X. (2011). The Steroid/Peptide Theory of Social Bonds: Integrating testosterone and peptide responses for classifying social behavioral contexts. *Psychoneuroendocrinology, 36*(9), 1265–1275.
van Anders, S. M., Hamilton, L. D., Schmidt, N., & Watson, N. V. (2007). Associations between testosterone secretion and sexual activity in women. *Hormones and Behavior, 51*(4), 477–482.
van Anders, S. M., Hamilton, L. D., & Watson, N. V. (2007). Multiple partners are associated with higher testosterone in North American men and women. *Hormones and Behavior, 51*(3), 454–459.
van der Meij, L., Almela, M., Buunk, A. P., Fawcett, T. W., & Salvador, A. (2012). Men with elevated testosterone levels show more affiliative behaviours during interactions with women. *Proceedings of the Royal Society B: Biological Sciences, 279*(1726), 202–208.
van der Meij, L., Buunk, A. P., van de Sande, J. P., & Salvador, A. (2008). The presence of a woman increases testosterone in aggressive dominant men. *Hormones and Behavior, 54*(5), 640–644.
van der Meij, L., Demetriou, A., Tulin, M., Méndez, I., Dekker, P., & Pronk, T. (2019). Hormones in speed-dating: The role of testosterone and cortisol in attraction. *Hormones and Behavior, 116*, 104555.
Wallen, K. (1990). Desire and ability: Hormones and the regulation of female sexual behavior. *Neuroscience & Biobehavioral Reviews, 14*(2), 233–241.
Wallen, K., & Tannenbaum, P. L. (1997). Hormonal modulation of sexual behavior and affiliation in rhesus monkeys. *Annals of the New York Academy of Sciences, 807*(1), 185–202.
Wallen, K., Winston, L. A., Gaventa, S., Davis-DaSilva, M., & Collins, D. C. (1984). Periovulatory changes in female sexual behavior and patterns of ovarian steroid secretion in group-living rhesus monkeys. *Hormones and Behavior, 18*(4), 431–450.
Wallen, K., & Zehr, J. L. (2004). Hormones and history: The evolution and development of primate female sexuality. *Journal of Sex Research, 41*(1), 101–112.
Warner, L. H. (1927). A study of sex behavior in the white rat by means of the obstruction method. *Comparative Psychology Monographs, 4, 22*, 58–58.
Welker, K. M., Lassetter, B., Brandes, C. M., Prasad, S., Koop, D. R., & Mehta, P. H. (2016). A comparison of salivary testosterone measurement using immunoassays and tandem mass spectrometry. *Psychoneuroendocrinology, 71*, 180–188.
Welling, L. L. M. (2013). Psychobehavioral effects of hormonal contraceptive use. *Evolutionary Psychology, 11*(3), 718–742.
Wilcox, A. J., Weinberg, C. R., & Baird, D. D. (1995). Timing of sexual intercourse in relation to ovulation—Effects on the probability of conception, survival of the pregnancy, and sex of the baby. *New England Journal of Medicine, 333*(23), 1517–1521.
Wingfield, J. C., Hegner, R. E., Dufty, Alfred M., & Ball, G. F. (1990). The "Challenge Hypothesis": Theoretical implications for patterns of testosterone secretion, mating systems, and breeding strategies. *American Naturalist, 136*(6), 829–846.
Xiao, K., Kondo, Y., & Sakuma, Y. (2004). Sex-specific effects of gonadal steroids on conspecific odor preference in the rat. *Hormones and Behavior, 46*(3), 356–361.
Yerkes, R. M., & Elder, J. H. (1936). The sexual and reproductive cycles of chimpanzee. *Proceedings of the National Academy of Sciences, USA, 22*(5), 276–283.
Zehr, J. L., Maestripieri, D., & Wallen, K. (1998). Estradiol increases female sexual initiation independent of male responsiveness in rhesus monkeys. *Hormones and Behavior, 33*(2), 95–103.
Zilioli, S., Caldbick, E., & Watson, N. V. (2014). Testosterone reactivity to facial display of emotions in men and women. *Hormones and Behavior, 65*(5), 461–468.

CHAPTER

6 Human Intersexual Courtship

Neil R. Caton, David M. G. Lewis, Laith Al-Shawaf, *and* Kortnee C. Evans

Abstract

From cockroaches and cuttlefish to crocodiles and chimpanzees, organisms across diverse taxa are equipped with physical and psychological systems for courting opposite-sex conspecifics. In this chapter, we focus on the colorful—literally and figuratively—collection of courtship ornaments, tactics, and strategies of one primate species: *Homo sapiens*. Humans use their vocal qualities—deep voices, soft voices, expressive voices—to show their dominance, kindness, and intelligence. They dance dynamically, kiss passionately, and offer caring (as well as deceptive) compliments. Humans' courtship signals and the psychophysical systems that detect them span the senses: visual, auditory, tactile, olfactory, and gustatory. We review research across these perceptual modalities and offer suggestions for future work into the many uncharted areas of this fascinating domain.

Key Words: courtship, human mating, sexual selection, honest signals, costly signals

A wide variety of organisms across diverse taxa possess physical and psychological systems shaped by sexual selection to promote their reproductive success (Darwin, 1871). Male fireflies attract their female counterparts in the language of light, intermittently shimmering their beams against the darkness of the night sky, whereas Madagascar hissing cockroaches take on a more musical approach through gesture and song. Lobsters spar with their prospective mates in a gentle boxing match to demonstrate their physical strength. Crocodiles bellow, cough, and blow bubbles at each other as part of their courtship ritual. Gentoo penguins begin their courtship ritual with bows and songs and conclude it with the presentation of smooth pebbles to their desired partners (see West, 2009). Like their invertebrate, reptilian, and avian counterparts, mammals deploy a diverse variety of courtship strategies that span sight, sound, and scent. Male humpback whales sing, female baboons' buttocks swell and become bright red when they are sexually available, and ring-tail lemurs secrete a fruity fragrance from their wrists (West, 2009). Another species of primate—*Homo sapiens*—boasts a similarly impressive and diverse set of courtship ornaments, tactics, and strategies.

Humans manage and manipulate their appearance, sing songs of love, and flaunt their financial resources by buying exorbitantly expensive items—from Rothko paintings to Gucci handbags and Rolex wristwatches. And people use their vocal qualities—deep voices, soft voices, expressive voices—to exhibit their dominance, kindness, and intelligence. Humans' psychophysical systems have evolved to pay attention to these courtship signals because they cue relevant underlying traits (such as health and resource-provisioning potential). These traits, and thus the neurocognitive programs that detect them, interface with the senses: visual, auditory, tactile, olfactory, and gustatory. Accordingly, we organize this chapter around the different perceptual modalities through which humans court each other.

Courtship in the Visual Modality

Because initial tactics in human courtship often revolve around visual signals (Morris, 1971; see also Miller & Todd, 1998), we first direct attention to the role of these visual cues in human courtship.

Facial Cues

In humans, information regarding physical attractiveness is first and foremost gauged from the face—the center of our visual attention and a primary source of information about a person's emotional, social, and physical state (Little, Jones, & Debruine, 2011).

SKIN TEXTURE AND COLORATION

Human skin texture and coloration convey distinct fitness-related information. Evidence suggests that sebum (which provides hydration and smoothness to the skin's surface; Wertz, 2009), carotenoid concentration (which may be visually detected via a combination of skin yellowness and redness; see Foo, Rhodes, et al., 2017), blood vascularization and oxygenation (visually detected in reddish skin pigments; Re et al., 2011), and melanin concentration (visually detected in darker skin pigments; Chung et al., 2010) are all positively associated with immune system functioning (see Chew & Soon Park, 2004; Lakaye et al., 2009; Re et al., 2011; Smith & Thiboutot, 2007). Moreover, carotenoid increases humans' visual capabilities, as the visual system's ability to correctly interpret wavelengths and produce color is dependent on carotenoid concentration (Toews et al., 2017). Blood vascularization and oxygenation also increase cardiovascular fitness (Re et al., 2011). Finally, melanin protects against ultraviolet damage (Brenner & Hearing, 2008), which was a powerful selective force throughout our species' evolutionary history (Greaves, 2014).

Evidence suggests that natural selection shaped humans' attractiveness-assessment systems to detect, process, and generate attraction to these cues linked with underlying physiological function. Specifically, people are attracted to others with smooth (Fink & Matts, 2008), yellow-orange (i.e., a combination of yellow and red; see Foo, Rhodes, et al., 2017), reddish (Re et al., 2011) and darker (Fink et al., 2001) skin. These preferences could motivate behaviors to manipulate these cues in order to enhance attractiveness (see Lewis & Buss, 2022).

Evidence across cultures, geographical regions, and time periods bears out this hypothesis. Cosmetic makeup (e.g., foundation and concealer) has long been used by people to manipulate perceptions of their skin's smoothness (Stewart, 2017). From 10,000 B.C.E., ancient Egyptians used scented oils and ointments (oils mimic the oily sebum compound; Wertz, 2009) to manipulate their skin's perceived smoothness (Stewart, 2017). Those in the modern courtship environment can now opt for nonsurgical cosmetic procedures (e.g., chemical peels and laser resurfacing) to manipulate perceptions of their skin's smoothness (Jacob et al., 2001). To manipulate perceptions of one's yellowish-orange skin pigmentation (see Foo, Rhodes, et al., 2017), ancient Egyptians applied yellow ochre, women in 17th-century England applied saffron (Stewart, 2017), and 21st-century humans can make use of modern makeup that has, as a central ingredient, carotenoid itself (Das et al., 2007). For reddish skin pigmentation, ancient Egyptians applied red ochre, English women in the 15th to 17th century applied red plant dyes (e.g., safflower, cochineal, vermillion, red sandalwood, and brazilwood), and many modern women make use of blush (Stewart, 2017). Finally, to create the perception of darker skin pigmentation, ancient Egyptians used brown ochre, whereas modern humans have a diverse set of resources at their disposal, ranging from bronzer that they can apply at home to professional services that they can seek at tanning salons and other facilities (see Stewart, 2017).

FACIAL SHAPE

Facial Masculinity in Men

There are several, sometimes competing, evolutionary hypotheses about what information is cued by androgen-linked facial features in men. One hypothesis is that masculine facial shape is an indicator of immune robustness (Foo, Nakagawa, et al., 2017; Foo et al., 2020; Phalane et al., 2017; Rhodes et al., 2003). Given that testosterone is an immunosuppressant, androgen-dependent masculine male facial features may cue an immune system strong enough to withstand the hormone's immunosuppressive effect (Foo, Nakagawa, et al., 2017; see also Al-Shawaf & Lewis, 2018; Al-Shawaf et al., 2018). An alternative hypothesis is that masculine facial structures cue *physical* robustness, specifically the ability to resist damage (e.g., facial fractures, lacerations, and knockouts) during combat. Lethal combat has been a powerful adaptive problem throughout hominin evolution, and has driven the evolution of sex-differentiated anatomical structures designed to inflict as well as resist damage in agonistic exchanges (Carrier & Morgan, 2014; Caton & Lewis, 2021a, 2021b; Sell et al., 2012). Larger bone structures are one form of defensive morphology that has evolved to solve this adaptive problem (Carrier & Morgan, 2014; Sell et al., 2012). The orbital (brow ridge), zygomatic (cheekbones), maxillary (midface), nasal (nose), and mandibular (jaw, chin) regions are most often struck and fractured during combat (see

Carrier & Morgan, 2014). Indeed, it is these specific facial regions that exhibit the greatest increases in robustness across hominin evolution, purportedly to protect against the impact of a punch (Carrier & Morgan, 2014). If either of these hypotheses is correct—if masculine facial structures in men cue immune robustness or if they confer an advantage in intrasexual competition—selection should have shaped psychological mechanisms in women to be attracted to masculine facial shape.

Consistent with this proposition, several studies have found that women are attracted to masculine facial features (see DeBruine, 2014; see also Little, Connely, et al., 2011). Other research, however, has shown that women are attracted to men with *feminine* facial features, which may influence perceptions of warmth, kindness, and paternal investment (see Marcinkowska et al., 2019). Some research suggests that variability in women's preferences may reflect adaptive calibration to local ecological harshness; in harsher environments, women are predicted to place greater value on cues to offspring survivability, whether indicated by a mate's immune or physical robustness. Consistent with this, DeBruine et al. (2010) found that women's preferences for facial masculinity were stronger in ecologically harsh environments (i.e., in countries where the national health indices are *lower*; DeBruine et al., 2010; see also Al-Shawaf et al., 2019 for a broader discussion of the context-sensitivity of evolved psychological mechanisms). Consistent specifically with the physical robustness hypothesis, evidence also suggests that women who perceive a greater risk of danger (e.g., experience of robberies/attacks in the past year and feelings of danger) have stronger preferences for men's facial masculinity (Borras-Guevara et al., 2017). However, more recent studies have found that preferences for masculinity are stronger in countries where the national health indices are *higher* (see Marcinkowska et al., 2019). Future research is needed to better understand precisely when and why women prefer masculine or feminine facial structures (see Lewis et al., in press). Nonetheless, existing studies suggest that women's attractiveness-assessment mechanisms attend to masculine facial features in men.

Facial Femininity in Women

In women, feminine facial shape (e.g., small jaw, small nose, and reduced interocular distance) is linked to higher estrogen (see Law Smith et al., 2006) and superior immune function (Foo et al., 2020). If feminine facial shape cued women's health, and thus the health of potential offspring, then selection should have shaped cognitive programs in men to attend to these cues. Numerous studies employing diverse methods have demonstrated that men perceive feminine facial features as attractive (see Bovet, 2018, for a brief review). The fact that men's attractiveness-assessment mechanisms attend to female-typical facial morphology could motivate women to engage in behavior to manipulate these cues. Makeup techniques, such as contouring, have been employed to manipulate the perceived size and definition of these facial features (e.g., to create the appearance of a small nose, jaw, and chin; Rozell, 2009).

Bodily Cues

While the face might be the center of our visual attention, the human body contains numerous morphological features – from neck musculature to lumbar curvature – that alter our perception of another's attractiveness.

CUES IN MEN'S BODIES

Upper-Body Musculature

Men's upper-body musculature has recurrently played an important role in contest competition and resource provisioning; it is a central predictor of their ability to inflict physical harm on adversaries and succeed in violent fights (Caton & Lewis, 2021a; Sell et al., 2012). These advantages would have selected for attractiveness-assessment mechanisms in women to attend to men's upper-body musculature (Sell et al., 2017). Indeed, men's upper-body strength explains most of the variance in women's perceptions of men's body attractiveness (Sell et al., 2017). Women's preferences for strength-based cues in men may drive men to engage in behaviors to manipulate their perceived physical formidability. Consistent with this hypothesis, men engage in many body expressions (e.g., muscle flexion, chest expansion, and space-taking) and behaviors (e.g., gait and dance) that manipulate perceivers' judgments of their upper-body strength, including in the courtship domain (see Tooke & Camire, 1991). In the modern environment, men's propensity to enhance the perception of their muscularity is perhaps best demonstrated by gym memberships and fitness centers (Jonason, 2007). It is also reflected by auxiliary practices such as the use of illegal and legal steroids and muscle implants, all of which manipulate perceptions of men's physical formidability and, consequently, their attractiveness (Bordo, 2000).

Neck Musculature

Neck musculature predicts both the capacity to inflict damage and the ability to resist it (Bauer et al., 2001; Collins et al., 2014; Illyés & Kiss, 2007). Neck musculature predicts punch-based force output: the size and strength of the upper trapezius fibers are key to force output because of their involvement in scapulae movement and elevation during striking (Illyés & Kiss, 2007). Neck musculature also contributes to increased damage *resistance* by reducing the risk of concussion. When combatants lose an agonistic exchange, it is most often due to an in-fight concussion (e.g., cognitive disorientation or knockout), suggesting that concussions may have been a recurrent adaptive problem throughout human evolution (Dixson et al., 2018). Larger neck musculature reduces concussions due to the increased head stabilization afforded by the sternocleidomastoid and upper trapezius muscles (Bauer et al., 2001; Collins et al., 2014). These muscles tighten at the time of impact to form a single, stable unit between the head and neck that dissipates kinetic energy and, in turn, reduces postimpact head acceleration and, ultimately, lowers the probability of concussion (Broglio et al., 2010; Gallagher et al., 2018). For these reasons, we might expect neck musculature to contribute to real-world fighting success.

By performing geometric morphometric analyses on a sample of 715 ultimate fighting championship (UFC) mixed-martial-arts fighters, Caton and Lewis (2021b) found that larger neck musculature was associated with greater fighting success, an effect that remained robust after controlling for numerous variables (e.g., weight, height, age, sex) and when specifically examining male fighters. Using geometric morphometrics, Caton and Lewis (2021b) isolated the allometric (bodily scaling) and non-allometric (non-bodily scaling) components of the neck, which allowed them to demonstrate that neck musculature specifically and independently contributed to increased fighting success (see Adams & Otárola-Castillo, 2013, for more detail on geometric morphometrics). If larger neck musculature was a recurrent cue to fighting success in ancestral men, we might expect women's attractiveness-assessment mechanisms to attend to men's neck musculature.

Consistent with this hypothesis, Caton and Lewis (2021b) found that men with larger neck muscles were perceived to be stronger, more masculine, more dominant, and more physically attractive. This feature of women's mate preferences—positive assessments of strong neck musculature—leads to the hypothesis that men will engage in behaviors to enhance these cues, including the prediction that, relative to women, men will focus more on training and enhancing their neck muscles. We encourage the interested reader to consult Lewis and Buss (2022) who articulate a number of novel hypotheses, including ones that posit sex differences in which women, more than men, are predicted to train specific muscle groups. These hypotheses do not just postulate intuitive or obvious overall sex differences in weight training; instead, they articulate specific predictions about male-biased and female-biased sex differences in behaviors to enhance specific muscle groups. Such specificity could give us a more nuanced understanding of the psychology of weight-based training, a domain of behavior that historically has been regarded as being a predominantly male enterprise but that needs to be investigated in a more fine-grained manner to detect interesting sex-differentiated patterns that are masked by the current focus on overall sex differences in weight training.

CUES IN WOMEN'S BODIES

Waist-to-Hip Ratio

The best evidence available at the time of writing suggests that the ratio of a woman's waist circumference to hip circumference (waist-to-hip ratio, or WHR) is a reliable cue to parity (see Bovet, 2019, for review; see also Lassek & Gaulin, 2006). Parity would have been fitness-relevant for several reasons. First, a woman's residual reproductive potential decreases with increased parity. Second, evidence suggests that increased parity is inversely related to the quality of future offspring, including their neural development (see Lassek & Gaulin, 2008; see also Lewis et al., in press, for review). If WHR is a reliable cue to a woman's parity, we should expect selection to have shaped men's attractiveness-assessment mechanisms to attend to this feature of women's bodies.

Evidence from numerous studies employing diverse methods and samples—from archival data and ancient artwork to 3D body scans and brain activity, and from Bakossiland to New Zealand—suggests that men's judgments of women's attractiveness are indeed influenced by women's WHR (see Lewis et al., in press, for review). The existence of a male preference for women with a WHR that is low relative to the local population distribution (Sugiyama, 2004; see also Sugiyama, 2015, for discussion) could motivate women to engage in behaviors that manipulate perceptions of their WHR. Behaviors consistent with this proposal include the historical use of corsets, bustles, and girdles, the contemporary use of lingerie and waist trainers (see Faries, 2015), and possibly the strategic adoption of specific poses, such as contrapposto, which may result in lower perceived WHR and greater attractiveness (see Pazhoohi et al., 2020).

Women's Lumbar Region

Women's lumbar curvature is a visible indicator of "wedging" in the vertebrae of the lower back (George et al., 2003). Wedged vertebrae refer to vertebrae that do not have parallel superior (top) and inferior (bottom) surfaces, result in a more acute angle of spinal curvature, and, crucially, helped ancestral women solve the adaptive problem of a forward-shifting center of mass during pregnancy (see Whitcome et al., 2007). Ancestral women who were unable to shift their center of mass back over the hips during pregnancy would have been subjected to an approximately eightfold increase in torque on the hips (Whitcome et al., 2007). This would have increased their likelihood of suffering a debilitating back injury and impaired their foraging capacity, thereby increasing the risk of malnutrition for them, their offspring, and other family members. Conversely, ancestral women with a beneficial degree of vertebral wedging would have been less likely to suffer these fitness-related costs. More specifically, a combination of medical orthopedic and biological anthropological literature suggests that women with a lumbar curvature angle of approximately 45.5° would have been best positioned to avoid these fitness threats (see Lewis et al., 2015). Consequently, men who were attracted to this lumbar curvature would have preferentially selected mates who were less likely to suffer debilitating back injury during pregnancy, more capable of sustaining multiple pregnancies, and able to forage longer into pregnancy, providing crucial calories for the family's metabolic budget. As a result, we would expect selection to have shaped psychological mechanisms in men to attend to women's lumbar curvature and to produce attractiveness judgments partly as a function of how much the angle of lumbar curvature deviates from this hypothesized biomechanical optimum. Consistent with this hypothesis, men's attraction to women peaks as women's lumbar curvature approaches this angle (Lewis et al., 2015; see also Semchenko et al., in press; Lewis, Russell, et al., 2017). In turn, the existence of this male mate preference may motivate women to engage in behaviors to strategically manipulate perceptions of their angle of lumbar curvature. In the modern courtship environment, this may be reflected in the use of high-heeled footwear, which has been shown to increase women's attractiveness precisely when it shifts their lumbar curvature closer to the proposed biomechanical optimum (see Lewis, Russell, et al., 2017).

There is also preliminary evidence suggesting that women might manipulate their angle of lumbar curvature through *lordosis behavior*. Lordosis behavior refers to the contraction of spinal muscles that results in the arching of the lower back. In other taxa, lordosis behavior is a demonstrated cue to sexual proceptivity (behaviors displayed by females to evoke male interest; see Semchenko et al., in press, for discussion). Among humans, research suggests that women believe that lordosis behavior influences male mating interest, especially in short-term mating contexts (Lewis et al., 2022). This view among women appears to be corroborated by men's mating psychology: lordosis behavior has stronger positive effects on men's perceptions of women's attractiveness as short-term mates than as long-term mates (Semchenko et al., in press; see also Goetz et al., 2012; Lewis et al., 2012 for context-dependent influences of visual cues to sexual availability). Further research is needed on men's preferences for the static cue of lumbar curvature and the dynamic cue of lordosis behavior, and on female behaviors that strategically manipulate these cues as part of intersexual courtship. The need for more research is especially pronounced for lordosis behavior, which some literature contends was lost long ago in humans' distant mammalian past (e.g., Wunsch, 2017), but which appears in vernacular dance in cultures across the globe (e.g., Kwassa Kwassa in Zimbabwe, Köçek in Turkey, 'ōte'a in Tahiti; see Semchenko et al., in press). The precise meanings and possible communicative functions of human lordosis behavior, in particular in the context of intersexual courtship, remain to be resolved by future work.

Auditory Courtship

The content of speech and the properties of sound are remarkably diverse in range, from the more than 150,000 words in the English language (Miller, 1995) to the 49 notes on a 24-fret guitar. An individual can make statements of love and affection or display their musical talents, mellifluous voice, sharp wit, or linguistic flair. Here, we separate auditory courtship strategies into two categories: auditory courtship concerned with content (e.g., verbal expressions of affection) and auditory courtship concerned with the acoustic properties of sound (e.g., deep voices and vocal inflection).

We consider written content to fall within the domain of auditory courtship. Although writing could be argued to fall outside this domain, written language is simply the recent (and extremely recent, at that: 70% of men in 17th-century England were unable to write their own names; Cressy, 1977) communication medium through which our evolved psychological mechanisms can transmit the content they evolved to communicate via spoken auditory courtship.

Communication of Content

From ambition and affection to income and education, humans use the power of the word to make statements of their qualities and court prospective mates.

STATUS

Across cultures, women value ambition, industriousness, and good earning capacity in a mate more than men do (Buss, 1989). This female preference for men's social standing and resource-provisioning potential (Buss, 1989) appears to motivate men to advertise and emphasize these attributes (e.g., status and education) in courtship interactions, which, in the modern world, can occur online and in speed-dating contexts (see Lee et al., 2019; Murphy et al., 2015; Sritharan et al., 2010). In speed-dating contexts, mentioning income and advanced education appear to be male courtship tactics (see Asendorpf et al., 2011), and men emphasize their social status in their online dating profiles (Lee et al., 2019; see also Murphy et al., 2015). Evidence suggests that these behaviors are linked to greater courtship success: women are more attracted to speed-dates who mention their high levels of education and income (Asendorpf et al., 2011) and are more likely to click on the online dating profiles of men who highlight their income and education (Ong, 2016).

AFFECTION

Communicating affection during courtship may serve as a cue that the speaker has the warmth, commitment, and positive emotion necessary to be a loving mate and parent (Floyd, 2006). Affectionate communication maintains intimate-partner (Floyd, 2006) and parent–infant pair-bonds (Hertenstein et al., 2006) and contributes to offspring reproductive success (Floyd, 2006).

Given these benefits associated with having a romantic partner who verbally communicates affection, it is reasonable to expect humans to have psychological machinery that generates attraction to such individuals. Although men have been traditionally thought to prefer affectionate tendencies in women more than women prefer these tendencies in men (Smith et al., 2012), both men and women across cultures strongly value kindness and warmth in a prospective mate (see Li et al., 2002, 2011), and recent speed-dating research has shown that women have even stronger preferences for warmth and trustworthiness in men than men do for such characteristics in women (Valentine et al., 2020). Consistent with this stronger female preference for affectionate communication, evidence suggests that men express more affection toward women (i.e., more other-focused questions and more appreciation comments) than women do toward men in modern speed-dating contexts (Ranganath et al., 2009). Future research is needed to more clearly determine whether this sex difference persists, disappears, or reverses at later stages in the formation and maintenance of mating relationships, and what factors may drive these possible changes.

INTELLIGENCE

Some researchers have hypothesized that humor is a signal of intelligence (Tornquist & Chiappe, 2020). Existing evidence suggests that humor *production* is indicative of verbal intelligence, vocabulary knowledge, fluid intelligence, broad retrieval ability, divergent thinking fluency, and crystallized intelligence (see Christensen et al., 2018). Similarly, humor *comprehension* is related to verbal and nonverbal intelligence (Willinger et al., 2017).

If humor production and comprehension reliably signal one's intellectual faculties, selection should have shaped mate assessment mechanisms to attend to humor production and comprehension in potential mates. Consistent with this hypothesis, both men and women prefer their partners to have a sense of humor (Li et al., 2002), with women specifically preferring humor-*producing* men, and men specifically preferring humor-*appreciating* women (Hone et al., 2015). Although future research is needed to better understand this sex difference, humor production and appreciation appear to demonstrate mental faculties that increase the romantic desirability of men and women (Tornquist & Chiappe, 2015). Future research should discriminatively test the hypothesis that humor production is a strategy for signaling intelligence against competing alternatives, such as the hypothesis that the primary function of humor production is to signal romantic interest (Tornquist & Chiappe, 2020). Future research should also more rigorously test the hypotheses that philosophizing, writing poetry, and artfully telling stories are strategies for displaying intelligence (see Miller, 2000). Finally, stronger empirical investigations need to be directed toward another hypothesized strategy for displaying intelligence: the production of music (see Miller, 2000), which may communicate information both through content and the property of sound.

Communication of Information Through Properties of Sound

Humans showcase their underlying qualities not only by communicating content but through their vocal properties as well. Human vocal properties communicate information about an individual's formidability and health.

PHYSICAL DOMINANCE

Human vocal properties can convey physical dominance and strength. Men's longer vocal folds and descended larynx produce deep, resonant vocalizations that serve as honest indicators of physical formidability (e.g., strength and fighting ability; Sell et al., 2010; see also Aung et al., 2021). Men appear to have psychological adaptations to use deep male vocalizations to produce intimidation in same-sex rivals (Sell et al., 2010), and women are attracted to these vocal properties (see Hodges-Simeon et al., 2010). This female mate preference may drive males to strategically alter their voices in mating contexts. Consistent with this proposal, Pisanski et al. (2018) found that speed-dating men lowered their voice pitch toward women they perceived to be desirable mates.

An alternative hypothesis is that deeper pitches serve as a cue to health. However, there is minimal evidence to support the link between masculine vocalizations and health status in men (see Arnocky et al., 2018). Arnocky et al. (2018) found no association between testosterone and men's masculinized vocalizations and small and inconsistent effects between men's masculinized vocalizations and immune function (measured using immunoglobulin-A concentration). If deep vocal pitches were an honest signal of men's health, then this would have driven the evolution of female tendencies to gauge men's health status from their voice. However, women do not accurately track men's self-reported health from their voice (but they do rate men's masculinized vocalizations as healthier; Albert et al., 2021). Future research using more comprehensive measures of health is needed to draw definitive conclusions about the health hypothesis.

Tactile Courtship

Touch is a crucial component of courtship, plays a major role in theories of intimacy and arousal, and serves as one of the strongest signals of emotional connection between two individuals (Gallace & Spence, 2010; Hertenstein et al., 2006). There are at least two important, overlapping functions of touch in romantic contexts. The first is the consolidation of pair-bonds. Romantic touch strengthens pair-bonds through increased oxytocin output (see Gallace & Spence, 2010). Oxytocin helps couples form lasting romantic bonds, with sexual contact being the most powerful means to induce oxytocin, followed by nonsexual physical affection (e.g., back-rubbing and hugs; see Gallace & Spence, 2010). The second, related function of touch-based romantic behaviors is to demonstrate affection, commitment, and positive emotion, which are valued components of a loving mate and parent (Floyd, 2006; Hertenstein et al. 2006; see also Caton & Horan, 2019, 2021).

Evidence suggests that men and women use touch as a strategy for courting and retaining mates, although Willis and Briggs (1992) found that the frequency with which touch is deployed varies as a function of the interaction between relationship stage and sex. In their public observations of 227 dating/engaged couples, they found that men used romantic touch more during the initial courtship stages of a relationship, but that this sex difference shifts as couples venture deeper into their relationship: women engage in romantic touch more than men in the later, noncourtship stages, such as marriage (Willis & Briggs, 1992). These findings highlight that both men and women use touch in courtship and mating but also underscore the need for more research—and theory—to identify when and why men and women use (or cease to use) touch as a courtship strategy.

Recent research has made important contributions to documenting patterns of affective touch across cultures. In their study of 14,478 individuals from 45 countries, Sorokowska et al. (2021) found that individuals use affective touch most toward romantic partners, followed by one's children, female friends, and, finally, male friends. Sorokowska et al. (2021) also found that participants were less likely to affectively touch their partner if they (the participants) had a greater history of suffering from contagious diseases. Drawing on parasite stress theory, the authors suggest that those who have had greater exposure to parasites have formed behavioral defenses designed to mitigate their risk of contagion, resulting in less affective touch toward their partner. Sorokowska et al.'s (2021) research makes important contributions in this largely uncharted area and begins to connect observed patterns of affective touch to theory. Future research would do well to continue to ask theoretically grounded questions about affective touch in the context of human courtship, including questions about temporal change and individual differences in affective touch.

Olfactory Courtship

Olfactory courtship is another emerging area of human courtship research. Humans use odor-based cues as both an indicator of health and personality in the courtship arena.

Odors as a Cue to Health

Evidence suggests that odor-based cues are a reliable indicator of bacterial load, and that humans have evolved to detect, process, and respond to these cues in prospective mates (Ferdenzi et al., 2020). A person's odor can cue their physiological health (Ferdenzi et al., 2020), as foul odor can indicate pathogen presence and disease (Olsson et al., 2014). Humans have cognitive mechanisms that respond to these odor-based cues to bacterial load (Olsson et al., 2014), and both men and women judge body odor as one of the most important components of attractiveness (Herz & Inzlicht, 2002). Olsson et al. (2014) found that men and women who were injected with an endotoxin, a component of the exterior cell wall of gram-negative bacteria, were rated as more unpleasant and unhealthier. Given the important role that body odor plays in assessments of attractiveness, we should expect people to engage in behaviors to conceal unpleasant odor-based cues. In modern environments, antiperspirants and deodorants are used to prevent or mask body odors resulting from bacteria breaking down chemical compounds on the skin (Shelley et al., 1953).

Human olfactory mechanisms were shaped to detect not only current bacterial load but also bacterial resistance, with odor cues serving as reliable indicators of ability to withstand future microbial invasions. Pleasant body odors have been hypothesized to be proxies of immune system functioning (see Ferdenzi et al., 2020). Consistent with this, people find odors linked to superior immune functioning more attractive (Rikowski & Grammer, 1999). Olsson et al. (2014) directly measured individuals' immune system strength and found that individuals with stronger immune systems are better able to guard against future bacterial invasions (measured by immune activation in response to an endotoxin injection), and these people's odors are perceived as healthier and more attractive.

Odors as a Cue to Psychological and Behavioral Variables

Odor cues have been most often studied as an indicator of health, but recent research has revealed a connection between odor and personality and emotionality (Sorokowska et al., 2012). Fear and anxiety are underpinned by the activation of the stress response system, which releases adrenaline and, in turn, activates apocrine sweat glands (Sorokowska et al., 2012). Sorokowska et al. (2016) asked participants to wear armpit cotton pads for 12 hours, and found that the odors of neurotic participants were rated as less neurotic and more pleasant when these participants were allowed (vs. not allowed) to wear scented cosmetics during this timeframe. Sorokowska et al. (2016) suggested that people can use these scented cosmetics to cover cues to undesirable personality traits such as high neuroticism and, in turn, manipulate their perceived attractiveness.

Body odor is also linked to men's masculinity and trait-level dominance (Sorokowska et al., 2012; Sorokowska et al., 2016). Dominance and masculinity are related to elevated androstadienone (a testosterone derivative) levels, a chemical compound to which human olfaction has been hypothesized to attend (for a detailed discussion, see Ferdenzi et al., 2020). Women's psychological mechanisms appear to produce an attraction to men's androstadienone-based odors (Saxton et al., 2008). Allen et al. (2016) asked male participants to wear armpit cotton pads for 24 hours, but asked one group of male participants to apply their own usual deodorant prior to the application of the armpit cotton pads (the "fragranced" condition) and asked another group to apply the armpit cotton pads without any deodorant (the "nonfragranced" condition). Women judged men with highly rated facial masculinity to have more masculine body odors, but only in the *nonfragranced* condition (Allen et al., 2016). When men applied their own usual deodorant, the discrepancy between odor ratings in men with high and low facial masculinity disappeared (Allen et al., 2016). Allen et al. (2016) suggested that men who already have desirable levels of masculinity may not derive much benefit from fragranced products, but men low in masculinity/dominance may be able to apply scented products to elevate perceptions of their masculinity/dominance and, in turn, their attractiveness.

Gustatory Courtship

Gustation may play an important role in human intersexual courtship, but it is one of the most unexplored perceptual modalities in research on human courtship and social psychology more broadly. Despite the paucity of research, there are theoretical and empirical reasons to believe that gustation is central to courtship behaviors such as mouth-to-mouth kissing and food provisioning.

Mouth-to-Mouth Romantic Kissing

Researchers have argued that mouth-to-mouth romantic kissing is a strategy used to (a) enhance pair bonds (Floyd, 2006) or (b) assess physiological health through olfactory cues (e.g., genetic MHC-based compatibility, general health, genetic fitness; see Wlodarski & Dunbar, 2013). However, there are shortcomings to these hypotheses. For the enhanced pair-bonding hypothesis, it is not clear why selection would favor mouth-to-mouth romantic kissing when tactile courtship (e.g., hugging) is a very effective means to enhance the pair-bond (see Gallace & Spence, 2010) and has often already occurred in earlier stages of interaction (Morris, 1971). For the hypothesis that kissing is used to assess health through olfactory cues, it is not clear why such a mechanism would evolve when it is unlikely to provide an additional advantage over existing mechanisms for olfactory assessment (see Wlodarski & Dunbar, 2013).

Here, we present an alternative possibility: that mouth-to-mouth romantic kissing evolved to gustatorily appraise a prospective mate's health status, in particular through the assessment of sebum, a bacteria-resistant compound (Smith & Thiboutot, 2007). This novel hypothesis awaits direct tests in future research, but several known features of sebum, gustation, and kissing are consistent with it. First, the antibacterial chemical compounds in sebum can be detected and assessed via taste (Wille & Kydonieus, 2003) but cannot be easily detected through other perceptual modalities; because sebum has no smell, it cannot be detected via olfaction (see Stoddart, 1990). Consequently, gustation may be the only means by which to reliably assess an individual's sebum composition and quality. Second, *mouth-to-mouth* kissing, as opposed to other forms of kissing—is best suited for assessing sebum; sebum is secreted via the sebaceous glands, which are most prominently aggregated inside the mouth and on the lips' borders (Montagna & Parakkal, 1974). Third, mouth-to-mouth kissing not only makes it possible to assess sebum but also appears to facilitate sebum production: sebum is hydrophilic (and therefore activated by kissing) as well as heat-activated (and therefore triggered by arousal; see Montagna & Parakkal, 1974). Fourth, sebum secretion increases precisely when mating effort is thought to increase and reach its peak: during adolescence and early adulthood (Montagna & Parakkal, 1974). Finally, mouth-to-mouth kissing is ubiquitous across cultures and time periods: it has been documented in 90% of known cultures (see Wlodarski & Dunbar, 2013), appears in humanity's earliest historical sources (e.g., Hindu Veda Sanskrit texts; see Wlodarski & Dunbar, 2013), and is observed in other branches of our recent phylogenetic lineage as well (e.g., bonobos and orangutans; de Waal, 2000). Collectively, these considerations suggest that the *sebum detection hypothesis* may be a plausible account of one reason why humans kiss. Nonetheless, as discussed in the section "Future Directions," this and other novel explanations for mouth-to-mouth kissing behavior await empirical testing.

Courtship Feeding

Malnutrition was a severe adaptive problem throughout our species' evolutionary history (Lukas & Campbell, 2000). To solve this adaptive problem, natural selection crafted adaptations for courtship feeding across a variety of taxa, from arthropods and birds to nonhuman primates (for a brief review, see Alley et al., 2013). Courtship feeding in humans is a relatively new area of investigation, but research so far has shown that human courtship feeding is an indicator of prosociality, provisioning ability, and romantic interest (Alley et al., 2013). In addition to reducing the likelihood of malnutrition, food sharing allows the provider to demonstrate their capacity for affection and commitment (components of mate value; Caton & Horan, 2019, 2021) and showcase their theory of mind (Hamburg et al., 2014). Consistent with the notion that food sharing is a courtship tactic, it appears to be associated with higher mating success (Alley et al., 2013). Recent analyses of outcomes from 792 dinner dates from the restaurant-based TV reality show "First Dates" found that couples who shared food were highly likely to agree to a second date: 93% of couples who shared food agreed to go on a second date, compared to 43% of couples who did not share food (Hendrie & Shirley, 2019). Given the nonexperimental nature of these findings, the direction of the causal arrow between food sharing and mating interest cannot be determined. However, regardless of whether food sharing leads to mating interest or mating interest leads to food sharing—or both—these findings suggest that food and gustation have an important but currently understudied place in human intersexual courtship.

Future Directions

While independent programs of research have laid the foundation for an understanding of human courtship, a great deal of further work is needed.

Visual Courtship

A substantial proportion of the evolutionary psychological literature on physical attractiveness has focused on men's facial masculinity. Surprisingly, few studies have focused on specific facial structures (e.g., jaw, chin, or browridge; Caton et al., 2022; see also Mogilski & Welling, 2018). This is a key future direction, as it is these specific structures that are the targets of natural and sexual selection (Caton et al., 2022). Existing research has devoted much attention to facial width-to-height ratio (fWHR). We have not discussed this ratio because its purported effects have often failed to replicate (Kosinski, 2017; but see Caton et al., *in* press), and because multivariate craniofacial morphology might be of greater theoretical relevance than this overall ratio (Caton et al., *in* press; Caton et al., 2022). We encourage future research on craniofacial morphology to deploy geometric morphometric analyses (e.g., for a detailed introduction, see Adams & Otárola-Castillo, 2013). Without these geometric analyses, and without a focus on specific features rather than overall ratios, researchers may continue to produce ratio-based studies that yield nonsignificant results and lead to the erroneous conclusion that facial features are irrelevant to human mating and courtship.

Auditory Courtship

An important limitation of existing auditory courtship research is its reliance on written communication (e.g., writing a hypothetical dating profile message; Murphy et al., 2015). Research focusing on spoken courtship (e.g., word-based linguistic analyses; Ranganath et al., 2009) is relatively sparse. Future research would benefit from directly examining *how* and *what* individuals verbally communicate during real-world courtship. For example, Ranganath et al. (2009) performed linguistic analyses on speed-dating participants and found that targets who were interested in a prospective mate asked more other-focused questions, and made more appreciation comments to their speed-dating partner. Their process involved microphone-recording speed-dating participants and analyzing their verbal expressions using the "Linguistic Inquiry and Word Count" (LIWC) software (Pennebaker et al., 2015). Future auditory research may profit from such software. Specifically, research can use these tools to examine whether certain fitness-relevant variables (e.g., physical formidability and sociosexuality) predict the use of specific verbal categories in real-world dating (e.g., explicit expressions of romantic and/or sexual interest and declarations of career ambitions), and whether these declarations predict courtship success.

Tactile Courtship

There is limited evolutionary research on courtship-oriented touch. Sorokowska et al.'s (2021) recent cross-cultural examination of affective touch makes several important contributions to our understanding of the use of affective touch, including similarities and differences between and within cultures. Future research could profitably explore precisely what information is communicated (or perceived to be communicated) by the distinct forms of affective touch studied by Sorokowska and colleagues (e.g., hugging vs. kissing vs. stroking), and how this depends on the context in which the touch occurs. Additionally, the *location* where one individual touches another almost certainly (a) influences the perceived meaning of that touch behavior and (b) interacts with the *timing* of that touch (e.g., before vs. after mutual expressions of interest) to predict the efficacy of that touch behavior as a courtship tactic. The relationship between these features of touch behavior and courtship success remain to be discovered. More broadly, touch appears to be fundamental to human courtship, but its precise functions—including variation in those functions across individuals, contexts, and cultures, as well as within relationships across time—remain largely uncharted.

Olfactory Courtship

Typically, olfactory courtship research has not directly examined the chemical compounds involved in attraction (e.g., Sorokowska et al., 2012; Sorokowska et al., 2016). For example, some studies have asked participants (targets) to complete a personality questionnaire and then wear cotton armpit pads for several hours (e.g., Sorokowska et al., 2012; Sorokowska et al., 2016). A separate set of participants (perceivers) then rates the attractiveness of targets' odors. The researchers then test for correlations between the targets' self-reported characteristics (e.g., neuroticism) and the perceivers' attractiveness ratings. Although such study designs have generated important new knowledge about the possible role of odor in the context of human mating, they cannot identify the actual chemical mediators of attraction—a key direction for future research. We therefore encourage future research to measure specific compounds and directly test their role in the psychology of interpersonal attraction (e.g., in speed-dating paradigms; see Ferdenzi et al., 2020).

Gustatory Courtship

Above, we suggested a novel hypothesis about mouth-to-mouth kissing behavior: the *sebum detection hypothesis* proposes that kissing functions to assess a mate's bacterial resistance capabilities by means of inducing the production of sebum and sampling it for antimicrobial chemical compounds. Future work is needed to test this hypothesis and to disentangle it from other new and untested hypotheses about the function of mouth-to-mouth kissing behavior. In testing and disentangling these hypotheses, it will be important for researchers to keep in mind both by-product hypotheses and adaptation hypotheses, including competing adaptation hypotheses (Al-Shawaf et al., 2020; Lewis, Al-Shawaf, et al., 2017).

To test the sebum detection hypothesis, future research should directly assess the chemical composition of individuals' sebum and test how the concentrations of specific antimicrobial compounds (e.g., lauric acid) predict increases or decreases in attraction and mating interest subsequent to the kissing behavior. It may be useful for researchers to measure not just sebum composition but also sebum volume, as both composition and volume appear to independently contribute to sebum's protective effects (see Wille & Kydonieus, 2003).

An alternative to the sebum detection hypothesis is that mouth-to-mouth kissing functions to gustatorily appraise an individual's overall health status but not sebum quality specifically. This could occur through assessment of the other person's oral microbiota; even if the presence of oral bacteria can be detected via olfaction, selection can shape psychological systems to attend to multiple cues to the same underlying information when the integration of these redundant cues increases inferential accuracy (see Johnstone, 1996). Another alternative is that mouth-to-mouth kissing is a costly signal of romantic interest; by engaging in this behavior, individuals can show a mutual willingness to incur the costs of exposing themselves to the pathogens that the other individual may be carrying (Goetz, 2012). We eagerly await future research that discriminatively tests these hypotheses about this important and near-universal courtship behavior.

Charting the Uncharted

In the arena of modern courtship, humans engage in a diverse array of behaviors ranging from serenades to seductive touches and from visual cosmetics (such as makeup and muscle implants) to olfactory cosmetics (such as deodorant). Independent programs of research traversing different perceptual modalities have begun to pave the way toward a more comprehensive understanding of human courtship, but a great deal of further work is needed—on each perceptual modality alone, and on how the human mind integrates cues from different modalities in order to produce an overall assessment. We hope this chapter offers a useful survey of the existing literature and serves as a launching point for new research into the many uncharted areas of human courtship.

References

Adams, D. C., & Otárola-Castillo, E. (2013). Geomorph: An R package for the collection and analysis of geometric morphometric shape data. *Methods in Ecology and Evolution, 4*(4), 393–399. https://doi.org/10.1111/2041-210X.12035

Albert, G., Arnocky, S., Puts, D. A., & Hodges-Simeon, C. R. (2021). Can listeners assess men's self-reported health from their voice? *Evolution and Human Behavior, 42*(2), 91–103. https://doi.org/10.1016/j.evolhumbehav.2020.08.001

Allen, C., Cobey, K. D., Havlíček, J., & Roberts, S. C. (2016). The impact of artificial fragrances on the assessment of mate quality cues in body odor. *Evolution and Human Behavior, 37*(6), 481–489.https://doi.org/10.1016/j.evolhumbehav.2016.05.001

Alley, T. R., Brubaker, L. W., & Fox, O. M. (2013). Courtship feeding in humans? *Human Nature, 24*(4), 430–443. https://doi.org/10.1007/s12110-013-9179-7

Al-Shawaf, L., & Lewis, D. M. G. (2018). The handicap principle. In T. K. Shackelford & V. A. Weekes-Shackelford (Eds.), *Encyclopedia of evolutionary psychological science*. Springer, Cham. https://doi.org/10.1007/978-3-319-16999-6_2100-1

Al-Shawaf, L., Lewis, D. M. G., Barbaro, N., & Wehbe, Y. S. (2020). The products of evolution: Conceptual distinctions, evidentiary criteria, and empirical examples. In T. K. Shackelford (Ed.), *SAGE handbook of evolutionary psychology* (pp. 70–95). SAGE.

Al-Shawaf, L., Lewis, D. M. G., & Buss, D. M. (2018). Sex differences in disgust: Why are women more easily disgusted than men? *Emotion Review, 10*(2), 149–160

Al-Shawaf, L., Lewis, D. M. G., Wehbe, Y. S., & Buss, D. M. (2019). Context, environment, and learning in evolutionary psychology. In T.K. Shackelford and V.A. Weekes-Shackelford (Eds.), *Encyclopedia of evolutionary psychological science*. Springer, Cham.

Arnocky, S., Hodges-Simeon, C. R., Ouellette, D., & Albert, G. (2018). Do men with more masculine voices have better immunocompetence? *Evolution and Human Behavior, 39*(6), 602–610. https://doi.org/10.1016/j.evolhumbehav.2018.06.003

Asendorpf, J. B., Penke, L., & Back, M. D. (2011). From dating to mating and relating: Predictors of initial and long-term outcomes of speed-dating in a community sample. *European Journal of Personality, 25*(1), 16–30. https://doi.org/10.1002/per.768

Aung, T., Goetz, S., Adams, J., McKenna, C., Hess, C., Roytman, S., Cheng, J. T., Zilioli, S., & Puts, D. (2021). Low fundamental and formant frequencies predict fighting ability among male mixed martial arts fighters. *Scientific Reports, 11*(1), 1–10. https://doi.org/10.1038/s41598-020-79408-6

Bauer, J. A., Thomas, T. S., Cauraugh, J. H., Kaminski, T. W., & Hass, C. J. (2001). Impact forces and neck muscle activity in heading by collegiate female soccer players. *Journal of Sports Sciences, 19*(3), 171–179. https://doi.org/10.1080/026404101750095312

Bordo, S. (2000). *The male body: A new look at men in public and in private*. Macmillan.

Borras-Guevara, M. L., Batres, C., & Perrett, D. I. (2017). Aggressor or protector? Experiences and perceptions of violence predict preferences for masculinity. *Evolution and Human Behavior, 38*(4), 481–489. https://doi.org/10.1098/rspb.2009.2184

Bovet, J. (2018). The evolution of feminine beauty. In Z. Kapoula, E. Volle, J. Renoult, & M. Andreatta (Eds.), *Exploring transdisciplinarity in art and sciences* (pp. 327–357). Springer. https://doi.org/10.1007/978-3-319-76054-4_17

Bovet, J. (2019). Evolutionary theories and men's preferences for women's waist-to-hip ratio: Which hypotheses remain? A systematic review. *Frontiers in Psychology*, *10*, Article 1221. https://doi.org/10.3389/fpsyg.2019.01221

Brenner, M., & Hearing, V. J. (2008). The protective role of melanin against UV damage in human skin. *Photochemistry and Photobiology*, *84*(3), 539–549. https://doi.org/10.1111/j.1751-1097.2007.00226.x

Broglio, S. P., Schnebel, B., Sosnoff, J. J., Shin, S., Feng, X., He, X., & Zimmerman, J. (2010). The biomechanical properties of concussions in high school football. *Medicine and Science in Sports and Exercise*, *42*(11), 2064–2071. https://doi.org/10.1249/MSS.0b013e3181dd9156

Buss, D. M. (1989). Sex differences in human mate preferences: Evolutionary hypotheses tested in 37 cultures. *Behavioral and Brain Sciences*, *12*(1), 1–14. https://doi.org/10.1017/S0140525X00023992

Carrier, D. R, & Morgan, M. H. (2014). Protective buttressing of the hominin face. *Biological Reviews of the Cambridge Philosophical Society*, *90*(1), 330–346. https://doi.org/10.1111/brv.12112

Caton, N. R., Hannan, J., & Dixson, B. J. (in press). Facial width-to-height ratio predicts fighting success: A direct replication and extension of Zilioli et al. (2014). *Aggressive Behavior*. https://doi.org/10.1002/ab.22027

Caton, N. R., & Horan, S. M. (2019). Deceptive affectionate messages: Mate retention deployed under the threat of partner infidelity. *Evolutionary Psychology*, *17*(3), Article 1474704919867902. https://doi.org/10.1177/1474704919867902

Caton, N. R., & Horan, S. M. (2021). Deceptive affection is strategically expressed under relational threat—but not towards partners with low mate value. https://doi.org/10.31234/osf.io/8wm9j

Caton, N. R., & Lewis, D. M. G. (2021a). Intrasexual selection for upper limb length in *Homo sapiens*. https://doi.org/10.31234/osf.io/fw6s9

Caton, N. R., & Lewis, D. M. G. (2021b). Intersexual and intrasexual selection for neck musculature in men: Attractiveness, dominance, and actual fighting success. https://doi.org/10.31234/osf.io/yez3t

Chew, B. P., & Soon Park, J. (2004). Carotenoid action on the immune response. *The Journal of Nutrition*, *134*(1), 257S–261S. https://doi.org/10.1093/jn/134.1.257S

Christensen, A. P., Silvia, P. J., Nusbaum, E. C., & Beaty, R. E. (2018). Clever people: Intelligence and humor production ability. *Psychology of Aesthetics, Creativity, and the Arts*, *12*(2), 136. https://doi.org/10.1037/aca0000109

Chung, V. Q., Gordon, J. S., Veledar, E., & Chen, S. C. (2010). Hot or not—Evaluating the effect of artificial tanning on the public's perception of attractiveness. *Dermatologic Surgery*, *36*(11), 1651–1655. https://doi.org/10.1111/j.1524-4725.2010.01713.x

Collins, C. L., Fletcher, E. N., Fields, S. K., Kluchurosky, L., Rohrkemper, M. K., Comstock, R. D., & Cantu, R. C. (2014). Neck strength: A protective factor reducing risk for concussion in high school sports. *The Journal of Primary Prevention*, *35*(5), 309–319. https://doi.org/10.1007/s10935-014-0355-2

Cressy, D. (1977). Levels of illiteracy in England, 1530-1730. *The Historical Journal*, *20*(1), 1–23.

Darwin, C. (1871). *The descent of man, and selection in relation to sex*. Murray.

Das, A., Yoon, S., Lee, S., Kim, J., Oh, D., & Kim, S. (2007). An update on microbial carotenoid production: Application of recent metabolic engineering tools. *Applied Microbiology and Biotechnology*, *77*(3), 505–512.

De Waal, F. B. (2000). Primates—A natural heritage of conflict resolution. *Science*, *289*(5479), 586–590. https://doi.org/10.1126/science.289.5479.586

DeBruine, L. M. (2014). Women's preferences for male facial features. In V. A. Weekes-Shackelford & T. K. Shackelford (Eds.), *Evolutionary psychology. Evolutionary perspectives on human sexual psychology and behavior* (pp. 261–275). Springer Science + Business Media. https://doi.org/10.1007/978-1-4939-0314-6_14

DeBruine, L. M., Jones, B. C., Crawford, J. R., Welling, L. L., & Little, A. C. (2010). The health of a nation predicts their mate preferences: Cross-cultural variation in women's preferences for masculinized male faces. *Proceedings of the Royal Society B: Biological Sciences*, *277*(1692), 2405–2410. https://doi.org/10.1098/rspb.2009.2184

Dixson, B. J., Sherlock, J. M., Cornwell, W. K., & Kasumovic, M. M. (2018). Contest competition and men's facial hair: Beards may not provide advantages in combat. *Evolution and Human Behavior*, *39*(2), 147–153. https://doi.org/10.1016/j.evolhumbehav.2017.11.004

Faries, M. D. (2015). Waist training: Squeezing out the truth. *Fitness Pudding*. https://www.fitnesspudding.com/entry/2-products/54-waist-training-squeezing-out-the-truth

Ferdenzi, C., Richard Ortegón, S., Delplanque, S., Baldovini, N., & Bensafi, M. (2020). Interdisciplinary challenges for elucidating human olfactory attractiveness. *Philosophical Transactions of the Royal Society B*, *375*(1800), Article 20190268. https://doi.org/10.1098/rstb.2019.0268

Fink, B., Grammer, K., & Thornhill, R. (2001). Human (Homo sapiens) facial attractiveness in relation to skin texture and color. *Journal of Comparative Psychology*, *115*(1), 92–99. http://doi.org/10.1037/0735-7036.115.1.92

Fink, B., & Matts, P. J. (2008). The effects of skin colour distribution and topography cues on the perception of female facial age and health. *Journal of the European Academy of Dermatology and Venereology*, *22*(4), 493–498. https://doi.org/10.1111/j.1468-3083.2007.02512.x

Floyd, K. (2006). *Communicating affection: Interpersonal behavior and social context*. Cambridge University Press.

Foo, Y. Z., Nakagawa, S., Rhodes, G., & Simmons, L. W. (2017). The effects of sex hormones on immune function: A meta-analysis. *Biological Reviews*, *92*(1), 551–571. https://doi.org/10.1111/brv.12243

Foo, Y. Z., Rhodes, G., & Simmons, L. W. (2017). The carotenoid beta-carotene enhances facial color, attractiveness and perceived health, but not actual health, in humans. *Behavioral Ecology*, *28*(2), 570–578. https://doi.org/10.1093/beheco/arw188

Foo, Y. Z., Simmons, L. W., Perrett, D. I., Holt, P. G., Eastwood, P. R., & Rhodes, G. (2020). Immune function during early adolescence positively predicts adult facial sexual dimorphism in both men and women. *Evolution and Human Behavior*, *41*(3), 199–209. https://doi.org/10.1016/j.evolhumbehav.2020.02.002

Gallace, A., & Spence, C. (2010). The science of interpersonal touch: An overview. *Neuroscience & Biobehavioral Reviews*, *34*(2), 246–259. https://doi.org/10.1016/j.neubiorev.2008.10.004

Gallagher, V., Kramer, N., Abbott, K., Alexander, J., Breiter, H., Herrold, A., Lindley, T., Mjaanes, J., & Reilly, J. (2018). The effects of sex differences and hormonal contraception on outcomes after collegiate sports-related concussion. *Journal of Neurotrauma*, *35*(11), 1242–1247. https://doi.org/10.1089/neu.2017.5453

George, S. Z., Hicks, G. E., Nevitt, M. A., Cauley, J. A., & Vogt, M. T. (2003). The relationship between lumbar lordosis and radiologic variables and lumbar lordosis and clinical variables in elderly, African-American women. *Journal of Spinal Disorders and Techniques*, *16*, 200–206.

Goetz, A. T. (2012, June). *Sexual conflict within mateships: Kissing as an honest signal and a commitment assessment mechanism* [Paper presentation]. 24th annual meeting of the Human Behavior and Evolution Society, Albuquerque, NM.

Goetz, C. D., Easton, J. A., Lewis, D. M. G., & Buss, D. M. (2012). Sexual exploitability: Observable cues and their link to sexual attraction. *Evolution & Human Behavior*, *33*, 417–426.

Greaves, M. (2014). Was skin cancer a selective force for black pigmentation in early hominin evolution? *Proceedings of the Royal Society. B, Biological Sciences*, *281*(1781), 1–10. https://doi.org/10.1098/rspb.2013.2955

Hamburg, M. E., Finkenauer, C., & Schuengel, C. (2014). Food for love: The role of food offering in empathic emotion regulation. *Frontiers in Psychology*, *5*, 1–9. https://doi.org/10.3389/fpsyg.2014.00032

Hendrie, C., & Shirley, I. (2019). Courtship-feeding in the "First Dates" restaurant is highly predictive of a second date. *Appetite*, *141*, Article 104329. https://doi.org/10.1016/j.appet.2019.104329

Hertenstein, M. J., Verkamp, J. M., Kerestes, A. M., & Holmes, R. M. (2006). The communicative functions of touch in humans, nonhuman primates, and rats: A review and synthesis of the empirical research. *Genetic, Social, and General Psychology Monographs*, *132*(1), 5–94. https://doi.org/10.3200/MONO.132.1.5-94

Herz, R. S., & Inzlicht, M. (2002). Sex differences in response to physical and social factors involved in human mate selection: The importance of smell for women. *Evolution and Human Behavior*, *23*(5), 359–364. https://doi.org/10.1016/S1090-5138(02)00095-8

Hodges-Simeon, C. R., Gaulin, S. J., & Puts, D. A. (2010). Different vocal parameters predict perceptions of dominance and attractiveness. *Human Nature*, *21*(4), 406–427. https://doi.org/ 10.1007/s12110-010-9101-5

Hone, L. S., Hurwitz, W., & Lieberman, D. (2015). Sex differences in preferences for humor: A replication, modification, and extension. *Evolutionary Psychology*, *13*(1), Article 147470491501300110.https://doi.org/10.1177/147470491501300110

Illyés, A., & Kiss, R. M. (2007). Electromyographic analysis in patients with multidirectional shoulder instability during pull, forward punch, elevation and overhead throw. *Knee Surgery, Sports Traumatology, Arthroscopy*, *15*(5), 624–631. https://doi.org/10.1007/s00167-006-0163-1

Jacob, C. I., Dover, J. S., & Kaminer, M. S. (2001). Acne scarring: A classification system and review of treatment options. *Journal of the American Academy of Dermatology, 45*(1), 109–117. https://doi.org/10.1067/mjd.2001.113451

Johnstone, R.A. (1996). Multiple displays in animal communication: "Backup signals" and "multiple messages." *Philosophical Transactions of the Royal Society B: Biological Sciences, 351*, 329–338.

Jonason, P. K. (2007). An evolutionary psychology perspective on sex differences in exercise behaviors and motivations. *The Journal of Social Psychology, 147*(1), 5–14. https://doi.org/10.3200/SOCP.147.1.5-14

Kosinski, M. (2017). Facial width-to-height ratio does not predict self-reported behavioral tendencies. *Psychological Science, 28*(11), 1675–1682. https://doi.org/ 10.1177/0956797617716929

Lakaye, B., Coumans, B., Harray, S., & Grisar, T. (2009). Melanin-concentrating hormone and immune function. *Peptides, 30*(11), 2076–2080. https://doi.org/10.1016/j.peptides.2009.05.004

Lassek, W. D., & Gaulin, S. J. C. (2006). Changes in body fat distribution in relation to parity in American women: A covert form of maternal depletion. *American Journal of Physical Anthropology, 131*(2), 295–302.

Lassek, W. D., & Gaulin, S. J. (2008). Waist-hip ratio and cognitive ability: Is gluteofemoral fat a privileged store of neurodevelopmental resources? *Evolution and Human Behavior, 29*(1), 26–34. https://doi.org/10.1016/j.evolhumbehav.2007.07.005

Law Smith, M. J., Perrett, D. I., Jones, B. C., Cornwell, R. E., Moore, F. R., Feinberg, D. R., Boothroyd, L. G., Durrani, S. J., Stirrat, M. R., Whiten, S., Pitman, R. M., & Hillier, S. G. (2006). Facial appearance is a cue to oestrogen levels in women. *Proceedings of the Royal Society B: Biological Sciences, 273*(1583), 135–140. https://doi.org/10.1098/rspb.2005.3296

Lee, A. J., Jones, B. C., & DeBruine, L. M. (2019). Investigating the association between mating-relevant self-concepts and mate preferences through a data-driven analysis of online personal descriptions. *Evolution and Human Behavior, 40*(3), 325–335. https://doi.org/10.1016/j.evolhumbehav.2019.01.005

Lewis, D. M. G., Al-Shawaf, L., Conroy-Beam, D., Asao, K., & Buss, D. M. (2017). Evolutionary psychology: A how-to guide. *American Psychologist, 72*(4), 353.

Lewis, D. M. G., & Buss, D. M. (2022). Appearance enhancement: A cue-based approach. *Archives of Sexual Behavior, 51*(1), 73–77. https://doi.org/10.1007/s10508-021-01957-2

Lewis, D. M. G., Easton, J. A., Goetz, C. D., & Buss, D. M. (2012). Exploitative male mating strategies: Personality, mating orientation, and relationship status. *Personality and Individual Differences, 52*, 139–143.

Lewis, D. M. G., Evans, K. C., & Al-Shawaf, L. (in press). The logic of physical attractiveness: What people find attractive, when, and why. In D. M. Buss (Ed.), *Handbook of human mating*. Oxford University Press.

Lewis, D. M. G., Russell, E. M., Al-Shawaf, L., & Buss, D. M. (2015). Lumbar curvature: A previously undiscovered standard of attractiveness. *Evolution and Human Behavior, 36*(5), 345–350.https://doi.org/10.1016/j.evolhumbehav.2015.01.007

Lewis, D. M. G., Russell, E. M., Al-Shawaf, L., Ta, V., Senveli, Z., Ickes, W., & Buss, D. M. (2017). Why women wear high heels: Evolution, lumbar curvature, and attractiveness. *Frontiers in Psychology, 8*, 1875. https://doi.org/10.3389/fpsyg.2017.01875

Li, N. P., Bailey, J. M., Kenrick, D. T., & Linsenmeier, J. A. W. (2002). The necessities and luxuries of mate preferences: Testing the tradeoffs. *Journal of Personality and Social Psychology, 82*(6), 947–955. https://doi.org/10.1037/0022-3514.82.6.947

Li, N. P., Valentine, K. A., & Patel, L. (2011). Mate preferences in the U.S. and Singapore: A cross-cultural test of the mate preference priority model. *Personality and Individual Differences, 50*, 291–294.

Little, A. C., Connely, J., Feinberg, D. R., Jones, B. C., & Roberts, S. C. (2011). Human preference for masculinity differs according to context in faces, bodies, voices, and smell. *Behavioral Ecology, 22*(4), 862–868. https://doi.org/10.1093/beheco/arr061

Little, A. C., Jones, B. C., & DeBruine, L. M. (2011). Facial attractiveness: Evolutionary based research. *Philosophical Transactions of the Royal Society B: Biological Sciences, 366*(1571), 1638–1659. https://doi.org/10.1098/rstb.2010.0404

Lukas, W. D., & Campbell, B. C. (2000). Evolutionary and ecological aspects of early brain malnutrition in humans. *Human Nature, 11*(1), 1–26. https://doi.org/10.1007/s12110-000-1000-8

Marcinkowska, U. M., Rantala, M. J., Lee, A. J., Kozlov, M. V., Aavik, T., Cai, H., Contreras-Garduño, J., David, O. A., Kaminski, G., Li, N. P., Onyishi, I. E., Prasai, K., Pazhoohi, F., Prokop, P., Rosales Cardozo, S. L., Sydney, N., Taniguichi, H., Krams, I., & Dixson, B. J. (2019). Women's preferences for men's facial masculinity are strongest under favorable ecological conditions. *Scientific Reports, 9*(1), 1–10. https://doi.org/10.1038/s41598-019-39350-8

Miller, G. (2000). *The mating mind: How sexual choice shaped the evolution of human nature.* Doubleday.

Miller, G. A. (1995). WordNet: A lexical database for English. *Communications of the ACM, 38*(11), 39–41. https://doi.org/10.1145/219717.219748

Miller, G. F. & Todd, P. M. (1998) Mate choice turns cognitive. *Trends in Cognitive Sciences, 2,* 190–198.

Mogilski, J. K., & Welling, L. L. M. (2018). The relative contribution of jawbone and cheekbone prominence, eyebrow thickness, eye size, and face length to evaluations of facial masculinity and attractiveness: A conjoint data-driven approach. *Frontiers in Psychology, 9,* Article 2428.

Montagna, W., & Parakkal, P. F. (1974). *The structure and function of skin.* Academic Press.

Morris, D. (1971). *Intimate behaviour.* Random House.

Murphy, S. C., von Hippel, W., Dubbs, S. L., Angilletta Jr, M. J., Wilson, R. S., Trivers, R., & Barlow, F. K. (2015). The role of overconfidence in romantic desirability and competition. *Personality and Social Psychology Bulletin, 41*(8), 1036–1052. https://doi.org/10.1177/0146167215588754

Olsson, M. J., Lundström, J. N., Kimball, B. A., Gordon, A. R., Karshikoff, B., Hosseini, N., Sorionen, K., Höglund, C. O., Soop, A., Axelsson, J., & Lekander, M. (2014). The scent of disease: Human body odor contains an early chemosensory cue of sickness. *Psychological Science, 25*(3), 817–823. https://doi.org/10.1177/0956797613515681

Ong, D. (2016). Education and income attraction: An online dating field experiment. *Applied Economics, 48*(19), 1816–1830. https://doi.org/10.1080/00036846.2015.1109039

Pazhoohi, F., Macedo, A. F., Doyle, J. F., & Arantes, J. (2020). Waist-to-hip ratio as supernormal stimuli: Effect of contrapposto pose and viewing angle. *Archives of Sexual Behavior, 49,* 837–847.

Pennebaker, J. W., Booth, R. J., Boyd, R. L., & Francis, M. E. (2015). *Linguistic Inquiry and Word Count: LIWC2015.* Pennebaker Conglomerates. Retrieved from https://www.LIWC.net

Phalane, K. G., Tribe, C., Steel, H. C., Cholo, M. C., & Coetzee, V. (2017). Facial appearance reveals immunity in African men. *Scientific Reports, 7*(1), 1–9. https://doi.org/10.1038/s41598-017-08015-9

Pisanski, K., Oleszkiewicz, A., Plachetka, J., Gmiterek, M., & Reby, D. (2018). Voice pitch modulation in human mate choice. *Proceedings of the Royal Society B, 285*(1893), Article 20181634. https://doi.org/10.1098/rspb.2018.1634

Ranganath, R., Jurafsky, D., & McFarland, D. (2009, August 6–7). It's not you, it's me: Detecting flirting and its misperception in speed-dates. Proceedings of the 2009 Conference on Empirical Methods in Natural Language Processing (pp. 334–342). Association for Computational Linguistics and Asian Federation of Natural Language Processing, Singapore. https://www.aclweb.org/anthology/D09-1035.pdf

Re, D. E., Whitehead, R. D., Xiao, D., & Perrett, D. I. (2011). Oxygenated-blood colour change thresholds for perceived facial redness, health, and attractiveness. *PLoS ONE, 6*(3), Article e17859. https://doi.org/10.1371/journal.pone.0017859

Rhodes, G., Chan, J., Zebrowitz, L. A. & Simmons, L. W. (2003). Does sexual dimorphism in human faces signal health? *Proceedings of the Royal Society. B, Biological Sciences, 270*(Suppl.1), S93–S95. https://doi.org/10.1098/rsbl.2003.0023

Rikowski, A., & Grammer, K. (1999). Human body odour, symmetry and attractiveness. *Proceedings of the Royal Society of London. Series B: Biological Sciences, 266*(1422), 869–874. https://doi.org/10.1098/rspb.1999.0717

Rozell, C. (2009). *Face time: The art of makeup* [Unpublished undergraduate thesis]. Retrieved from https://dspace.sunyconnect.suny.edu/bitstream/handle/1951/45359/rozell_cortney_2009_may.pdf?sequence=1

Saxton, T. K., Lyndon, A., Little, A. C., & Roberts, S. C. (2008). Evidence that androstadienone, a putative human chemosignal, modulates women's attributions of men's attractiveness. *Hormones and Behavior, 54*(5), 597–601. https://doi.org/10.1016/j.yhbeh.2008.06.001

Sell, A., Bryant, G. A., Cosmides, L., Tooby, J., Sznycer, D., Von Rueden, C., Krauss, A., & Gurven, M. (2010). Adaptations in humans for assessing physical strength from the voice. *Proceedings of the Royal Society B: Biological Sciences, 277*(1699), 3509–3518. https://doi.org/ 10.1098/rspb.2010.0769

Sell, A., Hone, L. S. E. & Pound, N. (2012). The importance of physical strength to human males. *Human Nature, 23,* 30–44. https://doi.org/10.1007/s12110-012-9131-2

Sell, A., Lukazsweski, A. W., & Townsley, M. (2017). Cues of upper body strength account for most of the variance in men's bodily attractiveness. *Proceedings of the Royal Society B: Biological Sciences, 284*(1869), Article 20171819. https://doi.org/10.1098/rspb.2017.1819" https://doi.org/10.1098/rspb.2017.1819

Semchenko, A. Y., Senveli, Z., Forrest, M. R. L., Flores, J., Fiala, V., Al-Shawaf, L., Buss, D. M., & Lewis, D. M. G. (in press). Lordosis in humans. *Personality and Social Psychology Bulletin.*

Shelley, W. B., Hurley, H. J., & Nichols, A. C. (1953). Axillary odor: Experimental study of the role of bacteria, apocrine sweat, and deodorants. *AMA Archives of Dermatology and Syphilology*, *68*(4), 430–446. https://doi.org/10.1001/archderm.1953.01540100070012

Smith, K. R., & Thiboutot, D. M. (2007). Thematic review series: Skin lipids. Sebaceous gland lipids: Friend or foe? *Journal of Lipid Research*, *49*(2), 271–281. https://doi.org/10.1159/000069757

Smith, M. J. L., Deady, D. K., Moore, F. R., Jones, B. C., Cornwell, R. E., Stirrat, M., Lawson, J. F., Feinberg, D. R., & Perrett, D. I. (2012). Maternal tendencies in women are associated with estrogen levels and facial femininity. *Hormones and Behavior*, *61*(1), 12–16. https://doi.org/ 10.1016/j.yhbeh.2011.09.005

Sorokowska, A., Saluja, S., Sorokowski, P., Frąckowiak, T., Karwowski, M., Aavik, T., Akello, G., Alm, C., Amjad, N., Anjum, A., Asao, K., Atama, C. S., Duyar, D. A., Ayebare, R., Batres, C., Bendixen, M., Bensafia, A., Bizumic, B., Boussena, M., . . . & Croy, I. (2021). Affective interpersonal touch in close relationships: A cross-cultural perspective. *Personality and Social Psychology Bulletin*, *47*(12), 1705–1721. https://doi.org/10.1177/0146167220988373

Sorokowska, A., Sorokowski, P., & Havlíček, J. (2016). Body odor based personality judgments: The effect of fragranced cosmetics. *Frontiers in Psychology*, *7*, Article 530. https://doi.org/10.3389/fpsyg.2016.00530

Sorokowska, A., Sorokowski, P., & Szmajke, A. (2012). Does personality smell? Accuracy of personality assessments based on body odour. *European Journal of Personality*, *26*(5), 496–503. https://doi.org/10.1002/per.848

Sritharan, R., Heilpern, K., Wilbur, C. J., & Gawronski, B. (2010). I think I like you: Spontaneous and deliberate evaluations of potential romantic partners in an online dating context. *European Journal of Social Psychology*, *40*(6), 1062–1077. https://doi.org/10.1002/ejsp.703

Stewart, S. (2017). *Painted faces: A colourful history of cosmetics*. Amberley.

Stoddart, D. M. (1990). *The scented ape: The biology and culture of human odour*. Cambridge University Press.

Sugiyama, L. S. (2004). Is beauty in the context-sensitive adaptations of the beholder? Shiwiar use of waist-to-hip ratio in assessments of female mate value. *Evolution and Human Behavior*, *25*(1), 51–62.

Sugiyama, L. S. (2015). Physical attractiveness: An adaptationist perspective. In D. M. Buss (Ed.), *The handbook of evolutionary psychology* (2nd ed., pp. 317–384). John Wiley& Sons.

Toews, D. P. L., Hofmeister, N. R., & Taylor, S. A. (2017). The evolution and genetics of carotenoid processing in animals. *Trends in Genetics*, *33*(3), 171–182. https://doi.org/10.1016/j.tig.2017.01.002

Tooke, W., & Camire, L. (1991). Patterns of deception in intersexual and intrasexual mating strategies. *Ethology and Sociobiology*, *12*(5), 345–364. https://doi.org/10.1016/0162-3095(91)90030-T

Tornquist, M., & Chiappe, D. (2015). Effects of humor production, humor receptivity, and physical attractiveness on partner desirability. *Evolutionary Psychology*, *13*(4), Article 1474704915608744.

Tornquist, M., & Chiappe, D. (2020). The role of humour production and humour receptivity in perceived romantic interest. *Psychology & Sexuality*, *11*(3), 212–224. https://doi.org/10.1080/19419899.2019.1668464

Valentine, K. A., Li, N. P., Meltzer, A. L., & Tsai, M. H. (2020). Mate preferences for warmth-trustworthiness predict romantic attraction in the early stages of mate selection and satisfaction in ongoing relationships. *Personality and Social Psychology Bulletin*, *46*(2), 298–311. https://doi.org/10.1177/0146167219855048

Wertz, P. W. (2009). Human synthetic sebum formulation and stability under conditions of use and storage. *International Journal of Cosmetic Science*, *31*(1), 21–25. https://doi.org/10.1111/j.1468-2494.2008.00468.x

West, K. (2009). *Animal courtship*. Infobase.

Whitcome, K. K., Shapiro, L. J., & Lieberman, D. E. (2007). Fetal load and the evolution of lumbar lordosis in bipedal hominins. *Nature*, *450*, 1075–1078.

Wille, J. J., & Kydonieus, A. (2003). Palmitoleic acid isomer (C16: 1Δ6) in human skin sebum is effective against gram-positive bacteria. *Skin Pharmacology and Physiology*, *16*(3), 176–187. https://doi.org/10.1159/000069757

Willinger, U., Hergovich, A., Schmoeger, M., Deckert, M., Stoettner, S., Bunda, I., Witting, A., Seidley, M., Moser, R., Kacena, S., Jaeckle, D., Loader, B., Mueller, C., & Auff, E. (2017). Cognitive and emotional demands of black humour processing: The role of intelligence, aggressiveness and mood. *Cognitive Processing*, *18*(2), 159–167. https://doi.org/10.1007/s10339-016-0789

Willis, F. N., & Briggs, L. F. (1992). Relationship and touch in public settings. *Journal of Nonverbal Behavior*, *16*(1), 55–63. https://doi.org/10.1007/BF00986879

Wlodarski, R., & Dunbar, R. I. (2013). Examining the possible functions of kissing in romantic relationships. *Archives of Sexual Behavior, 42*(8), 1415–1423. https://link.springer.com/article/10.1007/s10508-013-0190-1

Wunsch, S. (2017). Phylogenesis of mammal sexuality. Analysis of the evolution of proximal factors. *Sexologies, 26*(1), e1–e10.

CHAPTER

7

Intrasexual Mating Competition

Jaimie Arona Krems, Hannah K. Bradshaw, *and* Laureon A. Merrie

Abstract

In the mating domain, same-sex conspecifics can be competitors when pursuing, attracting, and retaining desirable partners. We provide (a) an overview of the major metatheories (e.g., obligate parental investment and biological markets) that bear on intrasexual competition for mates; (b) explore support for predictions derived from these metatheories in empirical research on females' and males' intrasexual mating competition; and also discuss (c) robust evidence consistent with the core premise of intrasexual mating competition—that members of each sex compete with rivals to gain and retain access to mates, and that this competition centers on features that the other sex finds particularly desirable. Moreover, the tactics of this competition often differ in revealing ways. Whereas examples in both human and nonhuman animals are considered, the current work focuses on the causes, consequences, and modes of intrasexual mating competition among heterosexual men and women, but we nevertheless conclude by highlighting important qualifiers and limitations in existing work with an eye toward future research (e.g., on women, non-heterosexual relationships, and parents) that challenges our current conceptualizations of the boundaries of intrasexual mating competition.

Key Words: intrasexual competition, mating competition, direct aggression, indirect aggression

The season of love is that of battle.
—Charles Darwin (1871, p. 48)

The mating domain contains many recurrent challenges, including competing with same-sex conspecifics to attract, secure, and maintain mating partners. For instance, consider the popular television shows *The Bachelor* and *The Bachelorette*. Each season features a group of young, single, and typically child-free women or men competing for one desirable other-sex partner. Although exaggerated and sensationalized for prime-time television, the content of these series provides a contemporary illustration of an important evolutionary phenomenon: intrasexual competition for mates.

There is a long and rich history of theorizing and empirical work on intrasexual mating competition in the evolutionary social sciences. Originally described by Charles Darwin in the late 19th century, intrasexual mating competition refers to the idea that members of one sex compete among themselves to gain access to desirable members of the other sex, with successful outcomes bolstering one's own fitness (Darwin, 1871). Although intrasexual competition was historically thought to be a male-specific or male-typical phenomenon, across species, females also compete for access to desirable mates (for review, see Benenson, 2013; Clutton-Brock, 2007; Vaillancourt, 2013). To explore existing work on both men's and women's intrasexual mating competition, this chapter first reviews and discusses predictions drawn from several metatheories that bear on the frequency, ferocity, and forms of intrasexual mating competition. In assessing those predictions, we illustrate prominent features of intrasexual mating competition, drawing on evidence from nonhuman animals, anthropological research from non-Western and small-scale societies, and other work on human psychology and behavior. We also note historical and more recent trends in this work, closing the chapter with qualifications about existing research and pointing out opportunities for future work that may challenge the current boundaries and traditional conceptualizations of intrasexual mating competition.

Evolutionary Metatheories and Related Predictions About Intrasexual Mating Competition

Men and women compete for desirable mates, with success in this intrasexual mating competition positively related to fitness. To understand why men and women compete in the ways that they do, we first consider several evolutionary metatheories that have helped direct research in this vein. Obligate parental investment, sexual strategies theory, and biological markets and their socioecological features all bear on the frequency and fierceness of intrasexual mating competition.

Obligate Parental Investment

Which sex is expected to exhibit more and perhaps fiercer intrasexual competition for mates? Parental investment theory (PIT; Trivers, 1972) suggests that the sex obligated to invest a greater minimum amount of resources (e.g., time and energy) in offspring will be more discriminating in choosing mates, and that the sex obligated to invest less will be more competitive in seeking mates. This asymmetry in minimum obligatory parental investment imposes a reproductive ceiling (i.e., the maximum number of possible lifetime offspring) on the greater-investing sex (typically females), and also implies greater reproductive variance (i.e., difference among individuals in the number of actual offspring) for the lesser-investing sex (typically males). Such asymmetry influences the costs and benefits of intrasexual competition. Moreover, as the reproductive success of the lesser-investing sex (typically males) is limited by the ability to gain access to other-sex mates, members of the lesser-investing sex (typically males) are expected to compete more frequently and ferociously among themselves to secure mating opportunities. Although recent theorizing challenges and updates this work (e.g., Kokko & Jennions, 2003, 2008), anisogamy-premised theorizing has nonetheless shaped the history of research on intrasexual mating competition.

Moreover, predictions regarding how this asymmetry in obligate parental investment bears on human cognition and behavior—including cognition and behavior surrounding intrasexual mating competition—have found robust support. In many species, including humans, females are obligated to invest more in offspring, from the level of the gamete (i.e., females' larger and finite eggs versus males' smaller and more numerous sperm) and beyond (i.e., pregnancy and lactation) (Butte & King, 2005; Melzer et al., 2010). Consistent with this, we see more frequent and often more fierce male–male mating competition across many species. For example, male chimpanzees exhibit high levels of intrasexual mating competition, whereas such competition among females is rarer (Muller, 2002; Sobolewski et al., 2013). Similar patterns can be seen in wolf packs (Derix et al., 1993). But perhaps the most compelling evidence for this PIT-derived prediction comes from species in which males invest heavily in offspring. In the avian Wattled Jacana, for example, males invest heavily in offspring care, and females exhibit more intrasexual competition for mates (Emlen & Wrege, 2004). Likewise, in the Mormon cricket, females compete more frequently and fiercely to access males and their nutrient-rich spermatophores (Gwynne, 1993; Trivers, 1985).

Although men exhibit high parental care compared to some other species, women are obligated to invest more in offspring than are men. In accordance with predictions derived from PIT, research in small-scale societies suggests that, compared to women, men have more combative interactions with same-sex others when competing for the same female partner (Chagnon, 1988; Flinn, 1988). A similar pattern emerges in industrialized nations: male–male homicides are drastically more frequent than other patterns (Daly & Wilson, 1988, 1990), and the theme of sexual rivalry is pervasive in these male–male homicides (Daly & Wilson, 1988; Wilson & Daly, 1998). Compared to women, men might also engage in more showy displays to attract other-sex attention—via physical risks, conspicuous consumption, or creation of cultural products (Andersson, 1994; Kruger, 2004; Miller, 2000; Ronay & von Hippel, 2010; Sundie et al., 2011). Consistent with predictions derived from PIT, men do seem to compete frequently and fiercely over female mates.

Given women's comparatively greater obligate investment, at first glance, it seems that PIT might predict that women would exhibit relatively low levels of intrasexual competition for mates. Indeed, historically, some viewed women as merely passively choosing male mates based on the outcomes of male–male competition (Darwin, 1871; for a review, see Milam, 2010). But male sexual drives do not imply female sexual passivity (Clutton-Brock & Huchard, 2013; Gowaty, 1997; Hrdy, 1981). We turn to another metatheory—sexual strategies theory (SST; Buss & Schmidt, 1993; see also Symons, 1979)—to help elucidate some of the further theoretical underpinnings that led researchers to expect female–female mating competition.

Sexual Strategies Theory

SST incorporates the foundational implications of PIT (Trivers, 1972) and greater male variance in reproductive success (Bateman, 1948; but see Gowaty et al., 2012). SST views human mating on a continuum from short term (e.g., one-off copulations) to long term (e.g., marriage) and details the costs and benefits of engaging in both—with obvious implications for sex similarities and differences in intrasexual mating competition. In doing so, SST points out that human mating strategies and related competition for mates is more complex than mere competing males and choosy females.

Short-term sex typically affords more potential benefits for men (than women) and more potential costs for women (than men). Again, because women's investment in any one offspring is typically higher than men's (Trivers, 1972), and men's reproductive potential is potentially higher but also more variable than women's (Bateman, 1948), men stand to experience greater gains in reproductive fitness via short-term mating. If a man has five short-term sex partners in a day, for example, he stands to potentially gain five offspring; a woman in the same situation can have just one pregnancy. As short-term sex is linked to greater net benefits for men, compared to women, men both exhibit greater desire and more competition for shorter-term sex (Buss & Schmitt, 1993, 2019; Schmitt, 2003, 2005).

Although much nonhuman animal research necessarily focuses on *short-term* mating, men engage in a great deal of parenting effort and can invest heavily in their offspring (Lovejoy, 1981). This parental investment is one notable feature of humans' longer-term mating relationships, which complicates the story of competitive males and choosy females. Indeed, that men and women have comparatively less asymmetry in the costs and benefits of longer-term relationships suggests that there should be intrasexual competition for long-term mates among both sexes. Support for this reasoning abounds. For example, romantic jealousy is part of the suite of psychological mechanisms promoting intrasexual competition to maintain—rather than simply attract—longer-term mates, and both sexes report high levels of jealousy (Buss, 2013; Scelza et al., 2020). Moreover, this is particularly evident in societies with high levels of paternal investment; when high investment is expected from men, men are more concerned with women's sexual infidelity and women are more concerned with the potential diversion of resources to a male's new mate—thus high jealousy (Scelza et al., 2020).

Although women's intrasexual competition has been studied systematically for a shorter time than men's, robust evidence also supports female–female mating competition for prospective mates (e.g., Benenson, 2014; Buss, 1988; Buss & Schmitt, 1993; Campbell, 2002; Krems et al., 2016; Vaillancourt, 2013; Vaillancourt & Krems, 2018).

Biological Markets and Ecological Factors

Whenever people have the ability to choose partners and partner quality varies, we should expect competition for more desirable partners. This competition for the "best" partners occurs in a biological market (e.g., Barclay, 2013, 2016; Noë & Hammerstein, 1994, 1995). In any market, supply and demand affect the value of a good (e.g., a romantic partner), and anything affecting supply and demand can also influence the mating market. This is clear in the case of socioecological factors and their effects on intrasexual mating competition in mating markets.

We noted above how paternal investment influences cross-societal patterns of romantic jealousy. But there are many other socioecological factors that bear on mate supply (e.g., sex ratio), mate demand (e.g., sex ratio and mating systems), mate quality (e.g., income inequality), and so on—thereby affecting intrasexual mating competition. Here, we focus on a few of the better-studied factors and their individual effects on intrasexual mating competition.

SEX RATIO

A prime example of a socioecological variable affecting the mating market and intrasexual competition for mates therein is the operational sex ratio (the number of males per females in the local environment; for review, see Kvarnemo & Ahnesjo, 1996). The operational sex ratio (OSR) specifically refers to the proportion of reproductively viable males to females in a given population (Emlen, 1976).

Evidence found across a wide variety of nonhuman animals supports theorizing about the influence of OSRs on intrasexual mating competition—and particularly the fact that biased sex ratios increase mating competition among the more numerous sex (e.g., Guttentag & Secord, 1983; Weir et al., 2011; for a review, see Maner & Ackerman, 2020). When the OSR is male-biased (i.e., more males than females) and females are scarce, the intensity of competition among males increases; more numerous males compete for mates and/or strive to embody those aspects females find desirable in order to be selected as a mate. This holds for nonhuman animals. In guppies, for example, the number of individual copulations for males decreases in male-biased sex ratios, and therein males interfere with the mating attempts of other males at higher rates (Jirotkul, 1999). Similar results are found in birds; in the Japanese medaka, each sex exhibits more competitive same-sex interactions when the sex ratio is biased against them (Clark & Grant, 2010). Increased competition is also found when the OSR is more female-biased (i.e., more females than males). In female-biased OSRs, females exhibit higher-intensity intrasexual competition than males. For example, although females engage in little overt competition for mating partners across many primate species, female-biased OSRs can cause increases in overt female–female mating competition in chacma baboons (Cheney et al., 2012). This same general pattern is seen among antelopes as well (Milner-Gulland et al., 2003).

In evolutionary social science focused on humans, sex ratio effects are among the best studied in terms of their impact on the mating market and related intrasexual mating competition (e.g., Griskevicius et al., 2012; Guttentag & Secord, 1983; Xing et al., 2016). Experimental research finds that when people are primed with unfavorable (vs. favorable) sex ratios, they become more intrasexually competitive (Arnocky et al., 2014; Griskevicius et al., 2012; Xing et al., 2016) and more aggressive toward desirable same-sex others who may be perceived as especially threatening potential rivals (Moss & Maner, 2016). Other research shows that unfavorable sex ratios can also influence people's economic decisions in ways concordant with the logic of biological markets. For instance, in unfavorable sex ratios, men report spending more on mating-related expenditures in an effort to compete with other men to attract women—buying women larger engagement rings and spending more on Valentine's Day dinners (Griskevicius et al., 2012).

Somewhat similarly, female-biased sex ratios lead women to be more wary of same-sex others (Vukovic et al., 2019) and to increase their desire to maximize their relative gain over same-sex others (Xing et al., 2016), which might be linked to female–female mating competition. Women in female-biased sex ratios also appear to enter the workforce in higher numbers and seek more lucrative careers, perhaps as a means to accrue resources via routes other than male mates (Durante et al., 2012; Guttentag & Secord, 1983). The notion that increased competition for traditionally desirable male mates leads some women to seemingly opt out of mating competition is especially intriguing, and it raises the question of what happens to those women in their romantic lives—do they pair with less traditionally desirable men, engage in single motherhood, remain single and child-free? Future research is needed to answer these and related questions.

MATING SYSTEMS

Another important factor that influences the intensity of intrasexual competition is the mating system. In mammals, the most common mating system is polygyny, where some males mate with multiple female partners (Kleiman, 1977). Given that one male can monopolize several female partners in such a mating system, less capable or desirable males are shut out of the mating market completely. This exacerbates males' reproductive variance and, as such, increases the expected intensity of male intrasexual competition. Supporting this reasoning, ceteris paribus, intrasexual competition occurs more frequently among polygynous male Savannah baboons (Drews, 1996) than among nonpolygynous male bonobos (Vervaecke & Van Elsacker, 2000). However, in polygynous species where males provide parental care, such as in birds, females also compete with same-sex rivals to monopolize the investment of male partners (Slagsvold & Lifjeld, 1994). Notably, females can also engage in amplified intrasexual mating competition when they mate with multiple other-sex partners (e.g., in butterflies; Charlat et al., 2007).

Human cultures and societies also vary in their mating systems, but the majority of societies across history have permitted some degree of polygyny (Murdock, 1967). Some have characterized the mating system in humans as "effective" polygyny (Daly & Wilson, 1983). Consistent with findings in the nonhuman animal literature, more prevalent polygyny is associated with increased intensity of male intrasexual competition both historically (for review, see Henrich et al., 2012) and across nations (Schmitt & Rohde, 2013). Concerning women, much work on intrasexual competition has taken place in Western populations where monogamy is the cultural norm. However, there is also a long history of excellent research on intrasexual mating competition among cowives in polygynous societies, wherein these cowives compete over access to resources from their shared male partner (Gibson & Mace, 2007; Hagen et al., 2001; Jankowiak et al., 2005; Madhavan, 2002; Shostak, 1981). In such contexts, we often see a hierarchy, such that first or senior wives typically have more power. Presumably in efforts to end the diversion of important, reproductively relevant resources to new wives, first or senior wives have been known to make life so miserable for new wives that those new wives leave (Shostak, 1981).

INCOME INEQUALITY

It is important to note that intrasexual competition not only involves direct competition for mates, per se but also competition for resources that influence the likelihood of successfully securing mating opportunities (Rosvall, 2011). In fact, some researchers go as far as to claim that resource competition and mating competition are too closely related to be considered separately (Wacker & Amundsen, 2014). This implies that resource competition may be mating competition—perhaps especially for males—and thus that any factors affecting resource availability and skew might influence mating competition.

Even more than the absolute availability of resources, income inequality—the disparity between the rich and the poor—may be particularly important in influencing the intensity of intrasexual competition. By exacerbating the disparity between the haves and the have-nots, high income inequality can increase reproductive variance and thus intrasexual competition over resources, status, and mating opportunities (Buttrick & Oishi, 2017; Krupp & Cook, 2018). If only a few men can command adequate resources, that should increase both men's intrasexual competition for resources as well as women's intrasexual competition for those resource-rich men.

In North America and across the globe, increased income inequality is associated with more lethal forms of male–male intrasexual competition, such as homicide (Daly et al., 2001; Krems & Varnum, 2017). Moreover, income inequality seems to be the strongest predictor of such homicide rates (Daly, 2010). Other research finds that economic inequality is found to be related to a greater male (vs. female) mortality rate, which might result from more homicides as well as riskier attempts by men to gain status—and thus mating opportunities (Kruger, 2010).

Recent research also suggests that income inequality could amplify women's intrasexual mating competition. For example, in areas with high income inequality, women post sexy selfies at a higher prevalence, presumably a means of competing with other women to entice those fewer male mates at the top of the income ladder (Blake & Brooks, 2019a; Blake, Bastian, et al., 2018). Indeed, we would also expect income inequality might increase some women's engagement in self-beautification practices (e.g., plastic surgery and increased exercise) to attract male mates or perhaps retain those they have. Other women, however, may opt out of this competition, pursuing briefcase over baby (see Durante et al., 2012).

We view income inequality as a primary ecological variable for future exploration in intrasexual mating competition research (see also Blake & Brooks, 2019b). There seem to be ready analogues in anthropological work; for example, some theorize that women would actually be better off as junior wives to very rich men than sole wives to poorer men when disparities in resources are especially great (Bensch & Hasselquist, 1992; Chisholm & Burbank, 1991; Hames, 1996; Orians, 1969), with implications for women's intrasexual mating competition. However, we emphasize the future study of income inequality not merely because studying the effects of income inequality is tractable but because it may have far-reaching and important practical applications, given the rise in income inequality in developed nations and its positive associations to negative outcomes (e.g., male–male violence and women's self-sexualization; Blake, Bastian, et al., 2018a; Daly & Wilson, 1988).

On What Dimensions Do Men and Women Engage in Intrasexual Mating Competition?

When men and women engage intrasexual mating competition, what are they competing over? By identifying men's and women's mate preferences, we can also identify the dimensions over which men and women compete for mates with same-sex others. Intrasexual mating competition often involves individuals competing with same-sex others to embody and/or excel on features desired by other-sex prospective mates. Although much work often—and understandably—focuses on sex differences in intrasexual competition to embody sex-differentiated mate preferences, the highest priorities for both sexes are kindness and intelligence (Buss, 1989). At the same time, there are prominent sex differences in the dimensions over which men and women engage in intrasexual mating competition. These differences can often elucidate the psychology and behavior of intrasexual mating competition.

These are not arbitrary preferences; an evolutionary approach posits that these sex differences in mate preference arise from sex-specific evolutionary pressures (e.g., Buss, 1989; Kenrick & Keefe, 1992; Symons, 1979; Trivers, 1972). Presumably, those males attracted to females displaying cues of fertility enjoyed greater reproductive fitness than those who did not. Men tend to place greater value on partners' reproductive potential and related characteristics than women. Thus, women tend to compete intrasexually over linked dimensions such as youth, physical attractiveness, and sexual fidelity. Similarly, females able to call on a male partner's ample formidability and/or resources were better able to become pregnant, birth children, and help those offspring thrive. As women tend to place greater value than men on a mate's resource provisioning ability, men often compete more than women over resources and status (Buss, 1989; Conroy-Beam & Buss, 2021; Walter et al., 2020).

Men's Preferences and Female–Female Mating Competition

Men's higher valuation of youth and physical attractiveness in mates is thought to arise because these characteristics cue women's reproductive viability (e.g., Kenrick et al., 1995; Rhodes, 2006), whereas men's valuation of women's sexual fidelity, particularly in prospective long-term mates, owes to paternity uncertainty. That is, whereas women can be certain the child they carry is theirs, men cannot; thus, men prize prospective long-term mates' sexual fidelity (though, also see Mogilski et al., 2014). As such, one should expect that women compete along these male-valued dimensions—and specifically over cues linked to fertility and fidelity.

And they do. Concerning physical attractiveness, women often compete via self-enhancement—making themselves more physically attractive than their rivals (e.g., Buss, 1988; Fisher & Cox, 2011; Mafra et al., 2020; Schmitt & Buss, 2001; Varella et al., 2017). Of course, women can engage in beautification for nonmating reasons as well (e.g., Blake et al., 2020). Women might also compete by derogating and/or manipulating their rivals' physical appearances, perhaps causing them to appear less physically attractive and/or sexually desirable to potential mates (Buss & Dedden, 1990; Fisher, 2004; Fisher & Cox, 2009). Some work even suggests that women prefer to take appearance-related advice from gay men (vs. female friends) because gay male friends are less likely to compete with women for access to particular mates—implying that female friends might sometimes give purposefully bad appearance-related advice as a means of mating competition (Russell et al., 2018). Concerning sexual fidelity, women typically compete by denigrating competitors' reputations, thereby making those rivals appear to be less desirable to prospective long-term mates (Buss & Dedden, 1990; Hess, 2006; Hess & Hagen, 2006a, 2006b; Krems, 2016).

Women's Preferences and Male–Male Competition

Women's higher minimum obligate parental investment is thought to be related to their greater valuation of resource provisioning from male mates (e.g., Buss, 1989; Buunk et al., 2002; Minervini & McAndrew, 2006; Li et al., 2002; Trivers, 1972; Walter et al., 2020). Among the Hiwi hunter–gatherers in Venezuela, for example, women's ability to acquire caloric resources drastically diminishes during pregnancy and lactation, even as resource needs increase (Hurtado & Hill, 1990); this increases the importance of securing a mate able and willing to invest resources. Indeed, the presence of a father—and presumably his resources—increases a mother's and her offspring's survivability across modern nations (Mortelmans & Defever, 2018; Radl et al., 2017; Yavorsky et al., 2019; though also see Sear & Mace, 2008).

Notably, however, women cannot always directly assess a prospective male mate's provisioning abilities and willingness. Women often rely on perceptually salient cues that a man is—or stands to be—adept in securing resources. For example, women prize certain traits linked to resource acquisition in prospective mates (e.g., larger size, masculinity, muscularity, and height; Andersson, 1994; Buss, 1989; Frederick & Haselton, 2007; Huntingford & Turner, 1987; Kenrick, 1987; Pawlowski et al., 2000) and are attracted to men whose clothing and job titles indicate high earning power (e.g., income and ambition; Minervini & McAndrew, 2006; Townsend & Levy, 1990a, 1990b). Other work on the indirect benefits women can derive from male mates points to some additional features that women might sometimes desire (e.g., genetic quality cued by low fluctuating asymmetry; Thornhill & Gangestad, 1994).

Just as women engage in intrasexual mating competition over youth, beauty, and fidelity (features prized by men), evidence suggests that men engage in intrasexual mating competition to control resources and gain status (features prized by women). For example, when competing for mates, men report displaying their financial resources (Buss, 1988; Griskevicius et al., 2012; Sundie et al., 2011; Walters & Crawford, 1994). Presumably to attract women, men also spend money on expensive cars and gifts (e.g., diamond rings) that ostensibly signal the resources they are able to "waste" and thus command in excess (e.g., Griskevicius et al., 2012; Sundie et al., 2011; Zahavi & Zahavi, 1999). Men even attempt to signal their physical prowess more in front of female audiences by taking physical risks to display their robustness (e.g., Ronay & von Hippel, 2010). That this status rivalry falls under the umbrella of intrasexual mating competition is suggested by work on men's aggression; when mating motivations are made salient, men (but not women) engaged in increased intrasexual (but not intersexual) aggression (Ainsworth & Maner, 2012). Men also report greater distress when a rival exceeds them on these characteristics (Buss et al., 2000). It should come as no surprise, then, that these same features prized by women are also the focus of men's competitor derogation, which is more likely to focus on rivals' (lack of) financial resources and/or fighting ability (Buss & Dedden, 1990).

Sex Differences in Intrasexual Mating Tactics

It stands to reason that if men and women are competing intrasexually on different dimensions, then men's and women's tactics of intrasexual mating competition might also be different. For example, theorizing informed by behavioral ecology suggests that males engage in contest competition (simultaneous, often face-to-face contests that are typically zero sum) and that females engage in scramble competition (obtaining widely dispersed resources via solitary and perhaps covert means; Benenson & Abadzi, 2020). Along with competing intrasexually on different dimensions (e.g., resource acquisition vs. beauty), these different kinds of competition likewise imply that different tactics of intrasexual competition might be more efficacious for men versus women. Moreover, men and women may experience different benefits and different costs from engaging in the same mode(s) of competition; the impact of physical aggression has been thought more harmful for women's fitness outcomes, for example (e.g., Campbell, 1999). Taken together, this work suggests that men and women might preferentially employ different tactics in the course of intrasexual mating competition.

Overt and Direct Aggression

Looking to the broader literature on sex differences in aggression, evidence suggests that, compared to girls and women, boys and men enact more physical, violent, and face-to-face tactics of intrasexual mating competition (e.g., Archer, 2004; Benenson, 2014; Björkqvist, Lagerspetz, & Kaukiainen, 1992; Campbell, 2002; Vaillancourt, 2013). For example, men engage in more intrasexual homicide than women do, especially in environments characterized by high income inequality (and thus increased mating competition). Lack of resources in such environments particularly limits males' mating competitiveness and is therefore thought to upregulate men's motivations to compete and take risks to gain precious status and therefore more mating opportunities (e.g., Ermer et al., 2008; Daly & Wilson, 1988).

The implications of men's direct aggression on their mating outcomes and even their physiology are rather clear. Anthropological evidence suggests that winning direct physical competition can be efficacious for winning in mating competition. Among the Yanamamo, men who have killed have more wives and children than those who have not (Chagnon, 1988). Indeed, men's physiology seems to reflect such competition (e.g., men's size; Arnocky & Carré, 2016; McElligott et al., 2001). For instance, taller men seem to have greater dating opportunities (Pawlowski, 2003). In all, then, the mating-related benefits of winning physical contests (e.g., resources, women's desire, and deterring other men from competing with them) seem to be comparatively greater for men than women. The zero-sum nature of men's contest competition underscores this, as a man's win is also his rival's loss. By contrast, injury related to physical aggression may be costlier for women (e.g., injury could make a woman unable to care for offspring, causing them to expire; Campbell, 1999, 2002), further facilitating this sex difference in overt and direct intrasexual mating competition.

Covert and Indirect Aggression

Both sexes engage in indirect aggression (e.g., gossip) and social exclusion (Benenson, 2014; Campbell, 1999, 2002; Crick & Grotpeter, 1995; Hess & Hagen, 2006a, 2006b, 2019; Underwood et al., 2001). Some work suggests that these tactics might be ideal tools for harming women, as it hits women where it can hurt the most—their social relationships and reputations (e.g., being deemed sexually unfaithful; Benenson, 2013, 2014). Reputation manipulation might be especially effective for harming female mating rivals because some features that men desire in women—particularly reputations for sexual fidelity—are difficult to assess, easy to impugn, and once denigrated, difficult to defend (Hess & Hagen, 2006a, 2006b). This is in stark contrast to men, as much of what women desire in men can be directly observed and/or objectively measured (e.g., if one man could best another in a fight or income).

The low-cost nature of indirect aggression may also be especially beneficial for female aggressors (Björkqvist et al., 1992; Campbell, 2002). The covert tactics characteristic of indirect aggression can harm victims without those victims ever realizing they have been aggressed against (e.g., via gossip). Thus, victims might be less likely to realize that harm has occurred—although they might still experience the costs—and, even when they do know that, say, a vicious rumor about them is making the rounds, they are less likely to find out where the rumor came from (as compared to where a punch came from); this implies less retaliation against aggressors. Compared to direct tactics of overt aggression, third parties can more easily dispute as to whether indirect, covert tactics were intentionally meant to harm (e.g., did the aggressor really *purposefully* forget to include the victim?). Thus, even when a victim complains of having been harmed, it is more difficult to recruit supporters to engage in third-party punishment of indirect aggressors.

In all, then, indirect, typically covert tactics are less likely to open aggressors up to revenge and third-party retaliation, making them ideal for actors aiming to avoid costly injury (Bjorkqvist, 1994; Krems, 2016; Vaillancourt, 2013). Indeed, female–female aggression is overwhelmingly likely to employ such subtle, covert, and/or behind-the-back tactics (Vaillancourt, 2013). This is not to say that males do not also glean benefits from covertly harming rivals—in fact, some work suggests that indirect tactics might be especially useful when women or men compete with their ingroup members (Hess & Hagen, 2019).

Additionally, whereas much has been made of men's harems—in which polygynous men keep multiple women (e.g., wives and concubines; Betzig, 1986, 2008; Campbell, 2002), sometimes under guard to preclude other reproductively viable men to encounter the women kept therein—evidence also suggests that women work to keep their mating rivals separate from their spouses or objects of desire, although they may do so by subtle means (Hurst et al., 2017; Krems et al., 2016; Vaillancourt & Sharma, 2011; Walters & Crawford, 1994). Social exclusion is one form of intrasexual mating competition (Buss & Shackelford, 1997), and girls and women exclude same-sex others more than men do (Benenson et al., 2009, 2013), with social exclusion potentially achieving separation of romantic partners from prospective rivals, and thus effective protection against rivals.

We also consider the possibility of coalitional *indirect* aggression. Whereas men's direct coalitional aggression is well documented (e.g., Wrangham, 2019), far less work has explored women's coalitional aggression. Hess (2006) intimates that female coalitions might be important in informational warfare, which involves, for example, gathering intelligence about female rivals, disseminating favorable information about oneself and allies and damaging information about rivals, and otherwise acting on this information. The ability to maintain a pristine reputation and also to denigrate rivals' reputations would seem ideal in female intrasexual competition for mates. Additionally, female coalitions (i.e., dyads or larger groups) would seem necessary to achieve social exclusion, a female-typical tactic of intrasexual aggression (Benenson, 2014; Benenson et al., 2013; Sheppard & Aquino, 2017; Williams & Tiedens, 2016).

Despite evidence that both women and men use indirect tactics in intrasexual mating competition (Arnocky & Carré, 2016; Buss & Dedden, 1990; Fisher & Cox, 2011; Schmitt & Buss, 2001), there is less work directly exploring the efficacy of gossip and/or social exclusion. For example, whereas work suggests Yanamamo men with more kills have greater mating success, there is little work showing that women who have ruined more rivals' reputations have greater mating success (though see Fisher & Cox, 2009; Vaillancourt, 2013). Compared to women, men do not seem to prefer mates who outcompete same-sex others in face-to-face contests—with the telling exception of beauty pageants, perhaps. Thus, effectively harming other women is not linked to female reproductive success in the same clear way as is winning physical fights for men.

However, nonhuman animal research suggests that female–female harassment can successfully diminish victims' reproductive capacities (e.g., Clutton-Brock & Huchard, 2013; Hrdy, 1977; Salmon, 2017; for a review, see Stockley & Bro-Jørgensen, 2011). For example, dominant female alpine marmots' harassment of same-sex subordinates increases those subordinates' glucocorticoids and thereby suppresses reproduction (Hackländer et al., 2003). Better understanding this suppression would have clear implications for our knowledge of women's intrasexual mating competition.

Suppressing rivals' reproductive capability—particularly insofar as diminishing perceptually salient cues that then render those women less desirable to men—would seem an important mode of women's mating competition. The extent to which girls and women are able to use reproductive suppression against mating rivals—and even how this works in better-studied species—is poorly understood. However, some research on reproductive suppression among nonhuman primates points out dominant females' ability to disrupt subordinates' mating (see Clutton-Brock & Huchard, 2013), which is a phenomenon that has existing parallels in research on humans. For example, Vaillancourt and Krems (2018) argued that more physically attractive girls become popular and use indirect aggression to maintain their social status. These girls often enjoy more dating opportunities than do lower-status girls (Bower et al., 2015; Lee et al., 2018; Smith et al., 2010; Vaillancourt & Hymel, 2006; Vaillancourt et al., 2003; Vaillancourt & Krems, 2018).

Other work on reproductive suppression in nonhuman animals implies that females might be best served by selectively directing their aggression toward sexually receptive, ovulating same-sex others to disrupt mating more directly. Work on women finds that ovulating women are at higher risk for incurring same-sex aggression (Hurst et al., 2017; Krems et al., 2016). Still other work on reproductive suppression attempts to explore the physiological mechanisms at play. It is unknown whether social stress from regular victimization (Wasser & Barash, 1983), the mere presence of more dominant females (e.g., French, 1997), and/or other factors might effectively suppress women's reproductive capacities, and if so, exactly how this occurs.

Somewhat similarly, the effects of men's intrasexual mating competition on their physiology—most notably with respect to studies of sexual dimorphism and men's body size, muscularity, and strength (e.g., Fessler et al., 2014; Lassek & Gaulin, 2009; Muñoz-Reye et al., 2012; see also Arnocky & Carré, 2016)—is comparatively better studied than are similar effects on women's physiology. One might speculate as to those effects, given the forms that women's aggression often takes (see Geary 2005, 2010). For example, women's aggression toward one another often takes the form of subtle facial expressions (Simmons, 2002; Underwood, 2003), with some suggesting that such nonverbal expressions may have special meanings for girls and women (Brown & Gilligan, 1993; LaFrance, 2002; Underwood, 2004). If this is the case, we might expect that women are especially apt at detecting even subtle negative emotional expressions, presumably to help them detect and avoid incoming aggression (Geary, 2010; Krems et al., 2015). Indeed, they seem to be (e.g., Geary, 2010; Goos & Silverman, 2002). Given other means by which women typically compete with same-sex rivals (e.g., informational warfare and social distancing; Benenson, 2014; Benenson et al., 2009, 2013; Campbell, 2002; Hess & Hagen, 2006b, 2019; Vaillancourt, 2013), we might also expect to find increased competences in other social arenas (e.g., some aspects of memory and sensitivity to impending exclusion).

Qualifications, Limitations, and Future Directions for Intrasexual Mating Competition

Much remains that we do not know about intrasexual mating competition. Here, we discuss some of the limitations of our current knowledge as well as related opportunities for future work. Most notably, whereas research on intrasexual mating competition had once discounted women as active agents competing for mates, more recent work demonstrates that women do actively compete for mates—and for other resources. If only because women's intrasexual mating competition has been systematically studied for less time than has men's, this is one area that might be especially fruitful for future work. We emphasize that here. We also consider which other groups might be less studied in the existing intrasexual mating competition canon, with an eye toward gaps in empirical study that evolutionary social scientists and other scholars will want to address.

Frequent Victims and Defenses against Intrasexual Mating Competition?

Men and women both engage in intrasexual mating competition, with each sex competing over different dimensions and tending to enact different tactics. Taken together, we can use this work to predict which men and women are likely to be most at risk for incurring intrasexual victimization. Given the potentially high costs of direct and indirect victimization (e.g., lethal violence and suicidal ideation) for both sexes (Daly & Wilson, 1988; Vaillancourt, 2013; Wrangham, 1999), this would seem an important undertaking. Additionally, we can use this work to generate novel research questions about the flexibility of men's and women's intrasexual mating competition, cognition, and behavior. We focus here on how this knowledge can guide predictions about how men and women might defend themselves against intrasexual aggression in the course of mating competition.

One sensible hypothesis would be that men and women both aggress disproportionately against those same-sex others who are perceived as especially threatening rivals. If so, women should preferentially engage in intrasexual mating competition against the most physically attractive and/or sexually desirable women in their social groups, whereas men should preferentially direct intrasexual mating competition toward the most formidable and/or wealthy men in their social groups. Krems et al. (2020) reviewed evidence supporting this hypothesis: physically attractive women are considered mating threats and are disproportionately aggressed against (Arnocky et al., 2012; Fink et al., 2014; Leenaars et al., 2008). However, other research suggests that this might not hold for men. That is, although formidable men engage in more physical fights in their lifetimes (Archer & Thanzami, 2007; Sell, 2006, Sell et al., 2009), this seems to be because more formidable men start those fights—engaging in proactive rather than reactive aggression (Archer & Thanzami, 2009). Put plainly, this could suggest that women are aggressed against by other women for simply being (physically attractive), whereas men are aggressed against by other men for acting (e.g., throwing the first punch). However, this is far from settled science and belies gaps in our knowledge of intrasexual mating competition. Perhaps those more formidable men do receive disproportionate amounts of specifically indirect aggression from mating rivals, for example.

This difference may have implications for intrasexual mating competition, including implications for men's and women's defenses against intrasexual aggression. Indeed, intrasexual mating competition is unlikely to be all attack (proactive) and no defense (reactive)—perhaps especially for those individuals more likely to be aggressed against. There are many possible reasons for why the defenses people, and perhaps particularly women, employ in the course of intrasexual mating competition are somewhat less studied. Given the lesser emphasis on female–female mating competition historically, it makes sense that there would be less work on its consequences. But if we consider female-typical indirect aggression between women, we realize that women must confront a difficult challenge: compared to men, women are less likely to show their anger and are more likely to engage in covert aggression against mating rivals, thus women might face greater difficulty detecting and mitigating incoming intrasexual aggression (Krems et al., 2015). Recent research has, however, begun to explore women's strategic defenses against intrasexual aggression, finding that especially those women who are frequent targets of same-sex aggression seem to possess tools for avoiding other women's slings and arrows (Krems et al., 2016; Krems et al., 2015; Krems et al., 2019). Nevertheless, much work remains to be done examining the impact of enacting and navigating indirect aggression in the course of mating competition on the physiology, cognition, and behavior of both sexes.

Further Work on Women's Intrasexual Mating Competition

Here, we also explore in depth one open, prominent direction for future work on women's intrasexual mating competition—status competition—to illustrate the importance of challenging current conceptualizations of what "counts" as intrasexual mating competition within existing mating competition research. Ostensibly, status has direct benefits for both sexes, such that competing with same-sex others for status should increase one's fitness (Alami et al., 2020; Clutton-Brock & Huchard, 2013; Majolo et al., 2012). But whereas most work understandably treats men's intrasexual competition for status as crucial to men's mating success, this does not seem to be the case for women (Buss, 1989; Cassar et al., 2016; Daly & Wilson, 1983; de Waal, 1989). We thus consider whether women's status bolsters (and/or harms) women's mating outcomes by focusing on its effects on attracting men and on competing with intrasexual rivals. (While women's status carries a myriad of benefits that are less obviously related to mating—e.g., Alami et al., 2020; Campbell, 2002; Cassar et al., 2016; Young et al., 2006—it is beyond the scope of the current chapter to discuss these.)

Because women are expected to compete on those dimensions that men find desirable, we first consider whether men's mating preferences imply that women should compete intrasexually for status to attract men. Notably, male status features (e.g., size, muscularity, and wealth) simultaneously help men engage in the intrasexual competition that garners them resources, makes them more attractive to prospective mates, and also aids in precluding further intrasexual attacks. But the confluence between status and mating success for women might not be so apparent, at least on first glance (Buss, 1989; Fisman et al., 2006).

Physical dominance, size, muscularity, and wealth are traditional cues or instantiations of status. These features are unlikely to help women attract men and may even render women less attractive as prospective mates. For example, being too tall can harm women's mating prospects; men typically prefer shorter women, and women typically prefer taller men (Pawlowski, 2003). As such, a taller woman (e.g., 6'4") must compete with shorter women (6'4" and below) for the few men taller than herself (6'4" and up). Similarly, being too intelligent, educated, or high-earning—other markers of what we typically think of as status—might also be considered potentially harmful to women's success in mating competition (Bertrand & Kamenica, 2015; Folke & Rickne, 2016). Although one could look at this as only an intersexual problem, these same preferences notably impact intrasexual mating competition; for example, just as women might compete to attract men by being more attractive than same-sex rivals, women could perhaps compete to attract men by downplaying their ambitions relative to same-sex rivals

(Bursztyn et al., 2017). This is obvious in the persistent anecdote of women "playing dumb" to attract men.

Recent work suggests, however, that this picture may be too simplistic. Rather than men wholly eschewing high-status women, men's preferences might be more nuanced. Whereas men are less attracted to *moderately* physically attractive women with a high-status job, having a high-status job increased men's attraction to *highly* physically attractive women (Fisher & Stinson, 2020). Many questions remain as to whether women's status is detrimental to this first facet of intrasexual mating competition—attracting men—for future research. For example, at what point(s) over the course of a relationship is a woman's status a potential stumbling block; that is, does it deter men from asking her out, from pursuing longer-term relationships, from retaining mates?

To fully explore the role of women's status in intrasexual mating competition, we must also ask whether having status might render women more effective intrasexual competitors. For instance, although women typically eschew physical aggression, perhaps women's size can help them impose physical harm on, or intimidate, other women. Beyond physical formidability, though, what aspects of status might help women against their mating rivals?

If we start to expand the traditional conceptualization of status beyond those male-typical features that first come to mind (e.g., physical size, muscularity, fighting ability, or wealth) and also include female-typical features (e.g., physical beauty, parenting ability, and fertility) associated with status, we might find that women's status can indeed be beneficial in their intrasexual mating competition. Physically attractive girls often garner and maintain high visibility, many friends, and thus high social status (Lee et al., 2018; Vaillancourt & Krems, 2018). Moreover, high social status puts women in social network positions that can be highly advantageous for effectively gathering and disseminating novel social information, which bears on women's abilities to thwart negative gossip about themselves and their reputations while spreading negative gossip about their rivals and those rivals' reputations (e.g., Hess & Hagen, 2006a; Mouttapa et al., 2004). (Another feature that would render women more adept mating competitors is the ability to effectively disseminate negative information about rivals.) Other work also suggests that more physically attractive women might be more effective derogators in intrasexual mating competition (Fisher & Cox, 2009). Indeed, some work does in fact consider women's beauty to be a form of status (e.g., Buss et al., 2020; Krems et al., 2022; Vaillancourt & Krems, 2018), and it has clear positive consequences for women's ability to effectively outcompete same-sex mating rivals (Fisher & Cox, 2009). Likewise, and as we discuss in some detail below, women's parenting abilities may be another form of status that helps women outcompete same-sex mating rivals (Fisher & Moule, 2013). Other work suggests that having had children can increase women's (and men's) status (e.g., Buss et al., 2020).

Work specifically addressing the importance of alloparents (e.g., Hrdy, 1999) could make a case for further broadening not just what we are willing to term "status" but also what we are willing to term "mating competition." Consider a straightforward anecdote: John's mother's friend helps to get him into a good school and helps him secure a high-paying job. Indeed, among humans and nonhuman primates, having a few close female allies is known to benefit one's offspring (Rucas, 2017; Silk et al., 2003; Silk et al., 2006). And whereas women may seem less competitive than men (Campbell, 1999), this does not seem to be the case when women are competing for friends or on behalf of offspring (Cassar et al., 2016; Krems et al., 2021; Krems et al., 2022; Owens et al., 2000; Tooby & Cosmides, 1996). To the extent that mating competition involves not just attracting a desirable mate in one's early adulthood—but also helping one's offspring survive, thrive, and outcompete others for desirable mates—perhaps we should consider women's (and men's) same-sex competition for allies and extended competition on behalf of offspring to be forms of intrasexual mating competition (e.g., Clutton-Brock & Huchard, 2013).

Lesser-Studied Groups

Here, we identify some of the groups lesser-studied within the mating competition literature. We shine a light on what research has been done on such group members and look forward to more work on these groups in the future.

IDENTITY FEATURES (E.G., NON-HETEROSEXUALS)

Research on intrasexual mating competition has been highly informed by sex similarities and differences in what men and women seek in other-sex mates, which itself has been highly informed by biological sex differences (e.g., in obligate parental investment; Trivers, 1972). This is a sensible trajectory for science—to build on strong metatheory and test related predictions. That this has been the trajectory of much work should not be construed as a conscious eschewing of people with transgender, LGBTQ+, and/or other understudied identities. Increasingly, however, people are less likely to be prohibited from expressing these identities; for example, those identifying as LGBT in Gallup polling increased even between 2012 and 2016, going from 3.5% to 4.1% (Gates, 2017; Nolan et al., 2019). As such groups become more visible, they are easier to study, and—visible or not—they are worthy of study.

It is high time for work to explore mating competition among members of such groups. Such work would aid in the discovery of how the mind works (Kenrick et al., 1995). It also has important implications for serving potentially lesser-studied and often lower-power groups. For example, Kenrick et al. (1995) found that homosexual men's age-related mate preferences were similar to heterosexual men's—both sought youth and beauty in prospective mates. This work not only addresses questions about the mind—is mating psychology wholly male- versus female-typical, or perhaps more modular?—but it also lays out important implications for intrasexual mating competition by identifying dimensions over which gay men compete for mates (physical attractiveness; e.g., Li et al., 2010). That is, if youth and beauty are important aspects of gay men's mate preference and mate competition, then we should expect that gay men engage in tactics of mating competition to augment their appearance and denigrate the appearance of rivals. We should also expect that, in contrast to the heterosexual mating market wherein men prefer younger women and women prefer older men, gay men's preferences for younger mates amplify intrasexual mating competition, in part because supply–demand dynamics mean that a large swath of (older) men will not be competitive. This dynamic might also be linked to some significant issues facing gay men (e.g., the loneliness epidemic; Hobbes, 2017), a population already at higher risk for physical and mental health issues (Graham et al., 2011; Pachankis et al., 2015, 2020).

Obviously, then, there has been some evolutionary-minded research on gay men, as well as on lesbians and bisexual individuals and their mating competition (e.g., Bailey, 2009; Bailey et al., 1994; Bailey et al., 1997; Kenrick et al., 1995; Li et al., 2010; Lippa, 2003). More recently, work has begun to explore intrasexual mating competition among transgendered persons as well. When confronted with romantic rivals, transgendered individuals respond in line with their gender identities (rather than biological sexes; Arístegui et al., 2019). Future work in this vein might benefit not only from continuing to study the cognition and behavior of those who are not young, single, cisgender, heterosexuals—but also from paying attention to variation within these understudied groups.

For example, we assert that work on homosexuals should pay greater attention to variation *within* non-heterosexual men and women, rather than simply comparing gay versus straight men. Some work on lesbians differentiates between "butch" (or more masculine) and "femme" (or more feminine) lesbians (e.g., Brown et al., 2002). But there is much more variation in these communities (see Valentova et al., Diamond & Alley, and Redlick, all in this volume), and being cognizant of this could aid in scientific discovery. To illustrate this, consider that, among gay men there is variation in sexual preferences (tops, bottoms, versatiles), gender presentation (e.g., more masculine), and even colloquial subtypes (e.g., twink, bear, jock, lumberjack, and otter). To the extent that gay men of any one subtype have similar mate preferences, a sensible prediction is that gay men might compete more for mates with same-subtype men versus other-subtype men; this remains an open question. We would also suggest that future work on these and other lesser-studied groups not attend to intrasexual competition for mate attraction at the expense of studying intrasexual competition for mate retention in the course of longer-term relationships.

PARENTS AND OLDER ADULTS

Much psychological research on mating competition focuses on mate attraction, and thus typically looks at young, single, and often child-free people. Likewise, the use of convenience samples of university students and online participant-workers cause this research to focus on people in their 20s, 30s, and perhaps 40s. At least in some countries, though, people's longer lives, the frequency of divorce, and even the surprising prevalence of sexually transmitted infections (and thus mating) in eldercare facilities all suggest that mating competition might take place long after one ages out of the typical study population (Centers for Disease Control and Prevention, 2017, 2018). This underscores the need to study intrasexual mating competition throughout the lifespan. Considering intrasexual mating competition and its possibly varied forms among less studied groups might aid in scientific discovery, perhaps in part by forcing scholars to broaden existing conceptualizations of what "counts" as mating competition.

Although an emphasis on parenting might cause a deemphasis on mate attraction or other linked motivations (Beall & Schaller, 2019; Krems et al., 2017; Marlowe, 1999), having children does not necessarily remove one from the mating market. Rather, there seem to be potentially highly nuanced, open questions about the mating market dynamics that parents experience. Parenthood itself can affect parents' own mating competition. For example, what an individual prioritizes in prospective mates can shift, depending on whether they are single and child-free versus a single parent (Gray et al., 2016; Gray, Reece, et al., 2015). Such work suggests that intrasexual mating competition might be largely segregated, with typically same-sex child-free individuals competing with one another and typically same-sex parents competing with one another, respectively.

This, of course, bears on parents' (and single people's) intrasexual competition. One implication is that the relative supply and demand, not just of females and males but perhaps particularly single mothers and fathers, should affect the intensity of intrasexual mating competition. In addition, single mothers of young children might experience especially strong mating market pressures. Given the heightened likelihood of children being abused by stepfathers (Daly & Wilson, 1988), single mothers of young children may be especially careful when choosing prospective mates. In light of other work suggesting that some single people would rather not date single parents (Escasa-Dorne et al., 2017; Goldscheider & Kaufman, 2006), this implies a possibly lower supply of desirable men willing to partner with single mothers, and thus heightened intrasexual mating competition for those men.

Moreover, both sexes might also be able to affect their own and others' (e.g., daughters and daughters-in-law) reproductive fitness—even after they themselves have ceased being reproductively viable (e.g., Dyble et al., 2018; Flinn et al., 2007; Gaulin & Boster, 1990). Indeed, having children can put a parent in the position of wanting to manipulate that market in their offspring's favor, suggesting the need to look beyond direct competition to attract novel mates. As such, intrasexual mating competition between parents might be a fruitful area for future work. Concerning parents' competition on behalf of their children's mating success, evidence suggests that parents' ideological support may be an instance of motivated reasoning, with parents supporting ideas and practices that benefit their offspring. For example, families with single, adult daughters are more likely to support women's reproductive rights, whereas families with more adult men are likely to oppose those rights (Betzig & Lombardo, 1992). Blake, Fourati, and Brooks (2018) somewhat similarly find that mothers with sons (vs. daughters) are more supportive of practices that suppress female sexuality (i.e., Muslim veiling), which might serve to control female sexuality and benefit male offspring. Indeed, that women invest so highly in each offspring suggests that this sort of second-order mating competition between mothers—competition on behalf of offspring—might be more frequent and/or fierce than that between fathers (Fisher & Moule, 2013; Linney et al., 2017).

Parents might also compete with their own same-sex offspring, as well as same-sex affinal kin (e.g., sons- or daughters-in-law; e.g., Dyble et al., 2018; Mace & Alvergne, 2012). For example, in rural Gambia, the presence of older women in a compound may cause younger women to suffer costs in the course of reproductive competition (Mace & Alvergne, 2012), supporting the notion that some intrasexual mating competition takes place within the biological and/or extended family network (e.g., Buunk et al., 2008). This is already recognized in work on cowives (Jankowiak et al., 2005). Thus, this is one arena in which thinking about intrasexual mating competition outside those narrow, traditional bounds—young, child-free single people competing to attract new mates—can lead us to expand our conceptualizations of intrasexual mating competition and perhaps motivate us to attend to understudied phenomena.

Summing up Intrasexual Mating Competition

In sum, there is a long history of theorizing and empirical work on intrasexual mating competition, beginning with Darwin himself and now including an increasing number of young researchers who are currently exploring the effects of intrasexual mating competition on the cognition, physiology, and behavior of lesser studied groups (e.g., women and non-heterosexuals). Even so, there remain updates and challenges to some of our most foundational metatheories (e.g., Kokko & Jennions, 2008; Trivers, 1972). We look forward to the new questions that will be raised and eventually solved in the course of investigating intrasexual mating competition and thereby elucidating how the (mating) mind works.

References

Ainsworth, S. E., & Maner, J. K. (2012). Sex begets violence: Mating motives, social dominance, and physical aggression in men. *Journal of Personality and Social Psychology, 103*(5), 819–829.

Alami, S., Von Rueden, C., Seabright, E., Kraft, T. S., Blackwell, A. D., Stieglitz, J., Kaplan, H., & Gurven, M. (2020). Mother's social status is associated with child health in a horticulturalist population. *Proceedings of the Royal Society B, 287*(1922), Article 20192783.

Andersson, M. (1994). *Sexual selection* (Vol. 72). Princeton University Press.

Archer, J. (2004). Sex differences in aggression in real-world settings: A meta-analytic review. *Review of General Psychology, 8*(4), 291–322.

Archer, J., & Thanzami, V. (2007). The relation between physical aggression, size and strength, among a sample of young Indian men. *Personality and Individual Differences, 43*(3), 627–633.

Archer, J., & Thanzami, V. (2009). The relation between mate value, entitlement, physical aggression, size and strength among a sample of young Indian men. *Evolution and Human Behavior, 30*(5), 315–321.

Arístegui, I., Solano, A. C., & Buunk, A. P. (2019). Do transgender people respond according to their biological sex or their gender identity when confronted with romantic rivals? *Evolutionary Psychology, 17*(2), Article 1474704919851139.

Arnocky, S., & Carré, J. M. (2016). Intrasexual rivalry among women. In T. K. Shackelford & V. A. Weekes-Shackelford (Eds.), *Encyclopedia of evolutionary psychological science* (p. 49). Springer.

Arnocky, S., Ribout, A., Mirza, R. S., & Knack, J. M. (2014). Perceived mate availability influences intrasexual competition, jealousy and mate-guarding behavior. *Journal of Evolutionary Psychology, 12*(1), 45–64.

Arnocky, S., Sunderani, S., Miller, J. L., & Vaillancourt, T. (2012). Jealousy mediates the relationship between attractiveness comparison and females' indirect aggression. *Personal Relationships, 19*(2), 290–303.

Bailey, J. M. (2009). What is sexual orientation and do women have one? In D. A. Hope (Ed.), *Contemporary perspectives on lesbian, gay, and bisexual identities* (pp. 43–63). Springer.

Bailey, J. M., Gaulin, S., Agyei, Y., & Gladue, B. A. (1994). Effects of gender and sexual orientation on evolutionarily relevant aspects of human mating psychology. *Journal of Personality and Social Psychology, 66*(6), 1081.

Bailey, J. M., Kim, P. Y., Hills, A., & Linsenmeier, J. A. (1997). Butch, femme, or straight acting? Partner preferences of gay men and lesbians. *Journal of Personality and Social Psychology, 73*(5), 960.

Barclay, P. (2013). Strategies for cooperation in biological markets, especially for humans. *Evolution and Human Behavior, 34*(3), 164–175.

Barclay, P. (2016). Biological markets and the effects of partner choice on cooperation and friendship. *Current Opinion in Psychology, 7*, 33–38.

Bateman, A. J. (1948). Intra-sexual selection in Drosophila. *Heredity, 2*(3), 349–368.

Beall, A. T., & Schaller, M. (2019). Evolution, motivation, and the mating/parenting trade–off. *Self and Identity, 18*(1), 39–59.

Benenson, J. F. (2013). The development of human female competition: Allies and adversaries. *Philosophical Transactions of the Royal Society B: Biological Sciences, 368*(1631), Article 20130079.

Benenson, J. F. (2014). *Warriors and worriers: The survival of the sexes*. Oxford University Press.

Benenson, J. F., & Abadzi, H. (2020). Contest versus scramble competition: Sex differences in the quest for status. *Current Opinion in Psychology, 33*, 62–68.

Benenson, J. F., Markovits, H., Fitzgerald, C., Geoffroy, D., Flemming, J., Kahlenberg, S. M., & Wrangham, R. W. (2009). Males' greater tolerance of same-sex peers. *Psychological Science, 20*(2), 184–190.

Benenson, J. F., Markovits, H., Hultgren, B., Nguyen, T., Bullock, G., & Wrangham, R. (2013). Social exclusion: More important to human females than males. *PLoS ONE, 8*(2), e55851.

Bensch, S., & Hasselquist, D. (1992). Evidence for active female choice in a polygynous warbler. *Animal Behaviour, 44*, 301–311.

Betzig, L. L. (1986). *Despotism and differential reproduction: A Darwinian view of history*. Aldine.

Betzig, L. (2008). Hunting kings. *Cross-cultural Research, 42*(3), 270–289.

Betzig, L., & Lombardo, L. H. (1992). Who's pro-choice and why. *Ethology and Sociobiology, 13*(1), 49–71.

Björkqvist, K. (1994). Sex differences in physical, verbal, and indirect aggression: A review of recent research. *Sex Roles, 30*(3), 177–188.

Björkqvist, K., Lagerspetz, K. M., & Kaukiainen, A. (1992). Do girls manipulate and boys fight? Developmental trends in regard to direct and indirect aggression. *Aggressive Behavior, 18*(2), 117–127.

Björkqvist, K., Österman, K., & Kaukiainen, A. (1992). The development of direct and indirect aggressive strategies in males and females. In K. Bjorkqvist & , P. Niemela (Eds.), *Of mice and women: Aspects of female aggression* (pp. 51–64). Academic Press.

Blake, K. R., Bastian, B., Denson, T. F., Grosjean, P., & Brooks, R. C. (2018). Income inequality not gender inequality positively covaries with female sexualization on social media. *Proceedings of the National Academy of Sciences, 115*(35), 8722–8727.

Blake, K. R., & Brooks, R. C. (2019a). Income inequality and reproductive competition: Implications for consumption, status-seeking, and women's self-sexualization. In J. Jetten & K. Peters (Eds.), *The social psychology of inequality* (pp. 173–185). Springer.

Blake, K. R., & Brooks, R. C. (2019b). Status anxiety mediates the positive relationship between income inequality and sexualization. *Proceedings of the National Academy of Sciences, 116*(50), 25029–25033.

Blake, K. R., Brooks, R., Arthur, L. C., & Denson, T. F. (2020). In the context of romantic attraction, beautification can increase assertiveness in women. *PLoS ONE, 15*(3), Article e0229162.

Blake, K. R., Fourati, M., & Brooks, R. C. (2018). Who suppresses female sexuality? An examination of support for Islamic veiling in a secular Muslim democracy as a function of sex and offspring sex. *Evolution and Human Behavior, 39*(6), 632–638.

Bower, A. R., Nishina, A., Witkow, M. R., & Bellmore, A. (2015). Nice guys and gals finish last? Not in early adolescence when empathic, accepted, and popular peers are desirable. *Journal of Youth and Adolescence, 44*(12), 2275–2288.

Brown, L. M., & Gilligan, C. (1993). Meeting at the crossroads: Women's psychology and girls' development. *Feminism & Psychology, 3*(1), 11–35.

Brown, W. M., Finn, C. J., Cooke, B. M., & Breedlove, S. M. (2002). Differences in finger length ratios between self-identified "butch" and "femme" lesbians. *Archives of Sexual Behavior, 31*(1), 123–127.

Bursztyn, L., Fujiwara, T., & Pallais, A. (2017). "Acting wife": Marriage market incentives and labor market investments. *American Economic Review, 107*(11), 3288–3319.

Buss, D. M. (1988). The evolution of human intrasexual competition: Tactics of mate attraction. *Journal of Personality and Social Psychology, 54*(4), 616.

Buss, D. M. (1989). Sex differences in human mate preferences: Evolutionary hypotheses tested in 37 cultures. *Behavioral and Brain Sciences, 12*(1), 1–14.

Buss, D. M. (2013). Sexual jealousy. *Psihologijske Teme, 22*(2), 155–182.

Buss, D. M., & Dedden, L. A. (1990). Derogation of competitors. *Journal of Social and Personal Relationships, 7*(3), 395–422.

Buss, D. M., Durkee, P. K., Shackelford, T. K., Bowdle, B. F., Schmitt, D. P., Brase, G. L., Choe, J. C., & Trofimova, I. (2020). Human status criteria: Sex differences and similarities across 14 nations. *Journal of Personality and Social Psychology, 119*(5) 979.

Buss, D. M., & Schmitt, D. P. (1993). Sexual strategies theory: An evolutionary perspective on human mating. *Psychological Review, 100*(2), 204.

Buss, D. M., & Schmitt, D. P. (2019). Mate preferences and their behavioral manifestations. *Annual Review of Psychology, 70*, 77–110.

Buss, D. M., & Shackelford, T. K. (1997). From vigilance to violence: Mate retention tactics in married couples. *Journal of Personality and Social Psychology, 72*(2), 346.

Buss, D. M., Shackelford, T. K., Choe, J. A. E., Buunk, B. P., & Dijkstra, P. (2000). Distress about mating rivals. *Personal Relationships, 7*(3), 235–243.

Butte, N. F., & King, J. C. (2005). Energy requirements during pregnancy and lactation. *Public Health Nutrition, 8*(7a), 1010–1027.

Buttrick, N. R., & Oishi, S. (2017). The psychological consequences of income inequality. *Social and Personality Psychology Compass, 11*(3), Article e12304.

Buunk, B. P., Dijkstra, P., Fetchenhauer, D., & Kenrick, D. T. (2002). Age and gender differences in mate selection criteria for various involvement levels. *Personal Relationships, 9*(3), 271–278.

Buunk, A. P., Park, J. H., & Dubbs, S. L. (2008). Parent–offspring conflict in mate preferences. *Review of General Psychology, 12*(1), 47–62.

Campbell, A. (1999). Staying alive: Evolution, culture, and women's intrasexual aggression. *Behavioral and Brain Sciences, 22*(2), 203–214.

Campbell, A. (2002). *A mind of her own: The evolutionary psychology of women*. Oxford University Press.

Cassar, A., Wordofa, F., & Zhang, Y. J. (2016). Competing for the benefit of offspring eliminates the gender gap in competitiveness. *Proceedings of the National Academy of Sciences, 113*(19), 5201–5205.

Centers for Disease Control and Prevention. (2017, January). *National marriage and divorce rate trends.* National Center for Health Statistics. https://www.cdc.gov/nchs/fastats/marriage-divorce.htm

Centers for Disease Control and Prevention. (2018, September). *Sexually transmitted disease surveillance 2017*. CDC. https://www.cdc.gov/std/stats17/2017-STD-Surveillance-Report_CDC-clearance-9.10.18.pdf

Chagnon, N. A. (1988). Life histories, blood revenge, and warfare in a tribal population. *Science, 239*(4843), 985–992.

Charlat, S., Reuter, M., Dyson, E. A., Hornett, E. A., Duplouy, A., Davies, N., Roderick, G. K., Wedell, N., & Hurst, G. D. D. (2007). Male-killing bacteria trigger a cycle of increasing male fatigue and female promiscuity. *Current Biology, 17*(3), 273–277.

Cheney, D. L., Silk, J. B., & Seyfarth, R. M. (2012). Evidence for intrasexual selection in wild female baboons. *Animal Behaviour, 84*(1), 21–27.

Chisholm, J. S., & Burbank, V. K. (1991). Monogamy and polygyny in Southeast Arnhem Land: Male coercion and female choice. *Ethology and Sociobiology, 12*(4), 291–313.

Clark, L., & Grant, J. W. (2010). Intrasexual competition and courtship in female and male Japanese medaka, Oryzias latipes: Effects of operational sex ratio and density. *Animal Behaviour, 80*(4), 707–712.

Clutton-Brock, T. (2007). Sexual selection in males and females. *Science, 318*(5858), 1882–1885.
Clutton-Brock, T. H., & Huchard, E. (2013). Social competition and selection in males and females. *Philosophical Transactions of the Royal Society B: Biological Sciences, 368*(1631), Article 20130074.
Conroy-Beam, D., & Buss, D. M. (2021). Mate preferences. In T. K. Shackelford & V. A. Weekes-Shackelford (Eds.), Encyclopedia of evolutionary psychological science (pp. 4850–4860). Springer.
Crick, N. R., & Grotpeter, J. K. (1995). Relational aggression, gender, and social-psychological adjustment. *Child Development, 66*(3), 710–722.
Daly, M. (2010, June). Income inequality (still) rules in explaining variations in homicide rates. In *Annual meeting of the Homicide Research Working Group.*
Daly, M., & Wilson, M. (1983). *Sex, evolution, and behavior* (2nd ed.). Willard Grant Press.
Daly, M., & Wilson, M. (1988). *Homicide.* Aldine de Gruyter
Daly, M., & Wilson, M. (1990). Killing the competition. *Human Nature, 1*(1), 81–107.
Daly, M., Wilson, M., & Vasdev, S. (2001). Income inequality and homicide rates in Canada and the United States. *Canadian Journal of Criminology, 43*(2), 219–236.
Darwin, C. (1871). *The descent of man and selection in relation to sex.* Murray.
Derix, R., Van Hooff, J., De Vries, H., & Wensing, J. (1993). Male and female mating competition in wolves: Female suppression vs. male intervention. *Behaviour, 127*(1–2), 141–174.
De Waal, F. B. (1989). Food sharing and reciprocal obligations among chimpanzees. *Journal of Human Evolution, 18*(5), 433–459.
Drews, C. (1996). Contexts and patterns of injuries in free-ranging male baboons (Papio cynocephalus). *Behaviour, 133*(5–6), 443–474.
Durante, K. M., Griskevicius, V., Simpson, J. A., Cantú, S. M., & Tybur, J. M. (2012). Sex ratio and women's career choice: Does a scarcity of men lead women to choose briefcase over baby? *Journal of Personality and Social Psychology, 103*(1), 121.
Dyble, M., Gardner, A., Vinicius, L., & Migliano, A. B. (2018). Inclusive fitness for in-laws. *Biology Letters, 14*(10), 20180515.
Emlen, S. T. (1976). Lek organization and mating strategies in the bullfrog. *Behavioral Ecology and Sociobiology, 1*(3), 283–313.
Emlen, S. T., & Wrege, P. H. (2004). Size dimorphism, intrasexual competition, and sexual selection in Wattled Jacana (Jacana jacana), a sex-role-reversed shorebird in Panama. *The Auk, 121*(2), 391–403.
Ermer, E., Cosmides, L., & Tooby, J. (2008). Relative status regulates risky decision making about resources in men: Evidence for the co-evolution of motivation and cognition. *Evolution and Human Behavior, 29*(2), 106–118.
Escasa-Dorne, M., Franco, C., & Gray, P. B. (2017). Sex differences: Mate preferences after having children. In T. K. Shackelford & V. A. Weekes-Shackelford (Eds.), *Encyclopedia of evolutionary psychological science.* Springer.
Fessler, D. M., Holbrook, C., & Gervais, M. M. (2014). Men's physical strength moderates conceptualizations of prospective foes in two disparate societies. *Human Nature, 25*(3), 393–409.
Fink, B., Klappauf, D., Brewer, G., & Shackelford, T. K. (2014). Female physical characteristics and intra-sexual competition in women. *Personality and Individual Differences, 58,* 138–141.
Fisher, A. N., & Stinson, D. A. (2020). Ambivalent attraction: Beauty determines whether men romantically desire or dismiss high status women. *Personality and Individual Differences, 154,* 109681.
Fisher, M. L. (2004). Female intrasexual competition decreases female facial attractiveness. *Proceedings of the Royal Society of London. Series B, Biological Sciences, 271,* S283–S285.
Fisher, M., & Cox, A. (2009). The influence of female attractiveness on competitor derogation. *Journal of Evolutionary Psychology, 7*(2), 141–155.
Fisher, M., & Cox, A. (2011). Four strategies used during intrasexual competition for mates. *Personal Relationships, 18*(1), 20–38.
Fisher, M. L., & Moule, K. R. (2013). A new direction for intrasexual competition research: Cooperative versus competitive motherhood. *Journal of Social, Evolutionary, and Cultural Psychology, 7*(4), 318.
Fisman, R., Iyengar, S. S., Kamenica, E., & Simonson, I. (2006). Gender differences in mate selection: Evidence from a speed dating experiment. *The Quarterly Journal of Economics, 121*(2), 673–697.
Flinn, M. V. (1988). Mate guarding in a Caribbean village. *Ethology and Sociobiology, 9*(1), 1–28.
Flinn, M. V., Quinlan, R. J., Coe, K., Ward, C. V. (2007). Evolution of the human family: Cooperative males, long social childhoods, smart mothers, and extended kin networks. In C. A. Salmon & T. K. Shackelford

(Eds.), Family relationships: An evolutionary perspective (pp. 16–38). Oxford University Press. https://doi.org/10.1093/acprof:oso/9780195320510.003.0002

Folke, O., & Rickne, J. (2016). The glass ceiling in politics: Formalization and empirical tests. *Comparative Political Studies, 49*(5), 567–599.

Frederick, D. A., & Haselton, M. G. (2007). Why is muscularity sexy? Tests of the fitness indicator hypothesis. *Personality and Social Psychology Bulletin, 33*(8), 1167–1183.

French, J. A. (1997). Proximate regulation of singular breeding in Callitrichid primates. In N. G. Solomon & J. A. French (Eds.), *Cooperative breeding in mammals* (pp. 34–75). Cambridge University Press.

Gates, G. J. (2017, January 11). In U.S., more adults identifying as LGBT. Retrieved from https://news.gallup.com/poll/201731/lgbt-identification-rises.aspx

Gaulin, S. J., & Boster, J. S. (1990). Dowry as female competition. *American Anthropologist, 92*(4), 994–1005.

Geary, D. C. (2005). *The origin of mind: Evolution of brain, cognition, and general intelligence*. American Psychological Association Press.

Geary, D. C. (2010). *Male, female: The evolution of human sex differences*. American Psychological Association Press.

Gibson, M. A., & Mace, R. (2007). Polygyny, reproductive success and child health in rural Ethiopia: Why marry a married man? *Journal of Biosocial Science, 39*(2), 287–300.

Goldscheider, F., & Kaufman, G. (2006). Willingness to stepparent: Attitudes about partners who already have children. *Journal of Family Issues, 27*(10), 1415–1436.

Goos, L. M., & Silverman, I. (2002). Sex related factors in the perception of threatening facial expressions. *Journal of Nonverbal Behavior, 26*(1), 27–41.

Gowaty, P. A. (1997). Sexual dialectics, sexual selection, and variation in mating behavior. In P. A. Gowaty (Ed.), *Feminism and evolutionary biology: Boundaries, intersections, and frontiers* (pp. 351–384). Springer.

Gowaty, P. A., Kim, Y. K., & Anderson, W. W. (2012). No evidence of sexual selection in a repetition of Bateman's classic study of Drosophila melanogaster. *Proceedings of the National Academy of Sciences, 109*(29), 11740–11745.

Graham, R., Berkowitz, B., Blum, R., Bockting, W., Bradford, J., de Vries, B., & Makadon, H. (2011). *The health of lesbian, gay, bisexual, and transgender people: Building a foundation for better understanding*. National Academies Press.

Gray, P. B., Franco, C. Y., Garcia, J. R., Gesselman, A. N., & Fisher, H. E. (2016). Romantic and dating behaviors among single parents in the United States. *Personal Relationships, 23*(3), 491–504.

Gray, P. B., Reece, J. A., Coore-Desai, C., Dinnall-Johnson, T., Pellington, S., & Samms-Vaughan, M. (2015b). Sexuality among fathers of newborns in Jamaica. *BMC Pregnancy and Childbirth, 15*(1), 1–9.

Griskevicius, V., Tybur, J. M., Ackerman, J. M., Delton, A. W., Robertson, T. E., & White, A. E. (2012). The financial consequences of too many men: Sex ratio effects on saving, borrowing, and spending. *Journal of Personality and Social Psychology, 102*(1), 69.

Guttentag, M., & Secord, P. F. (1983). *Too many women? The sex ratio question*. SAGE.

Gwynne, D. T. (1993). Food quality controls sexual selection in Mormon crickets by altering male mating investment. *Ecology, 74*(5), 1406–1413.

Hackländer, K., Möstl, E., & Arnold, W. (2003). Reproductive suppression in female Alpine marmots, Marmota marmota. *Animal Behaviour, 65*(6), 1133–1140.

Hagen, E. H., Hames, R. B., Craig, N. M., Lauer, M. T., & Price, M. E. (2001). Parental investment and child health in a Yanomamö village suffering short-term food stress. *Journal of Biosocial Science, 33*(4), 503–528.

Hames, R. B. (1996). Costs and benefits of monogamy and polygyny for Yanomamö women. *Ethology and Sociobiology, 17*(3), 181–199.

Henrich, J., Boyd, R., & Richerson, P. J. (2012). The puzzle of monogamous marriage. *Philosophical Transactions of the Royal Society B: Biological Sciences, 367*(1589), 657–669.

Hess, N. H. (2006). *Informational warfare: Female friendship and the coalitional manipulation of reputation*. University of California, Santa Barbara.

Hess, N. H., & Hagen, E. H. (2006a). Psychological adaptations for assessing gossip veracity. *Human Nature, 17*(3), 337–354.

Hess, N. H., & Hagen, E. H. (2006b). Sex differences in indirect aggression: Psychological evidence from young adults. *Evolution and Human Behavior, 27*(3), 231–245.

Hess, N. H., & Hagen, E. H. (2019). Gossip, reputation, and friendship in within-group competition. The *Oxford* handbook of gossip and reputation (p. 275). Oxford Handbooks Online. https://doi.org/10.1093/oxfordhb/9780190494087.013.15

Hobbes, M. (2017). *Together alone: The epidemic of gay loneliness.* Huffington Post Highline. https://highline.huffingtonpost.com/articles/en/gay-loneliness/

Hrdy, S. B. (1977). Infanticide as a primate reproductive strategy. *American Scientist, 65*(1), 40–49.

Hrdy, S. B. (1981). *The woman that never evolved.* Harvard University Press.

Hrdy, S. B. (1999). *Mother nature: A history of mothers, infants, and natural selection.* Pantheon Books.

Huntingford, F. A., & Turner, A. K. (1987). *Animal conflict.* Chapman and Hall.

Hurst, A. C., Alquist, J. L., & Puts, D. A. (2017). Women's fertility status alters other women's jealousy and mate guarding. *Personality and Social Psychology Bulletin, 43*(2), 191–203.

Hurtado, A. M., & Hill, K. R. (1990). Seasonality in a foraging society: Variation in diet, work effort, fertility, and sexual division of labor among the Hiwi of Venezuela. *Journal of Anthropological Research, 46*(3), 293–346.

Jankowiak, W., Sudakov, M., & Wilreker, B. C. (2005). Co-wife conflict and co-operation. *Ethnology, 44*(1), 81–98.

Jirotkul, M. (1999). Operational sex ratio influences female preference and male–male competition in guppies. *Animal Behaviour, 58*(2), 287–294.

Kenrick, D. T. (1987). Gender, genes, and the social environment: A biosocial interactionist perspective. In P. Shaver & C. Hendrick (Eds.), *Review of personality and social psychology: Vol. 7. Sex and gender* (pp. 14–43). SAGE.

Kenrick, D. T., & Keefe, R. C. (1992). Age preferences in mates reflect sex differences in human reproductive strategies. *Behavioral and Brain Sciences, 15*(1), 75–91.

Kenrick, D. T., Keefe, R. C., Bryan, A., Barr, A., & Brown, S. (1995). Age preferences and mate choice among homosexuals and heterosexuals: A case for modular psychological mechanisms. *Journal of Personality and Social Psychology, 69*(6), 1166.

Kleiman, D. G. (1977). Monogamy in mammals. *The Quarterly Review of Biology, 52*(1), 39–69.

Kokko, H., & Jennions, M. D. (2003). It takes two to tango. *Trends in Ecology & Evolution, 18*(3), 103–104.

Kokko, H., & Jennions, M. D. (2008). Parental investment, sexual selection and sex ratios. *Journal of Evolutionary Biology, 21*(4), 919–948.

Krems, J. A. (2016). Verbal derogation among women. In T. K. Shackelford & V. A. Weekes-Shackelford (Eds.), *Encyclopedia of evolutionary psychological science* (pp. 1–2). Springer.

Krems, J. A., Kenrick, D. T., & Neel, R. (2017). Individual perceptions of self-actualization: What functional motives are linked to fulfilling one's full potential? *Personality and Social Psychology Bulletin, 43*(9), 1337–1352.

Krems, J. A., Neel, R., Neuberg, S. L., Puts, D. A., & Kenrick, D. T. (2016). Women selectively guard their (desirable) mates from ovulating women. *Journal of Personality and Social Psychology, 110*(4), 551.

Krems, J. A., Neuberg, S. L., Filip-Crawford, G., & Kenrick, D. T. (2015). Is she angry? (Sexually desirable) women "see" anger on female faces. *Psychological Science, 26*(11), 1655–1663.

Krems, J. A., Rankin, A. M., & Northover, S. B. (2020). Women's strategic defenses against same-sex aggression: Evidence from sartorial behavior. *Social Psychological and Personality Science, 11*(6), 770–781.

Krems, J. A., & Varnum, M. E. (2010). More than just climate: Income inequality and sex ratio explain unique variance in qualitatively different types of aggression. *Behavioral and Brain Sciences, 49*(5), 1345–1365.

Krems, J. A., Williams, K. E. G., Kenrick, D. T., & Aktipis, A. (2021). Friendship jealousy: One tool for maintaining friendships in the face of third-party threats? *Journal of Personality and Social Psychology, 120*(4), 977.

Kruger, D. J. (2004). Sexual selection and the male: Female mortality ratio. *Evolutionary Psychology, 2*(1), Article 147470490400200112.

Kruger, D. J. (2010). Socio-demographic factors intensifying male mating competition exacerbate male mortality rates. *Evolutionary Psychology, 8*(2), Article 147470491000800205.

Krupp, D. B., & Cook, T. R. (2018). Local competition amplifies the corrosive effects of inequality. *Psychological Science, 29*(5), 824–833.

Kvarnemo, C., & Ahnesjo, I. (1996). The dynamics of operational sex ratios and competition for mates. *Trends in Ecology & Evolution, 11*(10), 404–408.

LaFrance, M. (2002). II. Smile boycotts and other body politics. *Feminism & Psychology, 12*(3), 319–323.

Lassek, W. D., & Gaulin, S. J. (2009). Costs and benefits of fat-free muscle mass in men: Relationship to mating success, dietary requirements, and native immunity. *Evolution and Human Behavior, 30*(5), 322–328.

Lee, K. S., Brittain, H., & Vaillancourt, T. (2018). Predicting dating behavior from aggression and self-perceived social status in adolescence. *Aggressive Behavior, 44*(4), 372–381.

Leenaars, L. S., Dane, A. V., & Marini, Z. A. (2008). Evolutionary perspective on indirect victimization in adolescence: The role of attractiveness, dating and sexual behavior. *Aggressive Behavior: Official Journal of the International Society for Research on Aggression, 34*(4), 404–415.

Li, N. P., Bailey, J. M., Kenrick, D. T., & Linsenmeier, J. A. (2002). The necessities and luxuries of mate preferences: Testing the tradeoffs. *Journal of Personality and Social Psychology, 82*(6), 947.

Li, N. P., Smith, A. R., Griskevicius, V., Cason, M. J., & Bryan, A. (2010). Intrasexual competition and eating restriction in heterosexual and homosexual individuals. *Evolution and Human Behavior, 31*(5), 365–372.

Linney, C., Korologou-Linden, L., & Campbell, A. (2017). Maternal competition in women. *Human Nature, 28*(1), 92–116.

Lippa, R. A. (2003). Are 2D: 4D finger-length ratios related to sexual orientation? Yes for men, no for women. *Journal of Personality and Social Psychology, 85*(1), 179.

Lovejoy, C. O. (1981). The origin of man. *Science, 211*(4480), 341–350.

Mace, R., & Alvergne, A. (2012). Female reproductive competition within families in rural Gambia. *Proceedings of the Royal Society: Biological Sciences, 279*(1736), 2219–2227.

Madhavan, S. (2002). Best of friends and worst of enemies: Competition and collaboration in polygyny. *Ethnology, 41*(1), 69–84.

Mafra, A. L., Varella, M. A. C., Defelipe, R. P., Anchieta, N. M., de Almeida, C. A. G., & Valentova, J. V. (2020). Makeup usage in women as a tactic to attract mates and compete with rivals. *Personality and Individual Differences,* 163, 110042.

Majolo, B., Lehmann, J., de Bortoli Vizioli, A., & Schino, G. (2012). Fitness-related benefits of dominance in primates. *American Journal of Physical Anthropology, 147*(4), 652–660.

Maner, J. K., & Ackerman, J. M. (2020). Ecological sex ratios and human mating. *Trends in Cognitive Sciences, 24*(2), 98–100.

Marlowe, F. (1999). Male care and mating effort among Hadza foragers. *Behavioral Ecology and Sociobiology, 46*(1), 57–64.

McElligott, A. G., Gammell, M. P., Harty, H. C., Paini, D. R., Murphy, D. T., Walsh, J. T., & Hayden, T. J. (2001). Sexual size dimorphism in fallow deer (Dama dama): Do larger, heavier males gain greater mating success? *Behavioral Ecology and Sociobiology, 49*(4), 266–272.

Melzer, K., Schutz, Y., Soehnchen, N., Girard, V. O., De Tejada, B. M., Pichard, C., Irion, O., Boulvain, M., & Kayser, B. (2010). Prepregnancy body mass index and resting metabolic rate during pregnancy. *Annals of Nutrition and Metabolism, 57*(3–4), 221–227.

Milam, E. L. (2010). *Looking for a few good males: Female choice in evolutionary biology.* JHU Press.

Miller, G. (2000). Evolution of human music through sexual selection. In N. L. Wallin, B. Merker, & S. Brown (Eds.), *The origins of music* (pp. 329–360). MIT Press.

Milner-Gulland, E. J., Bukreeva, O. M., Coulson, T., Lushchekina, A. A., Kholodova, M. V., Bekenov, A. B., & Grachev, I. A. (2003). Reproductive collapse in saiga antelope harems. *Nature, 422*(6928), 135.

Minervini, B. P., & McAndrew, F. T. (2006). The mating strategies and mate preferences of mail order brides. *Cross-Cultural Research, 40*(2), 111–129.

Mogilski, J. K., Wade, T. J., & Welling, L. L. (2014). Prioritization of potential mates' history of sexual fidelity during a conjoint ranking task. *Personality and Social Psychology Bulletin, 40*(7), 884–897.

Mortelmans, D., & Defever, C. (2018). Income trajectories of lone parents after divorce: A view with Belgian register data. In L. Bernardi & D. Mortelmans (Eds.), *Lone parenthood in the life course* (pp. 191–211). Springer.

Moss, J. H., & Maner, J. K. (2016). Biased sex ratios influence fundamental aspects of human mating. *Personality and Social Psychology Bulletin, 42*(1), 72–80.

Mouttapa, M., Valente, T., Gallaher, P., Rohrbach, L. A., & Unger, J. B. (2004). Social network predictors of bullying and victimization. *Adolescence, 39*(154), 315–335.

Muller, M. N. (2002). Agonistic relations among Kanyawara chimpanzees. In C. Boesch, G. Hohmann, & L. Marchant (Eds.), Behavioural diversity in chimpanzees and bonobos (pp. 112–124). Cambridge University Press.

Muñoz-Reye, J. A., Gil-Burmann, C., Fink, B., & Turiegano, E. (2012). Physical strength, fighting ability, and aggressiveness in adolescents. *American Journal of Human Biology, 24*(5), 611–617.

Murdock, G. P. (1967). Ethnographic atlas: A summary. *Ethnology, 6*(2), 109–236.

Noë, R., & Hammerstein, P. (1994). Biological markets: Supply and demand determine the effect of partner choice in cooperation, mutualism and mating. *Behavioral Ecology and Sociobiology, 35*(1), 1–11.

Noë, R., & Hammerstein, P. (1995). Biological markets. *Trends in Ecology & Evolution, 10*(8), 336–339.

Nolan, I. T., Kuhner, C. J., & Dy, G. W. (2019). Demographic and temporal trends in transgender identities and gender confirming surgery. *Translational Andrology and Urology, 8*(3), 184.

Orians, G. H. (1969). On the evolution of mating systems in birds and mammals. *American Naturalist, 103*(934), 589–603.

Owens, L., Shute, R., & Slee, P. (2000). "Guess what I just heard!": Indirect aggression among teenage girls in Australia. *Aggressive Behavior: Official Journal of the International Society for Research on Aggression, 26*(1), 67–83.

Pachankis, J. E., Clark, K. A., Burton, C. L., Hughto, J. M. W., Bränström, R., & Keene, D. E. (2020). Sex, status, competition, and exclusion: Intraminority stress from within the gay community and gay and bisexual men's mental health. *Journal of Personality and Social Psychology*, 119(3), 713.

Pachankis, J. E., Cochran, S. D., & Mays, V. M. (2015). The mental health of sexual minority adults in and out of the closet: A population-based study. *Journal of Consulting and Clinical Psychology, 83*(5), 890.

Pawlowski, B. (2003). Variable preferences for sexual dimorphism in height as a strategy for increasing the pool of potential partners in humans. *Proceedings of the Royal Society of London. Series B: Biological Sciences, 270*(1516), 709–712.

Pawlowski, R., Dunbar, R., & Lipwicz, A. (2000). Evolutionary fitness: Tall men have more reproductive success. *Nature*, 403(6766), 156. https://doi.org/10.1038/35003107

Radl, J., Salazar, L., & Cebolla-Boado, H. (2017). Does living in a fatherless household compromise educational success? A comparative study of cognitive and non-cognitive skills. *European Journal of Population, 33*(2), 217.

Rhodes, G. (2006). The evolutionary psychology of facial beauty. *Annual Review of Psychology, 57*, 199–226.

Ronay, R., & Hippel, W. V. (2010). The presence of an attractive woman elevates testosterone and physical risk taking in young men. *Social Psychological and Personality Science, 1*(1), 57–64.

Rosvall, K. A. (2011). Intrasexual competition in females: Evidence for sexual selection? *Behavioral Ecology, 22*(6), 1131–1140.

Russell, E. M., Babcock, M. J., Lewis, D. M., Ta, V. P., & Ickes, W. (2018). Why attractive women want gay male friends: A previously undiscovered strategy to prevent mating deception and sexual exploitation. *Personality and Individual Differences, 120*, 283–287.

Salmon, C. A. (2017). Is female competition at the heart of reproductive suppression and eating disorders? In M. L. Fisher (Ed.), The Oxford handbook of women and competition (p. 435). Oxford University Press.

Scelza, B. A., Prall, S. P., Blumenfield, T., Crittenden, A. N., Gurven, M., Kline, M., Koster, J., Kushnick, G., Mattison, S. M., Pillsworth, E., Shenk, M. K., Starkweather, K., Stieglitz, J., Sum, C., Yamaguchi, K., & McElreath, R. (2020). Patterns of paternal investment predict cross-cultural variation in jealous response. *Nature Human Behaviour, 4*(1), 20–26.

Schmitt, D. P. (2003). Universal sex differences in the desire for sexual variety: Tests from 52 nations, 6 continents, and 13 islands. *Journal of Personality and Social Psychology, 85*(1), 85.

Schmitt, D. P. (2005). Sociosexuality from Argentina to Zimbabwe: A 48-nation study of sex, culture, and strategies of human mating. *Behavioral and Brain Sciences, 28*(2), 247–275.

Schmitt, D. P., & Buss, D. M. (2001). Human mate poaching: Tactics and temptations for infiltrating existing mateships. *Journal of Personality and Social Psychology, 80*(6), 894.

Schmitt, D. P., & Rohde, P. A. (2013). The human polygyny index and its ecological correlates: Testing sexual selection and life history theory at the cross-national level. *Social Science Quarterly, 94*(4), 1159–1184.

Sear, R., & Mace, R. (2008). Who keeps children alive? A review of the effects of kin on child survival. *Evolution and Human Behavior, 29*(1), 1–18.

Sell, A. (2005). *Regulating welfare tradeoff ratios: Three tests of an evolutionary-computational model of human anger*. University of California, Santa Barbara.

Sell, A., Tooby, J., & Cosmides, L. (2009). Formidability and the logic of human anger. *Proceedings of the National Academy of Sciences, 106*(35), 15073–15078.

Sheppard, L. D., & Aquino, K. (2017). Sisters at arms: A theory of female same-sex conflict and its problematization in organizations. *Journal of Management, 43*(3), 691–715.
Shostak, M. (1981). *Nisa*. Harvard University Press.
Silk, J. B., Alberts, S. C., & Altmann, J. (2003). Social bonds of female baboons enhance infant survival. *Science, 302*(5648), 1231–1234.
Silk, J. B., Altmann, J., & Alberts, S. C. (2006). Social relationships among adult female baboons (Papio cynocephalus) I. Variation in the strength of social bonds. *Behavioral Ecology and Sociobiology, 61*(2), 183–195.
Simmons, R. (2002). *Odd girl out: The hidden culture of aggression in girls*. Houghton Mifflin Harcourt.
Slagsvold, T., & Lifjeld, J. T. (1994). Polygyny in birds: The role of competition between females for male parental care. *American Naturalist, 143*(1), 59–94.
Smith, R. L., Rose, A. J., & Schwartz-Mette, R. A. (2010). Relational and overt aggression in childhood and adolescence: Clarifying mean-level gender differences and associations with peer acceptance. *Social Development, 19*(2), 243–269.
Sobolewski, M. E., Brown, J. L., & Mitani, J. C. (2013). Female parity, male aggression, and the challenge hypothesis in wild chimpanzees. *Primates, 54*(1), 81–88.
Stockley, P., & Bro-Jørgensen, J. (2011). Female competition and its evolutionary consequences in mammals. *Biological Reviews, 86*(2), 341–366.
Sundie, J. M., Kenrick, D. T., Griskevicius, V., Tybur, J. M., Vohs, K. D., & Beal, D. J. (2011). Peacocks, porsches, and Thorstein Veblen: Conspicuous consumption as a sexual signaling system. *Journal of Personality and Social Psychology, 100*(4), 664.
Symons, D. (1979). *The evolution of human sexuality*. Oxford University Press.
Thornhill, R., & Gangestad, S. W. (1994). Human fluctuating asymmetry and sexual behavior. *Psychological Science, 5*(5), 297–302.
Tooby, J., & Cosmides, L. (1996). Friendship and the banker's paradox: Other pathways to the evolution of adaptations for altruism. In Proceedings-British Academy, *88*, 119–144.
Townsend, J. M., & Levy, G. D. (1990a). Effects of potential partners' costume and physical attractiveness on sexuality and partner selection. *The Journal of Psychology, 124*(4), 371–389.
Townsend, J. M., & Levy, G. D. (1990b). Effects of potential partners' physical attractiveness and socioeconomic status on sexuality and partner selection. *Archives of Sexual Behavior, 19*(2), 149–164.
Trivers, R. L. (1972). Parental investment and sexual selection. In B. Campbell (Ed.), *Sexual selection and the descent of man* (pp. 136–179). Aldine.
Trivers, R. (1985). *Social evolution*. Cummings Menlo Park.
Underwood, M. K. (2003). *Social aggression among girls*. Guilford Press.
Underwood, M. K. (2004). III. Glares of contempt, eye rolls of disgust and turning away to exclude: Nonverbal forms of social aggression among girls. *Feminism & Psychology, 14*(3), 371–375.
Underwood, M. K., Galen, B. R., & Paquette, J. A. (2001). Hopes rather than fears, admirations rather than hostilities: A response to Archer and Bjorqkvist. *Social Development, 10*(2), 275–280.
Vaillancourt, T. (2013). Do human females use indirect aggression as an intrasexual competition strategy? *Philosophical Transactions of the Royal Society B: Biological Sciences, 368*(1631), Article 20130080.
Vaillancourt, T., & Hymel, S. (2006). Aggression and social status: The moderating roles of sex and peer-valued characteristics. *Aggressive Behavior: Official Journal of the International Society for Research on Aggression, 32*(4), 396–408.
Vaillancourt, T., Hymel, S., & McDougall, P. (2003). Bullying is power: Implications for school-based intervention strategies. *Journal of Applied School Psychology, 19*(2), 157–176.
Vaillancourt, T., & Krems, J. A. (2018). An evolutionary psychological perspective of indirect aggression in girls and women. In S. M. Coyne & J. M. Ostrov (Eds.), *The development of relational aggression* (pp. 111–126). Oxford University Press.
Vaillancourt, T., & Sharma, A. (2011). Intolerance of sexy peers: Intrasexual competition among women. *Aggressive Behavior, 37*(6), 569–577.
Varella, M. A. C., Valentova, J. V., & Fernández, A. M. (2017). Evolution of artistic and aesthetic propensities through female competitive ornamentation. In M. L. Fisher (Ed.), *The Oxford handbook of women and competition* (pp. 757–783). Oxford University Press. https:// doi.org/10.1093/oxfordhb/978019 9376 377.013.46
Vervaecke, H., & Van Elsacker, L. (2000). Sexual competition in a group of captive bonobos (Pan paniscus). *Primates, 41*(1), 109–115.

Vukovic, J., Jean-Bart, R., Branson, D., Zephir, J., & Wright, A. (2019). Mate scarcity effects on women's wariness of other women. *EvoS Journal: The Journal of the Evolutionary Studies Consortium, 10*(1), 49–66.

Wacker, S., & Amundsen, T. (2014). Mate competition and resource competition are inter-related in sexual selection. *Journal of Evolutionary Biology, 27*(3), 466–477.

Walter, K. V., Conroy-Beam, D., Buss, D. M., Asao, K., Sorokowska, A., Sorokowski, P., Aavik, T., Akello, G., Alhababba, M. M., Alm, C., Amjad, N., Anjum, A., Atama, C. S., Duyar, D. A., Ayebare, R., Batres, C., Bendixen, M., Bensafia, A., Bizumic, B. . . . & Zupančič, M. (2020). Sex differences in mate preferences across 45 countries: A large-scale replication. *Psychological Science, 31*(4), 408–423.

Walters, S., & Crawford, C. B. (1994). The importance of mate attraction for intrasexual competition in men and women. *Ethology and Sociobiology, 15*(1), 5–30.

Wasser, S. K., & Barash, D. P. (1983). Reproductive suppression among female mammals: Implications for biomedicine and sexual selection theory. *The Quarterly Review of Biology, 58*(4), 513–539.

Weir, L. K., Grant, J. W., & Hutchings, J. A. (2011). The influence of operational sex ratio on the intensity of competition for mates. *American Naturalist, 177*(2), 167–176.

Williams, M. J., & Tiedens, L. Z. (2016). The subtle suspension of backlash: A meta-analysis of penalties for women's implicit and explicit dominance behavior. *Psychological Bulletin, 142*(2), 165.

Wilson, M., & Daly, M. (1998). Sexual rivalry and sexual conflict: Recurring themes in fatal conflicts. *Theoretical Criminology, 2*(3), 291–310.

Wrangham, R. W. (1999). Evolution of coalitionary killing. *American Journal of Physical Anthropology, 110*(S29), 1–30.

Wrangham, R. (2019). *The goodness paradox: The strange relationship between virtue and violence in human evolution.* Vintage Books.

Xing, C., Chen, J., & Du, C. (2016). Men and money: A scarcity of men leads women to care more about relative gain. *Evolutionary Psychology, 14*(4), Article 1474704916674726.

Yavorsky, J. E., Keister, L. A., Qian, Y., & Nau, M. (2019). Women in the one percent: Gender dynamics in top income positions. *American Sociological Review, 84*(1), 54–81.

Young, A. J., Carlson, A. A., Monfort, S. L., Russell, A. F., Bennett, N. C., & Clutton-Brock, T. (2006). Stress and the suppression of subordinate reproduction in cooperatively breeding meerkats. *Proceedings of the National Academy of Sciences, 103*(32), 12005–12010.

Zahavi, A., & Zahavi, A. (1999). *The handicap principle: A missing piece of Darwin's puzzle.* Oxford University Press.

CHAPTER

8 Initiation of Non-Heterosexual Relationships

Jaroslava Varella Valentova, Bruno Henrique Amaral, *and* Marco Antonio Correa Varella

Abstract

Human sexual orientation is an intriguing phenomenon, still poorly understood but with important evolutionary implications. Evolutionary-based studies mostly focus on heterosexual individuals and relationships, probably because non-heterosexuality concerns a minority of the population and decreases individual direct reproductive success. To better understand human nature, it is important to analyze whether the mating psychology of minorities exhibit specific evolved sexual/reproductive strategies. Here we review studies on partner preferences, mate choice, and flirting in non-heterosexual populations, to identify which patterns are similar to or different from heterosexuals. The general pattern supports the notion that sex differences are larger than within sex variation among people of different sexual orientations. However, although some mating strategies among non-heterosexuals resemble heterosexuals of the same sex, others resemble heterosexuals of the opposite sex, and yet in others, the pattern is different than among either heterosexual men or women. We point to limitations of the current state of this research, and we suggest possible future directions in the study of non-heterosexual relationship initiation.

Key Words: sexual orientation, homosexuality, relationships, sexuality, evolution

How universal is the initiation process for human romantic relationships? Does the same sequence of steps from mate preference to mate choice occur in each individual in a given population or just in the heterosexual majority? In this chapter, we organize and summarize the literature on relationship initiation among non-heterosexual individuals. We also compare each step of the initiation process with heterosexual people to assess which aspects are similar and which are specific to each group. Throughout, we discuss how adding non-heterosexuals into the evolutionary analysis of relationship dynamics provides a richer view of human mating. We hope to stimulate the development of new conceptual and experimental endeavors that integrate non-heterosexual individuals into mainstream evolutionary frameworks.

We first conceptualize and describe the non-heterosexual side of the sexual orientation continuum as evolved strategic variation in human mating. We present the main reasons why it is fruitful to approach non-heterosexuality from an evolutionary perspective. Then we discuss mating preferences, sexual strategies, and mate choice of non-heterosexuals compared to heterosexuals. We further discuss limitations of the current state of this research, highlight the measurement issues of sexual orientation, note the scarcity of cross-cultural comparisons, and point to future research directions.

Non-Heterosexual Individuals From the Evolutionary Perspective

Most men prefer women as sexual partners, while most women prefer men as sexual partners. Or is it so? Some studies show that a substantial proportion or even a majority of men and women do have also some level of same-sex attraction despite considering themselves heterosexual (Santtila et al., 2008; Savin-Williams & Vrangalova, 2013). Moreover, non-heterosexuality does not mean only exclusive homosexuality but rather a spectrum of non-heterosexual attractions and preferences (Valentova & Varella, 2016b). Thus, in general, non-heterosexuality encompasses bisexual and homosexual individuals exhibiting varying degrees of hetero and homosexuality.

Same-sex sexual behavior and preferences are widespread in nature and documented in nearly all human cultures, past and present, and in many vertebrate and invertebrate nonhuman animal species (Hames et al., 2017; Sommer & Vasey, 2006; Whitam, 1983). Same-sex sexuality also has genetic markers; high heritability; and psychological, neurological, hormonal, developmental, and anthropometric specificities (Bailey et al., 2016). Several plausible evidence-based evolutionary theories have attempted to explain its origins, functions, and adaptive advantages, including the theories of kin selection (Vasey et al., 2007), homosociality (Barron & Hare, 2020; Kirkpatrick, 2000), life history theory (Luoto et al., 2019), weak selection pressure hypothesis (Apostolou, 2017), and sexually-antagonistic selection (Gavrilets, Friberg, & Rice, 2018). Still, only a handful of evolutionary studies have addressed sexuality and relationships of non-heterosexual individuals, and the majority of these focus on homosexual men, while bisexual men, who were only recently embraced as an existing category (cf. Jabbour et al., 2020; Valentova et al., 2022a,b) and non-heterosexual women (Luoto et al., 2019; Semenyna et al., 2022) deserve more empirical and theoretical attention. Human sexual orientation is an intriguing phenomenon still relatively poorly understood, and it presents important evolutionary implications.

Why Same-Sex Relationships Are Important for Evolutionary Analysis

The general goal of human evolutionary psychological science is to ecologically situate and globally describe and understand the evolved psychology of human beings, their development, and their individual differences (Tooby, 2020; Buss, 2020). Focusing research on majorities is an intuitive and promising first step toward that goal. However, it is important to also include minorities, such as same-sex-attracted individuals, into the evolutionary framework to afford a universal understanding of human sexual diversity. Hence, in this chapter, we echo the plea for more research addressing relationship initiation in non-heterosexual orientations raised by many previous researchers (cf. Sprecher et al., 2018).

Evolutionary based studies mostly focus on heterosexual individuals or relationships, probably because non-heterosexuality concerns a minority of the population and logically decreases individual direct/exclusive reproductive success. Indeed, in traditional societies, direct reproductive success of some androphilic (i.e., attracted to men) males is virtually zero, although there is also evidence for indirect or inclusive fitness among these men (Vasey, Parker, & VanderLaan, 2014). At least in some modern Western societies, such as the United States, almost 40% of individuals who identify as LGBT report to have biological offspring (e.g., Gates, 2013). Other nationally representative studies, such as from New Zealand, show that in modern societies non-heterosexual women reproduce with the same frequency as heterosexual women, although non-heterosexual male reproductive success is significantly lower (e.g., Wells et al., 2011). The evidence for indirect and direct reproduction in non-heterosexual individuals together with the universality; antiquity; and genetic, hormonal, neurological, psychological, developmental, and anthropometric specificities (Bailey et al., 2016) makes a strong case for an evolutionary focus on these minorities per se (Valentova & Varella, 2016b). Therefore, it is important to have an evolutionary perspective of minority sexual orientations to increase knowledge about these minorities and whether their mating psychologies produce specific evolved reproductive strategies.

Besides the sexual and mating strategies of non-heterosexuals being of interest per se, there also are conceptual benefits of applying an evolutionary perspective to non-heterosexual individuals. The conceptual tools for describing and predicting the mating dynamics in reproductive populations were developed from heterosexual majorities. For instance, the mechanisms of intersexual selection and intrasexual competition describe the heterosexual mating market. However, for non-heterosexual individuals, researchers should approach "intrasexual selection" and in some cases "intersexual competition" (cf. Semenyna et al., 2020). In order to move forward in understanding human sexual diversity, it is paramount to expand the conceptual tools and metatheories to incorporate non-heterosexual individuals. By doing so, these updated models of sexuality and mating will exhibit greater ecological validity, because they will better explain real-life situations in which both heterosexual and non-heterosexual individuals interact in the general and operational mating market (cf. Whyte et al., 2019).

Another reason for applying an evolutionary perspective to non-heterosexuals is that they offer a unique methodological opportunity to compare effects of sex of the individual and of the partner, and thus shed light on psychological patterns of mating strategies (Howard & Perilloux, 2017). For example, heterosexual men tend to prefer relatively younger female partners (i.e., partners with higher residual fertility), while heterosexual women tend to prefer relatively older male partners (i.e., partners with higher status and more resources) (Grøntvedt, & Kennair, 2013; Kenrick & Keefe, 1992). Thus, if being female leads to preference for older partners and being male leads to preference for younger partners, then mate preferences should be sex-specific irrespective of sexual orientation. Conversely, if preferences are specific to the sex of the partner, homosexual men would be expected to show similarities to heterosexual women in preferring older male partners, while homosexual women should prefer younger female partners. Some previous studies show that compared to women, both heterosexual and homosexual men prefer younger partners (Hayes, 1995; Kenrick et al., 1995; Silverthorne & Quinsey, 2000) in both short- and long-term relationship contexts (Gobrogge et al., 2007). In the same vein, homosexual women are less likely to prefer younger partners than men (Silverthorne & Quinsey, 2000). This example suggests that at least some mechanisms of mating psychology are specific to the sex of the individual rather than their orientation. However, both homosexual men and women display a higher upper age tolerance and greater range of acceptable partner ages than both heterosexual men and women (Conway et al., 2015). Thus, despite the within-sex similarity of mating mechanisms across sexual orientations, there are some specificities in non-heterosexual relationship initiation. This demonstrates modularity of psychological mechanisms that produce mate preferences (Kenrick, 2011; Kenrick et al., 1995).

In several specific mating strategies and tactics, non-heterosexual individuals resemble heterosexual individuals of the same sex, whereas in others they are similar to heterosexual individuals of the other sex, and yet in others they show a pattern different from both heterosexual men and women. Some authors argue that because non-heterosexual individuals do not seek partners for reproductive reasons, their mating strategies might differ from heterosexual men and women (Gobrogge et al., 2007; Wood et al., 2014; Zheng, 2019a). However, the proximate subjective motivations for sexual relations usually do not include procreation (Meston & Buss, 2007; Wyverkens et al., 2018) or individual intention to spread their genes (Varella et al., 2013). On the contrary, evolutionary mechanisms can still be operative even in individuals who will eventually not reproduce (e.g., by infertility, homosexuality, asexuality, or chastity) (Dillon & Saleh, 2012). Thus, investigating whether mechanisms that operate in heterosexual, fertile, reproducing individuals also operate in sexual minorities is an important step to identifying whether and how such mechanisms are universal or group-specific.

We follow by reviewing studies on partner preferences and attractiveness in non-heterosexual populations and compare them with heterosexual populations, to identify which patterns are similar to or different from heterosexuals.

Attractiveness vs. Status vs. Personality

Sexual strategies theory (Buss, 1998; Buss & Schmitt, 1993, 2017) suggests that partly due to mammalian sex differences in the minimum necessary investment for reproduction (females invest more), and maximum potential number of offspring during lifetime (males can have more offspring) (cf. Janicke & Fromoteil, 2021; Janicke et al., 2016; Trivers, 1972), human males and females differ in what they find attractive in their potential sexual and romantic partners. Using divergent research methods, studies show that heterosexual men more than women value physical attractiveness and youth (i.e., cues to actual and residual fecundity), while women place more emphasis on status and earning capacity of their potential opposite-sex partners (i.e., cues to potential direct investments into offspring) (Buss & Schmitt, 2019; Shackelford, Schmitt, & Buss, 2005). Recently, this general sex difference in mate preferences pattern has been successfully replicated in a large-scale cross-cultural sample from 45 countries (Walter et al., 2020). For the same reasons, men, who can more than women increase their reproductive success by having more sexual partners, are also consistently and cross-culturally more interested in casual sexual relationships than women (Schmitt, 2005).

In one of the first studies on the topic, Bailey et al. (1994) investigated differences and similarities between heterosexual and homosexual men and women in several evolutionarily relevant aspects of mating strategies. In particular, they measured self-reported interest in uncommitted sex, interest in visual sexual stimuli, concern with partner's status, age preferences, importance of partner's physical attractiveness, and sexual versus emotional jealousy. In general, homosexual men reported similar mate preferences to heterosexual men, such as preferences for young and physically attractive partners, whereas homosexual women were more concerned with status, similar to heterosexual women. In the same vein, a more recent study found that, like heterosexual men, homosexual men value physical attractiveness more than status, while heterosexual and homosexual women value status more than physical attractiveness in their potential partners, although attractiveness was relatively more important than status for everyone (Ha et al., 2012).

Although overall the sex differences might be stronger, there is also some variation among individuals of the same sex and different sexual orientation. In a large scale survey, Lippa (2007) reported that both heterosexual and homosexual men ranked attractiveness of their ideal potential partners as more important than ambition or status. Still, heterosexual women emphasized male partner's status and financial prospects more than homosexual women. Moreover, homosexual men valued status cues as more important than heterosexual men. A more recent study analyzing personal advertisements revealed that compared to homosexual individuals, partner attributes offered and requested by heterosexual men and women revolved around status measures, with heterosexual women desiring status and heterosexual men offering status (Smith et al., 2011). Some studies, however, showed that financial resources of potential partners were more important for more feminine homosexual women ("femmes") than for more masculine homosexual women ("butches") (Bassett et al., 2001). This is an important finding that suggests that there is also variation among individuals of the same sex and sexual orientation (see below for details).

Although heterosexual men are concerned with the physical appearance of their potential and actual female partners, appearance and physical attractiveness might be of even higher value to homosexual men (e.g., Yelland & Tiggemann, 2003). However, homosexual men are more concerned with muscularity than with thinness, which is, in turn, of higher interest to heterosexual men (Levesque & Vichesky, 2006). This is a good example of how the general mechanism (i.e., focus on physical attractiveness) can be similar across sexual orientations among individuals of the same sex, but the importance of specific physical traits (here, muscularity versus thinness) can vary intra-sexually according to sexual orientation. Again, this example points to the modularity of each psychological aspect involved.

March et al. (2015) reported that homosexual and bisexual individuals consider the social status of a long-term mate more of a necessity than heterosexual individuals, while heterosexual individuals consider the physical attractiveness of a short-term mate more of a necessity than homosexual and bisexual individuals. Further, homosexual women value honesty above all other measured traits (Smith et al., 2010), and they also more frequently prefer partners of higher age than themselves and who are described as intelligent, which is similar to preferences of heterosexual women (Kenrick et al., 1995; Lippa, 2007).

When it comes to necessities in mate selection criteria, compared to a short-term sex partner who is expected to be physically attractive, for a long-term romantic partner both men and women of different sexual orientations value psychological characteristics, such as intellect, pro-sociality (e.g., interpersonal sensitivity), and family orientation (Lucas et al., 2011; Regan, et al., 2001). Similar to heterosexual men, homosexual men seeking long-term relationships mention their financial status on dating websites more than homosexual men or women seeking short-term encounters, and also than homosexual women seeking long-term partners (Dillon & Saleh, 2012). In one study, however, homosexual women valued physical attractiveness more than heterosexual women in both short- and long-term relationships, while heterosexual women valued other personal characteristics, mostly associated with good provisioning prospects and family/relationship orientation (Veloso et al., 2014). These studies were conducted in different populations, which might explain the difference in results.

There is limited evidence on preferences for personality characteristics in non-heterosexual individuals. In one cross-cultural study, heterosexual women desired partners higher on Extraversion, Conscientiousness and Emotional Stability than heterosexual men, non-heterosexual men, and non-heterosexual women (Valentova et al., 2016b). Further, heterosexual and non-heterosexual women desired partners higher on Agreeableness than both groups of men, and non-heterosexual women valued more Openness than heterosexual women. Thus, heterosexual and also partly non-heterosexual women showed higher standards for their ideal partners than heterosexual and non-heterosexual men. The only difference in men was greater preference for Conscientiousness among non-heterosexual men compared to heterosexual men. These results are in line with previous studies showing that women are more selective and have higher minimum standards than men (e.g., Buss, 1989; Regan, 1998; Schwarz & Hassebrauck, 2012), which could be attributable, at least in part, to the larger obligatory parental investment of women than men (Janicke et al., 2016; Schmitt & Buss, 1996; Trivers, 1972).

Interest in Casual Sex

Both homosexual and heterosexual men are more interested in visual sexual stimuli and casual sex than women of either sexual orientation (Bailey et al., 1994). However, realized casual sexual behavior is higher among homosexual men compared to heterosexual men (Howard & Perilloux, 2017; Schmitt, 2005, 2007). Some authors argue that heterosexual men's casual sexual behavior is limited by women, who are relatively more sexually restricted, whereas homosexual male partners are assortatively unrestricted, and thus their access to casual sex is less limited. Bisexual women (Luoto & Rantala, 2022) have been demonstrated to display elevated sex drive and desire when compared to both heterosexual and homosexual women (Lippa, 2006, 2007; Schmitt, 2007; Stief et al., 2014), and they also engage in more sexual behavior (Fethers et al., 2000; Hayes et al., 2011). Personality might play a role in elevated tendency for uncommitted sex among bisexual women. Stief et al. (2014) found that, in both men and women, bisexuality is associated with elevated sexual sensation seeking and sexual curiosity, but only among women with higher sexual excitability. Further, Semenyna et al. (2019) showed that this heightened sociosexuality observed in bisexual women is associated with personality traits known as the Dark Triad (Machiavellianism, sub-clinical narcissism, and sub-clinical psychopathy) and sexual competitiveness. It seems unsurprising that bisexual women report personality traits that enable them to pursue a sexually less restricted mating strategy (Schmitt et al., 2017; Valentova et al., 2020a), since such traits facilitate mate competition and offer psychological (i.e., emotional) protection in case this competition is not successful (Semenyna et al., 2018, 2019).

Thus, mating psychology seems to be rather sex-specific (i.e., similar among individuals of the same sex) with men being more sexually unrestricted than women, although some within-sex variation also exists. Intuitively, a more masculine individual should possess more male-typical traits because of the masculinizing role of androgens. For example, sociosexual orientation which refers to inclination toward short-term sexual relationships, is usually higher among men than women (Penke & Asendorpf, 2008). Indeed, a number of studies reported that more masculine women have more sexual partners than more feminine women (cf. Bártová et al., 2020; Mikach & Bailey, 1999; Varella et al., 2014). However, homosexual men are, on average, less masculine than heterosexual men (Bailey & Zucker, 1995), and their sociosexuality should thus be lower, which is not the case. Further, bisexual women are, on average, less masculine than homosexual women (Flanders & Hatfield, 2013), and yet have a more unrestricted sociosexuality (Schmitt, 2005, 2007). Moreover, a recent study found that gender non-conforming heterosexual and homosexual individuals (i.e., masculine women and feminine men) are more sexually unrestricted (Bártová et al., 2020). Similarly, non-heterosexual individuals are more often engaged in consensually nonmonogamous relationships (Valentova et al., 2020). Thus, a more proximate explanation might be that non-heterosexual and gender nonconforming individuals are more liberal, open-minded, and experimental, and thus willing to rebel against traditional gender roles (Schmitt, 2007). From the distal perspective, non-heterosexuality can be a part of a broader package, described by higher mating and lower parenting tendencies, sometimes conceptualized as a fast life history (Luoto et al., 2019).

When the first author of this chapter interviewed gay men about their sex life and attractiveness, she asked about lifetime number of sex partners. She received responses between 1 to several hundreds, but one respondent mentioned that he did not know what exactly it means "to have sex with someone"; he was thinking about what activities he should include into this definition. When asked with how many men he had anal sexual intercourse, he replied with around 40. When asked with how many partners he had oral sex, he said approximately 100. Mutual masturbation, he said, would not differ much from the oral sex partners. Thus, how this question is worded may produce unreliable estimates of sexual behavior, and can thus distort the numbers of sex partners reported. Different meanings of a 'sex partner' might be one of the reasons why different people or groups of people report different numbers of sex partners.

Preferences for Masculinity and Femininity (Hormonal Mechanisms)

Sex-typical morphological and behavioral characteristics that develop at least partly under the influence of sex hormones are presumed to cue to individual survival and reproductive abilities, such as fertility, immune system quality, capabilities of offspring protection, investments into offspring, or good partner abilities (cf. Thornhill & Gangestad, 2006). In general, heterosexual men find women with feminine sex-typical traits to be more attractive (e.g., Fraccaro et al., 2010), although there are exceptions, indicating that for long-term relationships and in harsh environments men prefer more masculine female partners (e.g., Little et al., 2007, but see Pereira et al., 2020). Women seem to vary more in their preference for masculinity-femininity. Such variation is partly due to genetic effects, and is also influenced by conditional factors, including personal and environmental characteristics (Zietsch et al., 2015).

Non-heterosexual individuals prefer sexual/romantic partners who are gender-typical, i.e., non-heterosexual men prefer rather masculine male partners, whereas non-heterosexual women prefer rather feminine female partners (Bailey et al., 1997; Bartholome et al., 2000; Boyden et al., 1984; Chen et al., 2019; Child et al., 1996; Glassenberg et al., 2010; Lippa, 2007; Phua, 2002; Zheng & Zheng, 2015a).

Masculine–Feminine Physical Traits and Behavior

Both heterosexual women and homosexual men prefer masculine, low-pitched voices (Valentova et al., 2013) and muscular, lean, and athletic body type (Bartholome et al., 2000; Štěrbová et al., 2018; Swami, & Tovée, 2008; Varangis et al., 2012), while homosexual men show stronger preferences for male facial masculinity than heterosexual women (Glassenberg et al., 2010; Zheng & Zheng, 2015a,b), and prefer partners either taller than themselves (similarly to heterosexual women) or with equal height (Valentova, Bártová et al., 2016; Valentova et al., 2014). Further, homosexual male preferences for their ideal partners' masculinity are consistent across different traits, including facial, bodily, and vocal cues (Zhang et al., 2018). Preferences for male masculinity may partly result from evolutionary processes (e.g., men with stronger bodies have higher mating and reproductive success; Lidborg et al., 2020) and, at the same time, can be emphasized and overstimulated by perpetuating the masculine ideal in social representations, thus leading to repeated exposure and, in turn, an increased preference (e.g., Pisanski & Feinberg, 2013).

Qualitative evidence suggests that a strong masculinity preference among homosexual men leads to preference for heterosexual or at least heterosexually looking and acting men not only among sexual partners but also among porn actors (Escoffier, 2009). There is a specific genre in gay pornography that is characterized by sex between two or more men who identify themselves as heterosexual: the "str8 sex"—or "gay for pay" (Burke, 2016; Ward, 2008). Further, it is estimated that around 30–40% of gay porn actors are heterosexually oriented, presumably because of a more masculine look and/or behavior (Escoffier, 2009). These straight performers are portrayed as taller, heavier, with a higher body mass index (BMI), and longer penises when compared to their homosexual counterparts. They also tend to have their masculinity and straightness exaggerated by their backstory and show signs of reluctance to engage in certain sexual acts (Burke, 2016; Kiss et al., 2019). A rich experience of the first author from interviews with gay men suggests that some gay men "specialize" as "straight men hunters." They value when the other man prefers women as sexual partners and has no previous same-sex experience. Some men further noticed that heterosexual men or at least men with a heterosexual experience are more caring and gentle in same-sex sexual relations. Thus, heterosexual men are preferred by some gay men because of their masculine characteristics, and at the same time because they need to be seduced into an intimate contact with other man. A hard-to-reach man might feel exciting, exotic and erotic.

Preferences for masculine, or even hypermasculine, traits within the homosexual male community can lead to distress and lower relationship satisfaction because homosexual men can be worried that their partner would lose interest if they acted in a more feminine way (Sanchez et al., 2009; Taywaditep, 2001; Wade & Donis, 2007; Wester et al., 2005). In an attempt to attend to the high masculinity demands, homosexual men also frequently suffer from eating disorders, alike to heterosexual women (Feldman & Meyer, 2007). Thus, men more than women report to value physical appearance in their partners (Walter et al., 2020), and this tendency seems to be even stronger in homosexual males. This might be a general pattern, but, of course, the specific physical traits that men prioritize can substantially differ according to the local sociocultural and historical habits.

Although homosexual women also prefer sex-typical (i.e., feminine) female sex partners, their preferences differ from those of heterosexual men. Similar to heterosexual men and women, non-heterosexual women tend to prefer a waist-to-hip ratio (WHR) of 0.7 (Cohen & Tannenbaum, 2001; Valentova et al., 2017a), although on average non-heterosexual women preferred bigger WHR than heterosexual men (Valentova et al., 2017a). Homosexual women show stronger preferences for female facial masculinity than heterosexual men (Glassenberg et al., 2010), and they prefer higher BMI than heterosexual men and women (Swami & Tovée, 2008). Inconclusive results appeared in preferences for breast size, as one study showed preferences for bigger breast size in non-heterosexual women (Cohen & Tannenbaum, 2001), while other research reported that non-heterosexual women showed preferences for smaller breasts and smaller buttocks than heterosexual men (Valentova et al., 2017a). However, both heterosexual men and non-heterosexual women preferred younger-looking female breasts (Valentova et al., 2017a). Thus, although homosexual women report preferences for feminine female partners, their preferences for specific physical traits are less sex-typical than in heterosexual men. Consequently, partner preferences of non-heterosexual individuals are not a mirror image of preferences of heterosexual individuals of the opposite sex (Glassenberg et al., 2010).

The tendency to prefer masculine male partners among non-heterosexual men and feminine female partners among homosexual women can be interpreted in two contrasting ways. On the one hand, preferences of non-heterosexual individuals can resemble those of heterosexual individuals of the opposite sex. In other words, homosexual male preferences for masculine partners may resemble those of heterosexual women, while non-heterosexual female preferences for feminine partners resemble those of heterosexual men. On the other hand, that gay men prefer rather masculine male partners while lesbian women prefer rather feminine partners can be a feature similar to heterosexual individuals of the same sex—both groups prefer rather sex-typical potential partners.

Importantly, heterosexual women do not show a clear preference for masculine traits, while homosexual men have stronger preferences for masculine traits than heterosexual women. For example, homosexual men prefer more masculine faces (Glassenberg et al., 2010) and more facial and body hair than women (Valentova et al., 2017b). On the contrary, heterosexual men have much clearer preference for feminine traits in their potential female partners (e.g., Fraccaro et al., 2010). This rather indicates, that the second interpretation is more plausible—homosexual male preferences for masculinity in their potential male partners and heterosexual male preferences for femininity in potential female partners (and vice versa in women) reflect the same pattern of preference for sex typicality. This might indicate a general tendency to pick up biological cues connected to sex typicality, such as sexual hormonal functioning, or social cues, such as group membership and/or status.

Further, not all studies found preferences for sex-typical partners in non-heterosexual individuals (e.g., Rieger et al., 2011; Valentova et al., 2013; Welling et al., 2013), suggesting that partner preferences of non-heterosexual men and women can be conditional, or they can vary according to different subgroups. Indeed, several contextual factors influence non-heterosexual male and female preferences for masculinity/femininity.

Preferences of Masculinity/Femininity for Short-Term vs. Long-Term Relationships

Preferences for masculinity/femininity in both heterosexual women and homosexual men are influenced by the temporal mating context. More specifically, both heterosexual and homosexual women and men prefer more sex-typical faces or bodies for short-term relationships than for long-term relationships (e.g., Li & Kenrick, 2006; Little et al., 2007; Provost et al., 2006; Varangis et al., 2012). The above mentioned high demands on physical appearance and masculinity among homosexual men might thus be associated with, or mediated by, an elevated search for short-term sexual partners, and thus a higher sociosexuality among homosexual men.

Influence of Sociosexuality on Preferences for Masculinity/Femininity

Heterosexual women and gay men who reported greater willingness to engage in uncommitted sexual relationships also reported stronger preferences for masculine faces (Glassenberg et al., 2010; Provost et al., 2006; Stower et al., 2020; Zheng, 2019a). Thus, both heterosexual women and homosexual men who seek short-term relationships tend to prefer more masculinized male faces. Masculine male characteristics could be cues to good health and other genetic qualities (Puts et al., 2012; but see Zaidi et al., 2019), and are thus sought in a short-term sexual partner to potentially pass these genetic qualities to a potential offspring. Although reproduction is reduced among same-sex sexual relationships, a similar psychological mechanism might work in androphilic individuals, irrespective of their own sex. It is yet to be answered whether this mechanism is at work also in homosexual women.

Influence of Relationship Status on Preferences for Masculinity/Femininity

Presumably, relationship status might also influence preferences for sex-typical traits. However, the results are rather ambiguous in both heterosexual and non-heterosexual individuals. One study found that single gay men preferred more masculine faces (Zheng, 2019a); another study found the opposite (Valentova et al., 2013); the most recent study did not find any effect of relationship status on preferences for facial masculinity/femininity in homosexual men (Cassar et al., 2020), suggesting that relationship status does not have a robust effect on gay men's masculinity preferences. In this case, the different results of these three studies might be attributable to assessment of distinct populations (Chinese, Czech, and British, respectively), calling for more cross-cultural comparisons of same-sex sexuality. As for homosexual women, more studies are needed to help understand any possible influence of partnership status on masculinity/femininity preferences.

Status, Sexism, and Dominance

Homosexual men who are more oriented to their potential partners' social status and health, and who report higher pathogen disgust prefer more masculine faces than men who value status less and have lower pathogen disgust (Zheng, 2019a; Zheng & Zheng, 2015a; although see Zheng et al., 2016). Further, homosexual men higher on hostile sexism (negative attitudes toward nontraditional women) prefer more masculine male faces, while homosexual men who score higher on benevolent sexism (tendency to protect women as a weaker sex) prefer more feminine male faces (Zheng & Zheng, 2015b). Similarly, in that study it was shown that heterosexual men with higher hostile sexism prefer more sex-typical female partners (i.e., more feminine), while more benevolently sexist women prefer potential male partners of higher status. These results indicate that preferences for "masculinity" may, in fact, rather mean preferences for social dominance and status. Rated facial and vocal masculinity is systematically associated with perceived dominance (Windhager et al., 2011; Wolff & Puts, 2010) and possibly also aggression, which is an important characteristic in intrasexual hierarchy, and thus of great significance in the context of intersexual selection (Lidborg et al., 2020) and also intrasexual competition (Puts et al., 2006).

Influence of Sexual Role on Preferences for Masculinity/Femininity

In some populations, individual roles during sexual activity are associated with hierarchy and gendered roles. Men who prefer the anal penetrative role in sex ("tops") prefer more feminized male faces than men who prefer the anal receptive role ("bottoms") (Zheng et al., 2013; Zhang et al., 2018). "Versatiles," who are willing to perform either role, did not show any specific preference (Zheng et al., 2013). In the same line, men who prefer to be dominant in both sexual activities and in the relationship also desire partners with shorter body stature, and vice versa (Valentova et al., 2014). Men who prefer the penetrative sexual role report being more masculine and having larger penises than bottoms (Moskowitz & Hart, 2011), suggesting complementarity among partners.

Among women, more feminine homosexual women ("femmes") do not differ much in preferred sexual roles from more masculine homosexual women ("butches"), although butches prefer to be slightly more sexually dominant and in the active penetrating position than femmes (Muscarella et al., 2004; Smith & Stillman, 2002). Also, most women, irrespective of their own masculinity/femininity, are attracted to femmes (Smith & Stillman, 2002), though there is some evidence that homosexual women who identify primarily as femmes prefer taller partners than butches (Muscarella et al., 2004).

Preferences for Self-Similarity Among Non-Heterosexual Individuals

In Western populations, heterosexual individuals couple most frequently with individuals of similar sociodemographic, physical, and some psychological characteristics. Besides the positive effect of similarity between partners on relationship quality, from the evolutionary point of view, some degree of self-similarity might increase reproductive success (for review, see Štěrbová & Valentova, 2012).

Preferences for self-similarity apply to preferences for masculinity/femininity (Bailey et al., 1997; Boyden et al., 1984). Bailey et al. (1997) analyzed personal ads of American heterosexual and homosexual men and women. Besides showing an overall preference for masculine male partners among gay men and a general preference for feminine female partners among homosexual women, they also reported that the partner preferences depended on own level of masculinity–femininity of the advertisers. More feminine men and more masculine women showed lower preferences for sex-typical potential partners. Similarly, Boyden et al. (1984) found that more masculine non-heterosexual men desired partners who would have higher analytical thinking (on average, a more masculine trait), while more feminine homosexual men desired ideal partners higher on expressive characteristics and dependency (on average, more feminine traits). Zheng & Zhang (2020) found that Chinese gay men with higher mental rotation abilities (on average, a more masculine cognitive trait) preferred more masculine male partners.

Interestingly, despite a preference for partners with similar degrees of masculinity/femininity, actual male–male couples are not alike in the degree of masculinity/femininity. However, partners who resemble each other in masculinity/femininity are more satisfied in their relationships, especially since masculinity/femininity in men can be a predictor for job and hobby preferences (Lippa, 2000, 2002; Lippa & Tan, 2001) and having them alike can improve time spent together and even emotional expression (Bártová et al., 2017). The self-similar preferences in masculinity/femininity domain are against a popular stereotype that imagine same-sex couples as gender stratified (i.e., one partner feminine and the other masculine).

Compared to heterosexual individuals, non-heterosexual women prefer female partners of a similar age (Boyden et al., 1984; Kenrick et al., 1995). However, male same-sex partners are less similar in age and education than their heterosexual counterparts and female same-sex partners (Andersson et al., 2006; Kurdek & Schmitt, 1987; Schwartz & Graf, 2009; Verbakel & Kalmijn, 2014). Similarly to masculinity/femininity, although same-sex male partners might not be more similar in age than random couples, they report higher relationship satisfaction when age similarity occurs (Todosijevic et al., 2005). Further, both heterosexual and non-heterosexual men and women preferred partners who would be similar in personality traits, although self-similarity between actual partners was significantly lower, particularly in homosexual men (Štěrbová et al., 2017). Interestingly, non-heterosexual men and women also prefer partners of similar body height (Valentova, Bártová, et al., 2016; Valentova et al., 2014), which dramatically differs from the "male-taller pattern" systematically reported among heterosexual men and women in Western populations (but see Sorokowski et al., 2015 for a different tendency in non-Western populations).

Some specific preferences for self-similarity in sex-dimorphic traits are impossible to be analyzed among heterosexual individuals, because they differ between the sexes. For example, we can only measure self-similarity in breast size among women who prefer women as sexual/romantic partners, while preferences for self-similarity in beards is measurable among men who are attracted to men. Indeed, preferences for self-similarity for sexually dimorphic traits appears in both men and women. In particular, non-heterosexual women prefer self-similar waist-to-hip ratio, buttock size, and breast size and shape in their ideal partners (Valentova, Bártová et al., 2017). Non-heterosexual men from one Latin American and one European population preferred self-similar degree of beardedness, although there was no such effect in body hair preferences (Valentova et al., 2017b). North American men, however, preferred self-similar amount of body hair, while in their ideal partners, men desired more facial hair than they had themselves (Muscarella et al., 2002). Finally, homosexual men showed a preference for a self-similar somatotype (body type)—in particular endomorphic dimension of the three-dimensional somatotype in their ideal partners (Štěrbová et al., 2018).

These findings provide some support for self-similarity preferences in some physical and personality traits among homosexual men and women across different populations, similar to heterosexual individuals. On first sight, homosexuality per se might be a part of preference for self-similarity.

To illustrate the self-similar preferences, the first author interviewed a highly masculine and dominant-looking gay man who looked so dominant that she was reluctant to ask him if he would agree with an interview. Luckily, he was very willing to talk, and during an almost three-hour interview he reported that he liked men who would be masculine, manly, with big hands, a masculine skull, broad chin and neck, prominent ears, deep voice, a manly gait, hairy chest, mustache, very short hair, tanned skin, physically fit and strong, using uniform-type clothes, smoking, using rough jewelry such as leather and steel (but no rings or small bracelets), being active and creative in bed, and men with a manly and creative profession, such as sculptor, architect, or car repairmen (but no waiter because that is a submissive type of job). As far as the first author could say, he basically described himself.

The above-mentioned interviewee might be characterized as a member of the leather gay community. There is limited research on sexuality, partner preferences, and relationships of specific subtypes of homosexual men. The gay community is often divided among several subcultural groupings, such as "bears" (more masculine, hairy, and heavy men), "twinks" (mostly young, slim, and rather feminine men), and many others (Maki, 2017; Prestage et al., 2015). These subgroups might help to understand better the variation among individuals of non-heterosexual orientation, including preferences for self-similarity. Among women, there seems to be rather a complementarity pattern in partner preferences among rather masculine ("butch") or feminine ("femme") subtypes of homosexual women (Muscarella et al., 2004), but more research is needed.

Further, self-similarity preferences might be specific to modern Western societies with the prevailing "gay" system, where both partners identify as homosexuals or gays and are of similar sociodemographic characteristics. In other historical periods and/or other populations, this picture can be profoundly different, mostly characterized by gender-stratified or age-stratified same-sex relationships, where one partner is significantly more masculine or older than the other, respectively (Hames et al., 2017; Murray, 2000; Werner, 2006; Whitam, 1983; Whitam & Mathy, 1986). Interestingly, in the sexual role (top vs. bottom), both men and women even in modern Western societies seek complementary partners; that is, men and women in the receptive/submissive sexual role prefer penetrative/active partners (Bailey et al., 1997; Moskowitz et al., 2008). This preference seems to be more universal, and in some populations the sexual role determines whether the individual is identified as homosexual (or a "third gender"), or not (e.g., Cardoso, 2005). The sexually, gender- or age-stratified partnering systems are suggested to reflect hierarchy between the partners and hierarchical structures of the given society (e.g., Werner, 2006).

Preferences for self-similarity can be partly a by-product of preferences for parent similarity, because of genetic relatedness between the individuals and their parents. A few studies, outlined in the next section, analyzed parent-similarity preferences in heterosexual and homosexual population.

Preferences for Parent Similarity (Imprinting-Like Effect)

Choosing a partner similar to one's own parents can be adaptive because parents have already proven that they can survive to adulthood and reproduce, in the given environment. Also, parent-similar partners might increase genetic compatibility of the partners (Helgason et al., 2008).

Several studies reported a possible influence of preferences for parent similarity (imprinting-like effect) in the ideal partners among the heterosexual population (for review, see Rantala & Marcinkowska, 2011). Non-heterosexual women prefer mother-similar WHR and buttock size in their ideal partners, but no mother influence has been found in their choice of actual partners (Valentova et al., 2017a). Homosexual men show a preference for men who wear glasses when either both parents or only father (but not only mother) wore glasses during the man's childhood (Aronsson et al., 2011). Non-heterosexual men also showed a preference for father-similar somatotype, which was similar to preferences of heterosexual women (Štěrbová et al., 2018). However, no father similarity has been found in preferences or actual mate choices based on father's facial and body hair (Valentova et al., 2017b). Mostly, actual partners did not resemble parents of both homosexual or heterosexual men and women.

Some studies reported that the quality of parent–child relationship positively influences preferences for parent similarity in their later sexual/romantic partners, particularly among women (e.g., Kocsor et al., 2016). No such effect was found in somatotype preferences of homosexual men (Štěrbová et al., 2018).

In general, the parent-similarity effect on partner preferences is still practically unknown, and in the studied traits it shows no or a very weak effect. However, other adaptive learning mechanisms can affect individuals of varying sexual orientations. One of the learning mechanisms people commonly use when choosing a partner is mate choice copying, when people rely on contextual information, such as another person, to evaluate a potential mate. In one recent study, participants judged photographs of individuals of their preferred sex surrounded by others who appeared to show interest in target individuals. Findings for gay and lesbian participants were inverted compared to heterosexual participants. In particular, lesbian women rated target women less desirable when surrounded by men compared to when surrounded by women. Gay men, on the other hand, rated target men surrounded by women as more desirable compared to male targets surrounded by other men (Scofield et al., 2020). Thus, some mating strategies are gender inverted in non-heterosexual individuals.

Partner Identification

"When I was younger I was trying to flirt with all men because I did not know who was gay," one interviewee told the first author. In a minority within the general population, it might be more difficult to identify an appropriate potential partner. Thus, during relationship initiation it is essential to focus efforts on maximizing the chances of finding a potential same-sex partner and to flirt appropriately. The universal solution seems to be defining specific places, such as bars, saunas, disco clubs, events and parades, parks, or even whole ghettos/neighborhoods, where like-minded people can easily detect and find a suitable mate. Most meeting points of non-heterosexual individuals are located in urban areas, several are even more specific, such as for singles only or "bears" only, and in some places heterosexual individuals or individuals of the nonpreferred sex are not permitted to enter. Flirting and short-term sexual relations are at a core of many non-heterosexual establishments, some of them offering specific places for rapid sexual encounters (e.g., in saunas, or in "dark rooms" in some nightclubs) (e.g., Guasch, 2011).

It is plausible that a similar social arrangement happened in ancestral times in which a specific location would be selected for gatherings where mating-motivated like-minded individuals could optimize mate search. Probably this gathering would also happen during the evening/nighttime, because the darkness makes it easier to conceal identity (Hirsh et al., 2011) and, because of tiredness, it is more difficult to self-regulate and thus easily succumb to immediate pleasures and vices (Millar et al., 2019). Indeed, Millar et al. (2019) conducted the only study that accessed tendency to nocturnal versus morning chronotype in gay and bisexual men; they found twice as many non-heterosexual participants in the "night owl" category (~1,600 individuals) than in the "early bird" one (~800 individuals), and only half of the latter in the "intermediate" chronocategory (+400). They also found that the non-heterosexual "night owl" chronotypes most used alcohol and club/party drugs after 9 p.m. Frequently, these substances also have disinhibitory effects (Hirsh et al., 2011), and thus help facilitate approaching a desirable mate during courtship.

Same-sex mating in such specific places and time periods is/was not exceptional to homosexually or bisexually identified individuals. These categories are quite recent, while same-sex attraction and behavior is very ancient. According to a recent model, bisexual behavior is probably the ancestral default (Monk et al., 2020), and as Kirkpatrick (2000) theorized, the capacity for both same-sex and other-sex sexuality seems to be adaptive. Homosociality might increase intrasexual cooperation and reduce competition, which is important in particular among societies aggregating non-kin individuals.

Little research has focused on describing the flirting methods and styles among non-heterosexuals. According to the Gersick and Kurzban (2014), human courtship/flirting behavior is uniquely covert due to second-party costs (e.g., an undesirable change in the nature of the relationship and loss of social capital) and third-party costs (e.g., a jealous partner or admirer intercepting or eavesdropping the dyad). They predict that courting individuals should strategically vary the overt intensity of their courtship signals to deal with the level of risk attached to the particular social configuration. An important cost to non-heterosexual courtship is incorrectly assessing the sexual orientation of a potential partner. To heterosexuals, this error would lead to not much more than a minor embarrassment; however, due to societal homophobic attitudes to non-heterosexuals, this might lead to a variety of risks to them, such as eliciting an offensive or violent reaction, and even revealing their non-heterosexual sexual identity, which could lead to losing their job, friends, or family (Custer et al., 2008). Thus, one of the great barriers in the relationship initiation process for non-heterosexuals is correctly identifying the sexual preference of a potential partner (Custer et al., 2008). Some studies suggest that non-heterosexual individuals are better at correctly recognizing other's sexual orientation, which can be partly due to familiarity with alikes (Valentova & Havlíček, 2013). Moreover, an ethnographic study of "gaydar" using participant observation and interviews with gay men and lesbians found that they tend to use the "gaydar gaze" to signal their homosexuality to other homosexual individuals (Nicholas, 2004). Besides, non-heterosexual orientation may be revealed by subtle arbitrary signals such as pins or rings of specific colors known only within the community. Thus, this ability greatly reduces the costs of courtship outside the specific community places which, in turn, could increase the overtness/directness of their approach according to Gersick and Kurzban's (2014) model. This model obviously applies in particular to societies with some degree of homophobia, although it seems that signals, language, and places specific to individuals with same-sex preferences were present in non-Western societies, such as the Tokugawa era in Japan (Leupp, 1997).

The same would apply to non-heterosexual flirting online. The risk of flirting with someone with an incompatible sexual orientation is attenuated, and hence the flirting could be more overtly erotic (Custer et al., 2008). Indeed, male and female homosexual couples use more sexually connoting words and phrases than their heterosexual counterparts;

though, admittedly this erotic/sexually laden vocabulary is used to arouse their partners (Wells, 1990). Moreover, White et al. (2018) found that heterosexual individuals pursuing a short-term mating strategy selected more atypical flirting behaviors. Given that non-heterosexual men and women are more prone to short-term mating (see above), we would expect that in gay/lesbian-friendly places, they would exhibit a high incidence of overt and atypical courtship displays. Indeed, both homosexual men and homosexual women show some differences in behavioral scripts during the first date than heterosexuals; in particular, they are freer from gendered schemas (Klinkenberg & Rose, 1994; Rose & Zand, 2002). Further, homosexual men use online dating apps (e.g., Grindr) to find uncommitted sexual encounters and avoid possible romantic involvement, or even conversation, while heterosexuals seem to be more socially involved, even though their primary motive is also casual sex (Licoppe, 2020). Moreover, homosexual men report to be more sexually oriented while homosexual women are more intimacy oriented (Klineberg & Rose, 1994). Interestingly, the boundaries between friendship and romantic relationship in lesbian women are less clear than in other individuals—intimacy being an integral part of lesbian relationships since their beginning (for review, Peplau & Fingerhut, 2007).

Ideal Preferences and Actual Partner Choice

Although partner preferences can influence actual partner choices (and vice versa, Kučerová et al., 2018), previous research shows some discrepancy between ideal and actual partners in personality and physical characteristics in heterosexual individuals (Courtiol et al., 2010; Valentova, Bártová et al., 2016; Valentova et al., 2016a) and also in non-heterosexual men and women (Valentova, Bártová et al., 2016a; Valentova, Štěrbová et al., 2016; Valentova et al., 2016b; Valentova et al., 2017b). For example, non-heterosexual men prefer slightly more beard than their actual partners have, and non-heterosexual women prefer narrower waists than their partners have (Valentova et al., 2017b).

Non-heterosexual men, on average, prefer masculine characteristics in their potential male partners (e.g., Bailey et al.,1997), but more masculine men did not have more masculine partners, in terms of self-reported gender nonconformity (Bártová et al., 2017). However, couples who were more alike in their level of masculinity/femininity indicated higher relationship satisfaction (Bártová et al., 2017). Further, participants of any sex and sexual orientation desired partners who would be more extraverted, open to new experiences, conscientious, agreeable, and emotionally stable (all the big five personality traits) than their actual partners were (Štěrbová et al., 2017).

These results indicate that people do compromise when it comes to actual partner choices (Eastwick & Neff, 2012; Figueredo et al., 2006; Todd et al., 2007). For example, one previous study on a heterosexual population did not find any correlation between preferred personality in an ideal partner and personality in the actual partner (Figueredo et. al., 2006). When people are choosing their actual partner, many factors and characteristics are considered, such as age, health, appearance, religion, political orientation and values, personality, and so on. However, only a few individuals would combine all preferred characteristics at the same time, and what is worse, the preferred partner can be unavailable. Thus, the optimal combination of all actual characteristics can differ from preferences for absolute traits. Interestingly, there is some evidence that the discrepancy between an ideal and actual partner is larger among non-heterosexual individuals, in particular, among non-heterosexual men (Valentova et al., 2016b). The bigger gap between ideal and actual partners might be influenced by a relatively smaller partner pool among non-heterosexual individuals, or non-heterosexual individuals might not be as demanding when it comes to real partner choices. The range between the ideal partner characteristics and minimal acceptable characteristics should be studied more both in heterosexual and non-heterosexual populations.

Nowadays, a majority of same-sex relationships are initiated through digital applications (Custer et al., 2008). LGBT people are more likely to find romantic partners online if they face a thin market for potential partners (Rosenfeld & Thomas, 2012). The impact of distal partner selection and first encounters on relationship formation has already received scientific attention and might reveal important insights into same-sex and opposite-sex mating initiation that face-to-face interactions do not.

We have already mentioned several studies analyzing online personal advertisements of people searching for long- or short-term sexual partners. In 2012, Dillon and Saleh analyzed photographs of personal profiles on a partner seeking website (i.e., Plenty of Fish) to investigate sex and sexual orientation variation in nonverbal displays. They found some similarities of homosexual men's and women's photographs with heterosexual men and women, respectively. For example, similarly to heterosexual women, homosexual women smiled more, displayed more skin, and downplayed their height by using a downward camera angle compared to gay men.

Limitations of the Existing Studies and Future Directions

Research investigating relationship initiation among non-heterosexual individuals has several limitations. As noted, long-term same-sex relationships between partners of the same age, education, status, and sexual orientation are rather recent and specific for Western populations. Same-sex relationships take many different forms in other populations. The anthropological and ethnographic literature reports three basic models of same-sex relationships that are based on age difference between the partners or gender roles established between partners (Murray, 2000). In the gender-stratified relationships, one of the partners is more masculine, while the other more feminine, which can also be connected to activity and passivity during sexual activities (e.g., Werner, 1998). In the age-stratified relationships, one partner is significantly older than the other. On the contrary, in egalitarian relationships the partners do not have strictly differentiated gender roles and are usually peers (Kurdek, 2004). Non-heterosexual individuals from Western populations mostly prefer self-similar and rather sex-typical characteristics in their potential partners, while in non-Western populations the pattern can be different. Gender stratified same-sex relationships are common in many distant populations, such as India, Malaysia, and Indonesia or among native North American tribes. In these populations, more than two genders traditionally exist or have existed, which means that, for example, biological males identified as either men or a specific third gender, who performed different rather than traditional male and female social roles. In some of these populations, sexual relationships between men and the third-gender males were or are quite common. In Samoa, a majority of men have sexual relations with both women and the third-gender males, called Fa'afafine (Semenyna et al., 2020). In Western and Westernized populations some people also prefer specifically transgendered men or women as sexual partners, rather than cisgender (e.g., Hsu et al., 2016). Preferences for partners of a very lower or higher age than oneself are also present in Western populations but have been overlooked in the scientific literature. Further, intersexual competition for partners also exists more in populations where people frequently have relations with individuals of both sexes and all genders (Semenyna et al., 2020). Mating strategies, including partner preferences, mate attraction and choice, and intrasexual and intersexual competition strategies, of these subgroups are practically unknown.

Further, stable same-sex preferences and long-term same-sex relationships are relatively rare among non-Western populations and among other species. Opportunistic short-term same-sex mating, though, is more frequent. However, most research cited in this chapter focuses on individuals who self-identify as non-heterosexuals and who systematically or even exclusively pursue same-sex mating. Mating psychology of individuals who do not identify as heterosexuals or homosexuals, or of individuals whose attraction is neither exclusively heterosexual nor homosexual is less known (Valentova et al., 2022b; Vrangalova & Savin-Williams, 2012).

One of the major limitations of previous studies is the definition and measurement of sexual orientation. Some studies did not measure sexual orientation but rather identification with sexual orientation labels (e.g., "Do you consider yourself heterosexual, bisexual, homosexual?"), other studies used a scale of sexual orientation anchored with explicit terms of sexual identification (ranging from "exclusively heterosexual" to "exclusively homosexual"), or used rather implicit terms of sexual preference or attraction (e.g., "exclusively attracted towards individuals of the opposite sex," etc.). Even if some studies used a scale of sexual orientation, they usually pooled exclusively and mostly heterosexual individuals into one category and mostly and exclusively homosexual into another; some pooled together bisexual and homosexual participants in order to analyze heterosexuals versus non-heterosexuals with bigger sample size, and only a handful of studies distinguished also bisexual individuals. Still, "bisexuals" is a broad category, that includes intermediate categories of "mostly heterosexuals" and "mostly homosexuals" who show some differences from both exclusively heterosexual/homosexual individuals and bisexuals (Savin-Williams & Vrangalova, 2013; Vrangalova & Savin-Williams, 2012). Individuals who are, for example, predominantly or mostly heterosexual, can adopt different mating strategies from other groups of sexual orientations and should be investigated further in future studies. Importantly, individuals who identify as bisexual might show some differences from pansexual or queer individuals, such as in a more dichotomous gender polarization of their preferred partners (e.g., Galupo et al., 2017).

Besides the importance of distinguishing better the bisexual and other non-heterosexual individuals, bisexual individuals are the only group that can decide the effect of sex of the partner. For example, if preference for younger age is typical for male sex, then bisexual men should prefer younger female and also younger male partners. On the contrary, bisexual women should prefer partners of both sexes who would be older than themselves. However, if age preference is rather influenced by sex of the partner, then we might expect bisexual men to be interested in younger female partners and older male partners, while bisexual women would show preference for older male partners and younger female partners. Of course, there can also be an interaction between own sex and sex of the partner, and again, only individuals who are attracted to both sexes can reliably show how these factors are interconnected.

Moreover, not only can bisexual individuals have partners of both sexes, they can also be threatened by rivals of both sexes, and can thus show whether sex of the rival makes some difference in their mating tendencies, such as jealousy (e.g., Scherer et al., 2013; Valentova et al., 2022a,b). Thus, future evolutionary-based research on mating strategies that involves sex differences should focus more on individuals with other than heterosexual orientation, in order to disentangle if there is any variation based on sex of the individual or their partner or even their rival.

Further, we have outlined a line of research that focuses on specific partner preferences and attractiveness in non-heterosexual individuals. Although important, there is still lack of systematic studies on specific evolutionary mechanisms in individuals of varying sexual orientations. For example, is there evidence for theories of "good genes," "sexy sons," imprinting-like effect, sensory exploitation, or social learning that would apply to or vary with different sexual orientations? Do non-heterosexual women's mating strategies (e.g., partner preferences and temporal context of sexual relationships) alter with ovulatory shift during their menstrual cycle? Or does the ovulatory shift affect female's variation in sexual attraction to one or the other sex? Mating mechanisms are sensitive to environmental conditions, such as pathogen threat or resource scarcity (e.g., Pereira et al., 2020), and they might thus also vary in respect to sexual orientation. We might infer that homosexual men value similar sex-typical characteristics in their male partners as heterosexual men do in their female partners. Thus, the mechanism of good genes or sexy sons might be active, although misplaced because the male partner with good genes will not provide these genes for the other male partner's offspring. There is also some scarce evidence of specific adaptive learning mechanisms that might function in non-heterosexual individuals, such as imprinting-like effect and social learning.

Further, what is mostly analyzed is an average tendency of some group of individuals, which is a valid quantitative approach but it does not capture the whole complexity and variability of individual mating strategies. To illustrate a more individual approach, one study discussed the distribution of preferences among different types of stimuli, in this case different levels of male facial hair, across two different populations (Valentova et al., 2017b). The pictorial stimuli comprised four pictures depicting the same man clean shaven, with a stubble after 5 days, after 10 days, and with a full beard. On average, non-heterosexual men preferred more bearded male faces than heterosexual women did. However, non-heterosexual male preferences in both populations were quite equally distributed among these four stimuli, whereas a vast majority of heterosexual women preferred either clean-shaven faces or a small stubble (depending on the population) and did not prefer full beards. This suggests that homosexual male preferences cannot be either stereotypically reduced to a gender atypical or heterosexual female pattern of preferences or to hypermasculine preferences for highly male typical traits. It rather seems that, at least in some characteristics, non-heterosexual partner preferences are not limited to a specific ideal form. It might also suggest that there are more subtypes of non-heterosexual individuals, some of them being rather sex typical, while others rather sex atypical.

Several studies suggest more subtypes of both homosexual women and homosexual men. In particular, homosexual women frequently divide themselves into femmes and butch, according to their feminine and masculine phenotype, respectively (e.g., Bailey et al., 1997). In men, only recently several subtypes have been taken into account, and associated with individual masculinity/femininity (Swift-Gallant, 2019). This indicates that homosexual individuals are a heterogeneous group composed of subtypes marked with different developmental, and potentially evolutionary, pathways (Swift-Gallant, 2019). Discrepancies in the mentioned studies and not an overall clear picture of partner preferences and sexual strategies may thus be, at least partly, caused by this heterogeneity within the non-heterosexual groups.

Gender (a)typicality can change over time, as it seems that homosexual men become more gender nonconforming after coming out (Daniele et al., 2020). Similarly, sexual preferences are also flexible and, particularly in women, fluid over time (Diamond et al., 2019). It is thus important to consider sexual preferences as a facultative (but not intentionally premeditated) trait, or as a mechanism that navigates sexuality of each individual toward partners of a determined sex, but the mechanism can sensitively respond to personal and environmental contexts (Valentova & Varella, 2016b).

Conclusions and future directions

We reviewed studies on mating strategies in non-heterosexual individuals. More specifically, we analyzed partner preferences, mate choice, and flirting to identify which patterns are similar to or different from heterosexuals. The more general mechanisms (e.g., focus on physical attractiveness, short-term mating and preferences for gender-typical partners) show differences between the sexes and are comparable among individuals of the same sex across different sexual orientations. Thus, at least some facets of the mating psychology seem to be rather sex-specific (i.e., similar among individuals of the same sex), but we also reported some within-sex variation.

- Physical attractiveness is valued especially for short-term sexual encounters, and on average more by men of any sexual orientation.
- Socioeconomic status, on the other hand, seems to be more important for women of any sexual orientation.
- Men, on average, are more prone to casual sex than women, and homosexual men and bisexual women score higher than their heterosexual counterparts.
- Heterosexual and non-heterosexual individuals prefer sexual/romantic partners who are gender-typical; that is, they prefer rather masculine male partners or rather feminine female partners.
- Partner preferences of heterosexual and non-heterosexual men and women can be conditional; they vary with the temporary context of the relationship, sociosexuality, relationship status, or dominance.
- Heterosexual and non-heterosexual individuals prefer some degree of self-similarity in their partners.
- There is some mismatch between ideal and actual romantic partners, in particular among non-heterosexual men.
- Among non-heterosexuals, the search for partners mostly happens in specific places designed for these purposes, and through digital social networks.

Thus, non-heterosexual individuals pursue similar sexual strategies as their heterosexual counterparts. This might indicate a general tendency to attend to biological cues connected to partner's reproductive quality, fertility, resource-holding potential, and/or partnering and parental abilities. Possibly, the mechanisms of good genes, sexy sons/daughters, the handicap principle, or the Fisherian runaway model or sensory exploitation may contribute, and there is scarce evidence of specific adaptive learning mechanisms that might function in non-heterosexual individuals, such as imprinting-like effect and social learning.

Importantly, we have demonstrated that although some aspects of mating psychology, such as partner preference, among non-heterosexuals resemble those of heterosexuals of the same sex, other aspects resemble those of heterosexuals of the opposite sex, and yet in others, the pattern is different than the one among either heterosexual men or heterosexual women. Thus, sexual strategies and partner preferences of non-heterosexual individuals are not a mirror image of preferences of heterosexual individuals of either sex. Non-heterosexuality may be a manifestation of adaptive homosociality, and their mating strategies, including relationship initiation processes and long-term relationship dynamics, may reflect an adaptive sexual strategy that is different from exclusively heterosexual strategy. Current and future theories of the evolutionary origins of homosexuality (and, ideally, non-heterosexuality more broadly) should account for the specific pattern of these relationships and try to explain their occurrence.

We have summarized, discussed, and criticized the sparse evolutionary literature on aspects of relationship initiation in non-heterosexuals. We also stressed the main reasons to approach non-heterosexuals from the evolutionary perspective and have highlighted many gaps in the current knowledge and offered new hypotheses and avenues for future research. We hope to have encouraged evolutionarily minded researchers to expand their research scope and help to systematically build the literature about sexual minorities, including the array of non-heterosexual, nonmonogamous, and nonbinary gendered people.

References

Andersson, G., Noack, T., Seierstad, A., & Weedon-Fekjaer, H. (2006). The demographics of same-sex marriages in Norway and Sweden. *Demography, 43*(1), 79–98.

Apostolou, M. (2017). Is homosexuality more prevalent in agropastoral than in hunting and gathering societies? Evidence from the Standard Cross-Cultural Sample. *Adaptive Human Behavior and Physiology, 3*(2), 91–100.

Aronsson, H., Lind, J., Ghirlanda, S., & Enquist, M. (2011). Parental influences on sexual preferences: The case of attraction to smoking. *Journal of Evolutionary Psychology, 9*(1), 21–41.

Bailey, J. M., Gaulin, S., Agyei, Y., & Gladue, B. A. (1994). Effects of gender and sexual orientation on evolutionarily relevant aspects of human mating psychology. *Journal of Personality and Social Psychology, 66*(6), 1081.

Bailey, J. M., Kim, P. Y., Hills, A., & Linsenmeier, J. A. (1997). Butch, femme, or straight acting? Partner preferences of gay men and lesbians. *Journal of Personality and Social Psychology, 73*(5), 960.

Bailey, J. M., Vasey, P. L., Diamond, L. M., Breedlove, S. M., Vilain, E., & Epprecht, M. (2016). Sexual orientation, controversy, and science. *Psychological Science in the Public Interest, 17*(2), 45–101.

Bailey, J. M., & Zucker, K. J. (1995). Childhood sex-typed behavior and sexual orientation: A conceptual analysis and quantitative review. *Developmental Psychology, 31*(1), 43.

Barron, A. B., & Hare, B. (2020). Prosociality and a sociosexual hypothesis for the evolution of same-sex attraction in humans. *Frontiers in Psychology, 10*, Article 2955.

Bartholome, A., Tewksbury, R., & Bruzzone, A. (2000). "I want a man": Patterns of attraction in all-male personal ads. *The Journal of Men's Studies, 8*(3), 309–321.

Bártová, K., Štěrbová, Z., Varella, M. A. C., & Valentova, J. V. (2020). Femininity in men and masculinity in women is positively related to sociosexuality. *Personality and Individual Differences, 152, 109575.* doi:10.1016/j.paid.2019.109575

Bártová, K., Štěrbová, Z., Nováková, L. M., Binter, J., Varella, M. A. C., & Valentova, J. V. (2017). Homogamy in masculinity–femininity is positively linked to relationship quality in gay male couples from the Czech Republic. *Archives of Sexual Behavior, 46*(5), 1349–1359.

Bassett, J., Pearcey, S., & Dabbs Jr, J. M. (2001). Jealousy and partner preference among butch and femme lesbians. *Psychology, Evolution & Gender, 3*(2), 155–165.

Boyden, T., Carroll, J. S., & Maier, R. A. (1984). Similarity and attraction in homosexual males: The effects of age and masculinity-femininity. *Sex Roles, 10*(11–12), 939–948.

Burke, N. B. (2016). Straight-acting: Gay pornography, heterosexuality, and hegemonic masculinity. *Porn Studies, 3*(3), 238–254.

Buss, D. M. (1989). Sex differences in human mate preferences: Evolutionary hypotheses tested in 37 cultures. *Behavioral and Brain Sciences, 12*(1), 1–14.

Buss, D. M., & Schmitt, D. P. (1993). Sexual strategies theory: An evolutionary perspective on human mating. *Psychological Review, 100*(2), 204.

Buss, D. M., & Schmitt, D. P. (2019). Mate preferences and their behavioral manifestations. *Annual Review of Psychology, 70*, 77–110.

Cardoso, F. L. (2005). Cultural universals and differences in male homosexuality: The case of a Brazilian fishing village. *Archives of Sexual Behavior, 34*(1), 103–109

Cassar, R., Shiramizu, V., DeBruine, L. M., & Jones, B. C. (2020). No evidence that partnered and unpartnered gay men differ in their preferences for male facial masculinity. *PLoS ONE, 15*(3), Article e0229133.

Chen, Q., Sui, L., Jiang, X., Zhou, Z., Han, C., & Hou, J. (2019). Facial attractiveness of Chinese college students with different sexual orientation and sex roles. *Frontiers in Human Neuroscience, 13*, 132.

Child, M., Low, K. G., McCormick, C. M., & Cocciarella, A. (1996). Personal advertisements of male-to-female transexuals, homosexual men, and heterosexuals. *Sex Roles, 34*(5–6), 447–455.

Cohen, A. B., & Tannenbaum, I. J. (2001). Lesbian and bisexual women's judgments of the attractiveness of different body types. *Journal of Sex Research, 38*(3), 226–232.

Conway, J. R., Noe, N., Stulp, G., & Pollet, T. V. (2015). Finding your soulmate: Homosexual and heterosexual age preferences in online dating. *Personal Relationships, 22*(4), 666–678.

Courtiol, A., Picq, S., Godelle, B., Raymond, M., & Ferdy, J. B. (2010). From preferred to actual mate characteristics: The case of human body shape. *PLoS ONE, 5*(9), e13010.

Custer, L., Holmberg, D., Blair, K., & Orbuch, T. L. (2008). So how did you two meet? Narratives of relationship initiation. In S. Sprecher, A. Wenzel, & J. Harvey (Eds.), *Handbook of relationship initiation* (pp. 453–470). Psychology Press.

Daniele, M., Fasoli, F., Antonio, R., Sulpizio, S., & Maass, A. (2020). Gay voice: Stable marker of sexual orientation or flexible communication device? *Archives of Sexual Behavior, 49*(7), 2585–2600. https://doi.org/10.1007/s10508-020-01771-2

Diamond, L. M., Alley, J., Dickenson, J., & Blair, K. L. (2019). Who counts as sexually fluid? Comparing four different types of sexual fluidity in women. *Archives of Sexual Behavior, 49*, 2389–2403. https://doi.org/10.1007/s10508-019-01565-1

Dillon, L. M., & Saleh, D. J. (2012). Sexual strategies theory: Evidence from homosexual personal advertisements. *Journal of Social, Evolutionary, and Cultural Psychology, 6*(2), 203–216. https://doi.org/10.1037/h0099214

Eastwick, P. W., & Neff, L. A. (2012). Do ideal partner preferences predict divorce? A tale of two metrics. *Social Psychological and Personality Science, 3*(6), 667–674.

Escoffier, J. (2009). *Bigger than life: The history of gay porn cinema from beefcake to hardcore.* Running Press Adult.

Feldman, M. B., & Meyer, I. H. (2007). Eating disorders in diverse lesbian, gay, and bisexual populations. *International Journal of Eating Disorders, 40*(3), 218–226.

Fethers, K., Marks, C., Mindel, A., & Estcourt, C. S. (2000). Sexually transmitted infections and risk behaviours in women who have sex with women. *Sexually Transmitted Infections, 76*(5), 345–349.

Figueredo, A. J., Sefcek, J. A., & Jones, D. N. (2006). The ideal romantic partner personality. *Personality and Individual Differences, 41*(3), 431–441.

Flanders, C. E., & Hatfield, E. (2013). Perceptions of gender and bisexuality: An exploration of the relationship between perceived masculinity, femininity, and sexual ambiguity. *Journal of Bisexuality, 13*(3), 374–389.

Fraccaro, P. J., Feinberg, D. R., DeBruine, L. M., Little, A. C., Watkins, C. D., & Jones, B. C. (2010). Correlated male preferences for femininity in female faces and voices. *Evolutionary Psychology, 8*(3), 147470491000800311.

Galupo, M. P., Ramirez, J. L., & Pulice-Farrow, L. (2017). "Regardless of their gender": Descriptions of sexual identity among bisexual, pansexual, and queer identified individuals. *Journal of Bisexuality, 17*(1), 108–124.

Gates, G.J. (2013). *LGBT parenting in the United States.* Williams Institute, UCLA School of Law.

Gavrilets, S., Friberg, U., & Rice, W. R. (2018). Understanding homosexuality: Moving on from patterns to mechanisms. *Archives of Sexual Behavior, 47*(1), 27–31.

Gersick, A., & Kurzban, R. (2014). Covert sexual signaling: Human flirtation and implications for other social species. *Evolutionary Psychology, 12*(3), Article 147470491401200305.

Glassenberg, A. N., Feinberg, D. R., Jones, B. C., Little, A. C., & DeBruine, L. M. (2010). Sex-dimorphic face shape preference in heterosexual and homosexual men and women. *Archives of Sexual Behavior, 39*(6), 1289–1296.

Gobrogge, K. L., Perkins, P. S., Baker, J. H., Balcer, K. D., Breedlove, S. M., & Klump, K. L. (2007). Homosexual mating preferences from an evolutionary perspective: Sexual selection theory revisited. *Archives of Sexual Behavior, 36*(5), 717–723.

Grøntvedt, T. V., & Kennair, L. E. O. (2013). Age preferences in a gender egalitarian society. *Journal of Social, Evolutionary, and Cultural Psychology, 7*(3), 239.

Guasch, O. (2011). Social stereotypes and masculine homosexualities: The Spanish case. *Sexualities, 14*(5), 526–543.

Ha, T., van den Berg, J.E.M., Engels, R.C.M.E. *et al.* (2012) Effects of Attractiveness and Status in Dating Desire in Homosexual and Heterosexual Men and Women. *Archives of Sexual Behavior* **41**, 673–682. https://doi.org/10.1007/s10508-011-9855-9

Hames, R., Garfield, Z., & Garfield, M. (2017). Is male androphilia a context-dependent cross-cultural universal? *Archives of Sexual Behavior, 46*(1), 63–71.

Hayes, A. F. (1995). Age preferences for same-and opposite-sex partners. *The Journal of Social Psychology, 135*(2), 125–133.

Hayes, J., Chakraborty, A. T., McManus, S., Bebbington, P., Brugha, T., Nicholson, S., & King, M. (2011). Prevalence of same-sex behavior and orientation in England: Results from a national survey. *Archives of Sexual Behavior, 41*, 631–639

Helgason, A., Palsson, S., Guobjartsson, D. F., Kristjánsson, Þ., & Stefánsson, K. (2008). An association between the kinship and fertility of human couples. *Science 319*, 813–816

Hirsh, J. B., Galinsky, A. D., & Zhong, C. B. (2011). Drunk, powerful, and in the dark: How general processes of disinhibition produce both prosocial and antisocial behavior. *Perspectives on Psychological Science, 6*(5) 415–427.

Howard, R. M., & Perilloux, C. (2017). Is mating psychology most closely tied to biological sex or preferred partner's sex? *Personality and Individual Differences, 115*, 83–89.

Hsu, K. J., Rosenthal, A. M., Miller, D. I., & Bailey, J. M. (2016). Who are gynandromorphophilic men? Characterizing men with sexual interest in transgender women. *Psychological Medicine, 46*(4), 819–827.

Jabbour, J., Holmes, L., Sylva, D., Hsu, K. J., Semon, T. L., Rosenthal, A. M., Safron, A., Slettevold, E., Watts-Overall, T. M., Savin-Williams, R. C., Sylla, J., Rieger, G., & Bailey, J. M. (2020). Robust evidence for bisexual orientation among men. *Proceedings of the National Academy of Sciences, 117*(31), 18369–18377.

Kenrick, D. T. (2011). *Sex, murder, and the meaning of life: A psychologist investigates how evolution, cognition, and complexity are revolutionizing our view of human nature.* Basic Books.

Kenrick, D. T., & Keefe, R. C. (1992). Age preferences in mates reflect sex differences in human reproductive strategies. *Behavioral and Brain Sciences, 15*(1), 75–91.

Kenrick, D. T., Keefe, R. C., Bryan, A., Barr, A., & Brown, S. (1995). Age preferences and mate choice among homosexuals and heterosexuals: A case for modular psychological mechanisms. *Journal of Personality & Social Psychology, 69*, 1166—1172.

Kirkpatrick, R. C. (2000). The evolution of human homosexual behavior. *Current Anthropology, 41*(3), 385–413.

Kiss, M., Morrison, T. G., & Parker, K. (2019). Understanding the believability and erotic value of 'heterosexual'men in gay pornography. *Porn Studies, 6*(2), 169–192.

Klinkenberg, D., & Rose, S. (1994). Dating scripts of gay men and lesbians. *Journal of Homosexuality, 26*(4), 23–35.

Kocsor, F., Saxton, T. K., Láng, A., & Bereczkei, T. (2016). Preference for faces resembling opposite-sex parents is moderated by emotional closeness in childhood. *Personality and Individual Differences, 96*, 23–27.

Kučerová, R., Csajbók, Z., & Havlíček, J. (2018). Coupled individuals adjust their ideal mate preferences according to their actual partner. *Personality and Individual Differences, 135*, 248–257.

Kurdek, L. A. (2004). Are gay and lesbian cohabiting couples really different from heterosexual married couples? *Journal of Marriage and Family, 66*(4), 880–900.

Kurdek, L. A., & Schmitt, J. P. (1987). Partner homogamy in married, heterosexual cohabiting, gay, and lesbian couples. *Journal of Sex Research, 23*(2), 212–232.

Leupp, G. (1997). *Male colors: The construction of homosexuality in Tokugawa Japan.* University of California Press.

Levesque, M. J., & Vichesky, D. R. (2006). Raising the bar on the body beautiful: An analysis of the body image concerns of homosexual men. *Body Image, 3*(1), 45–55.

Li, N. P., & Kenrick, D. T. (2006). Sex similarities and differences in preferences for short-term mates: What, whether, and why. *Journal of Personality and Social Psychology, 90*(3), 468.

Licoppe, C. (2020). Liquidity and attachment in the mobile hookup culture. A comparative study of contrasted interactional patterns in the main uses of Grindr and Tinder. *Journal of Cultural Economy, 13*(1), 73–90.

Lidborg, L. H., Cross, C. P., & Boothroyd, L. G. (2020). Does masculinity really matter? A meta-analysis of the relationships between sexually dimorphic traits in men and mating/reproduction. *bioRxiv*.
Lippa, R. A. (2000). Gender-related traits in gay men, lesbian women, andheterosexual men and women: The virtual identity of homosexual-heterosexual diagnosticity and gender diagnosticity. *Journal of Personality, 68*, 899–926.
Lippa, R. A. (2002). Gender-related traits of heterosexual and homosexual men and women. *Archives of Sexual Behavior, 31*, 83–98.
Lippa, R. A. (2006). Is high sex drive associated with increased sexual attraction to both sexes? It depends on whether you are male or female. *Psychological Science, 17*, 46–52.
Lippa, R. A. (2007). The relation between sex drive and sexual attraction to men and women: A cross-national study of heterosexual, bisexual, and homosexual men and women. *Archives of Sexual Behavior, 36*, 209–222.
Little, A. C., Cohen, D. L., Jones, B. C., & Belsky, J. (2007). Human preferences for facial masculinity change with relationship type and environmental harshness. *Behavioral Ecology and Sociobiology, 61*(6), 967–973.
Lippa, R. A., & Tan, F. D. (2001). Does culture moderate the relationship between sexual orientation and gender-related personality traits?. *Cross-Cultural Research, 35*(1), 65–87.
Lucas, M., Koff, E., Grossmith, S., & Migliorini, R. (2011). Sexual orientation and shifts in preferences for a partner's body attributes in short-term versus long-term mating contexts. *Psychological Reports, 108*(3), 699–710.
Luoto, S., Krams, I., & Rantala, M. J. (2019). A life history approach to the female sexual orientation spectrum: Evolution, development, causal mechanisms, and health. *Archives of Sexual Behavior, 48*(5), 1273–1308.
Luoto, S., & Rantala, M. (2022). Female bisexuality. In T. Shackelford (Ed.), *The Cambridge handbook of evolutionary perspectives on sexual psychology* (Cambridge Handbooks in Psychology, pp. 94–132). Cambridge University Press.
Maki, J. L. (2017). Gay subculture identification: Training counselors to work with gay men. *Vistas Online, 22*, 1–12.
March, E., Grieve, R., & Marx, E. (2015). Sex, sexual orientation, and the necessity of physical attractiveness and social level in long-term and short-term mates. *Journal of Relationships Research, 6*, Article E1.
Meston, C. M., & Buss, D. M. (2007). Why humans have sex. *Archives of Sexual Bbehavior, 36*(4), 477–507.
Mikach, S. M., & Bailey, J. M. (1999). What distinguishes women with unusually high numbers of sex partners? *Evolution and Human Behavior, 20*(3), 141–150.
Millar, B. M., Rendina, H. J., Starks, T. J., Grov, C., & Parsons, J. T. (2019). The role of chronotype, circadian misalignment, and tiredness in the substance use behaviors of gay and bisexual men. *Psychology of Sexual Orientation and Gender Diversity, 6*(1), 96.
Monk, J. D., Giglio, E., Kamath, A., Lambert, M. R., & McDonough, C. E. (2020). An alternative hypothesis for the evolution of same-sex sexual behaviour in animals. *Nature Ecology & Evolution, 3*, 1622–1631.
Moskowitz, D. A., & Hart, T. A. (2011). The influence of physical body traits and masculinity on anal sex roles in gay and bisexual men. *Archives of Sexual Behavior, 40*(4), 835–841.
Moskowitz, D. A., Rieger, G., & Roloff, M. E. (2008). Tops, bottoms and versatiles. *Sexual and Relationship Therapy, 23*(3), 191–202.
Murray, S. (2000). *Homosexualities*. University of Chicago Press.
Muscarella, F., Elias, V. A., & Szuchman, L. T. (2004). Brain differentiation and preferred partner characteristics in heterosexual and homosexual men and women. *Neuroendocrinology Letters, 25*(4), 299–303.
Nicholas, C. L. (2004). Gaydar: Eye-gaze as identity recognition among gay men and lesbians. *Sexuality & Culture, 8*, 60–86.
Penke, L., & Asendorpf, J. B. (2008). Beyond global sociosexual orientations: A more differentiated look at sociosexuality and its effects on courtship and romantic relationships. *Journal of personality and social psychology, 95*(5), 1113.
Peplau, L. A., & Fingerhut, A. W. (2007). The close relationships of lesbians and gay men. *Annual Review in Psychology, 58*, 405–424.
Phua, V. C. (2002). Sex and sexuality in men's personal advertisements. *Men and Masculinities, 5*(2), 178–191.
Pisanski, K., Feinberg, D. R. (2013). Cross-cultural variation in mate preferences for averageness, symmetry, body size, and masculinity. *Cross-Cultural Research, 47*(2), 162–197.
Prestage, G., Brown, G., De Wit, J., Bavinton, B., Fairley, C., Maycock, B., Batrouney, C., Keen, P., Down, I., Hammoud, M., & Zablotska, I. (2015). Understanding gay community subcultures: Implications for HIV prevention. *AIDS and Behavior, 19*(12), 2224–2233.
Provost, M. P., Kormos, C., Kosakoski, G., & Quinsey, V. L. (2006). Sociosexuality in women and preference for facial masculinization and somatotype in men. *Archives of Sexual Behavior, 35*(3), 305–312.

Puts, D. A., Gaulin, S. J., & Verdolini, K. (2006). Dominance and the evolution of sexual dimorphism in human voice pitch. *Evolution and Human Behavior, 27*(4), 283–296.
Puts, D. A., Jones, B. C., & DeBruine, L. M. (2012). Sexual selection on human faces and voices. *Journal of Sex Research, 49*(2–3), 227–243.
Rantala, M. J., & Marcinkowska, U. M. (2011). The role of sexual imprinting and the Westermarck effect in mate choice in humans. *Behavioral Ecology and Sociobiology, 65*(5), 859–873.
Regan, P. C. (1998). What if you can't get what you want? Willingness to compromise ideal mate selection standards as a function of sex, mate value, and relationship context. *Personality and Social Psychology Bulletin, 24*(12), 1294–1303.
Regan, P. C., Medina, R., & Joshi, A. (2001). Partner preferences among homosexual men and women: What is desirable in a sex partner is not necessarily desirable in a romantic partner. *Social Behavior and Personality: An International Journal, 29*(7), 625–633.
Rieger, G., Gygax, L., Linsenmeier, J. A., Siler-Knogl, A., Moskowitz, D. A., & Bailey, J. M. (2011). Sex typicality and attractiveness in childhood and adulthood: Assessing their relationships from videos. *Archives of Sexual Behavior, 40*(1), 143–154.
Rose, S. M., & Zand, D. (2002). Lesbian dating and courtship from young adulthood to midlife. *Journal of Lesbian Studies, 6*(1), 85–109.
Rosenfeld, M. J., & Thomas, R. J. (2012). Searching for a mate: The rise of the internet as a social intermediary. *American Sociological Review, 77*, 523–547
Sánchez, F. J., Greenberg, S. T., Liu, W. M., & Vilain, E. (2009). Reported effects of masculine ideals on gay men. *Psychology of Men & Masculinity, 10*(1), 73.
Santtila, P., Sandnabba, N. K., Harlaar, N., Varjonen, M., Alanko, K., & von der Pahlen, B. (2008). Potential for homosexual response is prevalent and enetic. *Biological Psychology, 77*(1), 102–105.
Savin-Williams, R. C., & Vrangalova, Z. (2013). Mostly heterosexual as a distinct sexual orientation group: A systematic review of the empirical evidence. *Developmental Review, 33*(1), 58–88.
Scherer, C. R., Akers, E. G., & Kolbe, K. L. (2013). Bisexuals and the sex differences in jealousy hypothesis. *Journal of Social and Personal Relationships, 30*(8), 1064–1071.
Schmitt, D. P. (2005). Sociosexuality from Argentina to Zimbabwe: A 48-nation study of sex, culture, and strategies of human mating. *Behavioral and Brain Sciences, 28*(2), 247–275.
Schmitt, D. P. (2007). Sexual strategies across sexual orientations. *Journal of Psychology and Human Sexuality, 18*, 183–214.
Schmitt, D. P., Alcalay, L., Allik, J., Alves, I. C. B., Anderson, C. A., Angelini, A. L., ... & Kökény, T. (2017). Narcissism and the strategic pursuit of short-term mating: Universal links across 11 world regions of the International Sexuality Description Project-2. *Psihologijske Teme, 26*, 89–137.
Schmitt, D. P., & Buss, D. M. (1996). Strategic self-promotion and competitor derogation: sex and context effects on the perceived effectiveness of mate attraction tactics. *Journal of personality and social psychology, 70*(6), 1185.
Schwartz, C. R., & Graf, N. L. (2009). Assortative matching among same-sex and different-sex couples in the United States, 1990–2000. *Demographic Research, 21*, 843.
Schwarz, S., & Hassebrauck, M. (2012). Sex and age differences in mate-selection preferences. *Human Nature, 23*(4), 447–466.
Scofield, J. E., Kostic, B., & Buchanan, E. M. (2020). How the presence of others affects desirability judgments in heterosexual and homosexual participants. *Archives of Sexual Behavior, 49*(2), 623–633.
Semenyna, S. W., Belu, C. F., Vasey, P. L., & Honey, P. L. (2018). Not straight and not straightforward: The relationships between sexual orientation, sociosexuality, and dark triad traits in women. *Evolutionary Psychological Science, 4*(1), 24–37.
Semenyna, S. W., Gómez Jiménez, F. R., VanderLaan, D. P., & Vasey, P. L. (2020). Inter-sexual mate competition in three cultures. *PLoS ONE, 15*(7), Article e0236549.
Semenyna, S. W., Vasey, P. L., & Honey, P. L. (2019). Replicating the relationships between dark triad traits and female mate-competition tactics in undergraduate women. *Personality and Individual Differences, 147*, 73–78.
Semenyna, S., Vasey, P., & Honey, P. (2022). The female sexual orientation spectrum in evolutionary perspective. In T. Shackelford (Ed.), *The Cambridge handbook of evolutionary perspectives on sexual psychology* (Cambridge Handbooks in Psychology, pp. 3–27). Cambridge University Press.
Shackelford, T. K., Schmitt, D. P., & Buss, D. M. (2005). Universal dimensions of human mate preferences. *Personality and Individual Differences, 39*(2), 447–458.

Silverthorne, Z. A., & Quinsey, V. L. (2000). Sexual partner age preferences of homosexual and heterosexual men and women. *Archives of Sexual Behavior, 29*(1), 67–76.

Smith, C. A., Konik, J. A., & Tuve, M. V. (2011). In search of looks, status, or something else? Partner preferences among butch and femme lesbians and heterosexual men and women. *Sex Roles, 64*(9–10), 658–668.

Smith, C. A., & Stillman, S. (2002). Butch/femme in the personal advertisements of lesbians. *Journal of Lesbian Studies, 6*(1), 45–51.

Sommer, V., & Vasey, P. L. (Eds.). (2006). *Homosexual behaviour in animals: An evolutionary perspective.* Cambridge University Press.

Sorokowski, P., Sorokowska, A., Butovskaya, M., Stulp, G., Huanca, T., & Fink, B. (2015). Body height preferences and actual dimorphism in stature between partners in two non-Western societies (Hadza and Tsimane'). *Evolutionary Psychology, 13*(2), Article 147470491501300209.

Sprecher, S., Wenzel, A., & Harvey, J. (Eds.). (2018). *Handbook of relationship initiation.* Psychology Press.

Štěrbová, Z., Bártová, K., Nováková, L. M., Varella, M. A. C., Havlíček, J., & Valentova, J. V. (2017). Assortative mating in personality among heterosexual and male homosexual couples from Brazil and the Czech Republic. *Personality and Individual Differences, 112,* 90–96.

Štěrbová, Z., Třebický, V., Havlíček, J., Tureček, P., Varella, M. A. C., & Valentova, J. V. (2018). Father's physique influences mate preferences but not the actual choice of male somatotype in heterosexual women and homosexual men. *Evolution and Human Behavior, 39*(1), 130–138.

Štěrbová, Z., & Valentova, J. (2012). Influence of homogamy, complementarity, and sexual imprinting on mate choice. *Anthropologie (1962-), 50*(1), 47–60.

Stief, M. C., Rieger, G., & Savin-Willaims, R. C. (2014). Bisexuality is associated with elevated sexual sensation seeking, sexual curiosity, and sexual excitability. *Personality and Individual Differences, 66,* 193–198.

Stower, R. E., Lee, A. J., McIntosh, T. L., Sidari, M. J., Sherlock, J. M., & Dixson, B. J. (2020). Mating strategies and the masculinity paradox: How relationship context, relationship status, and sociosexuality shape women's preferences for facial masculinity and beardedness. *Archives of Sexual Behavior, 49*(3), 809–820.

Swami, V., & Tovée, M. J. (2008). The muscular male: A comparison of the physical attractiveness preferences of gay and heterosexual men. *International Journal of Men's Health, 7*(1), 59–71.

Swift-Gallant, A. (2019). Individual differences in the biological basis of androphilia in mice and men. *Hormones and Behavior, 111,* 23–30.

Taywaditep, K. (2001). Marginalization among the marginalized. *Journal of Homosexuality, 42*(1), 1–28.

Todd, P. M., Penke, L., Fasolo, B., & Lenton, A. P. (2007). Different cognitive processes underlie human mate choices and mate preferences. *Proceedings of the National Academy of Sciences, 104*(38), 15011–15016.

Todosijevic, J., Rothblum, E. D., & Solomon, S. E. (2005). Relationship satisfaction, affectivity, and gay-specific stressors in same-sex couples joined in civil unions. *Psychology of Women Quarterly, 29*(2), 158–166.

Trivers, R. (1972). Parental investment and sexual selection. In B. Campbell (Ed.), *Sexual selection and the descent of man* (pp. 136–179). Aldine.

Valentova, J. V., Bártová, K., Štěrbová, Z., & Varella, M. A. C. (2016a). Preferred and actual relative height are related to sex, sexual orientation, and dominance: Evidence from Brazil and the Czech Republic. *Personality and Individual Differences, 100,* 145–150.

Valentova, J. V., Štěrbová, Z., Bártová, K., & Varella, M. A. C. (2016b). Personality of ideal and actual romantic partners among heterosexual and non-heterosexual men and women: A cross-cultural study. *Personality and Individual Differences, 101,* 160–166.

Valentova, J. V., Bártová, K., Štěrbová, Z., & Varella, M. A. C. (2017a). Influence of sexual orientation, population, homogamy, and imprinting-like effect on preferences and choices for female buttock size, breast size and shape, and WHR. *Personality and Individual Differences, 104,* 313–319.

Valentova, J. V., Varella, M. A. C., Bártová, K., Štěrbová, Z., & Dixson, B. J. W. (2017b). Mate preferences and choices for facial and body hair in heterosexual women and homosexual men: Influence of sex, population, homogamy, and imprinting-like effect. *Evolution and Human Behavior, 38*(2), 241–248.

Valentova, J. V., Junior, F. P. M., Štěrbová, Z., Varella, M. A. C., & Fisher, M. L. (2020a). The association between Dark Triad traits and sociosexuality with mating and parenting efforts: A cross-cultural study. *Personality and Individual Differences, 154,* 109613.

Valentova, J. V., de Moraes, A. C., & Varella, M. A. C. (2020b). Gender, sexual orientation and type of relationship influence individual differences in jealousy: A large Brazilian sample. *Personality and Individual Differences, 157,* 109805.

Valentova, J. V., Fernandez, A. M., Pereira, M., & Varella, M. A. C. (2022a). Jealousy is influenced by sex of the individual, their partner, and their rival. *Archives of Sexual Behavior, 51*(6), 2867–2877.

Valentova, J., Medrado, A., & Varella, M. (2022b). Male bisexuality. In T. Shackelford (Ed.), *The Cambridge handbook of evolutionary perspectives on sexual psychology* (Cambridge Handbooks in Psychology, pp. 52–93). Cambridge University Press.

Valentova, J. V., & Havlíček, J. (2013). Perceived sexual orientation based on vocal and facial stimuli is linked to self-rated sexual orientation in Czech men. *PLoS ONE, 8*(12), Article e82417.

Valentová, J., Roberts, S. C., & Havlíček, J. (2013). Preferences for facial and vocal masculinity in homosexual men: the role of relationship status, sexual restrictiveness, and self-perceived masculinity. *Perception, 42*(2), 187–197.

Valentova, J. V., Stulp, G., Třebický, V., & Havlíček, J. (2014). Preferred and actual relative height among homosexual male partners vary with preferred dominance and sex role. *PLoS ONE, 9*(1), Article e86534.

Valentova, J. V., & Varella, M. A. C. (2016a). Further steps toward a truly integrative theory of sexuality. *Archives of Sexual Behavior, 45*(3), 517–520.

Valentova, J. V., & Varella, M. A. C. (2016b). Sexual orientation and human sexuality. In T. K. Shackelford, & V. A. Weekes-Shackelford (Eds.), *Encyclopedia of evolutionary psychological science* (p. 253). Springer, Cham. https://doi.org/10.1007/978-3-319-16999-6_3622-1

Varangis, E., Lanzieri, N., Hildebrandt, T., & Feldman, M. (2012). Gay male attraction toward muscular men: Does mating context matter? *Body Image, 9*(2), 270–278.

Varella, M. A. C., Santos, I. B. C. dos, Ferreira, J. H. B. P., & Bussab, V. S. R. (2013). Misunderstandings in applying evolution to human mind and behavior and its causes: A systematic review. *EvoS Journal: The Journal of the Evolutionary Studies Consortium, 5*(1), 81–107.

Vasey, P. L., Parker, J. L., & VanderLaan, D. P. (2014). Comparative reproductive output of androphilic and gynephilic males in Samoa. *Archives of Sexual Behavior, 43*(2), 363–367.

Vasey, P. L., Pocock, D. S., & VanderLaan, D. P. (2007). Kin selection and male androphilia in Samoan fa'afafine. *Evolution and Human Behavior, 28*(3), 159–167.

Veloso, V., Brito, R., C. N. S. Câmara (2014). Comparison of partner choice between lesbians and heterosexual women. *Psychology, 5*(2), 134.

Verbakel, E., & Kalmijn, M. (2014). Assortative mating among Dutch married and cohabiting same-sex and different-sex couples. *Journal of Marriage and Family, 76*(1), 1–12.

Vrangalova, Z., & Savin-Williams, R. C. (2012). Mostly heterosexual and mostly gay/lesbian: Evidence for new sexual orientation identities. *Archives of Sexual Behavior, 41*(1), 85–101.

Wade, J. C., & Donis, E. (2007). Masculinity ideology, male identity, and romantic relationship quality among heterosexual and gay men. *Sex Roles, 57*(9–10), 775–786.

Ward, J. (2008). Dude-sex: White masculinities and authentic heterosexuality among dudes who have sex with dudes. *Sexualities, 11*(4), 414–434.

Welling, L. L., Singh, K., Puts, D. A., Jones, B. C., & Burriss, R. P. (2013). Self-reported sexual desire in homosexual men and women predicts preferences for sexually dimorphic facial cues. *Archives of Sexual Behavior, 42*(5), 785–791.

Wells, J. E., McGee, M. A., & Beautrais, A. L. (2011). Multiple aspects of sexual orientation: Prevalence and sociodemographic correlates in a New Zealand national survey. *Archives of Sexual Behavior, 40*(1), 155–168.

Wells, J. W. (1990). The sexual vocabularies of heterosexual and homosexual males and females for communicating erotically with a sexual partner. *Archives of Sexual Behavior, 19*(2), 139–147.

Werner, D. (2006). The evolution of male homosexuality and its implications for human psychological and cultural variations. In V. Sommer & P. L. Vasey (Eds.), *Homosexual behavior in animals: An evolutionary perspective* (pp. 316–346). Cambridge University Press.

Werner, D. W. (1998). Sobre a evolução e variação cultural na homossexualidade masculina [On evolution and cultural variation in male homosexuality]. In J. Pedro & M. Grossi (Eds.), *Masculino, feminino, plural* (pp. 99–130). Universidade Federal de Santa Catarina.

Wester, S. R., Pionke, D. R., & Vogel, D. L. (2005). Male gender role conflict, gay men, and same-sex romantic relationships. *Psychology of Men & Masculinity, 6*(3), 195.

Whitam, F. L. (1983). Culturally invariable properties of male homosexuality: Tentative conclusions from cross-cultural research. *Archives of Sexual Behavior, 12*(3), 207–226.

Whitam, F. L., & Mathy, R. M. (1986). *Male homosexuality in four societies: Brazil, Guatemala, the Philippines, and the United States*. Praeger.

White, J., Lorenz, H., Perilloux, C., & Lee, A. (2018). Creative casanovas: Mating strategy predicts using—but not preferring—atypical flirting tactics. *Evolutionary Psychological Science, 4*(4), 443–455.

Whyte, S., Brooks, R. C., & Torgler, B. (2019). Sexual economic theory & the human mating market. *Applied Economics, 51*(57), 6100–6112.

Windhager, S., Schaefer, K., & Fink, B. (2011). Geometric morphometrics of male facial shape in relation to physical strength and perceived attractiveness, dominance, and masculinity. *American Journal of Human Biology, 23*(6), 805–814.

Wolff, S. E., & Puts, D. A. (2010). Vocal masculinity is a robust dominance signal in men. *Behavioral Ecology and Sociobiology, 64*(10), 1673–1683.

Wood, J. R., Milhausen, R. R., & Jeffrey, N. K. (2014). Why have sex? Reasons for having sex among lesbian, bisexual, queer, and questioning women in romantic relationships. *Canadian Journal of Human Sexuality, 23*(2), 75–88.

Wyverkens, E., Dewitte, M., Deschepper, E., Corneillie, J., Van der Bracht, L., Van Regenmortel, D., Van Cleempoel, K., De Boose, N., Prinssen, P., & T'Sjoen, G. (2018). YSEX? A replication study in different age groups. *The Journal of Sexual Medicine, 15*(4), 492–501.

Yelland, C., & Tiggemann, M. (2003). Muscularity and the gay ideal: Body dissatisfaction and disordered eating in homosexual men. *Eating behaviors, 4*(2), 107–116.

Zaidi, A. A., White, J. D., Mattern, B. C., Liebowitz, C. R., Puts, D. A., Claes, P., & Shriver, M. D. (2019). Facial masculinity does not appear to be a condition-dependent male ornament and does not reflect MHC heterozygosity in humans. *Proceedings of the National Academy of Sciences, 116*(5), 1633–1638.

Zhang, J., Zheng, L., & Zheng, Y. (2018). Consistency in preferences for masculinity in faces, bodies, voices, and personality characteristics among homosexual men in China. *Personality and Individual Differences, 134*, 137–142.

Zheng, L. (2019a). Facial masculinity preferences according to relationship status and sociosexual orientation in gay and bisexual men in China. *Personality and Individual Differences, 138*, 243–246.

Zheng, L. (2019b). Relationships between disgust sensitivity and trait preferences in gay men in China. *Personality and Individual Differences, 146*, 58–61.

Zheng, L., Hart, T. A., & Zheng, Y. (2013). Attraction to male facial masculinity in gay men in China: Relationship to intercourse preference positions and sociosexual behavior. *Archives of Sexual Behavior, 42*(7), 1223–1232.

Zheng, L., Zhang, J., & Zheng, Y. (2016). Relationships between pathogen disgust sensitivity and preference for male facial masculinity in gay men in China. *Personality and Individual Differences, 92*, 33–36.

Zheng, L., & Zhang, J. (2021). Demographic and geographic differences in facial masculinity preferences among gay and bisexual men in China. *Archives of Sexual Behavior, 50*(8), 3711-3723.

Zheng, L., & Zheng, Y. (2015a). Correlated preferences for male facial masculinity and partner traits in gay and bisexual men in China. *Archives of Sexual Behavior, 44*(5), 1423–1430.

Zheng, L., & Zheng, Y. (2015b). Young gay men's sexism predicts their male facial masculinity preference in China. *Personality and Individual Differences, 76*, 183–186.

Zietsch, B. P., Lee, A. J., Sherlock, J. M., & Jern, P. (2015). Variation in women's preferences regarding male facial masculinity is better explained by genetic differences than by previously identified context-dependent effects. *Psychological Science, 26*(9), 1440–1448.

CHAPTER

9 Relationship Initiation Among Older Adults

Chaya Koren *and* Liat Ayalon

Abstract

Relationships are desired at any age including later in life among older adults. This chapter provides a broad overview of relationship initiation (i.e., entering a new relationship) in the second half of life among older persons. The chapter reviews sociocultural and inter/intrapersonal factors that shape relationship initiation among older adults, including the influence of individualistic/collectivistic cultural values, the presence of children and grandchildren, the living arrangement, and the health conditions of the partners. We frame our discussion using a psychosocial ecological framework and several contemporary theories of aging, including successful aging theory and socioemotional selectivity. We conclude the chapter with suggestions for future research, which take into account the lesbian, gay, bisexual, and transgender communities and explore the experiences of different older age groups (65–74; 75–84; and 85+). Moreover, although the use of technology for dating purposes among older adults has been studied extensively, what is still missing is information about the use of technology across different cultures and for purposes other than dating, such as sexual pleasure.

Key Words: relationship initiation, older adults, successful aging, late life repartnering, second couplehood, remarriage, cohabitation, living apart together, intimacy in later life, cultural diversity

"Interviewer: Tell me the story of your relationship initiation as an older person.

Man: Actually, I knew her when we were in our 20s [. . .] and then our paths separated. I married some girl and she married some other guy and that's it. We saw each other occasionally, through mutual friends, and we would visit sometimes, but there was nothing. After my wife died, I would sometimes visit my friend. Once, I had the brilliant idea of asking her if she wanted to grow old with me, and she [also widowed] said yes and that's it. We're growing old together." (man, interviewed for research at age 87, initiated the relationship at age 76). (Koren & Eisikovits, 2011, p. 52)

Definitions of relationship initiation refer to entering or starting a new relationship (e.g., Cambridge dictionary; Lexico Oxford dictionary; Merriam-Webster dictionary). However, such defininitions may also reflect an initiative, indicating an active rather than passive position in relationship formation. Entering a relationship involves "doing" and taking active responsibility to start, get into, and construct that relationship. Among older persons, it implies that two older adults are taking action to enter a new partnered relationship. Such action is easier to accomplish when the society it occurs in accepts it. Thus, using the concept "relationship initiation," in a way, frames the worldview it developed from, restricting it to societies with cultural values that accept relationship initiation among older adults.

Relationship initiation among older adults is a relatively new phenomenon. It is developing along with modernization processes that include increased life expectancy related to the advancement of health technology. This has resulted in changes in family structure and in older adults remaining alone due to widowhood or divorce (Koren, 2011). It coincides well with modernization (Marsh, 2014) because it emphasizes individualistic cultural values such as self-determination, as opposed to the collectivist familial cultural values of traditional societies (Koren & Simhi-Meidai, 2020). As such, relationship initiation among older adults reflects the modern, Western individualist cultural background of the phenomenon.

A major aspect shaping the phenomenon of relationship initiation among older adults is related to the social construction of old age, a period in life that is often perceived as a less desirable life stage (Erikson, 1998) and that is subject to ageism (i.e., stereotypes, prejudice, and discrimination toward people because of their age). In the present context, the term refers to the negative social construction of old age (Ayalon & Tesch-Römer, 2018). Ageist attitudes toward partnerships initiated in later life are reflected in the marginalization of older adults (Watson et al., 2010). Old age is usually associated with end of life, decline, and decay rather than with wisdom (Pachana & Mitchell, 2018), attractiveness (Clarke & Griffin, 2008), and an opportunity for new beginnings (e.g., Koren & Ayalon, 2019). As such, ageist attitudes (e.g., in this context, negative stereotypes toward older people because of their age) portray relationship initiation and old age as opposites that do not coincide (Koren, 2015). They raise the question of how relationship initiation that is associated with renewal, romance, and sexuality (Watson et al., 2010) can coincide with the commonly negative perceptions of old age. As an illustration, a brief search on APA PsycInfo conducted in January 2021 with the term "relationship initiation" in the search field, returned 175 items. When adding "older adults" to the search, it returned a single item, titled "Falling in Love" (Aron et al., 2008).

The experience of relationship initiation among older adults also relates to gender differences (e.g., Davidson, 2002; Watson & Stelle, 2021) and affects interpersonal relationships with family members, especially children and grandchildren (e.g., De Jong Gierveld & Peeters, 2003; De Jong Gierveld & Merz, 2013; Koren & Lipman Schily, 2014; Koren

& Simhi, 2016). Furthermore, intrapersonal aspects related to basic human conditions such as loneliness and to needs such as love, companionship, intimacy, friendship, emotional support, and mutual help (de Jong Gierveld, 2002) also shape the experience of relationship initiation among older adults.

The cultural, social, interpersonal, and intrapersonal aspects of relationship initiation among older adults mentioned above and how these intertwine (Koren, 2015; Watson, Bell, & Stelle, 2010) reflect a psychosocial ecological framework (Bronfenbrenner, 1994). In this chapter, we address the following issues: what old age is and who is considered an older adult; relationship initiation in diverse cultural contexts; motivations for relationship initiation among older women and men; features of partner relationships; sexuality experienced in relationships initiated among older adults; and the relationship these older adults experience with their offspring. We discuss the interplay of the phenomenon with major theories of aging and "successful aging." Finally, the chapter concludes with directions for future knowledge development on relationship initiation among older adults. We begin with introducing a diversity of forms of relationship initiation and their establishment among older adults.

Forms of Relationship Initiation and Establishment Among Older Adults

When relationship initiation among older adults leads to partnership, it is referred to in the empirical literature as a second couplehood in old age (Ayalon & Koren, 2015; Koren, 2011; 2015; Koren & Lipman-Schiby, 2014; Koren & Simhi, 2016) and as a late life repartnering (De Jong Gierveld, 2004; De Jong Gierveld & Peeters, 2003; Koren, 2014; 2016). These include remarriage (Brown & Lin, 2013; Watson et al., 2010), cohabitation (Brown et al., 2006), living apart together (LAT) (De Jong Gierveld, 2004), and dating (Brown & Shinohara, 2013; Bulcroft & O'Connor, 1986; Watson & Stelle, 2011). Other designations for the phenomenon of relationship initiation among older adults are "intimacy in later life" (Davidson & Fennell, 2002) and "new relationships in later life" (Bildtgård & Öberg, 2019), which include many of the above forms.

The aftermath of relationship initiation is the formation and establishment of relations among older adults, which can take multiple forms. Remarriage refers to older adults who have officially, by law of state or religion, initiated a marital relationship following a previous marriage (Watson et al., 2010). The estimate for the United States is that 20% of women and 25% of men remarry following later-life dissolutions (Carr & Utz, 2020). Cohabitation refers to older adults who are a couple and choose to live in the same household but without being officially married (Brown & Wright, 2017). Approximately 14% of U.S. persons ages 50 years and older are in a cohabiting union (Carr & Utz, 2020).

Living apart together (LAT) relationships refer to unmarried couples who live in separate homes. They are committed while the relationship lasts, but not necessarily expecting the relationship to be permanent (Benson & Coleman, 2016b). Nonetheless, LAT partners who are confronted with caregiving needs have been shown to provide care for their partner (De Jong Gierveld, 2015). An estimated 7% of older adults in the United States are in LAT relationships (Carr & Utz, 2020).

The term "dating" is the closest to relationship initiation because it is the stage that comes before one of the three forms of relationship establishment: remarriage, cohabitation, or LAT. It differs from the other forms mentioned above because it does not include the constraints of remarriage, cohabitation, and the type of commitments found in LAT relationships (Brown & Shinohhara, 2013). Participants in a qualitative research study defined LAT by contrasting it to dating and marital relationships, choosing terms to describe their relationship initiation through a process of meaning making. Terms associated with youth culture such as girl/boyfriend, although spurned, were commonly used for lack of age-appropriate alternatives (Benson & Coleman, 2016a). In other instances, older people negated the existence of the relationship, despite its objective presence (Koren & Ayalon, 2019). About 15% of unmarried older adults are currently dating, with rates considerably higher among men than women (Carr & Utz, 2020).

Old age and Older Adults

Old age is more than chronological age. There is a variability among older adults based on biological, physiological, and health aspects related to physical changes, illness, and adjustment to such changes. There also is variability in cognitive aspects related to memory, perception, and attention (Agogo et al., 2014) and functional aspects related to the ability to conduct activities of daily living (Devi, 2018). Old age also has an emotional aspect related to expectations for the future and to the regulation of emotions (Carstensen et al., 2003), whereby negative emotions decrease, and positive emotions increase (Verstaen et al., 2020). Furthermore, old age is affected by subjective age, referring to how old a person perceives him/herself (Kotter-Grühn et al., 2016) and how old a person feels, thinks, and appears (Lee et al., 2018). Research has found that being in a second couplehood relationship in old age helps to construct and maintain a younger image of the self (Koren, 2015).

Despite the subjective components associated with old age, chronological age is what determines who is considered old by the authorities. Although older adults are commonly referred to as aged 60 + or 65+ (World Health Organization, 2002), theoretical and empirical literature shows a wide range regarding who is considered an older adult. At times, older adults even refer to those age 50+, especially on issues related to relationship initiation (e.g., De Jong Gierveld, 2004). When relationship initiation refers to online dating profiles, as young as age 40 + is considered old; no differentiation is made between ages 40 + and 60+. This makes it difficult to focus on older dating adults age 60+ (Watson & Stelle, 2021).

In any case, with the increase in life expectancy, being an older adult age 60 + extends over several decades. Therefore, older adults age 60/65 + may be divided into three age groups: the young-old who are age 60/65–74; the old-old, age 75–84; and the oldest-old, age 85 and older (Lee et al., 2018), with each group having unique characteristics and needs. Older adults within each of these three age groups undergo biological, physiological, emotional, social, and health changes that impact everyday life experiences. However, changes differ in type, intensity, and importance within each age group.

Older adults may emphasize different aspects of life as they age (Carstensen, 2006), so that the same daily action or interpersonal relationship could assume different meanings for older adults as their age advances (Chen & Jordan, 2018). Despite experiencing changes in the various domains mentioned, young-old adults age 60/65–74 perceive having time left to fulfill their goals (Cicirelli, 2006) and are considered "third agers," denoting a life phase between middle-age working life and the frailty and dependence of the fourth age (Bildtgård & Öberg, 2019). As such, they are expected to remain active and productive contributors to society (Pavlova & Silbereisen, 2016). The middle group of older adults age 75–84 usually experiences further overall physical, cognitive, and functional declines. People in this group feel they have less time left to fulfill goals (Cicirelli, 2006). The oldest-old adults age 85+, who are closer to the end of life, focus on preparing for end of life, which in turn affects their relationship with self, others, and society (Freund & Smith, 1999). The next section addresses the broad age range of relationship initiation among older adults.

Relationship Initiation and the Age of Older Adults

Some studies restrict the phenomenon of relationship initiation among older adults to those who have initiated the relationship at the official retirement age or older (65+), after the termination of a long-term marriage due to death or divorce, in which both partners have previously raised families with children and grandchildren and are functionally independent, physically and cognitively (e.g., Koren, 2011). Yet other studies include those who have initiated their relationship at age 50 or above (e.g., De Jong Gierveld, 2004) and those who have divorced more than once (Brown & Wright, 2017).

The experience of relationship initiation is influenced by age of initiation and life course stage. Age 50 + is a life course stage in which the partners are expected to be part of the work force, and if they have children, at least some have not yet reached young adulthood and/or have not yet established a home. On the other hand, at age 65+, retirement is a common option and children have usually entered adulthood and most likely have launched home. Thus, at age 65+, older adults have fewer familial obligations (Carter & McGoldrick, 2005), leaving more time to invest in a new relationship. As such, the phenomenon is likely to be shaped differently within each life stage. At the same time, diversity in relationship initiation is also related to varied cultural contexts in which the initiation occurs.

Relationship Initiation in Diverse Cultural Contexts

Initiation is easier when the act of initiation is culturally acceptable. Thus, relationship initiation among older persons is more likely to develop in societies that culturally accept it. Cultural contexts refer to Western/Eastern; modern/traditional; individualist/collectivist values of self-determination versus familial values (Koren & Simhi Madai, 2020); and socioeconomic status (SES), class, and health, which are related to the culture of third-agers (Bildtgård & Öberg, 2019). Accordingly, relationship initiation among older adults occurs mainly among older persons from middle to high SES (Brown & Shinohara, 2013; Davidson, 2002) who are in good health (Bildtgård & Öberg, 2019; Brown & Shinohara, 2013). It is more common in modern Western societies living by individualist cultural values of self-determination (Koren & Eisikovits, 2011). Relationship initiation is less accepted in Eastern traditional societies living by collectivist values (Mehta, 2002). Further evidence of this can be drawn from a recent study conducted on the acceptance of love and remarriage among older adults in the Philippines. Only 17% of respondents reported acceptance. Thus, most older adults in the Philippines reported that love and remarriage in old age is unacceptable (Kim et al., 2021). However, in India, an Eastern Asian country, repartnering among adults age 50 + is increasing. Perhaps because the country is undergoing modernization processes. Thus, relationship initiation in India was found to serve as a platform that contradicts patriarchal family values of gender inequality within family structures (Samanta & Varghese, 2019).

In societies culturally located between tradition and modernity such as Israel (Lavee & Katz, 2003), the phenomenon occurs; however, it is not considered an acceptable option for older adults (Koren & Eisikovits, 2011). This conclusion is based on two factors. First, there is a lack of information in the official census records on the prevalence of older adults whose relationship initiation resulted in remarriage, cohabitation, or LAT (Simhi Meidani & Koren, 2018). This lack of information could indicate ignorance that such a phenomenon exists or a lack of interest in making the phenomenon visible as an acceptable option for older adults. The other is related to accounts of excuses and justifications (Scott & Lyman, 1968) provided by older adults in a late-life repartnering relationship in Israel who participated in a study on the phenomenon (Koren & Eisikovits, 2011). Accounts were provided to bridge the gap between relationship initiation as unacceptable behavior and the normative path (Scott & Lyman, 1968). Older, widowed people are expected to focus on relationships in the extended family and not on seeking out a new couplehood. Such accounts were expressed as justifying a behavior by taking responsibility for relationship initiation, in an attempt to convince that despite the behavior being unacceptable, the outcome is so good that it outweighs any disapproval. Excuses, however, involve withdrawing responsibility regarding relationship initiation by trying to convince that it happened unexpectedly. The need to withdraw responsibility indicates that perhaps such accounts are necessary in societies that do not accept relationship initiation among older adults as an option (Koren & Eisikovits, 2011).

Cultural diversity is also reflected in the forms of late-life repartnering, which differ according to country (Ayalon & Koren, 2015). In the Netherlands (De Jong Gierveld,

2004) and Scandinavian countries (Bildtgård & Öberg, 2017), Britain (Haskey & Lewis, 2006), and Israel (Koren, 2011), LAT and cohabitation are more common than remarriage among older adults who initiate a relationship in late life. Whereas in the United States remarriages, until recently, received more visibility in research than cohabitation (Ayalon & Koren, 2015) or LAT (e.g., Benson & Colman, 2016). A possible explanation for cultural diversity in the acceptance of relationship initiation among older adults could be related to the intersections between the individual, the family, and the state, influencing the way partner relationships and family are perceived (Bildtgård & Öberg, 2019), and the level of commitment each relationship form represents.

Remarriage is perceived as having the highest level of commitment and LAT the lowest (Lewin, 2017). Being less committed makes it easier to terminate the relationship when it is no longer fulfilling or when it becomes a burden. This is especially relevant because one of the main motivations for relationship initiation among older adults is to have fun and enjoy life (Koren, 2011). The United States is a modern nation that values individualist ideals such as self-determination (Bettache & Chiu, 2019), yet the state lacks in providing support and services to individuals and families. This results in a strong codependency between the individual and the family, strengthening familial values which continue into late life and are then manifested in officially remarrying (Bildtgård & Öberg, 2019) in order to ensure late-life caregiving when necessary among partners who initiated a relationship in old age. Furthermore, this may lead many in the United States to believe that older individuals should invest their time and resources in family rather than in fulfilling their personal desires for companionship.

In contrast to the United States, Scandinavian and Northern European countries provide state support and services to enable individual self-determination throughout the life course. Thus, individuals who are less dependent on their families can afford to establish relationships such as LAT, which are characterized by less commitment than remarriage because they can count on state support when necessary (Bildtgård & Öberg, 2019). In societies that rely more strongly on kinship networks, the formation of new relations might be more challenging. Israel is culturally located between tradition and modernity (Lavee & Katz, 2003), and between familial values and self-determination (Cohen, 2003). One manifestation of this is the state policy that supports individuals and couples, yet simultaneously relies on family members to care for their elders. Therefore, Israeli older couples prefer cohabitation or LAT over remarriage, because official remarriage among older adults increases commitment expectations. Furthermore, marriages and divorces are required to be performed through religious ceremonies (Simhi Meidani & Koren, 2018), thus complicating relationship dissolution if the relationship is no longer fulfilling and/or becomes a burden. Understanding when a relationship changes from being fulfilling to becoming a burden is related to the motivations or lack of motivation for relationship initiation among older adults.

Motivations/Lack of Motivation for Relationship Initiation Among Older Women and Men

Relationship initiation is a way to fulfill the third-age culture that promises opportunities to enjoy life in a variety of ways (Bildtgård & Öberg, 2019), besides being a way to deal with loneliness (Davidson, 2002; Koren, 2015). Motivations for relationship initiation among older adults are based on empirical research conducted on dating and online dating among older adults and on research among older adults living in such relationships. Both older men and women are motivated to initiate a relationship to have fun and to enjoy life (Koren, 2011) and are interested in a companion and someone fun-loving, kind, and compassionate (Watson & Stelle, 2021). Furthermore, third-agers are more like middle-agers seeking adventure, romance, sexual interests, and a soulmate and less likely to mention health, in comparison to fourth-agers (Alterovitz & Mendelsohn, 2013). When initiating relationships in the second half of life, both genders seek and convey youthful images (McWilliams & Barrett, 2014), are more likely to have had a college education, have more assets, are in better health, and are socially more connected (Brown & Shinohara, 2013).

Although the motivation to enjoy life refers to men and women alike, motivations also differ according to gender. Men were more likely to seek physical attractiveness in women, whereas women were more likely to seek men with financial and occupational accomplishments (McWilliams & Barrett, 2014). Furthermore, since Davidson's publication in the year 2002 on gender differences in new partnership choices, gender differences in motivations for relationship initiation among older adults have not changed much. Davidson (2002) found that women seek someone to go out with, whereas men look for someone to come home to. Consequently, women prefer LAT, whereas men prefer cohabitation or remarriage (De Jong Gierveld, 2002). The reasons are that older women seek to preserve their autonomy by avoiding housekeeping roles (Davidson, 2002; Spalter, 2010), they desire companionship without demanding caring roles (McWilliams & Barrett, 2014), and they prefer not to give up a recently gained lifestyle free of caregiving obligations (McIntosh et al., 2011). Older men, in contrast, seek committed relationships (McWilliams & Barrett, 2014). Men seek someone who can provide emotional support (Watson & Stelle, 2021) and the lost intimacy that women tend to find with friends and offspring (Davidson, 2002; Spalter, 2010). Men who are in a LAT relationship, despite preferring cohabitation or remarriage, justify it by emphasizing the benefits of constantly being in a courtship position, which preserves the romantic aspect of the relationship (Eisikovits & Koren, 2010). As in other contexts and situations, men in a LAT relationship externalize not being suitable to remarry, claiming remarriage does not suit them, whereas women internalize, claiming they are not suitable for remarriage. Thus, men blame the institution of marriage, whereas women blame themselves (Benson & Coleman, 2016b). In addition, late-life repartnered widows tend to be more resilient and thus able to get back to a relatively stable, healthy level of psychological and physical functioning. However, widowers are more vulnerable, having difficulty adapting after their wife's death. Thus, repartnering assists their adjustment (Koren, 2016).

Motivations among older adults to not initiate new relationships also have been investigated. Both older widows and widowers emphasize spouse sanctification and as such perceive relationship initiation among older widows and widowers as a betrayal of a lifelong spouse after death (Bennett et al., 2013; Koren & Ayalon, 2019; Van Den Hoonaard, 2002). Once the relationship is initiated and further established, it is characterized by several core elements. These features are addressed next.

Features of Couple Relationships: Together and Apart

Becoming a couple involves a shift from being two separate individuals to forming an interpersonal partner relationship unit (Seider et al., 2009). Based on theories of family dynamics (Bowen, 1978; Olson, 2000), a partner relationship involves the ability to be together and to be apart (Koren, 2014). It includes balancing "I-ness"/"we-ness," independence/codependence (Olson, 2000), autonomy/intimacy (Goodman, 1999), and separateness/togetherness (Bowen, 1978).

Being together and apart in a partner relationship has both emotional and physical aspects. Being physically together and/or apart refers to living arrangements, whether sharing the same home or living in separate homes. Being emotionally together includes intimacy, togetherness, "we-ness," and codependence, whereas being emotionally apart includes autonomy, separateness, "I-ness," and independence (Koren, 2014). Without being emotionally together, there is no partner relationship, and without being emotionally apart, the "self" might be erased (Ben-Ari, 2012). As such, a partner relationship requires inclusion of the other in the self (Aron et al., 1992), along with preserving a sense of self-identity (Gaine & La Guardia, 2009). As a result, balance between intimacy and autonomy (Goodman, 1999) can be achieved. Individuals differ in their needs to be together and to be apart, and this determines the compatibility between two individuals as partners. Furthermore, partners' differences in expectations from a couple relationship can derive from differences in cultural values (Koren, 2014).

Excessive emotional involvement in significant relationships with others, referred to as fusion (Bowen, 1978), appears to be sensitive to the differences among collectivist Asian cultures and individualistic Western cultures (Lampis et al., 2019). Individualistic Western cultures place high value on independence and autonomy (Cho, 2011), and as such perceive fusion as less desirable (Lampis et al., 2019), whereas Asian collectivistic cultures strive to achieve interdependence and harmony with others (Cho, 2011), and as such fusion is considered normative (Lampis et al., 2019). Partners also differ in their ability to be reflective (Ben-Ari, 2012). Hence, the match between partners is a together/apart balance of one partner with the other, and of the partners' awareness of these differences. The following section addresses the unique aspects of physical and emotional togetherness and apartness in relationship initiation among older adults.

Together and Apart in Relationship Initiation Among Older Adults

Studies indicate that late-life repartnering is a unique phenomenon with features that distinguish it from other partner relationships such as lifelong marriages (Ayalon & Koren, 2015), partner relationships in stepfamilies formed earlier in life (Ganong & Coleman, 2012), and young adult romantic relationships prior to marriage (e.g., Jamison & Ganong, 2010). Whereas lifelong marital relationships are formed for the purpose of raising a family with responsibilities, late-life repartnering is for enjoying life (Koren, 2011).

Emerging young adults usually perceive cohabitation as a phase toward marriage (Jamison & Ganong, 2010); however, late-life repartners who cohabitate or LAT usually do not wish to remarry (Benson & Coleman, 2016; Davidson & Fennell, 2002; King & Scott, 2005). Late-life repartnering is perceived as partners being exclusive to one another even if they do not have a sexual relationship (Koren, 2011). This is especially apparent in institutions such as continuing-care retirement communities (Koren & Ayalon, 2019).

Adult stepchildren who grew up most of their childhood with a stepparent have established an emotional bond with their parent's spouse and refer to them as a parent (Ganong et al., 2005). Yet, when a stepfamily is constructed late in life, adult stepchildren do not perceive their parent's new partner as a parent (Koren & Lipman-Schiby, 2014). These differences have the potential of influencing the experience of being together and apart physically and emotionally among late-life repartners.

A fourfold typology of physical and emotional togetherness and apartness in late-life repartnering was identified in a qualitative study by Koren (2014). The physical dimension refers to the form of living arrangement of residing in the same home—as in cohabitation or remarriage—or apart, as in LAT relationships. The emotional dimension relates to the experience of the following five abductive parameters: (a) living arrangement establishment; (b) togetherness/separateness: sharing, respecting being a part of the other's inner world; (c) intimacy and autonomy: balancing between we-ness and I-ness; (d) agreement on sexuality; and (e) influences of offspring on the relationship. The five parameters were examined on each of the following four unique types. The fourfold typology is mutually exclusive and collectively exhaustive (Bailey, 1994) as follows:

TYPE A

Type A, living together (physically and emotionally) (LT), repartners perceive that a "real" couple relationship is possible only when living physically together. Both partners have a mutual respect for their diverse inner worlds and can reach a balance between I-ness and we-ness. They both have a good sexual experience with each other; in some cases, it is even better than in their lifelong marriage (Koren, 2011). Both partners perceive that their offspring express satisfaction and accept the partner as part of the family.

TYPE B

Type B, living apart (physically) together (emotionally) (LAT), can bridge gender differences regarding living arrangements. Although their inner worlds are not shared as much as wanted, separate living arrangements make this less obvious. Thus, they need separate living arrangements to preserve an I-ness/we-ness balance. They perceive their sexual life as what makes them exclusive to one another, despite their separate living arrangements (Koren & Ayalon, 2019). Each partner helps the other overcome and address conflicts with children, contributing to emotional closeness.

TYPE C

Type C, living together (physically) apart (emotionally) (LTA), hold opposing worldviews that contribute to emotional distance. The way I-ness/we-ness should be balanced in a partner relationship remains unresolved. They have only seemingly resolved the gender differences regarding living arrangements. Living under the same roof intensifies emotional distance when only one of the partners is interested in sexuality. Furthermore, partner and children sanctify the deceased wife/mother (Bennett et al., 2013) and the other partner allows children to interfere, causing unresolved offense.

TYPE D

Type D, living apart (physically and emotionally) (LA), are openly unable to resolve gender differences regarding living arrangements. There is disrespect toward the partner's inner world. Besides disagreement regarding changes in their sexuality, there is disrespect and diverse interpretations of the nature of the relationship. For these partners, remaining a couple even when physically and emotionally apart is preferred over loneliness (Koren, 2014).

Sexuality and Relationship Initiation Among Older Adults

Sexuality is defined by the World Health Organization (WHO; 2002) as

> a central aspect of being human throughout life encompasses sex, gender identities and roles, sexual orientation, eroticism, pleasure, intimacy and reproduction. Sexuality is experienced and expressed in thoughts, fantasies, desires, beliefs, attitudes, values, behaviors, practices, roles and relationships. While sexuality can include all of these dimensions, not all of them are always experienced or expressed. Sexuality is influenced by the interaction of biological, psychological, social, economic, political, cultural, legal, historical, religious and spiritual factors (https://www.who.int/teams/sexual-and-reproductive-health-and-research/key-areas-of-work/sexual-health/defining-sexual-health).

Sexuality is considered an integral part of life and an important component of well-being and quality of life. Most older adults report that they continue to have sex and enjoy sex even in old and very old age. Nonetheless, men are more likely than women to report that they are sexually active and are interested in sex (Lindau & Gavrilova, 2010). The motivations of older people to engage in sex vary and are different from those of younger people. Past research has shown that older people have sex because they wish to maintain sexual functioning, to feel young again, and to feel attractive and desirable. They also reported their relationships moving from "lust to love" and their focus shifting from getting sex to giving sex (Gewirtz-Meydan & Ayalon, 2019).

For some older adults who initiate a relationship, sexuality is one of the motivations (Alterovitz & Mendelsohn, 2011, 2013). However, sexuality is not necessarily part of every late life repartnering relationship, although this does not prevent partner exclusivity (Koren, 2011; Koren & Ayalon, 2019). Sexuality and relationship initiation among older adults may be influenced by attitudes toward sexuality in old age (Bulcroft, 2019). When sexuality is part of the relationship, a range of sexual experiences is found. Some women shift from an emphasis on the importance of sexual intercourse and passion to a greater valuing of companionship, cuddling, affection, and intimacy (Hurd-Clarke, 2006). Others have emphasized that within the repartnering relationship, they experienced satisfaction from sexual intercourse for the first time (Koren, 2011). Finally, previous research indicates that middle-aged offspring at times take on the role of their parent's gatekeepers regarding sexual standards of conduct and cohabitation outside marriage (Bulcroft, 2019). Next, we address how offspring of older adults who initiate a relationship perceive the phenomenon.

Attitudes of Offspring and Repartnered Parent's Relationship With Offspring

It is possible to divide the research literature on relationship initiation in the second half of life into three phases. The first research phase focused on attitudes of widows and widowers toward relationship initiation (e.g., Bennett et al., 2013; Davidson, 2002; Mehta, 2002; Van Den Hoonaard, 2002). The second phase focused on the perspectives of older adults within such relationships on a variety of issues concerning the partners, such as motivations (De Jong Gierveld, 2004; Koren, 2011), relationship quality, being part of a dyad from a dyadic perspective (e.g., Koren, 2014), and partners' perspectives regarding their offspring's attitudes toward their relationship (De Jong Gierveld & Peeters, 2003; De Jong Gierveld & Merz, 2013). The third phase included research from the perspectives of the offspring (e.g., Koren & Lipman-Schiby; Koren & Simhi, 2016; Simhi Meidani, 2018). The current phase also focuses on relationship initiation among divorced older adults (Bildtgård & Öberg, 2019; Brown & Wright, 2017).

This section focuses on offspring's relationships with their older parents/grandparents and the offspring's attitudes toward their parent's/grandparent's relationship initiation from the perspectives of older parents, adult children, and grandchildren. Older adults in unmarried cohabitation and LAT relationships have the weakest bonds with their children (De Jong Gierveld & Peeters, 2003). A range of attitudes of adult children have been found. Some were positive and supportive, some were indifferent, and others were negative—refusing to accept the relationship and even sabotaging it. Negative attitudes were found to influence parents' choice of relationship form, whether to remarry, cohabitate, LAT, or not repartner at all. Parents preferred LAT or avoided initiating a relationship at all to reconcile with their adult children and be able to continue relationships with their grandchildren (De Jong Gierveld & Merz, 2013).

Experiences of grandchildren have scarcely been studied. They refer to the partners' role within the grandchild-grandparent relationship on a continuum. On one end, the grandchild expels the grandparent from the family for repartnering; on the other, the grandchild believes the new partner facilitates the intergenerational relationship with his grandparent and as such enhances closeness. Experiences of grandchildren also include complexity and ambivalence toward the relationship initiation of their grandparents. Interestingly, grandparents' relationship initiation was found to contribute to a change of attitude among grandchildren toward old age, perceiving it as an opportunity for innovation rather than something negative (Koren & Lipman-Schiby, 2018).

Adult children (Simhi Meidani & Koren, 2018) and grandchildren (Koren & Lipman-Schiby, 2018) who lost a parent to death were found to experience intertwining between the parental death of one parent/grandparent and the relationship initiation of the other, resulting in a loyalty conflict experienced in three ways. (a) For some adult children (Simhi Meidani & Koren, 2018) the experience of parental death and loss was their main experience. These adult children put more emphasis on loyalty toward their deceased parent rather than toward the wellbeing of their repartnered parent, thus sanctifying the deceased parent. (2) For others, the relationship initiation of the living parent was their main experience, showing that they understand the parent's need for a new partner. (3) For some, both loss and relationship initiation were experienced alongside each other by comparing between the deceased parent and the other parent's new partner (Simhi Meidani & Koren, 2018). In any case, parents' partners were not perceived by children or grandchildren as a replacement for their deceased parent or grandparent. However, offspring did perceive parents' partners as replacement for a couplehood relationship. The consequences of this were that offspring expected partners to know their place by not showing affection among partners in front of offspring and restricting partner participation in memorial ceremonies for their deceased parent/grandparent (Koren & Lipman-Schiby, 2014).

A common experience of offspring is the difficulty of accepting their parent's/grandparent's relationship initiation in old age as a social phenomenon or difficulty of accepting a specific partner. Offspring who objected to relationship initiation or objected to a specific partner were able to accept their parent's choice by seeing the dual benefits: for their parent as a way to decrease loneliness, and for themselves as a way to decrease the burden of care (Koren & Simhi, 2016). Some partners reported keeping relationship initiation a secret from offspring, particularly in Israel (Koren & Eisikovits, 2011) and North America (Bulcroft, 2019). Beyond the indication that such behavior is culturally related to society, it may also be related to intergenerational relationships in the family regarding concerns about the older parent's emotional vulnerability or concerns over inheritance. It may also be related to the intergenerational transmission of values regarding sexuality among older adults and outside wedlock (Bulcroft, 2019).

Gaps between repartnered parents and their adult children were found regarding caregiving expectations. Whereas parents prefer that their partners make caregiving decisions, adult children perceive themselves as the natural decision makers (Koren, Simhi, Lipman-Schiby, & Fogel, 2016). Accordingly, in comparison to married individuals, cohabiters who received caregiving from a partner received more hours of care from their partner than from other kin (Noël-Miller, 2011). Remarried wives to husbands in need of caregiving received more help from their own offspring than from their husband's offspring (Sherman, 2012). These findings are consistent with research on caregiving obligations in families, indicating that motivations to help stepparents are for helping the biological parent (Ganong & Coleman, 2006).

Relationship Initiation and Theories on Aging and "Successful Aging"

Relationship initiation among older adults and theories of successful aging are each developing within the context of modernization. Modernization processes include medical and technological development, processes of industrialization and internal migration, and advancing higher education. Medical and technological developments have contributed to increases in health and life expectancy (Cowgill, 1974). Living longer and healthier lives has developed the expectation to be more actively involved in life. Such expectations have set the foundations for the development of successful aging theories. Also, industrialization has encouraged internal migration of younger generations from rural to urban areas to obtain a higher education and increase employment opportunities (Cowgill, 1974). These processes have resulted in changes in family structures, from living in extended families that include several generations in one household to the nuclear family structure that includes two generations in a household when children are growing up and one generation when adult children launch home (Carter & McGoldrick, 2005). As spouses age, marriages end, either with widowhood or divorce, leaving the older person alone (de Jong Gierveld, 2001). Relationship initiation is a way to cope with this loneliness (de Jong Gierveld, 2002; Koren, 2011).

Relationship initiation is a phenomenon developing within the sociocultural attitudes of successful aging, namely, how aging should ideally be. The concept of successful aging and its theories have been developing for several decades. Pruchno (2015), in her editorial for a special issue on successful aging in the *The Gerontologist*, mentioned that successful aging includes a variety of definitions and theoretical models. The term itself, "successful aging," has been criticized for judgmentally dividing aging adults into those who succeed and those who do not. Furthermore, criteria for success put the upper socioeconomic strata at an advantage, because to achieve success, social and financial resources are required; conversely, the successful aging framework potentially discriminates marginalized groups in society. The concept is also criticized for reflecting Western modern perceptions of aging, while ignoring how aging is perceived in Eastern collective cultures.

One of the most referenced theories of successful aging is the biosociopsychological model of Rawe and Kahn (1987, 1997). It emphasizes the interplay between three main components that are important for older adults: avoiding disease and disability; having high cognitive and physical function; and being actively engaged with life (Rawe & Kahn, 1997). Dating profiles of older adults were found to emphasize high engagement with life while putting less emphasis on the two other components of this model for successful aging. This could be because most of the older adults who posted their profile did not think that the other two criteria were relevant, or perhaps they did not meet the criteria of avoiding health and functionality problems (Wada et al., 2016).

When theories of successful aging began to appear in the empirical and theoretical literature, they were referred to as follows:

> A theory of successful aging is a statement of the conditions of individual and social life under which the individual person gets a maximum of satisfaction and happiness and society maintains an appropriate balance among satisfactions for the various groups which make it up. (Havighurst, 1961 p. 8)

Such a definition is capable of including contrasting theories such as activity theory, which claims that successful aging is when older adults are capable of maintaining a middle-age lifestyle and as such continue to contribute to society, as well as disengagement theory, which claims that successful aging is achieved by a gradual withdrawal from an active life serving the needs of society in order to make room for younger generations and for the aging adult to relax and enjoy life (Havighurst, 1961).

Depending on the interpretation, relationship initiation coincides with disengagement theory regarding the opportunity to relax and have fun, and it also coincides well with activity theory and third-age culture, as it follows the principles of engaging with life and maintaining a young self-image (Koren, 2015).

Continuity theory of normal aging is characterized by the continuity of external social structures of familiar relationships and the continuity of internal psychological structures of the self (Atchely, 1989). Relationship initiation among older adults was experienced as a discontinuity from features of long-term marriages in several domains: the purpose of relationship initiation, which is mainly for enjoying life, in contrast to the purpose of lifelong marital relationships, which are constructed mainly for raising a family; the becoming of "the self" as possible within relationships initiated among older adults; caring based on a desire for a partner rather than caring based on the obligation to a spouse in a long-term marriage; and discovering sexuality for the first time within new relationships initiated in old age (Koren, 2011). Continuity as indicating normal aging (Atchley, 1988) and preferring familiar social relationships to newly formed network ties (Carstensen, 1992) may explain why some older adults decline forming new relationships and why others select a partner who was a past acquaintance (Bulcraft, 2019; Koren & Eisikovits, 2011) (see quote at the opening of the chapter).

According to the socioemotional selectivity theory, as people grow older, they are less interested in expanding their horizons and care more about experiencing meaningful social ties (Carstensen et al., 2003) and making the most of the time that is left (Carstensen et al., 1999). This coincides with the experience of late-life repartnering as influenced by the limited time left to live (Bildtgård & Öberg, 2015) for enjoying life while still possible (Koren, 2015). Furthermore, social-emotional selectivity theory found that older adults are more skilled at managing emotionally charged interactions. They are less engaged in upward social comparison motivated by future goals and more engaged in downward social comparison which better serves emotion regulation (Carstensen et al., 2003). Emotional well-being was found to improve with age (Carstensen et al., 2011). Moreover, as negative emotions decrease, positive emotions increase (Verstaen et al., 2020).

As such, older adults in a late-life repartnering relationship are expected to experience happiness. However, older people were surprised to find great happiness in late-life repartnering. A possible explanation could be related to the partners internalizing ageist attitudes toward relationship initiation among older adults (Koren, 2019). Another explanation could be that in everyday life, older adults prefer low-arousal positive emotions such as being satisfied and having a life filled with positive emotions. They are less likely to prefer high-arousal positive emotions such as feeling ecstatic or bursting with positive emotions (Bjalkebring et al., 2015). However, whereas experiences of happiness do not coincide with a preference for low-arousal emotions, experiences of love among partners who initiated a relationship as older adults do coincide. Love among partners is experienced as pleasant love that is not heated, as a parental love, meaning deep and quiet, as a "sibling" love with exclusivity, and as love characterized by compassion rather than passion (Koren, 2021).

Future Directions

Relationship initiation among older adults is a developing phenomenon both in real life and as a research field. The knowledge presented in this chapter is based on large databases such as the first wave of the National Social Life Health & Aging Project 2005–2006, which were used for secondary analyses (e.g., Lewin, 2017); on qualitative research (e.g., Koren, 2011, 2014, 2015, Koren & Lipman-Schiby, 2014; Koren & Simhi, 2016); and on mixed-methods studies that combined secondary analyses of large databases, such as the NESTOR longitudinal survey data from the Netherlands, with in-depth qualitative interviews (e.g., De Jong Gierveld, 2002; De Jong Gierveld & Peeters, 2003).

Studies based on large data sets can contribute information on prevalence, along with a variety of topics such as health and happiness (Lewin, 2017), the dilemma of repartnering

(De Jong Gierveld, 2002), or relationships with adult children (De Jong Gierveld & Peeters, 2003). Qualitative studies have revealed the in-depth experiences of older partners as individuals (Davidson, 2002; De Jong Gierveld, 2004; Spalter, 2010), as dyads (Koren & Eisikovits, 2011; Koren, 2011;2014; 2015), and of the stepfamilies constructed as a result of relationship initiation among older adults (e.g., Koren & Lipman Schiby, 2014).

Dyadic methodology (Eisikovits & Koren, 2010) and a methodology for analyzing intergenerational (step)families (Koren, 2017) have been developed. Due to the unique characteristics of intimate partner relationships initiated among older adults that have emerged from the empirical research of the phenomenon, the tools used at other life stages, such as the Couple's Relating to Each Other Questionnaires (CREOQ; Birtchnell et al., 2006) or the Relationship Assessment Scale (RAS; Hendrick, 1988), cannot capture the full experience of older adults who entered their relationship late in life. Therefore, the field needs to develop quantitative research tools to measure, for example, relationship quality based on the unique characteristics of the phenomenon.

Knowledge on sexuality among older adults is scarce (e.g., Gewirtz-Meydan & Ayalon, 2018), and on sexuality in relationships initiated among older adults is even scarcer (e.g., Koren, 2014). This field of knowledge needs to be developed in several ways. For example, to compare between sexual experiences of older spouses in long-term marriages with sexual experiences of older adults who recently initiated a relationship in order to understand if and how sexual experiences are related to age and/or to length of relationship. Another line of research could be to examine the relationship between internalized ageism, societal ageism, and sexuality among older adults who recently initiated a relationship.

Furthermore, a more refined distinction is required in research regarding the experience of relationship initiation among older adults within various age groups. Although relationship initiation is a way to fulfill the third-age culture of having fun and enjoying life (Bildtgård & Öberg, 2019), it requires health. Most of the knowledge addresses the phenomenon at the stage when both partners are independently functioning, physically and cognitively. However, knowledge on what happens to such relationships when third-agers become fourth-agers and health deteriorates and as a result partners lose capacity and become more dependent on others—is scarce (e.g., De Jong Gierveld, 2015; Koren et al., 2016). Expectations among LAT partners showed that about half of the LAT partners intended to exchange care if needed. The other half had ambiguous feelings or intentions to refuse care (De Jong Gierveld, 2015). When adult children's expectations were examined along with partners' expectations, the expectations of the two generations did not coincide. The parents preferred to rely on their partners to make caregiving decisions. However, the adult children perceived decision-making as their role, not the role of their parent's partner. Adult children perceived that the role of the partner is to carry out the decisions they, the adult children, make (Koren et al., 2016). However, LAT partners already confronted with illness in their current relationship were found to provide care to the partner in need. The minority of LAT partners who would not exchange care reciprocally are more likely to give care as opposed to receiving it (De Jong Gierveld, 2015). However, more knowledge is needed about caregiving expectations and intentions to provide care in LAT, cohabitation, and remarriage relationships among older adults as they transition from the third age to the fourth age, and what happens in practice.

The use of technology for relationship initiation has been studied quite extensively (McWilliams & Barrett, 2014). Research has shown that both older men and women use dating sites to establish new romantic relationships (Menkin et al., 2015). Nevertheless, even those dating sites that specifically cater to older people refrain from using terms that define the population as old and rely on visual images that portray youthfulness, actively striving to move away from the stigma of old age (Ayalon & Gewirtz-Meydan, 2017; Gewirtz-Meydan & Ayalon, 2018). Older adults themselves consistently attempt to present a youthful image on dating sites, and older men also tend to prefer substantially younger women for dating (Alterovitz & Mendelsohn, 2011). Although this line of research has received a considerable amount of attention, what is still missing is information about the use of technology across different cultures and for purposes other than dating, such as sexual pleasure in the second half of life.

Finally, research concerning relationship initiation among older lesbian, gay, transgender, and bisexual (LGBT) older adults is lacking. To date, research on older LGBT has been extremely scarce (e.g., Jönson & Siverskog, 2012; Siverskog & Bromseth, 2019), with a primary focus on older homosexual men and older lesbian women (Ayalon & Koren, 2015). Research on intimate relationships among older LGBTs started out regarding social support (Cooney & Dunne, 2001). Only at a later stage did research address older LGBT relationship initiation in the form of dating in Sweden, for instance (e.g., Jönson & Siverskog, 2012; Siverskog & Bromseth, 2019).

It is not surprising that the pioneer research on LGBT relationship initiation among older adults is developing in Sweden, as it has been a pioneer in LAT relationship initiation for younger and older adults alike (Levin & Trost 1999) and has moved farther from the typical nuclear family structure than any other industrial society. As such, it may be the groundbreaking model for understanding relationship initiation among older adults in the Western world (Bildtgård & Öberg, 2019), including older LGBTs.

Being an older LGBT is less common because in the past, the phenomenon was unaccepted. Although relationship initiation among heterosexual older adults is a challenge, homosexual dating suffers even more from ageist attitudes, making it much more difficult to find a suitable partner (Jönson & Siverskog, 2012; Siverskog & Bromseth, 2019). Self-mocking comments on old age, being overweight, impotence, and other age-related changes were part of a repertoire that displayed marketable characteristics such as humor, self-distance, and honesty among older LGBT advertisers (Jönson & Siverskog, 2012). Although old age could be a disadvantage for entering or participating in queer subcultures, especially when it comes to dating, the wisdom and experience that come with old age could serve as an advantage (Siverskog & Bromseth, 2019). Narratives of older gay men in Mumbai India indicate cultural differences between East and West. Findings indicate acceptance without threatening the heterosexual norm, as opposed to the Western cultural anxieties toward gay men (Sharma & Samanta, 2020).

Changes in societal norms in many Western societies allow older LGBTs to express their relationship preference and sexuality more freely nowadays, compared to the past. The limited research available has stressed the youth culture prevalent primarily in the gay community and contrasted it with the lesbian community, which has been less vested in physical appearance and an attractive youthful visual image (Kaufman & Phua, 2003). What is still missing is a much more refined differentiation within the LGBT community and a better understanding of relationship initiation and maintenance in the second half of life in this community.

Conclusion

In summary, this chapter has identified the concept and the actual experiences of relationship initiation in old age as occurring or at least being acknowledged primarily in Western modern societies. The present chapter suggests that several theoretical models, including the successful aging model and socioemotional selectivity theory, can be used to account for this phenomenon in the second half of life. We also point to currently unmet needs in research and theory, including a better cross-national and contextual understanding, as well as the development of methodological tools for an improved understanding of this phenomenon. Specific attention to unique segments of the population of older adults and to specific relationship issues is also required.

References

Agogo, D., Milne, G. & Schewe, C. (2014). Time benders: A model of subjective aging in aging adults. *Health Marketing Quarterly, 31*, 383–398. https://doi.org/10.1080/07359683.2014.966010.

Alterovitz, S., & Mendelsohn, G. (2011). Partner preferences across the life span: Online dating by older adults. *Psychology and Aging, 24*, 513–517. https://doi.org/10.1037/a0015897

Alterovitz, S., & Mendelsohn, G. (2013). Relationship goals of middle-aged, young-old, and old-old internet daters: An analysis of online personal ads. *Journal of Aging Studies, 27*, 159–165.

Aron, A., Aron, E. N., & Smollan, D. (1992). Inclusion of other in the Self Scale and the structure of interpersonal closeness. *Journal of Personality and Social Psychology, 63*(4), 596–612. https://doi.org/10.1037/0022-3514.63.4.596

Aron, A., Fisher, H. E., Strong, G., Acevedo, B., Riela, S., & Tsapelas, I. (2008). Falling in love. In S. Sprecher, A. Wenzel, & J. Harvey (Eds.), *Handbook of relationship initiation*. (pp. 315–336). Psychology Press.

Atchley, R.C. (1989). A continuity theory of normal aging, *The Gerontologist, 29*(2), 183–190.

Ayalon, L., & Gewirtz-Meydan, A. (2017). Senior, mature or single: A qualitative analysis of homepage advertisements of dating sites for older adults. *Computers in Human Behavior, 75*, 876–882.

Ayalon, L., & Koren, C. (2015). Marriage, second couplehood, divorce and singlehood in old age. I. P. Lichtenberg, B. Mast, & J. Werethel (Eds.), *APA Handbook of clinical geropsychology, Vol.2: Assessment, treatment and issues of later life* (pp. 617–644). APA Handbooks in Psychology. American Psychological Association Press.

Ayalon, L., & Tesch-Römer, C. (Eds.). (2018). *Contemporary perspectives on ageism*. Springer Open.

Bailey, K. D. (1994). *Typologies and taxonomies: An introduction to classification techniques*. SAGE.

Birtchnell, J., Voortman, S., Dejong, C., & Gordon, D. (2006). Measuring interrelating within couples: The Couple's Relating to Each Other Questionnaires (CREOQ). *Psychology and Psychotherapy: Theory, Research and Practice, 79*(3), 339–364. https://doi.org/10.1348/147608305X68787

Ben-Ari, A. (2012). Rethinking closeness and distance in intimate relationships: Are they really two opposites? *Journal of Family Issues, 33*(3), 391–412. https://doi.org/10.1177/0192513X11415357

Bennett, K. M., Arnott, L. & Soulsby, L. K. (2013). "You're not getting married for the moon and the stars": The uncertainties of older British widowers about the idea of new romantic relationships. *Journal of Aging Studies, 27*, 499–506.

Benson, J. J., & Coleman, M. (2016a). Older adult descriptions of living apart together. *Family Relations, 65*(3), 439–449. https://doi.org/10.1111/fare.12203

Benson, J. J. & Coleman, M. (2016b). Older adults developing a preference for living apart together. *Journal of Marriage and Family, 78*(3), 797–812. https://doi.org/10.1111/jomf.12292

Bettache, K., & Chiu, C. (2019). Why American conservatives and individuals from traditionalist cultures may share a preference for group uniformity. *Asian Journal of Social Psychology, 22*(3), 325–330. https://doi.org/ezproxy.haifa.ac.il/10.1111/ajsp.12356

Bildtgård, T., & Öberg, P. (2015). Time as a structuring condition behind new intimate relationships in later life. *Ageing & Society, 35*(7), 1505–1528. https://doi.org/10.1017/S0144686X14000452

Bildtgård, T., & Öberg, P. (2017). New intimate relationships in later life: Consequences for the social and filial network? *Journal of Family Issues, 38*(3), 381–405. https://doi.org/10.1177/0192513X15579503

Bildtgård T., & Öberg, P. (2019). *Intimacy and ageing: New relationships in later life.* Policy Press.

Bjalkebring, P., Västfjäll, D., & Johansson, B. E. A. (2015). Happiness and arousal: Framing happiness as arousing results in lower happiness ratings for older adults. *Frontiers in Psychology, 2015*(6), 706.

Bowen, M. (1978). *Family therapy in clinical practice.* Jason Aronson.

Bronfenbrenner, U. (1994). Ecological models of human development. In P. Peterson, E. Baker, & B. McGaw (Eds.), International *encyclopedia of education* (Vol. 3, 2nd ed., pp. xx–xx). Elsevier.

Brown S., Lee G., Bulanda J. (2006). Cohabitation among older adults: A national portrait. *Journal of Gerontology: Series B: Psychological Sciences and Social Sciences, 61*(2), S71–S79.

Brown, S. L., Lin, I. F. (2013). *Age variation in the remarriage rate, 1990–2011* (FP-13–17). National Center for Family & Marriage Research.

Brown, S., & Shinohara, S. (2013). Dating relationships in older adulthood: A national portrait. *Journal of Marriage and Family, 75*(5), 1194–1202.

Brown, S. L. & Wright, M. R. (2017). Marriage, cohabitation, and divorce in later life. *Innovation in Aging, 1*(2), 1–11. https://doi.org/10.1093/geroni/igx015

Bulcroft, K. A. (2019). Love and sexuality in later life: What your grandparents are not telling you. *Slovenský národopis* [Slovak Ethnology], *67*(2), 185–200. https://doi.org/10.2478/se-2019–0010

Bulcroft, K., & O'Connor, M. (1986). The importance of dating relationships on quality of life for older person. *Family Relations, 35*(3), 397–401.

Cambridge dictionary online. https://dictionary.cambridge.org/dictionary/english/initiation

Carr, D., & Utz, R. L. (2020). Families in later life: A decade in review. *Journal of Marriage and Family, 82*(1), 346–363. https://doi-org.ezproxy.haifa.ac.il/10.1111/jomf.12609

Carstensen, L. L. (1992). Social and emotional patterns in adulthood: Support for socioemotional selectivity theory. *Psychology and Aging, 7*(3), 331–338. https://doi.org/ezproxy.haifa.ac.il/10.1037/0882–7974.7.3.331

Carstensen, L. L. (2006). The influence of a sense of time on human development. *Science, 312*(5782), 1913–1915.

Carstensen, L. L., Fung, H. H., & Charles, S. T. (2003). Socioemotional selectivity theory and the regulation of emotion in the second half of life. *Motivation and Emotion, 27*(2), 103–123. https://doi.org/ezproxy.haifa.ac.il/10.1023/A:1024569803230

Carstensen, L. L., Isaacowitz, D. M., & Charles, S. T. (1999). Taking time seriously: A theory of socioemotional selectivity. *American Psychologist, 54*(3), 165–181. https://doi.org/ezproxy.haifa.ac.il/10.1037/0003–066X.54.3.165

Carter, B., & McGoldrick, M. (2005). *The expended family life cycle: Individual, family and the social perspectives.* Allyn and Bacon.

Chen, J., & Jordan, L. P. (2018). Intergenerational support and life satisfaction of young-, old- and oldest-old adults in China. *Aging and Mental Health, 22*(3), 412–420.

Cho, G. H. (2011). A psychological inquiry into the Confucian origins of East Asian collectivism. *Korean Social Sciences Review* (KSSR), *1*(1), 37–103.
Cicirelli, V. G. (2006). Fear of death in mid-old age. *The Journals of Gerontology: Series B: Psychological Sciences and Social Sciences*, *61*(2), P75–P81.
Clarke, L. H., & Griffin, M. (2008). Visible and invisible ageing: Beauty work as a response to ageism. *Ageing and Society*, *28*(5), 653.
Cohen, O. (2003). The Israeli family. In James J. Ponzetti (Ed.), *The international encyclopaedia of marriage and family* (Vol. 2, pp. 960–964). Macmillan.
Coleman, M., Ganong, L. H., Hans, J. D., Sharp, E. A., & Rothrauff, T. C. (2005). Filial obligations in post-divorce stepfamilies. *Journal of Divorce & Remarriage*, *43*(3–4), 1–27. https://doi.org/10.1300/J087v43n03_01
Cooney, T. M., & Dunne, K. (2001). Intimate relationships in later life. *Journal of Family Issues*, *22*(7), 838–858.
Cowgill, D.O. (1974). Aging and modernization: A revision of the theory. In J. E. Gubrium (Ed.), *Late life communities and environmental policy* (pp. 123–146). C. C. Thomas.
Davidson, K. (2002). Gender differences in new partnership choices and constraints for older widows and widowers. *Ageing International*, *27*, *4*, 43–60.
Davidson, K., & Fennell, G. (2002). New intimate relationships in later life. *Ageing International*, *27*(*4*), 3–10.
De Jong Gierveld, J. (2001). Unity and diversity in living arrangements of older adults in different regions of Europe. *EurAmerica*, *31*(3), 1–56.
De Jong Gierveld, J. (2002). The dilemma of repartnering: Considerations of older men and women entering new relationships in later life. *Ageing International*, *27*(4), 61–78.
De Jong Gierveld, J. (2004). Remarriage, unmarried cohabitation, living apart together: Partner relationships following bereavement or divorce. *Journal of Marriage and Family*, *66*, 236–243. https://doi.org/10.1111/j.0022-2445.2004.00017.x
De Jong Gierveld, J. (2015). Intra-couple caregiving of older adults living apart together: Commitment and independence. *Canadian Journal on Aging* [La Revue canadienne du vieillissement], *34*, 356–365 https://doi.org/10.1017/S0714980815000264
De Jong Gierveld, J., & Merz, E. M. (2013). Parents' partnership decision making after divorce or widowhood: The role of (step) children. *Journal of Marriage and Family*, *75*(5), 1098–1113.
De Jong Gierveld, J., & Peeters, A. (2003). The interweaving of repartnered older adults' lives with children and siblings. *Ageing and Society*, *23*, 187–205.
Devi, J. (2018). The scales of functional assessment of activities of daily living in geriatrics. *Age and Ageing*, *47*(4), 500–502.
Eisikovits, Z., & Koren, C. (2010). Approaches and outcomes of dyadic qualitative analysis. *Qualitative Health Research*, *20*(12), 1642–1655. https://doi.org/10.1177/1049732310376520
Erikson, E. H. (1998). *The life cycle completed*. Norton.
Freund, A. M., & Smith, J. (1999). Content and function of the self-definition in old and very old age. *The Journals of Gerontology: Series B: Psychological Sciences and Social Sciences*, 54(1), P55–P67.
Gaine, G. S., & La Guardia, J. G. (2009). The unique contributions of motivations to maintain a relationship and motivations toward relational activities to relationship well-being. *Motivation and Emotion*, *33*(2), 184–202. https://doi.org/10.1007/s11031-009-9120-x
Ganong, L., & Coleman, M. (2006). Patterns of exchange and intergenerational responsibilities after divorce and remarriage. *Journal of Ageing Studies*, *20*, 265–278.
Ganong, L., & Coleman, M. (2012). Relationships in older stepfamilies. In R. Blieszner, V. H. Bedford, R. Blieszner, V. H. Bedford (Eds.), *Handbook of families and aging* (2nd ed., pp. 213–242). Praeger/ABC-CLIO.
Gewirtz-Meydan, A., & Ayalon, L. (2018). Why do older adults have sex? Approach and avoidance sexual motives among older women and men. *Journal of Sex Research*, *56*(7), 870–881. https://doi.org/10.1080/00224499.2018.1543644
Goodman, C. (1999). Intimacy and autonomy in long term marriage. *Journal of Gerontological Social Work*, *32*(1), 83–97. https://doi.org/10.1300/J083v32n01_06
Haskey, J., & Lewis, J. (2006). Living-apart-together in Britain: Context and meaning. *International Journal of Law in Context*, *2*(01), 37–48.
Havighurst, R.J. (1961). Successful aging. *The Gerontologist*, *1*, 8–14.

Hendrick, S. S. (1988). A generic measure of relationship satisfaction. *Journal of Marriage and the Family*, *50*(1), 93–98. https://doi.org/10.2307/352430

Hurd-Clarke, L. (2006). Older women and sexuality: Experiences in marital relationships across the life course. *Canadian Journal on Aging*, *25*(2), 129–140.

Jamison, T.B., & Ganong, L. (2010). We're not living together: Stayover relationships among college-educated emerging adults, *Journal of Social and Personal Relationships*, *28*(4), 536–557.

Jönson, H., & Siverskog, A. (2012). Turning vinegar into wine: Humorous self-presentations among older GLBTQ online daters. *Journal of Aging Studies*, *26*(1), 55–64.

Jopp, D. S., Wozniak, D., Damarin, A. K., De Feo, M., Jung, S., & Jeswani, S. (2015). How could lay perspectives on successful aging complement scientific theory? Findings from a US and a German life-span sample. *The Gerontologist*, *55*(1), 91–106. https://doi.org/ezproxy.haifa.ac.il/10.1093/geront/gnu059

Karlsson, S.G. & Borell, K. (2002). Intimacy and autonomy, gender and ageing: Living apart together. *Ageing International*, *27*(4), 11–26.

Kaufman, G., & Phua, V.C. (2003). Is ageism alive in date selection among men? Age requests among gay and straight men in Internet personal ads. *The Journal of Men's Studies*, *11*(2), 225–235

Kim, J. Y., Xu, H., Cruz, G., Saito, Y., & Østbye, T. (2021). Acceptance of love and remarriage among older adults in the Philippines. *Journal of Aging and Health*, *33*(5–6), 331–339. https://doi.org/10.1177/08982 64320981246

King, V., & Scott, M. E. (2005). A comparison of cohabiting relationships among older and younger adults. *Journal of Marriage and Family*, *67*(2), 271–285.

Koren, C., & Eisikovits, Z. (2011). Life beyond the planned script: Accounts and secrecy of older persons living in second couplehood in old age in a society in transition. *Journal of Social and Personal Relationships*, *28*(1), 44. https://doi.org/10.1177/0265407510385430

Koren, C. (2011). Continuity and discontinuity: The case of second couplehood in old age. The Gerontologist, 51 (5), 687. https://doi.org/10.1093/geront/gnr018

Koren, C. (2014). Together and apart: A typology of re-partnering in old age. *International Psychogeriatrics*, *26*(8), 1327–1350. https://doi.org/10.1017/S1041610214000738

Koren, C. (2015). The intertwining of second couplehood and old age, *Ageing and Society*, *35*, 1864–1888. https://doi.org/10.1017/S0144686X14000294

Koren, C. (2016). Men's vulnerability—Women's resilience: From widowhood to late-life repartnering. *International Psychogeriatrics*, *28*(5), 719–731

Koren, C. (2017). Qualitative data analysis of the multigenerational family unit: The case of late-life stepfamilies. *Innovation in Aging*, *1*(Suppl. 1), 44.

Koren C. (2019). The experience of happiness in late-life repartnering: Surprise and disappointment. *Innovation in Aging*, *3*(Suppl. 1), S577. https://doi.org/10.1093/geroni/igz038.2138

Koren, C. (2021). Dyadic experiences of love in late-life repartnering relationships. *Journal of Family Issues*. Advance online publication. https://doi.org/10.1177/0192513X211031520

Koren, C., & Ayalon, L. (2019). "Not living together yet all the time together": The meaning of living-apart-together in continuing care retirement communities from perspectives of residents and healthcare professionals. *Journal of Social and Personal Relationships*, *36*(11–12), 3855–3874. https://doi.org/10.1177/0265407519840711

Koren, C., & Lipman-Schiby, S. (2014). "Not a replacement:" Emotional experiences and practical consequences of Israeli second couplehood stepfamilies constructed in old age. *Journal of Ageing Studies*, *31*, 70–82. https://doi.org/10.1016/j.jaging.2014.09.002

Koren, C., & Lipman-Schiby, S. (2018). The partners' place within the ongoing grandchild and late life repartnered grandparent relationship. *Innovation in Aging*, *2*(Suppl. 1), 7.

Koren, C., & Simhi, S. (2016). "As long as it's good": An intergenerational family perspective of bridging gaps between reality and ideality of second couplehood in old age as a problem and as a solution, *Ageing and Society* 36(4), 716–740 https://doi.org/10.1017/s0144686x14001482

Koren, C., Simhi, S., Lipman-Schiby, S., & Fogel, S. (2016). The partner in late-life repartnering: Caregiving expectations from an intergenerational perspective. *International Psychogeriatrics*, *28*(9), 1555–1565. https://doi.org/10.1017/S1041610215002240

Koren, C., & Simhi-Meidai, S. (2020). Integrating the familial and the cultural: An approach for analysing intergenerational family relationships in social work practice. *British Journal of Social Work*, *50*, 2152–2171. https://doi.org/10.1093/bjsw/bcaa005

Kotter-Grühn, D., Kornadt, A. E., & Stephan, Y. (2016). Looking beyond chronological age: Current knowledge and future directions in the study of subjective age. *Gerontology, 62*(1), 86–93. https://doi.org/ezproxy.haifa.ac.il/10.1159/000438671

Lampis, J., Cataudella, S., Agus, M., Busonera, A., & Skowron, E. A. (2019). Differentiation of self and dyadic adjustment in couple relationships: A dyadic analysis using the actor-partner interdependence model. *Family Process, 58*(3), 698–715. https://doi.org/10.1111/famp.12370

Lavee, Y. & Katz, R. (2003). The family in Israel: Between tradition and modernity. *Marriage & Family Review, 35*(1/2), 193–217.

Lee, S. B., Oh, J. H., Park, J. H., Choi, S. P., & Wee, J. H. (2018). Differences in youngest-old, middle-old, and oldest-old patients who visit the emergency department. *Clinical and Experimental Emergency Medicine, 5*(4), 249.

Levin, I., & Trost, J. (1999). Living apart together. *Community, Work and Family, 2(3),* 279–294.

Lewin, A. (2017). Health and relationship quality later in life: A comparison of living apart together (LAT), first marriages, remarriages, and cohabitation. *Journal of Family Issues 38*(12), 1754–1774. https://doi.org/10.1177/0192513X16647982

Lexico Oxford dictionary online. https://www.lexico.com/definition/initiation

Lindau, S. T., & Gavrilova, N. (2010). Sex, health, and years of sexually active life gained due to good health: Evidence from two US population based cross sectional surveys of ageing. *BMJ, 340,* Article c810.

Marsh, R. M. (2014). Modernization theory, then and now. *Comparative Sociology, 13*(3), 261–283.

McIntosh, W. D., Locker, L., Briley, K., Ryan, R., & Scott, A. J. (2011). What do older adults seek in their potential romantic partners? Evidence from online personal ads. *The International Journal of Aging and Human Development, 72*(1), 67–82. https://doi.org/10.2190/AG.72.1.d

McWilliams, S., & Barrett, A. (2014). Online dating in middle and later life: Gendered expectations and experiences. *Journal of Family Issues, 35,* 411–436. https://doi.org/10.1177/0192513X12468437

Mehta, K. K. (2002). Perceptions of remarriage by widowed people in Singapore. *Ageing International, 27,* 93–107.

Menkin, J. A., Robles, T. F., Wiley, J. F., & Gonzaga, G. C. (2015). Online dating across the life span: Users' relationship goals. *Psychology and Aging, 30*(4), 987.

Merriam-Webster dictionary online. https://www.merriam-webster.com/dictionary/initiation

Noël-Miller, C. M. (2011). Partner caregiving in older cohabiting couples. *The Journals of Gerontology Series B: Psychological Sciences and Social Sciences, 66B*(3), 341–353.

Olson, H. D. (2000). Circumplex-model of marital and family systems. *Journal of Family Therapy, 22*(2), 144–167.

Pachana, N. A., & Mitchell, L. K. (2018). Examining the unique wisdom of older adults. *International Psychogeriatrics, 30*(12), 1743–1744.

Pavlova, M. K., & Silbereisen, R. K. (2016). Perceived expectations for active aging, formal productive roles, and psychological adjustment among the young-old. *Research on Aging, 38*(1), 26–50. https://doi-org.ezproxy.haifa.ac.il/10.1177/0164027515573026

Pruchno, R. (2015). Successful aging: Contentious past, productive future. *The Gerontologist, 55*(1), 1–4. https://doi-org.ezproxy.haifa.ac.il/10.1093/geront/gnv002

Rowe, J. W., & Kahn, R. L. (1987). Human aging: Usual and successful. *Science, 237,* 143–149.

Rowe, J. W., & Kahn, R. L. (1997). Successful aging. *The Gerontologist, 37*(4), 433–440.

Samanta, T., &Varghese, S. S. (2019). Love in the time of aging: Sociological reflections on marriage, gender and intimacy in India. *Ageing International, 44,* 57–73. https://doi.org/ezproxy.haifa.ac.il/10.1007/s12126-018-9332-z

Scott, M. B., & Lyman, S. M. (1968). Accounts. *American Sociological Review, 33,* 46–62.

Seider, B. H., Hirschberger, G., Nelson, K. L., & Levenson, R. W. (2009). We can work it out: Age differences in relational pronouns, physiology, and behavior in marital conflict. *Psychology and Aging, 24,* 604–613.

Sharma, A., & Samanta, T. (2020). Crafting "youthful" desire, "doing" masculinity: Narratives of middle-aged to older men in grindr grid and offline spaces in Mumbai, India. *Ageing International, 45*(4), 361–379.

Sherman, C. W. (2012). Remarriage as context for dementia caregiving: Implications of positive and negative support for caregiver well-being, *Research in Human Development, 9,* 165–182.

Siverskog, A., & Bromseth, J. (2019). Subcultural spaces: LGBTQ aging in a Swedish context. *The International Journal of Aging and Human Development, 88*(4), 325–340. https://doi.org/10.1177/0091415019836923

Spalter, T. (2010). Social capital and intimate partnership in later life: A gendered perspective on 60+ year old Israelis. *Social Networks, 32*, 330–338.

Van Den Hoonaard, D. K. (2002). Attitudes of older widows and widowers in New Brunswick, Canada towards new partnerships. *Ageing International, 27*(4), 79–92.

Watson, W. K., Bell, N. J. & Stelle, C. (2010). Women narrate later life remarriage: Negotiating the cultural to create the personal. *Journal of Aging Studies, 24*, 302–312

Watson, W. K., & Stelle, C. (2011). Dating for older women: Experiences and meanings of dating in later life. *Journal of Women & Aging, 23*(3), 263–275. https://doi.org/ezproxy.haifa.ac.il/10.1080/08952841.2011.587732

Watson, W., & Stelle, C. (2021). Love in cyberspace: Self-presentation and partner seeking in online dating advertisements of older adults. *Journal of Family Issues, 42*(12), Article 0192513X2098202. https://doi.org/10.1177/0192513X20982024

Watson, W. K., Stelle, C., & Bell, N. (2017). Older women in new romantic relationships: Understanding the meaning and importance of sex in later life. *The International Journal of Aging & Human Development, 85*(1), 33–43. https://doi.org/ezproxy.haifa.ac.il/10.1177/0091415016680067

World Health Organization. (2002) Retrieved June 10, 2020, from https://www.who.int/healthinfo/survey/ageingdefnolder/en/#:~:text=Most%20developed%20world%20countries%20have,to%20the%20situation%20in%20Africa

CHAPTER

10 Cross-Cultural Variation in Relationship Initiation

Victor Karandashev

Abstract

Biological and cultural evolutionary perspectives complement each other to explain many processes in relationship initiation. The chapter shows how biological and social evolution interact to account for cultural variation in mate preferences and romantic relationship initiation. The influence of biological, ecological, socioeconomic, and cultural factors varies between and within types of societies. In isolated tribal, subsistence-based societies, biological and ecological factors play major roles. In traditional societies, besides these factors, socioeconomic and cultural factors play important roles. In modern societies, socioeconomic and cultural factors become dominant, with decreasing influences for biological and ecological factors. Ecological, socioeconomic, and cultural parameters, which affect practices of relationship initiation in subsistence-based, traditional, and modern societies, are propinquity, homogamy, social and relationship mobility, modernization of society, cultural values, cultural conception of individuality in interdependent versus independent societies, power distance and social equality, gender roles, and gender equality. The chapter addresses culturally evolved practices of relationship initiation, such as tribal gatherings, traditional courtship, dating, partnership, and social media and web-based communication and reviews the societal and cultural factors that affect these practices. The chapter concludes with a brief review of implications for future research on cultural variation in relationship initiation in terms of theoretical and empirical methodology.

Key Words: cultural evolution, traditional societies, modern societies, cultural affordances, propinquity, homogamy, relational mobility, arranged marriage, love marriage

1. Convergence of Evolutionary and Cultural Perspectives on Relationship Initiation

Humans are "social animals." Therefore, both biological and cultural evolutions influenced the ways of human mating through history. In this section, I show how biological, ecological, and cultural factors affected sexual selection and attraction of men and women.

SEXUAL SELECTION APPROACH TO MOTIVATION OF RELATIONSHIP INITIATION

In initiating romantic relationships, an individual strives to establish sexual and emotional connections with another. This process involves identifying the right person, approaching them, and engaging in interaction. Practices and forms of relationship initiation are driven by both biological and social-evolutionary mechanisms that have recurrently solved the challenges of survival and reproduction (Buss, 1988, 1994, 2004, 2006, 2019; Buss & Schmitt, 1993; Fisher, 1998, 2004; Gangestad, 2008; Schmitt, 2008; Thornhill & Gangestad, 1996).

People in subsistence-based, traditional, and modern societies have inherited the reproductive strategies that their ancestors successfully used. Evolved psychological mechanisms determine criteria for the choice of a fertile mate who is able and willing to produce and invest in offspring (Buss, 1989). An individual initiates a relationship with a potential mate who is high in mate value and, therefore, attractive and desirable (Buss, 1994). Various qualities can increase or decrease mate value, including youth, physical attractiveness, social status, and earning prospects.

MATING PREFERENCES FROM A BIOLOGICAL, SEXUAL SELECTION VIEW

Multiple studies have revealed that men and women across cultures share some preferences for mating partners but differ in others (e.g., Badahdah & Tiemann, 2005; Buss, 1989; Buss & Schmitt, 1993; Kamble et al., 2014; Karandashev et al., 2016, 2020; Khallad, 2005; Lei et al., 2011; Li et al., 2002). The major differences are that men are attracted by women's appearance and youth whereas women are attracted by men's status and earning prospects. Evolutionary theories have predicted and found that men value attractiveness in a prospective mate more than women because attractiveness is a better predictor of fertility of women than of men (see, for review, e.g., Buss, 1994; Buss et al., 1990; Buss & Barnes, 1986; Feingold, 1990). Other research, however, is less consistent and indicates differential effects depending on contexts and moderating variables. Meta-analysis of results across many studies (Langlois et al., 2000) showed no sex differences in the importance of attractiveness, with both men and women preferring physically attractive partners (e.g., Fletcher et al., 2004; Kenrick et al., 1993; Regan & Berscheid, 1997).

These discrepancies in findings on mate preferences and forms of relationship initiation can be resolved by integrating ecological and cultural perspectives into biological evolutionary theory. The following sections review the studies that have implemented this approach and discuss various cultural contexts and moderating cultural variables affecting relationship initiation.

MATING PREFERENCES FROM ECOLOGICAL VIEW

Sexual selection processes interact with ecological and social factors. An ecological approach (Cunningham & Barbee, 1991) proposes that individuals can adjust their mating preferences (e.g., valuation of attractiveness) depending on local ecological conditions (e.g., income, infant mortality, and sex ratio). Despite substantial similarities, standards of beauty vary across cultures and across time (see, for review, Cunningham et al., 1995; Fallon, 1990; Langlois et al., 2000; Marshall, 1971). According to the multiple fitness model of physical attractiveness (Cunningham et al., 2002), different attributes of physical appearance can vary in attractiveness across cultures. This ecological view also explains how people modify mating preferences and strategies of relationship initiation depending on the ratio of men to women in a local population (Guttentag & Secord, 1983; Maner & Ackerman, 2020; Moss & Maner, 2016). For example, analysis of data from 36 cultures (Stone et al., 2007) revealed that mate preferences vary with the number of potential mates in the social environment.

ATTRACTIVENESS PREFERENCES FROM CULTURAL VIEW

The stereotype "what is beautiful is good" is pervasive and influential (Dion et al., 1972; Hatfield & Rapson, 1996, 2005; Lemay et al., 2010; Lorenzo et al., 2010), yet it is less powerful and more culturally specific than previously believed (Eagly, Ashmore, et al., 1991; for review, Swami & Furnham, 2008). People in many cultures believe that physical attractiveness is associated with other good qualities of a person. Thus, this stereotype plays a signaling function. The value and content of this stereotype, however, vary across cultures. Besides signaling fertility in women, attractiveness can signal pleasing disposition, emotional stability, kindness, dependable character, and intelligence (Fugère et al., 2019; Yela & Sangrador, 2001).

The value of physical attractiveness for relationship initiation and standards of beauty vary across cultures. What is beautiful is culturally good (Anderson, 2019; Anderson et al., 2008; Wheeler & Kim, 1997). Although many cultures have stereotypes of interpersonal perception based on physical attractiveness, cultural values affect the importance and content of this stereotype. Attractiveness matters more in independent cultures, such as mainstream American society with high value on autonomy and where personal choice matters more for relationship initiation. Attractiveness matters less and implies different expectations in interdependent societies, such as Korea in Southeast Asia and Ghana in Africa. These cultures emphasize connections with social networks and place a high value on embeddedness. Limited societal affordances are associated with lower importance of physical attractiveness in everyday life and in relationship initiation. (Anderson et al., 2008; Wheeler & Kim, 1997).

Sex differences in mating preferences for attractiveness also vary depending on gender equality in societies and on cultural stereotypes. For instance, in the Netherlands—with greater gender equality—these differences are smaller in comparison with Germany—with more conventional norms of gender roles, and other countries in an international sample (Buss et al., 1990; De Raad & Doddema-Winsemius, 1992).

Cultural variation is observed also in which attributes of physical appearance people evaluate as attractive in a person for relationship initiation. This depends on local conditions of living. For example, in subsistence-based societies, in which hunters and gatherers produce products only for their survival and have high risk of food shortages, men prefer women with greater fat (e.g., Anderson et al., 1992; Brown and & Konnor, 1987;

Sugiyama, 2004). These mating preferences were observed in the forager, hunter, or horticultural cultures of the South African Zulu people (Tovée et al., 2006), the Hadza, an indigenous group in north-central Tanzania in East Africa (Wetsman & Marlowe, 1999), and Shiwiar (Achuar), an indigenous tribe of Ecuadorian Amazonia in South America (Sugiyama, 2004), and in the Yali of Papua—an indigenous tribal group in the mountainous terrain in Papua, Indonesia (Sorokowski & Sorokowska, 2012).

When ecological and social conditions of life change, people adjust their norms of attractiveness due to exposure to new cultural environments. The example of Zulu people of South Africa, who moved to the UK, have demonstrated such capability for adaptation (Tovée et al., 2006).

Cultures also differ in the attention that people pay to different modalities of physical appearance and expressive behavior of potential partners. In addition to visual preferences in the judgment of another person, auditory, tactile, kinesthetic, and olfactory sensory modalities of perception, as well as expressive behavior, contribute to mating attraction. The preferences for these parameters in a partner vary across cultures, especially between traditional and modern societies (Karandashev et al., 2016; Karandashev et al., 2020). In traditional societies, one's sensory preferences in romantic attraction are for *physical appearance* (body, facial features, skin, smell, etc.)—the stable biological and evolutionarily vital characteristics. In modern societies, one's sensory preferences in romantic attraction are for *expressive behavior* (facial expression, expressive behavior, dress, dance, etc.)—characteristics that are more flexible and easier to change (Karandashev et al., 2020), such as body movement, clothing, hairstyle, makeup, facial expression, and gestures.

INTERACTION OF CULTURAL AND BIOLOGICAL FACTORS IN RELATIONSHIP INITIATION

In the social world of human animals, biological, social, and cultural evolution interact. Therefore, evolutionary theories integrating biological, psychological, and cultural aspects of evolution have been advanced (e.g., Boyd & Richerson, 1985; Gangestad & Simpson, 2007) and may better explain the processes of mating, attraction, love, and relationship in humans (Fitness et al., 2003; Malach Pines, 2001; Tolman & Diamond, 2001).

People across cultures have the same basic needs. The universal motivational, cognitive, and emotional processes that they biologically inherited from their ancestors drive them to initiate romantic relationships according to their biologically and ecologically determined psychology. However, socioeconomic and cultural conditions of their environment determine how this inherited psychology develops to solve the unique challenges of the society in which people grow up and live.

The convergence of these biological and sociocultural perspectives can explain similarities and variation in the standards of physical attractiveness across cultures. In addition to universal sexual selection factors, the social and cultural variables, such as gender equality, gender stereotypes, the advisability of reproduction, and individual differences affect perception of some qualities of appearance (see, for reviews, Cunningham et al., 2002; Fallon, 1990) and other social scripts and cultural norms.

Evolutionary principles can explain not only *biological evolution* but also *cultural evolution* (e.g., Henrich & McElreath, 2003; Mace & Holden, 2005; Mead, 2017; Mesoudi, 2016; Mesoudi et al., 2006). For instance, intergroup competition has driven *cultural evolution* (Henrich, 2004) and shaped modern norms encouraging *monogamous marriage* (Henrich et al., 2012; Schacht & Kramer, 2019). The next section considers cultural variations of these practices across cultural history of societies and in modern cultural contexts in more detail.

2. *Cultural Evolution of Societies and Relationship Initiation*

The ways how men and women initiate their relationships evolved along with cultural evolution of societies. In this section, I show how cultural evolution of values in traditional and modern societies changed the norms and practices in mate preferences and relationship initiation.

SURVIVAL VS. SELF-EXPRESSION VALUES

The distinction between subsistence-based, traditional, and modern societies is important to understanding cultural variations in relationship initiation. These types of societies differ in their cultural values which in turn affect relationship motivation. Inglehart and colleagues (Inglehart 1997, Inglehart & Baker, 2000; Inglehart & Welzel, 2005) in their modernization theory distinguished *traditional* and *modern* societies based on social, economic, and cultural characteristics. Cultural norms of traditional societies place high value on survival and security, while cultural norms of modern societies place high value on self-expression and tolerance of minorities. The *survival values* emphasize physical and economic security (e.g., safety, food, and water). The *self-expression values* highlight quality of life, subjective well-being, and motivation to thrive. People in modern societies worry less about starvation and physical survival and therefore, they are more concerned about maximizing life quality.

Biological and cultural evolutionary processes work in both types of societies, but in different proportions. The more traditional a society is, the more its cultural norms conform to the principles of biological evolution. The more modern a society is, the more its cultural norms follow the new tendencies of cultural evolution. The findings of Buss and colleagues (Buss et al., 1990) about mate preference conform to this interpretation. The multidimensional scaling of the samples from 37 countries worldwide in terms of men's and women's mate preferences revealed that *traditional* versus *modern* is the major dimension differentiating these cultures. India, China, Iran, and Nigeria were on one end, with high value on resource provisioning, domestic skills, chastity, home, and children, and the Netherlands, Great Britain, Finland, and Sweden on the other end with low value of these traditional qualities (Buss et al., 1990).

TRADITIONAL VS. MODERN CULTURAL PRACTICES AND NORMS ASSOCIATED WITH RELATIONSHIP INITIATION

Social norms, psychological experiences, and expressions in many societies are frequently in accord with principles of biological evolution (e.g., encouraging extended reproduction of offspring and prohibiting incest). However, cultural evolution has modified some of them, adjusting to the modern social world. Let us consider some of these examples of interaction between biological and cultural evolution in more detail. People in modern societies often want to have fewer children. Population-based studies have shown decreasing reproductive rates in a majority of countries, except Africa. This decreasing reproductive rate is especially evident among wealthy people. High education delays women's motherhood, and childbearing is postponed until later age (e.g., Gonzalo et al., 2016; Lutz, 2007; Lutz et al., 2001; Mace, 2000). The new cultural norms decrease the desire of partners to have many children (e.g., Preston, 1986; Souza et al., 2016). In traditional societies, continued childbearing affords higher reproductive rates, but parental investment in existing children is more important in modern wealthy societies (e.g., Mace, 2000). Due to increasing overpopulation in some societies (and on the global scale), the modern culturally evolved norms frequently discourage extended reproduction of offspring and tolerate unhealthy offspring more than traditional societies. Subsequently, the norms value less the number of individuals but rather promote humanity and survival of everyone, regardless of their health perspective.

INTEGRATION OF EVOLUTIONARY AND CULTURAL APPROACHES TO MATE PREFERENCES

Modern societies rely on both biological and cultural evolution. Multiple studies on mate preferences are consistent in finding that men prefer physically attractive and younger women, whereas women prefer successful and older men. These gender differences have been replicated in the analysis of traditional folktales (Gottschall et al., 2004) and in the analysis of mating advertisements (Baber, 1936; Harrison & Saeed, 1977) across Western cultures between the 1930s and 1970s). This means that evolutionarily inherited mate preferences are persistent over time and supported or mediated by cultural factors.

Biological evolutionary principles sometimes suggest universality of mating preferences among individuals. In addition to biologically based sexual differences, one can also expect socially based gender differences in mate preferences. Later studies have found that these gender differences are not always consistent across populations and cultures (e.g., Badahdah & Tiemann, 2005; Malach Pines, 2001) and are prone to flux throughout cultural evolution (e.g., Kamble et al., 2014; Lei et al., 2011; Souza et al., 2016). For instance, Muslim men and women living in the United States expressed equal preference for a physically attractive mate (Badahdah & Tiemann, 2005).

Sociocultural perspectives proposed interpretation of these findings from social exchange theory, which explains that relationships entail the mutual exchange of rewards with a partner (e.g., Clark & Mills, 1979, 2011; Jagger, 1998; Nakonezny & Denton,

2008), and from gender-role stereotypes that present the social roles of men and women in a rigid conventional way (e.g., Blair & Madigan, 2016; Cameron et al., 1977; Hentschel et al., 2019). These gender differences and stereotypes are understandable because historically in many traditional societies, women had access to resources either via their father or via their husband as breadwinners. However, in subsistence-based societies (e.g., foraging, pastoralism, horticulture, and agriculture), women's labor was not a less important source of family sustainability compared to men's. The resources, which both men and women bring to family, were equally valuable. In modern societies, where women gained personal access to economic resources with their own labor and income, they place less value on the financial prospect of a prospective mate.

3. Cultural Evolution of Traditions in Relationship Initiation

The traditions of relationship initiation changed along with the cultural evolution of societies.

In this section, I show the ways how men and women initiate relationships in subsistence-based, traditional, and modern societies.

TRIBAL RITUALS OF MEETING MATES

Ecological, social, economic, and cultural contexts influence how potential mates meet and initiate a relationship. These contexts have changed over several historical periods, along with the development of societies, social mobility, equality, and gender roles. Social gatherings, traditional courtship, dating, and partnership are popular mating systems.

Social gatherings of communities (tribes, villages, etc.) living in relative proximity afford the opportunity to meet a prospective mating partner. These events might include dancing, listening to music, and singing (e.g., Bridges & Denisoff, 1986; Brown, 2000; Garfinkel, 2018; Horton, 1957; Leongómez et al., 2014; Savage et al., 2020). For example, dance is a joint activity rather than an individual action. Rhythmic movements in a circle, in pairs, or dancing together establish feelings of unity, connection, and synchrony between members of community. The dancing of indigenous populations in many parts of the world has been practiced for various purposes, including courtship (see, for review, Garfinkel, 2018). Traditional societies share many common rituals and experiences in this regard. Rhythmic music, playing musical instruments (e.g., rattles and drums), handclapping, and singing accompany dances. Such practices have been widely present across cultures (e.g., Loeb, 1950; Lockwood, 1983; Mu, 1994; Pitcairn & Schleidt, 1976).

Various symbols, metaphors, and rituals play a role during relationship initiation. They may be common or culturally specific. For example, wedding rings or bands is a widespread symbol of marriage across many cultures (Bingyao, 2017; Hamon & Ingoldsby, 2003). Partners exchange rings to symbolize their continuous and endless love. Metaphors of color, such as the color of flowers in a bouquet or a wedding dress, are among well-known symbols used in relationship initiation. The colors signify different meanings in societies according to folk cultural models. A white wedding is a cultural symbol in America that is pursued meticulously and obsessively by many middle- and upper-class people (Howard, 2008). Likewise, the cultures of Zulu in South Africa and Kaguru in Tanzania (Biyela, 2013) have several color metaphors associated with body, sex, love, and relationship. Among the Kaguru people, white color represents peace, safety, and normality. Among Zulu people, the white color symbolizes moral values, purity, and integrity. Among Chinese, the red color brings double happiness to a wedding (Qiang 2011).

TRADITIONAL COURTSHIP

The courtship patterns of communication and interaction differ in various respects (e.g., where mates meet, who initiates relationship, methods of communication, rules of interaction, and the length of courtship time). In Victorian England and the United States of the 19th century, traditional courtship took place at the home of the woman. When a daughter was approaching her mating age, her mother invited suitors, such as family acquaintances, neighbors, or other candidates from a close social circle (Karandashev, 2017; Lystra 1989).

Women usually regulated this calling system. Courtship occurred in the house of a woman and she could control this process. She could test patience, loyalty, faithfulness, and love of her wooer by setting obstacles in relationships. Men could also test her affection. A woman's parents commonly supervised communication and interaction of prospective mates. The mother was a primary figure who initially assessed whether a wooer has the good qualities for marriage (Bailey, 1989; Phegley, 2012). Such a *calling system* was typical in the cultures of England and America in the 1800s and the early 1920s (Bredow et al., 2008; Karandashev, 2017; Lystra 1989), being gradually replaced by new *dating culture*.

The practices of traditional courtship have been declined in many societies throughout the 20th century, in some cultural contexts, such as *traditional Zulu society* of South Africa, in recent years. In Zulu culture (Biyela, 2013), a man initiated the dating process and courtship took two years or more to let partners know how compatible they are before they committed to become a couple. A girl had the right to refuse her lover and wait "true love." Girls and boys refrained from their natural physical attraction and desire for immediate intimacy looking for a partner who is loving, trustworthy, and caring. They wanted partners who are, first, loving mates and, second, caring parents. A pair of birds called Hadadah Ibis (*amankankane*) symbolizes an ideal romantic couple.

In Zulu culture (Biyela, 2013), beads serves as messages in courtship communication. Girls communicate their desires to the loved boys with their beadwork to avoid the direct initial sensitive conversation. Boys ask their female relatives to explain beadwork symbols because the design and patterning of colors have special meanings. The white color embodies the values of integrity and ethical behavior that mates strive to follow in their romantic relationships.

> The white string is the first beaded communication that the girl sends to her lover. The red colour often follows the white string. A girl tells her partner that she is bursting with love for him. Before the girl suffers from "high blood pressure" of love, a responsible young man has to respond, either in person or ask his female relatives to make him a relevant token of love that he can send to his girlfriend. (Biyela, 2013, p. 39)

A girl may also send a *Zulu love letter* in green beads:

> I am yearning for you day and night. Come back soon, unless you will find me as thin as the grass that is being blown away by the winds. Thinness here stands for hunger for love and care while the wind represents rivals who keep on reminding her that she made a wrong choice by loving a man with a "cold heart." Temptations and confusion might flood the young girl's mind, which could be a reason for sending the wake-up calls to her partner. (Biyela, 2013, p. 39)

In Zulu culture, the white wedding is a beginning of marriage of young man and woman. The two white colors as uncontaminated bodies symbolize a double blessing. White color in the context of marriage expresses safety and fortune (Biyela, 2013).

Thus, traditional courtship rituals and symbols emerged in the societies where men and women had limited opportunities to communicate. Different methods to connect evolved. Cultural variation of courtship processes reflected social interdependence, traditional roles, and norms of gender-specific behavior and interaction. Low geographical and social mobility narrowed the array of opportunities for marital choices. Extended family arranged several aspects of relationship initiation. It appears, however, that the traditional *calling system* of courtship in European countries and the United States of the 19th century was more restrictive than the courtship in Zulu society.

DATING

In the 1870s–1920s, American and European societies were changing considerably, the *calling system* gradually eroded. Developing transportation increased social mobility. Industrialization and subsequent urbanization intensified migration of many people into the cities. Individuals in such dense populations became more independent of family ties, got more freedom in their actions and interpersonal and intergender communication. Increasing movement toward gender equality played an important role in transformation of *traditional courtship* into *dating*. Women received more freedom, better school education, and more financial independence due to participation in the paid labor force.

Due to these cultural transformations, a new *dating* system replaced the old courtship rituals among middle-class white population (Bailey, 1989; Karandashev, 2017). Both men and women had more opportunities to meet and interact with each other and initiate relationships on their own. Relationship activities relocated from homes—the places dominated by women—to external locations—the places dominated by men.

The gender positions switched: in dating, men took the active role in relationship initiation. The rules of dating etiquette suggested that men, rather than women, should initiate dating events. They should determine whether the potential woman was cleared for, open, and interested in a relationship; select an opening communication; and set up a second meeting. Men invited women to go out to have a good time together in interpersonal unsupervised settings: restaurant, dance halls, movie theaters, hotels, tourism, and mass-market entertainments. Such socialization required money. Men certainly paid for the restaurant or cinema. It was a gesture of the man's gallantry and care. Thus, the dating process was controlled by men rather than by women (Bredow et al., 2008; Illouz 1997; Rothman, 1987). Men often assured their commitment with the hope of having sex. Women largely took a gatekeeping role. They accepted or rejected overtures depending on their interest in the potential wooer. Women frequently did not behave passively but rather supported conversation.

Early in the 20th century, romantic relationships were commodified—gifts, candlelight dinners, romantic holidays, and sunsets have typically been associated with romantic relationship initiation. They became the symbols and rituals of romantic relationships (Illouz 1997; Murstein, 1974). The dating system was a common way of relationship initiation from the 1930s through the 1950s–1960s. Throughout the first part of the 20th century, initiation of romantic relationship with intention to marry became the aspiration of many women and men of the middle social class. Good marriage, with a good partner and having several adorable kids was the best dream for family life. Sexual pleasure became the key to ideal marriage. The 1950–1960s in the United States and Europe was the golden age of marriage; the majority of men and women strived to marry. Marriage became nearly universal in North America and Western Europe, with 95% of all persons marrying, as people married younger, and divorce rates fell or held steady (Coontz, 2005; Karandashev, 2017; Murstein, 1974).

Thus, the increased geographical and social mobility of Western European and North American societies, their shift to more independence of autonomous individuals afforded men and women more freedom from family ties. Gender inequality, however, still persisted. These factors caused the development of *traditional dating* as a new form of relationship initiation, which replaced the *traditional calling system* of courtship. Men and women were more independent from family influence in their intergender relationships. Yet, gender inequality and gender stereotypes still affected their interaction, and men played a leading role, while women played a supporting role.

PARTNERSHIP

The modern type of dating, which can be labeled *partnering*, emerged in the early 1970s (Bredow et al., 2008; Karandashev, 2017). Gender equality and sexual revolution were probably the most important cultural factors that promoted this transition. Equality of gender roles and companionship relations became widely acceptable in the United States, Canada, western and northern Europe, Australia, and New Zealand (e.g., Murstein, 1974; Ponxetti, 2003).

In *partnership dating*, both men and women could initiate a relationship, be active, and be relatively independent in behavior. This was different from *traditional courtship*, where a woman had an ability to control the courtship process, and *traditional dating*, where a man managed interaction. Many men became more sensitive and less detached, while many women became more self-assertive and less dependent on men than their predecessors (Karandashev, 2017). Therefore, initiation of a relationship by a woman became more acceptable than before. Yet, due to traditional gender stereotypes remaining in mind of many people, there was still a prejudice that a woman initiating relationships is cheap.

Dating as a path to relationship initiation was concomitant with flourishing of romantic love ideals. Although these cultural ideas were widely spread and shared in Europe and America, the real practices varied between generations and classes. Many people in the regional working class had a different experience of courtship, marriage, and love, with lack of mutual understanding and emotional intimacy between the sexes (e.g., Giles, 2004; Gillis, 1985, 1988; Szreter & Fisher, 2010).

In the 1960–1980s, in many European countries and the United States, the "sexual revolution" established sex as autonomous domain of pleasure and freedom of sexual self-expression (Karandashev, 2017; Murstein, 1974; Seidman, 1991). The discovery of effective oral contraceptives in the 20th century became one of the great human discoveries with important cultural consequences. Birth control spread in modernized nations, gradually expanding to developing countries. Dating partners became less afraid of sexual activity before marriage. They expected sex to be sensually and expressively pleasurable. Recreational sex became normal. Community and family cultural norms became more tolerant to premarital sex; chastity faded in its importance as a quality of partners. The discovery of effective contraceptives brought more sexual pleasure for women who were now free from fear of unwanted pregnancy. Gender equality assumed the equality of rights for sexual pleasure. Sexual pleasure for women was not only permissible but rather encouraged. The contemporary societies are quite permissible for premarital relationships between partners giving considerable freedom for trial and experimentation. Many potential partners have an opportunity to meet, talk, interact with each other, have sex, and cohabit before getting married.

Cultural norms considered romantic love a desirable and acceptable reason for relationship initiation and marriage (Coontz, 2005; Karandashev, 2017; Murstein 1974; Seidman, 1991). However, marriage itself lost its popularity. High expectations caused more frequent disappointment in relationships and increasingly early divorce. Cohabitation became acceptable in modern societies. Partnership and moving in to live together without many formal obligations made the initiation of a relationship simpler in some regards and easily reversable. Young men and women could hang out and date more than one person, avoiding exclusive commitment until they found a suitable partner.

PERSONAL ADS IN SOCIAL MEDIA (NEWSPAPERS, MAGAZINES, INTERNET)

Emerging matchmaking services (e.g., personal ads) opened the new paths to look for possible mating partners and facilitate the processes of relationship initiation. Since the 1970s in individualistic cultures of North America and west and north Europe, advertising in newspapers with an interest in finding marital partners became increasingly popular. The text was usually composed in terms of social exchange theory and negotiating process: self-description of personal characteristics—what a person offers—and a description of expectations from potential partners—what a person wants in them. Personal ads presented an offer—an advertiser's personal qualities—and requests—expectations of the qualities desired in a prospective partner. Advertisers usually preferred to present their image and abilities in a more positive way (Cameron et al., 1977). Despite the shifting of gender role expectations in the 1970s, people still put in advertisements traditional sex-related preferences and known expectations (e.g., physical attraction and earning prospect).

However, in the perception of many people across many traditional cultures (Darden & Koski, 1988), the dating advertisements in newspapers and magazines did not become widely acceptable and were considered a deviant activity. Therefore, individuals who searched for a partner through personal advertisements often felt embarrassment and, therefore, did this with caution to avoid stigma. The onset of the internet moved dating advertisements online, providing broader reach of potential partners and providing more confidentiality of a dater.

INTERNET AND ONLINE DATING

Internet websites have greatly expanded the landscape of dating and provided new opportunities for search and connection with potential partners in modern world. Websites and dating services give single individuals access to a number of potential partners. Computer-mediated online communication allows getting a first impression of a potential partner, learning some personal facts, and obtaining an initial experience of interaction before deciding to meet face-to-face in person (Finke et al., 2012; Rosenfeld & Thomas 2012; Smith & Duggan, 2013). Computer mediated online connection can promote initial interpersonal communication and healthy progression of romantic relationships (Cooper & Sportolari, 1997).

People view online dating favorably and without evident prejudice in many countries. (e.g., Finkel et al., 2012). For example, American society with individualistic values and highly developed information technology (IT) recognized this way to meet a partner in the early 2000s. Online dating became a common and acceptable idea (e.g., Lawrence, 2004; Smith & Duggan, 2013; Sprecher, 2009; Tracy, 2006).

In Australia (Couch & Liamputtong, 2008), people have also increasingly utilized internet dating to look for romantic and sexual partners. Men and women use multiple dating sites, chats, emails, and webcam to assess and validate the identity of their potential partners. They employ various filtering methods—the texts, chat, photographs, and webcam opportunities—before advancing to face-to-face meetings, or sexual encounters. They follow progressive personalized steps in communication and engagement in the lead-up to meeting in person.

Recent publications also shed light on the approaches to online dating and level of engagement in interaction in such countries as France, Portugal, Turkey, the United States, Cuba, China, Brazil, and India (Degim et al., 2015; Souza et al., 2016). From its introduction in the 1990s, this web-based way of dating has evolved acquiring some culturally specific goals and practices. As for the youth cultures, online methods of relationship initiation are utilized by modern youth less frequently than in-person encounters. Despite their interest in IT gadgets, the modern generation of adolescents and teens still prefers to use in-person methods to meet romantic partners while participating in activities with their peers (Korchmaros et al., 2015).

CULTURAL SENSITIVITY OF MATCHMAKING WEBSITES

Online dating provides new opportunities for seeking marriage partners. Some internet technologies, however, are not sensitive to cultural contexts of societies. Nevertheless, several dating websites focus on specific categories of people, such as Christian singles or ChristianMingle, targeted to Christians; Muslima, targeted to Muslims; Jdate, targeted to Jewish people; and Black Singles or Black People Meet, targeted at African American singles.

In modern multicultural India, marital websites have become a new and important medium to look for marriage partners. As of the late 1990s, such internet mating services were popular with millions of users (Titzmann, 2013). The web of dating media gradually replaced the traditional institution of arranged marriage. Internet-mediated services becomes a means of undertaking such "kin work" of matchmaking. The Indian cultural version of web-based matchmaking technology facilitates conventional marriage preferences and aids in the sustenance of caste- and community-based identities (Agrawal, 2015).

Due to profound changes in contemporary Indian society, these new opportunities of mate choice using IT media give young people more active role in their planning of relationship and family. This computer-mediated online marriage market becomes progressively more interactive (Titzmann, 2013). The notion of arranged marriages has been gradually changing, with less restrictive regulation of the mating process yet with respect to cultural traditions.

In Saudi Arabia, men know that their culture considers "online dating" inappropriate, associated with social stigma of nontraditional dating (Al-Dawood et al., 2017). Because of this, a low number of Saudi Arabians use such platforms. Engagement in these nontraditional routes of matchmaking can hurt a user's reputation, which is a high-stake value in the Saudi cultural context. Such websites should be culturally sensitive, reflect the traditional and religious conservative norms, and respect concerns for privacy. Flirting is viewed as culturally controversial (Al-Dawood et al., 2017).

Muslim emigrants in other countries also began to use the internet for the search of marriage partners. While confessing to a single article of faith, Muslims may come from a plethora of various ethnic backgrounds. Therefore, for them, it is difficult to overcome existing geographical and social barriers to find a suitable partner compatible in cultural attitudes. For example, American Muslims are increasing turning to the internet to look for a suitable mate matching them in religious and cultural aspects of life. However, the modern online dating services are challenging to their traditional practices of relationship initiation. Fortunately, some of the current online match-making websites are culturally sensitive and accommodate their needs in finding love and marriage partners (Lo & Aziz, 2009).

4. Ecological, Societal, and Cultural Factors Affecting Relationship Initiations

Cultural evolution changed ecological, socioeconomic, and cultural conditions of people' lives, also affecting the ways how men and women meet and initiate their relationships. In this section, I describe the roles of propinquity, social and relational mobility, homogamy, complementarity, and up-ward mobility in relationship initiation.

THE ROLE OF PROPINQUITY IN RELATIONSHIP INITIATION

Propinquity is the geographic proximity and physical closeness between individuals. Such spatial nearness is an important factor for the initiation of courtship, mating, and marital relationships (e.g., Alphonso, 2016; Schmitt, 2009) in isolated subsistence-based tribal communities and traditional and modern societies, yet to a different extent.

The factor of territorial propinquity is salient in the societies with limited relational mobility, such as the Lingāyats—a religious group in southern India. Interviews with heads of the Lingāyat families in a suburb of Dharwar City (Chekki, 1968) showed that kin marriage is preferential. In that culture, marriage within one's social ingroup (e.g., ethnic and religious) is a very important rule of mate selection that determines the geographical propinquity of their marital relationships.

The similar role of residential propinquity was found in the study of an urban Muslim community in Karachi—the largest city in Pakistan conducted in 1961–1964 (Korson, 1968). The results showed that among the lower class, the residential distance between husband and wife at the time of marriage was shorter; in the upper social class, the residential distance was higher.

Several studies conducted in the United States (Philadelphia; Pennsylvania; New Haven, Connecticut; Duluth, Minnesota) and New Zealand (Christchurch) (Bossard, 1932; Davie & Reeves, 1939; Marches & Turbeville, 1953; Morgan, 1981) showed that women and men living farther from each other before marriages less often initiated a relationship. This propinquity tendency was especially pronounced among American Jews, American Italians, and African Americans (Kennedy, 1943). The importance of residential propinquity was lower for initiation of marriage in Israel (with some variations) because young men and women frequently resided far from their permanent home regions (due to military service) for several years. Jews of Eastern origins were more affected by propinquity, compared to Jews of Western origins (Tabory & Weller, 1986).

The main factors explaining a stronger or weaker effect of residential propinquity on marriage partner selection are geographical location (low or high social mobility); ecological and social status segregation; homogamy of economic, social, and cultural traits; as well as ethnic endogamy. Residential organization of neighborhood according to socioeconomic class, race, and ethnicity can lead to segregation, while their self-sufficiency can limit communication between cultural groups. Such segregation, along with propinquity, can be a factor affecting marital choice. Propinquity usually leads to homogamy: partners are more favorable to one another in the same local community, church, city, and country. Due to these factors, partners initiating a relationship are often similar to each other in social class, culture, religious affiliation, and education.

PROPINQUITY AND ONLINE RELATIONSHIP INITIATION

Although propinquity means geographical proximity, modern online technologies of mating extend the concept and expand the opportunities for meeting potential partners. The reported level of intimacy in computer-mediated relationships is not related to the physical distance between partners. Geographical distance does not play the same role in this case as the level of self-disclosure (Merkle & Richardson, 2000).

Traditional face-to-face relationship initiation is dependent on the proximity of available partners. The emergent computer-mediated technologies (e.g., eHarmony and Match.com) and mobile dating applications (e.g. Tinder and Grindr) have changed the way men and women initiate and develop interpersonal relationships. This contemporary dating culture mediated by technology, internet, and smartphone evolves new relationship initiation strategies and selection processes (LeFebvre, 2018).

SOCIAL AND RELATIONAL MOBILITY

The factor of propinquity is more important in the societies with low social mobility, in which individuals have a limited opportunity to look for new prospective partners. Modern transportation—the improved road system, boating, and air connections—considerably boosted social mobility. Consequently, in societies high in population mobility, the pool of potential partners has expanded. People's migration from one region to another, from rural to urban residency, has extended the pool of potential mates.

Due to various geographical, economic, cultural circumstances, societies and local communities can afford individuals a different degree of autonomy for selecting their interpersonal relationships. Personal preferences or social affordances may have priorities. (Yuki, & Schug, 2012). This characteristic of society is called *relational mobility*—the number of opportunities, which are available for a person to select new relationship partners (Yuki et al., 2007). In low-mobility societies, a person is strongly connected with their local residence and existing social network. They have limited prospects for interaction with new partners. In high-mobility societies, a person may have numerous occasions to meet new partners and initiate relationships due to their personal choice, but not because of the constraints imposed by their isolated residency location or affordances of their family or community.

People may have fewer or more choices to select with whom to initiate a relationship. The pools of eligible candidates in urban and rural areas in traditional and modern countries differ. Countries, regions, and communities in history and modern time vary in the degree of such intergroup and interpersonal *mobility* and limitations (Adams, 2005; Chen et al., 2009; Oishi et al., 2007; Schug et al., 2009; Yamagishi & Yamagishi, 1994; Yuk et al., 2007). Accordingly, individuals initiate personal relationships depending on available *socioeconomic* and *cultural affordances—a* range of economic, social, and cultural constraints that social contexts and family impose on them. Society affords individuals a *personal choice,* yet it is assumed that this choice should be made by taking into account not only personal interests but also interests of family and society.

Relational mobility is higher in modern societies, for example, in northern and western European countries, in Canada, and in the United States. People in these modern societies have more possibilities to meet someone and initiate a romantic relationship. Availability, however, does not always lead to real encounters. This is what one may call being lonely in a city with plenty of possibilities. With a larger pool of potential acquaintances, people strive to find an ideal romantic partner. They tend to exhibit proactive interpersonal behavior (e.g., social support and self-disclosure) and psychological confidence (e.g., self-esteem, general trust, and intimacy) more frequently and openly (Thomson et al., 2018). For people in the United States (high relational mobility), it is acceptable and natural to express their passion and openness in communication (Yamada et al., 2017). This can reflect on expressive behavior during initiation of relationships. Individuals, however, differ in the degree of passionate expressiveness across multicultural population of the country.

Relational mobility is lower in traditional societies and isolated subsistence-based tribes, for example, in the regions of East Asia, Polynesia, and West Africa. In these societies, people have fewer opportunities to meet new acquaintances. Therefore, they have a limited pool of potential mating partners, especially in rural residence and working settings. In such conditions, young men and women initiate a relationship with a partner who is *good enough*.

In addition, by normative obligations, individuals are strongly tied to each other and to existing relationships in family and community. Physical and social environment, rather than their personal choice, determine their affordances in initiating new relationships (Wiseman, 1986; Yamagishi et al., 1998). In Japan (low relational mobility), it is culturally normative to be less passionate and less communicative (Yamada et al., 2017)—this can reflect on lower expressivity during initiation of relationships. Intensity of passion, however, varies across regions of the country.

COMPLEMENTARITY, HOMOGAMY, AND UPWARD MOBILITY IN RELATIONSHIP INITIATION

Socioeconomic and cultural factors may affect mating initiation in three possible ways: according to the principles of complementarity, homogamy, or upward mobility (Blossfeld & Timm, 2003). According to *complementarity model,* males and females are different by their nature, evolutionary functions, gender roles, and gender strengths. Due to these differences, men and women in many traditional societies complemented each other in mating relationships in their roles. Therefore, men and women prefer to initiate relationships with those who can be a good fit with their own roles.

According to the *homogamy model,* prospective mating partners are selected from the same or similar social circles with comparable economic and power standing, social status, and educational background. According to the *upward-mobility model,* also called hypergamy, partners from different social, economic, and educational classes can find each other attractive and initiate relationships. Individuals from a low socioeconomic class may prefer to initiate dating with a potential partner of high economic status because this relationship advances their status in a society. On the hand, a potential partner from the upper class can see in the individual of low social status some qualities, which overshadow social inequity. Prevalence of homogamous, downward, and upward marriages in societies depends on gender equality and the distributions of educational and social attainments of men and women (Blossfeld & Timm, 2003).

COMPLEMENTARITY MODEL IN RELATIONSHIP INITIATION

The *complementarity model* explains why women perceive men with wealthy standing or good economic prospects as attractive mates and offer in exchange something like good looks, good cooking, and good housekeeping. This cultural model fits very well with the early evolutionary explanation for sex differences in mate preferences. Across 37 cultural groups, the social status and earning prospects of their partners are more important for women compared to men for long-term mating. However, the resource prospect of a man was only of moderate importance for women in the list of men's qualities, compared to such highly valued traits as kindness, intelligence, and being lively (Buss et al., 1990; Buss, 1994; Buss & Barnes, 1986).

When a pool of mates consisted of individuals at the low end of social status, women selected male mates based on their social status. Furthermore, the individuals, who valued social status high in the survey also valued this quality in their actual choices. These gender differences in mate choices were greater in the context of choice for long-term relationships (Li et al., 2002). Several studies have shown that for initiation of long-term mating relationships, women highly value their male partner's wealth status and ability to secure economic resources (e.g., Buss, 1989; Buss et al., 2001; Feingold, 1992; Fletcher et al., 2004; Townsend & Wasserman, 1998).

HOMOGAMY MODEL IN RELATIONSHIP INITIATION

The *homogamy model* explains why similarities attract each other. The partners with similar background understand each other better, have more in common to talk about, and have similar interests and attitudes—all viewed as important for people in the modern culture of partnership. For instance, data collected from the Chicago area (United States; Burgess & Wallin, 1943) in the 1940s showed that engaged partners were likely to resemble each other not only in psychological traits but also in social characteristics, such as family backgrounds, religious affiliation, social participation, and so on. The extent of homogamy in the initiation of relationship varied in different social characteristics and cultural contexts depending on the value of social equality in a culture (Blossfeld & Timm, 2003; Burgess & Wallin, 1943; Kalmijn, 1991, 1994).

Homogamy of mating partners has been rising in several areas: economic and social status, educational background. Studies (see, for review, Gonalons-Pons & Schwartz, 2017) have shown that in America during the period of 1970s–2010s, assortative mating increased economic homogamy between newlyweds. In modern dual-earner societies, the economic role of women has grown, enhancing their contribution to the wealth-being of family. Equality of dating partners has increased in modern societies (Blossfeld & Drobnic, 2001). Women, being more economically independent, have become less interested than before in the earning prospect of their male partner.

5. The Role of Individual Choice and Social Affordances in Relationship Initiation

Cultural evolution of the norms and practices in relationship initiation and marriages occurred due to the influence of two major evolutionary factors. These are social affordances, which societies, communities, and families could afford for men and women in relationship initiation, and a freedom of individual choice to do so. In this section, I explain these two groups of factors and describe how they determined the well-known forms of relationship initiation: arranged marriages and love marriages, with transitional variations in between.

FREEDOM OF CHOICE IN RELATIONSHIP INITIATION

Personal understanding and value of freedom of choice and social responsibility in relationship initiation is noticeably different in collectivistic and individualistic societies because of several cultural factors. While the traditional collectivistic interdependent societies emphasize social responsibility, the modern individualistic independent societies emphasize personal freedom of choice. It is challenging to compromise a personal freedom of decision and social responsibility. Generally, collectivistic societies are characterized by interdependent and frequently hierarchical social organization; have low geographic, social, and relationship mobility; and allow limited freedom of choice to initiate new relationships independently. Individualistic societies are characterized by independent social and frequently egalitarian organization; have relatively high geographic, social, and relationship mobility; and allow greater freedom of choice to initiate new relationships independently (see, for review, Karandashev, 2021).

The differences in those societies emerge from the *conceptions of individuality* and corresponding cultural norms in those societies. For instance, in many collectivistic East-Asian cultures, social norms accentuate harmonious interdependence and social responsibility of individuals as a cultural value. An individual perceives *a personal self* as interdependent with others. The *personal self* includes the *selves of others.* This idea of *self-in-relationship-with-others* involves people's thoughts, emotions, motivations, and actions. Young men and women are driven to fit into the social roles, to seek interpersonal relations suitable for them, and to fulfill social obligations according to expectations (see, for review, Apostolou, 2013; Karandashev, 2021; Markus & Kitayama, 1991; Uchida et al., 2004; Weisz et al., 1984). Social survival and well-being of a group (e.g., family) is more important than independence of an individual. Besides, marriage is too serious matter to let youngsters make their own immature and blind decisions. Due to these socioeconomic and cultural factors, marriages in collectivistic societies are often arranged with larger or moderate engagement of relatives and friends, with lesser or moderate freedom of choice on behalf of mates.

The marriages arranged by parents or other specially designated members of family have been typical for many societies living according to the long-standing traditional norms, which highly value family and ethnic interests, think in the frame of rigid gender roles, and have low social mobility. This practice is quite persistent across traditional cultures. The practice of arranged marriages has been harshly criticized in modern societies, which value freedom of choice. However, these cultural practices have historical roots and traditions that should be taken into account. Since biological, economic, and social survival are among the top priorities in such traditional kinship-based societies, then attractive potential partners must be approved by seniors for arranged marriage. Well-matching, likable qualities of partners, as well as the potential for future survival of a couple, and extended family and community are sufficient in these cases. In modern cultural evolution, arranged marriages have also evolved into a variety of arrangements. Some of them may allow more freedom of choice than others.

In individualistic European American and West European cultures, social norms highlight autonomy, independence of individuals from others, and freedom of choice as cultural values. An individual perceives *a personal self* as *independent* and *separate from others.* The *independent model of self* inspires the individual to pursue their own preferences and beliefs and consider personal desire a priority. The cultural conception of individuality encourages free expression of the unique self, freedom of choice, and personal responsibility for making decision. The *individual self* is the main source of peoples' thoughts, emotions, motivations, and actions. Social interactions and interpersonal relationships, being valuable, still presume the independence of individual selves. Individuals have an option to initiate and withdraw the relationship (see, for review, Karandashev, 2021; Markus & Kitayama, 1991; Uchida et al., 2004; Weisz et al., 1984).

Due to these socioeconomic and cultural factors, typical marriages in individualistic societies are labeled *love marriages,* characterized by a free choice of mates and limited or moderate involvement of relatives and friends. In contemporary Western societies, such as in western European and European American countries, love marriages are viewed as culturally normative. According to these cultural conceptions, women and men are free to select their mates following their emotions of passionate romantic love. Parents cannot constrain such an individual choice in mate selection. Yet, research in American individualistic context showed that involvement of friends and family facilitates initiation of romantic relationships and help maintain them (see, for review, Clark et al., 1999; Wright & Sinclair, 2012). For example, in Southern states of the United States, friends' judgment was influential and predictive for dating preferences, while parental opinion was important in those dating choices when participants relied on their parents for resources (Wright & Sinclair, 2012). Thus, many love marriages, which normatively supposed to rely on a free independent choice, are not totally free from parental and practical affordances, from economic and social interests.

CULTURAL AND SOCIAL AFFORDANCES IN RELATIONSHIP INITIATION

These differences in the freedom of relationship initiation in interdependent and independent cultures are frequently deemed as a dichotomy of arranged marriages versus love marriages. As for the arranged marriages, it is believed that parents impose limitations on their sons' and daughters' selection of mates based on economic and social factors. Some scripts of arranged marriages describe circumstances in which young men and women have little influence on selection of their mates. Romantic love is regarded as a less important reason for relationship initiation. These limitations are usually due to low social mobility, tendency to social homogamy, and strong cultural stereotypes, which do not afford free choice of a mate partner for the sake of community interests. Cultural affordances are what a society can afford individuals to do in a specific cultural context to keep a balance of personal and social interests.

The discussion of arranged and love marriages usually revolves around availability or lack of availability of freedom of choice. Such stereotypical opposition of arranged and love marriages, however, is not always accurate; they are not mutually exclusive forms of relationships. For instance, despite cultural practice of arranged marriage in the South Asian country of Sri Lanka and Eastern Asian country of China, love still affects mate selection of young people (De Munck, 1998; Moore, 1998).

Some aspects of romantic love are similar across cultures, but courtship practices and social customs guide young men and women to navigate their path of attraction and initiate love relationship with a personally and socially right mate, with whom love, sexual desire, and kinship are harmonized. Cultural norms modify corresponding emotions, for example, discouraging publicly explicit display of love and encouraging filial piety (De Munck, 1998; Moore, 1998).

For men and women in these interdependent cultures, love may be not less important in their mate selection. However, people in the Eastern interdependent societies conceptualize love differently from the conceptions of romantic love portraited in Western independent cultures. The Eastern culturally normative conception of love assumes much greater subordination to family interests than in the Western societies. Many so-called arranged marriages can accommodate romantic love, attraction, and desire and become love marriages (Apostolou, 2013; De Munck, 1996; Epstein et al., 2013; Inhorn 2007; Moore, 1998). The traditional Eastern patterns of courtship, however, are in flux under the influence of Westernization (see, for review, Karandashev, 2017, 2019). In the following sections, I present several examples of cultural variations in relationship initiation in arranged and love marriages, which permit different degrees of affordance and freedom of choice.

ARRANGED MARRIAGES IN INDIA

Conceptions of individuality and consequently freedom of choice differ in individualistic and collectivistic societies. The modern American culture considers a free and independent will of an individual to choose a mating partner as primacy. This understanding of choice is individualistic.

Different from this, the Indian culture understands a choice of spouse from collectivistic perspective that involves a dialogue with a family in selection of mate. Matchmaking may also include professional matchmakers and matrimonial websites. Initiation of relationship goes beyond simplistic binaries of arranged versus love marriages. This dichotomy is not so clear now as before. Contemporary cultural practices do not separate the individual from the family but rather include consent of the family as an important and equal factor (Bhandari, 2018).

Indians generally consider getting married in their 20s. Formal relationship initiation between mating partners has been usually arranged by parents (Banerjee et al., 2013). A wedding is a very important event not only for partners but even more so for their families. Although it elicits the impassioned sentiments, the event draws out certain cultural norms and values, brings social obligations and kinship bonds, and takes into consideration economic resources (Heitzman & Worden, 1996). Cultural patterns of marriage are diverse in different parts of India, in rural and urban contexts, as well as across traditional Indian castes within the same geographical regions (Banerjee et al., 2013).

The upward economic mobility and proportion of the middle class in modern India have been expanding. Young and educated adults of the middle class have more control on their marriage initiation (Kamble et al., 2014). However, modern innovations vary since Indian society is culturally diverse in terms of religious and cultural traditions (Hindu, Buddhism, Christianity, Muslim, and others).

Nowadays, some women in urban India accommodate arranged marriage as the cultural practices in a modern meaning. Many of them are able to reconcile their cultural traditions of family-making with the desires of individual growth and find the way to live in an alternate modernity of Indian culture (Sharangpani, 2010).

Arranged marriage as the way to relationship initiation gradually declines due to increasing geographical mobility in population, changing social networks, and evolving the new paths to the search and choice of a marital partner. The kin and extended family are currently less willing and less capable to directly oversee matchmaking of their children, especially among the Indian urbanites and those living abroad (Agrawal, 2015; Allendorf & Pandian, 2016).

The increasing physical, social, and media mobilities have acted as cultural factors of social change. Subsequently, the perceptions of gender roles, love, and marriage, have been also gradually changing in accord with the new social realities and lifestyles. The evolving cultural reality is particularly visible regarding status of women and marriage. The gender image of *new Indian woman* is pervasive and influential in personal narratives and online representations. This role model connects cultural rootedness with a modern lifestyle in their relationships (Allendorf & Pandian, 2016; Titzmann, 2013).

ARRANGED MARRIAGES IN MUSLIM SOCIETIES

The Muslim country of Pakistan is the traditional society with high cultural dimension of *power distance* as a measure of inequality (Hofstede, 1998, 2001). Socioeconomic classes are strongly divided in social and interpersonal relations, and individuals recognize this social distance, the differences in social status, and hierarchy of power as important for interpersonal relationships. The study (Korson, 1968) of 1961–1964 conducted in an urban Muslim community in Karachi—Pakistan's largest city—showed high prevalence of arranged marriages. Relatives arranged selection of mates depending on a pool of eligible candidates in a community. The families from the lower social class selected mates for their sons and daughters from the local neighborhood. The families from the upper social classes could afford to select mates from broader regional community.

Saudi Arabian Muslim society is very conservative in attitudes toward gender roles, relationship initiation, and marriage arrangement. The cultural aspects of matchmaking and arranged marriage (Al-Dawood et al., 2017) include:

1. *Gender segregation*: a woman and a stranger man are not allowed to meet without a "*mahram*" for the woman to be protected.

2. *Family involvement: "bir al walidayn"* is a rooted principle stipulating that a son or a daughter need to involve their parents in the marriage process and obey their opinions . . .
3. *Khotobah*: The formal agreement between both the families that is necessary for the relationship to proceed . . . (p. 1022)

In Saudi Arabia, young men have some degree of freedom to choose a spouse, yet their choice is limited. The perceptions of relatives about suitability of a possible match are important in decision to marry. Men have the limited knowledge about a prospective bride; they can meet, but only in chaperoned settings (Al-Dawood et al., 2017).

The processes of marriage initiation in Saudi Arabian culture are similar to other Muslim countries, but more conservative. Matchmaking prefers *personal kinship connections* and *consanguinity* (El-Hazmi et al., 1995). They highly value *consanguinity* in relationship initiation—when a potential partner is a descent from the same ancestor as another person and belongs to the same kinship. Therefore, families often initiate a *consanguine marriage*, in which individuals are closely related as first cousins, first cousins once removed, second cousins, third cousins, or more distantly related persons.

Consanguineous marriage is also culturally favored in many societies in the Middle East, West Asia, and North Africa (El-Hazmi et al., 1995; Hamamy, 2012). And these cultural traditions have been enduring. Emigrants from these cultural regions currently residing in Europe, North America, and Australia, also frequently follow this practice of *consanguine* relationship initiation.

ARRANGED MARRIAGES IN CHINA

Traditional Chinese culture views marriage as a family responsibility, and matchmaking is a normal practice. When sons and daughters are grown, parents encourage them to marry. However, modern Chinese people, especially in major cities, tend to postpone their marriage (Gui, 2017). Many men and women in big cities remain single until later age. This fact is concerning for parents—they still feel the duty to arrange the marriage. Therefore, parents whose adult children are still single in their late 20s and beyond attempt to "help" their sons and daughters find a spouse. They organize in parks and other publicly available places in the matchmaking markets. They advertise and exchange personal information of their single adult children with other families. Significantly more parents of young women are present in such events compared to the parents of young men. The mate values are still traditional: good physical appearance and young age for women, and wealth, higher income, and better education for men (Gui, 2017).

LOVE MARRIAGES

Passionate love strongly motivates people to initiate a romantic relationship. The sparkling energy of passion is difficult to resist, romantic idealization is powerful and overlooks many shortcomings of a partner and overemphasizes their mating qualities beyond realistic expectations. According to evolutionary and cultural theories, passion of love is a universal experience across cultures and times that is conducive for relationship initiation (Fisher, 1992, 1998; Hatfield & Rapson, 1987; Karandashev, 2017, 2019).

However, it was believed that passionate love lives a short time and fades after the first years of marriage. As such, passionate love seemed incompatible with marriage. Therefore, in many traditional societies, love was not considered a prerequisite for marriage—as in love marriages but rather as a consequence of marriage—as in arranged marriages. Alternatively, love and necessity of social and economic arrangements were compromised.

The idea of love for marriage and in marriage appeared in modern Western cultures only in the 18th to 20th centuries: the courtship intertwined with passionate love. Love marriages became more frequent and spread widely in the Western world (Coontz, 2005; Karandashev, 2017; Singer, 1987).

In the 20th century, the increased mobility of population and urbanization gave more opportunities for men and women to mingle, interact, and dance in courtship. Young men and women received more economic and social independence from family in planning their life. These new possibilities brought more freedom from family influence and relative independence in mate selection. The economically and socially developed societies of the Western world were more willing to accept romantic love as an impractical reason for mating and marriage. Love feelings prior to marriage raised importance in marital decision. Free choice of partners and love began to play more important role in relationship initiation and selection of marital partner in middle and upper socioeconomic classes (Karandashev, 2017; Rosenblatt & Cozby, 1972).

In the second part of 20th century, this tendency became evident in many societies. Several studies (Buss, 1994; Buss et al., 1990; Buss & Barnes, 1986; Buss et al., 2001) revealed that thousands of respondents in more than 30 countries from various geographic, ethnic, religious, and cultural groups viewed the mutual attraction and love as the most desirable quality of the relationships with potential mates. In the early 2000s, this tendency also occurred in such countries as Jordan and India (Kamble et al., 2014; Khallad, 2005)—the societies with long tradition of arranged marriages. Young people even more than before wanted love in their marriages.

However, marriage itself has lost its popularity and importance for many people in modern societies. Singlehood, premarital and nonmarital sex, hook-up culture, "playboy" lifestyle, unmarried cohabitation, childlessness, relationship without commitment, divorce, and out-of-wedlock childbearing have become widely accepted in western and northern Europe, the United States, and Canada (e.g., Amato et al., 2007; Cherlin, 2004; Coontz, 2005; Heldman & Wade, 2010; Kalmijn, 2007; Kiernan, 2002). It seems that freedom of choice in relationship initiation has gone far beyond the freedom to love. It has brought freedom not only from family and kinship restrictions but also from any social obligations and responsibility. Striving for autonomy and independence from others, individuals often achieve freedom from relationship responsibility and freedom from commitment and care for a partner.

Thus, economic and social development of many societies in the 20th century upraised the values of self-expression, well-being, and rights for happiness. This cultural modernization reflected on evolution of relationship initiation from arranged to love marriages, shifting a priority of social responsibility to the priority of individual choice. The unrestrained free choice with diminished social responsibility, however, has produced the new reality of relationships with unlimited freedom. The cultures of postmodern societies encounter a new challenge: how to make freedom of choice and social responsibility compatible in relationship initiation.

6. *Integration of Biological and Cultural Evolutionary Perspectives for Future Research on Relationship Initiation*

This chapter has proposed the further integration of biological and cultural evolutionary perspectives on relationship initiation. The meme that humans are social animals characterizes their dual nature: as a species driven by biological factors—animals—and as a social individual driven by social factors—social. In this section, I summarize biological and cultural evolution as the two converging forces as well as the social factors shaping relationship initiation across cultures.

THE VALUE OF BIOLOGICAL AND CULTURAL FACTORS IN SUBSISTENCE-BASED, TRADITIONAL, AND MODERN SOCIETIES

Biological evolution, sexual selection, and striving for more and better offspring play important roles in procreation of humans because they are mammalians; they are (social) *animals*. The principles of biological evolution play their vital roles in the early stages of human evolution—in subsistence-based and some traditional societies where biological survival is a problem. Yet, they modify their roles in modern societies.

Humans are *social* (animals). The principles of social, economic, and cultural evolution play bigger roles in traditional societies, compared to isolated subsistence-based tribes. However, the biological problem of individual, family, and community survival is still challenging. Cultural evolution begins to play a drastically higher role in the modern societies where biological survival is not a problem anymore. The values of contemporary economics, parameters of social development, and cultural norms and practices substantially increase. An integrative theoretical framework, which merges biological, socioeconomic, and cultural perspectives is important to the study cross-cultural variation in relationship initiation.

SOCIAL FACTORS AFFECTING CULTURAL VARIATION IN RELATIONSHIP INITIATION

Cultural variation in relationship initiation is observed between and within subsistence-based, traditional, and modern cultures. Subsistence-based societies are characterized by relative isolation, propinquity, low geographical and social mobility, and priority of needs for survival. People adapt their personal choices, norms, and practices of relationship initiation reflecting biologically universal evolutionary principles and limited affordances of local socioecological conditions.

Cultural variation in relationship initiation is also present between and within societies of traditional and modern types. Traditional societies are characterized as collectivistic cultures with interdependent self-construal of individuals, while modern societies—as individualistic cultures with independent self-construal of individuals. The variations in these conceptions of individuality; degree of geographical, social, and relational mobility; endogamy, homogamy, and heterogamy; socioeconomic status, social equality versus power distance, rigidity versus flexibility of gender roles; and cultural values of survival or self-expression determine cultural affordances in relationship initiation. These affordances in traditional societies are limited and increase with modernization, thus providing more freedom of choice. The contemporary world presents many variations of the societies in transition and modernization (for detailed review of these cultural dimensions, see Karandashev, 2021).

7. *Methodology in Research of Cultural Variation in Relationship Initiation*

Cultural and cross-cultural research methodologies have provided scholars with an abundance of knowledge about relationship initiation across cultures. I have reviewed and summarized it in the sections above.

In this section, I highlight the future perspectives and directions of research on cultural variations in relationship initiation. I stress the importance of international and interdisciplinary approaches in this scholarly endeavor. I also address the promises and challenges of existing research methodology in this filed.

INTERDISCIPLINARY AND INTERNATIONAL APPROACH

Investigation of relationship initiation is and should be an interdisciplinary and international endeavor. Researchers from anthropology, sociology, psychology, and communication studies have explored the problem from different disciplinary perspectives and methodologies, with their strengths and limitations. Interdisciplinary integration of their findings enriches the knowledge on the topic.

Despite the increasing interest in cross-cultural findings, the long-standing ethnocentric approach in research of relationship initiation is still lingering. Authors of many publications neglect to indicate in a sample description the societal and cultural setting in which they collected data. Their results can be universal or culturally specific, but anyway to put those in cross-cultural perspective, it is important to know the country, ethnic, and some other cultural characteristics of a sample.

The number and diversity of samples in the studies should also be addressed. A cross-cultural study with 30 or 60 samples is impressive and valuable, yet not warranted to call the findings as universal. Scholars should be cautious in their generalizations, admitting limitations in sample size and representativeness. The sample of undergraduate students from the United States is not necessarily representative of Western culture, as well as of the multicultural population of the country. The same can be said about Japan and China as representative of Eastern culture. There is a great diversity of so-called Western and Eastern, individualistic, and collectivistic cultures (see more about this in Karandashev, 2021). International collaboration in the studies provides more comprehensive understanding of the topic.

METHODS OF RESEARCH OF RELATIONSHIP INITIATION

Descriptive, experimental, and comparative research methodologies are typical in cultural studies of emotions and relationships (see, for review, Karandashev, 2021). Antropological case studies present excellent illustrations of cultural variations in relationship initiation that "challenge cultural stereotypes" (Nelson & Jankowiak, September 2020, personal communication). Descriptive historical, literary, linguistic, systematic, or occasional observations of travelers also provide abundance of evidence for cross-cultural descriptions. Their scientific value increases when the number of such case studies and observations grows. Then, the comparative methodology becomes more valuable.

The studies in many disciplines include rating of stimulus figures (e.g., faces and bodies) in the photos, pictures, and drawings and self-report surveys of preferences or liking (e.g., preferences of mate qualities) (Cooper & Sheldon, 2002). These methods, however, have some limitations and may not measure what a researcher intends to measure. For example, rating of body shapes brings information about attractiveness of body, yet these depictions of bodies are out of context. They are not concrete and not directly related to the situation of relationship initiation. Besides, participants frequently rate static visual appearance, while real relationship initiation usually engages other sensory modalities of perception, as well as dynamic expressive behavior (Karandashev et al., 2016; Karandashev et al., 2020).

The surveys of mating preferences often use the words, which can be interpreted in various ways. For example, in the study of the value of physical appearance, a question remains how respondents interpreted the term "good looks" in the question "how important are good looks for me in a mate?" They can interpret this as a desire to have a mate with *better looks* or a desire to have a mate with *not bad looks*. Besides, is it necessity or luxury to have these qualities? That distinction is important to consider in future studies. The studies have shown that these subtle research contexts can make difference in results (e.g., Li et al., 2002). Multiple choice and ranking surveys limit the scope of information that a researcher obtains. Narrative approach can be a good methodological alternative to expand the knowledge beyond theoretical expectations (Custer et al., 2008). The storytelling can be short or long.

Studies have also shown that mating preferences, which people express in surveys, may not coincide with qualities, which really attract them in each other in relationship initiation (e.g., Eastwick & Finkel, 2008a; Eastwick et al., 2011; Karandashev & Evans, 2017; Kurzban & Weeden, 2005; Mafra et al., 2021; Malach Pines, 2001). Therefore, the studies of real interactive sessions with actual consequences and recorded behavioral evidence of people's real preferences in dating partners can bring more valid findings. Speed-dating is promising methodology in this regard (Eastwick & Finkel, 2008b; Kurzban & Weeden, 2005).

UNIVERSALITIES AND VARIATIONS IN RELATIONSHIP INITIATION ACROSS CULTURES

The factors of biological and cultural evolutions converge determining a cross-cultural variation in the processes of relationship initiation. Although people have the same basic needs and universal biological mechanisms of mating, the ecological, socioeconomical, and cultural conditions in which they live determine the specific approaches and methods to select partners and form their relationships. Being involved in an existing network of kinship and friendship, they have less or more freedom to initiate a new relationship. Low social mobility, interdependent social context, stringent social stratification, the tendency to homogamy, rigid gender roles, high value of embeddedness, and survival afford little personal freedom of choice yet impose social responsibility. On the other side, high social mobility, independent social context, equality of social organization, the tendency to heterogamy, flexible gender roles, high value of autonomy, and self-expression afford great personal freedom of choice yet impose little social responsibility. Distinguishing how these features differ across three major types of societies (i.e., isolated subsistence-based tribal societies, traditional societies, and modern societies) helps reveal the causes of cultural variation in relationship initiation.

References

Adams, G. (2005). The cultural grounding of personal relationship: Enemyship in North American and West African worlds. *Journal of Personality and Social Psychology, 88*(6), 948–968.

Agrawal, A. (2015). Cyber-matchmaking among Indians: Re-arranging marriage and doing "kin work." *South Asian Popular Culture, 13*(1), 15–30. https://doi.org/10.1080/14746689.2015.1024591

Al-Dawood, A., Abokhodair, N., el Mimouni, H., & Yarosh, S. (2017, June 14). "Against marrying a stranger": Marital matchmaking technologies in Saudi Arabia. In O. Mival, M. Smyth, & P. Dalsgaard (Eds.), *Proceedings of the 2017 Conference on Designing Interactive Systems* (pp. 1013–1024), Edinburgh, Scotland.

Allendorf, K., & Pandian, R. K. (2016). The decline of arranged marriage? Marital change and continuity in India. *Population and Development Review, 42*(3), 435–464.

Alphonso, C. (2016). Propinquity. In C.L. Shehan (Ed.), *Encyclopedia of family studies* (p. 103). Wiley-Blackwell. https://doi.org/10.1002/9781119085621.wbefs303

Amato, P. R., Booth, A., Johnson, D. R., Johnson, D. R., & Rogers, S. J. (2007). *Alone together: How marriage in America is changing.* Harvard University Press.

Anderson, S. L. (2019). The importance of attractiveness across cultures. In K. D. Keith (Ed.) *Cross-cultural psychology: Contemporary themes and perspectives* (pp. 598–613). John Wiley & Sons. https://doi.org/10.1002/9781119519348.ch29 https://doi.org/10.1002/9781119519348.ch29

Anderson, S. L., Adams, G., & Plaut, V. C. (2008). The cultural grounding of personal relationship: The importance of attractiveness in everyday life. *Journal of Personality and Social Psychology, 95*(2), 352–368

Anderson, J. L., Crawford, C. B., Nadeau, J., & Lindberg, T. (1992). Was the Duchess of Windsor right? A cross-cultural review of the socioecology of ideals of female body shape. *Ethology and Sociobiology, 13*, 197–277.

Apostolou, M. (2013). *Sexual selection under parental choice: The evolution of human mating behavior*. Psychology Press.

Badahdah, A. M., & Tiemann, K. A. (2005). Mate selection criteria among Muslims living in America. *Evolution and Human Behavior, 26*, 432–440.

Bailey, B. L. (1989). *From front porch to back seat: Courtship in twentieth-century America*. JHU Press.

Baber, R. E. (1936). Some mate selection standards of college students and their parents. *Journal of Social Hygiene, 22*, 115–125.

Banerjee, A., Duflo, E., Ghatak, M., & Lafortune, J. (2013). Marry for what? Caste and mate selection in modern India. *American Economic Journal: Microeconomics, 5*(2), 33–72.

Bhandari, P. (2018) Makings of modern marriage: Choice, family, and the matchmakers. In L. Choukroune & P. Bhandari (Eds.), *Exploring Indian modernities* (pp. 131–149). Springer. https://doi.org/10.1007/978-981-10-7557-5_7

Bingyao, H. U. (2017). A comparison study of wedding between China and Western Countries. *Cross-Cultural Communication, 13*(3), 21–26.

Biyela, N. G. (2013). Colour metaphor in Zulu culture: Courtship communication in beads. *American International Journal of Contemporary Research, 3*(10), 37–41.

Blair, S. L., & Madigan, T. J. (2016). Dating attitudes and expectations among young Chinese adults: An examination of gender differences. *The Journal of Chinese Sociology, 3*(1), 1–19.

Blossfeld, H. P., & Drobnic, S. (Eds.). (2001). *Careers of couples in contemporary society: From male breadwinner to dual-earner families*. Oxford University Press.

Blossfeld, H. P., & Timm, A. (Eds.). (2003). *Who marries whom? Educational systems as marriage markets in modern societies*. Springer Science & Business Media.

Bossard, J. H. (1932). Residential propinquity as a factor in marriage selection. *American Journal of Sociology, 38*(2), 219–224.

Boyd, R., & Richerson, P. J. (1985). *Culture and the evolutionary process*. University of Chicago Press.

Bredow, C. A., Cate, R. M., & Huston, T. L. (2008). Have we met before? A conceptual model of first romantic encounters. In S. Sprecher, A. Wenzel, & J. Harvey (Eds.), *Handbook of relationship initiation* (pp. 3–28). Psychology Press

Bridges, J., & Denisoff, R. S. (1986). Changing courtship patterns in the popular song: Horton and Carey revisited. *Popular Music & Society, 10*(3), 29–45.

Brown, P. J., & Konnor, M. (1987). An anthropological perspective on obesity. *Annals of the New York Academy of Sciences, 499*, 29–46.

Brown, S. (2000). Evolutionary models of music: From sexual selection to group selection. In F. Tonneau & N. S. Thompson (Eds.), *Perspectives in ethology* (pp. 231–281). Springer. https://doi.org/10.1007/978-1-4615-1221-9_9

Burgess, E. W., & Wallin, P. (1943). Homogamy in social characteristics. *American Journal of Sociology, 49*(2), 109–124.

Buss, D. M. (1988). Love acts. The evolutionary biology of love. In R. J. Sternberg & M. L. Barnes (Eds.), *Psychology of love* (pp. 100–118). Yale University Press.

Buss, D. M. (1989). Sex differences in human mate preferences: Evolutionary hypotheses tested in 37 cultures. *Behavioral and Brain Sciences, 12*, 1–49.

Buss, D. M. (1994). *The evolution of desire: Strategies of human mating*. Basic Books.

Buss, D. M. (2004). *Evolutionary psychology: The new science of the mind* (2nd ed.). Allyn & Bacon.

Buss, D. M. (2006). The evolution of love. In R. Sternberg & K. Weis (Eds.), *The new psychology of love* (pp. 65–86). Yale University Press.

Buss, D. M. (2019). *The evolution of love in humans*. In R. J. Sternberg & K. Sternberg (Eds.), *The new psychology of love* (p. 42–63). Cambridge University Press.

Buss, D. M., Abbott, A., Angleitner, A., Asherian, A., Biaggio, B., Blanco-Villasenor, A., Bruchon-Schweitzer, M., Ch'U, H-Y., Czapinski, J., Deraad, B., Ekehammar, B., El Lohamy, N., Fioravanti, M., Georgas, J., Gjerde, P., Guttman, R., Hazan, F., Iwawaki, S., Janakiramaiah, N., Khosroshani, F. . . . Yang, K-S. (1990). International preferences in selecting mates: A study of 37 cultures. *Journal of Cross-Cultural Psychology, 21*, 5–47.

Buss, D. M., & Barnes, M. (1986). Preferences in human mate selection. *Journal of Personality and Social Psychology, 50*(3), 559–570. https://doi.org/10.1037/0022-3514.50.3.559

Buss, D. M., & Schmitt, D.P. (1993). Sexual strategies theory: An evolutionary perspective on human mating. *Psychological Review, 100*, 204–232.

Buss, D. M., Shackelford, T. K., Kirkpatrick, L. A., & Larsen, R. J. (2001). A half century of mate preferences: The cultural evolution of values. *Journal of Marriage & Family, 63*, 491–503.

Cameron, C., Oskamp, S., & Sparks, W. (1977). Courtship American style: Newspaper ads. *The Family Coordinator, 26*(1), 27–30. https://doi.org/0.2307/581857

Chekki, D. A. (1968). Mate selection, age at marriage, and propinquity among the Lingayāts of India. *Journal of Marriage and the Family, 30*(4), 707–711.

Chen, J., Chiu, C-y., & Chan, F. S-F. (2009). The cultural effects of job mobility and the belief in a fixed world. *Journal of Personality and Social Psychology, 97*, 851–865

Cherlin, A. J. (2004). The deinstitutionalization of American marriage. *Journal of Marriage and Family, 66*(4), 848–861.

Clark, C. L., Shaver, P. R., & Abrahams, M. F. (1999). Strategic behaviors in romantic relationship initiation. *Personality and Social Psychology Bulletin, 25*(6), 709–722.

Clark, M. S., & Mills, J. (1979). Interpersonal attraction in exchange and communal relationships. *Journal of Personality and Social Psychology, 37*, 12–24.

Clark, M. S., & Mills, J. R. (2011). A theory of communal (and exchange) relationships. In P. A. M. Van Lange, A. W. Kruglanski, & E. T. Higgins (Eds.), *Handbook of theories of social psychology* (pp. 232–250). SAGE.

Coontz, S. (2005). *Marriage, a history: From obedience to intimacy, or how love conquered marriage*. Viking.

Cooper, M. L., & Sheldon, M. S. (2002). Seventy years of research on personality and close relationships: Substantive and methodological trends over time. *Journal of Personality, 70*, 783–812.

Cooper, A., & Sportolari, L. (1997). Romance in cyberspace: Understanding online attraction. *Journal of Sex Education and Therapy, 22*(1), 7–14.

Couch, D., & Liamputtong, P. (2008). Online dating and mating: The use of the internet to meet sexual partners. *Qualitative Health Research, 18*(2), 268–279.

Cunningham, M. R., & Barbee, A. P. (1991). Differential K-selection versus ecological determinants of race differences in sexual behavior. *Journal of Research in Personality, 25*, 205–217.

Cunningham, M. R., Barbee, A. P., & Philhower, C. L. (2002). *Dimensions of facial physical attractiveness: The intersection of biology and culture*. In G. Rhodes & L. A. Zebrowitz (Eds.), *Advances in visual cognition: Vol. 1. Facial attractiveness: Evolutionary, cognitive, and social perspectives* (pp. 193–238). Ablex.

Cunningham, M. R., Roberts, A. R., Barbee, A. P., Druen, P. B., & Wu, C. H. (1995). "Their ideas of beauty are, on the whole, the same as ours": Consistency and variability in the cross-cultural perception of female physical attractiveness. *Journal of Personality and Social Psychology, 68*(2), 261–279.

Custer, L., Holmberg, D., Blair, K., & Orbuch, T. L. (2008). "So how did you two meet?" Narratives of relationship initiation. In S. Sprecher, A. Wenzel, & J. Harvey (Eds.), *Handbook of relationship initiation* (pp. 453–470). Psychology Press.

Darden, D. K., & Koski, P. R. (1988). Using the personals ads: A deviant activity? *Deviant Behavior, 9*(4), 383–400.

Davie, M. R., & Reeves, R. J. (1939). Propinquity of residence before marriage. *American Journal of Sociology, 44*(4), 510–517.

Degim, I.A., Johnson, J., & Fu, T. (2015). *Online courtship: Interpersonal interactions across borders*. Institute of Network Cultures.

De Munck, V. C. (1996). Love and marriage in a Sri Lankan Muslim community: Toward a reevaluation of Dravidian marriage practices. *American Ethnologist, 23*(4), 698–716.

De Munck, V. C. (1998). Lust, love, and arranged marriages in Sri Lanka. In V. C. De Munck (Ed.), *Romantic love and sexual behavior: Perspectives from social sciences* (pp. 285–300). Praeger.

De Raad, B., & Doddema-Winsemius, M. (1992). Factors in the assortment of human mates: Differential preferences in Germany and the Netherlands. *Personality and Individual differences, 13*(1), 103–114.

Dion, K., Berscheid, & Walster, E. (1972). What is beautiful is good. *Journal of Personality and Social Psychology, 24*(3), 285–290. https://doi.org/10.1037/h0033731

Eagly, A. H., Ashmore, R. D., Makhijani, M. G., & Longo, L. C. (1991). What is beautiful is good, but. . . . A meta-analytic review of research on the physical attractiveness stereotype. *Psychological Bulletin, 110*(1), 109–128. https://doi.org/10.1037/0033-2909.110.1.109

Eastwick, P. W., Eagly, A. H., Finkel, E. J., & Johnson, S. E. (2011). Implicit and explicit preferences for physical attractiveness in a romantic partner: A double dissociation in predictive validity. *Journal of Personality and Social Psychology*, *101*(5), 993–1011. https://doi.org/10.1037/a0024061

Eastwick, P. W., & Finkel, E. J. (2008a). Sex differences in mate preferences revisited: Do people know what they initially desire in a romantic partner? *Journal of Personality and Social Psychology, 94*, 245–264.

Eastwick, P. W., & Finkel, E. J. (2008b). Speed-dating: A powerful and flexible paradigm for studying romantic relationship initiation. In S. Sprecher, A. Wenzel, & J. Harvey (Eds.), *Handbook of relationship initiation* (pp. 217–234). Guilford Press.

El-Hazmi, M. A., Al-Swailem, A. R., Warsy, A. S., Al-Swailem, A. M., Sulaimani, R., & Al-Meshari, A. A. (1995). Consanguinity among the Saudi Arabian population. *Journal of Medical Genetics*, *32*(8), 623–626.

Epstein, R., Pandit, M., & Thakar, M. (2013). How love emerges in arranged marriages: Two cross-cultural studies. *Journal of Comparative Family Studies*, *44*(3), 341–360.

Fallon, A. (1990). *Culture in the mirror: Sociocultural determinants of body image.* In T. F. Cash & T. Pruzinsky (Eds.), *Body images: Development, deviance, and change* (pp. 80–109). Guilford Press.

Feingold, A. (1990). Gender differences in effects of physical attractiveness on romantic attraction: A comparison across five research paradigms. *Journal of Personality and Social Psychology*, *59*(5), 981–993.

Feingold, A. (1992). Good-looking people are not what we think. *Psychological Bulletin*, *111*(2), 304–341.

Finkel, E. J., Eastwick, P. W., Karney, B. R., Reis, H. T., & Sprecher, S. (2012). Online dating: A critical analysis from the perspective of psychological science. *Psychological Science in the Public Interest*, *13*(1), 3–66.

Fisher, H. (1992). *Anatomy of love: A natural history of monogamy, adultery, and divorce.* W. W. Norton.

Fisher, H. (1998). Lust, attraction, and attachment in mammalian reproduction. *Human Nature, 9*, 23–52.

Fisher, H. (2004). *Why we love: The nature and the chemistry of romantic love.* Henry Holt.

Fitness, J., Fletcher, G. J. O., & Overall, N. (2003). Interpersonal attraction and intimate relationships. In M. Hogg & J. Cooper (Eds.), *Sage handbook of social psychology* (pp. 258–276). SAGE.

Fletcher, G. J., Tither, J. M., O'Loughlin, C., Friesen, M., & Overall, N. (2004). Warm and homely or cold and beautiful? Sex differences in trading off traits in mate selection. *Personality and Social Psychology Bulletin*, *30*(6), 659–672.

Fugère, M. A., Madden, S., & Cousins, A. J. (2019). The relative importance of physical attractiveness and personality characteristics to the mate choices of women and their fathers. *Evolutionary Psychological Science*, *5*(4), 394–404.

Gangestad, S. W. (2008). *Biological adaptations and human behavior.* In C. Crawford & D. Krebs (Eds.), *Foundations of evolutionary psychology* (pp. 153–172). Erlbaum.

Gangestad, S. W., & Simpson, J. A. (2007). An introduction to the evolution of mind: Why we developed this book. In S. W. Gangestad, & J. A. Simpson (Eds.), *The evolution of mind: Fundamental questions and controversies* (pp. 1–21). Guilford Press

Garfinkel, Y. (2018). The evolution of human dance: Courtship, rites of passage, trance, calendrical ceremonies and the professional dancer. *Cambridge Archaeological Journal*, *28*(2), 283.

Giles, J. (2004). *The parlour and the suburb: Domestic identities, class, femininity, and modernity*. Berg.

Gillis, J. R. (1985). *For better, for worse: British marriages, 1600 to the present.* Oxford University Press.

Gillis, J. R. (1988). From ritual to romance: Toward an alternative history of love. In C. Z. Stearns & P. N. Stearns (Eds.), *Emotion and social change toward a new psychohistory* (pp. 87–122). Holms and Meier.

Gonalons-Pons, P., & Schwartz, C. R. (2017). Trends in economic homogamy: Changes in assortative mating or the division of labor in marriage? *Demography*, *54*(3), 985–1005.

Gonzalo, J. A., Alfonseca, M., & Perez, F. F. M. (2016). *World population: Past, present, & future.* World Scientific.

Gottschall, J., Martin, J., Quish, H., & Rea, J. (2004). Sex differences in mate choice criteria are reflected in folktales from around the world and in historical European literature. *Evolution and Human Behavior, 25*, 102–112.

Gui, T. (2017). "Devalued" daughters versus "appreciated" sons: Gender inequality in China's parent-organized matchmaking markets. *Journal of Family Issues*, *38*(13), 1923–1948.

Guttentag, M., & Secord, P. (1983). *Too many women?* SAGE.

Hamamy, H. (2012). Consanguineous marriages. *Journal of Community Genetics*, *3*(3), 185–192.

Hamon, R. R., & Ingoldsby, B. B. (Eds.). (2003). *Mate selection across cultures.* SAGE.

Harrison, A. A., & Saeed, L. (1977). Let's make a deal: An analysis of revelations and stipulations in lonely hearts advertisements. *Journal of Personality and Social Psychology, 35*(4), 257–264. https://doi.org/10.1037/0022-3514.35.4.257

Hatfield, E., & Rapson, R. L. (1987). Passionate love: New directions in research. In W. H. Jones & D. Perlman (Eds.), *Advances in personal relationships* (Vol. 1, pp. 109–139). JAI Press.

Heitzman, J., & Worden, R. L. (1996). *India: A country study*. Bernan Press.

Heldman, C., & Wade, L. (2010). Hook-up culture: Setting a new research agenda. *Sexuality Research and Social Policy, 7*(4), 323–333.

Henrich, J. (2004). Cultural group selection, coevolutionary processes and large-scale cooperation. *Journal of Economic Behavior & Organization, 53*(1), 3–35.

Henrich, J., Boyd, R., & Richerson, P. J. (2012). The puzzle of monogamous marriage. *Philosophical Transactions of the Royal Society B: Biological Sciences, 367*(1589), 657–669.

Henrich, J., & McElreath, R. (2003). The evolution of cultural evolution. *Evolutionary Anthropology: Issues, News, and Reviews, 12*(3), 123–135.

Hentschel, T., Heilman, M. E., & Peus, C. V. (2019). The multiple dimensions of gender stereotypes: A current look at men's and women's characterizations of others and themselves. *Frontiers in Psychology, 10*, 11.

Hofstede, G. (1998). Attitudes, values and organizational culture: Disentangling the concepts. *Organization Studies, 19*(3), 477–493.

Hofstede, G. (2001). *Culture's consequences: Comparing values, behaviors, institutions, and organizations across nations* (2nd ed.). SAGE.

Horton, D. (1957). The dialogue of courtship in popular songs. *American Journal of Sociology, 62*(6), 569–578.

Howard, V. (2008). *Brides, Inc.: American weddings and the business of tradition*. University of Pennsylvania Press.

Illouz, E. (1997). *Consuming the romantic utopia: Love and the cultural contradiction of capitalism*. University of California Press.

Inglehart, R. (1997). *Modernization and postmodernization: Cultural, economic, and political change in 43 societies*. Princeton University Press.

Inglehart, R., & Baker, W. E. (2000). Modernization, cultural change, and the persistence of traditional values. *American Sociological Review, 65*(1), 19–51. https://doi.org/10.2307/26572 88.

Inglehart, R., & Welzel, C. (2005). *Modernization, cultural change, and democracy: The human development sequence*. Cambridge University Press.

Inhorn, M. C. (2007). Loving your infertile Muslim spouse. In M. B. Padilla, J. S. Hirsch, M. Munoz-Laboy, R. E. Sember, & R. G. Parker (Eds.), *Love and globalization: Transformations of intimacy in the contemporary world* (pp. 139–160). Vanderbilt University Press.

Jagger, E. (1998). Marketing the self, buying an other: Dating in a post modern, consumer society. *Sociology, 32*, 795–814.

Kalmijn, M. (1991). Status homogamy in the United States. *American Journal of Sociology, 97*(2), 496–523.

Kalmijn, M. (1994). Assortative mating by cultural and economic occupational status. *American Journal of Sociology, 100*(2), 422–452.

Kalmijn, M. (2007). Explaining cross-national differences in marriage, cohabitation, and divorce in Europe, 1990–2000. *Population Studies, 61*(3), 243–263.

Kamble, S., Shackelford, T. K., Pham, M. N., & Buss, D.M. (2014). Indian mate preferences: Continuity, sex differences, and cultural changes across a quarter of a century. *Personality and Individual Differences, 70*, 150–155.

Karandashev, V. (2017). *Romantic love in cultural contexts*. Springer.

Karandashev, V. (2019). *Cross-cultural perspectives on the experience and expression of love*. Springer.

Karandashev, V. (2021). *Cultural models of emotions*. Springer.

Karandashev, V., & Evans, N.D. (2017). *Test of Implicit Associations in Relationship Attitudes (TIARA): Manual for a new method*. Springer.

Karandashev, V., Zarubko, E., Artemeva, V., Evans, M., Morgan, K. A. D., Neto, F., Feybesse, C., Surmanidze, L., & Purvis, J. (2020). Cross-cultural comparison of sensory preferences in romantic attraction. *Sexuality & Culture, 24*(1), 23–53. https://doi.org/10.1007/s12119-019-09628-0

Karandashev, V., Zarubko, E., Artemeva, V. Neto, F. Surmanidze, L., & Feybesse, C. (2016). Sensory values in romantic attraction in four Europeans countries: Gender and cross-cultural comparison. *Cross-Cultural Research, 50* (5), 478–504. https://doi.org/10.1177/1069397116674446

Kennedy, R. J. R. (1943). Premarital residential propinquity and ethnic endogamy. *American Journal of Sociology, 48*(5), 580–584.

Kenrick, D. T., Groth, G. E., Trost, M. R., & Sadalla, E. K. (1993). Integrating evolutionary and social exchange perspectives on relationships: Effects of gender, self-appraisal, and involvement level on mate selection criteria. *Journal of Personality and Social Psychology, 64*(6), 951–969.

Khallad, Y. (2005). Mate selection in Jordan: Effects of sex, socio-economic status, and culture. *Journal of Social and Personal Relationships, 22*(2), 155–168.

Kiernan, K. (2002). Cohabitation in Western Europe: Trends, issues, and implications. In A. Booth & A. C. Crouter (Eds.), *Just living together: Implication of cohabitation on families, children, and social policy* (pp. 3–31). Erlbaum.

Korchmaros, J. D., Ybarra, M. L., & Mitchell, K. J. (2015). Adolescent online romantic relationship initiation: Differences by sexual and gender identification. *Journal of Adolescence, 40*, 54–64.

Korson, J. H. (1968). Residential propinquity as a factor in mate selection in an urban Muslim society. *Journal of Marriage and the Family, 30*(3), 518–527.

Kurzban, R., & Weeden, J. (2005). *HurryDate*: Mate preferences in action. *Evolution and Human Behavior, 26*(3), 227–244.

Langlois, J. H., Kalakanis, L., Rubenstein, A. J., Larson, A., Hallam, M., & Smoot, M. (2000). Maxims or myths of beauty? A meta-analytic and theoretical review. *Psychological Bulletin, 126*(3), 390–423.

Lawrence, R. (2004). Guest editorial: Overcoming the stigma of online dating—What are we embarrassed for? *Online Dating Magazine.* Retrieved from http://www.onlinedatingmagazine.com/columns/editorials/editorial10.html

LeFebvre, L. E. (2018). Swiping me off my feet: Explicating relationship initiation on Tinder. *Journal of Social and Personal Relationships, 35*(9), 1205–1229.

Lei, C., Wang, Y., Shackelford, T. K., & Buss, D. M. (2011). Chinese mate preferences: Cultural evolution and continuity across a quarter century. *Personality and Individual Differences, 50*, 678–683.

Lemay Jr, E. P., Clark, M. S., & Greenberg, A. (2010). What is beautiful is good because what is beautiful is desired: Physical attractiveness stereotyping as projection of interpersonal goals. *Personality and Social Psychology Bulletin, 36*(3), 339–353.

Leongómez, J. D., Binter, J., Kubicová, L., Stolařová, P., Klapilová, K., Havlíček, J., & Roberts, S. C. (2014). Vocal modulation during courtship increases proceptivity even in naive listeners. *Evolution and Human Behavior, 35*(6), 489–496.

Li, N. P., Bailey, J. M., Kenrick, D. T., & Linsemeier, J. A. W. (2002). The necessities and luxuries of mate preferences: Testing the tradeoffs. *Journal of Personality and Social Psychology, 82*, 947–955.

Lo, M., & Aziz, T. (2009). Muslim marriage goes online: The use of internet matchmaking by American Muslims. *The Journal of Religion and Popular Culture, 21*(3), 5–5.

Lockwood, Y. R. (1983). *Text and context: Folksong in a Bosnian Muslim village.* Slavica.

Loeb, E. M. (1950). Courtship and the love song. *Anthropos, 49*(4/6), 821–851.

Lorenzo, G. L., Biesanz, J. C., & Human, L. J. (2010). What is beautiful is good and more accurately understood: Physical attractiveness and accuracy in first impressions of personality. *Psychological Science, 21*(12), 1777–1782.

Lutz, W., Sanderson, W., & Scherbov, S. (2001). The end of world population growth. *Nature, 412*(6846), 543–545.

Lutz, W. (2007). The future of human reproduction: Will birth rates recover or continue to fall? *Ageing Horizons, 7*, 15–21.

Lystra, K. (1989). *Searching the heart: Women, men, and romantic love in nineteenth-century America.* Oxford University Press

Mace, R. (2000). Evolutionary ecology of human life history. *Animal Behaviour, 59*(1), 1–10.

Mace, R., & Holden, C. J. (2005). A phylogenetic approach to cultural evolution. *Trends in Ecology & Evolution, 20*(3), 116–121.

Mafra, A. L., Fisher, M. L., & Lopes, F. D. A. (2021). Does mate preference represent mate choice? A cross-cultural investigation. *Evolutionary Behavioral Sciences, 15*(1), 64–81. https://doi.org/10.1037/ebs0000221

Malach Pines, A. (2001). The role of gender and culture in romantic attraction. *European Psychologist, 6*(2), 96–102.

Maner, J. K., & Ackerman, J. M. (2020). Ecological sex ratios and human mating. *Trends in Cognitive Sciences, 24*(2), 98–100.

Marches, J. R., & Turbeville, G. (1953). The effect of residential propinquity on marriage selection. *American Journal of Sociology, 58*(6), 592–595.

Markus, H. R., & Kitayama, S. (1991). Culture and the self: Implications for cognition, emotion, and motivation. *Psychological Review*, 98, 224–253.

Marshall, D. S. (1971). Sexual behavior on Mangaia. In D. S. Marshall & R. C. Suggs (Eds.), *Human sexual behavior* (pp. 103–162). Basic Books.

Mead, M. (2017). *Continuities in cultural evolution.* Routledge. (Original work published 1964)

Merkle, E. R., & Richardson, R. A. (2000). Digital dating and virtual relating: Conceptualizing computer mediated romantic relationships. *Family Relations, 49*(2), 187–192.

Mesoudi, A. (2016). Cultural evolution: A review of theory, findings, and controversies. *Evolutionary Biology, 43*(4), 481–497.

Mesoudi, A., Whiten, A., & Laland, K. N. (2006). Towards a unified science of cultural evolution. *Behavioral and Brain Sciences, 29*(4), 329–347.

Moore, R. L. (1998). Love and limerence with Chinese characteristics: Student romance in the PRC. In V. C. De Munck (Ed.), *Romantic love and sexual behavior: Perspectives from social sciences* (pp. 251–283). Praeger.

Morgan, B. S. (1981). A contribution to the debate on homogamy, propinquity, and segregation. *Journal of Marriage and the Family, 43*(4), 909–921.

Moss, J. H., & Maner, J. K. (2016). Biased sex ratios influence fundamental aspects of human mating. *Personality and Social Psychology Bulletin, 42*(1), 72–80.

Mu, Y. (1994). Music and sexual customs in multi-ethnic China. *Asian Studies Review, 18*(2), 63–70.

Murstein, B. I. (1974). *Love, sex, and marriage through the ages.* Springer.

Nakonezny, P. A., & Denton, W. H. (2008). Marital relationships: A social exchange theory perspective. *The American Journal of Family Therapy, 36*(5), 402–412.

Oishi, S., Lun, J., & Sherman, G.D. (2007). Residential mobility, self-concept, and positive affect in social interactions. *Journal of Personality and Social Psychology, 93*, 131–141.

Phegley, J. (2012). *Courtship and marriage in Victorian England.* ABC-Clio.

Pitcairn, T. K., & Schleidt, M. (1976). Dance and decision an analysis of a courtship dance of the Medlpa, New Guinea. *Behaviour, 58*(3–4), 298–315.

Ponxetti, J. (Ed.). (2003). *International encyclopedia of marriage and family.* Macmillan Reference USA.

Preston, S. H. (1986). Changing values and falling birth rates. *Population and Development Review, 12*, 176–195.

Qiang, H. (2011). A study on the metaphor of «red» in Chinese culture. *American International Journal of Contemporary Research, 1*(3), 100–101.

Regan, P. C., & Berscheid, E. (1997). Gender differences in characteristics desired in a potential sexual and marriage partner. *Journal of Psychology & Human Sexuality, 9*(1), 25–37.

Rosenblatt, P. C., & Cozby, P. C. (1972). Courtship patterns associated with freedom of choice of spouse. *Journal of Marriage and the Family, 34*, 689–695.

Rosenfeld, M. J., & Thomas, R. J. (2012). Searching for a mate: The rise of the Internet as a social intermediary. *American Sociological Review, 77*(4), 523–547.

Rothman, E. K. (1987). *With hands and hearts: A history of courtship in America.* Harvard University Press.

Savage, P. E., Loui, P., Tarr, B., Schachner, A., Glowacki, L., Mithen, S., & Fitch, W. T. (2020). Music as a coevolved system for social bonding. *Behavioral and Brain Sciences, 44*, Article e59. https://doi.org/10.1017/S0140525X20000333

Schacht, R., & Kramer, K. L. (2019). Are we monogamous? A review of the evolution of pair-bonding in humans and its contemporary variation cross-culturally. *Frontiers in Ecology and Evolution, 7*, Article 230. https://doi.org/10.3389/fevo.2019.00230

Schmitt, A. (2009). *The propinquity effect: How relationships have enhanced my life.* AuthorHouse.

Schmitt, D. P. (2008). *An evolutionary perspective on mate choice and relationship initiation.* In S. Sprecher, A. Wenzel, & J. Harvey (Eds.), *Handbook of relationship initiation* (p. 55–74). Psychology Press.

Schug, J., Yuki, M., Horikawa, H., & Takemura, K. (2009). Similarity attraction and actually selecting similar others: How cross-societal differences in relational mobility affect interpersonal similarity in Japan and the USA. *Asian Journal of Social Psychology, 12*, 95–103.

Seidman, S. (1991). *Romantic longings: Love in America, 1830–1980.* Routledge.

Sharangpani, M. (2010). Browsing for bridegrooms: Matchmaking and modernity in Mumbai. *Indian Journal of Gender Studies, 17*(2), 249–276.

Singer, I. (1987). *The nature of love: Vol. 3. The modern world* (2nd ed.). University of Chicago Press.
Smith, A. W., & Duggan, M. (2013). *Online dating & relationship*. Pew Research Center.
Sorokowski, P., & Sorokowska, A. (2012). Judgments of sexual attractiveness: A study of the Yali tribe in Papua. *Archives of Sexual Behavior, 41*(5), 1209–1218.
Souza, A. L., Conroy-Beam, D., & Buss, D. M. (2016). Mate preferences in Brazil: Evolved desires and cultural evolution over three decades. *Personality and Individual Differences, 95*, 45–49.
Sprecher, S. (2009). Relationship initiation and formation on the Internet. *Marriage & Family Review, 45*(6–8), 761–782.
Stone, E. A., Shackelford, T. K., & Buss, D. M. (2007). Sex ratio and mate preferences: A cross-cultural investigation. *European Journal of Social Psychology, 37*(2), 288–296.
Sugiyama, L. S. (2004). Is beauty in the context-sensitive adaptations of the beholder? Shiwiar use of waist-to-hip ratio in assessments of female mate value. *Evolution and Human Behavior, 25*(1), 51–62.
Swami, V., Furnham, A. (2008). *The psychology of physical attraction*. Routledge.
Szreter, S., & Fisher, K. (2010). *Sex before the sexual revolution: Intimate life in England 1918–1963*. Cambridge University Press.
Tabory, E., & Weller, L. (1986). Residential propinquity and mate selection in an Israeli town. *International Journal of Sociology of the Family, 16*(2), 217–223.
Thomson, R., Yuki, M., Talhelm, T., Schug, J., Kito, M., Ayanian, A. H., Becker, J. C., Becker, M., Chiu, C-Y., Ferreira, C. M., Fülöp, M., Gul, P., Houghton-Illera, A. M., Joasoo, M., Jong, J., Kavanagh, C. M., Khutkyy, D., Manzi, C., Marcinkowska, U. M. . . . Visserman, M. L. (2018). Relational mobility predicts social behaviors in 39 countries and is tied to historical farming and threat. *Proceedings of the National Academy of Sciences, 115*(29), 7521–7526.
Thornhill, R., & Gangestad, S. W. (1996). The evolution of human sexuality. *Trends in Ecology & Evolution, 11*(2), 98–102.
Titzmann, F. M. (2013). Changing patterns of matchmaking: The Indian online matrimonial market. *Asian Journal of Women's Studies, 19*(4), 64–94.
Tolman, D. L., & Diamond, L. M. (2001). Desegregating sexuality research: Cultural and biological perspectives on gender and desire. *Annual Review of Sex Research, 12*(1), 33–74.
Tovée, M. J., Swami, V., Furnham, A., & Mangalparsad, R. (2006). Changing perceptions of attractiveness as observers are exposed to a different culture. *Evolution and Human behavior, 27*(6), 443–456.
Townsend, J. M., & Wasserman, T. (1998). Sexual attractiveness: Sex differences in assessment and criteria. *Evolution and Human Behavior, 19*(3), 171–191.
Tracy, J. (2006, January). Online dating stigma—Is the stigma gone? Online Dating Magazine. Retrieved from http://www.onlinedatingmagazine.com/columns/2006editorials/04-onlinedatingstigma.html
Uchida, Y., Norasakkunkit, V., & Kitayama, S. (2004). Cultural constructions of happiness: Theory and empirical evidence. *Journal of Happiness Studies, 5*(3), 223–239.
Weisz, J. R., Rothbaum, F. M., & Blackburn, T. C. (1984). Standing out and standing in: The psychology of control in America and Japan. *American Psychologist, 39*(9), 955–969.
Wetsman, A., & Marlowe, F. (1999). How universal are preferences for female waist-to-hip ratios? Evidence from the Hadza of Tanzania. *Evolution and Human Behavior, 20*(4), 219–228.
Wheeler, L., & Kim, Y. (1997). What is beautiful is culturally good: The physical attractiveness stereotype has different content in collectivistic cultures. *Personality and Social Psychology Bulletin, 23*(8), 795–800.
Wiseman, J. (1986). Friendship: Bonds and binds in a voluntary relationship. *Journal of Social and Personal Relationships, 3*(2), 191–211.
Wright, B. L., & Sinclair, H. C. (2012). Pulling the strings: Effects of friend and parent opinions on dating choices. *Personal Relationships, 19*(4), 743–758.
Yamada, J., Kito, M., & Yuki, M. (2017). Passion, relational mobility, and proof of commitment: A comparative socio–ecological analysis of an adaptive emotion in a sexual market. *Evolutionary Psychology, 15*(4), Article 1474704917746056.
Yamagishi, T., Jin, N., & Miller, A.S. (1998). In-group favoritism and culture of collectivism. *Asian Journal of Social Psychology, 1*, 315–328.
Yamagishi, T., & Yamagishi, M. (1994). Trust and commitment in the United States and Japan. *Motivation and Emotion, 18*, 129–166.
Yela, C., & Sangrador, J. L. (2001). Perception of physical attractiveness throughout loving relationships. *Current Research in Social Psychology, 6*(5), 57–75.

Yuki, M., & Schug, J. (2012). Relational mobility: A socioecological approach to personal relationships. In O. Gillath, G. Adams, & A. Kunkel (Eds.), *Decade of Behavior 2000–2010. Relationship science: Integrating evolutionary, neuroscience, and sociocultural approaches* (pp. 137–151). American Psychological Association Press. https://doi.org/10.1037/13489-007

Yuki, M., Schug, J., Horikawa, H., Takemura, K., Sato, K., Yokota, K., & Kamaya, K. (2007). *Development of a scale to measure perceptions of relational mobility in society.* CERSS Working Paper 75. Center for Experimental Research in Social Sciences, Hokkaido University.

PART II

Relationship Maintenance

In chapter 11, Kennair, Grøntvedt, Kessler, and Bendixen begin the section on relationship maintenance by outlining how sexual conflict has shaped the relationship challenges that men and women encounter in their attempt to preserve lasting, satisfactory relationships. They provide a review of historical and contemporary research directions in the evolutionary study of romantic relationships, with special emphasis on the sometimes incompatible strategies that men and women pursue in attempting to raise children and sustain a satisfying pair-bond dynamic. They highlight trade-offs in men's and women's reproductive optima and how these impact how often partners engage in sexual intercourse, how infidelity threat is managed (e.g., jealousy and mate retention), and how partners forgive each other's transgressions. They also consider how societies are structured (or not) to alleviate the stressors of sexual conflict and provide future directions for studying the evolved psychology of relationship maintenance outside modern couples and societies.

In chapter 12, Buunk and Massar distinguish possessive and reactive jealousy, the adaptations underlying each type, and how they uniquely guide how people recognize and respond to romantic rivals. They draw evidence from nonhuman and non-Western societies to argue that possessive jealousy is a culture-contingent expression of mate guarding meant to thwart potential rivals that varies with parental influence on mate choice, attachment and father absence, and domestic violence, whereas reactive jealousy has design features that prepare an individual to address their partner's actual extra-pair intimacy. Throughout, they emphasize sex differences and similarities in the experience of jealousy, in reactions to potential rivals, and within LGBTQ+ relationships. They conclude by summarizing the experimental procedures underlying jealousy research and outline which areas of study have yet to be examined.

In chapter 13, Denes, Crowley, Dhillon present the endocrinological bases of relationship maintenance processes, including peoples' reactions to relationship threat and motivations for relationship enhancement. They discuss how testosterone, oxytocin, and cortisol potentiate the evolved systems underlying how people experience commitment and competition in response to partner and rival conflict. In doing so, they distinguish individual versus interactive processes that give rise to relationship maintenance behaviors like forgiveness, sacrifice, social support and responsiveness, and joint leisure activities. They conclude by considering unresolved questions about testosterone's influence on relationship well-being, the contribution of oxytocin to pair-bonding and childrearing, and how cortisol interacts with situation variables (e.g., stress caused by workload) to influence relationship quality.

In chapter 14, Starratt outlines the adaptive logic by which people allocate and protect the investments they make into an intimate partnership. Drawing from sexual strategies theory, she considers differences in how men and women balance risk and reward, pursue long- versus short-term investments, and engage in behaviors that curtail investment loss (e.g., mate guarding). Throughout, she reviews the voluminous literature on mate retention behaviors and how individual differences (e.g., mate value and personality) and contextual factors (e.g., risk of partner defection, partner fertility, and presence of same-sex rivals) impact how these behaviors are deployed. The chapter concludes with a discussion of how mate retention tactics may differ in online environments, in nonmonogamous relationships, and within LGBTQ+ populations.

In chapter 15, Gallup and Burch defend their hypothesis that intimate partner violence (IPV) functions to increase paternity certainty and investment in genetically related children. They cite evidence for four mechanisms by IPV accomplishes this: prevention of insemination by rivals, rival semen displacement, pregnancy termination, and differential investment in offspring as a function of evidence of shared genes. Throughout, they highlight the role of paternal resemblance as a phenotypic indicator of paternity certainty and consider how this may impact relationship processes for adoptive parents and those who undergo artificial insemination. They close by discussing how knowledge of this logic may inform solutions to related social issues (e.g., deadbeat dads and differential investment in biological and nonbiological offspring).

In chapter 16, Westrupp, Marshal, Bennett, Benstead, King, and Karantzas consider the challenges that parenting can impose on successful relationship maintenance, with a particular focus on how individual differences impact mutual support and conflict between partners. They frame individual differences in relationship quality outcomes as a function of the evolved attachment system and its interaction with environmental stressors (e.g., work–family conflict, socioeconomic hardship, sleep quality, and quality of partner support). They support their argument with original data showing how factors related to COVID-19 have exacerbated relational difficulties for those with insecure relationship attachment. They conclude by highlighting the overrepresentation of research on initial rather than later stages of parenthood and the impact of parenthood on sexual relationship quality.

In chapter 17, Mogilski, Rodrigues, Lehmiller, and Balzarini address how people in multipartner relationships (i.e., consensual nonmonogamy, or CNM) (e.g., polyamory, swinging, and open relationships) maintain satisfaction and deter conflict with their partner(s). The authors begin by describing how CNM is an alternative strategy to infidelity for pursuing extra-pair intimacy and argue that CNM buffers against the interpersonal risks and relationship dissatisfaction that typically accompanies infidelity. They then review what is currently known about how people practice CNM, personality features associated with pursuit of CNM, and the barriers that prevent people from successfully maintaining CNM relationships. Mogilski and colleagues conclude by outlining what is currently unknown about CNM relationship maintenance and how the evolutionary study of CNM could reveal strategies for building positive-sum interactions between in- and extra-pair intimate partners.

In chapter 18, Diamond and Alley discuss relationship maintenance among sexual and gender diverse (SGD) individuals by reviewing how prominently social safety concerns (e.g., connection, nurturance, and protection) can feature within these relationships. They argue that SGD individuals may have a higher default stress reactivity by virtue of early and persistent adverse social experiences, and therefore a uniquely important feature of maintaining an SGD relationship may be to establish safety. They incorporate varied perspectives to support their claims, including evidence from minority stress theory and studies of stigma against SGD people, and conclude by outlining how evolutionary scientists might adopt social safety concerns into existing models relationship maintenance.

In chapter 19, Imami and Agnew review social and evolutionary psychological perspectives on relationship maintenance among older adults. Using interdependence theory, they describe how evolutionary concerns, such as status-striving and childcare priorities, interact with the increasing interdependence of older adults to predict relationship quality outcomes. They argue that conflict between the demands of a long-term bond and the inclusive fitness demands of relatives and other members of one's close network become more prominent with age, and that these factors may interact with other features of old age (e.g., declining health and need for care) to predict relationship quality. They identify several maintenance strategies (e.g., transformation of motivation, willingness to sacrifice, and positive illusions) that protect relationship well-being in older age by improving the quality of interdependence between partners.

In chapter 20, Adair and Ferenczi explore how relationship maintenance practices vary across cultures and the evolutionary logic that guides how these practices' help to resolve the unique challenges of one's local environment. In their review, they address how socio-cultural features, such as a community's historical subsistence type and residential mobility, shape how partners become interdependent or involve family in relationship decisions. Throughout, they incorporate research on motivational, perceptual, neurological, social, reasoning, and behavioral processes to explain how these variations help relationships to persist. They conclude by discussing the need to critically examine how current models of relationship persistence might better incorporate strategies from non-Western and non-heteronormative societies, and providing several suggestions that researchers may adopt to begin to decolonize relationship science.

CHAPTER

11 Sexual Conflict During Relationship Maintenance

Leif Edward Ottesen Kennair, Trond Viggo Grøntvedt, Andrea Melanie Kessler, *and* Mons Bendixen

Abstract

Sexual conflict is the conflict between the evolutionary interests of individuals of different sexes. Sexual conflict may result in sexually antagonistic coevolution, producing sex-specific adaptations that are involved in cooperation and conflict concerning sex and other mating-relevant aspects between individual men and women. Sexual conflict is studied in many species; however, human long-term relationship maintenance provides a special case. The current chapter introduces the concept of sexual conflict and considers sexual conflict in the context of species-specific and species-typical long-term relationship maintenance. Different expressions of this include phenomena such as parental investment conflict, relationship satisfaction, intercourse frequency in couples, mate retention tactics, jealousy, infidelity, threat to the relationship, breakup, and forgiveness. Evolutionary psychology theory and empirical findings from studies of these phenomena will be presented and discussed within a metanarrative of how human evolved psychology influences contemporary romantic relationships.

Key Words: relationship maintenance, sexual conflict, sex differences, mate retention tactics, relationship satisfaction

What Is Sexual Conflict?

Sexual conflict may be defined as conflict between the evolutionary interests of individuals of the two sexes (Parker, 1979, 2006). There are conflicts over resources that ensue because females and males follow different ideal strategies that may increase their own fitness at a cost to their mating partner.

Despite the often too prevalent perception of a war between the sexes in the social sciences (see special issue of *Sex Roles*, e.g., Vandermassen, 2011), to a large degree interdependent reproduction promotes cooperation rather than conflict (Buss, 2017; Mikulincer & Shaver, 2007). Still, the sexes differ in the minimal investment required to produce and secure the survival of offspring (Trivers, 1972), and there are differences in limiting factors for reproductive success between males and females, for instance, number of fertile partners or energy constraints. Parental investment theory provides a framework for when to expect sex differences in mating behavior and mating psychology. For instance, in mammalian species, the sex difference in required minimal parental investment is profound, with gestation, birth, and lactation exclusively provided by females, whereas males could (and often do) only contribute sperm. These differences in required parental investment create differences in optima for various aspects of mating and sexuality in humans (Buss, 2017). For instance, short-term, low-investment mating strategies yield larger fitness payoff for men than for women (Goetz & Shackelford, 2009b). Men more than women desire sexual variety, overperceive interactions with members of the opposite sex as sexual signals, are more sexually persistent, and more ready to consent to sexual intercourse—all psychological mechanisms related to short-term mating strategies in men (e.g., Bendixen et al., 2019; Buss & Schmitt, 1993, 2019; Clark & Hatfield, 1989; Goetz & Shackelford, 2009b; Hughes et al., 2020; Kennair et al., 2009). Women show greater regret after short-term sex, are more picky in choosing long-term mates, and value commitment more than men do (Bendixen et al., 2017; Kennair et al., 2016; Kennair et al., 2021; Kennair et al., 2018; Surbey & Conohan, 2000; Walter et al., 2020). In relationships or relationship formation, however, it takes two to tango. As such there are trade-offs between each sex's optima within the couple. There are instances where one sex can gain fitness benefits by inducing their partner to increase reproductive investment (Chapman, 2015); hence, there are areas of mating, relationship formation, and relationship maintenance that are subject to sexual conflict.

A strategy in one sex that interferes with the optima of the other sex, by for example causing increased investment, may in turn select for resistance to such exploitive attempts; hence, the sexes will have had conflicts of interest throughout evolutionary time, resulting in "sexually antagonistic coevolution" (Buss, 2017). Sexually antagonistic coevolution (i.e., an arms race between the sexes) produces adaptions and counteradaptations in sex-specific optima in given traits of conflict (Mulder & Rauch, 2009), much like the adaptions and counteradaptations in host/parasite coevolutionary processes. This antagonistic coevolution results in both cooperation and conflict as well as compromises and negotiations of states in between. In insects, for instance, there is substantial evidence for different mating-rate optima between females and males. Whereas females in various species secure increased fitness benefits from mating several times in the form of lifelong production of offspring, there are negative consequences of increased multiple matings, particularly in the form of reduced life expectancy for many insect species (see Arnqvist & Nilsson, 2000, for a review), possibly in part due to negative effects of substances injected during matings. Males' optima in mating rates are higher, and although the sexes have some similar negative fitness consequences for multiple matings, such as increased predatory risk, females seem to have a lower optima of number of matings than males. Sexual antagonistic coevolution is important in the evolution of mating systems and reproductive traits in insects (Arnqvist & Nilsson, 2000). One suggested example of sexual antagonistic coevolution in the morphology related to mating is found in a species of water strides (*Gerris incognitus*) with males having structures to clasp females during mating, and females having abdomen spines to hinder harassing males and as a consequence reduce the frequency of matings, which are costly for females (Arnqvist & Rowe, 1995).

In species where sex occurs not only for reproductive purposes, even more opportunities for conflict are present (Mulder & Rauch, 2009). In nonhuman primates, for instance, sexual coercion and mate guarding by males select for counterstrategies by females in the form of extra-pair matings and other behaviors that produce confusion of paternity and perhaps reduce the risk of infanticide by males (see Stumpf et al., 2011, for sexual conflict in primates). Adding extended parental care, and biparental care, to a mating system, there are additional conflicts of interest between parents of joint offspring, such as conflicts over allocation of resources to the partner and offspring in the ongoing relationship versus pursuit of new mating opportunities. Humans are no different from other sexually reproducing species with conflicts of interests and asymmetries between males and females. As sex-specific optima for mating traits are present, adaptations and counteradaptations related to mating traits are expected in human mating systems as well.

Initially, differences in parental certainty and minimal investment guided how researchers approached sexual conflict in humans (Buss, 2017; Goetz & Shackelford, 2009b); however, recent developments now also include phenomena such as sexual conflict in mating strategy (Li et al., 2012) and sexual conflict after conception (Wade et al., 2018). Considering current human mating psychology through the lens of sexual conflict theory addresses how the behavior and reproductive physiology of one sex poses adaptive challenges that members of the opposite sex must solve (Goetz & Shackelford, 2009b). Humans, unlike most species, have specific challenges due to both the species-specific and typical nature of long-term relationships. Further, due to sexual conflict, humans face specific sex differences related to the adaptive problems posed by these different aspects of long-term relationship maintenance. Sexual strategies theory offers a theoretical framework for analyzing human sexual psychology with specific predictions for women and men in different mating contexts (Buss, 1998) and identifies key challenges for modern couples, based on our evolved mating psychology.

What Is Relationship Maintenance?

Once a relationship has been initiated, partners can either stay and maintain the relationship or leave the relationship in hopes of finding a new and better mate. Relationships may be maintained in different ways—and all processes that prolong or improve the relationship between initiation and dissolution may be included in the definition of relationship maintenance. Scholars typically rely on four different definitions of relationship maintenance (Canary & Yum, 2015). These definitions cover (a) communication and corresponding behavior that protect the relationship and keep it stable; (b) preserving the status quo through protection of what exists in the present, which typically involves avoiding any changes to vital features of the relationship (e.g., level of intimacy); (c) keeping the relationship in a satisfactory condition through maintenance behaviors that sustain desired characteristics of the relationship (commitment, liking and loving the partner, etc.), and (d) reparative behaviors that restore the relationship after troubles or difficulties have occurred. These four conceptualizations highlight different aims and challenges to making a relationship both last and remain satisfactory in the face of differing individual relational needs, desires, and personalities. Ogolsky et al. (2017) reviewed the literature on relationship maintenance and concluded that humans use a large array of cognitive and behavioral tactics to attempt to improve or prolong relationships. Further, they conclude that these tactics have a moderate to strong relationship with vital relationship outcomes (e.g., dissolution and relationship satisfaction). They briefly address evolutionary approaches; however, they do not address sexual conflict theory specifically.

One line of work from a specific evolutionary psychology approach considers relationship maintenance from the perspective of mate retention tactics (Buss & Shackelford, 1997). Mate retention tactics are behavioral responses to perceived relationship threats and are used by one partner in ongoing relationships to keep the other partner in the relationship. As men have been found cross-culturally to rate physical appearance as more important in a mate than women do, and women have been found to emphasize resources more than men do (e.g., Buss, 1989; Kennair et al., 2011; Walter et al., 2020), mate retention tactics are expected to be influenced by different mate traits for women and men. This has also been found when investigating sex differences in mate retention tactics. For instance, men tend to use more mate retention behaviors when in a relationship with a highly attractive partner. The same is not true for women. Women, on the other hand, use more mate retention behaviors when their partners have higher income and are higher on status striving, whereas such traits and mate retention are uncorrelated in men (Buss & Shackelford, 1997). As such, the use of tactics to retain a mate is in line with mate preferences and the literature on jealousy and reactions to infidelity.

The Special Nature of Human Long-Term Mating

Defection from a mating pair to engage in new mating opportunities is a potential problem for sexually reproducing species that co-invest in offspring (Alvarez & Koene, 2018; Chapman, 2015; Parker, 2006). But unlike the majority of mammalian species, humans form and maintain long-term relationships (Buss & Schmitt, 1993; Conroy-Beam et al., 2015). This creates two specific areas of sexual conflict: (a) commitment to long-term relationship (including resource investment and sexual exclusivity), and (b) strategies for maintaining the relationship once it is formed (including making the relationship satisfactory, and lasting). In traditional, religious societies there are societal and religious norms and mores that enforce relationship maintenance, including influence and manipulation by parents (Apostolou, 2017). However, with fewer societal, parental, and religious controls in many modern societies, couples need to navigate the costs and benefits of forming and maintaining relationships on their own, aided in part by the evolved mating psychology described in this chapter—including possibly some mechanisms that evolved to counter effects of both parents and religion, potentially making this complex process mismatched to a time when these influences were stronger than they currently are in Western countries. This mismatch has received little attention; however, these social and technological changes (e.g., hormonal contraception and mass media exposure) might skew the output of our evolved sexual psychology. Nevertheless, relationship dyads are cross-culturally ubiquitous, have fitness consequences for individuals, and create specific areas of sexual conflict and selection (Conroy-Beam, Buss, et al., 2019; Conroy-Beam et al., 2015; Conroy-Beam et al., 2016; Conroy-Beam, Roney, et al., 2019; Walter et al., 2020).

The relationship will be constantly and dynamically a source of costs and benefits, including increased fitness, status, and companionship, as well as specific challenges such as spousal cost infliction (Shackelford & Buss, 2000). A relationship might reduce mating-related costs (particularly related to acquiring a new mate, such as time spent on searching for, evaluating, and seducing a partner), but investment and commitment in the relationship also brings costs, for instance, in the form of forgoing other mating opportunities or compromising genetic quality and resources. Such costs might be more or less relevant for either sex especially for sociosexually unrestricted individuals with preference for short-term sexual relationships, but perhaps more so for highly sexually attractive men, who are able to access new sexual partners and gain fitness benefits via increased number of offspring, compared to women. However, over evolutionary time, pair-bonding and relationship maintenance have solved adaptive problems associated with childrearing, such as investment, cultural transmission, protection, and forging social and marital alliances (Buss, 2017). In addition, there are adaptive aspects of marital dissatisfaction, too (Wade et al., 2018). Simply put, the benefits of long-term mateships need to be continually assessed and compared to costs. Relationship maintenance concerns increasing benefits and reducing costs, with dissolution being the potential result of costs outweighing benefits (Buss, 2017). And thus, to know when to break up, or to elicit reparative behavior within the dyad, mechanisms that dynamically are gauging satisfaction (Conroy-Beam et al., 2016) must also be able to consider when the cost of the spouse or partner exceeds any actual, current, or likely potential, future benefits (Shackelford & Buss, 2000).

From a sexual conflict perspective, the benefit of being with one partner also entails the cost of missing out on other possible partners. This is known as the commitment-problem (Frank, 1988, 2001; Hirshleifer, 1987). Intrasexual competition means that humans compete with others for the best possible mate—and, therefore, committing to a partner carries risk. Commitment ensures resources to the long-term partner and reduces the potential for diverting time and energy into pursuing other relations. Partners may provide better net benefits for us, but with changes throughout our lifetime in traits important in mate choice (e.g., physical attractiveness and social status), settling down with a partner is risky. Men, for example, value younger women (e.g., Conroy-Beam &

Buss, 2019; Grøntvedt et al., 2013), as younger women biologically have a better chance to produce healthy children (e.g., Bergh et al., 2019) and there is increased risk of miscarriage with age (e.g., Magnus et al., 2019). Women, on the other hand, to a larger degree value a partner's status and financial prospects (Walter et al., 2020), as a man high in status typically has resources to provide for her and her offspring. By committing to a partner, we take the risk of missing out on a younger or higher-status mate. Conroy-Beam et al. (2015) identified several sex-differentiated benefits from engaging in long-term pair-bonds: Men would gain status; by offering resources and commitment they would gain access to higher-quality mates and increased likelihood of paternity. Women would gain access to resources for self and offspring and protection from formidable partners. These benefits would be tied to sex differences in partner preferences and mate value (Buss, 1989; Walter et al., 2020; Walter et al., 2021) and also present specific challenges such as jealousy, relationship satisfaction, mate guarding, and mate retention. And differences in partner preferences, mate value, and sociosexuality would be relevant for male and female psychology tracking their dynamic relationship satisfaction (Conroy-Beam et al., 2016). We will be addressing these and other specific domains of sexual conflict within the domain of modern couples' long-term relationship maintenance in the next section.

Specific Examples of Sexual Conflict in Human Relationship Maintenance

Sexual conflict in human long-term relationship maintenance may place in several different domains, from conflict over parental investment to forgiveness of infidelity. There will be different aspects that influence what increases or decreases relationship satisfaction for women and men, and also what mate retention tactics that are employed. The following section will consider these domains of sexual conflict in greater detail.

Parental Investment Conflict

One of the functions of human long-term mating is investment in and rearing of common offspring. There are different approaches to why a long and expensive childhood and maturation period is necessary for humans. However, this increases bonding and long-term investment in offspring from both parents, and often also alloparents. There is a conflict underlying this arrangement though, despite both parents benefiting. As Trivers (1972, 1974) noted, there will be behavioral consequences of differential investment patterns in common offspring. There are asymmetries between the sexes, laying the ground for conflicts about entering committed relationships, which is mirrored by men's greater short-term orientation across cultures (Schmitt, 2005b). There are domains of sexual conflict confronted even before the relationship is initiated. And in modern Western societies, especially, the results may be evolutionarily mismatched behavior, or some groups may benefit more than others in achieving what they desire or in number of offspring, depending on which constraints are removed and which ecological settings are influencing relationship-forming behavior.

After the relationship is established there are further challenges associated with child raising that tax relationship satisfaction. Wade et al. (2018) consider sexual conflict after conception including topics such as divergent desire for sexual intercourse after pregnancy, the four-year itch, changes in sexual desire after birth, and transition to parenthood. The transition to parenthood is being delayed in modern couples. On average, the age of first birth for women in highly egalitarian, modern societies has been increasing since the 1970s, and is now approaching 30 years of age. This is potentially due to several reasons, including freedom to choose when to become pregnant (absence of religious and more traditional values), access to contraception, liberal abortion regulations, access to and completion of higher education, and women's workforce participation. Thus, having children is not prioritized, and the transition to parenthood may be more dramatic than during evolutionary history. There is a loss of some roles and liberties when having children, and child care regularly requires substantial resources and time. However, there are large differences between nations in how much parental leave, economic compensation, and child care support the couple and infant will receive, with Scandinavian welfare states being among those that lessen the burden of having children, compared to countries like the United States where a couple must make significantly larger financial sacrifices to raise a child (e.g., lack of paid parental leave (Organisation for Economic Cooperation and Development, 2017)). Societies also differ in how much time and resources fathers typically invest, which may factor into our sexual and mating psychologies (e.g., in explaining sex differences in jealousy responses; Bendixen et al., 2015; Buss et al., 1992; Scelza et al., 2020).

Further asymmetries that arise in couples after conception or childbirth include differences in sexual desire and the four-year itch (Wade et al., 2018). Frequency of sexual intercourse often drops after the birth of the child. This was found in the majority of cultures studied (Brewis & Meyer, 2005). Desire for sex shows greater reduction for women than for men as a function of childbirth (McNulty et al., 2019). Women's drop in desire might be because she has reduced fertility and also needs to divert time and attention toward nursing and caring for the child. It may also be that men have a more limited change in desire, which is tied to a drop in testosterone after becoming fathers, especially in men providing more daily child care (Gettler et al., 2011). The four-year itch is the fall in happiness couples experience after the time period needed to ensure the survival of the child (Fisher, 1989). Fisher (1989) suggests that female reproductive success is improved due to serial pair-bonding during their fertile years. For this to be an example of sexual conflict, and not just problems in relationship maintenance, one would need to suggest that men do not benefit from serial pair-bonding. However, for men who do have serial long-term pair-bonds, the pattern would suggest that it is the successful men who, albeit over a longer period of fertile years, have the greatest increased fecundity.

An evolutionarily novel aspect of modern relationship maintenance is that there often is a prolonged period without common offspring, despite the couple cohabiting and being sexually active. Thus, one of the major benefits of long-term relationships, and one of the most stabilizing maintenance factors, but also one of the greater sources of costs to the relationship, is typically not present. This probably creates a different dynamic in many modern relationships, providing modern mating psychology with novel challenges and perhaps increased instability. The U.S. Census Bureau statistics on marriage and divorce from 2001 shows that childless married couples divorce at a much higher rate than couples with children (Kreider, 2005). Thus, for many young couples there is a mismatch, where the absence of children might both be an evolutionarily novel benefit, with less strain on time, health, and resources but also present as a novel evolutionary stressor and challenge to relationship maintenance.

Mate Retention Tactics

A domain of relationship maintenance that has been addressed from a functional, adaptive perspective is that of mate retention tactics (Buss & Shackelford, 1997; Kaighobadi et al., 2010). In long-term mating species, guarding against mate poaching and avoiding breakup due to a dissatisfied partner are two different challenges that need to be solved once a couple is established. These behaviors may be collected under the rather unromantic header "mate retention tactics."

The first attempt to study what different behaviors are used in order to mate guard in humans was in the late 1980s (Buss, 1988). Buss found five categories of human mate-guarding tactics. Two of these broad categories of tactics are directed toward potential rivals; *signaling a relationship* by holding hands, wearing rings or introducing one's partner as boyfriend/girlfriend, and *negative inducements* such as telling potential rivals bad things about one's partner, threatening rivals, or being violent toward rivals. The list of movies, series, and songs that feature fist fights with people who present a threat to a current relationship is endless. The other three were directed toward the partner in various ways. *Positive inducements* refer to displays of resources, enhancing appearance, giving in to sexual requests, and focusing on love and caring. *Direct guarding* tactics are increased vigilance such as calling partner unexpectedly (or a more modern form using apps such as snapchat maps) to see where partner is, monopolizing time of partner, and keeping partner away from potential rivals. The final category of intersexual manipulation is *negative inducement,* which refers to threats of punishment or infidelity (flirting with rival or threats of breakup if partner flirts with someone else), emotional manipulation, commitment manipulation, and derogation toward competitors (see Buss, 2002, for a review of various tactics).

In an early a study of 214 married couples, Buss and Shackelford (1997) examined determinants of various forms of mate retention in men and women. Their findings were strongly supportive of an evolutionary psychology-informed hypothesis showing sex differences in what tactics men and women applied, with men displaying more resources (e.g., spending money on her), threatening rivals, and giving in to their partner's wishes than women did. Women, on the other hand, enhanced their appearance, signaled possession verbally (e.g., he's taken), and threatened to break up if their partner ever cheated on them more than men did. Length of relationship was positively associated with derogation of their mate and of same-sex competitors, but also with inducing jealousy in their partner. Discrepancies in age and attractiveness also affected the intensity of mate retention. Men married to women who were younger and more physically attractive than they were reported more use of derogation, possessiveness, emotional manipulation, and threats and violence toward other men. Correspondingly, women who were older and less attractive than their partners reported less use of verbal possession, ornamentation, and violence against rivals. Perceived likelihood of infidelity was positively associated with more use of mate retention for men in multivariate analyses (controlling for age, relationship length, and perceived attractiveness of spouse). In this context, within-couple violence seems to be evolutionary predictable, based on anxiety or uncertainty about partner being unfaithful or abandoning the dyad (Barbaro et al., 2018; Barbaro et al., 2019; Kaighobadi et al., 2008).

Relationship Satisfaction

Relationship satisfaction broadly refers to a person's overall evaluation of their relationship and may be measured uni- or multidimensionally. Thus, adaptations that dynamically gauge relationship satisfaction and dissatisfaction, are central to relationship maintenance (Conroy-Beam et al., 2016; Wade et al., 2018). These mechanisms provide feedback and emotional and motivational states that regulate maintenance or breakup behavior. And in the arms race that is sexual conflict, the two parts of the dyad seek sex-specific needs sated by their partner and provide at least a modicum of what the opposite sex desires to be satisfied enough not to leave.

To look at the complexity of relationship satisfaction and its evolutionary functions however, we must first look at long-term relationships. Put very bluntly: people who have a committed, long-term, romantic partner are together with the best person they could acquire—who could not find anyone better. This may sound harsh, but it is based on the reality that there is intrasexual competition for mates, where each competitor has different mate acquisition tactics, mate availability, personality traits, and current mate value. Especially with long-term partners, both sexes are relatively selective about their choices (Li et al., 2002; Thomas et al., 2020). Relationships include (at least) a dyad; and provided sex differences in partner preferences, available partners in the mating pool, the possibility for mate switching or infidelity, and changes in mate value, overall evaluation of relationships is prone to change over time. Thus, there is ample fuel for sexual conflict to cause the selection of different evaluative mechanisms.

Conroy-Beam et al. (2015) introduced three factors that influence relationship satisfaction. The first factor is the consideration of costs and benefits. Long-term relationships come with a number of benefits, such as support for the partner, shared responsibilities, and increased care for children (Marlowe, 2003). However, long-term relationships also include costs. High-maintenance partners cost resources, and abusive relationships may lead to physical or psychological damage. When in a long-term relationship, costs and benefits are considered—and one evaluates if the relative benefits of staying with a partner outweigh the relative benefits of leaving. With a higher number of benefits comes a higher relationship satisfaction. The second factor is manipulability of partner investment. How well one can elicit a partner's investment in the relationship may influence how satisfied one is with their relationship, making agreeableness a favored trait in partners (Walter et al., 2020). Experiencing that one's partner's investment has decreased causes dissatisfaction—some people are able to alter the situation and manipulate their partner to increase investments again. How well one is able alter those situations when they occur therefore influences how satisfied one is. The third factor is the signaling of relationship problems. Signaling to the public that there are problems occurring in a relationship may have certain costs. For one, private events are made public, even though one partner may not agree with that practice. Moreover, the relationship may become vulnerable to mate poachers (Buss & Duntley, 2008; Schmitt & Buss, 2001). This means that the knowledge of others that the relationship is unstable might motivate them to pose a threat to the relationship—and, ultimately, they may break up the relationship. When signaling relationship problems, one also risks displaying both parties as unstable relationship partners—therefore potentially lowering one's mate value. People who hide relationship problems may express less dissatisfaction to avoid sending those social signals to others—and therefore avoid the costs mentioned above. People who show their problems publicly may, on the other hand, experience greater dissatisfaction.

Another aspect that appears to influence relationship satisfaction is mate value. Mate value is an integration of desired preferences people may look for in a mate (Conroy-Beam, Buss, et al., 2019). We evaluate potential mates on different integrated dimensions, such as intelligence; health; a good sense of humor; or how interesting, kindhearted, physically attractive, wealthy, or of high status they are (Conroy-Beam, Buss, et al., 2019; Thomas et al., 2020; Walter et al., 2020). Different people put more emphasis on different features. To make good choices when choosing a mate, we must therefore integrate those desired preferences into an overall mate value (Conroy-Beam, Buss, et al., 2019). This integrated mate value influences how satisfied one is with a partner, and thus in a relationship. Overall, people in a long-term relationship with a partner who is higher in mate value than themselves are more satisfied (Conroy-Beam et al., 2016). However, this will vary across time because relationship costs and benefits, personal needs, and mate value are by no means stable. Income, interest from new partners, or desire to start a family are some examples of factors that changes within relationships.

Coming back to the sexual conflict perspective, relationship satisfaction influences competition for the best possible mate—or more precisely, relationship satisfaction motivates an individual to stay with a chosen partner or, through adaptive dissatisfaction, to leave that partner for a higher-value mate. It therefore also functions as a motivator. For example, relationship satisfaction is a motivation to make investments—either in the current satisfactory relationship or in extra-pair investments due to dissatisfaction with said relationship (Conroy-Beam et al., 2015). Extra-pair investments usually decrease the investments in a current relationship. However, low satisfaction does not necessarily lead to extra-pair investments. It can also motivate investment in relationship maintenance tactics such as repair strategies (Canary & Yum, 2015; Conroy-Beam et al., 2015). As relationship maintenance behavior covers behaviors used to improve an already good relationship and repair a possibly bad relationship (Canary & Yum, 2015), it seems that relationship maintenance behaviors are motivated both by high and low relationship satisfaction.

Relationship satisfaction is a dynamic concept. Therefore, it is natural for it to fluctuate over time, influenced by the individual partners and the situation they are in. If low relationship satisfaction would immediately lead to extra-pair investments, many more long-term relationships would (probably) end in breakup. Instead, there appear to be a number of psychological processes, such as immediate judgments and evaluations of attractive alternative mates, that may lead to people engaging in relationship maintenance behavior instead of extra-pair investments when faced with this choice (Campbell et al., 2001; Gonzaga et al., 2006; Lydon et al., 2003). This is in line with an evolutionary perspective, as commitment to a partner is necessary to experience relationship benefits such as shared responsibilities and emotional support. For example, a person who leaves a relationship every time a potentially better mate is available will not be able to experience the benefits of that long-term relationship—such as shared responsibilities or increased care for offspring. From an evolutionary perspective, it therefore does make sense to commit to one person long enough to benefit from that long-term relationship. Therefore, investing in relationship repair strategies instead of searching for other, possibly better mates can be beneficial (Conroy-Beam et al., 2015).

Relationship satisfaction is highly complex, even more so when the personal goals and needs of either partner are included. The equation seems to be simple; high relationship satisfaction makes partners stay in their relationship; low relationship satisfaction makes them see that they are better off rejoining the competition for a better mate. However, it is not that simple. Most people know a couple that was seemingly perfect but still broke up. Couples may break up, even though their relationship satisfaction is seemingly high and stable. They might decide to end their relationship and look for a mate better suited for them because the relationship, however good it was, was not consistent with specific personal needs (e.g., one partner desires children, while the other does not).

Most people also know couples who stay together even though at least one of them is not satisfied with the relationship. Aside from situations of financial or emotional dependence on the partner, those relationships may still function because of high investments that have already been made. High investment makes it more likely to continuously invest in a certain project or stay in a specific relationship. Another complex issue is mate value discrepancy. People who have partners with high mate value are more satisfied in their relationships. However, having a partner with mate value significantly higher may also lead to more jealousy in the relationship, and thus increased mate guarding (Barbaro et al., 2019; Sela et al., 2017). Therefore, just having a partner with high mate value is not the key to being satisfied, as every so often, it is a question of balance.

There are some sex differences in how humans experience relationship satisfaction. Men and women place higher value on slightly different aspects when choosing a mate and have different needs in relationships. Women are more focused on a partner's status, while men are likely to focus on physical attractiveness and youth (Walter et al., 2020). As such, the conflict between sexes might increase with relationship length because cues of youthfulness decrease and social status may change (e.g., due to job loss). These changes might trigger relationship termination. One possible example of this is serial monogamy among highly attractive, high-status men. Not only is there some evidence that they remarry progressively younger women and hence are able to attract partners similar to their mate preferences (e.g., Pollet et al., 2013), but there is also evidence for stronger selective advantage of serial monogamy in men than in women (Jokela et al., 2010). Provided that the relationship is maintained, there are still sex differences within long-term relationships. For example, men and women differ in sexual desire and sexual satisfaction—which of course may influence one's general satisfaction in a relationship (McNulty & Fisher, 2008).

Sexual Frequency

One of the major sources of conflict in relationships is tied to the question of how frequently one has sex. For individuals in relationships, there may be a sexual desire discrepancy—a difference between desired and actual frequency of sexual behavior (Willoughby & Vitas, 2012). Each partner in a relationship may experience this, and such discrepancies are related to higher levels of conflicts and less relationship satisfaction (Willoughby et al., 2014). Overall, men report stronger sexual desire than women (Baumeister et al., 2001), and within couples, men more often than women are likely to experience sexual desire discrepancy. Across the span of the relationship, women's desire for sex drops off faster than men's (McNulty et al., 2019), often resulting in a desire discrepancy despite high desire coordination in initial phases of the relationship. As touched upon above, childbirth accounts for some of these developing differences between the sexes. Also, there are sex-differentiated effects on changes in sexual frequency and satisfaction (McNulty & Fisher, 2008) and relationship discord is a function of a drop in her desire, not his (McNulty et al., 2019).

While sex with various partners has fitness benefits for men, within couples, sexual frequency desires might stem from the reoccurring adaptive problem of paternity uncertainty. With concealed female ovulation, males could increase the chance of conception by increasing frequency of matings in order to secure paternity. Thus, sperm competition may be driven by sexual conflict (Goetz & Shackelford, 2009b). In this regard, sperm competition has been suggested to play a part in human evolution (e.g., Shackelford & Goetz, 2007) and desired increased sexual frequency desire in males could hence be a product of intrasexual competition. Goetz and Shackelford (2006, 2009a) found that partnered men used more sexual coercion when in a relationship with women who had been or were likely to be unfaithful. In addition, several studies have found semen adjustment in humans, with positive association between time a couple spend apart since intercourse and sperm number ejaculation in next copulation, and men show increased sexual attraction and interest in intercourse with time spent apart from partner. These are hypothesized to be psychological adaptations to sperm competition (for a review, see Shackelford & Goetz, 2007). Further, men's sperm competition results in other psychological adaptations in men (including mate guarding and long-term relationship maintenance), and could also result in predictable counteradaptations in women (Shackelford & Goetz, 2007).

Whatever the ultimate explanation for the differences in sexual frequency desired arguments and friction over how frequently the couple ought to have sex are common. Peplau (2003) claimed that how often the couple has sex would involve some kind of compromise of their desire; meaning that both parties comply to some degree with the needs of the other. What factors that may affect this compromise is less studied. However, Grøntvedt et al. (2019) reported from a sample of Norwegian couples a positive association between intercourse frequency and women's sociosexuality, particularly their unrestricted attitudes toward uncommitted sex. No such effect was found for men. Apparently, the more women see sex as detached from love and commitment, the more they are willing to compromise, shifting the frequency toward their partner's ideal frequency. Thus, in this highly egalitarian sample, women's psychology influences frequency, although this finding considering sex and individual differences might have found other effects in less egalitarian societies, where her interest and desire to a lesser degree may influence frequency. The general finding is that men are more dissatisfied with frequency of intercourse within relationships compared to women (Baumeister et al., 2001), and this is found also in more gender-egalitarian samples (Kennair et al., 2009). In addition, men take the initiative to begin intercourse and regret forgoing sexual intercourse more than women (Baumeister et al., 2001; Kennair et al., 2009; Kennair et al., 2016).

Fascinatingly, and seemingly in conflict with other findings (Baumeister et al., 2001), Grøntvedt et al. (2015) found that women had more likely taken the initiative the last time the couple had intercourse, when couples had been together more than two years. However, considering who took the initiative the last time the couple had intercourse is different from who took the initiative to have sex last, whether or not intercourse occurred. If especially female sexual desire falls off as relationships last (McNulty & Fisher, 2008; McNulty et al., 2019), then it is possible that he accommodates to her initiatives more often than she does to his, resulting in the finding above.

Jealousy

There are a number of threats to a valued relationship, and some of these may activate jealousy responses. Jealousy is defined as a complex emotional state that evolved to solve adaptive problems of mating (Buss, 2013; Daly et al., 1982). When people are asked about their emotions following imagined, hypothetical infidelity by their partner, they report a vast array ranging from feeling abandoned and worthless to feeling vengeful and hatred toward their partner (Sagarin et al., 2012). The most commonly reported emotions besides jealousy are anger, distress/upset, and hurt. Although not having distinct facial expressions like those of anger, disgust, and sadness, Buss (2013) argues for jealousy being a basic emotion.

As outlined in the introduction, female internal fertilization and gestation has produced not only discrepancy in the minimal obligatory parental investment in offspring for men and women (Trivers, 1972) but has also had consequences for paternal uncertainty and the possibility of being cuckolded (i.e., investing in another man's child) (Goetz & Shackelford, 2009b). Female infidelity and cuckoldry have been recurrent features of human evolutionary history, and sexual conflict related to parental investment and paternity uncertainty is reflected in sex-differentiated reactions to infidelity, but also in sperm competition, and grandparental investment (For details, see Goetz & Shackelford, 2009b). Buss (2017) has identified several psychological and behavioral footprints of sexually antagonistic coevolution in human mating, including strategies of deception, exploitation, and their corresponding defenses (Buss, 2017). Sexual conflict within relationships revolve around infidelity and jealousy, and while the adaptive optimum for a man in a long-term committed relationship is to keep his partner 100% sexually faithful, the adaptive optimum for a potential mate poacher is to get sexual access to the woman or initiate a long-term relationship. The woman's adaptive optimum may be somewhere in between the two men's optimums (Buss, 2017), and she might strategically act unfaithful to test the mating "market" and her relative mate value, to get rid of a suboptimal mate, or to cultivate a backup mate (Buss et al., 2017). The coevolved defenses against infidelity is evident in sex-differentiated mate retention tactics and jealousy responses.

Mate retention tactics such as mate guarding (e.g., vigilance) are one class of several behavioral outcomes of jealousy; others may involve stalking an ex-partner and acts of violence and destruction toward one's current partner (e.g., Buss & Duntley, 2011; Buss & Shackelford, 1997; Duntley & Buss, 2012). The adaptive functions of jealousy are similar for women and men with regard to warding off potential mate poachers and preventing relationship defection and infidelity, and the intensity of jealousy responses may be equally strong for the two sexes. However, because only men historically have faced the adaptive problem of investing resources in another man's child, men more than women are expected to have adaptations that are particularly sensitive to sexual forms infidelity as opposed to emotional forms.

Generally, it is hard for evolutionary psychology to claim with certainty that any part of our psychology is a result of evolution. However, as the behaviorist Skinner (1981) pointed out, when there are no feedback mechanisms for conditioning, evolutionary selection must be the explanation of complex behavior. There is no proximate feedback mechanism of having been cuckolded, such as pain or observable hardship as the result, as women observing a partner leave may experience. For cuckoldry, the only source of distress is the cultural and individual understanding that it is painful and undesirable. But there is no feedback mechanism apart from reduced genetic fitness by investing in another man's offspring and not siring as many of one's own as one could have. The design of the male heterosexual sexual jealousy response must therefore be the result of selection. Across studies using the forced-choice or the continuous measures paradigms for measuring what aspect of the infidelity is more distressing or upsetting, heterosexual men regularly report that emotional forms of infidelity are less upsetting than sexual forms relative to the reports of women (Bendixen et al., 2015; Buss, 2013; Edlund & Sagarin, 2017; Frederick & Fales, 2016; Sagarin et al., 2012). This clearly links back to the different costs for men and women of having unfaithful partners. These effects are not an artifact of measurement paradigm, and the effects are expressed to a larger degree in cultures characterized by high levels of equality and high standard of living (Bendixen et al., 2015).

Jealousy-motivated mate retention tactics thus ultimately increase the likelihood of maintaining the relationship for both sexes, with emphasis on different aspects that might jeopardize the relationship—or if the relationship was maintained, would decrease the cheated partner's fitness.

Infidelity: Breakup or Forgiveness

The formation and maintenance of long-term relationships do create two specific areas of sexual conflict as outlined earlier in this chapter: (a) resource investment and sexual exclusivity as indicators of commitment to long-term relationship, and (b) strategies for preserving relationship satisfaction and stability once it is formed. Throughout history and culture by culture, polygyny is the most typical mating system. However, while consensual nonmonogamy is more frequent than many might be aware of (Balzarini et al., 2019; Haupert et al., 2017; Levine et al., 2018; Mogilski et al., 2017), the majority of modern, Western long-term relationships are founded on a mutual understanding of sexual and emotional exclusivity. This social contract is breached in cases of infidelity. Infidelity may therefore be considered a primary area of sexual conflict (Buss, 2017). Infidelity is considered functional to the extent that it is an adaptation to recurring problems men and women faced across deep time, such as increasing fitness for men through multiple partners and cuckolding competitors or for women increased access to resources, protection, or genetic quality. For infidelity, these adaptive problems have been to increase the number of reproductive opportunities, obtaining genes of higher quality to be transmitted to one's offspring, access to economic resources beyond those currently at hand,

and substituting one's current partner for an alternative one (Buss, 2017). Except for substituting one's partner, the above recurring problems have been different for men and women. For men the problem has been to increase his number of mating opportunities, and those few men who succeeded in mating many women over relatively short periods would have increased their reproductive fitness. However, this would come at a risk of their current long-term relationship or put them at risk of violent sanctions from other men. For women, extra-pair partners might be an avenue to secure superior genetic quality for their offspring or to gain access to additional recourses. However, the cost might be violence or death.

How prevalent is infidelity? The literature from extramarital affairs suggest that the problem of infidelity is prevalent in modern societies, ranging from 22–25% of men and 11–15% of women having had extramarital affairs during their lifetime (e.g., Atkins et al., 2001; Labrecque & Whisman, 2017; Wiederman, 1997). Occurrences of extramarital sex have also been found to be substantial in cross-cultural investigations of less modern societies (Broude & Greene, 1976. Another way of studying the cross-cultural prevalence of threats to sexual exclusivity in relationships is to investigate whether people ever have been tried lured away from an ongoing relationship or has tried to lure someone away from an ongoing relationship (Schmitt, 2004), what may be called mate poaching (Schmitt & Buss, 2001). The International Sexuality Description Project suggests that these behaviors are quite frequent, and that individuals can poach partners by seducing already-paired partners into new sexual or more long-term relationships (for a review on cross-cultural findings of mate poaching, see Schmitt, 2004).

The reproductive costs associated with defecting partners and the relative cross-cultural prevalence of mate poaching suggest that being vigilant and guarding partners has been relevant in our evolutionary history and still poses a problem for many relationships. Infidelity is possibly the most common reason for the breakup of relationships cross-culturally (Betzig, 1989), and the most commonly reported reason for breaking up for couples in retrospect (Amato & Previti, 2003). Still, breakup need not be a necessary outcome of infidelity as some are able to continue the relationship (e.g., Abrahamson et al., 2012). Because sexual conflict within relationships are so closely linked to infidelity and jealousy, we'll take a close look at factors that might increase the likelihood of maintaining relationship following infidelity in couples, and how these could differ for men and women.

FACTORS AFFECTING THE FORGIVENESS OF INFIDELITY

Because of the sex difference in minimal parental investment, the cost of a partner defecting from a long-term relationship is expectedly higher for women. This may influence the psychological processes involved in decisions to forgive infidelity or not differently for men and women. The path from infidelity to breakup or maintenance travels through several mediating psychological processes. First, it may matter if one's partner has been sexually or emotionally unfaithful for how threatening the infidelity is perceived to be for the relationship continuation, to what extent the partner is to blame, and the likelihood that one might forgive and move on. A separate line of thought stems from systematic biases in interpreting signals of forgiveness. When communicating forgiveness to one's partner, these signals may be subject to systematic misinterpretation that again may increase the likelihood of reparative behavior from the cheating part in an attempt to rectify the transgression.

Forgiveness comes in two forms: interpersonal and intrapsychic (Baumeister et al., Sommer, 1998). The first typically involves expressing verbal and physical signals (e.g., directly stating that one forgives, physical closeness, and touching), the second contains private feeling and thoughts (emotional and cognitive) that may not have any behavioral output. Expressed forgiveness without any internal transformation can best be described as "hollow" and may represent a particular problem to the cheating part with regard to interpretation. The defining act of forgiveness involves a transformation from wanting revenge and keeping one's distance (avoidance) to wanting to strengthen the relationship (McCullough et al., 1998; McCullough et al., 1997). However, forgiveness is contingent on judgment of responsibility/blameworthiness (Weiner, 1995), and nonbenign attributions in the form of blaming the transgressor predict less willingness to forgive (Boon & Sulsky, 1997; McCullough et al., 1998). However, the effect of blame on relationship dissolution seems to be indirect only. This is also found in studies of couples who report on past transgressions of various kinds (Friesen et al., 2005). In the above studies, the quality of the relationship seems to have a protective effect on blaming and forgiveness, although this may be due to methodological issues (Grøntvedt et al., 2020).

Studies using hypothetical scenarios or vignettes have reported that level of internal forgiveness fully accounted for the association between blaming partner and relationship dissolution in studies of noncoupled (Hall & Fincham, 2006; Shrout & Weigel, 2019) and coupled participants (Grøntvedt et al., 2020). In Grøntvedt et al.'s (2020) study, level of blame was associated with less forgiveness only for emotional infidelity. Further, the authors found that the perceived level of threat (i.e., how damaging) of the transgression was a strong and direct predictor of likelihood of breakup over and above the effect of forgiveness. Relative to avoidance (keeping distance), revenge motives were not so prevalent following imagined infidelity, and wanting revenge did not predict likelihood of breakup for either men or women in vignettes describing their partner being sexual or emotional unfaithful. The mediating psychological processes, or mechanisms, linking infidelity to breakup appear to be similar for coupled men and women. This was the case despite men being less concerned about the emotional part of their partner's infidelity. Relative to women, men report significantly lower levels of threat, less likelihood of keeping distance, and less likelihood of terminating the relationship following emotional but not sexual infidelity. So, how does infidelity and forgiveness relate to sexual conflict?

There is a level of uncertainty when it comes to being forgiven for one's transgression, and "hollow" forgiveness represents a particular problem. When forgiveness is communicated to one's partner, these signals may be subject to systematic perceptual biases that are predictable from error management theory (Haselton & Buss, 2000; Haselton & Nettle, 2006). Error management theory is an application of signal detection theory (e.g., Swets et al., 2000) for judgment under uncertainty. According to the theory, psychological adaptations designed by natural selection guide the organism to avoid costly errors when correct judgments were hard to reach. Two forms of errors can be made: A false positive (i.e., a person may falsely adopt a belief that is in fact not true) or a false negative (i.e., they may fail to adopt a belief that is in fact true). When making one type of error is more costly than the other within specific domains, natural selection favored designs that informed the organism to make the less costly even if more errors were made overall. Applied to transgressions in long-term relationships, the more costly error would be to falsely believe in signals of forgiveness. Hence, selection may have favored designs that lead to the tendency not to believe one's transgressions are forgiven. This tendency is known as negative forgiveness bias (Haselton & Nettle, 2006). The evolved function of this bias is to guide the individual toward reparative behavior securing that the transgressions are fully mended, and the relationship is secured. Strong support for such a bias has been found in a study of Norwegian couples using hypothetical vignettes where both parties reported on their reactions to emotional and sexual forms of infidelity (Bendixen et al., 2017). In separate scenarios, each part reported on their willingness to forgive their unfaithful partner as well on their belief in being forgiven if they had been cheating on their partner sexually or emotionally. For women across types of infidelity, and for men having been sexually unfaithful, there was a strong negative forgiveness bias effects suggesting that their partner's expressed and internal forgiveness was markedly higher than their beliefs in being forgiven. However, this bias was only moderate for men imagining themselves being emotionally unfaithful which suggests that men may not appreciate the possible threat their emotional infidelity represents for their partner and that men more than women fail to notice the underlying threat of infidelity that does not involve sex. This sex-differentiated bias represents a sexual conflict that presents a clear threat to relationship maintenance if adequate reparative behaviors do not follow.

Breakup

When couples fail to maintain their relationship and breakup is the only option left, the loss of a partner generates strong emotional reactions that we refer to as grief. According to Archer (1999), grief is a trade-off between costs and benefits. The benefits of a committed relationship are outlined earlier in this chapter, but there are also costs of commitment. A large-scale 96-country study finds that emotional reactions to romantic relationship dissolution are typically very strong in both men and women, but also physical symptoms such as weight loss, insomnia, and panic are commonly reported (Morris et al., 2015). The study specifically finds that responses to dissolution follow evolutionary informed predictions (i.e., sexual strategies theory) with women in general reporting more intense grief ("heartbreak") reactions than men. Despite women more often taking the initiative in the breakup, women reported higher intensity of anger, anxiety, and fear and all forms of physical reactions than men, while no sex difference was found for numbness, lost focus, and inability. Reactions were higher for dissolutions initiated by the partner compared to mutual and self-initiated breakups, suggesting that romantic rejection is particularly harmful. Lack of communication was reported to be the most common specific cause of breakup for both sexes, but women reported more often than men that partner's infidelity and "other" was the reason for the breakup. The stronger emotional and physical reactions in women alludes to the evolved sex differences found in romantic attachment and mating strategies (Schmitt, 2005a). Relative to women, men generally report more dismissing romantic attachment and stronger preferences for short-term sexual relationships, resulting in less grief on the male part over breakup, and a stronger inclination to rebound and to seek out a new partner. Hence, the adaptive strategies for the man and the woman following their breakup may be conflicting, particularly when the children are young and resources need to be allocated.

General Discussion: Relationship Maintenance and Sexual Conflict in a Modern World

One of the complicating aspects of considering sexual conflict in long-term relationships is the high degree of overlap in interest between the sexes. Men and women have a higher degree of similarity in long-term partner preferences, such as for healthy, kind, and agreeable partners (e.g.Buss & Barnes, 1986; Thomas et al., 2019). Nevertheless, even in these traits there are measurable differences between women and men (Walter et al., 2020). There are therefore possible asymmetries between the sexes, even where there seemingly are common and overlapping aims and similarities (Trivers, 1972, 1974). Jealousy, for example, shows a robust dimorphic sexual psychology, when addressing specific types of jealousy among heterosexual participants (Bendixen et al., 2015), and thus it is a prime example of sexual conflict (Buss, 2017). However, many other relationship-regulating psychological factors may seem less obviously a result of sexual conflict. If one primarily focuses on shared interest in maintaining the long-term relationship, love, and the specific human need for long-term investment in offspring, one might be blind to underlying adaptive sex differences. For instance, the sex difference in jealousy responses was not empirically studied before Buss et al. (1992) hypothesized the effect for two types of infidelity: emotional and sexual.

Partner preferences, though, are dimorphic to some degree (Walter et al., 2020), and these will regulate relationship satisfaction and dissatisfaction across time. Differences in reproductive biology and sex differences in strength will provide different areas of vigilance (e.g., sexual infidelity) and different tactics (indirect aggression vs. direct physical aggression). For instance, differences in reproductive benefits of multiple partners will exact a greater toll on men, while women suffer a greater cost from resources diverted from the relationship toward rivals. Therefore, from the initiation of the relationship, despite both parties benefiting from a long-lasting relationship, fueling the emotional bonds and motivating infatuation, love, and commitment in both partners, there are ongoing competing choices, all while the relationship is maintained and regulated.

Overall, long-term relationships are formed based on mutually beneficial aspects of increased investment in childrearing and the couples individual fitnesses. However, this seemingly overlapping interest will be sex differentiated in the manner in which individuals regulate the relationship, what they seek from their partner, and what thresholds they have for maintaining or dissolving the relationship. Thus, the seemingly similar behavior involved in relationship maintenance masks effects of sexual conflict and underlying sex differences. Therefore, although one might find smaller sex differences and more mutual dependency and cooperation within long-term relationship maintenance domains, there still are relevant sexual asymmetries and evolutionary arms races driven by sexual conflict between the sexes as outlined in this chapter.

The current chapter has considered how presumed evolved mental mechanisms help couples navigate challenges set by sexual conflict and maintain species-specific and species-typical long-term relationships. However, the research is performed mainly on modern couples, living in modern-day settings. The aim of evolutionary psychology is not to prove evolution; rather, it is to generate and empirically test original insights that improve our description of how our modern sexual psychology functions. Considering modern couples' behavior through the lens of sexual conflict theory highlights a specific set of adaptive problems and tasks that the couple must navigate behaviorally, emotionally, and relationally.

Mate retention tactics are a set of behaviors that solve the problem of keeping the relationship going and preventing the partner from straying or leaving. These tactics are deployed based upon a dynamic, adaptive evaluation of relationship satisfaction or dissatisfaction and the partner's mate value. They are also elicited by other emotional evaluations of the relationship and the partner's behavior, such as jealousy. If the cost of the relationship is too large, the relationship may result in dissolution. Modern couples must rely on mainly on their own evolved mating psychology, as family, religion, societal institutions, and traditions to a lesser degree regulate the relationship. Further, many couples today opt out of one of the evolutionary reasons for long-term relationships or have kids at a much later point in time due to family planning. However, this may cause some amount of mismatch, and probably makes relationship maintenance more challenging. A deeper understanding of sexual conflict and the mating psychology of men and women has coevolved as both challenges and solutions to sex-differentiated adaptive solutions may improve both couples' therapy and relationship quality.

References

Abrahamson, I., Hussain, R., Khan, A., & Schofield, M. J. (2012). What helps couples rebuild their relationship after infidelity? *Journal of Family Issues, 33*(11), 1494–1519. https://doi.org/10.1177/0192513x11424257

Alvarez, B., & Koene, J. M. (2018). Sexual conflict in nonhumans. In T. K. Shackelford & V. A. Weekes-Shackelford (Eds.), *Encyclopedia of evolutionary psychological science* (pp. 1–19). Springer International.

Amato, P. R., & Previti, D. (2003). People's reasons for divorcing. *Journal of Family Issues, 24*(5), 602–626. https://doi.org/10.1177/0192513x03254507

Apostolou, M. (2017). *Sexual selection in Homo sapiens: Parental control over mating and the opportunity cost of free mate choice.* Springer International.

Archer, J. (1999). *The nature of grief: The evolution and psychology of reactions to loss.* Routledge.

Arnqvist, G., & Nilsson, T. (2000). The evolution of polyandry: Multiple mating and female fitness in insects. *Animal Behaviour, 60*(2), 145–164. https://doi.org/10.1006/anbe.2000.1446

Arnqvist, G., & Rowe, L. (1995). Sexual conflict and arms races between the sexes: A morphological adaptation for control of mating in a female insect. *Proceedings of the Royal Society of London. Series B: Biological Sciences, 261*(1360), 123–127. https://doi.org/10.1098/rspb.1995.0126

Atkins, D. C., Baucom, D. H., & Jacobson, N. S. (2001). Understanding infidelity: Correlates in a national random sample. *Journal of Family Psychology, 15*(4), 735–749. https://doi.org/10.1037/0893-3200.15.4.735

Balzarini, R. N., Dharma, C., Kohut, T., Holmes, B. M., Campbell, L., Lehmiller, J. J., & Harman, J. J. (2019). Demographic comparison of American individuals in polyamorous and monogamous relationships. *The Journal of Sex Research, 56*(6), 681–694. https://doi.org/10.1080/00224499.2018.1474333

Barbaro, N., Holub, A. M., & Shackelford, T. K. (2018). Associations of attachment anxiety and avoidance with male- and female-perpetrated sexual coercion in romantic relationships. *Violence & Victims, 33*(6), 1176–1192. https://doi.org/10.1891/0886-6708.33.6.1176

Barbaro, N., Sela, Y., Atari, M., Shackelford, T. K., & Zeigler-Hill, V. (2019). Romantic attachment and mate retention behavior: The mediating role of perceived risk of partner infidelity. *Journal of Social and Personal Relationships, 36*(3), 940–956. https://doi.org/10.1177/0265407517749330

Baumeister, R. F., Catanese, K. R., & Vohs, K. D. (2001). Is there a gender difference in strength of sex drive? Theoretical views, conceptual distinctions, and a review of relevant evidence. *Personality and Social Psychology Review, 5*(3), 242–273. https://doi.org/10.1207/s15327957pspr0503_5

Baumeister, R. F., Exline, J. J., & Sommer, K. L. (1998). The victim role, grudge theory, and two dimensions of forgiveness. In E. L. Worthington, Jr. (Ed.), *Dimensions of forgiveness* (pp. 79–104). Templeton.

Bendixen, M., Asao, K., Wyckoff, J. P., Buss, D. M., & Kennair, L. E. O. (2017). Sexual regret in US and Norway: Effects of culture and individual differences in religiosity and mating strategy. *Personality and Individual Differences, 116*, 246–251. https://doi.org/10.1016/j.paid.2017.04.054

Bendixen, M., Kennair, L. E. O., Biegler, R., & Haselton, M. G. (2019). Adjusting signals of sexual interest in the most recent naturally occurring opposite-sex encounter in two different contexts. *Evolutionary Behavioral Sciences, 13*(4), 345–365. https://doi.org/10.1037/ebs0000162

Bendixen, M., Kennair, L. E. O., & Buss, D. M. (2015). Jealousy: Evidence of strong sex differences using both forced choice and continuous measure paradigms. *Personality and Individual Differences, 86*, 212–216. https://doi.org/10.1016/j.paid.2015.05.035

Bendixen, M., Kennair, L. E. O., & Grøntvedt, T. V. (2017). Forgiving the unforgivable: couples' forgiveness and expected forgiveness of emotional and sexual infidelity from an error management theory perspective. *Evolutionary Behavioral Sciences, 12*(4), 322–335. https://doi.org/10.1037/ebs0000110

Bergh, C., Pinborg, A., & Wennerholm, U.-B. (2019). Parental age and child outcomes. *Fertility and Sterility, 111*(6), 1036–1046. https://doi.org/10.1016/j.fertnstert.2019.04.026

Betzig, L. (1989). Causes of conjugal dissolution: A cross-cultural study. *Current Anthropology, 30*(5), 654–676. https://doi.org/10.2307/2743579

Boon, S. D., & Sulsky, L. M. (1997). Attributions of blame and forgiveness in romantic relationships: A policy-capturing study. Journal of Social Behavior & Personality, *12*(1), 19–44.

Brewis, A., & Meyer, M. (2005). Marital coitus across the life course. *Journal of Biosocial Science, 37*(4), 499–518. https://doi.org/10.1017/S002193200400690X" https://doi.org/10.1017/S002193200400690X

Broude, G. J., & Greene, S. J. (1976). Cross-cultural codes on twenty sexual attitudes and practices. *Ethnology, 15*(4), 409–429.

Buss, D. M. (1988). From vigilance to violence: Tactics of mate retention in American undergraduates. *Ethology and Sociobiology, 9*(5), 291–317. https://doi.org/10.1016/0162-3095(88)90010-6

Buss, D. M. (1989). Sex differences in human mate preferences: Evolutionary hypotheses tested in 37 cultures. *Behavioral and Brain Sciences, 12*, 1–49.

Buss, D. M. (1998). Sexual strategies theory: Historical origins and current status. *Journal of Sex Research, 35*(1), 19–31. https://doi.org/10.1080/00224499809551914" https://doi.org/10.1080/0022449980 9551914

Buss, D. M. (2002). Human mate guarding. *Neuroendocrinology Letters, 23*(4), 23–29.

Buss, D. M. (2013). Sexual jealousy. *Psychological Topics, 22*, 155–182.

Buss, D. M. (2017). Sexual conflict in human mating. *Current Directions in Psychological Science, 26*(4), 307–313. https://doi.org/10.1177/0963721417695559

Buss, D. M., & Barnes, M. (1986). Preferences in human mate selection. *Journal of Personality and Social Psychology, 50*, 559–570. https://doi.org/10.1037/0022–3514.50.3.559

Buss, D. M., & Duntley, J. D. (2008). Adaptations for exploitation. *Group Dynamics: Theory, Research, and Practice, 12*, 53–62.

Buss, D. M., & Duntley, J. D. (2011). The evolution of intimate partner violence. *Aggression and Violent Behavior, 16*(5), 411–419. https://doi.org/10.1016/j.avb.2011.04.015

Buss, D. M., Goetz, C., Duntley, J. D., Asao, K., & Conroy-Beam, D. (2017). The mate switching hypothesis. *Personality and Individual Differences, 104*, 143–149. https://doi.org/10.1016/j.paid.2016.07.022

Buss, D. M., Larsen, R. J., Westen, D., & Semmelroth, J. (1992). Sex differences in jealousy: Evolution, physiology, and psychology. *Psychological Science, 3*, 251–255. https://doi.org/10.1111/j.1467–9280.1992.tb00038.x

Buss, D. M., & Schmitt, D. P. (1993). Sexual strategy theory—An evolutionary perspective on human mating. *Psychological Review, 100*(2), 204–232. https://doi.org/10.1037/0033-295X.100.2.204

Buss, D. M., & Schmitt, D. P. (2019). Mate preferences and their behavioral manifestations. *Annual Review of Psychology, 17*, 77–110. https://doi.org/10.1146/annurev-psych-010418–103408

Buss, D. M., & Shackelford, T. K. (1997). From vigilance to violence: Mate retention tactics in married couples. *Journal of Personality and Social Psychology, 72*(2), 346–361. https://doi.org/10.1037/0022-3514.72.2.346

Campbell, L., Simpson, J. A., Kashy, D. A., Fletcher G.J.O. (2001). Ideal standards, the self, and flexibility of ideals in close relationships. *Personality and Social Psychology Bulletin, 27*, 447–462.

Canary, D. J., & Yum, Y. O. (2015). Relationship maintenance strategies. In C. R. Berger, M. E. Roloff, S. R. Wilson, J. P. Dillard, J. Caughlin, & D. Solomon (Eds.), *The international encyclopedia of interpersonal communication* (pp. 1–9). John Wiley & Sons.

Chapman, T. (2015). Sexual conflict and evolutionary psychology: Towards a unified framework. In T. K. Shackelford & R. D. Hansen (Eds.), *The evolution of sexuality* (pp. 1–28). Springer International.

Clark, R. D., & Hatfield, E. (1989). Gender differences in receptivity to sexual offers. *Journal of Psychology & Human Sexuality, 2*(1), 39–55.

Conroy-Beam, D., & Buss, D. M. (2019). Why is age so important in human mating? Evolved age preferences and their influences on multiple mating behaviors. *Evolutionary Behavioral Sciences, 13*(2), 127. https://doi.org/10.1037/ebs0000127

Conroy-Beam, D., Buss, D. M., Asao, K., Sorokowska, A., Sorokowski, P., Aavik, T., Grace Akello, Mohammad Madallh Alhabahba, Charlotte Alm, Naumana Amjad, Afifa Anjum, Chiemezie S. Atama, Derya Atamtürk Duyar, Richard Ayebare, Carlota Batres, Mons Bendixen, Aicha Bensafia, Boris Bizumic, Mahmoud Boussena, . . . Maja Zupančič (2019). Contrasting computational models of mate preference integration across 45 countries. *Scientific Reports, 9*(1), 1–13. https://doi.org/10.1038/s41598-019-52748-8

Conroy-Beam, D., Goetz, C. D., & Buss, D. M. (2015). Why do humans form long-term mateships? An evolutionary game-theoretic model. In J. M. Olson & M. P. Zanna (Eds.), *Advances in experimental social psychology* (Vol. 51, pp. 1–39). Academic Press.

Conroy-Beam, D., Goetz, C. D., & Buss, D. M. (2016). What predicts romantic relationship satisfaction and mate retention intensity: Mate preference fulfillment or mate value discrepancies? *Evolution and Human Behavior, 37*(6), 440–448. https://doi.org/10.1016/j.evolhumbehav.2016.04.003

Conroy-Beam, D., Roney, J. R., Lukaszewski, A. W., Buss, D. M., Asao, K., Sorokowska, A., Sorokowski, P., Aavik, T., Akello, G., Alhabahba, M. M., Alm, C., Amjad, N., Anjum, A., Atama, C. S., Duyar, D. A., Ayebare, R., Batres, C., Bendixen, M., Bensafia, A. . . . Zupančič, M. (2019). Assortative mating and the evolution of desirability covariation. *Evolution and Human Behavior, 40*(5), 479–491. https://doi.org/10.1016/j.evolhumbehav.2019.06.003

Daly, M., Wilson, M., & Weghorst, S. J. (1982). Male sexual jealousy. *Ethology and Sociobiology, 3*, 11–27.

Duntley, J. D., & Buss, D. M. (2012). The evolution of stalking. *Sex Roles, 66*(5), 311–327. https://doi.org/10.1007/s11199-010-9832-0

Edlund, J. E., & Sagarin, B. J. (2017). Sex differences in jealousy: A 25-year retrospective. In M. O. James (Ed.), *Advances in experimental social psychology* (Vol. 55, pp. 259–302). Academic Press.

Fisher, H. E. (1989). Evolution of human serial pairbonding. *American Journal of Physical Anthropology, 78*(3), 331–354. https://doi.org/10.1002/ajpa.1330780303

Frank, R. H. (1988). *Passions within reason: The strategic role of the emotions.* W. W. Norton.

Frank, R. H. (2001). Cooperation through emotional commitment. In R. M. Nesse (Ed.), *Evolution and the capacity for commitment* (pp. 57–76). Russell Sage.

Frederick, D. A., & Fales, M. R. (2016). Upset over sexual versus emotional infidelity among gay, lesbian, bisexual, and heterosexual adults. *Archives of Sexual Behavior, 45*(1), 175–191. https://doi.org/10.1007/s10508-014-0409-9

Friesen, M. D., Fletcher, G. J. O., & Overall, N. C. (2005). A dyadic assessment of forgiveness in intimate relationships. *Personal Relationships, 12*(1), 61–77. https://doi.org/10.1111/j.1350-4126.2005.00102.x

Gettler, L. T., McDade, T. W., Feranil, A. B., & Kuzawa, C. W. (2011). Longitudinal evidence that fatherhood decreases testosterone in human males. *Proceedings of the National Academy of Sciences, 108*(39), 16194–16199. https://doi.org/10.1073/pnas.1105403108

Goetz, A.T., & Shackelford, T. K. (2006). Sexual coercion and forced in-pair copulation as sperm competition tactics in humans. *Human Nature, 17*(3), 265–282. https://doi.org/10.1007/s12110-006-1009-8

Goetz, A. T., & Shackelford, T. K. (2009a). Sexual coercion in intimate relationships: A comparative analysis of the effects of women's infidelity and men's dominance and control. *Archives of Sexual Behavior, 38*(2), 226–234. https://doi.org/10.1007/s10508-008-9353-x

Goetz, A. T., & Shackelford, T. K. (2009b). Sexual conflict in humans: Evolutionary consequences of asymmetric parental investment and paternity uncertainty. *Animal Biology, 59*, 449–456. https://doi.org/10.1163/157075509X12499949744342

Gonzaga, G. C., Turner, R. A., Keltner, D., Campos, B., & Altemus, M. (2006), Romantic love and sexual desire in close relationships. *Emotion, 6*, 163–179

Grøntvedt ,T. V. and L. E. O. Kennair, L. E. O. (2013). Age preferences in a gender egalitarian society. *Journal of Social, Evolutionary, and Cultural Psychology*, 7(3), 239–249.

Grøntvedt, T. V., Kennair, L. E. O., & Bendixen, M. (2019). How intercourse frequency is affected by relationship length, relationship quality, and sexual strategies using couple data. *Evolutionary Behavioral Sciences, 14*(2), 147–159. https://doi.org/10.1037/ebs0000173

Grøntvedt, T. V., Kennair, L. E. O., & Bendixen, M. (2020). Breakup likelihood following hypothetical sexual or emotional infidelity: Perceived threat, blame, and forgiveness. *Journal of Relationships Research, 11*, Article e7. https://doi.org/10.1017/jrr.2020.5

Grøntvedt, T. V., Kennair, L. E. O., & Mehmetoglu, M. (2015). Factors predicting the probability of initiating sexual intercourse by context and sex. *Scandinavian Journal of Psychology, 56*(5), 516–526. https://doi.org/10.1111/sjop.12215

Hall, J. H., & Fincham, F. D. (2006). Relationship dissolution following infidelity: The roles of attributions and forgiveness. *Journal of Social and Clinical Psychology, 25*(5), 508–522. https://doi.org/10.1521/jscp.2006.25.5.508

Haselton, M. G., & Buss, D. M. (2000). Error management theory: A new perspective on biases in cross-sex mind reading. *Journal of Personality and Social Psychology, 78*(1), 81–91. https://doi.org/10.1037/0022-3514.78.1.81

Haselton, M. G., & Nettle, D. (2006). The paranoid optimist: An integrative evolutionary model of cognitive biases. *Personality and Social Psychology Review, 10*(1), 47–66. https://doi.org/10.1207/s15327957pspr1001_3

Haupert, M. L., Gesselman, A. N., Moors, A. C., Fisher, H. E., & Garcia, J. R. (2017). Prevalence of experiences with consensual nonmonogamous relationships: Findings from two national samples of single Americans. *Journal of Sex & Marital Therapy, 43*(5), 424–440. https://doi.org/10.1080/0092623X.2016.1178675

Hirshleifer, J. (1987). On emotions as guarantors of threats and promises. In J. Dupre (Ed.), *The latest on the best: Essays on evolution and optimality* (pp. 307–326). MIT Press.

Hughes, S. M., Aung, T., Harrison, M. A., LaFayette, J. N., & Gallup Jr., G. G. (2020). Experimental evidence for sex differences in sexual variety preferences: Support for the Coolidge Effect in humans. *Archives of Sexual Behavior, 50*(2), 495–509. https://doi.org/10.1007/s10508-020-01730-x

Jokela, M., Rotkirch, A., Rickard, I. J., Pettay, J., & Lummaa, V. (2010). Serial monogamy increases reproductive success in men but not in women. *Behavioral Ecology, 21*(5), 906–912.

Kaighobadi, F., Shackelford, T. K., & Buss, D. M. (2010). Spousal mate retention in the newlywed year and three years later. *Personality and Individual Differences, 48*(4), 414–418. https://doi.org/10.1016/j.paid.2009.11.008

Kaighobadi, F., Starratt, V. G., Shackelford, T. K., & Popp, D. (2008). Male mate retention mediates the relationship between female sexual infidelity and female-directed violence. *Personality and Individual Differences, 44*(6), 1422–1431. https://doi.org/10.1016/j.paid.2007.12.010

Kennair, L. E. O., Bendixen, M., & Buss, D. M. (2016). Sexual regret: Tests of competing explanations of sex differences. *Evolutionary Psychology, 14*(4), 1–9. http://doi.org/10.1177/1474704916682903

Kennair, L. E. O., Grøntvedt, T. V., & Bendixen, M. (2021). The function of casual sex action and inaction regret: A longitudinal investigation. *Evolutionary Psychology*. https://doi.org/10.1177/1474704921998333

Kennair, L. E. O., Nordeide, J., Andreassen, S., Strønen, J., & Pallesen, S. (2011). Sex differences in jealousy: A study from Norway. *Nordic Psychology, 63*(1), 20–34. https://doi.org/10.1027/1901-2276/a000025

Kennair, L. E. O., Schmitt, D. P., Fjeldavli, Y. L., & Harlem, S. K. (2009). Sex differences in sexual desires and attitudes in Norwegian samples. *Interpersona, 3*, 1–32. https://doi.org/10.5964/ijpr.v3isupp1.67 https://doi.org/10.1177/1474704916682903

Kennair, L. E. O., Wyckoff, J. P., Asao, K., Buss, D. M., & Bendixen, M. (2018). Why do women regret casual sex more than men do? *Personality and Individual Differences, 127*, 61–67. https://doi.org/10.1016/j.paid.2018.01.044

Kreider, R. M. (2005). Number, Timing, and Duration of Marriages and Divorces: 2001. Current Population Reports, P70-97. U.S. Census Bureau, Washington, DC.

Labrecque, L. T., & Whisman, M. A. (2017). Attitudes toward and prevalence of extramarital sex and descriptions of extramarital partners in the 21st century. *Journal of Family Psychology, 31*(7), 952.

Levine, E. C., Herbenick, D., Martinez, O., Fu, T. C., & Dodge, B. (2018). Open relationships, nonconsensual nonmonogamy, and monogamy among US adults: Findings from the 2012 National Survey of Sexual Health and Behavior. *Archives of sexual behavior, 47*(5), 1439–1450. https://doi.org/10.1007/s10508-018-1178-7

Li, N. P., Bailey, J. M., Kenrick, D. T., & Linsenmeier, J. A. W. (2002). The necessities and luxuries of mate preferences: Testing the tradeoffs. *Journal of Personality and Social Psychology, 82*(6), 947–955.

Li, N. P., Sng, O., & Jonason, P. K. (2012). Sexual conflict in mating strategies. In T. K. Shackelford & A. T. Goetz (Eds.), *The Oxford handbook of sexual conflict in humans*. Oxford University Press.

Lydon, J. E., Fitzsimons, G. M., & Naidoo, L. (2003). Devaluation versus enhancement of attractive alternatives: A critical test using the calibration paradigm. *Personality and Social Psychology Bulletin, 29*, 349–359

Magnus, M. C., Wilcox, A. J., Morken, N.-H., Weinberg, C. R., & Håberg, S. E. (2019). Role of maternal age and pregnancy history in risk of miscarriage: Prospective register based study. *British Medical Journal, 364*, Article I869. https://doi.org/10.1136/bmj.l869

Marlowe, F. W. (2003). A critical period for provisioning by Hadza men: Implications for pair bonding. *Evolution and Human Behavior, 24*(3), 217–229. https://doi.org/10.1016/S1090-5138(03)00014-X

McCullough, M. E., Rachal, K. C., Sandage, S. J., Worthington, E. L., Jr., Brown, S. W., & Hight, T. L. (1998). Interpersonal forgiving in close relationships: II. Theoretical elaboration and measurement. *Journal of Personality and Social Psychology, 75*(6), 1586–1603.

McCullough, M. E., Worthington Jr, E. L., & Rachal, K. C. (1997). Interpersonal forgiving in close relationships. *Journal of Personality and Social Psychology, 73*(2), 321–336. https://doi.org/10.1037/0022-3514.73.2.321

McNulty, J. K., & Fisher, T. D. (2008). Gender differences in response to sexual expectancies and changes in sexual frequency: A short-term longitudinal study of sexual satisfaction in newly married couples. *Archives of Sexual Behavior, 37*(2), 229–240. https://doi.org/10.1007/s10508-007-9176-1

McNulty, J. K., Maxwell, J. A., Meltzer, A. L., & Baumeister, R. F. (2019). Sex-differentiated changes in sexual desire predict marital dissatisfaction. *Archives of Sexual Behavior, 48*(8), 2473–2489. https://doi.org/10.1007/s10508-019-01471-6

Mikulincer, M., & Shaver, P. R. (2007). *Attachment in adulthood: Structure, dynamics, and change.* Guilford Press.
Mogilski, J. K., Memering, S. L., Welling, L. L. M., & Shackelford, T. K. (2017). Monogamy versus consensual non-monogamy: Alternative approaches to pursuing a strategically pluralistic mating strategy. *Archives of Sexual Behavior, 46*(2), 407–417. https://doi.org/10.1007/s10508-015-0658-2
Morris, C. E., Reiber, C., & Roman, E. (2015). Quantitative sex differences in response to the dissolution of a romantic relationship. *Evolutionary Behavioral Sciences, 9*(4), 270–282. https://doi.org/10.1037/ebs0000054
Mulder, M. B., & Rauch, K. L. (2009). Sexual conflict in humans: Variations and solutions. *Evolutionary Anthropology: Issues, News, and Reviews, 18*(5), 201–214. https://doi.org/10.1002/evan.20226
Ogolsky, B. G., Monk, J. K., Rice, T. M., Theisen, J. C., & Maniotes, C. R. (2017). Relationship maintenance: A review of research on romantic relationships. *Journal of Family Theory & Review, 9*(3), 275–306. https://doi.org/10.1111/jftr.12205
Parker, G. A. (1979). Sexual selection and sexual conflict. In M. S. Blum & N. A. Blum (Eds.), *Sexual selection and reproductive competition in insects* (pp. 123–166). Academic Press.
Parker, G. A. (2006). Sexual conflict over mating and fertilization: An overview. *Philosophical Transactions of the Royal Society B-Biological Sciences, 361*(1466), 235–259. https://doi.org/10.1098/rstb.2005.1785" https://doi.org/10.1098/rstb.2005.1785
Peplau, L. A. (2003). Human sexuality: How do men and women differ? *Current directions in psychological science, 12*(2), 37–40. https://doi.org/10.1111/1467-8721.01221
Pollet, T. V., Pratt, S. E., Edwards, G., & Stulp, G. (2013). The golden years: Men from the Forbes 400 have much younger wives when remarrying than the general US population. *Letters on Evolutionary Behavioral Science, 4*(1), 5–8.
Sagarin, B. J., Martin, A. L., Coutinho, S. A., Edlund, J. E., Patel, L., Skowronski, J. J., & Zengel, B. (2012). Sex differences in jealousy: A meta-analytic examination. *Evolution and Human Behavior, 33*(6), 595–614. https://doi.org/10.1016/j.evolhumbehav.2012.02.006
Scelza, B. A., Prall, S. P., Blumenfield, T., Crittenden, A. N., Gurven, M., Kline, M., Koster, J., Kushnick, G., Mattison, S. M., Pillsworth, E., Shenk, M. K., Starkweather, K., Stieglitz, J., Sum, C. Y., Yamaguchi, K., & McElreath, R. (2020). Patterns of paternal investment predict cross-cultural variation in jealous response. *Nature Human Behaviour, 4*(1), 20–26. https://doi.org/10.1038/s41562-019-0654-y
Schmitt, D. P. (2004). Patterns and universals of mate poaching across 53 nations: The effects of sex, culture, and personality on romantically attracting another person's partner. *Journal of Personality and Social Psychology, 86*(4), 560–584. https://doi.org/10.1037/0022-3514.86.4.560
Schmitt, D. P. (2005a). Is short-term mating the maladaptive result of insecure attachment? A test of competing evolutionary perspectives. *Personality and Social Psychology Bulletin, 31*(6), 747–768. https://doi.org/10.1177/0146167204271843
Schmitt, D. P. (2005b). Sociosexuality from Argentina to Zimbabwe: A 48-nation study of sex, culture, and strategies of human mating. *Behavioral and Brain Sciences, 28*(2), 247–311. https://doi.org/10.1017/s0140525x05000051
Schmitt, D. P., & Buss, D. M. (2001). Human mate poaching: Tactics and temptations for infiltrating existing mateships. *Journal of Personality and Social Psychology, 80*(6), 894. https://doi.org/10.1037/0022-3514.80.6.894
Sela, Y., Mogilski, J. K., Shackelford, T. K., Zeigler-Hill, V., & Fink, B. (2017). Mate value discrepancy and mate retention behaviors of self and partner. *Journal of Personality, 85*(5), 730–740. https://doi.org/10.1111/jopy.12281
Shackelford, T. K., & Buss, D. M. (2000). Marital satisfaction and spousal cost-infliction. *Personality and Individual Differences, 28*(5), 917–928. https://doi.org/10.1016/S0191–8869(99)00150–6
Shackelford, T. K., & Goetz, A. T. (2007). Adaptation to sperm competition in humans. *Current Directions in Psychological Science, 16*(1), 47–50. https://doi.org/10.1111/j.1467–8721.2007.00473.x
Shrout, M. R., & Weigel, D. J. (2019). "Should I stay or should I go?" Understanding the noninvolved partner's decision-making process following infidelity. *Journal of Social and Personal Relationships, 36*(2), 400–420. https://doi.org/10.1177/0265407517733335
Skinner, B. F. (1981). Selection by consequences. *Science, 213*(4507), 501–504.
Stumpf, R. M., Martinez-Mota, R., Milich, K. M., Righini, N., & Shattuck, M. R. (2011). Sexual conflict in primates. *Evolutionary Anthropology: Issues, News, and Reviews, 20*(2), 62–75. https://doi.org/10.1002/evan.20297

Surbey, M. K., & Conohan, C. D. (2000). Willingness to engage in casual sex: The role of parental qualities and perceived risk of aggression. *Human Nature, 11*, 367–386.

Swets, J. A., Dawes, R. M., & Monahan, J. (2000). Psychological science can improve diagnostic decisions. *Psychological Science in the Public Interest, 1*, 1–26. https://doi.org/10.1111/1529–1006.001

Thomas, A. G., Jonason, P. K., Blackburn, J. D., Kennair, L. E. O., Lowe, R., Malouff, J., Stewart-Williams, S., Sulikowski, D., & Li, N. P. (2020). Mate preference priorities in the East and West: A cross-cultural test of the mate preference priority model. *Journal of Personality, 88*, 606–620. https://doi.org/ 10.1111/jopy.12514.

Trivers, R. L. (1972). Parental investment and sexual selection. In B. Cambell (Ed.), *Sexual selection and the descent of man: 1871–1971* (pp. 139–179). Aldine.

Trivers, R. L. (1974). Parent-offspring conflict. *American Zoologist, 14*(1), 249–264. https://doi.org/10.1093/icb/14.1.249

Vandermassen, G. (2011). Evolution and rape: A feminist Darwinian perspective. *Sex Roles, 64*, 732–747.

Wade, T. J., Salerno, K., & Moran, J. (2018). Sexual conflict after conception. In T. K. Shackelford & V. A. Weekes-Shackelford (Eds.), *Encyclopedia of evolutionary psychological science* (pp. 1–8). Springer International.

Walter, K. V., Conroy-Beam, D., Buss, D. M., Asao, K., Sorokowska, A., Sorokowski, P., Aavik, T., Akello, G., Alhabahba, M. M., Alm, C., Amjad, N., Anjum, A., Atama, C. S., Duyar, D. A., Ayebare, R., Batres, C., Bendixen, M., Bensafia, A., Bizumic, B. . . . & Zupančič, M. (2020). Sex differences in mate preferences across 45 countries: A large-scale replication. *Psychological Science, 31*(4), 408–423. https://doi.org/10.1177/0956797620904154

Walter, K. V., Conroy-Beam, D., Buss, D. M., Asao, K., Sorokowska, A., Sorokowski, P., Aavik, T., Akello, G., Alhabahba, M. M., Alm, C., Amjad, N., Anjum, A., Atama, C. S., Duyar, D. A., Ayebare, R., Batres, C., Bendixen, M., Bensafia, A., Bizumic, B. . . . Zupančič, M. (2021). Sex differences in human mate preferences vary across sex ratios. *Proceedings of the Royal Society: B*, 288, Article 20211115.

Weiner, B. (1995). *Judgments of responsibility: A foundation for a theory of social conduct*. Guilford Press.

Wiederman, M. W. (1997). Extramarital sex: Prevalence and correlates in a national survey. *The Journal of Sex Research, 34*(2), 167–174. https://doi.org/10.1080/00224499709551881" https://doi.org/10.1080/00224499709551881

Willoughby, B. J., Farero, A. M., & Busby, D. M. (2014). Exploring the effects of sexual desire discrepancy among married couples. *Archives of Sexual Behavior, 43*(3), 551–562. https://doi.org/10.1007/s10508-013-0181-2

Willoughby, B. J., & Vitas, J. (2012). Sexual desire discrepancy: The effect of individual differences in desired and actual sexual frequency on dating couples. *Archives of Sexual Behavior, 41*(2), 477–486. https://doi.org/10.1007/s10508-011-9766-9

CHAPTER

12 Jealousy in Close Relationships From an Evolutionary and Cultural Perspective: Responding to Real and Feared Rivals

Abraham P. Buunk *and* Karlijn Massar

Abstract

Jealousy occurs when one feels an actual or potential intimate relationship is threatened by a real or imagined rival. This chapter shows that the psychological experience of jealousy is associated with physical and hormonal characteristics. Particularly, the focus is on the distinction between possessive jealousy and reactive jealousy in humans and other species. Possessive jealousy is a preventive reaction that often results in mate guarding. Among human males, possessive jealousy aims to prevent investment in offspring sired by another male, whereas among human females, it seems to have evolved to obtain and preserve the investment of males in offspring and for disease avoidance. Possessive jealousy is related to cultural factors, such as parental control of mate choice, life history (in particular attachment style and father absence), and domestic violence. Regarding reactive jealousy (i.e., the responses to actual sexual and emotional intimacy with a third person), we discuss sex differences in emotional versus sexual jealousy, how reactive jealousy is experienced, and the variables to which it is related. Jealousy implies by definition a rival, and assessing the threat of a rival is a basic, adaptive mechanism rooted in intrasexual competition. This aspect of jealousy may also occur when one has not yet established a relationship but is trying to obtain a mate. In the context of the evaluation of rivals, we focus in particular on sex differences and similarities in the rival characteristics that evoke jealousy among heterosexual, homosexual, and transgender men and women.

Key Words: possessive jealousy, reactive jealousy, rival characteristics, mate guarding, intrasexual competition

The adaptive value of jealousy

The desire to engage in extradyadic sex and romance is common in the human species. Hicks and Leitenberg (2001) found, in a diverse sample of university students and employees ages 18 to 70 years, that 87% of their respondents (98% of men and 80% of women) reported having had extradyadic sexual fantasies in the past two months. In a substantial number of cases, such fantasies are translated into actual extradyadic sexual involvement, including one-night stands, passionate love affairs, mate exchange, flirting, and sex with prostitutes (Buunk et al., 2018). Recent studies in representative Western samples suggest that only between 22% and 25% of men and 11% and 15% of women have ever engaged in extramarital sex, and in most cases only once (Allen et al., 2005). However, there are substantial cultural differences in the prevalence of extradyadic sexual behavior. For example, extramarital sex is more prevalent in African than in Asian and Western countries. One study showed that estimates of extramarital sex in the past year range from 38% for men and 19% for women in Guinea Bissau (e.g., Caraël et al., 1995), compared with 11% for men and 4.5% of women in China (Zhang et al., 2012). The incidence of extramarital sex seems especially low in Muslim countries, probably due to the severe sanctions on this behavior (Adamczyk & Hayes, 2012).

In recent years, due to the internet, it has become much easier for people to engage in all kinds of extradyadic sexual and erotic involvement (Mileham, 2007), including meeting new partners and engaging in sexualized conversations or sexual behaviors, with or without a webcam (e.g., Young et al., 2000). When discovered by a partner, such experiences may evoke—usually intense—feelings of jealousy in the partner, just as they do in offline extradyadic emotional or sexual/erotic involvement (cf. Whitty, 2003). From an evolutionary perspective, there has been an arms race between the desire to engage in extradyadic sexual and intimate relationships and partners' attempts to prevent or stop the realization of such desires. Jealousy is most often evoked in response to the actual, imagined, or suspected extradyadic involvement of one's partner, including nowadays contacting or communicating intimately through the internet and social media, with potential rivals (e.g., Dijkstra et al., 2010). Jealousy implies that one feels threatened by the loss of a partner's sexual or romantic exclusiveness, and it may involve feelings such as fear, suspicion, distrust, anxiety, and anger, betrayal, rejection, threat, and loneliness (e.g., Buunk & Dijkstra, 2004).

However, individuals may not only experience jealousy because of the appearance of a new rival but also because of a partner's contact with a previous partner (i.e., "ex")—especially if they were left by their ex and still have strong feelings for them. Jealousy can also arise when one does not currently have a close relationship but notices the apparent happiness that a previous partner is experiencing in a new relationship. Finally, jealousy does not imply necessarily the existence of a current or previous close relationship but may also occur when one vies for a partner and notices a rival to whom the desired partner is attracted. Although jealousy is probably most intense and volatile in close relationships, it may also occur in friendships and in relationships at work (e.g., Buunk et al., 2010; Zurriaga et al., 2018).

Although there are many examples of related behaviors elsewhere in the animal kingdom, human jealousy is special due to the unique reproductive strategies of the human species. Even though humans and chimpanzees evolved out of a common ancestor, their reproductive behaviors vary considerably: chimpanzees have promiscuous sexual relationships, whereas humans engage in more or less stable pair relationships. Human pair-bonding probably evolved because human offspring are relatively helpless during the first years of life, and unable to survive without the support of both parents. Unique to humans is the role of fathers: while investment in offspring is high for females in both species—in most mammals even—human males tend to invest more in their offspring than chimpanzee males. However, the evidence from hunter–gatherer societies suggests that in our ancestral past the contribution of males to child care and food provision to their mates and offspring must not be overrated. Probably, the benefit of a pair-bond for females was particularly that males protected their mates from predators, from other males, and from other hostile groups.

Types of Jealousy

Beginning with the work of Freud (1923), in the clinical literature a distinction has been made between normal or rational jealousy stemming from a realistic threat to the relationship, and abnormal, pathological, or morbid jealousy that is aroused in the absence of such a threat. Relatedly, within social psychology two typologies have been proposed each of which distinguishes among three types of jealousy. Pfeiffer and Wong (1989) made a distinction among *emotional* jealousy, which entails feelings such as fear, anger, insecurity, and sadness; *cognitive* jealousy, which consists of paranoid thoughts and worries about the behavior of one's partner; and *behavioral* jealousy, which involves jealous actions such as spying on one's partner or rummaging through their belongings. In a related vein, Buunk (1991, 1997) made a distinction among *reactive* jealousy, a direct response to an actual relationship threat, for instance, when one's partner is flirting or having sex with someone else; *anxious* jealousy, which refers to an active cognitive process in which the individual generates images of their partner becoming sexually or emotionally involved with someone else and experiences feelings of anxiety, suspicion, worry, distrust, and upset; and *possessive* or *preventive* jealousy, which is a manifestation of mate guarding and refers to the considerable effort jealous individuals may invest to prevent contact of their partner with a third person, such as by opposing their partner's contact with opposite-sex individuals. Thus, although reactive jealousy is a response to an actual threat, possessive jealousy is a response to a potential threat. Both Pfeiffer and Wong's and Buunk's typology takes into account that jealousy may not only occur in response to an actual threat to the relationship but also in the absence of such a threat. In the present chapter, we focus in particular on reactive jealousy and possessive jealousy as defined by Buunk, and on how these phenomena are related to, respectively, intrasexual competition and mate guarding.

Possessive Jealousy

From an evolutionary perspective, possessive jealousy among humans has its roots partly in mate guarding. Mate guarding is observed among both males and females in many species, and even the well-known tendency of many species to defend their territories may in fact be a consequence of individuals guarding the sexual rights to their mates (Barash & Lipton, 2002). Mate guarding among males has evolved because it is essential to guarantee paternity certainty: males who did not allow their partners to mate with other males were evidently reproductively more successful than males who did not pay attention to their mate's extradyadic sexual behavior. This explains why mate guarding has evolved in many species, even though it is an energetically costly activity and may co-opt psychological adaptations that assist in predator avoidance and foraging (e.g., Alberts et al., 1996).

In avian species, male mate guarding includes close following and surveilling the female. For example, the socially monogamous male bank swallows (*Riparia riparia*) who assist their mates in building a nest and incubating and feeding young, pursue the female for seven to nine days after pair formation whenever she leaves the nest, which may occur as often as 100 times a day (Barash & Lipton, 2002). Mate guarding may also be expressed through aggression toward other males, especially when they are an important threat (e.g., they are in the possession of prey; Mougeot et al., 2006). In species that live in multimale, multifemale groups, including savannah baboons (*Papio papio*) and chimpanzees (*Pan troglodytes*), mate guarding typically takes place in consortships, where males engage in frequent sexual activity and follow the female to exclude other males from access to the female. In this type of group, most of the mate guarding is done by high-status males, to prevent sneak copulations by other males. For example, one study showed that among mandrills (*Mandrillus sphinx*), high-status males accounted for 94% of periovulatory mate guarding, with apparent reproductive success, as these males accounted for 69% of the paternity (Setchell et al., 2005). In species where males invest much in their offspring, such as many bird species and humans, failure to mate guard becomes even more costly, as males risk investing their resources in the offspring of another male (Barash & Lipton, 2002). Nevertheless, according to parental investment theory (Trivers, 1972), all males should have some interest in controlling the fidelity of their mates, even under conditions of high female promiscuity.

There is abundant evidence for the occurrence of mate guarding by males in the human species (e.g., Buss, 1989). In his now-classic review, Murdock (1967) noted that only 4 of 849 societies did not show any sign of mate guarding (i.e., keeping close tabs on their mates, sometimes even when she is urinating or defecating). The absence of seasonality and the recurrence of ovulation at relatively short intervals make guarding of the female very important for males, as they have much to gain by the tremendous investment by a female in their offspring, and much to lose if she becomes pregnant through an extradyadic affair. Indeed, throughout history and in many cultures, all kinds of rules, behavioral practices, and physical measures—including veiling, walled courtyards, and genital mutilation—have been used to prevent contact between women and potential sexual partners (Dickemann, 1997). In claustrating societies, adulterous women may suffer severe penalties, including murder, which are considered "crimes of honor." According to Dickemann, one of the core social meanings of notions of "honor" and "shame" is the defense of the chastity and fidelity of female kin. Shackelford et al. (2006) showed that among humans, mate-guarding tactics such as vigilance, mate concealment, and monopolization of a mate's time were correlated with a higher frequency of intra-pair copulations, even when controlling for various potentially confounding variables such as relationship length, time spent together, and relationship satisfaction, suggesting that these constitute concurrent strategies of assuring paternity certainty.

It has sometimes been overlooked that in socially monogamous species, females may also engage in mate guarding for a number of reasons. Female burying beetles (*Nicrophorus vespilloides*) will "beat up" mates who attempt to attract other females. In socially monogamous birds, female mate guarding also occurs frequently and functions to avoid desertion, to prevent sperm depletion, or to reduce the risk of disease and parasite transmission as a consequence of the male's copulation with another female (Lazarus et al., 2004). Humans are no different: Burbank (1987) surveyed 137 societies in the Human Relations Area File and concluded that men were the single most frequent reason for female–female fights (121 of 297 for which reasons were recorded). Campbell (2013) has extensively documented that women often compete heavily with each other over access to males, which may result in assaults against other females. Although a woman does not suffer from uncertainty concerning the maternity of her offspring, a partner's infidelity may include other risks. First, she may contract a sexually transmitted disease, a considerable risk as more than 50% of the cases of infertility are the result of such a disease. Second, she may have to share her partner's resources with another woman, and, even more threatening, she runs the risk that her partner will direct all his support to another partner.

Possessive Jealousy and Freedom of Mate Choice

Despite the fact that the tendency to prevent one's spouse from becoming sexually involved with a rival seems to be a universal characteristic of males and females, it seems that there are considerable cultural differences in this regard (e.g., Hupka, 1981). For example, in Western cultures, most husbands do not actively and aggressively try to prevent contacts between their wife and other men, and a substantial minority of husbands accept a moderate degree of flirting by their wife (Buunk & Hupka, 1987). Although there are many cultural factors that may affect possessive jealousy, there is recent evidence that an important factor influencing this type of jealousy is the degree to which one can freely choose one's spouse. Freedom of mate choice is not a universal feature of human mating. Instead, there is considerable evidence that in most societies and historical periods, marriage has been at least partly arranged and has been based on a series of familial and community considerations rather than on the desires of the individuals concerned (e.g., Harris, 1995; Murstein, 1974; Reiss, 1980). Historical and anthropological evidence suggests that parents have often been wary of love-based unions among their children—indeed, they have been wary of their children's experience of love itself (e.g., Murstein, 1974; Reiss, 1980). In China, for example, love was historically condemned as a potential instigator of filial disobedience that could destroy the family (Theodorson, 1965). Cross-culturally, there is a substantial negative correlation between the presence of arranged marriage and emphasis on romantic love; that is, in cultures in which marriages are arranged, romantic love is viewed less positively (Williams et al., 1979). Apostolou (2007) reported data from 190 hunting and gathering societies and showed that in 70% of the societies, marriage was arranged by parents and other kin; only in 4% of societies was courtship the primary form of marriage. Further, Walker et al. (2011) conducted comparative phylogenetic analyses on modern hunter–gatherers and report a long history of regulated exchange of mates and resources between families, tracing back to early modern humans. These authors suggest that this influence on children's mate choice very likely functioned to regulate human metagroup social structures (e.g., forging coalitions and alliances across communities). Of course, the presence of arranged marriages does not rule out the possibility that children may exert their preferences—by influencing the parents' decisions, for example—but it does suggest that the tendency of parents to control the mate choice of their offspring was quite widespread in our evolutionary past.

In a setting where parents choose one's spouse, despite the vigilance of the community and family, people may experience more uncertainty that the other will not engage in an extradyadic sexual relationship than in a setting in which the partner is in the marriage by his or her own volition. Of course, in both settings one may have to be attentive to the possibility of rivals trying to lure away one's partner for either a long-term relationship or for casual sex (Dijkstra & Buunk, 2002). The rates of extradyadic sex are likely not higher in settings where one's parents choose one's spouse (see, e.g., Nowak et al. 2014). But in the case of an "assigned" spouse, infidelity of one's spouse may be perceived as more likely. There may be a mismatch in preferences and attitudes between the spouses, which would enhance relationship dissatisfaction, and in turn this could make individuals consider extradyadic sex or intimacy to resolve this dissatisfaction. If one knows that a spouse did not enter the marriage out of love, one may perceive a high risk that the spouse will become sexually involved or fall in love with someone else. When one knows one's spouse married one out of love, there is (especially in the early stages of the relationship) less reason to be concerned about him or her seeking passion or love elsewhere. Consider, for example, the situation of a man of the Yanomamö of Venezuela, where mate selection has been described as "a political process in which girls are promised in marriage at an early age by men who are attempting to create alliances with other men via marriage alliances" (Chagnon, 1992, p. 8). When married to a woman as part of an exchange between males, a man may feel he has to guard this "property" zealously, because she has not married out of her own volition. The man may not so much run the risk that she leaves him because in cultures with arranged marriages there are usually many sanctions against women who want to leave their husband. But he may yet run the risk, due to short-term sexual infidelity of his wife, of investing in the offspring of another man.

In arranged marriages, women may also engage in more mate guarding than in marriages that are the result of free mate choice. First, women in arranged marriages may perceive their husband in general as relatively more likely to engage in extradyadic sex. Second, women may have more to lose in societies with arranged marriages than in societies with love-based marriages. In both types of societies, women lose the support of their husband, who will invest his resources in another woman. However, in societies with arranged marriages, there is usually a severe societal stigma attached to divorced women, due to which women may obtain little support from other community members and become less attractive as a wife to a new man (Burbank, 1987). Thus, under high levels of parental influence on mate choice, both sexes may suffer in their reproductive opportunities when their spouse is unfaithful. In a study by Buunk and Castro Solano (2012) among international students in The Netherlands, clear support was found for this prediction. The level of possessive jealousy expressed by an individual was quite strongly related to the degree to which parents in his or her culture of origin had control over the mate choice of their children. That is, possessive jealousy was higher for those perceiving higher levels of parental control of mate choice. Of course, such an association may be due to the fact that both variables are influenced by another variable, such as cultural differences in collectivism and individualism. Generally, parental control over mate choice is higher in highly collectivistic cultures, but Buunk and Park (2010) found that when controlling for various forms of collectivism, the effect of parental control over mate choice on levels of possessive jealousy remained highly significant. Thus, individuals do indeed feel a need to possessively guard the behavior of their partner more when he or she is assigned to them rather than when he or she has chosen to marry them out of free choice. Put differently, freedom of mate choice seems to make possessive jealousy less necessary.

Possessive Jealousy and Domestic Violence

Possessive jealousy, or mate guarding more generally, has been linked in many studies and case reports to domestic violence among men. For example, already nearly 40 years ago, Martin (1983) described how a woman was locked up in her bedroom every morning by her husband before he left for work. He took away all her clothes, and just in case she might consider escaping into the street naked, he wired the door handle with electricity. In his classic book on intimate violence, Gelles (1974) noted that male jealousy often takes the form of interrogations with an aura of Gestapo violence. In one of the most extensive textbooks on family violence, Barnettet al. (2005) noted that "clinicians, researchers, social service agencies, police, and victims have all recognized that jealousy often becomes entwined . . ." with intimate partner violence (p. 438). In line with this, Graham-Kevan and Archer (2009) showed that in relationships where the woman was fecund, more controlling behaviors by the male partner were reported. These authors also showed, however, that both sexes—especially those of lower mate value—reported equal amounts of controlling behavior, which in turn predicted physical aggression toward their partner.

Some studies in convenience samples have supported a statistical association between male sexual jealousy and intimate partner violence (e.g., Russell & Wells, 2000), sometimes especially against pregnant partners (e.g., Chan et al., 2011), and other studies have found an association between women's reports of their partner's jealousy and being the victim of intimate partner violence (e.g., Hellmuth et al., 2013). In an extensive study among 453 representative couples, for both men and women controlling and jealous behaviors perpetrated by and experienced by each partner were together the strongest predictors of intimate partner violence (O'Leary et al., 2007). Nevertheless, few other studies in community samples have demonstrated correlations between self-reported jealousy and intimate partner violence. For example, in a study among 199 adult men and 201 women from the Rio San Juan Department in Nicaragua, one of the poorest areas in Latin America, possessive jealousy was *not* at all associated with intimate partner violence among men, while other factors such as a fast life history, intrasexual competitiveness, and a low mate value were. Among women, only intrasexual competitiveness was associated with intimate partner violence (Buunk & Massar, 2019). This finding is in line with the findings of Johnson et al. (2015), who showed that intimate partner violence among women peaks around age 20—which is also the age at which intrasexual competition peaks (e.g., Massar et al., 2012; Fernandez et al., 2014). Further, a systematic review by Bair-Merritt et al. (2010) indicates that not being able to get the partner's attention was a strong motivation for women to commit intimate partner violence. Other recent research has also not found an association between jealousy and intimate partner violence (e.g., Belus et al., 2014). These findings are noteworthy given the fact that jealousy is considered by many scholars and practitioners to be a major determinant of intimate partner violence, and may imply that the importance of jealousy in fostering intimate partner violence may have been somewhat overrated, and that other variables (e.g., intrasexual competition among women) may be better predictors.

Possessive Jealousy and Attachment

Attachment theory focuses on the effect of insecurity in the attachment to one's parents on one's relationship as an adult. According to this theory, particularly individuals with an anxious attachment style will more likely interpret extradyadic sexual behavior of their spouse in terms of abandonment, and will therefore have a lower threshold for jealousy. Intimate partner violence and jealousy are both associated with one's attachment style. For example, Holtzworth-Munroe et al. (1997) reported that compared to nonviolent husbands, violent men were more insecure, anxious, and preoccupied in their attachment style and reported more dependency on and preoccupation with their wives. Finally, they also reported higher levels of jealousy and less trust in their marriages. Few studies have examined the relationship between adult jealousy and attachment history in terms of objective indicators, such as separation from a parent during childhood. Using the scales developed by Buunk (1997), Van Brummen-Girigori et al. (2016) investigated jealousy among women on Curaçao, a Caribbean island where relatively many children grow up without a father in the home. This study showed that women who during childhood were abandoned by their father, reported significantly more possessive (as well as anxious) jealousy than females who grew up in the presence of their father.

Many other studies have shown that individuals with an insecure attachment style are more jealous than individuals with a secure attachment style (e.g., Miller et al., 2014), independently of the influence of personality characteristics such as self-esteem and neuroticism (Buunk, 1997). In particular, individuals with an anxious-ambivalent attachment style have been found to experience jealousy (e.g., Fleuriet et al., 2014; Marazitti et al., 2010), including jealousy aroused by a partner's use of Facebook (e.g., Hudson et al., 2015). As a consequence, such individuals tend to show a high level of possessive jealousy (e.g., tend to closely monitor their partner's activities on Facebook) (e.g., Muise et al., 2014; Marshall et al., 2013). As an anxious-ambivalent attachment style implies a "clinging" to the relationship out of fear of losing the partner, the link between this style and jealousy seems self-evident. Less self-evident is the fact that also avoidantly attached individuals are often relatively jealous (Buunk, 1997). A possible explanation is that such individuals *are* actually quite dependent on their partner but feel that they are not meeting the needs of their partner by their distant attitude and are therefore concerned with losing their partner.

Possessive Jealousy and Menstrual Cycle Effects

Finally, there is increasing evidence that possessive jealousy among women is associated with the stage of the menstrual cycle. For example, Geary et al. (2001) showed that among women, jealousy was positively associated with estrogen concentration assessed in the second week of the cycle (i.e., in the follicular phase and directly before ovulation). More recently, Cobey et al. (2012) found that in both single and partnered women, jealousy varied as a function of menstrual phase, with women reporting higher levels of jealousy when they were fertile than when nonfertile. In a study on the Caribbean island of Curaçao, it was found that this applied explicitly and mainly to possessive jealousy (Buunk & Van Brummen-Girigori, 2016). Interestingly, women seem to detect other women's fertility status as well (Hurst et al., 2017), and tend to exhibit increased jealousy and mate guarding in the presence of other women who are near peak fertility. For example, Krems et al. (2016) exposed partnered women to photographs of other women taken during their ovulatory cycle phase, and the participants reported they would try to avoid or even socially exclude these women, but only when they rated their own partners as highly desirable.

In light of our previous discussion of the function of possessive jealousy, these findings indicate that, given the importance of male investment, protection, and provisioning before, during, and after pregnancy (for a review, see Geary, 2005), when a woman is fertile, the risk of losing, or not receiving, the necessary investment from one's mate would be especially threatening for women. In line with this is research by Massar and Buunk

(2019), who showed that pregnant women were most jealous about a mate's emotional infidelity (rather than his sexual infidelity), whereas nonpregnant women considered both kinds of infidelity equally upsetting. The main evolutionary function of possessive jealousy for women thus seems to be preventing the involvement of their partner with another woman, to ensure his continued commitment and investment in both herself and her actual or future offspring.

Reactive Jealousy: Anticipated and "Fait-Accompli"

Whereas possessive jealousy is concerned with preventing extradyadic romantic, erotic, or sexual involvement of one's partner, reactive jealousy occurs in response to actual extradyadic romantic, erotic, or sexual behavior of one's partner. The stimuli that elicit jealousy may vary considerably between individuals and cultures. For example, in some cultures kissing is much more likely to evoke jealousy than in others, whereas in other cultures petting is a particularly salient jealousy-inducing event (Buunk & Hupka, 1987). Nonetheless, when looking at the themes that individuals from different cultures mention when asked to provide a description of a jealousy-evoking event, four common dominant themes emerge: fear of infidelity of one's partner, or actual infidelity; violated expectations concerning a partner's time and commitment; one's partner paying attention to a rival through social media; and loss of self-esteem due to one's partner paying attention to a rival (Zandbergen & Brown, 2015; see also Dijkstra et al., 2010).

In general, reactive jealousy is measured with scales assessing how one *would* respond to such behavior of a partner, as in the reactive jealousy scale of Buunk (1997), therefore we also take anticipated reactive jealousy into account here. It must be noted that many people confronted with extradyadic sexual behavior of one's partner do not consider jealousy their primary response but rather anger. Buunk (1995), in an early study, in a sample more or less typical for the Dutch population, asked people how they would respond when their partner would engage in extradyadic sex. He identified three main responses: *betrayal-anger* (e.g., angry, furious, and feeling betrayed); *disappointment* (e.g., feeling sad and feeling disappointed), and *self-doubt* (e.g., feeling powerless and full of self-doubt). In contrast to what is often assumed (e.g., Buss et al., 1992), men did not respond with more betrayal-anger than women, whereas women reacted with significantly more disappointment, and self-doubt than men did. However, the more often their partner had had extradyadic sex, the less disappointed and angry women were in response to a new extradyadic sexual event of their partner, whereas among men, these effects were far less pronounced. These findings confirm the conclusion of Kinsey et al. (1948) that "husbands are much less inclined to accept the non-marital activities of their wives. It has been so since the dawn of history" (p. 592), and are well compatible with parental investment and sexual investment theory: for men, *any* extradydyadic sexual contact of their wives is a potential threat to their reproductive success, whereas women may adapt more to their partner having sexual affairs as long as the investment of one's partner in the relationship is not threatened. It is also possible that women become as a consequence of their partner's recurrent extradyadic sexual behaviors, less invested in or dependent on the relationship.

Sexual vs. Emotional Reactive Jealousy

The most widely used paradigm in evolutionary psychology on anticipated jealousy is probably that developed by Buss et al. (1992) with their well-known dilemma asking individuals whether sexual or emotional infidelity would upset them more. As noted above, from an evolutionary perspective, over the course of evolution men faced the problem of paternity confidence, and women of securing the partner's investment of resources. Therefore, Buss et al. predicted that male jealousy would be specifically focused upon the sexual aspects of the partner's extradyadic activities. In contrast, for women an act of intercourse by her partner may especially be a threat when the investment of the partner in the relationship is in jeopardy (e.g., Buss et al., 2000; Bjorklund & Shackelford, 1999). To test the gender difference they predicted, Buss et al. (1992) developed a research paradigm in which participants were presented with dilemmas and had to choose whether a partner's sexual or emotional unfaithfulness was most upsetting. They found that more men than women selected a partner's sexual infidelity as the most upsetting event, whereas more women than men reported a partner's emotional infidelity as the most upsetting event. This pattern of results has since then been replicated several times across cultures, and for conventional as well as online infidelity (e.g., Buss et al., 1999; Buunk et al., 1996; Dunn & McLean, 2015; Groothof et al., 2009). Remarkably, in Sweden as well as in Norway, among the most egalitarian societies in the world, strong sex differences in response to emotional and sexual infidelity were found (Bendixen, Kennair, & Buss, 2015; Walum et al., 2013). Contradictory to what a learning perspective would predict—that is, an attenuation of the differences between men and women in the domain of jealousy—an evolutionary perspective holds that in these societies sex differences might be more pronounced, due to expected larger paternal investments. Bendixen, Kennair, and Buss (2015) argued that as men's investment in childrearing increases, for women the costs of losing these investments to another woman and for men the costs of paternal uncertainty also increase.

While findings with the paradigm developed by Buss et al. (1999) have been questioned (e.g., DeSteno & Salovey, 1996; Harris, 2003), assuming that most gender differences would disappear when actual infidelity experiences and responses on continuous measures (rather than forced-choice dilemmas) would be considered, a meta-analysis by Sagarin et al. (2012) showed that across 45 independent samples, the gender differences emerged on continuous measures and in response to experienced infidelities. Indeed, sex differences have been found in studies using different methods, such as reaction times (Schützwohl, 2005), recall of ambiguous cues (Schützwohl & Koch, 2004), spatial distance (Schützwohl et al., 2011), or audiorecords of partner interrogations in the face of an actual infidelity threat (Kuhle, 2011). In addition, twin research suggests that both types of jealousy have a strong genetic component (Walum et al., 2013). Nevertheless, when there is *no* risk of conception—such as when an infidelity between an opposite-sex partner occurs with a same-sex rival—the differences in jealousy tend to disappear (e.g., Harris, 2002; Sagarin et al., 2003; Valentova et al., 2022). There are several other factors that may moderate the gender difference in emotional versus sexual jealousy. For example, the gender difference has been found to be attenuated when controlling for variables such as personal experiences of being a victim or perpetrator of infidelity (e.g., Bendixen, Kennair, Ringheim, et al., 2015; Tagler, 2010), attachment style (Burchell & Ward, 2011; Levy & Kelly, 2009), participant age (IJzerman et al., 2014), and women's use of hormone-based birth control (Geary et al., 2001).

It must be noted that already long before the work by Buss et al, various studies had highlighted the sexual focus in male jealousy and the emotional focus in female jealousy. In a surprisingly relevant study, given that it was conducted more than 80 years ago, Gottschalk (1936; see Bohm, 1960) found that among men, jealousy manifested itself mainly as a shock of feeling sexually inadequate or sexually repulsive, resulting in a simultaneous and sudden release of rivalry feelings. Francis (1977), using a free association task, found that among men, sexual involvement with a third person was the most often mentioned situation evoking jealousy, whereas among women this was not mentioned at all. Rather, women indicated that their partner spending time or talking with a third person turned out to be of major importance. Teismann and Mosher (1978) found that men did experience jealousy primarily in terms of sexual issues, whereas issues of time and attention given to a third person evoked women's jealousy. In a study among 109 adult men and 109 adult women whose partner had engaged in extradyadic sex, among men, but not among women, jealousy correlated positively with the assumption that the partner had done so out of a need for sexual variety (Buunk, 1984). Even in cultures where it is acceptable for men to have multiple sexually committed relationships, especially women in these relationships often experience jealousy and a sense of competition over their spouse's attention and resources (e.g., Tabi et al., 2004).

Intrasexual Competition and the Role of the Rival

Intrasexual competition plays an important role in jealousy as, by definition, jealousy implies the presence of a potential or actual rival, with possessive jealousy often being expressed as a vigilance to *potential* rivals and reactive jealousy a response to the presence of an *actual* rival. Intrasexual competition refers to rivalry with same-sex others that is, ultimately, driven by the motive to obtain and maintain access to mates. Darwin (1871) had already recognized the importance of intrasexual competition for sexual selection, and he suggested that it led to important behavioral adaptation for attracting mates and for gathering the necessary resources for reproduction and offspring care. In species where males invest little in their offspring, they usually engage in fierce competition with other males for access to females, whereas females show few signs of intrasexual competition. As noted before, among humans, women may compete over men who are willing to invest considerably in their offspring, in terms of both resources and parental care. As a result, both sexes are discriminating in their choice of mates, and therefore both sexes will engage in competition with same-sex conspecifics.

Male Intrasexual Competition

Males tend to compete with other males for access to reproductive resources, including resources such as political influence and social status, which can be converted into reproductive opportunities, either because these are directly attractive to females or because these help conquer rival males (Sidanius & Pratto, 1999; Tooby & Cosmides, 1992). Male intrasexual competition often takes the form of a somewhat ritualized competition over the acquisition of those skills and resources that define status within a given culture (Sidanius & Pratto, 1999). In preindustrial societies in which male–male competition has been studied, it is consistently found that a man's status is directly related to his reproductive success (Betzig, 1986). Even in contemporary Western societies high-income men have more biological children than low-income men, whereas among women the opposite is true (Hopcroft, 2005; Nettle & Pollet, 2008). The presence of women tends to make men more aware of their status, and more eager to demonstrate that they can beat other men. For example, an experiment showed that men increased their cooperation in an economic game when observed by women (Iredale et al., 2008), reflecting competitive altruism: men compete with other men by being generous and foregoing individual benefits, and simultaneously impressing women with their ability to spend resources (Van Vugt et al., 2007). Behaving altruistically may improve one's reputation and social status: others often attribute charisma to those who sacrifice their own needs for those of others or the group (De Cremer & Van Knippenberg, 2004).

Female Intrasexual Competition

Females may also engage in fierce intrasexual competition, and in many socially living species, the rates of female–female aggression increase as the proportion of (fertile) females in the group increases, with pregnant females showing the highest rates of aggression. Research by Huchard and Cowlishaw (2011) showed that among wild chacma baboons (*Papio ursinus*), sexually receptive females received the most aggressive attacks from other females, whereas pregnant females initiated the most aggression against other females. Both these processes are likely driven by both mating competition—including suppression of other females' reproduction—as well as competition over access to resources. Among humans, given men's considerable parental investments, women compete with one another over access to those investments. However, given women's high physical and economic investments physical competition with other women is likely to engender high costs relative to its fitness benefits. Indeed, across human societies, children's survival depends almost exclusively on the mother's continued investment. Being harmed during physical competition would negatively affect a mother's ability to provision for herself and her (grand) offspring, and as a result of this selection pressure, women have evolved to be more risk-averse than men (e.g., Cross & Campbell, 2011; Massar, 2018). Women's intrasexual competition usually takes the form of self-promotion or rival derogation, and in the case of the latter, it includes actions such as social exclusion, gossiping, spreading rumors, and defamation of the rival (Campbell, 2013). Whereas men tend to compete within the domain of status and social reputation, women's intrasexual competition takes place within the domain of physical attractiveness and sexual reputation.

Jealousy and Rival Characteristics

Overall, a rival who possesses qualities that are believed to be important to the opposite sex or to one's partner (i.e., a rival with a high mate value) tends to evoke more feelings of jealousy than a rival who does not possess those qualities (e.g., Chung & Harris, 2018; DeSteno & Salovey, 1996; Dijkstra & Buunk, 1998). In general, men and women report comparable amounts of jealousy if their rivals possess more self-relevant attributes, such as intelligence, popularity, athleticism, and certain professional skills (e.g., DeSteno & Salovey, 1996; Rustemeyer & Wilbert, 2001). However, there are substantial sex differences in mate preferences, which translate to jealousy over rivals: men, more than women, value physical attractiveness in a partner, supposedly because a woman's physical attractiveness signals her reproductive value (Bovet, 2019; Lassek & Gaulin, 2019; Prokop et al., 2022; also see Buss, 1989; Buss & Barnes, 1986; Cunningham 1986; Feingold, 1990; Kenrick & Keefe, 1992; Mathes et al., 1985; Symons, 1979). Therefore, jealousy in women will be particularly driven by a rival's physical attractiveness. In contrast, women, more than men, value dominance and status in a partner, supposedly because these features are related to a man's ability to provide protection and resources (Barber, 1995; Buss, 1989; Buss & Barnes, 1986; Kenrick et al., 1990; Sadalla et al., 1987; Townsend & Levy, 1990; Townsend & Wasserman, 1998). Therefore, jealousy in men will be influenced particularly by the rival's dominance and status, and in women more by the rival's physical attractiveness.

QUESTIONNAIRE STUDIES

As is common in jealousy research, to evoke the sex-specific characteristics of a rival, participants are usually presented with a jealousy-evoking scenario (e.g., Buss et al., 1992; Buss et al., 2000; DeSteno & Salovey, 1996; Mathes et al., 1985; McIntosh & Tate, 1992; Wiederman & Algeier, 1992; Zammuner & Frijda, 1994). Although a hypothetical situation may not generate responses that 100% reliably reflect how individuals behave in "real" life, these "projected" responses may provide an index of how people tend to react to an actual comparable situation (Shettel-Neuber, Bryson, & Young, 1978). In an extensive research program, Dijkstra and Buunk (1998, 2002) developed a paradigm in which participants were confronted with a jealousy-evoking scenario in which one's partner engaged in heavy flirting with someone of the opposite sex and was then asked to indicate for 56 characteristics how much jealousy each would evoke if their rival possessed that characteristic. Dijkstra and Buunk (2002, Study 2 and Study 3) identified five dimensions underlying these 56 characteristics: (a) *social dominance* (more charisma, a better sense of humor, more self-confident, more intelligent, and more popular); (b) *physical attractiveness* (more slender, a better figure, a more attractive body, lighter body build, a more attractive face); (c) *seductive behavior* (more of a troublemaker, behaves more provocatively, more of a seducer, behaves more exaggeratedly); (d) *physical dominance* (more muscular, broader shoulders, is built heavier, taller, physically stronger); and (e) *social status* (a better job, more money, a better education, more successful). Consistent with evolutionary theorizing, it was found that in samples of students as well as adults, men experienced more jealousy than women when their rival was more socially or physically dominant or had a higher status than themselves, whereas women experienced more jealousy then men when their rival was more physically attractive. Men and women did not differ in the extent to which the seductive behavior of their rival evoked feelings of jealousy. Gay men and lesbian women appeared to respond in a similar way as heterosexual men and women (Dijkstra & Buunk, 2002, Study 4). Gay men reported more jealousy than lesbian women in response to a rival high in physical dominance, whereas lesbian women reported more jealousy than heterosexual women in response to a rival high in physical attractiveness. A recent study in Argentina in a large sample of transgender people showed similar effects of gender: female-to-male transgender individuals experienced more jealousy than male-to-female transgender individuals in response to a physically dominant rival, whereas male-to-female individuals experienced more jealousy than female-to-male individuals in response to a physically attractive rival (Aristegui et al., 2019).

Since earlier studies, subsequent research among heterosexuals has established similar sex differences in the rival characteristics that evoke jealousy (e.g., Yarab & Allgeier, 1999), and it has been found that these differences occur in different cultures like South Korea, Spain, and Argentina (Buss et al., 2000; Buunk et al., 2011). Interestingly however, in a study among young people in Iraqi Kurdistan (Buunk & Dijkstra, 2015), exactly the same five types of rival characteristics that evoke jealousy were found as in the Netherlands (Dijkstra & Buunk, 2002). However, although the level of jealousy was higher in Kurdistan than in the Netherlands, in contrast to the Dutch, the Kurdish men and women did *not* differ in which characteristics evoked most jealousy. Possible explanations for this lack of gender differences are that the overall high level of jealousy overruled the effect of specific rival characteristics, and that in The Netherlands men and women have much freedom to express their gender-related psychological characteristics.

There is evidence that the sex-specific responses to rivals are related to hormonal and physical characteristics. Although there is thus far no evidence that testosterone is associated with jealousy, prenatal exposure to male hormones seem to be clearly associated with jealousy in response to sex-specific rival characteristics. Such exposure affects the second-to-fourth digit ratio (2D:4D), with masculinity associated with a lower and femininity with a higher ratio. Park et al. (2008) found with the measure developed by Dijkstra and Buunk (2002) that men with more feminine 2D:4D ratios were most jealous in response to dominant rivals, whereas women with more masculine 2D:4D ratios were most jealous in response to physically attractive rivals. There is also increasing evidence that sex-specific differences in the jealousy-evoking nature of rival characteristics are associated with height. In general, tall men and women of medium height have the highest mate value and are considered the most attractive. For example, in speed-dating experiments, tall men and women of medium height receive the most positive responses from the opposite sex (Stulp et al., 2013). It seems self-evident that individuals with a high mate value will feel they have less to fear from rivals. Indeed, Buunk et al. (2008) found that as men were taller, they reported to be less jealous in general, but in particular in response to socially and physical dominant rivals, as well as physically attractive rivals. In contrast, average-height women reported in general lower levels of jealousy than short as well as tall women, but especially in response to physically attractive rivals.

EXPERIMENTAL STUDIES

From the survey studies described in the previous section, a rival's social and physical dominance and physical attractiveness emerged as the two domains of characteristics evoking clear sex differences in jealousy. In a number of experimental studies, these rival characteristics were experimentally manipulated by presenting participants with the jealousy-evoking flirting scenario developed by Dijkstra and Buunk (2002). Next, the participants received one of four profiles of the individual flirting with one's partner, consisting of a picture and a personality description. The picture showed an individual of either high or low physical attractiveness, and the personality description depicted someone who was either high or low in dominance. After they had read the scenario and the profile, participants were asked how they would respond to this situation. The hypothesized sex difference clearly emerged: jealousy in men was in particular influenced by the rival's dominance whereas jealousy in women was in particular influenced by the rival's physical attractiveness (Dijkstra & Buunk, 1998). Nevertheless, social dominance had a greater impact on men's jealousy scores when they were exposed to a physically unattractive rival than when they were exposed to an attractive rival, suggesting that it may depend on the salience of the rival's characteristics, such as his physical appearance, whether dominance affects men's jealousy. A subsequent study by Buunk and Dijkstra (2004) found that the gender differences found in many studies are confined to emotional infidelity, and that in the case of sexual infidelity, the sex difference is in part reversed, with men, and not women, responding with more jealousy to physically attractive rivals. This latter finding reflects the importance of physical attractiveness as an attribute for women in the context of casual sexual affairs (e.g., Buss, 1994; Gangestad & Simpson, 2000; Wiederman & Dubois, 1998).

There is evidence that the sex differences in the importance of rival characteristics reflect a sex-specific rival-oriented mechanism, in the sense that, independent of their sexual preference, when confronted with a rival, males and females seem to have developed different criteria to more or less automatically identify rivals that constitute a potential threat, Using the same experimental paradigm as in the Dijkstra and Buunk (1998) study, a study by Buunk and Dijkstra (2001) among homosexual and lesbian participants showed that lesbian women, but not gay men, reported more jealousy when they were exposed to a physically attractive rival as compared to a physically unattractive rival. Gay men, but not lesbian women, reported more jealousy when they were exposed to a rival high in dominance as compared to a rival low in dominance, especially when exposed to a physically unattractive rival. These findings strongly suggest that males and females possess an evolved mechanism through which they respond more or less automatically to those rival characteristics that have been important in sexual selection in our evolutionary past.

While the previous studies operationalized physical attractiveness as facial attractiveness, the study by Dijkstra and Buunk (2002) indicated that other physical features like having more beautiful legs, a better figure, a more attractive body, more beautiful hips, a lighter, and a more slender body build were also important rival characteristics. Indeed, many studies have shown that the body is at least as important in determining physical attractiveness as the face, in particular when individuals are observed from a distance (Alicke et al., 1986; Mueser et al., 1984; Pedersen et al., 1994). A series of studies employing different methods and examining various populations, including preadolescent Mexican-American, British, and Greek participants, have shown that particularly for women, a low (value of 0.7) waist-to-hip ratio (WHR) is an important determinant of attractiveness that is independent of weight (Furnham et al., 2002; Furnham et al., 1997; Henss, 1995; Markey et al., 2002; Singh, 1993, 1995; Streeter & McBurney, 2003). The ultimate reason that a low WHR is perceived as attractive, is that it is actually associated with health and fertility (though, see Bovet, 2019). Nevertheless, there is evidence that in many non-Westernized societies the attractiveness of a woman may be mainly determined by her weight (e.g., Wetsman & Marlowe, 1999; Yu & Shepard, 1998), supposedly because in cultures where few resources are available to provide adequate nutrition, being overweight and having a high WHR may be viewed as signs of high status, wealth, and prosperity. In contrast, males' attractiveness is determined more by the shoulder-to-waist ratio (SHR) as there is medical evidence that the pelvic–shoulder ratio correlates positively with beta-lipoproteins, hormones that are related to testosterone levels, and muscle development in men (e.g., Evans, 1972).

Using the line drawings of body shapes developed by Singh (1993, 1995), Dijkstra and Buunk (2001) found that rivals with a low as opposed to a high WHR evoked indeed more jealousy in women than in men. In contrast, rivals with a high as opposed to low SHR evoked more jealousy in men than in women, particularly when the rival had a high

WHR. In evaluating the rivals, women indicated that they had paid more attention to the rivals' waist, hips, and legs, and men indicated that they had paid more attention to the rivals' shoulders, chest, and belly. In a follow-up study Buunk and Dijkstra (2005) found that as men were older, the SHR of the rival tended to evoke less jealousy, assumedly because this affects the status of older men less than that of younger men. However, among women, the rival's WHR continued to evoke jealousy as the women got older, assumedly because, regardless of age, men tend to prefer women who signal health, youth, and fertility (e.g., Buunk et al., 2001; Kenrick & Keefe, 1992).

SUBLIMINAL PRIMING STUDIES

Given the importance of rival evaluation for reproductive success, it seems plausible that sensitivity to rival characteristics has evolved in such a way that these characteristics may be perceived even outside conscious awareness. A large body of evidence from the social cognition literature suggests that people may evaluate a target immediately as "good" or "bad," also without being consciously aware of the others' presence. Unobtrusively presenting participants with certain cues may nonconsciously influence their evaluations of others (Fazio et al., 1986; Devine, 1989; Ferguson et al., 2005). Some research using this paradigm has already been linked to evolutionary psychology. Focusing on the social cognitive aspects of mate attraction, Roney (2003) established that the mere visual exposure to young women caused young men to adopt more favorable attitudes toward material wealth than young men exposed to other men. These effects were found without men's awareness of the influence of the experimental manipulation, suggesting that visual stimuli from females act as input cues that are capable of priming mating-related constructs and behaviors in males.

Directly relevant to the present issue, recent research suggests that people not only evaluate others that are presented to them subliminally but also make social comparisons with these targets when these are presented subliminally (e.g., names of famous individuals; Mussweiler et al., 2004), and that these comparisons affect self-evaluations. Applying such findings to rival evaluation, Massar et al. (2009) hypothesized that the mere exposure to rival characteristics through subliminal priming would induce a comparison between oneself and the rival literally in the blink of an eye, and that the degree of jealousy would be based on the outcome of this comparison. In their study, words relating to attractiveness or social status were used as subliminal primes (Massar et al., 2009)—such as pretty, slender, success, and money. The results revealed the predicted sex differences in the characteristics that evoke jealousy: whereas women's jealousy increased after exposure to the attractiveness words, but not after priming with social dominance words, males showed the reverse pattern and reported increased jealousy after being primed with words relating to social dominance but not after priming with attractiveness words. A similar pattern was found in a study focusing on rivals' bodily features (Massar & Buunk, 2009a), where a parafoveal subliminal priming procedure was used to expose participants to silhouettes of bodies that were either attractive (a WHR of 0.7 for women and a SHR of 1.4 for men) or unattractive (a WHR of 0.9 for women and a SHR of 1.2 for men). The results showed that even though participants indicated not being aware of the content of the primes, their jealousy was influenced by the primes: Both men and women responded with the most jealousy after being exposed to the attractive body shapes. Finally, a study using photographs of an attractive or an unattractive female (Massar & Buunk, 2010) affected women's jealousy such that they reported significantly higher levels of jealousy after exposure to an attractive face than after priming with an unattractive face. However, in this study, men were not influenced by their rival's facial attractiveness: they reported equal amounts of jealousy after being exposed to the attractive or the unattractive male rival.

In a related experiment, Massar and Buunk (2009b) focused on the role of the infidelity context and examined if subliminally presenting sex-related versus intimacy-related words to men would affect responses to different types of rivals, moderated by individuals' sex drive. It was assumed that for individuals with a high sex drive, activating sex-related constructs would make intrasexual competition particularly salient, whereas for individuals with a low sex drive, activating intimacy-related constructs should make intrasexual competition particularly salient. That is, someone with a high sex drive will be more oriented to short-term mating and having sex with multiple partners, whereas someone with a low sex drive will be more oriented toward long-term mating and developing an intimate relationship with a single partner. In this experiment, participants were subliminally primed with words relating either to sex (*sex, passion, making out*, and *aroused*) or to intimacy (*warmth, intimate, attached*, and *committed*). After the priming procedure, the male participants were told to imagine their partner coming home one day and telling them "I found someone else." The results showed that for men who had been primed with intimacy, sex drive did not influence their feelings of upset over a rival's characteristics. However, when they had been primed with sex, sex drive did influence men's responses: men with a high sex drive reported feeling more upset over a rival's characteristics than men with a low sex drive. These results suggest that men with a high sex drive are more prone to engage in intrasexual competition, especially when they are confronted with the sexual infidelity of their partner (Massar & Buunk, 2009b).

Conclusion: The adaptive value of possessive and reactive jealousy

In the present chapter, we focused on the evolutionary relevance of two types of jealousy: possessive and reactive jealousy. Our review of the literature indicates that whereas both types of jealousy have in common that they function to alert an individual to the presence of a rival, they also differ in their adaptive value. Possessive jealousy functions mainly to prevent a possible extradyadic activity of one's partner, whereas reactive jealousy is evoked by an actual extra-pair transgression and may function mainly to keep the partner and to stop the extradyadic involvement. However, what they have in common is that the emotion of jealousy is evoked when a threat to the pair-bond is signaled, causing the individual to undertake actions to protect the relationship and, thus, one's reproductive investments. Further, both types of jealousy arise due to the presence of a real or imagined rival, and we emphasized that not all rivals evoke equal amounts of jealousy. Rather, the evolved motives serving men's and women's reproductive interests cause jealousy to be evoked mainly when paternity certainty and paternal investments are threatened by high-status men and physically attractive women, respectively. We further illustrate how these evolved motives and the experience and expression of jealousy interact with culture, for example, in the experience of jealousy in the context of parental mate choice. To conclude, we have, ideally, demonstrated that there are distinct forms of jealousy that may have different causes and consequences, and that it might be fruitful in future research to pay more attention to the factors specifically related to different types of jealousy.

References

Adamczyk, A., & Hayes, B. E. (2012). Religion and sexual behaviors: Understanding the influence of Islamic cultures and religious affiliation for explaining sex outside of marriage. *American Sociological Review, 77*, 723–746.

Alberts, S. C., Altmann, J., & Wilson, M. L. (1996). Mate guarding constrains foraging activity of male baboons. *Animal Behaviour, 51*, 1269–1277.

Alicke, M. D., Smith, R. H., & Klotz, M. L. (1986). Judgments of physical attractiveness: The role of faces and bodies. *Personality and Social Psychology Bulletin, 12*(4), 381–389.

Allen, E. S., Atkins, D. C., Baucom, D. H., Snyder, D. K., Gordon, K. C., & Glass, S. P. (2005). Intrapersonal, interpersonal, and contextual factors in engaging in and responding to extramarital involvement. *Clinical Psychology: Science and Practice, 12*(2), 101–130.

Apostolou, M. (2007). Sexual selection under parental choice: The role of parents in the evolution of human mating. *Evolution and Human Behavior, 28*, 403–409.

Aristegui, I., Castro Solano, A., & Buunk, A. P. (2019). Do transgender people respond according to their biological sex or their gender identity when confronted with romantic rivals? *Evolutionary Psychology, 17*(2), Article 147470491985113.

Bailey, K. G., Caffrey, J. V., & Hartnett, J. J. (1976). Body size as implied threat: Effects on personal space and person perception. *Perceptual and Motor Skills, 4*, 223–230.

Bair-Merritt, M. H., Shea Crowne, S., Thompson, D. A., Sibinga, E., Trent, M., & Campbell, J. (2010). Why do women use intimate partner violence? A systematic review of women's motivations. *Trauma, Violence, & Abuse, 11*(4), 178–189.

Barash, D. P., & Lipton, J. E. (2002). *The myth of monogamy: Fidelity and infidelity in animals and people*. Macmillan.

Barber, N. (1995). The evolutionary psychology of physical attractiveness: Sexual selection and human morphology. *Ethology and Sociobiology, 16*(5), 395–424.

Barnett, O., Miller-Perrin, C. L., & Perrin, R. D. (2005). *Family violence across the lifespan: An introduction*. SAGE.

Belus, J. M., Wanklyn, S. G., Iverson, K. M., Pukay-Martin, N. D., Langhinrichsen-Rohling, J., & Monson, C. M. (2014). Do anger and jealousy mediate the relationship between adult attachment styles and intimate violence perpetration? *Partner Abuse, 5*, 388–406.

Bendixen, M., Kennair, L. O., & Buss, D. M. (2015). Jealousy: Evidence of strong sex differences using both forced choice and continuous measure paradigms. *Personality and Individual Differences, 86*, 212–216.

Bendixen, M., Kennair, L. E. O., Ringheim, H. K., Isaksen, L., Pedersen, L., Svangtun, S., & Hagen, K. (2015). In search of moderators of sex differences in forced-choice jealousy responses: Effects of 2D: 4D digit ratio and relationship infidelity experiences. *Nordic Psychology, 67*, 272–284.

Betzig, L. (1986). *Despotism and differential reproduction: A Darwinian view of history*. Aldine.

Bjorklund, D. F., & Shackelford, T. K. (1999). Differences in parental investment contribute to important differences between men and women. *Current Directions in Psychological Science, 8*, 86–89.

Bohm, E. (1960). Jealousy. In A. Ellis & A. Arbarbanel (Eds.), *The encyclopedia of sexual behavior* (Vol. 1, pp. 567–571). Hawthorne.

Bovet, J. (2019). Evolutionary theories and men's preferences for women's waist-to-hip ratio: Which hypotheses remain? A systematic review. *Frontiers in Psychology, 10,* Article 1221.

Burbank, V. K. (1987). Female aggression in cross-cultural perspective. *Behavior Science Research,* 21, 70–100.

Burchell, J. L., & Ward, J. (2011). Sex drive, attachment style, relationship status and previous infidelity as predictors of sex differences in romantic jealousy. *Personality and Individual Differences, 51,* 657–661.

Buss, D. M. (1988). From vigilance to violence: Tactics of mate retention in American undergraduates. *Ethology & Sociobiology, 9*(5), 291–317.

Buss, D. M. (1989). Sex differences in human mate preferences: Evolutionary hypotheses tested in 37 cultures. *Behavioral and Brain Sciences, 12,* 1–49.

Buss, D. M. (1994). *The evolution of desire: Strategies of human mating.* Basic Books.

Buss, D. M., & Barnes, M. (1986). Preferences in human mate selection. *Journal of Personality and Social Psychology, 50*(3), 559–570.

Buss, D. M., Larsen, R. J., Westen, D., & Semmelroth, J. (1992). Sex differences in jealousy: Evolution, physiology, and psychology. *Psychological Science, 3,* 251–255.

Buss, D. M., Shackelford, T. K., Choe, J. A. E., Buunk, B. P., & Dijkstra, P. (2000). Distress about mating rivals. *Personal Relationships, 7*(3), 235–243.

Buss, D. M., Shackelford, T. K., Kirkpatrick, L. A., Choe, J. C., Lim, H. K., Hasegawa, M., Toshikazu Bennett, K. (1999). Jealousy and the nature of beliefs about infidelity: Tests of competing hypotheses about sex differences in the United States, Korea, and Japan. *Personal Relationships, 6,* 125–150.

Buunk, B. (1984). Jealousy as related to attributions for the partner's behavior. *Social Psychology Quarterly,* 47,107–112.

Buunk, B. P. (1991). Jealousy in close relationships: An exchange-theoretical perspective. In P. Salovey (Ed.), *The psychology of jealousy and envy* (pp. 148–177). Guilford Press.

Buunk, A. P. (1995). Sex, self-esteem, dependency and extradyadic sexual experiences as related to jealousy responses. *Journal of Social and Personal Relationships, 12,* 147–153.

Buunk, A. P. (1997). Personality, birth order, and attachment styles as related to various types of jealousy. *Personality and Individual Differences, 23,* 997–1006.

Buunk, A. P., Aan't Goor, J., & Castro Solano, A. (2010). Intrasexual competition at work: Sex differences in the jealousy-evoking effect of rival characteristics in work settings. *Journal of Social and Personal Relationships, 27,* 671–684.

Buunk, A. P., Angleitner, A., Oubaid, V., & Buss, D. M. (1996). Sex differences in jealousy in evolutionary and cultural perspective: Tests from the Netherlands, Germany, and the United States. *Psychological Science, 7,* 359–363.

Buunk, A. P., & Castro Solano, A. (2012). Mate guarding and parental influence on mate choice. *Personal Relationships, 19,* 103–112.

Buunk, A. P., Castro Solano, A., Zurriaga, R., & González, P. (2011). Gender differences in the jealousy-evoking effect of rival characteristics: A study in Spain and Argentina. *Journal of Cross-Cultural Psychology, 42*(3), 323–339.

Buunk, A. P., & Dijkstra, P. (2001). Evidence from a homosexual sample for a sex-specific rival-oriented mechanism: Jealousy as a function of a rival's physical attractiveness and dominance. *Personal Relationships, 8*(4), 391–406.

Buunk, B. P., & Dijkstra, P. (2004). Gender differences in rival characteristics that evoke jealousy in response to emotional versus sexual infidelity. *Personal Relationships, 11,* 395–408.

Buunk, B. P., & Dijkstra, P. (2005). A narrow waist versus broad shoulders: Sex and age differences in the jealousy-evoking characteristics of a rival's body build. *Personality and Individual Differences, 39*(2), 379–389.

Buunk, A. P., & Dijkstra, P. (2015). Rival characteristics that provoke jealousy: A study in Iraqi Kurdistan. *Evolutionary Behavioral Sciences, 9,* 116–127.

Buunk, B. P., Dijkstra, P., Kenrick, D. T., & Warntjes, A. (2001). Age preferences for mates as related to gender, own age and involvement level. *Evolution and Human Behavior, 22*(4), 241–250.

Buunk, A. P., Dijkstra, P., Massar, K. (2018). The universal threat and temptation of extradyadic affairs. In Vangelisti, A., Perlman, D. (Eds.), *The Cambridge handbook of personal relationships* (pp. 353–364). Cambridge, MA: Cambridge University Press.

Buunk, A. P., & Hupka, R. B. (1987). Cross-cultural differences in the elicitation of sexual jealousy. *Journal of Sex Research, 23*, 12–22.

Buunk, A. P., & Massar, K. (2019). Intimate partner violence in Nicaragua: The role of possessive jealousy, intrasexual competitiveness, life history, mate value, and stress. *Journal of Interpersonal Violence, 36*, 15–16. https://doi.org/10.1177/0886260519842854.

Buunk, A. P., & Park, J. H. (2010). Cultural variation in parental influence on mate choice. *Cross-Cultural Research, 44*, 23–40.

Buunk, A. P., Park, J. H., Zurriaga, R., Klavina, L., & Massar, K. (2008). Height predicts jealousy differently for men and women. *Evolution and Human Behavior, 29*, 133–139

Buunk, A. P., & Van Brummen-Girigori, O. (2016). Menstrual cycle effects on jealousy: A study in Curaçao. *Evolution, Mind and Behavior, 14*, 43–54.

Campbell, A. (2013). *A mind of her own: The evolutionary psychology of women*. Oxford University Press.

Caraël, M., Cleland, J., Deheneffe, J. C., Ferry, B., & Ingham, R. (1995). Sexual behaviour in developing countries: implications for HIV control. *AIDS, 9*,1171–1175.

Chagnon, N. A. (1992). *Yanomamö: The last days of Eden*. Harcourt Brace Jovanovich.

Chan, K. L., Brownridge, D. A., Tiwari, A., Fong, D. Y., Leung, W. C., & Ho, P. C. (2011). Associating pregnancy with partner violence against Chinese women. *Journal of Interpersonal Violence, 26*(7), 1478–1500.

Chung, M., & Harris, C. R. (2018). Jealousy as a specific emotion: The dynamic functional model. *Emotion Review, 10*(4), 272–287.

Cobey, K. D., Buunk, A. P., Roberts, C. S., Klipping, C., Appels, N., Zimmerman, Y., Herjan, J. T., Bennink, C., & Pollet, T.V. (2012). Reported jealousy differs as a function of menstrual cycle stage and contraceptive pill use: A within-subjects investigation. *Evolution and Human Behavior, 33*, 395–401.

Cross, C. P., & Campbell, A. (2011). Women's aggression. *Aggression and Violent Behavior, 16*, 390–398

Darwin, C. (1871). *The descent of man and selection in relation to sex*. Murray.

Deaux, K., & Hanna, R. (1984). Courtship in the personals column: The influence of gender and sexual orientation. *Sex Roles, 11*(5–6), 363–375.

De Cremer, D., & Van Knippenberg, D. (2004). Leader self-sacrifice and leadership effectiveness: The moderating role of leader self-confidence. *Organizational Behavior and Human Decision Processes, 95*(2), 140–155

Cunningham, M. R. (1986). Measuring the physical in physical attractiveness: Quasi-experiments on the sociobiology of female facial beauty. *Journal of Personality and Social Psychology, 50*(5), 925–935.

DeSteno, D. A., & Salovey, P. (1996). Evolutionary origins of sex differences in jealousy? Questioning the fitness of the model. *Psychological Science, 7*, 367–372.

Devine, P. G. (1989). Stereotypes and prejudice: Their automatic and controlled components. *Journal of Personality and Social Psychology, 56*(1), 5.

Dickemann, M. (1997). Paternal confidence and dowry competition: A biocultural analysis of Purdah. In L. Betzig (Ed.), *Human nature. A critical reader* (pp. 311–330). Oxford University Press.

Dijkstra, P., Barelds, D. P., & Groothof, H. A. (2013). Jealousy in response to online and offline infidelity: The role of sex and sexual orientation. *Scandinavian Journal of Psychology, 54*, 328–336.

Dijkstra, P., Barelds, D. P., & Groothof, H. A. (2010). An inventory and update of jealousy-evoking partner behaviours in modern society. *Clinical Psychology & Psychotherapy, 17*, 329–345.

Dijkstra, P., & Buunk, A. P. (1998). Jealousy as a function of rival characteristics: An evolutionary perspective. *Personality and Social Psychology Bulletin, 24*, 1158–1166.

Dijkstra, P., & Buunk, A. P. (2001). Sex differences in the jealousy-evoking nature of a rival's body build. *Evolution and Human Behavior, 22*(5), 335–341.

Dijkstra, P., & Buunk, A. P. (2002). Sex differences in the jealousy evoking effect of rival characteristics. *European Journal of Social Psychology, 32*, 829–852.

Dunn, M. J., & McLean, H. (2015). Jealousy-induced sex differences in eye gaze directed at either emotional- or sexual infidelity–related mobile phone messages. *Cyberpsychology, Behavior, and Social Networking, 18*, 37–40.

Evans, R. B. (1972). Physical and biochemical characteristics of homosexual men. *Journal of Consulting and Clinical Psychology, 39*, 140–147.

Fazio, R. H., Sanbonmatsu, D. M., Powell, M. C., & Kardes, F. R. (1986). On the automatic activation of attitudes. *Journal of Personality and Social Psychology, 50*, 229–238.

Feingold, A. (1990). Gender differences in effects of physical attractiveness on romantic attraction: A comparison across five research paradigms. *Journal of Personality and Social Psychology, 59*, 981–993.

Ferguson, M. J., Bargh, J. A., & Nayak, D. A. (2005). After-affects: How automatic evaluations influence the interpretation of subsequent, unrelated stimuli. *Journal of Experimental Social Psychology, 41*, 182–191.

Fernandez, A. M., Muñoz-Reyes, J. A., & Dufey, M. (2014). BMI, age, mate value, and intrasexual competition in Chilean women. *Current Psychology, 33*, 435–450.

Fleuriet, C., Cole, M., & Guerrero, L. K. (2014). Exploring Facebook: Attachment style and nonverbal message characteristics as predictors of anticipated emotional reactions to Facebook postings. *Journal of Nonverbal Behavior, 38*, 429–450.

Francis, J. L. (1977). Toward the management of heterosexual jealousy. *Journal of Marital and Family Therapy, 3*, 61–69.

Freud, S. (1923). Certain neurotic mechanisms in jealousy, paranoia and homosexuality. *International Review of Psycho-Analysis, 4*, 1–10.

Furnham, A., Moutafi, J., & Baguma, P. (2002). A cross-cultural study on the role of weight and waist-to-hip ratio on female attractiveness. *Personality and Individual Differences, 32*, 729–745.

Furnham, A., Tan, T., & McManus, C. (1997). Waist-to-hip ratio and preferences for body shape: A replication and extension. *Personality and Individual Differences, 22*, 539–549.

Gangestad, S. W., & Simpson, J. A. (2000). The evolution of human mating: Trade-offs and strategic pluralism. *Behavioral and Brain Sciences, 23*, 573–644.

Geary, D. C. (2005). Evolution of paternal investment. In D. M. Buss (Ed.), *The evolutionary psychology handbook* (pp. 483–505). John Wiley & Sons.

Geary, D. C., DeSoto, C. M., Hoard, M. K., Sheldon, M. S., & Cooper, L. M. (2001). Estrogens and relationship jealousy. *Human Nature, 12*, 299–320.

Gelfand, M. J., Bhawuk, D. P., Nishii, L. H., & Bechtold, D. J. (2004). Individualism and collectivism. In R. J. House, P. J. Hanges, M. Javidan, P. W. Dorfman, & V. Gupta (Eds.), *Culture, leadership, and organizations: The GLOBE study of 62 societies* (pp. 437–512). SAGE.

Gelles, R. J. (1974). *The violent home*. SAGE.

Gottschalk, H. (1936). *Skinsygens problemer* [Problems of jealousy]. Fremad.

Graham-Kevan, N., & Archer, J. (2009). Control tactics and partner violence in heterosexual relationships. *Evolution and Human Behavior, 30*, 445–452.

Groothof, H. A., Dijkstra, P., & Barelds, D. P. (2009). Sex differences in jealousy: The case of Internet infidelity. *Journal of Social and Personal Relationships, 26*, 1119–1129.

Harris, H. (1995). Rethinking heterosexual relationships in Polynesia: A case study of Mangaia, Cook Island. In W. Jankowiak (Ed.), *Romantic passion: A universal experience?* (pp. 95–127). Columbia University Press.

Harris, C. R. (2002). Sexual and romantic jealousy in heterosexual and homosexual adults. *Psychological Science, 13*, 7–12.

Harris, C. R. (2003). A review of sex differences in sexual jealousy, including self-report data, psychophysiological responses, interpersonal violence, and morbid jealousy. *Personality and Social Psychology Review, 7*, 102–128.

Hellmuth, J. C., Gordon, K. C., Stuart, G. L., & Moore, T. M. (2013). Risk factors for intimate partner violence during pregnancy and postpartum. *Archives of Women's Mental Health, 16*, 19–27.

Henss, R. (1995). Waist-to-hip ratio and attractiveness. Replication and extension. *Personality and Individual Differences, 19*, 479–488.

Hicks, T. V., & Leitenberg, H. (2001). Sexual fantasies about one's partner versus someone else: Gender differences in incidence and frequency. *Journal of Sex Research, 38*, 43–50.

Holtzworth-Munroe, A., Stuart, G. L., & Hutchinson, G. (1997). Violent versus nonviolent husbands: Differences in attachment patterns, dependency, and jealousy. *Journal of Family Psychology, 11*, 314–331

Hopcroft, R. L. (2005). Sex, status, and reproductive success in the contemporary United States. *Evolution and Human Behavior, 27*, 104–120.

Huchard, E., & Cowlishaw, G. (2011). Female–female aggression around mating: An extra cost of sociality in a multimale primate society. *Behavioral Ecology, 22*, 1003–1011.

Hudson, M. B., Nicolas, S. C., Howser, M. E., Lipsett, K. E., Robinson, I. W., Pope, L. J., ... & Friedman, D. R. (2015). Examining how gender and emoticons influence Facebook jealousy. *Cyberpsychology, Behavior, and Social Networking, 18*(2), 87–92.

Hurst, A. C., Alquist, J. L., & Puts, D. A. (2017). Women's fertility status alters other women's jealousy and mate guarding. *Personality and Social Psychology Bulletin, 43*, 191–203.

Hupka, R. B. (1981). Cultural determinants of jealousy. *Alternative Lifestyles, 4*, 310–356.

IJzerman, H., Blanken, I., Brandt, M. J., Oerlemans, J. M., Van den Hoogenhof, M. M., Franken, S. J., & Oerlemans, M. W. (2014). Sex differences in distress from infidelity in early adulthood and in later life. *Social Psychology, 45*, 202–208.

Iredale, W., Van Vugt, M., & Dunbar, R. I. M. (2008). Showing off in humans: Male generosity as mate signal. *Evolutionary Psychology, 6*, 386–392.

Jankowiak, W. R., Hill, E. M., & Donovan, J. M. (1992). The effects of sex and sexual orientation on attractiveness judgments: An evolutionary interpretation. *Ethology and Sociobiology, 13*, 73–85.

Johnson, W. L., Giordano, P. C., Manning, W. D., & Longmore, M. A. (2015). The age–IPV curve: Changes in the perpetration of intimate partner violence during adolescence and young adulthood. *Journal of Youth and Adolescence, 44*, 708–726.

Kenrick, D. T., & Keefe, R. C. (1992). Age preferences in mates reflect sex differences in human reproductive strategies. *Behavioral and Brain Sciences, 15*, 75–91.

Kenrick, D. T., Keefe, R. C., Bryan, A., Barr, A., & Brown, S. (1995). Age preferences and mate choice among homosexuals and heterosexuals: A case for modular psychological mechanisms. *Journal of Personality and Social Psychology, 69*, 1166–1172.

Kenrick, D. T., Groth, G. E., Trost, M. R., & Sadalla, E. K. (1993). Integrating evolutionary and social exchange perspectives on relationships: Effects of gender, self-appraisal, and involvement level on mate selection criteria. *Journal of Personality and Social Psychology, 64*(6), 951–969.

Kinsey, A. C., Pomeroy, W. B., & Martin, C. E. (1948). *Sexual behavior in the human male.* Saunders.

Krems, J. A., Neel, R., Neuberg, S. L., Puts, D. A., & Kenrick, D. T. (2016). Women selectively guard their (desirable) mates from ovulating women. *Journal of Personality and Social Psychology, 110*, 551.

Kuhle, B. X. (2011). Did you have sex with him? Do you love her? An in vivo test of sex differences in jealous interrogations. *Personality and Individual Differences, 51*, 1044–1047.

Lassek, W. D., & Gaulin, S. J. (2019). Evidence supporting nubility and reproductive value as the key to human female physical attractiveness. *Evolution and Human Behavior, 40*, 408–419.

Lazarus, J., Inglis, I. R., & Torrance, R. L. L. F. (2004). Mate guarding conflict, extra-pair courtship and signalling in the harlequin duck, histrionicus. *Behaviour, 141*, 1061–1078.

Levy, K. N., & Kelly, K. M. (2009). Sex differences in jealousy: A contribution from attachment theory. *Psychological Science, 21*, 168–173.

Marazziti, D., Consoli, G., Albanese, F., Laquidara, E., Baroni, S., & Dell'Osso, M. C. (2010). Romantic attachment and subtypes/dimensions of jealousy. *Clinical Practice and Epidemiology in Mental Health, 6*, 53–58.

Markey, C. N., Tinsley, B. J., Ericksen, A. J., Ozer, D. J., & Markey, P. M. (2002). Preadolescents' perceptions of females' body size and shape: Evolutionary and social learning perspectives. *Journal of Youth and Adolescence, 31*, 137–146.

Marshall, T. C., Bejanyan, K., Di Castro, G., & Lee, R. A. (2013). Attachment styles as predictors of Facebook-related jealousy and surveillance in romantic relationships. *Personal relationships, 20*(1), 1–22.

Martin, D. (1983). *Battered wives.* Simon & Schuster.

Massar. K. (2018). Contexts for women's aggression against women. In T. K. Shackelford & V. A. Weekes-Shackelford (Eds.), *Encyclopedia of evolutionary psychological science.* https://doi.org/10.1007/978-3-319-16999-6_877-1

Massar, K., & Buunk, A. P. (2009a). Rivals in the mind's eye: Jealous responses after subliminal exposure to body shapes. *Personality and Individual Differences, 46*, 129–134.

Massar, K., & Buunk, A. P. (2009b). The effect of a subliminally primed context on intrasexual competition depends on individual differences in sex drive. *Journal of Research in Personality, 43*, 691–694.

Massar, K., & Buunk, A. P. (2010). Judging a book by its cover: Jealousy after subliminal priming with attractive and unattractive faces. *Personality and Individual Differences, 49*, 634–638.

Massar, K., & Buunk, A. P. (2019). Expecting and competing? Jealous responses among pregnant and nonpregnant women. *Evolutionary Psychology, 17*(1), Article 1474704919833344

Massar, K., Buunk, A. P., & Dechesne, M. (2009). Jealousy in the blink of an eye: Jealous reactions following subliminal exposure to rival characteristics. *European Journal of Social Psychology, 39*, 768–779.

Massar, K., Buunk, A. P., & Rempt, S. (2012). Age differences in women's tendency to gossip are mediated by their mate value. *Personality and Individual Differences, 52*, 106–109.

Mathes, E. W., Adams, H. E., & Davies, R. M. (1985). Jealousy: Loss of relationship rewards, loss of self-esteem, depression, anxiety, and anger. *Journal of Personality and Social Psychology, 48*, 1552–1561

McIntosh, E. G., & Tate, D. T. (1992). Characteristics of the rival and the experience of jealousy. *Perceptual and Motor Skills, 74*, 369–370.

Mileham, B. L. A. (2007). Online infidelity in Internet chat rooms: An ethnographic exploration. *Computers in Human Behavior, 23*, 11–31.

Miller, M. J., Denes, A., Diaz, B., & Buck, R. (2014). Attachment style predicts jealous reactions to viewing touch between a romantic partner and close friend: Implications for internet social communication. *Journal of Nonverbal Behavior, 38*, 451–476.

Mougeot, F., Arroyo, B. E., & Bretagnolle, V. (2006). Paternity assurance responses to first-year and adult male territorial intrusions in a courtship-feeding raptor. *Animal Behaviour, 71*, 101–108.

Mueser, K. T., Grau, B. W., Sussman, S., & Rosen, A. J. (1984). You're only as pretty as you feel: Facial expression as a determinant of physical attractiveness. *Journal of Personality and Social Psychology, 46*, 469–478.

Muise, A., Christofides, E., & Desmarais, S. (2014). "Creeping" or just information seeking? Gender differences in partner monitoring in response to jealousy on Facebook. *Personal Relationships, 21*, 35–50.

Murdock, G. P. (1967). *Ethnographic atlas*. University of Pittsburgh Press.

Murstein, B. I. (1974). *Love, sex, and marriage through the ages*. Springer.

Mussweiler, T., Rüter, K., & Epstude, K. (2004). The man who wasn't there: Subliminal social comparison standards influence self-evaluation. *Journal of Experimental Social Psychology, 40*(5), 689–696.

Nettle, D., & Pollet, T. V. (2008). Natural selection on male wealth in humans. *American Naturalist, 172*, 658–666.

Nowak, N. T., Weisfeld, G. E., Imamoğlu, O., Weisfeld, C. C., Butovskaya, M., & Shen, J. (2014). Attractiveness and spousal infidelity as predictors of sexual fulfillment without the marriage partner in couples from five cultures. *Human Ethology Bulletin, 29*, 18–38.

O'Leary, K. D., Smith Slep, A. M., & O'leary, S. G. (2007). Multivariate models of men's and women's partner aggression. *Journal of Consulting and Clinical Psychology, 75*, 752–764.

Park, J. H., Wieling, M. B., Buunk, A. P., & Massar, K. (2008). Sex-specific relationship between digit ratio (2D: 4D) and romantic jealousy. *Personality and Individual Differences, 44*, 1039–1045.

Pedersen, E. L., Markee, N. L., & Salusso, C. J. (1994). Gender differences in characteristics reported to be important features of physical attractiveness. *Perceptual and Motor Skills, 79*(3_Suppl.), 1539–1544.

Pfeiffer, S. M., & Wong, P. T. (1989). Multidimensional jealousy. *Journal of Social and Personal Relationships, 6*, 181–196.

Prokop, P., Zvaríková, M., Zvarík, M., Fedor, P. (2022). Cues of pregnancy decrease female physical attractiveness for males. *Current Psychology, 41*, 697–704. https://doi.org/10.1007/s12144-020-00608-4

Reiss, I. L. (1980). *Family systems in America*. Holt, Rinehart & Winston.

Roney, J. R. (2003). Effects of visual exposure to the opposite sex: Cognitive aspects of mate attraction in human males. *Personality and Social Psychology Bulletin, 29*, 393–404.

Russell, R. J., & Wells, P. A. (2000). Predicting marital violence from the Marriage and Relationship Questionnaire: Using LISREL to solve an incomplete data problem. *Personality and Individual Differences, 29*, 429–440.

Rustemeyer, R., & Wilbert, C. (2001). Jealousy within the perspective of a self-evaluation maintenance theory. *Psychological Reports, 88*, 799–804.

Sadalla, E. K., Kenrick, D. T., & Vershure, B. (1987). Dominance and heterosexual attraction. *Journal of Personality and Social Psychology, 52*, 730.

Sagarin, B. J., Becker, V. D., Guadagno, R. E., Nicastle, L. D., & Millevoi, A. (2003). Sex differences (and similarities) in jealousy: The moderating influence of infidelity experience and sexual orientation of the infidelity. *Evolution and Human Behavior, 24*, 17–23.

Sagarin, B. J., Martin, A. L., Coutinho, S. A., Edlund, J. E., Patel, L., Skowronski, J. J., & Zengel, B. (2012). Sex differences in jealousy: A meta-analytic examination. *Evolution and Human Behavior, 33*, 595–614.

Schützwohl, A. (2005). Sex differences in jealousy: The processing of cues to infidelity. *Evolution and Human Behavior, 26*, 288–299.

Schützwohl, A., & Koch, S. (2004). Sex differences in jealousy: The recall of cues to sexual and emotional infidelity in personally more and less threatening context conditions. *Evolution and Human Behavior, 25*, 249–257.

Schützwohl, A., Morjaria, S., & Alvis, S. (2011). Spatial distance regulates sex-specific feelings to suspected sexual and emotional infidelity. *Evolutionary Psychology, 9*(3), Article 147470491100900310.

Setchell, J. M., Charpentier, M., & Wickings, E. J. (2005). Mate guarding and paternity in mandrills: Factors influencing alpha male monopoly. *Animal Behaviour, 70*, 1105–1120.

Shackelford, T. K., Goetz, A. T., Guta, F. E., & Schmitt, D. P. (2006). Mate guarding and frequent in-pair copulation in humans. *Human Nature, 17*, 239–252.

Sharpsteen, D. J. (1995). The effects of relationship and self-esteem threats on the likelihood of romantic jealousy. *Journal of Social and Personal Relationships, 12*, 89–101.

Shettel-Neuber, J., Bryson, J. B., & Young, L. E. (1978). Physical attractiveness of the "other person" and jealousy. *Personality and Social Psychology Bulletin, 4*, 612–615.

Sidanius, J., & Pratto F. (1999). *Social dominance*. Cambridge University Press.

Singh, D. (1993). Adaptive significance of female physical attractiveness: Role of waist-to-hip ratio. *Journal of Personality and Social Psychology, 65*, 293–307.

Singh, D. (1995). Female judgment of male attractiveness and desirability for relationships: Role of waist-to-hip ratio and financial status. *Journal of Personality and Social Psychology, 69*, 1089–1101.

Streeter, S. A., & McBurney, D. H. (2003). Waist–hip ratio and attractiveness: New evidence and a critique of "a critical test." *Evolution and Human Behavior, 24*, 88–98.

Stulp, G., Buunk, A. P., Kurzban, R., & Verhulst, S. (2013). The height of choosiness: Mutual mate choice for stature results in sub-optimal pair formation for both sexes. *Animal Behaviour, 86*, 37–46.

Symons, D. (1979). *The evolution of human sexuality*. Oxford University Press.

Tabi, M. M., Doster, C., & Cheney, T. (2004). A qualitative study of women in polygynous marriages. *International Nursing Review, 57*, 121–127.

Tagler, M. J. (2010). Sex differences in jealousy: Comparing the influence of previous infidelity among college students and adults. *Social Psychological and Personality Science, 1*, 353–360.

Teismann, M. W., & Mosher, D. L. (1978). Jealous conflict in dating couples. *Psychological Reports, 42*(3_ Suppl.), 1211–1216.

Theodorson, G. A. (1965). Romanticism and motivation to marry in the United States, Singapore, Burma and India. *Social Forces, 44*, 17–27.

Tooby, J., & Cosmides, L. (1992). The psychological foundations of culture. In J. Tooby (Ed.), *The adapted mind: Evolutionary psychology and the generation of culture* (pp. 19–136). Oxford University Press.

Townsend, J. M., & Levy, G. D. (1990). Effects of potential partners' physical attractiveness and socioeconomic status on sexuality and partner selection. *Archives of Sexual Behavior, 19*, 149–164.

Townsend, J. M., & Wasserman, T. (1998). Sexual attractiveness: Sex differences in assessment and criteria. *Evolution and Human Behavior, 19*, 171–191.

Trivers, R. L. (1972). Parental investment and sexual selection. In B. Campbell (Ed.), *Sexual selection and the descent of man: 1871–1971* (pp. 136–179). Aldine.

Valentova, J. V., Fernandez, A. M., Pereira, M., & Varella, M. A. C. (2022). Jealousy is influenced by sex of the individual, their partner, and their rival. *Archives of Sexual Behavior, 51*(6), 2867–2877.

Van Brummen-Girigori, O., Buunk, A. P., Dijkstra, P., & Girigori, A. (2016). Father abandonment and jealousy: A study among women on Curacao. *Personality and Individual Differences, 96*, 181–184.

Van Vugt, M., Roberts, G., & Hardy, C. (2007). Competitive altruism: Development of reputation-based cooperation in groups. In R. I. M. Dunbar & L. Barrett (Eds.), *Handbook of evolutionary psychology* (pp. 531–540). Oxford University Press.

Walker, R. S., Hill, K. R., Flinn, M. V., & Ellsworth, R. M. (2011). Evolutionary history of hunter-gatherer marriage practices. *PloS ONE, 6*(4), Article e19066. https://doi.org/10.1371/journal.pone.0019066

Walum, H., Larsson, H., Westberg, L., Lichtenstein, P., & Magnusson, P. E. (2013). Sex differences in jealousy: A population-based twin study in Sweden. *Twin Research and Human Genetics, 16*, 941–947.

Wetsman, A., & Marlowe, F. (1999). How universal are preferences for female waist-to-hip ratios? Evidence from the Hadza of Tanzania. *Evolution and Human Behavior, 20*, 219–228.

Whitty, M. T. (2003). Pushing the wrong buttons: Men's and women's attitudes toward online and offline infidelity. *Cyberpsychology & Behavior, 6*, 569–579.

Wiederman, M. W., & Allgeier, E. R. (1992). Gender differences in mate selection criteria: Sociobiological or socioeconomic explanation? *Ethology and Sociobiology, 13*, 115–124.

Wiederman, M. W., & Dubois, S. L. (1998). Evolution and sex differences in preferences for short-term mates: Results from a policy capturing study. *Evolution and Human Behavior, 19*, 153–170.

Williams, J. A., Jr., White, L. K., & Ekaidem, B. J. (1979). Romantic love as a basis for marriage. In M. Cook & G. Wilson (Eds.), *Love and attraction* (pp. 245–250). Pergamon.

Yarab, P. E., & Allgeier, E. R. (1999). Young adults' reactions of jealousy and perceived threat based on the characteristics of a hypothetical rival. *Journal of Sex Education and Therapy, 24*, 171–175.

Young, K. S., Griffin-Shelley, E., Cooper, A., O'Mara, J., & Buchanan, J. (2000). Online infidelity: A new dimension in couple relationships with implications for evaluation and treatment. *Sexual Addiction & Compulsivity: The Journal of Treatment and Prevention, 7*, 59–74.

Yu, D. W., & Shepard, G. H. (1998). Is beauty in the eye of the beholder?. *Nature, 396*(6709), 321–322.

Zammuner, V. L., & Frijda, N. H. (1994). Felt and communicated emotions: Sadness and jealousy. *Cognition & Emotion, 8*, 37–53.

Zandbergen, D. L., & Brown, S. G. (2015). Culture and gender differences in romantic jealousy. *Personality and Individual Differences, 72*, 122–127.

Zhang, N., Parish, W. L., Huang, Y., & Pan, S. (2012). Sexual infidelity in China: Prevalence and gender-specific correlates. *Archives of Sexual Behavior, 41*(4), 861–873.

Zurriaga, R., González-Navarro, P., Buunk, A. P., & Dijkstra, P. (2018). Jealousy at work: The role of rivals' characteristics. *Scandinavian Journal of Psychology, 59*, 443–450.

CHAPTER

13 Hormonal Mechanisms of In-Pair Mating and Maintenance

Amanda Denes, John P. Crowley, *and* Anuraj Dhillon

Abstract

The present chapter provides a review of research addressing the hormonal mechanisms of in-pair mating and maintenance. Using the integrative model of relationship maintenance as a guiding framework, the chapter explores relational maintenance processes at the interactive or relational level and their hormonal correlates. Specifically, the chapter explores interactive maintenance strategies aimed at mitigating relationship threat, which include conflict management, forgiveness, sacrifice, facilitation, and dyadic coping; and those aimed at relationship enhancement, which include communication, relationship talk, social support/responsiveness, humor, and joint leisure activities. Each of these strategies is then linked to research on three hormones of interest when exploring social relationships: testosterone, oxytocin, and cortisol. The chapter concludes with a summary of research on these three hormones and relationship maintenance, as well as by providing future directions for researchers interested in exploring the hormonal mechanisms of in-pair mating and maintenance.

Key Words: relationship maintenance, testosterone, oxytocin, cortisol, hormones, communication

Relationship researchers are increasingly identifying hormonal correlates of relationship-maintaining behaviors. Relational maintenance entails behaviors aimed at keeping relationships at a desired level or moving the relationship forward (Dindia, 2003; Duck, 1988; Stafford & Canary, 1991). From an evolutionary standpoint, relational maintenance helps individuals retain their relationships—which provide resources (e.g., food, money, and a reproductive partner) and protection (e.g., against threats and deprivation of basic human needs)—thereby contributing to human survival and reproduction (see Ogolsky et al., 2017; Tokunaga, 2016). Indeed, romantic love has been conceptualized as a "commitment device" that aids in sustaining pair-bonds and which has contributed to the evolution of humans' advanced social intelligence (Fletcher et al., 2015, p. 20). The evolution of pair-bonds is also understood through the hormonal mechanisms "by which social traits critical to life-history trade-offs are expressed" (van Anders et al., 2011, p.

1267). As such, a comprehensive understanding of in-pair mating requires an examination of the hormonal correlates of relational maintenance behaviors.

The present chapter examines three hormones that are key to a range of relationship maintaining behaviors: testosterone, oxytocin, and cortisol. The integrative model of relationship maintenance (Ogolsky et al., 2017), which identifies individual (i.e., processes driven by one partner or by internal motivations) and interactive (i.e., processes enacted by both relational partners or in response to one partner's behavior) relational maintenance processes, is used as a guiding framework for exploring the associations between testosterone, oxytocin, and cortisol and among key relational maintenance behaviors, such as conflict management, forgiveness, dyadic coping, communication, and social support. This chapter offers a review of research examining biosocial mechanisms in the context of relational maintenance and provides future directions for scholars seeking to further explore the hormonal mechanisms of in-pair mating and maintenance.

The Integrative Model of Relationship Maintenance

Relationships can be maintained in myriad ways, and as such, the literature on relational maintenance is vast. Whereas relational maintenance is often examined in response to negative relational events or relational transgressions, it can also include behaviors aimed at maintaining a positive relationship (Ogolsky et al., 2017). To address the expanse of research on relational maintenance, Ogolosky et al. (2017) proposed a conceptual model of relational maintenance that addresses it as both threat mitigation (i.e., keeping the relationship intact in the face of relational struggle or stress) and relational enhancement (i.e., improving or furthering the relationship). The *integrative model of relationship maintenance* (Ogolsky et al., 2017) identifies both individual and interactive processes that address threat mitigation and relationship enhancement. "Individual maintenance processes emerge from within the individual and may not be directly prompted," whereas interactive processes "are either triggered in response to the behavior of a partner or jointly enacted by both partners" (Ogolsky et al., 2017, p. 277). According to the model, threat-mitigation processes at the individual level include derogation of alternatives (i.e., devaluing alternative partners or relational threats), positive illusions/idealization (i.e., viewing one's relationship as superior or exaggerating a partner's strengths), and attributions (i.e., making attributions that benefit the relationship, such as more positive attributions); at the interactive level, they include conflict management (i.e., dealing with disagreements in a constructive manner), forgiveness (i.e., extending mercy and engaging in relational repair in response to a transgression), sacrifice (i.e., putting one's own needs aside for the sake of one's partner), facilitation (i.e., helping a partner achieve their goals, thereby reducing uncertainty), and dyadic coping (i.e., managing stressors together). The model presents relationship-enhancement processes at the individual level as including relationship thinking (i.e., reflecting upon one's relationship and partner), generosity (i.e., a willingness to give to one's partner), gratitude (i.e., showing appreciation for one's partner, relationship, and life), and prayer (i.e., praying for one's partner); at the interactive level, they include communication (i.e., relational messages meant to benefit the relationship), relationship talk (i.e., discussing one's relationship or aspects of it), social support/responsiveness (i.e., expressing care, concern, or interest for/in one's partner), humor (i.e., using humor to elicit positive emotions), and joint leisure (i.e., participating in leisure activities together). The model further posits that strategies originally intended to mitigate threats can eventually serve to enhance the relationship. For example, individuals may engage in positive illusions or facilitation in response to fears that their relationship is not special or to reduce uncertainty; however, over time, such behaviors may come to enhance the relationship by encouraging partners to continue to value their partnership and help one another meet their goals (Ogolsky et al., 2017). The next section reviews several hormones relevant to understanding relational maintenance.

Hormonal Mechanisms of Relationship Maintenance

Though not directly examined in the integrative model of relationship maintenance, several of the processes noted in the model are associated with hormonal markers. Given the emphasis of the present chapter on hormonal mechanisms of in-pair mating and maintenance, relational processes are the focal point and therefore the remainder of the chapter focuses on the linkages between hormones and the interactive relational-maintenance processes detailed in Ogolsky et al.'s (2017) model.

Testosterone

Testosterone (T) is a steroid hormone from the androgen family secreted by the testes in males and the ovaries in females. It plays an important role in physiological and psychological development and experiences. In terms of its effects on behavior, T is argued to influence psychological and neurological mechanisms (i.e., stress reduction, fear reduction, threat vigilance, and reward motivation) in ways that increase individuals' abilities to respond to competition (Eisenegger et al., 2011). Scholars have specifically conceptualized its influence on approach-related behaviors in service of superordinate goals to reclaim social status and dominance (Terberg & van Honk, 2013; van Anders et al., 2011). Other work identifies its role in fostering mating behavior (see the challenge hypothesis; Archer, 2006).

T plays an important role in risk-taking behavior during adolescence given changes in pubertal hormonal levels, particularly when circumstances involve status concerns and are subject to evaluation by peers (Ellis et al., 2012). Indeed, research has shown associations between T and adolescent girls' alcohol use (Martin et al., 1999) and risk-taking decision-making, and this relationship is most pronounced when social status is salient (Cardoos et al., 2017). In adolescent boys, T indirectly predicts alcohol use through activity in the amygdala and the orbitofrontal cortex (OFC; Peters et al., 2015). Furthermore, T is predictive of future alcohol consumption among adolescent/young adults (Braams et al.,

2016), as well as antisocial behavior (conceptualized as rule-breaking behavior; Chen et al., 2018), and cigarette smoking (Idris et al., 2016). In adult romantic relationships, T is also implicated in risk-taking. Higher T, for instance, is associated with greater incidence of infidelity in men (Klimas et al., 2019). For both men and women, research has shown that partnered individuals with T levels that are comparable to single individuals report desiring uncommitted sexual activity and behavior (Edelstein et al., 2011).

Oxytocin

Oxytocin is a neuropeptide that is produced in the hypothalamus and plays an important role in building and maintaining close relationships (Crespi, 2016). Thus, oxytocin exhibits adaptive functions that contribute to evolved social behavior in humans (Crespi, 2016; MacDonald & MacDonald, 2010). From the hypothalamus, oxytocin is released into the brain and peripheral circulation, where it influences and mediates a range of prosocial behavior, such as parent–infant bonding (including lactation), pair-bonding, social behavior, and stress and anxiety responses (for reviews, see Auyeung et al., 2013; Crespi, 2016; Ten Velden et al., 2014). In his social-evolution model of oxytocin and human cognition, Crespi (2016) notes that "the main cognitive-affective function of oxytocin is hormonally to indicate and quantify, to relevant regions of the brain, that some socially important event may happen, is happening, or has happened, and that one should focus on it, plan regarding it, and remember it because it is expected to influence one's social relationships and socially-mediated inclusive fitness, positively or negatively" (p. 395). In other words, oxytocin promotes the recognition and processing of social behavior.

One way that oxytocin influences prosocial outcomes is by increasing motivation for bonding and nurturing via its association with brain reward systems (see Crespi, 2016, for a review). From an evolutionary standpoint, "natural selection is expected to have favoured such reward systems as quantitative indicators of behaviour that is associated with increases in correlates and components of survival and reproduction" (Crespi, 2016, p. 91). Indeed, oxytocin is linked to maternal care, parent–infant bonding, sexual/romantic pair-bonding, kinship, and ingroup favoritism (Crespi, 2016), reinforcing its connection to the survival of individuals and their kin. However, it is worth noting that oxytocin is not purely prosocial, as it has also been linked to negative behavior directed at outgroups and more favoritism toward one's ingroup (De Dreu et al., 2011; see Crespi, 2016, for a review). Nonetheless, relationship researchers have taken a particular interest in oxytocin given its association with a range of relational and social outcomes, such as relationship quality, social connection, attachment, and pair-bonding (see Carter et al., 2008, for a review; Apter-Levi et al., 2014; Holt-Lunstad et al., 2014), making it a worthy hormone of interest when seeking to understand the hormonal mechanisms associated with sustaining relationships.

Cortisol

Released by the hypothalamic-pituitary-adrenal (HPA) axis, cortisol is a steroid hormone that is elevated in response to stress and/or anxiety (Burke et al., 2005). Cortisol serves myriad functions, including playing a role in metabolism, anti-inflammation, immune activity, the fight-or-flight response, and sensory acuity (Booth et al., 2000; Boren & Veksler, 2011). Variation in cortisol levels throughout the day (i.e., diurnal cortisol) reflects regulation of the HPA axis, such that a high degree of variation reflects healthy regulation, whereas flattened cortisol slopes (i.e., little changes) from morning to evening indicate dysregulation of the HPA axis or chronic stress (Giese-Davis et al., 2004). Cortisol is also released in response to acute stressors or stress tasks. It tends to peak approximately 10 minutes following a stressful task and then recovers back to homeostasis 30–40 minutes after the task (Gordis et al., 2006).

When experiencing stress, if a person's cortisol response is too high or low, delayed, or erratic, or the person is unable to sufficiently recover back to baseline (before stress) levels, it might be considered dysregulated (Dickerson & Kemeny, 2004). Dysregulation of the HPA axis/cortisol indicates that the body is having difficulty regulating the stress response. Although mixed findings have arisen when exploring the link between HPA axis activity and chronic stress, meta-analytic findings suggest that variability in cortisol response is a function of stressor and person features (Miller et al., 2007). In particular, cortisol secretion follows a flattened rhythm (or dysregulated) when stressors threaten physical integrity, involve trauma, and are uncontrollable. Additionally, HPA axis activity increases with individuals' report of greater subjective distress but decreases among those with posttraumatic stress disorder. Consequently, HPA axis activity is shaped by an individual's response to the situation (Miller et al., 2007).

Dysregulation is also associated with increased cortisol awakening response (CAR; 30–40 minutes after awakening), increased cortisol reactivity to a stressor, and other related illnesses (see Boren & Veksler, 2011, for review). CAR is positively associated with job stress and general life stress and negatively associated with fatigue, burnout, and exhaustion (Chida & Steptoe, 2009), suggesting that stress in personal and professional life can lead to dysregulation of cortisol responses. In addition, cortisol is released in response to those stressors that particularly warrant social self-preservation (see Boren & Veksler, 2011, for a review). Together, these reviews indicate that cortisol is relevant to relational communication processes that can both protect and threaten individuals' psychological and physiological health (Robles & Kiecolt-Glaser, 2003).

In the context of relationships, cortisol has been widely studied due to its ability to indicate the body's adaptability to stress (see Floyd & Afifi, 2011. Cortisol has been explored in a variety of communication processes, such as affectionate behavior, conflict, and stressful conversations (Aloia & Solomon, 2015a; Denes, Crowley, et al., 2020; Floyd & Riforgiate, 2008; Ha et al., 2016; Luecken et al., 2009; Priem & Solomon, 2011; Priem et al., 2010; Slatcher et al., 2015). Communication processes serve larger evolutionary goals, as "communication is a primary way in which human beings acquire resources, adapt to stressful situations, protect themselves and close others, and prolong their lives" (Afifi et al., 2015, p. 54). As such, understanding the physiological correlates of communication behavior can help to reveal the hormonal mechanisms related to maintaining pair-bonds and the resources that come with them. Communication research has found that supportive behaviors, received affection, and partner responsiveness buffer the effect of acute stressors on cortisol responses, whereas relational uncertainty, perceived sincerity of hurtful messages during conflict, and exposure to chronic conflict worsen the cortisol reactivity to stressors (Floyd & Riforgiate, 2008; Ha et al., 2016; Luecken et al., 2009; Priem & Solomon, 2011; Slatcher et al., 2015). Overall, dysregulation of cortisol slopes is positively associated with marital conflict and negatively associated with marital satisfaction (Barnett et al., 2005; Saxbe et al., 2008). The findings outlined here underscore the relevance of cortisol in understanding hormonal mechanisms of in-pair mating and maintenance.

Hormonal Mechanisms of Interactive Threat Mitigation

Each of the hormones detailed above has been associated with both threat-mitigating and relationship-enhancing maintenance processes. As noted earlier, at the interactive level, the integrative model of relationship maintenance (Ogolsky et al., 2017) identifies conflict management, forgiveness, sacrifice, facilitative behavior, and dyadic coping as threat-mitigating processes. Each of these five processes and their linkages to testosterone, oxytocin, and/or cortisol are detailed in the next sections.

Conflict Management, Sacrifice, and Forgiveness

Conflict management involves efforts couples make to resolve disagreements, solve problems that arise in the relationship, negotiate solutions, and/or live with conflicting opinions (Ogolsky et al., 2017). How couples manage conflict is indicative of the larger relational climate, suggesting that managing conflict is an important part of relational maintenance. For example, distressed couples tend to engage in less effective, less satisfying, and more aggressive conflict conversations (see Aloia & Solomon, 2015a, for a review). However, managing conflict effectively can benefit relationships and help couples mitigate threats, thereby keeping the relationship and the resources it provides intact and benefiting partners' shared goals related to reproduction and survival. In particular, integrative strategies (which prioritize the needs of both partners and focus on cooperation and collaboration; Sillars, 1980) and negotiation (which focuses on communication aimed at settling disputes; Straus et al., 1996) can help maintain pair-bonds. Integrative strategies and negotiation are associated with a range of positive relational outcomes, such as greater relationship satisfaction (Canary & Cupach, 1988; Canary & Spitzberg, 1989) and longer relationship duration (Shulman et al., 2006; Shulman et al., 2008), suggesting that both are key components of relational maintenance.

The integrative model of relationship maintenance also identifies accommodation as a valuable aspect of conflict management (Ogolsky et al., 2017). Accommodation is a constructive response to relational issues and linked to voicing one's concerns (i.e., an active response that promotes relational repair) and loyalty (i.e., maintaining commitment and hoping for relational change; Ogolsky et al., 2017; Rusbult et al., 1991). The model also notes that accommodation is linked to relationship outcomes that may benefit maintenance, such as commitment and satisfaction. Accommodation is also acknowledged in the context of sacrifice, another interactive threat-mitigation maintenance process within the integrative model of relationship maintenance (Ogolsky et al., 2017).

In the model, sacrifice is presented as the process of putting one's own needs and desires aside for the good of the relationship. When considering the motivations underlying sacrifice, Ogolsky et al. (2017) draw upon work on approach and avoidance goals. Approach and avoidance motivations are based within two systems of behavioral regulation—the behavioral activation system (BAS; approach) and the behavioral inhibition system (BIS; avoidance; Gray, 1990). Approach-oriented individuals enter situations with optimism and hope and recognize the potential for affiliation and connection with others in social situations. Avoidance-oriented individuals, conversely, worry about the potential negative outcomes of social interactions, including rejection by others (Gable, 2006). Approach motivations are linked with more positive social attitudes, more satisfaction, and less loneliness, whereas avoidance motivations are associated with greater loneliness, more negative social attitudes, less satisfaction with one's social life, and greater relationship anxiety (Gable, 2006). From the perspective of sacrifice, avoidance motivations entail putting one's needs aside due to a fear of rejection, disapproval, or relational harm and are linked to poorer relational outcomes, whereas approach motivations for sacrifice are more focused on relationship enhancement and bringing about positive relational outcomes, and as such tend to be more fulfilling and relationship-benefiting (Impett et al., 2005 and Impett et al., 2014, as summarized by Ogolsky et al., 2017).

Related to the management of conflict and the act of sacrificing for one's partner, forgiveness is another threat-mitigating behavior that may benefit in-pair bonding. Forgiveness as a threat mitigation relational maintenance process involves the reduction of motivations to exact revenge or avoid perpetrators and the introduction of benevolent responses (McCullough et al., 2006). In order for forgiveness to occur, a victim must both reduce negative responses and introduce positive responses oriented toward goodwill. Importantly, the reduction of avoidance or revenge motivations alone does not constitute forgiveness. Functionally, forgiveness is conceived as a relational maintenance behavior (Rusbult et al., 2005) that influences levels of investment in relationships (i.e., commitment, satisfaction, and relational investment) and that contributes evolutionarily by encouraging self-sacrifice and social harmony (Fitness & Peterson, 2008). Cognitive or psychological forgiveness is linked with a host of positive outcomes at numerous levels of health (see Lee & Enright, 2019 and Rasmussen et al., 2019 for reviews).

As a communicative construct, forgiveness is expressed directly, conditionally, and indirectly (Kelley, 1998). Direct forgiveness communication is an explicit pardoning of a relational offense that is expressed in both verbal (e.g., "I forgive you") and nonverbal (e.g., a hug that communicates forgiveness) ways. Conditional forgiveness, alternatively, involves a proviso where victims identify circumstances that must be met in order for perpetrators to receive forgiveness. Finally, individuals express indirect forgiveness through messages that minimize the transgression and nonexpressive or "silent" forgiveness (Merolla et al., 2013) by resuming relational roles and routines in ways that signal forgiveness. Research has linked direct forgiveness communication with more positive relational outcomes, including less negative outcomes (Merolla, 2014) and relationship strengthening (Waldron & Kelley, 2005), whereas conditional forgiveness is more consistently linked with more negative affect (Merolla, 2014) and relational weakening (Waldron & Kelley, 2005). Taken together, conflict management, sacrifice, and forgiveness play an important role in mitigating relational threats.

Aspects of the conflict management process, sacrificing for one's partner, and the forgiveness process have been linked to hormonal mechanisms. Regarding conflict and accommodative behavior (which is relevant to both conflict management and sacrifice), recent research has examined the role that T plays in attuning individuals to (non)accommodative behavior during conflict conversations. Specifically, Dhillon et al. (2020) discovered that, for females negotiating a difficult conversation with their male romantic partner, T levels were linked both to their perceptions that their partners were less accommodating during the conflict conversation and with their reports of being less satisfied with the discussion. These results are interesting when paired with recent findings on T reactivity in conflict. Makhanova et al. (2018), for instance, found that males who experienced oppositional behavior during discussions about marital problems experienced greater T reactivity. This finding is consistent with research that demonstrates higher T levels for fathers (and lower T levels for mothers) in conflict-laden marriages (Gettler et al., 2019). It appears that T likely plays an important role in inciting discord during conflicts for both men and women but may do so in different ways.

The findings that link T to perceptions of less partner accommodation and oppositional behavior coincide with prior research that has linked T with aggressive conflict. T is linked with aggressive conflict behaviors among adolescents (Kaiser & Powers, 2006) and adults (Manigault et al., 2019). A more aggressive and antisocial approach by individuals higher in T may be partially explained by T's limiting effects on empathy (Hermans, Putnam, & Van Honk, 2006). Prior research has shown that T administration compromises interpersonal trust through its impacts on neural mechanisms (Bos et al., 2012). It may be that individuals high in T are less capable of activating empathy in the throes of conflict because of superordinate goals to win (Geniole et al., 2017). As such, high T individuals may be more focused on quelling dominance and status threats than on achieving integrative and relational goals. Indeed, prior work has linked T levels to less desire for closeness and lower feelings of closeness (Ketay et al., 2017), as well as with less positive and intentional disclosures (Denes, Afifi, & Granger, 2017).

Oxytocin, on the other hand, has been linked with positive conflict management behaviors and outcomes, in part due to its effect on stress response systems. In certain contexts, oxytocin has been found to dampen the effects of stress via the HPA axis and sympathetic nervous system (SNS; e.g., Ditzen et al., 2009, 2013; Heinrichs et al., 2003). For example, Ditzen et al. (2009) found that couples administered intranasal oxytocin prior to discussing conflict-inducing topics exhibited more positive communication behaviors (e.g., disclosing their emotions and making eye contact) in relation to negative behaviors (e.g., defensiveness and contempt) during the conversation and experienced reduced cortisol levels following the discussion. Some studies suggest that oxytocin may have sex-specific effects on stress. For example, Ditzen et al. (2013) found that women who were given a dose of intranasal oxytocin experienced reduced autonomic nervous system activity, as indicated by salivary alpha-amylase (sAA) levels, during a conflict interaction, whereas men who were given intranasal oxytocin experienced increased sAA. Oxytocin is also associated with more cooperative behaviors among ingroup members, due to its influence on social categorization, fear/trust perceptions, and neural processes related to empathy (De Dreu, 2012). As such, the hormone may also be predictive of more integrative and negotiation-based conflict strategies, which involve a commitment to addressing both partners' needs and therefore require a certain degree of social awareness, trust in one's partner, and empathy for their goals.

Communication researchers have paid particular attention to cortisol reactivity as a physiological indicator of stress following a conflict discussion. The degree of uncontrollability and the possibility of a negative evaluation by a partner during a relational conflict triggers HPA axis activity (or cortisol reactivity), making it particularly relevant to understanding physiological responses to conflict (Dickerson & Kemeny, 2004). Aloia and Solomon (2015a) found that conflict interactions evoke a cortisol response among romantic partners, but that these responses are amplified due to greater intensity of conflict, suggesting that more intense conflict can lead to sharp increases in cortisol, making the body less adaptive to stress. Alongside these findings, other research demonstrates that the quality of communication during conflict is closely connected with cortisol dysregulation. For example, relational meanings attached to hurtful messages and feelings of hurt predict increases in cortisol following hurtful interactions (Priem et al., 2010).

Supporting these findings that link message features with cortisol, both avoidance and approach behaviors during disputes have been found to influence cortisol responses and their trajectory following conflict. For example, one study found that topic avoidance and withdrawal during conflict were positively associated with increased cortisol from preinteraction to after the conflict, whereas topic avoidance, indirectness, and withdrawal were positively associated with decreased cortisol following a cool-down period after the conflict (King & Theiss, 2016). Additionally, criticism and demandingness were negatively associated with decreased cortisol following the postconflict cool-down (King & Thiess, 2016). Stated another way, individuals who used avoidant behaviors during the conflict interaction recovered more quickly from the stressful episode, and individuals who were more confrontational saw a continued increase in their cortisol levels following the conflict and did not recover as quickly. Furthermore, heightened cortisol reactivity for husbands is associated with marital criticism during conflict discussions, whereas for wives, the positive association between cortisol reactivity and criticism is a function of experiencing high levels of marital aggression in the previous year (Rodriguez & Margolin, 2013). These findings suggest that men's cortisol responds to critical behaviors during a current conflict discussion, but women's physiological reactivity to a conflict discussion may be related to more chronic experiences of relational aggression (Rodriguez & Margolin, 2013). Apart from criticism, other qualities of the conflict interaction, namely, loudness and disagreement, are associated with both men's and women's amplified stress response postconflict, whereas sarcasm is only linked with men's cortisol responses (Aloia & Solomon, 2015b).

Sex differences in cortisol responses to conflict are illuminated elsewhere as well. For example, wife demand/husband withdrawal patterns (objectively observed) predict higher cortisol response in wives but not husbands, indicating a greater impact of negative conflict behaviors on women's physiological responses (Heffner et al., 2006; Kiecolt-Glaser et al., 1996). Additionally, husbands have heightened reactivity to conflict both when they are low in power and when couples share power in the marriage, whereas wives show healthier declines in cortisol when they are high in power and when the couple shares power (Loving et al., 2004). However, in older couples, perceptions (rather than objective observations) of wife demand/husband withdrawal behavior during conflict increased both husbands' and wives' cortisol reactivity (Heffner et al., 2006). Apparently, sex differences in cortisol reactivity to conflict may diminish in long-term relationships as perceptions of behaviors, rather than the actual behaviors, become more relevant.

Although negative or hostile behaviors during conflict heighten the cortisol response and impair the body's stress response, positive behaviors during conflict discussions can enhance physiological stress responses by amplifying the body's adaptability to the stress induced by such disagreements (Floyd, 2014). For example, Robles et al. (2006) found that, when couples displayed high levels of negative behavior during conflict, the more wives' engaged in positive behaviors (characterized by supportive communication, humor, and problem-solving behavior), the sharper wives' declines in cortisol responses to conflict, emphasizing that constructive engagement in conflict discussions promotes healthier physiological stress responses (Robles et al., 2006). Additional evidence suggests that satisfaction with spousal support during conflict also affects cortisol responses to conflict, such that newlywed wives and older husbands recorded healthier cortisol responses to conflict discussions when they perceived greater satisfaction with spousal support during the conflict (Heffner et al., 2004).

In summary, relational partners' positive/negative and approach/avoidance behaviors during conflict play a meaningful role in determining the body's stress regulation through the release of cortisol. The findings outlined above also reveal that women and men might respond in unique ways to a conflict episode. Given that conflict management is an integral relational maintenance behavior and constructive conflict management characterized by supportive behaviors is associated with healthier cortisol reactivity, cortisol is extremely relevant to understanding the aftermath of relational maintenance strategies used during conflict episodes. In the aftermath of conflict or relational transgressions, individuals may also need to engage in forgiveness to help repair the relationship.

Research on the physiological correlates of forgiveness has explored the potential role of T in the forgiveness communication process. Crowley et al. (2019) investigated the influence of expressive writing about relational transgressions on participants' willingness to forgive their current relational partners. Expressive writing refers to revealing deep thoughts and feelings in writing about a significant or troubling topic (Pennebaker, 1997). Expressive writing is robustly linked to a host of physical and mental benefits (Pennebaker & Chung, 2011) as well as relational well-being (Lepore & Greenberg, 2002) and, as such, Crowley et al. (2019) sought to examine whether it can help victims of relational transgressions to cope in ways that encourage relational maintenance. In addition to investigating the effects of expressive writing on forgiveness, the study investigated changes in victims' T levels, assuming that experiences with severe relational transgressions might result in elevated T levels given the threats they pose to individuals' feelings of dominance and social status in their relationship. That is, relational transgressions cannot only present an obstacle to individuals' sense of control and dominance in their relationship but can also threaten one's reputation and the reputation of their relationship, thus compromising the stability of their social status within the broader social network in which they are situated.

The findings identified differing associations between forgiveness communication and T. Specifically, levels of T were negatively associated with direct forgiveness and positively with conditional forgiveness (Crowley et al., 2019). These results underscore the notion that T influences approach-oriented behavior, which seeks to quell threats to dominance and social status and does so through neurological mechanisms such as fear and stress reduction (Eisenneger et al., 2011). Indeed, direct forgiveness communicates individuals' confidence about their relationship's future and a psychological sense of safety about the low likelihood of recurring transgressions (Waldron & Kelley, 2005). Conditional forgiveness, alternatively, is characterized by a lack of psychological safety and connotes concerns about future transgressions (Waldron & Kelley, 2005). Moreover, conditional forgiveness is avoidant behavior, as it functionally helps victims to establish a sense of security in their relationship in the wake of transgressions. Direct forgiveness, conversely, is approach behavior, as explicitly forgiving a transgression underscores hope, optimism, and importantly a lack of fear about the relationship's future.

In a manner similar to the mixed findings for T and its influence on forgiveness communication, research on T and disclosure, as yet another relational maintenance integrative strategy (discussed further below), also indicates heterogeneous findings. Recent work has shown, for instance, that T mediates the association between uncertainty levels and disclosure whereby uncertainty is negatively associated with T levels and T levels are positively associated with willingness to disclose (Crowley et al., 2018). Because uncertainty is characterized by feelings of anxiety and fear (Knobloch, Miller, Bond, et al., 2007), it makes sense that it would decrease with rising T levels, as research has shown that T functions to lessen worrisome feelings (Hermans, Putnam, Baas, et al., 2006). T's positive association with disclosure in the study by Crowley et al. (2018), however, is inconsistent with other research that has shown that T levels are associated with greater risk perceptions of disclosure during pillow talk (i.e., communication in the time period directly following sex; Denes, Afifi, & Granger, 2017). It is possible that, because T influences efforts toward mating and because pillow talk disclosures occur after sex, such disclosures are perceived as inconsequential to mating goals (which may have already been met). In fact, engaging in vulnerable self-disclosures may compromise feelings of dominance in relationships and therefore exist in contrast to T's underlying goals. With respect to the findings from Crowley et al. (2018), the positive association between T and disclosure manifests in the aftermath of relational transgressions, and thus disclosure, in this context, may be an effort to quell the particular status and dominance threats that emanated from the transgression. Future research is needed to reconcile these heterogeneous findings.

In sum, the research on T and conflict paints a complicated picture where T may influence behaviors that are approach-oriented and prosocial such as with forgiveness communication and disclosure, which are both central to relational maintenance processes (Rusbult et al., 2005; Stafford & Canary, 1991). On the other hand, it appears that, with respect to the actual communicative behaviors enacted within conflict, T may foster antisocial outcomes, as T is linked with aggressive behaviors and perceptions that others are relating more aggressively during conflict. It may be that T disrupts relationship maintenance if it triggers goals that are more self-oriented than relationally-oriented. That is, T may encourage self-serving goals to reclaim dominance and social status. Whereas those goals may coincide with relational maintenance goals, these two goals are not necessarily interwoven and thus T activation may create further discord in relational contexts, particularly within hierarchical romantic relationships or those that are already experiencing strife and conflict.

Facilitative Behavior and Dyadic Coping

Facilitative behavior involves actions that help partners achieve their goals and meet their needs (Knobloch & Solomon, 2004). As opposed to interference, which impedes or prevents goal achievement, facilitation "makes achieving goals or performing activities easier" and is associated with positive emotions (Knobloch & Solomon, 2004; Solomon et al., 2016, p. 514). As reviewed in the integrative model of relationship maintenance (Ogolsky et al., 2017), facilitative behavior is associated with a range of positive relational outcomes, such as greater adjustment, closeness, and affection (Jackman-Cram et al., 2006; Knobloch & Schmelzer, 2008; Knobloch & Solomon, 2004) and less uncertainty and turbulence (Knobloch, Miller, & Carpenter, 2007; McLaren et al., 2011). As such, helping a partner meet their goals via facilitative behaviors benefits the maintenance of one's relationship and can help mitigate relational threats.

Another maintenance process that couples employ to manage threats is dyadic coping, which is "the process by which an individual's stress elicits coping reactions from his or her partner" (Ogolsky et al., 2017, p. 283). One way that dyadic coping occurs is via supportive dyadic coping, in which one partner provides tangible and emotional support to the stressed partner (Ogolsky et al., 2017). Emotional support entails showing empathy, love, or affection for one's partner, whereas tangible support focuses on providing more concrete or instrumental forms of support, such as assisting with responsibilities or offering material assistance (Ogolsky et al., 2017; Xu & Burleson, 2001). A meta-analysis indicated the robust benefits of dyadic coping in relationships, finding that dyadic coping by either one member of the couple or both partners is strongly associated with relationship satisfaction (Falconier et al., 2015). Recent theories of resilience also note the value of providing a supportive relational environment when communicating about stressors, suggesting that couples who approach difficulties as a team are better able to manage the individual and relational impact of stress (Afifi et al., 2016).

Research on oxytocin and cortisol helps illuminate the hormonal mechanisms of facilitative behavior and dyadic coping. Oxytocin plays a key role in facilitative behavior associated with maternal care and nurturance (Galbally et al., 2011). The benefits of oxytocin to facilitative behavior have also been recognized in adult pair-bonds, as oxytocin has been identified as a hormone that promotes nurturing behavior, social bonding, and sexual intimacy (van Anders et al., 2011). As such, some scholars have suggested that therapies involving neurochemical enhancers, such as oxytocin administration, might "be used in *conjunction* with counseling and/or other controlled activities to facilitate communication and the pursuit of joint goals and ideals between couples experiencing conflict" (Wudarczyk et al., 2013, p. 3). Oxytocin has also been found to promote perceptions of an individual's own communal or other-oriented behavior, especially for individuals with an attachment style that may indicate a lack of connection or intimacy with others (Bartz et al., 2015). Such findings reinforce the hormone's linkages to relational maintenance, and facilitative behaviors specifically, as they emphasize oxytocin's effect on helping close others thrive. Taken together, oxytocin is implicated in in-pair mating and maintenance via its influence in contexts where social bonding goals are salient (van Anders et al., 2011). From an evolutionary perspective, oxytocin promotes pair-bonds, and in turn, pair-bonds provide benefits to health and safety, thereby promoting viability of individuals and their kin (Fletcher et al., 2015; van Anders et al., 2011).

Facilitation has also been explored in the context of relational turbulence, based on the idea that perceptions of partner facilitation or interference during relational transitions can lead to intensified emotions, in turn influencing relational turbulence (Solomon et al., 2016). Research on relational turbulence and relationship transitions posits that when partners are progressing in their relationship, they begin to question relational involvement (Solomon et al., 2016). In other words, romantic partners moving through transitions (such as casual to seriously dating and dating to engaged) experience relational uncertainty. During such transitions, conversations can become stressful and influence cortisol stress responses (Loving et al., 2009). Specifically, when dating partners discuss their potential for a future transition from dating to marriage, increases in marriage novelty (i.e., the extent to which they do not think or talk about marriage with their current partner, so the topic of marriage is novel) are associated with heightened cortisol reactivity (Loving et al., 2009). In other words, individuals with less prior experience with the transition topic experienced greater or elevated physiological stress responses. Loving et al. (2009) note that HPA axis reactivity during the interaction could be due to high conversational uncertainty.

As such, research underscores the role of relational uncertainty (which, as noted earlier, is negatively associated with facilitation; Knobloch, Miller, Bond, et al., 2007; McLaren et al., 2011) in physiological stress responses. Priem and Solomon (2011) conducted two separate studies to examine how relational uncertainty affects cortisol reactivity in response to a hurtful interaction with a partner, and cortisol recovery from a stressful task that was followed by a supportive interaction with a partner. In the context of a hurtful interaction, individuals who were more uncertain about their partner's involvement or feelings (i.e., higher partner uncertainty) demonstrated greater increases in cortisol compared to those who reported less partner uncertainty. In the context of a supportive interaction, partner uncertainty was associated with less cortisol recovery from a stressful episode following an interaction with the partner. Priem and Solomon (2011) also found that in the case of supportive messages, relational uncertainty attenuated the cortisol response to the stress induction task. These findings indicate that experiencing uncertainty is stressful and can have an effect on physiological responses to other stressors. Uncertainty about a partner can make a hurtful interaction more stressful and a supportive interaction less stress relieving, thus leading to maladaptive cortisol responses (Priem & Solomon, 2011).

Dyadic coping is also linked to cortisol and oxytocin responses. Parents are principal stress regulators for children during infancy, but as they move into adolescence, the buffering effect of parental support on HPA axis reactivity begins to fade and romantic partners assume the protective role of buffering HPA axis stress responses by adulthood (Gunnar & Hostinar, 2015). As such, communication in romantic relationships can alter individuals' responses to stressful situations and, therefore, influence cortisol responses and reactivity. Supporting this assertion, Merrill and Afifi (2017) found that partners vary in their ability to manage stress. The study revealed that perceived couple identity gaps (which emerged due to a difference in the couple's identity and how this identity was communicated) were positively associated with men's self-reported psychological stress and anxiety and baseline cortisol, as well as positively associated with women's cortisol reactivity to a conflict discussion (Merrill & Afifi, 2017).

One theory that is particularly relevant to understanding the hormonal mechanisms of coping and facilitative behaviors is the theory of resilience and relational load (TRRL; Afifi et al., 2016). The TRRL asserts that relational partners (or families) that maintain their relationships on a regular basis accumulate positive emotional reserves that aid in relationship protection during times of distress (Afifi et al., 2016). Specifically, the theory posits that investing in one's relationship over time via prosocial relational maintenance is key to managing stress and fostering resilience (Afifi et al., 2016). The theory was tested in couples with adolescent children who have type 1 diabetes (Afifi et al., 2019). Couples were randomly assigned to either an intervention where they were asked to increase their relational maintenance behaviors for two weeks or the control condition. The study revealed that maintenance is associated with less perceived and physiological stress (cortisol) following a stressful conversation. The intervention also helped improve women's thriving, communal orientation, and loneliness levels. As such, it may be the case that women in relationships characterized by high routine maintenance have healthier cortisol rhythms in response to everyday stressors.

As noted earlier, oxytocin has also been implicated in the context of couples' conflict and coping in relation to the hormone's stress-reducing effects (e.g., Ditzen et al., 2009, 2013). Such research has directly investigated the role of dyadic coping in the oxytocin-stress link. More specifically, Zietlow et al. (2019) found that individuals who reported low dyadic coping experienced greater benefits from receiving intranasal oxytocin in regard to their cortisol responses, perhaps suggesting that individuals who do not feel they provided adequate support stand to gain the most from oxytocin and its stress-dampening influence. In terms of supportive others, research has found that the presence of a support provider can also enhance the effects of oxytocin on stress. For example, one study revealed that social support and oxytocin combine to exert an anxiolytic effect on cortisol, such that individuals who received intranasal oxytocin and had the support of a close other during a stressful task exhibited the lowest cortisol levels, whereas those who did not receive oxytocin and did not have the support of a close other had the highest cortisol levels (Heinrichs et al., 2003). Social support in the form of dyadic coping is also linked with cortisol recovery. Specifically, stressed individuals who received positive dyadic coping from a partner recovered faster from stress (Meuwly et al., 2012). Taken together, both cortisol and oxytocin play a role in processes related to facilitation and dyadic coping, reinforcing that hormonal mechanisms are associated with various maintenance behaviors aimed at mitigating relational threats.

Hormonal Mechanisms of Interactive Relationship Enhancement

The integrative model of relationship maintenance also details interactive strategies that aim to enhance the relationship (Ogolsky et al., 2017). Such strategies include communicative relationship maintenance strategies, relationship talk, social support and responsiveness, humor, and joint activities. Each of these relational maintenance processes involves behaviors that individuals and couples enact to sustain and improve their relationships, and such processes have been linked in various ways to hormones and hormonal responses, as detailed next.

Communicative Relationship Maintenance Strategies and Relationship Talk

Within the area of communicative relationship maintenance strategies, researchers have identified a number of behaviors that aid in promoting and sustaining relationships (Canary & Stafford, 1992; Stafford & Canary, 1991). Work in this domain originally offered a typology of five communication-based strategies that couples enact to keep their relationship intact (Stafford & Canary, 1991). These strategies include (a) *positivity*, which involves maintaining a cheerful and pleasant relational environment; (b) *openness*, which entails sharing the details of one's feelings, thoughts, and life with a partner; (c) *assurances*, or behaviors that reinforce one's commitment to the relationship and its future; (d) *networks*, which focuses on maintaining connections with partners' social networks; and (e) *sharing tasks*, which involves managing responsibilities and commitments together (Stafford & Canary, 1991).

Further work on these strategies distinguished between routine and strategic behaviors (Dainton & Stafford, 1993). Routine behaviors include those that are more habitual and not necessarily enacted with relational maintenance goals in mind, whereas strategic behaviors are those enacted purposely and with the intent of keeping the relationship intact and/or enhancing the relationship (Dainton & Stafford, 1993; Stafford et al., 2000). Though communicative maintenance strategies can vary in their intention to meet maintenance needs (i.e., routine vs. strategic), a range of behaviors in both the strategic and routine realms are associated with greater relationship satisfaction and commitment (Dainton & Aylor, 2002). Research has also identified negative relational maintenance strategies, which entail antisocial behaviors aimed at keeping the relationship intact, such as inducing jealousy, avoiding one's partner or certain interactions, and spying (Dainton & Gross, 2008). From an evolutionary perspective, certain negative maintenance strategies, such as surveillance, may be adaptive in helping monitor the environment for potential relational threats (Tokunaga, 2016).

Relationship talk is another interactive relationship-enhancing process identified in the integrative model of relationship maintenance (Ogolsky et al., 2017). Relationship talk involves communication about aspects of the relationship, which can include identifying relational desires and goals, negotiating the relationship development process, and clarifying relational definitions (Ogolsky et al., 2017). In this way, relationship talk shares conceptual overlap with certain communicative strategies identified above, such as assurances and openness. Though relationship talk can be beneficial in reducing uncertainty and potentially moving the relationship forward, such talk can also be stress-inducing and threaten the relationship if partners are not in agreement (Ogolsky et al., 2017).

Hormonal mechanisms have been linked, both directly and indirectly, to communicative maintenance and relationship talk. For example, relational maintenance is associated with one's cortisol awakening response (Afifi et al., 2020). Research finds that reports of receiving greater relational maintenance from spouses is associated with a greater rise in cortisol awakening responses, indicating that consistent relational maintenance helps partners better manage daily stress due to work-life balance in dual-career families (Afifi et al., 2020). Because chronic stress, such as that created by the demands of balancing work and family, can slowly wear away the body's physiological stress responses, greater increases in CAR may indicate healthier (or less dysregulated) HPA axis functioning in response to daily stressors (Afifi et al., 2020). Findings by Afifi et al. (2020) revealed that routine relational maintenance buffers spouses' physiological responses to daily stress.

The communicative relationship maintenance strategy of openness, as well as relationship talk, involves the disclosing of one's thoughts and feelings. Self-disclosure is not only associated with intimacy, but it may also attenuate the effect of stressors or worries on cortisol reactivity (Slatcher et al., 2010). Intentionally holding back thoughts or emotions, or engaging in topic avoidance, can lead to adverse stress responses such as increased cortisol production, whereas disclosing thoughts and emotions in the form of expressive writing has been linked with healthier cortisol reactivity (Pennebaker & Chung, 2011; Smyth et al., 2008; Traue, & Deighton, 1999; van Middendorp et al., 2009). In the context of marital relationships, women reporting greater marital satisfaction and relational disclosure experienced a healthier cortisol rhythm in response to worries related to work (Slatcher et al., 2010). In other words, disclosing thoughts and feelings to a significant other facilitates the stress-buffering effect of a happy marriage for women. Similarly, in a lab interaction where partners were asked to intentionally respond in a disconfirming and hurtful manner to their dating partner's discussion of core traits and values, it was found that individuals who perceived their partners to be affiliative demonstrated an increase in "stability in cortisol change" (Priem et al., 2010). Stability in cortisol change "measures whether changes occurred over time is [sic] reflected in total hormonal output; therefore, it indexes stability in cortisol change" (Priem et al., 2010, p. 59). In other words, when a partner expresses liking or affiliation even during a negative interaction, receivers experience less increase in stress over time (Priem et al., 2010). Together, these findings suggest that openness and relationship talk, when coupled with positive and affiliative behavior, not only serve to enhance the relationship but may also garner physiological stress benefits.

Though yet to be directly tested, some scholars have suggested that individuals' hormone levels may also predict the enactment of relational maintenance behaviors (in the context of sexual activity, specifically; Denes, Dhillon, & Speer, 2017). More specifically,

Denes, Dhillon, and Speer (2017) tested whether experiencing orgasm is associated with the enactment of communicative relationship maintenance strategies, given that orgasm is linked with increases in oxytocin (Blaicher et al., 1999; Carmichael et al., 1987; for further explanation, see the section on "Joint Leisure Activities"). The study found that individuals who experienced orgasm during sexual activity reported enacting the strategy of assurances (i.e., confirming one's commitment to the relationship and its future) more than those who did not orgasm (Denes, Dhillon, & Speer, 2017). Though oxytocin levels were not directly tested in that study, Denes, Dhillon, and Speer (2017) suggest that orgasm may be a proxy for oxytocin increases, and thus the greater assurances enacted by individuals who orgasm may reflect oxytocin's enhancement of behaviors aimed at reinforcing pair-bonds between partners.

The orgasm-oxytocin link has also been applied to research examining positive relational disclosures immediately following sexual activity, sometimes referred to as pillow talk (Denes, 2012). Positive relational disclosures involve the expression of positive thoughts and feelings about one's partner (Denes, 2012), and as such, might be considered a form of relationship talk and affectionate communication. Models of post sex disclosure suggest that, because of oxytocin's fear-reducing and trust-enhancing effects (Kirsch et al., 2005; Kosfeld et al., 2005), individuals who orgasm (and therefore, are expected to experience a surge of oxytocin) should perceive fewer risks and greater benefits to engaging in relationship talk immediately following sexual activity (Denes, 2018). Several studies found support for the orgasm-pillow talk hypothesis, demonstrating that individuals who orgasm disclose more positive thoughts and feelings for their partners post sex (Denes, 2012, 2018; Denes & Afifi, 2014). Some support has also been found for the mediating role of risk-benefit assessments. Denes and Afifi (2014) found that individuals who orgasmed perceived greater benefits to disclosing postsex (but not fewer risks), and Denes (2018) found that orgasm predicted perceiving greater benefits/fewer risks, which in turn predicted more positive relational disclosures to one's partner postsex. Considering these findings, it seems that a bidirectional relationship likely exists between hormone levels and positive relational behaviors such as self-disclosure, affiliation, and relational maintenance. Such findings may also suggest that communicative relationship maintenance strategies and relationship talk exert stress buffering effects and that cortisol and oxytocin help explain the association between such behavior and relational well-being.

Social Support, Responsiveness, and Humor

As noted earlier, social support can serve the function of mitigating threat and stressors in relationships. However, it can also help to enhance relationships. From a relationship-enhancing perspective, social support and responsiveness can reinforce feelings of caring and concern for one's partner (Ogolsky et al., 2017). Indeed, responsiveness involves providing support in times of need, which can signal empathy and help reinforce and maintain pair-bonds (Ogolsky et al., 2017). Similarly, humor can be employed as a prosocial and positive way of coping with stress, as well as to communicate feelings of affection and intimacy; as such, it is unsurprising that the use of positive forms of humor in relationships is correlated with a range of indicators of relational well-being (see Ogolsky et al., 2017, for a review).

One way that individuals may signal support to their partners, enact responsiveness, and employ humor is by engaging in affectionate communication. Affectionate communication involves the sending and receiving of verbal and nonverbal messages that communicate feelings of closeness, love, fondness, caring, and/or positive regard (Floyd & Morman, 1998). As such, affectionate communication has been framed as a form of relational maintenance (e.g., Myers et al., 2011) and trait affectionate communication tendencies have been found to predict individuals' willingness to enact communicative relational maintenance strategies (Pauley et al., 2014). Affectionate communication is also associated with myriad positive outcomes in relationships (see Floyd et al., 2015, and Denes, Bennett, & Winkler, 2017, for reviews), reinforcing its role in building and sustaining close relationships (Floyd & Voloudakis, 1999).

Affectionate communication in relationships has a beneficial effect on both the psychological and physiological health of individuals (Boren & Veksler, 2011). Both the giving and receiving of affectionate communication has stress-buffering effects (see Floyd & Afifi, 2011, for a review), and like other social skills such as warmth, social support, and responsiveness, affection is a key moderator of stress reaction in the HPA axis (Floyd & Afifi, 2011). In fact, controlling for received affection, the propensity to engage in more affectionate communication (i.e., trait affection) is associated with average daily cortisol levels, waking cortisol, and decreases in diurnal variation of cortisol, indicating healthy regulation of the HPA axis (Floyd, 2006). Additionally, marital partners who receive greater affection from their spouses, manifested in verbal, nonverbal, and supportive affectionate behaviors, demonstrate higher CAR and a healthy diurnal change in cortisol (Floyd & Riforgiate, 2008). Humor is also likely to benefit individuals' stress levels, as humor and laughter have been linked to a range of positive health outcomes, including reduced cortisol levels (for a review, see Savage et al., 2017). Humor can also be used as a coping tool for managing life difficulties, and greater use of humor for coping has been associated with lower awakening cortisol levels in a study of older men (Lai et al., 2010). These findings underscore that expressing and receiving affection, as well as the use of humor, in relationships is pertinent to healthier regulation of cortisol in response to daily stress among relational partners.

Further revealing the moderating effect of affectionate communication on physiological stress responses, research has found that verbal and supportive affection in significant relationships predicted lower cortisol responses to acute stressors (Floyd et al., 2007b). Stated another way, individuals who reported a greater amount of verbal and supportive affectionate communication in their most significant relationship demonstrated faster stress recovery in response to a stress test. The moderating effect of affection has also been demonstrated even when affection is expressed in writing. For example, research found that those who express affectionate thoughts and feelings for a loved one in writing were able to downregulate their cortisol levels or recover from the stress tasks faster than those who merely thought about a loved one or sat quietly (Floyd et al., 2007a).

Affectionate communication manifested in touch and intimacy also has implications for HPA axis activity (Ditzen et al., 2009; Ditzen et al., 2008). More specifically, results of a diary study show that physical intimacy in romantic relationships is linked with average daily cortisol levels, such that romantic partners have lower cortisol levels on days that they report higher physical intimacy (e.g., holding hands and hugging; Ditzen et al., 2008). Further, receiving affectionate touch from a spouse or cohabiting partner prior to a stress induction task reduces women's cortisol responses to a stress test (Ditzen et al., 2009).

As noted earlier in regard to facilitation and dyadic coping, oxytocin and the presence of a support provider interact to buffer cortisol responses to stressful tasks (Heinrichs et al., 2003). Greater support from a partner has also been associated with increased oxytocin levels before and after a session of warm physical and emotional interaction between romantic partners (Grewen et al., 2005). Grewen et al. (2005) suggested that positive and supportive relational environments may have long-term cumulative effects by promoting oxytocin production. Oxytocin has also been linked to other supportive and warm relational behaviors, such as affectionate communication and touch. For example, Floyd et al. (2010) found that higher state and trait affectionate communication was associated with greater oxytocin reactivity in response to stress-induction tasks. Research examining affectionate forms of touch also finds that oxytocin is associated with hugging, warm touch, and massage, reinforcing the linkages between supportive and responsive behaviors and hormonal responses (Holt-Lundstad et al., 2008; Light et al., 2005; Morhenn et al., 2012). Taken together, affectionate behaviors—characterized by intimacy, warmth, touch, verbal and social affection, and writing affectionate thoughts and feelings—are an important form of communicating support and responsiveness and are linked with various hormonal mechanisms including but not limited to cortisol and oxytocin responses to stressful tasks and daily hormone levels.

Joint Leisure Activities

Joint leisure activities are identified in the integrative model of relationship maintenance as highly interactive activities that partners engage in together and are conceptualized as contributors to relational well-being (Ogolsky et al., 2017). Though perhaps a unique take on "leisure," sexual behavior between partners may be considered a leisure activity that helps partners maintain and enhance their relationship. Indeed, a sex-positive approach that acknowledges the importance of sexual desire and pleasure allows leisure scholars "to carve out a niche by advocating for and studying the roles of sex as leisure in the fulfillment of human rights and wellbeing" (Berdychevsky & Carr, 2020, p. 256).

Leisure scholars have increasingly recognized the ways in which sex constitutes a leisure activity and its ability to serve a range of leisure-related needs. More specifically, scholars acknowledge that "leisured sex" is about "having the time to give to exercise one's interest in sex, to engage in sex as a form of relaxation, entertainment, self-realization, self-gratification and gratification of others, and personal development" (Attwood & Smith, 2013, pp. 330–331). Satisfying sexual experiences may be particularly important in enhancing and sustaining pair-bonds by encouraging continued sexual activity and discouraging extradyadic relationships (Buss & Shackelford, 1997).

Oxytocin and testosterone are especially meaningful hormones to consider in the context of sexual activity, especially when considering aspects of sexual pleasure and desire. Oxytocin is released during sexual activity and has been associated with the intensity of orgasm and contentment after orgasm (Behnia et al., 2014; Carter, 1992; Zhang et al., 2015). Oxytocin has also been found to increase following orgasm (Blaicher et al., 1999; Carmichael et al., 1987; Murphy et al., 1987). Testosterone is responsive to sexual activity, and has been found to increase prior to sexual activity as well as the day following sexual activity (Dabbs & Mohammed, 1992; Hamilton & Meston, 2010). The link between testosterone and orgasm is less consistent, as the hormone has been positively associated with the frequency and likelihood of orgasm in some studies (Knussmann et al., 1986; van Anders et al., 2007), but not in others (Kruger et al., 1998; Lee et al., 1974). Such findings suggest that hormonal markers serve as both outcomes (e.g., of sexual satiation and bonding) and antecedents (e.g., of sexual desire and interest in sex) of leisured sex.

Hormonal mechanisms have also aided in understanding sexual communication processes. Communication in sexual contexts serves to enhance pair-bonds between sexual partners by reinforcing one's commitment to the future of the relationship (Denes, Afifi, & Granger, 2017), and various hormones may help explain individuals' propensity to engage in such behavior. As noted earlier, the links between oxytocin and testosterone have been theorized and tested in the context of sexual communication (for reviews, see Denes, Bennett, & DelGreco, 2020; Denes, Dhillon, et al., 2020). For example, Denes, Afifi, and Granger (2017) found that individuals' communication after sexual activity was predicted by individuals' T levels, such that the higher one's T levels, the fewer benefits and greater risks they perceived to disclosing to their partners postsex. In turn, those risk-benefit assessments predicted individuals disclosing less positive thoughts and feelings after sexual activity. The effect of T was also moderated by orgasm (Denes, Afifi, & Granger, 2017). In prior work, orgasm has been framed as a proxy for increased oxytocin and theorized to enhance postsex communication via its influence on perceptions of threat and reward. Denes, Afifi, and Granger (2017) found that for individuals who did not experience orgasm, T predicted postsex communication, but the same relationship was not significant for individuals who did experience orgasm, leading the researchers to suggest that orgasm and the assumed oxytocin surges that accompany it may nullify the negative effect of T on pair-bonding postsex. Additionally, men's oxytocin levels have been associated with the postsex disclosures process, such that the higher men's oxytocin levels after sexual activity, the greater benefits and fewer risks they perceived to disclosing postsex (Denes et al., 2021).

Finally, several studies examining cortisol in the context of sexual activity found that sexual arousal in women coincides with decreases in cortisol levels (Hamilton et al., 2008; Hamilton & Meston, 2011). Hamilton et al. (2008) found that the majority of women demonstrated reduced cortisol in response to watching a sexual film; however, genital arousal was not associated with cortisol levels. Another study revealed that anxiety does not influence physiological stress responses in women, whereas watching both sexual and humorous films was associated with decreased cortisol responses (Hamilton & Meston, 2011). Elsewhere, Goldey and van Anders (2011) found that imagining a sexual episode led to increases in T levels but did not affect cortisol levels, suggesting that sexual thoughts do not exhibit direct effects on cortisol responses. Taken together, the associations among oxytocin, T, cortisol, and social and sexual behaviors suggest that hormonal mechanisms may serve as cause and consequence of sexual behavior and the communication that accompanies it.

Conclusions and Future Directions

As detailed in this chapter, hormonal mechanisms are associated with in-pair mating and the maintenance of close relationships. This chapter focused on three key hormones (i.e., testosterone, oxytocin, and cortisol) and their linkages to the interactive relational maintenance processes detailed in the integrative model of relationship maintenance (Ogolsky et al., 2017). These processes are expected to together promote the longevity and success of one's relationship, and thus, it is unsurprising that, on a larger level, these hormones are linked to various indictors of relational well-being.

The review of T and relational maintenance with respect to integrative behaviors—such as forgiveness, disclosure, conflict, and accommodation—in this chapter has painted a somewhat complex picture where T is both associated with antisocial (e.g., perceptions of less partner accommodation and aggressive conflict behaviors) and prosocial (e.g., conditional forgiveness communication and disclosure) maintenance behaviors. With respect to its associations with romantic commitment and satisfaction, however, the role of T is much clearer. Given the predominant role that T plays in mating behavior (Slatcher et al., 2011) and in motivating sexual activity (van Anders et al., 2011), it follows that T is maladaptive for long-term relational maintenance with respect to fostering a sense of commitment to and satisfaction with one's partner and relationship (e.g., Edelstein et al., 2014; Gray et al., 2002; Julian & McHenry, 1989). The extant work on T and commitment largely supports this premise among men. Hooper et al. (2011) identified a negative association between T and commitment and satisfaction, but only among men. Other work has similarly shown significantly lower levels of T for men in committed relationships (Burnham et al., 2003). In an important extension of this work, Edelstein et al.

(2014) examined the dyadic associations between partners' commitment and satisfaction and their T levels. Both men's and women's T was negatively related to their own as well as their partner's satisfaction and commitment. The authors conclude, based on these findings, that T is therefore "incompatible with the maintenance of nurturant relationships" (Edelstein et al., 2014, p. 401).

In further support of the detrimental effects of T on relational maintenance, research has shown that both during pregnancy and postpartum, reduction in T promotes relational well-being. Fathers who experience greater reductions in T across pregnancy are also more likely to report greater levels of satisfaction and commitment postpartum (Saxbe et al., 2017). The role of T in explaining prosocial maintenance behaviors for men during pregnancy and postpartum is consistent across numerous studies. Lower T, for instance, explains greater relational quality and feelings of tenderness in new fathers (Perini et al., 2012) and less sensation-seeking in fathers compared with nonfathers (Perini et al., 2012). Future research would benefit from investigating the ways in which changes in T during pregnancy and postpartum influence the actual communication that occurs between parents. It would be interesting, for instance, to investigate whether messages that communicate dominance and submissiveness during conflict conversations lessen during pregnancy and postpartum and whether such changes coincide with hormonal fluctuations in T.

Scholars contend that such findings linking T positively with mating behavior and yet negatively with parenting behavior is evidence of the challenge hypothesis (see Archer, 2006, for a review). The challenge hypothesis posits that T plays an important role for men in encouraging responsiveness to sexual stimuli thereby promoting reproduction, and also argues that T facilitates vigilant responses to competition in both sexual and nonsexual (e.g., sports) contexts. Finally, the challenge hypothesis postulates that T reductions during fatherhood facilitate prosocial outcomes by dampening desires to engage in infidelity or mating behavior that somehow compromises the integrity of the family unit. The challenge hypothesis received mixed support in a meta-analysis (Meijer et al., 2019) and thus warrants further investigation. However, across the large corpus of findings investigating the link between T and commitment and satisfaction, the findings reveal that T functions in ways that promote mating behaviors in a manner that may also compromise investment and maintenance in long-term relationships.

Finally, it is important to note that T may encourage relational commitment indirectly through relational maintenance activities such as forgiveness. As noted earlier, T may motivate types of forgiveness communication (a tendency to communicate forgiveness directly), which may foster relational maintenance for couples negotiating during difficult times. It may also encourage individuals who have experienced transgressions to disclose their thoughts and feelings to their partners. Thus, an important direction for researchers is to try to ascertain the extent to which, and under which conditions, T encourages approach motivations indirectly (or directly) that amplify commitment in long-term relationships. Whereas it is possible that T is, in fact, incompatible with nurturant behaviors

(Edelstein et al., 2014), future research needs to reconcile previous findings that offer some possible prosocial relational pathways through which the activation of T is connected to commitment.

As noted throughout the chapter, the hormone oxytocin is also relevant to understanding the hormonal correlates of in-pair mating and maintenance. The hormone has long been associated with mechanisms related to childbirth and parent–child bonding (Apter-Levi et al., 2014; Galbally et al., 2011). Because human infants require care to survive, it is essential that pair-bonds are formed early and maintained, as such bonding "is a survival necessity on par with food and other basic elements" (MacDonald & MacDonald, 2010, p. 14). From an evolutionary perspective, oxytocin's effects on promoting social connection and bonding contribute to survival, and thus neural circuits related to social bonding (e.g., those that oxytocin is linked to) were selected over the course of human evolution (see MacDonald & MacDonald, 2010, for a review). The benefits of oxytocin and its social bonding effects for reproduction and survival extend to human adult relationships. As detailed throughout this chapter, oxytocin is associated with a range of prosocial behavior, including more positive communication between partners, cooperative behavior, greater trust, reduced fear perceptions, and stress mitigation (e.g., De Dreu, 2012; Ditzen et al., 2009, 2013; Heinrichs et al., 2003, Kirsch et al., 2005; Kosfeld et a1., 2005; see also IsHak et al., 2011). Although some mixed results arise when exploring the effects of intranasal oxytocin (calling the findings of studies employing such methods into question; e.g., Leppanen et al., 2018; Mierop et al., 2020), the body of research detailed throughout this chapter nonetheless suggests that oxytocin helps promote and reinforce bonds that contribute to in-pair mating and maintenance.

In their review of the prosocial effects of oxytocin, MacDonald and MacDonald (2010) also called attention to distinctions between (a) the oxytocin system, which considers both the hormone and its receptor, as well as its relation to other relevant neurochemicals such as cortisol; and (b) oxytocin's "dual roles as both a central neurotransmitter/neuromodulator and a peripheral hormone" and to the coevolution of these branches "to facilitate both the somatic and brain-based components of birth, nursing, and postbirth care" (p. 2). Recognition of these two systems acknowledges that oxytocin's effects on human brain activity are not only a product of the release of the hormone but also vary in relation to its receptors. Social scientists have explored the associations between various behavior and variation in the oxytocin receptor (OXTR) gene. For example, several studies have examined DNA variation in the single nucleotide polymorphism (SNP) rs53576, for which individuals can have one of three genotypes: AA, GG, or AG. Many studies investigating variation in this OXTR gene have compared individuals with an A allele (i.e., AA and AG individuals) to those who are homozygous for G (i.e., GG individuals). Given the consistent associations between the presence of an A allele and more detrimental social outcomes, some scholars have conceptualized it as the risk allele (Tost et al., 2010).

Research on rs53576 reveals that variation in this SNP on the OXTR gene is associated with a range of characteristics and behaviors that may help or hinder relational maintenance efforts. For example, individuals with an A allele have been found to engage in less prosocial and affiliative nonverbal behavior when listening to their romantic partner's experiences of hardship (Kogan et al., 2011) and are less adept at reading others' emotional states (Rodrigues et al., 2009) compared to GG individuals. Genotypic variation may be especially relevant for individuals lacking relational security. Similar to the finding by Bartz et al. (2015) that oxytocin can be especially beneficial in promoting communal behavior for individuals with attachment styles that indicate a lack of connection or intimacy with others, Floyd and Denes (2015) found that genotypic variation exhibited stronger effects on affectionate communication for individuals low in attachment security. More specifically, for individuals low in attachment security, those with a GG genotype reported expressing more affection than those with an A allele (Floyd & Denes, 2015). The moderating effect of attachment security was also supported by Denes (2015), who found that genotypic variation did not predict relational outcomes for securely attached individuals, but for those with an insecure attachment, GG individuals perceived fewer risks to disclosing to their romantic partner and felt closer to that partner compared to AA/AG individuals. Taken together, this body of research suggests that genetic factors interact with individual and/or relational factors to predict social behavior relevant to relational maintenance.

Despite the links between oxytocin, the OXTR gene, and social behavior, myriad avenues for future research exist in linking oxytocin to the relational maintenance processes detailed throughout this chapter. For example, though correlates of oxytocin (i.e., orgasm) have been linked to the enactment of communicative relational maintenance strategies in the context of sexual activity (Denes, Dhillon, & Speer, 2017), future work would benefit from directly testing whether oxytocin levels and/or variations in the OXTR gene predict the enactment of relational maintenance behaviors both within and beyond sexual episodes. Such work would help reveal whether oxytocin facilitates various forms of maintenance, either directly or as moderated by relational and individual factors such as attachment security. Much of the research on oxytocin and its association with social behavior has involved either the administration of intranasal oxytocin or blood draws in lab settings. However, given recent developments in the measurement of oxytocin via salivary samples (Salimetrics, 2018), researchers now have the opportunity to explore oxytocin levels in more naturalistic environments where individuals can collect saliva samples themselves, which can then be assayed for oxytocin. Collecting data in the home environment as individuals engage in everyday relationship work such as managing daily stressors, engaging in sexual activity, providing support, and helping facilitate each other's goals may provide greater clarity regarding the behaviors that both influence and are affected by individuals' own and their partners' oxytocin levels.

Finally, the hormone cortisol is imperative to understanding relational processes in light of its ability to indicate stress levels among humans. Negative relationship perceptions and/or processes intensify stress responses (Farrell & Simpson, 2017). For instance, individuals who have attachment insecurity in relationships perceive relationship situations as more stressful, have higher cortisol levels, and experience slower cortisol recovery in response to stress (Pietromonaco et al., 2013). Not only does frequency of conflict and marital distress predict flatter diurnal cortisol patterns (as cited in Farrell & Simpson, 2017), but furthermore, individuals who express greater hostility toward their partner during conflict report higher cortisol reactivity after the conflict (Miller et al., 1999). Alternatively, positive relationship perceptions and/or processes lead to healthier cortisol responses. Specifically, a longitudinal study revealed that perceiving partner responsiveness at the study's onset positively led to healthier waking cortisol and diurnal cortisol rhythms after 10 years (Slatcher et al., 2015), underscoring that higher-quality relational partners buffer stress responses over time, hence facilitating pair-bonding.

In light of these associations, it is reasonable to consider whether marital satisfaction and relational quality are linked with cortisol levels. Indeed, Saxbe et al. (2008) found that for women, greater marital satisfaction was associated with higher waking cortisol and sharper diurnal variation in cortisol, but for men, greater marital satisfaction augmented the positive association between high workload stress and evening cortisol levels. The study findings imply that women in satisfied relationships experience healthier morning cortisol and diurnal rhythms and recover faster from stress associated with high workload, whereas men in satisfied relationships experience slower recovery from stress on high workload days. As noted earlier, research on relational processes and cortisol reveal sex differences, but more research is needed to better understand these differences and how relational processes function as both predictors and outcomes of biomarkers of stress such as cortisol.

Despite the robust literature linking cortisol to relational quality, meta-analytic findings failed to support the association between cortisol slopes or cortisol reactivity and marital quality (Robles et al., 2014). Robles et al. (2014) cautioned that the studies included in their review sampled cortisol over one to two days, which might limit the ability of the meta-analysis to uncover the ongoing effect of marital satisfaction/quality on cortisol levels. Thus, future work should seek to tease apart the linkages between the relational maintenance processes detailed throughout this chapter and acute versus long-term physiological stress effects.

It is also important to highlight that partners' physiological responses may coregulate or become linked and, as such, have important implications for in-pair mating (see Timmons et al., 2015, for a review). In particular, Laws et al. (2015) found that couples' cortisol trajectories tended to converge across the early years of marriage. Especially as the relationship matured, couples showed greater similarity in cortisol rhythms during conflict discussions and their relational dissatisfaction was associated with a greater degree of convergence in cortisol responses during such conversations. Consequently, the findings suggest that partners shape each other's cortisol responses with increasing relational duration, and increased similarity in physiological responses to conflict may lead to poorer relationship functioning (Laws et al., 2015), thus hindering the couple's ability to maintain a satisfying relational bond. A review of previous research also finds that relationship satisfaction is negatively associated with linkage or coregulation of cortisol among romantic partners (Timmons et al., 2015), indicating that such linkages may put couples at risk if they become entrenched in patterns of conflict, as shown in Laws et al.'s (2015) study.

Overall, focusing future inquiry on positive relational indicators, processes, and/or constructive conflict behaviors may uncover an array of relational maintenance behaviors that foster the relational bond while leading to healthier cortisol recovery and rhythm, thereby supporting in-pair mating. Moreover, linkage in romantic partners' physiology may present an opportunity for researchers to develop interventions that focus on holistic approaches to stress management involving relational maintenance behaviors, such as affectionate communication, social support, responsiveness, and various forms of relationship talk.

In sum, the present chapter offered a review of research detailing the hormonal mechanisms of in-pair mating and maintenance, framed by the integrative model of relationship maintenance (Ogolsky et al., 2017). The review focused on hormonal mechanisms related to testosterone, oxytocin, and cortisol and their linkages to both threat-mitigating and relationship-enhancing relational maintenance processes occurring at the interactive level. By exploring the functions of testosterone, oxytocin, and cortisol as both cause and consequence of relational maintenance processes, it is clear that investigating the hormonal mechanisms of in-pair mating provides a more comprehensive understanding of the many biological, social, and relational factors that contribute to the viability of individuals and their relationships.

References

Afifi, T., Davis, S., & Denes, A. (2015). Evolutionary theories: Explaining the links between biology and interpersonal communication. In D. O. Braithwaite & P. Schrodt (Eds.), *Engaging theories of interpersonal communication* (2nd ed., pp. 51–62). SAGE.

Afifi, T., Granger, D., Ersig, A., Tsalikian, E., Shahnazi, A., Davis, S., Harrison, K., Acevedo Callejas, M., & Scranton, A. (2019). Testing the theory of resilience and relational load (TRRL) in families with type I diabetes. *Health Communication, 34*, 1107–1119. https://doi.org/10.1080/10410236.2018.1461585

Afifi, T. D., Harrison, K., Zamanzadeh, N., & Acevedo Callejas, M. (2020). Testing the theory of resilience and relational load in dual career families: Relationship maintenance as stress management. *Journal of Applied Communication Research, 48*, 5–25. https://doi.org/10.1080/00909882.2019.1706097

Afifi, T. D., Merrill, A. F., & Davis, S. (2016). The theory of resilience and relational load. *Personal Relationships, 23*, 663–683. https://doi.org/10.1111/pere.12159

Aloia, L. S., & Solomon, D. H. (2015a). Conflict intensity, family history, and physiological stress reactions to conflict within romantic relationships. *Human Communication Research, 41*, 367–389. https://doi.org/10.1111/hcre.12049

Aloia, L. S., & Solomon, D. H. (2015b). The physiology of argumentative skill deficiency: Cognitive ability, emotional competence, communication qualities, and responses to conflict. *Communication Monographs, 82*, 315–338. https://doi.org/10.1080/03637751.2014.989868.

Apter-Levi, Y., Zagoory-Sharon, O., & Feldman, R. (2014). Oxytocin and vasopressin support distinct configurations of social synchrony. *Brain Research, 1580*, 124–132. https://doi.org/10.1016/j.brainres.2013.10.052

Archer, J. (2006). Testosterone and human aggression: An evaluation of the challenge hypothesis. *Neuroscience & Biobehavioral Reviews, 30*, 319–345. https://doi.org/10.1016/j.neubiorev.2004.12.007

Attwood, F., & Smith, C. (2013). More sex! Better sex! Sex is fucking brilliant! Sex, sex, sex, SEX. In T. Blackshaw (Ed.), *Routledge handbook of leisure studies* (pp. 325–342). Routledge.

Auyeung, B., Lombardo, M. V., & Baron-Cohen, S. (2013). Prenatal and postnatal hormone effects on the human brain and cognition. *Pflügers Archiv-European Journal of Physiology, 465*, 557–571. https://doi.org/10.1007/s00424-013-1268-2

Barnett, R. C., Steptoe, A., & Gareis, K. C. (2005). Marital-role quality and stress-related psychobiological indicators. *Annals of Behavioral Medicine, 30*, 36–43. https://doi.org/10.1207/s15324796abm3001_5

Bartz, J. A., Lydon, J. E., Kolevzon, A., Zaki, J., Hollander, E., Ludwig, N., & Bolger, N. (2015). Differential effects of oxytocin on agency and communion for anxiously and avoidantly attached individuals. *Psychological Science, 26*, 1177–1186. https://doi.org/10.1177/0956797615580279

Behnia, B., Heinrichs, M., Bergmann, W., Jung, S., Germann, J., Schedlowski, M., Hartmann, U., & Kruger, T. H. (2014). Differential effects of intranasal oxytocin on sexual experiences and partner interactions in couples. *Hormones and Behavior, 65*, 308–318. https://doi.org/10.1016/j.yhbeh.2014.01.009

Berdychevsky, L., & Carr, N. (2020). Innovation and impact of sex as leisure in research and practice: Introduction to the special issue. *Leisure Sciences, 42*, 255–274. https://doi.org/10.1080/01490400.2020.1714519

Blaicher, W., Gruber, D., Bieglmayer, C., Blaicher, A. M., Knogler, W., & Huber, J. (1999). The role of oxytocin in relation to female sexual arousal. *Gynecological and Obstetric Investigation, 47*, 125–126. https://doi.org/10.1159/000010075

Booth, A., Carver, K., & Granger, D. A. (2000). Biosocial perspectives on the family. *Journal of Marriage and Family, 62*, 1018–1034. https://doi.org/10.1111/j.1741-3737.2000.01018.x

Boren, J. P. & Veksler, A. E. (2011). A decade of research exploring biology and communication: The brain, nervous, endocrine, cardiovascular, and immune systems. *Communication Research Trends*, 30, 1–31. https://doi.org/10.1111/j.1741-3737.2000.01018.x

Bos, P. A., Hermans, E. J., Ramsey, N. F., & Van Honk, J. (2012). The neural mechanisms by which testosterone acts on interpersonal trust. *Neuroimage, 61*, 730–737. https://doi.org/10.1016/j.neuroimage.2012.04.002

Braams, B. R., Peper, J. S., Van Der Heide, D., Peters, S., & Crone, E. A. (2016). Nucleus accumbens response to rewards and testosterone levels are related to alcohol use in adolescents and young adults. *Developmental Cognitive Neuroscience, 17*, 83–93. https://doi.org/10.1016/j.dcn.2015.12.014

Burke, H. M., Davis, M. C., Otte, C., & Mohr, D. C. (2005). Depression and cortisol responses to psychological stress: A meta-analysis. *Psychoneuroendocrinology, 30*(9), 846–856. https://doi.org/10.1016/j.psyneuen.2005.02.010

Burnham, T. C., Chapman, J. F., Gray, P. B., McIntyre, M. H., Lipson, S. F., & Ellison, P. T. (2003). Men in committed, romantic relationships have lower testosterone. *Hormones and Behavior, 44*, 119–122. https://doi.org/10.1016/S0018-506X(03)00125-9

Buss, D. M., & Shackelford, T. K. (1997). Susceptibility to infidelity in the first year of marriage. *Journal of Research in Personality, 31*, 193–221. https://doi.org/10.1006/jrpe.1997.2175

Canary, D. J., & Cupach, W. R. (1988). Relational and episodic characteristics associated with conflict tactics. *Journal of Social and Personal Relationships, 5*, 305–325. https://doi.org/10.1177/0265407588053003

Canary, D. J., & Spitzberg, B. H. (1989). A model of the perceived competence of conflict strategies. *Human Communication Research, 15*, 630–649. https://doi.org/10.1111/j.1468-2958.1989.tb00202.x

Canary, D. J., & Stafford, L. (1992). Relational maintenance strategies and equity in marriage. *Communications Monographs, 59*, 243–267. https://doi.org/10.1080/03637759209376268

Carmichael, M. S., Humbert, R., Dixen, J., Palmisano, G., Greenleaf, W., & Davidson, J. M. (1987). Plasma oxytocin increases in the human sexual response. *Journal of Clinical Endocrinology and Metabolism, 64*, 27–31. https://doi.org/10.1210/jcem-64-1-27

Cardoos, S. L., Suleiman, A. B., Johnson, M., van den Bos, W., Hinshaw, S. P., & Dahl, R. E. (2017). Social status strategy in early adolescent girls: Testosterone and value-based decision making. *Psychoneuroendocrinology, 81*, 14–21. https://doi.org/10.1016/j.psyneuen.2017.03.013

Carter, C. S. (1992). Oxytocin and sexual behavior. *Neuroscience & Biobehavioral Reviews, 16*, 131–144. https://doi.org/10.1016/S0149-7634(05)80176-9

Carter, C. S., Grippo, A. J., Pournajafi-Nazarloo, H., Ruscio, M. G., & Porges, S. W. (2008). Oxytocin, vasopressin and sociality. *Progress in Brain Research, 170*, 331–336. https://doi.org/10.1016/S0079-6123(08)00427-5

Chen, F. R., Dariotis, J. K., & Granger, D. A. (2018). Linking testosterone and antisocial behavior in at-risk transitional aged youth: Contextual effects of parentification. *Psychoneuroendocrinology, 91*, 1–10. https://doi.org/10.1016/j.psyneuen.2018.02.023

Chida, Y., & Steptoe, A. (2009). Cortisol awakening response and psychosocial factors: A systematic review and meta-analysis. *Biological psychology, 80*(3), 265–278. https://doi.org/10.1016/j.biopsycho.2008.10.004

Crespi, B. J. (2016). Oxytocin, testosterone, and human social cognition. *Biological Reviews, 91*, 390–408. https://doi.org/10.1111/brv.12175

Crowley, J. P., Denes, A., Makos, S., & Whitt, J. (2018). Threats to courtship and the physiological response: Testosterone mediates the relationship between relational uncertainty and disclosure for dating partner recipients of relational transgressions. *Adaptive Human Behavior and Physiology, 4*, 264–282. https://doi.org/10.1007/s40750-018-0092-5

Crowley, J. P., Denes, A., Makos, S., & Whitt, J. (2019). Expressive writing to cope with relational transgressions: Tests of a dual-process model of expressive writing and its effects on forgiveness communication and testosterone. *Health Communication, 34*, 628–630. https://doi.org/10.1080/10410236.2018.1431017

Dabbs Jr, J. M., & Mohammed, S. (1992). Male and female salivary testosterone concentrations before and after sexual activity. *Physiology & Behavior, 52*, 195–197. https://doi.org/10.1016/0031-9384(92)90453-9

Dainton, M., & Aylor, B. (2002). Routine and strategic maintenance efforts: Behavioral patterns, variations associated with relational length, and the prediction of relational characteristics. *Communication Monographs, 69*, 52–66. https://doi.org/10.1080/03637750216533

Dainton, M., & Gross, J. (2008). The use of negative behaviors to maintain relationships. *Communication Research Reports, 25*, 179–191. https://doi.org/10.1080/08824090802237600

Dainton, M., & Stafford, L. (1993). Routine maintenance behaviors: A comparison of relationship type, partner similarity and sex differences. *Journal of Social and Personal Relationships, 10*, 255–271. https://doi.org/10.1177/0265407593010000206

De Dreu, C. K. (2012). Oxytocin modulates cooperation within and competition between groups: An integrative review and research agenda. *Hormones and Behavior, 61*, 419–428. https://doi.org/10.1016/j.yhbeh.2011.12.009

De Dreu, C. K. W., Greer, L. L., Van Kleef, G. A., Shalvi, S., & Handgraaf, M. J. J. (2011). Oxytocin promotes human ethnocentrism. *Proceedings of the National Academy of the Sciences, 108*, 1262–1266. https://doi.org/10.1073/pnas.1015316108

Denes, A. (2012). Pillow talk: Exploring disclosures after sexual activity. *Western Journal of Communication, 76*, 91–108. https://doi.org/10.1080/10570314.2011.651253

Denes, A. (2015). Genetic and individual influences on predictors of disclosure: Exploring variation in the oxytocin receptor gene and attachment security. *Communication Monographs, 82*, 113–133. https://doi.org/10.1080/03637751.2014.993544

Denes, A. (2018). Toward a post sex disclosures model (PSDM): Exploring the associations among orgasm, self-disclosure, and relationship satisfaction. *Communication Research, 45*, 297–318. https://doi.org/10.1177/0093650215619216

Denes, A., & Afifi, T. D. (2014). Pillow talk and cognitive decision-making processes: Exploring the role of orgasm and alcohol on communication after sexual activity. *Communication Monographs, 81*, 333–358. https://doi.org/1080/03637751.2014.926377

Denes, A., Afifi, T. D., & Granger, D. A. (2017). Physiology and pillow talk: Relations between testosterone and communication post sex. *Journal of Social and Personal Relationships, 34*, 281–308. https://doi.org/10.1177/0265407516634470

Denes, A., Bennett, M., & DelGreco, M. (2020). Sexual communication and biology. In R. Weber & K. Floyd (Eds.), *Handbook of communication science and biology* (pp. 370–381). Routledge.

Denes, A., Bennett, M., & Winkler, K.L. (2017). Exploring the benefits of affectionate communication: Implications for interpersonal acceptance-rejection theory. *Journal of Family Theory & Review, 9*, 491–506. https://doi.org/10.1111/jftr.12218

Denes, A., Crowley, J. P., Winkler, K. L., Dhillon, A., Ponivas, A. L., & Bennett, M. (2020). Exploring the effects of pillow talk on relationship satisfaction and physiological stress responses to couples' difficult conversations. *Communication Monographs, 87*, 267–290. https://doi.org/10.1080/03637751.2020.1726424

Denes, A., Crowley, J. P., Dhillon, A., Bennett-Brown, M., Stebbins, J. L., & Granger, S. W. (2021). Exploring the role of oxytocin in communication processes: A test of the post sex disclosures model. *Communication Monographs*. Advance online publication. https://doi.org/10.1080/03637751.2021.1957490

Denes, A., Dhillon, A., Ponivas, A., & Winkler, K. L. (2020). The hormonal underpinnings of sexual communication. In L. S. Aloia, A. Denes, & J. P. Crowley (Eds.), *The Oxford handbook of the physiology of interpersonal communication* (pp. 235–260). Oxford University Press.

Denes, A., Dhillon, A., & Speer, A.C. (2017c). Relational maintenance strategies during the post sex time interval. *Communication Quarterly, 65*, 307–332. https://doi.org/10.1080/01463373.2016.1245206

Dhillon, A., Denes, A., Crowley, J. P, Ponivas, A., Winkler, K. L., & Bennett, M. (2020). Does testosterone influence young adult romantic partners' accommodation during conversations about stressors? *Human Communication Research, 46*(4), 444–469. https://doi.org/10.1093/hcr/hqaa008

Dickerson, S. S., & Kemeny, M. E. (2004). Acute stressors and cortisol responses: A theoretical integration and synthesis of laboratory research. *Psychological Bulletin, 130*(3), 355. https://doi.org/10.1037/0033-2909.130.3.355

Dindia, K. (2003). Definitions and perspectives on relational maintenance communication. In D. J. Canary & M. Dainton (Eds.), *Maintaining relationships through communication* (pp. 1–28). Erlbaum.

Ditzen, B., Hoppmann, C., & Klumb, P. (2008). Positive couple interactions and daily cortisol: On the stress-protecting role of intimacy. *Psychosomatic Medicine, 70*, 883–889. https://doi.org/10.1097/PSY.0b013e318185c4fc

Ditzen, B., Nater, U. M., Schaer, M., La Marca, R., Bodenmann, G., Ehlert, U., & Heinrichs, M. (2013). Sex-specific effects of intranasal oxytocin on autonomic nervous system and emotional responses to couple conflict. *Social Cognitive and Affective Neuroscience, 8*, 897–902. https://doi.org/10.1093/scan/nss083

Ditzen, B., Schaer, M., Gabriel, B., Bodenmann, G., Ehlert, U., & Heinrichs, M. (2009). Intranasal oxytocin increases positive communication and reduces cortisol levels during couple conflict. *Biological Psychiatry, 65*, 728–731. https://doi.org/10.1016/j.biopsych.2008.10.011

Duck, S.W. (1988). *Relating to others*. Open University Press.

Edelstein, R. S., Chopik, W. J., & Kean, E. L. (2011). Sociosexuality moderates the association between testosterone and relationship status in men and women. *Hormones and Behavior, 60*, 248–255. https://doi.org/10.1016/j.yhbeh.2011.05.007

Edelstein, R. S., van Anders, S. M., Chopik, W. J., Goldey, K. L., & Wardecker, B. M. (2014). Dyadic associations between testosterone and relationship quality in couples. *Hormones and Behavior, 65*(4), 401–407. https://doi.org/10.1016/j.yhbeh.2014.03.003

Eisenegger, C., Haushofer, J., & Fehr, E. (2011). The role of testosterone in social interaction. *Trends in Cognitive Sciences, 15*, 263–271. https://doi.org/10.1016/j.tics.2011.04.008

Ellis, B. J., Del Giudice, M., Dishion, T. J., Figueredo, A. J., Gray, P., Griskevicius, V., Hawley, P. H., Jacobs, W. J., James, J., Volk, A. A., & Wilson, D. S. (2012). The evolutionary basis of risky adolescent behavior: Implications for science, policy, and practice. *Developmental Psychology, 48*, 598. https://doi.org/10.1037/a0026220

Falconier, M. K., Jackson, J. B., Hilpert, P., & Bodenmann, G. (2015). Dyadic coping and relationship satisfaction: A meta-analysis. *Clinical Psychology Review, 42*, 28–46. https://doi.org/10.1016/j.cpr.2015.07.002

Farrell, A. K., & Simpson, J. A. (2017). Effects of relationship functioning on the biological experience of stress and physical health. *Current Opinion in Psychology, 13*, 49–53. https://doi.org/10.1016/j.copsyc.2016.04.014

Fitness, J., & Peterson, J. (2008). Punishment and forgiveness in close relationships: An evolutionary, social-psychological perspective. In J. P. Forgas, & J. Fitness (Eds.), *Social relationships: Vol. 10. Cognitive, affective, and motivational processes* (pp. 255–269). Sydney Symposium of Social Psychology. Psychology Press. https://doi.org/10.4324/9780203888124

Fletcher, G. J., Simpson, J. A., Campbell, L., & Overall, N. C. (2015). Pair-bonding, romantic love, and evolution: The curious case of Homo sapiens. *Perspectives on Psychological Science, 10,* 20–36. https://doi.org/10.1177/1745691614561683

Floyd, K. (2006). Human affection exchange: XII. Affectionate communication is associated with diurnal variation in salivary free cortisol. *Western Journal of Communication, 70,* 47–63. https://doi.org/10.1080/10570310500506649

Floyd, K. (2014) Humans are people, too: Nurturing an appreciation for nature in communication research. *Review of Communication Research, 2,* 1–29. http://doi.org/10.12840/issn.2255-4165.2014.02.01.001

Floyd, K., & Afifi, T. D. (2011). Biological and physiological perspectives on interpersonal communication. In M. L. Knapp & J. A. Daly (Eds.), *The handbook of interpersonal communication* (4th ed., pp. 87–127). SAGE.

Floyd, K., & Denes, A. (2015). Attachment security and oxytocin receptor gene polymorphism interact to influence affectionate communication. *Communication Quarterly, 63,* 272–285. https://doi.org/10.1080/01463373.2015.1039718

Floyd, K., Hesse, C., Generous, M.A. (2015). Affection exchange theory: A bio-evolutionary look at affectionate communication. In D. O. Braithwaite & P. Schrodt (Eds.), *Engaging theories of interpersonal communication* (2nd ed., pp. 309–319). SAGE.

Floyd, K., Mikkelson, A. C., Tafoya, M. A., Farinelli, L., La Valley, A. G., Judd, J., Davis, K. L., Haynes, M. T., & Wilson, J. (2007a). Human affection exchange: XIII. Affectionate communication accelerates neuroendocrine stress recovery. *Health Communication, 22*(2), 123–132. https://doi.org/10.1080/10410230701454015

Floyd, K., Mikkelson, A. C., Tafoya, M. A., Farinelli, L., La Valley, A. G., Judd, J., Davis, K. L., Haynes, M. T., & Wilson, J. (2007b). Human affection exchange: XIV. Relational affection predicts resting heart rate and free cortisol secretion during acute stress. *Behavioral Medicine, 32,* 151–156. https://doi.org/10.3200/BMED.32.4.151-156

Floyd, K., & Morman, M. T. (1998). The measurement of affectionate communication. *Communication Quarterly, 46,* 144–162. https://doi.org/10.1080/01463379809370092

Floyd, K., Pauley, P. M., & Hesse, C. (2010). State and trait affectionate communication buffer adults' stress reactions. *Communication Monographs, 77,* 618–636. https://doi.org/10.1080/03637751.2010.498792

Floyd, K., & Riforgiate, S. (2008). Affectionate communication received from spouses predicts stress hormone levels in healthy adults. *Communication Monographs, 75,* 351–368. https://doi.org/10.1080/03637750802512371

Floyd, K., & Voloudakis, M. (1999). Affectionate behavior in adult platonic friendships interpreting and evaluating expectancy violations. *Human Communication Research, 25,* 341–369. https://doi.org/10.1111/j.1468-2958.1999.tb00449.x

Gable, S.L. (2006). Approach and avoidance social motives and goals. *Journal of Personality, 74,* 175–222. https://doi.org/10.1111/j.1467-6494.2005.00373.x

Galbally, M., Lewis, A. J., IJzendoorn, M. V., & Permezel, M. (2011). The role of oxytocin in mother-infant relations: A systematic review of human studies. *Harvard Review of Psychiatry, 19,* 1–14. https://doi.org/10.3109/10673229.2011.549771

Gettler, L. T., Sarma, M. S., Lew-Levy, S., Bond, A., Trumble, B. C., & Boyette, A. H. (2019). Mothers' and fathers' joint profiles for testosterone and oxytocin in a small-scale fishing-farming community: Variation based on marital conflict and paternal contributions. *Brain and Behavior, 9,* Article e01367. https://doi.org/10.1002/brb3.1367

Geniole, S. N., Bird, B. M., Ruddick, E. L., & Carré, J. M. (2017). Effects of competition outcome on testosterone concentrations in humans: An updated meta-analysis. *Hormones and Behavior, 92,* 37–50. https://doi.org/10.1016/j.yhbeh.2016.10.002=

Giese-Davis, J., Sephton, S. E., Abercrombie, H. C., Durán, R. E., & Spiegel, D. (2004). Repression and high anxiety are associated with aberrant diurnal cortisol rhythms in women with metastatic breast cancer. *Health Psychology, 23,* 645. https://doi.org/10.1037/0278-6133.23.6.645

Goldey, K. L., & van Anders, S. M. (2011). Sexy thoughts: Effects of sexual cognitions on testosterone, cortisol, and arousal in women. *Hormones and Behavior, 59,* 754–764. https://doi.org/10.1016/j.yhbeh.2010.12.005

Gordis, E. B., Granger, D. A., Susman, E. J., & Trickett, P. K. (2006). Asymmetry between salivary cortisol and α-amylase reactivity to stress: Relation to aggressive behavior in adolescents. *Psychoneuroendocrinology, 31,* 976–987. https://doi.org/10.1016/j.psyneuen.2006.05.010

Gray, J. A. (1990). Brain systems that mediate both emotion and cognition. *Cognition and Emotion, 4*, 269–288. https://doi.org/10.1080/02699939008410799

Gray, P. B., Kahlenberg, S. M., Barrett, E. S., Lipson, S. F., & Ellison, P. T. (2002). Marriage and fatherhood are associated with lower testosterone in males. *Evolution and Human Behavior, 23*, 193–201. https://doi.org/10.1016/S1090-5138(01)00101-5

Grewen, K. M., Girdler, S. S., Amico, J., & Light, K. C. (2005). Effects of partner support on resting oxytocin, cortisol, norepinephrine, and blood pressure before and after warm partner contact. *Psychosomatic Medicine, 67*, 531–538. https://doi.org/10.1097/01.psy.0000170341.88395.47

Gunnar, M. R., & Hostinar, C. E. (2015). The social buffering of the hypothalamic–pituitary–adrenocortical axis in humans: Developmental and experiential determinants. *Social Neuroscience, 10*, 479–488. https://doi.org/10.1080/17470919.2015.1070747

Ha, T., Yeung, E. W., Rogers, A. A., Poulsen, F. O., Kornienko, O., & Granger, D. A. (2016). Supportive behaviors in adolescent romantic relationships moderate adrenocortical attunement. *Psychoneuroendocrinology, 74*, 189–196. https://doi.org/10.1016/j.psyneuen.2016.09.007

Hamilton, L. D., & Meston, C. M. (2010). The effects of partner togetherness on salivary testosterone in women in long distance relationships. *Hormones and Behavior, 57*, 198–202. https://doi.org/10.1016/j.yhbeh.2009.10.014

Hamilton, L. D., & Meston, C. M. (2011). The role of salivary cortisol and DHEA-S in response to sexual, humorous, and anxiety-inducing stimuli. *Hormones and Behavior, 59*, 765–771. https://doi.org/10.1016/j.yhbeh.2010.12.011

Hamilton, L. D., Rellini, A. H., & Meston, C. M. (2008). Cortisol, sexual arousal, and affect in response to sexual stimuli. *The Journal of Sexual Medicine, 5*, 2111–2118. https://doi.org/10.1111/j.1743-6109.2008.00922.x

Heffner, K. L., Kiecolt-Glaser, J. K., Loving, T. J., Glaser, R., & Malarkey, W. B. (2004). Spousal support satisfaction as a modifier of physiological responses to marital conflict in younger and older couples. *Journal of Behavioral Medicine, 27*, 233–254. https://doi.org/10.1023/B:JOBM.0000028497.79129.ad

Heffner, K. L., Loving, T. J., Kiecolt-Glaser, J. K., Himawan, L. K., Glaser, R., & Malarkey, W. B. (2006). Older spouses' cortisol responses to marital conflict: Associations with demand/withdraw communication patterns. *Journal of Behavioral Medicine, 29*, 317. https://doi.org/10.1007/s10865-006-9058-3

Heinrichs, M., Baumgartner, T., Kirschbaum, C., & Ehlert, U. (2003). Social support and oxytocin interact to suppress cortisol and subjective responses to psychosocial stress. *Biological Psychiatry, 54*, 1389–1398. https://doi.org/10.1016/S0006-3223(03)00465-7

Hermans, E. J., Putman, P., Baas, J. M., Koppeschaar, H. P., & van Honk, J. (2006). A single administration of testosterone reduces fear-potentiated startle in humans. *Biological Psychiatry, 59*, 872–874. https://doi.org/10.1016/j.biopsych.2005.11.015

Hermans, E. J., Putman, P., & Van Honk, J. (2006). Testosterone administration reduces empathetic behavior: A facial mimicry study. *Psychoneuroendocrinology, 31*, 859–866. https://doi.org/10.1016/j.psyneuen.2006.04.002

Holt-Lunstad, J., Birmingham, W. A., & Light, K. C. (2008). Influence of a "warm touch" support enhancement intervention among married couples on ambulatory blood pressure, oxytocin, alpha amylase, and cortisol. *Psychosomatic Medicine, 70*, 976–985. https://doi.org/10.1097/PSY.0b013e318187aef7

Holt-Lunstad, J., Birmingham, W. C., & Light, K. C. (2014). Relationship quality and oxytocin: Influence of stable and modifiable aspects of relationships. *Journal of Social and Personal Relationships, 32*, 472–490. https://doi.org/10.1177/0265407514536294

Hooper, A. E. C., Gangestad, S. W., Thompson, M. E., & Bryan, A. D. (2011). Testosterone and romance: The association of testosterone with relationship commitment and satisfaction in heterosexual men and women. *American Journal of Human Biology, 23*, 553–555. https://doi.org/10.1002/ajhb.21188

Idris, A., Ghazali, N. B., Said, N. M., Steele, M., Koh, D., & Tuah, N. A. (2016). Salivary testosterone as a potential indicator for risky behaviour associated with smoking-related peer pressure in adolescents. *International Journal of Adolescent Medicine and Health, 30*(1), 1-3. https://doi.org/10.1515/ijamh-2015-0125

Impett, E. A., Gable, S. L., & Peplau, L. A. (2005). Giving up and giving in: The costs and benefits of daily sacrifice in intimate relationships. *Journal of Personality and Social Psychology, 89*, 327–344. https://doi.org/10.1037/0022-3514.89.3.327

Impett, E. A., Gere, J., Kogan, A., Gordon, A. M., & Keltner, D. (2014). How sacrifice impacts the giver and the recipient: Insights from approach-avoidance motivational theory. *Journal of Personality, 82*, 390–401. https://doi.org/10.1111/jopy.12070

IsHak, W. W., Kahloon, M., & Fakhry, H. (2011). Oxytocin role in enhancing well-being: A literature review. *Journal of Affective Disorders, 130*(1-2), 1–9. https://doi.org/10.1016/j.jad.2010.06.001

Jackman-Cram, S., Dobson, K. S., & Martin, R. (2006). Marital problem-solving behavior in depression and marital distress. *Journal of Abnormal Psychology, 115*, 380–384. https://doi.org/10.1037/0021-843X.115.2.380

Julian, T., & McKenry, P. C. (1989). Relationship of testosterone to men's family functioning at mid-life: A research note. *Aggressive Behavior, 15*, 281–289. https://doi.org/10.1002/ab.2480150403

Kaiser, H., & Powers, S. (2006). Testosterone and conflict tactics within late-adolescent couples: A dyadic predictive model. *Journal of Social and Personal Relationships, 23*, 231–248. https://doi.org/10.1177/0265407506062473

Kelley, D. (1998). The communication of forgiveness. *Communication Studies, 49*, 255–271. https://doi.org/10.1080/10510979809368535

Ketay, S., Welker, K. M., & Slatcher, R. B. (2017). The roles of testosterone and cortisol in friendship formation. *Psychoneuroendocrinology, 76*, 88–96. https://doi.org/10.1016/j.psyneuen.2016.11.022

Kiecolt-Glaser, J. K., Newton, T., Cacioppo, J. T., MacCallum, R. C., Glaser, R., & Malarkey, W. B. (1996). Marital conflict and endocrine function: Are men really more physiologically affected than women? *Journal of Consulting and Clinical Psychology, 64*, 324. https://doi.org/10.1037/0022-006X.64.2.324

King, M. E., & Theiss, J. A. (2016). The communicative and physiological manifestations of relational turbulence during the empty-nest phase of marital relationships. *Communication Quarterly, 64*, 495–517. https://doi.org/10.1080/01463373.2015.1129353

Kirsch, P., Esslinger, C., Chen, Q., Mier, D., Lis, S., Siddhanti, S., Gruppe, H., Mattay, V.S., Gallhofer, B., & Meyer-Lindenberg, A. (2005). Oxytocin modulates neural circuitry for social cognition and fear in humans. *Journal of Neuroscience, 25*, 11489–11493. https://doi.org/10.1523/JNEUROSCI.3984-05.2005

Klimas, C., Ehlert, U., Lacker, T. J., Waldvogel, P., & Walther, A. (2019). Higher testosterone levels are associated with unfaithful behavior in men. *Biological Psychology, 146*, 107730. https://doi.org/10.1016/j.biopsycho.2019.107730

Knobloch, L. K., Miller, L. E., Bond, B. J., & Mannone, S. E. (2007). Relational uncertainty and message processing in marriage. *Communication Monographs, 74*, 154–180. https://doi.org/10.1080/03637750701390069.

Knobloch, L. K., Miller, L. E., & Carpenter, K. E. (2007). Using the relational turbulence model to understand negative emotion within courtship. *Personal Relationships, 14*, 91–112. https://doi.org/10.1111/j.1475-6811.2006.00143.x

Knobloch, L. K., & Schmelzer, B. (2008). Using the emotion-in-relationships model to predict features of interpersonal influence attempts. *Communication Monographs, 75*, 219–247. https://doi.org/10.1080/03637750802256300

Knobloch, L. K., & Solomon, D. H. (2004). Interference and facilitation from partners in the development of interdependence within romantic relationships. *Personal Relationships, 11*, 115–130. https://doi.org/10.1111/j.1475-6811.2004.00074

Knussmann, R., Christiansen, K., & Couwenbergs, C. (1986). Relations between sex hormone levels and sexual behavior in men. *Archives of Sexual Behavior, 15*, 429–445. https://doi.org/10.1007/BF01543113

Kogan, A., Saslow, L. R., Impett, E. A., Oveis, C., Keltner, D., & Saturn, S. R. (2011). Thin-slicing study of the oxytocin receptor (OXTR) gene and the evaluation and expression of the prosocial disposition. *Proceedings of the National Academy of Sciences (PNAS), 108*, 19189–19192. https://doi.org/10.1073/pnas.1112658108

Kosfeld, M., Heinrichs, M., Zak, P.J., Fischbacher, U., & Fehr1, E. (2005). Oxytocin increases trust in humans. *Nature, 435*, 673–676. https://doi.org/10.1038/nature03701

Kruger, T., Exton, M. S., Pawlak, C., von zur Muhlen, A., Hartmann, U., & Shedlowski, M. (1998). Neuroendocrine and cardiovascular response to sexual arousal and orgasm in men. *Psychoneuroendocrinology, 23*, 401–411. https://doi.org/10.1016/S0306-4530(98)00007-9

Lai, J. C., Chong, A. M., Siu, O. T., Evans, P., Chan, C. L., & Ho, R. T. (2010). Humor attenuates the cortisol awakening response in healthy older men. *Biological Psychology, 84*, 375–380. https://doi.org/10.1016/j.biopsycho.2010.03.012

Laws, H. B., Sayer, A. G., Pietromonaco, P. R., & Powers, S. I. (2015). Longitudinal changes in spouses' HPA responses: Convergence in cortisol patterns during the early years of marriage. *Health Psychology, 34*, 1076. https://doi.org/10.1037/hea0000235

Lee, R., Jaffe, R., & Midgley, A. (1974). Lack of alteration of serum gonadotropins in men and women following sexual intercourse. *American Journal of Obstetrics and Gynecology, 120,* 985–987. https://doi.org/10.1016/0002-9378(74)90351-2

Lee, Y. R., & Enright, R. D. (2019). A meta-analysis of the association between forgiveness of others and physical health. *Psychology & Health, 34,* 626–643. https://doi.org/10.1080/08870446.2018.1554185

Lepore, S. J., & Greenberg, M. A. (2002). Mending broken hearts: Effects of expressive writing on mood, cognitive processing, social adjustment and health following a relationship breakup. *Psychology and Health, 17,* 547–560. https://doi.org/10.1080/08870440290025768

Leppanen, J., Ng, K. W., Kim, Y. R., Tchanturia, K., & Treasure, J. (2018). Meta-analytic review of the effects of a single dose of intranasal oxytocin on threat processing in humans. *Journal of Affective Disorders, 225,* 167–179. https://doi.org/10.1016/j.jad.2017.08.041

Light, K. C., Grewen, K. M., & Amico, J. A. (2005). More frequent partner hugs and higher oxytocin levels are linked to lower blood pressure and heart rate in premenopausal women. *Biological Psychology, 69,* 5–21. https://doi.org/10.1016/j.biopsycho.2004.11.002

Loving, T. J., Gleason, M. E., & Pope, M. T. (2009). Transition novelty moderates daters' cortisol responses when talking about marriage. *Personal Relationships, 16,* 187–203. https://doi.org/10.1111/j.1475-6811.2009.01218.x

Loving, T. J., Heffner, K. L., Kiecolt-Glaser, J. K., Glaser, R., & Malarkey, W. B. (2004). Stress hormone changes and marital conflict: Spouses' relative power makes a difference. *Journal of Marriage and Family, 66,* 595–612. https://doi.org/10.1111/j.0022-2445.2004.00040.x

Luecken, L. J., Kraft, A., & Hagan, M. J. (2009). Negative relationships in the family-of-origin predict attenuated cortisol in emerging adults. *Hormones and Behavior, 55*(3), 412–417. https://doi.org/10.1016/j.yhbeh.2008.12.007

MacDonald, K., & MacDonald, T. M. (2010). The peptide that binds: A systematic review of oxytocin and its prosocial effects in humans. *Harvard Review of Psychiatry, 18,* 1–21. https://doi.org/10.3109/10673220903523615

Makhanova, A., McNulty, J. K., Eckel, L. A., Nikonova, L., & Maner, J. K. (2018). Sex differences in testosterone reactivity during marital conflict. *Hormones and Behavior, 105,* 22–27. https://doi.org/10.1016/j.yhbeh.2018.07.007

Manigault, A. W., Zoccola, P. M., Hamilton, K., & Wymbs, B. T. (2019). Testosterone to cortisol ratio and aggression toward one's partner: Evidence for moderation by provocation. *Psychoneuroendocrinology, 103,* 130–136. https://doi.org/10.1016/j.psyneuen.2019.01.018

Martin, C. A., Mainous, A. G., Curry, T., Martin, D. (1999). Alcohol use in adolescent females: Correlates with estradiol and testosterone. *American Journal on Addictions, 8,* 9–14. https://doi.org/10.1080/105504999306036

McCullough, M. E., Root, L. M., & Cohen, A. D. (2006). Writing about the benefits of an interpersonal transgression facilitates forgiveness. *Journal of Consulting and Clinical Psychology, 74,* 887–897. https://doi.org/10.1037/0022-006X.74.5.887

McLaren, R. M., Haunani Solomon, D., & Priem, J. S. (2011). Explaining variation in contemporaneous responses to hurt in premarital romantic relationships: A relational turbulence model perspective. *Communication Research, 38,* 543–564. https://doi.org/10.1177/0093650210377896

Meijer, W. M., van IJzendoorn, M. H., & Bakermans-Kranenburg, M. J. (2019). Challenging the challenge hypothesis on testosterone in fathers: Limited meta-analytic support. *Psychoneuroendocrinology, 110,* 104435. https://doi.org/10.1016/j.psyneuen.2019.104435

Merolla, A. J. (2014). Forgive like you mean it: Sincerity of forgiveness and the experience of negative affect. *Communication Quarterly, 62,* 36–56. https://doi.org/10.1080/01463373.2013.860903

Merolla, A. J., Zhang, S., & Sun, S. (2013). Forgiveness in the United States and China: Antecedents, consequences, and communication style comparisons. *Communication Research, 40,* 595–622. https://doi.org/10.1177/0093650212446960

Merrill, A. F., & Afifi, T. D. (2017). Couple identity gaps, the management of conflict, and biological and self-reported stress in romantic relationships. *Human Communication Research, 43,* 363–396. https://doi.org/10.1111/hcre.12110

Meuwly, N., Bodenmann, G., Germann, J., Bradbury, T. N., Ditzen, B., & Heinrichs, M. (2012). Dyadic coping, insecure attachment, and cortisol stress recovery following experimentally induced stress. *Journal of Family Psychology, 26,* 937. https://doi.org/10.1037/a0030356

Mierop, A., Mikolajczak, M., Stahl, C., Béna, J., Luminet, O., Lane, A., & Corneille, O. (2020). How can intranasal oxytocin research be trusted? A systematic review of the interactive effects of intranasal oxytocin on psychosocial outcomes. *Perspectives on Psychological Science, 15*(5), 1228–1242. https://doi.org/10.1177/1745691620921525

Miller, G. E., Chen, E., & Zhou, E. S. (2007). If it goes up, must it come down? Chronic stress and the hypothalamic-pituitary-adrenocortical axis in humans. *Psychological Bulletin, 133*(1), 25–45. https://doi.org/10.1037/0033-2909.133.1.25

Miller, G. E., Dopp, J. M., Myers, H. F., Stevens, S. Y., & Fahey, J. L. (1999). Psychosocial predictors of natural killer cell mobilization during marital conflict. *Health Psychology, 18*, 262. https://doi.org/10.1037/0278-6133.18.3.262

Morhenn, V., Beavin, L. E., & Zak, P. J. (2012). Massage increases oxytocin and reduces adrenocorticotropin hormone in humans. *Alternative Therapies in Health and Medicine, 18*, 11–18.

Murphy, M.R., Seckl, J.R., Burton, S., Checkley, S.A., & Lightman, S.L. (1987). Changes in oxytocin and vasopressin secretion during sexual activity in men. *Journal of Clinical Endocrinology and Metabolism, 65*(4), 738–741. https://doi.org/10.1210/jcem-65-4-738

Myers, S. A., Byrnes, K. A., Frisby, B. N., & Mansson, D. H. (2011). Adult siblings' use of affectionate communication as a strategic and routine relational maintenance behavior. *Communication Research Reports, 28*, 151–158. https://doi.org/10.1080/08824096.2011.565276

Ogolsky, B. G., Monk, J. K., Rice, T. M., Theisen, J. C., & Maniotes, C. R. (2017). Relationship maintenance: A review of research on romantic relationships. *Journal of Family Theory & Review, 9*, 275–306. https://doi.org/10.1111/jftr.12205

Pauley, P. M., Hesse, C., & Mikkelson, A. C. (2014). Trait affection predicts married couples' use of relational maintenance behaviors. *Journal of Family Communication, 14*, 167–187. https://doi.org/10.1080/15267431.2013.864292

Pennebaker, J. W. (1997). Writing about emotional experiences as a therapeutic process. *Psychological science, 8*, 162–166. https://doi.org/10.1111/j.1467-9280.1997.tb00403.x

Pennebaker, J. W., & Chung, C. K. (2011). Expressive writing: Connections to physical and mental health. In H. S. Friedman (Ed.), *The Oxford handbook of health psychology* (p. 417–437). Oxford University Press.

Perini, T., Ditzen, B., Fischbacher, S., & Ehlert, U. (2012). Testosterone and relationship quality across the transition to fatherhood. *Biological Psychology, 90*, 186–191. https://doi.org/10.1016/j.biopsycho.2012.03.004

Perini, T., Ditzen, B., Hengartner, M., & Ehlert, U. (2012). Sensation seeking in fathers: The impact on testosterone and paternal investment. *Hormones and Behavior, 61*, 191–195. https://doi.org/10.1016/j.yhbeh.2011.12.004

Peters, S., Jolles, D. J., Van Duijvenvoorde, A. C., Crone, E. A., & Peper, J. S. (2015). The link between testosterone and amygdala–orbitofrontal cortex connectivity in adolescent alcohol use. *Psychoneuroendocrinology, 53*, 117–126. https://doi.org/10.1016/j.psyneuen.2015.01.004

Pietromonaco, P. R., DeBuse, C. J., & Powers, S. I. (2013). Does attachment get under the skin? Adult romantic attachment and cortisol responses to stress. *Current Directions in Psychological Science, 22*, 63–68. https://doi.org/10.1177/0963721412463229

Priem, J. S., McLaren, R. M., & Haunani Solomon, D. (2010). Relational messages, perceptions of hurt, and biological stress reactions to a disconfirming interaction. *Communication Research, 37*, 48–72. https://doi.org/10.1177/0093650209351470

Priem, J. S., & Solomon, D. H. (2011). Relational uncertainty and cortisol responses to hurtful and supportive messages from a dating partner. *Personal Relationships, 18*, 198–223. https://doi.org/10.1111/j.1475-6811.2011.01353.x

Rasmussen, K. R., Stackhouse, M., Boon, S. D., Comstock, K., & Ross, R. (2019). Meta-analytic connections between forgiveness and health: The moderating effects of forgiveness-related distinctions. *Psychology & Health, 34*, 515–534. https://doi.org/10.1080/08870446.2018.1545906

Robles, T. F., & Kiecolt-Glaser, J. K. (2003). The physiology of marriage: Pathways to health. *Physiology & Behavior, 79*, 409–416. https://doi.org/10.1016/S0031-9384(03)00160-4

Robles, T. F., Shaffer, V. A., Malarkey, W. B., & Kiecolt-Glaser, J. K. (2006). Positive behaviors during marital conflict: Influences on stress hormones. *Journal of Social and Personal Relationships, 23*, 305–325. https://doi.org/10.1177/0265407506062482

Robles, T. F., Slatcher, R. B., Trombello, J. M., & McGinn, M. M. (2014). Marital quality and health: A meta-analytic review. *Psychological Bulletin, 140*, 140–187. https://doi.org/10.1037/a0031859

Rodrigues, S. M., Saslow, L. R., Garcia, N., John, O. P., & Keltner, D. (2009). Oxytocin receptor genetic variation relates to empathy and stress reactivity in humans. *Proceedings of the National Academy of Sciences, 106*, 21437–21441. https://doi.org/10.1073/pnas.0909579106

Rodriguez, A. J., & Margolin, G. (2013). Wives' and husbands' cortisol reactivity to proximal and distal dimensions of couple conflict. *Family Process, 52*, 555–569. https://doi.org/10.1111/famp.12037

Rusbult, C. E., Hannon, P. A., Stocker, S. L., & Finkel, E. J. (2005). Forgiveness and relational repair. In E. L. Worthington (Ed.), *Handbook of forgiveness* (pp. 185–205). Routledge.

Rusbult, C. E., Verette, J., Whitney, G. A., Slovik, L. F., & Lipkus, I. (1991). Accommodation processes in close relationships: Theory and preliminary empirical evidence. *Journal of Personality and social Psychology, 60*, 53. https://doi.org/10.1037/0022-3514.60.1.53

Salmetrics. (2018). *Salimetrics offers salivary oxytocin testing service*. Retrieved from https://salimetrics.com/salivary-oxytocin-testing-service/

Savage, B. M., Lujan, H. L., Thipparthi, R. R., & DiCarlo, S. E. (2017). Humor, laughter, learning, and health! A brief review. *Advances in Physiology Education, 41*, 341–347. https://doi.org/10.1152/advan.00030.2017

Saxbe, D. E., Edelstein, R. S., Lyden, H. M., Wardecker, B. M., Chopik, W. J., & Moors, A. C. (2017). Fathers' decline in testosterone and synchrony with partner testosterone during pregnancy predicts greater postpartum relationship investment. *Hormones and Behavior, 90*, 39–47. https://doi.org/10.1016/j.yhbeh.2016.07.005

Saxbe, D. E., Repetti, R. L., & Nishina, A. (2008). Marital satisfaction, recovery from work, and diurnal cortisol among men and women. *Health Psychology, 27*, 15. https://doi.org/10.1037/0278-6133.27.1.15

Shulman, S., Mayes, L. C., Cohen, T. H., Swain, J. E., & Leckman, J. F. (2008). Romantic attraction and conflict negotiation among late adolescent and early adult romantic couples. *Journal of Adolescence, 31*, 729–745. https://doi.org/10.1016/j.adolescence.2008.02.002

Shulman, S., Tuval-Mashiach, R., Levran, E., & Anbar, S. (2006). Conflict resolution patterns and longevity of adolescent romantic couples: A 2-year follow-up study. *Journal of Adolescence, 29*, 575–588. https://doi.org/10.1016/j.adolescence.2005.08.018

Sillars, A. L. (1980). Attributions and communication in roommate conflicts. *Communications Monographs, 47*, 180–200. https://doi.org/10.1080/03637758009376031

Slatcher, R. B., Mehta, P. H., & Josephs, R. A. (2011). Testosterone and self-reported dominance interact to influence human mating behavior. *Social Psychological and Personality Science, 2*, 531–539. https://doi.org/10.1177/1948550611400099

Slatcher, R. B., Robles, T. F., Repetti, R. L., & Fellows, M. D. (2010). Momentary work worries, marital disclosure and salivary cortisol among parents of young children. *Psychosomatic Medicine, 72*, 887. https://doi.org/10.1097/PSY.0b013e3181f60fcc

Slatcher, R. B., Selcuk, E., & Ong, A. D. (2015). Perceived partner responsiveness predicts diurnal cortisol profiles 10 years later. *Psychological Science, 26*, 972–982. https://doi.org/10.1177/0956797615575022

Smyth, J. M., Hockemeyer, J. R., & Tulloch, H. (2008). Expressive writing and post-traumatic stress disorder: Effects on trauma symptoms, mood states, and cortisol reactivity. *British Journal of Health Psychology, 13*, 85–93. https://doi.org/10.1348/135910707X250866

Solomon, D. H., Knobloch, L. K., Theiss, J. A., & McLaren, R. M. (2016). Relational turbulence theory: Explaining variation in subjective experiences and communication within romantic relationships. *Human Communication Research, 42*, 507–532. https://doi.org/10.1111/hcre.12091

Stafford, L., & Canary, D. J. (1991). Maintenance strategies and romantic relationship type, gender and relational characteristics. *Journal of Social and Personal Relationships, 8*, 217–242. https://doi.org/10.1177/0265407591082004

Stafford, L., Dainton, M., & Haas, S. (2000). Measuring routine and strategic relational maintenance: Scale revision, sex versus gender roles, and the prediction of relational characteristics. *Communications Monographs, 67*, 306–323. https://doi.org/10.1080/03637750009376512

Straus, M. A., Hamby, S. L., Boney-McCoy, S., & Sugarman, D. B. (1996). The revised conflict tactics scale (CTS2): Development and preliminary psychometric data. *Journal of Family Issues, 17*, 283–316. https://doi.org/10.1177/019251396017003001

Ten Velden, F. S., Baas, M., Shalvi, S., Kret, M. E., & De Dreu, C. K. (2014). Oxytocin differentially modulates compromise and competitive approach but not withdrawal to antagonists from own vs. rivaling other groups. *Brain Research, 1580*, 172–179. https://doi.org/10.1016/j.brainres.2013.09.013

Terburg, D., & van Honk, J. (2013). Approach–avoidance versus dominance–submissiveness: A multilevel neural framework on how testosterone promotes social status. *Emotion Review, 5,* 296–302. https://doi.org/10.1177/1754073913477510

Timmons, A. C., Margolin, G., & Saxbe, D. E. (2015). Physiological linkage in couples and its implications for individual and interpersonal functioning: A literature review. *Journal of Family Psychology, 29,* 720. https://doi.org/10.1037/fam0000115

Tokunaga, R. S. (2016). Interpersonal surveillance over social network sites: Applying a theory of negative relational maintenance and the investment model. *Journal of Social and Personal Relationships, 33,* 171–190. https://doi.org/10.1177/0265407514568749

Tost, H., Kolachana, B., Hakimi, S., Lemaitre, H., Verchinski, B. A., Mattay, V. S., Weinberger, D. R., & Meyer-Lindenberg, A. (2010). A common allele in the oxytocin receptor gene (OXTR) impacts prosocial temperament and human hypothalamic-limbic structure and function. *Proceedings of the National Academy of Sciences, 103,* 13936–13941. https://doi.org/10.1073/pnas.1003296107

Traue, H. C., & Deighton, R. (1999). Inhibition, disclosure, and health: Don't simply slash the Gordian knot. *Advances in Mind-Body Medicine, 15,* 184. https://doi.org/10.1054/ambm.1999.0086

van Anders, S. M., Goldey, K. L., & Kuo, P. X. (2011). The steroid/peptide theory of social bonds: Integrating testosterone and peptide responses for classifying social behavioral contexts. *Psychoneuroendocrinology, 36,* 1265–1275. https://doi.org/10.1016/j.psyneuen.2011.06.001

van Anders, S. M., Hamilton, L. D., Schmidt, N., & Watson, N. V. (2007). Associations between testosterone secretion and sexual activity in women. *Hormones and Behavior, 51,* 477–482. https://doi.org/10.1016/j.yhbeh.2007.01.003

Van Middendorp, H., Geenen, R., Sorbi, M. J., Van Doornen, L. J., & Bijlsma, J. W. (2009). Health and physiological effects of an emotional disclosure intervention adapted for application at home: A randomized clinical trial in rheumatoid arthritis. *Psychotherapy and Psychosomatics, 78,* 145–151. https://doi.org/10.1159/000206868

Waldron, V. R., & Kelley, D. L. (2005). Forgiving communication as a response to relational transgressions. *Journal of Social and Personal Relationships, 22,* 723–742. https://doi.org/10.1177/0265407505056445

Wudarczyk, O. A., Earp, B. D., Guastella, A., & Savulescu, J. (2013). Could intranasal oxytocin be used to enhance relationships? Research imperatives, clinical policy, and ethical considerations. *Current Opinion in Psychiatry, 26,* 474. https://doi.org/10.1097/YCO.0b013e3283642e10

Xu, Y., & Burleson, B. R. (2001). Effects of sex, culture, and support type on perceptions of spousal social support: An assessment of the "support gap" hypothesis in early marriage. *Human Communication Research, 27,* 535–566. https://doi.org/10.1111/j.1468-2958.2001.tb00792.x

Zhang, Y., Deiter, F., Jung, S., Heinrichs, M., Schedlowski, M., & Krüger, H. C. (2015). Differential effects of intranasal oxytocin administration on sexual functions in healthy females: A laboratory setting. *European Psychiatry, 30,* 264. https://doi.org/10.1016/S0924-9338(15)30215-7

Zietlow, A. L., Eckstein, M., Hernández, C., Nonnenmacher, N., Reck, C., Schaer, M., Bodenmann, G., Heinrichs, M., & Ditzen, B. (2019). Dyadic coping and its underlying neuroendocrine mechanisms–implications for stress regulation. *Frontiers in Psychology, 9,* Article 2600. https://doi.org/10.3389/fpsyg.2018.02600

CHAPTER

14 Mate Guarding and Partner Defection Avoidance

Valerie G. Starratt

Abstract

Successful mating requires the investment of resources, from genetic material and metabolic resources to time, money, and social support. This investment can be distributed across numerous low-investment short-term partnerships, concentrated on one high-investment long-term partnership, or some combination of partnerships of varying lengths and levels of investment. When the risks are low and the benefits are high, both men and women can be motivated to pursue a long-term strategy supplemented with short-term partnerships. While this can be beneficial for the person using this supplemented strategy, it can be costly for the long-term partner who is consequently at risk of losing their own investments in the event of their partner's defection. Therefore, both men and women have evolved motivations to protect against the loss of investment in a relationship via mate-guarding behaviors. These behaviors can function by enticing a partner's continued investment in the ongoing relationship, by reducing a partner's available alternatives to the ongoing relationship, or by punishing or threatening to punish a partner's defection from the ongoing relationship. Use of these mate-guarding strategies is moderated by individual difference and contextual factors that affect the costs and benefits of engaging in mate-guarding behaviors. In short, both men and women are most likely to engage in mate-guarding behaviors when the risk and cost of losing a partner—and so the risk of losing one's investment in the ongoing relationship—is comparatively high.

Key Words: mate guarding, mate retention, partner defection, cost-inflicting, benefit-provisioning, conditional mating strategies

Mating is a fundamental yet complex human behavior and, as such, is associated with myriad psychological adaptations. One constellation of such adaptations consists of those relevant to mate guarding and partner defection avoidance. Although these adaptations manifest in many ways and under many circumstances, they all serve the same function: to protect against the loss of investments in the development and maintenance of intimate relationships.

Investment in and Costs of Mating

Successful mating requires the investment of resources. These resources can take a variety of forms and can be comparatively inexpensive or relatively costly, depending on a number of factors. For example, for successful mating, both males and females must invest genetic and metabolic resources in the form of gametes, although even this basic form of investment is unequal between the sexes (Trivers, 1972). Across species, female metabolic investment in gamete production is roughly 3.5 orders of magnitude greater than male investment. That is, males devote 0.1% of basal metabolism to the production of sperm cells whereas females devote 300% of basal metabolism to the production of egg cells (Hayward & Gillooly, 2011).

For men, this nominal metabolic expenditure is near the total of the minimum investment required for successful reproduction. The only additional requirement is the time and effort of having sex. Reasonable estimates equate this effort to that expended during light housework (Hackett et al., 2018), or about 100 calories (Frappier et al., 2013). While of course there is substantial variation in the amount of energy men expend on this effort, this comparatively meager required investment is dwarfed by the minimum investment required of women.

In addition to the genetic and metabolic investment of gamete development and sexual activity, successful reproduction for women requires substantial investment in the processes of gestation, birth, and lactation. Pregnancy brings women to near the limits of what a human body can sustain in terms of energy expenditure (Thurber et al., 2019). This high metabolic cost continues throughout pregnancy and is extended beyond birth through the expenditure required for lactation (Butte & King, 2005; Dewey, 1997). Additionally, the risk of maternal morbidity and mortality is substantial (Hirshberg & Srinivas, 2017). Globally, 1 in 74 women will die of maternal causes. In some parts of the world, this risk is much larger, with 1 in 16 women dying of maternal causes (Ronsmans & Graham, 2006). The risk of morbidity, such as from pregnancy related hemorrhage, hypertension, stroke, sepsis, or other serious medical condition, is even higher (Geller et al., 2018). In contrast, paternal morbidity or mortality is essentially a null concept. The closest comparable risk would be the risk of suffering a significant cardiac event during sexual activity, which is not immaterial but sits at a substantially lower rate of roughly 2 in 10,000 and is not specific to men (Dahabreh & Paulus, 2011). It is safe to say, then, that the heft of the physical investment of reproduction, which is a risky investment, rests firmly on the shoulders (or in the wombs) of women.

Another cost of successful reproduction for women that is not incurred by men is the loss of alternative mating opportunities. A woman who has successfully mated with one man—that is, has mated with and become pregnant by him—is no longer capable of successfully conceiving with another man for up to 17 months or more (Bouchard et al., 2018). That is, for postpartum women who breastfeed their babies, it can take roughly eight months for the resumption of ovulation. While this return to fertility may be quickened under some circumstances, such as refraining from breastfeeding, women are capable of producing no more than one offspring over the course of a year (barring, of course, rare instances of superfetation). In short, women's reproductive opportunities are limited by their own reproductive biology with its high minimum investment. Men's reproductive opportunities, on the other hand, have no such biological limitations, and so men's ability to invest in reproductive opportunities is limited primarily by women's willingness to grant them sexual access.

Given this difference in minimum required investment in successful reproduction, females and males are often motivated to adopt different mating strategies. As a socially monogamous species, humans have evolved at least two fundamental mating strategies: a short-term strategy that involves less investment in each of a larger number of brief partnerships and a long-term strategy that involves a large investment in one permanent or semipermanent partnership (Buss, 2003, 2006). The extent to which each strategy results in a meaningful return on investment depends on a wide range of variables. However, there are circumstances under which both men and women can benefit from pursuing both strategies, sometimes simultaneously, and so people can and often do invest in developing and maintaining long-term partnerships while supplementing with extra-pair partnerships.

From an investment perspective, simultaneously investing in a long-term partnership and one or more short-term partnerships is akin to diversifying one's portfolio. The return on investment differs for each type of relationship, given that the return on investment in a relationship depends on the investment of one's partner. Ideally, one would choose a partner whose reciprocal investment in the relationship meets all of one's needs and wants. In reality, however, this is unlikely, and so people make trade-offs between the necessities and luxuries that can be obtained from any one relationship (Li et al., 2002). In these circumstances where one's needs or wants are left unmet by a long-term relationship partner, one may seek to meet those needs or wants with an extra-pair partner (Li & Kenrick, 2006). Although this may be valuable to the partner who engages in such a defection (i.e., extra-pair behavior), it can be costly to the partner from whom one is defecting. To protect against such costs, which can include loss of resources spent developing and maintaining the relationship up until the point of defection—or even after the defection, if the defection was not detected—both men and women have evolved adaptations that motivate the use of mate-guarding behaviors to protect against the costs of a partner's defection.

Mate-Guarding Tactics

All mate-guarding behaviors function to protect one's investment in an ongoing relationship by reducing the likelihood of a partner's defection, but these efforts can manifest in a number of ways. In a comprehensive assessment of the various mate-guarding tactics people use in the context of long-term committed relationships, 19 distinct mate-guarding tactics have been identified (Buss & Shackelford, 1997b; Buss et al., 2008):

- Vigilance over a partner's whereabouts and behavior;
- Concealment of a partner away from one's intrasexual rivals;
- Monopolization of a partner's time to reduce their opportunities to find another partner;
- Jealousy inducement;
- Punishment of a partner's infidelity;
- Emotional manipulation;
- Commitment manipulation;
- Derogation of one's intrasexual rivals so that they appear less enticing to a partner as a potential alternative to the ongoing relationship;
- Resource display;
- Sexual inducements;
- Enhancing one's own appearance;
- Providing a partner with love and care;
- Submitting to a partner's whims and wishes;
- Talking to others in a way that clearly marks a partner as being in a relationship;
- Engaging in physical behavior that clearly marks a partner as being in a relationship (e.g., holding hands);
- Encouraging a partner to wear/display ornaments that mark them as being in a relationship (e.g., a ring);
- Talking to others in a way that is derogatory about a partner, thus discouraging potential poachers;
- Presenting oneself as threatening to intrasexual rivals; and
- Engaging in violence against intrasexual rivals.

While this list includes a wide range of behaviors that operate in a variety of ways, they can be separated into two classes of mate guarding: benefit-provisioning behaviors and cost-inflicting behaviors (Miner et al., 2009). Benefit-provisioning behaviors are low-risk mate-guarding tactics that function as rewards or enticements for a partner to remain invested in the ongoing relationship. Cost-inflicting behaviors, on the other hand, are comparatively high-risk mate-guarding tactics that function as punishments to discourage a partner's defection from the relationship.

Benefit-Provisioning Mate Guarding

All benefit-provisioning mate-guarding behaviors function by offering to a partner something of value. Sometimes, this is as straightforward as giving a partner gifts. Although gift-giving is a common cultural practice that occurs under many circumstances, such as holidays or special social occasions like weddings and birthdays, evidence suggests that men are particularly likely to give gifts specifically as a mate-guarding tactic (Jonason et al., 2009). That is, although women are more generous in proffering gifts to friends and family, men may be more likely to target their gift-giving to the benefit of their long-term romantic partners for the purpose of securing that partner's investment in the ongoing relationship. This is consistent with the hypothesis that given women's relatively burdensome minimum parental investment, they prefer as partners men who are able and willing to make material investments in the relationship (Buss & Schmitt, 1993). Gift-giving could be one indication of such willingness and ability, which women may use to gauge the value of their current long-term partner against the value of seeking an alternative. This is demonstrated in the evidence that women who perceive an abundance of available alternatives to the ongoing relationship are more likely to expect their current long-term male partner to produce more materially valuable gifts than do women who perceive a comparative dearth of potential alternative partners (Locke et al., 2020). In essence, a woman who sees more viable alternatives to her ongoing relationship may expect her current long-term partner to provide her with bigger and better gifts to keep her from looking elsewhere.

Of course, not all benefit-provisioning mate-guarding tactics are so literal and direct. Some function by providing a partner with nonmaterial benefits. For example, efforts to enhance one's own physical appearance could function as a benefit-provisioning mate-guarding tactic (Arnocky et al., 2016; Atari et al., 2017b; Hill et al., 2012). Physical attractiveness is highly valued by both men and women in a romantic partner (Buss, 1989). In essence, then, enhancing one's physical appearance is akin to providing a partner with a more attractive, and therefore more valuable, partner. Additionally, evidence suggests that, at least among men, having a partner who is relatively attractive is associated with a reduced likelihood of defecting from that relationship (Starratt et al., 2017). Consequently, increasing one's own apparent attractiveness may decrease the likelihood that a partner will defect, thus functioning as an effective mate-guarding tactic.

A similar effect has been associated with the provision of sexual benefits to one's partner. Sexual satisfaction is positively related to relationship satisfaction, in a way that is bidirectional and mutually reinforcing (McNulty et al., 2016). The more sexually satisfied one is in a relationship, the more satisfied one is with that relationship, and the more satisfied one is with a relationship the more frequently one engages in sexual activity with one's partner. Sexual satisfaction is also bidirectionally positively related to sexual frequency (McNulty et al., 2016), and so it has been argued that in-pair copulation frequency could function as a mate-guarding tactic (Shackelford et al., 2006). In short, one could entice a partner's continued investment in an ongoing relationship by increasing their satisfaction with the relationship by providing abundant sex. Of course, abundant sex that is also satisfying may be a particularly enticing endorsement in favor of a current partner and the ongoing relationship (McKibbin et al., 2010). To that end, people who engage in sexual behavior that is more likely to lead to partner orgasm—such as oral sex (Richters et al., 2006)—may be employing a particularly valuable mate-guarding tactic (Pham & Shackelford, 2013; Sela et al., 2015).

Cost-Inflicting Mate Guarding

Rather unfortunately, not all mate-guarding tactics are as pleasant as buying gifts, making oneself attractive, and ensuring a partner's sexual satisfaction. Instead of enticing a partner's continued investment in the ongoing relationship, a large number of mate-guarding behaviors function by punishment or the reduction of a partner's perceived or actual alternatives to the ongoing relationship. For example, restricting a partner's social behavior such that they are prevented from spending time with other people effectively reduces a partner's actual alternatives to the ongoing relationship (Buss & Shackelford, 1997b). Such cloistering of a partner away from others, including potential intrasexual rivals who may attempt to poach that partner away from the ongoing relationship (Schmitt & Buss, 2001), is a mate-guarding strategy that may be bolstered by institutional rules and traditions (Grant & Montrose, 2018). For example, religion may help to serve the purpose of restricting a partner's mating opportunities outside an ongoing relationship (Buss, 2002; Moon et al., 2019). Many religions take a specific interest in regulating sexual behavior, to both promote reproductive efforts within the context of a long-term committed relationship and prohibit such efforts outside that context. Some of these religious traditions take specific aim at effectively cloistering women away from all men who are not their male partner. For example, it has been argued that religious veiling—which involves the obscuring of a woman's face and/or body via clothing such as the hijab, niqab, and burqa—functions as a mate-guarding device (Pazhoohi et al., 2017). Such veiling hides women from potential alternative mates and may therefore effectively reduce women's ability to defect from the ongoing relationship.

Intrasexual aggressive behavior may serve a similar purpose as veiling and cloistering, in that directing aggression toward potential intrasexual rivals may reduce a partner's alternatives to the ongoing relationship (Borau & Bonnefon, 2019; Buss, 1988; Fisher & Cox, 2010). Such rival-directed behavior can include both direct and indirect aggression. As an example of the latter, a person might engage in competitor derogation, whereby derogations contextualize a potential rival as being either unavailable or unworthy as a romantic partner (Bendixen & Kennair, 2014; Schmitt & Buss, 1996). Direct physical aggression against a same-sex rival, on the other hand, includes physical violence or the threat of physical violence to keep a potential poacher away from one's partner (Buss & Shackelford, 1997a).

Other forms of mate-guarding behaviors may function not by reducing a partner's actual available alternatives but rather by reducing a partner's *perceived* available alternatives. Partner-directed insults are one such behavior that serves this purpose (McKibbin et al., 2007). One of the things that may make partner-directed insults effective as a mate-guarding tactic is that the nature of the insults one directs at a partner are specific to those things that are mate-value relevant. Partner-directed insults targeted toward women, for example, include negative assessments of a physical attractiveness, value as a partner, mental competency, value as a person, and sexual fidelity (Goetz et al., 2006), while partner-directed insults targeted toward men include negative evaluations of his personality, value as a partner/attractiveness, resource potential, and masculinity (McKibbin et al., 2018). Such targeted insults suggest they are designed to reduce a partner's perception of their own value as a mate and, consequently, promote the belief that alternatives to the ongoing relationship are few. In short, partner-directed insults may function as effective mate-guarding behaviors by convincing a partner that they are not valuable as a partner, and should they choose to defect from the ongoing relationship they will likely be left without romantic relationship opportunities.

This kind of insulting verbal abuse has been associated with partner-directed physical violence (Kaighobadi et al., 2008) and partner-directed sexual violence (Lopes et al., 2019; Starratt et al., 2008), both of which have been linked to risk of a partner's defection and so have been identified as additional mate-guarding tactics (Burch & Gallup, 2020; Kaighobadi et al., 2009; Shackelford et al., 2005). These kinds of partner-directed assaults could be an effective form of mate guarding in that they inflict direct physical costs on a partner for even the threat of relationship defection.

While many of these mate-guarding behaviors are committed directly by the person who is protecting their investment in the ongoing relationship, people also routinely engage in coalitional mate guarding (Barbaro et al., 2015; Pham et al., 2015). That is, rather than performing these behaviors themselves, men and women might recruit the help of a friend or other allies to perform those behaviors on their behalf. For example, a friend who extolls the virtues of a person's current partner in that partner's absence or who aggresses against an intrasexual rival who demonstrates interest in a friend's partner is engaging in mate guarding on that friend's behalf. Such coalitions may be valuable in extending the reach of people's mate-guarding tactics to persist when they are not present.

It is worth noting that with the exception perhaps of religion and similarly unique human cultural traditions, the total collection of both benefit-provisioning and cost-inflicting mate-guarding tactics identified in humans is consistent with mate-guarding tactics observed across the animal kingdom. Gift-giving among mates, for example, is common among nonhuman animals, particularly from males to females (Lewis & South, 2012). These gifts include both biological resources and other material tools or trinkets and, as in humans, function to attract and retain a mate. Less pleasantly, intrasexual aggression is perhaps even more common. The sequestering of a mate and aggression toward intrasexual rivals is evident in species from porpoises (Willis & Dill, 2007) and octopuses (Huffard et al., 2010) to fruit flies (Baxter et al., 2015), and even coalitional mate guarding is observed in numerous species (e.g., King et al., 2019; Watts, 1998; Young et al., 2013). It seems, then, when it comes to mate guarding, human behavior is consistent with behaviors seen in other animals.

Mate Guarding as a Conditional Strategy

Although mate guarding does appear to be a universal component of human mating, it does not mean that mate-guarding behaviors are employed invariably. Rather, the extent to which any one person is motivated to employ a given mate-guarding strategy is moderated by a number of individual difference and contextual factors that relate to the risk of loss of one's investment. That is, mate-guarding tactics are most likely to be employed in circumstances where the actual or perceived risk of partner defection is high and where the costs of partner defection are great.

Individual Differences

Several individual difference traits are associated with the use of mate-guarding tactics, in terms of both the number and the types of tactics used. For example, men of higher mate value employ more benefit-provisioning mate-guarding behaviors, while men of lower mate value are more likely to employ cost-inflicting mate-guarding behaviors (Holden et al., 2014; Miner, Shackelford, & Starratt, 2009; Miner, Starratt, & Shackelford, 2009), although lower-value men may increase their provision of benefits to their partners during times when a partner's defection would be particularly costly to them (Pillsworth & Haselton, 2006). Similarly, conscientiousness and openness to experience, two personality traits associated with high mate value (Botwin et al., 1997; Strouts et al., 2017), are negatively related to use of cost-inflicting mate-guarding tactics (Atari et al., 2017a). On the other hand, digit ratio—the ratio of the length of the second digit to the fourth digit, a sexually dimorphic trait indicative of intrauterine testosterone exposure and related to mate value relevant traits (Ferdenzi et al., 2011)—is correlated with mate guarding such that men and women who display sex-atypical ratios are more likely to engage in certain cost-inflicting mate-guarding behaviors (Cousins et al., 2009).

It has been argued (Miner, Starratt, & Shackelford, 2009) that this relationship between mate value and mate-guarding behaviors demonstrates differences in investment patterns. Benefit-provisioning mate-guarding tactics require a comparatively large initial investment but are low risk. That is, being able to provide a partner with a benefit requires having the resources to do so. Higher mate value men, for example, may be more likely to have resources with which to provide a partner with benefits. Lower-value men may be less likely to have the resources with which to provide a partner with benefits, and so may be more likely to resort to a form of mate guarding that does not require a large initial investment of resources.

That said, additional evidence suggests there are some individual difference traits that may motivate a person to engage in cost-inflicting mate guarding even if they could afford a benefit-provisioning strategy. For example, people who score high on the dark triad traits of Machiavellianism, narcissism, and psychopathy are more likely to engage in mate guarding, including both benefit-provisioning and cost-inflicting behaviors (Chegeni et al., 2018; Jonason et al., 2010). While these dark triad traits are perceived as comparatively attractive in a potential mate (Carter et al., 2014), they are also inherently exploitative (Jonason et al., 2010). Consequently, a person high in these traits may be more willing to gain benefits for themselves at a partner's expense. Evidence has similarly related cost-inflicting mate-guarding behaviors to high levels of religiosity. That is, at least among men, increased religiosity is associated with an increased tendency to use cost-inflicting mate-guarding tactics (Chaudhary et al., 2018). As religion may function as a strategy to restrict women's mating opportunities, this may explain why the same relationship between religiosity and cost-inflicting mate guarding was not identified among women.

Contextual Factors

Outside of individual differences, in terms of contextual factors, people are more likely to be motivated to engage in mate-guarding behaviors when the risk of partner defection is high and when the costs of a partner's defection are high. In regard to the former, this is why increased mate guarding is associated with both perceived risk and actual risk of a partner's defection and relationship dissolution. For example, men and women who maintain a hyperawareness of threats to their relationship perform more mate-guarding behaviors than do people who are less attuned to such threats (Barbaro et al., 2016). Similarly, men are more likely to guard their female partners when those women demonstrate low relationship commitment (French et al., 2017) and when those female partners engage in behaviors that men interpret as sexual receptivity (Prokop & Pazda, 2016). Overall, when it seems as though a partner may be interested in alternatives to the ongoing relationship, people are more likely to engage in mate-guarding behaviors to prevent that defection.

Relatedly, for both men and women, the risk of partner defection and the costs of that defection are inextricably linked to female fertility. Even a partner's brief defection from an ongoing relationship can be catastrophic for men if that defection occurs when that partner is fertile and if that defection results in cuckoldry, wherein he unwittingly invests in the offspring of a rival man (Geary, 2006; Platek & Shackelford, 2006). Consequently, men may be most likely to guard their female partner when she is most fertile (Gangestad et al., 2007; Haselton & Gangestad, 2006). This may be a particularly valuable strategy for men, given that the time of peak fertility is when women are most likely to be attracted to men who are not their current long-term partners (Gangestad et al., 2002) and to demonstrate preferences for indicators of short-term value over long-term value in potential male partners (Gangestad et al., 2007). As women may be more likely to engage in short-term relationship defections when they have something to gain (Starratt et al., 2017)—like a short-term partner with higher-quality genes than her current long-term partner (Gangestad & Haselton, 2015) or a new and higher-value long-term partner (Buss et al., 2017; Moran et al., 2017)—it may be most valuable for men to engage in mate guarding at such times.

While women may be more likely to engage in short-term relationship defections when they have something to gain, men may be more likely to engage in such defections when provided the opportunity (Starratt et al., 2017). Consequently, women seem most motivated to guard their male mate when he is more likely to be presented with such opportunity. For example, women are more likely to be distrusting of other women and more likely to guard their own mates when intrasexual rivals are near peak fertility (Hurst et al., 2017), perhaps particularly so when the partners they are guarding are highly desirable (Krems et al., 2016). As a point of interest, this may be related to the effects that an intrasexual rival's fertility status has on women's testosterone levels and the subsequent increase in motivation to engage in intrasexual competition (Maner & McNulty, 2013).

In addition to an increased risk of partner defection, an increase in mate guarding may be motivated by factors indicating that the loss of a partner to defection would be particularly costly. One such indicator is having a partner who is of comparatively high value. The defection of a low-value partner might be no great loss, as the probability of obtaining a new partner of at least equal value to the one who defected is high. However, a high-value partner is not so easily replaced. Consequently, we see that men, for example, are more likely to engage in mate guarding, particularly benefit-provisioning mate guarding, when their current partner is high value (Miner, Starratt, & Shackelford, 2009; Starratt & Shackelford, 2012). Relatedly, both men and women engage in increased mate guarding when the availability of alternative mates is low (Arnocky et al., 2014), as even a low-value partner would be difficult to replace if the pool of available alternatives is shallow.

Resistance to Mate Guarding

Ultimately, people engage in mate-guarding behavior to protect their investments in an ongoing relationship. However, engaging in relationship defection can be a way to gain benefits from extra-pair partners outside the ongoing relationship, and so people may also be motivated to protect their own efforts at gaining those extra-pair benefits. That is, people can and do attempt to resist a partner's mate-guarding efforts to maintain their access to potential extra-pair partners. These resistance tactics include behaviors such as lying, engaging in clandestine behaviors, avoiding public displays of affection, and hampering a partner's efforts to engage in intrasexual competition (Cousins et al., 2015). Just as people are more likely to engage in mate-guarding behaviors when the cost of partner loss is high, people are more motivated to resist a partner's mate-guarding efforts when the value of the potential extra-pair benefits are high. For example, women are more likely to resist a partner's mate guarding when they perceive themselves to be more attractive than their partner (Fugere et al., 2015) and when they themselves are most fertile (Gangestad et al., 2014), likely because these are the circumstances in which a woman is most likely to benefit from engagement with an extra-pair partner. Additional evidence indicates that women who are most likely to find value in attempting to gain benefits from both a long-term partner and a short-term partner simultaneously, such as high Machiavellian women, are similarly more likely to resist a long-term partner's mate-guarding efforts (Abell & Brewer, 2016). Conversely, women may be less likely to resist mate guarding when the risk to such resistance would be higher, such as when the partner against whom she would be resisting may be particularly prone to costly aggression (Cousins et al., 2009). It is likely that men similarly engage in efforts to resist a partner's mate-guarding attempts, although such behavior appears to be as yet unstudied in men.

Future Directions

In addition to extending research on resistance to mate guarding to include assessments of men's behavior, future research should continue to evaluate how mate-guarding and resistance tactics may manifest differently given rapidly changing sociotechnological advances. There is evidence that mate-guarding behaviors extend to online environments (Bhogal et al., 2019; Guitar & Carmen, 2017) and that those behaviors, while functionally the same, may be structured differently than those performed in situ (Brem et al., 2015). As daily life becomes increasingly removed from the environment in which the adaptations motivating these behaviors evolved, our investigations of the manifestations of these adaptations must keep pace.

Another avenue for exploration is the extent to which the evidence for mate guarding generalizes to relationships other than exclusively monogamous heterosexual partnerships. Early evidence indicates that mate-guarding behaviors may be moderated (a) by a sex by sexual orientation interaction, such that homosexual men behave in a largely sex typical manner while homosexual women are more likely to demonstrate sex atypical behaviors (VanderLaan & Vasey, 2008); and (b) in the context of consensual nonmonogamy, whether the relationship in which the mate guarding occurs is with one's primary or secondary partner (Mogilski et al., 2017; Mogilski et al., 2019). These moderative effects may be a result of these variables' influence on the type and level of investment in the relationship and the differential costs of a partner's extra-pair sexual behavior, but further research is clearly needed to explore these possibilities.

Mate Guarding as Investment ProtectionHumans have evolved a collection of mating strategies whereby benefits can be gained both from investing in a long-term partnership and from defecting from that partnership to gain benefits from an extra-pair partner. The benefits one gains from one's own extra-pair partnerships, however, generally occur at a cost to one's long-term partner. Consequently, men and women have evolved motivations to protect against the loss of their investment in a long-term partnership by guarding against a partner's defection from the ongoing relationship. These mate-guarding behaviors can involve the enticement of a partner's continued investment through the provision of benefits, or through the infliction of costs that either reduce a partner's ability to engage in extra-pair partnerships or directly punish a partner for threatening to or actually engaging in such extra-pair partnerships. The extent to which one is motivated to engage in such mate-guarding behaviors depends on a wide range of both individual difference and contextual variables, all of which moderate the costs and benefits of engagement in such behavior and function to protect against the loss of one's relationship investments.

References

Abell, L., & Brewer, G. (2016). Machiavellianism, perceived quality of alternative mates, and resistance to mate guarding. *Personality and Individual Differences, 101*, 236–239.

Arnocky, S., Perrilloux, C., Cloud, J. M., Bird, B. M., & Thomas, K. (2016). Envy mediates the link between social comparison and appearance enhancement in women. *Evolutionary Psychological Science, 2*, 71–83.

Arnocky, S., Ribout, A., Mirza, R., & Knack, J. (2014). Perceived mate availability influences intrasexual competition, jealousy and mate-guarding behavior. *Journal of Evolutionary Psychology, 12*(1), 45–64.

Atari, M., Barbaro, N., Sela, Y., Shackelford, T. K., & Chegeni, R. (2017a). The Big Five personality dimensions and mate retention behaviors in Iran. *Personality and Individual Differences, 104*, 286–290.

Atari, M., Barbaro, N., Sela, Y., Shackelford, T. K., & Chegeni, R. (2017b). Consideration of cosmetic surgery as part of women's benefit-provisioning mate retention strategy. *Frontiers in Psychology, 8*, Article 1389.

Barbaro, N., Pham, M. N., & Shackelford, T. K. (2015). Solving problems of partner infidelity: Individual mate retention, coalitional mate retention, and in-pair copulation frequency. *Personality and Individual Differences, 82*, 67–71.

Barbaro, N., Pham, M. N., Shackelford, T. K., & Zeigler-Hill, V. (2016). Insecure romantic attachment dimensions and frequency of mate retention behaviors. *Personal Relationships, 23*, 605–618.

Baxter, C. M., Barnett, R., & Dukas, R. (2015). Agression, mate guarding and fitness in male fruit flies. *Animal Behavior, 109*, 235–241.

Bendixen, M., & Kennair, L. E. O. (2014). Revisiting judgments of strategic self-promotion and competitor derogation tactics. *Journal of Social and Personal Relationships, 32*, 1056–1082.

Bhogal, M. S., Rhead, C., & Tudor, C. (2019). Understanding digital dating abuse from an evolutionary perspective: Further evidence for the role of mate value discrepancy. *Personality and Individual Differences, 151*, Article 109552.

Borau, S., & Bonnefon, J.-F. (2019). The imaginary intrasexual competition: Advertisements featuring provocative female models trigger women to engage in indirect aggression. *Journal of Business Ethics, 157*, 45–63.

Botwin, M. D., Buss, D. M., & Shackelford, T. K. (1997). Personality and mate preferences: Five factors in mate selection and marital satisfaction. *Journal of Personality, 65*(1), 107–136. https://doi.org/10.1111/j.1467-6494.1997.tb00531.x

Bouchard, T. J., Blackwell, L., Brown, S., Fehring, R., & Parenteau-Carreau, S. (2018). Dissociation between cervical mucus and urinary hormones during the postpartum return of fertility in breastfeeding women. *The Linacre Quarterly, 85*, 399–411.

Brem, M. J., Spiller, L. C., & Vandehey, M. A. (2015). Online mate-retention tactics on Facebook are associated with relationship aggression. *Journal of Interpersonal Violence, 30*, 2831–2850.

Burch, R. L., & Gallup, G. G. (2020). Abusive men are driven by paternal uncertainty. *Evolutionary Behavioral Sciences, 14*, 197–209.

Buss, D. M. (1988). The evolution of human intrasexual competition: Tactics of mate attraction. *Journal of Personality and Social Psychology, 54*, 616–628.

Buss, D. M. (1989). Sex differences in human mate preferences: Evolutionary hypotheses tested in 37 cultures. *Behavioral and Brain Sciences, 12*(1), 1–14.

Buss, D. M. (2002). Sex, marriage, and religion: What adaptive problems do religious phenomena solve? *Psychological Inquiry, 13*, 201–238.

Buss, D. M. (2003). *The evolution of desire: Strategies of human mating*. Basic Books.

Buss, D. M. (2006). Strategies of human mating. *Psychological Topics, 15*, 239–260.

Buss, D. M., Goetz, C., Duntley, J. D., Asao, K., & Conroy-Beam, D. (2017). The mate switching hypothesis. *Personality and Individual Differences, 104*, 143–149.

Buss, D. M., & Schmitt, D. P. (1993). Sexual strategies theory: An evolutionary perspective on human mating. *Psychological Review, 100*(2), 204.

Buss, D. M., & Shackelford, T. K. (1997a). Human aggression in evolutionary psychological perspective. *Clinical Psychology Review, 17*, 605–619.

Buss, D. M., & Shackelford, T. K. (1997b). From vigilance to violence: Mate retention tactics in married couples. *Journal of Personality and Social Psychology, 72*(2), 346.

Buss, D. M., Shackelford, T. K., & McKibbin, W. F. (2008). The Mate Retention Inventory-Short Form (MRI-SF). *Personality and Individual Differences, 44*, 322–334.

Butte, N. F., & King, J. C. (2005). Energy requirements during pregnancy and lactation. *Public Health Nutrition, 8*, 1010–1027.

Carter, G. L., Campbell, A. C., & Muncer, S. (2014). The dark triad personality: Attractiveness to women. *Personality and Individual Differences, 56*, 57–61.

Chaudhary, N., Al-Shawaf, L., & Buss, D. M. (2018). Mate competition in Pakistan: Mate value, mate retention, and competitor derogation. *Personality and Individual Differences, 130*, 141–146.

Chegeni, R., Khodabakhsh Pirkalani, R., & Dehshiri, G. (2018). On love and darkness: The dark triad and mate retention behaviors in a non-Western culture. *Personality and Individual Differences, 122*, 43–46.

Cousins, A. J., Fugere, M. A., & Franklin, M. (2009). Digit ratio (2D:4D), mate guarding, and physical aggression in dating couples. *Personality and Individual Differences, 46*, 709–713.

Cousins, A. J., Fugere, M. A., & Riggs, M. L. (2015). Resistance to Mate Guarding Scale in Women: Psychometric properties. *Evolutionary Psychology, 2015*(13), 106–128.

Dahabreh, I. J., & Paulus, J. K. (2011). Association of episodic physical and sexual activity with triggering of acute cardiac events. *Journal of the American Medical Association, 305*, 1225–1233.

Dewey, K. G. (1997). Energy and protein requirements during lactation. *Annual Review of Nutrition, 17*, 19–36.

Ferdenzi, C., Lemaître, J.-F., Leongómez, J. D., & Roberts, S. C. (2011). Digit ratio (2D:4D) predicts facial, but not voice or body odour, attractiveness in men. *Proceedings of the Royal Society of London B: Biological Sciences, 278*, 3551–3557.

Fisher, M., & Cox, A. (2010). Four strategies used during intrasexual competition for mates. *Personal Relationships, 18*, 20–38.

Frappier, J., Toupin, I., Levy, J. J., Aubertin-Leheudre, M., & Kearelis, A. (2013). Energy expenditure during sexual activity in young healthy couples. *PLoS ONE, 8*, Article e79342.

French, J. E., Meltzer, A. L., & Maner, J. K. (2017). Men's perceived partner commitment and mate guarding: The moderating role of partner's hormonal contraceptive use. *Evolutionary Behavioral Sciences, 11*, 173–186.

Fugere, M. A., Cousins, A. J., & MacLaren, S. A. (2015). (Mis)matching in physical attractiveness and women's resistance to mate guarding. *Personality and Individual Differences, 87*, 190–195.

Gangestad, S. W., Garver-Apgar, C. E., Cousins, A. J., & Thornhill, R. (2014). Inersexual conflict across women's ovulatory cycle. *Evolution and Human Behavior, 35*, 302–308.

Gangestad, S. W., Garver-Apgar, C. E., Simpson, J. A., & Cousins, A. J. (2007). Changes in women's mate preferences across the ovulatory cycle. *Journal of Personality and Social Psychology, 92*, 151–163.

Gangestad, S. W., & Haselton, M. G. (2015). Human estrus: Implications for relationship science. *Current Opinion in Psychology, 1*, 45–51.

Gangestad, S. W., Thornhill, R., & Garver, C. E. (2002). Changes in women's sexual interests and their partner's mate-retention tactics across the menstrual cycle: Evidence for shifting conflicts of interest. *Proceedings of the Royal Society of London B: Biological Sciences, 269*, 975–982.

Geary, D. C. (2006). Coevolution of paternal investment and cuckoldry in humans. In T. K. Shackelford & S. M. Platek (Eds.), *Female infidelity and paternal uncertainty* (pp. 14–34). Cambridge University Press.

Geller, S. E., Koch, A. R., Garland, C. E., MacDonald, E. J., Storey, F., & Lawton, B. (2018). A global view of severe maternal morbidity: Moving beyond maternal mortality. *Reproductive Health, 15*, 98.

Goetz, A. T., Shackelford, T. K., Schipper, L. D., & Stewart-Williams, S. (2006). Adding insult to injury: Development and initial validation of the Partner-Directed Insults Scale. *Violence and Victims, 21*, 691–706.

Grant, R., & Montrose, T. (2018). It's a man's world: Mate guarding and the evolution of patriarchy. *Mankind Quarterly, 58*, 384–418.

Guitar, A. E., & Carmen, R. A. (2017). Facebook frenemies and selfie-promotion: Women and competition in the digital age. In M. L. Fisher (Ed.), *The Oxford handbook of women and competition* (pp. 681–697). Oxford University Press.

Hackett, G., Kirby, M., Wylie, K., Heald, A., Ossei-Gerning, N., Edwards, D., & Muneer, A. (2018). British Society for Sexual Medicine guidelines on the management of erectile dysfunction in men—2017. *The Journal of Sexual Medicine, 15*, 430–457.

Haselton, M. G., & Gangestad, S. W. (2006). Conditional expression of women's desires and men's mate guarding across the ovulatory cycle. *Hormones and Behavior, 49*, 509–518.

Hayward, A., & Gillooly, J. F. (2011). The cost of sex: Quantifying energetic investment in gamete production by males and females. *PLoS ONE, 6*, Article e16557.

Hill, S. E., Rodeheffer, C. D., Griskevicius, V., Durante, K., & White, A. E. (2012). Boosting beauty in an economic decline: Mating, spending, and the lipstick effect. *Journal of Personality and Social Psychology, 103*, 275–291.

Hirshberg, A., & Srinivas, S. K. (2017). Epidemiology of maternal morbidity and mortality. *Seminars in Perinatology, 41*, 332–337.

Holden, C. J., Shackelford, T. K., Zeigler-Hill, V., Miner, E. J., Kaighobadi, F., Starratt, V. G., Jeffery, A. J., & Buss, D. M. (2014). Husband's esteem predicts his mate retention tactics. *Evolutionary Psychology, 12*(3), Article 147470491401200311.

Huffard, C. L., Caldwell, R. L., & Farnis, B. (2010). Male-male and male-female aggression may influence mating associations in wild octopuses (*Abdopus aculeatus*). *Journal of Comparative Psychology, 124*, 38–46.

Hurst, A. C., Alquist, J. L., & Puts, D. A. (2017). Women's fertility status alters other women's jealousy and mate guarding. *Personality and Social Psychology Bulletin, 43*, 191–203.

Jonason, P. K., Cetrulo, J. F., Madrid, J. M., & Morrison, C. M. (2009). Gift-giving as a courtship or mate-retention tactic? Insights from non-human models. *Evolutionary Psychology, 7*, 89–103.

Jonason, P. K., Li, N. P., & Buss, D. M. (2010). The costs and benefits of the dark triad: Implications for mate poaching and mate retention tactics. *Personality and Individual Differences, 48*, 373–378.

Kaighobadi, F., Shackelford, T. K., & Goetz, A. T. (2009). From mate retention to murder: Evolutionary psychological perspectives on men's partner-directed violence. *Review of General Psychology, 13*, 327–334.

Kaighobadi, F., Starratt, V. G., Shackelford, T. K., & Popp, D. (2008). Male mate retention mediates the relationship between female sexual infidelity and female-directed violence. *Personality and Individual Differences, 44*, 1422–1431.

King, S. L., Allen, S. J., Krützen, M., & Connor, R. C. (2019). Vocal behaviour of allied male dolphins during cooperative mate guarding. *Animal Cognition, 22*, 991–1000.

Krems, J. A., Neel, R., Neuberg, S. L., Puts, D. A., & Kenrick, D. T. (2016). Women selectively guard their (desirable) mates from ovulating women. *Journal of Personality and Social Psychology, 110*, 551–573.

Lewis, S., & South, A. (2012). The evolution of animal nuptial gifts. *Advances in the Study of Behavior, 44*, 53–97.

Li, N. P., Bailey, J. M., Kenrick, D. T., & Linsenmeier, J. A. (2002). The necessities and luxuries of mate preferences: Testing the tradeoffs. *Journal of Personality and Social Psychology, 82*(6), 947.

Li, N. P., & Kenrick, D. T. (2006). Sex similarities and differences in preferences for short-term mates: What, whether, and why. *Journal of Personality and Social Psychology, 90*(3), 468.

Locke, A., Desrochers, J., & Arnocky, S. (2020). Induced mate abundance increases women's expectations for engagement ring size and cost. *Evolutionary Psychological Science, 6*, 188–194.

Lopes, G. S., Meneses, G. O., Cataldo, Q. F., Segundo, D. S. A., Fink, B., & Shackelford, T. K. (2019). Individual differences in men's use of partner-directed insults and sexual coercion: Replication and extension in a South American sample. *Personality and Individual Differences, 150*, Article 109480.

Maner, J. K., & McNulty, J. K. (2013). Attunement to the fertility status of same-sex rivals: Women's testosterone responses to olfactory ovulation cues. *Evolution and Human Behavior, 34*, 412–418.

McKibbin, W. F., Bates, V. M., Shackelford, T. K., Hafen, C. A., & LaMunyon, C. W. (2010). Risk of sperm competition moderates the relationship between men's satisfaction with their partner and men's interest in their partner's copulatory orgasm. *Personality and Individual Differences, 49*, 961–966.

McKibbin, W. F., Goetz, A. T., Shackelford, T. K., Schipper, L. D., Starratt, V. G., & Stewart-Williams, S. (2007). Why do men insult their intimate partners? *Personality and Individual Differences, 43*(2), 231–241.

McKibbin, W. F., Shackelford, T. K., & Lopes, G. S. (2018). Development and initial psychometric validation of the Women's Partner-Directed Insults Scale. *Personality and Individual Differences, 135*, 51–55.

McNulty, J. K., Wenner, C. A., & Fisher, T. D. (2016). Longitudinal associations among relationship satisfaction, sexual satisfaction, and frequency of sex in early marriage. *Archives of Sexual Behavior, 45*, 85–97.

Miner, E. J., Shackelford, T. K., & Starratt, V. G. (2009). Mate value of romantic partners predicts men's partner-directed verbal insults. *Personality and Individual Differences, 46*(2), 135–139.

Miner, E. J., Starratt, V. G., & Shackelford, T. K. (2009). It's not all about her: Men's mate value and mate retention. *Personality and Individual Differences, 47*, 214–218.

Mogilski, J. K., Memering, S. L., Welling, L. L. M., & Shackelford, T. K. (2017). Monogamy versus consensual non-monogamy: Alternative approaches to pursuing a strategically pluralistic mating strategy. *Archives of Sexual Behavior, 46*, 407–417.

Mogilski, J. K., Reeve, S. D., Nicolas, S. C., Donaldson, S. H., Mitchell, V. E., & Welling, L. L. (2019). Jealousy, consent, and compersion within monogamous and consensually non-monogamous romantic relationships. *Archives of Sexual Behavior, 48*(6), 1811–1828.

Moon, J. W., Krems, J. A., Cohen, A. B., & Kenrick, D. T. (2019). Is nothing sacred? Religion, sex, and reproductive strategies. *Current Directions in Psychological Science, 28*, 361–365.

Moran, J. B., Kuhle, B. X., Wade, T. J., & Seid, M. A. (2017). To poach or not to poach? Men are more willing to short-term poach mated women who are more attractive than their mates. *EvoS Journal: The Journal of the Evolutionary Studies Consortium, 2017*, 58–69.

Pazhoohi, F., Lang, M., Xygalatas, D., & Grammer, K. (2017). Religious veiling as a mate-guarding strategy: Effects of environmental pressures on cultural practices. *Evolutionary Psychological Science, 3*, 118–124.

Pham, M. N., Barbaro, N., & Shackelford, T. K. (2015). Development and initial validation of the Coalitional Mate Retention Inventory. *Evolutionary Psychological Science, 1*, 4–12.

Pham, M. N., & Shackelford, T. K. (2013). Oral sex as mate retention behavior. *Personality and Individual Differences, 55*, 185–188.

Pillsworth, E. G., & Haselton, M. G. (2006). Male sexual attractiveness predicts differential ovulatory shifts in female extra-pair attraction and male mate retention. *Evolution and Human Behavior, 27*(4), 247–258.

Platek, S. M., & Shackelford, T. K. (2006). *Female infidelity and paternal uncertainty: Evolutionary perspectives on male anti-cuckoldry* tactics. Cambridge University Press.

Prokop, P., & Pazda, A. D. (2016). Women's red clothing can increase mate-guarding from their male partners. *Personality and Individual Differences, 98*, 114–117.

Richters, J., de Visser, R., Rissel, C., & Smith, A. (2006). Sexual practices at last heterosexual encounter and occurrence of orgasm in a national survey. *Journal of Sex Research, 43*, 217–226.

Ronsmans, C., & Graham, W. J. (2006). Maternal mortality: Who, when, where, and why. *The Lancet, 368*, 1189–1200.

Schmitt, D. P., & Buss, D. M. (1996). Strategic self-promotion and competitor derogation: Sex and context effects on the perceived effectiveness of mate attraction tactics. *Journal of Personality and Social Psychology, 70*, 1185–1204.

Schmitt, D. P., & Buss, D. M. (2001). Human mate poaching: Tactics and temptations for infiltrating existing mateships. *Journal of Personality and Social Psychology, 80*, 894–917.

Sela, Y., Shackelford, T. K., Pham, M. N., & Euler, H. A. (2015). Do women perform fellatio as a mate retention behavior? *Personality and Individual Differences, 73*, 61–66.

Shackelford, T. K., Goetz, A. T., Buss, D. M., Euler, H. A., & Hoier, S. (2005). When we hurt the ones we love: Predicting violence against women from men's mate retention. *Personal Relationships, 12*, 447–463.

Shackelford, T. K., Goetz, A. T., Guta, F. E., & Schmitt, D. P. (2006). Mate guarding and frequent in-pair copulation in humans. *Human Nature, 17*, 239–252.

Starratt, V. G., Goetz, A. T., Shackelford, T. K., McKibbin, W. F., & Stewart-Williams, S. (2008). Men's partner-directed insults and sexual coercion in intimate relationships. *Journal of Family Violence, 23*, 315–323.

Starratt, V. G., & Shackelford, T. K. (2012). He said, she said: Men's reports of mate value and mate retention behaviors in intimate relationships. *Personality and Individual Differences, 53*(4), 459–462.

Starratt, V. G., Weekes-Shackelford, V. A., & Shackelford, T. K. (2017). Mate value both positively and negatively predicts intentions to commit an infidelity. *Personality and Individual Differences, 104*, 18–22.

Strouts, P. H., Brase, G. L., & Dillon, H. M. (2017). Personality and evolutionary strategies: The relationships between HEXACO traits, mate value, life history strategy, and sociosexuality. *Personality and Individual Differences, 115*, 128–132.

Thurber, C., Dugas, L. R., Ocobock, C., Carlson, B., Speakman, J. R., & Pontzer, H. (2019). Extreme events reveal an alimentary limit on sustained maximal human energy expenditure. *Science Advances, 5*, Article eaaw0341.

Trivers, R. (1972). *Parental investment and sexual selection* (Vol. 136). Biological Laboratories, Harvard University.

VanderLaan, D. P., & Vasey, P. L. (2008). Mate retention behavior of men and women in heterosexual and homosexual relationships. *Archives of Sexual Behavior, 37*, 572–585.

Watts, D. P. (1998). Coalitionary mate guarding by male chimpanzees at Ngogo, Kibale National park, Uganda. *Behavioral Ecology and Sociobiology, 44*, 43–55.

Willis, P. M., & Dill, L. M. (2007). Mate guarding in male Dall's porpoises (*Phocoenoides dalli*). *Ethology, 113*, 587–597.

Young, C., Hähndel, S., Majolo, B., Schülke, O., & Ostner, J. (2013). Male coalitions and female behaviour affect male mating success independent of dominance rank and female receptive synchrony in wild Barbary macaques. *Behavioral Ecology and Sociobiology, 67*, 1665–1677.

CHAPTER

15 Intimate Partner Violence and Relationship Maintenance

Gordon G. Gallup, Jr. *and* Rebecca L. Burch

Abstract

In a recent study of spouse abuse in the context of human reproductive competition, Burch and Gallup found that male sexual jealousy accounted for far more variance in different parameters of spouse abuse than the use of alcohol, drugs, or lack of financial resources combined. Coupled with these findings, our model of intimate partner violence centers around four evolved, sequentially dependent strategies that men use to increase the likelihood of paternity and investing in children that are genetically their own. These strategies include preventing partner insemination by rival males, counter insemination tactics such as sperm competition and semen displacement, pregnancy termination strategies, and differential investment in children as a function of phenotypic evidence for shared genes. By focusing on variation in paternal resemblance which includes differences in the degree to which fathers and children look, act, or think alike, we provide novel research predictions and specific recommendations for steps that can be taken to minimize family violence and promote paternal investment.

Key Words: paternal resemblance, spouse abuse, child abuse, adoption, artificial insemination, deadbeat dads

Until recently, most research on domestic violence focused on cultural and personality features of men who commit violent acts (Abramsky et al., 2011; Campbell 1992; Delgado et al., 1997; Huss & Langhinrichsen-Rohling, 2006; Murphy et al 1994), the specific behaviors that constitute abuse (Boulette & Anderson 1986; Jewkes et al., 2002), or merely identifying the signs of abuse (Riggs et al., 2000). However, research has begun to examine this problem from an evolutionary perspective (Archer, 2013; Burch & Gallup, 2000; Daly & Wilson, 1988; Peters et al., 2002; Wiederman & Allgeier 1993).

Predictions derived from evolutionary theory regarding spousal and child abuse (i.e., domestic violence) often stem from problems posed by questions about paternity (Burch & Gallup, 2020; Wilson & Daly, 1993, 1996). Females must contend with pregnancy and childbirth, but they rarely have reason to question their maternity. Males, however, must contend with the possibility that their children are not genetically their own. There is always a possibility that their female partner was unfaithful or forced into sexual intercourse and is carrying another man's child. A man who raises another man's child rather than his own invests in an individual who will add nothing to his genetic fitness (this is referred to as cuckoldry). Because of scarce resources in the ancestral environment and the high costs of rearing children, cuckoldry could have drastically reduced a man's inclusive fitness (i.e., his net genetic representation in subsequent generations). Therefore, as a product of natural selection men would be expected to deploy evolved paternal assurance tactics that function to increase the likelihood that the children they raise and invest in are their own. Because maternity is certain, women have not been selected to deploy such tactics (Gallup, Burch, & Berens Mitchell, 2006).

Although women cannot be cuckolded, they can be abandoned. In the ancestral environment, abandonment by a formerly committed, high-quality man who was providing for and protecting the female and her children could have had dire consequences. As a result, women have been selected to compete with one another to develop and maintain a pair-bond with a high-quality male and to take steps to reduce the risk of being abandoned (e.g., Gallup et al., 2012).

Paternal Assurance Strategies

In a review of the literature on the evolution of parental investment, Geary (2016) concluded that "the most remarkable feature of human reproduction is that many fathers show some degree of direct and indirect investment in their children" (p. 537). Indeed, human males invest far more in children than males of other species, and human children being highly altricial (i.e., parent-dependent) benefit in tangible ways from this investment (Marlowe, 2000). However, as is true of parental investment in other species, men's parenting is conditional upon high levels of paternal certainty (Geary, 2016). It is precisely because human infants need so much parental care and paternity is uncertain that men have been selected to make judicious choices about which children, they invest in.

Gallup and Burch (2006) were the first to compile and elaborate a list of four evolved categories of paternal assurance strategies which operate to minimize being duped into caring for other men's children. The first class of these tactics involves *insemination prevention strategies*, which include mate guarding (Buss, 2002; Haselton & Gangestad, 2006), male sexual jealousy (Daly & Wilson, 1982), and various other techniques (e.g., chastity belts and infibulation) used to discourage or preclude female infidelity (Daly et al., 1982). For example, Burch and Gallup (2020) found that among convicted spouse abusers, sexual jealousy was cited more often than any other factor in the instigation and escalation of conflict. When males were jealous, mate-guarding behaviors nearly doubled.

If these attempts should fail and the woman is inseminated by another man, there is a second class of *counterinsemination strategies*, which include sperm competition (e.g., Shackelford, 2003) and semen displacement (Baker & Bellis, 1993; Burch & Gallup, 2019; Gallup & Burch, 2006; Gallup et al., 2003) that function to reduce the likelihood of fertilization by the rival male. These strategies may escalate into sexual coercion. Burch and Gallup (2020) found that jealousy also triggered increases in sexual violence; when men were jealous pressuring the partner to have sex "in a way she didn't want" tripled, and forcing the partner to have sex more than quadrupled.

Should these mechanisms fail and the woman is impregnated by another man, the third category of paternal assurance strategies involves *pregnancy termination*, which can include pregnancy-induced domestic violence (Burch & Gallup, 2004) and coitus-induced uterine contractions that interfere with embryo implantation (see Gallup & Burch, 2006, for details). Finally, if a child sired by another man is born, the remaining class of paternal assurance strategies involves differential *postpartum investment* in the child by the resident male. There is growing evidence that men are sensitive to paternal resemblance and invest preferentially in children with whom they share facial features (Burch & Gallup, 2000; Burch et al., 2006; Platek et al., 2003).

According to this model, men use these four categories of paternal assurance tactics in their romantic and reproductive relationships throughout their lives, shifting and adjusting tactics according to different contexts. For example, men may have more paternity concerns regarding a particular child or within a particular relationship. They may also use tactics from different categories simultaneously, such as mate guarding their partner while also investing differentially in particular children. Burch and Gallup (2000, 2020) found that men who were jealous not only engaged in more mate guarding and abusive controlling behaviors toward their partner but also were more likely to engage in greater abuse and differential treatment of their children.

Paternal Resemblance

Paternal resemblance based on shared features between the resident male and the child is a phenotypic indicator of shared genes. A study inspired by this idea examined 55 men in a treatment program for domestic violence offenders who agreed to complete an anonymous survey that included questions about the types of abuse they had committed, along with the relationships, degree of relatedness, and perceived resemblance they shared with their children (Burch & Gallup, 2000). Severity of partner abuse and degree of injury as a result of the abuse was evaluated by independent raters. Burch and Gallup (2000) found these abusive males had worse marital relations, exhibited more abuse, and showed increased severity of abuse directed toward their mates as the degree of paternal resemblance to the children diminished. They also found that the presence of children who were explicitly unrelated to the resident male (e.g., children from the female partner's previous relationship or a stepchild) greatly increased the amount of violence in the home. This "mixed" family is common in such populations and appears to exacerbate instances of domestic violence. In the case of females with children from prior relationships, these sexually jealous resident men may be required not only to care for children who are not theirs but also sometimes to interact with their female partner's former mates. This can set the stage for further resentment, hostility, and jealousy, which can culminate in violence.

In the first experimental attempt to examine the effect of paternal resemblance Platek et al. (2002) studied the reactions of male and female college students to computer-generated images of children's faces. Without the students being told, the children's pictures were digitally morphed with either images of the subjects themselves or with images of one of four other people of the same sex. To measure the effect of shared facial features, the subjects were presented with hypothetical parental investment scenarios and asked to choose which pictured child they would invest in. Males chose their own morphed child's picture more often than females in almost every positive investment category and less often in almost every negative investment category. The greatest difference between males and females occurred in response to the question, "Which one of these children would you be most likely to adopt?" with 90% of the males but only 35% of the females selecting the child whose face had been morphed with their own. Likewise, none of the males selected children's faces that had been morphed with their own face as the child they would most likely punish.

In a follow-up study, Platek et al. (2003) tried to determine if there might simply be sex differences in the ability to detect resemblance and whether males were more prone to make investment decisions about children based on resemblance. The results showed no sex differences in the ability to detect resemblance, but males were far more likely than females to make hypothetical investment decisions that favored children they looked like. In a subsequent study using neuroimaging techniques, Platek et al. (2004) found sex differences in areas of the brain that were activated by viewing self-morphed baby pictures. Using a similar paradigm, Wu et al. (2013) also showed a stable male advantage in child face processing. Males showed higher detection of resembling child faces and self-referential processing in kin detection than did females. These effects originated from the anterior cingulate cortex and medial frontal gyrus, respectively. This supports the male advantage in paternity assessment, and it can be found in both early and late processing stages in different brain regions. These results are consistent with the idea that unlike women, men have been hard-wired by their evolutionary history to process children's faces based on the presence of shared features, particularly when making investment decisions.

DeBruine found a resemblance effect in cooperation and prosocial behaviors among adults but no sex difference (DeBruine 2002, 2005). However, she used adult faces, not children's faces. Platek and colleagues found sex differences in brain activation to resembling child faces (Platek et al., 2004) but not resembling adult faces (Platek & Kemp, 2009). Throughout this literature, sex differences are only found when children's faces are used. Thus, the different contexts in which previous studies investigated resemblance effects may account for this inconsistency. Platek and colleagues (2002, 2003) examined prosocial behavior toward children, and because of paternity uncertainty facial resemblance would be expected to have a greater effect on men's than women's parental investment. DeBruine (2002, 2005), on the other hand, assessed prosocial behavior toward peers. Both men and women have evolved to use resemblance as a cue for cooperation with others, but only men use resemblance as a cue for child investment. Studies showing patterns of greater paternal investment based on shared physical features have now been replicated many times by investigators all over the world. Males who commit infanticide also cite a lack of resemblance, implying nonpaternity as a reason (Daly & Wilson, 1984). Resemblance has been implicated in the father/child relationship (Apicella & Marlowe, 2004), with perceived child resemblance valued more highly by men (Volk & Quinsey, 2002).

Some of the most impressive work in this area has been done by Alvergne and colleagues. Alvergne et al. (2009) found that paternal investment was positively related to both face (visual) and odor (olfactory) similarities between fathers and children. This had a measurable effect on survival; children who received more investment had better growth and higher nutritional status. Alvergne et al. (2010) also found fathers reported the highest emotional proximity to children who displayed greater resemblance, but this relationship was not observed in mothers. Alvergne and colleagues have even examined which facial features have the greatest effect on resemblance ratings. By manipulating different parts of the face subjects were shown, they determined that the lower part of the face—which changes the most during the child's growth and development—does not contain paternity cues. Fathers were able to focus on specific resemblance cues even when the overall face was disrupted, and they ignored irrelevant unstable features. As a result, Alvergne et al. (2014) concluded "that environmental effects have little influence on the detection of paternity using facial similarities" (p. 1).

Another recent study shows that among couples, parents are happier than nonparents, but mothers are happier than fathers (Yu et al., 2019). For high parent–child resemblance both parents exhibited high levels of well-being, but for low parent–child resemblance the well-being of mothers was higher than fathers.

Thus, the literature overwhelmingly implicates a male-specific effect of resemblance on child investment. It is not surprising therefore that mothers and their relatives often try to convince ostensible fathers of this resemblance to increase paternal investment in offspring. Daly and Wilson (1982) recorded spontaneous remarks in maternity wards about the appearance of the newborn child. Mothers and her friends and relatives were more likely to comment on how children resemble their fathers. When fathers displayed any doubt, the mothers quickly reassured them of the child's resemblance. Regalski and Gaulin (1993) also found that women consistently ascribed resemblance of their children to their current male partner, and Alvergne et al. (2007) found that mothers ascribed resemblance to the father even when assessment by external judges revealed the opposite. As Alvergne et al. (2009) and Burch and Gallup (2000) pointed out, these perceptions have tangible consequences for children's survival.

Recently Gallup et al. (2016) extended this line of research by showing greater paternal investment in children based on shared psychological features (interests, attitudes, etc.). Indeed, while both physical and psychological features made a difference, they found that shared psychological features between fathers of adolescent and older children accounted for more variance in objective measures of paternal investment than did shared physical features.

Conditions Where the Probability of Paternity Drops to Zero

Whereas the probability of paternity is always less than 1.0, there are conditions at the other end of this continuum where the probability of paternity drops to zero. There are at least five conditions where this applies: adoption, artificial insemination with donor semen, becoming involved with a woman who has children from a prior union, conception as a result of rape or forced copulation by another man, and being cuckolded by a rival male. Because many conditions where the probability of paternity drops to zero make nonpaternity explicit, we predict that the risk of poor paternal investment as well as correspondingly poor marital outcomes will be higher.

We expect men and women to differ dramatically when it comes to mating and parental behavior. Women have been selected to show patterns of highly discriminate *mating* because the costs of reproduction are much higher for women and they have a strong vested interest in the other 50% of the genes being carried by their children. However, because maternity has always been certain, women have never been selected to invest preferentially in children based on maternal resemblance and as a result they show patterns of relatively indiscriminate *parenting*. For example, although women possess the ability to detect resemblance in children, they do not use this information to discriminate in child investment. In one study where women were directed to select the picture of one child out of several to invest in or punish, women attempted to spread the positive and negative investments across all the children and openly stated that this was a difficult and time-intensive task (Platek et al., 2003).

We predict, therefore, that women will be more likely to advocate and initiate caring for children who are not their own. However, because of the ever-present possibility of being cuckolded, men are expected to show patterns of highly discriminate parenting. Consistent with this prediction men are far more likely than women to answer hypothetical investment questions in the affirmative (e.g., "which of these children would you adopt?") when shown pictures of children whose faces contained some of their own features (Platek et al., 2002).

Decades of research show that children are more likely to experience abuse at the hands of their nonbiological parents than their biological parents (see Daly & Wilson, 1998, for a comprehensive review). Indeed, when it comes to the risk of infanticide as the most extreme case of child abuse, Daly and Wilson found that children are 100 times more likely to be killed by their nonbiological parents, and nonbiological fathers are far more prone to engage in killing and other forms of child abuse than nonbiological mothers. Although the work by Daly and Wilson is not without its critics, such criticisms have been effectively countered (Daly & Wilson, 2008), and their findings have been independently replicated and extended to unintentional fatalities among children living with a stepparent (Tooley et al., 2006).

Stepchildren receive less supervision (Amato, 1987), less attention (Cooksey & Fondell, 1996), less money for education (Zvoch, 1999), and lower amounts and quality of food (Case et al., 2000), and they are overrepresented in cases of incest (Russell, 1984). Children living with both biological parents achieve more in school and are better adjusted than children who have stepfathers (McLanahan & Sandefur, 1994).

Adoption

While some recent studies have failed to find appreciable differences between adoptive and biological parents in their relationship with their children (e.g., Werum et al., 2018), at the other extreme are reports of adopted children being killed by their adoptive parents (Miller et al., 2007). One reason for such discrepancies may be that most studies rely on surveys administered to adoptive parents rather than to adults who were adopted as children, and therefore such studies may be confounded by a social desirability reporting bias. Parents going through the adoptive process are also carefully screened in terms of time, effort, and finances. This creates a unique context in which the parents are vetted and have already committed to investing in the child. It is not surprising that this experience could affect investment in the child by screening out problematic parents.

Less than 2% of the U.S. population have adopted children (Jones, 2008), and Feigelman and Silverman (1977) found that women far outnumbered men in single-parent adoptions. Jones (2008) also found that adoptive mothers were more likely to be older or have fertility issues. Indeed, women who ever used infertility services were 10 times more likely to have adopted children, and those who never used infertility services were the least likely to have adopted children (Jones, 2009). This may imply that being unable to have biological children affects the likelihood to adopt unrelated children. Barash (1977) contended that human adoption is often a second choice, with biological children being the first. Thus, adoptive families may be fundamentally different from other families with unrelated children.

These studies also fail to distinguish between the treatment children receive from their adoptive fathers as opposed to that from their adoptive mothers. It is well known that women are more likely to adopt (Feigelman & Silverman, 1977), but when examining adoptive parents, it may not be easy or even possible to distinguish between mutual or solitary decisions to invest. Kirk (1984) found that men were more hesitant to adopt and that fathers of adoptive fathers—adoptive grandfathers—were especially resistant to the idea of adoption. Another important issue is the percentage of families with both biological and adopted children. In families with both adopted and biological children, Gibson (2009) found that biological children were less likely to be arrested, less likely to be on public assistance, and less likely to require treatment for substance abuse or other mental health problems. The contrast created by the presence of biological children in families with an adopted child can precipitate minor seemingly unintentional instances of favoring the biological children by the father that can negatively impact the self-esteem of the adopted children.

Still another reason why the incidence of mistreatment among families with adopted children may be lower than those with stepchildren or foster children (van Ijzendoorn et al., 2009) is that adoption can be used to codify an existing parental relationship with the child of a relative that the adoptive parents are already caring for on a regular basis. In that case, unlike stepchildren or foster children, one of the adoptive parents would share genes with the adoptive child (Jones, 2009). Child welfare services often preferentially send children into care with biological relatives rather than advocate for formal adoptions to unrelated families (Bartholet, 1999).

For other forms of adoption, we predict that one way of improving paternal investment would be to select adoptive children who share salient facial and other physical features in common with the to-be adoptive father. Although some people might argue that adoptive fathers already "know" that they are not the child's father, findings show that male college students who had no reason to think they were the fathers of the computer-generated child self-morphs they viewed were nonetheless far more likely than female students to select photos of self-morphs than other morphs when answering hypothetical investment questions. In fact, 90% of the men chose the child who most resembled them for "adoption" (Platek et al., 2002). Indeed, some of the females that participated in the original child morphing study had to be excused from the experiment because they found it impossible and too distressing to choose among different children to invest in.

Still another sophisticated psychological strategy for generating greater paternal investment in an adopted male child would be to give the adoptive father's name to the child (e.g., John Doe, "Jr."). Because cuckoldry is another instance in which the probability of shared genes drops to zero, mothers who cuckold their mates could also have a lot to gain in terms of generating paternal investment by advocating for "Junior" designations when it comes to picking baby boy names. Consistent with this logic, Johnson et al. (1991) found that adopted children were more likely to be named after relatives. While both male and female adopted children were more likely to be "namesakes," biological sons were more likely to be namesakes than daughters. In both cases, children were more likely to be named after patrilineal relatives. As the authors stated, "the more that parenthood was assured, the less likely the child was to be namesaked" (p. 373). Daly and Wilson (1982) found that new mothers were more likely to make comments about paternal resemblance and assert paternity when the newborn was named after the putative father (maternal relatives were also more insistent on paternal namesaking). Indeed, Furstenberg and Talvitie (1980) found that for children born out of wedlock, naming the child after the putative father was a strong predictor of a long-term supportive and close relationship between father and child: namesaked children spent more time with and had more financial assistance provided by their fathers. These children also had fewer behavioral problems and better cognitive skills.

Artificial Insemination

In response to problems posed by male infertility, an increasing number of couples are opting for artificial insemination as an alternative to adoption (Daniels & Golden, 2004). For instance, in 2014 there were 57,323 deliveries and 70,354 infants born in the United States using assisted reproductive technology (https://www.cdc.gov/art/artdata/index.html). Thompson (2005) estimated that 30,000 infants are born each year from donor insemination. Because artificial insemination with donor semen makes the absence of paternity for the infertile resident male explicit, we predict that paternal investment may be impaired. A number of studies suggest that men are threatened by this procedure and see donors as threats to their paternity (Cousineau & Domar, 2007; Dhillon et al., 2000; Fisher & Hammarberg, 2012). Wu (2011) examined fertility doctors in Taiwan where it was clear that nonpaternity was an issue for men in couples seeking donor insemination. The doctors stated that these men felt "threatened" and "needed to be won over." Several such studies (Burr 2009; Daniels, 2007; Wu, 2011) mentioned that some couples fear the donor insemination becoming publicly known, and Klock and Maier (1991) reported that couples were particularly concerned with how this would damage the father/child relationship.

There are several techniques that could be used to promote better parenting outcomes by infertile males with partners who conceive because of artificial insemination. One would be to inform the infertile resident male that his semen will be mixed with the donor's semen so that if conception occurs there is always the possibility that he would be the father. This sophisticated practice has existed for decades, often recommended by fertility doctors. Wu (2011) examined fertility practices in Taiwan over the past 60 years and reported that doctors would routinely mix donor and father semen to obscure paternity. Taylor (2005) described similar practices in England. Indeed, Klock and Maier (1991) found that a large percentage of couples have intercourse after insemination in an effort to obscure paternity themselves. Wu (2011) also mentioned that doctors ensure that donors remained anonymous to make the process easier for the fathers.

Paralleling the approach that we recommended for improving adoption outcomes, we also encourage couples who opt for artificial insemination to screen semen donors based on the presence of shared physical features with the resident/adoptive male. Indeed, a study in Israel (Birenbaum-Carmeli & Carmeli, 2002) found that prospective mothers and fathers often chose semen donors who resembled the fathers in terms of height and eye color. However, mothers and fathers differed when it came to skin color. The authors attributed this to issues of colorism (skin color indicating status or social class); where mothers wanted children with the most advantageous skin color but fathers wanted their own skin color reflected in the child. Wu (2011) found that in Taiwan, doctors would attempt to find donors who matched the fathers as much as possible, not only in blood type but also in race, body type, personality, and temperament.

Another and even more effective strategy would be to select semen donors who share genes in common with the resident male, such as his brother or his father. After all, shared genes would certainly promote shared features. If the woman conceived as a result of sperm donation from the husband's brother, the child would be carrying 25% of the resident male's genes and therefore would be either his niece or his nephew. Alternatively, if the woman was artificially inseminated by semen taken from the infertile male's father, the child would likewise be carrying 25% of the resident male's genes, but rather than being his niece or nephew the child would be the resident male's half-brother or half-sister.

Deadbeat Dads

There has been considerable news coverage of divorced males who default on making court-mandated child support payments, and these men have been dubbed "deadbeat dads" by the media (see also Shackelford et al., 2012). Although there are many reasons that may contribute to failures to make child support payments, we offer three testable predictions that ought to distinguish at least some estranged noncompliant men from compliant fathers. In the first instance, we predict that deadbeat dads will be more likely than compliant fathers to harbor suspicions and allegations of female infidelity concerning their former partners. In other words, some deadbeat dads may be deadbeats, but they may not be dads. Consistent with this, we also predict that some of the children of noncompliant fathers will show less evidence of paternal resemblance than the children of those making child support payments. Finally, we predict that an effective strategy for getting some deadbeat dads to become compliant and begin making child support payments would be to use DNA testing for paternity. In instances where paternity can be clearly demonstrated, we expect the incidence of compliance would increase dramatically.

We also predict that children who fail to show paternal resemblance will not only be at risk of paternal indifference and lack of support, the evidence shows that they and their mothers can be at an elevated risk of physical abuse (Burch & Gallup, 2020, 2000). One way to use the lack of paternal resemblance to reduce child abuse would be to develop proactive, early intervention strategies where social workers and other professionals could be trained to identify children who fail to look like their ostensible fathers and take steps designed to preclude or at least minimize ensuing family violence.

It is important to emphasize that not all deadbeat dads are necessarily unrelated to their children, or that all unrelated fathers or other men in a family setting are abusive. Even biological fathers are known to abandon their children and some unrelated men may be caring and conscientious toward children in their custody. But we expect that the incidence of estranged noncompliant fathers could be significantly reduced by adopting these recommendations.

Therapeutic Implications

Our discussion of strategies and techniques for improving paternal investment shows how evolutionary theory can be used to put poorly understood issues about paternal aggression and family violence into a more informed and coherent perspective. It can also be used to engineer outcomes that can have considerable redeeming psychological and social value. Contrary to popular opinion, a recent study of 258 men in a court-mandated domestic violence treatment facility found that the incidence of both child and spouse abuse had little to do with alcohol consumption, drug abuse, or financial hardship but instead was driven almost exclusively by male sexual jealousy (Burch & Gallup, 2020). Indeed, these findings are now being used by this facility to expand the duration and direction of the therapeutic program by focusing on the issues of male sexual jealousy and paternal assurance and addressing these effects on children in the home as well as the romantic partner.

References

Abramsky, T., Watts, C.H., Garcia-Moreno, C., Devries, K., Kiss, L., Ellsberg, M., Jansen, H.A., & Heise, L. (2011). What factors are associated with recent intimate partner violence? Findings from the WHO multi-country study on women's health and domestic violence. *BMC Public Health, 11*(1), 1.

Alvergne, A., Faurie, C., & Raymond, M. (2007). Differential facial resemblance of young children to their parents: Who do children look like more? *Evolution and Human Behavior, 28*(2), 135–144.

Alvergne, A., Faurie, C., & Raymond, M. (2009). Father–offspring resemblance predicts paternal investment in humans. *Animal Behaviour, 78*(1), 61–69.

Alvergne, A., Faurie, C., & Raymond, M. (2010). Are parents' perceptions of offspring facial resemblance consistent with actual resemblance? Effects on parental investment. *Evolution and Human Behavior, 31*(1), 7–15.

Alvergne, A., Perreau, F., Mazur, A., Mueller, U., & Raymond, M. (2014). Identification of visual paternity cues in humans. *Biology Letters, 10*(4), Article 20140063.

Amato, P. R. (1987). Family processes in one-parent, stepparent, and intact families: The child's point of view. *Journal of Marriage and the Family*, 49(2), 327–337.

Apicella, C. L., & Marlowe, F. W. (2004). Perceived mate fidelity and paternal resemblance predict men's investment in children. *Evolution and Human Behavior, 25*(6), 371–378.

Archer, J. (2013). Can evolutionary principles explain patterns of family violence? *Psychological Bulletin, 139*(2), 403.

Baker, R. R., & Bellis, M. A. (1993). Human sperm competition: Ejaculate adjustment by males and the function of masturbation. *Animal Behaviour, 46*(5), 861–885.

Barash, D. P. (1977). *Sociobiology and behavior*. Elsevier North-Holland.

Bartholet, E. (1999). *Nobody's children: Abuse and neglect, foster drift, and the adoption alternative*. Beacon Press.

Birenbaum-Carmeli, D., & Carmeli, Y. S. (2002). Physiognomy, familism and consumerism: Preferences among Jewish-Israeli recipients of donor insemination. *Social Science & Medicine, 54*(3), 363–376.

Boulette, T., & Andersen, S. (1986) "Mind control" and the battering of women. *Cultic Studies Journal, 3*, 25–35

Burch, R. L., & Gallup, Jr., G. G. (2000). Perceptions of paternal resemblance predict family violence. *Evolution and Human Behavior, 21*(6), 429–435.

Burch, R. L., & Gallup, Jr., G. G. (2004). Pregnancy as a stimulus for domestic violence. *Journal of Family Violence, 19*(4), 243–247.

Burch, R. L., & Gallup Jr., G. G. (2019). The other man: Knowledge of sexual rivals and changes in sexual behavior. *Evolutionary Behavioral Sciences, 13*(4), 376. https://doi.org/10.1037/ebs0000165

Burch, R. L., & Gallup, Jr., G. G. (2020). Abusive men are driven by paternal uncertainty. *Evolutionary Behavioral Sciences, 14*(2), 197–209. https://doi.org/10.1037/ebs0000163

Burch, R. L., Hipp, D., & Platek, S. M. (2006). Paternal investment, phenotypic resemblance, and the social mirror effect. In S. M. Platek & T. Shackelford (Eds.), *Female infidelity and paternal uncertainty evolutionary perspectives on male anti-cuckoldry tactics* (pp. 207–223). Cambridge University Press.

Burr, J. (2009). Fear, fascination and the sperm donor as "abjection" in interviews with heterosexual recipients of donor insemination. *Sociology of Health & Illness, 31*(5), 705–718.

Buss, D. M. (2002). Human mate guarding. *Neuroendocrinology Letters, 23*(Suppl. 4), 23–29.

Campbell, J. C. (1992). Prevention of wife battering: Insights from cultural analysis. *Response to the Victimization of Women and Children, 14*(3), 18–24.

Case, A., Lin, I. F., & McLanahan, S. (2000). How hungry is the selfish gene? *The Economic Journal, 110*(466), 781–804.

CDC.gov. (2017). Assisted reproductive technology (ART) data. Centers for Disease Control and Prevention, National Center for Chronic Disease Prevention and Health Promotion. Division of Reproductive Health. Accessed January 12, 2017, https://www.cdc.gov/art/artdata/index.html

Cooksey, E. C., & Fondell, M. M. (1996). Spending time with his kids: Effects of family structure on fathers' and children's lives. *Journal of Marriage and the Family, 58*(3), 693–707.

Cousineau, T. M., & Domar, A. D. (2007). Psychological impact of infertility. *Best Practice & Research Clinical Obstetrics & Gynaecology, 21*(2), 293–308.

Daly, M., & Wilson, M. I. (1982). Whom are newborn babies said to resemble? *Ethology and Sociobiology, 3*(2), 69–78.

Daly, M., & Wilson, M. I. (1984). A sociobiological analysis of human infanticide. In G. Hausfater & S. B. Hrdy (Eds.), *Infanticide: Comparative and evolutionary perspectives* (pp. 487–502). Routledge.

Daly, M., & Wilson, M. I. (1985). Child abuse and other risks of not living with both parents. *Ethology and Sociobiology, 6*(4), 197–210.

Daly, M., & Wilson, M. I. (1988). Evolutionary social psychology and family homicide. *Science, 242*(4878), 519–524.

Daly, M., & Wilson, M. I. (1996). Violence against stepchildren. *Current Directions in Psychological Science, 5*(3), 77–81.

Daly, M., & Wilson, M. I. (1998). *The truth about Cinderella: A Darwinian view of parental love*. Yale University Press.

Daly, M., & Wilson, M. I. (2008). Is the "Cinderella effect" controversial? A case study of evolution-minded research and critiques thereof. In C. Crawford & D. Krebs (Eds.), *Foundations of evolutionary psychology* (pp. 383–400). Erlbaum.

Daly, M., Wilson, M. I., & Weghorst, S. J. (1982). Male sexual jealousy. *Ethology and Sociobiology, 3*(1), 11–27.

Daniels, C. R., & Golden, J. (2004). Procreative compounds: Popular eugenics, artificial insemination and the rise of the American sperm banking industry. *Journal of Social History, 38*(1), 5–27.

Daniels, K. (2007). Donor gametes: Anonymous or identified? *Best Practice & Research Clinical Obstetrics & Gynaecology, 21*(1), 113–128.

DeBruine, L. M. (2002). Facial resemblance enhances trust. *Proceedings of the Royal Society of London B: Biological Sciences, 269*(1498), 1307–1312.

DeBruine, L. M. (2005). Trustworthy but not lust-worthy: Context-specific effects of facial resemblance. *Proceedings of the Royal Society of London B: Biological Sciences, 272*(1566), 919–922.

Delgado, A., Prieto, G., & Bond, R. (1997). The cultural factor in lay perception of jealousy as a motive for wife battery. *Journal of Applied Social Psychology, 20*, 1824–1841

Dhillon, R., Cumming, C. E., & Cumming, D. C. (2000). Psychological well-being and coping patterns in infertile men. *Fertility and Sterility, 74*(4), 702–706.

Feigelman, W., & Silverman, A. R. (1977). Single parent adoptions. *Social Casework, 58*(7), 418–425.

Fisher, J. R., & Hammarberg, K. (2012). Psychological and social aspects of infertility in men: An overview of the evidence and implications for psychologically informed clinical care and future research. *Asian Journal of Andrology, 14*(1), 121.

Furstenberg Jr, F. F., & Talvitie, K. G. (1980). Children's names and paternal claims: Bonds between unmarried fathers and their children. *Journal of Family Issues, 1*(1), 31–57.

Gallup, G. G., Jr., & Burch, R. L. (2006). The semen displacement Hypothesis: Semen hydraulics, double mating, adaptations to self-semen displacement, and the IPC proclivity model. In S. M. Platek & T. Shackelford (Eds.), *Female infidelity and paternal uncertainty evolutionary perspectives on male anti-cuckoldry tactics* (pp. 129–140). Cambridge University Press.

Gallup, G. G., Jr., Ampel, B. C., Matteo, D. Y., & O'Malley, E. E. (2016). Behavioral resemblance and paternal investment: Which features of the chip off the old block count? *Evolutionary Behavioral Sciences, 10*(1), 1.

Gallup. G. G. Jr., Burch, R. L., & Berens Mitchell, T. J. (2006). Semen displacement as a sperm competition strategy: Multiple mating, self-semen displacement, and timing of in-pair copulations. *Human Nature, 17*, 253–264. https://doi.org/10.1007/s12110-006-1008-9

Gallup, G. G., Jr., Burch, R. L. & Petricone, L. (2012). Sexual conflict, infidelity, and vaginal/semen chemistry. In T. Shackelford & A. Goetz (Eds.). *The Oxford handbook of sexual conflict in humans* (pp. 217–232). Oxford University Press.

Gallup, G. G., Jr., Burch, R. L., Zappieri, M., Parvez, R., & Stockwell, M. (2003). The human penis as a semen displacement device. *Evolution and Human Behavior, 24*, 277–289.

Geary, D. C. (2016). Evolution of paternal investment. In A. Figueredo, J. Sefcek, & G. Vasquez (Eds.), *The handbook of evolutionary psychology* (pp. 524–541). John Wiley & Sons.

Gibson, K. (2009). Differential parental investment in families with both adopted and genetic children. *Evolution and Human Behavior, 30*, 184–189.

Haselton, M. G., & Gangestad, S. W. (2006). Conditional expression of women's desires and men's mate guarding across the ovulatory cycle. *Hormones and Behavior, 49*(4), 509–518.

Huss, M. T., & Langhinrichsen-Rohling, J. (2006). Assessing the generalization of psychopathy in a clinical sample of domestic violence perpetrators. *Law and Human Behavior, 30*(5), 571–586.

Jewkes, R., Levin, J., & Penn-Kekana, L. (2002). Risk factors for domestic violence: Findings from a South African cross-sectional study. *Social Science and Medicine, 55*(9), 1603–1617.

Johnson, J. L., McAndrew, F. T., & Harris, P. B. (1991). Sociobiology and the naming of adopted and natural children. *Ethology and Sociobiology, 12*(5), 365–375.

Jones, J. (2008). Adoption experiences of women and men and demand for children to adopt by women 18-44 years of age in the United States, 2002. *Vital and Health Statistics. Series 23, Data from the National Survey of Family Growth, 23*, 1–36.

Jones, J. (2009). *Who adopts? Characteristics of women and men who have adopted children.* NCHS data brief no. 12. Centers for Disease Control and Prevention. https://stacks.cdc.gov/view/cdc/5324

Kirk, H. D. (1984). *Shared fate: A theory and method of adoptive relationships* (rev. ed.). Ben-Simon Publications.

Klock, S. C., & Maier, D. (1991). Psychological factors related to donor insemination. *Fertility and Sterility, 56*(3), 489–495.

Marlowe, F. (2000). Paternal investment and the human mating system. *Behavioural Processes, 51*(1–3), 45–61.

McLanahan, S., & Sandefur, G. (1994). *Growing up with a single parent. What hurts, what helps.* Harvard University Press.

Miller, L. C., Chan, W., Reece, R. A., Tirella, L., & Pertman, A. (2007). Child abuse fatalities among internationally adopted children. *Child Maltreatment, 12*, 378–379.

Murphy, C., Meyer, S., & O'Leary, K. (1994). Dependency characteristics of partner assaultive men. *Journal of Abnormal Psychology, 103*, 729–735

Peters, J., Shackelford, T. K., & Buss, D. M. (2002). Understanding domestic violence against women: Using evolutionary psychology to extend the feminist functional analysis. *Violence and Victims, 17*(2), 255–264.

Platek, S. M., Burch, R. L., Panyavin, I., Wasserman, B., & Gallup, Jr., G. G. (2002). Children's faces: Resemblance affects males but not females. *Evolution and Human Behavior 23*, 159–166.

Platek, S. M., Critton, S. R., Burch, R. L., Frederick, D. A., Myers, T. S. & Gallup, Jr., G. G. (2003). How much resemblance is enough? Sex differences in hypothetical investment decisions but not in the detection of resemblance. *Evolution and Human Behavior, 23*, 81–87.

Platek, S. M., & Kemp, S. M. (2009). Is family special to the brain? An event-related fMRI study of familiar, familial, and self-face recognition. *Neuropsychologia, 47*(3), 849–858.

Platek, S. M., Raines, D. M., Gallup, Jr., G. G., Mohamed, F. B., Thomson, J. W., Myers, T. E., Panyavin, I. S., Levin, S. L., Davis, J. A., Fonteyn, L. C., & Arigo, D. R. (2004). Reactions to children's faces: Males are more affected by resemblance than females are, and so are their brains. *Evolution and Human Behavior, 25*(6), 394–405.

Regalski, J. M., & Gaulin, S. J. (1993). Whom are Mexican infants said to resemble? Monitoring and fostering paternal confidence in the Yucatan. *Ethology and Sociobiology, 14*(2), 97–113.

Riggs, D. S., Caulfield, M. B., & Street, A. E. (2000). Risk for domestic violence: Factors associated with perpetration and victimization. *Journal of Clinical Psychology, 56*(10), 1289–1316.

Russell, D. E. (1984). The prevalence and seriousness of incestuous abuse: Stepfathers vs. biological fathers. *Child Abuse & Neglect*, *8*(1), 15–22.

Shackelford, T. K. (2003). Preventing, correcting, and anticipating female infidelity. *Evolution and Cognition, 9*, 1–7.

Shackelford, T. K., Weekes-Shackelford, V. A., Schmitt, D. P., & Salmon, C. (2012). Deadbeat dads: Evolutionary perspectives on providing child support. In T. Shackelford & A. Goetz (Eds.), *The Oxford handbook of sexual behavior in humans* (pp. 302–314). Oxford University Press.

Taylor, B. (2005). Whose baby is it? The impact of reproductive technologies on kinship. *Human Fertility, 8*(3), 189–195.

Thompson, C. (2005). *Making parents: The ontological choreography of reproductive technologies.* MIT Press.

Tooley, G. A., Karakis, M., Stokes, M., & Ozanne-Smith, J. (2006). Generalizing the Cinderella effect to unintentional childhood fatalities. *Evolution and Human Behavior, 27*, 224–230.

van IJzendoorn, M. H., Euser, E. M., Prinzie, P., Juffer, F., & Bakermans-Kranenburg, M. J. (2009). Elevated risk of child maltreatment in families with stepparents but not with adoptive parents. *Child Maltreatment, 14*, 369–375.

Volk, A., & Quinsey, V. L. (2002). The influence of infant facial cues on adoption preferences. *Human Nature, 13*(4), 437–455.

Werum, R., Davis, T., Cheng, S., & Browne, I. (2018). Adoption context, parental investment, and children's educational outcomes. *Journal of Family Issues, 39*(3), 720–746.

Wiederman, M., & Allgeier, E. (1993). Gender differences in sexual jealousy: Adaptionist or social learning explanation? *Ethology and Sociobiology,* 14, 115–140.

Wilson, M. I., & Daly, M. (1993). An evolutionary psychological perspective on male sexual proprietariness and violence against wives. *Violence and Victims, 8*(3), 271.

Wilson, M. I., & Daly, M. (1996). Male sexual proprietariness and violence against wives. *Current Directions in Psychological Science, 5*, 2–7.

Wilson, M. I., & Daly, M. (1998). Lethal and nonlethal violence against wives and the evolutionary psychology of male sexual proprietariness. *Sage Series on Violence Against Women, 9*, 199–230.

Wu, C. L. (2011). Managing multiple masculinities in donor insemination: Doctors configuring infertile men and sperm donors in Taiwan. *Sociology of Health & Illness, 33*(1), 96–113.

Wu, H., Yang, S., Sun, S., Liu, C., & Luo, Y. J. (2013). The male advantage in child facial resemblance detection: Behavioral and ERP evidence. *Social Neuroscience, 8*(6), 555–567.

Yu, Q., Zhang, J., Zhang, L., Zhang, Q., Guo, Y., Jin, S., & Chen, J. (2019). Who gains more? The relationship between parenthood and well-being. *Evolutionary Psychology, 17*(3), Article 1474704919860467.

Zvoch, K. (1999). Family type and investment in education: A comparison of genetic and stepparent families. *Evolution and Human Behavior, 20*(6), 453–464.

CHAPTER

16 Parenting and Relationship Maintenance

Elizabeth M. Westrupp, Emma M. Marshall, Clair Bennett, Michelle Benstead, Gabriella King, *and* Gery C. Karantzas

Abstract

The transition to parenthood represents one of the greatest potential stressors that the romantic couple relationship will experience. This chapter examines the role of individual vulnerability factors, environmental stressors, individual psychological responses, and couple relationship functioning in negatively impacting the maintenance and quality of the couple bond within the context of parenthood. We propose and then structure a summary of the current research evidence around a conceptual model of relationship maintenance that integrates an evolutionary psychology perspective—namely, attachment theory—to complement other relationship science and developmental perspectives. We show that individual differences in adult attachment are associated with relationship functioning (i.e., levels of support and conflict between partners), which, in turn, predict relationship outcomes related to the maintenance of romantic relationships (i.e., couple relationship quality and dissolution), and that the environmental stressors in and around parenthood can exacerbate these associations. Specifically, we highlight research showing that attachment insecurity (i.e., higher levels of attachment anxiety and avoidance) is associated with poorer relationship functioning and outcomes.

Key Words: parent, parenthood, attachment, relationships, diathesis-stress, couple conflict, partner support, life history theory

The Transition to Parenthood

The transition to parenthood marks considerable changes that have implications for the couple relationship. Couples must negotiate abrupt changes in their roles, responsibilities, and identities while having fewer opportunities to engage in their typical individual and couple recreation activities that serve a protective function. Each parent must also negotiate a range of stressors associated with parenthood, such as reductions or interruptions in their sleep, role and identity changes, and increased stress related to juggling work and family responsibilities. Overall, this transition places strain on the relationship and can be associated with a notable decline in couple relationship quality. Relationship quality has been found to have a significant impact on adult mental and physical health, with meta-analytic findings showing that low relationship quality can even predict earlier mortality (Robles et al., 2014). Moreover, the quality of the couple's relationship exerts a strong developmental influence on their child/children, conferring potential risk when there is couple conflict or a relationship breakdown, such as internalizing and externalizing problems and peer problems (Acock & Demo, 1999; Buehler et al., 1997; Westrupp et al., 2018).

We begin the chapter with a detailed outline of a conceptual model of couple relationship maintenance during parenthood, followed by a summary of empirical evidence characterizing the context and type of stressors associated with parenthood and their impacts on parents and the couple relationship. We then provide a detailed description of attachment theory, including the functioning of the attachment behavioral system and individual differences in adult attachment, and how it relates to another central evolutionary theory, life history theory. The chapter then discusses research on relationship functioning, focusing on two of the most important and widely studied processes, partner support and conflict processes, and how each mediates the association between attachment orientations and relationship outcomes. As a proof of concept for the proposed model, we examine it using baseline data from a large study of Australian parents during the COVID-19 pandemic. To conclude, we explore the implications and future directions for research investigating romantic relationships during parenthood from an evolutionary perspective.

Conceptual Model of Relationship Functioning During Parenthood

The conceptual model of relationship functioning that we propose is rooted in evolutionary theory—namely, attachment theory—a widely studied theory of human bonding that has been applied to relationship dynamics in adulthood. This conceptual model is presented in figure 16.1 and assumes that individual differences in people's

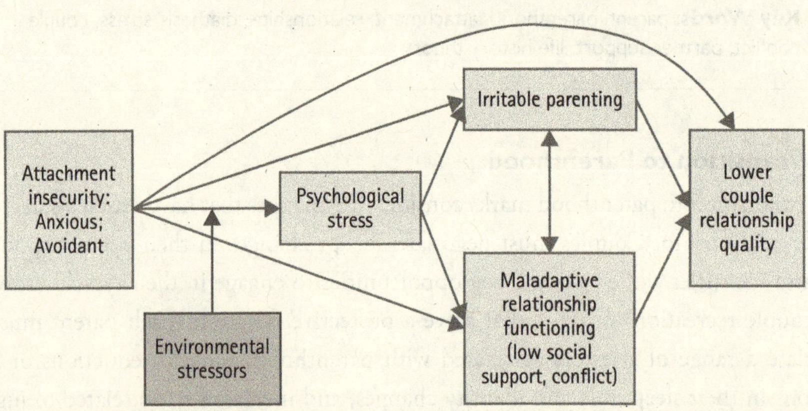

Figure 16.1 Conceptual diagram showing hypothesized associations between attachment insecurity, parent stress, irritable parenting, maladaptive relationship functioning, and couple relationship quality, with hypothesized moderation effects via environmental stressors.

cognition, affect, and behavior in close relationships (termed "attachment styles") differentially predict relationship outcomes (e.g., relationship quality) in romantic couples. Attachment styles are conceptualized as being the degree to which individuals vary along two semi-independent dimensions—attachment anxiety and attachment avoidance (Brennan et al., 1998; Gillath et al., 2016; Mikulincer & Shaver, 2016). Individuals characterized by attachment insecurity (i.e., high attachment avoidance or anxiety) are more likely to report poor relationship outcomes. For example, adults with high levels of attachment anxiety (characterized by a strong need for love and approval and a preoccupation with relationship partners) and/or attachment avoidance (characterized by a discomfort with closeness, a chronic distrust of others, and excessive self-reliance) (e.g., Brennan et al., 1998; KarantzasKarantza et al., 2010) typically experience relationship dissatisfaction and report low relationship intimacy and commitment (Brennan et al., 1998; Brennan & Shaver, 1995; Feeney & Noller, 1990; Karantzas et al., 2014).

In line with evolutionary theory, individual differences in attachment orientation are thought to arise from environmental adaption and ensure both personal and offspring survival (Szepsenwol & Simpson, 2019). However, in the conditions of modern society, attachment insecurity has consistently been found to be a vulnerability factor, associated with a wide range of interpersonal difficulties, including poorer relationship quality and relationship dissolution (Gillath et al., 2016; Mikulincer & Shaver, 2016). According to the diathesis-stress based model of attachment (Simpson & Rholes, 2012) and broad-based models of relationship functioning (see, e.g., Vulnerability Stress Adaptation Model; Karney & Bradbury, 1995), attachment insecurity is associated with a profile of cognitive, behavioral, and emotional strategies that are *triggered* in the face of stressful events (i.e., "stressors"), and that maintain or even exacerbate personal and relationship stress. Figure 16.1 outlines a conceptual schema showing how these processes may operate within the context of parenting. We hypothesize that environmental stressors exacerbate the influence of attachment insecurity on core relationship functioning, including how romantic couples handle conflict and the extent to which romantic partners provide support to one another to meet each other's socioemotional and physical needs, thus affecting the quality of the relationship. We review each of the proposed elements of the model in the following sections.

Parenting: A Chronic Stressor

Parents face numerous stressors at every stage of their parenting journey, including in the initial transition, and at each new transition across child and family developmental stages. Work-family conflict, socio-economic hardship, and parent sleep deprivation also have potential to place considerable strain on parents at any stage of the parenting life-cycle.

The Transition to Parenthood

There are few normative life events that are as significant as the transition to parenthood (Doss & Rhoades, 2017; Doss et al., 2009; Simpson & Rholes, 2019). Although, for many parents, the transition brings a host of new positive experiences and associated emotions, it is also invariably experienced as a significant and chronic stressor (Cowan & Cowan, 2000; Doss & Rhoades, 2017; Simpson & Rholes, 2019). When a couple become new parents, they are faced with significant role changes as they learn and negotiate new child care skills and responsibilities, while completely renegotiating the parameters of their couple relationship (Simpson & Rholes, 2019; Twenge et al., 2003). For many parents, these changes occur in the context of severe and often unprecedented sleep deprivation, physical changes (e.g., for women recovering from birth and/or engaging in breastfeeding), and threat to, or reduction of, individual and couple protective factors, such as constraints around their ability to engage in previously enjoyed social and recreation activities, physical activity, and independent time. Simultaneously, new parents may experience increases in household work, financial stress, and conflict in managing work and family roles and responsibilities (Cowan & Cowan, 2000; Simpson & Rholes, 2019).

In light of the life-altering and stressful nature of this transition to parenthood, it is perhaps not surprising that this period and its associated stressors can take a toll on individual well-being (Woolhouse et al., 2015), and the couple relationship (Doss & Rhoades, 2017; Mitnick et al., 2009). Indeed, while relationship satisfaction may be unaffected or even enhanced for some couples (Holmes et al., 2013), the majority of studies suggest that couples experience declines in their relationship quality during the transition to parenthood (Doss & Rhoades, 2017; Doss et al., 2009; Mitnick et al., 2009). A meta-analysis of 97 articles ($N = 47{,}692$) investigating couple satisfaction between parents and childless couples found that couples with children on average reported lower couple satisfaction compared to their childless counterparts (Twenge et al., 2003). To illustrate, findings from a longitudinal study following 218 couples every year for a total of eight years after the birth of their first child revealed that many mothers and fathers experience an abrupt decline in relationship functioning that persists over time, including reductions on measures of relationship satisfaction and confidence, poorer conflict management, and more negative communication patterns (Doss et al., 2009).

Ongoing Transitions Across Parenthood

For couples who stay together, there is evidence that the couple relationship may eventually recover, on average returning to reach equivalence of nonparents approximately 10 years postbirth of first child (Keizer & Schenk, 2012). However, the precise path and associated timelines are likely to vary considerably for different couples, whether it be a path of further decline and separation (Houts et al., 2008) or one of recovery (Keizer & Schenk, 2012). One certainty of parenthood is that the joys and challenges are never static, the nature of supporting a developing child means that the context and demands of parenting constantly change over time. For example, the context of parenting shifts with additional changes to the family structure, and research shows similar patterns of decline in couple outcomes following the birth of a second child (Figueiredo & Conde, 2015; Volling et al., 2015). As a child (or children) moves through key developmental stages (i.e., infancy, toddlerhood, preschool, school-age, and adolescence), parents must adapt their parenting strategies and adjust to multiple transitions as the children move through various child care, education, and healthcare systems; in addition, they must balance their own work life around the changing needs of their family.

Although a large literature documents the challenges faced by parents at the transition to parenthood, to date, research into the effects of ongoing transitions has been much more limited and requires further investigation. There is some evidence showing that parents' own mental health and well-being, and their management of stress in relation to juggling work and family roles, deteriorate in relation to various transitions in the family life cycle over time (Westrupp et al., 2016; Woolhouse et al., 2015). To further demonstrate how the transition to parenthood is a chronic stressor that impacts on an individual's well-being and the couples' romantic relationship, we expand on two common parenting experiences, work–family conflict and parent sleep deprivation/difficulties.

Work–Family Conflict

Work–family conflict refers to the difficulties that parents experience when combining work and family roles and responsibilities (Bianchi & Milkie, 2010). The entry to parenthood often marks a transition for a couple, where they may adopt more traditional gender roles, even in couples that had previously held egalitarian roles in their relationship (Twenge et al., 2003). The quantity and quality of child care and household responsibilities tends to be different for mothers versus fathers in many countries around the world (Lin & Burgard, 2018; Ruppanner et al., 2019). Women are more likely to give up or reduce paid employment in order to care for the infant, but even on return to part-time or full-time work when children are older, women are more likely to retain the greater portion of household duties (Lin & Burgard, 2018; Ruppanner et al., 2019). These changes in caregiving and unpaid work roles have a disproportionate effect on mothers. Meta-analytic findings demonstrate that mothers with children ages between 1 and 3 years are more likely to experience feelings of work–family guilt when balancing the competing roles than fathers, particularly in context of high work hours (Borelli et al., 2017). Findings from another meta-analysis show that women from more socioeconomic advantaged backgrounds, and who give up professional careers to care for their infants, report higher couple dissatisfaction compared to other women (Twenge et al., 2003).

The *crossover theory* suggests that a parent's experience of work–family conflict, and the associated experience of personal stress and distress, can cross over to affect close individuals such as partners or children within a family setting (Westman, 2002). For example, the increased level of distress and frustration accompanied by work–family conflict is associated with poorer relationship processes and outcomes, including increased negative interactions between partners (Westman, 2005), increases in negative affect, negative evaluations, and criticism directed toward a partner (Bakker et al., 2008; Dinh et al., 2017), and more irritable and less warm parenting practices (Cooklin, Westrupp, et al., 2015; Dinh et al., 2017). Much of the parent-focused research on work–family conflict is focused on the experience of mothers, with considerable evidence showing negative impacts for their mental health, parenting, and couple relationship outcomes (Chee et al., 2009; Cooklin, Westrupp, et al., 2015; Vahedi et al., 2019). However, there is also emerging evidence suggesting negative impacts for fathers' parenting practices and experiences in the couple relationship (Cooklin, Westrupp, et al., 2015; Dinh et al., 2017; Vahedi et al., 2019). Studies examining experiences of mothers and fathers in the same family also show similar themes between genders, where both parents' experiences of work–family conflict influence their own and their partners' perceived couple conflict and parenting irritability (Dinh et al., 2017; Vahedi et al., 2019).

Families must consider complex factors when balancing competing responsibilities associated with work and family roles. The task of juggling work and family responsibilities is a challenging task for many families, but there is considerable variation in the flexibility and options families have to draw on, and the type and range of potential supports and resources at their disposal, when making decisions about how they allocate their time between work and family responsibilities. Families particularly at risk are those facing financial and socioeconomic hardship.

Socioeconomic Hardship

Factors related to a person's social and economic context are strongly associated with every conceivable human outcome. Socioeconomic factors are so powerful, we now understand that they exert influences with impacts felt over multiple generations (McKnight & Nolan, 2012). Later in the chapter, we summarize the way in which evolutionary theory frames socioeconomic deprivation as determining human development and attachment outcomes; but first, in this section, we examine how socioeconomic hardship can be conceptualized as an environmental stressor; impacting parents' individual functioning, experience of stress, couple relationship functioning, and the quality of the couple relationship over the course of parenthood (Kinnunen & Feldt, 2004).

Socioeconomic disadvantage relates to differences in education, income, employment, wealth, government benefits, type and quality of housing, food supply, and neighborhood level disadvantage (Conger et al., 2010; Ensminger et al., 2003). Socioeconomic factors are often considered to be relatively stable, but they can change in response to stressful life events and major life transitions, including the transition to parenthood (Feldman et al., 2004), which often is associated with a reduction in maternal employment in order to prioritize caregiving and/or the increased household costs related to external child care fees. Thus, in context of the myriad other potential stressors associated with the transition to parenthood, parents may also experience increased economic hardship. Socioeconomic adversity, such as low income or unstable employment, influences the couple relationship by increasing adults' experience of psychological stress and other negative outcomes (Conger et al., 2010; Power et al., 2002; Whelan, 1994). Couples in socially disadvantaged circumstances are more likely to report relationship strain, conflict, less satisfied relationships, and more negative communication patterns within the relationship (Cutrona et al., 2003; Karney et al., 2005; Westrupp et al., 2015; Williamson et al., 2013).

Parent Sleep Deprivation and Sleep Quality

Parents' sleep quality and couple relationship processes and outcomes are closely interrelated during the transition to and throughout parenthood. Sleep can be conceptualized as an indicator of individual health, well-being, and quality of life, and both acute and chronic sleep problems have been consistently shown in meta-analyses to have negative impacts on functioning for children and adults (Bartel et al., 2015; Ju & Choi, 2013; Wu et al., 2014; Zhang & Wing, 2006). As described earlier in the chapter, the unique demands associated with caring for a child often threaten parents' ability to fulfill their sleep requirements (Montgomery-Downs et al., 2013; Stremler et al., 2013). This is well-documented for parents of infants (Montgomery-Downs et al., 2013), but there is evidence that sleep can continue to be threatened for parents of older children too (Keilty et al., 2015).

Evidence from meta-analyses and systematic reviews show reliable associations between parent sleep deprivation and increased risk for depression, anxiety, and mental health problems in the postpartum period and thereafter, both for mothers and fathers (Bei et al., 2015; Christian et al., 2019; Lawson et al., 2015; Montgomery-Downs et al., 2013). Sleep has also been shown to have a profound influence on the couple relationship (Hislop, 2007; Kiecolt-Glaser & Wilson, 2017; Richter et al., 2016; Troxel, 2010; Troxel et al., 2007). However, associations between sleep and the quality of the couple relationship are likely to be complex and multidirectional, involving numerous intermediatory relationship processes pertaining to relationship dysfunction such as destructive conflict processes (Kiecolt-Glaser & Wilson, 2017) and support processes (Cutrona & Russell, 2017).

We know from a large body of theoretical and empirical evidence that there is strong individual variation in adults' ability to cope with environmental stressors and their subsequent psychological stress. We also know that this individual variation is highly predictive of the downstream impact that the stressors have on couple maintenance processes, parenting, and subsequent couple relationship quality. The next section provides a detailed introduction to attachment theory and the specific individual-level vulnerability associated with insecure attachment styles.

Attachment Theory and Romantic Relationships in the Context of Parenting Attachment Theory

Attachment theory is a theory of human bonding based in biology and evolution (Bowlby, 1969, 1982; Simpson & Belsky, 2008; Simpson & Karantzas, 2019). The theory describes the tendency for humans to seek proximity to "stronger and wiser others" (termed "attachment figures") in times of stress to help achieve a state of physical and psychological safety known as *felt security*. This tendency is regulated by an innate psychobiological system—the attachment behavioral system (Bowlby, 1969, 1982; Gillath et al., 2016; Mikulincer & Shaver, 2016; Simpson & Rholes, 2012). Thus, the attachment system provides a survival advantage to altricial human offspring (Simpson & Belsky, 2008; Szepsenwol & Simpson, 2019). However, the evolutionary function of the attachment behavioral system extends beyond infancy and has important implications for evolutionary fitness during adulthood. These implications include mating strategies (Kirkpatrick, 1998; Simpson & Belsky, 2008; Szepsenwol & Simpson, 2019) but also the many and varied cognitive, affective, and behavioral outcomes associated with the maintenance of romantic relationships (e.g., Gillath et al., 2016), especially during stressful contexts such as parenthood. Although primary attachment figures are typically seen to be caregivers (e.g., parents) early in life, this switches to romantic partners during adulthood.

Attachment System Activation

According to the model of attachment system activation by Mikulincer and Shaver (2003, 2016), *normative* functioning involves activation of the attachment behavioral system in response to environmental signals of stress or threat. Once activated, individuals will engage in proximity-seeking behaviors to move within close vicinity of their attachment figure, or they will engage in attention-seeking behaviors to alert their attachment figure of their distress and thus render support. An attachment figure who is responsive and sensitive reduces the individual's feelings of distress, and thus the deactivation of the attachment system. Once the system is deactivated, an individual can engage in *exploration*, pursuing any number of goal-directed behaviors, challenges, life tasks, and activities. The provision of support by the attachment figure is internalized as an *internal working model* (Gillath et al., 2016; Mikulincer & Shaver, 2016)—that is, mental representations or schema that reflect the extent to which an individual views themself as worthy of love, care, and comfort (*model of self*), as well as trust that significant others can be reliably called upon to render support that responsively and sensitively meets their needs (*model of other*) (Gillath et al., 2016; Mikulincer & Shaver, 2016; Simpson & Rholes, 2012, 2017). Attachment security is characterized by a comfort with emotional closeness, confidence in depending on others, and willingness to provide support to others in need (Gillath et al., 2016; Karantzas et al., 2010; Mikulincer & Shaver, 2016).

Deviations from the normative function of the attachment system develop across childhood and adulthood when the quality of care and support received by an individual lacks sensitivity and responsiveness (Simpson & Karantzas, 2019). Individuals who experience consistent rejection and neglect by attachment figures develop deactivating behavioral strategies, entailing both physical and psychological escape-avoidance behaviors to either short-circuit or suppress distress. Moreover, these individuals internalize these negative experiences with attachment figures in the form of a fragile view of the self and negative views of others (Mikulincer & Shaver, 2016; Simpson & Karantzas, 2019). These deactivating behavioral strategies, together with negative internal working models, result in attachment avoidance. Attachment avoidance is characterized by a discomfort with closeness, a chronic distrust of others, and excessive self-reliance (Brennan et al., 1998; Gillath et al., 2016; Karantzas et al., 2010). Individuals who experience inept or inconsistent care from attachment figures develop hyperactivating behavioral strategies, reflecting an intensification of distress in context of persistent attempts to gain the attention and approval of an attachment figure (Mikulincer & Shaver, 2016). These individuals internalize interactions with attachment figures in the form of negative views of the self and ambivalent views of others (Arriaga & Kumashiro, 2019; Gillath et al., 2016; Simpson & Karantzas, 2019). Hyperactivating attachment behavioral strategies, coupled with these working models, result in attachment anxiety. Attachment anxiety is characterized by a strong need for love and approval and a preoccupation with relationship partners (Brennan et al., 1998; Karantzas et al., 2014).

From an evolutionary standpoint, the attachment behavioral system reflects an organized set of physiological and psychological mechanisms that encode and process early life experiences with attachment figures to produce phenotypes (i.e., attachment styles) that are more likely to increase fitness in particular environments (Simpson & Belsky, 2008; Szepsenwol & Simpson, 2019). In this respect, attachment styles reflect the adaptive calibration of life history strategies (Szepsenwol & Simpson, 2019). In the section that follows, we describe the associations between attachment styles and life history strategies but do so after providing a brief overview of life history theory (refer to Szepsenwol & Simpson, 2019, for a more detailed review).

Attachment Styles in Context of Life History Theory

Life history theory draws on evolutionary perspectives to explain individual differences in life trajectories across the life span, thought to be dependent on individuals' early environmental conditions (Del Giudice et al., 2016; Fletcher, 2002; Szepsenwol & Simpson, 2019). This theory suggests that individuals who are exposed to high levels of environmental deprivation and unpredictability show an accelerated mating strategy to ensure the survival of offspring, moving through key developmental milestones related to sexual maturation (e.g., first sexual experiences and dating) and reproduction at a quicker pace compared to their peers, prior to an earlier death. With the threat of earlier mortality, and to ensure reproduction success, it is not in their best interest to invest in longer-term resources. In contrast, individuals exposed to a safe and predictable childhood environment are not exposed to the threat of an earlier mortality and can therefore find the time to invest in resources that ensure survival of their (fewer) offspring and are more likely to adopt a "slower" life history strategy involving delayed sexual, romantic, and reproductive milestones, with capacity for much greater investment in each stage and in parenting offspring (Szepsenwol & Simpson, 2019).

Measures of environmental harshness tend to rely on socioeconomic indicators to measure deprivation in terms of individuals' access to all the factors and resources that support healthy growth and development. Recent theoretical and empirical work has advanced understanding of the association between life history strategies and attachment styles and the implications for romantic relationships. Although secure attachment is typically viewed as the most optimal and adaptive style within the developmental literature, an evolutionary perspective suggests that attachment security has an adaptive advantage in safe and predictable environments but not in harsh and unpredictable environments (Simpson & Belsky, 2008; Szepsenwol & Simpson, 2019). Hazan and Zeifman (1999) suggested that the primary evolutionary function of secure attachment in adult relationships is to increase the likelihood of stable and enduring pair-bonds. Enduring pair-bonds are inferred to enhance the reproductive fitness of both parents and their offspring. Thus, attachment security is thought to align with a slow life history strategy and long-term mating strategies that emphasize quality rather than quantity of investment in offspring when environment dangers and threats are low and predictability of future events is high (Geary, 2015; Hazan & Zeifman, 1999). Further, couples with stronger pair-bonds are thought to contribute to reproductive success by providing partners with greater support, in turn associated with better physical and mental health outcomes and more regular ovulation patterns (Zeifman & Hazan, 1997). Indeed, attachment security is consistently found to be associated with more committed and long-term romantic relationships (Mikulincer & Shaver, 2016; Szepsenwol & Simpson, 2019).

However, insecure attachment may have adaptive advantage over secure attachment in more harsh and unpredictable environments (Szepsenwol & Simpson, 2019). Attachment avoidance is assumed to reflect a relationship commitment minimization strategy (Del Giudice, 2019; Karantzas et al., 2019), in which parental investment is traded off against reproductive investment, thereby increasing the number of progeny (Szepsenwol & Simpson, 2019). Thus, attachment avoidance aligns with a fast life strategy and short-term mating strategies. In line with these assumptions, research has found attachment avoidance to be associated with low levels of relationship commitment, less parental investment in their own children, and less partner support provisioning, especially during parenthood (Szepsenwol et al., 2015). In contrast, attachment anxiety is assumed to reflect a relationship commitment maximization strategy (Del Giudice, 2019; Karantzas et al., 2019). Specifically, anxious people have a strong desire for long-term relationships; however, their need for approval and preoccupation with relationship partners is thought to result in relationships that are unstable and short-lived and deemed dissatisfying (Kirkpatrick,

1998). Thus, the relationships of anxiously attached individuals tend to be highly conflictual, and within the context of parenthood, anxiously attached parents are more likely to express frustration at their romantic partner due to perceptions of a lack of support (Kohn et al., 2012; Rholes et al., 2001).

Although attachment insecurity develops as a function of the environment to ensure survival, there are known trade-offs where particular styles are likely to be adaptive in some situations but maladaptive in others (Mikulincer & Shaver, 2016). For example, for a person with an avoidant attachment style, it is costly and maladaptive to invest precious resources in soliciting support when the relationship history suggests it is unlikely or impossible to achieve this function. Instead, it is adaptive to conserve or redirect resources for something more achievable, such as relying on the self. In context of low-level stress, individuals with avoidant attachment may experience lower levels of psychological distress as a result of a deactivation strategy to minimize distress. However, the trade-off is that this strategy will not have positive outcomes in all contexts. In context of high stress levels, they are not able to seek the support and resources needed to cope adaptively, resulting in higher levels of psychological stress and more maladaptive relationship outcomes (Mikulincer & Shaver, 2016).

Couple Relationship Functioning in Parenthood

Attachment insecurity can be conceptualized as a vulnerability that is triggered by parenting stressors, which activate internal working models and maladaptive coping strategies that spill into the couple relationship, resulting in poorer relationship maintenance and thus quality (Bowlby, 1979; Simpson & Rholes, 2012). Within this framework, parenthood—and the transition to parenthood in particular—is conceptualized as a chronic stressor (Simpson & Rholes, 2012). Chronic parenting stress is thought to lead to chronic activation of the attachment system (i.e., the respective internal working models and associated coping strategies), which in turn, influences adult psychological distress, relationship maintenance processes (e.g., partner interactions), parenting practices, and relationship quality (Simpson & Rholes, 2012). More specifically, the activation of insecure working models and associated coping strategies have a cascading effect resulting in greater psychological distress, which dovetails into poorer relationship processes and outcomes.

A number of studies have provided support for this theory. Specifically, adults with insecure attachment styles tend to report higher rates of stress in early parenthood compared to securely attached adults (Mazzeschi et al., 2015; Nygren et al., 2012; Vasquez et al., 2002). Parenthood is also associated with an increase in dysfunctional partner dynamics in insecurely attached couples, including couple conflict, destructive couple conflict patterns, and partner aggression (Eller et al., 2019; Gou & Woodin, 2017; Rholes et al., 2014; Rholes et al., 2001). Women high in attachment anxiety anticipate less support from their partners, and are more likely to report declines in relationship satisfaction in context of low perceived partner support (Kohn et al., 2012; Rholes et al., 2001). Furthermore, partners of highly anxious women report reductions in relationship satisfaction, and declines in perceptions of partner support (Kohn et al., 2012; Rholes et al., 2001). Avoidant individuals who perceive higher work–family conflict or higher child care and family demands report lower relationship satisfaction (Fillo et al., 2015; Kohn et al., 2012). High attachment avoidance in one partner has also been shown to lead to lower relationship commitment in both partners across the transition to parenthood (Ferriby et al., 2016).

Partner Support and Parenting

Prior to becoming parents, an adult couple function as a dyad within which each partner seeks to meet the other partner's needs and fulfill their own. In fact, romantic relationships are thought to involve the interplay and coordination of three complementary systems of behavior; the attachment (reviewed above), caregiving, and sexual behavioral systems (Bowlby, 1982). We now expand on the caregiving system and its function during parenthood, given that it is crucial within romantic relationships in times of stress.

As described above, normative functioning in the *attachment system* is characterized by romantic partners turning to one another for love, comfort, and security in times of threat and challenge (Doherty & Feeney, 2004; Gillath et al., 2019). In contrast, normative functioning of the *caregiving system* within a couple ensures that a partner meets another's physical needs through provision of protection, nurturance, and other support that is sensitive and responsive. While the attachment system drives an individual to *seek* care and support from an attachment figure when in need, the caregiving system drives them to *render* care and support when they perceive another to need care. Furthermore, securely attached adults are able to regulate their emotions when providing support to their partners, thereby ensuring that their own distress does not compromise the quality of care provided to their partner (Mikulincer & Shaver, 2016).

In regard to attachment avoidance, the lack of support-seeking from individuals high on attachment avoidance often fails to activate the caregiving system, so partners are unable to deliver the support needed. Moreover, when individuals with high attachment avoidance have an activated caregiving system, the support is often controlling or distant, withdrawn, or lacks warmth due to their tendency to suppress distress (Feeney & Collins, 2003; Kunce & Shaver, 1994). On the other hand, individuals higher on attachment anxiety have a caregiving system that is activated but functions ineffectively because they have difficulties in regulating their emotions, interfering with their ability to manage stressful situations (Mikulincer & Shaver, 2016). Attachment anxiety has shown to be associated with more compulsive or intrusive patterns of support provision, where the support provider maintains close proximity to their partner and renders care in a manner that is overbearing (Kunce & Shaver, 1994).

Prior to parenthood, couples act in caregiving roles reciprocally for one another. Thus, partners may elicit care when they feel in need through the activation of their own attachment system, but they may also provide care to their partner when they perceive that their partner is in need through the activation of their caregiving system. However, when adults become parents, they become attachment figures and caregivers to their children (Gillath et al., 2016; Mikulincer & Shaver, 2016). Thus, the transition to parenthood involves a significant shift in dynamics between parents. It is common for couples to prioritize the care and support of their children over and above the care needs of their partner. In this way, a new parent may have difficulty eliciting support from their partner when in need via their attachment system, and may also be less likely to notice the care needs of their partner via the caregiving system.

In addition to attachment behaviors, new parents must also work together to provide responsive, sensitive care to their child. In the face of parenting stressors, a parent's functioning as both a partner and a parent may be impaired, and they may experience difficulties in balancing their family responsibilities, potentially increasing their parenting irritability and couple conflict and reducing their ability to provide their partner with support (Dinh et al., 2017; Strazdins et al., 2006; Strazdins et al., 2013; Vahedi et al., 2019). There has been a dearth of empirical evidence elucidating the precise role that parenting plays in couple relationship maintenance during parenthood. However, it's likely that psychological stress experienced by one parent crosses over to affect the other parent, for example, where impairment in one parent's functioning at home may increase the pressure and caring responsibilities of the other parent and potentially affect that parent's irritability and perception of couple conflict and support (Karantzas et al., 2010; Simpson & Rholes, 2012).

Couple Conflict

A key threat to positive couple functioning and relationship maintenance is maladaptive couple conflict. Relationship conflict refers to interactions between couples involving an argument or disagreement (Buehler et al., 1994). Conflict is a normal part of life and frequent experiences of conflict are not necessarily a risk factor for poorer couple or family functioning (Krishnakumar & Buehler, 2000; Warmuth et al., 2019). Constructive conflict is characterized by problem-solving, resolution, or progression toward resolving conflict, support, and positive affection (Coln et al., 2013; McCoy et al., 2013; Warmuth et al., 2019), and is associated with improved family functioning and relationship quality (Feeney & Karantzas, 2017; Goeke-Morey et al., 2007; Sillars et al., 2002; Warmuth et al., 2019). On the other hand, maladaptive conflict exists on a spectrum of severity and patterns of conflict behavior and threatens relationship maintenance, leading to poor relationship quality and relationship dissolution, often because these patterns merely incite ongoing conflict rather than facilitate resolution (Feeney & Karantzas, 2017).

A very large body of research has investigated the associations between attachment styles and conflict patterns. In summarizing the literature, Feeney and Karantzas (2017) proposed an attachment-based model of relationship conflict in which attachment anxiety is assumed to be associated with physiological arousal and hyperactivating behaviors, designed to pressure a romantic partner to give more attention and support. This egoistic view involves neglecting a partner's needs and enacting blame, coercion, and other forms of destructive engagement. Attachment avoidance also predicts physiological arousal, but the deactivating strategies that underpin attachment avoidance manifest in suppressing conflict-related distress through conflict avoidance behaviors such as stonewalling and withdrawal. In contrast, attachment security is positively associated with constructive conflict patterns including greater problem-solving of relationship issues as well as providing and soliciting disclosure and accepting responsibility (Feeney & Karantzas, 2017; Feeney, et al., 1994; Simpson et al., 1992).

Testing Our Conceptual Model—Couple Adjustment in the COVID-19 Pandemic

So far, we have reviewed empirical evidence and theory showing how the stressful context of parenthood can affect adults' individual functioning by increasing psychological stress, which in turn impacts couple relationship maintenance functioning by increasing couple conflict, reducing partner support and caregiving, and increasing irritable parenting. We now describe an empirical study in which we test our conceptual model of relationship maintenance during parenthood using data collected from Australian parents during the COVID-19 pandemic, in April 2020, a time of unprecedented change and stress for many families.

The COVID-19 pandemic has had devastating effects around the world, and presents significant risks to mental health and well-being. Emerging research suggests that adult mental health symptoms during the early stages of pandemic were elevated compared to historical norms (Nelson et al., 2020). Stage three restrictions were in place in Australia throughout March–May 2020, requiring Australians to stay inside their homes, avoid contact with anyone outside their immediate family, avoid all nonessential travel, and maintain social distancing for essential nonfamily contact. As such, the pandemic presented threats to families in the form of reducing their ability to engage with protective factors, such as social and community connection; physical activity; access to greenspace and other co-curricular activities; and restricted access to clinical, community, family, and other supports and services.

Although Australia had early success in slowing the infection rate of the COVID-19 virus by the introduction of strict social distancing measures (Department of Health, 2020a; Department of Health, 2020b), its population has not been spared from the wider-ranging effects of the pandemic. For example, early data collected in March 2020 suggested that 27% of the Australian workforce were unemployed or underemployed

(Roy Morgan, 2020a). Furthermore, data collected in April suggested that a staggering two thirds of Australians reported that their employment was impacted by the COVID-19 pandemic (Roy Morgan, 2020b). As such, the impact of the pandemic has not been equal. Adults who lost jobs or experienced reductions in employment may have had to grapple with housing and economic uncertainty. Many families have experienced food and medication shortages. The pandemic has also presented another form of significant stressor in many families that are managing work from home while caring for young children, or homeschooling school-age children. In light of the evidence reviewed earlier in the chapter related to work–family conflict, we know that these changes represent significant potential stressors for parents in terms of their experience of psychological stress and distress, with potential downstream effects for their parenting practices and the couple relationship (Dinh et al., 2017; Strazdins et al., 2006; Strazdins et al., 2013; Vahedi et al., 2019).

We collected data to test the association between parent attachment insecurity and couple relationship quality during the COVID-19 pandemic in Australia. We drew on attachment theory and the diathesis-stress model (Simpson & Rholes, 2012) to propose a conceptual model (fig. 16.2) of the way in which the experience of COVID-19 pandemic stressors affect parents in couple relationships. We propose that attachment anxiety and avoidance will be associated with higher experiences of parent psychological stress. In line with the diathesis-stress model, we expect differential impacts of COVID-19 stressors. That is, compared to parents with low attachment avoidance and anxiety, we expect that parents with higher attachment avoidance and anxiety will report even greater psychological stress than parents low on these dimensions when faced with a greater number of COVID-19 stressors (i.e., job loss, housing and financial insecurity, COVID-19 illness,

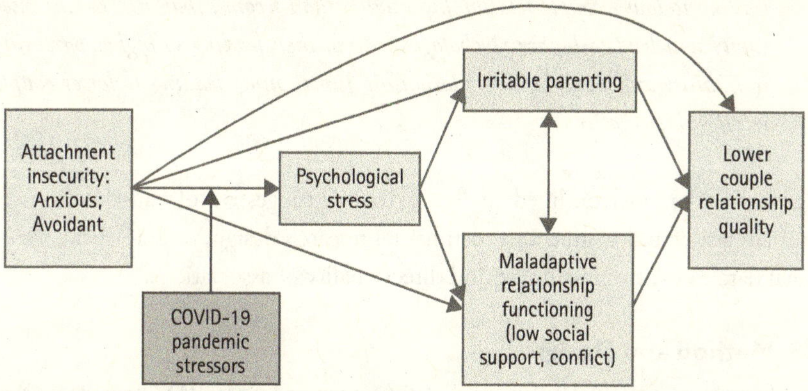

Figure 16.2 Conceptual diagram showing hypothesized associations between attachment insecurity, parent psychological stress, irritable parenting, maladaptive relationship functioning, and couple relationship quality, with hypothesized moderated associations for COVID-19 stressors.

hospitalization or death related the virus, and juggling child care or homeschooling while working from home).

The current study uses a cross-sectional study design, drawing on baseline data from the COVID-19 Pandemic Adjustment Study, a study of 2,365 Australian parents recruited to investigate the health and well-being impact of the pandemic on parents and children. Specifically, we aim to:

a. Investigate associations between attachment anxiety and avoidance, and parent psychological stress, parenting irritability, maladaptive relationship functioning, couple relationship quality. *As per figure 16.2, we expect that higher attachment anxiety and avoidance will be associated with higher levels of parent psychological stress, parenting irritability, maladaptive relationship functioning, and lower couple relationship quality.*
b. Test whether associations between attachment anxiety and avoidance, and parent stress, are moderated by COVID-19 pandemic stressors. *We expect that parents high on attachment anxiety and avoidance will show increased vulnerability to exposure to COVID-19 stressors compared to parents low on attachment avoidance and anxiety, with stronger associations between attachment insecurity and psychological stress in context of COVID-19 stressors compared to parents low on attachment anxiety and avoidance.*
c. Investigate whether associations between attachment insecurity (attachment anxiety and attachment avoidance) and couple relationship quality are mediated by parent psychological stress, parenting irritability, and maladaptive relationship functioning. *We expect that the associations between higher attachment anxiety and avoidance will be mediated according to two indirect paths; first, that attachment insecurity will lead to higher psychological stress, leading to lower couple relationship quality; and second, that attachment insecurity will lead to higher psychological stress, then leading to higher parenting irritability and maladaptive relationship functioning, leading to lower couple relationship quality.*

The proposed model outlined in figure 16.2 is suggestive of causal influences. An appropriate test would require an experimental research design, or at least the use of longitudinal data to control for timing and directionality of associations.

CPAS: Method and Design

Data from the COVID-19 Pandemic Adjustment Survey (CPAS) provide a pragmatic opportunity to test parent responses to the pandemic and potential influences on couple relationship quality, but the cross-sectional data limit our ability to make causal claims, and therefore findings must be interpreted with these limitations in mind.

Participants and Study Design

The current study drew on baseline data from a longitudinal cohort study of Australian parents of a child aged 0-18 years, the CPAS (N = 2,365). Participants were eligible to participate if they were an Australian resident, 18 years or over, and a parent of a child ages 0–18 years. Parents were recruited via paid and unpaid social media advertisements. Recruitment advertisements contained a web hyperlink which directed participants to an initial Qualtrics survey website. The study was approved by the Deakin University Human Ethics Advisory Group (Project number: HEAG-H 52_2020). Parents were invited to answer questions about their oldest child ages 0 to 18 years.

Measures

ADULT ATTACHMENT

The Experiences in Close Relationships Scale—Relationship Structures (ECR-RS; Fraley et al., 2011) has nine items in two subscales: Attachment anxiety (3 items) and attachment avoidance (6 items, 3 reverse-scored). An example item reads: "It helps to turn to people in times of need." The ECR-RS is rated on a 7-point scale from "strongly disagree" to "strongly agree." Items were averaged to form a total score.

RELATIONSHIP QUALITY

The Perceived Relationships Quality Component (PRQC) Questionnaire, developed by Fletcher et al. (2000) consists of six items. An example item reads: "How satisfied are you with your relationship?" The PRQC is rated on a 7-point scale from "not at all" to "extremely." Items were averaged to form a total score.

PSYCHOLOGICAL STRESS

We used the Stress subscale (7 items) of the Depression and Anxiety Scale (DASS) 21-item version (Lovibond & Lovibond, 1995). An example item reads: "I found it hard to wind down." It is rated on a 4-point scale from "did not apply to me at all" to "applied to me very much, or most of the time." Items were averaged to form a total score.

MALADAPTIVE RELATIONSHIP FUNCTIONING

This measure was formed from a composite of three measures assessing couple verbal conflict and low partner social support. Couple verbal conflict was assessed using the Argumentative Relationship Scale used in the Longitudinal Study of Australian Children (Australian Institute of Family Studies, 2005) (four items on verbal conflict). An example item reads: "How often do you and your partner disagree about basic household issues?" It is rated on a 5-point scale from "never" to "always." Items were averaged to form a total score. Partner social support was measured using two one-item measures: one item from the Social Provisions Scale (Cutrona & Russell, 1987), "When I am feeling stressed about a new or unknown situation, I can rely on my partner to comfort me," and one item from the Secure Base Characteristics Scale (Feeney & Thrush, 2010), "My partner encourages me to draw on my skills and abilities to deal with challenges." Both items were rated on a 7-point scale from "strongly disagree" to "strongly agree," and then reverse-scored and averaged to form a low partner social support score. To derive the composite measure for maladaptive relationship functioning, the verbal couple conflict and low partner social support scores were converted to z-scores and then averaged to form a total score.

PARENTING IRRITABILITY

This measure used five items from the Longitudinal Study of Australian Children (Zubrick et al., 2014). An example item reads: "In the past six months, how often would you say . . . I have raised my voice with or shouted at this child." It is rated on a 10-point scale from "not at all" to "all the time." Items were averaged to form a total score.

COVID-19 STRESSORS

Items were adapted from the CoRonavIruS Health Impact Survey (CRISIS) V0.1 (Merikangas & Stringaris, 2020): Household: COVID-19 diagnosis. About adult: Participant or family members affected by COVID-19 (hospitalized, passed away), financial problems or housing and food insecurity related to COVID-19, working from home; food shortages. Each of the eight COVID-19 risk factors was converted to a binary variable (0 = no risk; 1 = risk), and then summed to form a cumulative index score.

DEMOGRAPHIC CHARACTERISTICS

Parents reported on a range of demographic characteristics. About adult: Age, gender, country of birth, Aboriginal and Torres Strait Islander status, language other than English spoken at home, education, relationship status, whether living with partner, and number of children in the household. Demographics prior to COVID-19: employment, study, household income, source of income, shortage of money. About partner: Gender; partner's relationship to child, employment, education. About child: Age, gender, education setting.

Missing Data and Data Analysis

Data were prepared and cleaned in Stata version 16 (StataCorp, 2011). Analyses for Aims 1-3 were conducted in Mplus version 8.2 (Muthén & Muthén, 2012). All parents were included in the analyses if they had complete data on the exogenous variables in the model, that is, attachment anxiety and avoidance and COVID-19 stressors (N = 330 had missing data, final sample size, N = 2,035). Path analysis was conducted to simultaneously estimate associations between variables as specified in figure 16.1. Maximum likelihood estimation was used to handle missing data on dependent variables. To test Aims 1 and 2, relationship quality was regressed on irritable parenting and maladaptive relationship functioning. Relationship quality, irritable parenting, and

Table 16.1 Sample Characteristics for the Final Included Sample of Parents*

Variables	**N (%)**
Demographic characteristics	
Parent age (mean, sd)	38.52 (7.07)
Parent gender	
Female	1,582 (80%)
Male	395 (20%)
Nonbinary or not specified	1 (0.05%)
Parent not born in Australia	360 (18%)
Parent Aboriginal or Torres Strait Islander	41 (2%)
Single parent (no current partner)	203 (10%)
Parent did not complete high school	184 (9%)
Parent has university degree	1,610 (68%)
Child age (mean, SD)	8.73 (5.16)
Child age 0–5 years	823 (40%)
Child age 6–10 years	594 (29%)
Child age 11–18 years	618 (30%)
Child gender	
Female	994 (49%)
Male	1,028 (51%)
Nonbinary or not specified	9 (0.4%)
Number of children in the home	
1 child	575 (28%)
2 children	939 (46%)
3 children	375 (18%)
4 or more children	145 (7%)
Language other than English spoken at home most of the time	84 (4%)
COVID-19 stressors	
Financial problems associated with the pandemic	557 (27%)
Concerned about the stability of living situation	575 (28%)
Lost job due to the pandemic	155 (8%)
Experienced shortages of food related to the pandemic	970 (48%)
Caring for child while working from home (paid work)	1,113 (55%)
Parent or family member had a positive test for COVID-19	2 (0.1%)
Parent or family member hospitalized because of COVID-19	7 (0.3%)
Family member passed away due to COVID-19	7 (0.3%)
Cumulative number of COVID-19 stressors (mean, sd)	1.66 (1.19)

* *N* = 2,035.

maladaptive relationship functioning were regressed on attachment anxiety and avoidance. Irritable parenting and maladaptive relationship functioning were correlated. Finally, parent psychological stress was regressed on the exogenous model variables and interaction terms, including attachment anxiety, attachment avoidance, COVID-19 stressors, and the interaction terms between COVID-19 stressors and attachment anxiety/avoidance.

We report the chi-square goodness-of-fit statistic to determine model fit, but given that it is less informative with large sample sizes (Byrne, 2012), a model was deemed to have good fit if the root mean-square error of approximation (RMSEA) was < 0.05 (Byrne, 2012), standardized root-mean-square residual (SRMR) was < 0.05, and the comparative fit index (CFI) and/or the Tucker–Lewis index (TLI) had values > 0.95 (Hu & Bentler, 1999). The "Model Indirect" function in Mplus with bootstrapping was used to compare the contribution of unstandardized and standardized indirect and direct effects of parent attachment anxiety and avoidance on couple relationship quality. Given that the specified models examine paths between variables with negative correlations, we may find "inconsistent" mediation effects, that is, where two or more effects in a mediation model have opposite signs, causing the total effect to be null or reduced (MacKinnon et al., 2007). In this case, we interpret the direct and indirect effects separately from the total effect, and present only data for indirect effects in-text.

CPAS: Results

Sample characteristics, preliminary statistics, and model findings are reported below.

Sample Characteristics

Table 16.1 shows sample characteristics for parents participating in the CPAS. The majority of the participants were female parents with one or two children at home. There was a fairly equal distribution of child ages over 0–5 years, 6–10 years, and 11–18 years. On average, parents reported experiencing 1.7 stressful events related to the pandemic, with almost half reporting food shortages and more than half reporting supervising or homeschooling children while managing paid work from home.

Preliminary Statistics

Table 16.2 presents correlations between model variables. There was evidence for a large correlation between lower couple relationship quality and higher maladaptive relationship functioning, and small associations between lower couple relationship quality and higher verbal couple conflict and parent psychological stress. There were small-to-moderate associations between lower couple relationship quality and greater exposure to COVID-19 stressors, attachment anxiety, and attachment avoidance.

Table 16.2 Means, Standard Deviations, and Pairwise Correlations Between All Model Variables

	Mean	Sd	1	2	3	4	6	7	8
1. Couple relationship quality	33.95	6.60	1.00						
2. Maladaptive relationship functioning	−0.63	0.74	−0.73	1.00					
3. Irritable parenting	3.54	1.64	−0.08	0.16	1.00				
4. Psychological stress	15.46	8.87	−0.18	0.23	0.25	1.00			
5. COVID-19 stressors	1.66	1.19	−0.10	0.10	0.03	0.20	1.00		
6. Attachment anxiety	3.30	1.78	−0.26	0.28	0.19	0.37	0.16	1.00	
7. Attachment avoidance	3.31	1.31	−0.23	0.25	0.07	0.16	0.16	0.39	1.00

Note: SD = Standard deviation. p = values for all associations in the table were < 0.001.

AIM 1: PATH ANALYSIS

Figure 16.3 and Table 16.3 present regression coefficients results examining the direct and indirect associations in the final path analysis model. This model had excellent overall fit, x^2[df] = 8.095 [10], $p = 0.6196$; RMSEA = 0.000 [90% CI =.000, .020]; CFI = 1.000; TLI = 1.002; SRMR = 0.013. Starting at the left-hand side of the path diagram shown in figure 16.2, we found that higher levels of anxious attachment and avoidant attachment were directly associated with lower couple relationship quality. We also found that higher anxious attachment was associated with higher psychological stress, higher irritable parenting, and higher levels of maladaptive relationship functioning. In contrast, higher avoidant attachment was associated with lower psychological stress, was not associated with irritable parenting, but was associated with higher levels of maladaptive relationship functioning. We found that lower levels of irritable parenting and higher levels of maladaptive relationship functioning were associated with lower relationship quality.

AIM 2: MODERATION BY COVID-19 PANDEMIC STRESSORS

Greater numbers of COVID-19 stressors were not independently associated with higher stress, but we found evidence that the number of COVID-19 stressors moderated the associations between both attachment anxiety and stress and attachment avoidance and stress. We conducted simple slopes analysis to further investigate the moderation effects. We found a positive association between anxious attachment and parent stress at 1 standard deviation below the mean on the number of COVID-19 stressors (b = 2.06, $p < 0.001$); and a positive association 1 standard deviation above the mean (b = 1.46, $p < 0.001$); indicating that parents high on attachment anxiety were also high on parent stress, regardless of their number of COVID-19 stressors. In fact, higher attachment anxiety was associated with fewer COVID-19 stressors, and slightly lower stress with higher exposure to COVID-19 stressors. Parents low on attachment anxiety overall reported

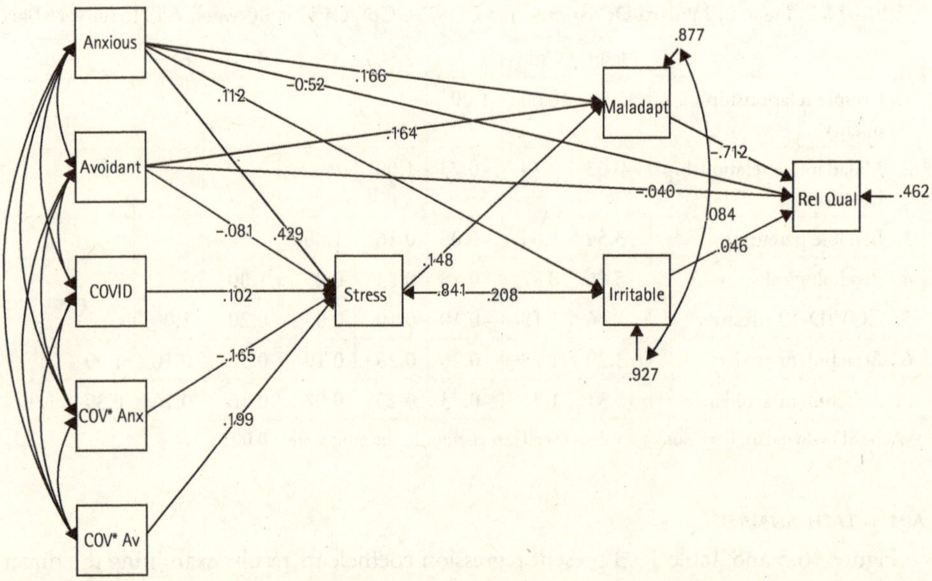

Figure 16.3 Findings from a path analysis involving $N = 2{,}365$ parents, showing standardized regression coefficients for significant ($p < 0.05$) direct and indirect paths between parent attachment anxiety and avoidance, and couple relationship quality. Anxious = Anxious attachment; Avoidant = Avoidance attachment; COVID = Number of COVID-19 pandemic stressors; COV*Anx = Interaction between COVID-19 stressors and anxious attachment; COV*Av = Interaction between COVID-19 stressors and avoidant attachment; Maladapt = Maladaptive relationship functioning; Irritable = Irritable parenting; Rel qual = couple relationship quality.

lower stress than parents high on attachment anxiety but were more likely to report stress when they experienced more COVID-19 stressors.

For the interaction between attachment avoidance and COVID-19 stressors, we found a nonsignificant association between attachment avoidance and parent stress at both low (b= −0.44, $p = 0.06$) and greater numbers of COVID-19 stressors (b = 0.38, $p = 0.053$). Parents high on avoidant attachment reported lower stress with fewer COVID-19 stressors compared to parents low on avoidant attachment. Parents high on avoidant attachment reported slightly higher stress with high numbers of COVID-19 stressors compared to parents low on avoidant attachment.

AIM 3: MEDIATION PATHS

We investigated the relative contribution of total, total indirect, and direct effects between attachment anxiety and avoidance, and relationship quality. We found evidence for a direct association (b = −0.19, $p = 0.001$), and four indirect paths between attachment anxiety and lower relationship quality; via (1) higher levels of maladaptive relationship functioning (indirect effect = b = −0.44, $p < 0.001$), (2) higher levels of irritable parenting (b = 0.02, $p = 0.03$), (3) higher levels of stress and higher levels of maladaptive relationship functioning (b = −0.17, $p < 0.001$), and (4) higher levels of stress and higher levels of irritable parenting (b = 0.02, $p = 0.02$). We found evidence for a direct association

Table 16.3 Direct and Indirect Relations Between Parent Attachment Anxiety and Avoidance, and Couple Relationship Quality

Regression paths	Unstandardized regression coefficient (SE)		Standardized regression coefficient (SE)		p
Rel quality on maladaptive rel processes	**-6.33**	**0.15**	**-0.71**	**0.01**	**0.000**
Rel quality on irritable parenting	**0.18**	**0.07**	**0.05**	**0.02**	**0.005**
Rel quality on anxious attachment	**-0.19**	**0.07**	**-0.05**	**0.02**	**0.004**
Rel quality on avoidant attachment	**-0.20**	**0.09**	**-0.04**	**0.02**	**0.021**
Maladaptive functioning on parent stress	**0.01**	**0.00**	**0.15**	**0.02**	**0.000**
Maladaptive functioning on anxious attachment	**0.07**	**0.01**	**0.17**	**0.03**	**0.000**
Maladaptive functioning on avoidant attachment	**0.09**	**0.01**	**0.16**	**0.02**	**0.000**
Irritable parenting on parent stress	**0.04**	**0.00**	**0.21**	**0.02**	**0.000**
Irritable parenting on anxious attachment	**0.10**	**0.02**	**0.11**	**0.03**	**0.000**
Irritable parenting on avoidant attachment	0.00	0.03	0.00	0.02	0.926
Maladaptive functioning with irritable parenting	**0.09**	**0.03**	**0.08**	**0.02**	**0.000**
Parent stress on anxious attachment	**2.14**	**0.19**	**0.43**	**0.04**	**0.000**
Parent stress on avoidant attachment	**-0.55**	**0.27**	**-0.08**	**0.04**	**0.040**
Parent stress on COVID-19 stressors	0.76	0.44	0.10	0.06	0.087
Parent stress on COVID-19 stressors*anxious attachment	**-0.24**	**0.09**	**-0.17**	**0.06**	**0.007**
Parent stress on COVID-19 stressors*avoidant attachment	**0.33**	**0.12**	**0.20**	**0.07**	**0.007**

Note. SE = standard error; Rel quality = Relationship quality; Maladaptive functioning = Maladaptive relationship functioning. Font is presented in boldface where there was evidence for associations ($p < 0.05$).

(b = -0.20, p = 0.03), and one indirect path between attachment avoidance and lower relationship quality, via higher levels of maladaptive relationship functioning (indirect effect = b = −0.59, $p < 0.001$).

CPAS: Discussion

The current empirical study sought to test our conceptual model of parenting maintenance during parenthood, by investigating whether environmental stressors related to the COVID-19 pandemic in Australia exacerbated associations between attachment vulnerability and individual, parenting, and couple relationship outcomes in a large study of Australian parents of a child 0–18 years. Our findings are summarized in a schema (fig. 16.4) for illustrative purposes and show that we found a different set of associations for parents reporting higher levels of anxious attachment compared to avoidant attachment.

Our hypotheses were almost all supported in regard to the results related to attachment anxiety. We found that attachment anxiety was associated with increased psychological stress, more irritable parenting, higher levels of maladaptive relationship functioning, and overall, lower couple relationship quality. In contrast to expectation, higher attachment avoidance was associated with lower psychological stress and was not associated with irritable parenting. However, as expected, higher attachment avoidance was associated with higher levels of maladaptive relationship functioning and, overall, lower couple relationship quality.

Our second aim tested the diathesis-stress model, conceptualizing attachment insecurity as a vulnerability factor (Simpson & Rholes, 2012). In line with our conceptual model, we found evidence that the association between attachment anxiety and psychological stress was moderated by COVID-19 stressors, but this was in an unexpected direction. We found that parents with high attachment anxiety reported more psychological stress compared to other parents, but they reported the highest levels of stress in the context of fewer COVID-19 stressors. It is not surprising that parents who reported being high on attachment anxiety also reported higher levels of psychological stress even in the face of a low stressor exposure; this is consistent with theory and research evidence showing that adults high on attachment anxiety tend to be hypervigilant to threat (Gillath et al., 2016; Mikulincer & Shaver, 2016). It may be that the difference in levels of stress between parents high on anxiety is accounted for by the external support they received. For example, perhaps parents high on anxious attachment who also experienced a high number of COVID-19 stressors were able to successfully elicit recognition of their care needs from others around them, resulting in sufficient supports and resources and thus reducing their experience of psychological stress. That is, perhaps these adults were viewed by others as facing a difficult situation and therefore were provided the support that they required to cope with the situation. In contrast, it's possible that for other parents high on anxious attachment but who experienced fewer COVID-19 stressors, their attachment system may have also been hyperactivated in the context of the pandemic; however, perhaps their needs for additional support were not recognized or met, resulting in their experiencing higher levels of psychological stress.

We also found evidence that COVID-19 stressors moderated the association between attachment avoidance and psychological stress. This finding is in line with the diathesis-stress model (Simpson & Rholes, 2012), where parents high on avoidance deactivate their attachment system, which results in more adaptive outcomes in context of few stressors (Mikulincer & Shaver, 2016). However, the same deactivation response crumbles with more extreme stressors, which is borne out in our results, where these adults reported higher psychological stress compared to parents low on avoidance with greater exposure to COVID-19 stressors. We have not included the moderated association between attachment avoidance and stress in the schema outlined in figure 16.4, since we did not find an indirect association between attachment avoidance and relationship quality via

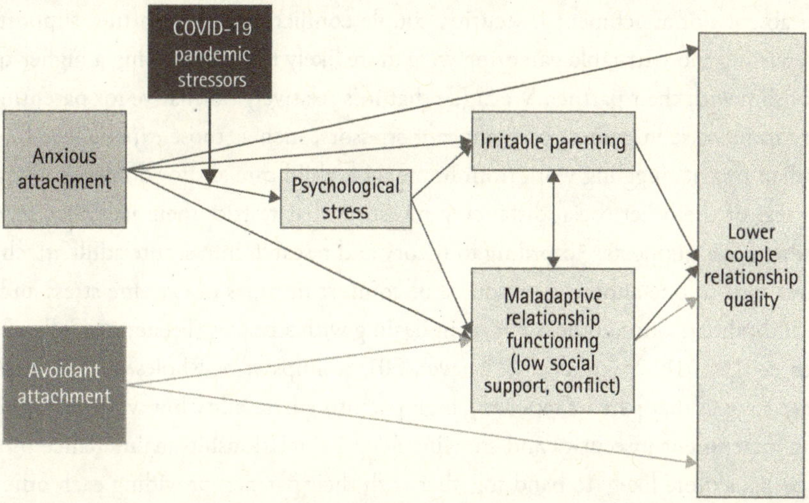

Figure 16.4 Schema showing a summary of the key associations related to attachment anxiety (see dark gray paths) and attachment avoidance (see light gray paths).

psychological stress. Further, we found that attachment avoidance was not associated with irritable parenting. It is possible that parents high on avoidant attachment withdraw from the parent–child relationship in times of stress, rather than engaging and interacting negatively. This is consistent with research showing that avoidance is unrelated to other negative parenting outcomes such as spanking and intrusiveness, but related to lower synchronicity, discomfort with contact, less sensitivity, and lower supportiveness (Jones et al., 2015).

In relation to our third aim testing mediation, we found evidence for a number of indirect paths explaining the association between higher attachment anxiety and lower couple relationship quality: via psychological stress, irritable parenting, and maladaptive relationship functioning. We found just one indirect association between higher attachment avoidance and lower relationship quality, via higher levels of maladaptive relationship functioning. These findings are broadly consistent with the extant theory and empirical evidence reviewed in the chapter, suggesting a number of downstream effects associated with attachment insecurity in the context of parenting stressors, including increased irritable parenting, higher couple conflict, lower partner support, and lower relationship quality (Adamsons, 2013; Campbell et al., 1992; Doss & Rhoades, 2017; Mitnick et al., 2009; Simpson & Rholes, 2019).

We had an unexpected finding in our final model, where higher levels of irritable parenting were associated with higher couple relationship quality. The bivariate association between irritable parenting and couple relationship quality was negative, where higher levels of irritable parenting were associated with poorer relationship quality. However, once attachment insecurity and maladaptive relationship functioning were accounted for in the fully adjusted model, the direction of the association was reversed. This means that in the absence of attachment insecurity, couple conflict, and low partner support, parents reporting more irritable parenting were more likely to report having a higher-quality relationship with their partner. We argue that it is relatively normative for parenting irritability to increase in context of significant stressors, such as those experienced by many Australian parents juggling work from home with child care and/or homeschooling, and in context of the other social distancing measures that restrict their access to child care and other social supports. According to theory and research into secure adult attachment, partners turn to one another as a source of comfort in times of extreme stress and challenge and validate one another's efforts in dealing with stressors (Feeney & Collins, 2019; Gillath et al., 2016; Mikulincer & Shaver, 2016; Simpson & Rholes, 2012). Thus, our findings suggest that parents reporting high parenting irritability but who were otherwise low on attachment insecurity and showing adaptive relationship maintenance processes were perhaps more likely to band together with their partner, providing each other with mutual support and thus increasing their relationship quality.

The COVID-19 pandemic presents significant risks to the mental health and well-being of Australian families. This study investigated the manifold impacts of the pandemic, including the impacts for families in regard to job loss, employment conditions, and homeschooling, as well as unprecedented lifestyle changes associated with social distancing measures. Chronic stress and social isolation have potential risks for adult mental health, couple and family relationships as well as children's health and development (Bakusic et al., 2017; Leigh-Hunt et al., 2017). Our findings suggest that parents high on attachment avoidance and anxiety are at increased risk of experiencing reductions in couple relationship quality in context of the pandemic. Given known associations between relationship quality and outcomes for children (Dinh et al., 2017; Strazdins et al., 2006; Strazdins et al., 2013; Vahedi et al., 2019), these results suggest that these parents require additional supports. Our findings, in relation to the way in which COVID-19 stressors moderate the association between attachment anxiety and psychological stress, suggest that parents with higher levels of attachment anxiety may particularly benefit from addition support.

As mentioned previously, the cross-sectional design of this research study was not adequate for testing causal processes. This means that associations between variables may have been reciprocal or they may have been caused by influences from other unmeasured variables. It is likely that reciprocal influences do exist in reality; for example, there is evidence in the work–family literature showing reciprocal influences between individual adult functioning in terms of well-being, experiences of psychological stress and mental health, and other couple and family processes (Demerouti et al., 2004; Innstrand et al., 2008; Westrupp et al., 2016). In the current study, it's possible that there might be reciprocal influences between parents' experience of psychological stress, the couple relationship functioning, and also irritable parenting. Further, as mentioned earlier in the chapter, relationship quality has been found to have important and significant downstream impacts on adult's mental and physical health, with meta-analytic findings showing that low relationship quality can even predict earlier mortality (Robles et al., 2014). Thus, future research should examine these associations with an appropriate research design to investigate the precise nature, timing, and direction of associations between individual functioning and functioning of the couple relationship over time.

Future Directions

In the current chapter, we reviewed current theory and empirical evidence in relation to relationship maintenance during parenthood. Altogether, we have summarized a large and well-established field of study. However, our review also highlighted some key gaps in knowledge that would benefit from further research investigation. Although there is a large literature regarding adult attachment in the context of parenting, it tends to focus on the initial transition to parenthood. Thus, validation of the diathesis-stress process model in later stages of parenthood is still needed. Future research should explore the relationship between partners' attachment insecurity and relationship quality across other stressful childrearing phases in order to shed further light on the generalizability of the diathesis-stress model, as well as investigate in more detail the psychological processes that influence the maintenance of the couple relationship during parenthood. The current chapter includes the attachment system and the caregiving system given that they are both relevant in the face of stressors. However, we do acknowledge that the sexual system is also important during parenting and will have important relationship outcome implications.

Empirical Support for Our Conceptual Model ofOf Parenting

The current chapter reviewed theory and evidence related to key couple relationship processes relevant to parenthood. The transition to parenthood represents one of the greatest potential stressors that the romantic couple relationship will experience over the lifetime, and can be associated with a notable decline in couple relationship quality (Doss & Rhoades, 2017; Doss et al., 2009; Simpson & Rholes, 2019). Further, although there is evidence that the couple relationship may eventually recover, families move through multiple transitions over the family life cycle, as children move through developmental stages and start child care, school, and so on. Parents must juggle these transitions as they manage their own transitions in their career, as well as other major life events.

Our chapter examined the role of attachment insecurity, conceptualized as an individual vulnerability factor, in line with the diathesis-stress model, and investigated how environmental stressors, individual psychological responses, and couple relationship processes can negatively impact the maintenance and quality of the couple bond within the context of parenthood. We proposed and then structured a summary of the current research evidence around a conceptual model of relationship maintenance, integrating an evolutionary psychology perspective; namely, attachment theory, to complement other relationship science and developmental perspectives. We tested our conceptual model using cross-sectional data from a large study of Australian parents facing an unprecedented stressful event, that of the COVID-19 pandemic and the associated social distancing restrictions. Our findings provide support to our conceptual model. Specifically, findings show that individual differences in adult attachment are associated with relationship functioning (i.e., levels of support and conflict between partners) and irritable parenting, which in turn, predict relationship outcomes (i.e., couple relationship quality), and that the environmental stressors in and around parenthood can exacerbate these associations. Developing an understanding of these mechanisms is important as it can highlight important areas for targeted prevention and intervention efforts, via bolstering couple relationships, strengthening positive parenting practices, and thus improving overall family functioning. Our findings suggest a role for targeted intervention to support adults with insecure attachment, but also adults facing significant increases in environment stressors related to the COVID-19 crisis.

References

Acock, A. C., & Demo, D. H. (1999). Dimensions of family conflict and their influence on child and adolescent adjustment. *Sociological Inquiry, 69*(4), 641–658. https://doi.org/10.1111/j.1475-682X.1999.tb00890.x

Adamsons, K. (2013). Predictors of relationship quality during the transition to parenthood. *Journal of Reproductive and Infant Psychology, 31*(2), 160–171. https://doi.org/10.1080/02646838.2013.791919

Arriaga, X. B., & Kumashiro, M. (2019). Walking a security tightrope: Relationship-induced changes in attachment security. *Current Opinion in Psychology, 25*, 121–126.

Australian Institute of Family Studies. (2005). *Growing up in Australia: The Longitudinal Study of Australian Children: 2004 annual report*. Author.

Bakker, A. B., Demerouti, E., & Dollard, M. F. (2008). How job demands affect partners' experience of exhaustion: Integrating work-family conflict and crossover theory. *Journal of Applied Psychology, 93*(4), 901.

Bakusic, J., Schaufeli, W., Claes, S., & Godderis, L. (2017). Stress, burnout and depression: A systematic review on DNA methylation mechanisms. *Journal of Psychosomatic Research, 92*, 34–44. https://doi.org/10.1016/j.jpsychores.2016.11.005

Bartel, K. A., Gradisar, M., & Williamson, P. (2015). Protective and risk factors for adolescent sleep: A meta-analytic review. *Sleep Medicine Reviews, 21*, 72–85.

Bei, B., Coo, S., & Trinder, J. (2015). Sleep and mood during pregnancy and the postpartum period. *Sleep Medicine Clinics, 10*(1), 25–33.

Bianchi, S. M., & Milkie, M. A. (2010). Work and family research in the first decade of the 21st century. *Journal of Marriage and Family, 72*(3), 705–725. https://doi.org/10.1111/j.1741-3737.2010.00726

Borelli, J. L., Nelson, S. K., River, L. M., Birken, S. A., & Moss-Racusin, C. (2017). Gender differences in work-family guilt in parents of young children. *Sex Roles, 76*(5–6), 356–368.

Bowlby, J. (1969). *Attachment and loss: Attachment*. Hogarth Press.

Bowlby, J. (1979). *The making and breaking of affectional bonds*. Tavistock.

Bowlby, J. (1982). Attachment and loss: Retrospect and prospect. *American Journal of Orthopsychiatry, 52*(4), 664–678. https://doi.org/10.1111/j.1939-0025.1982.tb01456.x

Brennan, K. A., Clark, C. L., & Shaver, P. R. (1998). Self-report measurement of adult attachment: An integrative overview. In J. A. Simpson, & W. S. Rholes (Eds.), *Attachment theory and close relationships* (pp. 46–76). Guilford Press.

Brennan, K. A., & Shaver, P. R. (1995). Dimensions of adult attachment, affect regulation, and romantic relationship functioning. *Personality and Social Psychology Bulletin, 21*(3), 267–283.

Buehler, C., Anthony, C., Krishnakumar, A., Stone, G., Gerard, J., & Pemberton, S. (1997). Interparental conflict and youth problem behaviors: A meta-analysis. *Journal of Child and Family Studies, 6*(2), 233–247. https://doi.org/10.1023/a:1025006909538

Buehler, C., Krishnakumar, A., Anthony, C., Tittsworth, S., & Stone, G. (1994). Hostile interparental conflict and youth maladjustment. *Family Relations, 60*(1), 409–416.

Byrne, B. (2012). *Structural equation modeling with Mplus*. Routledge.

Campbell, S. B., Cohn, J. F., Flanagan, C., Popper, S., & Meyers, T. (1992). Course and correlates of postpartum depression during the transition to parenthood. *Development and Psychopathology, 4*(1), 29–47.

Chee, K. H., Conger, R. D., & Elder, G. H. (2009). Mother's employment demands, work-family conflict, and adolescent development. *International Journal of Sociology of the Family, 35*(2), 189–202.

Christian, L. M., Carroll, J. E., Teti, D. M., & Hall, M. H. (2019). Maternal sleep in pregnancy and postpartum Part I: Mental, physical, and interpersonal consequences. *Current psychiatry reports, 21*(3), 20.

Coln, K. L., Jordan, S. S., & Mercer, S. H. (2013). A unified model exploring parenting practices as mediators of marital conflict and children's adjustment. *Child Psychiatry & Human Development, 44*(3), 419–429.

Conger, R., Conger, K. J., & Martin, M. J. (2010). Socioeconomic status, family processes, and individual development. *Journal of Marriage and Family, 72*(3), 685–704. https://doi.org/10.1111/j.1741-3737.2010.00725

Cooklin, A. R., Westrupp, E. M., Strazdins, L., Giallo, R., Martin, A., & Nicholson, J. M. (2015). Mothers' work-family conflict and enrichment: Associations with parenting quality and couple relationship. *Child: Care, Health & Development, 41*(2), 266–277. https://doi.org/10.1111/cch.12137

Cowan, C. P., & Cowan, P. A. (2000). *When partners become parents: The big life change for couples*. Erlbaum.

Cutrona, C. E., & Russell, D. W. (1987). The provisions of social relationships and adaptation to stress. *Advances in Personal Relationships, 1*(1), 37–67.

Cutrona, C. E., & Russell, D. W. (2017). Autonomy promotion, responsiveness, and emotion regulation promote effective social support in times of stress. *Current Opinion in Psychology, 13*, 126–130.

Cutrona, C. E., Russell, D. W., Abraham, W. T., Gardner, K. A., Melby, J. N., Bryant, C., & Conger, R. D. (2003). Neighborhood context and financial strain as predictors of marital interaction and marital quality in African American couples. *Personal Relationships, 10*(3), 389–409.

Del Giudice, M. (2019). Sex differences in attachment styles. *Current Opinion in Psychology, 25*, 1–5. https://doi.org/10.1016/j.copsyc.2018.02.004

Del Giudice, M., Gangestad, S. W., & Kaplan, H. S. (2016). Life history theory and evolutionary psychology. In D. Buss (Ed.), *The handbook of evolutionary psychology* (2nd ed.) (pp. 88–114). John Wiley & Sons.

Demerouti, E., Bakker, A. B., & Bulters, A. J. (2004). The loss spiral of work pressure, work–home interference and exhaustion: Reciprocal relations in a three-wave study. *Journal of Vocational Behavior, 64*(1), 131–149. https://doi.org/10.1016/S0001-8791(03)00030-7

Department of Health. (2020a). Coronavirus (COVID-19) current situation and case numbers. Retrieved from internet archive https://web.archive.org/web/20200601192704/https://www.health.gov.au/news/health-alerts/novel-coronavirus-2019-ncov-health-alert/coronavirus-covid-19-current-situation-and-case-numbers

Department of Health. (2020b). Coronavirus (COVID-19) current situation and case numbers. Retrieved from internet archive https://web.archive.org/web/20200529160019/https://www.health.gov.au/news/health-alerts/novel-coronavirus-2019-ncov-health-alert/how-to-protect-yourself-and-others-from-coronavirus-covid-19/physical-distancing-for-coronavirus-covid-19

Dinh, H., Cooklin, A. R., Leach, L. S., Westrupp, E. M., Nicholson, J. M., & Strazdins, L. (2017). Parents' transitions into and out of work-family conflict and children's mental health: Longitudinal influence via family functioning. *Social Science & Medicine, 194*, 42–50.

Doherty, N. A., & Feeney, J. A. (2004). The composition of attachment networks throughout the adult years. *Personal Relationships, 11*(4), 469–488.

Doss, B. D., & Rhoades, G. K. (2017). The transition to parenthood: Impact on couples' romantic relationships. *Current Opinion in Psychology, 13*, 25–28.

Doss, B. D., Rhoades, G. K., Stanley, S. M., & Markman, H. J. (2009). The effect of the transition to parenthood on relationship quality: An 8-year prospective study. *Journal of Personality and Social Psychology, 96*(3), 601.

Eller, J., Marshall, E. M., Rholes, W. S., Vieth, G., & Simpson, J. A. (2019). Partner predictors of marital aggression across the transition to parenthood: An I3 approach. *Journal of Social and Personal Relationships, 36*(5), 1491–1508.

Ensminger, M. E., Fothergill, K. E., Bornstein, M., & Bradley, R. (2003). A decade of measuring SES: What it tells us and where to go from here. *Socioeconomic Status, Parenting, and Child Development, 13*, 27.

Feeney, B. C., & Collins, N. L. (2003). Motivations for caregiving in adult intimate relationships: Influences on caregiving behavior and relationship functioning. *Personality and Social Psychology Bulletin, 29*(8), 950–968.

Feeney, B. C., & Collins, N. L. (2019). The importance of relational support for attachment and exploration needs. *Current Opinion in Psychology, 25*, 182–186.

Feeney, B. C., & Thrush, R. L. (2010). Relationship influences on exploration in adulthood: The characteristics and function of a secure base. *Journal of Personality and Social Psychology, 98*(1), 57.

Feeney, J. A., & Karantzas, G. C. (2017). Couple conflict: Insights from an attachment perspective. *Current Opinion in Psychology, 13*, 60–64.

Feeney, J. A., & Noller, P. (1990). Attachment style as a predictor of adult romantic relationships. *Journal of Personality and Social Psychology, 58*(2), 281.

Feeney, J. A., Noller, P., & Callan, V. J. (1994). Attachment style, communication and satisfaction in the early years of marriage. In K. Bartholomew & D. Perlman (Eds.), *Attachment processes in adulthood* (pp. 269–308). Jessica Kingsley.

Feldman, R., Sussman, A. L., & Zigler, E. (2004). Parental leave and work adaptation at the transition to parenthood: Individual, marital, and social correlates. *Journal of Applied Developmental Psychology, 25*(4), 459–479.

Ferriby, M., Kotila, L., Dush, C. K., & Schoppe-Sullivan, S. (2016). Dimensions of attachment and commitment across the transition to parenthood. *Journal of Family Psychology, 29*(6), 938–944. https://doi.org/10.1037/fam0000117

Figueiredo, B., & Conde, A. (2015). First- and second-time parents' couple relationship: From pregnancy to second year postpartum. *Family Science, 6*(1), 346–355. https://doi.org/10.1080/19424620.2015.1075894

Fillo, J., Simpson, J. A., Rholes, W. S., & Kohn, J. L. (2015). Dads doing diapers: Individual and relational outcomes associated with the division of childcare across the transition to parenthood. *Journal of Personality and Social Psychology, 108*(2), 298.

Fletcher, G. J. (2002). Attachment and intimacy. In G. J. Fletcher, *The new science of intimate relationships* (pp. 149–168). John Wiley & Sons.

Fletcher, G. J., Simpson, J. A., & Thomas, G. (2000). The measurement of perceived relationship quality components: A confirmatory factor analytic approach. *Personality and Social Psychology Bulletin, 26*(3), 340–354.

Fraley, R. C., Heffernan, M. E., Vicary, A. M., & Brumbaugh, C. C. (2011). The experiences in close relationships—Relationship Structures Questionnaire: A method for assessing attachment orientations across relationships. *Psychological Assessment, 23*(3), 615.

Geary, D. C. (2015). Evolution of paternal investment. In D. M. Buss (Ed.), The handbook of evolutionary psychology (1st ed.) (pp. 483–505). John Wiley & Sons.

Gillath, O., Karantzas, G. C., & Fraley, R. C. (2016). *Adult attachment: A concise introduction to theory and research*. Academic Press.

Gillath, O., Karantzas, G. C., & Lee, J. (2019). Attachment and social networks. *Current Opinion in Psychology, 25*, 21–25.

Goeke-Morey, M. C., Cummings, E. M., & Papp, L. M. (2007). Children and marital conflict resolution: Implications for emotional security and adjustment. *Journal of Family Psychology, 21*(4), 744.

Gou, L. H., & Woodin, E. M. (2017). Relationship dissatisfaction as a mediator for the link between attachment insecurity and psychological aggression over the transition to parenthood. *Couple and Family Psychology: Research and Practice, 6*(1), 1.

Hazan, C., & Zeifman, D. (1999). Pair bonds as attachments. In C. Hazan & D. Zeifman Handbook of attachment: Theory, research, and clinical applications (pp. 336–354). Guilford Press.

Hislop, J. (2007). A bed of roses or a bed of thorns? Negotiating the couple relationship through sleep. *Sociological Research Online, 12*(5), 146–158. https://doi.org/10.5153/sro.1621

Holmes, E. K., Sasaki, T., & Hazen, N. L. (2013). Smooth versus rocky transitions to parenthood: Family systems in developmental context. *Family Relations, 62*(5), 824–837.

Houts, R. M., Barnett-Walker, K. C., Paley, B., & Cox, M. J. (2008). Patterns of couple interaction during the transition to parenthood. *Personal Relationships, 15*(1), 103–122. https://doi.org/10.1111/j.1475-6811.2007.00187.x

Hu, L., & Bentler, P. M. (1999). Cutoff criteria for fit indexes in covariance structure analysis: Conventional criteria versus new alternatives. *Structural Equation Modeling: A Multidisciplinary Journal, 6*(1), 1–55. https://doi.org/10.1080/10705519909540118

Innstrand, S. T., Langballe, E. M., Geir, A. E., Falkum, E., & Olaf, G. W. A. (2008). Positive and negative work–family interaction and burnout: A longitudinal study of reciprocal relations. *Work & Stress, 22*(1), 1–15. https://doi.org/10.1080/02678370801975842

Jones, J. D., Cassidy, J., & Shaver, P. R. (2015). Parents' self-reported attachment styles: A review of links with parenting behaviors, emotions, and cognitions. *Personality and Social Psychology Review, 19*(1), 44–76.

Ju, S., & Choi, W. (2013). Sleep duration and metabolic syndrome in adult populations: A meta-analysis of observational studies. *Nutrition & Diabetes, 3*(5), e65–e65.

Karantzas, G. C., Evans, L., & Foddy, M. (2010). The role of attachment in current and future parent caregiving. *Journals of Gerontology Series B: Psychological Sciences and Social Sciences, 65*(5), 573–580.

Karantzas, G. C., Feeney, J. A., Goncalves, C. V., & McCabe, M. P. (2014). Towards an integrative attachment-based model of relationship functioning. *British Journal of Psychology, 105*(3), 413–434.

Karantzas, G. C., Feeney, J. A., & Wilkinson, R. (2010). Is less more? Confirmatory factor analysis of the Attachment Style Questionnaires. *Journal of Social and Personal Relationships, 27*(6), 749–780.

Karantzas, G. C., Simpson, J. A., Overall, N. C., & Campbell, L. (2019). The association between attachment orientations and partner evaluations: An ideal standards perspective. *Personal Relationships, 26*(4), 628–653. https://doi.org/10.1111/pere.12297

Karney, B. R., & Bradbury, T. N. (1995). The longitudinal course of marital quality and stability: A review of theory, methods, and research. *Psychological Bulletin, 118*(1), 3.

Karney, B. R., Story, L. B., & Bradbury, T. N. (2005). Marriages in context: Interactions between chronic and acute stress among newlyweds. In T. A. Revenson, K. Kayser, & G. Bodenmann (Eds.), *Couples coping with stress: Emerging perspectives on dyadic coping* (pp. 13–32). American Psychological Association Press.

Keilty, K., Cohen, E., Ho, M., Spalding, K., & Stremler, R. (2015). Sleep disturbance in family caregivers of children who depend on medical technology: A systematic review. *Journal of Pediatric Rehabilitation Medicine, 8*, 113–130. https://doi.org/10.3233/PRM-150325

Keizer, R., & Schenk, N. (2012). Becoming a parent and relationship satisfaction: A longitudinal dyadic perspective. *Journal of Marriage and Family, 74*(4), 759–773.

Kiecolt-Glaser, J. K., & Wilson, S. J. (2017). Lovesick: How couples' relationships influence health. *Annual Review of Clinical Psychology, 13*(1), 421–443. https://doi.org/10.1146/annurev-clinpsy-032816-045111

Kinnunen, U., & Feldt, T. (2004). Economic stress and marital adjustment among couples: Analyses at the dyadic level. *European Journal of Social Psychology, 34*(5), 519–532. https://doi.org/10.1002/ejsp.213

Kirkpatrick, L. A. (1998). Evolution, pair-bonding, and reproductive strategies: A reconceptualization of adult attachment. In J. A. Simpson & W. S. Rholes (Eds.), *Attachment theory and close relationships* (pp. 353–393). Guilford Press.

Kohn, J. L., Rholes, S. W., Simpson, J. A., Martin III, A. M., Tran, S., & Wilson, C. L. (2012). Changes in marital satisfaction across the transition to parenthood: The role of adult attachment orientations. *Personality and Social Psychology Bulletin, 38*(11), 1506–1522.

Krishnakumar, A., & Buehler, C. (2000). Interparental conflict and parenting behaviors: A meta-analytic review. *Family Relations, 49*(1), 25–44.

Kunce, L. J., & Shaver, P. R. (1994). *An attachment-theoretical approach to caregiving in romantic relationships* [Paper presentation]. 6th International Conference on Personal Relationships, Orono, ME.

Lawson, A., Murphy, K. E., Sloan, E., Uleryk, E., & Dalfen, A. (2015). The relationship between sleep and postpartum mental disorders: A systematic review. *Journal of Affective Disorders, 176*, 65–77.

Leigh-Hunt, N., Bagguley, D., Bash, K., Turner, V., Turnbull, S., Valtorta, N., & Caan, W. (2017). An overview of systematic reviews on the public health consequences of social isolation and loneliness. *Public Health, 152*, 157–171. https://doi.org/https://doi.org/10.1016/j.puhe.2017.07.035

Lin, K. Y., & Burgard, S. A. (2018). Working, parenting and work-home spillover: Gender differences in the work-home interface across the life course. *Advances in Life Course Research, 35*, 24–36.

Lovibond, P. F., & Lovibond, S. H. (1995). The structure of negative emotional states: Comparison of the Depression Anxiety Stress Scales (DASS) with the Beck Depression and Anxiety Inventories. *Behaviour Research and Therapy, 33*(3), 335–343.

MacKinnon, D. P., Fairchild, A. J., & Fritz, M. S. (2007). Mediation analysis. *Annual Review of Psychology, 58*, 593–614.

Mazzeschi, C., Pazzagli, C., Radi, G., Raspa, V., & Buratta, L. (2015). Antecedents of maternal parenting stress: The role of attachment style, prenatal attachment, and dyadic adjustment in first-time mothers. *Frontiers in Psychology, 6*, Article 1443.

McCoy, K. P., George, M. R., Cummings, E. M., & Davies, P. T. (2013). Constructive and destructive marital conflict, parenting, and children's school and social adjustment. *Social Development, 22*(4), 641–662.
McKnight, A., & Nolan, B. (2012). Social impacts of inequalities. *Intermediate Work Package, 4.* Retrieved from https://www1feb-uva.nl/aias/IntermediateWorkPackage4Report.pdf
Merikangas, K., & Stringaris, A. (2020). The CoRonavIruS Health Impact Survey (CRISIS) V0.1. Retrieved from https://github.com/nimh-mbdu/CRISIS
Mikulincer, M., & Shaver, P. R. (2003). The attachment behavioral system in adulthood: Activation, psychodynamics, and interpersonal processes. *Advances in Experimental Social Psychology, 35*, 53–152.
Mikulincer, M., & Shaver, P. (2016). Adult attachment and emotion regulation. In J. Cassidy & P. Shaver (Eds.), Handbook of attachment: Theory, research, and clinical applications (3rd ed., pp. 507–533). Guilford Press.
Mitnick, D. M., Heyman, R. E., & Smith Slep, A. M. (2009). Changes in relationship satisfaction across the transition to parenthood: A meta-analysis. *Journal of Family Psychology, 23*(6), 848.
Montgomery-Downs, H., Stremler, R., & Insana, S. (2013). Postpartum sleep in new mothers and fathers. *The Open Sleep Journal, 6*(Suppl. 1: M11), 87–97.
Muthén, L. K., & Muthén, B. O. (2012). *Mplus user's guide.* Muthén & Muthén.
Nelson, B. W., Pettitt, A. K., Flannery, J., & Allen, N. B. (2020). Psychological and epidemiological predictors of COVID-19 concern and health-related behaviors. *PsyArXiv.* https://doi.org/10.31234/osf.io/jftze
Nygren, M., Carstensen, J., Ludvigsson, J., & Sepa Frostell, A. (2012). Adult attachment and parenting stress among parents of toddlers. *Journal of Reproductive and Infant Psychology, 30*(3), 289–302.
Power, C., Stansfeld, S. A., Matthews, S., Manor, O., & Hope, S. (2002). Childhood and adulthood risk factors for socio-economic differentials in psychological distress: Evidence from the 1958 British birth cohort. *Social Science & Medicine, 55*(11), 1989–2004. https://doi.org/10.1016/S0277-9536(01)00325-2
Rholes, S. W., Kohn, J. L., & Simpson, J. A. (2014). A longitudinal study of conflict in new parents: The role of attachment. *Personal Relationships, 21*(1), 1–21.
Rholes, W. S., Simpson, J. A., Campbell, L., & Grich, J. (2001). Adult attachment and the transition to parenthood. *Journal of Personality and Social Psychology, 81*(3), 421.
Richter, K., Adam, S., Geiss, L., Peter, L., & Niklewski, G. (2016). Two in a bed: The influence of couple sleeping and chronotypes on relationship and sleep. An overview. *Chronobiology International, 33*(10), 1464–1472. https://doi.org/10.1080/07420528.2016.1220388
Robles, T. F., Slatcher, R. B., Trombello, J. M., & McGinn, M. M. (2014). Marital quality and health: A meta-analytic review. *Psychological Bulletin, 140*(1), 140.
Roy Morgan. (2020a). Article No. 8363: Extra 1.4 million Australians out of work in wake of COVID-19 pandemic—3.92 million (27.4% of workforce) now unemployed or under-employed [Press release]. Retrieved from https://www.roymorgan.com/findings/8363-roy-morgan-unemployment-and-under-employment-march-2020-202004080900
Roy Morgan. (2020b). Article No. 8383: Over two-thirds of working Australians have had their employment impacted by the "Coronavirus Crisis" [Press release]. Retrieved from https://www.roymorgan.com/findings/8383-roy-morgan-coronavirus-crisis-impact-on-employment-april-24-2020-202004240654
Ruppanner, L., Perales, F., & Baxter, J. (2019). Harried and unhealthy? Parenthood, time pressure, and mental health. *Journal of Marriage and Family, 81*(2), 308–326. https://doi.org/10.1111/jomf.12531
Sillars, A., Leonard, K. E., Roberts, L. J., & Dun, T. (2002). Cognition and communication during marital conflict: How alcohol affects subjective coding of interaction in aggressive and nonaggressive couples. In P. Noller & J. A. Feeney (Eds.), Understanding marriage: Developments in the study of couple interaction (pp. 85–112). Cambridge University Press.
Simpson, J. A., & Belsky, J. (2008). Attachment theory within a modern evolutionary framework. In J. Cassidy & P. R. Shaver (Eds.), Handbook of attachment: Theory, research, and clinical applications (pp. 131–157). Guilford Press.
Simpson, J. A., & Karantzas, G. C. (2019). Editorial overview: Attachment in adulthood: A dynamic field with a rich past and a bright future. *Current Opinion in Psychology, 25*, 177–181.
Simpson, J. A., & Rholes, W. S. (2012). Adult attachment orientations, stress, and romantic relationships. In *Advances in experimental social psychology* (Vol. 45, pp. 279–328). Elsevier.
Simpson, J. A., & Rholes, W. S. (2017). Adult attachment, stress, and romantic relationships. *Current Opinion in Psychology, 13*, 19–24.

Simpson, J. A., & Rholes, W. S. (2019). Adult attachment orientations and well-being during the transition to parenthood. *Current Opinion in Psychology, 25*, 47–52.
Simpson, J. A., Rholes, W. S., & Nelligan, J. S. (1992). Support seeking and support giving within couples in an anxiety-provoking situation: The role of attachment styles. *Journal of Personality and Social Psychology, 62*(3), 434.
StataCorp. (2011). *Stata Statistical Software (V.12)*. StataCorp LP.
Strazdins, L., Clements, M. S., Korda, R. J., Broom, D. H., & D'Souza, R. M. (2006). Unsociable work? Nonstandard work schedules, family relationships, and children's well-being. *Journal of Marriage and Family, 68*(2), 394–410.
Strazdins, L., OBrien, L. V., Lucas, N., & Rodgers, B. (2013). Combining work and family: Rewards or risks for children's mental health? *Social Science & Medicine, 87*, 99–107. https://doi.org/10.1016/j.socscimed.2013.03.030
Stremler, R., Hodnett, E., Kenton, L., Lee, K., Weiss, S., Weston, J., & Willan, A. (2013). Effect of behavioural-educational intervention on sleep for primiparous women and their infants in early postpartum: Multisite randomised controlled trial. *BMJ: British Medical Journal, 346*, Article f1164. https://doi.org/10.1136/bmj.f1164
Szepsenwol, O., & Simpson, J. A. (2019). Attachment within life history theory: An evolutionary perspective on individual differences in attachment. *Current Opinion in Psychology, 25*, 65–70. https://doi.org/10.1016/j.copsyc.2018.03.005
Szepsenwol, O., Simpson, J. A., Griskevicius, V., & Raby, K. L. (2015). The effect of unpredictable early childhood environments on parenting in adulthood. *Journal of Personality and Social Psychology, 109*(6), 1045.
Troxel, W. M. (2010). It's more than sex: Exploring the dyadic nature of sleep and implications for health. *Psychosomatic Medicine, 72*(6), 578–586. https://doi.org/10.1097/PSY.0b013e3181de7ff8
Troxel, W. M., Robles, T. F., Hall, M., & Buysse, D. J. (2007). Marital quality and the marital bed: Examining the covariation between relationship quality and sleep. *Sleep Medicine Reviews, 11*(5), 389–404. https://doi.org/10.1016/j.smrv.2007.05.002
Twenge, J. M., Campbell, W. K., & Foster, C. A. (2003). Parenthood and marital satisfaction: A meta-analytic review. *Journal of Marriage and Family, 65*(3), 574–583.
Vahedi, A., Krug, I., Fuller-Tyszkiewicz, M., & Westrupp, E. M. (2019). Maternal work–family experiences: Longitudinal influences on child mental health through inter-parental conflict. *Journal of Child and Family Studies, 28*(12), 3487–3498.
Vahedi, A., Krug, I., & Westrupp, E. M. (2019). Crossover of parents' work-family conflict to family functioning and child mental health. *Journal of Applied Developmental Psychology, 62*, 38–49.
Vasquez, K., Durik, A. M., & Hyde, J. S. (2002). Family and work: Implications of adult attachment styles. *Personality and Social Psychology Bulletin, 28*(7), 874–886.
Volling, B. L., Oh, W., Gonzalez, R., Kuo, P. X., & Yu, T. (2015). Patterns of marital relationship change across the transition from one child to two. *Couple and Family Psychology: Research and Practice, 4*(3), 177.
Warmuth, K. A., Cummings, E. M., & Davies, P. T. (2019). Constructive and destructive interparental conflict, problematic parenting practices, and children's symptoms of psychopathology. *Journal of Family Psychology, 34*(3), 301–311.
Westman, M. (2002). Crossover of stress and strain in the family and in the workplace. In P. L. Perrewe & D. C. Ganster (Eds.), *Historical and current perspectives on stress and health: Research in occupational stress and well-being* (pp. 143–181). Emerald Group.
Westman, M. (2005). Cross-cultural differences in crossover research. In S. Poelmans (Ed.), Work and family: An international research perspective (pp. 241–260). Erlbaum.
Westrupp, E. M., Brown, S., Woolhouse, H., Gartland, D., & Nicholson, J. M. (2018). Repeated early-life exposure to inter-parental conflict increases risk of preadolescent mental health problems. *European Journal of Pediatrics, 177*(3), 419–427.
Westrupp, E. M., Rose, N., Nicholson, J. M., & Brown, S. J. (2015). Exposure to inter-parental conflict across 10 years of childhood: Data from the longitudinal study of Australian children. *Maternal and Child Health Journal, 19*(9), 1966–1973.
Westrupp, E. M., Strazdins, L., Martin, A., Cooklin, A. R., Zubrick, S., & Nicholson, J. M. (2016). Maternal work-family conflict and psychological distress: Reciprocal relationships over 8 years. *Journal of Marriage and Family, 78*(1), 107–126.

Whelan, C. T. (1994). Social class, unemployment, and psychological distress. *European Sociological Review, 10*(1), 49–61. https://doi.org/10.1093/oxfordjournals.esr.a036315

Williamson, H. C., Karney, B. R., & Bradbury, T. N. (2013). Financial strain and stressful events predict newlyweds' negative communication independent of relationship satisfaction. *Journal of Family Psychology, 27*(1), 65.

Woolhouse, H., Gartland, D., Mensah, F., & Brown, S. (2015). Maternal depression from early pregnancy to 4 years postpartum in a prospective pregnancy cohort study: Implications for primary health care. *BJOG: An International Journal of Obstetrics & Gynaecology, 122*(3), 312–321.

Wu, Y., Zhai, L., & Zhang, D. (2014). Sleep duration and obesity among adults: A meta-analysis of prospective studies. *Sleep Medicine, 15*(12), 1456–1462. https://doi.org/10.1016/j.sleep.2014.07.018

Zeifman, D., & Hazan, C. (1997). Attachment: The bond in pair-bonds. In J. A. Simpson & D. Kenrick (Eds.), *Evolutionary social psychology* (pp. 237–263). Erlbaum.

Zhang, B., & Wing, Y.-K. (2006). Sex differences in insomnia: A meta-analysis. *Sleep, 29*(1), 85–93.

Zubrick, S. R., Lucas, N., Westrupp, E. M., & Nicholson, J. M. (2014). *Parenting measures in the Longitudinal Study of Australian Children: Construct validity and measurement quality, Waves 1 to 4.* (LSAC Technical Paper No. 12). Australian Government Department of Social Services.

CHAPTER

17

Maintaining Multipartner Relationships: Evolution, Sexual Ethics, and Consensual Nonmonogamy

Justin K. Mogilski, David L. Rodrigues, Justin J. Lehmiller, *and* Rhonda N. Balzarini

Abstract

Humans maintain romantic relationships for sexual gratification, child care assistance, intimate friendship, and a host of other interpersonal benefits. In monogamous relationships (i.e., exclusive courtship between two people), individuals agree that certain benefits of the relationship (i.e., sexual contact, material resources, and emotional support) may only be shared within the pair-bond. That is, each partner is expected to maintain the relationship by provisioning sufficient benefits to satisfy the needs and desires of their partner. By comparison, consensual nonmonogamy (CNM) is a collection of relationship practices and structures whereby partners agree that it is permissible to have sexual contact or form intimate attachments with other people to satisfy these interpersonal needs and desires. In this chapter, we review literature examining who pursues CNM, how people who practice CNM derive and maintain satisfaction within their relationship(s), and when and how these relationships persist. We consider the role of CNM relationship maintenance practices, personality features that predispose people to CNM, and psychological and social barriers (e.g., jealousy, interpersonal conflict, sexual health anxiety, and condemnation) that prevent people from pursuing or maintaining CNM. Throughout, we consider how CNM compares to infidelity as an alternative strategy for pursuing multiple, concurrent romantic or sexual relationships. We close by discussing current directions in the scientific study of CNM and highlight which gaps in the literature are most pressing to address.

Key Words: consensual nonmonogamy, infidelity, relationship maintenance, relationship quality, relationship investment, stigma, personality

Multipartner mating refers to romantic, sexual, or otherwise intimate behavior between an individual and two or more concurrent people. Monogamy (i.e., intimate behavior between only two people) characterizes the majority of romantic relationships worldwide, but multipartner mating is observed in every known society (Henrich et al., 2012; Schacht & Kramer, 2019). Multipartner mating has been a core focus of study in the evolutionary sciences because having several concurrent partners introduces different reproductive opportunities and challenges for the two dominant sex morphs (i.e., women and men) (Trivers, 1972; also see Mogilski, 2021). By mating with more than one partner, men are able to produce more children because their inexpensive gametes (i.e., sperm) are readily dispersed. Thus, they can increase their number of children by having sex with multiple female partners. Women, on the other hand, are obligated to commit gestational resources to a single, fertilized egg for nine months and therefore do not benefit from mating with multiple partners in the same way. Nevertheless, women may pursue multipartner mating for other reasons, such as to sample and secure better partners (i.e., mate switch; see Buss et al., 2017), to produce offspring with diverse genes (see Buss & Schmitt, 1993; Gangestad & Simpson, 2000), or to secure investment from several partners at once (Hrdy, 1995). These divergent motives for men and women can cause conflict when one partner's pursuit of an extra-pair romantic or sexual relationship is at odds with the other partner's reproductive interests (i.e., sexual conflict; see Kennair et al., this volume; also see Buss, 2017). For example, if a man's female partner becomes sexually involved with other men, he risks cuckoldry (i.e., unwitting investment in genetically unrelated offspring). If a woman's male partner becomes involved with other women, she risks her partner diverting his time and resources to children who are genetically unrelated to her. Men and women are thus both motivated (a) to pursue multipartner mating (albeit for different reasons), and (b) to restrict their partner from doing the same.

Infidelity

Organisms have diverse strategies for resolving the sexual conflict caused by multipartner mating (Clutton-Brock, 1989; Selander, 1965; Setchell, 2008), but infidelity is one of the most well-studied (Haseli et al., 2019; Selterman et al., 2019). Infidelity is when extra-pair courtship occurs within an exclusively single-partner (i.e., monogamous) relationship. In monogamous relationships, partners mutually agree (though often implicitly; see Badcock et al., 2014) to refrain from extra-pair sex and romance. This is reasonable because there are persistent threats to reproduction caused by multipartner mating (see Shackelford & Buss, 1997), such as cuckoldry (see Anderson, 2006; Scelza, 2020; Voracek et al., 2008), domestic violence (Buunk & Massar, 2019), lethal intrasexual competition (e.g., homicide; Daly & Wilson, 2001), and sexual disease transmission (Kokko et al., 2002; Nunn et al., 2000). If both partners faithfully commit to this social contract, these risks are prevented, thus mutually benefiting each partner. Infidelity is thus when one partner defects from this social contract (i.e., forms an extra-pair relationship) while deceiving their partner into believing otherwise. Strategically, this causes the duped partner to restrict their own, but not their partner's, extra-pair behavior. In other words, by subverting a partner's consent to engage in an extra-pair relationship, those who practice infidelity reap the benefits of having multiple partners (e.g., access to sexual or romantic partner variety) while avoiding the costs of their partner doing the same (e.g., cuckoldry and resource diversion).

The absence of a partner's informed consent is a key feature of infidelity. If an individual were to know about an in-pair partner's current or potential extra-pair relationship(s), this would permit them to calculate the impact of these additional relationships on in-pair relationship quality. For example, someone who knows that their partner is having sexual contact with another person can assess the likelihood of potential pregnancy or sexual disease transmission and take precaution if necessary (e.g., by ensuring that their partner uses safe sexual practices). Likewise, someone who knows that their partner is forming other emotionally intimate attachments can anticipate how that partner might allocate time, effort, or resources among each attachment—and perhaps decide that they should form their own extra-pair relationship(s) and/or leave that partner if the relationship becomes inequitable or costly. At the heart of consent, then, is freedom of association, whereby people are not inhibited from leaving an inauspicious relationship. This freedom of association creates a biological mating market based on partner choice (see Barclay, 2013; Noë & Hammerstein, 1994; Whyte et al., 2019) wherein partners compete for each other's commitment rather than coerce it. It is unsurprising, then, that non-consensual extra-pair relationships tend to be secretive: those who successfully convince their partner to adhere to an exclusivity contract that they themselves do not follow are able to subvert the mating market—and thereby their partner's choice.

In this sense, infidelity is a solution to sexual conflict—albeit a risky one. Evidence suggests that forming a romantic or sexual relationship outside an established pair-bond without the consent of one's partner increases sexual disease transmission (Hirsch et al., 2007; Lehmiller, 2015), psychological distress (e.g., major depressive disorder, anxiety, and post-traumatic stress; Roos et al., 2019), relational instability and dissatisfaction (Betzig, 1989; Previti & Amato, 2004; Spanier & Margolis, 1983), financial hardship (Crouch & Dickes, 2016), and family disruption (Lusterman, 2005; Negash & Morgan, 2016). Discovering an infidelity is often experienced as betrayal or "attachment injury" (see Warach & Josephs, 2019), whereby a previously reliable partner subsequently appears less predictable, trustworthy, or fair. Infidelity may also prompt revenge in the form of physical aggression, property damage, or retributive infidelity (Yoshimura, 2007), and in extreme but not infrequent circumstances it can lead to intimate partner violence and homicide (Pichon et al., 2020). Infidelity may thereby promote a vengeful cycle of deception, contest, and injury between partners (see Boon et al., 2009) that escalates mutual reprisal until the cost of maintaining multiple partnerships (or the pair-bond) overwhelms the benefit.

Thus—as a strategy for satisfying the motive to mate with multiple partners, infidelity is decidedly zero-sum. Certainly, there are advantages to long-term cooperative partnerships in which each individual sacrifices a personal optimum for a relatively higher net collaborative yield (i.e., positive-sum relationships; Axelrod, 1997), such as when children are afforded security and environmental stability by multiparent care (Abraham & Feldman, 2018; Geary, 2000). But the greater net individual benefit of defecting in a trust game (i.e., when one partner cheats but the other does not) suggests that human's evolved mating psychology is configured to motivate calculated deception (i.e., infidelity) (see McNally & Jackson, 2013; Mokkonen & Lindstedt, 2016).

Consensual Nonmonogamy: An Alternative to Infidelity

Consensual nonmonogamy (CNM) is an alternative strategy for resolving the challenges of multipartner mating. CNM is a collection of romantic relationship practices and structures (e.g., polyamory, open relationships, swinging, solo poly, and relationship anarchy) whereby partners agree that it is permissible to have sexual contact or form intimate attachments with other people (see Loue, 2006). Rather than entirely restrict a partner's extra-pair behavior, partners develop and follow guidelines to minimize the harmful or unpleasant consequences of managing multiple partners (Anapol, 1997; Hardy & Easton, 2017). Some studies suggest that about 3–7% of adults in the United States and Canada are in a CNM relationship, and up to 25% have had a CNM relationship in their lifetime (e.g., Fairbrother et al., 2019; Levine et al., 2018; Rubin et al., 2014; Séguin et al., 2017; Haupert, Gesselman, et al., 2017; Haupert, Moors, et al., 2017). Several studies have identified demographic differences between people in CNM and monogamous relationships. Drawing from nationally representative samples in the United States, Haupert, Gesselman, et al. (2017) and Levine et al. (2018) found that CNM relationships were more likely among men and among people identifying as gay, lesbian, or bisexual (see also Moors et al., 2014; Rubin et al., 2014), with prevalence especially high (33%) among people who identify as bisexual (Haupert, Moors et al., 2017).

Swinging, open, and polyamorous relationships have received the most attention from relationship researchers (Barker, 2011; Matsick et al., 2014; Rubel & Bogaert, 2015). Swinging relationships involve couples who engage in extra-pair sexual activity together, and these sexual experiences typically occur without emotional attachment or love for their extra-pair partners (Klesse, 2006; Matsick et al., 2014). Open relationships involve extra-pair sex without love and without a romantic partner's participation (Adam, 2006; Barker & Langdridge, 2010; Jenks, 1998; Matsick et al., 2014). Polyamorous relationships permit loving more than one person, and typically consist of multiple, emotionally intimate relationships (Barker & Langdridge, 2010; Matsick et al., 2014). Although CNM has different structures, research on polyamorous relationships suggests that most people report having two concurrent partners and that it is more common for one partner to be primary and the other(s) to be secondary (Balzarini et al., 2019; Veaux, 2011). Within this configuration, a primary relationship is between two partners who typically have shared investments (e.g., household finances), live together, and/or who are married, whereas relationships with partners beyond the primary relationship are referred to as secondary, nonprimary, or tertiary relationships (Balzarini et al., 2017; Balzarini, Dharma, Kohut, et al., 2019; Klesse, 2006). Although less research has examined partner configurations in open and swinging relationships, they likely adhere to a similar structure where one (or a few) partners are more interdependent (i.e., they share property, are married, or have a high degree of intimacy) and may thus be given relationship affordances that nonprimary partners do not receive (e.g., Buchanan, Poppen, & Reisen, 1996; Poppen et al., 2004).

Compared to infidelity, people in CNM relationships seek and secure, rather than subvert, a partner's informed consent (thus "consensual" nonmonogamy). That is, rather than hide extra-pair attractions, they acknowledge them, allowing partners to discuss and negotiate the boundaries of their relationship. Researchers and practitioners have noted that the relationship maintenance practices of CNM, such as communication and honesty about extra-pair attraction and jealousy (de Visser & McDonald, 2007; McLean, 2004), sexual health practices (Conley et al., 2012; Lehmiller, 2015; Rodrigues, Lopes, & Conley, 2019; Rodrigues, Prada, & Lopes, 2019), and friendliness among romantic partners (Al-Krenawi, 1998), may help minimize the harmful or unpleasant consequences of multipartner mating (see Mogilski et al., 2020). For example, Cohen (2016) found that those practicing CNM consider lying or withholding information to be more indicative of infidelity than extra-pair interactions that have been discussed explicitly. Open communication between partners promotes perceptions of equity in the relationship and trust in one another and commitment (Hangen et al., 2020; McLean, 2004; Moors, Matsick, & Schechinger, 2017a) is helpful in processing jealousy (de Visser & McDonald, 2007) and may help people feel more comfortable discussing the terms of their relationship agreement (e.g., Philpot et al., 2018). Brooks et al. (2021) likewise found that people practicing CNM reported using compromise and negotiation to address relationship conflict more often than those in monogamous relationships. Thus, by refusing to subvert a partner's consent, people practicing CNM may avoid the challenges of multipartner mating and thereby create higher quality or more stable relationships than infidelity.

Existing evidence suggests that people who practice CNM have some success in preventing and/or resolving the potential conflicts introduced by multipartner mating. For example, people practicing CNM report similar or safer sexual health practices on average compared to unfaithful monogamous individuals (Conley et al., 2012; Lehmiller, 2015; though some exceptions exist; Platteau et al., 2017; Rodrigues, Lopes, & Conley, 2019; Rodrigues, Prada, & Lopes, 2019), often establish agreements with partners to facilitate comfort with extra-pair relationships (Wosick-Correa, 2010), and report unique benefits (e.g., more expansive social networks) from forming multiple intimate relationships (see Moors, Matsick, & Schechinger, 2017; see also Balzarini, Dharma, Muise, et al., 2019; Manley et al., 2015; Muise et al., 2019; Murphy et al., 2020). Furthermore, people who practice CNM report relationship outcomes that are comparable to or better than those reported within monogamous relationships (e.g., Conley, Ziegler, et al., 2013; Lehmiller, 2015; Rubel & Bogaert, 2015; Rodrigues et al., 2016; Rodrigues et al., 2017; Rodrigues, Lopes, Pereira, et al., 2019). However, the quality of these relationships seems to depend on whether individuals who pursue CNM benefit from its unique advantages, such as the freedom to form several concurrent intimate partnerships (see Moors, Matsick, & Schechinger, 2017), diversify their relationship need fulfillment with different partners (Balzarini, Dharma, Kohut, et al., 2019; Balzarini, Dharma, Muise, 2019; Mitchell et al., 2014; Muise et al., 2019), have more frequent social interaction and network diversity

(Moors, Matsick, & Schechinger, 2017), and experiment with sexual expression (Manley et al., 2015). Indeed, CNM appears to improve relationship satisfaction more than monogamy for some people (Levine et al., 2018; Rubel, & Bogaert, 2015). People who practice CNM and those who commit infidelity are thus each pursuing multipartner relationships, but CNM appears to produce more positive relationship outcomes. However, it should be noted that the prevalence of infidelity and other challenges to relationship quality (e.g., cuckoldry and partner abandonment) within CNM relationships has not been established.

Although people practicing CNM do not perceive extra-pair involvement as infidelity—if partners adhere to the rules and boundaries of their relationship agreement—they appear to share with monogamous individuals the motive to preserve valuable relationships. Mogilski et al. (2017) found no difference between CNM and monogamous relationships in relationship satisfaction or frequency of mate retention (though only if people practicing CNM reported about their primary partner). They also reported being in a relationship with their primary partner for a longer period of time, and viewed this partner as a more desirable long-term mate, compared to their nonprimary partners. Mogilski et al. (2019) also found that those in CNM relationships were more confident that their primary (compared to secondary) partner would not engage in infidelity (i.e., extra-pair behavior that violates the bounds of their relationship agreement), were more distressed when thinking about that possibility, and mate guarded these partners more often. Other research has shown that within polyamorous relationships, people report more relationship quality (e.g., more commitment and better communication) with their primary partner, even though they spend more time on sexual activity with secondary partners (Balzarini et al., 2017; Balzarini, Dharma, Kohut et al., 2019; Balzarini & Muise, 2020). This suggests that those who are both monogamous and nonmonogamous maintain partnerships (e.g., primary relationships) that satisfy their relationship needs and desires. However, rather than depend on a single partner, people practicing infidelity or CNM share the responsibility of need fulfillment across networks of people, as opposed to concentrating it on a single pair-bond. The difference between infidelity and CNM, then, is a matter of ethics: people who practice CNM secure their partner(s)' consent to form these relationship networks—which helps each partner account and adjust for the impact of extra-pair relationships on in-pair relationship quality—whereas those who commit infidelity do not.

Factors That Impact CNM Relationship Maintenance

Aside from CNM's ethical practices, which appear to discourage the deception and reprisal caused by infidelity (though it should be noted that individual differences in adherence to these practices have not yet been studied), there are several intra- and interpersonal factors associated with peoples' experiences of CNM that may also explain how those who practice CNM manage to peacefully maintain multiple partnerships.

Individual Differences

Although people practicing monogamy and CNM appear to share relational motives, personality may shape a person's willingness to forgo relationship exclusivity. People scoring higher in openness to experience and lower on conscientiousness have more positive attitudes and greater desire for CNM (Moors, Selterman, & Conley, 2017). Moors et al. (2015) found that CNM people were less likely than monogamous people to have an avoidant attachment style. Attachment is defined as an internal working model developed in childhood that can influence relationship experiences and outcomes in adulthood (for reviews, see Mikulincer & Shaver, 2007; Shaver & Hazan, 1987, 1988). To the extent that people low in avoidance do not emotionally distance themselves from their partner (e.g., Mikulincer et al., 2003), these findings suggest that CNM people may better express intimacy, feel closer to their partner, and practice open communication with them (Domingue & Mollen, 2009; Edelstein & Shaver, 2004; Pistole et al., 2010).

Likewise, people who are more willing to have a CNM relationship have more positive attitudes toward CNM (Sizemore & Olmstead, 2018), and both willingness and positive attitudes are associated with sociosexuality (i.e., the tendency to seek out and engage in uncommitted sex; Simpson & Gangestad, 1991). Despite consistent sex differences in sociosexuality, with men reporting a more unrestricted sociosexuality than women (Lippa, 2009; Schmitt, 2005), women and men with positive attitudes toward nonmonogamy, and those who are willing to engage in nonmonogamy, are more unrestricted (Balzarini et al., 2020; Cohen & Wilson, 2017; Sizemore & Olmstead, 2017b). Compared to monogamous people, those who practice CNM are not only more interested in casual sex but also less interested in long-term, committed relationships (Mogilski et al., 2020), have more permissive sexual attitudes, and are more apt to seek out sexual stimulus (see Balzarini et al., 2020). In a monogamous relationship, people with unrestricted sociosexuality are more likely to experience relationship distress (e.g., Webster et al., 2015), report extradyadic behaviors (e.g., Barta & Kiene, 2016; Rodrigues & Lopes, 2017; Rodrigues et al., 2017) and end their relationship (e.g., French et al., 2019). For example, Penke and Asendorpf (2008) found that monogamous people with a restricted sociosexuality were more likely to remain in their relationship one year later, whereas those with an unrestricted sociosexuality were more likely to change romantic partners. This does not necessarily mean that having an unrestricted sociosexuality is at odds with relationship longevity—rather, it might depend on whether partners' sociosexualities are assortatively matched. For example, Markey and Markey (2013) conducted a dyadic study and found that partners with restricted sociosexualities were the most committed, followed by partners with unrestricted sociosexualities. However, the lowest relationship commitment was reported by partners with unmatched sociosexuality. This suggests that partners with similar sociosexualities might be better able to accommodate each other's needs and desires because they share a preferred style of mating. Likewise, CNM may enhance relationship satisfaction for those who wish to act on their desire for extra-pair sexuality. This is supported by data showing that those in CNM relationships who act upon their unrestricted sociosexuality report feeling more satisfied and committed to their relationship (Rodrigues et al., 2016; Rodrigues et al., 2017) and better overall quality of life (Rodrigues, Lopes, Pereira, et al., 2019). For example, when those with greater interest in having sex with multiple partners engage in CNM, they report higher relationship satisfaction (Rodrigues et al., 2017; Rodrigues, Lopes, Pereira, et al., 2019). This suggests that people who form CNM relationships may avoid the fallout of infidelity by choosing a relationship structure that better matches their (and their partner's) mating motives and personalities.

Age may also influence how successfully people manage CNM. Emerging adults are in a developmental period in which they are exploring their identity and experimenting with sexuality (Arnett, 2015). Despite having implicit positive attitudes toward monogamy, these people have neutral implicit and explicit attitudes toward nonmonogamy (Thompson et al., 2018; Thompson, Moore, et al., 2020). By not rejecting nonmonogamy, emerging adults might be more predisposed to try it. Indeed, Sizemore and Olmstead (2018) found that 21% of emerging adults were willing or open-minded about the possibility of having a CNM experience, and Stephens and Emmers-Sommer (2020) found that 48% of emerging adults in their sample were currently in polyamorous, monogamish, open, negotiable, swinging, or other type of CNM relationship. Nevertheless, interest in CNM is higher among adults in mid versus emerging adulthood (Lehmiller, 2018). Hangen et al. (2020) showed that younger individuals in multipartner relationships report lower levels of consent, comfort, and communication and experience more relationship distress than those who are older. This suggests that younger populations may be more susceptible to interpersonal conflict caused by multipartner mating, possibly because they have not yet had time to learn how to navigate these experiences.

Sexual and gender diversity may also correlate with the proclivity or capacity to practice CNM. Compared to heterosexuals, LGBTQ+ individuals have more positive attitudes toward CNM (Currin et al., 2016), are more likely to report being in a CNM relationship (Haupert, Moors, et al., 2017; Moors et al., 2014; Rubin et al., 2014), report different experiences with jealousy (de Visser et al., 2020; Dijkstra et al., 2001; Harris, 2002; Valentova et al., 2020), and report more diverse romantic relationship experiences and structures (see Valentova et al., this volume; Holland, this volume). One factor that may explain these differences is the degree to which individuals within sexually diverse relationships (i.e., those involving one or more individuals who experience same-sex attraction) compromise about sex-typical relationship motives and preferences (see Sagarin et al., 2012). That is, sexual conflict may be less common if partners' sex/gender are matched. For example, Scherer et al. (2013) found that bisexual men in monogamous relationships with women were more concerned about their partner's sexual infidelity than those who were with male partners. Partners with a similar sex or gender may also have a better understanding of the other's sex-typical mating preferences and anxieties. Thus, LGBTQ+

individuals may be more likely to share attraction to extra-pair partners, have relatable jealousy experiences, or hold similar interest in extra-pair sex or romance. Lippa (2020) found that in a diverse U.S. sample (1,437 men, 1,474 women), non-heterosexual men and women reported a similarly higher sex drive and more unrestricted sociosexuality than heterosexual people. Gender diverse relationships (i.e., those with one or more individuals whose pattern of gender identity or expression does not match their birth-assigned sex/gender) may likewise differ to the degree that sex and gender are (in)congruent between partners, and therefore whether sexual conflict is a prominent concern (see Arístegui et al., 2018, 2019). That said, intrasexual competitive concerns may yet feature prominently in same-sex romantic relationships and affect relationship functioning (Pachankis et al., 2020; Semenyna et al., 2020; also see Buunk & Dijkstra, 2001). Likewise, the compounding social condemnation of being LGBTQ+ and CNM could further expose sexually and gender diverse people to the interpersonal challenges of stigma, reputation management, and wrongful discrimination (see Diamond & Alley, this volume).

Social Stigma

Stigma has been shown to affect the quality and practice of CNM. Stigma against CNM is robust, with 26 to 43% of people in polyamorous relationships reporting experiences of stigma and discrimination. Illustrating stigma's pervasiveness, Conley, Moors et al. (2013) found that monogamous targets were rated more positively than polyamorists in relationship-relevant and relationship-irrelevant domains. For example, monogamous people were perceived not only to be more trustworthy and passionate but also more likely to pay their taxes on time, to floss their teeth, and to walk their dog. Balzarini et al. (2018) asked participants to make a series of judgments about romantic partners in monogamous, open, polyamorous, and swinging relationships. Monogamous participants reported wanting more social distance from all CNM groups and perceived them as more promiscuous and more likely to have sexually transmitted infections. To a lesser extent, this negative appraisal was also observed when CNM participants evaluated relationship agreements that were different from their own, thus evidencing some in-group favoritism (Marques et al., 1998). Indeed, CNM peoples' perceptions conformed to how monogamous people perceive different CNM relationships. For example, Grunt-Mejer and Campbell (2016) presented participants with vignettes describing partners in monogamous, polyamorous, open, swinging, or cheating relationships and asked them to rate those partners on several attributes. Participants perceived monogamous partners as the most satisfied and moral, and as having superior cognitive abilities. Cheating partners—those who wanted to maintain their relationships, but at the same time engaged in affairs that they suspected would end their marriage if the other knew—received the most negative appraisals. Interestingly, participants evaluated polyamorous partners more positively than open or swinging partners, possibly because polyamorous people are motivated to establish an emotional connection with other people, instead of solely casual sex (Matsick et al., 2014), and are perceived to be less likely to have a sexually transmitted infection (Balzarini et al., 2018), which may explain why they are stigmatized to a lesser extent (but see also Séguin et al., 2017).

Accordingly, it has been argued that monogamy is the "gold standard" of romantic relationships, with the assumption being that sexual and emotional exclusivity is ideal (Conley et al., 2017; Ziegler et al., 2015). Moral stigma against CNM, then, may be caused by the perception that CNM undermines monogamy (Emens, 2004). Indeed, CNM could threaten monogamy by offering monogamous partners the opportunity to leave an exclusive relationship if it becomes unpropitious. If CNM were predominant over monogamy, this could drastically increase a partner's pool of available alternative mates. It should then be observed that those for whom an open mating market is advantageous will have more favorable attitudes toward CNM. That is, CNM may be preferred by those who are well-suited or motivated to compete with others for access to romantic/sexual partners, while those who are not might attempt to publicly enforce monogamy to restrict intrasexual competition.

Restricting intrasexual competition is a reasonable moral aim. Higher rates of intrasexual competition may lead to public and personal health risks, such as higher rates of mortality and homicide (Daly & Wilson, 2001; Kruger, 2010), anabolic steroid use among men (Harris et al., 2019), interpersonal antagonism and/or social ostracism (Vaillancourt & Sharma, 2011), problematic eating habits among women (Li et al., 2010), and risky medical procedures (Dubbs et al., 2017). In this sense, those who condemn CNM may be attempting to curtail the harms caused by rivalry within multipartner mating systems. Mogilski et al. (2020) likewise suggested that people might assume that those who practice CNM engage in riskier, more competitive interpersonal behaviors that strain social cooperation. Indeed, they found that people in CNM compared to monogamous relationships reported higher social and ethical risk-taking, along with several other traits that are characteristic of a "fast life history" (e.g., earlier pubertal development, less aversion to germs, and greater interest in short-term [and less interest in long-term] relationships) (reviewed in Figueredo et al., 2006; see also Del Giudice et al., 2016). Therefore, people may publicly endorse orthodox monogamy if they believe that doing so will protect them (or their social networks) from the harms of intrasexual competition.

However, intrasexual competition can also improve well-being. People who compete for partners may spend more time enhancing their mating market value by self-beautifying (Wang et al., 2021), engaging in regular exercise (Jonason, 2007), or otherwise improving qualities that a partner might find desirable (musical ability, intelligence, etc.) (Miller, 2000). If these efforts are extreme or pose a health risk, then they are clearly harmful. But a moderate amount of rivalry between partners could motivate physical or mental health improvement—perhaps especially if their rivalry is mutually respectful. Indeed, showing respect for a rival in nonromantic contexts has been shown to ease tension and promote affiliation after conflict (see Wolf, 2011; also see Pham et al., 2017). In this sense, CNM practices which encourage friendship or collaboration between in- and extra-pair partners may be particularly effective at reducing the conflict often associated multipartner mating. In other words, people who practice CNM may be harnessing the self-enhancement of intrasexual competition while suppressing the zero-sum feuds that it can produce.

There is also evidence that CNM people are dehumanized (Rodrigues et al., 2018; Rodrigues et al., 2021). Dehumanization occurs when people are not credited with attributes that are uniquely human (Haslam, 2006). This phenomenon is observed between people from different countries, ethnicities, or social groups (for a review, see Haslam & Loughnan, 2014). For example, people dehumanize others when they perceive them to lack secondary emotions which are putatively unique to humans (e.g., love and embarrassment), and instead only experience primary emotions that are shared with other nonhuman animals (e.g., anger and desire) (Demoulin et al., 2004; Leyens et al., 2000, 2001; Vaes et al., 2012). Dehumanization has been associated with negative psychological and physical consequences, such that dehumanized people are victims of verbal and physical abuse (e.g., Rai et al., 2017), including in romantic relationships (Pizzirani et al., 2019; Pizzirani & Karantzas, 2019). In a cross-national study, Rodrigues et al. (2018) presented participants with vignettes depicting partners in a committed monogamous relationship or in a committed CNM relationship, and then asked them to attribute primary and secondary emotions to those partners. Portuguese, Croatian, and Italian participants attributed more secondary emotions (e.g., fear and pleasure) to monogamous partners and more primary emotions (e.g., guilt and compassion) to CNM partners. These findings were independent of the sexual orientation of the partners depicted in the vignettes (see also Moors et al., 2013), suggesting that departures from mononormativity (rather than heteronormativity) were more important in determining stigmatization. In a follow-up study, Rodrigues et al. (2021) showed that participants attributed more secondary emotions to monogamous partners, and more primary emotions to open or polyamorous partners (no differences were found between the latter). Additional analysis suggested that the dehumanization of CNM partners occurred because participants perceived them as more immoral and less committed to their relationship. Neither perceived promiscuity nor perceived sexual satisfaction emerged as significant mediators. Much like other groups that are dehumanized, CNM people are also at risk of negative psychological, physical, and social outcomes. For example, the experience of stigma may affect whether CNM people disclose their identity to close others (Valadez et al., 2020), trust the healthcare system to address their specific health needs (e.g., increased sexual health screening; Vaughan et al., 2019), or maintain their therapeutic relationships after seeking psychological help (Schechinger et al., 2018).

Stigma may thereby shape whether or how someone engages in CNM. The threat of admonishment from friends and family may lead people with an interest in multipartner mating to form these relationships secretively. For example, people report maintaining secondary/tertiary partners in secrecy more often than CNM primary and monogamous partners (Balzarini et al., 2017; Balzarini, Dharma, Kohut, et al., 2019). People report lower relationship quality and satisfaction with secret partners (Foster & Campbell, 2005), and people in CNM relationships report greater stigma, more secrecy, and less satisfaction with secondary compared to primary partners (Balzarini et al., 2017; Balzarini, Dharma, Kohut, et al., 2019). Indeed, it is possible that secrecy explains observed differences between primary and nonprimary partners. People may feel less committed to a nonprimary relationship if its public discovery would make the relationship costly to maintain. Partners may therefore spend more time in private with this person, allowing more time for sex, and less time engaging in public activities that might reinforce commitment (family gatherings, work events, etc.). Secrecy may also undermine commitment between partners by constraining how close partners feel (Lehmiller, 2009). Stigma may thus interfere with how well CNM is maintained. The cost of a hidden relationship is that actions may occur within the relationship that impact the person (or people) from whom the relationship is hidden. Without explicit knowledge of the relationship (i.e., consent), hidden courtship could bias resource allocation (e.g., time spent together, living situation, financial interdependence) away from a partner who expects otherwise.

There is reason to believe that stigma against CNM will diminish as people become more aware of its practices. Moors (2017) found a significant increase in searches containing words related to nonmonogamy (particularly polyamory and open relationship) over a 10-year period in the United States. Based on the contact hypothesis, whereby knowledge and contact with a given social group can buffer negative appraisals toward that group (Allport, 1954; Paluck et al., 2019; Pettigrew & Tropp, 2006), an increased interest in or knowledge of CNM might help buffer stigma. Hutzler et al. (2016), for example, found that people who were experimentally provided information about polyamorous practices reported more positive attitudes toward it than those for whom polyamory was simply defined. Similarly, Rodrigues et al. (2021) found that CNM partners were dehumanized to a lesser extent by participants with more positive (vs. more negative) attitudes toward nonmonogamy. If stigma against CNM diminishes over time, this may help alleviate the harms of secretive multipartner mating.

Future Directions

Together, this research suggests that CNM is an alternative strategy to infidelity for satisfying the motives that drive multipartner mating. We have outlined how one's success in maintaining stable, cooperative, and satisfying bonds with multiple concurrent partners will depend on several intersecting variables: (a) which multipartner relationship maintenance practices (jealousy regulation, disclosure of extra-pair relationships, etc.) are adopted in these relationships, (b) whether one's personal features are suited to a nonmonogamous relationship structure (e.g., sociosexuality and current life stage), and (c) whether external pressures (e.g., social stigma) shape how people communicate about their extra-pair relationship experiences and impact relationship processes (commitment, investment into partners, etc.). However, it must be noted that extant literature on CNM is limited in several important respects. In this section, we suggest an agenda for future research that aims to address these limitations and enhance our understanding of CNM.

First, most studies on nonmonogamy in relationships have conflated nonconsensual nonmonogamy (i.e., infidelity and cheating) with CNM (for a review, see Lehmiller & Selterman, 2022). This has several unfortunate implications, one of which is that it is difficult to establish the population prevalence of each form of nonmonogamy. For example, it is common practice on nationally representative surveys to conceptualize "infidelity" as engaging in sexual activity with a person other than one's spouse (e.g., Atkins et al., 2001). Use of broad operational definitions such as this has had the effect of overstating the prevalence of infidelity and rendering CNM invisible. It is vital that future work disentangles various forms of nonmonogamy, with the goal of identifying which practices predict lower relationship satisfaction and/or commitment (see Rodrigues et al., 2017). Related to this, little work has explored the factors that predict engagement in consensual versus nonconsensual nonmonogamy and the degree to which they are similar or different. Some work suggests that the predictors are distinct—for example, low sexual satisfaction is linked to more fantasies of infidelity, whereas sexual satisfaction is unrelated to fantasies about practicing CNM (Lehmiller, 2020). This suggests the possibility that what drives people to cheat versus pursue some type of open relationship may be unique.

Second, most research has treated CNM as a monolithic category, failing to distinguish between the forms these relationships can take, including polyamory, swinging, open relationships, and "cuckolding" (a variant of swinging that involves a relationship in which one partner watches or listens while their partner has sex with another person; Lehmiller et al., 2018). The result is that it is unclear which types of CNM are more versus less common. In addition, it is unclear whether there are differences in the demographic characteristics of people attracted to different types of CNM, the relationship maintenance strategies that are most common or effective for each arrangement, and the relationship outcomes of each type of CNM. This is important to explore because research suggests that there are likely differences in which types of CNM are most common and the characteristics of persons attracted to each form. For example, in a study of people in monogamous romantic relationships who were asked to report on the frequency with which they fantasized about various types of CNM, 68% reported having ever fantasized about being in an open relationship, 58% had fantasized about being polyamorous, 57% had fantasized about swinging, and 51% had fantasized about cuckolding their partner (Lehmiller, 2020). Those who identified as men or as nonbinary were more likely to report fantasizing about all forms of CNM compared to those who identified as women; however, open relationships were the one variant of CNM that a majority of participants—regardless of sex or gender identity—reported having fantasized about, suggesting that this might be the most commonly pursued form of CNM. Furthermore, different personality traits, attachment styles, and sexual orientations uniquely predicted fantasies about each type of CNM, suggesting that different groups of people are likely drawn to each variant.

Third, most studies of CNM have been based on reports from one, rather than all, partners' perspectives of their relationship. Increasingly, research on monogamous relationships has recognized the value of surveying both partners, given that there are often cross-over effects, with each partner's perceptions contributing unique variance to outcome predictions (e.g., Barr & Simons, 2014). It is unclear to what extent such effects also occur in relationships among more than two partners. This is important because we also know that people practicing CNM sometimes have different perceptions of the "rules" and structure of their relationship, which could reasonably be expected to affect their relational outcomes. For example, in Hoff and Beougher's (2010) study of sexual agreements among men in same-sex relationships, 5% reported discrepant understandings of their arrangement (e.g., one partner believed the relationship was open while the other did not). In CNM, it is vital to know not just what the structure of the relationship is but also whether partners are abiding by the same set of rules. Of course, the same is true for research on monogamous relationships—monogamous partners often do not agree when it comes to their relational boundaries, which can have implications for whether they even agree that infidelity occurred (Warren et al., 2012).

Fourth, more longitudinal research on CNM is needed. Most work to date has been cross-sectional, which makes it difficult to understand how CNM relationships might change over time, as well as what happens when people in monogamous relationships decide to open their relationship to some degree. Murphy et al. (2020) conducted the first prospective study of monogamous people who were considering opening their relationship in some way. Most participants (67%) who thought about doing so did in fact open their relationship before the two-month follow-up assessment. The researchers did not find any changes in relationship satisfaction for openers and nonopeners; however, those who opened their relationships reported an increase in sexual satisfaction, whereas the nonopeners experienced a decline. This suggests that studying the transition from monogamy to CNM could reveal how people evaluate their intimate lives, particularly in terms of their sexual satisfaction. However, the time frame in this study was quite limited (i.e., two months), the researchers did not take into account how gender and sexual orientation might impact perceptions, and they did not consider whether different types of CNM might have different trajectories. More research is therefore needed to better understand the complexities and nuances of how opening a relationship might change the course of the relationship itself. Certainly, this is a tall order—funding for relationship research in general is scarce, especially relationships that deviate from what is considered "normal" by many funding agencies. Thus, securing funding to recruit a sample with each partner in a CNM that also has sufficient statistical power is likely to be challenging; however, there is much to be learned from such lines of inquiry. Furthermore, it is common for people pursuing CNM to change or adjust the rules or structure of their relationship over time, in part, because nonmonogamy agreements are sometimes broken (Hoff & Beougher, 2010; Prestage et al., 2006). For example, partners in CNM relationships may have various rules (e.g., condom usage is required with some partners but not others, kissing and/or other intimate activities may be off-limits with certain partners) but fail to abide by them. This raises the more general question of what "infidelity" means in a CNM relationship. Generally speaking, it is defined relative to the unique set of rules that partners negotiate; however, little research has explored how those practicing CNM navigate instances of infidelity, the prevalence of infidelity in CNM, and what ultimately happens in CNM relationships when transgressions are discovered.

Fifth, research on multipartner sex (e.g., threesomes, orgies, and other forms of group sex) has traditionally been separate from research on CNM. Research on CNM rarely makes mention of group sex (Thompson, Cipriano, et al., 2020); however, group encounters are often permitted within CNM, including swinging (Houngbedji & Guilem, 2016), open relationships (Hosking, 2014), and polyamory (Wosick-Correa, 2010). Likewise, in a recent study of mixed-gender threesomes (MGTs), two thirds (65%) of those who identified as being in a CNM relationship reported having experienced an MGT previously (Thompson, Cipriano, et al., 2020). All this suggests that multipartner sex is a common part of relationships that are consensually nonmonogamous (although, of course, not everyone practicing CNM is interested in or has experience with group sex). Future research would do well to explore the degree to which multipartner sex is permitted within CNM, as well as how group sexual activity affects CNM relationship dynamics. For example, group sex might be a way by which all partners sexually engage and intimately bond at the same time, thereby strengthening the relationships between everyone. Likewise, those in swinging, cuckolding, or open relationships might also engage in group activities—but the dynamic and impact on relationship quality or stability might be quite different in these relationships, particularly if everyone does not equally desire a multipartner encounter or if partners are pursuing it for different reasons.

Sixth, most theories and models of romantic relationships are premised on the assumption that everyone is or wants to be monogamous. For example, Rusbult's (1980) investment model of commitment posits that one of the three key factors predicting high relationship commitment is the perception of undesirable romantic alternatives. In other words, the idea that one might find alternative partners to be sexually or romantically appealing is presumed to undermine commitment to one's existing relationship. Generally speaking, research (primarily based on monogamous samples) has found that the perception of desirable alternatives is consistently linked to lower commitment (Rusbult et al., 1998); however, in a study of polyamorous relationships, quality of alternatives emerged as the weakest commitment predictor, it did not predict commitment to primary partners at all, and greater quality of alternatives actually predicted *more* commitment to a secondary partner (Balzarini et al., 2017). These results imply that the concept of relationship alternatives may be perceived differently in a CNM context: rather than viewing alternatives as all-or-nothing replacements for a given partner, they may be perceived as relationship additions. This suggests that key premises of many popular models of relationships may not apply to CNM. Multiple relationship theories, from commitment to jealousy to attachment, are therefore ripe for expansion. Many of the principles widely believed to be characteristic of healthy relationships may be flawed because they are based on an assumption of monogamy.

Finally, it is unclear to what extent the existing research on CNM is globally generalizable. Most academic research on CNM is limited to WEIRD (Western, educated, industrialized, rich, and democratic) cultures. Moreover, this research is usually limited to online convenience samples, which may select for those who are more "out" or open about their relationship status. Many people practicing CNM may be underrepresented in extant work due to the pervasive stigma that exists against these relationships (Conley, Moors, et al., 2013; Rodrigues et al., 2018, 2021), and this may be especially true for those who live in rural and/or politically or religiously conservative areas. Obtaining representative samples of people practicing CNM is another tall order and one that poses significant funding challenges; however, it is vital for ensuring the generalizability of this body of research. At the very least, it is important that those who are collecting nationally representative data are not just attentive to the existence of CNM but are also equipped to ask sufficiently nuanced questions that disentangle the diverse array of CNM practices and characteristics.

Final Considerations

We have argued that it may be fruitful to view CNM as a collection of "alternative strategies" (Clutton-Brock, 1989; Selander, 1965; Setchell, 2008) for overcoming the challenges and conflicts of human mating (see Buss & Schmitt, 2019). Sexual subcultures like CNM have developed sophisticated relationship maintenance and conflict resolution strategies for managing multipartner mating. Though certain personalities and sexualities are drawn to different variations of CNM (e.g., polyamory, swinging, and open relationships), partners who practice CNM commonly communicate their extra-pair attractions and negotiate how or whether partners will act on these attractions. This empowers each partner to make relationship decisions based on informed knowledge of a partner's current or potential extra-pair sexual/emotional relationships. This may prevent or resolve relationship conflict caused by multipartner mating because partners are afforded a more accurate estimate of each other's current and anticipated relationship investments. Partners can thus work together to deliberately avoid costly, zero-sum relationship outcomes—or independently decide to leave their relationship. By comparison, infidelity subverts a partner's agency to likewise pursue multipartner mating. It is this difference in relationship maintenance philosophy, in combination with other dispositional (e.g., sociosexuality, attachment, age, and sexual orientation) and situational factors (e.g., the propitiousness of an open mating market and third-party condemnation or stigma), that appears to yield more positive relationship outcomes for those who pursue multimating by CNM rather than infidelity.

If CNM is a more stable or satisfactory relationship structure for some people, then it may be harmful to believe or legislate that people should be uniformly monogamous. Instead, social policy about sexual behavior might focus on regulating and preventing the conflict caused by infidelity and intrasexual competition, rather than restrict multipartner mating altogether. An important step in achieving effective prevention might be to legalize plural marriage or recognize domestic partnerships between more than two people. This has already happened in several areas of the United States. If multipartner mating is publicly recognized and permitted, then people who pursue nonmonogamy secretly will have less reason to hide it. In turn, social acceptance may encourage those who are experiencing poor relationship outcomes (e.g., domestic violence and partner abandonment) to share their experiences, seek support, and learn about other styles of relating with their partner(s). Indeed, research in nonhuman primates, for example, suggests that normalizing and supporting alloparental care networks could help buffer struggling mothers against the temptation to deliberately harm their children (Hrdy, 2016).

Evolutionary biological research on sexual conflict has considered how reproductive partners with different mating optima negotiate sexual cooperation (Servedio et al., 2019). We predict that by developing more ethical strategies for resolving the adaptive problems caused by multipartner mating, CNM practitioners may do a better job of achieving sexual cooperation than those who commit infidelity—insofar as they adhere to their relationship agreement. Research that identifies how people in CNM relationships manage their extra-pair attractions, whether these strategies resolve the recurrent challenges of sexual conflict (e.g., cuckoldry and in-pair divestment), and how faithfully people engage in its best ethical practices is yet to be demonstrated (also see Mogilski et al., 2020). But this research promises to reveal affiliative strategies for resolving conflict caused extra-pair partnerships that may, in some cases, also be applicable to monogamy. If the scientific community could produce an evidence-based, data-driven, theoretically coherent framework that describes which multipartner relationship maintenance practices produce better relationship outcomes for different people and relationship structures, this information could help people navigate the complexities of maintaining positive-sum relationships with multiple concurrent partners.

References

Abraham, E., & Feldman, R. (2018). The neurobiology of human allomaternal care: Implications for fathering, coparenting, and children's social development. *Physiology & Behavior, 193*, 25–34.

Adam, B. D. (2006). Relationship innovation in male couples. *Sexualities, 9*, 5–26.

Al-Krenawi, A. (1998). Family therapy with a multiparental/multispousal family. *Family Process, 37*(1), 65–81.

Allport, G. (1954). *The nature of prejudice*. Perseus Books.

Anapol, D. (1997). *Polyamory: The new love without limits*. IntiNet Resource Center.

Anderson, K. (2006). How well does paternity confidence match actual paternity? Evidence from worldwide nonpaternity rates. *Current Anthropology, 47*(3), 513–520.

Arístegui, I., Castro Solano, A., & Buunk, A. P. (2018). Mate preferences in Argentinean transgender people: An evolutionary perspective. *Personal Relationships*, *25*(3), 330–350.

Arístegui, I., Castro Solano, A., & Buunk, A. P. (2019). Do transgender people respond according to their biological sex or their gender identity when confronted with romantic rivals? *Evolutionary Psychology*, *17*(2), Article 1474704919851139.

Arnett, J. J. (2015). *The Oxford handbook of emerging adulthood*. Oxford University Press.

Atkins, D. C., Baucom, D. H., & Jacobson, N. S. (2001). Understanding infidelity: Correlates in a national random sample. *Journal of Family Psychology*, *15*(4), 735–749.

Axelrod, R. (1997). *The complexity of cooperation: Vol. 3. Agent-based models of competition and collaboration*. Princeton University Press.

Badcock, P. B., Smith, A. M., Richters, J., Rissel, C., de Visser, R. O., Simpson, J. M., & Grulich, A. E. (2014). Characteristics of heterosexual regular relationships among a representative sample of adults: The Second Australian Study of Health and Relationships. *Sexual Health*, *11*(5), 427–438.

Balzarini, R. N., Campbell, L., Kohut, T., Holmes, B. M., Lehmiller, J. J., Harman, J. J., & Atkins, N. (2017). Perceptions of primary and secondary relationships in polyamory. *PLoS ONE*, *12*(5), e0177841.

Balzarini, R. N., Dharma, C., Kohut, T., Campbell, L., Lehmiller, J. J., Harman, J. J., & Holmes, B. M. (2019). Comparing relationship quality across different types of romantic partners in polyamorous and monogamous relationships. *Archives of Sexual Behavior*, *48*(6), 1749–1767.

Balzarini, R. N., Dharma, C., Muise, A., & Kohut, T. (2019). Eroticism versus nurturance: How eroticism and nurturance differ in polyamorous and monogamous relationships. *Social Psychology*, *50*, 185–200.

Balzarini, R. N., & Muise, A. (2020). Beyond the dyad: A review of the novel insights gained from studying consensual non-monogamy. *Current Sexual Health Reports*, *12*, 398–404.

Balzarini, R. N., Shumlich, E. J., Kohut, T., & Campbell, L. (2018). Dimming the "halo" around monogamy: Re-assessing stigma surrounding consensually non-monogamous romantic relationships as a function of personal relationship orientation. *Frontiers in Psychology*, *9*, Article 894. https://doi.org/10.3389/fpsyg.2018.00894

Balzarini, R. N., Shumlich, E., Kohut, T., & Campbell, L. (2020). Sexual attitudes, opinions, and sociosexual orientation differ based on relationship orientation. *Journal of Sex Research*, *57*, 458–469.

Barclay, P. (2013). Strategies for cooperation in biological markets, especially for humans. *Evolution and Human Behavior*, *34*(3), 164–175.

Barker, M. (2011). Monogamies and non-monogamies—A response to: "The challenge of monogamy: Bringing it out of the closet and into the treatment room" by Marianne Brandon. *Sexual and Relationship Therapy*, *26*, 281–287.

Barker, M., & Langdridge, D. (2010). Whatever happened to non-monogamies? Critical reflections on recent research and theory. *Sexualities*, *13*, 748–772.

Barr, A. B., & Simons, R. L. (2014). A dyadic analysis of relationships and health: Does couple-level context condition partner effects? *Journal of Family Psychology*, *28*(4), 448.

Barta, W. D., & Kiene, S. M. (2016). Motivations for infidelity in heterosexual dating couples: The roles of gender, personality differences, and sociosexual orientation. *Journal of Social and Personal Relationships*, *22*(3), 339–360. https://doi.org/10.1177/0265407505052440

Betzig, L. (1989). Causes of conjugal dissolution: A cross-cultural study. *Current Anthropology*, *30*(5), 654–676.

Boon, S. D., Deveau, V. L., & Alibhai, A. M. (2009). Payback: The parameters of revenge in romantic relationships. *Journal of Social and Personal Relationships*, *26*(6–7), 747–768.

Brooks, T. R., Shaw, J., Reysen, S., & Henley, T. B. (2021). The vices and virtues of consensual non-monogamy: A relational dimension investigation. *Psychology & Sexuality*.

Buchanan, D. R., Poppen, P. J., & Reisen, C. A. (1996). The nature of partner relationship and AIDS sexual risk-taking in gay men. *Psychology and Health*, *11*, 541–555.

Buss, D. M. (2017). Sexual conflict in human mating. *Current Directions in Psychological Science*, *26*(4), 307–313.

Buss, D. M., Goetz, C., Duntley, J. D., Asao, K., & Conroy-Beam, D. (2017). The mate switching hypothesis. *Personality and Individual Differences*, *104*, 143–149.

Buss, D. M., & Schmitt, D. P. (1993). Sexual strategies theory: An evolutionary perspective on human mating. *Psychological Review*, *100*(2), 204–232.

Buss, D. M., & Schmitt, D. P. (2019). Mate preferences and their behavioral manifestations. *Annual Review of Psychology*, *70*, 77–110.

Buunk, B. P., & Dijkstra, P. (2001). Evidence from a homosexual sample for a sex-specific rival-oriented mechanism: Jealousy as a function of a rival's physical attractiveness and dominance. *Personal Relationships, 8*(4), 391–406.

Buunk, A. P., & Massar, K. (2019). Intimate partner violence in Nicaragua: The role of possessive jealousy, intrasexual competitiveness, life history, mate value, and stress. *Journal of Interpersonal Violence*, Article 0886260519842854.

Clutton-Brock, T. H. (1989). Review lecture: Mammalian mating systems. *Proceedings of the Royal Society of London. B. Biological Sciences, 236*(1285), 339–372.

Cohen, M. T. (2016). An exploratory study of individuals in non-traditional, alternative relationships: How "open" are we? *Sexuality & Culture, 20*(2), 295–315. https://doi.org/10.1007/s12119-015-9324-z

Cohen, M. T., & Wilson, K. (2017). Development of the Consensual Non-Monogamy Attitude Scale (CNAS). *Sexuality & Culture, 21*(1), 1–14. https://doi.org/10.1007/s12119-016-9395-5

Conley, T. D., Matsick., J., Moors., A. C., & Ziegler, A. (2017). Investigation of consensually nonmonogamous relationships: Theories, methods, and new directions. *Perspectives on Psychological Science, 12*, 205–232.

Conley, T. D., Moors, A. C., Matsick, J. L., & Ziegler, A. (2013). The fewer the merrier? Assessing stigma surrounding consensually non-monogamous romantic relationships. *Analyses of Social Issues and Public Policy, 13*(1), 1–30. https://doi.org/10.1111/j.1530-2415.2012.01286.x

Conley, T. D., Moors, A. C., Ziegler, A., & Karathanasis, C. (2012). Unfaithful individuals are less likely to practice safer sex than openly nonmonogamous individuals. *Journal of Sexual Medicine, 9*, 1559–1565. https://doi.org/10.1111/j.1743-6109.2012.02712.x

Conley, T. D., Ziegler, A., Moors, A. C., Matsick, J., & Valentine, B. (2013). A critical examination of popular assumptions about the benefits and outcomes of monogamous relationships. *Personality and Social Psychology Review, 2*, 124–141.

Crouch, E., & Dickes, L. (2016). Economic repercussions of marital infidelity. *International Journal of Sociology and Social Policy, 36*(1/2), 13.

Currin, J. M., Hubach, R. D., Brown, C., & Farley, S. (2016). Impact of non-heterosexual impulses on heterosexuals' attitudes towards monogamy and casual sex. *Psychology & Sexuality, 7*(3), 197–210.

Daly, M., & Wilson, M. (2001). *Risk-taking, intrasexual competition, and homicide.* In J. A. French, A. C. Kamil, & D. W. Leger (Eds.), *Nebraska symposium on motivation. Evolutionary psychology and motivation* (Vol. 47, pp. 1–36). University of Nebraska Press.

Del Giudice, M., Gangestad, S. W., & Kaplan, H. S. (2016). Life history theory and evolutionary psychology. In D. M. Buss (Ed.), The handbook of evolutionary psychology: *Foundations* (pp. 88–114). John Wiley and Sons.

Demoulin, S., Leyens, J.-P., Paladino, M.-P., Rodriguez-Torres, R., Rodriguez-Perez, A., & Dovidio, J. (2004). Dimensions of "uniquely" and "non-uniquely" human emotions. *Cognition and Emotion, 18*, 71–96. https://doi.org/10.1080/02699930244000444

de Visser, R., & McDonald, D. (2007). Swings and roundabouts: Management of jealousy in heterosexual "swinging" couples. *British Journal of Social Psychology, 46*(2), 459–476. https://doi.org/10.1348/014466606X143153

de Visser, R., Richters, J., Rissel, C., Grulich, A., Simpson, J., Rodrigues, D. L., & Lopes, D. (2020). Romantic jealousy: A test of social cognitive and evolutionary models in a population-representative sample of adults. *The Journal of Sex Research, 57*(4), 498–507. https://doi.org/10.1080/00224499.2019.1613482

Dijkstra, P., Groothof, H. A., Poel, G. A., Laverman, E. T., Schrier, M., & Buunk, B. P. (2001). Sex differences in the events that elicit jealousy among homosexuals. *Personal Relationships, 8*(1), 41–54.

Domingue, R., & Mollen, D. (2009). Attachment and conflict communication in adult romantic relationships. *Journal of Social and Personal Relationships, 26*(5), 678–696. https://doi.org/10.1177/0265407509347932

Dubbs, S. L., Kelly, A. J., & Barlow, F. K. (2017). Ravishing rivals: Female intrasexual competition and cosmetic surgery. *The Oxford handbook of women and competition* (pp. 597–615). Oxford University Press.

Edelstein, R. S., & Shaver, P. R. (2004). Avoidant attachment: Exploration of an oxymoron. In D. J. Mashek & A. P. Aron (Eds.), *Handbook of closeness and intimacy* (pp. 397–412). Erlbaum.

Emens, E. F. (2004). Monogamy's law: Compulsory monogamy and polyamorous existence. *NYU Review of Law & Social Change, 29*, 277–376

Fairbrother, N., Hart, T. A., & Fairbrother, M. (2019). Open relationship prevalence, characteristics, and correlates in a nationally representative sample of Canadian adults. *Journal of Sex Research, 56*, 695–704.

Figueredo, A. J., Vásquez, G., Brumbach, B. H., Schneider, S. M., Sefcek, J. A., Tal, I. R., Hill, D., & Wenner, C. J., & Jacobs, W. J. (2006). Consilience and life history theory: From genes to brain to reproductive strategy. *Developmental Review, 26*(2), 243–275.

Foster, C. A., & Campbell, W. K. (2005). The adversity of secret relationships. *Personal Relationships, 12*(1), 125–143.

French, J. E., Altgelt, E. E., & Meltzer, A. L. (2019). The implications of sociosexuality for marital satisfaction and dissolution. *Psychological Science, 30*(10), 1460–1472. https://doi.org/10.1177/0956797619868997

Gangestad, S. W., & Simpson, J. A. (2000). The evolution of human mating: Trade-offs and strategic pluralism. *Behavioral and Brain Sciences, 23*(4), 573–587.

Geary, D. C. (2000). Evolution and proximate expression of human paternal investment. *Psychological Bulletin, 126*(1), 55.

Grunt-Mejer, K., & Campbell, C. (2016). Around consensual nonmonogamies: Assessing attitudes toward nonexclusive relationships. *The Journal of Sex Research, 53*(1), 45–53. https://doi.org/10.1080/00224499.2015.1010193

Hangen, F., Crasta, D., & Rogge, R. D. (2020). Delineating the boundaries between nonmonogamy and infidelity: Bringing consent back into definitions of consensual nonmonogamy with latent profile analysis. *The Journal of Sex Research, 57*(4), 438–457. https://doi.org/10.1080/00224499.2019.1669133

Hardy, J. W., & Easton, D. (2017). *The ethical slut: A practical guide to polyamory, open relationships, and other adventures* (3rd ed.). Penguin Random House.

Harris, C. R. (2002). Sexual and romantic jealousy in heterosexual and homosexual adults. *Psychological Science, 13*(1), 7–12.

Harris, M., Dunn, M., & Alwyn, T. (2019). Intrasexual competition as a potential influence on anabolic-androgenic steroid use initiation. *Journal of Health Psychology, 24*(9), 1210–1220.

Haseli, A., Shariati, M., Nazari, A. M., Keramat, A., & Emamian, M. H. (2019). Infidelity and its associated factors: A systematic review. *The Journal of Sexual Medicine, 16*(8), 1155–1169.

Haslam, N. (2006). Dehumanization: An integrative review. *Personality and Social Psychology Review, 10*, 252–264. https://doi.org/10.1207/s15327957pspr1003_4

Haslam, N., & Loughnan, S. (2014). Dehumanization and infrahumanization. *Annual Review of Psychology, 65*, 399–423. https://doi.org/10.1146/annurev-psych-010213-115045

Haupert, M., Gesselman, A., Moors, A., Fisher, H., & Garcia, J. (2017). Prevalence of experiences with consensual non-monogamous relationships: Findings from two nationally representative samples of single Americans. *Journal of Sex & Marital Therapy, 43*, 424–440.

Haupert, M. L., Moors, A. C., Gesselman, A. N., & Garcia, J. R. (2017). Estimates and correlates of engagement in consensually non-monogamous relationships. *Current Sexual Health Reports, 9*(3), 155–165. https://doi.org/10.1007/s11930-017-0121-6

Henrich, J., Boyd, R., & Richerson, P. J. (2012). The puzzle of monogamous marriage. *Philosophical Transactions of the Royal Society: Series B: Biological Sciences, 367*, 657–669.

Hirsch, J. S., Meneses, S., Thompson, B., Negroni, M., Pelcastre, B., & Del Rio, C. (2007). The inevitability of infidelity: Sexual reputation, social geographies, and marital HIV risk in rural Mexico. *American Journal of Public Health, 97*(6), 986–996.

Hoff, C. C., & Beougher, S. C. (2010). Sexual agreements among gay male couples. *Archives of Sexual Behavior, 39*(3), 774–787.

Hosking, W. (2014). Australian gay men's satisfaction with sexual agreements: The roles of relationship quality, jealousy, and monogamy attitudes. *Archives of Sexual Behavior, 43*, 823–832.

Houngbedji, A., & Guillem, E. (2016). Profiles and sexual practices of current and past swingers interviewed on French websites. *Sexologies, 25*, e1–e4.

Hrdy, S. B. (1995). The primate origins of female sexuality, and their implications for the role of nonconceptive sex in the reproductive strategies of women. *Human Evolution, 10*(2), 131–144.

Hrdy, S. B. (2016). Variable postpartum responsiveness among humans and other primates with "cooperative breeding": A comparative and evolutionary perspective. *Hormones and Behavior, 77*, 272–283.

Hutzler, K., Giuliano, T., Herselman, J., & Johnson, S. (2016). Three's a crowd: Public awareness and (mis)perceptions of polyamory. *Psychology & Sexuality, 7*, 69–87. https://doi.org/10.1080/19419899.2015.1004102

Jenks, R. J. (1998). Swinging: A review of literature. *Archives of Sexual Behavior, 27*, 507–521.

Jonason, P. K. (2007). An evolutionary psychology perspective on sex differences in exercise behaviors and motivations. *The Journal of Social Psychology, 147*(1), 5–14.

Klesse, C. (2006). Polyamory and its "others": Contesting the terms of non-monogamy. *Sexualities, 9*, 565–583.

Kokko, H., Ranta, E., Ruxton, G., & Lundberg, P. (2002). Sexually transmitted disease and the evolution of mating systems. *Evolution, 56*(6), 1091–1100.

Kruger, D. J. (2010). Socio-demographic factors intensifying male mating competition exacerbate male mortality rates. *Evolutionary Psychology, 8*(2), Article 147470491000800205.

Lehmiller, J. J. (2009). Secret romantic relationships: Consequences for personal and relational well-being. *Personality and Social Psychology Bulletin, 35*(11), 1452–1466.

Lehmiller, J. J. (2015). A comparison of sexual health history and practices among monogamous and consensually nonmonogamous sexual partners. *Journal of Sexual Medicine, 12*, 2022–2028. https://doi.org/10.1111/jsm.12987

Lehmiller, J. J. (2018). *Tell me what you want: The science of sexual desire and how it can help you improve your sex life.* Da Capo Press.

Lehmiller, J. J. (2020). Fantasies about consensual nonmonogamy among persons in monogamous romantic relationships. *Archives of Sexual Behavior, 49*, 2799–2812. https://doi.org/10.1007/s10508-020-01788-7

Lehmiller, J. J., Ley, D .J., & Savage, D. (2018). The psychology of gay men's cuckolding fantasies. *Archives of Sexual Behavior, 47*, 999–1013. https://doi.org/10.1007/s10508-017-1096-0

Lehmiller, J. J., & Selterman, D. (2022). The nature of infidelity in non-heterosexual relationships. In T. DeLecce & T. Shackelford (Eds.), *The Oxford handbook of infidelity*. Oxford University Press.

Levine, E. C., Herbenick, D., Martinez, O., Fu, T.-C., & Dodge, B. (2018). open relationships, nonconsensual nonmonogamy, and monogamy among U.S. adults: Findings from the 2012 National Survey of Sexual Health and Behavior. *Archives of Sexual Behavior, 47*(5), 1439–1450. https://doi.org/10.1007/s10508-018-1178-7

Leyens, J.-P., Paladino, P. M., Rodriguez-Torres, R., Vaes, J., Demoulin, S., Rodriguez-Perez, A., & Gaunt, R. (2000). The emotional side of prejudice: The attribution of secondary emotions to ingroups and outgroups. *Personality and Social Psychology Review, 4*, 186–197. https://doi.org/10.1207/S15327957PSPR0402_06

Leyens, J.-P., Rodriguez-Perez, A., Rodriguez-Torres, R., Gaunt, R., Paladino, M.-P., Vaes, J., & Demoulin, S. (2001). Psychological essentialism and the differential attribution of uniquely human emotions to ingroups and outgroups. *European Journal of Social Psychology, 31*, 395–411. https://doi.org/10.1002/ejsp.50

Li, N. P., Smith, A. R., Griskevicius, V., Cason, M. J., & Bryan, A. (2010). Intrasexual competition and eating restriction in heterosexual and homosexual individuals. *Evolution and Human Behavior, 31*(5), 365–372.

Lippa, R. A. (2009). Sex differences in sex drive, sociosexuality, and height across 53 nations: Testing evolutionary and social structural theories. *Archives of Sexual Behavior, 38*(5), 631–651. https://doi.org/10.1007/s10508-007-9242-8

Lippa, R. A. (2020). Interest, personality, and sexual traits that distinguish heterosexual, bisexual, and homosexual individuals: Are there two dimensions that underlie variations in sexual orientation? *Archives of Sexual Behavior, 49*(2), 607–622.

Loue, S. (2006). Multi-bonding: Polygamy, polygyny, polyamory. In S. Loue, Sexual *partnering, sexual practices, and health* (pp. 27–53). Springer.

Lusterman, D. D. (2005). Helping children and adults cope with parental infidelity. *Journal of Clinical Psychology, 61*(11), 1439–1451.

Manley, M. H., Diamond, L. M., & van Anders, S. M. (2015). Polyamory, monoamory, and sexual fluidity: A longitudinal study of identity and sexual trajectories. *Psychology of Sexual Orientation and Gender Diversity, 2*(2), 168.

Markey, P., & Markey, C. (2013). Sociosexuality and relationship commitment among lesbian couples. *Journal of Research in Personality, 47*(4), 282–285. https://doi.org/10.1016/j.jrp.2013.02.002

Marques, J., Abrams, D., Paez, D., & Martinez-Taboada, C. (1998). The role of categorization and in-group norms in judgments of groups and their members. *Journal of Personality and Social Psychology, 75*(4), 976–988. https://doi.org/10.1037/0022-3514.75.4.976

Matsick, J. L., Conley, T. D., Ziegler, A., Moors, A. C., & Rubin, J. D. (2014). Love and sex: Polyamorous relationships are perceived more favourably than swinging and open relationships. *Psychology and Sexuality, 5*, 339–348.

McLean, K. (2004). Negotiating (non)monogamy. *Journal of Bisexuality, 4*(1–2), 83–97. https://doi.org/10.1300/J159v04n01_07

McNally, L., & Jackson, A. L. (2013). Cooperation creates selection for tactical deception. *Proceedings of the Royal Society B: Biological Sciences, 280*(1762), Article 20130699.

Mikulincer, M., & Shaver, P. R. (2007). *Attachment in adulthood: Structure, dynamics, and change.* Guilford Press.

Mikulincer, M., Shaver, P. R., & Pereg, D. (2003). Attachment theory and affect regulation: The dynamics, development, and cognitive consequences of attachment-related strategies. *Motivation and Emotion, 27*(2), 77–102. https://doi.org/10.1023/A:1024515519160

Miller, G. (2000, January). Sexual selection for indicators of intelligence. In *Novartis Foundation Symposium* (pp. 260–270). John Wiley & Sons.

Mitchell, M. E., Bartholomew, K., & Cobb, R. J. (2014). Need fulfillment in polyamorous relationships. *The Journal of Sex Research, 51*(3), 329–339.

Mokkonen, M., & Lindstedt, C. (2016). The evolutionary ecology of deception. *Biological Reviews, 91*(4), 1020–1035.

Mogilski, J. K. (2021). Parental investment theory. In T. K. Shackelford (Ed.), *The SAGE handbook of evolutionary psychology* (pp. 137-154). SAGE.

Mogilski, J. K., Memering, S. L., Welling, L. L. M., & Shackelford, T. K. (2017). Monogamy versus consensual non-monogamy: Alternative approaches to pursuing a strategically pluralistic mating strategy. *Archives of Sexual Behavior, 46*(2), 407–417. https://doi.org/10.1007/s10508-015-0658-2

Mogilski, J. K., Mitchell, V. E., Reeve, S. D., Donaldson, S. H., Nicolas, S. C. A., & Welling, L. L. M. (2020). Life history and multi-partner mating: A novel explanation for moral stigma against consensual non-monogamy. *Frontiers in Psychology, 10,* 3033. https://doi.org/10.3389/fpsyg.2019.03033

Mogilski, J. K., Reeve, S. D., Nicolas, S. C. A., Donaldson, S. H., Mitchell, V. E., & Welling, L. L. M. (2019). Jealousy, consent, and compersion within monogamous and consensually non-monogamous romantic relationships. *Archives of Sexual Behavior, 48*(6), 1811–1828. https://doi.org/10.1007/s10508-018-1286-4

Moors, A. C. (2017). Has the American public's interest in information related to relationships beyond "the couple" increased over time? *The Journal of Sex Research, 54*(6), 677–684. https://doi.org/10.1080/00224499.2016.1178208

Moors, A. C., Conley, T. D., Edelstein, R. S., & Chopik, W. J. (2015). Attached to monogamy? Avoidance predicts willingness to engage (but not actual engagement) in consensual non-monogamy. *Journal of Social and Personal Relationships, 32*(2), 222–240. https://doi.org/10.1177/0265407514529065

Moors, A. C., Matsick, J. L., & Schechinger, H. A. (2017). Unique and shared relationship benefits of consensually non-monogamous and monogamous relationships: A review and insights for moving forward. *European Psychologist, 22,* 55–71. https://doi.org/10.1027/1016-9040/a000278

Moors, A. C., Matsick, J., Ziegler, A., Rubin, J., & Conley, T. (2013). Stigma toward individuals engaged in consensual nonmonogamy: Robust and worthy of additional research. *Analyses of Social Issues and Public Policy, 13,* 52–69. https://doi.org/10.1111/asap.12020

Moors, A. C., Rubin, J., Matsick, J., Ziegler, A., & Conley, T. (2014). It's not just a gay male thing: Sexual minority women and men are equally attracted to consensual non-monogamy. *Journal Für Psychologie, 22,* 38–51.

Moors, A. C., Selterman, D. F., & Conley, T. D. (2017). Personality correlates of desire to engage in consensual non-monogamy among lesbian, gay, and bisexual individuals. *Journal of Bisexuality, 17*(4), 418–434. https://doi.org/10.1080/15299716.2017.1367982

Muise, A., Laughton, A. K., Moors, A., & Impett, E. A. (2019). Sexual need fulfillment and satisfaction in consensually nonmonogamous relationships. *Journal of Social and Personal Relationships, 36*(7), 1917–1938. https://doi.org/10.1177/0265407518774638

Murphy, A., Joel, S., & Muise, A. (2020). A prospective investigation of the decision to open up a romantic relationship. *Social Psychological and Personality Science, 12*(2), 194–201.

Negash, S., & Morgan, M. L. (2016). A family affair: Examining the impact of parental infidelity on children using a structural family therapy framework. *Contemporary Family Therapy, 38*(2), 198–209.

Noë, R., & Hammerstein, P. (1994). Biological markets: Supply and demand determine the effect of partner choice in cooperation, mutualism and mating. *Behavioral Ecology and Sociobiology, 35*(1), 1–11.

Nunn, C. L., Gittleman, J. L., & Antonovics, J. (2000). Promiscuity and the primate immune system. *Science, 290*(5494), 1168–1170.

Pachankis, J. E., Clark, K. A., Burton, C. L., Hughto, J. M. W., Bränström, R., & Keene, D. E. (2020). Sex, status, competition, and exclusion: Intraminority stress from within the gay community and gay and bisexual men's mental health. *Journal of Personality and Social Psychology, 19*(3), 713–740. https://doi.org/10.1037/pspp0000282

Paluck, E. L., Green, S. A., & Green, D. P. (2019). The contact hypothesis re-evaluated. *Behavioural Public Policy, 3*(2), 129–158. https://doi.org/10.1017/b2018.25

Penke, L., & Asendorpf, J. B. (2008). Beyond global sociosexual orientations: A more differentiated look at sociosexuality and its effects on courtship and romantic relationships. *Journal of Personality and Social Psychology, 95*(5), 1113–1135. https://doi.org/10.1037/0022-3514.95.5.1113

Pettigrew, T. F., & Tropp, L. R. (2006). A meta-analytic test of intergroup contact theory. *Journal of Personality and Social Psychology, 90*(5), 751–783. https://doi.org/10.1037/0022-3514.90.5.751

Pham, M. N., Barbaro, N., Mogilski, J. K., Shackelford, T. K., & Zeigler-Hill, V. (2017). Post-fight respect signals valuations of opponent's fighting performance. *Personality and Social Psychology Bulletin, 43*(3), 407–417.

Philpot, S. P., Duncan, D., Ellard, J., Bavinton, B. R., Grierson, J., & Prestage, G. (2018). Negotiating gay men's relationships: How are monogamy and non-monogamy experienced and practised over time? *Culture, Health & Sexuality, 20*(8), 915–928. https://doi.org/10.1080/13691058.2017.1392614

Pichon, M., Treves-Kagan, S., Stern, E., Kyegombe, N., Stöckl, H., & Buller, A. M. (2020). A mixed-methods systematic review: Infidelity, romantic jealousy and intimate partner violence against women. *International Journal of Environmental Research and Public Health, 17*(16), Article 5682.

Pistole, M. C., Roberts, A., & Chapman, M. L. (2010). Attachment, relationship maintenance, and stress in long distance and geographically close romantic relationships. *Journal of Social and Personal Relationships, 27*(4), 535–552. https://doi.org/10.1177/0265407510363427

Pizzirani, B., & Karantzas, G. C. (2019). The association between dehumanization and intimate partner abuse. *Journal of Social and Personal Relationships, 36*(5), 1527–1541. https://doi.org/10.1177/0265407518811673

Pizzirani, B., Karantzas, G. C., & Mullins, E. R. (2019). The development and validation of a dehumanization measure within romantic relationships. *Frontiers in Psychology, 10*, 2754. https://doi.org/10.3389/fpsyg.2019.02754

Platteau, T., van Lankveld, J., Ooms, L., & Florence, E. (2017). Sexual behavior and sexually transmitted infections among swingers: Results from an online survey in Belgium. *Journal of Sex & Marital Therapy, 43*(8), 709–719.

Poppen, P. J., Reisen, C. A., Zea, M. C., Bianchi, F. T., & Echeverry, J. J. (2004). Predictors of unprotected anal intercourse among HIV-positive Latino gay and bisexual men. *AIDS Behavior, 8*, 379–389.

Prestage, G., Mao, L., McGuigan, D., Crawford, J., Kippax, S., Kaldor, J., & Grulich, A. E. (2006). HIV risk and communication between regular partners in a cohort of HIV-negative gay men. *AIDS Care, 18*(2), 166–172.

Previti, D., & Amato, P. R. (2004). Is infidelity a cause or a consequence of poor marital quality? *Journal of Social and Personal Relationships, 21*(2), 217–230.

Rai, T. S., Valdesolo, P., & Graham, J. (2017). Dehumanization increases instrumental violence, but not moral violence. *Proceedings of the National Academy of Sciences, 114*(32), 8511–8516. https://doi.org/10.1073/pnas.1705238114

Rodrigues, D. L., Fasoli, F., Huic, A., & Lopes, D. (2018). Which partners are more human? Monogamy matters more than sexual orientation for dehumanization in three European countries. *Sexuality Research and Social Policy, 15*(4), 504–515. https://doi.org/10.1007/s13178-017-0290-0

Rodrigues, D. L., & Lopes, D. (2017). Sociosexuality, commitment, and sexual desire for an attractive person. *Archives of Sexual Behavior, 46*(3), 775–788. https://doi.org/10.1007/s10508-016-0814-3

Rodrigues, D. L., Lopes, D., & Conley, T. (2019). Non-monogamy agreements and safer sex behaviors: The role of perceived sexual self-control. *Psychology & Sexuality, 10*, 338–353. https://doi.org/10.1080/19419899.2019.1649299

Rodrigues, D. L., Lopes, D., & Huic, A. (2021). What drives the dehumanization of consensual non-monogamous partners? *Archives of Sexual Behavior, 50*(4) 1587–1597. https://doi.org/10.1007/s10508-020-01895-5

Rodrigues, D. L., Lopes, D., & Pereira, M. (2016). "We agree and now everything goes my way": Consensual sexual nonmonogamy, extradyadic sex, and relationship satisfaction. *Cyberpsychology, Behavior, and Social Networking, 19*, 373–379. https://doi.org/10.1089/cyber.2016.0114

Rodrigues, D. L., Lopes, D., Pereira, M., de Visser, R., & Cabaceira, I. (2019). Sociosexual attitudes and quality of life in (non)monogamous relationships: The role of attraction and constraining forces among users of the Second Love web site. *Archives of Sexual Behavior, 48*, 1795–1809. https://doi.org/10.1007/s10508-018-1272-x

Rodrigues, D. L., Lopes, D., & Smith, C. V. (2017). Caught in a "bad romance"? reconsidering the negative association between sociosexuality and relationship functioning. *The Journal of Sex Research, 54*(9), 1118–1127. https://doi.org/10.1080/00224499.2016.1252308

Rodrigues, D. L., Prada, M., & Lopes, D. (2019). Perceived sexual self-control and condom use with primary and casual sex partners: Age and relationship agreement differences in a Portuguese sample. *Psychology & Health, 34*, 1231–1249. https://doi.org/10.1080/08870446.2019.1603384

Roos, L. G., O'Connor, V., Canevello, A., & Bennett, J. M. (2019). Post-traumatic stress and psychological health following infidelity in unmarried young adults. *Stress and Health, 35*(4), 468–479.

Rubel, A. N., & Bogaert, A. F. (2015). Consensual nonmonogamy: Psychological well-being and relationship quality correlates. *Journal of Sex Research, 52*, 961–982.

Rubin, J., Moors, A., Matsick, J., Ziegler, A., & Conley, T. (2014). On the margins: Considering diversity among consensually non-monogamous relationships. *Journal Für Psychologie, 22*(1), 19–37.

Rusbult, C. E. (1980). Commitment and satisfaction in romantic associations: A test of the investment model. *Journal of Experimental Social Psychology, 16*(2), 172–186.

Rusbult, C. E., Martz, J. M., & Agnew, C. R. (1998). The investment model scale: Measuring commitment level, satisfaction level, quality of alternatives, and investment size. *Personal Relationships, 5*(4), 357–387.

Sagarin, B. J., Becker, D. V., Guadagno, R. E., Wilkinson, W. W., & Nicastle, L. D. (2012). A reproductive threat-based model of evolved sex differences in jealousy. *Evolutionary Psychology, 10*(3), Article 147470491201000307.

Scelza, B. A., Prall, S. P., Swinford, N., Gopalan, S., Atkinson, E. G., McElreath, R., Sheehama, J., & Henn, B. M. (2020). High rate of extrapair paternity in a human population demonstrates diversity in human reproductive strategies. *Science Advances, 6*(8), Article eaay6195.

Schacht, R., & Kramer, K. L. (2019). Are we monogamous? A review of the evolution of pair-bonding in humans and its contemporary variation cross-culturally. *Frontiers in Ecology and Evolution, 7*, 230.

Schechinger, H. A., Sakaluk, J. K., & Moors, A. C. (2018). Harmful and helpful therapy practices with consensually non-monogamous clients: Toward an inclusive framework. *Journal of Consulting and Clinical Psychology, 86*(11), 879–891.

Scherer, C. R., Akers, E. G., & Kolbe, K. L. (2013). Bisexuals and the sex differences in jealousy hypothesis. *Journal of Social and Personal Relationships, 30*(8), 1064–1071.

Schmitt, D. P. (2005). Sociosexuality from Argentina to Zimbabwe: A 48-nation study of sex, culture, and strategies of human mating. *Behavioral and Brain Sciences, 28*(2), 247–275. https://doi.org/10.1017/S0140525X05000051

Séguin, L. J., Blais, M., Goyer, M.-F., Adam, B. D., Lavoie, F., Rodrigue, C., & Magontier, C. (2017). Examining relationship quality across three types of relationship agreements. *Sexualities, 20*(1–2), 86–104. https://doi.org/10.1177/1363460716649337

Selander, R. K. (1965). On mating systems and sexual selection. *American Naturalist, 99*(906), 129–141.

Selterman, D., Garcia, J. R., & Tsapelas, I. (2019). Motivations for extradyadic infidelity revisited. *The Journal of Sex Research, 56*(3), 273–286.

Semenyna, S. W., Gómez Jiménez, F. R., VanderLaan, D. P., & Vasey, P. L. (2020). Inter-sexual mate competition in three cultures. *PloS ONE, 15*(7), Article e0236549.

Servedio, M. R., Powers, J. M., Lande, R., & Price, T. D. (2019). Evolution of sexual cooperation from sexual conflict. *Proceedings of the National Academy of Sciences, 116*(46), 23225–23231.

Setchell, J. M. (2008). *Alternative reproductive tactics in primates.* Cambridge University Press.

Shackelford, T. K., & Buss, D. M. (1997). Cues to infidelity. *Personality and Social Psychology Bulletin, 23*(10), 1034–1045. https://doi.org/10.1177/01461672972310004

Shaver, P. R., & Hazan, C. (1987). Being lonely, falling in love: Perspectives from attachment theory. *Journal of Social Behavior & Personality, 2*(2, Pt 2), 105–124.

Shaver, P. R., & Hazan, C. (1988). A biased overview of the study of love. *Journal of Social and Personal Relationships*, *5*(4), 473–501. https://doi.org/10.1177/0265407588054005

Simpson, J. A., & Gangestad, S. W. (1991). Individual differences in sociosexuality: Evidence for convergent and discriminant validity. *Journal of Personality and Social Psychology*, *60*(6), 870–883. https://doi.org/10.1037/0022-3514.60.6.870

Sizemore, K. M., & Olmstead, S. B. (2017). Testing the validity and factor structure of the willingness to engage in consensual non-monogamy scale among college men and women. *Sexuality Research and Social Policy*, *14*(2), 182–191. https://doi.org/10.1007/s13178-016-0263-8

Sizemore, K. M., & Olmstead, S. B. (2018). Willingness of emerging adults to engage in consensual non-monogamy: A mixed-methods analysis. *Archives of Sexual Behavior*, *47*(5), 1423–1438. https://doi.org/10.1007/s10508-017-1075-5

Stephens, A. K., & Emmers-Sommer, T. M. (2020). Adults' identities, attitudes, and orientations concerning consensual non-monogamy. *Sexuality Research and Social Policy*, *17*, 469–485. https://doi.org/10.1007/s13178-019-00409-w

Spanier, G. B., & Margolis, R. L. (1983). Marital separation and extramarital sexual behavior. *Journal of Sex Research*, *19*(1), 23–48.

Thompson, A. E., Bagley, A. J., & Moore, E. A. (2018). Young men and women's implicit attitudes towards consensually nonmonogamous relationships. *Psychology & Sexuality*, *9*(2), 117–131. https://doi.org/10.1080/19419899.2018.1435560

Thompson, A. E., Cipriano, A. E., Kirkeby, K. M., Wilder, D., & Lehmiller, J. J. (2020). Exploring variations in North American adults' attitudes, interest, experience, and outcomes related to mixed-gender threesomes: A replication and extension. *Archives of Sexual Behavior*, *15*(4), 1433–1448. https://doi.org/10.1007/s10508-020-01829-1

Thompson, A. E., Moore, E. A., Haedtke, K., & Karst, A. T. (2020). Assessing implicit associations with consensual non-monogamy among U.S. early emerging adults: An application of the single-target Implicit Association Test. *Archives of Sexual Behavior*, *49*(8), 2813–2828. https://doi.org/10.1007/s10508-020-01625-x

Trivers, R. (1972). Parental investment and sexual selection. In B. Campbell (Ed.), *Sexual selection and the descent of man* (pp. 136–179). Aldine.

Vaes, J., Leyens, J.-P., Paladino, M. P., & Miranda, M. P. (2012). We are human, they are not: Driving forces behind outgroup dehumanisation and the humanisation of the ingroup. *European Review of Social Psychology*, *23*, 64–106. https://doi.org/10.1080/10463283.2012.665250

Vaillancourt, T., & Sharma, A. (2011). Intolerance of sexy peers: Intrasexual competition among women. *Aggressive Behavior*, *37*(6), 569–577.

Valadez, A. M., Rohde, J., Tessler, J., & Beals, K. (2020). Perceived stigmatization and disclosure among individuals in consensually nonmonogamous relationships. *Analyses of Social Issues and Public Policy*, *20*(1), 143–165. https://doi.org/10.1111/asap.12194" https://doi.org/10.1111/asap.12194

Valentova, J. V., de Moraes, A. C., & Varella, M. A. C. (2020). Gender, sexual orientation and type of relationship influence individual differences in jealousy: A large Brazilian sample. *Personality and Individual Differences*, *157*, Article 109805.

Vaughan, M. D., Jones, P., Taylor, B. A., & Roush, J. (2019). Healthcare experiences and needs of consensually non-monogamous people: Results from a focus group study. *The Journal of Sexual Medicine*, *16*(1), 42–51. https://doi.org/10.1016/j.jsxm.2018.11.006

Veaux, F. (2011). Care and feeding of polyamorous secondary relationships. *More Than Two*. Retrieved from https://www.morethantwo.com/primarysecondary.html

Voracek, M., Haubner, T., & Fisher, M. L. (2008). Recent decline in nonpaternity rates: A cross-temporal meta-analysis. *Psychological Reports*, *103*(3), 799–811.

Wang, X., Chen, H., Chen, Z., & Yang, Y. (2021). Women's intrasexual competition results in beautification. *Social Psychological and Personality Science*, *12*(5):648–657.

Warach, B., & Josephs, L. (2019). The aftershocks of infidelity: A review of infidelity-based attachment trauma. *Sexual and Relationship Therapy*, *36*(4), 1–23.

Warren, J. T., Harvey, S. M., & Agnew, C. R. (2012). One love: Explicit monogamy agreements among heterosexual young adult couples at increased risk of sexually transmitted infections. *Journal of Sex Research*, *49*(2-3), 282–289.

Webster, G., Laurenceau, J.-P., Smith, C., Mahaffey, A., Bryan, A., & Brunell, A. (2015). An investment model of sociosexuality, relationship satisfaction, and commitment: Evidence from dating, engaged, and newlywed couples. *Journal of Research in Personality, 55*, 112–126. https://doi.org/10.1016/j.jrp.2015.02.004

Wolf, R. (2011). Respect and disrespect in international politics: The significance of status recognition. *IT, 3*, 105–142.

Wosick-Correa, K. (2010). Agreements, rules, and agentic fidelity in polyamorous relationships. *Psychology & Sexuality, 1*, 44–61.

Whyte, S., Brooks, R. C., & Torgler, B. (2019). Sexual economic theory & the human mating market. *Applied Economics, 51*(57), 6100–6112.

Yoshimura, S. (2007). Goals and emotional outcomes of revenge activities in interpersonal relationships. *Journal of Social and Personal Relationships, 24*(1), 87–98.

Ziegler, Ali, A., Conley, T., Moors, A., Matsick, J., & Rubin, J. (2015). Monogamy. In C. Richards & M. Barker (Eds.), *The Palgrave handbook of the psychology of sexuality* (pp. 219–235). Palgrave Macmillan.

CHAPTER

18

Evolutionary Perspectives on Relationship Maintenance Across the Spectrum of Sexual and Gender Diversity

Lisa M. Diamond *and* Jenna Alley

Abstract

Most evolutionary models of relationship functioning have focused on heterosexual pairings (i.e., male–female) and on cisgender individuals (i.e., individuals whose gender identity corresponds to their birth-assigned sex/gender). Yet in the modern world, humans have the freedom to pursue a much broader range of intimate ties, including same-gender relationships as well as relationships in which one or more partners identify as transgender, gender nonconforming, or nonbinary. In this chapter we argue that evolutionary theory can help us understand the unique features of these relationships by highlighting the evolved significance of *social safety*. Perhaps the most important difference between cisgender/heterosexual couples and other types of couples (i.e., those of lesbian, gay, bisexual, or transgender individuals) is that the latter group faces persistent stigmatization and social marginalization. As a result, they do not have the same access to *social safety* (i.e., connection, nurturance, security, and protection) that is available to cisgender/heterosexual couples, and this creates a new source of burden that can impede the development and maintenance of these relationships. We show how a focus on the evolutionary significance of social safety can elucidate the unique hurdles facing couples confronting social stigma.

Key Words: couples, cisgender, transgender, sexual orientation, minority stress, stigma

Most evolutionary models of sexual and romantic relationships have focused on heterosexual, cisgender relationships (i.e., relationships containing one man and one woman, and in which both individuals' gender identities match their birth-assigned sex). Throughout human history, these types of dyads have been the predominant and socially approved context for reproduction and childrearing, and hence a range of psychological and behavioral processes and mechanisms (many of them based in the human attachment system) have evolved to establish and preserve these dyads. Yet as with many psychological and behavioral phenomena, contemporary humans have expanded beyond ancestral practices, and we now have more diverse forms of sexual and romantic partnering and more diverse patterns of gender identity and expression. Do evolutionary models have anything to tell us about these new practices? On the one hand, contemporary romantic pairings demonstrate the capacity for humans to break free from the constraints of our ancestral past and to make novel life choices that directly challenge prior norms. Survival and reproduction no longer pose the overarching challenges that they once did, and so humans enjoy a broader range of options for sexual and romantic relationships. On the other hand, we cannot "undo" our evolutionary past, and we still retain psychological and behavioral tendencies that may have little direct relevance to our contemporary context.

Accordingly, what might evolutionarily informed perspectives on intimate relationships tell us about the diverse spectrum of intimate relationships that we now see in the modern age, which includes same-gender relationships as well as relationships among individuals with diverse modes of gender identity and expression? We refer to this broad spectrum as "sexual and gender diversity." We define sexually diverse relationships as those involving one or more individuals who are lesbian, gay, or bisexual or who have same-gender attractions; we define gender-diverse relationships as those with one or more individuals who are transgender, nonbinary, genderqueer, or gender fluid or who have a pattern of gender identity or expression that does not match their birth-assigned sex/gender. We use the abbreviation "SGD" for expediency (to refer to both sexually diverse and gender-diverse individuals and relationships), but we want to highlight that there are multiple forms of sexual diversity and gender diversity, and the experiences of individuals in this broader category vary widely. What they all share, despite this diversity, is chronic exposure to social stigma and marginalization, although in different forms and within different contexts (Flanders et al., 2017; Layland et al., 2020; Pachankis, Hatzenbuehler, et al., 2018; Pachankis, Sullivan, et al., 2018; Puckett et al., 2017; Valente et al., 2020). Same-gender relationships are perhaps the most widely studied type of SGD relationship, but they are by no means the only type. The pairing of a heterosexual man and a bisexual woman is an SGD relationship by virtue of the woman's sexual diversity. Similarly, the pairing of a transgender man and a heterosexual woman is also an SGD relationship because of the man's gender identity and expression. Studies investigating basic relationship processes within these couples (relationship formation, maintenance, conflict resolution, etc.) find few differences between SGD relationships and cis/hetero relationships (reviewed in Diamond & Dehlin, 2021), and hence one might conclude that our evolved relationship "programming" operates similarly for all relationship forms.

The Role of Social Safety

Yet this is not exactly the case. There is one thing that renders SGD relationships different, in a manner that is evolutionarily significant: *lack of social safety* (Diamond & Alley, 2022). SGD individuals inhabit a social world that reliably denigrates, rejects, excludes, isolates, and stigmatizes them. The psychological ramifications of this systemic social marginalization have received extensive attention over the past several decades and have been conceptualized as minority stress (Meyer, 2003). Minority stress has been conceptualized as the stress experienced by sexually diverse and gender-diverse individuals as a result of their chronic exposure to social stigma and marginalization, which includes overt discrimination, institutional invisibility, violence and harassment, the need to conceal one's sexual or gender identity, anxiety and chronic hypervigilance to signs of social rejection and inclusion, and the psychological internalization of homophobia and transphobia. Numerous studies have documented the deleterious effects of minority stress on individual well-being (Chodzen et al., 2019; Dyar et al., 2020; Lefevor et al., 2019; Parra et al., 2016; Timmins et al., 2018) as well as couple-functioning (Cao et al., 2017; Green, 2008; LeBlanc et al., 2015; Rostosky et al., 2007).

Although the concept of minority stress has been important for drawing attention to the enduring psychological consequences of social stigma and marginalization, phrasing this phenomenon in terms of "stress" does not do justice to its evolutionary significance. The core experience underlying all forms of minority stress is *social threat,* defined as experiences of exclusion, rejection, isolation, shame, neglect, and ostracization (Diamond, Dehlin, & Alley, 2021). Although social threat causes psychological "stress," its significance to human health and well-being is more fundamental. Humans are a group-living species, for which stable group membership and the reliable assistance of social partners is critical for survival (Kemeny, 2009; Kemeny & Shestyuk, 2008; Slavich, 2020; Slavich & Irwin, 2014). Exclusion from the social group, hostility and harassment by fellow group members, and chronic isolation could lead to injury and death. Social threats are so dangerous for human survival that our immune systems respond to social threats in the same way they respond to *physical* threats such as infection and injury, with the production of inflammatory cytokines aimed at healing the physical wounds that accompanied social rejection in our ancestral environment (Slavich, 2020).

Hence, one advantage of an evolutionary approach to the relationships of SGD individuals is that it underscores the significance of social marginalization and stigmatization. From a species-wide perspective, exposure to chronic stigma and marginalization is more than "stressful"; it initiates a broad range of integrated neurobiological and behavioral "alarms" that temporarily suspend other goal-directed behavior. Within the domain of general psychology, Maslow articulated this basic concept in terms of a "hierarchy of needs" (Maslow, 1943), which anticipated later developments in evolutionary psychology focusing on differences in the immediate and long-term functional significance of different human behaviors (eating vs. mating). For Maslow, immediate physical needs (food and housing) were the top priority, followed by safety and then affiliation. Later evolutionary theorists have retained this basic ordering (Kenrick et al., 2010). The major insight proposed by Slavich (2020) is that affiliation, in the form of social belongingness, is a fundamental component of the need for safety (rather than a separate domain). For a group-living species such as humans, inclusion in the social group plays a critical role for both survival and reproduction (reviewed in Kenrick et al., 2010). Accordingly, as reviewed by

Slavich (2020), humans evolved a sophisticated neurobiological "threat-detection" system, involving the amygdala, the mentalizing network, the empathy network, and the mirror neuron system (Kennedy & Adolphs, 2012), to continuously monitor the level of social threat and safety in the immediate environment.

Yet in our contemporary cultural context, psychologists rarely consider "safety" to be a core relationship issue. Rather, we focus on interpersonal processes such as communication, commitment, conflict resolution, and relationship maintenance (reviewed in Diamond et al., 2010). From an evolutionary perspective, these are secondary concerns. Because social safety is a cognitive "priority" (Kenrick et al., 2010), no attentional, energetic, or emotional resources can be directed to other goals until it is established. Research on differences between high-income and low-income couples provides a modern example of this idea. Ross et al. (2019) pointed out that resolving competing demands is a form of relationship maintenance for all couples, but that this process may be especially challenging for couples facing chronic stress due to external and uncontrollable factors (such as socioeconomic disadvantage). As they reviewed, studies of well-resourced, economically secure couples find that emotional and behavioral withdrawal during conflict discussions (as opposed to calm engagement) are detrimental to couple-functioning. Yet they noted that for couples facing chronic isolation and stress (such as low-income couples), withdrawal might be the more *adaptive* strategy. They explain this pattern as follows: individuals with low social capital will have more difficulty meeting their partner's needs (especially if they have little power to change the circumstances causing conflict), and in such cases it might be more relationship-enhancing to *disengage and withdraw* from the conflict than to engage in a problem they are powerless to solve. Numerous other studies support this view, showing that couples coping with external stressors that are beyond their immediate control have fewer psychological and social resources available to deal with everyday relationship maintenance (Neff & Karney, 2017).

The notion that *immediate threats* to a relationship take priority over other concerns has been acknowledged by scholars studying relationship maintenance. Ogolsky et al. (2017) argued that there are two categories of relationship maintenance: threat mitigation and relationship enhancement. In their formulation, threat mitigation behaviors include phenomena such as conflict resolution, forgiveness, derogating alternatives, and sacrifice, whereas relationship enhancement behaviors include communication, social support, responsiveness, and shared positive activities. Yet both processes center on phenomena that are *dyadic* relationship (disagreements, violations of trust, etc.). An evolutionary perspective suggests that the most important form of "threat mitigation" might be *individual* rather than dyadic. To the extent that either member of the couple experiences a lack of safety on an *individual* level, they may not be able to have the necessary resources to compromise, sacrifice, and make other efforts to maintain the relationship on a dyadic level (Doyle & Molix, 2014).

For the majority of individuals within cisgender and heterosexual couples, social safety can be taken for granted. When a cisgender heterosexual couple goes to a restaurant for their anniversary, applies for a marriage license, reserves a honeymoon suite at a hotel, attends a parent–teacher conference for their child, or holds hands at the movies, they can usually be confident that they will not be harassed, victimized, shamed, or rejected for these actions. This is not true for all SGD couples. Some of them might escape social rejection and hostility because they are presumed to be "average heterosexual couples" by outside observers (e.g., couples in which a heterosexual woman is paired with a bisexual man). This does not imply that the couples feel protected from outside scrutiny—to the contrary, they might experience heightened vigilance regarding "who knows" and "who does not know." Yet in cases where SGD individuals are consistently visible to the world as sexually diverse or gender diverse, they face heightened potential for social rejection. The consequences of this rejection can vary widely, from momentary annoyance to job loss to physical violence.

One of the unique challenges faced by couples with only one gender-diverse partner (e.g., a cisgender woman paired with a transman) is that they may have divergent experiences moving through the world as a couple, because one partner has more social privilege and power than the other. The transman may experience chronic concerns about rejection and mistreatment, and his partner may fail to appreciate the psychological toll that this takes and the degree to which her own feelings of security and safety (with family, with friends, at work) do not "carry over" to her partner. Whereas same-gender couples often feel that they are bonded together in a shared "fight" against oppression, misunderstanding, and marginalization, partners with one cisgender and one gender-diverse individual may not have the same sense of shared experience and may also have divergent *histories* of exposure to trauma, violence, and stigma. This can prove daunting if the cisgender partner views the other partner as "overreacting" to day-to-day stigma experiences, or if the trans partner feels that the cisgender partner does not "stand up" for them in public.

Even within the relationship itself, feelings of safety may be difficult to establish or maintain. One study by Iantaffi and Bockting (2011) found that half of gender-diverse individuals were uncomfortable talking about their bodies with their partner, and nearly a quarter preferred to have the lights off while engaging in sexual intimacy with their partners, due to their own self-consciousness and anxiety. Such examples show how the persistent stigma and shame experienced by gender-diverse individuals may rob them of a sense of safety even in their own bedrooms. Additional unique struggles may arise when one partner begins a gender transition *during* the course of the relationship. Depending on the initial gender identities of each partner, this may involve becoming an altogether different *type* of couple (i.e., from a lesbian couple to a couple containing one lesbian and one transman, or from a heterosexual couple to a couple containing one heterosexual woman and one transwoman). In addition to the relationship challenges that these couples face when renegotiating and rethinking their identity *as a couple*, they also find themselves exposed to notably different forms of stigmatization and differential treatment that introduce new threats, both individually and as a couple, and may erode their sense of safety and security. Friends, family members, and workplaces that previously provided them with validation and affirmation may not extend the same affirmation to their "new" couple status. In some cases, these stressors lead to the dissolution of the relationship (Meier et al., 2013). In highlighting these examples, we do not mean to suggest that cisgender or heterosexual couple *always* feel safe: To the contrary, interracial couples routinely face social threats due to persistent racism, which threaten their individual and relationship functioning (Bratter & Eschbach, 2006; Bratter & King, 2008; Schueths, 2014; Zhang & Van Hook, 2009). Hence, although the lack of social safety is a pressing concern for SGD couples, it takes a variety of different manifestations, for different reasons, among many other types of couples, and it deserves more attention across different domains.

Threat Vigilance as an Adaptive Default

Given that social attitudes regarding sexual diversity and gender diversity have become more accepting over the past few decades (Twenge et al., 2016), one might expect that social safety is less of a concern for SGD individuals and relationships *now,* compared to several decades ago. Yet although attitudes and social policies regarding SGD individuals and relationships have unquestionably advanced, these individuals continue to face widespread family rejection (Koken et al., 2009; Ryan et al., 2009; Willoughby et al., 2010), physical violence (Brenner, 1995; National Coalition of Anti-Violence Programs, 2011), and workplace and housing discrimination (Becker, 2014; Herek, 2009; Reisner et al., 2016. Hence, the fact that a same-gender couple can now legally marry in the United States and many other countries, and that gender-diverse children have expanded access to gender-affirmative counseling and medical care, has not obviated the importance of social threat for their day-to-day functioning.

Perhaps more importantly, recent research on stress and health suggests that stressors do not need to be directly experienced to be detrimental. Brosschot et al. (2017; Brosschot et al., 2018) have pointed out that a long-standing weakness of conventional models of psychological stress is the presumption that our "default" neurobiological state is one of safety and security. According to this view, we remain in a calm and relaxed state until we encounter a discrete environmental threat, which activates the complex chain of neurobiological, autonomic, endocrine, and immunological processes involved in stress reactivity. Yet Brosschot and colleagues note that this model makes little evolutionary sense. Danger and uncertainty were regular features of the human ancestral environment, and hence humans evolved to chronically *expect* danger and to continuously monitor the environment for cues of safety (Brosschot, 2017; Brosschot et al., 2016; Carleton, 2016). Hence, our neurobiological "threat-detection" system is not so much *activated* by threats as it is *deactivated* by cues of safety (Amat et al., 2005; Carleton, 2016; Maier, 2015). Without sufficient cues of safety, generalized unsafety is presumed by our brain's neural networks and tonic psychological stress becomes the default state. Accordingly, Brosschot and colleagues have argued that the more appropriate question, for stress researchers, is not what *starts* stress reactivity but what *stops* it.

This view has implications for the study of SGD relationships. Instead of assuming that stigma and marginalization are added stressors for SGD relationships (and also for interracial and lower-income relationships), it is more appropriate to assume that chronic social safety is an "added benefit" for cisgender and heterosexual relationships (especially among White, middle-class individuals). The fact that social safety has been presumed to be a "default state" for contemporary relationships may reflect the fact that the majority of research on close relationships has been conducted by contemporary Western scholars who tend to study White, middle-class, heterosexual couples (Karney & Bradbury, 1995). The degree to which such individuals enjoy plentiful access to social safety across multiple levels (institutional, cultural, and interpersonal) is a novelty, in evolutionary terms, similar to the ways in which access to high-quality plentiful food in the contemporary industrialized West is an evolutionary novelty.

In the same way that the average cisgender, heterosexual couple might not be consciously aware of their plentiful access to social safety, many individuals in SGD relationships may not be consciously aware of their chronic vigilance for threat. As reviewed by Brosschot (2017), a growing body of research indicates that our brains and bodies respond to cues of threat and stress outside our conscious awareness. For example, neurobiological studies have detected threat-related activation in the amygdala even when the threat-inducing stimuli are presented below the threshold of conscious awareness (Critchley et al., 2002; LeDoux, 2000; Pessoa, 2005). This activation extends to peripheral autonomic activation: Levy et al. (2000) elicited blood pressure elevations in elderly adults by subliminally exposing them to words that communicated denigrating views of aging (such as "demented," "sick," and "frail"). Subsequent studies have successfully triggered autonomic stress reactivity through subliminal exposure to threats (van der Ploeg, Brosschot, Verkuil, et al., 2017), fear stimuli (reviewed in van der Ploeg, Brosschot, Versluis, & Verkuil, 2017) and aversive interpersonal relationships (Carlisle et al., 2012).

Brosschot and colleagues (Brosschot, 2010; Brosschot et al., 2010) have argued for greater attention to the role of nonconscious stress and worry in eliciting forms of prolonged physiological activity that may engender long-term health risks. We argue that nonconscious stress and worry also pose notable risks for interpersonal functioning. Specifically, chronic exposure to sexual/gender stigma may intrude upon SGD individuals' close relationships in ways that they do not consciously perceive or understand. SGD individuals may approach their intimate relationships with a degree of chronic worry, hypersensitivity, hypervigilance, fatalistic thinking, and anxiety that they cannot consciously name, identify, or explain. Given the chronicity of SGD exposure to social threat, many SGD individuals may have become acclimated to chronic stress as a "regular" state of being. As Brosschot (2010) points out, "it is often only through the relief we feel when after receiving a positive examination outcome or a benign medical diagnosis that we realize how 'stressed' we actually were" (p. 48). For SGD individuals who have never had an opportunity to experience intimate social ties *outside* the context of pervasive social stigmatization, the legacies of chronic threat exposure may be difficult to identify and alter.

Legacies of Early Threat Exposure

Childhood adversity has implications for evolutionary perspectives on SGD relationships, although the topic receives little discussion by relationship researchers. Extensive research using nationally representative samples has found that SGD individuals have disproportionate rates of childhood and adolescent exposure to emotional, sexual, and physical abuse, as well as adversity related to parental mental health and household instability (Austin et al., 2016; Baams, 2018; Fergusson et al., 1999; McGeough & Sterzing, 2018; McLaughlin et al., 2012; Merrick et al., 2018; Schnarrs et al., 2019; Schneeberger et al., 2014; Tobin & Delaney, 2019; Xu et al., 2019; Zietsch et al., 2012). The differences in prevalence rates are stark: The prevalence of physical, sexual, and emotional abuse among cisgender heterosexuals in the United States is 12%, 17%, and 35%, respectively (Merrick et al., 2018), but among sexually diverse individuals, these figures are approximately *doubled* (Merrick et al., 2018; Schneeberger et al., 2014).

Scholars studying the relationships of SGD individuals rarely discuss the high rates of early adversity in this population, perhaps to avoid giving credence to the long-standing but false myth that early maltreatment "causes" sexual and/or gender diversity. There is no evidence for such a causal pathway (see Rind, 2013), and in fact, there is extensive evidence that for many SGD individuals, the early expression of sexual or gender diversity *elicits* maltreatment (reviewed in Corliss et al., 2002). McGeough et al. (2018) systematically reviewed research on family victimization and sexual identity development and found higher rates of family victimization among youths who became aware of their same-gender attractions at earlier ages and who made earlier disclosures about their sexuality to peers and family members. Childhood gender nonconformity is a known risk factor for parental abuse (Roberts et al., 2012) as well as peer victimization (D'Augelli et al., 2006; Roberts et al., 2013). One study examined the relative roles of gender nonconformity and early trauma in predicting adult sexual victimization and found that for men, early gender nonconformity predicted experiences of adult trauma from an adult family member, which in turn predicted men's subsequent experiences with sexual victimization (Bo et al., 2019). The fact that these effects were found for men but not women is consistent with the fact that parents often react more negatively to gender nonconformity among boys than among girls (Spivey et al., 2018).

Childhood adversity among SGD populations deserves greater attention by scholars interested in understanding how their life paths and intimate relationships differ from those of cisgender and heterosexual individuals. Childhood adversity is a well-established predictor of mental health problems in adolescence and adulthood (Ford et al., 2011;

Fritz et al., 2018; Sheikh et al., 2016), along with a variety of interpersonal challenges such as distrust of others, difficulty maintaining appropriate boundaries, discomfort with closeness, and chronic isolation (Beitchman et al., 1992; Briere & Elliott, 1994; Busby et al., 1993; Larson & Lamont, 2005; Mullen et al., 1994). These long-term effects may explain why individuals exposed to early adversity have greater risks for later intimate partner violence (Hammett et al., 2020), relationship stress and dysfunction (Donnelly et al., 2018; Wheeler et al., 2020), and relationship dissolution (Dayoung et al., 2019). Furthermore, individuals exposed to physical and sexual victimization in childhood have disproportionate rates of *revictimization* in their adolescent and adult relationships (Arata, 2002; Roodman & Clum, 2001; Widom et al., 2008), which further increases risks for mental health problems, substance use, suicide, violence, intimate partner violence, sexual risk behaviors, and chronic conditions (Hatchel et al., 2019; Johns et al., 2019; King et al., 2019; Newcomb et al., 2020; Peitzmeier et al., 2020; Scheer et al., 2020; Woulfe & Goodman, 2020). Hence, there is no way to understand the unique dynamics of relationship maintenance among SGD couples without taking into account the long-term psychosocial effects of childhood adversity.

Some studies have specifically adopted an evolutionary perspective on links between early adversity and later interpersonal dysfunction. Figueredo et al. (2020) argued that early childhood adversity (particularly, the combination of resource instability and maternal insensitivity) alters youths' developing cognitive schemas regarding social vulnerability and shifts them onto a "fast" life history strategy characterized by early reproduction, impulsiveness, and aggression. The notion of "fast" versus "slow" life history strategies comes from life history theory, an evolutionary theory that posits that early life experiences calibrate a child's physical and neurobiological development in a manner to promote future adaptation. According to this model, early life experiences (harshness vs. warmth, unpredictability vs. stability, nurturance vs. neglect) provide cues to the developing organism regarding what types of environments they are likely to confront in the future. Early adversity is a potent cue that the child's future is likely to be difficult, unpredictable, and dangerous (Brumbach et al., 2009). In such environments, the most adaptive developmental strategy is for the child to mature quickly, to take risks to meet immediate needs, and to be constantly wary of danger, given the multiple environmental threats to both survival and reproduction (Del Giudice et al., 2011). This is not to suggest that traits such as threat vigilance, impulsiveness, and aggression are wholly environmentally determined. Research using behavioral genetics increasingly indicates a role for genetic factors in shaping features of the child's psychosocial and biological development (such as attachment style and pubertal maturation) that have been traditionally attributed to environmental factors (Barbaro et al., 2017a, 2017b). Hence, some of the association between a child's exposure to adversity and the child's later psychosocial development may stem from shared genetic factors that underlie both maladaptive parenting *and* psychological vulnerabilities, such as impulsivity and aggression (Anokhin et al., 2015; Niv et al., 2012; Porsch et al., 2016). Diathesis-stress models and epigenetic models suggest that environmental factors (ranging from the uterine environment to early household characteristics) *interact* with certain genetic predispositions to augment the child's developmental profile and trait expression (Essex et al., 2013; Meaney, 2010; Monroe & Simons, 1991; Murgatroyd & Spengler, 2011). In other cases, adversity may directly compete with genetic influences. For example, one twin study examined genetic and environmental influences on children's cortisol reactivity to stress. They found that among children raised without family adversity, genetic factors significantly contributed to individual differences in cortisol stress reactivity, but genetic factors did *not* contribute to cortisol stress reactivity among children exposed to familial adversity (Ouellet-Morin et al., 2008).

A number of studies have investigated the implications of "fast" life history strategies among adversity-exposed individuals for later sexual behavior, substance use, and rule-breaking (reviewed in Alley and Diamond, 2021). Yet from the perspective of romantic relationship functioning, some of the most important implications of early adversity and "fast" life history strategies may concern stress reactivity and regulation. The adaptive calibration model of stress responsivity (Del Giudice et al., 2011) builds on life history theory by positing that the child's developing stress reactivity systems are "calibrated" by early life experiences in a manner that fosters adaptation to future expectable environments. According to this model, environmental features such as danger, unpredictability, and neglect trigger the development of distinct patterns of stress responsivity that should increase the child's eventual survival and reproduction. For example, early experiences of adversity and threat foster "hyperreactive" stress response systems (specifically within the hypothalamic-pituitary-adrenocorticol axis, the autonomic nervous system, and the immune system) which assist the developing child in detecting and responding to future threats, even in the absence of parental nurturance.

Hyperreactivity to threat among adversity-exposed individuals has also been observed with regard to cognitive and emotional processes. Adversity-exposed individuals show heightened sensitivity to emotionally negative information, particularly in the context of their intimate relationships (Miano et al., 2018), and fatalistic expectations about the future (Brumley et al., 2017). Although these patterns might be adaptive in an evolutionary sense (by preparing individuals to confront the same types of harsh social environments they faced in childhood), they are maladaptive from the perspective of adult relationship functioning. Hence, SGD individuals who have faced childhood and adolescent adversity may be endowed with enduring patterns of emotional and physiological stress reactivity that make it more difficult to cope with the larger social threats of stigma *in concert with* the day-to-day threats of relationship conflict and management. Adopting an evolutionary perspective on the legacy of early life adversity helps to frame such patterns within a broader context, highlighting the fact that hypervigilance to threat and hypersensitivity to negative emotions are not fundamental deficits but in fact complex *adaptations* that have the ultimate goal of fostering survival and well-being. From this perspective, SGD couples that struggle with emotion regulation and conflict resolution are not inherently "damaged" or "dysfunctional" but instead are coping with a complex array of evolved biopsychosocial adaptations that may have served them well in the ancestral environment but are ill-suited to our contemporary context. For this reason, "routine" relationship maintenance may be both more challenging and more important.

Directions for Future Research

There has already been a fair amount of empirical research on relationship processes (including relational maintenance) in sexually diverse couples and a small but growing body of research on gender-diverse couples. How can the evolutionary-theoretical perspective introduced in this chapter make a novel contribution in these areas? We see three promising areas for future research.

First, how might relationship partners assist one another in establishing and maintaining *safety* in the face of the chronic threats that these couples face due to their stigmatized status? Most studies of relational maintenance focus on within-couple processes such as sharing tasks or expressing affection (Dainton & Aylor, 2002; Haas, 2003; McNulty et al., 2008; Rusbult et al., 2004), but within SGD couples the basic establishment of social and psychological safety may be the most important form of relational maintenance. Yet, what types of behaviors "count" as safety signals and safety maintenance? Because most research on relational maintenance has been conducted with cisgender, heterosexual couples, conventional assessments of relational maintenance may be ill suited to capturing the dynamics involved in establishing and maintaining safety in SGD couples. For example, public expressions of affection are a routine form of relational maintenance for cisgender, heterosexual couples, but for SGD couples it might be the *lack* of public displays of affection that fosters a sense of safety, given that public displays of affection might lead to harassment and violence. SGD couples report less comfort with public displays of affection (compared to cisgender, heterosexual couples) and higher threat-vigilance during such activities (Blair, McKenna, & Holmberg, 2022). Consider, also, interactions with in-laws: For cisgender, heterosexual couples, maintaining regular contact with in-laws might serve relational maintenance goals by engaging broader systems of social support and affirmation for their partnership. Yet many SGD individuals have troubled relationships with their own families and with their partner's families. In such cases, *not* spending time with in-laws and taking active steps to *protect* one another from family rejection may prove to be the most adaptive strategies.

The notion of adaptation is helpful here: As evolutionary theorizing teaches us, there is no single strategy for maximizing health and well-being. Rather, individuals must constantly tailor their goals and behavior for their current (and future environment). In the threatening social environment facing SGD couples, adaptive relational maintenance strategies may diverge notably from the strategies employed by cisgender, heterosexual couples in ways that have not yet been fully appreciated by relationship scientists. Perhaps the most important task for future research is to broaden our perspective on the nature of adaptive forms of relational maintenance—especially for individuals exposed to environmental adversity—and to bring a deeper appreciation of threat and safety into our assessments of SGD couples.

Perhaps the most important relational maintenance challenge for SGD involves negotiating relationship behaviors and practices that serve each partner's individual needs. Consider, for example, a study by Iantaffi and Bockting (2011), which found that almost one fourth of transgender participants reported preferring to have the lights off when they engaged in sexual contact with their partners, to cope with their own self-consciousness and body-related anxiety. Although this study did not provide any information about the *partners'* responses to such requests, it is interesting to consider how couples might go about establishing and maintaining such arrangements. On one hand, it might be maladaptive for a partner to "go along" with such an arrangement rather than helping the transgender partner to become more comfortable and accepting of their body. Yet maybe not: feelings of body dysmorphia and self-consciousness can be enduring challenges for gender-diverse individuals, and it might be naïve or insensitive to assume that with a little support, individuals can simply "get over" their body concerns.

A more relationship-enhancing and relationship-maintaining approach might be to respect and defend one's partner's boundaries and work together to establish practices around physical intimacy that feel safe for both individuals. Individuals with different histories of social threat (in adulthood as well as childhood) may have different safety needs, and reconciling these differences may be one of the most challenging aspects of SGD relationship functioning. The fact that SGD individuals have twice the rate of childhood maltreatment, compared to cisgender, heterosexual individuals, suggests that SGD individuals may have enduring issues with safety and intimacy that both partners will need to carefully navigate. The adaptive calibration model suggests that for such individuals, their stress response systems have been "tuned" to expect and prepare for threat even within environments that "appear" safe (such as a couple's own bedroom). These patterns are not pathologies but simply the legacy of our own evolved developmental programming that treats childhood threat as a precursor to lasting adult danger.

Along the same lines, some scholars have noted that "microaffirmations" may be particularly important aspects of relational maintenance in gender-diverse couples (Pulice-Farrow et al., 2019). Microaffirmations denote everyday actions that serve to affirm the other person's identity and well-being. From our perspective, microaffirmations also represent powerful *safety signals* that communicate to one's partner that they are not alone, and that you will protect them from harassment and danger. Examples of microaffirmations might include correcting other individuals who misgender your partner, helping your partner choose clothing that affirm their sense of self, or even finding subtle ways to escort your partner out of social environments that become uncomfortable or threatening. These actions are not just affirming for the partner's identity and security but inherently *relationship enhancing* and *relationship maintaining.* Future research on relationship maintenance in SGD couples should attend more carefully to the preeminent role of *safety* for such couples, and for the importance of dyadic approaches to fostering and maintaining safety for both partners.

In closing, we reiterate that SGD individuals are not the only individuals for whom social safety is a pressing individual and relationship concern. Interracial couples, interfaith couples, couples coping with disability, and other stigmatized groups are also likely to struggle with fundamental issues of safety and danger. Heightened attention to these dynamics, from an evolutionary perspective, is likely to enhance our understanding of relationship diversity more broadly. Couples navigating intersecting forms of stigma and oppression have been particularly understudied and deserve much greater attention. Consider, for example, a couple containing a Latina cisgender woman and a White transgender woman—how might their intersecting experiences of marginalization and privilege due to gender and ethnicity shape their experiences as individuals and as a couple? How might these experiences shift if they choose to live in a diverse urban area versus an isolated rural town? What types of practices might they adopt, as a couple, to cope with their individual and joint experiences of danger and marginalization? Greater appreciation of the importance of safety can inform and advance our conceptualization of "relational maintenance" and provide a deeper understanding of couple-functioning across the full spectrum of sexual and gender diversity.

References

Alley, J. C. and Diamond, L. M. (2021). Early childhood adversity and women's sexual behavior: The role of sensitivity to sexual reward. *Developmental Review, 61*, 100982.

Amat, J., Baratta, M. V., Paul, E., Bland, S. T., Watkins, L. R., & Maier, S. F. (2005). Medial prefrontal cortex determines how stressor controllability affects behavior and dorsal raphe nucleus. *Nature Neuroscience, 8*(3), 365–371. https://doi.org/10.1038/nn1399

Anokhin, A. P., Grant, J. D., Mulligan, R. C., & Heath, A. C. (2015). The genetics of impulsivity: Evidence for the heritability of delay discounting. *Biological Psychiatry, 77*(10), 887–894. https://doi.org/10.1016/j.biopsych.2014.10.022

Arata, C. M. (2002). Child sexual abuse and sexual revictimization. *Clinical Psychology: Science and Practice, 9*(2), 135–164. https://doi.org/10.1093/clipsy.9.2.135

Austin, A., Herrick, H., & Proescholdbell, S. (2016). Adverse childhood experiences related to poor adult health among lesbian, gay, and bisexual individuals. *American Journal of Public Health, 106*(2), 314–320. https://doi.org/10.2105/ajph.2015.302904

Baams, L. (2018). Disparities for LGBTQ and gender nonconforming adolescents. *Pediatrics, 141*(5), Article e20173004. https://doi.org/10.1542/peds.2017-3004

Barbaro, N., Boutwell, B. B., Barnes, J. C., & Shackelford, T. K. (2017a). Genetic confounding of the relationship between father absence and age at menarche. *Evolution and Human Behavior, 38*(3), 357–365. https://doi.org/10.1016/j.evolhumbehav.2016.11.007

Barbaro, N., Boutwell, B. B., Barnes, J. C., & Shackelford, T. K. (2017b). Rethinking the transmission gap: What behavioral genetics and evolutionary psychology mean for attachment theory: A comment on Verhage et al (2016). *Psychological Bulletin, 143*(1), 107–113. https://doi.org/10.1037/bul0000066

Becker, A. B. (2014). Employment discrimination, local school boards, and LGBT civil rights: Reviewing 25 years of public opinion data. *International Journal of Public Opinion Research, 26*(3), 342–354. https://doi.org/10.1093/ijpor/edu003

Beitchman, J. H., Zucker, K. J., Hood, J. E., DaCosta, G. A., Akman, D., & Cassavia, E. (1992). A review of the long-term effects of child sexual abuse. *Child Abuse & Neglect, 16*(1), 101–118. https://doi.org/10.1016/0145-2134(92)90011-F" https://doi.org/10.1016/0145-2134(92)90011-F

Blair, K. L., McKenna, O., & Holmberg, D. (2022). On guard: Public versus private affection-sharing experiences in same-sex, gender-diverse, and mixed-sex relationships. *Journal of Social and Personal Relationships*, 02654075221090678. https://doi.org/10.1177/02654075221090678

Bos, H., de Haas, S., & Kuyper, L. (2019). Lesbian, gay, and bisexual adults: Childhood gender nonconformity, childhood trauma, and sexual victimization. *Journal of Interpersonal Violence, 34*(3), 496–515. https://doi.org/10.1177/0886260516641285

Bratter, J. L., & Eschbach, K. (2006). "What about the couple?" Interracial marriage and psychological distress. *Social Science Research, 35*(4), 1025–1047. https://doi.org/10.1016/j.ssresearch.2005.09.001

Bratter, J. L., & King, R. B. (2008). "But will it last?" Marital instability among interracial and same-race couples. *Family Relations, 57*(2), 160–171. https://doi.org/10.1111/j.1741-3729.2008.00491.x

Brenner, C. (1995). *Eight bullets: One woman's story of surviving anti-gay violence.* Firebrand Books.

Briere, J. N., & Elliott, D. M. (1994). Immediate and long-term impacts of child sexual abuse. *The Future of Children, 4*(2), 54–69. https://doi.org/10.2307/1602523

Brosschot, J. F. (2010). Markers of chronic stress: Prolonged physiological activation and (un)conscious perseverative cognition. *Neuroscience and Biobehavioral Reviews, 35*(1), 46–50. https://doi.org/10.1016/j.neubiorev.2010.01.004

Brosschot, J. F. (2017). Ever at the ready for events that never happen. *European Journal of Psychotraumatology, 8*(1), 1309934–1309934. https://doi.org/10.1080/20008198.2017.1309934

Brosschot, J. F., Verkuil, B., & Thayer, J. F. (2010). Conscious and unconscious perseverative cognition: Is a large part of prolonged physiological activity due to unconscious stress? *Journal of Psychosomatic Research, 69*(4), 407–416. https://doi.org/10.1016/j.jpsychores.2010.02.002

Brosschot, J. F., Verkuil, B., & Thayer, J. F. (2016). The default response to uncertainty and the importance of perceived safety in anxiety and stress: An evolution-theoretical perspective. *Journal of Anxiety Disorders, 41*, 22–34. https://doi.org/10.1016/j.janxdis.2016.04.012

Brosschot, J. F., Verkuil, B., & Thayer, J. F. (2017). Exposed to events that never happen: Generalized unsafety, the default stress response, and prolonged autonomic activity. *Neuroscience and Biobehavioral Reviews, 74*(Pt. B), 287–296. https://doi.org/10.1016/j.neubiorev.2016.07.019

Brosschot, J. F., Verkuil, B., & Thayer, J. F. (2018). Generalized unsafety theory of stress: Unsafe environments and conditions, and the default stress response. *International Journal of Environmental Research and Public Health, 15*(3), 464. https://doi.org/10.3390/ijerph15030464

Brumbach, B. H., Figueredo, A. J., & Ellis, B. J. (2009). Effects of harsh and unpredictable environments in adolescence on development of life history strategies: A longitudinal test of an evolutionary model. *Human Nature, 20*(1), 25–51. https://doi.org/10.1007/s12110-009-9059-3

Brumley, L. D., Jaffee, S. R., & Brumley, B. P. (2017). Pathways from childhood adversity to problem behaviors in young adulthood: The mediating role of adolescents' future expectations. *Journal of Youth and Adolescence, 46*(1), 1–14. https://doi.org/10.1007/s10964-016-0597-9

Busby, D. M., Glenn, E., Steggell, G. L., & Adamson, D. W. (1993). Treatment issues for survivors of physical and sexual abuse. *Journal of Marital and Family Therapy, 19*(4), 377–391. https://doi.org/10.1111/j.1752-0606.1993.tb01000.x

Cao, H., Zhou, N., Fine, M., Liang, Y., Li, J., & Mills-Koonce, W. R. (2017). Sexual minority stress and same-sex relationship well-being: A meta-analysis of research prior to the U.S. nationwide legalization of same-sex marriage. *Journal of Marriage and the Family, 79*(5), 1258–1277. https://doi.org/10.1111/jomf.12415

Carleton, R. N. (2016). Into the unknown: A review and synthesis of contemporary models involving uncertainty. *Journal of Anxiety Disorders, 39*, 30–43. https://doi.org/10.1016/j.janxdis.2016.02.007

Carlisle, M., Uchino, B. N., Sanbonmatsu, D. M., Smith, T. W., Cribbet, M. R., Birmingham, W., Light, K. C., & Vaughn, A. A. (2012). Subliminal activation of social ties moderates cardiovascular reactivity during acute stress. *Health Psychology, 31*(2), 217–225. https://doi.org/10.1037/a0025187

Chodzen, G., Hidalgo, M. A., Chen, D., & Garofalo, R. (2019). Minority stress factors associated with depression and anxiety among transgender and gender-nonconforming youth. *Journal of Adolescent Health, 64*(4), 467–471. https://doi.org/10.1016/j.jadohealth.2018.07.006

Corliss, H. L., Cochran, S. D., & Mays, V. M. (2002). Reports of parental maltreatment during childhood in a United States population-based survey of homosexual, bisexual, and heterosexual adults. *Child Abuse & Neglect, 26*(11), 1165–1178. https://doi.org/10.1016/S0145-2134(02)00385-X

Critchley, H. D., Mathias, C. J., & Dolan, R. J. (2002). Fear conditioning in humans: The influence of awareness and autonomic arousal on functional neuroanatomy. *Neuron, 33*(4), 653–663. https://doi.org/10.1016/s0896-6273(02)00588-3

D'Augelli, A. R., Grossman, A. H., & Starks, M. T. (2006). Childhood gender atypicality, victimization, and PTSD among lesbian, gay, and bisexual youth. *Journal of Interpersonal Violence, 21*(11), 1462–1482. https://doi.org/10.1177/0886260506293482

Dainton, M., & Aylor, B. (2002). Routine and strategic maintenance efforts: Behavioral patterns, variations associated with relational length, and the prediction of relational characteristics. *Communication Monographs, 69*(1), 52–66.

Dayoung, B., Wickrama, K. A. S., & Bae, D. (2019). Pathways linking early socioeconomic adversity to diverging profiles of romantic relationship dissolution in young adulthood. *Journal of Family Psychology, 33*(1), 23–33. https://doi.org/10.1037/fam0000465

Del Giudice, M., Ellis, B. J., & Shirtcliff, E. A. (2011). The adaptive calibration model of stress responsivity. *Neuroscience and Biobehavioral Reviews, 35*(7), 1562–1592. https://doi.org/10.1016/j.neubiorev.2010.11.007" https://doi.org/10.1016/j.neubiorev.2010.11.007

Diamond, L. M. & Alley, J. C. (2022). Rethinking minority stress: A social safety perspective on the health effects of stigma in sexually-diverse and gender-diverse populations. *Neuroscience & Biobehavioral Reviews,* 104720.

Diamond, L. M., Dehlin, A. J., & Alley, J. C. (2021). Systemic inflammation as a driver of health disparities among sexually-diverse and gender-diverse individuals. *Psychoneuroendocrinology, 129,* 105215

Diamond, L. M., & Dehlin, A. J. (2021). Sexual and gender diversity and family relationships. In A. L. Vangelisti (Ed.), *The Routledge handbook of family communication* (3rd ed., pp. 173–186). Routledge.

Diamond, L. M., Fagundes, C. P., & Butterworth, M. R. (2010). Intimate relationships across the lifespan. In M. E. Lamb, L. White, & A. Freund (Eds.), *Handbook of lifespan development* (Vol. 2, pp. 379–433). John Wiley & Sons.

Donnelly, R., Umberson, D., & Kroeger, R. A. (2018). Childhood adversity, daily stress, and marital strain in same-sex and different-sex marriages. *Journal of Family Issues, 39*(7), 2085–2106. https://doi.org/10.1177/0192513X17741177

Doyle, D. M., & Molix, L. (2014). Perceived discrimination as a stressor for close relationships: Identifying psychological and physiological pathways. *Journal of Behavioral Medicine, 37*(6), 1134–1144. https://doi.org/10.1007/s10865-014-9563-8

Dyar, C., Sarno, E. L., Newcomb, M. E., & Whitton, S. W. (2020). Longitudinal associations between minority stress, internalizing symptoms, and substance use among sexual and gender minority individuals assigned female at birth. *Journal of Consulting and Clinical Psychology, 88*(5), 389–401. https://doi.org/10.1037/ccp0000487

Essex, M. J., Boyce, W. T., Hertzman, C., Lam, L. L., Armstrong, J. M., Neumann, S. M. A., & Kobor, M. S. (2013). Epigenetic vestiges of early developmental adversity: Childhood stress exposure and DNA methylation in adolescence. *Child Development, 84*(1), 58–75. https://doi.org/10.1111/j.1467-8624.2011.01641.x

Fergusson, D. M., Horwood, L. J., & Beautrais, A. L. (1999). Is sexual orientation related to mental health problems and suicidality in young people? *Archives of General Psychiatry, 56,* 876–880.

Figueredo, A. J., Black, C. J., Patch, E. A., Heym, N., Ferreira, J. H. B. P., Varella, M. A. C., Defelipe, R. P., Cosentino, L. A. M., Castro, F. N., Natividade, J. C., Hattori, W. T., Pérez-Ramos, M., Madison, G., & Fernandes, H. B. F. (2020). The cascade of chaos: From early adversity to interpersonal aggression. *Evolutionary Behavioral Sciences, 15*(3), 231–250. https://doi.org/10.1037/ebs0000241

Flanders, C. E., Dobinson, C., & Logie, C. (2017). Young bisexual women's perspectives on the relationship between bisexual stigma, mental health, and sexual health: A qualitative study. *Critical Public Health, 27*(1), 75–85. https://doi.org/10.1080/09581596.2016.1158786

Ford, E., Clark, C., & Stansfeld, S. A. (2011). The influence of childhood adversity on social relations and mental health at mid-life. *Journal of Affective Disorders, 133*(1–2), 320–327. https://doi.org/10.1016/j.jad.2011.03.017

Fritz, J., de Graaff, A. M., Caisley, H., van Harmelen, A. L., & Wilkinson, P. O. (2018). A systematic review of amenable resilience factors that moderate and/or mediate the relationship between childhood adversity and mental health in young people. *Frontiers of Psychiatry, 9*, Article 230. https://doi.org/10.3389/fpsyt.2018.00230

Green, R.-J. (2008). Gay and lesbian couples: Successful coping with minority stress. In M. McGoldrick & K. V. Hardy (Eds.), *Re-visioning family therapy: Race, culture, and gender in clinical practice* (2nd ed., pp. 300–310). Guilford Press.

Haas, S. M. (2003). Relationship maintenance in same-sex couples. In D. J. Canary (Ed.), *Maintaining relationships through communication: Relational, contextual, and cultural variations* (pp. 209–230). Erlbaum.

Hammett, J. F., Karney, B. R., & Bradbury, T. N. (2020). Adverse childhood experiences, stress, and intimate partner violence among newlywed couples living with low incomes. *Journal of Family Psychology, 34*(4), 436–447. https://doi.org/10.1037/fam0000629

Hatchel, T., Valido, A., De Pedro, K. T., Huang, Y., & Espelage, D. L. (2019). Minority stress among transgender adolescents: The role of peer victimization, school belonging, and ethnicity. *Journal of Child and Family Studies, 28*(9), 2467–2476. https://doi.org/10.1007/s10826-018-1168-3

Herek, G. M. (2009). Hate crimes and stigma-related experiences among sexual minority adults in the United States: Prevalence estimates from a national probability sample. *Journal of Interpersonal Violence, 24*(1), 54–74. https://doi.org/10.1177/0886260508316477

Iantaffi, A., & Bockting, W. O. (2011). Views from both sides of the bridge? Gender, sexual legitimacy and transgender people's experiences of relationships. *Culture, Health & Sexuality, 13*(3), 355–370. https://doi.org/10.1080/13691058.2010.537770

Johns, M. M., Lowry, R., Andrzejewski, J., Barrios, L. C., Demissie, Z., McManus, T., Rasberry, C. N., Robin, L., & about:blankUnderwood, J. M. (2019). Transgender identity and experiences of violence victimization, substance use, suicide risk, and sexual risk behaviors among high school students—19 states and large urban school districts, 2017. *MMWR: Morbidity and Mortality Weekly Report, 68*(3), 67–71. https://doi.org/10.15585/mmwr.mm6803a3

Karney, B. R., & Bradbury, T. N. (1995). The longitudinal course of marital quality and stability: A review of theory, methods, and research. *Psychological Bulletin, 118*, 3–34.

Kemeny, M. E. (2009). Psychobiological responses to social threat: Evolution of a psychological model in psychoneuroimmunology. *Brain, Behavior, and Immunity, 23*(1), 1–9.

Kemeny, M. E., & Shestyuk, A. (2008). Emotions, the neuroendocrine and immune systems, and health. In M. Lewis, J. M. Haviland-Jones, & L. F. Barrett (Eds.), *Handbook of emotions* (3rd ed., pp. 661–675). Guilford Press.

Kennedy, D. P., & Adolphs, R. (2012). The social brain in psychiatric and neurological disorders. *Trends in Cognitive Sciences, 16*(11), 559–572. https://doi.org/10.1016/j.tics.2012.09.006

Kenrick, D. T., Griskevicius, V., Neuberg, S. L., & Schaller, M. (2010). Renovating the pyramid of needs: Contemporary extensions built upon ancient foundations. *Perspectives on Psychological Science, 5*(3), 292–314. https://doi.org/10.1177/1745691610369469

King, W. M., Restar, A., & Operario, D. (2019). Exploring multiple forms of intimate partner violence in a gender and racially/ethnically diverse sample of transgender adults. *Journal of Interpersonal Violence, 36*(19–20), NP10477–NP10498. https://doi.org/10.1177/0886260519876024

Koken, J. A., Bimbi, D. S., & Parsons, J. T. (2009). Experiences of familial acceptance-rejection among transwomen of color. *Journal of Family Psychology, 23*(6), 853–860. https://doi.org/10.1037/a0017198

Larson, J. H., & Lamont, C. (2005). The relationship of childhood sexual abuse to the marital attitudes and readiness for marriage of single young adult women. *Journal of Family Issues, 26*(4), 415–430. https://doi.org/10.1177/0192513X04270474

Layland, E. K., Carter, J. A., Perry, N. S., Cienfuegos-Szalay, J., Nelson, K. M., Bonner, C. P., & Rendina, H. J. (2020). A systematic review of stigma in sexual and gender minority health interventions. *Translational Behavioral Medicine, 10*(5), 1200–1210. https://doi.org/10.1093/tbm/ibz200

LeBlanc, A. J., Frost, D. M., & Wight, R. G. (2015). Minority stress and stress proliferation among same-sex and other marginalized couples. *Journal of Marriage and Family, 77*(1), 40–59. https://doi.org/10.1111/jomf.12160

LeDoux, J. E. (2000). Emotion circuits in the brain. *Annual Review of Neuroscience, 23*(1), 155–184. https://doi.org/10.1146/annurev.neuro.23.1.155

Lefevor, G. T., Boyd-Rogers, C. C., Sprague, B. M., & Janis, R. A. (2019). Health disparities between genderqueer, transgender, and cisgender individuals: An extension of minority stress theory. *Journal of Counseling Psychology, 66*(4), 385–395. https://doi.org/10.1037/cou0000339

Levy, B. R., Hausdorff, J. M., Hencke, R., & Wei, J. Y. (2000). Reducing cardiovascular stress with positive self-stereotypes of aging. *The Journals of Gerontology: Psychological Sciences and Social Sciences, 55*(4), P205–213. https://doi.org/10.1093/geronb/55.4.p205

Maier, S. F. (2015). Behavioral control blunts reactions to contemporaneous and future adverse events: Medial prefrontal cortex plasticity and a corticostriatal network. *Neurobiology of Stress, 1*, 12–22. https://doi.org/10.1016/j.ynstr.2014.09.003

Maslow, A. H. (1943). A theory of human motivation. *Psychological Review, 50*(4), 370–396. https://doi.org/10.1037/h0054346

McGeough, B. L., & Sterzing, P. R. (2018). A systematic review of family victimization experiences among sexual minority youth. *The Journal of Primary Prevention, 39*(5), 491–528. https://doi.org/10.1007/s10935-018-0523-x

McLaughlin, K. A., Hatzenbuehler, M. L., Xuan, Z., & Conron, K. J. (2012). Disproportionate exposure to early-life adversity and sexual orientation disparities in psychiatric morbidity. *Child Abuse & Neglect, 36*(9), 645–655. https://doi.org/10.1016/j.chiabu.2012.07.004

McNulty, J. K., O'Mara, E. M., & Karney, B. R. (2008). Benevolent cognitions as a strategy of relationship maintenance: "Don't sweat the small stuff". . . But it is not all small stuff. *Journal of Personality and Social Psychology, 94*(4), 631–646.

Meaney, M. J. (2010). Epigenetics and the biological definition of gene x environment interactions. *Child Development, 81*(1), 41–79. https://doi.org/10.1111/j.1467-8624.2009.01381.x

Meier, S. C., Pardo, S. T., Labuski, C., & Babcock, J. (2013). Measures of clinical health among female-to-male transgender persons as a function of sexual orientation. *Archives of Sexual Behavior, 42*(3), 463–474. https://doi.org/10.1007/s10508-012-0052-2

Merrick, M. T., Ford, D. C., Ports, K. A., & Guinn, A. S. (2018). Prevalence of adverse childhood experiences from the 2011-2014 Behavioral Risk Factor Surveillance System in 23 states. *JAMA Pediatrics, 172*(11), 1038–1044. https://doi.org/10.1001/jamapediatrics.2018.2537

Meyer, I. H. (2003). Prejudice, social stress, and mental health in lesbian, gay, and bisexual populations: Conceptual issues and research evidence. *Psychological Bulletin, 129*(5), 674–697. https://doi.org/10.1037/0033-2909.129.5.674

Miano, A., Weber, T., Roepke, S., & Dziobek, I. (2018). Childhood maltreatment and context dependent empathic accuracy in adult romantic relationships. *Psychological Trauma, 10*(3), 309–318. https://doi.org/10.1037/tra0000296

Monroe, S. M., & Simons, A. D. (1991). Diathesis-stress theories in the context of life stress research: Implications for the depressive disorders. *Psychological Bulletin, 110*(3), 406–425. https://doi.org/10.1037/0033-2909.110.3.406

Mullen, P. E., Martin, J. L., Anderson, J. C., Romans, S. E., & Herbison, G. P. (1994). The effect of child sexual abuse on social, interpersonal and sexual function in adult life. *The British Journal of Psychiatry, 165*(1), 35–47. https://doi.org/10.1192/bjp.165.1.35

Murgatroyd, C., & Spengler, D. (2011). Epigenetic programming of the HPA axis: Early life decides. *Stress: The International Journal on the Biology of Stress, 14*, 581–589.

National Coalition of Anti-Violence Programs. (2011). *Hate violence against lesbian, gay, bisexual, transgender, queer, and HIV-affected communities in the United States, 2010.* Retrieved from http://www.ncdsv.org/images/ncavp_hateviolencereport_2011.pdf

Neff, L. A., & Karney, B. R. (2017). Acknowledging the elephant in the room: How stressful environmental contexts shape relationship dynamics. *Current Opinion in Psychology, 13*, 107–110. https://doi.org/10.1016/j.copsyc.2016.05.013

Newcomb, M. E., Hill, R., Buehler, K., Ryan, D. T., Whitton, S. W., & Mustanski, B. (2020). High burden of mental health problems, substance use, violence, and related psychosocial factors in transgender, non-binary, and gender diverse youth and young adults. *Archives of Sexual Behavior, 49*(2), 645–659. https://doi.org/10.1007/s10508-019-01533-9

Niv, S., Tuvblad, C., Raine, A., Wang, P., & Baker, L. A. (2012). Heritability and longitudinal stability of impulsivity in adolescence. *Behavior Genetics, 42*(3), 378–392. https://doi.org/10.1007/s10519-011-9518-6

Ogolsky, B. G., Monk, J. K., Rice, T. M., Theisen, J. C., & Maniotes, C. R. (2017). Relationship maintenance: A review of research on romantic relationships. *Journal of Family Theory & Review, 9*(3), 275–306. https://doi.org/10.1111/jftr.12205

Ouellet-Morin, I., Boivin, M., Dionne, G., Lupien, S. J., Arsenault, L., Barr, R. G., Pérusse, D., & Tremblay, R. E. (2008). Variations in heritability of cortisol reactivity to stress as a function of early familial adversity among 19-month-old twins. *Archives of General Psychiatry, 65*(2), 211–218. https://doi.org/10.1001/archgenpsychiatry.2007.27

Pachankis, J. E., Hatzenbuehler, M. L., Wang, K., Burton, C. L., Crawford, F. W., Phelan, J. C., & Link, B. G. (2018). The burden of stigma on health and well-being: A taxonomy of concealment, course, disruptiveness, aesthetics, origin, and peril across 93 stigmas. *Personality and Social Psychology Bulletin, 44*(4), 451–474. https://doi.org/10.1177/0146167217741313

Pachankis, J. E., Sullivan, T. J., Feinstein, B. A., & Newcomb, M. E. (2018). Young adult gay and bisexual men's stigma experiences and mental health: An 8-year longitudinal study. *Developmental Psychology, 54*(7), 1381–1393. https://doi.org/10.1037/dev0000518

Parra, L. A., Benibgui, M., Helm, J. L., & Hastings, P. D. (2016). Minority stress predicts depression in lesbian, gay, and bisexual emerging adults via elevated diurnal cortisol. *Emerging Adulthood, 4*(5), 365–372. https://doi.org/10.1177/2167696815626822

Peitzmeier, S. M., Malik, M., Kattari, S. K., Marrow, E., Stephenson, R., Agénor, M., & Reisner, S. L. (2020). Intimate partner violence in transgender populations: Systematic review and meta-analysis of prevalence and correlates. *American Journal of Public Health, 110*(9), e1–e14. https://doi.org/10.2105/AJPH.2020.305774

Pessoa, L. (2005). To what extent are emotional visual stimuli processed without attention and awareness? *Current Opinion in Neurobiology, 15*(2), 188–196. https://doi.org/10.1016/j.conb.2005.03.002

Porsch, R. M., Middeldorp, C. M., Cherny, S. S., Krapohl, E., van Beijsterveldt, C. E. M., Loukola, A., Korhonen, T., Pulkkinen, L., Corley, R., Rhee, S., Kaprio, J., Rose, R. R., Hewitt, J. K., Sham, P., Plomin, R., Boomsma, D. I., & Bartels, M. (2016). Longitudinal heritability of childhood aggression. *American Journal of Medical Genetics Part B: Neuropsychiatric Genetics, 171*(5), 697–707. https://doi.org/10.1002/ajmg.b.32420

Puckett, J. A., Newcomb, M. E., Ryan, D. T., Swann, G., Garofalo, R., & Mustanski, B. (2017). Internalized homophobia and perceived stigma: A validation study of stigma measures in a sample of young men who have sex with men. *Sexuality Research and Social Policy, 14*(1), 1–16. https://doi.org/10.1007/s13178-016-0258-5

Pulice-Farrow, L., Bravo, A., & Galupo, M. P. (2019). "Your gender is valid": Microaffirmations in the romantic relationships of transgender individuals. *Journal of LGBT Issues in Counseling, 13*(1), 45–66. https://doi.org/10.1080/15538605.2019.1565799

Reisner, S. L., White Hughto, J. M., Gamarel, K. E., Keuroghlian, A. S., Mizock, L., & Pachankis, J. E. (2016). Discriminatory experiences associated with posttraumatic stress disorder symptoms among transgender adults. *Journal of Counseling Psychology, 63*(5), 509–519. https://doi.org/10.1037/cou0000143

Rind, B. (2013). Homosexual orientation—From nature, not abuse: A critique of Roberts, Glymour, and Koenen (2013). *Archives of Sexual Behavior, 42*(8), 1653–1664. https://doi.org/10.1007/s10508-013-0080-6

Roberts, A. L., Rosario, M., Corliss, H. L., Koenen, K. C., & Austin, S. B. (2012). Childhood gender nonconformity: A risk indicator for childhood abuse and posttraumatic stress in youth. *Pediatrics, 129*(3), 410–417. https://doi.org/10.1542/peds.2011-1804

Roberts, A. L., Rosario, M., Slopen, N., Calzo, J. P., & Austin, S. B. (2013). Childhood gender nonconformity, bullying victimization, and depressive symptoms across adolescence and early adulthood: An 11-year longitudinal study. *Journal of the American Academy of Child and Adolescent Psychiatry, 52*(2), 143–152. https://doi.org/10.1016/j.jaac.2012.11.006

Roodman, A. A., & Clum, G. A. (2001). Revictimization rates and method variance: A meta-analysis. *Clinical Psychology Review, 21*(2), 183–204. https://doi.org/10.1016/s0272-7358(99)00045-8

Ross, J. M., Karney, B. R., Nguyen, T. P., & Bradbury, T. N. (2019). Communication that is maladaptive for middle-class couples is adaptive for socioeconomically disadvantaged couples. *Journal of Personality and Social Psychology, 116*(4), 582–597. https://doi.org/10.1037/pspi0000158

Rostosky, S. S., Riggle, E. D. B., Gray, B. E., & Hatton, R. L. (2007). Minority stress experiences in committed same-sex couple relationships. *Professional Psychology: Research and Practice, 38*(4), 392–400.

Rusbult, C. E., Olsen, N., Davis, J. L., & Hannon, P. A. (2004). Commitment and relationship maintenance mechanisms. In H. T. Reis & C. E. Rusbult (Eds.), *Close relationships: Key readings* (pp. 287–303). Taylor & Francis.

Ryan, C., Huebner, D., Diaz, R. M., & Sanchez, J. (2009). Family rejection as a predictor of negative health outcomes in white and latino lesbian, gay, and bisexual young adults. *Pediatrics, 123*, 346–352. https://doi.org/10.1542/peds.2007-3524

Scheer, J. R., Harney, P., Esposito, J., & Woulfe, J. M. (2020). Self-reported mental and physical health symptoms and potentially traumatic events among lesbian, gay, bisexual, transgender, and queer individuals: The role of shame. *Psychology of Violence, 10*(2), 131–142. https://doi.org/10.1037/vio0000241

Schnarrs, P. W., Stone, A. L., Salcido, R., Jr., Baldwin, A., Georgiou, C., & Nemeroff, C. B. (2019). Differences in adverse childhood experiences (ACEs) and quality of physical and mental health between transgender and cisgender sexual minorities. *Journal of Psychiatric Research, 119*, 1–6. https://doi.org/10.1016/j.jpsychires.2019.09.001

Schneeberger, A. R., Dietl, M. F., Muenzenmaier, K. H., Huber, C. G., & Lang, U. E. (2014). Stressful childhood experiences and health outcomes in sexual minority populations: A systematic review. *Social Psychiatry and Psychiatric Epidemiology, 49*(9), 1427–1445. https://doi.org/10.1007/s00127-014-0854-8

Schueths, A. M. (2014). "It's almost like white supremacy": Interracial mixed-status couples facing racist nativism. *Ethnic & Racial Studies, 37*(13), 2438–2456. https://doi.org/10.1080/01419870.2013.835058

Sheikh, M. A., Abelsen, B., & Olsen, J. A. (2016). Clarifying associations between childhood adversity, social support, behavioral factors, and mental health, health, and well-being in adulthood: A population-based study. *Frontiers of Psychology, 7*, 727. https://doi.org/10.3389/fpsyg.2016.00727

Slavich, G. M. (2020). Social safety theory: A biologically based evolutionary perspective on life stress, health, and behavior. *Annual Review of Clinical Psychology, 16*, 265–295. https://doi.org/10.1146/annurev-clinpsy-032816-045159

Slavich, G. M., & Irwin, M. R. (2014). From stress to inflammation and major depressive disorder: A social signal transduction theory of depression. *Psychological Bulletin, 140*(3), 774–815. https://doi.org/10.1037/a0035302

Spivey, L. A., Huebner, D. M., & Diamond, L. M. (2018). Parent responses to childhood gender nonconformity: Effects of parent and child characteristics. *Psychology of Sexual Orientation and Gender Diversity, 5*(3), 360–370. https://doi.org/10.1037/sgd0000279

Timmins, L., Rimes, K. A., & Rahman, Q. (2018). Minority stressors, rumination, and psychological distress in monozygotic twins discordant for sexual minority status. *Psychological Medicine, 48*(10), 1705–1712. https://doi.org/10.1017/s003329171700321x

Tobin, V., & Delaney, K. R. (2019). Child abuse victimization among transgender and gender nonconforming people: A systematic review. *Perspectives in Psychiatric Care, 55*(4), 576–583. https://doi.org/10.1111/ppc.12398

Twenge, J. M., Sherman, R. A., & Wells, B. E. (2016). Changes in American adults' reported same-sex sexual experiences and attitudes, 1973–2014. *Archives of Sexual Behavior, 44*(8), 2273–2285. https://doi.org/10.1007/s10508-016-0769-4

Valente, P. K., Schrimshaw, E. W., Dolezal, C., LeBlanc, A. J., Singh, A. A., & Bockting, W. O. (2020). Stigmatization, resilience, and mental health among a diverse community sample of transgender and gender nonbinary individuals in the U.S. *Archives of Sexual Behavior, 49*(7), 2649–2660. https://doi.org/10.1007/s10508-020-01761-4

van der Ploeg, M. M., Brosschot, J. F., Verkuil, B., Gillie, B. L., Williams, D. P., Koenig, J., Vasey, M. W., Thayer, J. F. (2017). Inducing unconscious stress: Cardiovascular activity in response to subliminal presentation of threatening and neutral words. *Psychophysiology, 54*(10), 1498–1511. https://doi.org/10.1111/psyp.12891

van der Ploeg, M. M., Brosschot, J. F., Versluis, A., & Verkuil, B. (2017). Peripheral physiological responses to subliminally presented negative affective stimuli: A systematic review. *Biological Psychology, 129*, 131–153. https://doi.org/10.1016/j.biopsycho.2017.08.051

Wheeler, N. J., Barden; S. M., & Daire, A. P. (2020). Mediation of childhood adversity and health by relationship quality in diverse couples. *Family Process, 59*(3), 1243–1260. https://doi.org/10.1111/famp.12467

Widom, C. S., Czaja, S. J., & Dutton, M. A. (2008). Childhood victimization and lifetime revictimization. *Child Abuse & Neglect, 32*(8), 785–796. https://doi.org/10.1016/j.chiabu.2007.12.006

Willoughby, B. L. B., Doty, N. D., & Malik, N. M. (2010). Victimization, family rejection, and outcomes of gay, lesbian, and bisexual young people: The role of negative GLB identity. *Journal of GLBT Family Studies, 6*(4), 403–424.

Woulfe, J. M., & Goodman, L. A. (2020). Weaponized oppression: Identity abuse and mental health in the lesbian, gay, bisexual, transgender, and queer community. *Psychology of Violence, 10*(1), 100–109. https://doi.org/10.1037/vio0000251

Xu, Y., Norton, S., & Rahman, Q. (2019). Early life conditions and adolescent sexual orientation: A prospective birth cohort study. *Developmental Psychology, 55*(6), 1226–1243. https://doi.org/10.1037/dev0000704

Zhang, Y., & Van Hook, J. (2009). Marital dissolution among interracial couples. *Journal of Marriage & Family, 71*(1), 95–107. https://doi.org/10.1111/j.1741-3737.2008.00582.x

Zietsch, B. P., Verweij, K. J. H., Heath, A. C., Madden, P. A. F., Martin, N. G., Nelson, E. C., & Lynskey, M. T. (2012). Do shared etiological factors contribute to the relationship between sexual orientation and depression? *Psychological Medicine, 42*(3), 521–532. https://doi.org/10.1017/S0033291711001577

CHAPTER

19 Relationship Maintenance in Older Adults: Considering Social and Evolutionary Psychological Perspectives

Ledina Imami *and* Christopher R. Agnew

Abstract

Relationship maintenance processes refer to a wide range of cognitive and behavioral strategies that serve to protect and enhance the quality and stability of romantic relationships. As romantic partners share more aspects of their lives together, their goals become increasingly coordinated and they become especially motivated to care for each other's welfare. However, even established romantic relationships face times of difficulty, including problems with action coordination. As interdependence between partners grows, partners face challenges distinct from those that surround relationships in which interdependence is low. In this chapter, we review the current social psychological literature on relationship maintenance processes and discuss how these strategies may change as evolutionary priorities (e.g., striving for success in the workplace or caring for children and parents) become more prominent over the course of long-term involvements. In this regard, we focus on strategies that are more prevalent among older adults and discuss how these strategies may reflect adaptations to the constraints that romantic partners face at later stages in life. We conclude our discussion with recommendations for future research and a call for integrative work that combines evolutionary and social psychological perspectives to refine our understanding of maintenance processes among older adults.

Key Words: relationship maintenance processes, interdependence theory, relationship stability across lifespan, interdependence in older adults, evolutionary perspectives on aging and relationship maintenance

Relationship maintenance processes refer to a wide range of cognitive and behavioral strategies that romantic partners employ to protect and enhance the quality and stability of their relationships. As romantic partners share more aspects of their lives together over time, their actions and desires become increasingly coordinated and they become especially motivated to care for each other's welfare. Of course, even established romantic relationships face times of difficulty, including problems with action and preference coordination. As interdependence between partners grows, partners face goals and challenges that are distinct from those that surround relationships in which interdependence is low. In this chapter, we review the current social psychological literature on relationship maintenance processes and discuss how these strategies may change as evolutionary priorities (e.g., striving for success in the workplace, caring for children and parents, and expanding one's sphere of influence through social networks) become more prominent over the course of long-term involvements. First, we present our underlying theoretical perspective, based on the notion that romantic relationships should not be viewed as events with a discrete beginning and ending but as interpersonal bonds which vary over time in their degree of interdependence. Based on this perspective, we categorize relationship maintenance processes as strategies that help to maintain or increase current levels of interdependence, and we summarize the latest advances in relationship science with regard to these processes. Second, we discuss how relationship maintenance processes are used at various stages of interdependence as romantic partners' priorities in their relationship change with time. In this regard, we focus on strategies that are more prevalent among older adults and discuss how these strategies may reflect adaptations to the constraints that romantic partners face at this stage of life. We conclude our discussion with recommendations for fruitful directions in future research and a call for more integrative work that combines evolutionary and social psychological perspectives.

Relationship Maintenance Processes From an Interdependence Perspective

Perhaps more than any other type of close tie, romantic relationships often require partners to think and act like one. When a person enters a romantic relationship, their everyday actions begin to coordinate with the desires, goals, and behaviors of their partner (Thibaut & Kelley, 1959). One of the key features of interdependence theory (IT; Kelley & Thibaut, 1978; Thibaut & Kelley, 1959; VanderDrift & Agnew, 2020) is its usefulness in examining how people navigate the inevitable dilemmas that arise from such coordination. Interdependence theory recognizes explicitly that relational bonds are built and evolve based on the partners' ability to fulfill each other's needs. One of the key challenges relationship partners face is to find ways to maintain and expand their bonds, even in those circumstances when the desires and actions of one partner do not necessarily benefit the other. Relationship maintenance processes help with this coordination task. They refer to a wide range of cognitive and behavioral strategies that romantic partners employ to protect and enhance the quality of their relationship (Linardatos & Lydon, 2011; Rusbul et al., 1991; Van Lange et al., 1997).

There is significant empirical research on relationship maintenance processes (Agnew & VanderDrift, 2015; Canary & Dainton, 2003; Dainton & Stafford, 1993; Van Lange et al., 1997), with much of it tending to label "maintenance" as what happens in between the beginning and end of a relationship. From an interdependence theory perspective, however, romantic relationships are not most fruitfully characterized as events with a discrete beginning and end. Rather, romantic relationships are relational bonds featuring varying degrees of interdependence between partners over time. For example, when partners dissolve a relationship, they do not invariably become strangers to one another. Rather, as often happens, they may continue to maintain their ties but rely less on one another for fulfilling their needs (Tan et al., 2015). This view has important implications. First, it recognizes that the underlying processes that bring people together across various types of relationships (e.g., romantic relationships, friendships, and extended family) are probably the same. Second, it implies that the more interdependent partners are, the more difficult it is to dissolve a relationship. As a result, the default option in romantic relationships is to protect one's investments, persist in maintenance efforts, and preserve the state of the relationship, a point we return to later in this chapter (VanderDrift & Agnew, 2020). Finally, this view also allows us to organize maintenance processes in two broad categories: those strategies that (a) serve to maintain interdependence, and (b) help to increase interdependence.

Below, we review how the strategies that help to maintain and enhance interdependence may change as partners transition into older adulthood. Because some of these shifts are systematically triggered by developmental processes and have held adaptive value throughout our ancestral history, we first begin by considering some key insights from evolutionary psychology to inform our review.

Relationship Maintenance Processes From an Evolutionary Perspective

Insights from evolutionary psychology offer a useful framework for understanding the priorities that emerge as romantic partners reach older adulthood. One key assumption of this perspective is that some of the psychological traits that guide human behavior have been transmitted through evolution because they helped to enhance the fitness of our ancestors. As a result, this view implies that relationship maintenance strategies over the course of long-term bonds should vary in ways that help partners maximize their reproductive success (Griskevicius et al., 2015). One important point to note about this assumption is that reproductive success does not simply require the survival of an individuals' genes but rather the achievement of *inclusive fitness,* or the survival of many individuals who share the same genes (e.g., immediate family members and more distant relatives; Hamilton, 1964).

To achieve this goal, humans must overcome some of the same challenges our ancestors had to face, such as securing physical safety, procuring needed resources, finding a mate, caring for genetic relatives, and gaining status (Griskevicius et al., 2015; Liberman et al., 2007). Each of these challenges may become more or less prominent at various points in life, and individuals devote resources and form various relational bonds to meet each of them (Griskevicius et al., 2015). For example, scholars have argued that long-term romantic bonds in humans have evolved to increase the survival of their offspring, who require intense resources from others to reach maturity (Fletcher et al., 2015). However, the attention that partners devote to these long-term bonds may be challenged over time due to other priorities they have to meet (e.g., contributing to the well-being of relatives or other network members to increase reproductive payoffs; Apicella & Crittenden, 2016).

Research from both relationship science and evolutionary psychology has contributed data that illustrate how these priorities may influence the relationship maintenance strategies that romantic partners employ to build and preserve their long-term bonds. For example, to overcome the challenge of attracting mates, humans engage in strategies that help to bind people to one another. Self-disclosure is one of the most important processes that helps to accomplish this goal (Altman & Taylor, 1973; Dindia, 2000), and research has found that levels of self-disclosure are higher during the relationship initiation phase than any other subsequent phases (Sprecher et al., 2015). Studies have also found gender differences in the use of self-disclosure. When initiating a relationship, men are more likely than women to rely on humor (Wilbur & Campbell, 2011), to engage in higher levels of self-disclosure (Davis, 1978), to offer intimate information (Derlega et al., 1985), and to confess their love first (Ackerman et al., 2011). Altogether, these findings align with an evolutionary perspective that argues that men are more motivated than women to detect and secure mating opportunities (Haselton & Buss, 2000), which is why they may be more likely to show more intense efforts in self-disclosure.

Once bonds are formed, humans have to meet the challenge of retaining their partner, which helps to increase chances of offspring survival. This may be a prototypical challenge for married couples (e.g., Griskevicius et al., 2015) but also to any other couple in a committed relationship. Again, studies show that several relationship maintenance strategies are more typical at this stage of interdependence. In this regard, researchers have identified several perceptual or attentional biases which help individuals process information in ways that favor their romantic partners. For example, newlyweds possess positively inflated views about their partners, which result in their perceiving their partner in an idealized fashion (Murray et al., 1996). Relative to singles, individuals who are involved in a relationship have been found to rate highly attractive others as less attractive (Simpson et al., 1990), and the same bias has also been observed in those who were highly committed versus less committed to their relationship partners (Lydon et al., 1999). Evolutionary psychologists have also proposed that displays of jealousy may serve as a maintenance strategy at this stage (Buss et al., 1996).

Other lines of research have shown that highly committed individuals think about and describe their relationships by spontaneously using a higher degree of plural pronouns (e.g., "we," "us," and "our"; Agnew et al., 1998; Agnew, 2000). Although this finding reflects the extent to which participants perceive themselves as part of a merged unit with their partner, it is also possible that this spontaneous behavior may be used as a signaling strategy intended to communicate one's relationship status to others. Finally, research has also shown that partners who are motivated to maintain interdependence actively engage in behaviors intended to demonstrate their unique value to their partner, in hopes of solidifying their commitment (Murray et al., 2009).

These examples illustrate how specific priorities that dominate individuals' attention at particular points in time may influence the array of maintenance strategies that partners use in their relationships. As partners continue to face other challenges while their interdependence grows (such as those of securing alliances by expanding their social networks or striving for status in the workplace), the degree to which they engage in binding and protective strategies might change. Unfortunately, current research in this regard is limited. However, some data suggest that, with time, couples engage in maintenance effortlessly and without required planning or conscious intent (Dainton & Stafford, 1993). If this is the case, this shift toward routine maintenance behaviors in established couples would prove adaptive, allowing them to reserve regulatory resources for meeting other important life demands (Dindia, 2003).

Interdependence in Older Adults

As romantic partners age, they face several constraints that should make relationship maintenance difficult. Most notably, older adults have to cope with declining health, which increases strain and imposes the burden of caregiving. Furthermore, older adults have smaller social networks than younger people, which makes it more difficult to seek and obtain support (Morgan, 1988; Wrzus et al., 2013). Although these circumstances are associated with lower relationship satisfaction and well-being in younger adults (Keneski et al., 2018; Sprecher et al., 2002), research depicts a different picture for older couples. In contrast to these expectations, older adults are more satisfied with their relationships than younger adults (Birditt & Fingerman, 2003; Brubaker, 1990; Fitzpatrick & Vinick, 2003; Levenson et al., 1993; but also see Bushfield et al., 2008). As much as this finding may appear paradoxical, it may be the result of a series of adaptive responses to the constraints that characterize life in older age.

Arguably, one of the greatest constraints that older adults face is the absence of an open-ended future. The awareness that time is limited can have important implications for human motivation. Scholars have argued that reminders that the end of life is near can influence the way in which older adults process information and the type of goals they prioritize (Carstensen, 2006).

One influential framework in this domain is socioemotional selectivity theory (Carstensen, 1992; Carstensen & Löckenhoff, 2003), which states that older adults prefer to focus on goals that bring immediate rewards and make them feel good in the moment, as opposed to goals whose benefits will materialize in the distant, and, hence, uncertain, future. This tendency to focus on immediate rewards may explain a series of findings which show that older adults are biased toward processing and selecting positive, intrinsically rewarding information. For example, older adults show greater attention and memory for emotionally positive relative to emotionally negative information, which is starkly different from younger adults who are more likely to focus on negative than positive information (Charles et al., 2003; Mather et al., 2004). Other studies have found that older adults show a preference for advertisements that promised savoring special moments versus exploring the unknown (Fung & Carstensen, 2003), and when asked to recall a formative experience from their past, they were more likely to recall a positive experience relative to younger adults (Quackenbush & Barnett, 2001).

This motivational shift to an appreciation for positive and immediately gratifying experiences has implications for the way in which older adults approach their social relationships and the maintenance strategies they use with their romantic partners. For example, experimental studies have shown that when given the choice between forming a new relationship or spending time with a familiar, close other, older adults have a stronger preference for the familiar partner (Fung et al., 1999). These data are in line with observations that relative to younger people, older adults are more likely to have smaller, but more intimately close social networks (Fung et al., 2001). Furthermore, studies suggest that older people selectively exclude peripheral ties from their social networks (Lang, 2001), a strategy that would allow them to devote more of their remaining time and energy to their close ties. Altogether, this body of work suggests that as romantic partners become even more salient in older adults' daily lives, older couples should be particularly motivated to maintain their interdependence with their partners.

Maintaining Interdependence

Building interdependence requires resource investment and comes with cost. Quite often, romantic partners face situations in which their own needs and desires may lead to benefits for themselves but not for their partner or their relationship (Fitzsimons et al., 2015). In classic IT terms, these situations are known as "noncorrespondent" outcomes (Kelley & Thibaut, 1978) and may introduce conflict and destabilize a relationship. Maintaining interdependence requires partners to navigate these delicate situations, and the tools involved vary as a function of both motivational and individual-level factors (e.g., ability to exercise self-control). Although research on maintenance strategies in older adults is limited, existing evidence suggests that older adults engage in several strategies that keep their levels of interdependence stable. In part, this may be facilitated by the fact that some threats to the relationship, such as the presence of potential alternative partners, may be lower given that older adults have smaller social networks. However, relative to younger romantic partners, older partners are more likely to actively engage in several important strategies. In the next sections, we review some of the most well-researched relationship maintenance processes that help to maintain interdependence in romantic relationships and discuss how older adults use these processes.

Transformation of Motivation

Transformation of motivation is a cornerstone IT process that allows partners to think and act in ways that are beneficial to their romantic relationship (Kelley & Thibaut, 1978). This process involves a motivational shift so that partners find value in goals and desires that benefit the long-term interests of their relationship and forgo their own immediate preferences, desires, or needs. Given that romantic partners may help to fulfill a multitude of important needs, researchers from many perspectives have emphasized that people involved in romantic relationships become especially motivated to care for and attend to their partners' welfare (Hazan & Shaver, 2004; Kelley & Thibaut, 1978; Murray & Holmes, 2011). Some have even claimed that romantic relationships provide a context in which partners develop an automatic tendency to think and behave in partner-oriented ways (e.g., Righetti et al., 2013; Wieselquist et al., 1999). Experiencing this motivational shift is critical for the long-term stability of relationships, and many of the other maintenance processes described here depend on this essential shift.

As we have already noted, research on older adults suggests that they are, perhaps, more likely than younger adults to show this motivational shift, given that older adults prioritize their close relationships over other types of ties and try to avoid conflict with their romantic partners (Jensen & Rauer, 2015; Verstaen et al., 2020). In fact, some evidence suggests that other-oriented, prosocial behaviors (key markers of transformation of motivation) may generally increase as a function of age (Mayr & Freund, 2020). This pattern of behavior is likely to have been adaptive to our ancestors in their postreproductive years. In this vein, scholars have argued that the presence of grandparents throughout evolutionary history has played an important role in helping with the survival of offspring and contributing to inclusive fitness (Apicella & Crittenden, 2016). According to the "grandmother hypothesis" (Hawkes et al., 1997), grandmothers secure food and help with child care, which allow parents to invest in other offspring, thus increasing their reproductive success (Apicella & Crittenden, 2016). Older adults' emphasis on selectively devoting attention and care to members of their close social network would have resulted in favorable outcomes for them throughout evolutionary history (Carstensen & Löckenhoff, 2003), motivating younger members of their network to reciprocate and care for them in return. Moreover, just as romantic love in younger adults may help forge commitment and facilitate offspring care, keeping these bonds intact in older adulthood would have given our ancestors an advantage in promoting inclusive fitness.

Willingness to Sacrifice

Willingness to sacrifice involves individuals foregoing their own immediate self-interest by either engaging in an otherwise undesirable behavior or refraining to engage in a desirable behavior that undermines the partners' wishes or best interests. Willingness to sacrifice is similar to transformation of motivation. Scholars have shown that commitment to one's partner promotes sacrifice (Rusbult et al., 2012) given that partners have developed a strong goal of maintaining their relationship. However, unlike transformation of motivation, sacrifice does not always occur automatically (in other words, partners are aware that they are giving up something valuable). Recent work has shown that the visibility of a partner's sacrifice is important for relationship well-being (Visserman et al., 2019) and the partner's reactions to sacrifice provide an important feedback loop in promoting further sacrifice and satisfaction within the relationship (Righetti & Visserman, 2018). We are unaware of extant research that has focused on sacrifice in romantic relationships among older adults. However, given the strong body of research showing a stronger prosocial orientation in older age (Mayr & Freund, 2020), one could expect older adults to show higher levels of willingness to sacrifice than younger adults.

Positive Illusions

Motivated reasoning in the form of positive illusions constitutes another process through which romantic partners maintain their relationships. Given that interdependence comes with cost and may leave partners vulnerable to getting hurt, one way to mitigate these threats is to avoid doubts about a partner's questionable behavior or undesirable qualities. In this vein, people idealize their partners, perceiving them in even more positive ways than the partners see themselves (Murray et al., 1996). These idealizations, in turn, are associated with greater satisfaction and relationship longevity (Murray et al., 1996; Le et al., 2010). Studies have also provided some evidence that this process is more likely to take place once individuals have built up at least some degree of interdependence. For example, individuals do not always initiate relationships with people who match their ideal partner standards; however, once in a relationship, people perceive their partners' qualities as quite close to their ideals (Fletcher et al., 1999). Finally, the idealization process might also work by adjusting one's standards to the partner's qualities. For example, a longitudinal study of married couples found that, relative to couples who divorced, those who maintained their relationships showed shifts in their ideal standards over time. Specifically, these partners' standards changed in such a way that reflected the ways in which their partners' characteristics had also changed (Neff & Karney, 2005).

Although it may appear difficult for couples to continue to see themselves in an idealized fashion in older age, research has shown that this is not the case. Indeed, positive illusions are prevalent even in long-term marriages (O'Rourke & Cappeliez, 2003; O'Rourke et al., 2010), and may continue to serve important adaptive functions. For example, research has shown that partner idealization has been associated with lower levels of distress among those who care for a spouse with Alzheimer disease (O'Rourke & Wenaus, 1998; O'Rourke et al., 2011) as well as, more generally, higher levels of physical well-being (O'Rourke, 2005). Considering that older adults have a smaller social network than younger adults, and, therefore, fewer sources of social support available to them, this strategy may prove particularly useful in helping them cope with the burden of caregiving which is one of the most prominent challenges romantic partners face in older age. In this way, positive illusions may constitute an important strategy for helping older adults to maintain their relationship stable.

Accommodation

One interesting finding in romantic relationship research is that conflict in the relationship does not show a strong association with relationship dissolution (Le et al., 2010). In part, this may be because partners engage in specific patterns of thought and behavior that help to mitigate the deleterious effects of conflict and other harmful actions. These processes are called accommodation, and they are categorized along two dimensions: passive–active reactions and constructive–destructive reactions (Rusbult et al., 1982). Neglect and loyalty are both passive strategies but differ such that neglect is destructive to the relationship whereas loyalty is constructive. Partners who employ neglect avoid discussing the issues at hand and may, instead, criticize their partner on unrelated matters. Those who engage in loyalty also avoid facing issues directly, but they embrace patience, have faith in their partner, and forgive and forget. Exit and voice constitute active strategies, with exit being a destructive reaction and voice a constructive one. Those who engage in exit derogate and criticize the partner, threaten to end the relationship, and take action toward dissolution. Those who engage in voice, on the other hand, face the issues at hand, suggest solutions, and try to change problematic behaviors. Behaving destructively is particularly harmful to relationships (Rusbult et al., 1986) as it promotes a cycle of negativity and retaliation (Gottman, 1998). However, recent work suggests that in some contexts, passive strategies that share some features with neglect (such as withdrawing from an argument) may not always lead to negative outcomes. For example, a longitudinal study revealed that withdrawal was associated with lower relationship satisfaction among wives who enjoyed higher socioeconomic status, but not among those who were economically disadvantaged (Ross et al., 2019.

When comparing younger and older adults, researchers have found marked differences in their use of accommodation strategies. The key finding in this domain is that older adults are more likely to engage in strategies that have the purpose of either avoiding conflict or deescalating it (Holley et al., 2013; Verstaen et al., 2020), which is in line with the idea that older adults are motivated to behave in ways that help them keep their close relationships intact. As we mentioned before, several factors may contribute to these findings. For one, research shows that older adults have better emotion regulation skills, which can be crucial in helping them navigate conflict. Older adults not only experience lower levels of negative emotions in response to stress (Almeida et al., 2006) but also recover more quickly from negative moods (Carstensen et al., 2000). During conflict discussions with their partners, older adults show lower levels of physiological reactivity (Levenson et al., 1994). Furthermore, early research showed that compared to their younger counterparts, older adults were less likely to rely on active destructive strategies such as exit (Carstensen et al., 1995), as they expressed lower levels of anger, belligerence, and disgust during arguments. Instead, this study found that older adults engaged in higher levels of accommodative strategies that resembled loyalty and voice, showing more affection for their partner regardless of the degree of severity of the argument. Recent research supports these early findings. One investigation that followed middle-aged and older adult couples over 13 years found that the use of avoidance behaviors such as hesitating to discuss a problem, changing the topic, or diverting attention increased over time (Holley et al., 2013). Furthermore, research from this sample also found that emotional reactions in response to conflict that typically characterize exit and neglect (e.g., belligerence, defensiveness, and whining) tended to decline with age, whereas positive reactions such as humor, enthusiasm, and validation tended to increase (Verstaen et al., 2020).

Forgiveness

Forgiveness is among the most well-researched relationship maintenance processes. Although traditionally conceptualized as a deliberate decision-making process, forgiveness is manifested in the reduction of negative feelings toward an offender and often occurs unconsciously and automatically (Karremans & Van Lange, 2008). Enduring motivational factors such as commitment play an important role in promoting forgiveness (Finkel et al., 2002). However, forgiveness with regard to a particular transgression can also easily change over time depending on the momentary goals that guide individuals' behavior in a particular situation. For example, Karremans and colleagues have demonstrated that people are more likely to forgive an offender when prosocial values and motives are subtly primed through experimental procedures (Karremans & Aarts, 2007; Karremans & Van Lange, 2008). As is the case for other maintenance processes, nonmotivational factors also play a role. For example, self-regulatory resources such as self-control (Karremans et al., 2015), personality traits such as agreeableness (Exline et al., 2004), and characteristics related to the transgression itself (e.g., severity; McCullough et al., 1998) may intertwine to determine how quickly partners reduce negative feelings toward transgressors. Not surprisingly, research has shown that forgiveness tends to increase with age (Steiner et al., 2012). For one, some of the personality characteristics that are positively associated with forgiveness, such as agreeableness, tend to be more prevalent among older adults (Roberts et al., 2006). Furthermore, older adults' tendency to underestimate the intensity of negative emotions experienced in the past (Levine & Bluck, 1997; Steiner et al., 2011) may be instrumental with this regard.

Staving Off Alternatives

The presence of romantic alternatives to one's current partner constitutes one of the most powerful forces to threaten an interdependent relationship. The most threatening alternatives are characterized by desirable traits such as physical attractiveness, high status, or (in the case of women) the presence of fertility cues (Buss, 1989; S. L. Miller & Maner, 2010). Nonetheless, committed partners are able to employ several conscious and unconscious processes that allow them to deflect this threat. Motivated partners modulate their attention in ways that facilitates their commitment. For example, highly committed individuals (Linardatos & Lydon, 2011), those who are in satisfying relationships (Johnson & Rusbult, 1989), or those who have just been reminded of their love for their partner (Maner et al., 2008) shield their relationships from the temptation of alternative partners by directing their attention away (Linardatos & Lydon, 2011; Maner et al., 2008), or by rating them less attractive (Johnson & Rusbult, 1989; Lydon et al., 2003). In this way, individuals ignore or downplay the importance of information (e.g., attractiveness of alternatives) that may interfere with their desire to maintain interdependence with their current partner.

Typically, the threat of alternative partners is considered to be a key challenge for younger or middle-age adults rather than older adults (Griskevicius et al., 2015; Li & Fung, 2011). This may be, in large part, because younger adults face a greater number of demands that compete for their attention simultaneously, such as caring for children, trying to achieve growth in the workplace, and also caring for older relatives. These competing goals may take a toll on relationship satisfaction. For example, researchers have documented declines in relationship satisfaction after the birth of the first child (e.g., Johnson & Bradbury, 1999) but also in contexts where partners face stressors outside the marriage, such as difficulties at work (Karney & Bradbury, 2005). These factors may lead partners to be more receptive toward romantic alternatives which may offer better prospects and higher satisfaction. These pressures tend to decrease in older age, reducing the threat of alternative partners (Li & Fung, 2011). However, the cognitive biases that help partners protect their relationships from attractive alternatives continue to operate in older adulthood but with regard to different threats. One example of this is the tendency that older adults have to ignore or undermine the intensity of negative information (Charles et al., 2003; Steiner et al., 2011), which, as we have discussed, may play an important role during conflict resolution.

In this section, we discussed some of the key processes that romantic partners employ to maintain their interdependent ties and the manifestation of these processes among older adults. Although empirical evidence on relationship maintenance in older adults is limited, most of the existing work suggests that older adults rely particularly on accommodation, forgiveness, and idealization to maintain satisfaction and stability within their romantic relationships. These findings are in agreement with the core arguments of the socioemotional selectivity theory (Carstensen, 1992), which emphasizes how the developmental constraints that characterize older age (e.g., smaller social networks and limited time prospects) may cause older adults to concentrate their limited resources (in terms of time and effort) in ways that guarantee immediate satisfaction. As such, older adults are motivated not only to maintain and nurture their most meaningful relationships but also to use maintenance strategies that avoid dwelling on negative emotions. For example, older adults continue to idealize their spouses despite many years of partnership, and, instead of engaging in conflict, they tend to avoid it or to engage in behaviors that help to deescalate it.

Next, we turn our attention to processes that serve to bolster interdependence. These processes are also diverse and can be further categorized in terms of behaviors that help to bring partners together initially (e.g., self-disclosure and self-expansion), as well as behaviors that help to deepen ongoing interdependence further (e.g., investment and capitalization). Of course, we should note that these categorizations are to a certain extent arbitrary and that many of these processes can serve both maintenance and enhancement (or binding and bolstering) functions. For example, not only do positive illusions help to maintain interdependence, but they also play a critical role in enhancing it through a cycle of mutual self-perception processes. Once an individual engages in positive illusions about their partner, these perceptions can transform as self-fulfilling prophecies which may result in the partner changing for the better (Murray et al., 1996).

Enhancing Interdependence

Maintenance processes that serve to mitigate threats and maintain interdependence have been widely researched. However, as we alluded to at the beginning of this chapter, the forces that can destabilize a highly interdependent relationship will have to be quite strong given that partners often engage in maintenance processes automatically and efficiently (VanderDrift & Agnew, 2020). This could be particularly the case for older adults (Dindia, 2003). Perhaps for this reason, researchers have recently called for a greater focus on understanding processes that not only give rise to interdependence but also make romantic bonds even more deep, pleasurable, and rewarding as interdependence grows (Ogolsky et al., 2017). Below we turn our attention to some of those key interdependence enhancement processes.

Self-Disclosure

Just as transformation of motivation is considered a cornerstone process in guiding partners efficiently toward keeping their relationship intact, so is self-disclosure considered a cornerstone process in bringing partners together (Altman & Taylor, 1973; Reis & Shaver, 1988). Scholars have argued that disclosing one's thoughts, emotions, and feelings constitutes one of the building blocks in the development of intimacy (e.g., Reis & Shaver, 1988; Rime, 2009), as it gives rise to a reciprocal process of information exchange which ultimately increases liking and closeness (Graham et al., 2008). For example, studies have found that not only do people disclose to people they like, but they also like them more after having shared information with them (Collins & Miller, 1994). With time, this process contributes to a sense of belonging among partners and is associated with higher relationship satisfaction (Laurenceau et al., 1998). Unlike most other maintenance processes, however, self-disclosure appears to decline over time, being most frequent at the initial stages of relationships (Hays, 1985; Rubin et al., 1980). This may occur because partners ultimately reach limits of information to exchange as the duration of their partnership increases and/or believe that the partner already must know how they feel, thus obviating the need for further disclosures. Research in older adults has shown that not only are they less likely to engage in self-disclosure but also that certain forms of self-disclosure may harm relationship well-being at this stage of life. For example, older adults do not appear to benefit as much as younger adults from discussing marital problems with one another (Jensen & Rauer, 2015), a finding that is in alignment with work showing that older adults prefer to avoid rather than confront conflict (Holley et al., 2013).

Self-Expansion

Echoing humanistic notions of human development (Maslow, 1971), self-expansion refers to a basic motivation that guides human behavior: To continuously expand one's sense of self by widening one's influence, knowledge, and identity (Aron & Aron, 1996). According to this theoretical perspective, the main purpose of love is to expand oneself by merging one's identity with that of a romantic partner. Furthermore, this process is mainly achieved by engaging in novel and arousing experiences that increase attraction and bind partners together (Dutton & Aron, 1974; Aron et al., 2000). As a result, self-expanding activities serve a maintenance function as they benefit relationships by increasing positive affect and reducing boredom (Aron et al., 2000). In this vein, longitudinal and experimental studies have shown that couples who engage in novel and exciting activities report higher relationship satisfaction relative to couples in a control group (Coulter & Malouff, 2013; Muise et al., 2019).

Of note, self-expansion is also reflected in a cognitive merging of the concept of the partner with the concept of self (Agnew et al., 1998; Aron et al., 1991), which is typically reflected in couples using pronouns such as "we" rather than "you/me" when describing their relationship to others or when discussing marital issues with one another. In line with the large body of work showing that older adults are more other-oriented than younger adults (Mayr & Freund, 2020), research has found that older adults are also more likely than younger adults to use "we"-words during conflict discussions (Seider et al., 2009), which was related to better coping. Furthermore, this aspect of self-expansion has also been associated with transformation of motivation, which facilitates threat-mitigating actions (Aron et al., 2004) and may provide another explanation for why older adults are more motivated than younger adults to focus and invest their effort on their intimate relationships.

Investments and Plans

One key insight derived from IT theory is that interdependence grows by increasing one's investments in a relationship (Rusbult, 1980; Rusbult et al., 1998). Investments refer to a variety of resources that partners devote to their relationship, including material, social, and psychological. As investments increase, partners become more reliant on one another for fulfilling their needs and they also become more comfortable in continuing to invest in the relationship (Fitzsimons et al., 2015). As a result, the value of the relationship increases and the magnitude of loss from a potential dissolution increases as well, making investments a strong predictor of commitment and relationship longevity (Le et al., 2010). Investments have also been characterized not just with respect to "sunken cost" but also with respect to the future plans that couple members make (Goodfriend & Agnew, 2008). Just as relationship dissolution would end the accumulation of past investments, so too would it thwart the achievement of envisioned plans. In this way, couples are bound together by both their past investments and their future plans (Agnew et al., 2008). To date, we don't have direct empirical evidence on the importance of future plans in enhancing interdependence in older adults. However, experimental work shows that older adults have a strong preference to spend their time with a familiar relationship figure rather than an admired stranger (e.g., their preferred novelist; Fung et al., 1999), suggesting that, when making plans about the future, older adults may be more likely than younger adults to continue to invest their effort on further enhancing their ties with their romantic partner.

Altogether, research on enhancing interdependence suggests that, although older adults are less likely than their younger counterparts to share their thoughts and feelings with partners, they still engage in self-expansion and may be more likely to have a merged identity with their partner.

Next Steps for Understanding Relationship Maintenance Processes in Older Adults

Relationship maintenance strategies have been the subject of great deal of attention by researchers over the years (e.g., Canary & Stafford, 1992; Lydon & Quinn, 2013; Ogolsky & Monk, 2020). Based on an interdependence perspective, in this chapter we have made the case that partners can use strategies in ways that help them respond and adapt to the major challenges that their relationships face as they become increasingly interdependent with each another. We have also noted that some of these challenges (e.g., taking care of offspring, expanding one's social network to build alliances and strive for higher status, and taking care of older relatives; Griskevicius et al., 2015) may vary normatively over the life course and reflect the key challenges that our ancestors had to face throughout our evolutionary history.

Most of the knowledge that we have on relationship maintenance strategies comes from studying young couples or middle-age adults. Less research has addressed partner dynamics in older age, and those who do concentrate on this population are primarily interested in understanding the processes of coping with the stress of disease burden (Korporaal et al., 2013). However, as developmental psychologists have argued (Carstensen, 2006), older adults enact a series of cognitive and behavioral adaptations which help them to maintain satisfactory relationships and a generative life (Carstensen & Löckenhoff, 2003).

A better understanding of the processes through which older adults maintain their romantic bonds would help us understand (a) which relationship maintenance strategies help to preserve relationship satisfaction in the face of limited resources, and (b) how these strategies contribute to the well-being of older adults and their close network members. In addition, some attention also needs to be paid to methodological issues to disentangle the effects of relationship duration from the effects of age, although a functional perspective such as interdependence theory can help with this task.

In addition to more research on older adult relationships, future social psychological work would benefit from integrating insights from other perspectives, including developmental and evolutionary psychology. Similar to interdependence theory, evolutionary psychology focuses on a functional approach when explaining human behavior. Scholars who work at the intersection of these two fields have already made important contributions that have advanced our knowledge. For example, scholars have argued about the value of romantic love as a commitment device that, throughout evolution, helped to keep partners together and provide better care for their offspring (Fletcher et al., 2015). Other researchers have pointed out how environmental features related to scarcity or the presence of caregiving figures can influence reproductive patterns among female youth (Griskevicius et al., 2011). One fruitful area for investigation along these lines would be to understand how the motivations that we have inherited from our evolutionary past (e.g., need to achieve status) interact with momentary goals (e.g., desire to obtain a promotion or difficulties with handling conflict in work environments) to influence the ways in which people use relationship maintenance strategies to maintain and/or deepen interdependence. For example, in the case of older adults, more work could be done to understand how these motives (e.g., need for safety, desire to care for grandchildren or other younger relatives, etc.) interact to determine when and how older adults decide to prune their social networks and focus their energy on their romantic partner and other intimate ties.

Romantic relationships can be central to the well-being of individuals, as they can help people accomplish their goals, cope with setbacks, and live a generative life (Baumeister & Leary, 1995; Fitzimons et al., 2015). Investigating the processes that bring and keep romantic partners together has been a central goal of relationship science since its early days. Now it is time for more work to be done to understand these processes not only among younger couples but also at the other end of the life spectrum where close relationships appear to be resilient and satisfying.

References

Ackerman, J. M., Griskevicius, V., & Li, N. P. (2011). Let's get serious: Communicating commitment in romantic relationships. *Journal of Personality and Social Psychology, 100*(6), 1079–1094.

Agnew, C. R. (2000). Cognitive interdependence and the experience of relationship loss. In J. H. Harvey & E. D. Miller (Eds.), *Loss and trauma: General and close relationship perspectives* (pp. 385–398). Brunner-Routledge.

Agnew, C. R., Arriaga, X. B., & Wilson, J. E. (2008). Committed to what? Using the bases of relational commitment model to understand continuity and changes in social relationships. In J. P. Forgas & J. Fitness (Eds.), *Social relationships: Cognitive, affective and motivational processes* (pp. 147–164). Psychology Press.

Agnew, C. R., & VanderDrift, L. E. (2015). Relationship maintenance and dissolution. In M. Mikulincer & P. R. Shaver (Eds.), *APA handbook of personality and social psychology: Vol. 3. Interpersonal relations* (pp. 581–604). American Psychological Association Press.

Agnew, C. R., Van Lange, P. A., Rusbult, C. E., & Langston, C. A. (1998). Cognitive interdependence: Commitment and the mental representation of close relationships. *Journal of Personality and Social Psychology, 74*(4), 939–954.

Almeida, D. M., Mroczek, D. K., & Neiss, M. (2006). Can self-regulation explain age differences in daily, weekly, and monthly reports of psychological distress? In L. Carstensen & K. W. Schaie (Eds.), *Social structure, aging and self-regulation* (pp. 95–122). Springer.

Altman, I., & Taylor, D. A. (1973). *Social penetration: The development of interpersonal relationships.* Holt, Rinehart & Winston.

Apicella, C.L. & Crittenden, A. (2016). Hunter-gatherer families and parenting. In D. Buss (Ed.), *The handbook of evolutionary psychology* (578–592). John Wiley & Sons.

Aron, A., & Aron, E. N. (1996). Self and self-expansion in relationships. In G. J. O Fletcher & J. Fitness (Eds.), *Knowledge structures in close relationships: A social psychological perspective* (pp. 325–344). Erlbaum.

Aron, A., Aron, E. N., Tudor, M., & Nelson, G. (1991). Close relationships as including other in the self. *Journal of Personality and Social Psychology, 60*(2), 241–253.

Aron, A. P., Mashek, D. J., & Aron, E. N. (2004). Closeness as including other in the self. In D. J. Mashek & A. Aron (Eds.), *Handbook of closeness and intimacy* (pp. 37–52). Psychology Press.

Aron, A., Norman, C. C., Aron, E. N., McKenna, C., & Heyman, R. E. (2000). Couples' shared participation in novel and arousing activities and experienced relationship quality. *Journal of Personality and Social Psychology, 78*(2), 273–284.

Baumeister, R. F., & Leary, M. R. (1995). The need to belong: Desire for interpersonal attachments as a fundamental human motivation. *Psychological Bulletin, 117*(3), 497–529.

Birditt, K. S., & Fingerman, K. L. (2003). Age and gender differences in adults' descriptions of emotional reactions to interpersonal problems. *The Journals of Gerontology Series B: Psychological Sciences and Social Sciences, 58*(4), 237–245.

Brubaker, T. H. (1990). Families in later life: A burgeoning research area. *Journal of Marriage* and the Family, *52*(4), 959–981.

Bushfield, S. Y., Fitzpatrick, T. R., & Vinick, B. H. (2008). Perceptions of "impingement" and marital satisfaction among wives of retired hus- bands. *Journal of Women & Aging, 20*, 199–213.

Buss, D. M. (1989). Sex differences in human mate preferences: Evolutionary hypotheses tested in 37 cultures. *Behavioral and Brain Sciences, 12*(1), 1–14.

Buss, D. M., Larsen, R. J., & Westen, D. (1996). Sex differences in jealousy: Not gone, not forgotten, and not explained by alternative hypotheses. *Psychological Science, 7*(6), 373–375.

Canary, D. J., & Dainton, M. (2003). *Maintaining relationships through communication: Relational, contextual, and cultural variations.* Routledge.

Canary, D. J., & Stafford, L. (1992). Relational maintenance strategies and equity in marriage. *Communication Monographs*, 59, 243–267.

Carstensen, L. L. (2006). The influence of a sense of time on human development. *Science, 312*(5782), 1913–1915.

Carstensen, L. L. (1992). Social and emotional patterns in adulthood: Support for socioemotional selectivity theory. *Psychology and Aging, 7*(3), 331–338.

Carstensen, L. L., Gottman, J. M., & Levenson, R. W. (1995). Emotional behavior in long-term marriage. *Psychology and Aging, 10*(1), 140–149.

Carstensen, L. L., & Löckenhoff, C. E. (2003). Aging, emotion, and evolution: The bigger picture. In P. Ekman, J. J. Campos, R. J. Davidson, & F. B. M. de Waal (Eds.), *Annals of the New York Academy of Sciences: Vol. 1000. Emotions inside out: 130 years after Darwin's: The expression of the emotions in man and animals* (p. 152–179). New York Academy of Sciences.

Carstensen, L. L., Pasupathi, M., Mayr, U., & Nesselroade, J. R. (2000). Emotional experience in everyday life across the adult life span. *Journal of Personality and Social Psychology, 79*(4), 644–655.

Charles, S. T., Mather, M., & Carstensen, L. L. (2003). Aging and emotional memory: The forgettable nature of negative images for older adults. *Journal of Experimental Psychology: General, 132*(2), 310–324.

Collins, N. L., & Miller, L. C. (1994). Self-disclosure and liking: A meta-analytic review. *Psychological Bulletin, 116*(3), 457–475.

Coulter, K., & Malouff, J. M. (2013). Effects of an intervention designed to enhance romantic relationship excitement: A randomized-control trial. *Couple and Family Psychology: Research and Practice, 2*(1), 34–44.

Davis, J. D. (1978). When boy meets girl: Sex roles and the negotiation of intimacy in an acquaintance exercise. *Journal of Personality and Social Psychology, 36*(7), 684–692.

Dainton, M., & Stafford, L. (1993). Routine maintenance behaviors: A comparison of relationship type, partner similarity and sex differences. *Journal of Social and Personal Relationships, 10*(2), 255–271.

Derlega, V. J., Winstead, B. A., Wong, P. T., & Hunter, S. (1985). Gender effects in an initial encounter: A case where men exceed women in disclosure. *Journal of Social and Personal Relationships, 2*(1), 25–44.

Dindia, K. (2000). Relational maintenance. In C. Hendrick & S. S. Hendrick (Eds.), *Close relationships: A sourcebook* (pp. 286–299). SAGE.

Dindia, K. (2003). Definitions and perspectives on relational maintenance communication. In D. J. Canary & M. Dainton (Eds.), *Maintaining relationships through communication: Relational, contextual, and cultural variations* (pp. 1–28). Psychology Press.

Dutton, D. G., & Aron, A. P. (1974). Some evidence for heightened sexual attraction under conditions of high anxiety. *Journal of Personality and Social Psychology, 30*(4), 510–517.

Exline, J. J., Baumeister, R. F., Bushman, B. J., Campbell, W. K., & Finkel, E. J. (2004). Too proud to let go: Narcissistic entitlement as a barrier to forgiveness. *Journal of Personality and Social Psychology, 87*(6), 894–912. https://doi.org/10.1037/0022-3514.87.6.894

Finkel E. J., Rusbult, C. E., Kumashiro, M., & Hannon, P. A. (2002). Dealing with betrayal in close relationships: Does commitment promote forgiveness? *Journal of Personality and Social Psychology, 82*, 956–974.

Fitzpatrick, T. R., & Vinick, B. (2003). The impact of husbands' retirement on wives' marital quality. *Journal of Family Social Work, 7*(1), 83–100.

Fitzsimons, G. M., Finkel, E. J., & vanDellen, M. R. (2015). Transactive goal dynamics. *Psychological Review, 122*(4), 648–673.

Fletcher, G. J., Simpson, J. A., Campbell, L., & Overall, N. C. (2015). Pair-bonding, romantic love, and evolution: The curious case of Homo sapiens. *Perspectives on Psychological Science, 10*(1), 20–36.

Fletcher, G. J., Simpson, J. A., Thomas, G., & Giles, L. (1999). Ideals in intimate relationships. *Journal of Personality and Social Psychology, 76*(1), 72–89.

Fung, H. H., & Carstensen, L. L. (2003). Sending memorable messages to the old: Age differences in preferences and memory for advertisements. *Journal of Personality and Social Psychology, 85*(1), 163–178.

Fung, H. H., Carstensen, L. L., & Lang, F. R. (2001). Age-related patterns in social networks among European Americans and African Americans: Implications for socioemotional selectivity across the life span. *The International Journal of Aging and Human Development, 52*(3), 185–206.

Fung, H. H., Carstensen, L. L., & Lutz, A. M. (1999). Influence of time on social preferences: Implications for life-span development. *Psychology and Aging, 14*(4), 595–604.

Haselton, M. G., & Buss, D. M. (2000). Error management theory: A new perspective on biases in cross-sex mind reading. *Journal of Personality and Social Psychology, 78*(1), 81–91.

Goodfriend, W., & Agnew, C. R. (2008). Sunken costs and desired plans: Examining different types of investments in close relationships. *Personality and Social Psychology Bulletin, 34*, 1639–1652.

Gottman, J. M. (1998). Psychology and the study of marital processes. *Annual Review of Psychology, 49*(1), 169–197.

Graham, S. M., Huang, J. Y., Clark, M. S., & Helgeson, V. S. (2008). The positives of negative emotions: Willingness to express negative emotions promotes relationships. *Personality and Social Psychology Bulletin, 34*, 394–406.

Griskevicius, V., Haselton, M. G., & Ackerman, J. M. (2015). Evolution and close relationships. In M. Mikulincer & P. R. Shaver (Eds.), *APA handbook of personality and social psychology: Vol. 3. Interpersonal relations* (pp. 3–32). American Psychological Association Press.

Griskevicius, V., Tybur, J. M., Delton, A. W., & Robertson, T. E. (2011). The influence of mortality and socioeconomic status on risk and delayed rewards: A life history theory approach. *Journal of Personality and Social Psychology, 100*(6), 1015–1026.

Hamilton, W. D. (1964). The genetical evolution of social behaviour. II. *Journal of Theoretical Biology, 7*(1), 17–52.

Hays, R. B. (1985). A longitudinal study of friendship development. *Journal of Personality and Social Psychology, 48*(4), 909–924.

Hazan, C., & Shaver, P. R. (2004). Attachment as an organizational framework for research on close relationships. *Psychological Inquiry, 5*, 1–22.

Hawkes, K., O'Connell, J. F., & Blurton Jones, N. G. (1997). Hadza women's time allocation, offspring provisioning, and the evolution of long postmenopausal life spans. *Current Anthropology, 38*(4), 551–577.

Holley, S. R., Haase, C. M., & Levenson, R. W. (2013). Age-related changes in demand-withdraw communication behaviors. *Journal of Marriage and Family, 75*(4), 822–836.

Jensen, J. F., & Rauer, A. J. (2015). Marriage work in older couples: Disclosure of marital problems to spouses and friends over time. *Journal of Family Psychology, 29*(5), 732–743.

Johnson, M. D., & Bradbury, T. N. (1999). Marital satisfaction and topographical assessment of marital interaction: A longitudinal analysis of newlywed couples. *Personal Relationships, 6*(1), 19–40.

Johnson, D. J., & Rusbult, C. E. (1989). Resisting temptation: Devaluation of alternative partners as a means of maintaining commitment in close relationships. *Journal of Personality and Social Psychology, 57*(6), 967–980.

Karney, B. R. & Bradbury, T. N. (1995). The longitudinal course of marital quality and stability: A review of theory, method, and research. *Psychological Bulletin*, 118, 3–34.

Karney, B. R., & Bradbury, T. N. (2005). Contextual influences on marriage: Implications for policy and intervention. *Current Directions in Psychological Science, 14*(4), 171–174.

Karremans, J. C., & Aarts, H. (2007). The role of automaticity in determining the inclination to forgive close others. *Journal of Experimental Social Psychology, 43*(6), 902–917.

Karremans, J. C., & Van Lange, P. A. (2008). Forgiveness in personal relationships: Its malleability and powerful consequences. *European Review of Social Psychology, 19*(1), 202–241.

Karremans, J. C., Pronk, T. M., & van der Wal, R. C. (2015). Executive control and relationship maintenance processes: An empirical overview and theoretical integration. *Social and Personality Psychology Compass, 9*(7), 333–347.

Kelley, H. H., & Thibaut, J. W. (1978). *Interpersonal relations: A theory of interdependence.* John Wiley & Sons.

Keneski, E., Neff, L. A., & Loving, T. J. (2018). The importance of a few good friends: Perceived network support moderates the association between daily marital conflict and diurnal cortisol. *Social Psychological and Personality Science, 9*(8), 962–971.

Korporaal, M., Broese van Groenou, M. I., & Tilburg, T. G. V. (2013). Health problems and marital satisfaction among older couples. *Journal of Aging and Health, 25*, 1279–1298.

Lang, F. R. (2001). Regulation of social relationships in later adulthood. *The Journals ofGerontology Series B: Psychological Sciences and Social Sciences, 56*(6), 321–326.

Laurenceau, J. P., Barrett, L. F., & Pietromonaco, P. R. (1998). Intimacy as an interpersonal process: The importance of self-disclosure, partner disclosure, and perceived partner responsiveness in interpersonal exchanges. *Journal of Personality and Social Psychology, 74*(5), 1238–1251.

Le, B., Dove, N. L., Agnew, C. R., Korn, M. S., & Mutso, A. A. (2010). Predicting nonmarital romantic relationship dissolution: A meta-analytic synthesis. *Personal Relationships, 17*(3), 377–390.

Levenson, R. W., Carstensen, L. L., & Gottman, J. M. (1993). Long-term marriage: Age, gender, and satisfaction. *Psychology and Aging, 8*(2), 301–313.

Levenson, R. W., Carstensen, L. L., & Gottman, J. M. (1994). Influence of age and gender on affect, physiology, and their interrelations: A study of long-term marriages. *Journal of Personality and Social Psychology, 67*(1), 56–68.

Levine, L. J., & Bluck, S. (1997). Experienced and remembered emotional intensity in older adults. *Psychology and Aging, 12*(3), 514–523.

Li, T., & Fung, H. H. (2011). The dynamic goal theory of marital satisfaction. *Review of General Psychology, 15*(3), 246–254.

Lieberman, D., Tooby, J., & Cosmides, L. (2007). The architecture of human kin detection. *Nature, 445*(7129), 727–731.

Linardatos, L., & Lydon, J. E. (2011). Relationship-specific identification and spontaneous relationship maintenance processes. *Journal of Personality and Social Psychology, 101*(4), 737–753.

Lydon, J. E., Fitzsimons, G. M., & Naidoo, L. (2003). Devaluation versus enhancement of attractive alternatives: A critical test using the calibration paradigm. *Personality and Social Psychology Bulletin, 29*(3), 349–359.

Lydon, J. E., Meana, M., Sepinwall, D., Richards, N., & Mayman, S. (1999). The commitment calibration hypothesis: When do people devalue attractive alternatives? *Personality and Social Psychology Bulletin, 25*(2), 152–161.

Lydon, J. E., & Quinn, S. (2013). Relationship maintenance processes. In J. A. Simpson & L. Campbell (Eds), *Oxford handbook of close relationships* (pp. 573–588). Oxford University Press.

Mayr, U., & Freund, A. M. (2020). Do we become more prosocial as we age, and if so, why? *Current Directions in Psychological Science, 29*(3), 248–254.

Maner, J. K., Rouby, D. A., & Gonzaga, G. C. (2008). Automatic inattention to attractive alternatives: The evolved psychology of relationship maintenance. *Evolution and Human Behavior, 29*(5), 343–349.

Maslow, A. H. (1971). *The farther reaches of human nature.* Viking.

Mather, M., Canli, T., English, T., Whitfield, S., Wais, P., Ochsner, K., Ochsner, K., Gabrieli, J. D. E., & Carstensen, L. L. (2004). Amygdala responses to emotionally valenced stimuli in older and younger adults. *Psychological Science, 15*(4), 259–263.

McCullough, M. E., Rachal, K. C., Sandage, S. J., Worthington, E. L., Jr., Brown, S. W., & Hight, T. L. (1998). Interpersonal forgiving in close relationships: II. Theoretical elaboration and measurement. *Journal of Personality and Social Psychology, 75*(6), 1586–1603.

Miller, S. L., & Maner, J. K. (2010). Evolution and relationship maintenance: Fertility cues lead committed men to devalue relationship alternatives. *Journal of Experimental Social Psychology, 46*(6), 1081–1084.

Morgan, D. L. (1988). Age differences in social network participation. *Journal of Gerontology, 43*(4), S129–S137.

Muise, A., Harasymchuk, C., Day, L. C., Bacev-Giles, C., Gere, J., & Impett, E. A. (2019). Broadening your horizons: Self-expanding activities promote desire and satisfaction in established romantic relationships. *Journal of Personality and Social Psychology, 116*, 237–258.

Murray, S. L., Aloni, M., Holmes, J. G., Derrick, J. L., Stinson, D. A., & Leder, S. (2009). Fostering partner dependence as trust insurance: The implicit contingencies of the exchange script in close relationships. *Journal of Personality and Social Psychology, 96*, 324–348.

Murray, S. L., & Holmes, J. G. (2011). *Interdependent minds: The dynamics of close relationships.* Guilford Press.

Murray, S. L., Holmes, J. G., & Griffin, D. W. (1996). The self-fulfilling nature of positive illusions in romantic relationships: Love is not blind, but prescient. *Journal of Personality and Social Psychology, 71*(6), 1155–1180.

Neff, L. A., & Karney, B. R. (2005). To know you is to love you: The implications of global adoration and specific accuracy for marital relationships. *Journal of Personality and Social Psychology, 88*(3), 480–497.

Ogolsky, B. G., & Monk, J. K. (Eds.). (2020). *Relationship maintenance: Theory, process, and context.* Cambridge University Press.

Ogolsky, B. G., Monk, J. K., Rice, T. M., Theisen, J. C., & Maniotes, C. R. (2017). Relationship maintenance: A review of research on romantic relationships. *Journal of Family Theory & Review, 9*(3), 275–306.

O'Rourke, N. (2005). Personality, cognitive adaptation, and marital satisfaction as predictors of well-being among older married adults. *Canadian Journal on Aging, 24*, 211–224.

O'Rourke, N., & Cappeliez, P. (2003). Intra-couple variability in marital aggrandizement: Idealization and satisfaction within enduring relationships. *Current Research in Social Psychology, 8*, 206–224.

O'Rourke, N., Claxton, A., Kupferschmidt, A. L., Smith, J. Z., & Beattie, B. L. (2011). Marital idealization as an enduring buffer to distress among spouses of persons with Alzheimer disease. *Journal of Social and Personal Relationships, 28*(1), 117–133.

O'Rourke, N., Neufeld, E., Claxton, A., & Smith, J. Z. (2010). Knowing me-knowing you: Reported personality and trait discrepancies as predictors of marital idealization between long-wed spouses. *Psychology and Aging, 25*(2), 412–421.

O'Rourke, N., & Wenaus, C. A. (1998). Marital aggrandizement as a mediator of burden among spouses of suspected dementia patients. *Canadian Journal on Aging, 17*(4), 384–400.

Quackenbush, S. W., & Barnett, M. A. (2001). Recollection and evaluation of critical experiences in moral development: A cross-sectional examination. *Basic and Applied Social Psychology, 23*(1), 55–64.

Reis, H. T., & Shaver, P. (1988). Intimacy as an interpersonal process. In S. Duck (Ed.), *Handbook of personal relationships* (pp. 367–389). John Wiley & Sons.

Rime, B. (2009). Emotion elicits the social sharing of emotion: Theory and empirical review. *Emotion Review, 1*, 60–85.

Righetti, F., Finkenauer, C., & Finkel, E. J. (2013). Low self-control promotes the willingness to sacrifice in close relationships. *Psychological Science, 24*(8), 1533–1540.

Righetti, F., & Visserman, M. (2018). I gave too much: Low self-esteem and the regret of sacrifices. *Social Psychological and Personality Science, 9*(4), 453–460.

Roberts, B. W., Walton, K. E., & Viechtbauer, W. (2006). Patterns of mean-level change in personality traits across the life course: A meta-analysis of longitudinal studies. *Psychological Bulletin, 132*(1), 1–25.

Ross, J. M., Karney, B. R., Nguyen, T. P., & Bradbury, T. N. (2019). Communication that is maladaptive for middle-class couples is adaptive for socioeconomically disadvantaged couples. *Journal of Personality and Social Psychology, 116*(4), 582–597.

Rubin, Z., Hill, C. T., Peplau, L. A., & Dunkel-Schetter, C. (1980). Self-disclosure in dating couples: Sex roles and the ethic of openness. *Journal of Marriage and the Family, 42*(2), 305–317.

Rusbult, C. E. (1980). Commitment and satisfaction in romantic associations: A test of the investment model. *Journal of Experimental Social Psychology, 16*(2), 172–186.

Rusbult, C. E., Agnew, C., R., & Arriaga, X. B. (2012). The investment model of commitment processes. In P. A. M. Van Lange, A. W. Kruglanski, & E. T. Higgins (Eds.), *Handbook of theories of social psychology* (Vol. 2, pp. 218–231). SAGE.

Rusbult, C. E., Johnson, D. J., & Morrow, G. D. (1986). Impact of couple patterns of problem solving on distress and nondistress in dating relationships. *Journal of Personality and Social Psychology, 50*(4), 744–753.

Rusbult, C. E., Martz, J. M., & Agnew, C. R. (1998). The investment model scale: Measuring commitment level, satisfaction level, quality of alternatives, and investment size. *Personal Relationships, 5*(4), 357–387.

Rusbult, C. E., Verette, J., Whitney, G. A., Slovik, L. F., & Lipkus, I. (1991). Accommodation processes in close relationships: Theory and preliminary empirical evidence. *Journal of Personality and Social Psychology, 60*(1), 53–78.

Rusbult, C. E., Zembrodt, I. M., & Gunn, L. K. (1982). Exit, voice, loyalty, and neglect: Responses to dissatisfaction in romantic involvements. *Journal of Personality and Social Psychology, 43*(6), 1230–1242.

Seider, B. H., Hirschberger, G., Nelson, K. L., & Levenson, R. W. (2009). We can work it out: Age differences in relational pronouns, physiology, and behavior in marital conflict. *Psychology and Aging, 24*(3), 604–613.

Simpson, J. A., Gangestad, S. W., & Lerma, M. (1990). Perception of physical attractiveness: Mechanisms involved in the maintenance of romantic relationships. *Journal of Personality and Social Psychology, 59*(6), 1192–1201.

Sprecher, S., Felmlee, D., Metts, S., & Cupach, W. (2015). Relationship initiation and development. In M. Mikulincer & P. R. Shaver (Eds.), *APA handbook of personality and social psychology: Volume 3. Interpersonal relations* (pp. 211–245). American Psychological Association Press.

Sprecher, S., Felmlee, D., Orbuch, T. L., & Willetts, M. C. (2002). Social networks and change in personal relationships. In A. L. Vangelisti, H. T. Reis, & M. A. Fitzpatrick (Eds.), *Stability and change in relationships* (pp. 257–284). Cambridge University Press.

Steiner, M., Allemand, M., & McCullough, M. E. (2011). Age differences in forgivingness: The role of transgression frequency and intensity. *Journal of Research in Personality, 45*(6), 670–678.

Steiner, M., Allemand, M., & McCullough, M. E. (2012). Do agreeableness and neuroticism explain age differences in the tendency to forgive others? *Personality and Social Psychology Bulletin, 38*(4), 441–453.

Tan, K., Agnew, C. R., VanderDrift, L. E., & Harvey, S. M. (2015). Committed to us: Predicting relationship closeness following non-marital romantic relationship breakup. *Journal of Social and Personal Relationships, 32*, 456–471.

Thibaut, J. W., & Kelley, H. H. (1959). *The social psychology of groups*. John Wiley & Sons.

VanderDrift, L. E., & Agnew, C. R. (2020). Interdependence perspectives on relationship maintenance. In B. G. Ogolsky & J. K. Monk (Eds.), *Relationship maintenance: Theory, process, and context* (pp. 15–28). Cambridge University Press.

Van Lange, P. A., Rusbult, C. E., Drigotas, S. M., Arriaga, X. B., Witcher, B. S., & Cox, C. L. (1997). Willingness to sacrifice in close relationships. *Journal of Personality and Social Psychology, 72*(6), 1373–1395.

Verstaen, A., Haase, C. M., Lwi, S. J., & Levenson, R. W. (2020). Age-related changes in emotional behavior: Evidence from a 13-year longitudinal study of long-term married couples. *Emotion, 20*(2), 149–163.

Visserman, M. L., Impett, E. A., Righetti, F., Muise, A., Keltner, D., & Van Lange, P. A. (2019). To "see" is to feel grateful? A quasi-signal detection analysis of romantic partners' sacrifices. *Social Psychological and Personality Science, 10*(3), 317–325.
Wieselquist, J., Rusbult, C. E., Foster, C. A., & Agnew, C. R. (1999). Commitment, pro-relationship behavior, and trust in close relationships. *Journal of Personality and Social Psychology, 77*(5), 942–966.
Wilbur, C. J., & Campbell, L. (2011). Humor in romantic contexts: Do men participate and women evaluate? *Personality and Social Psychology Bulletin, 37*(7), 918–929.
Wrzus, C., Hänel, M., Wagner, J., & Neyer, F. J. (2013). Social network changes and life events across the life span: A meta-analysis. *Psychological Bulletin, 139*(1), 53–80.

CHAPTER

20 Cultural Variation in Relationship Maintenance

Lora Adair *and* Nelli Ferenczi

Abstract

Romantic love appears to be a part of the shared human experience—with nearly all studied cultures evidencing intimate and romantic pair-bonding. This work focuses on a growing area of research on romantic relationship maintenance, employing an evolutionary perspective and positioning the maintenance and longevity of romantic relationships as important for survival and reproduction throughout human history. This chapter explores which evolved psychological mechanisms help to preserve our relationships, how individuals from various cultures maintain relationship satisfaction and longevity, and how local environments interact with our evolved psychologies to produce unique relationship maintenance behaviors and cognitions. We use sociocultural and socioecological perspectives contextualize research findings on relationship maintenance behaviors and cognitions across cultures—investigating the relationships among ecology, culture, and romantic relationship behaviors and outcomes. Specifically, we use factors like historical subsistence type and residential mobility to explain sources of cultural variability in relationship maintenance mechanisms. For example, historical rice subsistence creates ecological demands for coordinated and collaborative efforts among social group members, which in turn favor the development of specific cultural practices and norms, such as the interdependent self. In these contexts, families become sources of romantic advice, and familial approval is situated as an essential criterion for relationship persistence. We acknowledge the dynamic relationship between ecologies, cultures, and romantic relationships as we review contemporary literature about motivational processes. We discuss future research directions with an emphasis on critically evaluating the Euro-American, heteronormative, and patriarchal biases present in relationship research and theory.

Key Words: romantic relationships, relationship maintenance, relationship longevity, relationship satisfaction, cross-cultural variability, decolonization

"Love is divine only and difficult always. If you think it is easy you are a fool. If you think it is natural you are blind."

—Toni Morrison, Paradise

Romantic love and relationship dissolution are part of the human experience, with ethnographic accounts providing evidence for romantic love, divorce, and nonmarital romantic breakups in most studied cultures and societies (Betzig, 1989; Jankowiak & Fischer, 1992). This suggests that attempting to preserve and maintain romantic relationships and navigating romantic conflict were recurrent adaptive problems throughout human history. If we consider that relationship breakups are universal, and that breakups are associated with significant personal and interpersonal costs, then it is likely that selection favored the evolution of adaptations to assist in avoiding these costs. We propose that evolution has provided humans with a toolbox of behavioral, cognitive, and perceptual tools to aid in relationship maintenance: only a fool would believe that the act of loving is easy. Throughout this chapter, we explore how humans in various cultures and societies avoid these painful breakup experiences, and what evolved psychological architecture might help us in preserving our relationships, even in the face of relationship challenges and conflict.

An Evolutionary Perspective on Relationship Maintenance

Humans' environment of evolutionary adaptedness was characterized by struggle, competition, and survival threats, including ecological events, pathogens and disease, aggressive conspecifics, access to clean water, and finding and consuming sufficient calories and nutrients. In this ancestral environment, survival and reproduction was enhanced by establishing and maintaining long-term pair-bonds (Lukas & Clutton-Brock, 2013). To construct an argument regarding the evolution of psychological mechanisms designed to maintain romantic relationships, it is critical to first demonstrate that building and maintaining long-term pair-bonds was advantageous to ancestral humans.

Fitness Benefits of Staying Together

Long-term, monogamous mating is rare among primates (with a few exceptions, including owl monkeys and white-handed gibbons; Fernandez-Duque & Huck, 2013; Reichard, 1995). Considering other *Hominoidea*, chimpanzee and bonobo sexual strategies are characterized by short-term, multipartnered sexual encounters (Dixson, 2015). Human societies are characterized by flexible mating systems (including monogamy, polygyny, and polyandry; Walker et al., 2011), with certain departures from monogamy increasing in representation in a given community in accordance with shifting ecological conditions, such as sex ratio, male mortality, and female economic opportunity (Starkweather & Hames, 2012). However, examples of polygynous and polyandrous mating systems in humans are still characterized by a significant proportion (Haddix, 2001) of monogamous long-term relationships wherein multiple partners are only secured by individuals with sufficient wealth or social power (Ember et al., 2007). Why might have selection pressures favored the evolution of preference for long-term pair-bonds among humans?

Selection should favor evolved psychological architecture designed to build and maintain long-term relationships when the benefits of long-term bonds outweigh their costs. These costs and benefits are defined in terms of inclusive fitness—the survival and reproductive success of individuals and their genetic relatives. Thus, adaptations for long-term relationship building and maintenance would evolve if they reliably contributed to the solution of a recurrent (throughout human history) adaptive problem with a high impact on fitness. There is much evidence suggesting that, in both industrial and hunter–gatherer societies, the presence of a long-term romantic partner provides myriad fitness benefits, such as additional support for offspring and increased offspring survivability (Hewlett & Mcfarlan, 2010). This can help to explain the selection pressures favoring adoption of long-term pair-bonding in humans, as human offspring require significant time and investment before they reach sexual maturity and independence. This means that humans, particularly those raising multiple children, would suffer tremendous costs of rearing and child care compared to other primates.

Among humans, the effect of long-term relationship persistence on offspring success and survival is particularly strong in certain ecologies where women have limited opportunities to acquire resources on their own and are therefore dependent on men for support. For example, due to the sex-differentiated nature of provisioning in hunter–gatherer societies, in colder climates where there is less edible plant food for women to acquire, daily energetic needs are much more dependent on hunting success and thus men contribute more to daily caloric intake than women. In these kinds of contexts, provisioning provided by male romantic partners is more strongly tied to women's reproductive success (and therefore, fitness), specifically earlier weaning, higher overall parity, and shorter interbirth intervals (Marlowe, 2001). These findings are bolstered by modeling approaches to the evolution of long-term mating in humans, which finds that female preferences for provisioning may have coevolved with male propensity to engage in provisioning to produce mating systems where long-term, monogamous pair-bonding is favored over polygynous mating systems (Gavrilets, 2012). However, male provisioning in nonmonogamous primate species does suggest that male infant care can evolve in the absence of long-term pair-bonding (Rosenbaum et al., 2018). Given that human societies have traditionally been characterized by social hierarchy, the fitness benefits associated with provisioning would be different for low-ranked versus high-ranked males. Males with low social rank may have difficulty "winning" direct intrasexual competition for access to mates and would therefore differentially increase their own fitness—likelihood of attracting a mate—by acquiring and sharing physical resources with potential mates. However, stronger males with higher social rank could simply physically overpower, steal resources and mates from, and/or expel low-ranked males from their nomadic group. Therefore, the evolution of male provisioning and monogamous mating systems would also be dependent on female *preference* for males that could collect, hoard, and share physical resources. Female attraction to provisioning would ensure that male efforts to acquire and defend physical resources would produce fitness benefits, even for low-ranked males. Taken together, this suggests that not only male provisioning but female mating preferences have worked in concert to produce mating systems favoring long-term, stable romantic relationships.

While the majority of the evolutionary psychological literature focuses on attraction and relationship initiation, maintaining romantic relationships poses an equally important adaptive challenge. We can find evidence illustrating how our ancestors solved this adaptive challenge in our contemporary evolved psychological toolbox. We will synthesize evolutionary and cultural perspectives to evaluate why, when, and how individuals engage in relationship maintenance behaviors and cognitions.

A Cross-Cultural Perspective on Relationship Maintenance

Our presentation of relationship maintenance behaviors and cognitions relies on sociocultural and socioecological lenses to examine how cultures shape adaptive relationship maintenance processes. For example, there are contrasting findings for the links between collectivism and relationship maintenance and romantic beliefs. Collectivist cultures such as India and Japan focus on maintaining group harmony and social cohesion (Imada & Yussen, 2012) and are more likely to emphasize the importance of pragmatic aspects of love relationships, including one's material contributions to a relationship (Jankowiak et al., 2015). On the other hand, collectivism mediates the link between culture and increased idealistic romantic beliefs, with (collectivist) Indian participants reporting more idealistic love beliefs than (individualist) American participants (Bejanyan et al., 2014). Additionally, relational mobility—the extent to which the social context provides individuals opportunities to leave relationships and form new ones (Yuki & Schug, 2012)—is linked with increased passion, and in turn, commitment (Yamada et al., 2017), as well as active engagement in relationship maintenance behaviors such as self-disclosure and social support (Kito et al., 2017, Thomson et al., 2018). Here, we will synthesize these approaches to highlight cross-cultural variability and similarity in relationship maintenance in contemporary romantic relationships.

To contextualize findings relevant to relationship maintenance behaviors and cognitions across cultures, we propose a model linking ecology, culture, and love beliefs. This model relies on a concept termed "evoked culture" (Tooby & Cosmides, 1992), which refers to the ways in which different environmental cues and contexts interact with evolved psychology—which is highly responsive to context—to produce behaviors and cognitions that fit the current environmental constraints and demands. In short, culture likely reflects the relationship between specific social and ecological conditions and the psychological adaptations that respond to those conditions (Gangestad et al., 2006). Consider the threat of disease: pathogens and infectious diseases have posed a significant survival threat to humans throughout our evolutionary history. However, the threat of infectious disease differs according to region, with areas closest to the equator

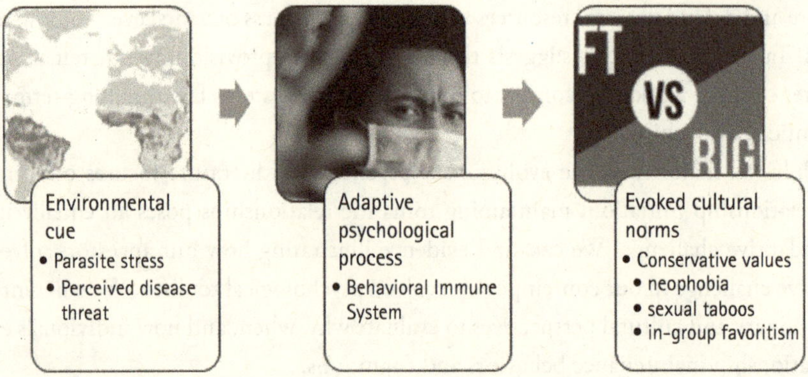

Figure 20.1 Evoked Culture

This concept provides an evolutionary account of cultural variability, proposing that unique environmental demands interact with our highly adaptive human psychologies to produce various elements of culture. From Tooby and Cosmides (1992).

possessing more prevalent disease and more pathogen diversity (Fincher & Thornhill, 2008). Given that the threat of disease is species universal, but the immediate likelihood of infection is ecology-dependent, humans should possess a malleable psychology which can produce certain behaviors, cognitions, and even cultural norms and rituals, dynamically in response to the demands of their environment. Evidence supports this prediction of evoked culture in response to disease threat, with societies located in environments characterized by greater pathogen load also less likely to disperse and relocate and more likely to promote collectivistic values and ethnocentrism and even possess greater religious richness and diversity (Fincher & Thornhill, 2008). All these behavioral dispositions and elements of culture encourage in group cooperation and favoritism; detection and avoidance of outgroup members; and strict adherence to sexual, food, and social norms that can reduce the likelihood that an individual comes into contact with contaminated food or human-borne pathogens. See Figure 20.1 for an example of how cultural differences can be perceived as resulting from evoked culture (i.e., ecological and sociological demands).

We propose that cultures characterized by increased ecological threats, high pathogen load, and historical rice subsistence—would differentially benefit from cultural norms encouraging the prioritization of group duties, responsibilities, and relational concerns. The rice theory of subsistence (Talhelm et al., 2014) posits that as rice requires more cooperative and coordinated labor to sow, irrigate, and harvest relative to other crops such as wheat, societies that were primarily rice-subsistent are more likely to be collectivistic. Additionally, low residential mobility societies—characterized by stable social groups (Oishi, 2010) are also more likely to be collectivistic. In these environments, relationships are difficult to replace and resource stability is highly dependent on a group's ability to agree upon and collectively pursue a goal. These environmental pressures increase the adaptive value of norms encouraging the prioritization of group responsibilities and shared group concerns, as individuals conforming to these norms will provide the group with survival and reproductive benefits. These environmental pressures also increase the adaptive value of pragmatic love beliefs—the belief that long-term partners should provide stable and sufficient material contributions to the relationship, should be "willing to work" to support one's family, and that in-pair relationship problems and conflict will improve over time and with effort (i.e., thus relationships characterized by conflict/disagreement should be invested in to resolve said conflict).

On the other hand, we propose that cultures characterized by high residential mobility and historical wheat subsistence would differentially benefit from cultural norms encouraging the prioritization of individual and personal goals, attitudes, needs, rights, and contracts. High residential mobility societies—characterized by unstable social groups—and societies with a historical reliance upon wheat subsistence which requires individual efforts to sow and harvest—are more likely to be individualistic in nature. In these environments, relationships are relatively easy to replace and resource stability is highly dependent on an individual's ability to pursue their own goals and defend their own provisions. These environmental pressures increase the adaptive value of norms encouraging the prioritization of individual responsibilities and personal concerns, as individuals conforming to these norms under these environmental constraints will enjoy survival and reproductive benefits. These environmental pressures also increase the adaptive value of idealistic love beliefs—the belief that long-term partners should contribute to an individual's personal development and growth, partners should be emotionally supportive and uphold their marital/relational contracts, and relationship problems and conflict will not improve over time (i.e., thus relationships characterized by conflict/disagreement should be dissolved rather than invested in and improved).

Relationship Maintenance Adaptations

Contemporary literature on romantic relationship maintenance focuses on the perceptual, motivational, neurological, and social processes that facilitate the persistence of a relationship over time; the persistence and quality of relationship satisfaction; and the mitigation of relationship threats. We review cross-cultural variability and similarity in these relationship maintenance mechanisms.

Motivational Mechanisms

Motivational mechanisms refer to a broad suite of conscious and subconscious processes that promote goal-directed behaviors. These motivation mechanisms can facilitate both approach and avoidance behaviors. Specifically, motivation can promote attraction to positive outcomes (approach of stimuli associated with satisfaction of hunger, sexual drives, etc.) or the avoidance of negative outcomes (avoidance of stimuli associated with pain or discomfort).

One of the most significant threats to romantic relationship longevity is the presence of alternative mates in one's current environment. In a survey of British relationships, infidelity was a common cause of marital and nonmarital relationship dissolution—with 36.6% of participants reporting experience with a romantic breakup due to infidelity (Lampard, 2014). However, there appear to be sociocultural and environmental effects on the role that infidelity plays in relationship dissolution. Some research suggests that women living in areas characterized by resource instability and relative poverty are more likely to cite physical abuse, psychological abuse, and partner drug and alcohol use, as well as financial problems as reasons for relationship dissolution (Fine & Harvey, 2006). Alternatively, women living in higher socioeconomic strata are more likely to cite a partner's lack of love, emotional commitment, and fidelity as reasons for relationship dissolution (Savaya & Cohen, 1998). And while infidelity has been reported as immoral and even "unforgivable" by Americans (Jones, 2008), and has been identified as a leading cause of relationship dissolution for Americans (Amato & Previti, 2003), this does not reliably replicate in non-Western samples. For example, in a sample of first-generation Korean immigrants living in America, an ex-partner's financial irresponsibility, unemployment, and inability to financially provide were the most oft-cited reasons for relationship dissolution (Chang, 2004). An inability to provide and a perceived lack of commitment to the family also appear as common reasons for relationship dissolution among Palestinian women (Cohen & Savaya, 2003). In sum, it seems as though interpersonal competence and compatibility—fidelity, communication, problem solving, emotional support—are more critical to relationship maintenance among Western samples (e.g., America, Germany, Italy, and Switzerland; Bodenmann et al., 2007). On the other hand, commitment to the family and provisioning ability—financial responsibility, consistent employment, ability to support one's family, interest and dedication to childrearing responsibilities—are more critical to relationship maintenance in non-Western samples (e.g., Korea, Palestine, and Turkey; Demir, 2013).

These findings are consistent with our model (see fig. 20.2), which proposes that individualistic cultures should be characterized by more idealistic love beliefs and collectivistic cultures should be characterized by more pragmatic love beliefs. This should be particularly likely in those cultures also characterized by cultural "tightness," where greater importance is placed on compliance with social norms and expectations (Gelfand et al., 2011). The prioritization of fidelity and emotional support in Western society is consistent with idealistic love beliefs such as the belief that romantic relationships should be personally fulfilling and enriching, and that romantic relationships should involve nearly perfect interpersonal dynamics (e.g., the belief that you should know each other's inner feelings; Hefner & Wilson, 2013). Likewise, cultural differences in the positioning of romantic attachment within the relationship hierarchy (i.e., relative to other social connections and commitments) shape relationship standards, or the expectations and beliefs of what relationships should be (Epstein & Baucom, 2002). Specifically, the relative decentering

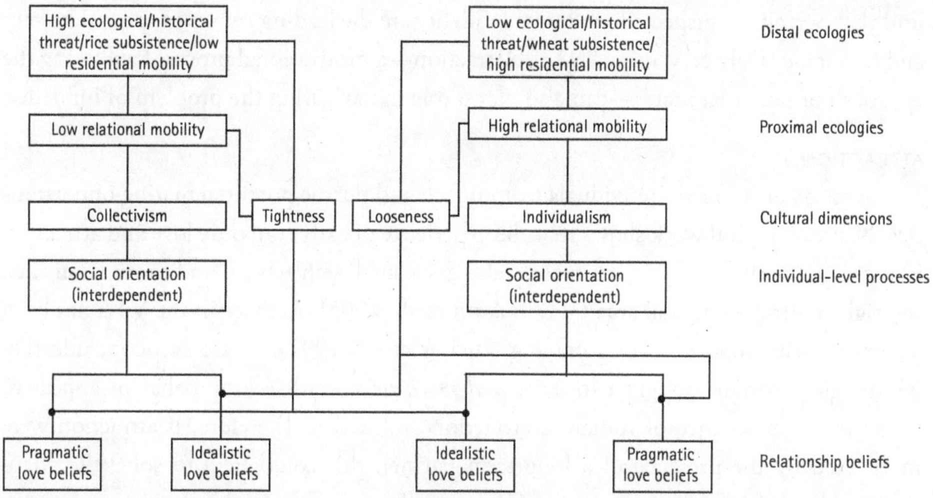

Figure 20.2 This model illustrates our proposed relationship between ecology, culture, and love beliefs. We propose that cultures characterized by high ecological and historical threats, low residential mobility, and historical rice subsistence would shape socioecologies which promote low relational mobility. Individuals in these contexts differentially benefit from cultural norms encouraging an interdependent self-construal as well as romantic relationship values which emphasize responsibility for, dedication to, and support of the family. Alternatively, cultures characterized by low ecological and historical threats, high residential mobility, and historical wheat subsistence would shape high relational mobility socioecologies. Individuals in these contexts differentially benefit from cultural norms encouraging independent self-construal as well as romantic relationship values which emphasize personal fulfilment and personal contracts.

of romantic relationships within collectivist cultures, which emphasize the importance of family and social relationships, promotes relationship standards, which emphasize relational harmony, relations with extended family, and face maintenance (i.e., maintaining a positive social image; Hiew et al., 2015), paralleling pragmatic love beliefs. In contrast, the decrease of kin networks as a result of the rise of individualism has positioned romantic relationships as the most prominent relationship in adulthood within Western cultures, demonstrated in the transition of primary attachment figures from parents/caregivers to romantic partners. To the extent that romantic relationships function as integral social groups from which we can gain social belonging, meaning, and identity within Western societies (Lindholm, 1995), the relationship standards of intimacy and showing care and love are valued more (Hiew et al., 2015), reflecting idealistic love beliefs.

Acknowledging the role that culture and resource stability likely play in this relationship, we can conclude that the presence of attractive alternative mates poses a threat to an individual's long-term romantic relationship. Indeed, infidelity does appear as a reason for breakups in both Western and non-Western samples (e.g., and a leading cause of divorce in 43 cultures; Betzig, 1989). Attraction to and pursuit of relationship alternatives is associated with a host of fitness costs, including the diversion of resources, potential social and reputational costs of infidelity, as well as relational conflict and intimate partner violence (Negash et al., 2014). Cross-cultural investigations of intimate partner violence find that perceived, suspected, or actual infidelity are the leading causes of spousal battery and homicide (Daly & Wilson, 1988). Attraction—a motivational process facilitating the approach of potential mates—can also play a role in navigating the problem of infidelity.

ATTRACTION

Attraction encourages individuals to approach and pursue potential mating opportunities. Neurobiological work shows that the experience of early romantic love and attraction is associated with activity in brain areas also associated with reward and motivation (i.e., the right ventral tegmental area (VTA); Aron et al., 2005). Activity in the VTA has been associated with food and drug craving (Breiter et al., 1997), so we can conclude that neurological systems designed to *drive and motivate* reward-seeking behavior appear to underlie the experience of romantic attraction and desire. Therefore, if attraction were moderated by the presence of a long-term partner, this could help to solve the adaptive problem of infidelity. Cues of one's current long-term partner's fertility can trigger the activation of motivational relationship maintenance mechanisms (Miller & Maner, 2010). In a sample of young adult men, Miller and Maner (2010) created an experimental scenario wherein participants completed cooperative tasks with a confederate. This confederate was a naturally cycling woman (i.e., not using hormonal contraceptives), instructed to avoid appearance-enhancing tools (e.g., she did not wear makeup or perfume) and trained to engage in standardized and neutral interactions with participants (i.e., minimizing direct eye contact and conversation). Overall, men without a partner rated the confederate as more attractive—suggesting that *attraction is suppressed by the presence of a long-term partner*. What is interesting is that ovulation cues further moderate this motivational mechanism: unpartnered men's attraction was *upregulated* when the confederate was experiencing peak fertility, and partnered men's attraction was *downregulated* even further when the confederate was experiencing peak fertility. This derogation effect—perceiving alternative mates as less attractive when committed—has even been found to bias memory for potential mates, with partnered individuals remembering potential mates as less attractive than they actually are, compared to single individuals (Karremans et al., 2011).

MATE PREFERENCES

Mating preferences and desires also serve as motivational processes—encouraging individuals to preferentially seek out and pursue mates with traits associated with various survival and reproductive benefits. Cross-cultural evidence supports the existence of sex-differentiated mating preferences, with men being more likely to prioritize traits signaling youth and reproductive potential (e.g., slightly younger age and physical attractiveness) in potential mates, and women being more likely to prioritize traits signaling stability and resource acquisition abilities (e.g., good financial prospects, slightly older age, and intelligence) in potential mates (Buss, 1989; Walter et al., 2020). Given that females in mammalian species incur greater obligatory minimum parental investment, considering internal gestation and subsequent lactation, women may enjoy survival and reproductive benefits if they preferentially select and pursue reliable, stable, industrious mates. Similarly, males' reproductive potential is constrained by the health and fertility of the mates they choose; preferentially choosing and seeking mates with reliable indicators of health, like facial symmetry (Shackelford & Larsen, 1997) and larger waist-to-hip ratios (Singh, 2002) would be associated with fitness benefits for ancestral men. Notably, our mating psychologies are highly responsive to changing environmental challenges and demands, and evidence suggests that greater competition for resources and greater resource demands in one's local ecology *upregulates* women's preference for earning capacity and *downregulates* women's preference for emotional stability and compatibility of interests and values when evaluating potential mates (McGraw, 2002). Further, individuals appear to be sensitive to cultural-level patterns in mating preferences, with individuals high on communal traits (i.e., integrating oneself within a larger social unit) more likely to demonstrate mating preferences similar to those valued by other individuals in their society (Gebauer et al., 2012). Agentic individuals (i.e., those who seek to differentiate themselves from the larger social unit), however, tend to prioritize physical attractiveness and status at the expense of traits valued by individuals in their culture. This work also supports our model and the proposed relationship between ecology, culture, and love beliefs (see fig. 20.2)—finding that cultural-level mating preferences reflect a prioritization of pragmatic traits in cultures relatively high in endorsement of collectivistic values (e.g., a strong preference for social status in Turkey) and a prioritization of idealistic traits in cultures relatively high in endorsement of individualistic values (e.g., a strong preference for interpersonal warmth in Australia). How might specific mating preferences help us solve the adaptive problem of mate retention?

A large body of literature suggests that partner similarity is critical to relationship satisfaction, maintenance, and longevity. Specifically, romantic relationships wherein partners are similar on dimensions such as religiosity, personal interests, likes and values, education level, sex drive, personality, and relationship standards tend to enjoy greater relationship satisfaction and relationship longevity (Gaunt, 2006; Hiew et al., 2015; Wilson & Cousins, 2003), with similar couples being more likely to still be together at time 2 in longitudinal investigations (Bleske-Rechek, et al., 2009). Cross-cultural evidence supports the proposition that couple similarity is associated with relationship satisfaction and reduced marital conflict (Dyrenforth et al., 2010). This is particularly true for couples where similarity on a given dimension (e.g., religion) is rated as subjectively more important (Lutz-Zois et al., 2006). If partners that are more alike report higher relationship satisfaction and have romantic relationships that persist over time, *then a mating preference for and attraction to individuals like oneself might solve the adaptive problem of relationship preservation and maintenance*. While we're all familiar with the adage "opposites attract," the majority of existing evidence suggests that "similarity attracts." Humans are more attracted to individuals that are like themselves on a variety of dimensions, including height, age, physical attractiveness, personality, weight, and even intelligence (Stulp et al., 2017). When asked to describe one's ideal partner, individuals often describe someone similar to themselves on multiple personality dimensions (Botwin et al., 1997). Cross-cultural investigations support this similarity-attracts model, finding that individuals prefer mates similar to themselves on dimensions like physical attractiveness, interpersonal warmth, and status in 11 sampled countries (Gebauer et al., 2012). By the same token, similarity on personality-related domains was linked with increased marital quality in newlyweds, with similarity in attachment orientations serving as the strongest predictor of satisfaction (Luo & Klohnen, 2005). Collectively, these findings support the existence of assortative mating in humans, suggesting that individuals tend to prefer mates who are more similar to themselves. A preference for similarity, in turn, likely facilitates relationship satisfaction and longevity.

ATTACHMENT

Bowlby (1969) described attachment as a universal affiliative human motivation; moreover, interactions with one's caregiver during critical periods of development predisposes an individual to form specific kinds of psychological connections with other individuals throughout their lifetime (Bretherton, 1994). These childhood attachment experiences form the basis for our attachment system functioning in adulthood. Romantic love in adulthood has been conceptualized as a biosocial process which parallels infant attachment (Hazan & Shaver, 1987).

There are both individual differences and cultural differences in attachment system functioning. On an individual level, reliable and responsive caregivers promote secure attachment, or a positive view of self, others, and relationships, characterized by a sense of safety and security in interpersonal relationships (Mikulincer & Shaver, 2007). Alternatively, unreliable or unresponsive caregivers promote insecure attachment (i.e., avoidant and anxious attachment), or a negative view of self, others, and relationships, characterized by a sense of insecurity and instability in interpersonal relationships. These individual differences in attachment system functioning produce unique patterns in subsequent relational behaviors, with secure and anxiously attached individuals reporting more desire to seek out relationships with others for social support and mutual enjoyment (Schwartz et al., 2007). Cultural-level differences in attachment patterns have also been identified, with environments characterized by high mortality rates, as well as high pathogen load and disease threat, facilitating the development of dismissing attachment patterns—a greater interest in short-term romantic relationships, and less desire for emotional closeness with romantic partners—particularly among women (Schmitt et al., 2004). This sensitivity of attachment style to broader ecological conditions promotes individual fitness, as short-term mating strategies would produce greater reproductive benefits for women in harsh and high mortality ecologies, compared to long-term mating strategies. These benefits include earlier reproduction and thus greater familial support of offspring, the ability to attract more attractive mates with "good genes" that can be passed to offspring, and the ability to garner resources from multiple mates (Hrdy, 1981; Gangestad & Simpson, 2000).

However, it must be noted that some sex-specific relationships between dismissive attachment and sexual permissiveness (e.g., infidelity and short-term mating orientation) do not replicate in African and Asian samples (Schmitt & Jonason, 2015), further demonstrating that the function of attachment and its impact on relationship behaviors is adaptable. Conversely, preoccupied attachment, or holding positive models of others and a negative model of self, was prevalent with East Asian samples (Schmitt et al., 2004); this pattern may reflect the socialization of an interdependent self-construal within a collectivist societal framework. A positive model of others and negative model of self may aid in promoting relational harmony and self-improvement motives, which characterize interdependent self-construals. Self-improvement is important for relationship maintenance and may be driven by extrinsic relational demands, such as perceived partner disapproval as opposed to intrinsic motivation within collectivist cultures (Ming Hui & Harris Bond, 2009). Therefore, preoccupied attachment may encourage specific adaptive relationship maintenance strategies within collectivist contexts, such as prioritizing relational harmony, minimizing conflict, and increased focus on extrinsic self-improvement to avoid perceived partner disapproval.

Of all human motivational systems, attachment may play the most critical role in relationship maintenance and longevity. This motivational system shapes an individual's propensity to seek out, form, and maintain affectionate bonds with caregivers, friends, and romantic relationship partners (Hazan & Shaver, 1987), and thus likely has implications for an individual's ability to navigate relational challenges and avoid the negative outcomes associated with relationship dissolution. Specifically, research suggests that securely attached individuals are more likely to engage in romantic relationship maintenance behaviors, such as providing care for one's romantic partner, self-disclosing to partners, actively assuring a partner of one's commitment to the relationship, fostering common friendships and social networks with a partner, sharing responsibilities with a partner (Adams & Baptist, 2012), and forgiving a partner and compromising when conflict occurs (Kachadourian et al., 2004). Among samples of gay men, securely attached individuals are more likely to talk openly about sex with their partner and report higher levels of both sexual and relationship satisfaction (Starks & Parsons, 2014). Attachment security is related to romantic relationship satisfaction (Erol & Orth, 2013), and in turn, relationship persistence and longevity (Carnelley et al., 1996). Cross-cultural evidence suggests a stable relationship between secure romantic attachment and relationship satisfaction in both Western and non-Western cultures (Ho et al., 2012; Wongpakaran et al., 2012). Research further suggests that not only secure but also anxious attachment patterns may facilitate relationship longevity. Securely and anxiously attached individuals are more likely to talk about sources of relational conflict with their partner, and more likely to remain with a romantic partner after experiencing conflict (Jang et al., 2002). Individuals high in anxious attachment may maintain relationships as a result of elevated fear of being alone and, in turn, a fear of change (George et al., 2020). Anxious attachment may therefore serve as a drive to remain even within unsatisfying romantic relationships. Together, this work suggests that attachment—specifically secure and anxious attachment—motivates individuals to perform various relationship maintenance behaviors, and thus cultivates greater romantic relationship satisfaction and persistence over time.

Perceptual and Cognitive Mechanisms

Perceptual mechanisms refer to a broad suite of both conscious and subconscious processes that collect, organize, and interpret sensory information. These perceptual mechanisms shape the way we understand and experience the world around us, and even the way we understand ourselves. Specifically, perception makes use of incoming sensory information (e.g., attending to and ignoring or habituating to certain forms of stimulation) as well as higher-order cognitive processes (e.g., previous knowledge, experiences, memories, and even schema, assumptions, and beliefs) to construct our subjective experiences (Teufel & Nanay, 2017). For example, research suggests that attachment style can affect individuals' basic perception of emotion in facial stimuli (Fraley et al., 2006) with anxiously attached individuals more quickly—but less accurately—perceiving changes in emotion based on gradually changing facial stimuli, compared to securely attached individuals. These findings suggest that attachment experiences and affiliative motivation may shape various perceptual mechanisms, including attention and vigilance to social and emotional stimulation in one's immediate environment.

ATTENTION

Attention guides which sensory information is processed and interpreted. Our world is full of information, and at any given moment humans are exposed to more information and stimulation than we can possibly process and interpret (Dukas, 2002). So, attention is an important first step in the perceptual process—determining (consciously or unconsciously) what information to organize, interpret, and utilize. Attention can help individuals identify recurrent ancestral survival threats (e.g., spiders) in their immediate environment (New & German, 2015), identify potential sources of infectious disease (Ackerman et al., 2009), and identify aggressive conspecifics in their social group (van Honk et al., 1999). It is obvious that automatic attentional processes can guide us to acquire life-sustaining information in our environment, but perhaps less clear how attention might promote relationship maintenance. Addressing the problem of attraction to and pursuit of alternative mates, evolved relationship maintenance mechanisms could regulate attention to alternative mates as a function of long-term partner presence. Decreased attention to alternative mates, therefore, would assist in solving the adaptive problem of infidelity.

It is fitness-enhancing for an individual to experience attentional bias toward attractive alternatives until that individual encounters cues that reliably signal the possibility of relationship initiation and commitment. Such evolved cognitive architecture facultatively adjusting the allocation of attentional resources can promote attention toward and pursuit of attractive potential mates when single but selective inattention to attractive conspecifics when courting or satisfactorily partnered. For example, after being asked to think about someone they are attracted to as a romantic partner who reciprocates their interest (i.e., asks participants to "go out with" them), participants were better able to quickly divert their visual attention away from attractive potential mates, compared to individuals simply asked to imagine someone they were attracted to (i.e., without any cues of reciprocated interest; Koranyi & Rothermund, 2012). This suggests that specific cues of relationship and commitment possibilities—like reciprocal interest and liking—shape basic perceptual mechanisms directing social attention. Similarly, when asked to view magazine advertisements, participants with higher relationship satisfaction spent less time visually attending to the attractive targets, compared to participants with lower relationship satisfaction (Miller, 1997). Further, individuals involved in committed romantic relationship devoted less visual attentional resources to attractive alternative mates, particularly following exposure to a mating prime (i.e., exposure to words like "kiss" and "lust"; Maner et al., 2009). This effect seems specific to potential mates in one's environment, rather than social targets more broadly, as individuals in committed heterosexual relationships more quickly diverted their visual attention away from attractive opposite-sex, but not same-sex, targets (Maner et al., 2008). Attention appears to be an effective relationship maintenance mechanism, as attention to attractive relationship alternatives was associated with a greater likelihood of relationship dissolution at time 2 in longitudinal investigations of this effect (Miller, 1997). Inattention to relationship alternatives has been demonstrated in both American (Maner et al., 2009) and Chinese samples (Ma et al., 2019; Zhang et al., 2017), providing initial evidence that this may be a culturally invariant relationship maintenance mechanism, yet more work in this area with diverse samples and cultures is needed.

REASONING AND BELIEF

Patterns of cognition that are most salient to us are shaped by differences in social orientation—the extent to which individuals report an independent or interdependent self-concept (for a review, see Varnum et al., 2010). As Hong and Choi (2019) described, "thinking styles vary in the degree to which they are oriented toward interconnections in the universe" (p. 1076). Holistic cognition, fostered by collectivist values, promotes attentional, perceptual, and reasoning tendencies which are field dependent (e.g., objects are perceived as being part of the field within which they appear, are linked to other objects, and are not differentiated), are broad, and focus on background and relationship elements (Nisbett et al., 2001). Further, holistic cognition is dialectical and is linked with categorization of objects according to theme and function and increased situational attribution. In contrast, analytic cognition, fostered by individualist values, promotes a different set of attentional, perceptual, and reasoning tendencies which are field independent (e.g., objects are perceived as discrete and separate from their contexts and other objects), are narrow, and focus on salient, central objects; analytic cognition is taxonomic, grounded in linearity (trends will continue as they are), and is linked with increased dispositional attribution (Nisbett et al., 2001). In this vein, Hong and Choi (2019) investigated individual differences in cognition type and their impact on relational decisions. Cyclic perceivers (holistic thinkers) possess the worldview that situations change, and relationships have their ups and downs. Conversely, linear perceivers (analytic thinkers) tend to believe in the continuation of a trend; for example, if a linear perceiver experiences relationship difficulties, one would expect that they would terminate it to end the troubles in the moment, as they would believe that the relationship will only continue the (downward) trend. Notably, linear perception mirrors features emblematic of *idealistic love beliefs*—for example, the belief that soul mate relationships should be easy, characterized by little or no conflict and a partner's ability to intuitively know and understand an individual's needs (Knobloch-Fedders & Knudson, 2009). Cyclic perceivers were more likely to tolerate relational transgressions, reported less willingness to break up and fewer breakups, and Were more likely to stay in relationships over the course of one year (Hong & Choi, 2019). Cyclic perception shares features with *pragmatic love beliefs*—for example, the belief that relationships require work and investment, and that relationships are built rather than fated (Knobloch-Fedders & Knudson, 2009).

Relatedly, lay theories (Dweck et al., 1995; Dweck & Leggett, 1988) can guide motivation and attribution of events (Hong et al., 1999). Entity theory encompasses lay beliefs that qualities (e.g., intelligence) are fixed, whereas incremental theory encompasses lay beliefs that qualities can change through effort. In keeping with effort beliefs, incremental theorists are more likely to persist in the face of negative feedback or failure relative to entity theorists (Hong et al., 1999). Cross-cultural variation exists in the extent to which incremental or entity lay beliefs are chronically salient through the socialization of cultural norms and values of collectivism or individualism, respectively (Heine, 2001). These differences are exemplified in goal pursuit following failure: Japanese (collectivist) participants were more likely to persevere on a follow-up task after failing and receiving feedback, relative to American (individualist) participants; this effect was driven, in part, by differences in beliefs about the utility of effort (Heine et al., 2001). Additionally, these lay theories can be expanded to understand relational goal pursuit and motivation. Specifically, individuals can hold lay beliefs that relational qualities are fixed (entity theory) or that they can change (incremental lay theory; Knee, 1998). Within the context of relationship maintenance, incremental theorists report more hope in overcoming relational difficulties (Knee et al., 2003). Thus, we posit that cultural dimensions that promote incremental lay beliefs (collectivism), coupled with norm adherence (tightness), would foster greater relational maintenance in the face of relationship challenges. Taken together with findings regarding cognition types, we would expect cyclic perception to further bolster persistence in relationship maintenance strategies and behaviors.

Social Mechanisms

The extent of social support, expectation, and influence of various social contexts shapes the dynamics of romantic relationships. The maintenance of relationships can extend beyond the pair-dyad to include close others such as family and friends.

SOCIAL SUPPORT

Perceived social network support for one's romantic relationship (friends, acquaintances, family) is associated with increased relationship satisfaction and persistence (Blair & Holmberg, 2008). The ways that we relate to others, define ourselves, and interact with our social environment is shaped by our socialization within overarching cultural dimensions (Triandis, 1995). In this respect, the extent to which individuals expect and accept social support and influence in romantic relationship initiation and maintenance outside the pair-dyad is shaped by cultural norms. Specifically, collectivism engenders interdependent self-construals, which rely on the fundamental connectedness between individuals. Interdependent self-construals are characterized by a focus on harmonious interdependence, attending to others, and fitting into the social milieu (Imada, 2010). The interdependent self may behave in different ways across differing situations depending on what is deemed appropriate (Markus & Kitayama, 1991), directing control inward to ensure that private emotions do not displace the equilibrium of harmonious interpersonal interaction. Awareness of others and their needs is inherent in the interdependent self, with the implicit assumption that attendance to the needs and goals of others is a reciprocal endeavor. Pro-relationship traits and caring behaviors form a stronger basis for their self-esteem than they do for independent selves (Goodwin et al., 2012). Because close others actively participate in the construction and definition of the self, the interdependent self is constantly aware of others' needs, goals, and expectations. Self-esteem is contingent on fitting into the in group and living up to their standards (Hannover et al., 2006).In contrast, individualism, which values development of and attendance to one's inner attributes (e.g., motives, traits, and values) and personal goals (van Horen et al., 2008), promotes independent self-construals, which are characterized by personal agency (Imada & Ellsworth, 2011) and perceptions of a distinct inner self (Markus & Kitayama, 1991). Individuals rely on their inner self—which is perceived as being consistent (Suh, 2002)—to interpret and imbue behavior with meaning (Morris & Peng, 1994). Culture and the resulting socialized self-construal concepts (interdependent vs. independent) play a role in shaping not only how individuals see themselves but also how they perceive and rely on others in their broader social support network. Thus, social support mechanisms for relationship maintenance are flexible and responsive to cultural norms and constraints.

For example, some assumptions about the universality of attachment hierarchies—the network of attachment relationships arranged by the extent to which they fulfill attachment functions, with primary attachment figures at the top—have recently been questioned (e.g., Flicker et al., 20209). Particularly, individuation from parents and prioritization of romantic partners as the primary figure may be context dependent and an artifact of individualist cultural norms as opposed to collectivist cultural norms such as reliance on extended family, filial piety, and attending to close others to maintain relationship harmony. In a study of Bangladeshi married women, Flicker et al. (2020) reported that across both arranged and couple-initiated marriages, participants were more likely to name parents as primary attachment figures rather than spouses, implying that parents can continue to fulfill attachment functions in adulthood. By the same token, differences in family and extended family social support of romantic relationships were found between Chinese and U.S. participants, with Chinese participants reporting fewer relational boundaries in terms of information sharing and acceptance of advice from others about their romantic relationship (Epstein, et al., 2005).

On the other hand, reliance on social support systems can also hinder relationship maintenance processes and motivation if the romantic relationship does not receive approval. For example, Indonesian participants who perceived that their family did not approve of their relationship partner were more likely to withdraw from their partner by withholding intimacy and commitment relative to Australian participants, who only withdrew if they felt their dating partner did not hold them in high regard (MacDonald & Jessica, 2006). This reflects the differing goals of interdependent and independent selves, respectively. Indonesian participants withheld relationship maintenance behaviors and downregulated their relationship maintenance motivation because it is functional and self-protective within the collectivist context that prioritizes relational harmony with in groups such as family. If familial approval is crucial for a long-term relationship within collectivist settings, then overinvestment is costly if there is a lack of social support; instead, it might be better to withdraw and cease relationship maintenance. The perceived disapproval of a romantic relationship by one's social network was linked with decreased love and commitment and an increased likelihood of relationship dissolution (Lehmiller & Agnew, 2007; Sinclair et al., 2014). This effect was enhanced in collectivist cultures, with family disapproval of a romantic relationship more strongly associated with decreased relationship quality in more collectivist cultures such as Indonesia and Japan relative to more individualist cultures such as Canada and Australia (MacDonald et al., 2012). Furthermore, social network influence predicted relationship commitment and intentions to marry for Chinese students, reflecting the cultural values of *Xiao* (filial piety) and *Guanxi* (network) which underpin collectivism, relative to their U.S. counterparts (Zhang & Kline, 2009). Collectivism may pit romantic relationships against other social relationships, thereby driving social support down. For example, a study that interviewed Hindu men about their relationship beliefs and hierarchies found that 60% of the participants believed that individuals should avoid spending too much time with romantic partners, as prioritization of one's romantic relationship could result in neglecting family relations and cultural duties (Derné, 1994). Taken together, we can conclude that relationship maintenance behaviors are adaptively adjusted to meet the social and cultural demands of one's current environment—with collectivist values and interdependent self-construal increasing the likelihood that relationship maintenance behaviors will be deployed only if an individual's kin network approves of their romantic partner.

FAMILY ALLOCENTRISM AND PARENTAL INFLUENCE

The countervailing effects of social support as both bolstering and curtailing relationship maintenance can be understood within the context of family allocentrism and parental influence. These two attributes reflect the extent to which individuals accept and expect close others to support and exert influence within the romantic domain. Family allocentrism represents the strength of devotion, loyalty, and closeness between family members (Lay et al., 1998), while parental influence represents acceptance of parental involvement in romantic relationships, with both attributes more prominent in collectivist cultures. Bejanyan et al. (2015) found that collectivism was linked with *both* increased and decreased commitment and passion. These associations were mediated by parental influence, which drove commitment and passion down, and family allocentrism, which drove both passion and commitment up. *The opposing relationships indicate that social support can either promote or decrease relationship maintenance mechanisms.* Accordingly, although the experience of passion is a human universal (de Munck et al., 2011), the expression of passion is *culturally moderated.* The expression of passion may be restricted within some cultural settings (e.g., cultures that value collectivism) because it can unbalance family dynamics and disrupt the relational harmony of other relationships and because it deviates from culturally sanctioned norms regarding marriage and romantic relationship maintenance (Netting, 2010; Sandhya, 2009). We posit that this restriction is particularly enhanced within collectivist cultures which are also tight—possessing a rigid framework of well-defined social norms and allowing for little deviation—relative to loose cultures, which have weak norms and high tolerance for deviant behavior (Gelfand et al., 2011). Although there is some correlation between the dimensions of collectivism-individualism and tightness-looseness (please see Figure 20.3), they are theoretically and

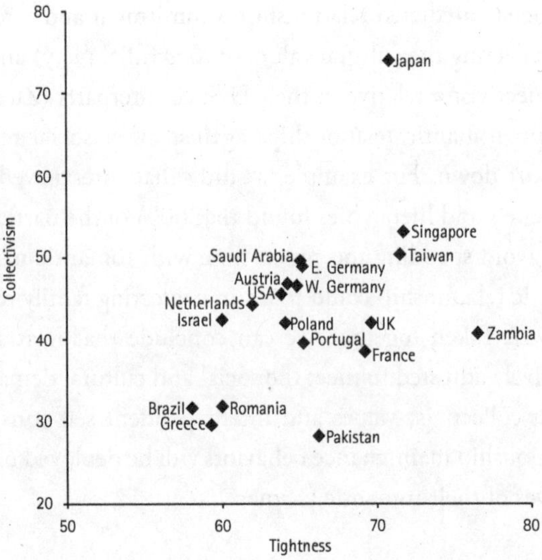

Figure 20.3 Variation of countries across the intersection of two cultural dimensions (collectivism-individualism and tightness-looseness). This is taken from Stamkou et al.,'s work (2019) which collected data from 2,369 participants in 19 countries. This illustrates how cultural dimensions interact within socioecologies and provides a meaningful setting in which we can understand the variation of relationship maintenance mechanisms. From Cultural Collectivism and Tightness Moderate Responses to Norm Violators: Effects on Power Perception, Moral Emotions, and Leader Support, by Stamkou et al., 2019, *Personality and Social Psychology Bulletin, 45*(6), p. 950.

empirically distinct (Gelfand et al., 2006). By intersecting these two continua, contradictory findings regarding the role of social support and increased relationship maintenance can be understood. We propose that collectivist values and cultural tightness likely combine to create an environment where familial support and approval are more heavily weighted in romantic relationship dynamics. Thus, in this specific cultural and social context (i.e., collectivism and cultural tightness), familial approval of a romantic partner strongly facilitates the deployment of relationship maintenance behaviors. Additionally, through crossing over these two dimensions, we can further explore why collectivism promotes both pragmatic and idealistic love beliefs (Bejanyan et al., 2015). In sum, social support provides a resource for relationship quality and maintenance, which can be both buffering in times of relationship difficulty or might encourage individuals to disengage—particularly in contexts where individuals are socialized to more strongly value and rely on kinship approval and support.

Behavioral Mechanisms

Individuals can enact relationship maintenance through engaging in prosocial relationship behaviors, including the display of intimacy, self-disclosure, social support, and gift-giving. Such interpersonal behaviors can communicate relationship commitment and intention. Costly signaling theory (Grafen, 1990; Zahavi & Zahavi, 1997) suggests that the costliness of producing a signal—in this case, a relationship maintenance behavior—provides information about the honesty of the signal; this approach has been applied to interpersonal behaviors (Ohtsubo & Watanabe, 2009; Yamaguchi et al., 2015). Through expending resources (e.g., time and money) or potentially endangering status (e.g., self-disclosure places the individual within a position of vulnerability if their partner discloses their secrets), to maintain a relationship, an individual forgoes other opportunities the same resources could be invested in, thereby honestly signaling their intention to commit to the relationship.

The extent to which individuals engage in costly relationship maintenance behaviors varies across cultures. We situate our discussion of the cross-cultural variation in relationship maintenance behaviors within a sociecological approach (Nisbett & Cohen, 1996), and specifically, the relational mobility framework (Kito et al., 2017; Thomson et al., 2018; Yuki et al., 2007). Social ecologies (or social environments) refer to the patterns of behavior of others within society, which informs and constrains one's own behavior display and what can be acquired or learned. This approach acknowledges that the actual characteristics of a social environment (e.g., divorce rate and migration) meaningfully intersects with the beliefs and norms about these characteristics within a given society (e.g., what we believe about divorce; Nisbett & Cohen, 1996) to create socioecologies. Socioecologies define the adaptive tasks for social flourishing in terms of developing and maintaining desirable social relationships. That is, the norms, expectations, and content of what a socially desirable relationship should be are influenced by culture. Observed behaviors and psychological processes (e.g., relationship maintenance behaviors and processes) can be interpreted as those which are best fit to achieve specific adaptive tasks (e.g., mate acquisition and retention in the presence of attractive relationship alternatives and maintaining relational harmony) defined by the socioecologies within which they occur (Kito et al., 2017).

Relational mobility is the degree to which individuals perceive that they may select relationship partners based on their personal preferences and sever existing interpersonal relationships (Yuki et al., 2007). Relational mobility bridges distal ecologies (e.g., subsistence practices and ecological and historical threats) and the resulting cultural and individual-level factors through functioning as a proximal socioecology (Kito et al., 2017). Within this proximal socioecology, humans form communities with differing levels of freedom within relational domains in response to distal ecologies (Kito et al., 2017). For example, a study of 39 societies (N = 16,939) found that relational mobility is lower in societies with greater ecological and historical threats and settled societies with interdependent subsistence practices such as rice production (Thomson et al., 2018). Low relational mobility ecologies, such as societies in Asia, Africa, or the Middle East, select for relationships which are stable, exclusive, and relatively prescribed by circumstance (e.g., geographic or social network location); in contrast, high relational mobility ecologies, exemplified by societies in Latin America, North America, and Western Europe, are defined by increased opportunities for relationship partners and the ability to sever relationships, selecting for active investment behaviors (e.g., gift-giving or self-disclosure; Thomson et al., 2018). By intersecting relational mobility with cultural dimensions such as tightness–looseness, we can gain a more holistic overview of variation within relationship maintenance behaviors. Thus, relational mobility prescribes adaptive tasks for social relationships (e.g., overt and active mate retention strategies, particularly in high relational mobility societies), while tightness–looseness shapes the social norms that provide the instructions for achieving these tasks and outline the degree of acceptance of deviation in pursuing these tasks (Thomson et al., 2018). Within the context of romantic relationships, relational mobility accounted for 18% of the societal variance in amount of past romantic partners reported, with participants from societies high in relational mobility reporting a greater amount of past romantic partners (Thomson et al., 2018). Next, we address the impact of relational mobility on specific relationship maintenance behaviors.

INTIMACY AND SELF-DISCLOSURE

Literature suggests that individuals residing in individualistic cultures tend to report engaging more in romantic relationship maintenance behaviors (e.g., increased displays of intimacy; Marshall, 2008). According to Kito et al. (2017), this relationship between culture (i.e., individualism/collectivism) and relationship maintenance behaviors is mediated by relational mobility. Specifically, because individualistic cultures tend to be higher in relational mobility, relationships are seen as more fragile and there is greater perceived availability of potential new relationships; thus, active engagement (e.g., displays of intimacy and overt commitment cues) helps to impress potential new partners and retain existing ones. Further, it is argued that psychological mechanisms aid individuals in accomplishing these adaptive tasks, and that some of these mechanisms are moderated by culture. Some of the features of the independent self, such as self-enhancement—or the motivation for elevated positive regard of the self from oneself and others (Heine et al., 1999; Kitayama et al., 2009; Markus & Kitayama, 1991)—are argued to be selected for within specific socioecologies as it facilitates the achievement of adaptive tasks (Kito et al., 2017). Self-enhancement allows individuals to make use of the large mating marketplace in high relational mobility contexts and gain and retain desirable social relationships through portraying the self in an elevated status (e.g., "punching above one's weight"). In this vein, costly relationship maintenance behaviors, such as increased intimacy and self-disclosure, can help demonstrate commitment and investment within high relational mobility ecologies, reminding others that one is a useful partner and avoiding relationship termination (Schug et al., 2010). Higher intimacy in Canadians compared to Japanese individuals was mediated by relational mobility (Yamada et al., 2015). Conversely, active retention is not a priority relationship maintenance strategy within low relational mobility socioecologies as relationships are more stable and less likely to be terminated due to fewer perceived opportunities. Thus, where partner-dyads are unlikely to dissolve, the adaptive task is to maintain the relationship without creating conflict (Kito et al., 2017), reflecting the focus on relational harmony (Imada, 2010) and the prevention-focused orientation (Lee et al., 2000) of the interdependent self-concept. Thus, behavioral relationship maintenance can be understood as adaptive tendencies (e.g., active and overt commitment cues and behaviors to resolve conflict and restore harmony) shaped by the socio-ecological environment. Furthermore, relationship behavioral mechanisms can also be regulated *within* relationships through shared relationship norms (e.g., communication and benefit-giving) which outline the expectations and prescriptions within a relationship (Sakaluk, et al., 2020). The strength of established shared relationship norms in terms of norm consistency, punishment expectancy and enforcement, and agreement within the dyad is linked with increased relationship quality. Thus, beyond cultural norms and expectations—partner-shared norms can further direct relationship maintenance behaviors within the context of social ecologies and cultural tightness–looseness.

GIFT-GIVING

Partners can also engage in gift-giving as a signal of commitment (Komiya et al., 2019). Commitment signals seem to be integral for romantic relationships; forgoing commitment signals is more detrimental for romantic relationships relative to friendships (Yamaguchi et al., 2015). Komiya et al. (2019) conducted two studies using self-report and secondary data to investigate gift-giving in the United States (high in relational mobility) and Japan (low in relational mobility). Relational mobility was operationalized as national divorce rates, with the United States reporting higher divorce rates compared to Japan (crude divorce rate of 2.9 compared to 1.7, respectively, per 1,000 people; Organisation for Economic Co-operation and Development, 2019). Married couples in the United States reported more gift-giving relative to married couples in Japan. Taken together with findings regarding the use of intimacy, self-disclosure, and promoting relational harmony, we surmise that individuals have an expansive toolkit which they can rely on for behavioral strategies with which they can maintain relationships; which tools, however, meet the adaptive tasks of making and retaining socially desirable relationships, are moderated by cultural, ecological, and socioecological contexts.

Future Research Directions: A Call to Action and Decolonization of Knowledge and Practice

We would like to position our suggestions for future research directions within a call to action which reflects increasing practices to move away from Euro-American-centric epistemologies and knowledge production (MacLeod, 2018) and psychological research that is "ahistorical, acultural, and decontextualised" (Sonn et al., 2020, p. 40). We posit that to understand the real-world experiences and contemporary concerns of romantic relationships, an overarching framework that incorporates *all* relationships must be constructed, particularly with awareness of the historical practices that have served to marginalize others and position the Euro-American (Western) perspectives versus the "Other" in a dichotomous and reductionist approach. The decolonization standpoint values and promotes "a plurality of epistemologies and dialogical ethics and, importantly, is committed to affirming the experiences and knowledge of those who have been marginalized and oppressed" (Sonn et al., 2020, p. 39). Here we outline several research directions we hope will contribute to incorporating active decolonization practices, including emic approaches to uncovering preferred mate characteristics, investigating within-culture (Euro-American) heteronormative patriarchal cultural artifacts and their impact on knowledge production in research, the inclusion of non-Western relationship practices such as arranged marriages, and relationship maintenance in intercultural relationships.

First, we turn to decolonizing research practices and methodologies. For example, a study of mate preferences in 1,260 never-married heterosexual adults in China and the United States found that Chinese participants selected more general and abstract mate characteristics, such as "personality" or "character," without specifying a particular personality or character dimension (Chen et al., 2015). The authors used a selection of validated measures of mate criteria (e.g., Buss & Barnes, 1986, Toro-Morn & Sprecher, 2003), as well as open-ended questions. The combination of these etic and emic approaches yielded insight in the need for more culturally informed research practices in replication and cross-cultural approaches, with one participant noting that "in fact, many criteria you listed are not important" (Chen et al., 2015, p. 115); this extends further than traditional practices of testing measurement invariance and validity. As argued by Chen et al. (2015), adopting a culturally appropriate standpoint requires the evaluation of pan-cultural items using an emic approach, acknowledging that the expression of shared underlying constructs is shaped by cultural context. For example, Chen et al. (2015) evaluated whether the underlying trait of emotional stability as a mate preference is captured by the word "mature" in China but "confident" in the United States (Chen et al., 2015); this can be interpreted within the framework of the self-concept, with "mature" reflecting increased relational attention and focus on maintaining relational harmony that characterizes the interdependent self. Conversely, "confident" reflects the promotion orientation of the independent self with a focus on self-expression and uniqueness goals (Markus & Kitayama, 1991; Varnum et al., 2010). In turn, the extent to which one self-concept is made more salient than the other is grounded within cultural values (i.e., individualism/collectivism), which can be rooted in socioecological contexts such as relational mobility. By taking these environmental demands and cultural practices into account, we can conduct more culturally informed (and less Euro-American-centric) romantic relationship research.

Relatedly, part of the decolonization work to be done is through critical appraisal of the Euro-American structures which perpetuate epistemologies that are purported to be objective and universal and are, in turn, applied to understanding psychological processes from a biased lens. Within the context of relationship maintenance research, we argue that particular attention should be given to embedded cultures which propagate what Garlen and Sandlin (2017) termed the "supremacy of a white heteropatriarchal family ideal" (p. 957) and which limit female agency through the socialization of norms to maintain relationships even when they are harmful, and the reinforcement of ideals such as long-term mating institutions (e.g., marriage) as the highest ideals. This knowledge structure is propagated through cultural artifacts (various types of media, including literature, film, adverts, etc.) and corporate cultures such as Disney. Garlen and Sandlin (2017) positioned Disney as a macrocurriculum through which we all learn and which embodies social and cultural norms from which it emerges (e.g., individualism). Thus, gender differences in relationship maintenance might be a reflection of the differing goals promoted by embedded cultures, where for women a relationship is presented as the highest goal, which must be maintained: even if it is painful, demands sacrifice, and requires taking on the burdens transforming the self and one's partner (Garlen & Sandlin, 2017). Thus, it places responsibility in women's hands to engage in relationship maintenance and shapes its practice through perpetuating "bridal fiction." Mounting evidence makes plain the harm associated with perpetrating these relationship ideals, as romantic myth endorsement predicts romanticizing controlling and psychologically abusive behaviors, which (in turn) predicts experiences of intimate partner violence (Papp et al., 2017). To decolonize knowledge, romantic relationship researchers must acknowledge the systemic biases and perpetuations of White heteropatriarchal power that have shaped relationship research's participants and practitioners. For example, cross-cultural research incorporates the development, testing, and application of non-Euro-American frameworks and hypotheses (e.g., Chinese Culture Connection, 1987; Joshanloo, 2014; Li, 2002; Minkov & Hofstede, 2010), rather than solely relying on cross-cultural comparisons of Euro-American theories and constructs. Furthermore, emerging work uniting feminist and evolutionary perspectives calls for evolutionary psychologists to position women as active forces, working to shape and promote their inclusive fitness and also acting (historically) in ways that have shaped the evolution of our species. As Sarah Hrdy (2013) explains, "much of the scholarship pertaining to women and evolution has been directed toward what happens to women rather than how women actively influence . . . human evolution" (p. 7). Future work in relationship science should take care to recognize persistent narratives and Western-centric biases about romantic relationships and love, particularly those that position women as passive—rather than active—agents.

Our second future research recommendation is driven by the trend that we know little about relationship outcomes in relationship practices that are not rooted in Western traditions, such as arranged marriages. We risk applying a Western lens if we adapt Euro-American-centric approaches and knowledge to their investigation. Much of relationship research has focused on "couple-initiated" (or "love marriages") rather than arranged marriages (Regan et al., 2012). Notably, anthropological work suggests that for the majority of our shared evolutionary history, long-term mateships have been arranged by kin rather than initiated by individuals for "love" (Walker et al., 2011). As such, evolutionary accounts of romantic relationship dynamics may erroneously rely on the assumption that humans have evolved to select their own romantic partners, apart from kin approval and interventions. Although arranged marriages are a cross-cultural practice, we will focus on the experiences of arranged marriage within India, where it is estimated that approximately 90–95% of marriages have some degree of parental arrangement (Lall, 2006; Uberoi, 2006). A recently emerging body of research has investigated satisfaction within arranged marriages. For example, an investigation of Indian couples living in the United States in arranged or couple-initiated marriages found that there were no differences in ratings of love, satisfaction, and commitment between the two groups (Regan et al., 2012). Additionally, Madathil and Benshoff (2008) investigated four domains of marital satisfaction (loving, loyalty, finance, and shared values) in Asian Indians in arranged marriages living in India, Asian Indians in arranged marriages living in the United States, and monocultural Americans in couple-initiated marriages living in the United States. Asian Indians in arranged marriages living in the United States reported the highest satisfaction across all domains. The authors interpreted these findings as couples benefiting from being grounded in an intersection of both individualist and collectivist contexts: possessing and having been socialized within the cultural values of collectivism (stability of marriage, ensured compatibility between individuals and family and focus on relational harmony) without the pressure or presence of extended families. Little is known about the relationship maintenance strategies that individuals use in arranged marriages and within cultures with different relationship scripts, as dating (in the Euro-American conceptualization) is not part of the relationship trajectory in most contemporary societies where arranged marriages are common (Walker et al., 2011). Future researchers are encouraged to combine cultural, evolutionary, and social perspectives to explore how ultimate (e.g., psychological adaptations) and proximate (e.g., environmental and cultural demands) forces work together to shape relationship maintenance and longevity in couple- and family-initiated romantic partnerships.

We also call for research focusing not only on cross-cultural differences and similarities in relationship dynamics (broadly) but also on the effect and operation of cultural differences within an intimate partnership. Although little published work has investigated intercultural couple (i.e., partners having different cultural or ethnic identities, or partners residing in a mainstream culture different to their shared cultural identities) dynamics, Hiew et al. (2015) examined the relationship standards of Australian and Chinese monocultural couples (both members of the relational dyad reporting the same cultural identity) and Chinese–Australian couples. Although there were differences in Chinese and Australian monocultural couples' relationship standards, Chinese–Australian couples reported relationship standards which fell on the continuum between the Chinese and Australian couples, demonstrating an interaction between cultural values. Furthermore,

Chinese–Australian couples reported within-dyad similarity *to the same level* as mono-cultural couples, providing further evidence of the flexibility of relationship maintenance strategies within relational dyads and a convergence effect. In a study of Mexican American married couples, more acculturated partners reported being more open with their emotions and expressing conflict more directly compared to less acculturated partners, reflecting a shift in cultural conflict resolution strategies and emotional display rules (Flores et al., 2004). Thus, sociocultural changes impact relationship dynamics as a result of shifts in cultural identity. Exploration of relationship maintenance mechanisms within intercultural relationships can provide us with a richer understanding of the flexibility of tools at our disposal to maintain relationships. It can also provide further insight into the ways that the cultural, ecological, and socioecological environments that shaped individuals' relationship maintenance strategies can impact and shape their partner, who may have had little to no influence from the same contexts.

Building bridges: Relationship maintenance research going forward

To fully understand the ways that humans maintain relationships, we must adopt a holistic and transdisciplinary approach which incorporates evolutionary, cross-cultural, and social perspectives. Part of this work will rely on addressing our systemic knowledge structures and practices as a discipline. What we set out here is the beginning of what we hope echoes wider calls for a transformative effort for opening up research, practice, and knowledge. To love is not easy, and we hope that our synthesized approach to relationships highlights that lovers do not meet—they are made, within their cultural, ecological, and socioecological contexts, and through continuous, mutual, and active engagement in maintaining loving relationships.

References

Ackerman, J. M., Becker, D. V., Mortensen, C. R., Sasaki, T., Neuberg, S. L., & Kenrick, D. T. (2009). A pox on the mind: Disjunction of attention and memory in the processing of physical disfigurement. *Journal of Experimental Social Psychology, 45*(3), 478–485.

Adams, R. D., & Baptist, J. A. (2012). Relationship maintenance behavior and adult attachment: An analysis of the actor-partner interdependence model. *The American Journal of Family Therapy, 40*(3), 230–244.

Amato, P. R., & Previti, D. (2003). People's reasons for divorcing: Gender, social class, the life course, and adjustment. *Journal of Family Issues, 24*(5), 602–626.

Aron, A., Fisher, H., Mashek, D.J., Strong, G., Li, H. and Brown, L.L. (2005) Reward, motivation, and emotion systems associated with early-stage intense romantic love. *Journal of Neurophysiology, 94*, 327–337.

Bejanyan, K., Marshall, T. C., & Ferenczi, N. (2014). Romantic ideals, mate preferences, and anticipation of future difficulties in marital life: A comparative study of young adults in india and america. *Frontiers in Psychology, 5*, 1355–1355.

Bejanyan, K., Marshall, T. C., & Ferenczi, N. (2015). Associations of collectivism with relationship commitment, passion, and mate preferences: Opposing roles of parental influence and family allocentrism. *PloS ONE, 10*(2), Article e0117374.

Betzig, L. (1989). Causes of conjugal dissolution. *Current Anthropology, 30*, 654–676.

Blair, K. L., & Holmberg, D. (2008). Perceived social network support and well-being in same-sex versus mixed-sex romantic relationships. *Journal of Social and Personal Relationships, 25*(5), 769–791.

Bleske-Rechek, A., Remiker, M. W., & Baker, J. P. (2009). Similar from the start: Assortment in young adult dating couples and its link to relationship stability over time. *Individual Differences Research, 7*(3), 142–158.

Bodenmann, G., Charvoz, L., Bradbury, T. N., Bertoni, A., Iafrate, R., Giuliani, C., Banse, R., & Behling, J. (2007). The role of stress in divorce: A three-nation retrospective study. *Journal of Social and Personal Relationships, 24*(5), 707–728.

Botwin, M., Buss, D. M. & Shackelford, T. K. (1997). Personality and mate preferences: Five factors in mate selection and marital satisfaction. *Journal of Personality, 65*, 107–136.

Bowlby J. (1969). *Attachment and loss*. Basic Books.

Breiter, H. C., Gollub, R. L., Weisskoff, R. M., Kennedy, D. N., Makris, N., Berke, J. D., Goodman, J. M., Kantor, H. L., Gastfriend, D. R., Riorden, J. P., Mathew, R. T., Rosen, B. R., & Hyman, S. E. (1997). Acute effects of cocaine on human brain activity and emotion. *Neuron, 19*(3), 591–611.

Bretherton, I. (1994). Developmental psychology. In R. Parke, P. Ornstein, J. Reiser, & C. Zahn-Waxler (Eds.), *A century of developmental psychology* (pp. 431–471). American Psychological Association Press.

Buss, D. M. (1989). Sex differences in human mate preferences: Evolutionary hypotheses tested in 37 cultures. *Behavioral and Brain Sciences, 12*(1), 1–14.

Buss, D. M., & Barnes, M. (1986). Preferences in human mate selection. *Journal of Personality and Social Psychology, 50*(3), 559–570.

Carnelley, K. B., Pietromonaco, P. R., & Jaffe, K. (1996). Attachment, caregiving, and relationship functioning in couples: Effects of self and partner. *Personal Relationships, 3*(3), 257–278.

Chang, J. (2004). Self-reported reasons for divorce and correlates of psychological well-being among divorced Korean immigrant women. *Journal of Divorce & Remarriage, 40*(1–2), 111–128.

Chen, R., Austin, J. P., Miller, J. K., & Piercy, F. P. (2015). Chinese and American individuals' mate selection criteria: Updates, modifications, and extensions. *Journal of Cross-Cultural Psychology, 46*(1), 101–118.

Chinese Culture Connection. (1987). Chinese values and the search for culture-free dimensions of culture. *Journal of Cross-Cultural Psychology, 18*(2), 143–164.

Cohen, O., & Savaya, R. (2003). Lifestyle differences in traditionalism and modernity and reasons for divorce among Muslim Palestinian citizens of Israel. *Journal of Comparative Family Studies, 34*(2), 283–302.

Daly, M., & Wilson, M. (1988). Evolutionary social psychology and family homicide. *Science, 242*(4), 519–524.

Demir, S. A. (2013). Attitudes toward concepts of marriage and divorce in Turkey. *American International Journal of Contemporary Research, 3*(12), 83–88.

De Munck, V. C., Korotayev, A., de Munck, J., & Khaltourina, D. (2011). Cross-cultural analysis of models of romantic love among U.S. residents, Russians, and Lithuanians. *Cross-Cultural Research, 45*(2), 128–154.

Derné, S. (1994). Hindu men talk about controlling women: Cultural ideas as a tool of the powerful. *Sociological Perspectives, 37*, 203–22.

Dixson, A. (2015). Primate sexuality. In P. Whelehan & A. Bolin (Eds.) *The international encyclopedia of human sexuality* (pp. 861–1042). John Wiley & Sons.

Dukas, R. (2002). Behavioural and ecological consequences of limited attention. *Philosophical Transactions of the Royal Society, Series B: Biological Sciences, 357*, 1539–1547.

Dweck, C. S., Chiu, C, & Hong, Y. (1995). Implicit theories: Elaboration and extension of the model. *Psychological Inquiry, 6*, 322–333.

Dweck, C. S., & Leggett, E. L. (1988). A social-cognitive approach to motivation and personality. *Psychological Review, 95*, 256–273.

Dyrenforth, P. S., Kashy, D. A., Donnellan, M. B., & Lucas, R. E. (2010). Predicting relationship and life satisfaction from personality in nationally representative samples from three countries: The relative importance of actor, partner, and similarity effects. *Journal of Personality and Social Psychology, 99*(4), 690–702.

Ember, M., Ember, C. R., & Low, B. S. (2007). Comparing explanations of polygyny. *Cross-Cultural Research, 41*(4), 428–440.

Epstein, N. B., & Baucom, D. H. (2002). Cognitive and emotional factors in couples' relationships. In N. B. Epstein & D. H. Baucom, *Enhanced cognitive-behavioral therapy for couples: A contextual approach* (pp. 65–104). American Psychological Association.

Epstein, N. B., Chen, F., & Beyder-Kamjou, I. (2005). Relationship standards and marital satisfaction in Chinese and American couples. *Journal of Marital and Family Therapy, 31*, 59–74.

Erol, R. Y., & Orth, U. (2013). Actor and partner effects of self-esteem on relationship satisfaction and the mediating role of secure attachment between the partners. *Journal of Research in Personality, 47*(1), 26–35.

Fernandez-Duque, E., & Huck, M. (2013). Till death (or an intruder) do us part: Intrasexual-competition in a monogamous primate. *PloS ONE, 8*(1). https://doi.org/10.1371/journal.pone.0053724

Fine, M. A., & Harvey, J. H. (2006). *Handbook of divorce and relationship dissolution*. Routledge.

Fincher, C. L., & Thornhill, R. (2008). Assortative sociality, limited dispersal, infectious disease and the genesis of the global pattern of religion diversity. *Proceedings of the Royal Society B: Biological Sciences, 275*(1651), 2587–2594.

Flicker, S. M., Sancier-Barbosa, F., Afroz, F., Saif, S. N., & Mohsin, F. (2020). Attachment hierarchies in Bangladeshi women in couple-initiated and arranged marriages. *International Journal of Psychology, 55*(4), 638–646. https://doi.org/10.1002/ijop.12619

Flores, E., Tschann, J. M., Marin, B. V., & Pantoja, P. (2004). Marital conflict and acculturation among Mexican American husbands and wives. *Cultural Diversity & Ethnic Minority Psychology, 10*, 39–52. https://doi.org/10.1037/1099-9809.10.1.39

Fraley, C. R., Niedenthal, P. M., Marks, M., Brumbaugh, C., & Vicary, A. (2006). Adult attachment and the perception of emotional expressions: Probing the hyperactivating strategies underlying anxious attachment. *Journal of Personality, 74*(4), 1163–1190.

Gangestad, S. W., Haselton, M. G., & Buss, D. M. (2006). Evolutionary foundations of cultural variation: Evoked culture and mate preferences. *Psychological Inquiry, 17*(2), 75–95.

Gangestad, S. W., & Simpson, J. A. (2000). The evolution of human mating: Trade-offs and strategic pluralism. *Behavioral and Brain Sciences, 23*(4), 573–587.

Garlen, J. C., & Sandlin, J. A. (2017). Happily (n)ever after: The cruel optimism of Disney's romantic ideal. *Feminist Media Studies, 17*(6), 957–971.

Gaunt, R. (2006). Couple similarity and marital satisfaction: Are similar spouses happier? *Journal of Personality, 74*(5), 1401–1420.

Gavrilets S. (2012). Human origins and the transition from promiscuity to pair-bonding. *Proceedings of the National Academy of Sciences of the United States of America, 109(25)*, 9923–9928.

Gebauer, J. E., Leary, M. R., & Neberich, W. (2012). Big Two personality and Big Three mate preferences: Similarity attracts, but country-level mate preferences crucially matter. *Personality and Social Psychology Bulletin, 38*(12), 1579–1593.

Gelfand, M. J., Nishii, L. H., & Raver, J. L. (2006). On the nature and importance of cultural tightness-looseness. *Journal of Applied Psychology, 91*(6), 1225–1244.

Gelfand, M. J., Raver, J. L., Nishii, L., Leslie, L. M., Lun, J., Lim, B. C., Duan, L., Almaliach, A., Ang, S., Arnadottir, J., Aycan, Z., Boehnke, K., Boski, P., Cabecinhas, R., Chan, D., Chhokar, J., D'Amato, A., Ferrer, M., Fischlmayr, I. C. . . . Yamaguchi, S. (2011). Differences between tight and loose cultures: A 33-nation study. *Science, 332*, 1100–1104.

George, T., Hart, J., & Rholes, W. S. (2020). Remaining in unhappy relationships: The roles of attachment anxiety and fear of change. *Journal of Social and Personal Relationships, 37*(5), 1626–1633.

Goodwin, R., Marshall, T., Fülöp, M., Adonu, J., Spiewak, S., Neto, F., & Hernandez Plaza, S. (2012). Mate value and self-esteem: Evidence from eight cultural groups. *PloS ONE, 7*(4). https://doi.org/10.1371/journal.pone.0036106

Grafen, A. (1990). Biological signals as handicaps. *Journal of Theoretical Biology, 144*, 517–546.

Haddix, K. A. (2001). Leaving your wife and your brothers: When polyandrous marriages fall apart. *Evolution and Human Behavior, 22*, 47–60.

Hannover, B., Birkner, N., & Pöhlmann, C. (2006). Ideal selves and self-esteem in people with independent or interdependent self-construal. *European Journal of Social Psychology, 36*, 119–133.

Hazan, C., & Shaver, P. (1987). Romantic love conceptualized as an attachment process. *Journal of Personality and Social Psychology, 52*(3), 511–524.

Hefner, V., & Wilson, B. J. (2013). From love at first sight to soul mate: The influence of romantic ideals in popular films on young people's beliefs about relationships. *Communication Monographs, 80*(2), 150–175.

Heine, S J. (2001). Self as cultural product: An examination of East Asian and North American selves. *Journal of Personality, 69*(6), 881–906.

Heine, S J, Lehman, D. R., Ide, E., Leung, C., Kitayama, S., Takata, T., & Matsumoto, H. (2001). Divergent consequences of success and failure in Japan and North America: An investigation of self-improving motivations and malleable selves. *Journal of Personality and Social Psychology, 81*, 599–615.

Heine, S. J., Lehman, D. R., Markus, H. R., & Kitayama, S. (1999). Is there a universal need for positive self-regard? *Psychological Review, 106*(4), 766–794.
Hewlett, B. S., & Macfarlan, S. J. (2010). Fathers' roles in hunter-gatherer and other small-scale cultures. In M. E. Lamb (Ed.), *The role of the father in child development (pp. 413–434)*. John Wiley & Sons Inc.
Hiew, D. N., Halford, W. K., van de Vijver, F. J. R., & Liu, S. (2015). Relationship Standards and satisfaction in Chinese, Western, and intercultural Chinese–Western couples in Australia. *Journal of Cross-Cultural Psychology, 46*(5), 684–701.
Ho, M. Y., Chen, S. X., Bond, M. H., Hui, C. M., Chan, C., & Friedman, M. (2012). Linking adult attachment styles to relationship satisfaction in Hong Kong and the United States: The mediating role of personal and structural commitment. *Journal of Happiness Studies, 13*(3), 565–578.
Hong, E. K., & Choi, I. (2019). Oh darling, this too shall pass: Cyclic perceptions of change keep you in romantic relationships longer during difficult times. *Journal of Cross-Cultural Psychology, 50*(9), 1075–1090.
Hong, Y. Y., Chiu, C. Y., Dweck, C. S., Lin, D. M. S., & Wan, W. (1999). Implicit theories, attributions, and coping: A meaning system approach. *Journal of Personality and Social Psychology, 77*, 588–599.
Hrdy, S. (1981*). The woman that never evolved.* Harvard University Press.
Hrdy, S. (2013). Introduction to Evolution's Empress. M. Fisher, J. Garcia, & R. Chang (Eds.), *Evolution's empress: Darwinian perspectives on the nature of women.* Oxford University Press.
Imada, T. (2010). Cultural narratives of individualism and collectivism: A content analysis of textbook stories in the United States and Japan. *Journal of Cross-Cultural Psychology, 43*, 576–591.
Imada, T., & Ellsworth, P. C. (2011). Proud Americans and lucky Japanese: Cultural differences in appraisal and corresponding emotion. *Emotion, 11*(2), 329–345.
Imada, T., & Yussen, S. R. (2012). Reproduction of cultural values: A cross-cultural examination of stories people create and transmit. *Personality and Social Psychology Bulletin, 38*(1), 114–128.
Jankowiak, W. R., & Fischer, E. F. (1992). A cross-cultural perspective on romantic love. *Ethnology, 31*(2), 149–155.
Jankowiak, W. R., Shen, Y., Yao, S., Wang, C., & Volsche, S. (2015). Investigating love's universal attributes: A research report from China. *Cross-Cultural Research, 49*(4), 422–436.
Joshanloo, M. (2014). Eastern conceptualizations of happiness: Fundamental differences with Western views. *Journal of Happiness Studies, 15*(2), 475–493.
Jones, J.M. (2008). *Most Americans not willing to forgive unfaithful spouse.* Gallup. https://news.gallup.com/poll/105682/most-americans-willing-forgive-unfaithful-spouse.aspx
Kachadourian, L. K., Fincham, F., & Davila, J. (2004). The tendency to forgive in dating and married couples: The role of attachment and relationship satisfaction. *Personal Relationships, 11*(3), 373–393.
Karremans, J. C., Dotsch, R., & Corneille, O. (2011). Romantic relationship status biases memory of faces of attractive opposite-sex others: Evidence from a reverse-correlation paradigm. *Cognition, 121*(3), 422–426.
Kitayama, S., Park, H., Sevincer, A. T., Karasawa, M., & Uskul, A. K. (2009). A cultural task analysis of implicit independence: Comparing North America, Western Europe, and East Asia. *Journal of Personality and Social Psychology, 97*(2), 236–255.
Kito, M., Yuki, M., & Thomson, R. (2017). Relational mobility and close relationships: A socioecological approach to explain cross-cultural differences. *Personal Relationships, 24*(1), 114–130.
Knee, C. R. (1998). Implicit theories of relationships: Assessment and prediction of romantic relationship initiation, coping, and longevity. *Journal of Personality and Social Psychology, 74*, 360–370.
Knee, C. R., Patrick, H., & Lonsbary, C. (2003). Implicit theories of relationships: Orientations toward evaluation and cultivation. *Personality and Social Psychology Review, 7*, 41–55.
Knobloch-Fedders, L. M., & Knudson, R. M. (2009). Marital ideals of the newly-married: A longitudinal analysis. *Journal of Social and Personal Relationships, 26*(2-3), 249–271.
Komiya, A., Ohtsubo, Y., Nakanishi, D., & Oishi, S. (2019). Gift-giving in romantic couples serves as a commitment signal: Relational mobility is associated with more frequent gift-giving. *Evolution and Human Behavior, 40*(2), 160–166.
Koranyi, N., & Rothermund, K. (2012). When the grass on the other side of the fence doesn't matter: Reciprocal romantic interest neutralizes attentional bias towards attractive alternatives. *Journal of Experimental Social Psychology, 48*(1), 186–191.

Lampard, R. (2014). Stated reasons for relationship dissolution in Britain: Marriage and cohabitation compared. *European Sociological Review, 30*(3), 315–328.

Lay, C., Fairlie, P., Jackson, S., Ricci, T., Eisenberg, J., Sato, T., et al. (1998). Domain-specific allocentrism-idiocentrism. *Journal of Cross-Cultural Psychology, 29*, 434–460.

Lee, A. Y., Aaker, J. L., & Gardner, W. L. (2000). The pleasures and pains of distinct self-construals: The role of interdependence in regulatory focus. *Journal of Personality and Social Psychology, 78*(6), 1122–1134.

Lehmiller, J. J., & Agnew, C. R. (2007). Perceived marginalization and the prediction of romantic relationship stability. *Journal of Marriage and Family, 69*, 1036–1049.

Li, J. (2002). A cultural model of learning: Chinese "heart and mind for wanting to learn." *Journal of Cross-Cultural Psychology, 33*, 248–269.

Lindholm, C. (2006). Romantic love and anthropology. *Etnofoor, 19*(1), 5–21.

Lukas, D., & Clutton-Brock, T. H. (2013). The evolution of social monogamy in mammals. *Science, 341*(6), 526–530.

Luo, S., & Klohnen, E. C. (2005). Assortative mating and marital quality in newlyweds: A couple-centred approach. *Journal of Personality and Social Psychology, 88*, 304–326.

Lutz-Zois, C. J., Bradley, A. C., Mihalik, J. L., & Moorman-Eavers, E. R. (2006). Perceived similarity and relationship success among dating couples: An idiographic approach. *Journal of Social and Personal Relationships, 23*(6), 865–880.

Ma, Y., Xue, W., Zhao, G., Tu, S., & Zheng, Y. (2019). Romantic love and attentional biases toward attractive alternatives and rivals: Long-term relationship maintenance among female Chinese college students. *Evolutionary Psychology, 17*(4), Article 1474704919897601.

MacDonald, G., & Jessica, M. (2006). Family approval as a constraint in dependency regulation: Evidence from Australia and Indonesia. *Personal Relationships, 13*, 183–194.

MacDonald, G., Marshall, T. C., Gere, J., Shimotomai, A., & Lies, J. (2012). Valuing romantic relationships: The role of family approval across cultures. *Cross-Cultural Research, 46*(4), 366–393.

Macleod, C. I. (2018). The case for collation to inform debate and transform practice in decolonising Psychology. *South African Journal of Psychology, 48*(3), 372–378.

Madathil, J., & Benshoff, J. M. (2008). Importance of marital characteristics and marital satisfaction: A comparison of Asian Indians in arranged marriages and Americans in marriages of choice. *The Family Journal, 16*(3), 222–230.

Maner, J. K., Gailliot, M. T., & Miller, S. L. (2009). The implicit cognition of relationship maintenance: Inattention to attractive alternatives. *Journal of Experimental Social Psychology, 45*(1), 174–179.

Maner, J. K., Rouby, D. A., & Gonzaga, G. C. (2008). Automatic inattention to attractive alternatives: The evolved psychology of relationship maintenance. *Evolution and Human Behavior, 29*(5), 343–349.

Marlowe, F. (2001). Male contribution to diet and female reproductive success among foragers. *Current Anthropology, 42*(5), 755–759.

Markus, H. R., & Kitayama, S. (1991). Culture and the self: Implications for cognition, emotion, and motivation. *Psychological Review, 98*, 224–253.

Marshall, T. C. (2008). Cultural differences in intimacy: The influence of gender-role ideology and individualism—collectivism. *Journal of Social and Personal Relationships, 25*, 143–168.

McGraw, K. J. (2002). Environmental predictors of geographic variation in human mating preferences. *Ethology, 108*(4), 303–317.

Mikulincer, M., & Shaver, P. R. (2007). Contributions of attachment theory and research to motivation science. In J. Shah & W. Gardner (Eds.), *Handbook of motivation science* (pp. 201–216). Guilford Press.

Miller, R. S. (1997). Inattentive and contented: Relationship commitment and attention to alternatives. *Journal of Personality and Social Psychology, 73*(4), 758–766.

Miller, S. L., & Maner, J. K. (2010). Evolution and relationship maintenance: Fertility cues lead committed men to devalue relationship alternatives. *Journal of Experimental Social Psychology, 46*(6), 1081–1084.

Ming Hui, C., & Harris Bond, M. (2009). To please or to neglect your partner? Attachment avoidance and relationship-driven self-improvement. *Personal Relationships, 16*(1), 129–145.

Minkov, M., & Hofstede, G. (2010). Hofstede's fifth dimension: New evidence from the world values survey. *Journal of Cross-Cultural Psychology, 43*, 3–14.

Morris, M. W., & Peng, K. (1994). Culture and cause: American and Chinese attributions for social and physical events. *Journal of Personality and Social Psychology, 67*, 949–971.

Negash, S., Cui, M., Fincham, F. D., & Pasley, K. (2014). Extradyadic involvement and relationship dissolution in heterosexual women university students. *Archives of Sexual Behavior, 43*(3), 531–539.

Netting, N. S. (2010). Marital ideoscapes in 21st-century India: Creative combinations of love and responsibility. *Journal of Family Issues, 31*(6), 707–726.

New, J. J., & German, T. C. (2015). Spiders at the cocktail party: An ancestral threat that surmounts inattentional blindness. *Evolution and Human Behavior, 36*(3), 165–173.

Nisbett, R. E., & Cohen, D. (1996). *Culture of honor: The psychology of violence in the South*. Westview Press.

Nisbett, R. E., Peng, K., Choi, I., & Norenzayan, A. (2001). Culture and systems of thought: Holistic versus analytic cognition. *Psychological Review, 108*(2), 291–310.

OECD (2019), Society at a Glance 2019: OECD Social Indicators, OECD Publishing, Paris, https://doi.org/10.1787/soc_glance-2019-en.

Ohtsubo, Y., & Watanabe, E. (2009). Do sincere apologies need to be costly? Test of a costly signaling model of apology. *Evolution and Human Behavior, 30*, 114–123.

Oishi, S. (2010). The psychology of residential mobility: Implications for the self, social relationships, and well-being. *Perspectives on Psychological Science, 5*(1), 5–21.

Papp, L. J., Liss, M., Erchull, M. J., Godfrey, H., & Waaland-Kreutzer, L. (2017). The dark side of heterosexual romance: Endorsement of romantic beliefs relates to intimate partner violence. *Sex Roles: A Journal of Research, 76*(1-2), 99–109.

Regan, P. C., Lakhanpal, S., & Anguiano, C. (2012). Relationship outcomes in Indian-American love-based and arranged marriages. *Psychological Reports, 110*(3), 915–924.

Reichard, U. (1995). Extra-pair copulations in a monogamous gibbon (Hylobates lar). *Ethology, 100*(2), 99–112.

Rosenbaum, S., Vigilant, L., Kuzawa, C. W., & Stoinski, T. S. (2018). Caring for infants is associated with increased reproductive success for male mountain gorillas. *Scientific Reports, 8*(1), 15223–8.

Sakaluk, J. K., Biernat, M., Le, B. M., Lundy, S., & Impett, E. A. (2020). On the strength of ties that bind: Measuring the strength of norms in romantic relationships. *Journal of Social and Personal Relationships, 37*(3), 906–931.

Sandhya, S. (2009). The social context of marital happiness in urban Indian couples: Interplay of intimacy and conflict. *Journal of Marital and Family Therapy, 35*, 74–96.

Savaya, R., & Cohen, O. (1998). Qualitative cum quantitative approach to construct definition in a minority population: Reasons for divorce among Israeli Arab women. *Journal of Sociology and Social Welfare, 25*, 157–202.

Schmitt, D. P., Alcalay, L., Allensworth, M., Allik, J., Ault, L., Austers, I., Bennett, K. L., Bianchi, G., Boholst, F., Borg Cunen, M. A., Braeckman, J., Brainerd, E. G., Caral, L. G. A., Caron, G., Martina Casullo, M., Cunningham, M., Daibo, I., De Backer, C., De Souza, E. . . . Shackelford, T. K. (2004). Patterns and universals of adult romantic attachment across 62 cultural regions: Are models of self and of other pancultural constructs? *Journal of Cross-Cultural Psychology, 35*, 367–402.

Schmitt, D. P., & Jonason, P. K. (2015). Attachment and sexual permissiveness: Exploring differential associations across sexes, cultures, and facets of short-term mating. *Journal of Cross-Cultural Psychology, 46*(1), 119–133.

Schug, J., Yuki, M., & Maddux, W. (2010). Relational mobility explains between- and within-culture differences in self-disclosure to close friends. *Psychological Science, 21*, 1471–1478.

Schwartz, J. P., Lindley, L. D., & Buboltz Jr, W. C. (2007). Adult attachment orientations: Relation to affiliation motivation. *Counselling Psychology Quarterly, 20*(3), 253–265.

Shackelford, T. K., & Larsen, R. J. (1997). Facial asymmetry as an indicator of psychological, emotional, and physiological distress. *Journal of Personality and Social Psychology*, 72(2), 456–466.

Sinclair, H. C., Hood, K. B., & Wright, B. L. (2014). Revisiting the Romeo and Juliet effect (Driscoll, Davis, & Lipetz, 1972): Reexamining the links between social network opinions and romantic relationship outcomes. *Social Psychology, 45*(3), 170–178.

Singh, D. (2002). Female mate value at a glance: Relationship of waist-to-hip ratio to health, fecundity and attractiveness. *Neuroendocrinology Letters, 23*(4), 81–91.

Sonn, C. C., Rua, M. R., & Quayle, A. F. (2020). Decolonising applied social psychology: Culture, indigeneity and coloniality. In K. C. O. Doherty & D. Hodgetts (Eds.), *The SAGE handbook of applied social psychology (pp. 39-59)*. SAGE.

Starks, T. J., & Parsons, J. T. (2014). Adult attachment among partnered gay men: Patterns and associations with sexual relationship quality. *Archives of Sexual Behavior, 43*(1), 107–117.

Stamkou, E., van Kleef, G. A., Homan, A. C., Gelfand, M. J., van de Vijver, F. J. R., van Egmond, M. C., Boer, D., Phiri, N., Ayub, N., Kinias, Z., Cantarero, K., Treister, D. E., Figueiredo, A., Hashimoto, H., Hofmann, E. B., Lima, R. P., & Lee, I-C. (2019). Cultural collectivism and tightness moderate responses to norm violators: Effects on power perception, moral emotions, and leader support. *Personality and Social Psychology Bulletin*, 45(6), 947–964.

Starkweather, K. E., & Hames, R. (2012). A survey of non-classical polyandry. *Human Nature, 23*(2), 149–172.

Stulp, G., Simons, M. J., Grasman, S., & Pollet, T. V. (2017). Assortative mating for human height: A meta-analysis. *American Journal of Human Biology, 29*(1), Article e22917.

Talhelm, T., Zhang, X., Oishi, S., Shimin, C., Duan, D., Lan, X., & Kitayama, S. (2014). Large-scale psychological differences within china explained by rice versus wheat agriculture. *Science (American Association for the Advancement of Science), 344*(6184), 603–608.

Teufel, C., & Nanay, B. (2017). How to (and how not to) think about top-down influences on visual perception. *Consciousness and Cognition, 47*, 17–25.

Thomson, R., Yuki, M., Talhelm, T., Schug, J., Kito, M., Ayanian, A. H., Becker, J. C., Becker, M., Chiu, C. Y., Choi, H. S., Ferreira, C. M., Fülöp, M., Gul, P., Houghton-Illera, A. M., Joasoo, M., Jong, J., Kavanagh, C. M. Khutkyy, D., Manzi, C. . . . Visserman, M. L. (2018). Relational mobility predicts social behaviors in 39 countries and is tied to historical farming and threat. *Proceedings of the National Academy of Sciences of the United States of America, 115*(29), 7521–7526.

Tooby, J., & Cosmides, L. (1992). The psychological foundations of culture. In J. H. Barkow, L. Cosmides, & J. Tooby (Eds.), *The adapted mind: Evolutionary psychology and the generation of culture* (pp. 19–136). Oxford University Press.

Toro-Morn, M., & Sprecher, S. (2003). A cross-cultural comparison of mate preferences among university students: The United States vs. the People's Republic of China (PRC). *Journal of Comparative Family Studies, 34*(2), 151–170.

Triandis, H. C. (1995). *Individualism and collectivism*. Westview.

Uberoi, P. (2006). *Freedom and destiny: Gender, family, and popular culture in India*. Oxford University Press.

van Honk, J., Tuiten, A., Verbaten, R., van den Hout, M., Koppeschaar, H., Thijssen, J., & de Haan, E. (1999). Correlations among salivary testosterone, mood, and selective attention to threat in humans. *Hormones and Behavior, 36*(1), 17–24.

van Horen, F., Pöhlmann, C., Koeppen, K., & Hannover, B. (2008). Importance of personal goals in people with independent versus interdependent selves. *Social Psychology, 39*, 213–221.

Varnum, M. E. W., Grossmann, I., Kitayama, S., & Nisbett, R. E. (2010). The origin of cultural differences in cognition: Evidence for the social orientation hypothesis. *Current Directions in Psychological Science, 19*(1), 9–13.

Walter, K. V., Conroy-Beam, D., Buss, D. M., Asao, K., Sorokowska, A., Sorokowski, P., Aavik, T., Akello, G., Alhabahba, M. M., Alm, C., Amjad, N., Anjum, A., Atama, C. S., Duyar, D. A., Ayebare, R., Batres, C., Bendixen, M., Bensafia, A., Bizumic, B. . . . & Zupančič, M. (2020). Sex differences in mate preferences across 45 countries: A large-scale replication. *Psychological Science, 31*(4), 408–423.

Walker, R. S., Hill, K. R., Flinn, M. V., & Ellsworth, R. M. (2011). Evolutionary history of hunter-gatherer marriage practices. *PloS ONE, 6*(4). https://doi.org/10.1371/journal.pone.0019066

Wilson, G., & Cousins, J. (2003). Partner similarity and relationship satisfaction: Development of a compatibility quotient. *Sexual and Relationship Therapy, 18*(2), 161–170.

Wongpakaran, T., Wongpakaran, N., & Wedding, D. (2012). Gender differences, attachment styles, self-esteem and romantic relationships in Thailand. *International Journal of Intercultural Relations, 36*(3), 409–417.

Yamada, J., Kito, M., & Yuki, M. (2015). Relational mobility and intimacy in friendships and romantic relationships: A cross-societal study between Canada and Japan. *Japanese Journal of Experimental Social Psychology, 55*(1), 18–27.

Yamada, J., Kito, M., & Yuki, M. (2017). Passion, relational mobility, and proof of commitment: A comparative socio-ecological analysis of an adaptive emotion in a sexual market. *Evolutionary Psychology, 15*(4), Article 147470491774605. https://doi.org/10.1177/1474704917746056

Yamaguchi, M., Smith, A., & Ohtsubo, Y. (2015). Commitment signals in friendship and romantic relationships. *Evolution and Human Behavior, 36*(6), 467–474.

Yuki, M., & Schug, J. (2012). Relational mobility: A socioecological approach to personal relationships. In O. Gillath, G. Adams, & A. Kunkel (Eds.), *Relationship science: Integrating evolutionary, neuroscience, and sociocultural approaches* (pp. 137–151). American Psychological Association Press.

Yuki, M., Schug, J., Horikawa, H., Takemura, K., Sato, K., Yokota, K., & Kamaya, K. (2007). *Development of a scale to measure perceptions of relational mobility in society* (CERSS Working Paper 75). Center for Experimental Research in Social Sciences, Hokkaido University.

Zahavi, A., & Zahavi, A. (1997). *The handicap principle: A missing piece of Darwin's puzzle.* Oxford University Press.

Zhang, S., & Kline, S. L. (2009). Can I make my own decision? A cross-cultural study of perceived social network influence in mate selection. *Journal of Cross-Cultural Psychology, 40*(1), 3–23.

Zhang, Q., Maner, J. K., Xu, Y., & Zheng, Y. (2017). Relational motives reduce attentional adhesion to attractive alternatives in heterosexual university students in China. *Archives of Sexual Behavior, 46*(2), 503–511.

PART III

Relationship Dissolution

In chapter 21, Wade, Moran, and Fisher begin the final section on relationship dissolution by discussing how insufficient access to a partner and the relational resources they provide can prompt relationship dissatisfaction. They argue that when partners do not equitably contribute to a partnership, perceived deficits in need or desire fulfillment may prompt partner conflict or relationship renegotiation. They review evidence of the proximate and ultimate causes of relationship dissatisfaction to support their claims and outline the scientific and humanitarian merits of studying partner access deficits in LGBTQ+, consensually nonmonogamous, and non-Western samples.

In chapter 22, Sciara and Pantaleo adopt emotional intensity theory (EIT) to describe how partners emotionally disinvest according to an adaptive energy conservation principle. They present evidence that when faced with relationship obstacles, called deterrents, the intensity of a partner's emotional attachment will coincide with the minimum effort needed to preserve the relationship. They argue that too weak or too strong deterrents may both cause partners to functionally reduce love, but for two different reasons. In the first case, it is because intense feelings are no longer needed to face little obstacles, while, in the second case, excess obstacles render the relationship too costly and, thereby, not worth additional investment. They conclude by highlighting how EIT may be used to reconcile presently disunited findings in relationship dissolution research.

In chapter 23, Ryan and Lemay detail how peoples' motivations for seeking and securing extra-pair partnerships have produced mating strategies where people disinvest in one relationship to nurture an alternative (e.g., mate poaching, infidelity, and switching). They review evidence for how these strategies have been shaped by the recurrent challenges of sexual conflict and vary adaptively with personality features (e.g., preference for novelty, sociosexuality, and attachment). They conclude by highlighting how researchers might incorporate interdisciplinary methods and sample characteristics to improve the quality of existing research.

In chapter 24, Havlíček and Roberts recount and critique the history of research on menstrual cycle shifts in human mating psychology. They outline the nuanced predictions that cycle researchers have proposed and tested to address whether fluctuations in sex hormones during the fertile phase impact mate preferences, courtship behavior, sociosexuality, and sexual desire and behavior. They then compare the strength of evidence for several competing explanations for these patterns including the ovulatory shift, spandrel, and motivational priorities hypotheses. They conclude by urging future researchers to incorporate direct measures of hormone fluctuation, control for more confounding variables (e.g., mood), and study the entire, rather than only the fertile phase of, the menstrual cycle.

In chapter 25, Brodbeck and Znoj review the antecedents, mechanisms, and outcomes of divorce and partner death. They frame their discussion using attachment theory, suggesting that affective reactions to partner loss (e.g., grief, anger, and anxiety) result from an active reorganization of one's attachment to a lost partner, including one's identity without the partner. They argue that research on partner loss would benefit from unifying findings from studies of divorce and spousal death using the dual process model of coping with bereavement into a broader framework of separation and loss. They conclude by noting the practical and therapeutic applications of this approach and the promise of incorporating new technologies to help people overcome partner loss.

In chapter 26, LeFebvre and Rasner tackle how people regulate emotion after an intimate relationship dissolves. They identify the myriad factors that impact dissolution strategies, such as who initiates a breakup, sex differences in the reasons for breakup, relationship length, age, and the processes for redefining one's relationship with an ex-partner. They use evolutionary reasoning to extend current conceptualizations of relationship dissolution processes and emotions and conclude by suggesting how such a perspective might unify current research on distress and adjustment after breakup.

In chapter 27, Langlais and Xiao review the factors influencing how people form romantic relationships after divorce. They use evolutionary theory to frame the unique processes and challenges of these relationships, including men's and women's decisions to date after divorce, how many people they date, the features they seek in a potential partner, the challenges of having existing children, and how postmarital relationships can buffer the hardships of partner loss. They outline several areas within this literature that need development, including how people manage stepfamily relationships, how divorce experiences shape peoples' partner preferences, and reasons for remaining single after relationship dissolution.

In chapter 28, Moloney and Smyth review the empirical and historical research on post-separation parenting to reveal the evolutionary reasoning that underlies how people navigate the parenting disputes that arise after divorce. They argue that the emotions motivating this conflict have historically helped parents to adapt to the breakdown of their co-parenting relationship and its consequences on children. They contrast this with research on "no fault" divorce proceedings which they argue can interrupt how these emotions help parents and children adjust to post-separation parenting. They conclude by outlining how divorce and child custody proceedings might benefit from an evolutionary understanding of these processes to improve outcomes for parents and children.

In chapter 29, Holland and Lannutti consider the experiences of LGBTQ+ individuals undergoing relationship dissolution and the unique causes and consequences of breakup within these relationships. They highlight the challenges caused by discrimination against sexually and gender-diverse people, including barriers to LGBTQ+ marriage, social structural challenges to division of labor, devaluation of consensual nonmonogamy, and other sources of minority stress. They adopt social script theory to explain how concepts like "chosen family" and the incomplete institutionalization of same-sex marriage (and thus divorce) can further complicate relationship dissolution. They conclude by identifying several future directions including the need to incorporate experimental designs, account for intermediate stages of breakup (i.e., deescalation, cyclic relationship formation, and breakup), and distinguish the contributions of sex/gender and sexual orientation to account for the spectrum of diverse sexualities that comprise LGBTQ+ populations.

In chapter 30, Mortelmans examines how uncoupling occurs among older adults. He frames this discussion from a legal perspective, arguing that the processes and consequences of breakup in old age are shaped by historical trends in divorce law and child custody arrangements. He reviews how these legal processes intersect with other social and individual factors (e.g., divorce taboos, level of education, and financial interdependence between partners) to influence personal outcomes (e.g., physical and mental health, social network adjustments, and parenting challenges) of older adults going through divorce. He likewise incorporates theoretical perspectives, including social exchange, attachment, and evolutionary theory, to explain these patterns. He concludes by highlighting how future research might address unresolved aspects of later-life divorce including the unique challenges of LGBTQ+ and "living apart together" relationships, or how recent technology might be used to mitigate stress and poor relationship outcomes.

CHAPTER

21 Relationship Dissatisfaction and Partner Access Deficits

T. Joel Wade, James B. Moran, *and* Maryanne L. Fisher

Abstract

In this chapter, we discuss how partners' feelings about relationship inequity (i.e., unequal access to relationship resources, such as sex, emotional investment, finances, and family-size decisions) can cause relationship dissatisfaction. Individuals may initiate a romantic relationship with the desire to create a long-term committed relationship that is emotionally and sexually fulfilling. However, romantic relationships do not always fulfill both partners' needs and desires, and couples often experience conflict and dissatisfaction when this happens. In this chapter, we explore both the proximate and ultimate reasons for why individuals experience dissatisfaction in their relationships. Proximate reasons include issues such as finances, cultural backgrounds, and ascribed sex roles whereas ultimate causes encompass issues of sexual conflict with others, reproduction-related conflict, and jealousy. Further, we also survey a promising area of research that suggests dissatisfaction in a romantic relationship may arise from a deficit in emotional and sexual access for one of the partners in the relationship. We conclude by suggesting that researchers explore how relationship deficits affect couples who identify as LGBTQ, pursue consensual nonmonogamy and investigate how relationship access deficits affect couples from non-WEIRD samples. Additionally, we suggest that future research examine how relationship access deficits affect abuse in relationships because such research may help deter or end abuse.

Key Words: relationship deficits, access, relationship satisfaction, sex differences, gender roles, marriage, couples, evolutionary psychology

"When I'm riding round the world, and I'm doing this and I'm signing that, and I'm trying to make some girl who tells me baby, better come back, maybe next week. . . . I can't get no satisfaction!"

—Rolling Stones

The Importance of Relationship Satisfaction

Being involved in a satisfying romantic and sexual relationship is, at least for most people, the ideal. Byers (2005) defines sexual and relationship satisfaction as the extent to which sexual and romantic relationship needs are fulfilled. People who feel highly satisfied with their romantic relationships experience a stronger sense of relationship stability and are less likely to face relationship dissolution (Gottman & Levenson, 1992). People in satisfied relationships are happier, feel more positive, state their life has meaning, report higher levels of well-being, and experience greater mental and physical health (Prigerson et al., 1999; see Tummala, 2007, for a review). Indeed, the importance of sexual and relationship satisfaction cannot be overstated, given that they are major contributors to overall life satisfaction (Sprecher, 2002; Yeh, et al., 2006).

General relationship satisfaction (i.e., including sexual behavior) tends to be related to passion and, to a lesser degree, feeling altruistic love toward one's partner. It is negatively correlated with game-playing, uncommitted love, and manipulative sexuality (Hendrick et al., 1988). It may also be linked with trait perspective-taking (i.e., the tendency to comprehend another's feelings, thoughts, or situation). Those who engage in perspective-taking experience higher satisfaction, regardless of whether they rate their own ability to take perspective or that of their partner, or even if it was in general terms or specific to the relationship (Cahill et al., 2020).

Many factors contribute to how satisfied partners are within their romantic relationships. Two areas that are well investigated are the connections between sexuality and relationship satisfaction, and the influence of personality. Sexual and relationship satisfaction are strongly associated, regardless of one's sexual orientation (i.e., found in both mixed and same-sex couples), age, or whether one is dating or in a long-term marriage (see, for review, Vowels & Mark, 2020). When relationships are evaluated based on costs and rewards, individuals may consider being sexually satisfied as a reward, leading them to feel high relationship satisfaction (Fletcher et al., 1999). However, as Vowels and Mark (2020) report, the relationship appears to be the opposite, such that one's perceived quality of the relationship may influence sexual satisfaction.

Personality is another key component, as it may impact on how one perceives the relationship, or it may be seen as a fundamental part of the process of establishing and maintaining the relationship. It can play a role in how people chose their partner, how they behave within the relationship, and even how satisfied their partner is with the relationship. Indeed, it is key to acknowledge that one can examine satisfaction either within an individual or among the partners. Those who self-report higher emotional stability, agreeableness, conscientiousness, and extroversion also report greater marital satisfaction (Heller et al., 2004). Similarly, the presence of these factors in one partner correlates with higher satisfaction in the other partner (although openness is not significant; Malouff et al., 2010). Other characteristics, such as neuroticism, are linked with decreased sexual satisfaction, which may be associated with lower marital satisfaction (see McNulty, 2013, p. 537, for a review).

The underlying factors that lead to satisfaction have been studied for decades, with evolutionary arguments typically resting on the idea that it is based on one's evaluation of the benefits and costs of the union with a particular person (e.g., Zainah et al., 2012). This cognitive assessment includes whether one could "do better" by ending the relationship and initiating a relationship with someone new (e.g., Dillon et al., 2016). From this perspective, satisfaction may index an individual's assessment of whether they are receiving what they want from their relationship.

An alternative view is that satisfaction is the outcome of a relationship, such that researchers may use feelings of love, or one's investment in the relationship, to predict satisfaction (Hendrick et al., 1988). This argument is problematic, though, when one considers that satisfaction is likely part of a feedback loop, such that satisfaction is connected to feelings of love or investment (Hendrick et al., 1988). Moreover, there are notable sex differences. Investment by a partner is linked to satisfaction, but only for women; this pattern is similarly observed for self-disclosure, as well as the ability to elicit a partner's disclosures (Hendrick et al., 1988). Work on parental investment theory (Trivers, 1972) in humans suggests that women have an evolutionary heritage of relying on men's resources and investment in the well-being of their children, such that it would be expected that investment is linked to satisfaction for women. Men have a different set of relationship needs (i.e., desire for sexual access) that better predicts their satisfaction. Therefore, satisfaction is about need fulfillment rather than investment, per se.

The reverse situation, dissatisfaction within a relationship, is also noteworthy, especially given feelings of dissatisfaction often lead to relationship dissolution. However, it must be noted that although marital dissatisfaction increases over the length of the relationship for most individuals, the majority do not end their marriages (Hirschberge et al., 2009). Hence, it is not plausible to draw a causal relationship between relationship satisfaction and relationship dissolution; for many people, dissolution does not typically result from dissatisfaction. The lack of a causal link has led some researchers to propose that there is a complex connection between satisfaction and dissolution (Hirschberger et al., 2009). Indeed, Hirschberger et al. (2009) conducted a longitudinal study and reported that marital satisfaction immediately before divorce did not predict divorce, and neither did satisfaction at the beginning of the relationship predict divorce. The remainder of the chapter explores the various factors that are part of this complex connection.

What Makes Individuals in a Relationship Dissatisfied?

These findings lead to the question: what is driving relationship dissolution or divorce? It is important to first examine the prevalence of divorce, as rates in many countries are falling, and likewise the numbers of marriages. The mainstream idea that about half of all marriages in the United States end in divorce is inaccurate: current rates tend to be 6.5

marriages per 1,000 total population, and 2.9 divorces per 1,000 population (National Center for Health Statistics, 2020), whereas, in 2000, the rate was 8.2 marriages per 1,000 totally population (National Center for Health Statistic, 2000). In a popular press column in *Time*, Luscombe (2018) argued that the approximately 39% divorce rate in the United States should not be seen as positive, because it may reflect the economic hardships involved in divorce, leading many to simply avoid marrying. Likewise, the rates should not be seen as indicating that people are avoiding cohabitating or common-law relationships. Both have steadily increased (12% in 2008 to 15% in 2018) for the last decade, at least among those ages 25 to 34 years, according to census data (U.S. Census, 2018). Thus, marriage may represent an unmet goal for many people; more than half of those who have never married want to be married, although this figure is decreasing (Pew Research Center, 2014).

These thoughts aside, it is interesting to consider what mediators and moderators influence marriages resulting in divorce. Amato and Previti (2003) reported that infidelity is the leading cause, followed by incompatibility, drinking or drug use, and feelings related to growing apart. They also documented that people blame their spouses more so than themselves for problems that lead to divorce. The act of initiating a divorce may be seen as the penultimate move resulting from dissatisfaction, which leads to the question: what causes an individual in a romantic relationship to shift from feeling satisfied to dissatisfied?

Although satisfaction in a relationship is something couples strive for, there are often periods when couples experience dissatisfaction in the relationship. Some of the issues that cause dissatisfaction in a relationship arise from proximate causes or societal influences. However, others could stem from ultimate or evolutionary causes.

Societal Moderators

The foundation of relationship satisfaction may be considered as resting on proximate versus ultimate reasons. Proximate causes are primarily descriptive, accounting for the shape of the relationship, how the variables function toward satisfaction, for instance. Many of these are also societal causes, or linked to social norms, cultural constraints, or similar. Societal or proximal influences that may relate to one's relationship satisfaction include finances of those involved in the relationship, culture and religion, and ascribed gender roles. We next describe each of these in detail.

FINANCES

Discussing and managing shared finances are common relationship challenges. Finances is a significant contributor to overall marital conflict (Papp et al., 2009), because it can cascade into other problems such as how the couple discusses money. For example, wives who stated they had fights over money, reported the fights lasting longer (γ = .41), and husbands reported fights occurring more often (γ = .46). These dialogues often focus on issues about who makes the money and power inequalities within a relationship (Fincham, 2003; Papp et al., 2009).

Further, discourses about money are the most recurrent conversation in long-term romantic relationships (Papp et al., 2009). Couples who are better at communicating about their money tend to be more satisfied with their relationship (Archuleta, 2013). Research suggests that a couple's style of communicating also influences their general satisfaction. In one study, Afifi et al. (2018) coded couples' themes of communicating and found that couples who use more uplifting speech, known as unified couples, have more satisfied relationships. Besides the type of communication couples use, their mindset toward money may also be a predictor of satisfaction. For instance, clinicians often work to adjust couples' financial communication to change their mindset from "money is everything" to "money is not everything," which leads to an increase in the couples' well-being (Romo & Abetz, 2016).

Second, inequity in earning power causes dissatisfaction in relationships. For instance, when women are the breadwinners (e.g., make more than her opposite-sex partner), they are less likely to engage in sexual infidelity; however, men in these relationships are more likely to cheat on their breadwinning partner. Moreover, when women earn more money than their opposite-sex partner, the latter are more likely to emotionally distance themselves (Munsch, 2015). Those couples with high socioeconomic inequality experience increased negative emotions and strong relationship dissatisfaction (Cho et al., 2020).

CULTURE AND RELIGION

Another moderator that influences relationship satisfaction is one's identification with a particular culture or religion (Boiger, 2019). How individuals self-identify via their self-construal might influence how they interact with others in their group (Markus & Kitayama, 1991). For example, when a person identifies as harmonious with their group, they are participating in an interdependent group. In contrast, if an individual identifies as fundamentally different from their group, they are in independent cultures (Markus & Kitayama, 1991), and these cultural differences can change how relationships are viewed and lived.

Thus, culture may affect how couples interact with one another and enjoy one another's time. For example, Turkish (interdependent) and Euro-Canadian (independent) individuals both report wanting to be close with their romantic partners; however, Turkish individuals tend to want to be closer to their family and friends, too (Usku et al., 2004). Similarly, Japanese couples are less likely to disclose their thoughts and feelings and instead hope their partner is equipped to understand or "mind-read" their emotions and thoughts (Rothbaum et al., 2000). These findings suggest that interdependent cultures may expect greater interdependence from their partner compared to those with independent cultural norms.

Besides one's immediate culture shaping their relationships, issues can arise when the partners in the couple do not identify with the same culture. For example, heterosexual couples where the woman is Chinese and the man is Western (i.e., European ancestry) display fewer positive behaviors during a conflict, which suggests that when a culturally interdependent and independent individual form a union, their conflict is harder to resolve (Hiew et al., 2016). Furthermore, Chinese couples tend to report that their relationship satisfaction depends on intimacy and commitment but not passion, which is discrepant with the fact that these three relationship features are together considered ideals among U.S. couples (Sakalli-Ugurlu, 2003). Thus, when a culturally independent and an interdependent individual form a couple, their definitions of relationship satisfaction may not be aligned, which could cause significant stress (Hiew et al., 2016).

Besides culture, the couple's religious beliefs may influence how satisfied they are with their relationship. For example, firmer religious beliefs are often associated with forgiveness, which increases relationship quality (David & Stafford, 2013). The connections between religion, relationship quality, and stability have been examined extensively, with the data showing that shared religion increases relationship quality, helps to define commitment to the relationship, and aids parenting (see Henderson et al., 2018).

ASCRIBED GENDER ROLES

Societal pressures have also shaped specific gender roles (i.e., social constructions about how men and women should behave, their identities and how biological sex is expressed; Fisher & Burch, in press); these roles determine many features of romantic relationships. For example, men's traditional masculinity is negatively related to their romantic satisfaction (Burn & Ward, 2005). This effect is found in both straight and gay couples, where men who have more traditional masculine ideology tend to have lower romantic satisfaction (Wade & Donis, 2007). Researchers speculate that this effect may stem from financial concerns. For instance, men who are more masculine and who have higher-earning opposite-sex partners are more likely to have lower relationship quality (Coughlin & Wade, 2012). Thus, these gender roles are not only ingrained in society but also are cornerstones of relationships.

The distinction between gender, biological sex, and the newly coined idea of gender/sex is still unclear (see Fisher & Burch, in press). Further, though, how gender roles arise is uncertain, particularly in light of the potential for biological influences. These gender roles, outlined in the preceding section, may have some biological underpinnings that are driven by evolutionary forces, which we turn to in the next section.

Evolutionary-Driven Moderators

The research previously mentioned may lead to the conclusion that when there is an inequality in the relationship (whether it originates from lack of financial communication, resource earning potential, differences in cultural and religious expectations, or gender roles), couples may experience relationship dissatisfaction. These reasons are *proximate* ones, in that they are concerned with how the relationship works or the mechanisms underpinning the functioning of the relationship. There also are *ultimate* reasons for why couples may experience romantic dissatisfaction, and these pertain to the overall fitness of individuals. That is, ultimate reasons, such as rivalry with an outsider or sexual competitor, may influence relationship satisfaction.

COMPETITION BY POACHERS

One way that individuals may experience dissatisfaction from outside competitors is in the form of mate poaching (Schmitt & Buss, 2001). Mate poaching is a mating strategy where a person external to the romantic relationship attempts to lure one of the partners away (Schmitt & Buss, 2001). Mate poaching is a frequent behavior and involves evolved tactics to perform successfully (Fisher & Wade, in press; Moran & Wade, 2017; Wade & Fisher, 2022).

For example, opposite-sex friendships are perceived to be a successful way for mate poachers to gain sexual access to their targets (Mogilski & Wade, 2013). Besides using friendship as a tactic to infiltrate a relationship, similar flirtatious tactics are often utilized to seduce a member of a romantic relationship (Schmitt & Buss, 2001). For instance, men who are interested in mate poaching someone for a short-term relationship (i.e., one-time sexual experience) tend to use tactics that deceptively display their potential of being a committed partner (Moran & Wade, 2017). Moreover, poachers seem to use the outward characteristics of the couple to determine which individuals could be successfully poached. One feature that is easily assessed is the physical attractiveness of the involved individuals. When the two members of a couple are significantly different in their levels of attractiveness, the couple is perceived as a desirable target in that the poaching attempt will more likely be successful (Moran, et al., 2017; Moran & Wade, 2019b). Further, couples where the man is less attractive than the woman are perceived as easier targets for poaching (Moran & Wade, 2019a). Due to the actions of these poachers, who may be perceived as potential mating competitors, different types of jealousy may arise. Jealousy has been well documented to elicit negative feelings and, consequently, cause people in a relationship to feel dissatisfied (Foster & Misra, 2013; Green & Sabini, 2006; Tchalova & Eisenberger, 2015).

COMPETITION ELICITS SEXUAL JEALOUSY

Sexual jealousy is experienced more often by men than women (Buss, 2013). It indicates to men that a mate may be behaving in a way that communicates to other men that she is available. Men's sexual jealousy is pervasive and important to understand, as it is a contributor to men's homicides (as the perpetrator and as the target; Daly et al., 1982). For instance, the Detroit police crime record in 1972, concluded that of "social conflicts" that lead to homicides, 19.0% were caused by jealousy, 4.2% were from business conflicts, 32.4% were from family, and 44.4% were from friends (Daly et al., 1982). Furthermore, men are more likely to be murdered by another man due to mate poaching or intrasexual mating competition (Duntley & Buss, 2011). Men are also more likely to kill and abuse romantic partners due to sexual jealousy. Although murder does not always occur, sexual jealousy can increase the engagement of other types of behaviors that result in dissatisfaction.

Before sexual jealousy motivates murder, men are more likely to check up on their mates and punish them for behaving flirtatiously (Buss, 2013). As mentioned, there is a sex difference such that whereas women also experience sexual jealousy, it is argued to be less distressing and rarely leads to homicidal outcomes (Buss, 2013). In evolutionary terms, the complex emotion of jealousy serves to alert men and women that they are at risk of their mate cheating on them. Adaptively, feelings of jealousy signal that they should check to see if their partners are engaging in infidelity or behaviors that may signal an infidelity may occur. If jealousy draws attention to relationship inequities (e.g., cheating behavior), it may cause men and women to feel less satisfied in their relationship.

COMPETITION ELICITS EMOTIONAL JEALOUSY

Besides sexual jealousy, individuals may also experience jealousy if a partner provides insufficient emotional investment or commitment (i.e., emotional infidelity-based jealousy). There are sex differences in reactions to a partner's emotional infidelity. Women report greater jealousy due to a partner falling in love with another woman rather than only engaging in sex with another woman (Buss et al., 1992). This difference does not imply that men are immune to feeling distressed about emotional infidelity, and researchers suggest that men and women both engage in behaviors that may be construed as checking on the emotional commitment of a mate. For example, Elphinston and Noller (2011) documented that men and women engage in snooping on social media *Facebook* profiles, which may lead individuals to have more negative experiences in their romantic relationships.

Ultimately, these evolutionary reasons for why people experience romantic dissatisfaction are connected to one's fitness. If a mate poacher infiltrates a relationship, the remaining (now single) mate experiences significant loss; there is the loss of a romantic partner and their resources (love, companionship, etc.). In other words, they experience a decrease in their fitness in the form of reduced mate value (via potential reputational damage), possible mental health impairment (e.g., depression, anxiety, and distress), and the loss of their partner's support (Shrout & Wiegel, 2018). If their goal was to raise a family, there is also the potential loss or delay in having children, or the removal of parental care and shared resources for parenting. For example, people evaluate their partners on the instrumentality of obtaining specific goals (e.g., Orehek et al., 2018). An example of how relationships are transactional is reflected in how one's partner fulfills emotional needs and/or sexual needs. Thus, when one is not being fulfilled, it could lead to deficits in a relationship.

Partner Access Deficits

A partner's fulfillment of one's emotional and sexual needs plays a major role in relationship satisfaction. It is therefore not surprising that problems arise when there are deficits in sexual and emotional access in a relationship. Buss (1989) documented that when men are denied sexual access by a partner, they can become enraged. Conversely, when men pressure women for sexual access, women can become enraged. This pattern is significant in terms of relationship prognosis, given Regan (2000) posited the sexual desire partners feel for one another affects their relationship satisfaction and thoughts about ending the relationship. Additionally, Norona et al. (2017) reported that a lack of opportunities to fulfill sexual needs leads to relationship dissolution. Clearly, sexual access is important for both men and women. But, what about emotional needs? Emotional needs play a role in men and women's relationship dissolution decisions also. Findings indicate that when women's emotional needs are not met by a partner, women may engage in emotional infidelity with another man to resolve the deficit (see Fisher, 2016; Tsapelas et al., 2010).

Researcher have found that these emotional and sexual access deficits can lead to decisions regarding relationship dissolution. In the first evolutionary based study on how sexual and emotional access deficits affect these decisions, Wade et al. (2008) presented individuals with scenarios where a partner was either 100% emotionally inaccessible or 100% sexually inaccessible. They found that a lack of emotional access was more likely to lead to a breakup than a lack of sexual access. This result was surprising because the sexes differ with respect to emotional and sexual access needs and reactions. However, Wade et al.'s research did not exhibit high ecological validity, given individuals are rarely 100% emotionally inaccessible or 100% sexually inaccessible. Indeed, intermediate degrees of the respective types of access more accurately reflect real-life situations. To resolve this, Wade and Brown (2012) presented individuals with nine scenarios that represented incremental deficits in both sexual and emotional accessibility ranging from 90% to 10% emotional accessibility with corresponding sexual accessibility. They found that women were more likely to expel their mates due to emotional accessibility deficits of 90% to 60% while men were more likely to expel a mate when there were sexual access deficits of 60%. An examination of how the demographic variables measured affect mate expulsion decisions revealed that this sexual accessibility deficit was also true for individuals who had sexual relationship experience, meaning that they had personally relevant life experiences that may allow them to better imagine the experimental scenarios. These access deficit findings were explained in two ways. First, the authors proposed women desire partners who are willing to emotionally commit to and invest in them, given women's reliance on men to help provide support and resources, especially for raising children (e.g., Buss, 1989). Second, they argued that men desire women who are not prudish, which means that there will be heightened probability of their having children. Third, those with sexual experience desire partners willing to fulfill their sexual desires.

Wade and Brown (2012) also examined how the "Big 5" personality dimensions affect mate expulsion decisions based on deficits in sexual and emotional access. They found that individuals who are less agreeable are more concerned with sexual accessibility. Specifically, those low in agreeableness were more likely to expel a mate when the mate was sexually inaccessible 60% and 70% of the time. Also, they discovered that individuals who are less emotionally stable are more concerned about a partner's emotional accessibility. Specifically, they were more likely to expel a mate when the mate was emotionally inaccessible 80–90% of the time. No other dimensions of the Big-5 were associated with mate expulsion decisions.

More recent research develops this finding by using a methodology (i.e., conjoint analysis; Wade & Mogilski, 2018) that accounts for limitations associated with incremental and forced choice measures that can bias the emergence of a different mate expulsion pattern for deficits in sexual and emotional access. Using a conjoint research design, researchers asked individuals to rank a collection of scenarios which revealed how people trade off characteristics of those scenarios. Wade and Mogilski (2018) presented individuals with nine profiles that varied in three levels of emotional and sexual accessibility: high, medium, and low. They found that men were more likely to break up with a partner due to sexual access deficits and women were more likely to break up with a partner due to emotional access deficits. However, regardless of the sex of the participant, a lack of emotional accessibility was most likely to lead to mate expulsion. Further supporting the importance of emotional access and relationship satisfaction, Wade et al. (2018) reported that actions suggesting emotional commitment are perceived as most effective for relationship reconciliation after a couple undergoes conflict. They also found sex differences consistent with evolutionary theory, such that men perceive sexual acts as more effective reconciliation actions than women. Overall, emotional accessibility is most important for relationships, but sex differences consistent with evolutionary-based research on mate preferences are present. While sexual access deficits are less important than emotional access deficits overall, reproductive deficits (i.e., a partner wanting to have a child while the other prevents this possibility) are worthy of note. They are a sexual access related deficit that affects relationship satisfaction and outcomes.

Reproductive Access Deficits

One of the challenges couples negotiate is whether to have children, which includes compromises about the timing of having children and the number of children to parent. Modern sex roles for men and women have changed now that more women are in the workforce, meaning that the decision of whether to have children, and when, might be more of a problem today than in the past. Traditional social scripts about women as primary caretakers and remaining at home to tend children are less applicable for many families today. In Canada, for example, in 1976, 51% of families with at least one child under 16 years were single-earner families composed exclusively of working fathers and nonworking mothers (i.e., so-called stay-at-home mothers; there were only 2% with working mothers and stay-at-home fathers). Women's (including nonmothers) employment rates dramatically increased; among those ages 15 to 64 years, it rose from 47% in 1976 to 69% in 2014. Meanwhile, the single-earner pattern of fathers working and stay-at-home mothers changed dramatically, declining from the 51% in 1976 to 17% in 2014 (Statistics Canada, 2015).

Indeed, in today's society, finances are among the top reasons why people are forgoing having children, or having fewer children than they desire. The *New York Times* reported on their 2018 survey of 1,858 men and women (aged 20 to 45 years) about the reasons why Americans are having fewer children than ever before (Miller, 2018). Near the bottom of the rather extensive list, after issues such as wanting more leisure time, issues of work-life balance, concerns about population growth or environmental matters, and only above one item, concerns about one's parenting ability, is the statement "partner does not want children, 19%."

Evolutionary-based research points out that reproduction is important for both sexes (see, Buss, 1989), although women bear far greater costs associated with childbearing (Duvander et al., 2020). Therefore, due to their disproportionate effort, one might expect women to have a greater say in the decision-making. However, prior research indicates that men and women have an equal say (Bauer & Kneip, 2013; Jansen & Liefbroer, 2006, Testa, 2012; Thomson & Hoem, 1998, 2014), as does recent longitudinal research (Duvander et al., 2020). What happens, though, when there is disagreement about having children (i.e., a reproductive access deficit)? Miller and Pasta (1996) reported that fertility conflict leads to a delay in decision-making which favors the partner who does not want to have children. Thomson (1997) found that when parents' childbearing intentions are in disagreement, childbearing intentions and births fall below the average number of children that would be otherwise expected.

These conflicts may be resolved in a variety of ways. For example, Testa et al. (2012) reported that individuals can resolve the conflict via three rules. Couples can utilize a *golden mean rule* where each partner has an equal say in the decision and the couple tries to reach a compromise. This rule highlights a communal perspective of relationships, where individuals in a relationship want the best for one another, and focus on the other's needs (Clark & Mills, 1979). Conversely, couples may also use a *sphere of interest rule* where the individual who makes the decision is the individual whose sphere of interest involves childbearing and childrearing. Finally, couples may use a *social drift rule* where the individuals want to maintain the status quo, and, consequently, the decision favors the individual who does not want to have children.

If the conflict stemming from reproductive access is not resolved, does it lead to relationship dissolution? The answer is, sometimes, "yes." Betzig (1989) reported that failure to produce a child is a cause of divorce in 75 of 186 societies. More recently, Kjaer et al. (2014) reported that a lack of having common children (i.e., fully genetically related) might contribute to a couple's decision to dissolve a marriage or a relationship. Clearly, deficits in reproductive access can create pernicious problems for relationships.

Number of Children and Family Size

According to Thomson and Hoem (1998), the number of children to have is an issue decided by both parents in collaboration. They also found that when disagreements occur either partner can exercise veto power over the decision. However, recent longitudinal research (Duvander et al., 2020) showed that women have more influence over the decision to have a second or third child than do their heterosexual partners. This bias in favor of women is explained as a product of women assuming more responsibility for childcare and childrearing (see Duvander et al., 2020). Given reproductive conflict and sexual conflict affect relationship satisfaction (see Gorelik & Shackleford, 2012; Wade, 2012), one can surmise that deficits in these areas may cause conflicts, which if not resolved, may lead to lower relationship satisfaction.

Long-Term Mate Preferences Deficits

Long and Li (2019) specify that mate preferences that individuals possess are not always fulfilled by the mates that they initially select, such that over time mate preference deficits occur. These deficits may stem from inaccuracy in a partner's initial mate choice, decline in a partner's mate value, and sexual conflict (see Kennair et al., this volume) among partners. Consequently, individuals can be left with deficits in what they receive from their long-term partners. The initial assessment might be incorrect because the desired traits may be hard to observe and/or individuals may misrepresent their traits (Long & Li, 2019). Tooke and Camire (1991) reported that misrepresentation may have been selected for over evolutionary time because it can successfully promote one's (i.e. the deceiver's) fitness. Additionally, a man's mate value may deteriorate due to a job loss which violates a woman's preference for a high-status mate, and a woman's fertility can decline over time due to advancing age violating a man's preference for a fertile mate (Long & Li, 2019). Long and Li (2019) also proposed that sex ratios may decrease a partner's mate value if there are more mates available and less within-sex competition to access these potential mates. Moreover, partaking in extra-pair sex may also lead to decreases in one's mate value as a long-term mate, given it is associated with a lack of sexual or emotional fidelity and investment.

When these long-term mate preference deficits occur, the individual whose partner shows the deficit in their long-term mate value may decide to expel that mate and seek a replacement partner. The individuals whose mate value is in deficit in relation to their partner may also engage in mate retention actions to try to maintain their relationship (Long & Li, 2019). Specifically, individuals whose long-term mate value is lower than their partner's may resort to inflicting negative costs on their partners in an attempt to retain them. Daly and Wilson (1993) reported that men with deficits are more likely to inflict physical harm on their partners. However, women with deficits are more likely to use more direct mate guarding and intersexual negative inducement to reduce the chances that their male partners will cheat on them (Long & Li, 2019). Positive benefit-provisioning mate retention tactics (Miner et al., 2009) such as positive enticements and possession signals can be used also in an attempt to satisfy and retain the partner whose mate value has not declined (Long & Li, 2019).

Further, actions may be taken by the partner whose mate value has not declined. Long and Li (2019) reported that the higher mate value partner may encourage the partner in deficit to increase their mate value by getting a higher-status job (for men) or changing their physique in healthy nonsurgical ways (for women). While the deficits and their consequences can be upsetting for the partners, Baker and McNulty (2015) reported that engaging in actions to change aspects of the relationship without breaking up can be positively associated with relationship satisfaction over time. If the efforts to ameliorate the deficits fail, individuals may expel their mates or they may engage in polyamorous relationships or open relationships (Long & Li, 2019).

Deficits in Time Spent Together

Love is important for most relationships. Evolutionary theorists suggest that love likely evolved about 1.8 million years ago (Fuentes, 2002) out of our need to establish bonds with one another to facilitate our ability to survive, and to direct aspects of reproduction (see Buss, 1988; Fisher, 1998; Wade et al., 2009; Wade & Vanartsdalen, 2013). One of the three characteristic feelings associated with love is attachment, which is wanting to spend time with a partner and being happiest when one is together with them (Rubin, 1970). Thus, one would assume that spending time with a partner is paramount for relationship satisfaction such that deficits in time spent together would lead to dissatisfaction and relationship dissolution. Prior research indicates that spending time together is the second most commonly used maintenance strategy for married couples (Dindia & Baxter, 1987) and is often suggested as a primary therapeutic strategy (Guldner & Swensen, 1995; Stuart, 1980). So, do deficits in time spent together lead to less satisfaction and eventually relationship dissolution? This question is hard to address experimentally as there are ethical problems associated with manipulating the amount of time a couple spends together. However, examining couples where individuals naturally spend less time together, such as couples in long-distance relationships (LDRs), allows one to ascertain whether or not deficits in time spent together affect relationship quality and decisions about relationship dissolution. The majority of research examining LDRs finds that mate expulsion rates in LDRs are equal to or less than their non-LDR counterparts with less time spent together (Guldner, 1992; Pavalko & Elder, 1990; Stafford & Reske, 1990; Stephen, 1984a, 1984b). Similarly, Sahlstein (2000, 2004; see also Guldner & Swensen,

1995) found that deficits in time spent together did not affect LDRs' marital commitment and satisfaction, trust, intimacy, or commitment. These findings collectively suggest that relationships can endure deficits in time spent together.

Future Directions for Inquiry

There are many future directions that researchers could potentially pursue. Understanding how a couples' romantic satisfaction is affected by their partner's nonfulfillment of their needs, both sexual needs or emotional needs, provides a background for a diverse set of future studies that need to be conducted. For example, explorations of how relationship deficits affect couples who identify with the LGBTQ+ community and CNM (i.e., consensual nonmonogamy) relationships are needed. Additionally, the effects of deficits in non-WEIRD (i.e., Western, educated, industrial rich, and democratic; Henrich et al., 2010) cultures should be examined. There is also a vast area of study to be done on how deficits may influence levels of domestic, sexual, or other forms of abuse.

LGBTQ+ Relationships

First, many of the studies that have been conducted on relationships in terms of deficits have focused on heterosexual unions. However, understanding how non-heterosexual couples experience deficits could be a fruitful area of research. Pepping et al. (2018) documented that most lesbian, gay, and bisexual individuals desire stable, satisfying romantic relationships, parallel to findings from heterosexual populations. However, although satisfaction, and presumably access deficits, are similar among groups, same-sex couples are presented with additional challenges related to being a minority, due to stigmatization. Pepping et al. (2018) found internalized homophobia and hardship in accepting one's minority identity led to a greater motivation to conceal one's relationship, which negatively influences relationship satisfaction. Instead, affirmation of one's identity predicted increased satisfaction. There is far less research on minority relationships' satisfaction, and there is a need to examine access deficits among these groups. Additionally, whereas previous work leads to the conclusion that straight and gay women share aspects of mating psychology, there is more variability between straight and gay men (Howard & Perilloux, 2017). Thus, one could hypothesize that gay women may endure the same distress that straight women do when facing emotional and sexual deficits, but that there may be differences among gay and straight men.

Consensual Nonmonogamy Relationships

Although most research on relationship satisfaction focusses on monogamous couples, some relationships are not monogamous yet remain consensual (Conley et al., 2017). These CNM relationships need to be investigated as well. Within these relationships, additional partners are involved and they may also perceive, or produce, further emotional or sexual access-related deficits. For example, previous researchers have discovered that individuals in CNM relationships tend to report greater relationship satisfaction with their primary partner compared to their secondary partner (Mogilski et al., 2017), and individuals in CNM relationships express more distress when thinking about their primary partner cheating on them than when thinking about their secondary partner cheating on them (Mogilski et al., 2019). Therefore, one could hypothesize that individuals in CNM relationships may feel more upset if they are not achieving sexually related or emotionally related access from their primary partner compared to their secondary partner.

Cross-Cultural Understanding

Like much of psychological research, many of the studies mentioned in this chapter have focused on Western cultures (Henrich, Heine, & Norenzayan, 2010). Therefore, future work should begin to explore how cultures vary with respect to how sexual and emotional access deficits affect the individuals in the relationships (Boiger, 2019). For example, in a small-scale society such as the Himba, men tend to be more upset if their partner sexually cheated on them; however, this effect changes if the relationship is a love match—not an arranged marriage—in which case emotional infidelity is more upsetting (Scelza, 2014). However, a large cross-cultural study, pertaining to how men and women differ in their response to sexual and emotional infidelity, led to the finding that in cultures where men invest more in their children, those men are more upset by emotional infidelity (Scelza et al., 2020). Thus, sociological factors may influence how men and women respond to deficits in their relationships. For example, if the culture is interdependent (e.g., more group focused and connected), they may not experience as much upset from receiving less than their desired amount of sexual and emotional access from their partner because they are part of a collective unit within a much larger group, compared to the classically studied independent Westernized cultures.

Abuse

Intimate partner violence has implications for public health. Specifically, withholding sexual and emotional access may increase the probability that one member of the couple receives abuse, or engages in violence directed toward the other partner. Future work is needed to further our understanding of how these deficits can foster emotional and physical abuse. Indeed, there is a lack of research that connects social psychological findings with abuse, particularly in terms of access deficits, as compared to abuse stemming from more proximate issues such as alcoholism. Internet searches for reasons for domestic abuse, for example, primarily yield explanations about the abuser wanting power, as well as proximal causes such as economic matters including poverty, media influences, systemic family abuse patterns, and substance abuse. Those working to help deter or end abuse need tools based on findings stemming from evolutionary perspectives of human behavior.

Last Thoughts to Move Forward

Deficits in sexual and emotional access can exert pernicious effects on relationships. Such deficits can lead to mate expulsion, diminutions in relationship satisfaction, delays in fertility and family size decisions, and jealousy. The research we reviewed leads to the conclusion that emotional and sexual access provide adaptive benefits for relationships. The results from the numerous reviewed studies indicate that a deficit or disagreement can be detrimental to relationships and lead to dissatisfaction that may result in dissolution. Furthermore, relationship deficits depict a relationship that is not communal. Communal relationships are those where the individuals in the couple engage in behaviors that benefit their partner's needs rather than their own. Those involved in this form of relationship are more responsive to each other's needs, and congruent with achieving their goals as a couple (Lemay et al., 2007). Therefore, based on the research presented in this chapter, we suggest that one effective way for couples to move past their deficits, whether sexual or emotional, is by being more communal with one another.

Deficits create potholes in relationships that can grow over time. If the couple starts their relationship from a place of strong communication and satisfaction, the research we reviewed indicates they will be able to weather some deficits and remain together. However, once feelings about emotional unavailability, especially if connected with a lack of sexual access, become entrenched, relationship dissolution becomes more probable. Our conclusions are not necessarily surprising; the value of this chapter lies in the distinction between proximate and ultimate causes for relationship dissolution, as connected to emotional and sexual access deficits in romantic relationships. This novel way of examining reasons for ending a relationship may lead to new lines of inquiry and practical solutions to be used by those hoping to maintain their relationships.

In this chapter, we reviewed the importance of feeling satisfied within a romantic relationship, and how dissatisfaction may arise. Dissatisfaction may lead to relationship dissolution, which has the potential to cause meaningful losses for both individuals. One area of research that has been recently explored is the influence of sexual and emotional access and, in particular, access deficits, on the potential for relationship dissolution. Much more research is needed to connect the ways access deficits lead to the ending of relationships, or at least dissatisfaction, but the findings to date are promising. While there remain many unknown topics to explore, such as how those in nonmonogamous relationships, LGBTQ+ relationships, or residing in diverse cultures experience access deficits, there are critical avenues that must be explored, such as how access deficits may be related to relational abuse.

References

Afifi, T. D., Davis, S., Merrill, A. F., Coveleski, S., Denes, A., & Shahnazi, A. F. (2018). Couples' communication about financial uncertainty following the great recession and its association with stress, mental health and divorce proneness. *Journal of Family and Economic Issues*, *39*(2), 205–219.

Amato, P. R., & Previti, D. (2003). People's reasons for divorcing: Gender, social class, the life course, and adjustment. *Journal of Family Issues, 24*(5), 602–626.

Archuleta, K. L. (2013). Couples, money, and expectations: Negotiating financial management roles to increase relationship satisfaction. *Marriage & Family Review, 49*(5), 391–411.

Baker, L. R., & McNulty, J. K. (2015). Adding insult to injury partner depression moderates the association between partner-regulation attempts and partners' motivation to resolve interpersonal problems. *Personality and Social Psychology Bulletin, 41*(6), 839–852

Bauer, G., & Kneip, T. (2013). Fertility from a couple perspective: A test of competing decision rules on proceptive behaviour. *European Sociological Review, 29*(3), 535–548.

Betzig, L. (1989). Causes of conjugal dissolution: A cross-cultural study. *Current Anthropology, 30*(5), 654–676.

Boiger, M. (2019). Close relationships and culture: Understanding cultural variation and re-thinking what we thought we knew. In D. Schoebi & B. Campos (Eds.), *New directions in the psychology of close relationships*. Routledge.

Burn, S. M., & Ward, A. Z. (2005). Men's conformity to traditional masculinity and relationship satisfaction. *Psychology of Men & Masculinity, 6*(4), 254–263.

Buss, D. M., (1988). *Love acts: The evolutionary biology of love*. In R. J. Sternberg & M. L. Barnes (Eds.). *The psychology of love*. (pp. 100–118). Yale University Press.

Buss, D. M. (1989). Conflict between the sexes: Strategic interference and the evocation of anger and upset. *Journal of Personality and Social Psychology, 56*(5), 735–747.

Buss, D. M. (2013). Sexual jealousy. *Psychological Topics*, I, 155–182.

Buss, D. M., Larsen, R. J., Westen, D., & Semmelroth, J. (1992). Sex differences in jealousy: Evolution, physiology, and psychology. *Psychological Science, 3*(4), 251–256.

Byers, S. (2005). Relationship satisfaction and sexual satisfaction: A longitudinal study of individuals in long-term relationships. *Journal of Sex Research, 42*(2), 113–118. https://doi.org/10.1080/00224490509552264.

Cahill, V. A., Malouff, J. M., Little, C. W., & Schutte, N. S. (2020). Trait perspective taking and romantic relationship satisfaction: A meta-analysis. *Journal of Family Psychology*. Advance online publication. https://doi.org/ 10.1037/fam0000661

Cho, M., Impett, E. A., Campos, B., Chen, S., & Keltner, D. (2020). Socioeconomic inequality undermines relationship quality in romantic relationships. *Journal of Social and Personal Relationships, 37*(5), 1722–1742.

Clark, M. S., & Mills, J. (1979). Interpersonal attraction in exchange and communal relationships. *Journal of Personality and Social Psychology, 37*(1), 12–24. https://doi.org/10.1037/0022-3514.37.1.12

Conley, T. D., Matsick, J. L., Moors, A. C., & Ziegler, A. (2017). Investigation of consensually nonmonogamous relationships: Theories, methods, and new directions. *Perspectives on Psychological Science, 12*(2), 205–232.

Coughlin, P., & Wade, J. C. (2012). Masculinity ideology, income disparity, and romantic relationship quality among men with higher earning female partners. *Sex Roles, 67*(5–6), 311–322.

Daly, M., & Wilson, M. (1993). An evolutionary perspective on male sexual proprietariness and violence against wives. *Violence and Victims, 8*, 271–294.

Daly, M., Wilson, M., & Weghorst, S. J. (1982). Male sexual jealousy. *Ethology and Sociobiology, 3*(1), 11–27.

David, P., & Stafford, L. (2015). A relational approach to religion and spirituality in marriage: The role of couples' religious communication in marital satisfaction. *Journal of Family Issues, 36*(2), 232–249. https://doi.org/10.1177/0192513X13485922

Dillon, H. M., Adair, L. E., Geher, G., Wang, Z., & Strouts, P. H. (2016). Playing smart: The mating game and mating intelligence. *Current Psychology, 35*, 414–420.

Dindia, K., & Baxter, L. A. (1987). Strategies for maintaining and repairing marital relationships. *Journal of Social and Personal Relationships, 4*(2), 143–158.

Duntley, J. D., & Buss, D. M. (2011). Homicide adaptations. *Aggression and Violent Behavior, 16*(5), 399–410.

Duvander, A. Z., Brandén, M., Ohlsson Wijk, S., & Fahlén, S. (2018). Who decides about having children? Couples' childbearing intentions and actual childbearing. *Advances in Life Course Research, 43*, Article 100286.

Elphinston, R. A., & Noller, P. (2011). Time to face it! Facebook intrusion and the implications for romantic jealousy and relationship satisfaction. *Cyberpsychology, Behavior, and Social Networking, 14*(11), 631–635.

Fincham, F. D. (2003). Marital conflict: Correlates, structure, and context. *Current Directions in Psychological Science, 12*(1), 23–27. https://doi.org/10.1111/1467-8721.01215

Fisher, H. E. (1998). Lust, attraction, and attachment in mammalian reproduction. *Human Nature, 9*(1), 23–52.
Fisher, H. E. (2016). *Anatomy of love: A natural history of mating, marriage, and why we stray (completely revised and updated with a new introduction)*. W. W. Norton.
Fisher, M. L., & Burch, R. L. (in press). Evolutionary psychology and gender. In T. K. Shackelford (Ed.), *The SAGE handbook of evolutionary psychology*. SAGE.
Fisher, M. L., & Wade, T. J. (in press). Mate poaching. In T. K. Shackelford & V. A. Weekes-Shackelford (Eds.), *Encyclopedia of evolutionary psychological science*. Springer.
Fletcher, G. J. O., Simpson, J. A., Thomas, G., & Giles, L. (1999). Ideals in intimate relationships. *Journal of Personality and Social Psychology, 76*, 72–89.
Foster, J. D., & Misra, T. A. (2013). It did not mean anything (about me) Cognitive dissonance theory and the cognitive and affective consequences of romantic infidelity. *Journal of Social and Personal Relationships, 30*(7), 835–857. https://doi.org/10.1177/0265407512472324
Fuentes, A. (2002). Patterns and trends in primate pair bond. *International Journal of Primatology, 23*(5), 953–978.
Gorelik, G., & Shackelford, T. K. 2012. Spheres of sexual conflict. In T. K. Shackelford & A. T. Goetz (Eds.), *The Oxford handbook of sexual conflict in humans* (pp. 1–25). Oxford University Press.
Gottman, J. M., & Levenson, R. W. (1992). Marital processes predictive of later dissolution: Behavior, physiology, and health. *Journal of Personality and Social Psychology, 63*, 221–233.
Green, M. C., & Sabini, J. (2006). Gender, socioeconomic status, age, and jealousy: Emotional responses to infidelity in a national sample. *Emotion, 6*(2), 300–334. https://doi.org/10.1037/1528-3542.6.2.330
Guldner, G. T. (1992). *Propinquity and dating relationships: Toward a theory of long-distance romantic relationships including an exploratory study of college students' relationships at-a-distance* [Unpublished doctoral dissertation]. Purdue University.
Guldner, G. T., & Swensen, C. H. (1995). Time spent together and relationship quality: Long-distance relationships as a test case. *Journal of Social and Personal Relationships, 12*(2), 313–320.
Heller, D., Watson, D., & Ilies, R. (2004). The role of person versus situation in life satisfaction: A critical examination. *Psychological Bulletin, 130*, 574–600.
Hendrick, S. S., Hendrick, C., & Adler, N. L. (1988). Romantic relationships: Love, satisfaction, and staying together. *Journal of Personality and Social Psychology, 54*(6), 980–988.
Henderson, A. K., Ellison, C. G., & Glenn, N. D. (2018). Religion and relationship quality among cohabiting and dating couples. *Journal of Family Issues, 39*(7), 1904–1932.
Henrich, J., Heine, S. J., & Norenzayan, A. (2010). Most people are not WEIRD. *Nature, 466*(7302), 29–29.
Hiew, D. N., Halford, W. K., van de Vijver, F. J. R., & Liu, S. (2016). Communication and relationship satisfaction in Chinese, Western, and intercultural Chinese–Western couples. *Journal of Family Psychology, 30*(2), 193–202. https://doi.org/10.1037/fam0000144
Hirschberger, G., Srivastava, S., Marsh, P., Cowan, C. P., & Cowan, P. A. (2009). Attachment, marital satisfaction, and divorce during the first fifteen years of parenthood. *Personal Relationships, 16*(3), 401–420.
Howard, R. M., & Perilloux, C. (2017). Is mating psychology most closely tied to biological sex or preferred partner's sex? *Personality and Individual Differences, 115*, 83–89.
Jansen, M., & Liefbroer, A. C. (2006). Couples' attitudes, childbirth, and the division of labor. *Journal of Family Issues, 27*(11), 1487–1511.
Kjaer T., Albieri V., Jensen A., Kjaer, S. K., Johansen C., & Dalton S. O. (2014). Divorce or end of cohabitation among Danish women evaluated for fertility problems. *ACTA Obstetricia et Gynecologica Scandinavica, 93*, 269–276.
Lemay, E. P., Jr., Clark, M. S., & Feeney, B. C. (2007). Projection of responsiveness to needs and the construction of satisfying communal relationships. *Journal of Personality and Social Psychology, 92*(5), 834–853. https://doi.org/10.1037/0022-3514.92.5.834
Long, M., & Li, N. P. (2019). Violation of long-term mate preferences. In T. K. Shackelford & V. A. Weekes-Shackelford (Eds.), *Encyclopedia of evolutionary psychological science*. Springer.
Luscombe, B. (2018). The divorce rate is dropping. That may not actually be good news. *Time*. Retrieved June 10, 2020, from https://time.com/5434949/divorce-rate-children-marriage-benefits/
Malouff, J. M., Thorsteinsson, E. B., Schutte, N. S., Bhullar, N. & Rooke, S. E. (2010). The five-factor model of personality and relationship satisfaction of intimate partners: A meta-analysis. *Journal of Research in Personality, 44*, 124–127.

Markus, H. R., & Kitayama, S. (1991). Culture and the self: Implications for cognition, emotion, and motivation. *Psychological Review, 98*(2), 224–253. https://doi.org/10.1037/0033-295X.98.2.224

McNulty, J. K. (2013). Personality and relationships. In J. A. Simpson & L. Campbell (Eds.), *The Oxford handbook of close relationships* (pp. 535–552). Oxford University Press.

Miller, C. C. (2018). American are having fewer babies. They told us why. *The New York Times.* https://www.nytimes.com/2018/07/05/upshot/americans-are-having-fewer-babies-they-told-us-why.html

Miller, W. B., & Pasta, D. J. (1996). Couple disagreement: Effects on the formation and implementation of fertility decisions. *Personal Relationships, 3*(3), 307–336.

Miner, E., Starratt, V., & Shackelford, T. (2009). It's not all about her: Men's mate value and mate retention. *Personality and Individual Differences, 47*(3), 214–218.

Mogilski, J. K., Memering, S. L., Welling, L. L., & Shackelford, T. K. (2017). Monogamy versus consensual non-monogamy: Alternative approaches to pursuing a strategically pluralistic mating strategy. *Archives of Sexual Behavior, 46*(2), 407–417.

Mogilski, J. K., Reeve, S. D., Nicolas, S. C., Donaldson, S. H., Mitchell, V. E., & Welling, L. L. (2019). Jealousy, consent, and comparison within monogamous and consensually non-monogamous romantic relationships. *Archives of Sexual Behavior, 48*(6), 1811–1828.

Mogilski, J. K., & Wade, T. J. (2013). Friendship as a relationship infiltration tactic during human mate poaching. *Evolutionary Psychology, 11*(4), 926–943.

Moran, J. B., Kuhle, B. X., Wade, T. J., & Seid, M.A. (2017). To poach or not to poach? Men are more willing to short-term poach mated women who are more attractive than their mates [Special issue]. *EvoS Journal: The Journal of Evolutionary Studies Consortium, 8*(3), 58–69.

Moran, J. B., & Wade, T. J. (2017). Sex and perceived effectiveness of short-term mate poaching acts in college aged men. *Human Ethology Bulletin*, 32(*3*), 109–128

Moran, J. B., & Wade, T. J. (2019a). Perceptions of a mismatched couple: The role of attractiveness on mate poaching and copying. *Evolutionary Behavioral Science.* Advance online publication.

Moran, J. B., & Wade, T. J. (2019b). Self-perceived success in mate poaching: How a couple's attractiveness and relationship duration impact men's short-term poaching intentions. *Human Ethology Bulletin, 34*, 26–40.

Munsch, C. L. (2015). Her support, his support: Money, masculinity, and marital infidelity. *American Sociological Review, 80*(3), 469–495.

National Center for Health Statistics. (2000). Marriage and divorce. Retrieved August 31, 2020, from https://www.cdc.gov/nchs/data/dvs/national-marriage-divorce-rates-00-18.pdf

National Center for Health Statistics. (2020). Marriage and divorce. Retrieved June 10, 2020, from https://www.cdc.gov/nchs/fastats/marriage-divorce.htm#:~:text=Number%20of%20divorces%3A%20782%2C038%20(45,45%20reporting%20States%20and%20D.C.)

Norona, J. C., Olmstead, S. B., & Welsh, D. P. (2017). Breaking up in emerging adulthood: A developmental perspective of relationship dissolution. *Emerging Adulthood, 5*(2), 116–127.

Orehek, E., Forest, A. L., & Barbaro, N. (2018). A people-as-means approach to interpersonal relationships. *Perspectives on Psychological Science, 13*(3), 373–389. https://doi.org/10.1177/1745691617744522

Papp, L. M., Cummings, E. M., & Goeke-Morey, M. C. (2009). For richer, for poorer: Money as a topic of marital conflict in the home. *Family Relations*, 58, 91–103. https://doi.org/10.1111/j.1741-3729.2008.00537.x

Pavalko, E. K., & Elder Jr, G. H. (1990). World War II and divorce: A life-course perspective. *American Journal of Sociology, 95*(5), 1213–1234.

Pepping, C. A., Cronin, T. J., Halford, W. K., & Lyons, A. (2018). Minority stress and same-sex relationship satisfaction: The role of concealment motivation. *Family Process, 58*(2), 496–508.

Pew Research Center. (2014). Fewer never-married adults now say they hope to wed. Retrieved June 10. 2020. from https://www.pewsocialtrends.org/2014/09/24/record-share-of-americans-have-never-married/st-2014-09-24-never-married-11/

Prigerson, H. G., Maciejewski, P. K., & Rosenheck, R. A. (1999). The effects of marital dissolution and marital quality on health and health service use among women. *Medical Care, 37*, 858–873.

Regan, P. C. (2000). The role of sexual desire and sexual activity in dating relationships. *Social Behavior and Personality, 28*, 51–60.

Romo, L. K., & Abetz, J. S. (2016). Money as relational struggle: Communicatively negotiating cultural discourses in romantic relationships. *Communication Studies, 67*(1), 94–110.

Rothbaum, F., Weisz, J., Pott, M., Miyake, K., & Morelli, G. (2000). Attachment and culture: Security in the United States and Japan. *American Psychologist, 55*(10), 1093–1104. https://doi.org/10.1037/0003-066X.55.10.1093

Rubin, Z. (1970). Measurement of romantic love. *Journal of Personality and Social Psychology, 16*(2), 265–273.

Sahlstein, E. (2000). Relating at a distance: Being together and being apart in long-distance relationships [Doctoral dissertation, University of Iowa]. *Dissertation Abstracts International, 61*, 2105.

Sahlstein, E. M. (2004). Relating at a distance: Negotiating being together and being apart in long-distance relationships. *Journal of Social and Personal Relationships, 21*(5), 689–710.

Sakalli-Ugurlu, N. (2003). How do romantic relationship satisfaction, gender stereotypes, and gender relate to future time orientation in romantic relationships? *The Journal of Psychology, 137*(3), 294–303.

Scelza, B. A. (2014). Jealousy in a small-scale, natural fertility population: The roles of paternity, investment and love in jealous response. Evolution and Human Behavior, 35(2), 103–108.

Scelza, B. A., Prall, S. P., Blumenfield, T., Crittenden, A. N., Gurven, M., Kline, M., Koster, J., Kushnick, G., Mattison, S. M., Pillsworth, E., Shenk, M. K., Starkweather, K., Stieglitz, J., Sum, C.-Y., Yamaguchi, K., & McElreath, R. (2020). Patterns of paternal investment predict cross-cultural variation in jealous response. *Nature Human Behaviour, 4*(1), 20–26.

Schmitt, D. P., & Buss, D. M. (2001). Human mate poaching: Tactics and temptations for infiltrating existing mateships. *Journal of Personality and Social Psychology, 80*(6), 894–917.

Shrout, M. R., & Weigel, D. J. (2018). Infidelity's aftermath: Appraisals, mental health, and health-compromising behaviors following a partner's infidelity. *Journal of Social and Personal Relationships, 35*(8), 1067–1091.

Sprecher, S. (2002). Sexual satisfaction in premarital relationships: Associations with satisfaction, love, commitment, and stability. *Journal of Sex Research, 39*(3), 190–196. https://doi.org/10.1080/00224490209552141

Stafford, L.; & Reske, J. R. (1990). Idealization and communication in long-distance premarital relationships. *Family Relations, 39*(3), 274–279.

Statistics Canada. (2015). Employment patterns of families with children. Retrieved July 15, 2020, from https://www150.statcan.gc.ca/n1/pub/75-006-x/2015001/article/14202-eng.htm#a3

Stephen, T. D. (1984a). A symbolic exchange framework for the development of intimate relationships. *Human Relations, 37*(5), 393–408.

Stephen, T. D. (1984b). Symbolic interdependence and post-break-up distress: A reformulation of the attachment construct. *Journal of Divorce, 8*(1), 1–16.

Stuart, R. B. (1980). *Helping couples change: A social learning approach to marital therapy*. Guilford Press

Tchalova, K., & Eisenberger, N. I. (2015). How the brain feels the hurt of heartbreak: Examining the neurobiological overlap between social and physical pain. *Brain Mapping: An Encyclopedic Reference, 3*, 15–20.

Testa, M. R. (2012). Couple disagreement about short-term fertility desires in Austria: Effects on intentions and contraceptive behaviour. *Demographic Research, 26*, 63–98.

Testa, M. R., Cavalli, L., & Rosina, A. (2012). *The decision of whether to have a child: Does couple disagreement matter?* (Vienna Institute of Demography Working Papers, No. 7). Austrian Academy of Sciences (ÖAW), Vienna Institute of Demography (VID).

Thomson, E. (1997). Couple childbearing desires, intentions, and births. *Demography, 34*(3), 343–354.

Thomson, E., & Hoem, J. M. (1998). Couple childbearing plans and births in Sweden. *Demography, 35*(3), 315–322.

Tooke, W., & Camire, L. (1991). Patterns of deception in intersexual and intrasexual mating strategies. *Ethology and Sociobiology, 12*(5), 345–364.

Trivers, R. (1972). Parental investment and sexual selection. In B. Campbell (Ed.), *Sexual selection and the descent of man: 1871–1971* (pp. 136–179). Aldine.

Tsapelas, I., Fisher, H. E., & Aron, A. (2010). Infidelity: When, where, why. In W. R. Cupach & B. H Spitzberg (Eds.), *The dark side of close relationships II* (pp. 175–196). Routledge.

Tummala A. (2007). Marital satisfaction. In S. J. Loue & M. Sajatovic (Eds.), *Encyclopedia of aging and public health*. Springer. https://doi.org/10.1007/978-0-387-33754-8_280

United States Census. (2018). Living arrangements of adults ages 25-34. Retrieved June 10, 2020, fromhttps://www.census.gov/library/visualizations/2018/comm/living-arrangements-25-34.html

Uskul, A. K., Hynie, M., & Lalonde, R. N. (2004). Interdependence as a mediator between culture and interpersonal closeness for Euro-Canadians and Turks. *Journal of Cross-Cultural Psychology, 35*(2), 174–191.

Vowels, L. M., & Mark, K. P. (2020). Relationship and sexual satisfaction: A longitudinal actor-partner interdependence model approach. *Journal of Sexual and Relationship Therapy, 35*(1). 46–59.

Wade, J. C., & Donis, E. (2007). Masculinity ideology, male identity, and romantic relationship quality among heterosexual and gay men. *Sex Roles, 57*(9–10), 775–786.

Wade, T. J. (2012). Mate expulsion and sexual conflict. In T. K. Shackleford & A. T. Goetz (Eds.), *The Oxford handbook of sexual conflict in humans* (pp. 315–327). Oxford University Press.

Wade, T. J., Auer, G., & Roth, T. M. (2009). What is love: Further investigation of love acts. *Journal of Social, Evolutionary, and Cultural Psychology, 3*(4), 290–304.

Wade T. J., & Brown, K. (2012). Recent mate expulsion research. In T. Shackelford & A. Goetz (Eds.), *The Oxford handbook of sexual conflict in humans* (pp. 320–323). Oxford University Press.

Wade, T. J., & Fisher, M. L. (2022). Male mate poaching. In T. K. Shackelford (Ed.), *The Cambridge handbook of evolutionary perspectives on sexual psychology.*

Wade, T. J., & Mogilski, J. (2018). Emotional accessibility is more important than sexual accessibility in evaluating romantic relationships–especially for women: A conjoint analysis. *Frontiers in Psychology, 9*, 632. https://doi.org/10.3389/fpsyg.2018.00632

Wade, T. J., Mogilski, J., & Schoenberg, R. (2018). Sex differences in reconciliation behavior after romantic conflict. *Evolutionary Psychological Science, 4*(1), 1–7.

Wade, T. J., Palmer, R., DiMaria, M., Johnson, C., & Multack, M. (2008). Deficits in sexual access versus deficits in emotional access and relationship termination decisions. *Journal of Evolutionary Psychology, 6*(4), 309–319.

Wade, T. J., & Vanartsdalen, J. (2013). The Big-5 and the perceived effectiveness of love acts. *Human Ethology Bulletin, 28*(2), 3–12.

Yeh, H. C., Lorenz, F. O., Wickrama, K. A., Conger, R. D., & Elder, G. H., Jr. (2006). Relationships among sexual satisfaction, marital quality and marital instability at midlife. *Journal of Family Psychology, 20*(2), 339–343. https://doi.org/10.1037/0893-3200.20.2.339

Zainah, A. Z., Nasir, R. Rozy, S. H., & Noraini, M. Y. (2012). Effects of demographic variables on martial satisfaction. *Asian Social Science, 8*(9). Retrieved June 10, 2020, from http://www.ccsenet.org/journal/index.php/ass/article/view/18537

CHAPTER 22

In-Pair Divestment

Simona Sciara *and* Giuseppe Pantaleo

Abstract

How do in-pair obstacles and difficulties affect the intensity of love? Why do people at some point in their romantic relationships emotionally disinvest? Does a reduction in the intensity of romantic feelings always result in relationship breakup? Core assumptions of emotional intensity theory suggest that feelings of love vary in strength according to an adaptive "energy conservation" principle. To save energy, romantic partners automatically adapt the intensity of their feelings to the *minimum* level needed to overcome the obstacles and difficulties the couple encounters daily (e.g., reciprocal partners' flaws, relational stress, and perceived risk of breakup), because *small* relationship obstacles and difficulties only demand the investment of correspondingly *small* quantities of motivational/emotional resources to be surmounted. Thus, romantic feelings appear to diminish when obstacles are almost absent and, by contrast, to augment when obstacles grow stronger—with emotional strength reflecting the magnitude of what challenges the stability of the relationship. This specific *fine-tuning* of emotion intensity holds up, however, only to the point where maintaining the relationship is still worth the effort. Beyond this point, actual in-pair divestment occurs, because any further investment of energy would represent a useless (i.e., *nonfunctional*) waste of energy. In adopting the perspective of emotional intensity theory, this chapter reviews the most relevant empirical evidence on romantic relationships in light of a unitary, single-process explanation that reconciles past conflicting findings while also addressing new theoretical and practical implications for contemporary romantic partnerships.

Key Words: emotional intensity, motivation, romantic feelings, romantic relationships, relationship breakup, in-pair divestment, energy conservation, emotional adaptation, deterrence, relational obstacles and difficulties

People commonly consider in-pair divestment as the main signal of a romantic relationship's breakup. According to core assumptions of emotional intensity theory (EIT; Brehm, 1999), however, a reduction in the intensity of romantic feelings may not necessarily represent the first step of an imminent dissolution but rather an *adaptive* response in stable couples who face relatively small difficulties. Looking more closely, a reduction in romantic feelings may result from a *functional* process that leads the couple to adjust reciprocal emotional intensity to the *minimum* level needed to maintain the relationship.

According to EIT, in fact, such a reduction in the intensity of romantic feelings obeys an energy conservation principle, whereby *small* relationship obstacles and difficulties will only require the investment of correspondingly *small* quantities of motivational/emotional resources to be surmounted—this resulting, of course, in an apparent reduction in the intensity of those romantic feelings (i.e., the drop). From a functional point of view, by obeying such an energy conservation principle the emotional/motivational system efficiently allows the organism to save precious and vital resources to be employed later and/or in different activities.

In this sense, emotional disengagement and breakup are not necessarily contiguous, even if they represent similar outcomes of the same process. In this chapter, we illustrate how this process works, consider why such a reflex-like lessening and adaptation of emotional intensity may be functional for the relationship, and discuss when in-pair divestment becomes a synonym for relationship breakup.

What Is Emotional Divestment?

In-pair divestment is a reduction in the intensity of affect toward the partner that may involve romantic feelings, such as love, affection, and reciprocal commitment (Gonzaga et al., 2001; Kelley, 1983; Miron et al., 2009; Miron et al., 2012), as well as time spent together, shared pursuit of goals, or resource sharing (cf. Felmlee et al., 1990; Meuwly & Schoebi, 2017). At some point in their relationship, romantic partners may appear to be less interested in each other (Gottman, 1999; Kayser, 1993, 1996; Snyder & Regts, 1982). Most frequently, they experience a reduction in the intensity of passion and romance (Hatfield & Rapson, 1993; Hatfield et al., 1982). In more severe cases, however, partners *fall out of love*, with reciprocal daily life becoming increasingly dissatisfying and stressful (Kayser, 1993). When it comes to married couples, this outcome has been called "marital disaffection" (Barry et al., 2008; Kayser, 1993), to refer to a specific phase in marriage characterized by a gradual and progressive loss of emotional attachment, accompanied by a growing sense of *indifference* toward the spouse—that is, a sensation that apparently represents the opposite of feelings of love (e.g., Abbasi & Alghamdi, 2017). Emotional divestment also concerns negative feelings as it reduces not only the intensity of love but also the strength of jealousy, guilt, and even anger (Gottman, 1999). The result, then, is a widespread flattening of any kind of emotional intensity, whereby former emotions give way to indifference that, at a cognitive and behavioral level, soon translates into active forms of distancing between partners (Barry et al., 2019; Barry et al., 2008; Hess, 2002).

For all the above reasons, people often consider emotional divestment as one of the first steps of relationship dissolution, and research supports this idea as well (Barry et al., 2019). Data from two separate studies by VanderDrift et al. (2009) highlight the critical role of dissolution considerations in mediating reduced relationship commitment (i.e., a form of emotional divestment), on the one hand, and the enactment of *actual* leave behavior, on the other. More specifically, building on the behavioral, goal, and implementation intention literatures (e.g., Ajzen, 1985; Armitage & Conner, 2001; Fishbein & Ajzen, 1975; Gollwitzer, 1996; Gollwitzer & Sheeran, 2006), VanderDrift and colleagues predicted and found that psychologically *salient* (i.e., consciously accessible to mind) dissolution considerations were indeed linking reduced commitment (expressed as strength of psychological and material investment in the relationship) to leave behaviors (expressed as the proportion of participants who were no longer in the relationship after a time period of four months). These results, especially if considered alone, add to the idea that emotional divestment precedes relationship dissolution.

Also, scholars describe affective disengagement as a crucial part of relationship decline, from which few couples recover (Barry et al., 2008; Gottman, 1999). Also in line with other commonly mentioned reasons for relationship breakup, habitually reported by former married couples, this phase usually leads to an actual relationship dissolution (Amato & Previti, 2003; Baxter, 1986; Sprecher, 1994). Further invoked reasons that cause spouses to terminate their relationship include labeling the marriage as stale and boring, preferring alternative stimuli, and diffusely feeling that partners are neglectful of their needs (Kayser & Rao, 2006; see also Betzig, 1989).

A reduction in the intensity of romantic feelings, however, does not necessarily result in relationship breakup. Changes and fluctuation in the intensity of love and passion usually occur within romantic relationships (Hatfield et al., 2008; Hatfield & Rapson, 1993; Hatfield et al., 1982). Sometimes, a substantial decrease in partners' emotional intensity appears to be *natural* within the couple, as it takes the form of a decay due to the mere passing of time—or, at least, of an emotional waning not constituting in itself a threat to the relationship (Lieberman & Long, 2018).

A stable couple in which the partners have been together for several years represents a good example in this respect. Let us imagine what these two partners may be experiencing, emotionally, at some point in their relationship. We can easily imagine that the partners may have found some form of inner stability and balance; perhaps they no longer find stimulating experiences and events, but neither they do have considerable troubles to face in their shared daily life. Thus, it is plausible that the intensity of their reciprocal feelings of love, attraction, and passion, but also of jealousy and anger, may appear to have been reduced if compared to their initial intensity, when the two partners were at the beginning of their union. In other words, as relationships grow older, romantic feelings tend to give way to less passionate but more pragmatic bonds (e.g., *pragmatic love*; Kelley, 1983; see also the concept of *companionate love*, Hatfield et al., 2008, in this respect; Hatfield & Rapson, 1993; Hatfield et al., 1982). From the above example, we can easily assume that a high *intensity* of passion and love might no longer be essential for the stability of a relationship after some time has passed from the start of the union (Lieberman & Long, 2018). At the same time, this reduction in the intensity of passionate love may not constitute a sufficient reason for partners to break up (Schoenfeld, 2013).

Also from an evolutionary perspective, and perhaps even more cogently from such a theoretical point of view, the above reduction in partners' feelings would be "normal." According to classic evolutionary analyses, feelings such as love evolved to serve several functions—such as providing sexual access, displaying commitment, or promoting relationship exclusivity (Buss, 1988, 2019)—that a stable couple, whose members have reached some form of enduring relationship, does not need any more or, at least not with the same initial urgency and intensity. In our example, the bond that stable partners developed in the course of their years-long relationship is established and relatively permanent, so that all the primary functions of their initial romantic feelings (e.g., sexual access, commitment, and exclusivity) appear now to be of less importance, as the couple has already reached the main goals (e.g., the pursuing of a satisfying and stable relationship) served by those functions (Lieberman & Long, 2018).

Natural Reduction in the Intensity of Romantic Feelings

The above reasoning leads us to an important derivation: when a couple has found its stability, and lives in an absence of threatening obstacles, high intensity of love becomes *superfluous*. Previous research (e.g., Hatfield et al., 2008; Lieberman & Long, 2018) has shown that *intense* romantic feelings, as for instance passionate love, are crucial in the first phase of the relationship—that is, when the partners are dating, when the couple is at its very beginning, or when a relational stability is yet to be found. In all these circumstances, intense love represents the fundamental drive that encourages individuals to direct their energy and resources toward the primary common goals of (a) selecting the mate and (b) cultivating the relationship (Fisher, 2006; Fisher et al., 2005; Leckman et al., 2006), because by securing those goals romantic partners ensure sexual reproduction (Buss, 1988, 2006). Partners within stable long-term relationships, however, do not need to experience the same levels of passionate love to make their relationship endure (e.g., Hatfield et al., 2008). For this reason, reciprocal romantic feelings naturally tend to decrease with the passing of time (e.g., Schoenfeld, 2013)—this representing an outcome that finds support not only in research spelled out above, but also in our daily experiences.

The same, of course, should happen in the case of *negative* romantic feelings. Passionate love is not the only feeling that decreases in intensity. From an evolutionary perspective, jealousy is another good example of an emotion that may no longer be essential if the couple is stable and does not face obstacles and threats to the relationship. Jealousy is defined as the emotional reaction to a threat that puts partners at risk of losing their relationship (Buss, 2019; Buss & Haselton, 2005). Then, if in a couple there are no signs and indicators that might otherwise bring the partners to suspect infidelity—such as, for instance, the presence of romantic rivals—high intensity of jealousy is unessential. In other words, a reduction in emotional intensity seems to be justified with respect to both negative and positive feelings.

Two Instances of Reduction in the Intensity of Romantic Feelings

Nevertheless, *none* of the described "natural" declines in strength of emotional intensity is a signal *in itself* of an imminent dissolution. We should then distinguish between two different instances that qualify the reduction in the intensity of romantic feelings. On the one hand, the emotional divestment that results in a breakup; on the other, a more *functional* reduction of feelings that occurs in normal relationships, and even seems to make them last. At some point in their romantic relationships, people begin to emotionally disinvest, without feeling compelled to end the relationship. In our view, this is intriguing.

Why should that be the case? To what extent, and how, are in-pair obstacles and difficulties—or even the clear *absence* of such obstacles and difficulties—responsible for such a lessening in the intensity of romantic feelings? And, most important, how can we predict and explain what kind of emotional divestment will occur in specific couples and romantic relationships?

Causes of In-Pair Divestment: The Perspective of Emotional Intensity Theory

Several studies have addressed what causes romantic partners to emotionally disinvest. As common sense would suggest, in-pair obstacles and difficulties are among the most cited motivations in research. Marital conflicts and stressful events, such as repeated attempts at controlling the partner's deeds and actions, a lack of intimacy, workaholic tendencies, financial problems, or a variety of pressures from the social context, all represent barriers that demonstrated to lead directly to marital disaffection (Kayser, 1993, 1996; Kayser & Rao, 2006; Robinson, et al., 2006; Sadati et al., 2015). Also, when considering unmarried couples, a host of obstacles—such as a lack of social support, social disapproval, or parental interference (e.g., Sinclair & Ellithorpe, 2014; Sinclair et al., 2014; see also Levinger, 1999; Rusbult, 1980)—diminishes the intensity of reciprocal romantic feelings within the couple.

A growing body of empirical evidence, however, also shows the opposite effects. The same obstacles that lead partners to reduce romantic feelings become, in some circumstances, *beneficial* for the couple. A moderate degree of parental interference (Driscoll et al., 1972; see also Driscoll, 2014), a certain amount of social disapproval or lack of support by the family (Felmlee, 2001; Parks, et al., 1983; Sprecher, 2011), as well as living in marginalized relationships (e.g., homosexual, interracial, age-gap, or consensually nonmonogamous relationships; Lehmiller & Agnew, 2006), are all examples of obstacles that, under some conditions, may *enhance* attraction and commitment between romantic partners. A reduction in emotional intensity might not derive from the fact that couples are facing obstacles and barriers. Rather, it may originate in the fact that the couple is gradually and "naturally" adapting the intensity of romantic feelings and emotions to the magnitude of those obstacles and barriers—an adaptation that may occur in the *absence* of substantial difficulties. Put differently, the idea that romantic emotional divestment is caused by in-pair obstacles and barriers appears insufficient to explain the observed phenomena.

In this respect, the perspective of EIT (Brehm, 1999; Brehm & Brummett 1998; Brehm & Miron, 2006) provides a coherent and integrative theoretical explanation for the above conflicting findings. According to the theory, a relatively *low intensity of love*, usually observed in stable couples and *actual relationship breakup* are two different outcomes of the same process. They are only apparently similar, as in both cases partners evidently show a *reduction* in the intensity of the affect they manifest within the relationship. These two conditions, however, are causally determined by different combinations of theoretically unambiguous and well-specified factors and may lead to different consequences.

Emotional Intensity Theory

Brehm's emotional intensity theory (Brehm, 1999; Brehm & Brummett, 1998; Brehm & Miron, 2006), or EIT, rests on the assumption that emotions have a *motivational function*. This is because any emotional state—whether it is a basic emotion, an empathetic reaction, or even a basic, sensory affect—motivates specific classes of behavior that originally solved precise adaptive problems (e.g., Brehm et al., 2009; see also Al-Shawaf et al., 2016, for a review). The resulting behavior depends on the goal of the emotion. Anger, for instance, usually urges the person to aggress against whomever or whatever instigated the emotion, while sadness urges the person to withdraw (Lazarus, 1991). Even when its primary goal is unclear, an emotion involves an *urge* to act (or to refrain from acting) in specific ways. Thus, as *emotions function as motivational states*, emotional intensity must be affected by the same factors that affect motivational intensity (Brehm, 1999; see also Miron & Brehm, 2012, on EIT's cardiovascular impications for emotional states).

As demonstrated by more than three decades of research on motivational intensity, motivational systems are designed to save energy (see the core assumptions of *motivational intensity theory*, or MIT, in this respect: Brehm & Self, 1989; Gendolla & Wright, 2005; see also the original theoretical formulation on core principles of "motivational suppression": Brehm, 1975; for reviews: Gendolla et al., 2019; Richter et al., 2016b; Richter, 2013; Silvestrini & Gendolla, 2019; Silvestrini et al., in press; Silvia & Brehm, 2001). When people strive to achieve a goal, they do not mobilize all the energy at their disposal but only the amount *just needed* to overcome the obstacles they encounter while performing a given action. Thus, great obstacles will cause people to exert relatively high motivational effort, while small obstacles will let them exert correspondingly less effort, even when the pursued goal is important to them. Also, people invest motivational energy only when the required effort is justified by the importance they attribute to the goal; when the goal is not attractive, small obstacles will be sufficient to cause them to give up and disinvest. In other words, the greater the obstacles, the more energy (corresponding to greater motivational intensity) will be mobilized by the motivational system, up to the point where obstacles become too great to be surmounted, and the importance attributed to the goal no longer justifies further energy expenditure. From this perspective, motivational intensity is determined by two factors: the *importance* of reaching an outcome (i.e., the goal) and the *obstacles* that stand between the person and the attainment of the outcome. In this process, the importance of the goal sets the maximum *potential* effort a person will be willing to exert to overcome the obstacles, while the perceived magnitude of the obstacles will determine the *actual* effort the person will exert (Brehm, 1975; Brehm & Self, 1989; Brehm et al., 1983; for reviews and qualifications: Gendolla et al., 2019; Richter et al., 2016a,b; Silvestrini et al., in press; R. A. Wright, 2008; Wright & Pantaleo, 2013).

In light of the fundamental analogy that links emotions to motivational processes, variations in the intensity of emotions must obey the same energy conservation principle that controls the intensity of motivation (e.g., Richter, 2013; Silvestrini & Gendolla, 2019; Silvia & Brehm, 2001). The intensity of an emotion is thus determined by a combination of two factors: (a) the *importance* of the event that instigated the emotion (e.g., a painful event)—also understandable as the importance of experiencing that specific emotion at a given strength to secure the attainment of the emotional primary goal (e.g., the urgency of withdrawing into oneself as determined by the feeling of sadness)—and (b) the magnitude of *deterrence* to that emotional expression—that is, the counterforce exerted by any obstacle or barrier qualifying as a reason for not feeling the emotion (e.g., receiving a gift, as a counterforce to sadness, as established in Brehm et al., 1999). To clarify and better understand this process, let us look at the theoretical curve described in figure 22.1.

As in the case of motivation, the importance attributed to the event that instigated the emotion sets the maximum level of emotional intensity that a person can experience in a given situation, called the level of *potential intensity* (see fig. 22.1). As depicted in the figure, the level of potential intensity works as a *threshold* under which actual emotional intensity will be controlled by a single factor: the magnitude of "deterrence." Thus, when the event that instigated the emotion is important to the person, and the person therefore

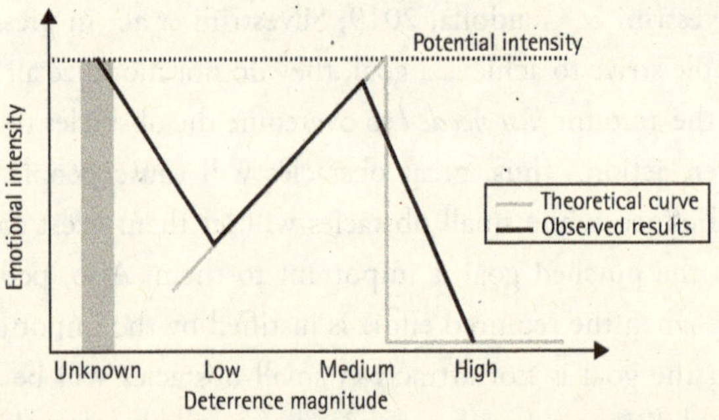

Figure 22.1 The effect of deterrence magnitude (unknown *vs.* low *vs.* medium *vs.* high) on the intensity of instigated emotions as predicted by EIT (*theoretical curve*) and as observed in results coming from studies designed to test the theory (*observed results*).

acutely feels the urge to express the emotion (e.g., the sadness resulting from failure at the final examination for graduation), then emotional intensity must be only determined by obstacles, with the emotion (e.g., sadness) growing more intense as the obstacles to the possibility of feeling and/or expressing that emotion increase in magnitude (e.g., with the increasing value of the gift—i.e., the counterforce or *deterrent*—the person has just received). Both in our example and more generally, this happens because feeling and expressing that given emotion are experienced as worthy and necessary, and the emotion's urgency justifies the mobilization of the energy needed to express/enact the emotion *despite* its deterrents. Emotional intensity will then mirror the magnitude of deterrence, with the person automatically investing only the quantity of energy strictly needed to counteract the magnitude of the deterrent. This amounts to experiencing/expressing low emotional intensity when the deterrent is little and comparatively higher emotional intensity when the deterrent becomes bigger (*low* to *medium deterrence* conditions; fig. 22.1).

Remarkably, however, obstacles will cause emotional intensity to augment only up to the point where strength of deterrence outweighs the importance of the event that instigated the emotion (in our example, receiving a gift of inestimable value). After this point (*high deterrence* condition; fig. 22.1), when deterrents become too great and a further emotional increase is no longer justified by the importance of expressing/enacting the emotion, emotional intensity drops to zero (e.g., the person will no longer experience sadness or feel any further impulse toward the enactment of sadness-motivated behaviors).

Finally, in a circumstance in which deterrents are unknown or unspecified (e.g., no gift has been given to contrast sadness, or the value of the gift is unknown), the intensity of the emotional state will correspond to the importance/strength of the instigating event (this is the *unknown deterrence* condition, as depicted in fig. 22.1). According to the theory, keeping a high level of emotional intensity when people are unaware of what obstacle/barrier will contrast with the emotion they are feeling has an adaptive value: experiencing the highest intensity possible will let the person endure and overcome counterforces of any magnitude, at least within the limits of the person's maximum potential intensity (Brehm, 1999; Silvia & Brehm, 2001).

In sum, according to EIT, the intensity of an emotional state varies as a *cubic* function of increasing levels of deterrence (fig. 22.1). Emotional intensity will thus be (a) relatively strong in the presence of unknown deterrents; (b) substantially reduced in the presence of relatively weak deterrents; (c) relatively strong in the presence of moderately strong deterrents; and (d) drastically reduced in the presence of too strong deterrents (i.e., deterrents that either objectively or subjectively cannot be overcome).

To date, several experiments have documented the predicted cubic effects of deterrence on the intensity of emotions and affective states, all reporting the same pattern of results (see the *observed results* in fig. 22.1). In particular, EIT's predictions have been substantiated with respect to emotional and affective states such as happiness (e.g., Miron et al., 2007), sadness (e.g., Brehm et al., 1999; Silvia & Brehm, 2001), anger (e.g., Miron et al., 2008), and positive and negative basic sensory affect (Brehm et al., 2009). On a more sociorelational level, the same cubic effects of deterrence have been documented for prejudiced and attitude-related affect (Fuegen & Brehm, 2004; Miron et al., 2011; Pantaleo & Contu, 2021, 2022), and political justification (Contu et al., 2021), as well as for affective social identification (Pantaleo et al., 2014). Also, the same cubic trend has been reported even with respect to the intensity of emotions such as collective guilt (Schmitt et al., 2008), vicarious empathy (Pantaleo, 2011), and the affective component of intentions (Miron & Pantaleo, 2010, for a review).

In the domain of romantic relationships, a series of experimental/controlled studies designed to test predictions of EIT confirmed the anticipated *cubic* effects of deterrence on the intensity of partners' feelings (e.g., Miron et al., 2009; Sciara & Pantaleo, 2018). These experiments not only have provided further and converging support for EIT but also a unitary and coherent theoretical explanation for all the *contrasting* findings that have been accumulating on the causes of in-pair divestment (e.g., Driscoll, 2014; Driscoll et al., 1972; Felmlee, 2001; Lehmiller & Agnew, 2006; Sinclair & Ellithorpe, 2014). In the next section, we review and discuss the most relevant empirical evidence at our disposal in this respect.

The Surprising Effects of Obstacles on the Intensity of Romantic Feelings

According to EIT (Brehm, 1999; Brehm & Brummett 1998; Brehm & Miron, 2006), since feelings of affect toward a person are motivational states (see Brehm et al., 2009), the intensity of love, affection, attraction, or any other feeling toward the romantic partner must be controlled by the same factors that control the intensity of motivation, namely, by the magnitude of *obstacles* or any other *counterforces*, renamed *deterrents* in EIT's theoretical language, to those feelings of affect (see also Brehm & Brummett, 1998, on the emotional control of behavior). Therefore, any reason *not* to feel a specific affect will qualify as a *deterrent* to that affect, as a dynamic counterforce able to either *augment* or *reduce* the intensity of the affect (Brehm, 1999; Brehm & Brummett, 1998; Fuegen & Brehm, 2004). In the context of romantic relationships, several different in-pair obstacles and barriers have proven to act systematically and precisely as predicted by EIT, that is, as deterrents to romantic feelings (e.g., Donato et al., 2018; Miron et al., 2009; Sciara & Pantaleo, 2018; see also Miron et al., 2012; Wright et al., 1985).

Miron and her colleagues were the first to provide empirical support for what they termed "the surprising effects" of obstacles on the intensity of romantic feelings (Miron et al., 2009). To test the hypothesis that the severity of *partners' flaws* can deter romantic feelings according to the *cubic* function predicted by EIT, they created an experimental procedure in which the increasing magnitude of partner's flaws (i.e., the deterrent) was experimentally manipulated. Working with young partners and lovers, the researchers first instigated feelings of positive affect and commitment toward the partner/beloved. Then, they assigned participants to one of four conditions of increasing magnitude of deterrence—that is, the four indispensable conditions for detecting the hypothesized cubic effect of deterrence magnitude (control *vs.* minor *vs.* medium *vs.* major flaws). Deterrence was manipulated in two steps, by first asking participants (a) to name some positive characteristics of their partner/significant other—this amounting to the experimental induction, through an explicit recall procedure, of positive affect toward the partner (i.e., the affect to be deterred)—and, right after (b) to list and rank-order three important *negative* partner's characteristics (i.e., partner' flaws). Depending on experimental (i.e., *deterrence*) conditions, participants were thus asked to elaborate (explain or give examples) either (a) on the most important (*high deterrence*), (b) the second most important (*moderate deterrence*), or (c) the third most important *negative* partner's characteristic (*low deterrence*). In the two control conditions, participants either limited themselves (only) to the listing of positive partner's characteristics or to listing both positive *and* negative characteristics *without* any further explicit focus, elaboration, or reference to those characteristics. Finally, the experimenters measured the intensity of feelings toward the romantic partner/beloved. Across two experiments, the researchers were able to show that romantic positive affect and commitment toward the partner was *intense* in the two control conditions; paradoxically *reduced* by a minor salient partner's flaw, maintained *intense* by a moderately important flaw, and again *reduced* by an important flaw. This pattern of results perfectly corresponds to the cubic trend originally predicted by the theory and depicted in figure 22.1.

A variety of subsequent experiments, all testing the effects of distinct deterrents, replicated these surprising though predictable effects. Reysen and Katzarska-Miller (2013), for instance, tested whether the manipulated *degree of reciprocation* of a potential partner acted as a deterrent to romantic feelings by producing cubic effects of deterrence on the intensity of attraction (Reysen & Katzarska-Miller, 2013). To test their hypothesis, the researchers asked participants to imagine a potential romantic partner who reciprocated either a strong, moderate, weak, or unspecified personal feeling of attraction (this latter condition instantiating the control condition of "reciprocation unmentioned"). Results revealed that potential partners' reciprocation of attraction acted as a deterrent to participants' actual intensity of attraction to the potential partner. Specifically, the intensity of attraction varied as a cubic function of increasing degrees of reciprocation: it was *intense* when reciprocation was unspecified; paradoxically *reduced* when participants' feelings of attraction were highly reciprocated; *intense*, again, when attraction was only moderately reciprocated; and eventually substantially *reduced* when attraction was, instead, only scarcely reciprocated. Again, this pattern of observed results fits perfectly the pattern of expected results, as one can easily anticipate from figure 22.1.

Some years later, Sciara and Pantaleo (2018) tested EIT predictions from different theoretical and empirical angles by experimentally manipulating the *risk of relationship breakup* of one's own romantic relationship, whereby the "manipulated risk" represented the counterforce (deterrent) to feelings of romantic affect and commitment toward the partner. The procedure admitted only partners who were in actual medium- to long-term romantic relationships, and after bringing each participant to focus on *positive* aspects of his or her relationship (this amounting to the *instigation* of positive romantic emotions), then asked participants to complete a test which was introduced as essential to provide them later (false) feedback on their *own* personal risk of terminating the relationship. Participants were then randomly assigned to one of the four usual experimental conditions of increasing deterrence, that is, to conditions in which they, respectively, did not receive any feedback (*unknown* risk of breakup condition), received positive feedback (*low* risk of breakup), received less comforting feedback (*medium* risk of breakup), or received negative feedback (*high* risk of breakup). The results were, again, counterintuitive and—one more time—perfectly congruent with EIT's theoretical predictions. Participants' feelings of affect and commitment toward their respective romantic partners resulted *strong* when the risk of breakup was not mentioned; substantially *reduced* when the risk was low; *strong*, again, when the risk was moderate; and, eventually, significantly *reduced* again when the risk was high. In other words, once more, the intensity of romantic feelings followed exactly—and systematically—the cubic pattern predicted by the theory (see figure 22.1).

Donato et al. (2018) replicated these findings with one more experiment, this time showing that even the recall of *stressful events* can act as a deterrent of romantic affect toward the partner (Donato et al., 2018). By implementing the established experimental paradigm and design described above, they experimentally manipulated stress (the deterrent) across four distinct levels of intensity by asking young partners—all involved in real romantic relationships—to recall three stressful events in their current romantic relationship, each characterized by a different burden of stress for the relationship. Participants in the control condition did not receive any further instructions, while participants in the remaining three experimental conditions were asked to focus, and further elaborate, either on the least stressful event ("low stress" condition), on the moderately stressful event ("moderate stress" condition), or on the most stressful event ("high stress" condition). In line with previous findings, results substantiated EIT's predictions: feelings of romantic affect resulted *strong* in the control condition, *reduced* in the "low stress" condition, maintained *intense* in the "moderate stress" condition, and eventually *reduced*, again, in the "high stress condition"' (again, a configuration of results perfectly in line with the pattern of results depicted in fig. 22.1). Recently, analogous deterrence effects of stress on the intensity of romantic affect have been replicated—with some further important qualifications—also among adults engaged in long-term romantic relationships (Sciara et al., 2020).

A first consequence of the accumulating evidence described above is given by the possibility of interpreting the previous conflicting findings of in-pair obstacles on the intensity of romantic feelings in light of a *unitary, single-process explanation*. By adopting the perspective of EIT (Brehm, 1999), we can realize that obstacles and barriers—traditionally conceptualized as detrimental for in-pair feelings and the fate of the relationship (e.g.,

Levinger, 1999; Rusbult, 1980)—can function, rather, as "motivators" and be even beneficial for partners' reciprocal feelings of romantic attachment (Brehm, 1999; Brehm & Self, 1989; H. F. Wright, 1937). In light of this perspective, all of the *mixed* effects accidentally found by previous research—that is, empirical evidence not purposely designed to test Brehm's EIT (e.g., Driscoll et al., 1972; Driscoll, 2014)—appear now to be plausible and coherent. As we have seen, the effects of obstacles on romantic feelings depend on a combination of detailed circumstances. As such, they can either systematically *decrease* emotional intensity (when obstacles are either too weak or exert an excessive deterrence effect), or even sharply *increase* the intensity of those feelings (when obstacles exert just a moderate deterrence effect; e.g., Donato et al., 2018; Miron et al., 2009, 2012; Reysen & Katzarska-Miller, 2013; Sciara & Pantaleo, 2018).

Moreover, EIT's conceptual lenses allow us to derive precise implications also for those previous models that, at a more theoretical level, have always considered obstacles and barriers as the main causes of in-pair emotional divestment. Rusbult's investment model (Rusbult, 1980, 1983; Rusbult et al., 2012; Rusbult & Buunk, 1993), for instance, predicts that in-pair negative factors (i.e., low levels of satisfaction, the presence of viable alternatives to the relationship, and a few investments in the relationship) can be all antecedents of a *linear decrease* in the intensity of partners' romantic commitment. Similarly, the risk regulation model (RRM; Murray et al., 2006, 2008) predicts that the perceived risk of rejection (i.e., an in-pair barrier) should *impair* the strength of romantic cognitions and then *linearly reduce* romantic involvement (i.e., the stronger the barrier, the more pronounced the *lessening* of romantic feelings toward the partner). Therefore, from our perspective, both Rusbult's investment model and the RRM can neither predict nor explain the *drop* in the intensity of romantic feelings that has been repeatedly observed, instead, when partners face *only little obstacles* (e.g., Miron et al., 2009). This drop, as we have seen, shapes the *cubic* function predicted by the energy conservation principle and is coherent with core assumptions of Brehm's EIT (Brehm & Self, 1989; Gendolla et al., 2019; Richter et al., 2016b; see also Richter, 2015; Stanek & Richter, 2016).

Finally, a further relevant implication—and the most important for what concerns us here—is that, according to EIT, a substantial reduction in the intensity of romantic feelings can occur as a result of *two* different theoretical conditions. The process as specified by EIT predicts that romantic partners will emotionally divest in two apparently similar cases which, in daily life, even risk to be mistaken for the same condition, as both view partners experiencing less involvement, love, attraction, and affection. In the first case, however, the person is facing obstacles of low magnitude to his or her romantic feelings and, for this reason, is *adapting* to a relatively "low challenging" environment through emotional divestment (see the "energy conservation principle"). In the second scenario, the person is instead facing obstacles beyond what the person can handle. For this reason, such big deterrents will make the person feel overwhelmed and, eventually, divest. In the next section, we will see why and how these two cases of in-pair divestment have different implications, and also can produce opposite consequences.

The Energy Conservation Principle and Its Implications for Romantic Relationships

The basic assumption of EIT is the principle for which people would tend, both at a motivational and an emotional level, to save energy (i.e., the *energy conservation principle*; Brehm & Self, 1989; Brehm, 1999; Gendolla et al., 2019; Richter et al., 2016b; Silvestrini & Gendolla, 2019; see also Richter, 2015; Stanek & Richter, 2016). An early version of the theory described the process using an expression that leaves no room for misunderstanding, with the principle originally termed as the "suppression of excess motivational energy" (Brehm, 1975). Also within romantic relationships, researchers consistently observe a *fine-tuning* process for which romantic partners make the intensity of their reciprocal feelings correspond to the *minimum level* required to overcome reasons not to feel those feelings (i.e., the deterrents; Donato et al., 2018; Miron et al., 2009; Reysen & Katzarska-Miller, 2013; Sciara & Pantaleo, 2018). From this point of view, the most surprising implication of this process might not be the fact that obstacles stimulate an increase in felt attraction and feelings of love (as notably remarked by Miron et al., 2009) but, instead, the consequent reduction in emotional feelings we observe when, in normal stable couples, there are no great obstacles to handle—one of our contentions in this chapter. Why do romantic feelings obey an "energy conservation" principle?

To reach the primary and ultimate goal of any romantic feeling such as jealousy, love, attraction, affection, and commitment of *maintaining the relationship* over time, romantic partners spontaneously react emotionally by mirroring the magnitude of whatever challenges the stability of their relationship at a given time and, as long as the emotional investment is justified by the importance attributed to the beloved person. By adapting emotional intensity to the actual magnitude of obstacles, partners invest only the minimum amount of energy that is *sufficient* to overcome the challenge (i.e., the magnitude of the deterrent to romantic feelings). The primary advantage of such adaptation is that partners are allowed to invest, on the whole, *less* energy than they would without such an adaptation mechanism at work. This constant *saving* of energy and common emotional resources will allow the couple to invest (superior) amounts of energy only when effectively needed, to overcome (bigger) relational obstacles that are still both possible to surmount and also worth the effort. Conserved energy may, in fact, be used later when the perceived utility of energy expenditure is greatest (e.g., when a threat is unknown or moderate). This flexibility is clearly *functional* to make romantic relationships last. What are the central implications of such a functional emotional reduction for romantic relationships? And, perhaps most important, how can we predict actual relationship dissolution?

A first implication, in this respect, regards the difference between the consequences of (a) the functional in-pair divestment due to adaptation to a *low* deterrence magnitude, on the one hand, and (b) the emotional drop stemming from the depletion of potential emotional resources due to the couple's complete emotional "surrender" in front of too *high* deterrence, on the other. In the first case, partners are not likely to break up because in-pair conflicts, obstacles, and barriers are almost absent, and, for this reason, feelings are just *momentarily* reduced in strength. Such a reduction is justified when in-pair conflicts (i.e., the deterrents) remain circumscribed and not particularly demanding. Once the magnitude of deterrence grows stronger, however, partners will react by adjusting the emotional intensity of their romantic feelings to the challenges posed by the new relationship's demands (see fig. 22.1). Consider, for example, the case of a long-term marriage that has been relatively stable for several years. In the absence of challenging obstacles—which would pose a threat to the stability of the relationship—partners should show a reduction in the intensity of love. This reduction, however, would only depend on the *absence* of challenging obstacles; if a new challenge emerges (e.g., an attractive new neighbor), the couple should promptly respond with an intensification of in-pair love and attraction that will help the partners to surmount the challenge. In this example, in other words, the partners' feelings are reduced only temporarily, and the couple is definitely far away from an actual relationship dissolution.

In the second case, the scenario is turned around: the partners have drastically reduced their emotional investment almost to zero because in-pair problems and the difficulties they met in the past were already too great and well beyond the limit that the couple could successfully withstand. For this reason, if compared with the first case, in which greater obstacles were able to awaken romantic feelings, in the present situation greater obstacles would cause exactly the *opposite* consequences: dealing with challenges that are even more demanding than one can reasonably handle *would not make romantic feelings magically reappear.* In such a scenario, actual relationship dissolution is reasonably likely to occur.

To illustrate and elaborate further on this point, let us think about a couple in which the partners decided to remain together, forcibly, to raise their children. Great obstacles of the past, such as frequent and repeated relationship troubles, or incompatibility between the partners, may have all caused romantic feelings to rise excessively, such that they surpass the maximum allowed level of intensity, the level beyond which intense feelings of love are *no longer* functional and justified in the relationship. In such a scenario, romantic feelings would of course be *reduced* in intensity, exactly as with a long-term spouse, but for a different reason. In this second illustration, in fact, both partners have presumably reduced their feelings almost to zero *because of* the *too great obstacles* they were dealing with—not because of an absence of relevant challenges, or because of the mere passing of time. In such a scenario, obstacles of even greater magnitude (e.g., a new, attractive neighbor) would only worsen the situation, with actual relationship breakup becoming increasingly more likely, if not unavoidable.

There is a further implication of our general reasoning on resource conservation, which follows directly from the consideration that the two conditions of in-pair divestment described above, due either to low *or* too high deterrence strength, are *by no means contiguous*. First, the two kinds of divestment within the couple are not necessarily sequential, because one condition does not determine the other, and vice versa. We cannot predict one reaction from the other, as those reactions simply stem, as we already know, from different crossings of two factors—the magnitude of deterrence (the obstacles) *and* the level of potential emotional intensity (i.e., the importance of the person who instigated the affect) (fig. 22.1). Second, moving from one kind of emotional divestment to the other should represent, at least, an infrequent event. This is because it is rather seldom that couples quickly move from situations in which they face "very low" deterrence (e.g., just some little occasional quarrel) to situations in which they abruptly face "very high" deterrence (e.g., reciprocal incompatibility on every front).

A third and final implication could help us guess what kind of in-pair divestment a given romantic relationship is facing. The reaction to obstacles in itself can be considered—at least potentially—as a fair indicator of which part of the Brehmian theoretical curve (fig. 22.1) the couple is dealing with at a certain time. Are the couple's feelings reacting to some *increasing* in-pair difficulties, obstacles, and barriers? If yes, then we would infer that those feelings originate, probably, in the first left part of the theoretical curve, where emotional divestment is a *functional* reaction to low deterrence magnitude (see fig. 22.1). This not being the case, if the couple is *not* emotionally mirroring the magnitude of new, bigger in-pair obstacles, we would then have to infer that partners are finding themselves, *psychologically*, in the second right part of the curve, where emotional disengagement is, again, a *functional* reaction to too strong deterrents. To try to render these two different scenarios more graphically, let us think for a moment about a popular commonplace. It is frequent to hear that "a bit of jealousy is good for the couple," meaning that some occasional jealousy reactions are good indicators that the partner is still having feelings for their counterpart or is still feeling some romantic involvement. So, if the partner finds himself or herself in the first left part of the theoretical curve (i.e., the "low deterrence" region in fig. 22.1), then some evidence of a possible betrayal will *stimulate* and raise an emotional reaction of jealousy. In contrast, however, if the partner finds himself or herself far away, toward the end of the second right part of the theoretical curve (i.e., in the too "high deterrence" region), even the most unmistakable sign of betrayal will no longer touch the person, at least not in terms of jealousy or any other relationship-maintaining romantic feeling.

Implications and Directions for Future Research and Professional Practice

Although numerous studies have provided substantial support, in the past, for EIT's predictions, some important theoretical implications in the context of close relationships have never been spelled out or systematically tested yet and *are* in need of further investigation. To date, little research has explored the predicted effects of deterrence on the intensity of romantic *negative* feelings (e.g., jealousy, envy, and rancor). So far, only an experiment by Miron et al. (2009, Study 3) started to investigate the effects of deterrence on negative romantic emotions. In a nutshell, this experiment outlined how the increasing relevance of positive partner's *qualities* (i.e., the deterrent) shaped the intensity of *anger* within romantic couples so that, once instigated, anger was high in the control and moderate deterrence conditions and significantly reduced in both the low and high deterrence conditions—a pattern conforming, again, to the predicted cubic trend depicted in figure 22.1.

Also, at first glance, results such as those obtained by Miron et al. (2009, Study 3) could perhaps sound somewhat counterintuitive—like almost any other well-established hypothesis coming from EIT—but, at the same time, they may also prove extremely useful for a number of practical reasons. In the case of jealousy, for example, EIT would predict that one partner's—and/or any other persons' (friends, acquaintances, etc.)—benevolent attempts at *reassuring* and *comforting* the other partner about his or her (perhaps mistaken) feelings of jealousy within the relationship would unintentionally (and *paradoxically*) act as *deterrents* to the strength of those feelings of jealousy, and alter its intensity accordingly, in line with the predicted cubic pattern. From results such as these, our community of researchers, professionals, counselors, practitioners, or any other interested person, would learn that certain levels of "reassurance" (i.e., those substantially corresponding to moderate deterrence) might (as predicted) surprisingly *augment* the partner's worries and, thereby, even be detrimental for the relationship. Such a discovery would of course not only lead researchers to deepen and expand their understanding of the dynamics of emotional regulation within the couple but also let a vast array of psychological professionals be in a better—and well-documented/sustainable—position to efficiently help partners find their balance within the relationship. Further empirical testing of such and similar theoretical derivations, however, is needed.

Another aspect of the theory that would need further investigation regards the study of what determines the level, or threshold, of *potential* emotional intensity in general, and of romantic emotions in particular. As we have seen in the course of this chapter, EIT states that the threshold of potential intensity is a direct function of strength of emotional instigation, that is, the subjective importance of whatever—or *whomever*, in the case of romantic feelings—instigated the emotion (Brehm, 1999). In this sense, the maximum *potential* level an emotion can reach (i.e., the threshold) is not fixed a priori but is assumed to be a direct function of the subjective importance of the ultimate *goal* of a given romantic feeling (e.g., staying with the beloved person and maintaining the relationship over time). Although the theory unambiguously predicts such an upward/downward shift of potential intensity (i.e., the threshold), to date no study has yet tested this important facet of the theory—certainly not within the context of close/romantic relationships.

The reader can easily imagine how relevant such a new line of research could be. Let us imagine for a moment what would happen if the ultimate goal of some reciprocal romantic feelings was *not* the maintenance of the relationship. What should happen if feelings of affection were no longer directed at maintaining the relationship over time? What parallel implications would we then derive with respect to other kinds of dyadic relationships (e.g., casual dating) and, of course, with respect to related emotional feelings (so-called "affective states"; e.g., Fuegen & Brehm, 2004) *not* directly oriented at maintaining the bond (e.g., mere physical attraction)? Further, what would happen to emotional intensity if a certain positive affect would aim at keeping two persons together (as it *should*) when, in reality, those two persons *must* stay together because the bond cannot be resolved for some other, external technical reason such as, for instance, in the case of co-parenting relationships? Similarly, what would happen in the case of parental affect toward one's child, when relationship maintenance is, to some extent, constantly ensured/secured, regardless of obstacles? Parents usually try hard for their offspring. Thus, if the goal of achieving a solid bond has already been reached and secured within the parent–child relationship, we would expect no special/unusual emotional reactions (i.e., any abrupt diminishing or intensification of emotions) as a sheer function of obstacles (i.e., deterrence magnitude), because those obstacles—in *those kinds* of relationships—no longer act as real psychological barriers to feelings of affect toward the other person (e.g., the child, in the case of the parental relationship).

Some evidence in this respect has already been collected in a recent study on the intensity of parental feelings of affect in parent–children relationships—more specifically, in a controlled experiment deliberately constructed to test some core predictions of EIT (1999) in the context of those specific parent–child relationships (Sciara et al., 2020). The authors assumed that the ultimate goal of positive affect was to maintain the relationship and, also, that parental relationships should be among the most difficult/impossible relationships to break (their maintenance should be relatively secured because the emotional goal of relationship maintenance has *already* been reached). In line with this reasoning, Sciara et al. (2020) found that traditional obstacles and relationship barriers, comprising various stressful events for the relationship, did *not* deter the intensity of parents' positive feelings of love and affection toward their own children (all parental feelings remained invariably intense). Again, however, future research should explore more systematically such new directions, and possibly also clarify what for the moment, in our view, remains little more than a fascinating set of interrelated questions and stimulating hypotheses.

Aside from which particular aspects of the theory still need to be tested, a close reading of EIT (Brehm, 1999; Brehm & Brummett, 1998; Brehm & Miron, 2006) also suggests a number of practical implications that have the clear potential to benefit, in many respects, a vast array of professionals in the field of interpersonal relationships. A first implication in this respect regards, for instance, the possibility to practically determine and/or regulate the intensity of romantic affect between couples/partners by assessing those known (i.e., theoretically specified) parameters, or factors, which are central in shaping the intensity of partners' feelings: (a) the magnitude of *deterrence*, and (b) the level of *potential intensity* at which a given emotion can be experienced/expressed at its level of maximal intensity (i.e., the threshold of potential intensity). An accurate prediction of resultant variations in the intensity of reciprocal emotions, made on the basis of the above-identified factors, would enable professionals and couples to prevent unwanted negative and automatic consequences of the emotion regulation process, among which—of course—is actual relationship breakup. In this respect, the theory represents a genuinely good guide, as it shows exactly which factors should be identified—and possibly controlled—to avoid the negative consequences of in-pair divestment or, more precisely, to prevent the kind of in-pair divestment that, in the end, typically leads partners to break up. Under EIT's theoretical guide, thus, interested professionals could venture to find out (and also help the couple to maintain) the best perfect *match* between partners' emotional *potential*, on the one hand, and the appropriate range of deterrence magnitude the couple is able to handle at a given time, on the other hand, without disengaging. Certainly not an easy task to accomplish but, for sure, a feasible enterprise.

Even when a certain couple appears to have already infringed the limit that usually brings the partners to definitive emotional divestment (i.e., the threshold of potential intensity), and begins to no longer be able to tolerate further increments in the magnitude of in-pair obstacles, EIT still lets us hope that—to use a common expression—"all is not lost." At a theoretical level, a couple that has already drastically divested, perhaps after having significantly grappled with too great obstacles, still has the chance to *reverse* the process. What caused partners' reciprocal feelings of love to drop to a level of *minimum* intensity? There are at least two possible answers to this crucial question. First, "an insufficient level of potential intensity of feelings." In other words, if the threshold of potential intensity (i.e., importance attributed to the relationship and/or partner) would have hypothetically been just a little bit higher, then emotional intensity would have *not* dropped to zero, because it would have adapted to the intensity level necessary to *overcome* obstacles of great entity (and, of course, it would have theoretically made feelings of romantic attraction grow paradoxically stronger!). In such a case, a good solution to give the couple another chance would consist in intensifying partners' reciprocal levels of *potential* intensity, by emphasizing—and thereby heightening—the subjective importance of their respective mate (e.g., this could be achieved by bringing the partners to rediscover and consequently attach, again, more subjective value and positive qualities to the other person). In so doing, a new intensification of romantic feelings would be fully justified, even in the face of relatively strong obstacles. The couple would then not only merely survive but even intensify reciprocal romantic strivings.

A second way to answer the question of "what caused partners' feelings of love to drop to a *minimum* level of intensity" could consider, instead, the decisive role of in-pair obstacles. If, again in our hypothetical reasoning, obstacles had been just a little bit smaller than they were, then partners' feelings would have *not* dropped to zero: those feelings would have adapted in strength to the intensity level needed to overcome such (comparatively smaller) difficulties. In such a case, then, a good alternative and recommended solution would be to remove—or, at least, to try to adjust the perception of—the obstacles that caused reciprocal romantic feelings to encroach the limit of *potential* intensity (i.e., EIT's theoretical threshold; see fig. 22.1) and thereby visibly drop to a minimum level of intensity.

Before moving to the conclusion of this chapter, we still need clarification on a further intriguing theoretical possibility, the chance of *inverting* the unfolding of the emotional intensity-regulation process specified by EIT to bring romantic relationships to last longer than they normally would in normal/typical circumstances. The process described by EIT, and in particular the emotional divestment that results from a drastic drop in emotional intensity, is an *adaptive* process (Brehm, 1999; Richter, 2013)—that is, it evolved to prevent people wasting resources while they were striving to reach goals that were either *unattainable* or else *not worth* the effort. This means that, to some extent, romantic breakups also should be seen as *adaptive* outcomes of a functional process. In keeping with this reasoning, then, a clear advantage of adopting the perspective of EIT is the possibility to recognize those cases in which the process of energy mobilization is, instead, *not* functioning properly (i.e., in a nonadaptive way). In some cases, for example, misperceiving a certain situation by either *underestimating obstacles* or *overestimating the importance* attributed to one's partner (or to the relationship) may directly lead a person to continue to invest *even when* such emotional investments are dysfunctional, deleterious, and harmful both for the person and the relationship. Closely related to this, a better understanding of how the intensity of romantic feelings can be effectively regulated in specific circumstances, then, would help professionals also in preventing the unwanted effects of *extreme feelings* (i.e., either too feeble or too intense romantic feelings).

In this respect, researchers, as well as practitioners, counselors, and other professionals, should all carefully consider the probable emergence of a parallel ironic side effect due to a rapid intensification of strivings and feelings within the couple. This effect amounts to an emotionally driven *cognitive narrowing* of one's own perceptual and social abilities—a severe limitation to relational skills stemming from the sudden intensification of emotions (Easterbrook, 1959; Pantaleo et al., 2014, p. 863; Silvia & Brehm, 2001). In such a scenario, an abrupt reduction in partners' reciprocal cognitive abilities, and related perspective-taking skills, is expected just when each member of the couple would do better, instead, to continue entertaining and bearing in mind the full array of standpoints, needs, desires, and requests made by the other partner *and* by the broader societal context/situation—an ability that normally guarantees relatively high flexibility in a changing physical and social world (Pantaleo et al., 2014; Silvia & Brehm, 2001). According to the theory of multiple perspectives (TMP; Pantaleo, 1997; Pantaleo & Wicklund, 2000; Wicklund & Pantaleo, 2012; Wicklund, 1999), such a strong and abrupt reduction in partners' capacity and competence to entertain a *multiplicity* of social standpoints and perspectives (i.e., the cognitive narrowing) is part of a so-called *orienting* reaction, a response that brings people to manifest social "blindness" vis-à-vis the different social perspectives, standpoints, and opinions typically present in the public arena (cf. Sciara et al., 2022).

In our case, such an orienting reaction would bring us, the researchers, to observe both partners acting, thinking, and feeling in a social *vacuum*, as if they were de facto "shielded" and isolated—by their own strong private goals and motivations—from other potential sources of influence or inspiration, even if those sources could turn out, one day, to be helpful to the couple. According to predictions of the theory of multiple perspectives, then, such an *orienting* reaction would easily bring the two partners to an unwanted forgetfulness and consequent paradoxical disregard of their reciprocal needs, desires, and declared preferences within the couple, as well as to a more general neglect of the broader societal perspective and related social input and suggestions (Pantaleo, 1997; Pantaleo & Wicklund, 2000, pp. 233–234; Wicklund & Pantaleo, 2012, pp. 364–367; see also Wicklund & Steins, 1996). This being the case, then, it would be true, once again—and this time also from a different theoretical angle—that "(*strong*) love blinds."

Finally, professionals may find it useful to combine EIT's practical implications with more fine-grained assessments of the distinctive, idiosyncratic characteristics of the particular romantic relationship they are dealing with. Decades of research have constantly shown that people can be grouped easily in terms of some fundamental dispositional differences in the way in which they tend to perceive obstacles and other potential sources of stress (e.g., Lazarus, 1993; Lazarus & Folkman, 1984). For this reason, any systematic (i.e., dispositional or character-related) *overestimation* or *underestimation* of in-pair obstacles and difficulties made by one or both the romantic partners will interact with all the predictions of Brehm's theory (i.e., the *cubic trend*; Brehm, 1999; see fig. 22.1). In other words, people will emotionally respond according to (a) the predictions of EIT *in combination* with (b) their personal tendencies in perceiving obstacles and barriers (see Brinkmann & Franzen, 2015; Gendolla, 2018; Gendolla et al., 2007; Richter et al., 2016b; Wright, 2014; Wright & Franklin, 2004; Wright et al., 2019; and Wright & Pantaleo, 2013, for a rationale and reviews of analogous moderating factors affecting perception of obstacles and barriers from the perspective of MIT). Thus, a specific kind of emotional divestment (be it functional and transitory vs. drastic and radical) will happen depending on whether obstacles are, for whatever reason (e.g., personality, circumstances, or a combination thereof), *perceived* as "too little" (i.e., unchallenging) or "too great" (i.e., excessively challenging). Again, implementing the perspective offered by EIT also in the arena of romantic relationship will enormously help perceptive professionals—as any other interested scholar, of course—to responsibly identify those crucial factors that may, under circumstances, lead a particular couple to emotionally divest.

In sum, we are persuaded that EIT—together with a number of related research findings—may represent a clear, dependable, and integrative guide to anyone interested in emotional dynamics. In our view, this theory will easily keep the promise of bringing every interested person—scholars, researchers, professionals, practitioners, or any other genuinely attentive person worth his or her professional salt—to understand, with clarity and simplicity, the subtleties of emotional investment and regulation and the dynamics that lie at the heart of different, yet unitary romantic and love processes.

Acknowledgments

We owe a debt of gratitude to Justin Mogilski and Todd Shackelford for their outstanding editorial guidance. This chapter is dedicated to the memory of Jack W. Brehm and Robert A. Wicklund.

References

Abbasi, I. S., & Alghamdi, N. G., (2017). Polarized couples in therapy: Recognizing indifference as the opposite of love. *Journal of Sex & Marital Therapy, 43*(1), 40–48. https://doi.org/10.1080/0092623X.2015.1113596

Ajzen, I. (1985). From intentions to actions: A theory of planned behavior. In J. Kuhl & J. Beckmann (Eds.), *Action control: From cognition to behavior* (pp. 11–39). Springer-Verlag.

Al-Shawaf, L., Conroy-Beam, D., Asao, K., & Buss, D. M. (2016). Human emotions: An evolutionary psychological perspective. *Emotion Review, 8*(2), 173–186. https://doi.org/10.1177/1754073914565518

Amato, P. R., & Previti, D. (2003). People's reasons for divorcing: Gender, social class, the life course, and adjustment. *Journal of Family Issues, 24*, 602–626. https://doi.org/10.1177/0192513X0-3024005002

Armitage, C. J., & Conner, M. (2001). Efficacy of the theory of planned behaviour: A meta-analytic review. *British Journal of Social Psychology, 40*, 471–499. https://doi.org/10.1348/014466601164939

Barry, R. A., Lawrence, E., & Langer, A. (2008). Conceptualization and assessment of disengagement in romantic relationships. *Personal Relationships, 15*, 297–315. https://doi.org/10.1111/j.1475-6811.2008.00200.x

Barry R.A., Lorenzo J.M., Singh R. (2019) Romantic disengagement. In J. L. Lebow, A. L. Chambers, & D. C. Breunlin (Eds.), *Encyclopedia of couple and family therapy* (pp. 2532–2535). Springer. https://doi.org/10.1007/978-3-319-49425-8_795

Baxter, L.A. (1986). Gender differences in the heterosexual relationship rules embedded in break-up accounts. *Journal of Social and Personal Relationship, 3*, 289–306. https://doi.org/10.1177/0265407586033003

Betzig, L. (1989). Causes of conjugal dissolution: A cross-cultural study. *Current Anthropology, 30*, 654–676. https://doi.org/10.1086/203798

Brehm, J. W. (1975). *Research on motivational suppression* [Grant proposal]. University of Kansas.

Brehm, J. W. (1999). The intensity of emotion. *Personality and Social Psychology Review, 3*, 2–22. https://doi.org/10.1207/s15327957pspr0301_1

Brehm, J. W., & Brummett, B. H. (1998). The emotional control of behavior. In M. Kofta, G. Weary, & G. Sedek (Eds.), *Personal control in action* (pp. 133–154). Plenum Press.

Brehm, J. W., Brummett, B. H., & Harvey, L. (1999). Paradoxical sadness. *Motivation and Emotion, 23*, 31–44. https://doi.org/10.1023/A:1021379317763

Brehm, J. W., & Miron, A. M. (2006). Can the simultaneous experience of opposing emotions really occur? *Motivation and Emotion, 30*, 13–30. https://doi.org/10.1007/s11031-006-9007-z

Brehm, J. W., Miron, A. M., & Miller, K. (2009). Affect as a motivational state. *Cognition and Emotion, 23*, 1069–1089. https://doi.org/10.1080/02699930802323642

Brehm, J. W., & Self, E. A. (1989). The intensity of motivation. *Annual Review of Psychology, 40*, 109–131. https://doi.org/10.1146/annurev.ps.40.020189.000545

Brehm, J. W., Wright, R. A., Solomon, S., Silka, L., & Greenberg, J. (1983). Perceived difficulty, energization, and the magnitude of goal valence. *Journal of Experimental Social Psychology, 19*, 21–48. https://doi.org/10.1016/0022-1031(83)90003-3

Brinkmann, K., & Franzen, J. (2015). Depression and self-regulation: A motivational analysis and insights from effort-related cardiovascular reactivity. In G. H. E. Gendolla, M. Tops, & S. Koole (Eds.), *Handbook of biobehavioral foundations of self-regulation* (pp. 333–347). Springer.

Buss, D. M. (1988). Love acts: The evolutionary biology of love. In R. J. Sternberg & M. L. Barnes (Eds.), *The psychology of love* (pp. 100–118). Yale University Press.

Buss, D. M. (2006). The evolution of love. In R. J. Sternberg & K. Weis (Eds.), *The new psychology of love* (pp. 65–86). Yale University Press.

Buss, D. M. (2019). The evolution of love in humans. In R. J. Sternberg & K. Sternberg (Eds.), *The new psychology of love* (pp. 42–63). Cambridge University Press.

Buss, D. M., & Haselton, M. (2005). The evolution of jealousy: Comment. *Trends in Cognitive Sciences, 9*(11), 506–507. https://doi.org/10.1016/j.tics.2005.09.006

Contu, F., Sciara, S., & Pantaleo, G. (2021, May 26th – 27th). *Paradoxical justification of Government's mistakes during the Covid-19 pandemic in Italy: Emotion intensity theory goes political* [Poster]. 2021 APS Virtual Convention of the Association for Psychological Science (APS), virtually hosted. https://www.psychologicalscience.org/conventions/archive/2021-virtual

Donato, S., Parise, M., Pagani, A. F., Sciara, S., Iafrate, R., & Pantaleo, G. (2018). The paradoxical influence of stress on the intensity of romantic feelings towards the partner. *Interpersona: An International Journal on Personal Relationships, 12*(2), 215–231. https://doi.org/10.5964/ijpr.v12i2.310

Driscoll, R. (2014). Commentary and rejoinder on Sinclair, Hood, and Wright (2014): Romeo and Juliet through a narrow window. *Social Psychology, 45*, 312–314. https://doi.org/ 10.1027/1864-9335/a000203

Driscoll, R., Davis, K. E., & Lipetz, M. E. (1972). Parental interference and romantic love: The Romeo and Juliet effect. *Journal of Personality and Social Psychology, 24*, 1–10. https://doi.org/ 10.1037/h0033373

Easterbrook, J. A. (1959). The effect of emotion on cue utilization and the organization of behavior. *Psychological Review, 66*, 183–201. https://doi.org/ 10.1037/h0047707

Felmlee, D. (2001). No couple is an island: A social network perspective on dyadic stability. *Social Forces, 79*, 1259–1257. https://doi.org/10.1353/sof.2001.0039

Felmlee, D., Sprecher, S., & Bassin, E. (1990). The dissolution of intimate relationships: A hazard model. *Social Psychology Quarterly, 53*, 13–30. https://doi.org/10.2307/2786866.

Fishbein, M., & Ajzen, I. (1975). *Belief, attitude, intention, and behavior: An introduction to theory and research.* Addison-Wesley.

Fisher, H. E. (2006). The drive to love: The neural mechanism for mate selection. In R. J. Sternberg & K. Weis (Eds.), *The new psychology of love* (pp. 87–115). Yale University Press.

Fisher, H. E., Aron, A., & Brown, L. L. (2005). Romantic love: An fMRI study of a neural mechanism for mate choice. *The Journal of Comparative Neurology, 493*, 58–62. https://doi.org/10.1002/cne.20772

Fuegen, K., & Brehm, J. W. (2004). The intensity of affect and resistance to social influence. In E. S. Knowles & J. A. Linn (Eds.), *Resistance and persuasion* (pp. 39–63). Erlbaum.

Gendolla, G. H. E. (2018). Implicit affect and the intensity of motivation: From simple effects to moderators. *Polish Psychological Bulletin* (Special issue on perception and motivation), *49*, 56–65. https://doi.org/10.24425/119472

Gendolla, G. H. E., Brinkmann, K., & Richter, M. (2007). Mood, motivation, and performance: An integrative theory, research, and application. In A.M. Lane (Ed.), *Mood and human performance: Conceptual, measurements, and applied issues* (pp. 35–62). Nova Science.

Gendolla, G. H. E., & Wright, R. A. (2005). Motivation in social settings: Studies of effort-related cardiovascular arousal. In J. P. Forgas, K. D. Williams, & S. M. Laham (Eds.), *Social motivation: Conscious and unconscious processes* (pp. 71–90). Cambridge University Press.

Gendolla, G. H. E., Wright, R.A., & Richter, M. (2019). Advancing issues in motivation intensity research: Updated insights from the cardiovascular system. In R.M. Ryan (Ed.), *The Oxford handbook of human motivation* (2nd ed., pp. 373–392). Oxford University Press.

Gollwitzer, P. M. (1996). The volitional benefits of planning. In P. M. Gollwitzer & J. A. Bargh (Eds.), *The psychology of action: Linking cognition and motivation to behavior* (pp. 287–312). Guilford Press.

Gollwitzer, P. M., & Sheeran, P. (2006). Implementation intentions and goal achievement: A meta-analysis of effects and processes. In M. P. Zanna (Ed.), *Advances in experimental social psychology* (Vol. 38, pp. 69–119). Academic Press.

Gonzaga, G. C., Keltner, D., Londahl, E. A., & Smith, M. D. (2001). Love and the commitment problem in romantic relations and friendship. *Journal of Personality and Social Psychology, 81*, 247–262. https://doi.org/10.1037/0022-3514.81.2.247.

Gottman, J. M. (1999). *The marriage clinic: A scientifically-based marital therapy*. W. W. Norton.

Hatfield, E., Nerenz, D., Greenberger, D., Lambert, P., & Sprecher, S. (1982). *Passionate and companionate love in newlywed couples* [Unpublished manuscript]. University of Wisconsin, Madison. Retrieved from http://www2.hawaii.edu/~elaineh/60.pdf

Hatfield, E., Pillemer, J. T., O'Brien, M. U., & Le, Y.-C. L. (2008). The endurance of love: passionate and companionate love in newlywed and long-term marriages. *Interpersona: An International Journal on Personal Relationships 2*(1), 35–64. https://doi.org/10.5964/ijpr.v2i1.17

Hatfield, E., & Rapson, R. L. (1993). *Love, sex, and intimacy: Their psychology, biology, and history*. HarperCollins.

Hess, J. A. (2002). Distance regulation in personal relationships: The development of a conceptual model and a test of representational validity. *Journal of Social and Personal Relationships, 19*(5), 663–683. https://doi.org/10.1177/0265407502195007

Kayser, K. (1993). *When love dies: The process of marital disaffection*. Guilford Press.

Kayser, K. (1996). The Marital Disaffection Scale: An inventory for assessing emotional estrangement in marriage. *American Journal of Family Therapy, 24*, 83–88. https://doi.org/10.1080/01926189508251019

Kayser, K., & Rao, S. S. (2006). Process of disaffection in relationship breakdown. In M. A. Fine & J. H. Harvey (Eds.), *Handbook of divorce and relationship dissolution* (pp. 201–221). Erlbaum.

Kelley, H. H. (1983). Love and commitment. In H. H. Kelley, E. Berscheid, A. Christensen, J. H. Harvey, T. L. Huston, G. Levinger, E. McClintock, L. A. Peplau, & D. R. Peterson (Eds.), *Close relationships* (pp. 265–314). Freeman.

Lazarus, R. S. (1991). *Emotion and adaptation*. Oxford University Press.

Lazarus, R. S. (1993). Coping theory and research: Past, present, and future. *Psychometric Medicine, 55*, 234–247.

Lazarus, R. S., & Folkman, S. (1984). *Stress, appraisal and coping*. Springer.

Leckman, J. F., Hrdy, S. B., Eric, B., & Carter, C. S. (2006). A biobehavioral model of attachment and bonding. In R. J. Sternberg & K. Weis (Eds.), *The new psychology of love* (pp. 116–145). Yale University Press.

Lehmiller, J. J., & Agnew, C. R. (2006). Marginalized relationships: The impact of social disapproval on romantic relationship commitment. *Personality and Social Psychology Bulletin, 32*, 40–51. https://doi.org/10.1177/014616720527871

Levinger, G. (1999). Duty toward Whom? Reconsidering attractions and barriers as determinants of commitment in a relationship. In W. H. Jones & J. M. Adams (Eds.). *Handbook of interpersonal commitment and relationship stability* (pp. 37–52). Plenum Press.

Lieberman, D. Z., & Long, M. E. (2018). *The molecule of more: How a single chemical in your brain drives love, sex, and creativity—And will determine the fate of the human race*. BenBella Books.

Meuwly, N., & Schoebi, D. (2017). Social psychological and related theories on long-term committed romantic relationships. *Evolutionary Behavioral Sciences, 11*, 106–120. https://doi.org/10.1037/ebs0000088

Miron, A., & Brehm, J. W. (2012). Emotional intensity theory and its cardiovascular implications for emotional states. In R. A. Wright & G. H. E. Gendolla (Eds.), *How motivation affects cardiovascular response: Mechanisms and applications* (pp. 121–137). American Psychological Association.

Miron, A. M., Brummett, B., Ruggles, B., & Brehm, J. W. (2008). Deterring anger and anger-motivated behaviors. *Basic and Applied Social Psychology, 30*, 326–338. https://doi.org/10.1080/0197353080250225

Miron, A. M., Ferguson, M. A., & Peterson, A. (2011). Difficulty of refusal to assist the outgroup nonmonotonically affects the intensity of prejudiced affect. *Motivation and Emotion, 45*, 484–498. https://doi.org/10.1007/s11031-011-9220-2

Miron, A. M., Knepfel, D., & Parkinson, S. K. (2009). The surprising effect of partner flaws and qualities on romantic affect. *Motivation and Emotion, 33*, 261–276. https://doi.org/10.1007/s11031-009-9138-0

Miron, A. M., & Pantaleo, G. (2010). *The paradoxical effect of deterrence on emotional intensity: Why less can be better than more* [Unpublished manuscript]. University of Wisconsin, Oshkosh.

Miron, A. M., Parkinson, S. K., & Brehm, J. W. (2007). Does happiness function like a motivational state? *Cognition and Emotion, 21*, 248–267. https://doi.org/10.1080/02699930600551493

Miron, A. M., Rauscher, F. H., Reyes, A., Gavel, D., & Lechner, K. K. (2012). Full-dimensionality of relating in romantic relationships. *Journal of Relationships Research, 3*, 67–80. https://doi.org/10.1017/jrr.2012.8

Murray, S. L., Derrick, J. L., Leder, S., & Holmes, J. G. (2008). Balancing connectedness and self-protection goals in close relationships: A levels of-processing perspective on risk regulation. *Journal of Personality and Social Psychology, 94*, 429–459. https://doi.org/10.1037/0022-3514.94.3.429

Murray, S. L., Holmes, J. G., & Collins, N. L. (2006). Optimizing assurance: The risk regulation system in relationships. *Psychological Bulletin, 132*, 641–666. https://doi.org/10.1037/0033-2909.132.5.641

Pantaleo, G. (1997). *Explorations in orienting vs. multiple perspectives*. Pabst Science.

Pantaleo, G. (2011). Enjoying multiplicity: From familiarity to 'multiple perspectives'. In M. Cadinu, S. Galdi, & A. Maass (Eds.), *Social perception, cognition, and language in honour of Arcuri* (pp. 51–65). Cleup.

Pantaleo, G., & Contu, F. (2021). The dissociation between cognitive and emotional prejudiced responses to deterrents. *Psychology Hub, 38*(1), 39–50. https://doi.org/10.13133/2724-2943/17436.

Pantaleo, G., & Contu, F. (2022). Emozioni e pregiudizio [Emotions and prejudice]. In M. Brambilla & S. Sacchi (Eds.), *Psicologia sociale del pregiudizio* [Social psychology of prejudice] (pp. 121–142). Cortina Editore.

Pantaleo, G., Miron, A., Ferguson, M., & Frankowski, S. (2014). Effects of deterrence on intensity of group identification and efforts to protect group identity. *Motivation and Emotion, 38*, 855–865. https://doi.org/10.1007/s11031-014-9440-3

Pantaleo, G., & Wicklund, R. A. (2000). Multiple perspectives: Social performance beyond the single criterion. *Zeitschrift für Sozialpsychologie, 31*, 231–242. doi.org/10.1024//0044-3514.31.4.231

Parks, M. R., Stan, C. M., & Eggert, L. L. (1983). Romantic involvement and social network involvement. *Social Psychology Quarterly, 46*, 116–131. http://www.jstor.org/stable/3033848

Reysen, S., & Katzarska-Miller, I. (2013). Playing moderately hard to get. An application of Brehm's emotion intensity theory. *Interpersona, 7*, 260–271. https://doi.org/10.5964/ijpr.v7i2.128

Richter, M. (2013). A closer look into the multi-layer structure of motivational intensity theory. *Social and Personality Psychology Compass, 7*, 1–12. https://doi.org/10.1111/spc3.12007

Richter, M. (2015). Goal pursuit and energy conservation: Energy investment increases with task demand but does not equal it. *Motivation and Emotion, 39*, 25–33. https://doi.org/10.1007/s11031-014-9429-y

Richter, M., Brinkmann, K., & Carbajal, I. (2016a). Effort and autonomic activity: A meta-analysis of four decades of research on motivational intensity theory. *International Journal of Psychophysiology, 108*, 34. https://doi.org/10.1016/j.ijpsycho.2016.07.113

Richter, M., Gendolla, G. H. E., & Wright, R. A. (2016b). Three decades of research on motivational intensity theory: What we have learned about effort and what we still don't know. *Advances in Motivation Science, 3*, 149–186. https://doi.org/10.1016/bs.adms.2016.02.001

Robinson, B. E., Flowers, C., & Kok-Mun, N. (2006). The relationship between workaholism and marital disaffection: Husbands' perspective. *Family Journal, 14*(3), 213–220. https://doi.org/10.1177/1066480706287269

Rusbult, C. E. (1980). Commitment and satisfaction in romantic associations: A test of the investment model. *Journal of Experimental Social Psychology, 16*, 172–186. https://doi.org/10.1016/0022-1031(80)90007-4

Rusbult, C. E. (1983). A longitudinal test of the investment model: The development (and deterioration) of satisfaction and commitment in heterosexual involvements. *Journal of Personality and Social Psychology, 45*, 101–117. https://doi.org/10.1037/0022-3514.45.1.101

Rusbult, C. E., Agnew, C. R., & Arriaga, X. B. (2012). The investment model of commitment processes. In A. Van Lange, A. W. Kruglanski, & E. T. Higgins (Eds.), *Handbook of theories of social psychology* (Vol. 2, pp. 218–231). SAGE.

Rusbult, C. E., & Buunk, B. P. (1993). Commitment processes in close relationships: An interdependence analysis. *Journal of Social and Personal Relationships, 10*, 175–204. https://doi.org/10.1177/026540759301000202

Sadati, S. E., Honarmand, M. M., & Soodani, M. (2015). The causal relationship of differentiation, neuroticism, and forgiveness with marital disaffection through mediation of marital conflict. *Journal of Family Psychology, 1*(2), 55–68.

Schmitt, M. T., Miller, D. A., Branscombe, N. R., & Brehm, J. W. (2008). The difficulty of making reparations affects the intensity of collective guilt. *Group Processes and Intergroup Relations, 11*, 267–279. https://doi.org/10.1177/1368430208090642

Schoenfeld, E., (2013). *The temporal course of love: The developmental trajectories of passionate and companionate love and their connections to relationship dissolution* [Unpublished doctoral dissertation]. University of Texas at Austin. Retrieved from http://hdl.handle.net/2152/22963

Sciara, S., & Pantaleo, G. (2018). Relationships at risk: How the perceived risk of ending a romantic relationship influences the intensity of romantic affect and relationship commitment. *Motivation and Emotion, 42*, 137–148. https://doi.org/10.1007/s11031-017-9650-6

Sciara, S., Regalia, C., & Gollwitzer, P. M. (2022). Resolving incompleteness on social media: Online self-symbolizing reduces the orienting effects of incomplete identity goals. *Motivation Science*, Advance online publication. https://doi.org/10.1037/mot0000267

Sciara, S., Resta, E., Pirola, V., & Pantaleo, G. (2020). *Parental vs. romantic affect: Why and how relational stress deters the intensity of affect in romantic but not in parental relationships* [Unpublished manuscript]. Vita-Salute San Raffaele University of Milan.

Silvestrini, N., & Gendolla, G. H. E. (2019). Affect and cognitive control: Insights from research on effort mobilization. *International Journal of Psychophysiology, 143*, 116–125. https://doi.org/10.1016/j.ijpsycho.2019.07.003

Silvestrini, N., Musslick, S., Berry, A., & Vassena, E. (in press). An integrative effort: Bridging motivational intensity theory and recent neurocomputational and neuronal models of effort and control allocation. *Psychological Review*. https://doi.org/10.1037/rev0000372

Silvia, P. J., & Brehm, J. W. (2001). Exploring alternative deterrents to emotional intensity: Anticipated happiness, distraction, and sadness. *Cognition and Emotion, 15*, 575–592. https://doi.org/10.1080/02699930125985

Sinclair, H. C., & Ellithorpe, C. N. (2014). The new story of Romeo and Juliet. In C. R. Agnew (Ed.). *Social influences on romantic relationships: Beyond the dyad* (Advances in Personal Relationships) (pp.148–170). Cambridge University Press. https://doi.org/10.1017/CBo9781139333640.010

Sinclair, H. C., Hood, K., & Wright, B. (2014). Revisiting the Romeo and Juliet effect (Driscoll, Davis, & Lipetz, 1972): Reexamining the links between social network opinions and romantic relationship outcomes. *Social Psychology, 45*, 170–178. https://doi.org/10.1027/1864-9335/a000181

Snyder, D. K., & Regts, J. M. (1982). Factor scales for assessing marital disharmony and disaffection. *Journal of Consulting and Clinical Psychology, 50*, 736–743. https://doi.org/10.1037/0022-006X.50.5.736

Sprecher, S. (1994). Two sides to the breakup of dating relationships. *Personal Relationships, 1*, 199–222. https://doi.org/10.1111/j.1475-6811.1994.tb00062.x

Sprecher, S. (2011). The influence of social networks on romantic relationships: Through the lens of the social network. *Personal Relationships, 18*, 630–644. https://doi.org/10.1111/j.1475-6811.2010.01330.x

Stanek, J. C., & Richter, M. (2016). Evidence against the primacy of energy conservation: Exerted force in possible and impossible handgrip tasks. *Motivation Science, 2*, 49–65. https://doi.org/10.1037/mot0000028

VanderDrift, L. E., Agnew, C., & Wilson, J. E. (2009). Non-marital romantic relationship commitment and leave behavior: The mediating role of dissolution consideration. *Personality and Social Psychology Bulletin, 35*, 1220–1232. https://doi.org/10.1177/0146167209337543

Wicklund, R. A. (1999). Multiple perspectives in person perception and theorizing. *Theory & Psychology, 9*, 667–678. https://doi.org/10.1177/0959354399095005

Wicklund, R. A., & Pantaleo, G. (2012). The role of the professor. *Psicologia Sociale, 3*, 355–376. https://doi.org/10.1482/38441

Wicklund, R. A., & Steins, G. (1996). Person perception under pressure: When motivation brings about egocentrism. In P. M. Gollwitzer & J. A. Bargh (Eds.), *The psychology of action: Linking cognition and motivation to behavior* (pp. 511–528). Guilford Press.

Wright, H. F. (1937). *The influence of barriers upon strength of motivation*. Duke University Press.

Wright, R. A. (2008). Refining the prediction of effort: Brehm's distinction between potential motivation and motivation intensity. *Social and Personality Psychology Compass: Motivation and Emotion, 2*, 682–701. https://doi.org/10.1111/j.1751-9004.2008.00093.x.

Wright, R. A. (2014). Presidential address 2013: Fatigue influence on effort—Considering implications for self-regulatory restraint. *Motivation and Emotion, 38*, 183–195. https://doi.org/10.1007/s11031-014-9406-5

Wright, R. A., & Franklin, J. (2004). Ability perception determinants of effort-related cardiovascular response: Mood, optimism, and performance resources. In R. A. Wright, J. Greenberg, & S. S. Brehm (Eds.), *Motivational analyses of social behavior: Building on Jack Brehm's contributions to psychology* (pp. 187–204). Erlbaum.

Wright, R. A., Mlynski, C., & Carbajal, I. (2019). Outsiders' thoughts on generating self-regulatory-depletion (fatigue) effects in limited-resource experiments. *Perspectives on Psychological Science, 14*, 469–480. https://doi.org/ 10.1177/174569161881565

Wright. R. A., & Pantaleo, G. (2013). Effort processes in achieving performance outcomes: Interrelations among and roles of core constructs. *Behavioral and Brain Sciences, 36*, 661–726. https://doi.org/10.1017/S0140525X13001180

Wright, R. A., Toi, M., & Brehm, J. W. (1985). Difficulty and interpersonal attraction. *Motivation and Emotion, 8*, 327–341. https://doi.org/10.1007/BF00991871

CHAPTER

23 Mate Poaching, Infidelity, and Mate Switching

Joshua Everett Ryan *and* Edward P. Lemay, Jr.

Abstract

Most humans today practice social monogamy, characterized by exclusive, long-term attachments with a single other individual with whom they share emotional and sexual intimacy. However, people are prone to stray from these bonds. We review research on infidelity, mate poaching, and mate-switching behaviors. Infidelity entails the intimate (i.e., sexual, emotional, or both) involvement of one individual with another while in an exclusive relationship. Mate poaching entails attempts to seduce an individual who is already mated to another with the intention to usurp their partner, and mate switching consists of dissolving one relationship to form a new relationship with another. We review theory and empirical findings related to these phenomena, with a focus on evolved psychological mechanisms that explain why and how people engage in these behaviors, and what consequences they have. This research suggests that infidelity, mate poaching, and mate switching are influenced by sex differences in desire for emotional investment and in sexual frequency and variety, and by individual differences in preferences for novel experiences, antisocial tendencies, sexual permissiveness, and attachment orientation. It also suggests that relationship attributes, including relationship satisfaction, and situational factors, including quality of alternatives and opportunity, relate to why and how people pursue extradyadic partners, poach, and switch mates. We describe the evolutionary significance of these mechanisms, assess the extent to which research findings relate to these mechanisms, and discuss future research directions to increase our understanding of why and how these behaviors have been selected for over human evolutionary history.

Key Words: infidelity, mate poaching, mate switching, evolved psychological mechanisms, monogoamy, sex differences, attachment, sociosexual orientation

Most humans today practice social monogamy, characterized by exclusive, long-term attachments with a single other individual with whom they share emotional and sexual intimacy (Schact & Kramer, 2019). The value ascribed to monogamy is evidenced by the adoption of marriage in many cultures—a lifelong monogamous attachment characterized by promises of fidelity and commitment (e.g., "till death do us part"). However, although monogamy presents an elegant (if simple) portrait of a relationship between two people, real-life relationship contexts are often more complex. Romantic relationships do not occur within a vacuum but instead take place within larger social networks, allowing for outside agents to exert influence on these relationships. These influences may be explicit and direct or subtle and indirect. For instance, someone may actively try to seduce another away from their existing relationship until they are embroiled in a sexual or emotionally intimate affair—or until their presence tempts them to break the rules of monogamy or dissolve their existing relationship in favor of a mate switch.

This chapter explores the phenomena of infidelity, mate poaching, and mate switching. Infidelity entails the intimate (i.e., sexual, emotional, or both) involvement of someone in an exclusive relationship with a partner outside of that relationship. Mate poaching entails seducing an individual who is already paired with another with the intention to usurp their partner, and mate switching consists of dissolving one relationship to form a new relationship with another. Each of these behaviors requires at least three people: two involved in a romantic relationship and at least one outsider with whom a paired individual shares emotional or sexual intimacy. For each of these focal behaviors, we will discuss how and why these behaviors occur, including qualities of actors (i.e., the person enacting the behavior), qualities of existing romantic relationships, and other environmental factors that impact infidelity, mate poaching, and mate switching. We devote special attention to qualities that have appeared to evolve over time to influence these human mating behaviors. We also discuss the consequences of these behaviors—for the actor, for relationship partners, and for others, such as children, or the outsiders who have exerted influence on a relationship.

Infidelity

Most people have negative attitudes toward infidelity. Poll results from the Pew Research Center (2014) found that 84% of Americans disapprove of infidelity. Further, these negative attitudes have been found in several cultures (Widmer et al., 1998). However, infidelity is fairly common. Approximately 21% of married men and 10–15% of married women in the United States engage in infidelity, according to polls over the last 20 years by the nonpartisan research organization NORC at the University of Chicago (Smith et al., 1972–2018).

Thus, despite their negative attitudes toward infidelity, people nevertheless are sometimes unfaithful. Evolutionary perspectives offer some insight into this paradox. On the one hand, researchers have proposed arguments as to why and how monogamy has evolved in humans, outlining the benefits that long-term pair bonds offered, including more reliable access to copulation, protection from infanticide or rape from rival males, increased provision of security and resources to help family units, or reduced intersexual competition over mates and territories (Rooker & Gavrilets, 2021). People may have an evolved preference for monogamy and deep socioemotional attachments with particular individuals. On the other hand, individuals are also motivated to engage in strategies that ancestrally propagated genes, wherein men desire sexual frequency and variety and women desire emotional intimacy (Symons, 1979). Thus, people may be oriented toward establishing long-term bonds with specific partners to benefit from the arsenal of rewards such a monogamous system may offer, but may deviate from this path in certain ways (e.g., infidelity, stealing, or switching mates) if such strategies promise benefits.

Person-Level Predictors of Infidelity

In the following sections, we discuss several evolved psychological mechanisms of infidelity. Evolved psychological mechanisms are complex cognitive or affective mental processes that promote behaviors that ancestrally offered adaptive benefits (Davies et al., 2007). Below, we describe a number of evolved psychological mechanisms of infidelity, including the adaptive problems they may solve, how they relate to human infidelity, and recent empirical work that supports their significance.

SEX DIFFERENCES

Parental investment theory suggests that men and women have different minimum obligations toward offspring investment (Trivers, 1972), and these differences in investment yield different sexual strategies for men and women (Buss & Schmitt, 1993, 2019). For men, sex is a relatively low-risk venture due to low gamete cost (i.e., the production of sperm). Given that the benefits of gene propagation outweigh this relatively low cost, men desire to copulate frequently. Beyond frequency, men also value sexual diversity: procreating with multiple females diversifies their genetic lineage, allowing for a greater possibility that their sons or daughters' genes will enhance survival. Evidence of the "Coolidge effect" (i.e., the shortening of a male's refractory period when introduced to a novel sexual partner) in humans suggests that males evolved a preference for sexual variety (Ventura-Aquino et al., 2018). Thus, men should find the prospect of having sex frequently, and with a variety of partners, desirable. Further, this desire may serve as a powerful mechanism for infidelity in men: for men who are already partnered, an opportunity for sex with a novel partner might serve as a powerful motivator for some men to be unfaithful.

Sex requires more investment and risk from women. Women's gametes are costlier to produce, and internal fertilization and gestation make females more vulnerable during and after pregnancy (Trivers, 1972), increasing their dependence on others for the survival of infants and themselves. Given the nature of these investments and risks of sex, women have evolved discerning tastes when selecting mates. Specifically, women have evolved preferences for men with signifiers of good genes, because such genes will be conducive to an offspring's survival, and preferences for men who are emotionally invested in the relationship, as such men might be inclined to provide long-term protection and support to help rear young. Such benefits would improve women's life expectancies and infant survival rates relative to women who chose partners of poor quality, or partners who abandoned them. Thus, selection pressures may have favored women's preferences for good genes and emotional attachment, and such preferences may further serve as compelling motivators for infidelity. That is, women might be especially inclined to be unfaithful if an existing partner is of poor quality, if the partner is not a good means of emotional support, or if a male who offers more emotional fulfillment or higher gene quality becomes available (Buss, 2000).

A number of empirical findings support such sex differences. Mark et al. (2011) examined predictors of infidelity for men and women and found that sexual excitation was a stronger predictor of infidelity for men relative to women, while relationship satisfaction and relationship happiness were stronger predictors for women relative to men. Brand et al. (2007) found that, in a sample of 2,313 undergraduates and 233 community members in the United States, men engaged in more sexual intercourse with their affair partners than women, while relationship dissatisfaction and attraction to alternative partners were stronger motivators for infidelity for women relative to men. Martins et al. (2016) examined infidelity behaviors in both face-to-face and online contexts. They found that men were more likely to report physical and sexual infidelity in both face-to-face and online contexts relative to women. Barta and Kiene (2005) also examined motivations for infidelity for men and women and found that the motivation for sexual frequency and variety were more powerful motivators of infidelity for men relative to women, while relationship dissatisfaction and emotional attachment to affair partners were more powerful motivators for women relative to men. These findings further align with past work that demonstrates that men are more likely to initiate a sexual affair (Allen & Baucom, 2004; Atkins et al., 2001) than women, while the frequency and intensity of women's affairs are related to the degree of dissatisfaction that they experience with their primary relationship partner (Prins et al., 1993). These results suggest that men are likely to be unfaithful to acquire sex, while women are likely to be unfaithful in pursuit of emotional intimacy.

PERSONALITY TRAITS

Certain evolved personality characteristics may relate to human infidelity. Preferences for novelty may be such a characteristic. A number of findings from animal research show that exploratory behaviors are adaptive in some contexts (e.g., when resources are abundant or predators are few) but maladaptive in others (e.g., when resources are scarce or predators are many; Dingemanse et al., 2004; Dugatkin, 1992; O'Steen et al., 2002). Such preferences for novel experiences are also assumed to be adaptive in humans, such that people who continuously seek novelty may reap rewards from their environment that are untapped by their less adventurous peers, and such rewards may include sexual benefits (Zuckerman, 1994), such as liaisons with novel and rewarding sexual partners. Research suggests that many people indeed have an ingrained attraction to novel sex partners, as evidenced by the Coolidge effect (Ventura-Aquino et al., 2018), as well as additional research which suggests that familiarity tends to decrease sexual arousal, while the novelty of a sexual partner tends to increase both desire and arousal (see Morton & Gorzalka,

2015, for a review). Further, people who strongly desire novel stimulation may become easily bored in long-term relationships and may be unfaithful to recapture the excitement of a new relationship or novel experience. Empirical work suggests that such tendencies are indeed associated with infidelity. People higher in extroversion or openness to new experiences (Altgelt et al., 2018; Orzeck & Lung, 2005; Yeniceri & Kökdemir, 2006), or those who are higher in sensation seeking (Lalasz & Weigel, 2011) are more likely to be unfaithful. People who have poor impulse control (i.e., low self-regulation) may also enact more infidelity, as evidenced by findings from Brady et al. (2020), that when attractive outsiders were available, people with poor self-regulation were more unfaithful relative to those with greater self-regulation.

Antisocial tendencies may also shape sexuality. While such tendencies are presumed to be maladaptive because they are counterproductive for cooperation (Tomasello & Vaish, 2013), antisocial qualities have nevertheless persisted over time. One explanation for this persistence is that personality traits are the result of mutations across thousands of genes that underlie human behavior (Buss, 2006). Further, these genes are passed along to descendants because selection pressures are ineffective at weeding out characteristics that result from the mutations of many genes rather than the mutation of a single gene. Thus, meanness and selfishness are hard to eradicate. Alternatively, these qualities could be adaptive. Just as drivers who use illegal traffic lanes to bypass other cars might arrive at their destinations sooner, people willing to use unsavory means such as lying, exploiting, stealing, or injuring others might be successful in advancing their goals, thus securing benefits from these behaviors. Among such benefits may be the procurement of sexual partners considered unattainable to many lovers due to their commitments to existing long-term partners. Antisocial people may be less hesitant to engage in infidelity due to their selfishness and/or apathy about how their actions affect others. Empirical findings suggest that antisocial people (e.g., those low in agreeableness) (Miller et al., 2003) are more likely to be unfaithful to their partners (Shackelford et al., 2008)—an effect that has been found across many world regions (Schmitt, 2004). Other antisocial tendencies captured in the "dark triad" traits (i.e., narcissism, psychopathy, and Machiavellianism; Paulhus & Williams, 2002) have been positively linked with infidelity (Jones & Weiser, 2014). Brewer et al. (2015) found that among women, dark triad traits predicted both past infidelity and intentions to be unfaithful, whereas Brewer et al. (2020) found that women high in these traits are more likely to acknowledge alternative partners—a potential mechanism explaining infidelity risk—relative to women lower on these qualities. Thus, women who lack empathy and emotional warmth or are manipulative exhibit more interest in suitors and become involved in affairs at greater rates relative to other women. Altogether, these findings suggest that both antisocial people and those who desire novelty and excitement are prone to infidelity.

SEXUAL PERMISSIVENESS

Permissiveness reflects one's willingness to engage in sexual activity and serves as a powerful mechanism within sexual selection. This trait is adaptive, affording individuals the motivation to copulate and propagate genes. However, issues can arise if permissiveness is too low (i.e., too few copulations) or too high (i.e., unplanned pregnancy or transmission of sexually transmitted illnesses). High sexual permissiveness is associated with risky forms of health and sexual behaviors (Corbin et al., 2016), and thus, people who are more sexually permissive may be more inclined to be unfaithful. Unrestricted sociosexuality (i.e., greater willingness to engage in sexual activity outside a committed relationship context) is a powerful predictor of infidelity (Barta & Kiene, 2005; Rodrigues et al., 2017). Jackman (2015) examined the infidelity intentions of 512 users of social media outlets, including Twitter and Facebook. She examined a number of predictors that serve as proxies for sexual permissiveness, including favorable attitudes toward infidelity, beliefs that one could effectively seduce alternative partners if one tried (i.e., self-efficacy), existence of a social support network that would support one's infidelity, and past infidelity experiences. Each predicted intentions to be unfaithful to their partner. Conversely, religiosity was associated with reduced intentions to be unfaithful, presumably due to the link between many practiced religions and monogamy. Other research suggests that people who attend religious services (and thus, may be less sexually permissive) were less likely to engage in sexual infidelity (Amato & Rogers, 1997), while less religious people were more likely to be unfaithful (Whisman et al., 2007).

ATTACHMENT ORIENTATION

In proposing attachment theory, Bowlby (1969) suggested that infants form a socioemotional attachment with caregivers. Further, this attachment is adaptive. For instance, infants in need who signal for attention (e.g., cry) enhance their safety and security by soliciting a caregiver's investment. Infants who do not signal their needs risk neglect. According to attachment theory, people construct mental representations of the self and others based on prior experiences, which reflect the extent to which others can be relied on to protect and support the self, as well as whether the self is worthy of love and care from others. Variations in these mental representations produce differential patterns of behaviors, each of which is adaptive in the context of one's prior experiences: secure people have positive experiences with caregivers, facilitating trust and beliefs that one is worthy of love and care, and that others will provide it, whereas insecure people respond to unpredictable or uncaring caregivers by signaling for attention and affection (e.g., anxious attachment) or championing self-sufficiency and withdrawal from intimacy (e.g., avoidant attachment) (Cassidy & Shaver, 2016). Features of attachment persist through adulthood and influence people's experiences in adult relationships (Hazan & Shaver, 1987), though attachment may also be shaped through experience (Doyle & Cicchetti, 2017; Jones et al., 2018). Attachment insecurities influence sexual behaviors as well (Cassidy & Shaver,

2016; Cooper et al., 2006), and people insecure in their attachments to others may engage in infidelity more, though the motivations and behaviors may differ based on the type of insecure attachment people exhibit (i.e., whether they are avoidant or anxiously attached).

Avoidant people fear intimacy with others and prioritize autonomy and self-reliance. Consequently, they tend to be low on relationship commitment (Birnie et al., 2009), and may also be prone to infidelity. Empirical findings support such assertions. DeWall et al. (2011) found that, across eight studies with data from more than 2,500 participants, paired people with an avoidant attachment style exhibited greater interest and attraction for alternative partners, less relationship commitment, and more permissive attitudes for, and enactment of, infidelity over time. Allen and Baucom (2004) explored associations between attachment orientation and infidelity in a sample of 504 undergraduate students and 251 community participants in the United States. They found that dismissive-avoidant people (i.e., those uncomfortable with intimacy) reported engaging in infidelity for autonomy reasons (i.e., due to wanting space and freedom from their primary partner) at greater rates relative to secure and anxious people, consistent with their general desire for independence. They also found that dismissive men had more affairs than all other categories of men and women of varying attachment styles. This finding might be explained by simultaneous forces of both avoidant tendencies to devalue commitment and intimacy, and men's desire for sexual frequency and variety, motivating individuals to be more unfaithful relative to others.

Anxiously attached people crave intimacy and affection but fear rejection from others. Therefore, anxiously attached people might be unfaithful because they worry a partner will reject or leave them, and they seek to secure a "backup" partner, or because they believe an affair will grant them the love and affection they crave but don't experience in an existing relationship. Davis et al. (2004) found that anxiously attached people used sex as a means of facilitating a connection with others, or to feel safe and loved. Thus, they might be unfaithful to achieve these same goals. Indeed, Allen and Baucom (2004) found that anxious-preoccupied and fearful-avoidant people were more likely to report a need for intimacy or self-esteem as motivations for their infidelity relative to secure or dismissive-avoidant people.

Sex differences in the association between anxious attachment and infidelity are noteworthy. Bogaert and Sadava (2002) found that, in a sample of 792 Canadian adults, more anxiously attached people viewed themselves as less physically attractive, had sex at an earlier age, and engaged in more infidelity relative to more securely attached people. However, these effects were stronger for women. Further, anxious men engaged in less infidelity, whereas anxious women engaged in more infidelity, relative to secure adults (Allen & Baucom, 2004). One explanation for this discrepancy may be that both anxiously attached men and women desire sex to feel loved, but anxious women are propositioned for sex more than men. According to traditional sexual scripts, women are the "gatekeepers" of sex, and men often must initiate courtship (Jozkowski & Peterson, 2013;

LaPlante et al., 1980). However, anxious men may fear rejection from extradyadic partners in ways that mirror their fear of rejection from current partners. Thus, they may not pursue sex out of fear. By contrast, anxious women may be the recipients of overtures by extradyadic partners and may conflate sex and love (Birnbaum, 2007; Birnbaum et al., 2006), opting to pursue sex with their suitors to achieve the feelings of affection and love that they crave from others.

Attachment style also appears to have implications for the types of affairs people have. Allen and Baucom (2004) found that people with anxious attachment styles (i.e., fears of abandonment and rejection) were more likely to exhibit obsessive neediness and greater desires for attention and reassurance from affair partners relative to secure or dismissive people. Fearful-avoidant people were also more likely to have extradyadic relationships characterized by a desire for closeness yet fears of rejection when partners were intimate and open with them. Given that such insecurities are characterized by an intense desire for affection coupled with fear of rejection, it is unsurprising that these insecure people would desire affirmation from partners yet feel apprehensive when partners are open with them—as they may anticipate rejection lurking around the corner. Altogether, these results suggest that attachment orientation has diverse effects on infidelity—including on frequency of, and motivation for, infidelity and the type of affair that results.

Relationship-Level Predictors of Infidelity

Certain facets of an existing relationship may also contribute to infidelity. Specifically, people who feel dissatisfied with a primary relationship may be more inclined to be unfaithful. Buss and Shackelford (1997) found that people dissatisfied with their marriages anticipated that they might engage in infidelity in the future—and that their spouses would do the same. Lewandowski and Ackerman (2006) examined the role of self-expansion (i.e., the incorporation of others' identities, perspectives, and resources into one's own self-concept, thereby expanding the margins of one's own identity) and self-reported infidelity intentions. They found that when romantic relationships did not fulfill people's needs (e.g., for intimacy, companionship, sex, security, or emotional involvement) or did not provide ample opportunities for self-expansion (e.g., relationships which stagnate and lack growth or become devoid of novel stimulation), their susceptibility to infidelity increased. Further, relationship dissatisfaction also appears to be correlated with the number of extradyadic partners one has (Wiggins & Lederer, 1984) and one's emotional and sexual involvement with extradyadic partners (Allen & Baucom, 2004).

The quality of sexual relations also appears to be a significant factor in predicting infidelity. For instance, Scott et al. (2017) examined aspects of a sexual relationship (e.g., sexual satisfaction, sex frequency, comfort in communicating about sex, and sexual closeness) of unmarried, opposite-sex dyads over time. They found that people who engaged in infidelity tended to experience declines in sexual-relational adjustment leading up to their infidelity, while people who were faithful experienced relatively stable sexual-relational adjustment. Other research suggests that within a relationship, people may engage in retaliatory infidelity. That is, when one person within a dyad has been unfaithful, their partners initiate an affair in order to "get back" at their partner (Greiling & Buss, 2000). Indeed, Warach et al. (2018) found that sexual betrayal was the single best predictor of sexual infidelity of the personality dimensions they examined.

A number of proxies for relationship fulfillment are associated with increased infidelity as well, including lack of emotional support (Allen et al., 2005) or love and commitment (Selterman et al., 2019), or poor communication and frequency of negative interactions with partners (Allen et al., 2008). Previti and Amato (2004) conducted a 17-year study with 1,475 married participants to examine the nature of the relationship between divorce and infidelity, and found that low relationship quality predicted infidelity, but infidelity subsequently predicted reduced marital happiness and increased likelihood of divorce, suggesting that infidelity is both a cause and consequence of relationship deterioration.

Research also suggests gender differences in the association between relationship satisfaction and infidelity. For instance, some research suggests that relationship satisfaction is a more powerful predictor of infidelity for women relative to men (Prins et al., 1993), and that women are more likely than men to report feeling neglect or rejection, or a desire for closeness, as reasons for infidelity (Allen & Baucom, 2004). Conversely, men's sexual dissatisfaction in a relationship has been found to correlate with participation in short-term affairs (Buss & Shackelford, 1997). These findings together are consistent with the notion that women who are dissatisfied with their existing relationships engage in infidelity because they wish to establish a powerful emotional connection with another partner, such that they might "trade up" to a partner who will be more gratifying to them (Buss, 2000). Men, by contrast, are more motivated to be unfaithful due to sexual dissatisfaction.

Situational Predictors of Infidelity

Contextual factors that determine opportunities for desirable affairs may also influence infidelity. For instance, people may be inclined to be unfaithful when high-quality alternative partners are available. The quality of these alternatives is reflected by the rewards that such extradyadic partners may offer. People are motivated to secure high-quality mates when possible, such that their offspring (and the self) may benefit from the reward of securing a better mate. Thus, people who believe they have high-quality alternatives to their current partner(s) may be motivated to pursue them to reap the rewards of a new partnership. If instead only equally or lower-quality mates are available relative to one's current partner, individuals may refrain from infidelity. Empirical work supports this. Emmers-Sommer et al. (2010) found that, among 220 students in the United States, men and women were more likely to be unfaithful when they had higher-quality alternative partners, while Martins et al. (2016) examined infidelity in both face-to-face and online settings. They found that the quality of alternatives was generally associated with greater infidelity, though alternative quality predicted emotional infidelity for women more than men, consistent with theorizing that women enact affairs to establish deep emotional bonds with partners. Further, self-regulation may also moderate the effects of the quality of alternative partners on infidelity, such that people with more self-control may not be as prone to infidelity as those with low self-control (Brady et al., 2020). Self-control, in part, reflects people's ability to resist situational temptations, which could include available and attractive alternative partners. Other factors may also attenuate people's risk of infidelity. McNulty et al. (2018) found that some people are predisposed to attentional and evaluative biases, such that they divert attention from, or devalue the quality of, extradyadic partners, thereby decreasing their temptation to pursue attractive outsiders and, consequently, their likelihood of committing infidelity.

Other factors beyond quality of alternatives may also determine the opportunity for infidelity. For instance, people who work outside their home report higher rates of infidelity relative to people who work at home (Atkins et al., 2001). Certain job characteristics serve as opportunities for infidelity—such as physical contact with clients, working alone with coworkers, or personal conversations with colleagues or clients—thereby increasing the risk of infidelity (Treas & Giesen, 2000). Further, Wiggins and Lederer (1984) found that men and women who had an affair with a coworker had higher relationship satisfaction with their primary partners relative to people who sought out affair partners through other means. These results suggest that working alongside others presents opportunity for infidelity that tempts individuals despite happiness with their primary relationship. Conversely, people who have affairs with noncoworkers may exert more effort to find extradyadic partners, and such effort is motivated by deep dissatisfaction with primary relationships.

Importantly, sociotechnological advancements, such as social media and dating websites and applications, suggest that opportunity for infidelity is on the rise. For instance, Weisser et al. (2018) found that many people know at least one friend who used the dating app Tinder for the purposes of infidelity, while some websites have been designed specifically for the purpose of facilitating infidelity. Such is the case with "Ashley Madison," a dating site designed to allow paired people to initiate discreet extradyadic relationships (Wysocki & Childers, 2011). Altogether, these findings suggest that the opportunity and quality of alternatives are important facets of why and how people are unfaithful, and access to opportunities and alternatives may be on the rise with technological advancements.

Consequences of Infidelity

Research suggests that infidelity has a number of important consequences—both to the people within the primary relationship (i.e., the unfaithful individual and their regular partner) as well as others—including the paramour, offspring, and beyond.

CONSEQUENCES FOR UNFAITHFUL INDIVIDUALS

The actor (i.e., the person who engages in infidelity) may experience a number of personal consequences. Some of these consequences may be positive, including sexual excitement and variety, and the possible fulfillment of an emotional bond with a new partner—consistent with theorizing as to why men and women may engage in infidelity in the first place. Other consequences may be negative, including the experience of guilt or remorse for having betrayed the trust of a close relationship partner—a mechanism that may have evolved to facilitate cooperation and monogamous attachments by deterring future betrayals of close others. Fisher et al. (2008) examined sex differences in feelings of guilt due to imagined infidelity. They found that men felt guiltier after imagining sexual infidelity while women felt guiltier after imagining emotional infidelity, though both men and women believed partners would be less forgiving of sexual, relative to emotional, infidelity. Similarly, research also suggests that there are sex differences in the disclosure and concealment of infidelity. Hughes and Harrison (2019) found that women were likely to disclose their relationship status to affair partners while men were likely to conceal this status. One explanation for this difference is that women may disclose their relationship status to male paramours because it appeals to men's desire for short-term mating. By contrast, men may conceal their relationship commitments from mistresses to avoid advertising their other commitments, as these may suggest that they are unable to provide the emotional or material support their mistress might desire.

People who are unfaithful also risk retaliation. For instance, actual or perceived infidelity is a precipitating factor for intimate partner violence (Daly & Wilson, 1998), and people who suspect or discover a partner's infidelity may respond with psychological (Buss & Duntley, 2006) or sexual (Goetz & Shackelford, 2006) aggression. Further, Brewer et al. (2015) found that women high in dark triad traits were both more vulnerable to a partner's infidelity but also more likely to enact revenge on these partners in response to that infidelity, suggesting that the risk of aggression to adulterers is relatively high. Beyond partners, it is also possible that the actor's extradyadic partner could act aggressively toward an actor. For instance, if actors do not disclose their relationship status, or if they use other forms of obfuscation of their intent, such as promising to leave spouses that they have no intention of abandoning, extradyadic partners could become aggressive as well, such as by threatening blackmail, telling one's primary partner about the affair, or enacting other means of revenge.

IMPACT ON PARTNERS

An actor's infidelity also puts a partner in jeopardy in a variety of ways. Individuals whose partner has been unfaithful often experience sexual or romantic jealousy—an emotion presumed to have evolved to solve adaptive problems in mating, including warding off mate poachers and retaining mates (Buss, 2013). A partner's infidelity is threatening to both men and women, though some reasons may vary. For men, infidelity increases the risk of sperm competition and cuckoldry (i.e., the rearing of a child who does not carry his genes). For women, a man's infidelity may communicate risk that he will allocate resources to the "other woman," putting her fitness—and the fitness of offspring—in jeopardy. These coincide with sex differences in response to a partner's infidelity: men exhibit more distress over sexual infidelity, while women exhibit more distress over emotional infidelity (Shackelford et al., 2002). Infidelity also inflicts other deleterious effects on partners, including impaired self-esteem (Goldenberg et al., 2003) and increased risk of depression and anxiety (Cano & O'Leary, 2000). As with higher rates of sexual activity in general, sexual infidelity also confers greater risk of partners contracting a sexually transmitted illness via their unfaithful partner (Conley et al., 2012). Partners of unfaithful individuals are also sometimes at risk for violence, even murder—as unfaithful individuals or their lovers seek to harm partners to eliminate competition so that they can be together in a more formalized relationship (Wells, 2003).

Research also suggests that some of the evolved psychological mechanisms that influence infidelity also influence the way that they experience their partner's infidelity. For instance, Miller and Maner (2008) examined people's responses to imagined partner infidelity and found evidence of sex differences. Men were prone to anger and desired violence—particularly against mate poachers—while women were prone to seek social and emotional support from others. Further, Treger and Sprecher (2011) conducted a longitudinal study evaluating data regarding reactions to infidelity from 3,879 college students across 14 years. They found that sexual permissiveness was associated with greater distress in response to a partner's sexual infidelity, a finding suggesting that permissiveness may have a contradictory nature in that it makes people more prone to infidelity themselves but increases distress when a partner is unfaithful. Further, attachment orientation also impacted the type of infidelity that was most distressing to men and women: anxious-preoccupied men reported emotional infidelity as more distressing relative to other men, perhaps due to fears that a partner lacks affection or commitment, while avoidant women reported sexual infidelity more distressing relative to other women, perhaps because avoidant women value their own sexual allure as an indicator of self-reliance and independence. These results suggest that beyond motivating people's enactment of infidelity, sex differences, sexual permissiveness, and attachment orientation also inform the way people respond to a partner's infidelity.

Another important consequence of infidelity is relationship dissolution. Infidelity is a leading cause of divorce worldwide (Betzig, 1989), and thus, relationships where one partner is unfaithful often fail, perhaps because infidelity is experienced as a betrayal of trust that is difficult to forgive. Forgiveness appears to play an integral link in the relationship between infidelity and breakup or divorce. Hall and Fincham (2006) found that forgiveness was a powerful predictor of whether people stayed in relationships or not after infidelity. In fact, when partners were unable to forgive actors for infidelity, relationships were more likely to dissolve.

IMPACTING CHILDREN

Relationship infidelity may impact children as well. Platt et al. (2008) examined the associations between parental infidelity and adult children's attachment and behaviors. They found that adult children who knew of their father's infidelity were more likely to engage in infidelity themselves relative to adult children with no knowledge of father infidelity. One explanation for these results is that children may inherit a genetic predisposition for infidelity. A second explanation is that, to some extent, infidelity may produce intergenerational effects that lead children to enact some of the same destructive behaviors that their parents have modeled for them, yielding consequences for them, and their own partners, further down the line.

Summary

Infidelity confers advantages, such as the opportunity for sexual frequency and variety, better genes for offspring, or the grooming of a new long-term partner. Certain people seem more inclined to be unfaithful than others: antisocial people and people who prefer new experiences, those who are sexually permissive, those with attachment insecurities, and people who are unsatisfied in their existing relationships are all inclined toward infidelity more than people without such qualities. Importantly, the associations of these traits with infidelity may be explained by different motivations. For instance, men, people who prefer novelty, or those who are sexually permissive may desire sexual frequency and variety, and infidelity may serve as a means to advancing such a goal. Avoidant or antisocial people, or people who are dissatisfied in an existing relationship, may pursue infidelity because they devalue an existing relationship, while women or people who are anxiously attached may pursue infidelity as a means of feeling valuable and worthy of affection from others. Beyond these individual differences, situational factors also influence infidelity: people are more prone to infidelity when there is increased opportunity or higher-quality partners for affairs. However, infidelity confers negative consequences, too, including guilt (for the unfaithful partner) and distress, reduced self-esteem, and depression (for the individual whose partner is unfaithful). Infidelity prompts other risks for partners, including sperm competition for men, risk of abandonment, and the contraction of sexually transmitted illnesses. Aggression and violence are also possible, toward unfaithful actors (for betraying partners) or partners (to eliminate competition with extradyadic partners). Infidelity is also a powerful predictor of relationship dissolution, though partner's forgiveness may be an important protective factor against breakup and divorce. Such an array of findings suggest that infidelity has far-reaching implications that ripple out to one's close social network, resulting in consequences not just for the unfaithful partner but for their relationship partners and offspring as well (Platt et al., 2008).

Mate Poaching

Mate poaching occurs when an individual attempts to seduce someone who is already paired with a partner. Mate poaching attempts appear relatively common, as 50% of a college and community sample report attempting to poach someone else, while 80% reported someone else's attempt to poach them from an existing relationship (Schmitt & Buss, 2001). Further, mate poaching has been reported in many cultures (Schmitt & International Sexuality Description Project, 2004), and attempts are relatively successful: Schmitt and Buss (2001), in their examination of mate-poaching behaviors, found that the success rate across men and women was more than 35%. Of note, prevalence rates vary depending upon which definitions researchers use to measure mate poaching—such as whether poachers must be aware that their target of affection is in a relationship or not for it to be described as "poaching" (Davies et al., 2019).

Evolutionary perspectives offer suggestions as to why mate poaching may be adaptive. In monogamous mating systems, individuals pair off and establish long-term, exclusive attachments. Importantly, as people pair off, some individuals may remain alone with no desirable means of copulation other than pursuing individuals who are already partnered. Thus, seducing mates from existing partners may serve as a viable strategy to secure a mate. Paired people may also attempt to poach for reasons similar to those underlying infidelity, described in the previous section of this chapter (e.g., sexual frequency and variety, better genes for offspring, or the opportunity to "trade up" to a higher quality long-term partner).

Who Poaches, and Who Is Poached?

Certain qualities may make people more inclined to mate poach than others. Poaching shares conceptual overlap with infidelity (and mate switching), such that paired people who attempt to poach other paired people from relationships are, in essence, practicing infidelity, while unpaired people who attempt poaching a paired partner seek to entice this target to be unfaithful or to switch mates. Given such conceptual similarities, mate poaching may share many of the same antecedents to and consequences of these other behaviors. To avoid redundancy, we focus our attention on distinct empirical findings related to the decision to poach partnered individuals and to the susceptibility of being poached.

SEX DIFFERENCES

Sexual strategies theory suggests that men are more motivated to engage in multiple matings relative to women, as they may procure many more offspring through this strategy relative to women (Buss & Schmitt, 1993, 2019). Thus, men may enact more mate-poaching attempts than do women. Empirical findings support this assertion. Schmitt and the International Sexuality Description Project (2004) examined mate-poaching behaviors of nearly 17,000 participants in 53 nations and found that men were indeed more likely than women to both enact, and to succumb to, mate-poaching attempts.

Some research has also found differences in the motivations that men and women have for poaching. For instance, Davies et al. (2010) explored the costs and benefits that men and women consider when deciding whether to poach. They found that men seemed to view some benefits of poaching that women did not endorse, while women saw costs to poaching that men did not endorse. For instance, men identified the feeling of accomplishment of attracting someone away from an existing partner, and the ego boost associated with it, as a benefit of mate poaching that predicted their intentions to poach—whereas women did not strongly value such benefits. Importantly, these benefits were influential in only short-term contexts and not predictive for poaching partners for a long-term relationship. On the other hand, women found certain costs, including suffering shame and injured reputation, or risk of physical harm from a partner of the poached, as costs of poaching that deterred them—costs that did not persuade men.

PERSONALITY TRAITS

Most people appear to view poaching unfavorably and as a costly means to an end (Davies et al., 2010). However, certain personality traits may be more strongly associated with poaching than others. For instance, antisocial people may be inclined to poach—or to be poached—to pursue self-interest, and because they are unconcerned about social norms or harming established relationships. Indeed, Schmitt and Buss (2001) examined the personality characteristics of both poachers and their targets and found that both the people who were likely to attempt to poach a mate, and the people who were most likely to be poached, self-reported as disagreeable and unconscientious. Further, "dark triad" traits are also positively associated with mate poaching (Jonason et al., 2010; Kardum et al., 2015). Other research also suggests that antisocial and impulsive tendencies are associated with more mate poaching. Mitchell et al. (2019) found that more antagonistic and emotionally detached people were more likely to have poached relationships, and that male poachers who had physical relations with a paired partner and female poachers who were in poached relationships each exhibited more ethical risk-taking relative to their nonpoacher counterparts.

Such antisocial tendencies may actually offer some adaptive advantage, whereby willingness to poach mates affords antisocial people copulations from a pool of possible mates that other individuals dare not dive into due to monogamous norms or ethical concerns about poaching. Of note, although antisocial people were most susceptible to poaching attempts, they are not the most frequent targets of these attempts. Instead, highly extroverted, open, attractive, and loving people are the most sought-after targets of poaching (Schmitt & Buss, 2001), consistent with people's general tendencies to find these qualities attractive (Fletcher et al., 1999). Further, although they attempt poaching frequently, antisocial people are also not the most successful poachers. That recognition goes to people who are self-described as open to new experiences, sexually attractive, and sexually unrestrained.

ATTACHMENT ORIENTATION

Attachment insecurities may relate to poaching behaviors. Avoidant people might poach because they devalue intimacy and do not mind disrupting existing relationships. However, avoidant people are generally wary of long-term commitments and thus may only enact poaching in short-term relationship contexts. Empirical findings offer some support for this notion. Schmitt and Jonason (2015) investigated the associations between attachment and mate poaching for 17,837 participants across 10 world regions and found that dismissive-avoidant men were marginally more likely to attempt to poach an individual for a short-term relationship relative to anxious-preoccupied men. Further, Schachner and Shaver (2002) found that highly avoidant people were both more likely to attempt mate poaching and to be more susceptible to another's mate-poach attempts for short-term relationships but not for long-term contexts.

Attachment insecurity also appears to inform people's concerns about a partner's susceptibility to mate poaching. Specifically, anxiously attached people tend to believe that their partners could be poached for long-term relationships, and that these partners have succumbed to poaching attempts in the past (Shachner & Shaver, 2002). These results may be explained by the fact that relationships with anxious people are emotionally challenging due to difficulties navigating their anxieties, or the fact that anxiety involves a fear of abandonment.

SITUATIONAL PREDICTORS

People may be inclined to attempt mate poaching if they believe that there is an opportunity. For instance, if a paired individual expresses dissatisfaction with their existing relationship partner, would-be poachers might do well to derogate this partner, thereby increasing this suitor's susceptibility to an affair. Poachers may also see opportunity in the form of misalignment between the attractiveness of an existing couple. For instance, Moran and Wade (2019) found that men tend to attempt to poach women when they appear to be more attractive than their existing partners, perhaps because her commitments to a comparatively less attractive partner mean her standards are low or that she might be easy prey for seduction.

People generally see mate poaching as costly (Davies et al., 2010), and thus, people may only resort to poaching, or to being poached, if the rewards it offers are quite high. Davies and Shackelford (2015) had 215 people imagine they were single, in a dating, cohabitating, or married relationship, and asked them how attractive and wealthy (i.e., proxies for mate value) a mate would need to be to seduce them. They found that people reported that suitors would need to be considerably higher in mate value if they were in an existing relationship, relative to if they were single. As commitment increased, so too did the attractiveness and wealth that was necessary to seduce them. Together, these results suggest that both opportunity and quality of alternative partners are significant factors in mate poaching.

Strategies for Mate Poaching and Their Effectiveness

People may utilize various strategies in order to attract a mate who is already committed to another. Schmitt and Buss (2001) examined the tactics people employed in mate poaching, and offered three categories of strategies. One such category reflects self-enhancement tactics, whereby individuals attempt to embody the desires of potential mates. Past work has demonstrated that men desire signals of a woman's reproductive value, such as her youth and physical attractiveness, while women desire signals of a man's status and resources, such as his material wealth, masculinity, investment, and dominant personality (Buss & Schmitt, 2019; Li et al., 2002; Walter et al., 2020). Thus, women should be motivated to advertise youth, beauty, and sexual access, while men should be motivated to advertise masculinity, dominance, resource wealth, and emotional investment, as each of these qualities should enhance their appeal to prospective mates. Importantly, mate preferences vary in accordance with the desired mating context (i.e., whether a short or long term relationship is desired) (Buss & Schmitt, 2019). Thus, men and women's advertisements might depend upon the desired relationship context. For instance, men and women who desire only short-term "flings" may advertise masculinity or ease of sexual access, respectively, given the other sex's preferences for these qualities in short-term affairs. A second category of poaching tactics includes competitor derogation tactics, whereby poachers vie for affections from paired targets by denigrating their target's partner, such as by questioning a partner's commitment, implying that a partner is unfaithful, or otherwise deriding the value of the target's partner. Schmitt and Buss (2001) found that such tactics are indeed useful in poaching. Men were evaluated as better poachers by women when they were seen as both willing and able to provide resources for her, when they exhibited dominance, or when they manipulated the emotional commitment of male rivals (i.e., convinced rivals to invest less in their relationship). Alternatively, women were evaluated as better poachers by men if they enhanced their physical appearance, stroked the man's ego (i.e., through flattery), or provided easy access to sex, though this strategy was effective primarily for short-term relationship contexts.

A third category of mate-poaching strategies captures insinuation tactics, which include presenting the self as a friend to both a target and their partner in efforts to earn trust, allay suspicion of one's true intentions, and thus poach more effectively from within the target's social network. Mogilski and Wade (2013) examined the role of friendship in mate-poaching behaviors. They assessed the success and costs of imagined mate-poaching scenarios, where the poacher in the scenario was either an acquaintance or a friend to the target. They found that friendship increased the perceived probability of successful poaching and mitigation of risks, but at the cost of more punitive judgments by evaluators on their interpersonal warmth. That is, acting as one's friend in order to steal a mate appears to be viewed by others as an effective, though dubious, strategy, perhaps because it violates social norms of communal motivations and supportiveness within close relationships, such as friendships (Clark & Lemay, 2010; Mills et al., 2004).

Lemay and Wolf (2016) examined the mate poaching behaviors of 47 pairs of opposite-sex friends across a five-week period utilizing a dyadic, longitudinal design. They found that when people used the mate-poaching tactics described above on their friends, they were effective in reducing their friend's commitments to their romantic partners and increased their friend's perceptions of the actor's mate value and their romantic attraction to these actors over time. That is, people who employed self-enhancement, competitor derogation, and insinuation tactics within an opposite-sex friendship lowered their target's commitment to existing partners and garnered romantic attraction from these friends over time. Such findings suggest that these psychologically sophisticated tactics are indeed adaptive in that they provide advantages within the context of sexual selection, allowing individuals to poach high-quality mates from others, and affording them the associated benefits.

Other research has looked at "mate-poaching enticement," which are acts designed to get others to attempt to poach them from existing relationships, indicating high susceptibility to poaching. Schmitt and Shackelford (2003) outlined a number of such tactics to entice a poacher's attempts, and these include an array of behaviors similar to poaching tactics described earlier, such as enhancing one's mate quality (e.g., appearance and resources), facilitating an emotional connection, ingratiating oneself with another by being friendly or generous, or arranging easy sexual access. They found that women offering sexual access and physical beauty and men advertising dominance and resources were perceived as more effective for enticing poachers. They also found that certain strategies, such as inviting the meddling of a poacher in one's relationship affairs, or mentioning that a partner constantly derogates the self, are perceived as more effective. Men and women were also found to engage in certain strategies to disguise their enticement to avoid partners discovering their adulterous desires. For instance, men spend more money on and display emotional investment in existing partners, while women initiate more sex with existing partners and maintain their physical appearance in order to avoid suspicions regarding infidelity. Together, these results demonstrate sophisticated strategies people use to attempt poaching, or to entice poachers, that are indeed effective, or are perceived as effective, in eliciting attraction from others.

Consequences of Mate Poaching

Mate poaching may yield a number of consequences. Of course, one such consequence is rather obvious: as described in the preceding section, some mate-poaching attempts are indeed effective at poaching mates, garnering adaptive advantages for certain individuals. Arnocky et al. (2013) found that men and women who poach indeed had more lifetime sex, casual sex, and dating partners relative to people who did not poach, suggesting that poaching offers a pool of potential sexual partners that nonpoachers do not benefit from.

Mate poaching also affords a number of possible negative consequences. For instance, poaching attempts, if suspected or discovered, may incite sexual jealousy and anger from partners. Indeed, Miller and Maner (2008) found that men's response to a partner's infidelity often entailed anger and a desire for retribution toward mate poachers. Further, the finding by Davies et al. (2010) that women are dissuaded to mate poach due to fear of physical harm from the target's partners may evidence that violence in response to mate-poaching attempts are a phenomena that has evolved to retain mates by fending off the poacher's advances.

If poachers are able to seduce targets and form a relationship with them, there is also evidence that this union may be tumultuous. For instance, Foster et al. (2014) examined the qualities of relationships that form via mate poaching. They found that individuals who had been poached by existing partners tended to have poorer-quality relationships, including less satisfaction, commitment, and investment. Poached individuals also reported being more attentive to alternative partners, perceiving their alternatives to be of higher quality, and engaged in more infidelity relative to nonpoached individuals.

Summary

Mate poaching is adaptive (i.e., it allows individuals to mate with high-quality partners regardless of whether the self or the partner are already paired, or it allows unpaired individuals to copulate when prospects are few), yet people view it unfavorably and seem to generally avoid poaching. However, certain people are more inclined to poach than others. Men and antisocial people are more likely to poach or to be poached than women or prosocial people. Avoidant people are prone to poach and to be poached, but only for short-term affairs, while anxiously attached people fear losing their partners to poachers. People also poach when there is a strong opportunity, such as when a paired individual appears disaffected with an existing relationship, and tend to only poach if the paired individual seems particularly rewarding (e.g., high in mate value), perhaps to ensure poaching is worth the risks, which include threat of violence from partners and the possibility of low-quality relationships that form from poaching. When people have decided to poach, though, a number of strategies appear effective, including advertising desirable qualities, derogating a paired individual's existing relationship or partner, or inserting oneself into a target's social network to gain their trust and wreak havoc on their relationship from a privileged position. When people are unhappy in their relationships, rather than initiating an affair themselves, they may also enact similar strategies to entice would-be poachers to make a move and vie for their affections, and such seduction strategies are also effective in eliciting poaching efforts.

Mate Switching

Mate switching occurs when an individual dissolves a relationship with one partner to form a new bond with another. This should generally occur when the switcher believes they stand to gain from this transition. For example, if a once promising relationship now seems mired in misunderstandings, conflict, and other difficulties, one or more partners may wish to replace their partner with someone more gratifying. Mate switching may be prompted by relationship dissatisfaction or the introduction of a highly attractive alternative partner. Importantly, mate switching need not reflect a clean break from a partner. That is, people may not smoothly terminate one relationship, then form another. Indeed, switches could be decidedly messier. For instance, a would-be switcher might initiate an affair to better assess the rewards they would receive from an alternative partner and may only terminate the current relationship if the affair partner seems promising.

It is difficult to pinpoint how prevalent mate switching truly is, as both infidelity and relationship dissolution are difficult to study (e.g., due to social desirability or logistical concerns) and are often measured through self-report. However, there is indirect evidence of its incidence. For instance, South and Lloyd (1995) found that of approximately 855 divorced adults, between 14% of women and 17% of men had been romantically involved with another person prior to the finalization of a divorce with their spouse. Further, perceived quality of alternative partners has been found to be an important predictor of relationship dissolution for both married (South, 1995) and unmarried (Le et al., 2010) individuals, suggesting some individuals may terminate one relationship in favor of a switch to an alternative one. In this section, we discuss why and how people switch mates, and what consequences exist for mate switching. Importantly, mate switching is related to both infidelity and mate poaching: some switches may employ infidelity or poaching as a means by which to attract mates that people might then switch to. As such, some theorizing and empirical findings from these behaviors are relevant to mate switching as well, and will not be repeated. Instead, in this section, we focus attention on literature uniquely related to why and how people switch, and what impact it has on those involved.

Why Switch?

Buss et al. (2017) originally proposed a theory that explains why people might switch mates. We first examine their theory as to what motivates a switch, then discuss factors that may make individuals more prone to switch.

RELATIONSHIP LOAD

Relationship load refers to how costly a particular relationship is—but such costs may not always be apparent from the outset. Partners sometimes surprise us. These surprises can either be helpful or destructive, and some surprises may shift the calculus people employ to determine whether a relationship is worthwhile or not. Importantly, people often hide their flaws during courtship (Haselton et al., 2005), and thus, people may only learn some intimate details about partners over time and through experiences, and some of this information may be consequential to assessing a partner's true mate value. People tend to be dissatisfied when partners fail to meet their expectations (McNulty & Karney, 2004), and such dissatisfaction may motivate a mate switch.

EQUITY

People generally desire to obtain mates with maximum mate value. However, not everyone is capable of attracting such a high-value mate. Thus, people tend to pair up with individuals whose mate value reflects their own (Conroy-Beam, 2018; Conroy-Beam et al., 2019). However, mate value may fluctuate over time as people change, and with these fluctuations, discrepancies may arise. These mate value discrepancies could serve as powerful predictors of relationship quality (Sela et al., 2017). Sidelinger and Booth-Butterfield (2007) found that within a romantic relationship, people who believe their partners to be of higher mate value than themselves are both more forgiving of a partner's transgressions and more jealous of perceived threats to their relationship relative to people who did not perceive such a discrepancy. Further, Buss and Shackelford (1997) found that women who believed they were of lower mate value than their husbands also believed that their husbands were more prone to infidelity, which prompted these women to report a higher likelihood that they, themselves, would be unfaithful to their husbands. Further, as people's mate value increases, their standards increase as well (Buss & Shackelford, 2008), and when partners fail to meet one's expectations for mate value, they are likely to experience relationship dissatisfaction, which further predicts engagement in infidelity (Buss & Shackelford, 1997). These results suggest both that people are uncomfortable with inequity of mate value within relationships and that mate value discrepancy can be a powerful factor in predicting relationship infidelity, a strategy people sometimes use to switch mates (described below).

IDENTIFICATION OF A NEW AND DESIRABLE ALTERNATIVE PARTNER

Quality of alternative partners is positively associated with infidelity, as this chapter has described earlier. Further, people who pay greater attention to alternative partners tend to be less committed to their existing partners (Miller, 1997), while low commitment is associated with greater risk of relationship dissolution (Drigotas & Rusbult, 1992). Thus, another reason that people may switch mates is because they identify a high-value alternative that seems worth the cost of a breakup. Alternatively, people may initiate an affair with this alternative to get a closer inspection of this alternative's quality and ascertain whether the alternative is really a suitable candidate for a relationship.

Who Switches?

Certain people may be more inclined to switch mates than others. Of note, many of the findings described for infidelity and mate poaching are relevant to switches as well. For instance, avoidant people (DeWall et al., 2011) and women high in "dark triad" traits (Brewer et al., 2020) pay greater attention to alternative partners, a risk factor for infidelity and mate switching. Evidence also suggests that relationship satisfaction informs people's relationship commitment (Rusbult, 1980), suggesting that dissatisfied people may be likely to switch partners. Further, findings related to susceptibility to mate poaching also yield valuable insights into switchers. For instance, anxiously attached people view their partners as susceptible to being poached for a long-term relationship (Schachner & Shaver, 2002), suggesting they fear their partners may switch mates. One explanation is that their fears are justified, and partners may seek to switch mates due to the demanding and ungratifying nature of their relationship with an anxious partner (Birnbaum, 2007; Birnbaum et al., 2006). However, a second explanation is that anxiously attached people have inaccurate views of a partner's susceptibility to mate poaching due to their fears of abandonment.

Buss et al. (2017) asserted that men and women may mate switch differently. In their view, men's evolved desire for sexual frequency and variety explains their willingness to abandon partners in pursuit of attractive alternatives. However, switching for women is not so straightforward. Women may switch if they believe an alternative partner has better genes—thus granting better fitness for potential offspring—or because he possesses other desirable qualities, such as cues of emotional investment or material wealth, allowing them to "trade up" to this better alternative. Women may also facilitate an emotional bond with a partner to serve as a "backup" in case an existing partner dies or abandons her. These theories are supported by sex differences in infidelity and mate poaching described earlier in this chapter. Further, Brand et al. (2007) examined sex differences in infidelity and found that women, relative to men, were more likely to begin new relationships with extradyadic partners after infidelity (in Study 2), and were also more likely to report a desire to switch long-term mates as a reason for infidelity. This finding is consistent with the notion that women pursue infidelity as a means of switching mates more than males do.

How People Switch

Mate switching may not look the same for everyone. Some people may make a clean break from an old partner, then aggressively court a new partner to form a relationship. Other people may begin the process of switching earlier, resorting to infidelity to evaluate a lover to ensure they can replace a primary partner when the time comes to switch.

BREAKUP AND REMATING

In the words of the popular American songwriter Neil Sedaka, "breaking up is hard to do." Research suggests that this is true: people remain in unsatisfying, and even sometimes abusive, relationships for long periods of time before they break up—and sometimes, may not break up at all (Rusbult & Martz, 1995). Thus, people may not leave a partner unless there is a sufficiently good reason to do so—for instance, if the rewards offered by an alternative partner outweigh the costs of a breakup. Such a notion is supported by evidence that the perceived quality of alternatives is a powerful predictor of relationship dissolution (Le et al., 2010; South, 1995), suggesting that many people may only leave partners if they believe they can replace them. After a breakup, people may then seek to remate.

Remating strategies may vary. For instance, although some people may have a suitor "lined up" who they may pursue, others must reenter the mate marketplace and attempt to both find and court a mate. Still others may opt for a "rebound" relationship—that is, a new relationship initiated shortly after a breakup that is typically short in duration. People use rebound relationships to distract themselves from unresolved attachments to previous partners (Barber & Cooper, 2014). Further, rebounds may have positive effects. Brumbaugh and Fraley (2015) found that people who entered into rebound relationships had more confidence and felt more at peace with their previous relationships relative to people who did not.

INFIDELITY FIRST, THEN SWITCH

A potentially easier route to a new mate might be through infidelity. Buss (2000) argued that infidelity is advantageous because it allows people to secure "backup" mates to which they can switch, provided an existing partner becomes unavailable (i.e., leaves or dies) or diminishes in mate value. By being unfaithful to a partner, one might foster an attachment with another lover who can then be turned to and relied upon once it is time to leave a primary partner. Buss et al. (2016) argued that this strategy should be particularly effective for women because it communicates less risk: women may establish a relationship with a partner who can provide for them and potential offspring that she can switch to, reducing the time between relationships when she might otherwise be vulnerable. Such theorizing is consistent with findings related to women's reasons for infidelity, including the pursuit of emotional intimacy, and due to poor satisfaction with an existing relationship (Allen & Baucom, 2004), among other findings described in the section "Infidelity," earlier in this chapter.

Consequences of Mate Switching

A clear consequence of mate switching entails the dissolution of one relationship and the formation of another. Ideally, this will suggest a reward for the switcher and their new partner in the form of a new attachment with a rewarding partner. For the former partner, however, this switch might invite psychological distress that is typical of breakups (Boutwell et al., 2015). Importantly, the quality of these relationships that form from a switch may depend upon the context of the switch. For instance, people who used infidelity to facilitate a switch may be subject to poor-quality relationships, given that people who have prior experience with infidelity also are more likely to engage in infidelity in the future (Rodrigues et al., 2017). Further, people who are lured away from existing relationships by a poacher might also be at risk of an ungratifying relationship, given that relationships formed from poaching are characterized by poorer relationship quality, less investment, and higher risk of infidelity (Foster et al., 2014).

Summary

People who switch mates may experience rewards in the form of a more satisfying relationship. People may switch for a variety of reasons, including changes or revelations that lead them to believe an existing partner has diminished in mate value, or when they are introduced to an alternative who is more rewarding than an existing partner. Certain factors may make people more inclined to switch, including antisocial tendencies, attachment avoidance, relationship dissatisfaction, and high-quality alternatives. When people do switch, they may opt to break up and remate, or engage in infidelity to facilitate a switch. However, these strategies may yield different outcomes: while evaluating a partner during infidelity may result in a more informed mate switch, relationships that start as infidelity may be less gratifying and more tumultuous (e.g., characterized by poorer satisfaction and commitment and more infidelity).

Future Directions

We have examined theory and empirical data related to infidelity, mate poaching, and mate switching, including why and how these behaviors occur and the consequences of these behaviors. Although great strides have been made to enhance understanding of these important domains of human sexuality, we believe future work might reveal even more important insights into these phenomena.

Dyadic longitudinal design (e.g., Lemay & Wolf, 2016) is a powerful methodology that captures the experiences of both individuals involved in a relationship over time, yet most of the studies reviewed in this chapter are cross-sectional in nature and do not involve dyads. Future work might utilize longitudinal dyadic methods to examine temporal patterns and associations of these behaviors. For example, such methods might offer insights into how much time poaching campaigns require to entice targets into a relationship, or whether affair length is associated with mate-switching probabilities or resulting relationship quality. Such research might also shed light on the cognitive and affective processes underlying people's decisions and experiences when actively engaging in these behaviors or succumbing to temptation and provide insights into the concealment strategies people use to hide these behaviors, or how people disclose these behaviors to partners. For instance, longitudinal studies might reveal how much time elapses, or how many rendezvous have been enacted, before adulterers disclose affairs to partners, and partner's cognitive and affective experiences before and after disclosure. Such designs might also enhance understanding of existing findings. For instance, relationships that form as a result of mate poaching appear to be dissatisfying and fraught with problems (Foster et al., 2014). Longitudinal studies that examine relationship origins and trace them across time might help decipher whether there is something unique about a relationship formed from poaching that prompts dissatisfaction and infidelity—or whether individuals who are likely to be poached simply have less satisfying attachments.

Other recent work offers promising directions for research as well. For instance, Ueda et al. (2017) found that activity in the orbitofrontal cortex of the brain—a region associated with value-based decision-making—was associated with romantic preferences for people with partners. Future research might clarify the role of this brain region on infidelity and active mate-poaching behaviors. Foo et al. (2019) found that people could detect men's, but not women's, infidelity simply by looking at their faces. Future research might explore the scope and limits of this detection mechanism to discern whether it could help individuals detect variations in partner commitment and other sexual behaviors, such as poacher enticement or risk of mate switching.

Additional research may also examine the experience of outside agents that exert influence on relationships. Some work has been done in this regard. For instance, Weisser and Weigel (2015) examined aspects of the "other" man or woman who serve as affair partners for individuals engaging in infidelity. They found that these outsiders tended to be anxiously attached and sexually permissive, and that low agreeableness was associated with both knowledge of their role as an affair partner and a low likelihood of revealing their transgressions to others. However, future research might explore additional qualities that might motivate outsiders to participate in illicit arrangements, such as infidelity, a poached relationship, or a mate switch.

Our chapter focused on infidelity, mate poaching, and mate switching in the context of monogamous, heterosexual relationships. Importantly, infidelity, mate poaching, and mate switching may operate differently in multipartner mating systems (e.g., polygamy and consensual nonmonogamy; see Mogilski et al., 2017; Mogilski et al., 2019; Mogilski et al., 2020). Not all humans practice monogamy, and even within monogamous societies, there is evidence of substantial minorities of polygamous individuals (Haupert et al., 2017), and research suggests that certain evolved mechanisms, such as jealousy in response to an unfaithful partner's extradyadic involvement, may differ between people in monogamous and multipartner relationships (Mogilski et al., 2019). Further, Frederick and Fales (2014) found that distress over sexual and emotional infidelity deviated from typical gender patterns for gay, lesbian, and bisexual individuals. Thus, we believe that important insights may be garnered by assessing infidelity, mate-poaching, and mate-switching behaviors in these contexts, as individuals may react to, and even define, these behaviors differently than those in the studies described in this chapter that have assumed a heterosexual, monogamous context.

Concluding Remarks on Infidelity, Mate Poaching, and Mate Switching

Evolved psychology helps explain why and how people engage in infidelity, mate poaching, and mate switching. For instance, differences in sexual proclivities for men and women lead each to be unfaithful, poach, and switch mates, though for potentially distinct reasons: relative to women, men often appear to be more motivated by the pursuit of sex, by a desire for diverse sexual partners, or both. By contrast, women appear to be more motivated to enact these behaviors in pursuit of emotional intimacy and fulfillment relative to men. Likewise, attachment insecurity and sexual permissiveness are associated with these behaviors: people who are avoidant or who have more positive views of casual sex are each inclined to be unfaithful and poach mates, and they are also more easily seduced into affairs. Anxiously attached people desire intimacy but fear rejection, and thus may be likely to be unfaithful, poach, or switch mates primarily if they believe this behavior will facilitate connection, or if they believe that existing partners have rejected them. Relationship and situational factors are yet additional predictors of these behaviors: people dissatisfied with existing relationships, or those with ample opportunities to participate in these behaviors, are also more likely to be unfaithful, poach, and switch mates relative to people more satisfied or with less opportunity, while the quality of suitors (i.e., the person that actors would initiate a relationship with) also positively predicts infidelity and mate poaching and switching. Certain personality dimensions, such as openness and extroversion, are also associated with increased success when attempting to be unfaithful or poach mates, while antisocial personality traits, including disagreeableness and psychopathy, are associated with both increased tendency to be unfaithful and poach mates, as well as susceptibility to temptation from others.

We have demonstrated that outside agents sometimes exert influence on relationships, prompting infidelity, mate poaching, and mate switching. These behaviors are adaptive, in that they afford individuals some benefits, including sex, transmission of good genes to offspring, or the opportunity for a higher-quality partner. We have further described the mechanisms that drive these behaviors, including sex differences in sexuality, attachment insecurities, personality traits such as preference for novelty or antisocial tendencies, sexual permissiveness, relationship satisfaction, and opportunity and quality of alternatives. We have also described the consequences of these behaviors, including relationship tumult, distress, and risk of violence, among others, which impact not just actors, but also others. The information in this chapter demonstrates the importance of understanding the effects that outside agents have on relationships, either directly or indirectly, through infidelity, mate poaching, and mate switching. Still, although much important work has been done, the future may yet yield important discoveries utilizing more sophisticated methodologies that offer insights into the complexities of these relational phenomena.

References

Allen, E. S., Atkins, D. C., Baucom, D. H., Snyder, D. K., Gordon, K. C., & Glass, S. P. (2005). Intrapersonal, interpersonal, and contextual factors in engaging in and responding to extramarital involvement. *Clinical Psychology: Science and Practice, 12*(2), 101–130.

Allen, E. S., & Baucom, D. H. (2004). Adult attachment and patterns of extradyadic involvement. *Family Process, 43*(4), 467–488.

Allen, E. S., Rhoades, G. K., Stanley, S. M., Markman, H. J., Williams, T., Melton, J., & Clements, M. L. (2008). Premarital precursors of marital infidelity. *Family Process, 47*(2), 243–259.

Altgelt, E. E., Reyes, M. A., French, J. E., Meltzer, A. L., & McNulty, J. K. (2018). Who is sexually faithful? Own and partner personality traits as predictors of infidelity. *Journal of Social and Personal Relationships, 35*(4), 600–614. https://doi.org/10.1177/0265407517743085

Amato, P. R., & Rogers, S. J. (1997). A longitudinal study of marital problems and subsequent divorce. *Journal of Marriage and the Family, 59*(3), 612–624.

Arnocky, S., Sunderani, S., & Vaillancourt, T. (2013). Mate-poaching and mating success in humans. *Journal of Evolutionary Psychology, 11*(2), 65–83.

Atkins, D. C., Baucom, D. H., & Jacobson, N. S. (2001). Understanding infidelity: Correlates in a national random sample. *Journal of Family Psychology, 15*(4), 735–749.

Barber, L. L., & Cooper, M. L. (2014). Rebound sex: Sexual motives and behaviors following a relationship breakup. *Archives of Sexual Behavior, 43*(2), 251–265.

Barta, W. D., & Kiene, S. M. (2005). Motivations for infidelity in heterosexual dating couples: The roles of gender, personality differences, and sociosexual orientation. *Journal of Social and Personal Relationships, 22*(3), 339–360.

Betzig, L. (1989). Causes of conjugal dissolution: A cross-cultural study. *Current Anthropology, 30*(5), 654–676.

Birnbaum, G. E. (2007). Attachment orientations, sexual functioning, and relationship satisfaction in a community sample of women. *Journal of Social and Personal Relationships, 24*, 21–35.

Birnbaum, G. E., Reis, H. T., Mikulincer, M., Gillath, O., & Orpaz, A. (2006). When sex is more than just sex: Attachment orientations, sexual experience, and relationship quality. *Journal of Personality and Social Psychology, 91*, 929–943.

Birnie, C., Joy McClure, M., Lydon, J. E., & Holmberg, D. (2009). Attachment avoidance and commitment aversion: A script for relationship failure. *Personal Relationships, 16*(1), 79–97.

Bogaert, A. F., & Sadava, S. (2002). Adult attachment and sexual behavior. *Personal Relationships, 9*(2), 191–204.

Boutwell, B. B., Barnes, J. C., & Beaver, K. M. (2015). When love dies: Further elucidating the existence of a mate ejection module. *Review of General Psychology, 19*(1), 30–38.

Bowlby, J. (1969). *Attachment and loss* (Vol. 1). Random House.

Brady, A., Baker, L. R., & Miller, R. S. (2020). Look but don't touch? Self-regulation determines whether noticing attractive alternatives increases infidelity. *Journal of Family Psychology, 34*(2), 135–144.

Brand, R. J., Markey, C. M., Mills, A., & Hodges, S. D. (2007). Sex differences in self-reported infidelity and its correlates. *Sex Roles, 57*(1–2), 101–109.

Brewer, G., Erickson, E., Whitaker, L., & Lyons, M. (2020). Dark triad traits and perceived quality of alternative partners. *Personality and Individual Differences, 154*, Article 109633.

Brewer, G., Hunt, D., James, G., & Abell, L. (2015). Dark triad traits, infidelity and romantic revenge. *Personality and Individual Differences, 83*, 122–127.

Brumbaugh, C. C., & Fraley, R. C. (2015). Too fast, too soon? An empirical investigation into rebound relationships. *Journal of Social and Personal Relationships, 32*(1), 99–118.

Buss, D. M. (2000). Desires in human mating. *Annals of the New York Academy of Sciences, 907*(1), 39–49.

Buss, D. M. (2006). The evolutionary genetics of personality: Does mutation load signal relationship load? *Behavioral and Brain Sciences, 29*(4), 409–409.

Buss, D. M. (2013). Sexual jealousy. *Psihologijske teme, 22*(2), 155–182.

Buss, D. M., & Duntley, J. D. (2006). The evolution of aggression. In M. Schaller, & J. A. Simpson, & D. T. Kenrick (Eds.), *Evolution and social psychology* (pp. 263–286). New York: Psychology Press.

Buss, D. M., Goetz, C., Duntley, J. D., Asao, K., & Conroy-Beam, D. (2017). The mate switching hypothesis. *Personality and Individual Differences, 104*, 143–149.

Buss, D. M., & Schmitt, D. P. (1993). Sexual strategies theory: An evolutionary perspective on human mating. *Psychological Review, 100*(2), 204–232.

Buss, D. M., & Schmitt, D. P. (2019). Mate preferences and their behavioral manifestations. *Annual Review of Psychology, 70*, 77–110.

Buss, D. M., & Shackelford, T. K. (1997). Susceptibility to infidelity in the first year of marriage. *Journal of Research in Personality, 31*(2), 193–221.

Buss, D. M., & Shackelford, T. K. (2008). Attractive women want it all: Good genes, economic investment, parenting proclivities, and emotional commitment. *Evolutionary Psychology, 6*(1), Article 147470490800600116.

Cano, A., & O'Leary, K. D. (2000). Infidelity and separations precipitate major depressive episodes and symptoms of nonspecific depression and anxiety. *Journal of Consulting and Clinical Psychology, 68*(5), 774–781.

Cassidy, J., & Shaver, P. R. (Eds.). (2016). *Handbook of attachment: Theory, research, and clinical applications.* Third edition. New York: Guildford Press.

Clark, M. S., & Lemay, E. P. (2010). Close relationships. In S. T. Fiske, D. T. Gilbert, & G. Lindzey (Eds.), Handbook of social psychology, vol. 2 (5th edition) (pp. 898–940). John Wiley & Sons.

Conley, T. D., Moors, A. C., Ziegler, A., & Karathanasis, C. (2012). Unfaithful individuals are less likely to practice safer sex than openly nonmonogamous individuals. *The Journal of Sexual Medicine, 9*(6), 1559–1565.

Conroy-Beam, D. (2018). Euclidean mate value and power of choice on the mating market. *Personality and Social Psychology Bulletin, 44*(2), 252–264.

Conroy-Beam, D., Roney, J. R., Lukaszewski, A. W., Buss, D. M., Asao, K., Sorokowska, A., Sorokowski, P., Aavik, T., Akello, G., Alhabahba, M. M., Alm, C., Amjad, N., Anjum, A., Atama, C. S., Atamtürk Duyar, D., Ayebare, R., Batres, C., Bendixen, M., Bensafia, A. . . . Zupančič, M. (2019). Assortative mating and the evolution of desirability covariation. *Evolution and Human Behavior, 40*(5), 479–491.

Cooper, M. L., Pioli, M., Levitt, A., Talley, A. E., Micheas, L., & Collins, N. L. (2006). Attachment styles, sex motives, and sexual behavior: Evidence for gender-specific expressions of attachment dynamics. In M. Mikulincer & G. S. Goodman (Eds.), *Dynamics of romantic love: Attachment, caregiving, and sex* (pp. 243–274). Guilford Press.

Corbin, W. R., Scott, C. J., & Treat, T. A. (2016). Sociosexual attitudes, sociosexual behaviors, and alcohol use. *Journal of Studies on Alcohol and Drugs, 77*(4), 629–637.

Daly, M., & Wilson, M. (1998). The evolutionary social psychology of family violence. In C. B. Crawford & D. L. Krebs (Eds.), *Handbook of evolutionary psychology: Ideas, issues and applications*, (431-456). Lawrence Erlbaum.

Davies, A. P., & Shackelford, T. K. (2015). Comparisons of the effectiveness of mate-attraction tactics across mate poaching and general attraction and across types of romantic relationships. *Personality and Individual Differences, 85*, 140–144.

Davies, A. P., Shackelford, T. K., & Goetz, A. T. (2007). An evolutionary psychological perspective on infidelity. In P. Peluso (Ed.), *Infidelity* (pp. 49–69). Routledge.

Davies, A. P., Shackelford, T. K., & Hass, R. G. (2010). Sex differences in perceptions of benefits and costs of mate poaching. *Personality and Individual Differences, 49*(5), 441–445.

Davies, A. P., Tratner, A. E., & Shackelford, T. K. (2019). Not clearly defined, not reliably measured, and not replicable: Revisiting the definition and measurement of human mate poaching. *Personality and Individual Differences, 145*, 103–105.

Davis, D., Shaver, P. R., & Vernon, M. L. (2004). Attachment style and subjective motivations for sex. *Personality and Social Psychology Bulletin, 30*(8), 1076–1090.

DeWall, C. N., Lambert, N. M., Slotter, E. B., Pond Jr, R. S., Deckman, T., Finkel, E. J., Luchies, L., B., & Fincham, F. D. (2011). So far away from one's partner, yet so close to romantic alternatives: Avoidant attachment, interest in alternatives, and infidelity. *Journal of Personality and Social Psychology, 101*(6), 1302.

Dingemanse, N. J., Both, C., Drent, P. J., & Tinbergen, J. M. (2004). Fitness consequences of avian personalities in a fluctuating environment. *Proceedings of the Royal Society of London Series B-Biological Sciences, 271*, 847–852.

Doyle, C., & Cicchetti, D. (2017). From the cradle to the grave: The effect of adverse caregiving environments on attachment and relationships throughout the lifespan. *Clinical Psychology: Science and Practice, 24*(2), 203–217.

Drigotas, S. M., & Rusbult, C. E. (1992). Should I stay or should I go? A dependence model of breakups. *Journal of Personality and Social Psychology, 62*(1), 62–87.

Dugatkin, L. A. (1992). Tendency to inspect predators predicts mortality risk in the guppy (Poecilia reticulate). *Behavioral Ecology, 3*, 124–127.

Emmers-Sommer, T. M., Warber, K., & Halford, J. (2010). Reasons for (non) engagement in infidelity. *Marriage & Family Review, 46*(6-7), 420–444.

Fisher, M., Voracek, M., Rekkas, P. V., & Cox, A. (2008). Sex differences in feelings of guilt arising from infidelity. *Evolutionary Psychology, 6*(3), Article 147470490800600308.

Fletcher, G. J., Simpson, J. A., Thomas, G., & Giles, L. (1999). Ideals in intimate relationships. *Journal of Personality and Social Psychology, 76*(1), 72–89.

Foo, Y. Z., Loncarevic, A., Simmons, L. W., Sutherland, C. A., & Rhodes, G. (2019). Sexual unfaithfulness can be judged with some accuracy from men's but not women's faces. *Royal Society Open Science*, *6*(4), 181552.

Foster, J. D., Jonason, P. K., Shrira, I., Campbell, W. K., Shiverdecker, L. K., & Varner, S. C. (2014). What do you get when you make somebody else's partner your own? An analysis of relationships formed via mate poaching. *Journal of Research in Personality, 52*, 78–90.

Frederick, D. A., & Fales, M. R. (2016). Upset over sexual versus emotional infidelity among gay, lesbian, bisexual, and heterosexual adults. *Archives of Sexual Behavior, 45*(1), 175–191.

Goetz, A. T., & Shackelford, T. K. (2006). Sexual coercion and forced in-pair copulation as sperm competition tactics in humans. *Human Nature, 17*(3), 265–282.

Goldenberg, J. L., Landau, M. J., Pyszczynski, T., Cox, C. R., Greenberg, J., Solomon, S., & Dunnam, H. (2003). Gender-typical responses to sexual and emotional infidelity as a function of mortality salience induced self-esteem striving. *Personality and Social Psychology Bulletin, 29*(12), 1585–1595.

Greiling, H., & Buss, D. M. (2000). Women's sexual strategies: The hidden dimension of extra-pair mating. *Personality and individual Differences*, *28*(5), 929–963.

Hall, J. H., & Fincham, F. D. (2006). Relationship dissolution following infidelity: The roles of attributions and forgiveness. *Journal of Social and Clinical Psychology*, *25*(5), 508–522.

Haselton, M. G., Buss, D. M., Oubaid, V., & Angleitner, A. (2005). Sex, lies, and strategic interference: The psychology of deception between the sexes. *Personality and Social Psychology Bulletin, 31*(1), 3–23.

Haupert, M. L., Gesselman, A. N., Moors, A. C., Fisher, H. E., & Garcia, J. R. (2017). Prevalence of experiences with consensual nonmonogamous relationships: Findings from two national samples of single Americans. *Journal of Sex & Marital Therapy*, *43*(5), 424–440.

Hazan, C., & Shaver, P. (1987). Romantic love conceptualized as an attachment process. *Journal of Personality and Social Psychology, 52*(3), 511–524.

Hughes, S. M., & Harrison, M. A. (2019). Women reveal, men conceal: Current relationship disclosure when seeking an extrapair partner. *Evolutionary Behavioral Sciences, 13*(3), 272–277.

Jackman, M. (2015). Understanding the cheating heart: What determines infidelity intentions? *Sexuality & Culture, 19*(1), 72–84.

Jonason, P. K., Li, N. P., & Buss, D. M. (2010). The costs and benefits of the dark triad: Implications for mate poaching and mate retention tactics. *Personality and Individual Differences*, *48*(4), 373–378.

Jones, D. N., & Weiser, D. A. (2014). Differential infidelity patterns among the dark triad. *Personality and Individual Differences, 57*, 20–24.

Jones, J. D., Fraley, R. C., Ehrlich, K. B., Stern, J. A., Lejuez, C. W., Shaver, P. R., & Cassidy, J. (2018). Stability of attachment style in adolescence: An empirical test of alternative developmental processes. *Child Development, 89*(3), 871–880.

Jozkowski, K. N., & Peterson, Z. D. (2013). College students and sexual consent: Unique insights. *Journal of Sex Research, 50*(6), 517–523.

Kardum, I., Hudek-Knezevic, J., Schmitt, D. P., & Grundler, P. (2015). Personality and mate poaching experiences. *Personality and Individual Differences, 75*, 7–12.

Lalasz, C. B., & Weigel, D. J. (2011). Understanding the relationship between gender and extradyadic relations: The mediating role of sensation seeking on intentions to engage in sexual infidelity. *Personality and Individual Differences*, *50*(7), 1079–1083.

LaPlante, M. N., McCormick, N., & Brannigan, G. G. (1980). Living the sexual script: College students' views of influence in sexual encounters. *Journal of Sex Research, 16*(4), 338–355.

Le, B., Dove, N. L., Agnew, C. R., Korn, M. S., & Mutso, A. A. (2010). Predicting nonmarital romantic relationship dissolution: A meta-analytic synthesis. *Personal Relationships, 17*(3), 377–390.

Lewandowski, G. W., & Ackerman, R. A. (2006). Something's missing: Need fulfillment and self-expansion as predictors of susceptibility to infidelity. *The Journal of Social Psychology, 146*(4), 389–403.

Lemay, E. P., & Wolf, N. R. (2016). Human mate poaching tactics are effective: Evidence from a dyadic prospective study on opposite-sex "friendships." *Social Psychological and Personality Science*, *7*(4), 374–380.

Li, N. P., Bailey, J. M., Kenrick, D. T., & Linsenmeier, J. A. (2002). The necessities and luxuries of mate preferences: Testing the tradeoffs. *Journal of Personality and Social Psychology, 82*(6), 947–955.

Mark, K. P., Janssen, E., & Milhausen, R. R. (2011). Infidelity in heterosexual couples: Demographic, interpersonal, and personality-related predictors of extradyadic sex. *Archives of Sexual Behavior, 40*(5), 971–982.

Martins, A., Pereira, M., Andrade, R., Dattilio, F. M., Narciso, I., & Canavarro, M. C. (2016). Infidelity in dating relationships: Gender-specific correlates of face-to-face and online extradyadic involvement. *Archives of Sexual Behavior, 45*(1), 193–205.

McNulty, J. K., & Karney, B. R. (2004). Positive expectations in the early years of marriage: Should couples expect the best or brace for the worst? *Journal of Personality and Social Psychology, 86*, 729–743. https://doi.org/10.1037/0022-3514.86.5.729

McNulty, J. K., Meltzer, A. L., Makhanova, A., & Maner, J. K. (2018). Attentional and evaluative biases help people maintain relationships by avoiding infidelity. *Journal of Personality and Social Psychology, 115*(1), 76–95.

Miller, J. D., Lynam, D., & Leukefeld, C. (2003). Examining antisocial behavior through the lens of the five factor model of personality. *Aggressive Behavior: Official Journal of the International Society for Research on Aggression, 29*(6), 497–514.

Miller, R. S. (1997). Inattentive and contented: Relationship commitment and attention to alternatives. *Journal of Personality and Social Psychology, 73*(4), 758–766.

Miller, S. L., & Maner, J. K. (2008). Coping with Romantic Betrayal: Sex Differences in Responses to Partner Infidelity. *Evolutionary Psychology, 6*(3), 413–426.

Mills, J., Clark, M. S., Ford, T. E., & Johnson, M. (2004). Measurement of communal strength. *Personal Relationships, 11*(2), 213–230.

Mitchell, V. E., Mogilski, J. K., Zeigler-Hill, V., & Welling, L. L. M. (2019). Mate poaching strategies are differentially associated with pathological personality traits and risk-taking in men and women. *Personality and Individual Differences, 142*, 110–115.

Mogilski, J. K., Memering, S. L., Welling. L. L. M., & Shackelford, T. K. (2017). Monogamy versus consensual non-monogamy: Alternative approaches to pursuing a strategically pluralistic mating strategy. *Archives of Sexual Behavior, 46*, 407–417.

Mogilski, J. K., Mitchell, V. E., Reeve, S. D., Donaldson, S. H., Nicolas, S. C. A., & Welling, L. L. M. (2020). Life history and multi-partner mating: A novel explanation for moral stigma against consensual nonmonogamy. *Frontiers in Psychology, 10*, Article 3033.

Mogilski, J. K., Reeve, S. D., Nicolas, S. C., Donaldson, S. H., Mitchell, V. E., & Welling, L. L. (2019). Jealousy, consent, and compersion within monogamous and consensually non-monogamous romantic relationships. *Archives of Sexual Behavior, 48*(6), 1811–1828.

Mogilski, J. K., & Wade, T. J. (2013). Friendship as a relationship infiltration tactic during human mate poaching. *Evolutionary Psychology, 11*(4), Article 147470491301100415.

Moran, J. B., & Wade, T. J. (2019). Perceptions of a mismatched couple: The role of attractiveness on mate poaching and copying. *Evolutionary Behavioral Sciences, 16*(1), 94–99. https://doi.org/10.1037/ebs0000187

Morton, H., & Gorzalka, B. B. (2015). Role of partner novelty in sexual functioning: A review. *Journal of Sex & Marital Therapy, 41*(6), 593–609.

Orzeck, T., & Lung, E. (2005). Big-five personality differences of cheaters and non-cheaters. *Current Psychology, 24*(4), 274–286.

O'Steen, S., Cullum, A. J., & Bennett, A. F. (2002). Rapid evolution of escape ability in Trinidadian guppies (Poecilia reticulate). *Evolution, 56*, 776–784.

Paulhus, D. L., & Williams, K. M. (2002). The dark triad of personality: Narcissism, Machiavellianism, and psychopathy. *Journal of Research in Personality, 36*(6), 556–563.

Pew Research Center (2014). Extramarital affairs topline. https://www.pewresearch.org/global/2014/01/14/extramarital-affairs-topline/

Platt, R. A., Nalbone, D. P., Casanova, G. M., & Wetchler, J. L. (2008). Parental conflict and infidelity as predictors of adult children's attachment style and infidelity. *The American Journal of Family Therapy, 36*(2), 149–161.

Previti, D., & Amato, P. R. (2004). Is infidelity a cause or a consequence of poor marital quality? *Journal of Social and Personal Relationships, 21*(2), 217–230.

Prins, K. S., Buunk, B. P., & VanYperen, N. W. (1993). Equity, normative disapproval and extramarital relationships. *Journal of Social and Personal Relationships, 10*(1), 39–53.

Rodrigues, D., Lopes, D., & Pereira, M. (2017). Sociosexuality, commitment, sexual infidelity, and perceptions of infidelity: Data from the second love web site. *The Journal of Sex Research, 54*(2), 241–253.

Rooker, K., & Gavrilets, S. (2021). Evolution of long-term pair-bonding in humans. *Encyclopedia of Evolutionary Psychological Science, 10*(1), 20–36.

Rusbult, C. E. (1980). Commitment and satisfaction in romantic associations: A test of the investment model. *Journal of Experimental Social Psychology, 16*(2), 172–186.

Rusbult, C. E., & Martz, J. M. (1995). Remaining in an abusive relationship: An investment model analysis of nonvoluntary dependence. *Personality and Social Psychology Bulletin, 21*(6), 558–571.

Schachner, D. A., & Shaver, P. R. (2002). Attachment style and human mate poaching. *New Review of Social Psychology, 1*, 122–129.

Schmitt, D. P. (2004). The Big Five related to risky sexual behaviour across 10 world regions: Differential personality associations of sexual promiscuity and relationship infidelity. *European Journal of Personality, 18*(4), 301–319.

Schmitt, D. P., & Buss, D. M. (2001). Human mate poaching: Tactics and temptations for infiltrating existing mateships. *Journal of Personality and Social Psychology, 80*(6), 894–917.

Schmitt, D. P., & International Sexuality Description Project. (2004). Patterns and universals of mate poaching across 53 nations: The effects of sex, culture, and personality on romantically attracting another person's partner. *Journal of Personality and Social Psychology, 86*(4), 560–584.

Schmitt, D. P., & Jonason, P. K. (2015). Attachment and sexual permissiveness: Exploring differential associations across sexes, cultures, and facets of short-term mating. *Journal of Cross-Cultural Psychology, 46*(1), 119–133.

Schmitt, D. P., & Shackelford, T. K. (2003). Nifty ways to leave your lover: The tactics people use to entice and disguise the process of human mate poaching. *Personality and Social Psychology Bulletin, 29*(8), 1018–1035.

Scott, S. B., Post, K. M., Stanley, S. M., Markman, H. J., & Rhoades, G. K. (2017). Changes in the sexual relationship and relationship adjustment precede extradyadic sexual involvement. *Archives of Sexual Behavior, 46*(2), 395–406.

Sela, Y., Mogilski, J. K., Shackelford, T. K., Zeigler-Hill, V., & Fink, B. (2017). Mate value discrepancy and mate retention behaviors of self and partner. *Journal of Personality, 85*(5), 730–740.

Selterman, D., Garcia, J. R., & Tsapelas, I. (2019). Motivations for extradyadic infidelity revisited. *The Journal of Sex Research, 56*(3) 273–286.

Shackelford, T. K., Besser, A., & Goetz, A. T. (2008). Personality, marital satisfaction, and probability of marital infidelity. *Individual Differences Research, 6*(1), 13–25.

Shackelford, T. K., Buss, D. M., & Bennett, K. (2002). Forgiveness or breakup: Sex differences in responses to a partner's infidelity. *Cognition & Emotion, 16*(2), 299–307.

Sidelinger, R. J., & Booth–Butterfield, M. (2007). Mate value discrepancy as predictor of forgiveness and jealousy in romantic relationships. *Communication Quarterly, 55*(2), 207–223.

Smith, T. W. (Principal Investigator), Davern, M., Freese, J., & Morgan, S. (Co-Principal Investigators). 1972–2018 [machine-readable data file]. *General social surveys* [Grant]. National Science Foundation (NORC ed.). NORC at the University of Chicago [producer and distributor].

South, S. J. (1995). Do you need to shop around? Age at marriage, spousal alternatives, and marital dissolution. *Journal of Family Issues, 16*(4), 432–449.

South, S. J., & Lloyd, K. M. (1995). Spousal alternatives and marital dissolution. *American Sociological Review, 60*(1), 21–35.

Symons, D. (1979). *The evolution of human sexuality*. Oxford University Press.

Tomasello, M., & Vaish, A. (2013). Origins of human cooperation and morality. *Annual Review of Psychology, 64*, 231–255.

Treas, J., & Giesen, D. (2000). Sexual infidelity among married and cohabiting Americans. *Journal of Marriage and Family, 62*(1), 48–60.

Treger, S., & Sprecher, S. (2011). The influences of sociosexuality and attachment style on reactions to emotional versus sexual infidelity. *Journal of Sex Research, 48*(5), 413–422.

Trivers, R. (1972). Parental investment and sexual selection. In B. Campbell (Ed.), *Sexual selection and the descent of man: 1871-1971* (pp. 136–179). Aldine.

Ueda, R., Yanagisawa, K., Ashida, H., & Abe, N. (2017). Implicit attitudes and executive control interact to regulate interest in extra-pair relationships. *Cognitive, Affective, & Behavioral Neuroscience, 17*(6), 1210–1220.

Ventura-Aquino, E., Fernández-Guasti, A., & Paredes, R. G. (2018). Hormones and the Coolidge effect. *Molecular and Cellular Endocrinology, 467*, 42–48.

Walter, K. V., Conroy-Beam, D., Buss, D. M., Asao, K., Sorokowska, A., Sorokowski, P., Aavik, T., Akello, G., Alhababha, M. M., Alm, C., Amjad, N., Anjum, A., Atama, C. S., Duyar, D. A., Ayebare, R., Batres, C., Bendixen, M., Bensafia, A., Bizumic, B. . . . & Zupančič, M. (2020). Sex differences in mate preferences across 45 countries: A large-scale replication. *Psychological Science, 31*(4), 408–423.

Warach, B., Josephs, L., & Gorman, B. S. (2018). Pathways to infidelity: The roles of self-serving bias and betrayal trauma. *Journal of Sex & Marital Therapy, 44*(5), 497–512.

Weiser, D. A., Niehuis, S., Flora, J., Punyanunt-Carter, N. M., Arias, V. S., & Baird, R. H. (2018). Swiping right: Sociosexuality, intentions to engage in infidelity, and infidelity experiences on Tinder. *Personality and Individual Differences, 133*, 29–33.

Weiser, D. A., & Weigel, D. J. (2015). Investigating experiences of the infidelity partner: Who is the "other man/woman"?. *Personality and Individual Differences, 85*, 176–181.

Wells, G. L. (2003). Murder, extramarital affairs, and the issue of probative value. *Law and Human Behavior, 27*(6), 623–627.

Whisman, M. A., Gordon, K. C., & Chatav, Y. (2007). Predicting sexual infidelity in a population-based sample of married individuals. *Journal of Family Psychology, 21*(2), 320–324.

Widmer, E. D., Treas, J., & Newcomb, R. (1998). Attitudes toward nonmarital sex in 24 countries. *Journal of Sex Research, 35*(4), 349–358.

Wiggins, J. D., & Lederer, D. A. (1984). Differential antecedents of infidelity in marriage. *American Mental Health Counselors Association Journal, 6*(4), 152–161.

Wysocki, D. K., & Childers, C. D. (2011). "Let my fingers do the talking": Sexting and infidelity in cyberspace. *Sexuality & Culture, 15*(3), 217–239.

Yeniceri, Z., & Kökdemir, D. (2006). University student perceptions of, and explanations for, infidelity: The development of The Infidelity Questionnaire (INFQ). *Social Behavior & Personality: An International Journal, 34*(6), 639–650.

Zuckerman, M. (1994). *Behavioral expressions and biosocial bases of sensation seeking*. Cambridge University Press.

CHAPTER

24

Menstrual Cycle Variation in Women's Mating Psychology: Empirical Evidence and Theoretical Considerations

Jan Havlíček *and* S. Craig Roberts

Abstract

Humans engage in sex year-round, but women can conceive only during a brief fertile window each month. The ovulatory shift hypothesis predicts that women will show stronger preferences and sexual desire for men with markers of genetic quality during this window. This hypothesis has stimulated an enormous body of research which has generated conflicting findings. Here we review recent evidence on cyclic fluctuations in (a) mate preferences, (b) courtship behavior, (c) sexual desire, (d) sociosexuality, and (e) sexual behavior. Studies on mate preferences provide limited evidence for robust changes across the cycle. In contrast, there appears to be subtle but systematic increase in sexual desire and behavior during the high-fertility phase. Nevertheless, these changes are similar for in-pair and extra-pair sexual desire, thus contradicting the ovulatory shift hypothesis. Hormonal mechanisms underpinning these fluctuations are not fully understood. Progesterone appears to be negatively associated with sexual desire, but the role of estradiol might be more complex than previously expected. We discuss methodological issues and emphasize the need for direct hormonal assays to determine ovulation timing. Finally, we suggest that future research should broaden its scope, from focusing solely on the fertile phase to more fully studying the entire menstrual cycle, taking into account variables such as fluctuations in mood, well-being, and body image. Factors contributing to variation in cyclic changes, both within and between women, should be a focus of future studies.

Key Words: estrus, estradiol, extra-pair copulation, fertility, masculinity, mate preferences, ovulation, ovulatory shift hypothesis, progesterone, sexual desire

Human mating is characterized by mutual choice and relatively long-term relationships. The length of such relationships and whether they are monogamous or polygamous vary across societies. Sexual activities are frequently restricted to the primary partner, and penalties for engaging in intimate activities beyond the primary relationship are frequently biased against women (Betzig, 1989). Nevertheless, people occasionally engage in extra-pair sex, which may lead to procreation. How often this happens in different societies, and how important this was during human evolution, is hotly debated (Larmuseau et al.,

2016; Scelza, 2011). Indeed, reliably estimating the frequency of extra-pair paternity is difficult due to social sensitivity on the side of respondents and ethical issues in obtaining unbiased data on the researchers' side (Anderson, 2006).

Another distinct feature of human mating is that sexual activities are not restricted to a mating season, occurring instead throughout the year. Conception may occur only during a short fertile window preceding ovulation, and most sexual activities, therefore, do not lead to procreation. Given this fact, evolutionary psychologists have suggested that women show stronger mate preferences and sexual attraction to men expressing markers of genetic quality when conception is more likely (Gangestad et al., 2005a; Gangestad & Thornhill, 2008; Thornhill & Gangestad, 2008). In other words, one may expect menstrual cycle fluctuations in various aspects of mating psychology. During the last two decades, this idea has attracted enormous interest, and numerous studies have tested cyclical changes in women's mating psychology. However, they have produced inconsistent results and there are contrasting views on their significance (Gangestad & Haselton, 2015; Jones, Hahn, & DeBruine, 2019). Any fresh student of human evolutionary sciences or a scholar from a different field must find the literature on cyclical changes confusing. This perception is further bolstered by heated debates, which often seem to focus on technical details (Gangestad et al., 2019; Jones, Marcinkowska, & DeBruine, 2019; Stern et al., 2019). Outsiders may thus wonder: what is all the fuss about? They may further feel that there must be something of substance behind this idea, if so many excellent brains have invested time and energy into this area, but be at a loss to know how to navigate the huge literature.

In response to these frustrations, we offer this chapter. Thus, the main aim is to provide an overview of this complex area of research. We take advantage of the fact that we have been closely following research on cyclical changes for the past two decades, even occasionally adding some empirical evidence (e.g., Cobey et al., 2015; Havlicek et al., 2005) or entering the theoretical debate ourselves (Havlíček et al., 2015). We try to take a balanced perspective, but because we were partly involved, we may not succeed entirely. We leave it to the reader to judge.

We start with a brief sketch of historical developments in the research on cycle changes, and we introduce the leading theoretical framework. Subsequently, we review empirical evidence on various aspects of mating psychology. We divide the research on cyclical changes into the following sections: (a) mate preferences, (b) courtship behavior, (c) sexual desire, (d) sociosexuality, and (e) sexual behavior. We focus on studies that used hormonal assessment of the cycle and more recent studies using considerably larger samples than was typical of early studies. A review of the main body of evidence is followed by a section on methodological issues, which are relevant here as they may affect the validity of the individual studies. We then discuss current support for the main theoretical predictions (i.e., ovulatory shift hypothesis) and introduce alternative views. Finally, we interpret the findings of cyclical changes in the context of human life-history.

Historical Overview

Research on cyclic changes in women's sexuality dates back at least as far as the 1960s and was inspired by findings from animal studies indicating that experimental treatment with steroid hormones can have dramatic effects on female sexual behavior (Wallen, 2001). Because levels of steroid hormones such as estradiol and progesterone fluctuate across the menstrual cycle, researchers explored how this might affect women's sexual desire and behavior (Bancroft et al., 1983; Udry & Morris, 1968). A parallel line of research in psychosomatic medicine investigated physical pain and psychological distress preceding menstrual bleeding, so-called premenstrual syndrome (Kiesner et al., 2020; van Goozen et al., 1997). Both lines of research were concerned with hormonal mechanisms of cyclic fluctuations and were mostly performed by sexologists and medical researchers.

With an influx of evolutionary thinking into the behavioral sciences and psychology, interest in cyclic changes dramatically changed. The focus became the periovulatory period, the only part of the cycle when conception is possible. It was argued that mating psychology evolved to be sensitive to cues of the genetic quality of partners during this time. The first trigger for the subsequent boom in cycle studies on mate preferences was an influential paper published in *Nature* in 1999, which reported heightened preferences for facial masculinity during the fertile phase of the cycle (Penton-Voak et al., 1999). Another milestone in the history of cycle research was reached in 2008, with publication of the book *Evolution of Human Female Sexuality* (Thornhill & Gangestad, 2008) and a theoretical review paper entitled "Human Oestrus" (Gangestad & Thornhill, 2008). These provided the most comprehensive reviews of, and a detailed theoretical framework for, cyclic changes in mating psychology. During the same decade, several key studies testing cyclic changes in sexual desire toward extra-pair men appeared (e.g., Gangestad et al., 2005b; Haselton & Gangestad, 2006). This golden era culminated with the publication of two meta-analyses (Gildersleeve et al., 2014; Wood et al., 2014) on cyclic changes in mate preferences which came to different conclusions (see below). This started several rounds of heated debate about the validity of the assessment of the fertile period (Wood & Carden, 2014) and theoretical implications of the findings (Gangestad & Grebe, 2015; Havlíček et al., 2015), which continue to the present (Gangestad et al., 2019; Jones, Marcinkowska, & DeBruine, 2019; Stern et al., 2019). These debates should be seen against the background of more general discussion in psychology and related sciences on false-positive results, publication bias, and other issues related to the so-called reproducibility crisis (McNutt et al., 2016; Munafò et al., 2017). As a result of these debates, several independent labs collected large-scale data sets with more precise methods of fertility assessment. These are the studies we focus on in our literature review. Further, several methodological studies recently provided guidelines for quality research on cyclic fluctuations (Blake et al., 2016; Gangestad et al., 2016; Lobmaier & Bachofner, 2018; Marcinkowska, 2020).

Theoretical Foundations

Cyclical changes in women's mating psychology and their hormonal underpinning are of interest in their own right, but the main driver for the boom in cycle studies appears to be evolutionary theorizing. It should be noted that there are several overlapping versions of the hypothesis described below, and they are labeled inconsistently as there is no clearly defined terminology. To further complicate matters, some authors have developed their views as time has passed (for comparison, see Gangestad et al., 2005a; Gangestad & Haselton, 2015). The main theoretical concept is usually labeled the "ovulatory shift hypothesis" (Gangestad et al., 2005a). Building on the facts that conception is possible only during the so-called fertile window and that humans form long-term relationships, the hypothesis predicts that women will express enhanced preferences for markers of genetic quality in potential partners when conception is more likely. In contrast, it is expected that cyclic changes in cues to long-term investment will be absent (Grebe et al., 2013). There are several subsidiary predictions: (a) preferences for markers of genetic quality will be more pronounced in a short-term mating context than in a long-term mating context, (b) cyclic changes will be more substantial in coupled than in single women, and (c) cyclic changes will be more substantial in women paired with men who lack cues of genetic quality. The most elaborated version of the ovulatory shift hypothesis is the dual sexuality hypothesis, which argues that women have two functionally distinct sexualities: (a) extended sexuality—expressed during the nonfertile phase and which functions in attachment to the primary partner, and (b) estrus—expressed during the fertile window and which functions to increase the likelihood of conceiving with genetically high-quality men (Gangestad & Thornhill, 2008; Thornhill & Gangestad, 2008). The hypothesis relies on the fact that primary partners vary in genetic quality, and many women have below-average-quality partners. The authors argue that women were selected to decouple markers of direct and indirect benefits and to more strongly prefer markers of genetic quality during the fertile phase. As a consequence, coupled women will show an increase in sexual desire toward extra-pair men during the fertile phase of the cycle but will show no changes in sexual desire toward their primary partner. More recently, this view was reevaluated, with Gangestad and Haselton (2015) suggesting that coupled women are in fact expected to show a decrease in sexual desire toward their primary partner during the fertile phase.

In subsequent sections, we review the evidence for cyclic changes in various aspects of mating psychology. Because the ovulatory shift hypothesis predicts that these changes will be modulated by mating context, relationship status, and partner's quality, we provide this information when it is available. Further, a reliable estimation of the fertile phase is critical, and counting methods are notoriously unreliable (Blake et al., 2016; Gangestad et al., 2016). Thus, we focus on research that employed direct hormonal assessments and specify the method used. Finally, multiple studies ran analyses using the same sample; to account for this fact, we named the individual studies according to the city of the principal investigator.

Mate Preferences

Most studies on cyclical changes have tested fluctuations in mate preferences, using stimuli such as facial or body images, behavioral displays, voice recordings, and body odor samples. Some researchers use verbal descriptors of male characteristics (e.g., muscular, arrogant) (Gangestad et al., 2007). Importantly, the early research was frequently based on a between-subject design and imprecise measures of menstrual cycle phase such as counting methods. The results of these studies were summarized in two meta-analyses published in 2014. Despite being based on an overlapping set of studies, they reached contrasting conclusions. One reported no systematic cycle effect on preferences (Wood et al., 2014), whereas the other found heightened preferences for markers of genetic quality during the follicular phase (Gildersleeve et al., 2014). The main difference between the two is that Wood et al. (2014) analyzed individual traits separately (e.g., masculinity, dominance) while Gildersleeve et al. (2014) pooled categories of traits. The observed cyclic effects tend to be small (overall: $g = 0.15$; facial symmetry: $g = 0.07$; scents associated with symmetry: $g = 0.83$; facial masculinity: $g = 0.13$; body masculinity: $g = 0.21$; vocal masculinity: $g = 0.28$; behavioral dominance: $g = 0.04$; facial cues to testosterone: $g = 0.20$) (Gildersleeve et al., 2014). Note that except for facial masculinity, the cyclical change in preference for individual traits did not reach statistical significance. However, Gildersleeve et al. also separately analyzed studies according to mating context, finding that cycle effects were stronger in the short term ($g = 0.21$) compared to the long-term context ($g = 0.06$), particularly for body masculinity and behavioral dominance. In light of mostly nonsignificant results for the individual traits, the results of the two meta-analyses do not differ substantially.

What does differ, however, is the interpretation of these findings. Gildersleeve et al. (2014) based their reasoning on the ovulatory shift hypothesis and increased statistical power to find the effects by pooling the categories of traits. In contrast, Wood et al. (2014), who were skeptical of cyclical change effects, did not pool the studies. As was pointed out in the heated discussion that followed, meta-analyses can rarely resolve ideological debates (Ferguson, 2014). We embrace this view. As shown above, the design of a meta-analysis includes decisions such as the study inclusion criteria, which moderating factors are included, and so on. None of these decisions are free from the theoretical perspective that authors may use and favor. Furthermore, the debate about these meta-analyses included accusations of p-hacking and hidden degrees of freedom in data analysis, as well as several methodological issues (Wood & Carden, 2014). It should be noted that most studies included in the meta-analyses used counting methods of cycle assessment that vary in how well they characterize the fertile period (for details, see the section "Methodological Considerations"). They only rarely used within-subject designs and hormonal measures to estimate ovulation (see Roney & Simmons, 2008, for an exception). In the following paragraphs, we therefore focus on studies which did so. Most were published after the meta-analyses, but we occasionally refer to some of the earlier studies as well.

Facial Masculinity

The most frequently studied characteristic in cycle studies is facial masculinity. As shown above, the overall meta-analytic effect size of the cyclic shift in facial masculinity preferences was g = 0.13. However, it was close to zero in both short- (g = -0.02) and long-term (g = -0.01) contexts and was thus primarily driven by studies that did not specify the mating context (g = 0.17) (Gildersleeve et al., 2014).

Several large-scale studies using hormonal assays recently have been conducted to address shortcomings in imprecise ovulation assessment. Marcinkowska et al. (2016) employed a large sample of women (*n* = 115) with daily measures of estradiol and progesterone levels. Each woman performed a masculinity preference test only once, and their fertility status was computed based on three different approaches (a fertility window of either three, seven, or nine days). They found no differences in masculinity preference between high- and low-fertility groups in any of the three approaches. Average levels of estradiol also showed no association with masculinity preferences.

A subsequent study by the same team employed a within-subject design (Krakow sample, *n* = 90), collecting hormonal assays across the complete cycle and confirming ovulation by the luteinizing hormone (LH) test (Marcinkowska et al., 2018). The authors found no cyclic changes in preferences for facial masculinity and symmetry or for body masculinity. They also analyzed average hormonal levels across the cycle and found that progesterone was positively associated with facial masculinity preferences in single women, but negatively so in partnered women. In contrast, the interaction between facial symmetry preference and estradiol showed the opposite pattern, being negatively associated in single women and positively associated in partnered women. There were no statistically significant associations between estradiol and facial masculinity preferences, between progesterone and symmetry preferences, and between either of the two steroid hormones and body masculinity preferences.

Another recent study tested cyclic changes in preferences for facial masculinity and whether these are affected by psychosocial stress which may affect mate selectiveness (Ditzen et al., 2017). The authors tested a sample of 56 women across two cycles and ovulation was assessed by the LH test. The women were tested during the late follicular and midluteal phases, and saliva samples for assessing estradiol, progesterone, testosterone, and cortisol were collected. During each session, participants were exposed either to a psychosocial stress test, which consisted of a public-speaking task, or to a control task which also involved speaking but without an audience. There was a statistically significant but subtle increase in masculinity preferences during the high-fertility period. Psychosocial stress decreased masculinity preferences during both high- and low-fertility periods. Further, the increase in masculinity preferences was mediated by estradiol, but no effect of progesterone or testosterone was detected.

Human faces are not only characterized by structural sexual dimorphism but also show differences in facial hair growth. In a series of studies, Dixson et al. (2018) investigated cyclic fluctuations in short-term mate preferences for faces varying in masculinity and in levels of hair, ranging from clean-shaven to a full beard. The first study used a between-subject design and a very large sample of women (n = 2161). The likelihood of conception was estimated using the forward counting method. The results showed no association between the likelihood of conception and preferences for the male faces. In the second study, the authors again assessed mate preferences for facial masculinity and hair in a sample of women (n = 68) across the cycle, with ovulation assessed with the LH test. In the high-fertility phase, women gave higher attractiveness ratings in both short- and long-term contexts. Nevertheless, there was no effect of fertility on preferences for more masculine faces or faces with more hair. The within-subject analysis further found a positive association between estradiol and preferences for unmanipulated faces, and an opposite association with progesterone. Between-subject analysis showed that women with higher levels of estradiol gave higher attractiveness ratings only in the short-term context. No effect of progesterone was found.

Cyclic changes in preferences for men's beards were further tested in the Krakow sample (n = 52) using a forced-choice test of 10 pairs of clean-shaven and full-bearded composite facial images (Dixson, Lee, Blake, Jasienska, & Marcinkowska, 2018). Ovulation was confirmed either using the brief decrease in estradiol or by a positive LH test. There was a systematic preference for full-bearded images, but no cyclic changes were found.

As the menstrual cycle is regulated by hormonal mechanisms, it is thought that cyclic changes in mate preferences are also under the influence of sex hormones. Several previous studies, therefore, focused on possible hormonal correlates of masculinity preferences. Bobst et al. (2014) tested facial masculinity preferences in 27 women not using hormonal contraception during the early follicular phase (cycle days 3–8). They found no association between masculinity preferences and levels of estradiol and progesterone, but there was a positive association with testosterone levels. To date, the largest study testing hormonal correlates of masculinity preferences was conducted by Jones, Hahn, Wang, Fisher, Kandrik, Han, et al. (2018), who repeatedly assessed steroid hormone levels and preferences for facial masculinity in 351 women not using hormonal contraception (Glasgow sample). They found no significant link between masculinity preference and estradiol, progesterone, or estradiol-to-progesterone ratio, and these were not modulated by the relationship status of the participants. Note that this study did not test the effect of fertility or cyclic changes in masculinity preferences. Instead, the study tested possible hormonal underpinning of the masculinity preferences. While no hormonal markers for within-subject fluctuations in masculinity preferences were initially detected, further analysis of this data set showed that between-individual differences in masculinity preferences are associated with progesterone levels, depending on relationship status. The association between masculinity preferences and progesterone was positive in single women and negative in partnered women (DeBruine et al., 2019). A similar interaction was reported in the study by Marcinkowska et al. (2018).

Body Masculinity

Another large study (Göttingen sample, n = 157) tested cyclic changes in preferences for male behavior (Stern et al., 2020). Women were asked to rate the attractiveness of videos of men displaying various levels of competitive and flirtatious behavior. All women were tested during low- and high-fertility sessions, which was confirmed by the LH test. The authors also collected saliva samples to assess estradiol and progesterone levels. There were no cyclic changes in preferences for either type of behavior. Also, no within-cycle changes in estradiol and progesterone were associated with the preferences for competitive and flirtatious behavior.

Using the same set of women, preferences for masculine bodies were tested (Jünger et al., 2018). Women rated a set of 3D male body torsos for attractiveness during low- and high-fertility periods. Ratings of both sexual and long-term attractiveness were higher during the high-fertility period. Nevertheless, preferences for individual predictors of body masculinity, such as shoulder-to-chest ratio, body mass index (BMI), and physical strength did not vary across the cycle. The authors further found that the cyclic changes were driven by partnered women. Cyclic changes in sexual and long-term attractiveness were predicted by a high estradiol-to-progesterone ratio. Sexual attractiveness was negatively associated with estradiol and cortisol, and long-term attractiveness was positively associated with progesterone levels. The data from this study were subsequently reanalyzed by Gangestad et al. (2019b), who reported that log-transformed estradiol-to-progesterone ratio predicts preferences for muscularity when rated for a short-term relationship. This paper was followed by another round of heated debate focusing on the validity of different analytical methods, such as log transformations (Gangestad et al., 2019; Jones, Marcinkowska, & DeBruine, 2019; Roney, 2019; Stern et al., 2019).

To provide independent evidence, another data set was collected to test preferences for male bodies (Stern et al., 2021). This was based on a large sample of women (n = 200) who, in each week across the cycle, rated the same set of 3D male body torsos as in the previous study as well as a set of female bodies and inanimate objects. Fertility was assessed using LH kits, and levels of estradiol and progesterone were recorded during the four rating sessions. There was a small increase in attractiveness ratings of male bodies related to conception risk. The only preference for a marker of quality that showed an association with conception risk was a preference for masculinity, but the effect size was close to zero. No association was found between preference and either estradiol-to-progesterone ratio or estradiol or progesterone alone. Importantly, there were also no observed changes in ratings of female bodies or objects, and no effect of relationship status was detected.

Vocal Masculinity

Changes in preference for voice masculinity were tested in two within-subject studies (Shirazi et al., 2018). The first used voices manipulated in fundamental frequency and formant dispersion, while the second employed a set of naturally varying vocal recordings.

The first study (n = 202) found a negative effect of progesterone on the attractiveness of voices with lower fundamental frequency. No effect of estradiol or estradiol-to-progesterone ratio was observed. The second study (Göttingen sample, n = 157) found an increase in ratings of sexual attractiveness but not long-term attractiveness during high-fertility sessions. There were no cyclic changes for specific vocal cues such as fundamental frequency, formant dispersion, shimmer, and jitter. Again, there was a negative effect of progesterone levels on sexual attractiveness ratings but no effect of estradiol and estradiol-to-progesterone ratio.

Taken together, numerous earlier studies suggested cyclic changes in mate preferences for markers of genetic quality. Based on these results, the meta-analysis by Gildersleeve et al. (2014) concluded that there is a relatively modest, but robust, cycle effect. Nevertheless, many of these studies were criticized for several methodological shortcomings, such as using a between-subjects design to test a within-subjects effect, having low power, and relying on inaccurate counting methods to assess ovulation (Wood & Carden 2014). To address these shortcomings, several recent studies used considerably larger data sets and assessed ovulation via hormonal assays. Overall, the results of these studies indicate that either there are no cyclic changes or the changes are very subtle. Most studies on cyclic fluctuations in preferences for facial masculinity show null results (Dixson, Lee, Blake, Jasienska, & Marcinkowska, 2018; Marcinkowska et val., 2018). The studies on preferences for body and vocal masculinity show a small but consistent nonspecific increase in attractiveness ratings during the high-fertility phase (Shirazi et al., 2018; Stern et al., 2021). However, no increase for specific markers such as muscularity was detected. It is, therefore, an open question of how important they are in real-life settings. Many studies also did not detect a consistent association with ovarian hormones or their ratios (Marcinkowska et al., 2018; Stern et al., 2021). If there is an association, it explains only a small proportion of within-individual variation in mate preferences.

Courtship Behavior

Another area of women's mating psychology which has been extensively investigated is courtship behavior. The ovulatory shift hypothesis proposes that selection shaped courtship behavior to maximize the probability of conception by the best available partner. One should thus expect to see cyclical variation in behavior that attracts partners, and this may even extend to ornamentation, such as choice of more appealing clothes or colors. Two previous studies focused on cyclic changes in dressing. In a pioneering study, the authors obtained full-body photographs from 30 coupled women during low- and high-fertility periods, with ovulation being assessed by the LH test (Haselton et al., 2007). An independent panel of raters was subsequently asked to choose which of the two images from each woman looked more attractive. Raters judged images taken during high-fertility sessions as more attractive, in 59.5% of the images. In a follow-up study, a similar design was employed. Participants (n = 88) arrived during low- and high-fertility periods, assessed by the LH test, and full-body photographs were taken (Durante et al., 2008). They were further asked to draw how they would dress for a party. No cycle effects were observed in ratings of photographs taken on the testing day. However, the women's drawings were found to reveal a greater amount of skin during high-fertility sessions, and this effect was driven by women who had previous sexual experience. It was further found that there were no cyclic changes in the outfit drawings in coupled women, and the cyclic changes were restricted to single women.

Apart from the amount of revealed skin, several studies tested whether women more frequently wear red or pink clothing during the high-fertility period. The rationale behind these studies is that individuals wearing the color red are rated as more attractive when compared to other colors because it may mimic cues of health, such as epidermal vascular blood flow in human skin (Elliot & Niesta, 2008; Roberts et al., 2010). In the original study, two sets of women ($n = 24$, $n = 100$) reported in an online survey the shirt color they were currently wearing and how many days had elapsed from the onset of their last menses (Beall & Tracy, 2013). Across the samples, women estimated to have high conception risk (days 6–14) reported wearing red 3.5 times more often than those estimated to have low conception risk. The same authors aimed to replicate their study using the same procedure and recruitment via Mechanical Turk ($n = 116$), but here found no differences in wearing red between high- and low-fertility groups (Tracy & Beall, 2014). They argued that the increase in wearing red might be apparent only in cold weather: in warm weather, women have other ways to express their fertility status, such as revealing more skin. To test this claim, they again recruited women during a warm winter's day ($n = 101$) and on a cold winter's day ($n = 108$). They found a higher frequency of wearing a red shirt at high fertility on the cold day but no similar effect on the warm day. In another between-subjects study ($n = 81$), no higher frequency in wearing red during high conception risk days (9–14) was reported (Prokop & Hromada, 2013). This contrasts with findings of a within-subjects study (Santa Barbara sample) based on daily measures of ovarian hormones (Eisenbruch et al., 2015). Here, it was observed that the probability of wearing red was higher during the fertile window and was predicted by estradiol-to-progesterone ratio but not by the levels of the two hormones alone. Finally, in the most recent study on wearing red clothing, 82 women came for the rating session during both fertile and nonfertile phases of the cycle, while another 82 women attended only a single session (Blake et al., 2017). LH kits were used to assess ovulation. Overall, 16% of women wore red during the nonfertile session and 14.5% during the fertile session. In the combined data set, it was found that estradiol-to-progesterone ratio predicted wearing red, but this effect was restricted to younger women (18–22 years). It was not seen in a group of older women (23–36 years), but this might also be related to a higher likelihood of being in a relationship, which the authors did not report. No associations between wearing red and either estradiol or progesterone levels were found.

In sum, the studies on various aspects of ornamentation show rather inconsistent patterns. Both studies on dressing show some, but conflicting, cycle-related effects. An effect in actual dressing was reported in coupled women. In contrast, another study found no effect on actual dressing and a cyclic effect was apparent only in drawings of potential dress and was restricted to single women. The studies on cyclic changes in dress color are similarly conflicting. Furthermore, most are based on a between-subjects design and many use unreliable forward-counting methods. It was shown that to achieve adequate power (80%) using forward-counting methods to detect a medium-size effect ($d = 0.5$), one should sample 1,200 individuals (Gangestad et al., 2016). All between-subjects studies are underpowered, which dramatically increases the chances of false-positive results (Krzywinski & Altman, 2013). Importantly, however, even the two remaining within-subjects studies that used hormonal assays to assess fertility status show conflicting results. One found a high frequency of wearing red during the high-fertility period but the other did not. There is some consensus that the frequency of wearing red is positively predicted by the estradiol-to-progesterone ratio, but this applies only to younger women (Blake et al., 2017). As noted above, an effect of age might be confounded by the age-dependent probability of being in a relationship. Furthermore, color preferences are associated with mood, which also fluctuates during a cycle (for a review, see Kiesner et al., 2020). Therefore, the observed effect might be an epiphenomenon of these mood fluctuations and might be related to mating only indirectly. Clearly, there is space for further investigation.

Sexual Desire

The study of cyclic changes in sexual desire has a long history (for review, see Pawłowski, 1999). Numerous studies aimed to test fluctuations in female sexuality across the cycle, preceding the ovulatory shift hypothesis. Consequently, some studies specify the target of the sexual desire while others evaluate any change in sexual desire. As in previous sections, we review studies that rely on hormonal assays to assess the fertility phase.

Changes in attraction to the primary partner and extra-pair men were tested by Gangestad et al. (2002). The authors collected data from 31 partnered women in low- and high-fertility sessions and assessed ovulation by the LH kit. Women reported an increase in attraction to both primary partners and extra-pair men during the follicular phase, although only the change in preference for extra-pair men was statistically significant. However, it should be noted that, on average, attraction to the primary partner was several times higher than attraction to other men.

A similar research design was adopted by Pillsworth and Haselton (2006), who compared sexual attraction during the high- and low-fertility sessions, with ovulation confirmed by the LH kit. The researchers asked 37 coupled women (15 had no sexual experience) about their attraction to their primary partner and to other men. They found that the magnitude of change in extra-pair attraction between high- and low-fertility sessions was negatively correlated with the sexual attractiveness of their primary partner. In other words, women coupled with less attractive men showed an increase in attraction to extra-pair men during high-fertility sessions. A similar cyclic change was not observed in sexual desire to primary partner.

To further investigate whether cyclic effects are dependent on the attractiveness of the primary partner, Haselton and Gangestad (2006) performed a study using diary reports of 25 coupled women (seven broke up during the study). They assessed in-pair and extra-pair sexual desire and created composite measures for low- and high-fertility periods. They further created a difference score between sexual and investment attractiveness for the primary partner. There was a nonsignificant increase in attraction to extra-pair men during the fertile period. However, when the quality of the primary partner was taken into account, the difference between high- and low-fertility periods in attraction to other men was negatively associated with a difference in sexual versus investment attractiveness (Haselton & Gangestad, 2006). These results were interpreted as evidence for a higher cyclic increase of extra-pair attraction in women with partners low in sexual versus investment attractiveness.

Another study tested whether the quality of the primary partner modulates cyclic changes. Gangestad et al. (2005b) studied 54 paired women in low- and high-fertility periods. Ovulation was assessed by the LH kit. As a proxy for partner quality, the authors used fluctuating asymmetry (FA), which is considered to be a marker of developmental instability (Thornhill & Moller, 1997). The results showed an increase in attraction to other men during the fertile phase, which was modulated by their primary partner's FA. More specifically, women partnered with men with a high level of FA showed higher attraction to other men when fertile. No cyclic change was found in the attraction to the primary partner, but again it should be noted that values for in-pair attraction were considerably higher compared to extra-pair attraction. Gangestad et al. (2010) similarly found, apparently based on the same sample, that a primary partner's facial masculinity affects cyclic changes in attraction to other men.

Finally, how a partner's attractiveness affects cycle-related fluctuations was explored in a study of 41 heterosexual women who reported their in-pair and extra-pair attraction during the low- and high-fertility period (Larson et al., 2012). The occurrence of ovulation was confirmed by the LH kit. The male partner's attractiveness was assessed by their partners and also by an independent panel of female raters based on facial and full-body photographs. Overall, there were no changes in in-pair or extra-pair attraction across the cycle. Nevertheless, women who rated their partners as less sexually attractive reported lower in-pair attraction during high-fertility sessions. No cyclic changes in extra-pair attraction were observed. The subsequent analysis employed a composite measure of partner's attractiveness as assessed by the third-party raters. The cyclic changes in in-pair attraction were not modulated by the partner's attractiveness, but extra-pair attraction was higher during the high-fertility session in women coupled with men perceived by others as less attractive. It should be noted that in all the above-reviewed studies, in-pair attraction was assessed by fewer items than extra-pair attraction, thus allowing for greater variation in extra-pair ratings.

Shimoda et al. (2018) aimed to test cyclic changes in in-pair and extra-pair sexual desire. They asked 35 coupled women to keep a diary about their sexual desire, commitment, and mood. Ovulation was assessed by the LH kit. There was a statistically significant increase in extra-pair desire during the periovulatory period. In-pair sexual desire followed a similar pattern, but the differences were not statistically significant. None of the cyclic changes were modulated by the partner's physical attractiveness. Importantly, in-pair desire was considerably higher than extra-pair desire in all cycle phases.

Most of the above-reviewed studies suggested an interaction between cycle phase and quality of the partner on attraction to extra-pair men, but most also were based on small samples ($n < 50$). To address this, Arslan et al. (2018) used an online diary method to assess changes in sexual desire across the cycle in a large set of partnered women. Altogether, they collected data from 428 naturally cycling women and 628 women using hormonal contraception. The fertile phase was assessed using the backward-counting method. They found an increase during the fertile window in in-pair sexual desire but also in several measures of extra-pair sexual motivations such as sexual desire and fantasies. Both in-pair and extra-pair fluctuations were of similar size and were robust to different methods of fertility assessment. Importantly, these changes were independent of the attractiveness of the primary partner.

Some studies suggested that the cyclic fluctuations in sexual desire might differ between single women and women in a relationship. This was tested in an early study using a between-subject design and a backward-counting method for assessing conception probability (Pillsworth et al., 2004). The study found a positive association between a composite measure of sexual desire and conception probability in paired women ($n = 88$) but not in single women ($n = 85$). A follow-up analysis separately assessed in-pair and extra-pair sexual desire and found greater in-pair sexual desire when the probability of conception was high, but no differences in extra-pair sexual desire. Roney and Simmons (2016) reanalyzed data from their Santa Barbara sample ($n = 52$) and found an increase in sexual desire during the fertile window in partnered women but a more balanced distribution of sexual desire in single women.

Several other studies investigated cyclic fluctuations in sexual desire without differentiating the target of the desire. In one, van Stein et al. (2019) collected reports about sexual desire as measured by a revised version of the Sexual Desire Inventory (SDI-2) from 78 women (Jena sample) during the menstrual, late follicular, and luteal phases of the cycle. Ovulation was assessed by LH kits. Women, on average, reported an increase in sexual desire during the late follicular phase as compared to the menstrual and luteal phases. Similarly, Roney and Simmons (2013) asked 52 women (Santa Barbara sample) to report daily their sexual desire (single item measure) and found an increase during the fertile window (defined as five days preceding ovulation). Importantly, the changes in desire were associated positively with estradiol levels and negatively with progesterone levels. These results were partly confirmed by a much larger study (Glasgow sample, n = 375), in which the researchers repeatedly collected data on sexual desire (measured by SDI-2) and ovarian hormone levels (Jones, Hahn, Fisher, Wang, Kandrik, & DeBruine, 2018). The results showed a negative effect of progesterone on sexual desire, but a positive effect of estradiol was found only for the solitary sexual desire subscale. Another recent study collected data on sexual desire (measured by SDI-2) and hormonal samples of estradiol, progesterone, and testosterone from 353 women not using hormonal contraception, 78 of whom were tested twice (Shirazi et al., 2019). The results showed that between-individual differences in sexual desire (both solitary and dyadic) were predicted by testosterone but not by estradiol and progesterone levels. The analysis of within-subject changes found no association between changes in sexual desire and changes in estradiol, progesterone, or testosterone.

It has been proposed that in-pair and extra-pair sexual desire might be regulated by different hormonal mechanisms. Grebe et al. (2016) collected data on attraction to their partner and to other men from 33 women in a relationship during the fertile and non-fertile phases. They found that estradiol was negatively related to attraction to the primary partner, while progesterone showed a positive association. No hormonal correlates of attraction to extra-pair men were detected. Roney and Simmons (2016), in an attempt to replicate these findings (Santa Barbara sample), found a positive effect of estradiol and a negative effect of progesterone for both in-pair and extra-pair attraction. This was further supported by analysis focusing on the fertile window (five days preceding ovulation): in-pair attraction was significantly higher in this period, and this was to a lesser extent mirrored by extra-pair attraction.

To summarize the section on cyclic changes in sexual desire, prevailing evidence indicates an increase in sexual desire during the high-fertility period. Several studies also suggested that such an increase in sexual desire might be specific to extra-pair men, and this might particularly apply to women coupled with men lacking putative markers of genetic quality. Nevertheless, a recent large-scale study did not replicate the effect of the partner's quality on changes in sexual desire toward extra-pair men (Arslan et al., 2018). It should be further emphasized that studies that showed cyclic changes only in extra-pair attraction also show that in-pair attraction was several times higher than extra-pair attraction, irrespective of the cycle. The available evidence further suggests that cyclic changes in sexual desire might be more pronounced in or perhaps limited to coupled women, with single women showing flatter patterns. The possible hormonal mechanism behind these fluctuations is still unclear. Some studies indicate a positive association between estradiol and sexual desire (Roney & Simmons, 2013). However, several highly powered studies did not detect this association (Jones, Hahn, Fisher, Wang, Kandrik, & DeBruine, 2018; Shirazi et al., 2019). Similarly, some studies found a positive link between testosterone and sexual desire, but others did not, and its role in fluctuating sexual desire is not well understood. On the other hand, a negative association with progesterone appears to be consistently reported across the studies (Jones, Hahn, Fisher, Wang, Kandrik, & DeBruine, 2018; Roney & Simmons, 2013). Finally, it was proposed that in-pair attraction is driven by progesterone while extra-pair attraction is influenced by estradiol (Grebe et al., 2016). Based on current evidence, we find such complex mechanisms very unlikely, as changes in in-pair and extra-pair desire are usually correlated (Arslan et al., 2018).

Sociosexuality

Although sexual desire conceptualizes the drive to pursue sexual activity, another important aspect of mating psychology is sociosexuality, which refers to the tendency to desire or have sex with various partners. To assess interindividual differences in sociosexuality, the most frequently used tool is the Sociosexuality Orientation Index-Revised (SOI-R; Penke & Asendorpf, 2008). It consists of three main dimensions: (a) attitudes—assessing one's views about uncommitted sexual activities, (b) desire—assessing how much one wishes to have various sexual partners, and (c) behavior—experience with sexual activities with various partners. While the SOI-R score is considered to reflect a trait with high stability across time, it has also been successfully used to assess short-term fluctuations.

Several large-scale studies have investigated whether cyclic fluctuations can be detected in sociosexuality. In a sample of 78 women (Jena sample), van Stein et al. (2019) found no cyclic changes in overall SOI-R score. Similarly, no significant cycle effect in SOI desire or attitudes was observed in a study based on data from 102 women (Krakow sample) who were studied across the entire cycle (Marcinkowska et al., 2021). Nevertheless, there was a significant increase in combined SOI score when analyses were restricted to women with a confirmed LH assay. The cyclic fluctuations appear to be similar in single and partnered women. The authors also found that combined desire/attitude SOI scores were positively associated with estradiol levels and negatively associated with progesterone levels.

These results are consistent with another study (n = 78) which found a positive association between change in estradiol and change in SOI desire, and a negative interaction between estradiol and progesterone (i.e., increase in SOI desire was observed when estradiol increased and progesterone simultaneously decreased) (Shirazi et al., 2019). In contrast, no association between steroid hormones (estradiol, progesterone, and testosterone), and SOI score was reported by Jones, Hahn, Fisher, Wang, Kandrik, Han, et al., (2018). Although the latter study comprised a large sample (Glasgow sample, n = 351), it also employed a 5-point scale (other studies used a more sensitive 9-point scale) for assessing SOI, which might not be sensitive enough to detect these small-scale fluctuations.

In sum, it was predicted that the desire for uncommitted sex would be stronger during the high-fertility phase, and this tendency would be particularly pronounced in coupled women. Nevertheless, there is currently little evidence that sociosexuality fluctuates across the cycle. There seems to be a positive association between sociosexuality and estradiol, and a negative association with progesterone (Marcinkowska et al., 2021; Shirazi et al., 2019). However, the largest study so far did not find any association with ovarian hormones, so it is unclear how robust the above-mentioned associations are (Jones, Hahn, Fisher, Wang, Kandrik, & DeBruine, 2018). Considering that cyclic fluctuations in other domains are rather subtle, it is not surprising that the SOI, which primarily measures interindividual differences, shows no cyclic shifts.

Sexual Behavior

As discussed in the previous section, there appear to be cycle-related changes in sexual desire. However, sexual motivation might not directly translate into sexual behavior as it is restricted by both internal and external factors which may interfere with the motivation to have sex. The external factors include partner availability, lack of free time and privacy, and many others. In this section, we review studies on cyclic changes in sexual behavior and once again focus on those using a within-subjects design and hormonal measures to assess fertility.

Several previous studies reported a significant increase in sexual activity during the late follicular phase. Wilcox et al. (2004) asked 68 women to keep a diary of their sexual activities and collected urine samples for hormonal assays (ovulation was determined from urinary levels of estrone 3-glucuronide and pregnanediol 3-glucuronide—the main metabolites of estradiol and progesterone). All women used nonhormonal contraception, and therefore they did not need to change their sexual behavior to avoid unwanted pregnancy. The authors found a 24% increase in the frequency of sexual intercourse during a six-day fertile window as compared to other parts of the cycle (menstruation excluded). In an additional analysis, using data from 285 women, the authors found an increase in sexual intercourse on Saturdays and Sundays, of about 35%. An increase in the frequency of sexual activity in high-fertility sessions was also found in a sample of 31 coupled women (Gangestad et al., 2002). Women further reported initiating sexual activity with their partners more often during this period. Importantly, none of the women claimed to have sex with other men than their primary partner.

Another large-scale study was based on 1,180 women who kept a diary of their sexual activity across a cycle, and whose serum levels of sex hormones were assessed (Caruso et al., 2014). The authors observed a robust increase in sexual activity in single women during the late follicular phase (more than 65% of all sexual activities occurred during this period). An increase in sexual activity during the late follicular phase was also found in partnered women, although the size of the change was considerably smaller (more than 30% of all sexual activities), and sexual activities were more equally distributed across the cycle. There was also a strong day-of-week effect, especially in partnered women: almost 30% of sexual activities in partnered women occurred on a Saturday.

Burleson et al. (2002) explored whether cycle-related changes in sexual activity differ between homosexual and heterosexual women. In all, 147 heterosexual and 89 homosexual coupled women were asked to keep a diary of their autosexual activity and sexual activities with their partner. The timing of ovulation was determined based on a change in basal body temperature and changes in cervical mucus. Sexual activities with the partner showed a cyclic pattern, with an increase during the follicular phase. The data also showed a peak in autosexual activity during the follicular and ovulatory phases in both homosexual and heterosexual women who were not cohabiting with their partner, while this was more equally distributed over the cycle in women who lived with their partner. Although on average heterosexual women reported more sexual activities than homosexual women, the cyclic pattern was similar in both groups.

No cyclic fluctuations in overall or self-initiated sexual activity were found in a recent study based on 78 women (Jena sample) (van Stein et al., 2019). Nevertheless, an increase in autosexual activity was observed during the fertile window. A large diary study (n = 428) found no overall increase in the frequency of sex or female-initiated sex during the fertile window (Arslan et al., 2018). However, when the sample was restricted to women who cohabited with their partner, there was an increase in sexual activity during the fertile window. The authors also recorded rare cases of actual extra-pair behavior; however, these were not related to the fertility window.

Roney and Simmons (2013) explored hormonal predictors of sexual activity using a diary study (Santa Barbara sample). They found no increase in the frequency of overall sexual activity, female-initiated sex, or autosexual activity during the fertile window. However, there was a positive association between estradiol and sexual activity, and a trend for autosexual activity, but no effect of progesterone or testosterone. There was also a strong day-of-week effect, with a 22% probability of sex during the weekend as compared to 9% on other days.

Overall, there seems to be an increase in sexual activities during the high-fertility period. Nevertheless, the size of the effect depends on several external factors such as partner availability. This limitation does not apply to autosexual activities, which show a more consistent pattern. The cyclic shifts in sexual activities are higher in single women, and sexual activities in partnered women are more equally distributed across the cycle with a minor peak around the time of ovulation. If we compare the size of cyclic fluctuations with other relevant factors such as weekend days, the latter show a much stronger effect.

Methodological Considerations

As we have just described, even small differences in methodology can substantially affect results and their interpretation, so it is worth noting here two of the most influential methodological issues in the cycle literature: appropriate scheduling of data collection and the nature of the methods used to assess behavioral change.

Cycle Assessment

Research into cyclic variation in mating psychology assumes that these changes are related to actual fertility. Therefore, the reliability of fertility assessment is of key importance. One way to study differences between high- and low-fertility periods is to use a

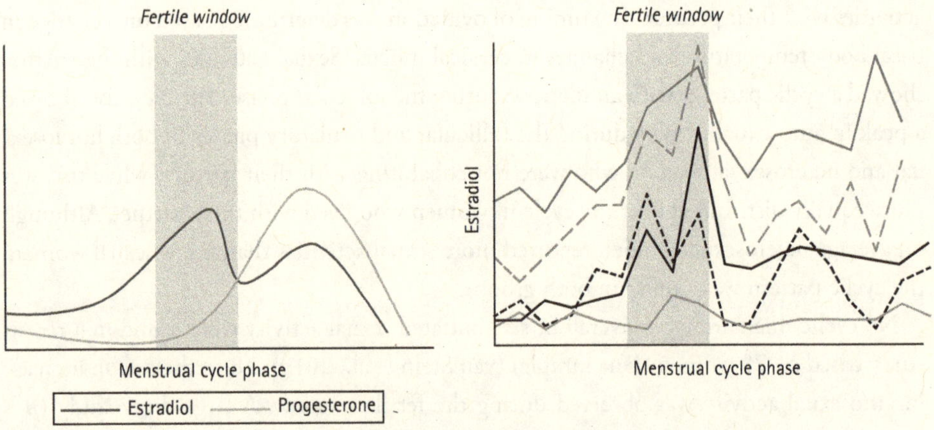

Figure 24.1 *Schematic Depiction of Cyclic Changes in Estradiol and Progesterone*

Note. The left panel shows population average levels of estradiol (dark line) and progesterone (light line) while the right panel shows individual variation in salivary estradiol levels. Right panel adapted from "Human Reproduction and Health: An Evolutionary Perspective," by G. Jasienska, R. G. Bribiescas, A. S. Furberg, S. Helle, and A. Núñez-de la Mora, 2017, *The Lancet, 390* (10093), p. 511 (https://doi.org/10.1016/S0140-6736(17)30573-1).

between-subjects design by comparing women in the high-fertility phase with women in low-fertility phases. The main advantage of such an approach is that it is less time-consuming, and therefore such a design was adopted in numerous early studies (for review, see Gildersleeve et al., 2014). Nevertheless, due to large interindividual differences in mating psychology between women, coupled with small effect sizes of cyclic fluctuations, researchers who opt for such a design require very large data sets to have sufficient statistical power (Gangestad et al., 2016). It is therefore recommended to use a within-subjects design that is considerably more sensitive.

However, even the use of a within-subjects design is not a guarantee of precise assessment of the cycle. There is high variation in cycle length, both between women and across cycles of individual women, even among those who report having cycles of a regular length (Jasienska et al., 2017; Marcinkowska 2020) (fig. 24.1). Until recently, the most common way to assess the timing of ovulation was by one of several counting methods. The forward-counting method assumes that ovulation occurs on the 14th day after the onset of the last menstrual bleeding (day 1). There is an agreement that ovulation, *on average,* occurs in the middle of a 28-day cycle. However, cycle length varies considerably and the follicular phase is the most variable part of the menstrual cycle (Jasienska et al., 2017). Therefore, forward-counting estimations are extremely unreliable (Blake et al., 2016; Gangestad et al., 2016). The backward-counting method is based on a prediction of the next onset of menstrual bleeding, calculated by adding the normal cycle length to the date of the onset of the last menstrual bleeding. From that predicted date, 14 days are subtracted to obtain the predicted date of ovulation. The basis for this approach is that the luteal phase is usually of more standard length than the follicular phase. Nonetheless, most studies do not focus on the exact timing of ovulation but are concerned rather with the fertility window, which is the period in which sexual intercourse may lead to conception. It was shown that only 60% of fertile days are correctly classified as such by using the backward-counting method (Blake et al., 2016). Interestingly behavioral studies vary in the definition of the fertile window or high-fertility period. Some use the complete follicular phase (days 6–14) (e.g., Penton-Voak et al., 1999), while others restrict it to a narrower number of days preceding predicted ovulation (e.g., Havlicek et al., 2005). Usually, no justifications are provided for this decision. Studies assessing the probability of conception show that chances to conceive after a single incidence of sexual intercourse can be restricted to the five days preceding the ovulation and the day of the ovulation (Wilcox et al., 2001). Such a six-day period is commonly referred to as a fertile window (fig. 24.1).

For these reasons, it is currently agreed that cycle studies should use hormonal assays to obtain a reliable assessment of ovulation and fertility window. The simplest way is to use LH kits that detect the LH surge which precedes ovulation by 24 to 48 hours. Importantly, the LH kit is designed to give positive results when LH is higher than a certain threshold (e.g., 25mIU/ml). This cutoff point is based on populational levels and may thus not show a positive result in some ovulatory cycles. Marcinkowska (2020) has recently found that in 81% of women with an LH negative test, there was an estradiol drop indicating that the given cycle might be ovulatory. It was also argued that scheduling behavioral tests after a positive LH test may misclassify fertility status in some women and the authors recommend complementing hormonal assessment with cervical mucus quality test (Bachofner & Lobmaier, 2018). A more reliable way of estimating ovulation is thus a daily measurement of estradiol and progesterone and assessing the day of ovulation based on a drop in estradiol followed by a rise in progesterone. This can be further confirmed by an LH surge. However, it should be noted that obtaining daily measures of hormones provides logistical challenges, greater financial demands for researchers, and more inconvenience for participants. Of course, the only direct method of detecting ovulation is using ultrasound, but it is also the most invasive method and is thus rarely employed in behavioral studies (for an exception, see Cobey et al., 2013).

Behavioral Measures

Most cycle studies do not rely on direct behavioral measures or outcomes but instead use various stimuli to assess mate preferences, self-reports of sexual psychology, and behavior. Because numerous and diverse measures are used in cycle-related research, a detailed discussion on their validity is beyond the scope of this chapter. Instead, we focus on two widely employed measures to illustrate this issue.

The most frequently tested characteristic is facial masculinity. Research can make use of natural variation in facial masculinity, which can be either measured or assessed by an independent panel. It should be noted that the correlation between measured and perceived masculinity usually shows only a medium correlation and should not be conflated without due caution (Mitteroecker et al., 2015). Furthermore, perceptions of masculinity vary cross-culturally (Kleisner et al., 2021). However, the most common method for testing masculinity preferences is to digitally manipulate the sexual dimorphism of the images. The manipulation is based on the average shape of female and male images, and the shape coordinates of these average faces are used to create a feminized and masculinized version (called transforms) of an original image. The software to do this uses a linear algorithm to create the manipulated images; however, it is not clear whether the manipulated images mirror natural variation in facial masculinity. Most important, it is assumed that level of sexual dimorphism is a reliable marker of genetic quality in general, and immune system functioning in particular. Nevertheless, the evidence that a high level of sexual dimorphism is closely related to genetic quality and immune system functioning is equivocal at best (for discussion, see Jones, Marcinkowska, & DeBruine, 2019; Marcinkowska et al., 2018).

A second, widely studied aspect of mating psychology is sexual desire. Many studies used a unidimensional measure of sexual desire, not differentiating between the target of the desire (Roberts et al., 2013). This is of key importance as it has been hypothesized that sexual desire for a primary partner might not fluctuate across the cycle as much as during the high-fertility phase for extra-pair partners. For this reason, several studies separately asked about sexual desire for an in-pair partner and extra-pair men. Interestingly, the scale used is not analogously constructed for the partner and extra-pair men (Gangestad et al., 2005b; Haselton & Gangestad, 2006) and the section about extra-pair attraction consists of more items than the section on in-pair attraction. This is important as the items are summed, and the extra-pair part is thus more sensitive to detect fluctuations.

Assessing the Ovulatory Shift Hypothesis

In this section, we aim to evaluate evidence in relation to the ovulatory shift hypothesis. In its simple form, it predicts that women's mate preferences for markers of genetic quality fluctuate across a cycle as a function of fertility. The changes are expected to be stronger in preferences for a short- compared to a long-term partner. As we have discussed, the most frequently studied characteristic—facial masculinity—shows no cyclic fluctuation in most of the highly powered, within-subjects studies. Also, no cyclic fluctuations were detected in preference for facial hair (Dixson et al., 2018b). In contrast, preference for male bodies seems stronger in the high-fertility phase (Jünger et al., 2018). A similar nonspecific increase was also reported in a study on vocal preferences (Shirazi et al., 2018). Nevertheless, no changes for specific markers of quality such as muscularity or shoulders-to-chest ratio were detected. Overall, these findings show little support for the idea that cyclic changes in mate preferences are adaptations to enhance the likelihood of short-term mating with men possessing markers of genetic quality during the high-fertility period.

The elaborated version of the ovulatory shift hypothesis—the dual sexuality hypothesis—predicts a set of adaptations in relation to the fertile phase of the menstrual cycle (Gangestad & Thornhill, 2008; Thornhill & Gangestad, 2008). It is hypothesized that women's sexuality consists of two distinct parts. Sexuality during the fertile phase is labeled estrus, and sexuality during nonfertile phases is extended sexuality. The main function of estrus sexuality is to conceive with an individual providing high genetic benefits. In contrast, the main function of extended sexuality is to maintain a relationship with an invested long-term partner. It is therefore predicted that in partnered women, there is a decrease in sexual desire for a long-term partner and an increase in sexual desire for extra-pair men with markers of genetic quality (Gangestad & Haselton, 2015) (see fig. 24.2). Do the data support such a complex fine-tuned pattern? Several early studies interpreted their results in support of the dual sexuality hypothesis as they found an increase in extra-pair attraction during the high-fertility period (Gangestad et al., 2005b; Haselton & Gangestad, 2006; Larson et al., 2012). No changes in attraction to the primary partner were observed in most of these studies. Nevertheless, the theory predicts higher extra-pair than in-pair attraction during the high-fertility period. The data show a very different picture—in-pair attraction is several times higher than extra-pair attraction, irrespective of the comparatively minute cyclic fluctuations (fig. 24.2). Furthermore, several large-scale within-subjects studies investigated cyclic changes in sociosexuality, which should show a significant increase in interest in extra-pair sex in the high-fertility phase. However, most of these studies did not show cyclic changes in sociosexuality (Marcinkowska et al., 2021; van Stein et al., 2019), and the largest study (Glasgow sample), which investigated hormonal predictors of sociosexuality, did not find any association between ovarian hormones and SOI scores (Jones, Hahn, Fisher, Wang, Kandrik, & DeBruine, 2018).

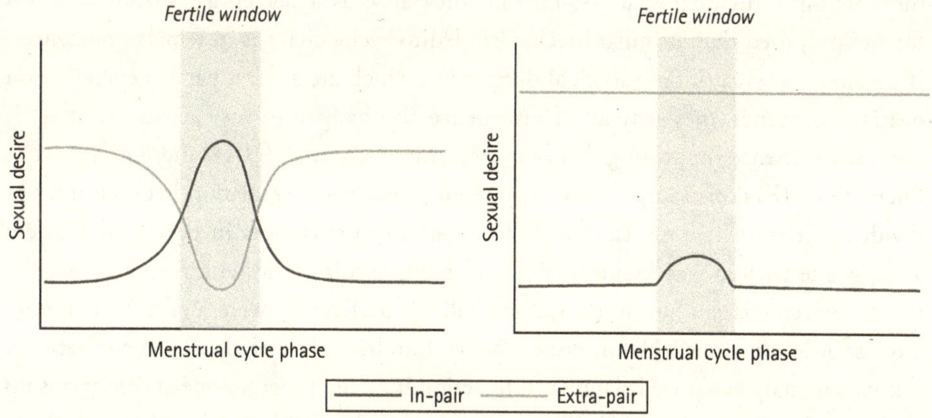

Figure 24.2 *Schematic Depiction of the Cyclic Changes in Sexual Desire*

Note. The left panel shows in-pair (light line) and extra-pair (dark line) sexual desire as predicted by the dual sexuality hypothesis. The right panel shows in-pair (light line) and extra-pair (dark line) sexual desire as found by several empirical studies. Left panel adapted from "Human Estrus: Implications for Relationship Science," by S. W. Gangestad and M. G. Haselton, 2015, *Current Opinion in Psychology, 1*, p. 47 (https://doi.org/10.1016/j.copsyc.2014.12.007).

The most stringent test of the dual sexuality hypothesis is whether we observe changes not only in desire but also in actual behavior. Most studies on cyclic changes in sexual behavior show that there is a higher frequency of sexual interactions at high fertility (Burleson et al., 2002; Wilcox et al., 2004). Nevertheless, the size of these changes is larger in single women than in partnered women (Caruso et al., 2014), contrary to what the dual sexuality hypothesis predicts. Furthermore, the changes appeared to be similar in heterosexual and homosexual women and were also observed in autosexual activities (Burleson et al., 2002; van Stein et al., 2019). These patterns are again contradictory to the dual sexuality hypothesis, which predicts that an increase in sexuality is related to the probability of conception, and this is not an issue in homosexual or autosexual activities.

Alternative Views

Although the ovulatory shift hypothesis has dominated thinking of researchers for a considerable time, several other ideas have been proposed to explain cyclic changes in mating psychology.

Spandrel Hypothesis

The spandrel hypothesis proposed that cyclic changes are a by-product of interindividual differences, due to a shared underlying mechanism. It was formulated to explain mechanisms involved in the male perception of female cyclic changes in appearance. Havlíček et al., (2015) argued that male perception of female attractiveness was selected to be sensitive to interindividual differences in ovarian hormone-dependent traits such as facial appearance or body odor quality. Then, because estradiol and progesterone fluctuate during the menstrual cycle, it will also affect male ratings of female attractiveness. However, the model does not expect direct selection for the perception of these within-individual changes; instead, they arise as a perceptual spandrel. It was further proposed that a similar mechanism led to cyclic changes in female preferences. If preferences reveal interindividual differences, which are at least partly dependent on ovarian hormones, they may as a consequence also happen to vary across the cycle. Is there any evidence supporting this view? Marcinkowska et al. (2018) did not find cyclic fluctuations (Krakow sample), but they report a negative association between interindividual variation in progesterone and masculinity preferences in partnered women; an opposite pattern was found in single women. Similarly, no within-subject associations between ovarian hormones and masculinity preferences were reported in another large-scale study (Jones, Hahn, Fisher, Wang, Kandrik, Han, et al., 2018) but between individual analyses showed a similar interaction between progesterone and relationship status (DeBruine et al., 2019). These results are in line with the spandrel hypothesis which predicts that interindividual differences in ovarian hormones will affect mate preferences. Nevertheless, future studies should clarify why the observed association varies as a function of relationship status.

Motivational Priorities Hypothesis

While the spandrel hypothesis predicts mate preferences, it has little to say regarding changes in sexual desire and behavior. This is targeted by the motivational priorities hypothesis, which proposes that when conception is most likely, there will be enhanced motivation for sexual activity, because at this time the potential fitness benefits are higher than the potential costs (Roney, 2018; see also Jones, Hahn, & DeBruine, 2019). It was further suggested that, at the proximate level, heightened sexual motivation will be positively influenced by estradiol and negatively by progesterone. If ovarian hormones affect motivation toward sexual activities, then they should also have negative effects on conflicting motivations, such as feeding. Several studies have found evidence for lower food intake during ovulation (for review, see Fessler, 2003). Current studies on sexual desire support the motivational priorities hypothesis as they show that in-pair and extra-pair increases in sexual desire during the high-fertility period are correlated (Arslan et al., 2018). Further, periovulatory increase in sexual behavior also includes autosexual activities (van Stein et al., 2019), which again supports the motivational priorities hypothesis, but is difficult to reconcile with the dual sexuality hypothesis. Concerning hormonal mechanisms, there is robust evidence concerning a negative effect of progesterone on sexual desire, but the effect of estradiol is more mixed. One reason might be that, on average, levels of estradiol steadily increase during the follicular phase and it might be thus more difficult to detect the changes if the sampling is not performed on a daily basis (see also Roney, 2018). In contrast, progesterone levels are comparatively stable during the luteal phase and its effect thus might be more easily detected. In any case, the proportion of variation in sexual desire and behavior explained by hormonal levels is small, and other factors such cohabitation, the day of the week, communication with partner, and many others might have stronger effects. To be clear, we do not mean to suggest that ovarian hormones do not influence female sexuality. They do, and there appears to be a threshold effect, such that if ovarian hormones drop below a certain level this may have enormous influence on women's sexual desire, as shown in some medical conditions or after menopause (for reviews, see Parish & Hahn, 2016; Pfaus, 2009). Nonetheless, in view of their subtle effects on sexual desire and behavior, human sexual motivations seem to be somewhat decoupled from hormonal fluctuations and are much more influenced by social context.

Broader Context

The dual sexuality hypothesis is further based on two major assumptions: (a) existence of distinct short-term and long-term mating strategies in women, and (b) men providing direct and indirect benefits are two distinct groups pursuing different mating (or sexual) strategies. Although we see such models as theoretically heuristic, we also think they should not be mistaken with phenomena they aim to explain (i.e., the reification fallacy). The concept of short-term versus long-term mating strategies was originally formulated as a part of sexual strategies theory, which aims to explain evolutionary causes of sex differences in mating psychology (Buss, 1994; Buss & Schmitt, 1993). The authors also argued that not only men but also women can benefit from pursuing short-term mating (i.e., having an uncommitted sexual liaison), and labeled these as mating/sexual strategies. Since then, the distinction became popular among evolutionary psychologists and especially within mate preferences studies (for review, see Marzoli et al., 2018). Thus, scholars frequently ask their participants: "Would you find this characteristic attractive in a short-term (or long-term) partner?" Studies employing this concept have produced insightful findings. However, to our knowledge, there is no clear evidence showing how these categories are interpreted by participants and whether scholars are not transferring their theoretical concepts to the participants. It is frequently noted that mating strategies need not be deliberate and that people may pursue them nonconsciously. This may be the case, but as the bulk of research on mating strategies relies on self-reporting, understanding how respondents interpret these research questions is a key issue.

Even if we leave aside these methodological ambiguities and assume that the short-/long-term concept makes good sense to the Western participants on whose reports these studies are predominantly based, it does not automatically imply relevance to ancestral conditions. In the same vein, Henrich et al. (2010) advocated cautious generalizations of psychological research based on participants from Western populations. Studies on social dynamics in hunter–gatherer societies, which are seen as models for our ancestral social structure, demonstrate that individuals most commonly encountered are either those who live in the same group (which frequently have fission-fusion dynamics, mostly of a seasonal form) and are thus seen on a daily basis or members of the neighboring communities who are seen somewhat less often. Thus, people know the majority of people they meet over a long period (mostly since childhood). Such a social environment makes the evolution of distinct short-term mating strategies highly unfavorable. This should not be mistaken for an absence of sexual affairs, as was, for instance, vividly depicted by Shostak (2009), who conducted her fieldwork with San women of Botswana. They reported frequently to have long-term parallel sexual relationships (i.e., lovers). A similar distinction between formal and informal relationships in Himba of Namibia was observed by Scelza and Prall (2018). These are, however, different from the one-night stands, hook-ups, and other casual relationships that are usually typified as short-term mating activities by Western researchers (Wentland & Reissing, 2014).

The second major assumption of the dual sexuality hypothesis is that men who can provide indirect benefits (i.e., men with high-quality genes) pursue mainly a short-term mating strategy as it allows them to increase their reproductive success (Gangestad & Thornhill, 2008). As a consequence, their willingness to provide direct benefits (e.g., in the form of paternal care) is low. This assumes that qualities responsible for direct benefits are of different origin than qualities of indirect benefits. In other words, men who can provide paternal care lack cues of genetic quality. Such an assumption is, however, likely to be unfounded. Indirect benefits in humans can take various forms such as food provisioning, direct care for children, protection against other humans and predators, and teaching local craft knowledge and cultural values (Geary, 2000). Analysis of available data from various societies shows that involvement of fathers varies greatly among communities (Marlowe, 2000). However, and irrespective of form and amount of care provided, most of the listed activities can be performed only by individuals who are healthy, physically fit, and competent. All these characteristics are partly dependent on the genetic makeup of such individuals. Low relevance of separating direct and indirect benefits in the case of human mating systems is also mirrored in female mate preferences. Even women with a high number of casual partners (i.e., suggesting a short-term sexual strategy) do not show lower appreciation of partner's social status as compared to more sexually restricted women (Mikach & Bailey, 1999).

Future Directions

The two contradictory meta-analyses on cyclic changes in mate preferences were followed by a critique concerning the methods used in menstrual cycle-related research. Since then, several studies with more precise methodology and considerably larger samples have been performed and reported. One may therefore think that our understanding of cyclic changes is almost complete. In this section, we aim to show that at this point, we do not so much need further replications but rather a change in research strategy to close remaining knowledge gaps. Most previous research focused on answering whether fertility-related changes in mating psychology exist, and on the size of this effect. Some studies also investigated modulating factors, such as relationship status or mating context. What has been neglected so far is the huge variation in several aspects of the menstrual cycle, both between and within individual women. Although it is theorized that any expected changes are related to ovulation, there is currently no evidence to show that ovulatory and anovulatory cycles differ in the size of changes in mating psychology. Furthermore, some women show large fluctuations in somatic pain or irritation, while others hardly notice in what phase of their cycle they are in. It is currently not clear how such variation is related to changes in mating psychology. The approach focusing solely on fertility was recently criticized for neglecting other phases of the cycle, which may introduce various biases (Kiesner et al., 2020). For instance, changes in well-being may have an impact on self-perception and consequently also on mate preferences and sexual desire. Studies only rarely control for potentially confounding variables such as changes in mood (for an exception, see Stern et al., 2021).

Furthermore, most studies are based on young women in their early 20s, mostly college students (for exceptions, see Blake et al., 2017; Marcinkowska et al., 2016). Studies testing the use of hormonal contraception on sexuality show that effects are often different between young women and older women who often have children (for review, see Pastor et al., 2013). Similarly, cyclic changes in mating psychology might not be generalizable to reproducing women. In addition, all studies on cyclic changes in mating psychology so far are based on women from Western societies. There is evidence that levels of ovarian hormones are, on average, considerably lower in women from non-Western countries (Jasienska et al., 2017), which may again have a significant impact on cyclic changes in mating psychology. Moreover, many women in non-Western societies experience considerably fewer cycles during their reproductive life, because of repeated pregnancies and longer periods of breastfeeding. Long-term data from Dogon women in Mali show that they (on average) experience 109 menstrual cycles over the course of their lives, compared to around 400 in U.S. women (Strassmann, 1997). We therefore believe research addressing some of the outlined issues would significantly contribute to a more systematic knowledge in this fascinating field.

What have we learned?

Although the story is not over and we will surely be confronted with exciting findings in the future, we think we have reached the point where we can make some provisional conclusions. So what are the lessons we have learned from the burgeoning research on cyclic changes in mating psychology? We divide them into four main areas: (a) empirical, (b) theoretical, (c) methodological, and (d) epistemological.

First, there is currently robust evidence, from large and thorough studies, suggesting that cyclic fluctuations in mate preferences are very subtle for certain characteristics and nonexistent for other characteristics. Relatedly, there is no robust evidence that within-individual variation in ovarian hormones is related to fluctuations in preferences. On the other hand, there might be a between-individual association between progesterone and some aspects of mate preferences, as predicted by the spandrel hypothesis. The evidence for cyclic changes in sexual desire and behavior seems to be robust, although the effects are small and might be overridden by other factors such as relationship status or quality, cohabitation, and day of the week. There is also systematic evidence that progesterone is negatively related to sexual desire and mixed evidence for positive association with estradiol. Again, these associations are rather small and contextual factors may play a more pronounced role.

Second, current evidence does not support several predictions for adaptive design related to ovulation. The fluctuations in in-pair and extra-pair desire are correlated and do not show the opposite pattern predicted by the dual sexuality hypothesis. These changes also do not seem to depend on the partner's quality. Instead, the findings provide more consistent support for the motivational priority hypothesis, which predicts that during the high-fertility phase there is heightened motivation for sexual encounters, as only at this time may sex lead to conception and thus increase female fitness.

Third, there has been enormous progress in methodological rigor in cyclic studies. This particularly applies to sample size and to ovulation assessment, where use of counting methods is extremely unreliable and repeated sampling of ovarian hormonal assays should be the gold standard, with use of LH kits as an acceptable minimum. In addition, using between-subjects approaches to study what is a within-subject phenomenon should soon become a thing of the past, unless one incorporates an extremely large sample and controls for numerous confounding variables. Much less effort has been dedicated to establishing the ecological validity of mate preference stimuli (e.g., natural variability in face shape sexual dimorphism), and this should also be targeted by future studies.

Finally, the story of research on cyclic changes convincingly shows how well-formulated theories may become a mainstream view, even though their empirical support is weak and their assumptions unrealistic (e.g., the role of extra-pair copulations). Relatedly, it shows how science often operates in waves of fashion, following a pattern of sporadic interest followed by introduction of an influential theory, an outbreak of empirical activity, and then gradual decline and sporadic interest. This is not restricted to menstrual cycle studies. Other areas such as research on fluctuating asymmetry, waist-to-hip ratio, and second-to-fourth digit ratio (to name just a few) have followed a similar pattern. Over a decade ago, in his critical review of the foundational book *Evolution of Human Female Sexuality* by Thornhill and Gangestad (2008), A. F. Dixson (2009, p. 1069) noted: "Time will tell if I am mistaken about all of this; thankfully, the truth usually emerges in the end, at least in science." The remaining question is whether we needed to experience the whole journey or whether there was a short-cut that might have saved our time and effort, freeing us to explore other exciting aspects of mating psychology.

Acknowledgements

J.H. is supported by the Czech Science Foundation grant (no.18-15168S) and by the Charles University Research Centre (UNCE) programme UNCE/HUM/025(204056). We are indebted to Dagmar Schwambergová for creating the figures and to Jitka Třebická Fialová, Zsófia Csajbók, Zuzana Štěrbová, Justin K. Mogilski, and Todd K. Shackelford for their extremely valuable comments on an earlier version of this chapter.

References

Anderson, K. G. (2006). How well does paternity confidence evidence match actual paternity? *Current Anthropology*, *47*(3), 513–520. https://doi.org/10.1086/504167

Arslan, R. C., Schilling, K. M., Gerlach, T. M., & Penke, L. (2018). Using 26,000 diary entries to show ovulatory changes in sexual desire and behavior. *Journal of Personality and Social Psychology, 121*(2), 410–431. https://doi.org/10.1037/pspp0000208

Bachofner, L. M., & Lobmaier, J. S. (2018). Towards a more holistic view of fertility: The need to consider biological underpinnings rather than only data. *Hormones and Behavior, 106*, A10–A11. https://doi.org/10.1016/j.yhbeh.2018.07.004

Bancroft, J., Sanders, D., Davidson, D., & Warner, P. (1983). Mood, sexuality, hormones, and the menstrual cycle. III. Sexuality and the role of androgens. *Psychosomatic Medicine*, *45*(6), 509–516. https://doi.org/10.1097/00006842-198312000-00005

Beall, A. T., & Tracy, J. L. (2013). Women more likely to wear red or pink at peak fertility. *Psychological Science*, *24*(9), 1837–1841. https://doi.org/10.1177/0956797613476045

Betzig, L. (1989). Causes of conjugal dissolution: A cross-cultural study. *Current Anthropology*, *30*(5), 654. https://doi.org/10.1086/203798

Blake, K. R., Dixson, B. J. W., O'Dean, S. M., & Denson, T. F. (2016). Standardized protocols for characterizing women's fertility: A data-driven approach. *Hormones and Behavior, 81*, 74–83. https://doi.org/10.1016/j.yhbeh.2016.03.004

Blake, K. R., Dixson, B. J. W., O'Dean, S. M., & Denson, T. F. (2017). No compelling positive association between ovarian hormones and wearing red clothing when using multinomial analyses. *Hormones and Behavior, 90*, 129–135. https://doi.org/10.1016/j.yhbeh.2017.03.005

Bobst, C., Sauter, S., Foppa, A., & Lobmaier, J. S. (2014). Early follicular testosterone level predicts preference for masculinity in male faces—But not for women taking hormonal contraception. *Psychoneuroendocrinology, 41*, 142–150. https://doi.org/10.1016/j.psyneuen.2013.12.012

Burleson, M. H., Trevathan, W. R., & Gregory, W. L. (2002). Sexual behavior in lesbian and heterosexual women: Relations with menstrual cycle phase and partner availability. *Psychoneuroendocrinology, 27*(4), 489–503. https://doi.org/10.1016/S0306-4530(01)00066-X

Buss, D. M. (1994). The strategies of human mating. *American Scientist, 82*(3), 238–249. http://www.jstor.org/stable/29775193

Buss, D. M., & Schmitt, D. P. (1993). Sexual strategies theory—An evolutionary perspective on human mating. *Psychological Review, 100*(2), 204–232. https://doi.org/10.1037/0033-295X.100.2.204

Caruso, S., Agnello, C., Malandrino, C., Lo Presti, L., Cicero, C., & Cianci, S. (2014). Do hormones influence women's sex? Sexual activity over the menstrual cycle. *Journal of Sexual Medicine, 11*(1), 211–221. https://doi.org/10.1111/jsm.12348

Cobey, K. D., Buunk, A. P., Pollet, T. V., Klipping, C., & Roberts, S. C. (2013). Men perceive their female partners, and themselves, as more attractive around ovulation. *Biological Psychology, 94*(3), 513–516. https://doi.org/10.1016/j.biopsycho.2013.09.011

Cobey, K. D., Little, A. C., & Roberts, S. C. (2015). Hormonal effects on women's facial masculinity preferences: The influence of pregnancy, post-partum, and hormonal contraceptive use. *Biological Psychology, 104*, 35–40. https://doi.org/10.1016/j.biopsycho.2014.11.002

DeBruine, L. M., Hahn, A. C., & Jones, B. C. (2019). Does the interaction between partnership status and average progesterone level predict women's preferences for facial masculinity? *Hormones and Behavior, 107*, 80–82. https://doi.org/10.1016/j.yhbeh.2018.12.004

Ditzen, B., Palm-Fischbacher, S., Gossweiler, L., Stucky, L., & Ehlert, U. (2017). Effects of stress on women's preference for male facial masculinity and their endocrine correlates. *Psychoneuroendocrinology, 82*, 67–74. https://doi.org/10.1016/j.psyneuen.2017.05.006

Dixson, A. F. (2009). The evolutionary biology of human female sexuality. Book review. *Archives of Sexual Behavior, 38*(6), 1067–1069. https://doi.org/10.1007/s10508-009-9584-5

Dixson, B. J. W., Blake, K. R., Denson, T. F., Gooda-Vossos, A., O'Dean, S. M., Sulikowski, D., Rantala, M. J., & Brooks, R. C. (2018). The role of mating context and fecundability in women's preferences for men's facial masculinity and beardedness. *Psychoneuroendocrinology, 93*, 90–102. https://doi.org/10.1016/j.psyneuen.2018.04.007

Dixson, B. J. W., Lee, A. J., Blake, K. R., Jasienska, G., & Marcinkowska, U. M. (2018). Women's preferences for men's beards show no relation to their ovarian cycle phase and sex hormone levels. *Hormones and Behavior, 97*, 137–144. https://doi.org/10.1016/j.yhbeh.2017.11.006

Durante, K. M., Li, N. P., & Haselton, M. G. (2008). Changes in women's choice of dress across the ovulatory cycle: Naturalistic and laboratory task-based evidence. *Personality & Social Psychology Bulletin, 34*(11), 1451–1460. https://doi.org/10.1177/0146167208323103

Eisenbruch, A. B., Simmons, Z. L., & Roney, J. R. (2015). Lady in red: Hormonal predictors of women's clothing choices. *Psychological Science, 26*(8), 1332–1338. https://doi.org/10.1177/0956797615586403

Elliot, A. J., & Niesta, D. (2008). Romantic red: Red enhances men's attraction to women. *Journal of Personality and Social Psychology, 95*(5), 1150–1164. https://doi.org/10.1037/0022-3514.95.5.1150

Ferguson, C. J. (2014). Comment: Why meta-analyses rarely resolve ideological debates. *Emotion Review, 6*(3), 251–252. https://doi.org/10.1177/1754073914523046

Fessler, D. M. T. (2003). No time to eat: An adaptationist account of periovulatory behavioral changes. *Quarterly Review of Biology, 78*(1), 3–21. https://doi.org/10.1086/703580

Gangestad, S. W., Dinh, T., Grebe, N. M., Del Giudice, M., & Emery Thompson, M. (2019). Psychological cycle shifts redux, once again: Response to Stern et al., Roney, Jones et al., and Higham. *Evolution and Human Behavior, 40*(6), 537–542. https://doi.org/10.1016/j.evolhumbehav.2019.08.008

Gangestad, S. W., Garver-Apgar, C. E., Simpson, J. A., & Cousins, A. J. (2007). Changes in women's mate preferences across the ovulatory cycle. *Journal of Personality and Social Psychology, 92*(1), 151–163. https://doi.org/10.1037/0022-3514.92.1.151

Gangestad, S. W., & Grebe, N. M. (2015). Are within-cycle variations in women's sexual interests mere by-products? A comment on Havliček et al. *Behavioral Ecology, 26*(5), 1262–1263. https://doi.org/10.1093/beheco/arv113

Gangestad, S. W., & Haselton, M. G. (2015). Human estrus: Implications for relationship science. *Current Opinion in Psychology, 1*, 45–51. https://doi.org/10.1016/j.copsyc.2014.12.007

Gangestad, S. W., Haselton, M. G., Welling, L. L. M., Gildersleeve, K., Pillsworth, E. G., Burriss, R. P., Larson, C. M., & Puts, D. A. (2016). How valid are assessments of conception probability in ovulatory cycle research? Evaluations, recommendations, and theoretical implications. *Evolution and Human Behavior, 37*(2), 85–96. https://doi.org/10.1016/j.evolhumbehav.2015.09.001

Gangestad, S. W., & Thornhill, R. (2008). Human oestrus. *Proceedings of the Royal Society B-Biological Sciences, 275*(1638), 991–1000. https://doi.org/10.1098/rspb.2007.1425

Gangestad, S. W., Thornhill, R., & Garver, C. E. (2002). Changes in women's sexual interests and their partners' mate-retention tactics across the menstrual cycle: Evidence for shifting conflicts of interest. *Proceedings of the Royal Society B-Biological Sciences, 269*(1494), 975–982. https://doi.org/10.1098/rspb.2001.1952

Gangestad, S. W., Thornhill, R., & Garver-Apgar, C. E. (2005a). Adaptations to ovulation:Implications for sexual and social behavior. *Current Directions in Psychological Science, 14*(6), 312–316. https://doi.org/10.1111/j.0963-7214.2005.00388.x

Gangestad, S. W., Thornhill, R., & Garver-Apgar, C. E. (2005b). Women's sexual interests across the ovulatory cycle depend on primary partner developmental instability. *Proceedings of the Royal Society B-Biological Sciences, 272*(1576), 2023–2027. https://doi.org/10.1098/rspb.2005.3112

Gangestad, S. W., Thornhill, R., & Garver-Apgar, C. E. (2010). Men's facial masculinity predicts changes in their female partners' sexual interests across the ovulatory cycle, whereas men's intelligence does not. *Evolution and Human Behavior, 31*(6), 412–424. https://doi.org/10.1016/j.evolhumbehav.2010.06.001

Geary, D. C. (2000). Evolution and proximate expression of human paternal investment. *Psychological Bulletin, 126*(1), 55–77. https://doi.org/10.1037/0033-2909.126.1.55

Gildersleeve, K., Haselton, M. G., & Fales, M. R. (2014). Do women's mate preferences change across the ovulatory cycle? A meta-analytic review. *Psychological Bulletin, 140*(5), 1205–1259. https://doi.org/10.1037/a0035438

Grebe, N. M., Emery Thompson, M., & Gangestad, S. W. (2016). Hormonal predictors of women's extra-pair vs. in-pair sexual attraction in natural cycles: Implications for extended sexuality. *Hormones and Behavior, 78*, 211–219. https://doi.org/10.1016/j.yhbeh.2015.11.008

Grebe, N. M., Gangestad, S. W., Garver-Apgar, C. E., & Thornhill, R. (2013). Women's luteal-phase sexual proceptivity and the functions of extended sexuality. *Psychological Science, 24*(10), 2106–2110. https://doi.org/10.1177/0956797613485965

Haselton, M. G., & Gangestad, S. W. (2006). Conditional expression of women's desires and men's mate guarding across the ovulatory cycle. *Hormones and Behavior, 49*(4), 509–518. https://doi.org/10.1016/j.yhbeh.2005.10.006

Haselton, M. G., Mortezaie, M., Pillsworth, E. G., Bleske-Rechek, A., & Frederick, D. A. (2007). Ovulatory shifts in human female ornamentation: Near ovulation, women dress to impress. *Hormones and Behavior, 51*(1), 40–45. https://doi.org/10.1016/j.yhbeh.2006.07.007

Havlíček, J., Cobey, K. D., Barrett, L., Klapilová, K., & Roberts, S. C. (2015). The spandrels of Santa Barbara? A new perspective on the peri-ovulation paradigm. *Behavioral Ecology, 26*(5), 1249–1260. https://doi.org/10.1093/beheco/arv064

Havlicek, J., Roberts, S. C., & Flegr, J. (2005). Women's preference for dominant male odour: Effects of menstrual cycle and relationship status. *Biology Letters, 1*(3), 256–259. https://doi.org/10.1098/rsbl.2005.0332

Henrich, J., Heine, S. J., & Norenzayan, A. (2010). The weirdest people in the world. *Behavioral and Brain Sciences, 33*(2–3), 61–83. https://doi.org/10.1017/S0140525X0999152X

Jasienska, G., Bribiescas, R. G., Furberg, A. S., Helle, S., & Núñez-de la Mora, A. (2017). Human reproduction and health: An evolutionary perspective. *The Lancet, 390*(10093), 510–520. https://doi.org/10.1016/S0140-6736(17)30573-1

Jones, B. C., Hahn, A. C., & DeBruine, L. M. (2019). Ovulation, sex hormones, and women's mating psychology. *Trends in Cognitive Sciences, 23*(1), 51–62. https://doi.org/10.1016/j.tics.2018.10.008

Jones, B. C., Hahn, A. C., Fisher, C. I., Wang, H., Kandrik, M., & DeBruine, L. M. (2018). General sexual desire, but not desire for uncommitted sexual relationships, tracks changes in women's hormonal status. *Psychoneuroendocrinology, 88*, 153–157. https://doi.org/10.1016/j.psyneuen.2017.12.015

Jones, B. C., Hahn, A. C., Fisher, C. I., Wang, H., Kandrik, M., Han, C., Fasolt, V., Morrison, D., Lee, A. J., Holzleitner, I. J., O'Shea, K. J., Roberts, S. C., Little, A. C., & DeBruine, L. M. (2018). No compelling evidence that preferences for facial masculinity track changes in women's hormonal status. *Psychological Science, 29*(6), 996–1005. https://doi.org/10.1177/0956797618760197

Jones, B. C., Marcinkowska, U. M., & DeBruine, L. M. (2019). Assessing the evidentiary value of secondary data analyses: A commentary on Gangestad, Dinh, Grebe, Del Giudice, and Thompson (2019). *Evolution and Human Behavior, 40*(6), 531–532. https://doi.org/10.1016/j.evolhumbehav.2019.08.004

Jünger, J., Kordsmeyer, T. L., Gerlach, T. M., & Penke, L. (2018). Fertile women evaluate male bodies as more attractive, regardless of masculinity. *Evolution and Human Behavior, 39*(4), 412–423. https://doi.org/10.1016/j.evolhumbehav.2018.03.007

Kiesner, J., Eisenlohr-Moul, T., & Mendle, J. (2020). Evolution, the menstrual cycle, and theoretical overreach. *Perspectives on Psychological Science, 15*(4), 1113–1130. https://doi.org/10.1177/1745691620906440

Kleisner, K., Tureček, P., Roberts, S. C., Havlíček, J., Valentova, J. V., Akoko, R. M., Leongómez, J. D., Apostol, S., Varella, M. A. C., & Saribay, S. A. (2021). How and why patterns of sexual dimorphism in human faces vary across the world. *Scientific Reports, 11*, 5978. https://doi.org/10.31234/osf.io/7vdmb

Krzywinski, M., & Altman, N. (2013). Points of significance: Power and sample size. *Nature Methods, 10*(12), 1139–1140. https://doi.org/10.1038/nmeth.2738

Larmuseau, M. H. D., Matthijs, K., & Wenseleers, T. (2016). Cuckolded fathers rare in human populations. *Trends in Ecology and Evolution, 31*(5), 327–329. https://doi.org/10.1016/j.tree.2016.03.004

Larson, C. M., Pillsworth, E. G., & Haselton, M. G. (2012). Ovulatory shifts in women's attractions to primary partners and other men: Further evidence of the importance of primary partner sexual attractiveness. *PloS ONE, 7*(9), e44456. https://doi.org/10.1371/journal.pone.0044456

Lobmaier, J. S., & Bachofner, L. M. (2018). Timing is crucial: Some critical thoughts on using LH tests to determine women's current fertility. *Hormones and Behavior, 106*, A2–A3. https://doi.org/10.1016/j.yhbeh.2018.07.005

Marcinkowska, U. M. (2020). Importance of daily sex hormone measurements within the menstrual cycle for fertility estimates in cyclical shifts studies. *Evolutionary Psychology, 18*(1), 1–8. https://doi.org/10.1177/1474704919897913

Marcinkowska, U. M., Ellison, P. T., Galbarczyk, A., Milkowska, K., Pawlowski, B., Thune, I., & Jasienska, G. (2016). Lack of support for relation between woman's masculinity preference, estradiol level and mating context. *Hormones and Behavior, 78*, 1–7. https://doi.org/10.1016/j.yhbeh.2015.10.012

Marcinkowska, U. M., Galbarczyk, A., & Jasienska, G. (2018). La donna è mobile? Lack of cyclical shifts in facial symmetry, and facial and body masculinity preferences—A hormone based study. *Psychoneuroendocrinology, 88*, 47–53. https://doi.org/10.1016/j.psyneuen.2017.11.007

Marcinkowska, U. M., Mijas, M., Koziara, K., Grebe, N. M., & Jasienska, G. (2021). Variation in sociosexuality across natural menstrual cycles: Associations with ovarian hormones and cycle phase. *Evolution and Human Behavior, 42*(1), 35–42. https://doi.org/10.1016/j.evolhumbehav.2020.06.008

Marlowe, F. (2000). Paternal investment and the human mating system. *Behavioural Processes, 51*(1–3), 45–61. https://doi.org/10.1016/S0376-6357(00)00118-2

Marzoli, D., Havlíček, J., & Roberts, S. C. (2018). Human mating strategies: From past causes to present consequences. *Wiley Interdisciplinary Reviews: Cognitive Science, 9*(2), 1–18. https://doi.org/10.1002/wcs.1456

McNutt, M., Lehnert, K., Hanson, B., Nosek, B. A., Ellison, A. M., & King, J. L. (2016). Liberating field science samples and data. *Science, 351*(6277), 1024–1026. https://doi.org/10.1126/science.aad7048

Mikach, S. M., & Bailey, J. M. (1999). What distinguishes women with unusually high numbers of sex partners? *Evolution and Human Behavior, 20*(3), 141–150. https://doi.org/10.1016/S1090-5138(98)00045-2

Mitteroecker, P., Windhager, S., Müller, G. B., & Schaefer, K. (2015). The morphometrics of "masculinity" in human faces. *PLoS ONE, 10*(2), e0118374. https://doi.org/10.1371/journal.pone.0118374

Munafò, M. R., Nosek, B. A., Bishop, D. V. M., Button, K. S., Chambers, C. D., Percie du Sert, N., Simonsohn, U., Wagenmakers, E.-J., Ware, J. J., & Ioannidis, J. P. A. (2017). A manifesto for reproducible science. *Nature Human Behaviour, 1*(1), 0021. https://doi.org/10.1038/s41562-016-0021

Parish, S. J., & Hahn, S. R. (2016). Hypoactive sexual desire disorder: A review of epidemiology, biopsychology, diagnosis, and treatment. *Sexual Medicine Reviews, 4*(2), 103–120. https://doi.org/10.1016/j.sxmr.2015.11.009

Pastor, Z., Holla, K., & Chmel, R. (2013). The influence of combined oral contraceptives on female sexual desire: A systematic review. *The European Journal of Contraception & Reproductive Health Care, 18*(1), 27–43. https://doi.org/10.3109/13625187.2012.728643

Pawłowski, B. (1999). Loss of oestrus and concealed ovulation in human evolution: The case against the sexual-selection hypothesis. *Current Anthropology, 40*(3), 257–276. https://doi.org/10.1086/200017

Penke, L., & Asendorpf, J. B. (2008). Beyond global sociosexual orientations: A more differentiated look at sociosexuality and its effects on courtship and romantic relationships. *Journal of Personality and Social Psychology, 95*(5), 1113–1135. https://doi.org/10.1037/0022-3514.95.5.1113

Penton-Voak, I. S., Perrett, D. I., Castles, D. L., Kobayashi, T., Burt, D. M., Murray, L. K., & Minamisawa, R. (1999). Menstrual cycle alters face preference. *Nature, 399*(6738), 741–742. https://doi.org/10.1038/21557

Pfaus, J. G. (2009). Pathways of sexual desire. *Journal of Sexual Medicine, 6*(6), 1506–1533. https://doi.org/10.1111/j.1743-6109.2009.01309.x

Pillsworth, E. G., & Haselton, M. G. (2006). Male sexual attractiveness predicts differential ovulatory shifts in female extra-pair attraction and male mate retention. *Evolution and Human Behavior, 27*(4), 247–258. https://doi.org/10.1016/j.evolhumbehav.2005.10.002

Pillsworth, E. G., Haselton, M. G., & Buss, D. M. (2004). Ovulatory shifts in female sexual desire. *Journal of Sex Research, 41*(1), 55–65. https://doi.org/10.1080/00224490409552213

Prokop, P., & Hromada, M. (2013). Women use red in order to attract mates. *Ethology, 119*(7), 605–613. https://doi.org/10.1111/eth.12102

Roberts, S. C., Cobey, K. D., Klapilová, K., & Havlíček, J. (2013). An evolutionary approach offers a fresh perspective on the relationship between oral contraception and sexual desire. *Archives of Sexual Behavior, 42*(8), 1369–1375. https://doi.org/10.1007/s10508-013-0126-9

Roberts, S. C., Owen, R. C., & Havliček, J. (2010). Distinguishing between perceiver and wearer effects in clothing color-associated attributions. *Evolutionary Psychology, 8*(3), 350–364. https://doi.org/10.1177/147470491000800304

Roney, J. R. (2018). Functional roles of gonadal hormones in human pair bonding and sexuality. In O. C. Schultheiss & H. Mehta Pranjal (Eds.), *Routledge international handbook of social neuroendocrinology* (pp. 239–255). Routledge.

Roney, J. R. (2019). On the use of log transformations when testing hormonal predictors of cycle phase shifts: Commentary on Gangestad, Dinh, Grebe, Del Giudice, and Emery Thompson (2019). *Evolution and Human Behavior, 40*(6), 526–530. https://doi.org/10.1016/j.evolhumbehav.2019.08.006

Roney, J. R., & Simmons, Z. L. (2008). Women's estradiol predicts preference for facial cues of men's testosterone. *Hormones and Behavior, 53*(1), 14–19. https://doi.org/10.1016/j.yhbeh.2007.09.008

Roney, J. R., & Simmons, Z. L. (2013). Hormonal predictors of sexual motivation in natural menstrual cycles. *Hormones and Behavior, 63*(4), 636–645. https://doi.org/10.1016/j.yhbeh.2013.02.013

Roney, J. R., & Simmons, Z. L. (2016). Within-cycle fluctuations in progesterone negatively predict changes in both in-pair and extra-pair desire among partnered women. *Hormones and Behavior, 81*, 45–52. https://doi.org/10.1016/j.yhbeh.2016.03.008

Scelza, B. A. (2011). Female choice and extrapair paternity in a traditional human population. *Biology Letters, 7*(6), 889–891. https://doi.org/10.1098/rsbl.2011.0478

Scelza, B. A., & Prall, S. P. (2018). Partner preferences in the context of concurrency: What Himba want in formal and informal partners. *Evolution and Human Behavior, 39*(2), 212–219. https://doi.org/10.1016/j.evolhumbehav.2017.12.005

Shimoda, R., Campbell, A., & Barton, R. A. (2018). Women's emotional and sexual attraction to men across the menstrual cycle. *Behavioral Ecology, 29*(1), 51–59. https://doi.org/10.1093/beheco/arx124

Shirazi, T. N., Bossio, J. A., Puts, D. A., & Chivers, M. L. (2018). Menstrual cycle phase predicts women's hormonal responses to sexual stimuli. *Hormones and Behavior, 103*, 45–53. https://doi.org/10.1016/j.yhbeh.2018.05.023

Shirazi, T. N., Self, H., Dawood, K., Rosenfield, K. A., Penke, L., Carré, J. M., Ortiz, T., & Puts, D. A. (2019). Hormonal predictors of women's sexual motivation. *Evolution and Human Behavior, 40*(3), 336–344. https://doi.org/10.1016/j.evolhumbehav.2019.02.002

Shostak, M. (2009). *Nisa: The life and words of a !Kung woman*. Harvard University Press.

Stern, J., Arslan, R. C., Gerlach, T. M., & Penke, L. (2019). No robust evidence for cycle shifts in preferences for men's bodies in a multiverse analysis: A response to Gangestad, Dinh, Grebe, Del Giudice, and Emery Thompson (2019). *Evolution and Human Behavior, 40*(6), 517–525. https://doi.org/10.1016/j.evolhumbehav.2019.08.005

Stern, J., Gerlach, T. M., & Penke, L. (2020). Probing ovulatory-cycle shifts in women's preferences for men's behaviors. *Psychological Science, 31*(4), 424–436. https://doi.org/10.1177/0956797619882022

Stern, J., Kordsmeyer, T. L., & Penke, L. (2021). A longitudinal evaluation of ovulatory cycle shifts in women's mate attraction and preferences. *Hormones and Behavior, 128*, 104916. https://doi.org/10.1016/j.yhbeh.2020.104916

Strassmann, B. I. (1997). The biology of menstruation in *Homo sapiens*: Total lifetime menses, fecundity, and nonsynchrony in a natural-fertility population. *Current Anthropology, 38*(1), 123–129. https://doi.org/10.1086/204592

Thornhill, R., & Gangestad, S. W. (2008). *The evolutionary biology of human female sexuality.* Oxford University Press.

Thornhill, R., & Moller, A. P. (1997). Developmental stability, disease and medicine. *Biological Reviews, 72*(4), 497–548.

Tracy, J. L., & Beall, A. T. (2014). The impact of weather on women's tendency to wear red or pink when at high risk for conception. *PLoS ONE, 9*(2), e88852. https://doi.org/10.1371/journal.pone.0088852

Udry, J. R., & Morris, N. M. (1968). Distribution of coitus in the menstrual cycle. *Nature, 220*(5167), 593–596. https://doi.org/10.1038/220593a0

van Goozen, S. H. M., Wiegant, V. M., Endert, E., Helmond, F. A., & Van de Poll, N. E. (1997). Psychoendocrinological assessment of the menstrual cycle: The relationship between hormones, sexuality, and mood. *Archives of Sexual Behavior, 26*(4), 359–382. https://doi.org/10.1023/A:1024587217927

van Stein, K. R., Strauß, B., & Brenk-Franz, K. (2019). Ovulatory shifts in sexual desire but not mate preferences: An LH-test-confirmed, longitudinal study. *Evolutionary Psychology, 17*(2), 1–10. https://doi.org/10.1177/1474704919848116

Wallen, K. (2001). Sex and context: Hormones and primate sexual motivation. *Hormones and Behavior, 40*, 339–357. https://doi.org/10.1006/hbeh.2001.1696

Wentland, J. J., & Reissing, E. (2014). Casual sexual relationships: Identifying definitions for one night stands, booty calls, fuck buddies, and friends with benefits. *Canadian Journal of Human Sexuality, 23*(3), 167–177. https://doi.org/10.3138/cjhs.2744

Wilcox, A. J., Day Baird, D., Dunson, D. B., McConnaughey, D. R., Kesner, J. S., & Weinberg, C. R. (2004). On the frequency of intercourse around ovulation: Evidence for biological influences. *Human Reproduction, 19*(7), 1539–1543. https://doi.org/10.1093/humrep/deh305

Wilcox, A. J., Dunson, D. B., Weinberg, C. R., Trussell, J., & Baird, D. D. (2001). Likelihood of conception with a single act of intercourse: Providing benchmark rates for assessment of post-coital contraceptives. *Contraception, 63*(4), 211–215. https://doi.org/10.1016/S0010-7824(01)00191-3

Wood, W., & Carden, L. (2014). Elusiveness of menstrual cycle effects on mate preferences: Comment on Gildersleeve, Haselton, and Fales (2014). *Psychological Bulletin, 140*(5), 1265–1271. https://doi.org/10.1037/a0036722

Wood, W., Kressel, L., Joshi, P. D., & Louie, B. (2014). Meta-analysis of menstrual cycle effects on women's mate preferences. *Emotion Review, 6*(3), 229–249. https://doi.org/10.1177/1754073914523073

CHAPTER

25 Affective Reactions to Divorce or Spousal Death

Jeannette Brodbeck *and* Hans Joerg Znoj

Abstract

This chapter explores similarities and differences in emotional reactions, physical and mental health consequences, and coping after the breakup of a long-term romantic relationship and spousal death. We employ an attachment perspective and argue that the core of both events is the activation of the attachment system and a separation reaction that result in similar affective reactions including grief, anger, and anxiety. Even though the most frequent long-term adaptation to partner loss is resilience, both events increase the risk for mental and physical health problems and higher mortality. Separation/divorce and spousal death require an attachment reorganization and share adaptation tasks such as creating a new life and identity without the partner and transforming the bond with the lost person. Furthermore, the established dual process model of coping with bereavement is applicable for both events. This is supported by the results of an online self-help program for prolonged grief that indicate that separated and widowed individuals benefit from the same interventions. Despite these similarities, theory and research related to separation/divorce and spousal death have traditionally been separate. We argue that it is fruitful to integrate these research traditions into a broader conceptual framework of separation and loss. Future research should empirically test similarities and differences in affective reactions, challenges, and coping strategies and identify optimal ways of intervention and prevention. For this purpose, we discuss how social media or virtual reality offer new opportunities for coping but also how they may prolong the process of adaptation.

Key Words: bereavement, separation/divorce, emotions, grief, coping, intervention

An attachment perspective on partner loss

Humans share with other social animals the capacity to bond and to build long-lasting social relationships. The need to belong is a fundamental human motivation (Baumeister & Leary, 1995) that drives attachment to others in various ways (e.g., as dependent children, lovers, or because people share the same living circumstances). Long-term romantic relationships are among the strongest bonds in human life and the breakup of a romantic relationship or death of a spouse are major, stressful life events. Still, in Western countries, up to half of marriages end in divorce. According to recent statistics from the Office for National Statistics (2020), 42% of marriages in England and Wales ended in divorce. The average age for divorce among opposite-sex couples in 2018 was 46.9 years for men and 44.5 years for women. In Switzerland in 2018, 40% of marriages ended in divorce; 45% of the divorces occurred after 15 or more years (Federal Statistical Office, 2020). In 2019, 4.7% of the population was widowed, 8.6% divorced. Up to the age of 70, more individuals were divorced than widowed.

Many studies show that separation/divorce and spousal death have a negative impact on psychological, social, and physical well-being (e.g., Hughes & Waite, 2009; Luhmann et al., 2012; Stroebe et al., 2007). However, there are large individual differences in the duration and severity of these consequences and it is not well understood through which mechanisms of action the loss of a partner is linked to these health outcomes. Bowlby's attachment theory (Bowlby, 1969, 1980) provides a useful framework for understanding the consequences and reactions to partner loss due to divorce or spousal death (e.g., Feeney & Monin, 2016; Fletcher et al., 2019; Sbarra & Borelli, 2019; Sbarra & Coan, 2017; Shear & Shair, 2005). Attachment theory is an evolutionary theory of social and personality development across the lifespan and was originally developed to describe infant reactions after separation from their caregiver. The attachment figure represents a safe haven to where the infant can turn for comfort and support when distressed and a secure base for exploration and play. Bowlby assumes that the attachment system was evolutionarily designed and shaped by natural selection when survival and reproductive fitness increased in infants who forged stronger emotional bonds with their caregivers, maintained closer physical contact with them, and later successfully transferred these attachment functions to close friends and/or romantic partners (Bowlby, 1969; Fletcher et al., 2019). Shaver and Hazan (1987) proposed that the attachment system is co-opted to facilitate bonding in adult romantic relationship. These romantic relationships have similarities to the relationship between an infant and caregiver, including the desire for proximity and security.

Bowlby's theory of loss, grief, and mourning describes how children and adults respond to separations from an attachment figure (Bowlby, 1980). This separation reaction consists of active distress, sorrow, anger, and passive-depressive behavior, which assists in maintaining important social bonds and limiting long-term separations. It is adaptive in the case of a temporal separation but not flexible enough to be suppressed in the case of death. Archer (2001) concluded that grief is not adaptive for survival or reproductive fitness and that the poor health outcomes related to grief can even lower fitness. Nevertheless, grief is a consequence of how emotional bonds are maintained.

This chapter aims to link two strands of theory and research related to separation/divorce and spousal loss due to death. The core of both experiences is the separation from the spouse and the loss of an attachment figure who is no longer emotionally available and not part of one's daily life. We explore the similarities and differences in the characteristics and the consequences of separation/divorce and spousal death and discuss whether theoretical models for the adaptation and coping for one of the events can be applied to the other. Table 25.1 provides a summary of the similarities and differences between the

Table 25.1 Summary of Similarities and Differences Between Separation/Divorce and Spousal Death

	Separation/divorce	Spousal death
Characteristics of the event		
- Finality	Potentially reversible	Final
- Initiator	One of the partners	Destiny, illness, age
- Temporal dynamics	Long-term uncoupling process	Discrete event (sudden or foreseeable)
- Preloss history	Conflict or estrangement	Not per se interpersonally problematic
- Postloss history	Ongoing real-world relationship with the partner, probably interfering with daily life	Transition to a symbolic relationship with the deceased partner
- Average age and life perspective	Younger age and longer life perspective	Older age and shorter life perspective
Cultural and societal aspects		
- Cultural/religious rituals as formats of mourning	No cultural aids/religious rituals or religious exclusion, disenfranchised grief	Established and elaborated shared rituals
- Societal attribution	Failure	Fate
- Traditional cultural reactions	Blame, condemnation, social exclusion	Compassion and support
Consequences for attachment system		
- Loss of attachment figure and activated attachment system	Attachment figure no more emotionally available, not there in daily life	Attachment figure no more emotionally available, not there in daily life
- Separation reaction	Large individual differences	Large individual differences
- Attachment reorganization for adaptive grief response	Shift from an interdependent regulation to independent regulation	Shift from an interdependent regulation to independent regulation
Social and psychological consequences		
- Changes in social and financial resources and daily life	Reorganization required for both events	Reorganization required for both events
- Loneliness	Frequent reaction	Frequent reaction
- Affective reactions	Similar reactions possible but broader range; frequent troubles accepting the loss and difficulties trusting others; reactions may be indicative of different severity level of grief	Similar reactions possible, frequent longing and yearning, emotional pain
- Posttraumatic growth	Possible	Possible

(continued)

Table 25.1 *Continued*

	Separation/divorce	Spousal death
- Long-term adaptation patterns	Resilience as most frequent pattern, more diverse maladaptive pattern after divorce?	Resilience as most frequent pattern
Grief		
- Specific diagnosis	No specific diagnosis after divorce	Grief-related disorders listed in psychiatric classification systems (DSM-5 and ICD-11)
- Separation distress	Possible	Possible, more pronounced?
- Reactive distress	Possible (e.g., difficulties accepting the loss, self-blame, avoidance of reminders of the loss)	Possible (e.g., difficulties accepting the loss, self-blame, avoidance of reminders of the loss)
- Social/identity disruption	Possible	Possible
Distal health outcomes		
- Risk for physical and mental health problems and mortality	Increased	Increased
- Health risk behaviors	Increased	Increased
- Mechanisms of action linking event to distal helth outcomes	Similar for both events; that is, changes of social and financial resources, cognitive and affective experiences and changes in health behaviors leading to health-relevant biological changes	Similar for both events; that is, changes of social and financial resources, cognitive and affective experiences and changes in health behaviors leading to health-relevant biological changes
Tasks of mourning sensu Worden (2009)		
- Accepting the reality of the loss	Required, more difficult as reunion might be possible?	Required
- Processing the pain	Required	Required
- Creating new identify, finding new roles	Required	Required
- New definition of the relationship to the lost partner	Renegotiate new relationship with the ex-partner in real life	Transform continuing bonds or ending the bond
Dual process model for coping with bereavement		
- Loss-oriented coping	Applicable if grief is present, large individual differences	Required
- Restoration-oriented coping	Required	Required

Table 25.1 *Continued*

	Separation/divorce	Spousal death
- Oscillation between loss-, and restoration-oriented coping	Applicable if grief is present	Required
Interventions		
- Established treatments	No specific established interventions	Well validated treatments for prolonged grief
- Online self-help program LIVIA for coping with the loss of a partner	Efficacy established, similar effects	Efficacy established, similar effects

two events. In addition to attachment theory, we refer to other theoretical models which employ a cognitive stress perspective with a focus on coping with stressors, meaning making, and identity disruption (e.g., Amato, 2000; Stroebe & Schut, 1999), as well as grief as a reaction to partner loss. Finally, we investigate whether there is a need for different interventions for grief and adaptation problems after separation/divorce or spousal death.

Some findings reported in this chapter stem from a project that is part of the Swiss National Centre of Competence in Research: "LIVES—Overcoming vulnerability: life course perspectives: IP 212 Relationships in later life." More than 2,000 older adults were recruited based on a random sample stratified by age group, gender, and marital status supplied by the Swiss Federal Office of Statistics. The three-wave survey study aims to gain insight into the trajectories of psychological adaptation to divorce or spousal death in the second half of life. A further subproject consists of the development and evaluation of the guided online self-help intervention LIVIA for divorced and widowed older adults for coping with prolonged grief and adaptation problems after the loss of a partner.

Partner Loss due to Divorce or Spousal Death

Many differences between divorce and spousal death are related to the cultural context and the societal appraisal of the events. Although legal divorce is a relatively new phenomenon which has increased considerably during the last 30 years (Perrig-Chiello et al., 2015), mourning the death of a spouse has been a human experience since the emergence of committed relationships. Not surprisingly, religious belief systems, rituals, and social coping strategies for death-related losses have been developed in many cultures. Rites of passage from the state of living to the state of death are major topics in religious contexts as well as in ancestor cults. In ancient Egypt and Greece, the passage from life to death was considered dangerous. To be safe, people performed elaborate funerary practices and made provisions for the afterlife. Examples are the physical preservation of the body, grave goods, or a coin placed in the mouth of the deceased to pay Charon, the ferryman who carried souls across the river that divided the world of the living from the world of the dead. Being a member of one's culture, individuals can cope with the death of a person with the help of a common belief system and by sharing the grief with members of the community. Rituals give both structure and solace to the bereaved and are at the same time reminder of the own mortality.

In contrast to a loss due to death, a romantic breakup has no or fewer cultural aids or rituals (Doka, 2008). A separation or divorce is often seen as a sign of a failed life and many cultures condemn divorce or tolerate it only among privileged members of the society (e.g., Encyclopaedia Britannica, 2020; Rowlandson & Bagnall, 1998). Although the effects of a marital separation or divorce can be stressful and a health risk (Sbarra et al., 2011), no format for mourning exists for divorce. Divorcees have to cope by themselves and often will experience social exclusion. Thus, grief after a divorce has also been called disenfranchised grief (Doka, 2008).

In addition to these cultural distinctions, further differences between a separation/divorce and spousal death include the preloss history and temporal dynamics of the loss. The divorce-stress-adaptation model (Amato, 2000) highlights that a divorce is not a discrete event in time but an uncoupling process. In most cases, this process involves conflicts or feelings of estrangement before the separation, the legal act of divorce itself, the immediate post-divorce period perhaps with custody over children or loss of contact with children, moving from the family home, and maybe longer-lasting conflicts with the ex-partner. Finally, a new relationship with the ex-partner has to be negotiated. In the case of spousal death, many losses are sudden and not foreseeable. Still, preloss history is important as prior conflicts or unfinished business with the deceased are risk factors for intensifying or prolonging grief reactions and even grief-related disorders (Field, 2006; Holland et al., 2020).

A main difference between spousal death and separation/divorce is the finality of the loss. The death of a spouse is irreversible and facilitates idealizing the lost relationship and the lost partner (Yárnoz-Yaben, 2017). In contrast, a separation/divorce is the end of a marriage but often not the end of a relationship. The loss may be uncertain and potentially recoverable and uncertain losses often lead to complicated forms of bereavement (Znoj, 2016a). Contact between former partners can be intense and long-lasting, especially when divorcees have young children together (Symoens et al., 2014). Conflictual contacts between ex-partners have been associated with poorer emotional adaptation over time (Amato & Hohmann-Marriott, 2007; Symoens et al., 2014). However, positive relationships between former partners can also represent a possible resource for adaptation to divorce (Kulik & Heine-Cohen, 2011).

Apart from these differences, separation/divorce and spousal death show many similarities. In both events, the attachment system is affected by the loss of an attachment figure. Spousal death and a romantic breakup can cause separation distress with symptoms such as longing for and preoccupation with the lost person. In addition, there can be reactions such as difficulties accepting the loss; avoidance of reminders or activities related to the lost spouse; inability to trust others, feelings of detachment, bitterness, and anger toward the lost spouse; difficulties moving on with life; numbness; and the belief that life is unfulfilling, empty, meaningless, or unbearable since the loss (Znoj, 2016b).

Znoj (2016a) posited that after spousal death as well as after separation/divorce, many reactions are related to a still active attachment system and active internal working model, which have not yet adapted to the new situation and still expect signals from the lost attachment figure. Grief reactions after partner loss can be explained by missing the expected signals of the partner and slowly adapting to the fact that they will remain out of reach. Reminders of the person are everywhere and during the first weeks and months of the separation, the anticipation system has to be adapted to the new circumstances. The symptoms involve feeling the presence of the partner and the resulting realization of loneliness which stresses the organism and calls for specific coping abilities and adaptation to the loss. Grief and grief work could be labeled simply a habituation process up to the point where the attachment system ceases to "expect" the appearance of the formally attached object. The perspective that reactions to the loss of a partner are strongly related to the breakdown of the attachment system and the expectations of signals from the lost partner has implications for therapeutic intervention (Znoj, 2016b).

Physical and Mental Health Consequences of Partner Loss

It is well established that, on average, separation/divorce and spousal death are stressful events and present psychological challenges that can affect physical, psychological, and social well-being (e.g., Hughes & Waite, 2009; Luhmann et al., 2012; Stroebe et al., 2007). Loss is related to decrements in physical health, indicated by presence of symptoms and illnesses and the use of medical services. There is a clear association between spousal loss and nutritional risk, involuntary weight loss, poor sleep, smoking, increased alcohol consumption and alcohol dependence, chronic pain, inflammation, and cardiovascular risks (Ennis & Majid, 2021; Parisi et al., 2019; Stahl & Schulz, 2014). Stroebe at al. (2007) summarized the risks of spousal death to include excess risk of mortality, particularly in the early weeks and months after loss. Men suffered more adverse health outcomes than women. Mortality was also heightened after a divorce, in men more so than in women (Malgaroli et al., 2017; Shor et al., 2012).

In addition to the risks to physical health, both spousal death and separation/divorce are related to a higher risk of psychiatric disorders. Two large Swedish population-based studies using register information on psychiatric care showed that the loss of a spouse through divorce or death increased the risk of psychiatric disorders compared to married individuals. Divorcees had a higher risk of psychiatric disorders in the year after a divorce (Björkenstam, et al., 2013). This risk was even higher for short-term marriages of less than five years where the risk of psychiatric disorders was six times higher. Similarly, widowed older adults more often received psychiatric care, took psychotropic medication, and had increased mortality (Möller et al., 2011). Even though the analyses of the two studies are not directly comparable, the risk of receiving psychiatric care was considerably higher for divorced individuals than for widowed older adults.

Grief is a frequent reaction after spousal death but can also occur after a separation or divorce. It lies on a dimension from mild, temporary feelings of grief to a debilitating psychological disorder that impairs important areas of functioning (e.g., Shear et al., 2011). Following attachment theory, grief is the individual response to separation distress caused by a genetically provided subcortical network leading to emotional responses such as panic, sadness, and a diminished pursuit for dopamine-driven activities (Panksepp & Watt, 2011). Indeed, many bereaved parents express their grief in metaphors relating to bodily loss (Znoj, 2016a). The interruption of the bond with an attached person (sometimes the attachment figure may also be a beloved animal) leaves the bereft in a state of loss, often including a breakdown of the world that was taken for granted. Hence, loss can be a traumatic experience with signs and symptoms known to this condition, such as a sense of unreality; physiological reactions such as great tension, anxiety, and panic; and a loss of plans and motives.

Most mourners find a way of coping with the loss; however, for a few individuals complications in the grieving process emerge. For disturbed forms of grief, the literature uses terms such as "complicated" or "prolonged" grief. About 10% of bereaved individuals develop a prolonged grief disorder that last more than six months (Kersting et al., 2011; Lundorff et al., 2017). The prevalence of prolonged grief is higher among older adults. Among Dutch older adults who experienced current grief, 25.4% developed prolonged grief and among them 10% also had a current major depression and 17% an anxiety disorder (Newson et al., 2011). Also comorbid posttraumatic distress and suicidal ideation were frequent (Molina et al., 2019). According to the study of Simon et al. (2007), 75% of those with complicated grief also fulfilled criteria for another disorder, mostly depression or an anxiety disorder such as panic disorder or posttraumatic stress disorder.

Symptoms of prolonged or complicated grief consist of (a) separation distress, including, for example, yearning and longing for the deceased and emotional pain as a result of the desired but unfulfilled reunion with the lost person; (b) reactive distress such as difficulties accepting the loss, self-blame, avoidance of reminders of the loss; and (c) social/identity disruption, for example, loneliness, meaninglessness, or role confusion, which can lead to impairments in important life domains (Boelen et al., 2018).

Impairing prolonged grief after the death of a close person has been included in classification systems for psychiatric disorders as prolonged grief disorder in the 11th revision of the *International Classification of Diseases* (ICD-11) or persistent complex bereavement disorder, defined as a condition for further study in the fifth edition of *Diagnostic and Statistical Manual of Mental Disorders* (DSM-5). Daily or disabling separation distress is one required group of symptoms of a prolonged grief disorder or a persistent complex bereavement disorder. Furthermore, multiple cognitive, emotional, and behavioral symptoms must be present which relate to reactive distress or social or identity disruption. Several symptoms must persist for at least 6 (ICD 11) or 12 months (DSM-5) after the loss. Both psychiatric classification systems require that the individual experienced the death of a close person. Even if all criteria are present after a divorce, they do not qualify for the psychiatric diagnosis of a grief disorder.

In summary, separation/divorce as well as spousal death is associated with risk to physical and mental health. The loss, or more precisely the separation, can have similar effects on mental and physical health including heightened mortality independent of the cause of the loss. Although no specific disorder has been associated with divorce, psychological disorders related to prolonged grief after the death of a close person have been listed as disorders in psychiatric classification systems.

Affective and Cognitive Experiences After the Loss of a Partner

Negative health consequences of the loss of a partner have been well established; however, pathways linking loss with physical and mental health disorders are less clear. According to the divorce-stress-adaptation model (Amato, 2000), the uncoupling process can set into motion numerous stressful events which in turn can lead to negative emotional, behavioral, and health outcomes. Sbarra and Coan (2017) identified three major domains of life as mechanisms of action linking divorce with distal health outcomes, (a) changes of social and financial resources, (b) cognitive and affective experiences, and (c) changes in health behaviors. These proximal consequences together affect health-relevant biological changes which then lead to distal health outcomes after a divorce.

Considering the similar distal and proximal health outcomes of separation/divorce and spousal death and similar adaptation tasks, we argue that the same domains are affected after separation/divorce and spousal death and that the same mechanisms of action link the loss to adverse health outcomes. To substantiate this claim, we focus in the next sections on cognitive and affective experiences after a loss and compare them between separated/divorced and widowed older adults. The following two studies (Brodbeck et al., 2016; Burger et al., 2020) used data from the LIVES project and are among a few which directly compare the frequency of affective reactions or the association of symptoms in separated/divorced or widowed individuals in the same sample.

In a direct comparison of emotional reactions in 759 separated/divorced and widowed older adults, Brodbeck et al. (2016) explored similarities and differences in the expression of grief or posttraumatic growth after separation/divorce or spousal death. After a separation/divorce or spousal death, individuals report a range of psychological reactions, including sadness, longing and yearning, or embitterment. However, the same affective reaction may be differently related to grief or, in statistical terms, display differential item functioning. This has to be accounted for when comparing symptoms and levels of grief or growth in divorced and widowed participants. The results showed that among separated/

divorced individuals, trouble accepting the loss and difficulties with trusting others since the loss were the most common reactions. These reactions were not related to high levels of underlying grief. High levels of grief were indicated by feeling stunned, the impression that life is empty, as well as longing, yearning, and emotional pain. Such reactions may suggest that additional social or professional support for coping with grief is needed.

Among widowed participants, longing or yearning for the lost person and trouble accepting the loss and intense feelings of emotional pain or sorrow were frequent reactions to partner loss. These reactions were related to lower grief levels. In contrast, bitterness over the loss, trying to avoid reminders of loss, and difficulties trusting others were associated with higher levels of underlying grief and may indicate a need for help. When taking into account that the same reaction was sometimes differently related to grief in both groups, separated/divorced participants reported significantly lower levels of prolonged grief compared to widowed older adults. Thus, even though separated/divorced and widowed individuals reported similar affective reactions, item characteristic curves showed that some symptoms represented different severity levels on the underlying grief trait.

Unlike grief symptoms, the expression of personal growth after separation/divorce and death was similar with one exception. Widowed participants who reported that they had established a new path for their lives had a higher level of posttraumatic growth than divorced participants who endorsed the same response categories. Accounting for this, separated/divorced and widowed older adults reported the same levels of posttraumatic growth. This is in line with other studies that established psychological growth in bereavement (Znoj, 2006). In parents who lost a child, a sense of having grown into a better human being may be accompanied by more adaptive emotion regulation (Znoj & Keller, 2002).

Burger et al. (2020) conducted two network analyses for depressive symptoms among widowed and separated/divorced older adults in the LIVES sample. About 18% of the widowed and 30% of the separated/divorced individuals met the criteria for a diagnosis of depression (Lehr et al., 2008). Network analyses showed that in both groups, the loss was primarily associated with loneliness, which in turn was associated with other depressive symptoms. Among widowed participants, the loss was also related to sadness. One important difference between the two groups was that separated/divorced individuals reported more intense feelings of experiencing an unfriendly environment and of oneself as a failure compared to widowed older adults.

To summarize, separation/divorce and spousal bereavement resulted in similar affective reactions, including loneliness, longing, yearning, and troubles accepting the loss. These findings suggest that losses due to separation/divorce or death are associated with similar psychological mechanisms such as a separation reaction after the loss of the attachment figure described in the attachment theory. Differences between the separated/divorced and widowed individuals were related to aspects of social appraisal: separated/divorced individuals reported more intense feelings of experiencing an unfriendly environment and of oneself as a failure. Also, difficulties trusting others were frequent and related to lower levels of grief among separated/divorced individuals but high levels of grief among widowed older adults. Differences in affective and cognitive reactions may be associated with characteristics of the events such as different cultural and social appraisals or the different preloss history and not with a separation reaction.

Duration and Individual Differences in Adaptation to Partner Loss

The loss of a partner and grief are often an experience shared with others, but it is rarely the same for different individuals. It is well established that there are large individual differences in the reactions toward a separation/divorce and spousal death, and in the severity and duration of symptoms (Kersting et al., 2011; Lundorff et al., 2017; Malgaroli et al., 2017; Mancini et al., 2011; Perrig-Chiello et al., 2015; Spahni et al., 2015). Explaining these differences is an ongoing line of research. One approach to shed light on adaptation patterns and trajectories are latent class or growth mixture models. These models are person- and not variable-based and capture inter-and intraindividual change over time. They identify subgroups with distinct adaptation patterns and trajectories and allow the analysis of predictors of membership in each group. In contrast to other models, they do not assume that one average trajectory adequately represents the adaptation to grief for all individuals.

Results of studies employing latent class or growth mixture models show that the majority of separated/divorced or widowed individuals are resilient after the loss of the spouse. Over time, they do not substantially change their high life satisfaction, low depression level, or overall positive psychological adaptation. Some individuals, however, show a different trajectory. Malgaroli et al. (2017), for example, analyzed depression after divorce and found that 67% were resilient, about 10% showed emergent or decreasing depression and 12% chronic pre- and post-divorce depression. Mancini et al. (2011) analyzed life satisfaction over four years prior and four years after divorce as well as spousal death in Germans under the age of 75 years. After adjusting for age, health dysfunction, and changes in income, the majority of divorced and widowed participants reported a stable high life satisfaction. About 15% of the widowed participants reported stable low life satisfaction, and 21% showed an acute decline in life satisfaction and then recovery one year after the event. No group was found with a permanent decrease in life satisfaction. In divorced participants 9% reported a slow increase in life satisfaction prior to the divorce, a peak, and then a stable trajectory after the divorce. About 19% reported a slow decline in life satisfaction over the eight years.

Based on the LIVES project, Spahni et al. (2015) and Perrig-Chiello et al. (2015) used a similar statistical approach to identify adaptation patterns after spousal death and separation/divorce. They used a multidimensional construct for psychological adaptation including health, life satisfaction, loneliness, hopelessness, and depression in a random sample of older adults who lost their spouse to death or divorce within the last five years prior to the assessment. Among widowed participants, 54% of the participants were resilient with positive values in all indicators; 39% were in the "coper" group with minor psychological difficulties; and 7% were in the vulnerable group that reported severe psychological problems. High psychological resilience, personality traits such as high extroversion and low neuroticism, spousal support during the marriage, a longer time since the loss and the emotional valence of the death predicted class membership in the resilient group (Spahni et al. 2015).

Compared to spousal death, the adaptation patterns after a divorce were more diverse (Perrig-Chiello et al., 2015). About half of the divorcees were labeled "average copers" (49%) and 29% were resilient with positive outcomes. About 20% of the divorced older adults reported maladaptive outcomes with distinct patterns of negative adaptation: the group of "malcontents" (12%) and "vulnerables" (6%) both showed a low life satisfaction and high hopelessness with the "vulnerables" also reporting high depression scores and low subjective health. The smallest group with "resigned individuals" (4%) included older divorcees with high levels in depression and mourning and relatively low subjective health. Class membership was, for example, predicted by the emotional experience of the separation, psychological resilience, neuroticism, and being in a new relationship.

In summary, adaptation patterns or trajectories after separation/divorce or spousal death are similar and the most frequent pattern is resilience with no substantial long-term changes in life satisfaction, depression, or psychological adaptation, in general. However, there is some evidence that after a divorce, responses are more diverse, including distinct maladaptive classes as well as a group of individuals with an improvement in positive adaptation.

Attachment Theory as Explanation for Individual Differences in Adaptation to Partner Loss

Apart from explaining immediate grief reactions after the loss of a partner, attachment theory also clarifies individual differences in the response to partner loss through separation/divorce (e.g., Feeney & Monin, 2016; Sbarra & Borelli, 2019) or spousal death (Fraley & Bonanno, 2004; Mikulincer & Shaver, 2008). Individuals differ in their attachment styles which influence internal working models of the self, of others, and of how social relationships work. Thus, attachment styles affect the behavior of individuals in social relationships, how someone interprets the behaviors and intentions of others, and how relationships are experienced. Although adult attachment styles may have their origins in early caregiving experiences, these associations are weak and inconsistent (Fraley & Roisman, 2019). In early childhood, socialization effects are predominant and the environment plays a greater role. Later, selection processes become more important and individuals select and shape their environments. They select relationships that agree with their expectations and preferences and evoke specific responses from others.

Individuals with a secure attachment style are comfortable in close interaction with others, maintain their autonomy, and can meet their and other's needs. Secure attachment is associated with greater acceptance of a loss and less grief after a divorce (Yárnoz-Yaben, 2010, 2017). Individuals with a secure attachment are also assumed to be better able to update their internal working model and to redefine the relationship with the lost partner as well as to benefit more from social support after spousal death (Shaver & Tancredy, 2001). Individuals with an avoidant attachment style find it difficult to trust others or to depend on others, and they feel uncomfortable when others get too close. They are less likely to use their partner as an attachment figure and may deny the importance of intimacy. In the case of a loss, they tend to suppress or avoid attachment-related emotions. Evidence shows that in general, individuals with an avoidant attachment style adapt well to loss (Fraley & Bonanno, 2004; Mikulincer & Shaver, 2008). Adults with an anxious/ambivalent attachment style are worried that their partners don't really love them and desire more closeness than their partners which may scare the partners away (Shaver & Hazan, 1987). They tend to be very emotional, expressive, and preoccupied after the loss but unable to cope well with attachment-related feelings after the loss of a partner (Shaver & Tancredy, 2001).

Sbarra and Coan (2017) applied attachment theory to divorce and underlined that attachment theory can explain individual differences, which first lead to an increased risk of divorce and second to affect mechanisms of action that link a divorce with distal health outcomes. Sbarra and Borelli (2019) pointed out that early attachment, internal working models, history of loss, and the individual risk for psychopathology in both partners shape emotional experiences, such as yearning, love, jealousy, anger, or fear when a romantic relationship breaks up. They suggest that attachment reorganization is crucial for an adaptive grief response. This involves a shift from an interdependent regulation of psychological and biological responses within a couple to an independent regulation which is not dependent on interactions with one specific person. They identify two dimensions that are relevant for successful attachment reorganization: self-concept clarity and narrative coherence. In addition, cognitive adaptation and changes in the appraisal of the loss are required (Sbarra & Hazan, 2008).

Regarding spousal death, we argue that Sbarra and Coan (2017) and Sbarra and Borelli (2019) highlighted processes that are also relevant for individual differences in spousal bereavement. We posit that attachment style and working models influence the mechanisms of action that link spousal death with distal health outcomes and that attachment reorganization is important for an adaptive grief response. Thus, the models developed for divorce can be adapted and extended to spousal death and the outlined processes can be addressed in therapeutic interventions for separated/divorced as well as widowed individuals.

Coping With Partner Loss

After the loss of a spouse due to death or the breakup of a romantic relationship, a person has to cope with similar interpersonal and intrapersonal challenges and stressors.

The loss requires similar adaptation tasks such as reorganizing aspects of daily life, creating a new identity without the partner, as well as attachment reorganization and transforming the bond with the lost person. With the exception of Sbarra and Borelli (2019), most models for coping with divorce emphasize interpersonal stressors and predictors of positive adaptation while models for grief after bereavement often focus on intrapersonal coping with the loss.

The divorce-stress-adaptation model (Amato, 2000) elaborates that the reorganization of one's life and the related affective reactions and distress lead to an increase of stressors. He identifies stressors after a divorce such as sole parenting responsibility or loss of custody of children, the loss of emotional support, continuing conflicts and/or renegotiating the ongoing relationship with the ex-spouse, and financial hardship. These stressors, together with the individual availability of resources, protective factors, and coping strategies, affect the quality of the adjustment after the divorce and determine whether individuals can succeed in recovering faster or show enduring difficulties in adaptation.

Coping research has investigated various coping styles and their outcomes but does not specify the role of the stressor since it is not the stressor that calls for the response but the individual appraisal of the situation (e.g., Lazarus & Folkman, 1984). Coping with separation distress due to death or separation/divorce and the regulation of intensive emotional states such as anger, anxiety, or unwelcome weeping is important because dysregulation of emotional states often leads to health risks (Aldao et al., 2010). Avoidant coping or rumination, for example, can lead to elevated depression and higher distress levels. In contrast, a problem-oriented coping predicts better adaptation and includes distractive coping, even cognitive avoidance (e.g., Bonanno, 2004). Maladaptive coping strategies consist, for example, of the isolation of affective states, the negation of the impact of the loss, avoidance of the consequences, or trying to escape the situation through the use of drugs or behavioral stimuli such as sex or thrill seeking. This is maladaptive if it causes diminution of resources to adapt to the new situation. Positive meaning and meaning reconstruction following bereavement have been linked to positive outcomes following loss; the capacity to display positive emotions during bereavement predicts better outcomes after the loss of a spouse (Bonanno & Keltner, 1997). Taken together, these results may indicate that too much avoidance as well as too much confrontation is detrimental to adaptation following loss.

Two widely applied models of coping with grief after spousal death are the task model by Worden (2009) and the dual process model of coping with bereavement by Stroebe and Schut (1999). The task model identifies four tasks to adjust to spousal death: accepting the reality of the loss, experiencing the pain, adjusting to an environment without the deceased person, and finally finding a new understanding with the deceased. It underlines the importance of actively coping with the challenges instead of passively experiencing the loss. Stroebe and Schut (1999) proposed the dual process model, which integrates both stress and coping theories as well as psychosocial models. The integrative dual process model considers the empirical evidence and postulates that oscillation between loss-oriented coping and restoration-oriented coping is key for a positive adaptation to the loss. Loss-oriented coping includes positive reappraisal versus rumination and wishful thinking, revisions of personal goals, positive and negative event interpretation, and expressing emotions and mood states such as dysphoria or expressing positive affect toward the deceased. On the other hand, restoration-oriented coping is focused on attending to life changes, engaging in new activities, distraction from grief, and finding new roles and identities.

Models for coping with bereavement as illustrated by Worden (2009) and Stroebe and Schut (2001) are helpful in understanding the challenges that both separated and widowed are confronted with. However, only a few studies have applied the dual process model for coping with a romantic breakup or divorce (e.g., McKiernan et al., 2018).

Interventions for Adaptation Problems and Grief After Partner Loss

The medicalization of grief after the death of a close person includes the definition of specific diagnoses for prolonged grief and the development of specific treatments. There is broad evidence that psychological interventions for prolonged severe grief after bereavement are effective (Currier et al., 2008; Neimeyer, 2000; Wittouck et al., 2011). They generally include exposure to the experience of the loss, cognitive reappraisal of the loss, and integration and restoration of the experience of the loss into daily life (Boelen et al., 2007; Shear & Shair, 2005). Recently, internet interventions have complemented traditional face-to-face treatment.

New technologies, such as internet-based self-help interventions (e-health) or interventions delivered on smartphones (mobile- or m-health), are scalable; affordable; and a convenient, user-friendly, low-threshold, and immediate way of delivering interventions in daily life. Thus, they have a great potential for expanding the reach of interventions. Internet-based interventions for different disorders have been widely evaluated and often show similar effect sizes as traditional face-to-face interventions (Andersson, 2016; Andersson et al., 2014). Also for treating grief after bereavement, internet-based interventions have complemented traditional face-to-face grief counseling or therapy and have proven to be effective (Eisma et al., 2015; Litz et al., 2014; van der Houwen et al., 2010; Wagner et al., 2006).

In contrast to grief after the death of a close person, there is no specific diagnosis for adaptation problems after a divorce and few specific interventions. Exceptions are, for example, the "Divorce Counseling Homework Planner" (Rich, 2002) or specific interventions for aspects of divorce—for example, a group intervention to facilitate forgiveness of an ex-spouse (Rye et al., 2005). In the context of a divorce, specific counseling and mediation may focus on custody issues and co-parenting children, living arrangements, or property ownerships.

Considering the similarities in psychological consequences for the attachment system and the tasks regarding the reorganization of one's life, we assumed that interventions developed for coping with bereavement are also effective for coping with divorce. This was tested in the LIVIA project. LIVIA is a guided online self-help program for prolonged grief after spousal bereavement as well as grief and adaptation problems after separation/divorce (Brodbeck et al., 2017; Brodbeck et al., 2019). LIVIA was based on evidence and theoretical models related to grief after bereavement—that is, the task model by Worden (2009) and the dual process model by Stroebe and Schutt (1999), and employed therapeutic intervention principles for coping with bereavement as well as generic interventions for activating resources. We hypothesized that the same topics and intervention strategies would be relevant for bereaved as well as separated/divorced older adults. The majority of the participants were divorced (77% of the 110 participants) which also underlined that prolonged grief or other adaptation problems were relevant for them.

The cognitive-behavioral online self-help program consisted of ten text-based modules of which eight were by and large identical for separated/divorced and widowed participants. Two loss-related modules had an identical structure but were adapted to the specific event. Module 1 was event-specific and provided information about bereavement or separation reactions and the treatment of complicated grief. For both groups, we presented the dual process model for coping with the loss as two sides of coping with a loss and introduced Worden's tasks of accepting the reality of the loss, accepting and processing the pain of the loss, adapting to an environment where the lost person is not there anymore, and the new definition of the relationship with the lost partner. In module 2, we presented information on emotional reactions in the context of interpersonal loss and assessed the emotional state of the participants. Writing tasks assessed changes in the life of the participants and obstacles for a successful adaptation as well as possibilities to overcome them. Modules 3 to 5 focused on emotion regulation and fostering positive thoughts and emotions, finding comfort and self-care. We introduced the emotion regulation model by Gross (2002, 2014) and presented examples of adaptive strategies, possibilities to find comfort and writing tasks for becoming aware of the own strategies, and applying the presented model to their own life. A checklist for physical and emotional self-care assessed the current state, as well as goals for improving self-care. Work sheets for practicing these strategies in daily life complemented the module.

Modules 6 and 7 covered loss-related content. Telling the story of the loss was the second of the two event-specific modules. The goal was to integrate painful memories of the loss into the autobiographical memory using writing tasks. While the overall structure for both groups was similar, these writing tasks covered event-specific questions related to the death of the spouse, the funeral and the days after or in the case of a separation/divorce, to the uncoupling process (Amato, 2000). The next module, again similar for bereaved and separated/divorced participants, encompassed the identification of unfinished business, regrets and writing tasks to find possibilities to put these issues at rest.

Modules 8 and 9 were restoration-oriented and focused on creating a new life without the partner. Topics were sources of support and strengths before and after the loss, activating resources in daily life and information about posttraumatic growth. Module 9 was dedicated to social relationships, clarifying current relationships, improving existing relationships, and building up new social contacts. Finally, the last module aimed at redefining the relationship with the lost partner. Participants wrote a farewell letter to the lost partner in which they described how life will continue without them and what meaning the loss will have in the future.

Results supported the hypothesis that the intervention based on evidence and literature for bereavement would also be effective for separated or divorced older adults with prolonged grief or adaptation problems after the loss and demonstrated that the same intervention principles worked for both groups (Brodbeck et al., 2019). Separated/divorced as well as widowed participants improved grief, psychopathological distress, depression, loneliness, embitterment, and life satisfaction compared to a wait-list control group.

Mediation analyses suggested that improvements in emotion-regulation skills and loss-related coping self-efficacy during the intervention acted as mechanisms of change (Brodbeck et al., 2022). LIVIA improved emotion-regulation skills and loss-related self-efficacy which both correlated with improvements in grief and psychopathology. Path models including both mediators simultaneously indicated that emotion regulation was directly associated with improvements in grief symptoms but not psychopathology. In contrast, loss-related self-efficacy was directly related to improvements in psychopathology but not grief. Emotion regulation was confirmed as mediator for improvement in grief; self-efficacy showed a trend as mediator for improvement in psychopathology.

Thus, emotion regulation appears to be more important for enabling grief processing whereas loss-related coping self-efficacy might be more relevant for improving psychopathology in general. Emotion regulation skills, self-soothing and self-care could facilitate loss-oriented tasks and also directly modulate cognitive and affective experiences after the loss, a mechanism of action that links the separation/divorce with distal health outcomes (Sbarra & Coan, 2017). High loss-related coping self-efficacy may facilitate creating a new life without the spouse and addressing the changes caused by the loss. The belief in the ability to be able to cope with these tasks may render them less threatening and alleviate stress and anxiety as well as promote the engagement in coping behavior and sustain coping efforts (Benight & Bandura, 2004).

Building up on the evaluation of LIVIA, the LEAVES project is an example for taking text-based self-help interventions a step further and using new technologies for providing a more comprehensive support for mourners (van Velsen et al., 2020). LEAVES integrates the LIVIA self-help intervention into an online bereavement support service for older adults who lost their partner. Older adults who sign up for the service will have access to a platform, where a customized virtual agent leads them through the dialogue-based program. The program monitors grief and psychopathological symptoms, can detect persons at risk for complications, and can uncover negative trends in their emotional life. Those who struggle with coping with the loss will be encouraged to use the self-help program. If they need more help, blended counseling will be offered with telephone calls, video conferences, or face-to-face sessions with a psychotherapist. The LEAVES service aims to strengthen resilience and well-being, to soften the mourning process and to prevent or treat complicated grief, depression symptoms, or social isolation. A similar service may be developed for divorced participants who seek help for adaptation problems after a separation.

Future Directions

In this chapter, we linked two strands of research and theory related to divorce and spousal death. Key characteristics of separation/divorce and spousal death are that the attachment system is impaired and that the loss requires the reorganization of many aspects of daily life. We highlighted similarities in the physical and mental health consequences as well as cognitive and affective reactions to the loss of a partner and argued that the loss or more specifically the separation can have similar effects on mental and physical health independent of the cause of whether the loss is due to separation/divorce or death. Furthermore, we presented models for psychological adjustment and coping with divorce and bereavement and investigated whether these models can be applied to both events. We also demonstrated that an online intervention based on models for coping with bereavement worked for divorced participants.

We argue that it is fruitful to combine both research traditions, to integrate their common and specific findings into a broader conceptual framework of separation and loss. This fosters the development of comprehensive models of psychological functioning and reactions after partner loss and refines and expands conceptual thinking in this field. An attachment perspective can help to integrate models and findings on reactions to the loss and offers opportunities for future research. Based on these findings and conceptual thoughts, further studies are needed to systematically examine similarities and differences in the reactions to romantic breakup, divorce, and spousal bereavement; to address the question of specificity in grief reactions after bereavement; and to clarify the uniqueness of the experiences of romantic breakups, separation/divorce, and spousal bereavement.

There is ample evidence that, independent of the event, there are individual differences in the reactions to social losses and that only a subset of individuals shows persistent adverse health consequences. The tasks of adaptation after social loss may differ and vary but even more so between individuals and not necessarily between the types of loss. A more systematic view on predictors and moderators of individual differences in the reactions to a social loss is required which focuses more on the personal characteristics or social context and less on the type of the loss.

The extensive tradition in grief research and theories on coping with bereavement can inspire models and specific interventions for coping with romantic breakups or divorce without an implicit tendency to pathologize the reactions. Specifically, the dual process model could easily be applied to divorce as well as bereavement. Overall, a common conceptual framework for coping with social losses may be helpful to develop more parsimonious generic interventions for grief and adaptation problems, which may primarily be tailored to the individual needs of the clients and only if necessary to the different types of losses.

Apart from the integration of divorce and bereavement research, there are more specific areas of future research. The role of the attachment figure for the personal development and striving after the loss is an open question (Fraley, 2019). In the case of personal loss one has not only the task to overcome the "emotional hole" but to revise one's goals, social environment, and other aspects of orientation in life. The revision of the working model after the loss implies also how future relationships may be integrated in the "network" of social relations.

Intriguing questions also concern new challenges such as social media or virtual reality, which offer opportunities for coping but also for prolonging the process of adaptation. New technologies, especially the development of the internet, virtual services, and last but not least robotics and virtual reality, offer a multiplicity of possibilities of coping and memorials. The case of Eugenia Kuyda and Roman Mazurenko illustrates what types of challenges may come in the future (Newton, n.d). After the death of her friend in a traffic accident, Kuyda programmed a bot using artificial intelligence with whom she was able to communicate as if he was still alive. How this affected her grieving is not documented, but it may impede the transition of the internal working model and the completion of the tasks of mourning (Worden, 2009)—that is, accepting the reality of the loss, accepting and processing the pain of the loss, and adapting to an environment where the lost person is not there anymore. Thus, the question is whether these possibilities facilitate a peaceful closure of the grief experience or whether they rather prolong it.

A perhaps more common way to grieve will be websites that allow transmitting messages to relatives and friends even after one's own death (e.g., https://www.welcome.ai/eternime). New technologies will allow keeping memories alive. In a sense, this is not just keeping memories but creating life in a virtual room. This is different from, for example, graveyards as places to visit, to mourn and to keep in touch with people long gone. It is an open question how new possibilities of remembering affect the way bereaved can cope with loss. Memories are important, but it is also important not to expect guidance and signs of attachment from the lost person.

In conclusion, Bowlby's attachment theory offers a helpful framework for explaining affective reactions after a romantic breakup and spousal death. A major challenge after both events is to cope with the separation from the attachment figure, the transition of the inner working model into a state of peace and to reorient oneself to a life without the connection to the lost person. Risks and protective factors that influence the nature and course of grief following spousal loss are becoming clearer. Separation distress is one of the major risk factors for prolonged grief and adaptation problems even more so than the predictability of the event or traumatic circumstances. Social support from family and friends seems to be more important for a positive adaptation than professional help. This is well established for loss due to death but less clear for separation or divorce.

Acknowledgements

We thank the editors for their very helpful comments on the chapter. We also thank Sarah Madoerin and Bettina Mooser for their help with preparing the manuscript.

References

Aldao, A., Nolen-Hoeksema, S., & Schweizer, S. (2010). Emotion-regulation strategies across psychopathology: A meta-analytic review. *Clinical Psychology Review, 30*, 217–237.

Amato, P. R. (2000). The consequences of divorce for adults and children. *Journal of Marriage and Family, 62*(4), 1269–1287.

Amato, P. R., & Hohmann-Marriott, B. (2007). A comparison of high- and low-distress marriages that end in divorce. *Journal of Marriage and Family, 69*, 621–638.

Andersson, G. (2016). Internet-delivered psychological treatments. *Annual Review of Clinical Psychology, 12*, 157–179.

Andersson, G., Cuijpers, P., Carlbring, P., Riper, H., & Hedman, E. (2014). Guided internet-based vs. face-to-face cognitive behavior therapy for psychiatric and somatic disorders: A systematic review and meta-analysis. *World Psychiatry, 13*(3), 288–295.

Archer, J. (2001). Grief from an evolutionary perspective. In M. S. Stroebe, R. O. Hansson, W. Stroebe, & H. Schut (Eds.), *Handbook of bereavement research: Consequences, coping, and care* (pp. 263–283). American Psychological Association.

Baumeister, R. F., & Leary, M. R. (1995). The need to belong: Desire for interpersonal attachments as a fundamental human motivation. *Psychological Bulletin, 117*(3), 497.

Benight, C. C., & Bandura, A. (2004). Social cognitive theory of posttraumatic recovery: The role of perceived self-efficacy. *Behaviour Research and Therapy, 42*(10), 1129–1148.

Björkenstam, E., Hallqvist, J., Dalman, C., & Ljung, R. (2013). Risk of new psychiatric episodes in the year following divorce in midlife: Cause or selection? A nationwide register-based study of 703,960 individuals. *International Journal of Social Psychiatry, 59*(8), 801–804.

Boelen, P. A., de Keijser, J., van den Hout, M. A., & van den Bout, J. (2007). Treatment of complicated grief: A comparison between cognitive-behavioral therapy and supportive counseling. *Journal of Consulting and Clinical Psychology, 75*(2), 277.

Boelen, P. A., Lenferink, L. I., Nickerson, A., & Smid, G. E. (2018). Evaluation of the factor structure, prevalence, and validity of disturbed grief in DSM-5 and ICD-11. *Journal of Affective Disorders, 240*, 79–87.

Bonanno, G. A. (2004). Loss, trauma, and human resilience: Have we underestimated the human capacity to thrive after extremely aversive events? *American Psychologist, 59*(1), 20.

Bonanno, G. A., & Keltner, D. (1997). Facial expressions of emotion and the course of conjugal bereavement. *Journal of Abnormal Psychology, 106*(1), 126.

Bowlby, J. (1969). *Attachment and loss: Vol. 1. Attachment.* Basic Books.

Bowlby, J. (1980). *Attachment and loss: Vol. 3. Loss: Sadness and depression.* Basic Books.

Brodbeck, J., Berger, T., Biesold, N., Rockstroh, F., Schmidt, S. J., & Znoj, H. J. (2022). Emotion regulation and self-efficacy are mediators in an internet intervention for grief. *JMIR Mental Health, 9*(5), e27707.

Brodbeck, J., Berger, T., Biesold, N., Rockstroh, F., & Znoj, H. J. (2019). Evaluation of a guided internet-based self-help intervention for older adults after spousal bereavement or separation/divorce: A randomised controlled trial. *Journal of Affective Disorders, 252*, 440–449.

Brodbeck, J., Berger, T., & Znoj, H. J. (2017). An internet-based self-help intervention for older adults after marital bereavement, separation or divorce: Study protocol for a randomized controlled trial. *Trials, 18*(1), 21.

Brodbeck, J., Knöpfli, B., Znoj, H., & Perrig-Chiello, P. (2016, July 12). *Expression of grief and personal growth in divorced and widowed older adults* [Poster presentation]. 24th Biennial Meeting of the International Society for the Study of Behavioural Development, Vilnius, Lithuania.

Burger, J., Stroebe, M. S., Perrig-Chiello, P., Schut, H. A., Spahni, S., Eisma, M. C., & Fried, E. I. (2020). Bereavement or breakup: Differences in networks of depression. *Journal of Affective Disorders, 267*, 1–8.

Currier, J. M., Neimeyer, R. A., & Berman, J. S. (2008). The effectiveness of psychotherapeutic interventions for bereaved persons: A comprehensive quantitative review. *Psychological Bulletin, 134*(5), 648–661.

Doka, K. J. (2008). Disenfranchised grief in historical and cultural perspective. In M. S. Stroebe, R. O. Hansson, H. Schut, & W. Stroebe (Eds.), *Handbook of bereavement research and practice: Advances in theory and intervention* (pp. 223–240). American Psychological Association Press.

Eisma, M. C., Boelen, P. A., van den Bout, J., Stroebe, W., Schut, H. A., Lancee, J., & Stroebe, M. (2015). Internet-based exposure and behavioral activation for complicated grief and rumination: A randomized controlled trial. *Behavior Therapy, 46*(6), 729–748.

Encyclopaedia Britannica. (n.d.). *Divorce.* Retrieved July 21, 2020, from https://www.britannica.com/topic/annulment

Ennis, J., & Majid, U. (2021). "Death from a broken heart": A systematic review of the relationship between spousal bereavement and physical and physiological health outcomes. *Death Studies, 45*(7), 538–551.

Federal Statistical Office. (2020, May 29). *Divorces, divortiality.* https://www.bfs.admin.ch/bfs/en/home/statistics/population/marriages-partnerships-divorces/divortiality.html

Feeney, B. C., & Monin, J. K. (2016). Divorce through the lens of attachment theory. In J. Cassidy & P. R. Shaver (Eds.), *Handbook of attachment* (pp. 941–965). Guilford Press.

Field, N. (2006). Unresolved grief and continuing bonds: An attachment perspective. *Death Studies, 30*(8), 739–756.

Fletcher, G. J., Simpson, J. A., Campbell, L., & Overall, N. C. (2019). *The science of intimate relationships.* John Wiley & Sons.

Fraley, R. C. (2019). Attachment in adulthood: Recent developments, emerging debates, and future directions. *Annual Review of Psychology, 70*, 401–422.

Fraley, R. C., & Bonanno, G. A. (2004). Attachment and loss: A test of three competing models on the association between attachment-related avoidance and adaptation to bereavement. *Personality and Social Psychology Bulletin, 30*(7), 878–890.

Fraley, R. C., & Roisman, G. I. (2019). The development of adult attachment styles: Four lessons. *Current Opinion in Psychology, 25*, 26–30.

Gross, J. J. (2002). Emotion regulation: Affective, cognitive, and social consequences. *Psychophysiology, 39*, 281–291.

Gross, J. J. (2014). *Handbook of emotion regulation* (2nd ed.). Guilford Press.

Holland, J. M., Plant, C. P., Klingspon, K. L., & Neimeyer, R. A. (2020). Bereavement-related regrets and unfinished business with the deceased. *Death Studies, 44*(1), 42–47.

Hughes, M. E., & Waite, L. J. (2009). Marital biography and health at mid-life. *Journal of Health and Social Behavior, 50*(3), 344–358.

Kersting, A., Brähler, E., Glaesmer, H., & Wagner, B. (2011). Prevalence of complicated grief in a representative population-based sample. *Journal of Affective Disorders, 131*(1–3), 339–343.

Kulik, L., & Heine-Cohen, E. (2011). Coping resources, perceived stress and adjustment to divorce among Israeli women: Assessing effects. *The Journal of Social Psychology, 151*, 5–30.

Lazarus, R. S., & Folkman, S. (1984). *Stress, appraisal, and coping.* Springer.

Lehr, D., Hillert, A., Schmitz, E., & Sosnowsky, N. (2008). Screening depressiver Störungen mittels Allgemeiner Depressions-Skala (ADS-K) und State-Trait Depressions Scales (STDS-T) eine vergleichende Evaluation von Cut-off-Werten. *Diagnostica, 54*(2), 61–70.

Litz, B. T., Schorr, Y., Delaney, E., Au, T., Papa, A., Fox, A. B., Morris, S. E., Block, S., & Prigerson, H. (2014). A randomized controlled trial of an internet-based therapist-assisted indicated preventive intervention for prolonged grief disorder. *Behaviour Research and Therapy, 61*, 23–34.

Luhmann, M., Hofmann, W., Eid, M., & Lucas, R. E. (2012). Subjective well-being and adaptation to life events: A meta-analysis. *Journal of Personality and Social Psychology, 102*(3), 592.

Lundorff, M., Holmgren, H., Zachariae, R., Farver-Vestergaard, I., & O'Connor, M. (2017). Prevalence of prolonged grief disorder in adult bereavement: A systematic review and meta-analysis. *Journal of Affective Disorders, 212*, 138–149.

Malgaroli, M., Galatzer-Levy, I. R., & Bonanno, G. A. (2017). Heterogeneity in trajectories of depression in response to divorce is associated with differential risk for mortality. *Clinical Psychological Science, 5*(5), 843–850.

Mancini, A. D., Bonanno, G. A., & Clark, A. E. (2011). Stepping off the hedonic treadmill: Individual differences in response to major life events. *Journal of Individual Differences, 32*(3), 144–152.

McKiernan, A., Ryan, P., McMahon, E., Bradley, S., & Butler, E. (2018). Understanding young people's relationship breakups using the dual processing model of coping and bereavement. *Journal of Loss and Trauma, 23*(3), 192–210.

Mikulincer, M., & Shaver, P. R. (2008). An attachment perspective on bereavement. In M. S. Stroebe, R. O. Hansson, H. Schut, & W. Stroebe (Eds.), *Handbook of bereavement research and practice: Advances in theory and intervention* (pp. 87–112). American Psychological Association Press.

Molina, N., Viola, M., Rogers, M., Ouyang, D., Gang, J., Derry, H., & Prigerson, H. G. (2019). Suicidal ideation in bereavement: A systematic review. *Behavioral Sciences, 9*(5), 53.

Möller, J., Björkenstam, E., Ljung, R., & Åberg Yngwe, M. (2011). Widowhood and the risk of psychiatric care, psychotropic medication and all-cause mortality: A cohort study of 658,022 elderly people in Sweden. *Aging & Mental Health, 15*(2), 259–266.

Neimeyer, R. A. (2000). Searching for the meaning of meaning: Grief therapy and the process of reconstruction. *Death Studies, 24*(6), 541–558.

Newson, R. S., Boelen, P. A., Hek, K., Hofman, A., & Tiemeier, H. (2011). The prevalence and characteristics of complicated grief in older adults. *Journal of Affective Disorders, 132*(1–2), 231–238.

Newton, C. (n.d.). Speak, memory. When her best friend died, she rebuilt him using artificial intelligence. *The Verge*. https://www.theverge.com/a/luka-artificial-intelligence-memorial-roman-mazurenko-bot.

Office for National Statistics. (2020, May 29). https://www.ons.gov.uk/ https://www.ons.gov.uk/peoplepopulationandcommunity/birthsdeathsandmarriages/divorce/bulletins/divorcesinenglandandwales.

Panksepp, J., & Watt, D. (2011). Why does depression hurt? Ancestral primary-process separation-distress (PANIC/GRIEF) and diminished brain reward (SEEKING) processes in the genesis of depressive affect. *Psychiatry: Interpersonal & Biological Processes, 74*(1), 5–13.

Parisi, A., Sharma, A., Howard, M. O., & Wilson, A. B. (2019). The relationship between substance misuse and complicated grief: A systematic review. *Journal of Substance Abuse Treatment, 103*, 43–57.

Perrig-Chiello, P., Hutchison, S., & Morselli, D. (2015). Patterns of psychological adaptation to divorce after a long-term marriage. *Journal of Social and Personal Relationships, 32*(3), 386–405.

Rich, P. (2002). *Divorce counseling homework planner*. John Wiley & Sons.

Rowlandson, J., & Bagnall, R. S. (Eds.). (1998). *Women and society in Greek and Roman Egypt: A sourcebook.* Cambridge University Press.

Rye, M. S., Pargament, K. I., Pan, W., Yingling, D. W., Shogren, K. A., & Ito, M. (2005). Can group interventions facilitate forgiveness of an ex-spouse? A randomized clinical trial. *Journal of Consulting and Clinical Psychology, 73*(5), 880–892.

Sbarra, D. A., & Coan, J. A. (2017). Divorce and health: Good data in need of better theory. *Current Opinion in Psychology, 13*, 91–95.

Sbarra, D. A., & Borelli, J. L. (2019). Attachment reorganization following divorce: Normative processes and individual differences. *Current Opinion in Psychology, 25*, 71–75.

Sbarra, D. A., & Hazan, C. (2008). Coregulation, dysregulation, self-regulation: An integrative analysis and empirical agenda for understanding adult attachment, separation, loss, and recovery. *Personality and Social Psychology Review, 12*(2), 141–167.

Sbarra, D. A., Law, R. W., & Portley, R. M. (2011). Divorce and death: A meta-analysis and research agenda for clinical, social, and health psychology. *Perspectives on Psychological Science, 6*(5), 454–474.

Shaver, P., & Hazan, C. (1987). Being lonely, falling in love. *Journal of Social Behavior and Personality, 2*(2), 105.

Shaver, P. R., & Tancredy, C. M. (2001). *Emotion, attachment, and bereavement: A conceptual commentary.* In M. S. Stroebe, R. O. Hansson, W. Stroebe, & H. Schut (Eds.), *Handbook of bereavement research: Consequences, coping, and care* (pp. 63–88). American Psychological Association Press.

Shear, K., & Shair, H. (2005). Attachment, loss, and complicated grief. *Developmental Psychobiology: The Journal of the International Society for Developmental Psychobiology, 47*(3), 253–267.

Shear, M. K., Simon, N., Wall, M., Zisook, S., Neimeyer, R., Duan, N., Reynolds, C., Lebowitz, B., Sung, S., Ghesquiere, A., Gorscak, B., Clayton, P., Ito, M., Nakajima, S., Konishi, T., Melhem, N., Meert, K., Schiff, M., O'Connor, M. F., . . . Keshaviah, A. (2011). Complicated grief and related bereavement issues for DSM-5. *Depression and Anxiety, 28*(2), 103–117.

Shor, E., Roelfs, D. J., Bugyi, P., & Schwartz, J. E. (2012). Meta-analysis of marital dissolution and mortality: Reevaluating the intersection of gender and age. *Social Science & Medicine, 75*(1), 46–59.

Simon, N. M., Shear, K. M., Thompson, E. H., Zalta, A. K., Perlman, C., Reynolds, C. F., Frank, E., Melhem, N. M., & Silowash, R. (2007). The prevalence and correlates of psychiatric comorbidity in individuals with complicated grief. *Comprehensive Psychiatry, 48*, 395–399.

Spahni, S., Morselli, D., Perrig-Chiello, P., & Bennett, K. M. (2015). Patterns of psychological adaptation to spousal bereavement in old age. *Gerontology, 61*(5), 456–468.

Stahl, S. T., & Schulz, R. (2014). Changes in routine health behaviors following late-life bereavement: A systematic review. *Journal of Behavioral Medicine, 37*(4), 736–755.

Stroebe, M., & Schut, H. (1999). The dual process model of coping with bereavement: Rationale and description. *Death Studies, 23*(3), 197–224.

Stroebe, M., Schut, H., & Stroebe, W. (2007). Health outcomes of bereavement. *The Lancet, 370*(9603), 1960–1973.

Symoens, S., Colman, E., & Bracke, P. (2014). Divorce, conflict, and mental health: How the quality of intimate relationships is linked to post-divorce well-being. *Journal of Applied Social Psychology, 44*, 220–233.

van der Houwen, K., Schut, H., van den Bout, J., Stroebe, M., & Stroebe, W. (2010). The efficacy of a brief internet-based self-help intervention for the bereaved. *Behaviour Research and Therapy, 48*(5), 359–367.

van Velsen, L., Cabrita, M., op den Akker, H., Brandl, L., Isaac, J., Suárez, M., Gouveia, A., de Sousa, R. D., Rodrigues, A. M., Canhão, H., Evans, N., Blok, N., Alcobia, C., & Brodbeck, J. (2020). LEAVES (optimizing the mentaL health and resiliencE of older Adults that haVe lost thEir spouSe via blended, online therapy): A proposal. *JMIR Research Protocols, 9*(9), Article e19344.

Wagner, B., Knaevelsrud, C., & Maercker, A. (2006). Internet-based cognitive-behavioral therapy for complicated grief: A randomized controlled trial. *Death Studies, 30*(5), 429–453.

Wittouck, C., van Autreve, S., De Jaegere, E., Portzky, G., & van Heeringen, K. (2011). The prevention and treatment of complicated grief: A meta-analysis. *Clinical Psychology Review, 31*(1), 69–78.

Worden, J. W. (2009). *Grief counseling and grief therapy: A handbook for the mental health professional* (4th ed.). Springer.

Yárnoz-Yaben, S. (2010). Attachment style and adjustment to divorce. *The Spanish Journal of Psychology, 13*(1), 210–219.

Yárnoz-Yaben, S. (2017). El duelo ante el divorcio: Relación con el Estilo de apego y efectos en el bienestar subjetivo y el ejercicio de la co-parentalidad [Grief due to divorce: Relationship with attachment style and effects on subjective well-being and co-parenting]. *Estudios de Psicología, 38*(3), 667–688.

Znoj, H. (2006). Bereavement and posttraumatic growth. In L. Calhoun & R. Tedeschi (Eds.), *The handbook of posttraumatic growth: Research and practice* (pp. 176–196). Erlbaum.

Znoj, H. (2016a). *Komplizierte Trauer: Fortschritte der Psychotherapie.* Hogrefe Verlag.

Znoj, H. J. (2016b). *Trennung, Tod und Trauer—Geschichten zum Verlusterleben und zu dessen Transformation.* Hogrefe Verlag.

Znoj, H. J., & Keller, D. (2002). Mourning parents: Considering safeguards and their relation to health. *Death Studies, 26*(7), 545–565.

CHAPTER

26 Affective Self-Regulation After Relationship Dissolution

Leah E. LeFebvre *and* Ryan D. Rasner

Abstract

Breakups are among the most distressing occurrences in life. The affective responses to and recovery from relationship dissolution are multifaceted. Scholarship investigating relationship dissolution and the ensuing processes that follow has come a long way in facilitating a more holistic understanding of affect. These findings have driven empirical and theoretical research exploring important intersections around distress and adjustment, while illuminating the need to replicate and expand findings to more diverse populations. This chapter highlights common variables and questions in empirical relationship dissolution research including dissolution strategies (unilateral and bilateral), breakup roles (initiator and noninitiator), sex differences (reasons and roles), time (relationship length and adjustment), age (life span), and relationship redefinition (continuance or termination). These moderating variables have been studied to understand affective responses to relationship dissolution, yet they fail to fully delineate the complex structures that individuals and couples encounter. This chapter concludes by outlining and discussing gaps in prior scholarship and providing evolutionary extensions for relationship dissolution related to contemporary dating practices. The emergent lexicon of the dissolution process extends conventional metrics stability regarding development, intimacy, and commitment of interpersonal relationships. We discuss future areas for applying an evolutionary psychological perspective and offer a unifying narrative around distress, adjustment, and the moderating variables that call attention to the complex process of romantic relationship dissolution.

Key Words: breakup, relationship dissolution, distress, adjustment, initiator, dating, affection

Relationship dissolution is the transition from couplehood to singlehood, or the detachment of pair bonding. This relational change includes many labels, such as breaking up, dissolving, ending, and terminating (Rollie & Duck, 2006). Breakups force individuals to redefine and clarify who they are in absence of their partner (Slotter et al., 2010). Breakups account for varying degrees of psychological and emotional anguish in individuals' lives. Most individuals will dissolve a romantic relationship at least once in their lifetime (Buss, 2016; Morris, 2015). Many adults consider their romantic relationships a prominent aspect of their life and experience at least one nonmarital break prior to marriage (Battaglia et al., 1998); therefore, the impact of romantic breakups cannot be understated (see Berscheid & Reis, 1998). Commonly, breakups are considered one of the most distressing psychological events in life (Kendler et al., 2003; Monroe et al., 1999; Sbarra, 2006; Tashiro & Frazier, 2003).

With regard to the dissolution process, dating (nonmarital or premarital) relationships have been argued to differ, with greater assignments of responsibility, commitment, investment, and interdependence attributed to marital relationships (Agnew & VanderDrift, 2015; Cupach & Metts, 1986; Rhoades et al., 2012). These presumptions suggest that nonmarital relationships often occur casually and with much less stress because less stigma surrounds their dissolution (Rollie & Duck, 2006; Sorenson et al., 1993). This assumes individuals can more fluidly begin and end relationships with less external pressures; however, these generalizations concentrate on claims that responsibility, commitment, investment, and interdependence differ and change along with social and institutional permanency. Our perspective of dissolution is based on claims put forth by Duck (1982), in that termination processes are the same across various types of romantic relationships. Prior scholarship offers few direct comparative assessments of dissolution versus divorce, especially since only particular relationships have been allowed or afforded marital rights. Also, this binary has been complicated because frequently nonmarital and marital dissolution may be conflated within study samples. This false dichotomy between nonmarital and marital relationships hinder the ability to approach romantic relationship dissolution more comprehensively. With the societal parameters imposed around marriage, this binary separates this body of scholarship. We can incorporate greater understanding across the life span with an evolutionary psychological lens around the mechanisms rather than marital distinction. Dissolution offers a process to understand uncoupling. Although, we primarily discuss nonmarital dissolution research, the insights should broadly apply to the process for both nonmarital and marital romantic relationship dissolution.

We examine evolutionarily relevant factors of emotional distress and adjustment (negative and positive) that determine what happens in the dissolution process and highlight associated benefits and mitigating risks during and after romantic relationship dissolution. We address affective regulation surrounding factors, strategies (unilateral and bilateral), roles (initiator and noninitiator), sex differences (reasons and roles), time (relationship length and time since breakup), age (life span), and relationship redefinition (continuance or termination) that determine how and why individuals dissolve romantic relationships. To conclude, we offer future directions for empirical and theoretical work.

Distress and Adjustment

The distress of romantic relationship dissolution refers to how upset individuals are at the time of their breakup and how long it takes to recover or adjust (see Frazier & Cook, 1993; Kellas & Manusov, 2003). Emotional responses to relationship dissolution depend on moderating variables, such as: initiator role, sex differences, relationship length, time since the breakup, and relationship costs (see Field et al., 2009). Time often relates to commitment, since commitment commonly increases as the relationship investment and value increases (Rusbult, 1980). The ability to adapt to change is reflected through distress and adjustment. Contrary evidence highlights how time and commitment produce distress after a breakup. Moreover, relationship dissolution can lead to negative and positive emotions. We delineate the relationship chronology in accordance with relationship length, time since breakup, and emotional consequences from dissolving.

Often individuals inquire "How long will it take to get over this breakup?" (Sbarra & Emery, 2005, p. 228). Dissolution distress may have different timelines and adaptive adjustments. Distress relates to individual and relationship-level indicators. Consequently, distress may be mitigated depending on how dissolution perceptions relate to individual mate value and potential for alternative mate acquisition. Distress may also relate to the potential tangible costs, such as status, resource investments, protection, cohabitation, children, or emotional commitments that accompany relational closeness and investment, such as "expression of love, sacrifices of time, allocation of resources, and public declarations of commitment" (Perilloux & Buss, 2008, p. 166). Over time, distress diminishes from a relationship ending, thus contributing to the uncoupling adjustment. Adjustment refers to emotional, psychological, behavioral, and communicative changes that do not produce restrictive or maladaptive functioning based on a former and/or previous relationship (see Duck, 1982; Zhang & Chen, 2017). Frequently, distress, adjustment, and time operate as interrelated facets in that when individuals experience less distress, they are able to adjust faster. Adjustment can refer to mental or physical health conditions that occur as a result of relationship dissolution and relate to the sense of coming to terms with the relationship dissolution (see Frazier & Cook, 1993; Kellas et al., 2008; Rhoades et al., 2012; Simpson, 1987; Sprecher et al., 1998).

The distress individuals feel following a breakup is directly related to: closeness, satisfaction, investment, or commitment during the relationship; the duration of the relationship; and the ability to find a suitable alternative mate (Collins & Clark, 1989; Chung et al., 2003; Fine & Sacher, 1997). The most intense distress occurs immediately following a breakup and decreases over time (see Dailey et al., 2020; Field et al., 2009; Knox et al., 2000; LeFebvre, Rasner, et al., 2020; Moller et al., 2003; Slotter et al., 2010). People who most recently dissolved a relationship are less likely to begin a new relationship (Brumbaugh & Fraley, 2015). Greater recency of a breakup causes individuals to believe that they can try harder to rekindle the relationship, and females are more likely to exhibit this form of thought (Priest et al., 2009). Conversely, people experiencing less distress during the breakup exhibit positive emotions such as (including but not limited to) freedom, happiness, and relief (Carter et al., 2018; Tashiro & Frazier, 2003). These emotions also accompany decreased feelings of anxiousness and stress and promotion of increased confidence, growth, independence, and optimism. Individuals who originally initiated the relationship, and who were more emotionally involved experienced greater distress (Sprecher et al., 1998).

Distress may manifest as a complicated mixture of emotional, psychological, and physical negative and positive health implications. Following a relationship breakup, negative emotions are more common than positive feelings (Monroe et al., 1999). People reported experiencing poorer physical health and an associated host of stress-induced diseases and feelings (Fine & Harvey, 2006). Distress may exhibit as a lowering of self-esteem, being pessimistic, appearing preoccupied, or representing negative emotions such as anxiety, anger, bitterness, depression, guilt, fear, frustration, hopelessness, hurt, insecurity, jealousy, loneliness, regret, and sadness (see Carter et al., 2018; Choo et al., 1996; LeFebvre & Fan, 2020; Mearns, 1991; Moller et al., 2003; Sprecher, 1994). Dissolution distress can lead to appetite loss, insomnia, weight loss, social withdrawal, and suicidal thoughts (Carter et al., 2018; Chung et al., 2003; Knox et al., 2000; Priest et al., 2009).

Distressed individuals who relied upon the romantic relationship for a sense of self-worth may engage in unwanted pursuit behaviors (Park et al., 2011). People, especially females, experience physical and emotional indirect stress from their former partners including aggression, stalking, and violence when rejecting or dissolving relationships (Buss, 2016). Initiators, often with a higher mate value, are more likely to end the relationship since other alternatives or higher-quality mates are available. Noninitiators must often recalibrate their perception of their mate value, and often in a downward direction (see Perilloux & Buss, 2008). Individuals who cannot accept the breakup may continue to desire a relationship with their former partner and exhibit increased ruminating processes over time (Cupach et al., 2011). Noninitiators may experience cycling of love, anger, and sadness. Typically, the process unfolds with dramatic anger decreases, followed by sadness and eventually love (Sbarra, 2006; Sbarra & Emery, 2005). The actual distress decreases over time except less so for noninitiators. Often noninitiators felt the relationship dissolution was more abrupt, were more in love with their partners, and were less likely to have available alternatives (Eastwick et al., 2008). Greater inequity caused more distress (Huesmann & Levinger, 1976); however, individuals who exhibited more perceived control and optimism predicted better adjustment (Helgeson, 1994).

Two Sides to the Breakup

There usually are two sides to a breakup with limited agreement about the execution including the bilateralness and timing (Baxter, 1984). Distinct dissolution roles accompany the dissolution process (Doering, 2010). This dissolution decision-making process can occur as unilateral (self- or other-oriented) or bilateral (mutual-oriented). The unilateral dissolution refers to one person instigating with distinct roles for initiator and noninitiator. The bilateral dissolution, sometimes referred to as mutual disengagement, refers to both partners instigating the dissolution and each partner containing both roles.

Unilateral dissolution frequently occurs, whereas bilateral breakups are rare (Hill et al., 1976; Sprecher, 1994).

The conceptualization of dissolution orientation is primarily focused on individuals rather than couples (see Hill et al., 1976; Sprecher, 1994; Stephen, 1987). Previous relationship termination research found that those who experience relationship termination may not accurately report who initiated the relationship dissolution. Often the same number of participants indicated that their partner instigated the breakup as those who say that they themselves instigated it (Helgeson, 1994; Metts et al., 1989). When combining both breakup accounts from partners, prior findings reflect minimal agreement about bilateral breakups (Hill et al., 1976; Sprecher, 1994). The methodological constraints surrounding dyadic data collection have hindered replication. These studies used longitudinal analyses (two years: Hill et al., 1976; four years: Sprecher, 1994) to ascertain both perspectives from romantic relationships, and subsamples were then observable. Contemporary scholarship explores unilateral and bilateral perspectives; however, these findings are situated around only one partner due to methodological difficulties in securing both partners. When partners' perceptions are compared, they agree about who wanted the breakup more, thus confirming few cases of bilateral dissolution (see Drigotas & Rusbult, 1992; Helgeson, 1994; Metts et al., 1989; Sprecher, 1994). Both partners appear to have similar rationales for breaking up and experiencing change after breaking up (Sprecher, 1994). If the decision was made by one partner (either who terminated the relationship or who had to accept the other's decision), the process will be more disconcerting or intense than in circumstances where the decision was bilateral (Agnew, 2000).

We begin with the most frequent dissolution process—unilateral dissolution—and highlight the distinctive functions of each role, initiator and noninitiator. We then discuss functions for bilateral dissolution, although in reality bilateral dissolutions are rare. The initiation and rationale for the unilateral or bilateral dissolution often signals a discrepancy of rationale, roles, and thereby emotional reactions, behaviors, and adaptive responses.

Unilateral Dissolution

Unilateral dissolution causes divergence in partners' emotional reactions to dissolution. These feelings may include guilt, remorse, freedom, longing, and/or happiness for both initiators and noninitiators (Kellas, 2006). Often the distress that accompanies relationship dissolution occurs at varying times for initiator and noninitiator roles rather than happening concurrently. Unilateral initiators often experience the least emotional and physical distress, followed by bilateral dissolvers and then unilateral noninitiators (Morris, 2015). Initiators and noninitiators have been described with many variations: disengager and disengagee, dumper and dumpee, leaver and left, and rejector and rejectee or rejected (Aronson et al., 2005; Baxter, 1984; Cody, 1982; Perilloux & Buss, 2008; Sbarra & Emery, 2005; Sprecher, 1994; Tong & Walther, 2010). The various terms highlight the difference in roles and agency that causes partners to be in different places of the dissolution process. Often varying levels of trauma accompany each role. In unilateral dissolution, initiators operate as the agent who enacted dissolution and often experience emotional intensity prior to the breakup event or action, and the noninitiator responds to the event and process afterward (LeFebvre et al., 2019; Sbarra & Emery, 2005).

INITIATORS

Unilaterality, or nonmutuality, advantageously serves the initiator yet has unique challenges (Baxter, 1985). Initiators tend to have less distress following a breakup than noninitiators, and may display more positive emotions, including a sense of happiness, relief, and freedom (Hill et al., 1976; Sprecher et al., 1998). Public and private accounts are created to help establish control of the event and its account (Duck, 2011; LeFebvre et al., 2020). Frequently, initiators bear responsibility to justify their actions for breakup attribution and ownership (Blackburn et al., 2014; Lloyd & Cate, 1985). Initiators are often those who are less dependent on or committed to the relationship, and typically guide the relationship trajectory and determine its relational stability or continuance (Attridge et al., 1995). Initiators maintain more control over the event and are agents of the action. Often initiators are under the presumption that they can reject their partner because the cost of retaining their partner is too high, and they might secure a higher-value mate (Perilloux & Buss, 2008). A frequent cause for dissolution is infidelity either by self or by partner (see Buss & Schmitt, 1993; Schmitt et al., 2001). Initiators may have already begun enacting preemptive strategies to secure additional resources, sexual access, or an alternative mate (see Buss & Schmitt, 1993). As such, initiators more rapidly begin new relationships following the breakup (Brumbaugh & Fraley, 2015).

Positive emotions commonly accompany initiators allowing for the opportunity to increase their mate value, predict the speed of recovery, and/or obtain a new mate. Consequently, initiators endure fewer costs. Initiators report certain negative emotions including guilt, regret, or shame associated with the dissolved relationship (Blackburn et al., 2014; Emery, 1994). Initiators are responsible for the relationship ending and may experience reputational damage from noninitiators and/or their personal network (Perilloux & Buss, 2008). Couples create investments, which also include shared personal networks and have the ability to help or hinder relationship development and maintenance (Knobloch & Donovan-Kicken, 2006). Consequently, these perceptions influence reputations in dissolution. Initiators should consider adopting a sympathetic or caring outward appearance that may reduce reputational damage, especially with embeddedness or overlap of shared personal networks. The shared networks increase the costs of breaking up, especially since networks become intertwined, overlapping, and interdependent over time (Felmlee, 2001; Sprecher et al., 2006). The overlap in networks can cause turbulence as network members may choose sides. Reputational damage can diminish mate value to other alternative mates within shared personal networks (Buss & Dedden, 1990);

therefore, the implications of renegotiating boundaries during disentanglement need to be navigated delicately to avoid negative short- and long-term ramifications.

Additionally, initiators may experience distress, particularly if noninitiators are interested in reducing uncertainty with pursuit, displaying unwanted attention toward them, and pushing for continuance of the relationship (see Baumeister & Dhavale, 2001; LeFebvre, Rasner, et al., 2020; Tokunaga, 2011, 2015). Unilateral dissolution creates a nonmutual, or disjunctive structure to a relationship. The divergence in goals may result in further contact, and potentially unwanted contact and communication. Distress caused by unilateral dissolution leads individuals to enact unwanted pursuit behaviors (Dutton & Winstead, 2006). As a result, intrusive contact (i.e., stalking, surveilling, creeping, or obsessive relational intrusion and other violations of personal space, ownership of information, and encroached boundaries) may be pursued by noninitiators (see Brody et al., 2017; Spitzberg & Cupach, 2014). Stalking is an evolved adaptation to problems of mating and intrasexual competition (Duntley & Buss, 2010). Individuals who stalk initiators (or former partners) are attempting to salvage lost benefits of the previous relationship, ensure rivals do not acquire those benefits, and decrease the likelihood of the partner disclosing status-damaging information (Duntley & Buss, 2010). The frequency of interaction and object of pursuit becomes affected by the process of the pursuit creating difficulty in starting new relationships (Spitzberg & Cupach, 2014).

NONINITIATORS

Noninitiators commonly experience more negative emotions, lower moods, and decreased self-concept compared to initiators (LeFebvre, Rasner, et al., 2020; Perilloux & Buss, 2008; Wilmot et al., 1985). Noninitiators who are caught off guard or surprised by a breakup indicate having a more difficult time adjusting and perform more surveillance behaviors (Belu et al., 2016). Usually noninitiators face a greater deficit from relationship loss. Noninitiators experience distress with a wide array of negative emotional responses, such as anxiety, embarrassment, guilt, hurt, loneliness, sadness, and shame, which may emerge when trying to understand or resolve the breakup (Leary et al., 2001). Individuals craft accounts that assist in acknowledging their role, eventually helping them to cope with the causes and consequences (Blackburn et al., 2014; Sorenson et al., 1993). Negative emotions commonly accompany narratives, or accounts that explain the cause of the event or behaviors (Blackburn et al., 2020; Weiss, 1975). The accounts suggest mixed responses to managing emotional coping, feelings of control over the breakup, and attempts to achieve catharsis (Kellas, 2006).

While managing their outward expressions, noninitiators often reflect on what went wrong in order to reassess and avoid future relationship failures. Often rumination (Collins & Clark, 1989; Saffrey & Ehrenberg, 2007) that manifests as brooding or preoccupation may result. Individuals may become preoccupied by rumination, which leads to self-blame, increased depression, and an inability to ameliorate these negative consequences

(Honeycutt, 2010). Individuals who consistently ruminate over a past relationship remain vigilant about reinstating the relationship (Cupach et al., 2011). Displays of outward distress, such as crying, may promote sympathy and protection from their social network. Many individuals seek out others to help support and cope with relationship breakups (Duck, 1982). To respond, noninitiators may express grief toward kin and nonkin allies to signal help (Perilloux & Buss, 2008). The process for noninitiators unfolds as they respond to the action of the breakup and then to the relational consequences of problems they face after a breakup.

Noninitiators must face rejection and may be hurt. Acknowledgment of these feelings requires noninitiators to determine how they want to respond to the rejection (LeFebvre & Fan, 2020). Hurt feelings may cause noninitiators to engage in relational distancing. In the process of distancing, noninitiators can protect themselves from greater harm, decrease vulnerability to further harm, and build support and alliances. Variations in the affective processing responses to dissolution pain or their degree of hurt may manifest in four response combinations: reactive, suppressed, protective, and indifferent (see Vangelisti, 2006). *Reactive responses* indicate that noninitiators want to distance themselves from their previous partner, thereby opting to remove prior commitment, intimacy, and investment. Although noninitiators have not been found to appear less desirable (Perilloux & Buss, 2008), the perception is that noninitiators may feel as if they are less desirable as the rejected or undesired partners. For noninitiators who exhibit or demonstrate *suppressed* reactions, they experience a similar high degree of hurt yet opt to maintain their relationships with initiators. Suppressed reactions do not result in further distancing from their partners or relationship because they do not want to incur further loss to resources, cost to reputation, and protection through association. These noninitiators may also have few relational alternatives and the dissolution places them in worse positions (see Thibaut & Kelley, 1959). Conversely, noninitiators' *protective* responses operate to distance themselves from their partners due to increased recurring relationship costs. Their decision indicates that any emotional pain and hurt, even small amounts, is not worth any associated benefits. Noninitiators may also employ an *indifferent response,* by which they have subdued emotional and relational responses. These individuals may attempt to remain close to the partner and maintain the relational benefits associated with resources and access. These variations demonstrate varying tendencies of non-initiators to navigate hurt and distancing.

Bilateral Dissolution

This dissolution strategy infrequently occurs within breakups; however, this mutual account offers a way by which people can share responsibility (Blackburn et al., 2014; Cupach & Metts, 1986; Dailey et al., 2009; Hill et al., 1976; Sprecher, 1994). Discrepancies in perception cause confusion about who enacted the relationship termination. Although the individuals may indicate that mutuality occurred, it is difficult to observe because breakup responsibility and overall dissolution do not indicate mutuality or equity. The intimacy, involvement, and length of the relationship can cause partners to consider how they recount the breakup to others. Accounts allow for attribution (or blame) of the breakup. Bilateral dissolution provides coalition building among previous partners. The mutual account does not allow for the complete denigration of either partner and thereby may decrease negative impact on both partners since both are to blame. Amicable termination allows for each partner and their networks to prepare for the acceptance of the dissolution (Cupach et al., 2011) and continued desirability of partners in enmeshed networks (Baxter, 1985; Rollie & Duck, 2006).

Bilateral dissolution may present to their personal networks and public audiences (potential mates and rivals) as more empathetic and supportive (Blackburn et al., 2014). Bilateral dissolution is accompanied by more positive outcomes (e.g., less bitterness or feeling damaged) and less stress than unilateral dissolution (Carter al., 2018). Outwardly, bilateral dissolution may display a unified dissolution that communicates a positive outcome and wards off costs for both initiators and noninitiators. This public display most likely meets normative expectations of emotion for each sex. Maintaining the mutual construction provides individuals with social rewards (Cohen & Wills, 1985). However, these displays may vary by whether they are communicated in public (potential mates and rival mates) or private (kin) (see LeFebvre, Brody, et al., 2020). This function enables decreased cost for each partner within their peer network, especially with similar social networks and alliances, ability to retain respect (self, other, and relationship), manage intimate information, and maintain access to resources (e.g., cohabitation, children, and pets). Attaining social support allows opportunity for increased adjustment because social network members are not forced to choose sides. The social environment aids in recovery and bilateral dissolution affords individuals access to shared social network members and their resources (Felmlee et al., 1990; Yıldırım & Demir, 2015). This neutral consensus formulated as the bilateral account (even if fabricated by one or both partners) may prime indications of sympathetic, cooperative, and beneficial conflict-resolution skills as well as mitigate attributes reserved for initiators or noninitiators. Additionally, the bilateral account may allow for former partners to become reintegrated into the social network (Duck, 1982; Lannutti & Cameron, 2002).

Bilateral dissolution may provide for an intermediate step as both partners adjust to their new separation. Individuals may use bilateral dissolution to circumvent the inevitability of relationship termination. However, mutual agreement and amicable dissolution may not permit future access to sexual or emotional intimacy or reengagement in a romantic relationship with investment, commitment, and duration. Using mutuality when dissolving a relationship reduces the likelihood of reconciliation (Dailey et al., 2020). Individuals who dissolved the relationship mutually were less likely to reconcile and reinitiate or renew any form of romantic relationship, even on-again/off-again relationships or cycling (see Dailey et al., 2009; Dailey et al., 2011), and simultaneously negatively impacted future relationships. Previous closeness in past relationships negatively impacts future relationship commitment and satisfaction in bilateral dissolution (Merolla et al., 2004). Although, loyalty and guilt may cause individuals to maintain communication, this closeness inhibits other potential partners and relationships (Weiss, 1975). The mutuality of dissolution, therefore, may hinder individual's ability to acquire resources (sexual access, economic resource, protection, etc.) lost from previous and potential future partners. Consequently, rivals will gain access instead to resources. As a by-product, bilateral dissolution prevents third-party judges from attributing roles (and their presumed character associations, e.g., initiators are relatively higher-quality mates than noninitiators) to each person, unlike unilateral dissolution, which delineates the initiator and noninitiator roles and subsequently may allow for differing relationship power, breakup ownership, and reconnection opportunities. The ability to assign roles allows for a discrepancy and inequity in blame, responsibility, and power that might be more equitable in bilateral dissolution. With equal assignments, each partner has the ability to rekindle (yet may restrict) responsibility in the dissolution. Unilateral dissolution often assigns blame in an effort to rekindle the relationship. In bilateral dissolutions both partners must admit individual deficiencies to insinuate relationship change. Resultingly, bilateral dissolutions facilitate less attributable ownership for the dissolution, more enduring dissolution, and lasting finality with partners (Dailey et al., 2011).

Sex Differences

The interaction between the initiator role and sex (as an extension of varying mating strategies) relates to who ends the relationship and the rationale for termination. Contradictory evidence occurs around who is responsible, how disengagement occurred, and reasons surrounding the dissolution. Sex refers to differences between females and males determined through primarily biological processes (e.g., genetics and hormone exposure), whereas gender refers to differences between men and women due to social factors (e.g., culture norms and identity formation; Duck & Wood, 2011). Sex and gender have been utilized synonymously in relationship dissolution; however, clear conceptual differences between sex and gender offer different adaptive functionality in understanding an evolutionary perspective. Prior relational scholarship often conflates and misuses sex and gender. The amalgamation of terminology and conceptualizations lead to varying arguments for evolution versus social constructivism (see LeFebvre, Brody, et al., 2020). Often, the misuse of sex versus gender does not distinguish the two concepts. We delineate the differences as articulated by various scholars and scholarship (if possible); however, these findings may have become conflated or misconstrued until recent scholarship. Contemporary distinctions have begun to unpack and acknowledge the biological and social differences between sex and gender (see Muehlenhard & Peterson, 2011, for the history, conceptualizations, and implications).

Evolutionary psychology argues that females and males have recurrently faced different adaptive problems that hinder reproduction and survival. Sex differences in optimal mating strategies, including short- and long-term goals, has been backed by robust research (Buss, 2016; Buss & Schmitt, 1993, 2019). The theory of sexual selection and parental investment provides a powerful basis for sex differences in mating (Mogilski, 2021; Trivers, 1972). Mating strategies may generally be divided into two categories: short- and long-term. *Short-term mating* relates to fleeting sexual encounters, with brief affairs, intermediate-term relationships, and prolonged romances. *Long-term mating* focuses on extended courtship, greater investment, and dedication of resources. These mating strategies have helped individuals overcome the ancestrally recurrent challenges of mating and reproduction. Short- and long-term mating distinctions are descriptive rather than explanatory for understanding the functionality of the pair-bonding system (Eastwick et al., 2019). Both categories have their strengths and weaknesses for enhancing reproductive success and decreasing costs.

This coevolutionary struggle (i.e., sexual conflict; see Kennair et al., this volume) has substantial impact on both sexes and their mating strategies. We explore sex differences as contingent and complementary functions influenced by short- and long-term mating strategies in relationship dissolution (Bleske-Rechek & Buss, 2006). Relationship dissolution scholarship (e.g., Baxter, 1986; Choo et al., 1996; Hill et al., 1976; Le et al., 2010; LeFebvre, Brody, et al., 2020; Mearns, 1991; Rubin et al., 1981; Sorenson et al., 1993; Sprecher, 1994; Sprecher et al., 1998; Tashiro & Frazier, 2003) has reached various, sometimes conflicting, conclusions about ways in which females and males respond to relationship termination. Although some scholars have argued that sex differences are relatively unimportant in interpersonal communication research (e.g., Canary & Hause, 1991; Dindia & Canary, 2006), others argue there are more similarities than differences. We acknowledge the similarities yet highlight significant sex differences.

Differences in both the number and types of reasons were observed between the sexes (Baxter, 1986; Hill et al., 1976; Rubin et al., 1981). Many dissolution strategies have been identified and employed to end relationships (see Banks et al., 1987; Cody, 1982). Direct versus indirect strategies lead to different outcomes and strategies for maintaining, retaining, or dissolving resources. The *justification* strategy utilized in dissolution employs direct honest dissolution (see Cody, 1982), by which the initiator expresses a positive tone and openness to dissolve the relationship. This strategy may include emotions about grief over the intention to disengage, attention on the noninitiator through the demonstration of care given by the initiator, and discussion about a fair or appropriate course of action (Cody, 1982). This strategy allows for reasons for dissolution, often expectations or rules of permanence, and assignment of blame. See Cody, 1982, for other dissolution strategies. Findings have indicated that females report consideration for both themselves and their partner, whereas, males only consider themselves when they initiate the breakup (Helgeson, 1994). Reasons for breaking up may be explicit or implicit depending on strategy.

Sex differences should lead to differences reported as reasons for breakups. The three most common reasons were boredom in the relationship, differences of interests, and desires for independence by at least one partner (Hill et al., 1976). Fewer contemporary studies (see adolescents: Connolly & McIsaac, 2009; Norona, Oberson, et al., 2017; Norona, Roberson, et al., 2017; on-again/off-again: Dailey et al., 2009) have focused on reasons for romantic breakups. Dissolution studies commonly suggest loyalty and (in) fidelity as the primary reason for dissolution and rejection (Betzig, 1989; McKiernan et al., 2018). Females are at risk of males committing emotional infidelity and losing resources, and males are at risk of sexual infidelity and being cuckolded, or investing resources in another's offspring (Schmitt & Buss, 2001). Baxter (1986) allowed participants (females and males) to openly report their reasons for dissolving their relationships. They found (in)fidelity as the primary reason for dissolution as well as many other reasons including autonomy, similarity display, supportiveness, openness, shared time, equity, romance, and miscellaneous. Importantly, it is not only the initiator role that equates to blame or impetus; rather, sex differences further illuminate dissolution reasons and effects.

Following relationship dissolution (see Rollie & Duck, 2006), most people formulate private and public accounts, or reasons for their breakups, and females and males differ in their conceptualization and articulation of emotional distress and adjustment. Females utilize more negative emotions in their private accounts compared to males who utilize similar negative emotional expressions for either private or public audiences (Blackburn et al., 2014; LeFebvre, Brody, et al., 2020). Females might regulate emotional use regarding former partners and previous relationships, especially for public audiences to avoid demonstrating distress, appearing as adjusted, and creating opportunities to display greater desirability for other potential long-term partners. In comparison, male emotional displays are less contingent on mate value relegated to a specific age and life span and therefore, the ability to engage with similar emotional use in both private and public audiences can be afforded to them. The evolutionary differences in accordance with short- and long-term mating as well as age may cause different adaptive responses for managing emotion.

Females

Females are more often the breakup initiators (Baumeister et al., 1993; DeLecce & Weisfeld, 2016; Sprecher, 1994; Tong & Walther, 2010) and precipitate unilateral breakups (perceive breakups as gradual rather than abrupt) than do males. These findings may evidence greater awareness and relationship appraisal granted to females due to their heavier investment costs. Often females are perceived to work harder to maintain their relationships and are more aware of relationship problems, and when the costs become greater than rewards, females may opt to dissolve those relationships (Baxter, 1984; Choo et al., 1996; Cupach & Metts, 1986; Rusbult, 1987). Some findings suggest that females and males warrant similar controllability or blame of the breakup (Choo et al., 1996; Frazier & Cook, 1993); however, females frequently still blame males more than themselves and have more negative attitudes toward their former partners (Athenstaedt et al., 2020; Sprecher, 1994). Although females were perceived as initiators more often, females who were noninitiators reported higher instances of feeling sad, confused, and scared in comparison to males who reported feeling more happy or indifferent following the dissolution (Perilloux & Buss, 2008). Females felt slightly more negative toward their previous partner (Stephen, 1987).

Females are often involved or invested partners (Hill et al., 1976), first to fall out of love (Rubin et al., 1981), and more likely to move to alternative mates (Blau, 1964). Consequently, females perceived more positive consequences by rebounding from the relationship when they had initiated the breakup (Buss et al., 2017; Helgeson, 1994; Rubin et al., 1981). Females also possess a greater need to maintain their image, mate value, and self-presentation as desirable relationship-oriented individuals (Baxter, 1986). The ability for females to initiate the dissolution allows for greater control of the breakup reasoning. Females are more likely to mention autonomy, openness, and equity, whereas males frequently mention a lack of romance as rationale for breaking up among college students (Baxter, 1986). Females articulate more reasons than males for justifying relationship termination. Initiators from intimate relationships felt greater obligation to justify dissolution intentions (Cody, 1982). Specifically, autonomy and interdependence generated tension. Females must be selective in their mate selection process to warrant quality selection; therefore, in the dating process they may find evidence that they will incur greater costs than rewards for maintaining the relationship. This selection process suggests females are usually the latter to commit, first out for pragmatic reasons (e.g., last in, first out), and pursue long-term mating strategies (see Baxter, 1986; Hendrick et al., 1984). Moreover, these findings indicate that females experience more positive emotions and less initial distress following a breakup than males. Often these females encounter a foreboding inclination of relationship termination and relief when enacting the initiator role. Their decision to terminate the relationship allows for greater opportunity to procure a more advantageous mate.

Males

Conversely, males appeared to initiate romantic overtones more often, fall in love easier, and, therefore, experience more rejection (Hendrick & Hendrick, 1986; Rubin et al., 1981; Tong & Walther, 2010). Males often reported having been in love more often (Kephart, 1967; Sprecher, 1994) suggesting that they are afforded more opportunities to pursue the *luxury of love* since they commonly incur fewer costs with commitment (Rubin et al., 1981). The ability to incur less of the cost allows males to initiate more frequently and with a more diverse range of potential alternative mates. Male initiators retain a sense of confidence in the ability to acquire a better mate (Perilloux & Buss, 2008). Furthermore, males retain the ability to present themselves to other males as more sexually promiscuous than females (Seto et al., 1997) and appear less discriminating in their mate-seeking behaviors due to incurring fewer mating costs (Buss, 2016).

Males are typically considered to be responsible for the relationship termination; however, they are less likely to initiate the breakup and denigrate their partners (Baumeister et al., 1993; Choo et al., 1996; Sprecher, 1994; Tong & Walther, 2010). Often they are reactive to the dissolution operating as noninitiators rather than initiators (Rubin et al., 1981), and they claim they do not know the cause of their relationship dissolutions (Amato & Previti, 2003). Males commonly report attempting to prevent dissolution by increasing the level of commitment or investment (Helgeson, 1994; Perilloux & Buss, 2008). When males are initiators, males and females are more likely to indicate that the dissolution was abrupt (Rubin et al., 1981). Consequently, males fall in love faster and experience more emotional reactions from breakups (Rubin et al., 1981). Accordingly, males indicated feeling more depressed, lonely, less happy and less free after the breakup and engaged in more harmful behaviors following breakups (Athenstaedt et al., 2020; Rubin et al., 1981). Males are often less willing to break ties with former partners especially since they have more positive perceptions of their partners, rely on them for emotional support, and experience longer recovery than females (Athenstaedt et al., 2020; Morris, 2015). Males, therefore, may exhibit less emotional distress following a breakup, yet they are more likely to engage in damaging behaviors.

Relationship Length and Time since Breakup

Distress is contingent on relationship length (Tashiro & Frazier, 2003), relationship investment (Field et al., 2009), and time since breakup (Sprecher et al., 1998). Relationship length and investment have covarying functions since both demonstrate interdependence and serve as forms of commitment (see Morris & Reiber, 2011). Those individuals who put in more time maintaining the relationship incur more costs and experience more distress following a breakup (Sprecher et al., 1998). Relationship length is often assessed in scholarship; however, this metric has not been determined to independently cause greater distress in dissolution. Instead, stronger emotional ties (evidenced as investment, satisfaction, or commitment) result in greater distress upon relationship dissolution (Kelley et al., 1983). Strong emotional ties reflect changes in the needs fulfilled by the relationship; therefore, as the relationship becomes redefined it may or may not allow for emotional and/or sexual intimacy between previous partners. Distress lessens over time after a relationship ends (Slotter et al., 2010); thus, time since the breakup often plays a stronger (significant) determining factor in whether previous partners continue their relationship.

Contradictory findings indicate varying responses to dissolution based on the characteristics of the relationship including length and/or investment. When individuals have been in longer relationships where they reported higher commitment, satisfaction, and investment, they experienced greater distress (Simpson, 1987). Similarly, individuals who reported higher levels of satisfaction and closeness to their former partner experienced greater distress following the breakup, along with greater perceived difficulty in finding a future mate (Frazier & Cook, 1993). Additionally, individuals with higher investments had more difficulty adjusting after breakups (Stanley et al., 2006). Other studies have observed that individuals who had longer relationships appeared to have lower emotional distress and reduced emotional and sexual intimacy after the breakup (Lannutti & Carmeron, 2002; Sbarra & Emery, 2005). These contradictory findings may relate to disparity in short- and long-term costs and rewards that are not measured and that may become more apparent with repeated assessments and longitudinal analyses. Findings may relate more to actual and potential costs which may not be as observable through relationship length. Additionally, adaptations and acceptance of a breakup can occur prior to the event; therefore, adjustment may occur without accounting for relationship length.

Relationship length and time since the breakup negatively predict whether individuals maintain a relationship after dissolution (Lannutti & Carmeron, 2002). Daily communication with former partners increases sadness (Sbarra & Emery, 2005), and remaining close after a breakup may obstruct emotional recovery by prolonging the distress (Tan et al., 2015). Individuals who longed for their former partners experienced lower relationship quality in future relationships (Spielmann et al., 2012). For noninitiators, maintaining sexual access with a former partner is negatively associated with ability to recover after a breakup (Spielmann, Joel, et al., 2019) and more likely to cause the desire for vengeance on their former partners (Brumbaugh & Fraley, 2015). Individuals motivated by distress from prior relationships seek relief through short-term mating strategies with casual sexual encounters by *getting it on, to get over* a relationship (Hadden & Agnew, 2020). Initial sexual access (that decreases over time) is utilized to cope with distress, attempt to rekindle relationships, and as revenge (Barber & Cooper, 2014). Besides sex encounters, males are adapted to overcome stress by using distraction (e.g., sports and hobbies), whereas females opt to utilize their social networks to recover (Choo et al., 1996; Sprecher et al., 1998). New partners and friends can help individuals in the short term get over their former partners (Spielmann et al., 2009); however, people tend to become more distressed, if they believe they will never find a long-term relationship and love (Berscheid et al., 1989). People who remain single demonstrate unresolved feelings about their previous relationships which are compounded by difficulty exhibiting confidence to seek alternative mating options (Brumbaugh & Fraley, 2015).

The ability to find suitable alternative mates highlights different emotional responses. Individuals who view their former partner and previous relationship as providing an enhanced life and increased mate value display decreased sense of self-concept and self-esteem (Lewandowski et al., 2006; Morris, 2015) and sought out future partners similar to their previous partner to fill the sense of self that was lost (Lewandowski & Sahner, 2005). Individuals who are more distressed from their previous relationship may provide further emotional commitments and resources available to the new romantic relationship (Haggen & Agnew, 2020). Once both females and males have begun new (less strictly sexual-oriented, noncommittal, or rebound) romantic relationships, they hold less favorable views about their former partners (Athenstaedt et al., 2020). Rebound relationships indicate that distress remains from the previous relationship and the initiation of relationships toward short-term mating to provide healing, and that time is necessary before individuals are ready to pursue further long-term mating strategies (see Brumbaugh & Fraley, 2015).

Dissolution Across the Life Span

The adage *time heals all wounds* indicates that distress may lessen but fails to account for substantial fitness costs associated with age. Moving forward after dissolution initially causes the greatest distress, then distress diminishes as individuals seek and find alternative mates. Successful adaptation and navigation of distress allow individuals to avoid fewer pending costs with age. Despite understanding dissolution strategy, initiator role, and sex differences, minimal information is known about how specific life span age affects self-regulation in relationship dissolution. We speculate how age corresponds to reproduction and survival and how sex difference highlights different costs over the life span. Age corresponds to relationship development across the life span. Specifically, puberty in adolescence and access to numerous potential partners in emerging adulthood sparks exploration of romantic relationship behavior and selection of partners. Adolescence and emerging adulthood entail similar reasons (affiliation, intimacy, and need for autonomy) for breaking up with partners (Bravo et al., 2017); however, minimal research speculates how relationship dissolution influences mating throughout the life span. Personal timing relates to biology, sexual behavior, and pair-bonding. Mate value for each sex presents distinct coevolutionary processes depending on age and life stage.

The majority of relationship dissolution scholarship uses samples of adolescents or emerging adults. Individuals typically follow a sequence of relationship progression to correspond with their age and life stage. Often adolescents begin with soft stages demonstrating interest but have no romantic relationships, then build to one casual relationship, followed by multiple casual relationships, and finally one steady relationship (Davies & Windle, 2000; Meier & Allen, 2009). The time of early adolescence socializes individuals into understanding their mate value in romantic relationships. Timing is important since individuals who spend too much time in short-term mating may incur costs, and simultaneously those in long-term mating that dissolves will lose out on potential alternatives. Adolescents' and emerging adults' romantic relationships may end frequently and afford opportunity to test the mating market and secure alternative partners (Rollie & Duck, 2011), whereas older people have fewer expectations or vital opportunities to secure replacements. Timing within the life span may influence viability as a romantic partner.

Dissolution effects become stronger during reproductive viability (Morris, 2015). Females have a smaller window for fertility and therefore to achieve reproduction, whereas males have the opportunity to continue to choose from an array of females for a longer duration. Fertility and reproductive value, as measured by mate value, correspond with age and physical attractiveness (see Bech-Sørensen & Pollet, 2016; Buss, 1989;

Sprecher et al., 1994). Mate value based on these criteria operates on a curvilinear function which peaks as teenagers (after puberty) and emerging adults (18 to 29 years old) and declines throughout the 30s and 40s (Buss & Shackelford, 1997). Even among adolescents, females are more interested in long-term committed relationships, conceptualized as marriage (Bech-Sørensen & Pollet, 2016), although they are less likely or more reluctant to commit. With each dissolution, females focused on what not to do or how not to behave in relationships while males, in contrast, framed lessons about what to do (Norona, Roberson, et al., 2017).

Females are more likely to select mates based on partners' willingness to invest time and resources in the relationship and potential. Females incur greater costs with a longer reproductive process; pregnant females and females with young children experience the greatest costs upon dissolution (Kelly et al., 2016). Therefore, distress associated with relationship dissolution may become more contingent on age, costs incurred with childbearing and children, and alternative mate viability. As females age, their mate value may concurrently decrease along with more limited access to viable alternatives, greater rejection, and less opportunity to secure long-term partners. Furthermore, as females age, they tend to become more interested in older males, greater earning potential, less on physical attractiveness, and mates who have children from prior relationships (Sprecher et al., 1994).

Males have the opportunity to produce more offspring from an array of females enabling them to more frequently exhibit short- and long-term mating strategies (Buss, 2016). The mate value of males relies on physical attractiveness and resource acquisition. Male attractiveness gradually decreases with age (Kelly et al., 2016). Males have more time and potential to increase their mate value, since their value peaks later in life (Buss, 2016; Perilloux & Buss, 2008), and varying values oscillate between attractiveness with dominance in physical prowess and resource acquisition. At every age, males are more interested than females in physical attractiveness and multiple sexual partners (Bleske-Rechek et al., 2009). Age-specific benefits outweighed the costs to younger males (Perilloux & Buss, 2008). As a result, males experience more rejections and romantic relationship involvement similarly at any age throughout their lifetime (Rubin et al., 1981). However, with each dissolution, males focus more on their own feelings (self-focused) and their independence and become more attuned to establishing connectedness with potential future partners compared to females (Norona, Roberson, et al., 2017). Males may approach and value romantic relationships differently—especially the experience of romantic relationships and their meaning. Therefore, males are more likely to respond to breakups consistently regardless of age (Buss, 1989; Morris, 2015; Sprecher et al., 1994). When males evidence long-term mating strategies, they are more likely to have long-term relationships with females who are younger, to have fewer resource acquisitions (e.g., employment or earning potential), and to express more reluctance to start a relationship with females who have children (Bech-Sørensen & Pollet, 2016; Sprecher et al., 1994).

Sex-differentiated costs of reproduction suggest that short-term mating strategies are utilized less frequently by females, and that long-term mating strategies that dissolve create compounded effects for females, reducing their ability to secure long-term committed male partners. Therefore, earlier dissolutions may not result in distressing effects for females, unless increased costs have been encumbering. In comparison, male fertility and reproduction is not limited as much by age, and they often commit to long-term mating strategies with younger females. Therefore, males may face more rejection and dissolution throughout their lifetimes; however, their mate value is less contingent on traits that senesce (e.g., physical attractiveness). Sex differences vary by age throughout the life span to influence relationship investment and varying self-regulation throughout relationship dissolution.

Redefining the Post-Dissolution Relationship

Dissolution constitutes the end to a romantic relationship; however, some form of relationship may remain or emerge (Kellas, 2006). The dissolution process focuses on the psychological, emotional, and communicative effects of individuals, whereas, post-dissolution highlights the relationships between previous partners (Dragon & Duck, 2005; Vangelisti, 2006). In the process of initiating dissolution, individuals may consider the implications for relationship deescalation versus termination and the implications to social networks. Individuals list a number of reasons for retaining a friendship after dissolution: reliability, practicality, continued attraction, children/shared resources, decreased attraction, maintaining a social relationship, and sexual access (Mogilski & Welling, 2017). Post-dissolution relationships (PDR) redefined following a breakup highlight the complexity surrounding the breakup adjustment and relational satisfaction (see Kellas et al., 2008, for visual PDR trajectories for premarital relationships). Nascent scholarship has begun to explore PDR communication and outcomes; however, further understanding of the processes and functions suggest that costs of the breakup may suggest relationships change to face different adaptive problems in an attempt to achieve reproduction and survival. The fundamental changes to the relationship can result in a process whereby the decrease in intimacy level leads to severance or termination, or prompts a complete reversal in a relationship (Orbuch, 1992). Individuals, therefore, navigate the dissolution process to match their own reproduction and survival needs, which may represent turning points in their relationship redefinition rather than relationship endings.

The dissolution process allows individuals the opportunity to redefine the relationship in a way that benefits each person (Baxter, 1984). A redefined relationship that allows individuals the opportunity to retain their status within the social network and to be viewed as kind and compassionate to potential future mates benefits both individuals, thus securing the likelihood of a future relationship with individuals of high mate value. Individuals who invested considerable resources often seek to maintain a relationship following dissolution as the relationship is a perceived wellspring of resources (Tan et al., 2015). The closeness of individuals following a breakup may be viewed by others as a signal of commitment within relationships. However, particularly successful romantic relationship recovery from a breakup indicates reflecting on the past relationship and its negative attributes, starting a new relationship, focusing on other demands, or seeking support from network and alliances (Carter et al., 2018). People who reported higher levels of commitment during the relationship will remain closer following a breakup (for a short time). These individuals may yearn for their former partner and seek out a sexual relationship with them following a breakup (Spielmann, Joel, et al., 2019). Sexually pursuing a former partner is a common occurrence as individuals navigate redefining the PDR.

Continued contact with former partners often makes moving on after a breakup more difficult for some individuals (Rhoades et al., 2010). Maintaining contact may foster lingering feelings individuals are not able to manage and thus affect movement into new relationships. The continued feelings for previous partners are associated with ambiguity about the dissolution (Rhoades et al., 2010). People who were less invested in the romantic relationship will seek out a platonic relationship and those more invested want to maintain a romantic relationship following a divorce (Emery & Dillon, 1994). The redefinition of a relationship from romantic to friendship constitutes a transference of goals and expectations where commitment is renegotiated into compatibility (Metts et al, 1989). Where previous commitments to one another and the relationship were prominent, individuals must now focus on their ability to remain platonically compatible. The redefinition process is ambiguous and lacks conventional scripts for how individuals should proceed (Foley & Fraser, 1998), thus creating difficulties and anxiety for both individuals when navigating the redefinition process.

Fear may emerge as individuals leave the comfort of a relationship for the uncertainty found in singledom (Spielmann, Maxwell, et al., 2019). Males may seek out a continued relationship following a breakup as a means to maintain sexual access (Mogilski & Welling, 2017), while females may seek out a continued relationship with a past partner for the purpose of protection (Bleske-Rechek & Buss, 2001). Findings regarding sex differences and the propensity for women to seek a continued relationship for protection have been contradictory where some sex differences failed to emerge in connection with protection (see Mogilski & Welling, 2017). The scriptless nature of relationship redefinition poses unique problems for these individuals and differing accounts for the motivations behind remaining friends (see Foley & Fraser, 1998). Therefore, individuals may resort to behaviors indicative of mate retention rather than redefinition.

Mate Retention

The process of mate retention dissuades and guards against potential rivals to retain acquired mates (Buss, 1988). As individuals seek out and acquire new mates and mating opportunities, the redefined relationships become less relevant and important. These relationships are constructed and sought out for social support and resources provided by the former partner, assuming those resources were satisfactory during the relationship (Busboom et al., 2002). Individuals who provided more resources and value are often sought out for friendship following a breakup. For example, an individual who perceives their partner as highly desirable is more likely to seek out friendship after a breakup (Banks et al., 1987). Moreover, when a previous partner is more desirable than possible alternative partners, or if the relationship was perceived as highly satisfactory (Bullock et al., 2011), individuals may seek out a continued friendship following a breakup (Banks et al., 1987). However, once that relationship need is fulfilled by a new partner, the reliance upon a former partner subsides along with the previously redefined relationship.

Engaging in post-relationship friendship may benefit individuals by decreasing anxiety through the possibility of continued support and/or the possibility of future romantic involvement (Mogilski & Welling, 2017). However, these post-relationship friendships are often the result of individuals who were friends prior to the romantic relationship (Metts et al., 1989). Retaining a relationship after a breakup has evolutionary benefits through the continuation of a social alliance (DeScioli & Kurzban, 2009) where individuals can continue to share and benefit from each other's support (Mogilski & Welling, 2017). Individuals may not wish to lose the resources previously afforded to them in the relationship or lose what they invested in the relationship. Those who invested more in the relationship may have a higher propensity to maintain the relationship following a breakup, therefore retaining their previous investments (Tan et al., 2015). Regardless of initiator role, individuals retain certain benefits through friendships. Individuals seek out continued friendship following a breakup if the benefits are more substantial than the costs.

Mate value has been directly related to the propensity to reinstate a relationship and individuals seeking the reestablishment with a partner of high mate value would benefit from maintaining some form of relationship (i.e., friendship) after the breakup (Kelly et al., 2016). Initiators whose previous partner was high in mate value could create an opportunity for the relationship to be reinstated by maintaining a friendship following a breakup. Males high in mate value are those with an ability to acquire resources, while youth and attractiveness are indicators of female mate value (Buss, 2016). Therefore, initiators dissolving a relationship with a partner of higher mate value in this sense should leave an opportunity for the relationship to reemerge.

Initiators and noninitiators differ in the form and number of behaviors following a breakup. Noninitiators typically utilize both low-cost behaviors, such as pleading, and high-cost behaviors, such as threats of self-harm. Initiators, on the other hand, focused on creating a compassionate reputation for themselves by increasing the noninitiators' self-esteem (Perilloux & Buss, 2008). Initiators, therefore, focus on preparing themselves for future relationships, while noninitiators concentrate their efforts toward salvaging the relationship. The difference in behaviors between initiators and noninitiators may be partially explained by the perceived mate value of each individual based on initiator status. Noninitiators often attempt to salvage the relationship and retain their mate with either low- or high-cost behaviors. Mate-retention behaviors utilized in marriage by noninitiators include negativity, alignment, commitment, and harm building on behaviors utilized in marriage (Buchanan et al., 2006). The four behaviors employed by noninitiators can be understood in the context of low- or high-cost behaviors. Low-cost retention behaviors include emotional manipulation (inducing guilt, derogating others, using sex), commitment manipulation (cohabitation, monogamy, marriage), and verbalized signs of possession (possessive ornamentation or cock-blocking). Conversely, high-cost behaviors would include harm in the form of violence, such as physical harm directed at the partner and/or rivals. Initiators retain control over how the relationship progresses or terminates and their own social image, while noninitiators focus energy toward mate retention or regaining lost access. The redefinition of a PDR commonly relates to social benefits and continued access to resources. Overall, the redefinition of relationships in post-dissolution (see Metts et al., 1989) is frequently a short-lived experience that lacks continuance when romantic relationships end.

Future Directions

The majority of relationship dissolution scholarship investigates adolescents or collegiate, homogeneous, heterosexual emerging adults. Utilizing initiator role and sex differences provides a framework for understanding distress from dissolution. Further investigations must determine the dissolution impact corresponding to age. The depiction of time—relationship length and time since breakup—offers a singular perspective of breakups in adolescence or emerging adults (i.e., the episodic level). Prior studies primarily measured participants' retrospective understanding of their most recent breakup. These cross-sectional surveys fail to provide a comprehensive (i.e., global level) depiction of the evolution of relationship dissolution and PDRs throughout the life span. Global-level depictions utilizing an evolutionary psychological lens may offer insight into the individual and cumulative changes that occur for individuals throughout their lifetime depending on differing adaptive needs. These findings ignore or neglect the potential compounding influence of breakups on sexual selection and mating strategies corresponding to age and repeated occurrence. Future relationship dissolution scholarship should consider the global implications of dissolution in conjunction with age and relationship history: How many relationship dissolutions should occur throughout a lifetime? What are the compounding effects of many breakups, and do they lead to evidence of lower mate value and greater emotional distress? Does experiencing relationship dissolution increase reputational value more than single individuals who never seemed desirable? Is experience with numerous breakups (regardless of initiator or non-initiator status) viewed as a beneficial trait in mate selection? What are the associated sex differences that accompany the dissolution experience(s)? Further investigations should highlight age-related variation (e.g., early adolescent development, later emerging adults, or adulthood interaction with dissolution distress) or differences within LGBTQ+ populations (see Holland

& Lannutti, this volume). Future research must replicate prior findings and expand the investigations to more diverse populations.

Additionally, relationship dissolution delineates the primary use of unilateral dissolution and therefore illuminates the process for initiators and noninitiators. Although several scholars (see Sprecher, 1994) call into question whether bilateral dissolution truly exists, numerous investigations continue to investigate self, partner, and mutual dissolution. Current metrics primarily utilize individual perspectives as either nominal variable, such as self, partner, or mutual (see Belu et al., 2016; Blackburn et al., 2014; LeFebvre et al., 2015), or as a Likert scale (see Dailey et al., 2009; Sprecher et al., 1998). The Likert 7-point scale anchors self and partner at opposite ends and mutual at the center. These variations delineate metrics for perceptions surrounding dissolution roles outlining different outcomes; however, they neglect to understand the perceptions available from both partners in a dissolved relationship. Bilateral dissolution remains infrequently observed; future investigations should examine their functionality and offer explicit predictions about their evolutionary benefits and costs (e.g., retaining respect or managing third-party judgment). Moreover, the mutuality of bilateral dissolution blurs blames and responsibility for the dissolution; therefore, the post-dissolution ownership may suggest a variety of relationship trajectories. The amicable consensus about termination allows both parties to accept yet complicate the dissolution distress (Cupach et al., 2011), leading to a number of alternative relationship outcomes that function to split the costs incurred and benefits received between partners.

The modern relationship lexicon illuminates new vocabulary to challenge and change interpersonal communication and relationship formation processes including maintenance and dissolution. These conceptualizations highlight some of the emergent lexicons which include booty calls, one-night stands, on-again/off-again, hooking-up, fuck buddies, relationship churning, friends with benefits, friendzone, asymmetrical committed relationships, back-burner relationships, rebound relationships, nonrelationships, ghosting, and breadcrumbing. Utilizing an evolutionary psychology approach, the nexus for conventional stability and normative parameters regarding development, intimacy, and commitment may offer additional insight into these modern relationship processes. Relationship dissolution may emerge when pluralistic mating strategies are employed causing confusion and ambiguity surrounding cost and benefit allocation during relationship continuance. For instance, friends-with-benefits relationships (see Lewis, Al-Shawaf, et al., 2012; Lewis, Conroy-Beam, et al., 2012; Mongeau et al., 2019) offer both individuals the benefit of a sexual relationship while allowing each person to seek out other mating opportunities. Friends-with-benefits relationships may be a relational destination following a breakup. Individuals who continue to yearn for a past partner will often seek out a continued sexual relationship with that person (Spielmann, Joel, et al., 2019). Among the motivations for seeking out friends-with-benefits relationships is a desire for sex and emotional connection (Hughes et al., 2005). One way to achieve is to examine the expectations afforded in a romantic relationship but negate the problem of relationship dissolution. Therefore, the nonnormative relationships may allow for less distress without explicit commitment and adjustment after its disengagement. Future research would benefit from exploring the nuances of bilateral dissolution and nonnormative relationships through evolutionary psychology perspectives.

As an outgrowth of changing technologies, contemporary relationship behaviors become observable on mediated platforms. Mediated communication provides people a platform for creating social bonds unconstrained by proximity or propinquity. Online and mobile dating applications permit new affiliations redefining propinquity yet eliminate common sexual selection and mating strategies that rely on kinship and social alliances. Many relationships begin through technologies, and people utilize these same features to dissolve relationships. How is relationship dissolution enacted through mediated communication? (LeFebvre, Rasner, et al., 2020). Furthermore, online dating has leveled out the mating pool sex ratio by allowing users the opportunity to seek out greater potential mates and alternatives (see Buss, 2016; Perilloux & Buss, 2008). Emergent technology decreases the difference in the mating pool sex ratio. How does this impact mating strategies and dissolution? How do different sexes apply short-term mating strategies, thus increasing the propensity for dissolution in romantic relationships? As mediated communication is more frequently employed, the social norms and features may become strategically impersonal, facilitate social distance, cause rejection, and employ dissolution (Tong & Walther, 2010). Questions arise surrounding dissolution strategies, mating retention, emotional distress, and predation (see Brody et al., 2017; LeFebvre, Rasner, et al., 2020; Tokunaga, 2011, 2015) as people consider how to dissolve relationships, uncover what their partners were thinking, and attempt to control what and when individuals learn about their breakup (Gershon, 2020). People utilized the similar dissolution processes engrained through mating strategies; however, this emergent context may highlight underrecognized strategies for romantic pursuit and dissolution. The changes to modern romantic relationships offer further important opportunities to understand the interwoven complexities and adaptive mechanisms.

Conclusion

Breakups are distressing. Many facets affect how individuals respond to and recover from breakups. This chapter provides a unifying narrative for understanding relationship dissolution as it relates and applies to evolutionary psychology and highlights the processes and functions individuals undergo as they breakup, traverse, and move on. We delineate each moderating variable—strategies (unilateral and bilateral), roles (initiator and non-initiator), sex differences (reasons and roles), time (relationship length and adjustment), age (life span), and relationship redefinition (continuance or termination)—that has been used frequently to investigate relationship dissolution and its implications in regard to distress and adjustment.

The ability to adapt to change is reflected through distress and adjustment. The unilateral dissolution process tends to favor the initiator who experiences less distress, retains more control over the process, and is able to move on to other relationships more quickly. Noninitiators, on the other hand, find it more difficult to adjust, ruminate over the dissolution, and engage in intrusive contact following the dissolution. Occurring less frequently, some partners opt for bilateral dissolution where the initiator roles are blurred, and termination becomes more amicable. These individuals share responsibility for the dissolution and mutually retain a more positive public presentation, and the dissolution becomes more finalized. Sex also matters. Unilaterally, females typically initiate breakups and consider both sides (theirs and their partner's) during the process. They are first to fall out of love and to move on to alternative mates faster, yet they experience feelings of sadness, fear, and confusion surrounding the dissolution more intensely. Conversely, males fall in love easier and are less likely to initiate a breakup. However, when dissolution occurs, males are typically viewed as responsible for the breakup, are less willing to break ties with their former partner, and experience longer recovery time. Individuals may also seek to ameliorate negative feelings and public presentation of self and partner through relationship redefinition. Redefining the relationship allows individuals the opportunity to retain access to previous partners and project themselves in a more positive light to potential mates and social networks. However, this redefinition or post-dissolution may also prolong the recovery period for one or both partners.

These findings accentuate significant and interacting aspects of how individuals adjust to changes in relationship status. The plethora of scholarship suggests important overlaps while also highlighting the necessity to further replicate and expand prior findings to new populations. These prior moderating variables have been used to understand distress and adjustment in relationship dissolution yet fail to capture all the complex changes those individuals and couples undergo. Therefore, we suggest future investigation is vital to understanding the complex process of relationship dissolution that expands beyond traditional perceptions, variables, and adaptations.

References

Agnew, C. R. (2000). Cognitivie interdependence and the experience of relationship loss. In J. H. Harvey & E. D. Miller (Eds.), *Loss and Trauma* (pp. 385–398). Routledge.

Agnew, C. R., & VanderDrift, L. E. (2015). Relationship maintenance and dissolution. In M. Mikulincer, P. R. Shaver, J. A. Simpson, & J. F. Dovidio (Eds.), *APA handbook of personality and social psychology: Vol. 3. Interpersonal relations* (pp. 581–604). American Psychological Association Press. https://doi.org/10.1037/14344-021

Amato, P. R., & Previti, D. (2003). People's reasons for divorcing: Gender, social class, the life course, and adjustment. *Journal of Family Issues, 24*(5), 602–626. https://doi.org/10.1177/0192513X03254507

Aronson, E., Wilson, T. D., & Akert, R. M. (2005). *Social psychology* (5th ed.). Prentice Hall.

Athenstaedt, U., Brohmer, H., Simpson, J. A., Muller, S., Schindling, N., Bacik, A., & Van Lange, P. A. M. (2020). Men view their ex-partners more favorably than women do. *Social Psychological and Personality Science, 11*(4), 483–491. https://doi.org/10.1177/1948550619876633

Attridge, M., Berscheid, E., & Simpson, J. A. (1995). Predicting relationship stability from both partners versus one. *Journal of Personality and Social Psychology, 69*(2), 254–268. https://doi.org/10.1037/0022-3514.69.2.254

Banks, S. P., Altendorf, D. M., Greene, J. O., & Cody, M. J. (1987). An examination of relationship disengagement: Perceptions, breakup strategies and outcomes. *Western Journal of Speech Communication, 51*(1), 19–41. https://doi.org/10.1080/10570318709374250

Barber, L. L., & Cooper, M. L. (2014). Rebound sex: Sexual motives and behaviors following a relationship breakup. *Archives of Sexual Behavior, 43*(2), 251–265. https://doi.org/10.1007/s10508-013-0200-3

Battaglia, D. M., Richard, F. D., Datteri, D. L., & Lord, C. G. (1998). Breaking up is (relatively) easy to do: A script for the dissolution of close relationships. *Journal of Social and Personal Relationships, 15*(6), 829–845. https://doi.org/10.1177/0265407598156007

Baumeister, R. F., & Dhavale, D. (2001). Two sides of romantic rejection. In M. R. Leary (Ed.), *Interpersonal rejection* (pp. 55–72). Oxford University Press.

Baumeister, R. F., Wotman, S. R., & Stillwell, A. M. (1993). Unrequited love: On heartbreak, anger, guilt, scriptlessness, and humiliation. *Interpersonal Relations and Group Processes, 64*(3), 377–394. https://doi.org/10.1037/0022-3514.64.3.377

Baxter, L. A. (1984). Trajectories of relationship disengagement. *Journal of Social and Personal Relationships, 1*(1), 29–48.

Baxter, L. A. (1985). Accomplishing relationship disengagement. In S. Duck & D. Perlman (Eds.), *Understanding personal relationships: An interdisciplinary approach* (pp. 243–265). SAGE.

Baxter, L. A. (1986). Gender differences in the hetero-sexual relationship rules embedded in break-up accounts. *Journal of Social and Personal Relationships, 3*(3), 289–306. https://doi.org/10.1177/0265407586033003

Bech-Sørensen, J., & Pollet, T. V. (2016). Sex differences in mate preferences: A replication study, 20 years later. *Evolutionary Psychological Science, 2*(3), 171–176. https://doi.org/10.1007/s40806-016-0048-6

Belu, C. F., Lee, B. H., & O'Sullivan, L. F. (2016). It hurts to let you go: Characteristics of romantic relationships, breakups and the aftermath among emerging adults. *Journal of Relationships Research, 7*(e11), 1–11. https://doi.org/10.1017/jrr.2016.11

Berscheid, E., & Reis, H. T. (1998). Attraction and close relationships. In D. T. Gilbert, S. T. Fiske, & G. Lindzey (Eds.), *The handbook of social psychology* (4th ed., pp. 193–281). McGraw-Hill.

Berscheid, E., Snyder, M., & Omoto, A. M. (1989). The Relationship Closeness Inventory: Assessing the closeness of interpersonal relationships. *Journal of Personality and Social Psychology, 57*(5), 792–807. https://doi.org/10.1037/0022-3514.57.5.792

Betzig, L. (1989). Causes of conjugal dissolution: A cross-cultural study. *Current Anthropology, 30*(5), 654–676. https://doi.org/10.1086/203798

Blackburn, K., Brody, N., & LeFebvre, L. (2014). The I's, we's and she/he's of breakups: Public and private pronoun usage in relationship dissolution accounts. *Journal of Language and Social Psychology, 33*(2), 202–213. https://doi.org/10.1177/0261927X13516865

Blau, P. M. (1964). *Exchange and power in social life.* Wiley.

Bleske-Recheck, A. L., & Buss, D. M. (2001). Opposite-sex friendship: Sex differences and similarities in initiation, selection, and dissolution. *Personality and Social Psychology Bulletin, 27*(10), 1310–1323. https://doi.org/10.1177/01461672012710007

Bleske-Recheck, A. L., & Buss, D. M. (2006). Sexual strategies pursued and mate attraction tactics deployed. *Personality and Individual Differences, 40*(6), 1299–1311. https://doi.org/10.1016/j.paid.2005.11.014

Bleske-Recheck, A., Remiker, M. W., & Baker, J. P. (2009). Similar from the start: Assortment in young adult dating couples and its link to relationship stability over time. *Individual Differences Research, 7*(3), 142–158.

Bravo, V., Connolly, J., & McIsaac, C. (2017). Why did it end? Breakup reasons of youth of different gender, dating stages, and ages. *Emerging Adulthood, 5*(4), 230–240. https://doi.org/10.1177/2167696817700261

Brody, N., LeFebvre, L. E., & Blackburn, K. G. (2017). Post-dissolution surveillance on social networking sites. In N. Punyanunt-Carter & J. S. Wrench (Eds.), *Swipe right for love: The impact of social media in modern romantic relationships* (pp. 237–258). Rowman & Littlefield.

Brumbaugh, C. C., & Fraley, R. C. (2007). Transference of attachment patterns: How important relationships influence feelings toward novel people. *Personal Relationships, 14*(4), 369–386. https://doi.org/10.1111/j.1475-6811.2007.00169.x

Brumbaugh, C. C., & Fraley, R. C. (2015). Too fast, too soon? An empirical investigation into rebound relationships. *Journal of Social and Personal Relationships, 32*(1), 99–118. https://doi.org/10.1177/0265407514525086

Buchanan, M. C., O'Hair, H. D., & Becker, A. H. (2006). Strategic communication during marital relationship dissolution: Disengagement resistance strategies. *Communication Research Reports, 23*(3), 139–147. https://doi.org/10.1080/08824090600796351

Bullock, M., Hackathorn, J., Clark, E. M., & Mattingly, B. A. (2011). Can we be (and stay) friends? Remaining friends after dissolution of a romantic relationship. *Journal of Social Psychology, 151*(5), 662–666. https://doi.org/10.1080/00224540903536162

Busboom, A. L., Collins, D. M., Givertz, M. D., & Levin, L. A. (2002). Can we still be friends? Resources and barriers to friendship quality after romantic relationship dissolution. *Personal Relationships, 9*(2), 215–223. https://doi.org/10.1111/1475-6811.00014

Buss, D. M. (1988). From vigilance to violence: Tactics of mate retention in American undergraduates. *Ethology and Sociobiology, 9*(5), 291–317. https://doi.org/10.1016/0162-3095(88)90010-6

Buss, D. M. (1989). Sex differences in human mate preferences: Evolutionary hypotheses tested in 37 cultures. *Behavioral and Brain Sciences, 12*(1), 1–49. https://doi.org/10.1017/S0140525X00023992

Buss, D. M. (2016). *The evolution of human desire: Strategies of human mating.* Basic Books.

Buss, D. M., & Dedden, L. A. (1990). Derogation of competitors. *Journal of Social and Personal Relationships, 7*(3), 395–422. https://doi.org/10.1177/0265407590073006

Buss, D. M., Goetz, C., Duntley, J. D., Asao, K., & Conroy-Beam, D. (2017). The mate switching hypothesis. *Personality and Individual Differences, 104*, 143–149. https://doi.org/10.1016/j.paid.2016.07.022

Buss, D. M., & Schmitt, D. P. (1993). Sexual strategies theory: An evolutionary perspective on human mating. *Psychological Review, 100*(2), 204–232. https://doi.org/10.1037/0033-295X.100.2.204

Buss, D. M., & Schmitt, D. P. (2019). Mate preferences and their behavioral manifestations. *Annual Review of Psychology, 70*, 77–110. https://doi.org/10.1146/annurev-psych-010418-103408

Buss, D. M., & Shackelford, T. K. (1997). From vigilance to violence: Mate retention tactics in married couples. *Journal of Personality and Social Psychology, 72*(2), 346–361. https://doi.org/10.1037/0022-3514.72.2.346

Canary, D. J., & Hause, K. S. (1993). Is there any reason to research sex differences in communication? *Communication Quarterly, 41*(2), 129–144. https://doi.org/10.1080/01463379309369874

Carter, K. R., Knox, D., & Hall, S. S. (2018). Romantic breakup: Difficult loss for some but not for others. *Journal of Loss and Trauma, 23*(8), 698–714. https://doi.org/10.1080/15325024.2018.1502523

Choo, P., Levine, T., & Hatfield, E. (1996). Gender, love schemas, and reactions to romantic breakups. *Journal of Social Behavior & Personality, 11*(5), 143–160.

Chung, M. C., Farmer, S., Grant, K., Newton, R., Payne, S., Perry, M., & Stone, N. (2003). Coping with post-traumatic stress symptoms following relationship dissolution. *Stress and Health, 19*(1), 27–36. https://doi.org/10.1002/smi.956

Cody, M. (1982). A typology of disengagement strategies and an examination of the role intimacy, reactions to inequity and relational problems play in strategy selection. *Communication Monographs, 49*(3), 148–170. https://doi.org/10.1080/03637758209376079

Cohen, S., & Wills, T. A. (1985). Stress, social support, and the buffering hypothesis. *Psychological Bulletin, 98*(2), 310–357. https://doi.org/10.1037/0033-2909.98.2.310

Collins, J. E., & Clark, L. F. (1989). Responsibility and rumination: The trouble with understanding the dissolution of a relationship. *Social Cognition, 7*(2), 152–173. https://doi.org/10.1521/soco.1989.7.2.152

Connolly, J., & McIsaac, C. (2009). Adolescents' explanations for romantic dissolutions: A developmental perspective. *Journal of Adolescence, 32*(5), 1209–1223. https://doi.org/10.1016/j.adolescence.2009.01.006

Cupach, W. R., & Metts, S. (1986). Accounts of relational dissolution: A comparison of marital and non-marital relationships. *Communication Monographs, 53*(4), 311–334. https://doi.org/10.1080/03637758609376146

Cupach, W. R., Spitzberg, B. H., Bolingbroke, C. M., & Tellitocci, B. S. (2011). Persistence of attempts to reconcile a terminated romantic relationship: A partial test of relational goal pursuit theory. *Communication Reports, 24*(2), 99–115. https://doi.org/10.1080/08934215.2011.613737

Dailey, R. M., Jin, B., Pfiester, R. A., & Beck, G. (2011). On-again/off-again relationships: What keeps partners coming back? *Journal of Social Psychology, 151*(4), 417–440. https://doi.org/10.1080/00224545.2010.503249

Dailey, R. M., Pfiester, A., Jin, B., Beck, G., & Clark, G. (2009). On-again/off-again dating relationships: How are they different from other dating relationships? *Personal Relationships, 16*(1), 23–47. https://doi.org/10.1111/j.1475-6811.2009.01208.x

Dailey, R. M., Zhong, L., Pett, R., & Varga, S. (2020). Post-dissolution ambivalence, breakup adjustment, and relationship reconciliation. *Journal of Social and Personal Relationships, 37*(5), 1604–1625. https://doi.org/10.1177/0265407520906014

Davies, P. T., & Windle, M. (2000). Middle adolescents' dating pathways and psychosocial adjustment. *Merrill-Palmer Quarterly, 46*(1), 90–118.

DeLecce, T., & Weisfeld, G. (2016). An evolutionary explanation for sex differences in nonmarital breakup experiences. *Adaptive Human Behavior and Physiology, 2*, 234–251. https://doi.org/10.1007/s40750-015-0039-z

DeScioli, P., & Kurzban, R. (2009). The alliance hypothesis for human friendship. *PloS ONE, 4*(6), 1–8. https://doaj-org.article/7beade0dcd47401eaadc4c027bc6591f

Dindia, K., & Canary, D. J. (Eds.). (2006). *Sex differences and similarities in communication*. Routledge.

Doering, J. (2010). Face, accounts, and schemes in the context of relationship breakups. *Symbolic Interaction, 33*(1), 71–95. https://doi.org/10.1525/si.2010.33.1.71

Dragon, W., & Duck, S. (2005). *Understanding research in personal relationships: A text with readings*. SAGE.

Drigotas, S. M., & Rusbult, C. E. (1992). Should I stay or should I go? A dependence model of breakups. *Journal of Personality and Social Psychology, 62*(1), 62–87. https://doi.org/10.1037/0022-3514.62.1.62

Duck, S. W. (1982). A topography of relationship disengagement and dissolution. In S. W. Duck (Ed.), *Personal relationship: Vol. 4. Dissolving personal relationships* (pp. 1–30). Academic Press.

Duck, S. W. (2011). The language of relationships in a social order. In S. W. Duck (Ed.), *Rethinking relationships* (pp. 171–192). SAGE.

Duck, S., & Wood, J. T. (2011). What goes up may come down: Sex and gendered patterns in relationship dissolution. In M. A. Fine & J. H. Harvey (Eds.), *Handbook of divorce and relationship dissolution* (pp. 169–188). Erlbaum.

Dunntley, J. D., & Buss, D. M. (2010). The evolution of stalking. *Sex Roles, 66*(5–6), 311–327. https://doi.org/10.1007/s11199-010-9832-0

Dutton, L. B., & Winstead, B. A. (2006). Predicting unwanted pursuit: Attachment, relationship satisfaction, relationship alternatives, and break-up distress. *Journal of Social and Personal Relationships, 23*(4), 565–586. https://doi.org/10.1177/0265407506065984

Eastwick, P. W., Finkel, E. J., Krishnamurti, T., & Loewenstein, G. (2008). Mispredicting distress following romantic breakup: Revealing the time course of the affective forecasting error. *Journal of Experimental Social Psychology, 44*(3), 800–807. https://doi.org/10.1016/j.jesp.2007.07.001

Eastwick, P. W., Finkel, E. J., & Simpson, J. A. (2019). The relationship trajectories framework: Elaboration and explanation. *Psychological Inquiry, 30*(1), 48–57. https://doi.org/10.1080/1047840X.2019.1585740

Emery, R. E. (1994). *Renegotiating family relationships: Divorce, child custody, and mediation*. Guildford Press.

Emery, R. E., & Dillon, P. (1994). Conceptualizing the divorce process: Renegotiating boundaries of intimacy and power in the divorced family system. *Family Relations, 43*(4), 374–379. https://www.jstor.org/stable/585367

Felmlee, D. H. (2001). No couple is an island: A social network perspective on dyadic stability. *Social Forces, 79*(4), 1259–1287. https://doi.org/10.1353/sof.2001.0039

Felmlee, D., Sprecher, S., & Bassin, E. (1990). The dissolution of intimate relationships: A hazard model. *Social Psychology Quarterly, 53*(1), 13–30. https://doi.org/10.2307/2786866

Field, T., Diego, M., Pelaz, M., Deeds, O., & Delgado, J. (2009). Breakups distress in university students. *Adolescence, 44*(176), 705–727. https://doi.org/10.4236/psych.2010.13023

Fine, M. A., & Sacher, J. A. (1997). Predictors of distress following relationship termination among dating couples. *Journal of Social and Clinical Psychology, 16*, 381–388.

Fine, M. A., & Harvey, J. H. (2006). Divorce and relationship dissolution in the 21st century. In M. A. Fine & J. H. Harvey (Ed.), *Handbook of Divorce and Relationship Dissolution* (pp. 3-11). Lawrence Erlbaum Associates, Publishers.

Foley, L., & Fraser, J. (1998). A research note on post-dating relationships: The social embeddedness of redefining romantic couplings. *Sociological Perspectives, 41*(1), 209–219. https://doi.org/10.2307/1389360

Frazier, P. A., & Cook, S. W. (1993). Correlates of distress following heterosexual relationship dissolution. *Journal of Social and Personal Relationships, 10*(1), 55–67. https://doi.org/10.1177/0265407593101004

Gershon, I. (2020). The breakup 2.1: The ten-year update. *The Information Society, 36*(5), 279–289. https://doi.org/10.1080/01972243.2020.1798316

Hadden, B. W., & Agnew, C. R. (2020). Commitment readiness: Timing, the self, and close relationships. In B. Mattingly, K. McIntyre, & G. Lewandowski, Jr. (Eds.), *Interpersonal relationships and the self-concept* (pp. 53–67). Springer. https://doi.org/10.1007/978-3-030-43747-3_4

Helgeson, V. S. (1994). Long-distance romantic relationships: Sex differences in adjustment and breakup. *Personality and Social Psychology Bulletin, 20*(3), 254–265. https://doi.org/10.1177/0146167294203003

Hendrick, C., & Hendrick, S. (1986). A theory and method of love. *Journal of Personality and Social Psychology, 50*(2), 392–402. https://doi.org/10.1037/0022-3514.50.2.392

Hendrick, C., Hendrick, S., Foote, F., & Slapion-Foot, M. (1984). Do men and women love differently? *Journal of Social and Personal Relationships, 1*(2), 177–195. https://doi.org/10.1177/0265407584012003

Hill, C. T., Rubin, Z., & Peplau, L. A. (1976). Breakups before marriages: The end of 103 affairs. *Journal of Social Issues, 32*(1), 147–168. https://doi.org/10.1111/j.1540-4560.1976.tb02485.x

Honeycutt, J. M. (2010). Forgive but don't forget: Correlates of rumination about conflict. In J. M. Honeycutt (Ed.), *Imagine that: Studies in imagined interactions* (pp. 17–29). Hampton Press.

Huesmann. L. R., & Levinger, G. (1976). Incremental exchange theory: A formal model for progression in dyadic social interaction. In L. Berkowitz & E. Walster (Eds.), *Advances in experimental social psychology* (pp. 151–193). Academic Press.

Hughes, M., Morrison, K., & Asada, K. J. K. (2005). What's love got to do with it? Exploring the impact of maintenance rules, love attitudes, and network support on friends with benefits relationships. *Western Journal of Communication, 62*(1), 49–66. https://doi.org/10.1080/10570310500034154

Kellas, J. K. (2006). "The worst part is, we don't even talk anymore": Post-dissolutional communication in break up stories. In K. M. Galvin & P. J. Cooper (Eds.), *Making connections: Readings in relational communication* (pp. 281–291). Oxford University Press.

Kellas, J. K., Bean, D., Cunningham, C., & Cheng, K. Y. (2008). The ex-files: Trajectories, turning points, and adjustment in the development of post-dissolutional relationships. *Journal of Social and Personal Relationships, 25*(1), 23–50. https://doi.org/10.1177/0265407507086804

Kellas, J. K., & Manusov, V. (2003). What's in a story? The relationship between narrative completeness and tellers' adjustment to relationship dissolution. *Journal of Social and Personal Relationships, 20*(3), 285–307. https://doi.org/10.1177/0265407503020003002

Kelley, H. H., Berscheid, E., Christensen, A., Harvey, J. H., Huston, T. L., Levinger, G., McClintock, E., Peplau, L. A., & Peterson, D. R. (1983). Analyzing close relationships. In H. H. Kelley, E. Berscheid, A. Christensen, J. H. Harvey, T. L. Huston, G. Levinger, E. McClintock, L. A. Peplau, & D. R. Peterson (Eds.), *Close relationships* (pp. 20–67). Freeman.

Kelly, A. J., Dubbs, S. L., & Barlow, F. K. (2016). An evolutionary perspective on mate rejection. *Evolutionary Psychology, 14*(4), Article 1474704916678626.

Kendler, K. S., Hettema, J. M., Butera, F., Gardner, C. O., & Prescott, C. A. (2003). Life event dimensions of loss, humiliation, entrapment, and danger in the prediction of onsets of major depression and generalized anxiety. *Archives of General Psychiatry, 60*(8), 789–796. http://doi.org/10.1001/archpsyc.60.8.789

Kephart, W. M. (1967). Some correlates of romantic love. *Journal of Marriage and the Family, 29*(3), 470–474. https://doi.org/10.2307/349585

Knobloch, L. K., & Donovan-Kicken, E. (2006). Perceived involvement of network members in courtships: A test of the relational turbulence model. *Personal Relationships, 13*(3), 281–302. https://doi.org/10.1111/j.1475-6811.2006.00118.x

Knox, D., Zusman, M. E., Kaluzny, M., & Cooper, C. (2000). College student recovery from a broken heart. *College Student Journal, 34*(3), 322–324.

Lannutti, P. J., & Cameron, K. A. (2002). Beyond the break-up: Heterosexual and homosexual post-dissolutional relationships. *Communication Quarterly, 50*(2), 153–170. https://doi.org/10.1080/01463370209385654" https://doi.org/10.1080/01463370209385654

Le, B., Dove, N. L., Agnew, C. R., Korn, M. S., & Mutso, A. A. (2010). Predicting nonmarital romantic relationship dissolution: A meta-analytic synthesis. *Personal Relationships, 17*(3), 377–390. https://doi.org/10.1111/j.1475-6811.2010.01285.x

Leary, M. R., Koch, E. J., & Hechenbleiker, N. R. (2001). Emotional responses to interpersonal rejection. In M. R. Leary (Ed.), *Interpersonal rejection* (pp. 145–166). Oxford University Press.

LeFebvre, L. E., Allen, M., Rasner, R., Garstad, S., Wilms, A., & Parrish, C. (2019). Ghosting in emerging adults' romantic relationships: The digital disappearance dissolution strategy. *Imagination, Cognition, and Personality, 39*(2), 125–150. https://doi.org/10.1177/0276236618820519

LeFebvre, L. E., Brody, N., & Blackburn, K. (2020). Account-making following relationship dissolution: Exploring sex as a moderator in public and private breakup accounts. *Discourse Process, 57*(3), 224–241. https://doi.org/10.1080/0163853X.2019.1627647

LeFebvre, L. E., & Fan, X. (2020). Ghosted? Navigating strategies for reducing uncertainty and implications surrounding ambiguous loss. *Personal Relationships, 27*(2), 433–459.

LeFebvre, L. E., Rasner, R. D., & Allen, M. (2020). "I guess I'll never know . . .": Non-initiators account-making after being ghosted. *Journal of Loss and Trauma: International Perspectives on Stress & Coping, 25*(5), 395–415. https://doi.org/10.1080/15325024.2019.1694299

Lewandowski, G. W., Jr., Aron, A., Bassis, S., & Kunak, J. (2006). Losing a self-expanding relationship: Implications for the self-concept. *Personal Relationships, 13*(3), 317–331. https://doi.org/10.1111/j.1475-6811.2006.00120.x

Lewandowski, G. W., Jr., & Sahner, D. F. (2005). The influence of past relationships on subsequent relationships: The role of the self. *Individual Differences Research, 3*(4), 269–275.

Lewis, D. M. G., Al-Shawaf, L., Conroy-Beam, D., Asao, K., & Buss, D. M. (2012). Friends with benefits II: Mating activation in opposite-sex friendships as a function of sociosexual orientation and relationship status. *Personality and Individual Differences, 53*(5), 622–628. http://dx.doi.org/10.1016/j.paid.2012.04.040

Lewis, D. M. G., Conroy-Beam, D., Al-Shawaf, L., Raja, A., DeKay, T., & Buss, D. M. (2012). Friends with benefits: The evolved psychology of same- and opposite-sex friendship. *Evolutionary Psychology, 9*(4), 543–563. https://doi.org/10.1177/147470491100900407" https://doi.org/10.1177/147470491100900407

Lloyd, S. A., & Cate, R. M. (1985). Attributions associated with significant turning points in premarital relationship development and dissolution. *Journal of Social and Personal Relationships, 2*(4), 419–436. https://doi.org/10.1177/0265407585024003

McKiernan, A., Ryan, R., McMahon, E., Bradley, S., & Butler, E. (2018). Understanding young people's relationship breakups using the dual processing model of coping and bereavement. *Journal of Loss and Trauma, 23*(3), 192–210. https://doi.org/10.1080/15325024.2018.1426979

Mearns, J. (1991). Coping with a breakup: Negative mood regulation expectancies and depression following the end of a romantic relationship. *Journal of Personality and Social Psychology, 60*(2), 327–334. https://doi.org/10.1037/0022-3514.60.2.327" https://doi.org/10.1037/0022-3514.60.2.327

Meier, A., & Allen, G. (2009). Romantic relationships from adolescence to young adulthood: Evidence from the National Longitudinal Study of Adolescent Health. *The Sociological Quarterly, 50*(2), 308–335. https://doi.org/10.1111/j.1533-8525.2009.01142.x

Merolla, A. J., Weber, K. D., Myers, S. A., & Booth-Butterfield, M. (2004). The impact of past dating relationship solidarity on commitment, satisfaction, and investment in current relationships. *Communication Quarterly, 52*(3), 251–264. https://doi.org/10.1080/01463370409370196

Metts, S., Cupach, W. R., & Bejlovec, R. A. (1989). "I love you too much to ever start liking you": Redefining romantic relationships. *Journal of Social and Personal Relationships, 6*(3), 259–274. https://doi.org/10.1177/0265407589063002

Mogilski, J. K. (2021). Parental investment theory. In T. K. Shackelford (Ed.), *The SAGE handbook of evolutionary psychology: Foundations of evolutionary psychology* (pp. 137–154). SAGE.

Mogilski, J. K., & Welling, L. L. M. (2017). Staying friends with an ex: Sex and dark personality traits predict motivations for post-relationship friendship. *Personality and Individual Differences, 115*(1), 114–119. https://doi-org/10.1016/j.paid.2016.04.016

Moller, N., Fouladi, R., McCarthy, C., & Hatch, K. (2003). Relationship of attachment and social support to college students' adjustment following a relationship break-up. *Journal of Counseling & Development, 81*(3), 354–370. https://doi.org/10.1002/j.1556-6678.2003.tb00262.x

Mongeau, P. A., van Raalte, L. J., Bednarchik, L., & Generous, M. (2019). Investigating and extending variation among friends with benefits relationships: Relational maintenance and social support. *Southern Journal of Communication, 84*(5), 275–286. https://doi.org/10.1080/1041794X.2019.1641837

Monroe, S. M., Rohde, P., Seeley, J. R., & Lewinsohn, P. M. (1999). Life events and depression in adolescence: Relationship loss as a prospective risk factor for first onset of major depressive disorder. *Journal of Abnormal Psychology, 108*(4), 606–614. https://doi.org/10.1037/0021-843X.108.4.606

Morris, C. E. (2015). *The breakup project: Using evolutionary theory to predict and interpret responses to romantic relationship dissolution* (Publication No. 3713604). [Doctoral dissertation, Binghamton University]. ProQuest Dissertations.

Morris, C. E., & Reiber, C. (2011). Frequency, intensity and expression of post-relationship grief. *Journal of the Evolutionary Studies Consortium, 3*(1), 1–11.

Muehlenhard, C., & Peterson, Z. D. (2011). Distinguishing between sex and gender: History, current conceptualizations, and implications. *Sex Roles, 64*, 791–803. https://doi.org/10.1007/s11199-011-9932-5

Norona, J. C., Olmstead, S. B., & Welsh, D. P. (2017). Breaking up in emerging adulthood: A developmental perspective of relationship dissolution. *Emerging Adulthood, 5*(2), 116–127. https://doi.org/10.1177/2167696816658585

Norona, J. C., Roberson, P. N. E., & Welsh, D. P. (2017). "I learned things that make me happy, things that bring me down": Lessons from romantic relationships in adolescence and emerging adulthood. *Journal of Adolescent Research, 32*(2), 155–182. https://doi.org/10.1016/j.adolescence.2009.01.006

Orbuch, T. L. (1992). *Close relationship loss: Theoretical approaches*. Springer-Verlag.

Park, L. E., Sanchez, D. T., & Brynildsen, K. (2011). Maladaptive responses to relationship dissolution: The role of relationship contingent self-worth. *Journal of Applied Psychology, 41*(7), 1749–1773. https://doi.org/10.1111/j.1559-1816.2011.00769.x

Perilloux, C., & Buss, D. M. (2008). Breaking up romantic relationships. Costs experienced, and coping strategies deployed. *Evolutionary Psychology, 6*(1), 164–181. https://doi.org/10.1177/147470490800600119

Priest, J., Burnett, M., Thompson, R., Vogel, A., & Schvaneveldt, P. L. (2009). Relationship dissolution and romance and mate selection myths. *Family Science Review, 14*, 48–57.

Rhoades, G. K., Dush, C. K., Atkins, D. C., Stanley, S. M., & Markman, H. J. (2012). Breaking up is hard to do: The impact of unmarried relationship dissolution on mental health and life satisfaction. *Journal of Family Psychology, 25*(3), 366–374. https://doi.org/10.1037/a0023627

Rhoades, G. K., Stanley, S. M., & Markman, H. J. (2010). Should I stay or should I go? Predicting dating relationship stability from four aspects of commitment. *Journal of Family Psychology, 24*(5), 543–550. https://doi.org/10.1037/a0021008

Rollie, S. S., & Duck, S. W. (2006). Divorce and dissolution of romantic relationships: Stage models and their limitations. In M. A. Fine & J. H. Harvey (Eds.), *Handbook of divorce and relationship dissolution* (pp. 223–240). Erlbaum.

Rubin, Z., Peplau, L. A., & Hill, C. T. (1981). Loving and leaving: Sex differences in romantic attachments. *Sex Roles, 7*(8), 821–835. https://doi.org/10.1007/BF00287767

Rusbult, C. E. (1980). Commitment and satisfaction in romantic associations: A test of the investment model. *Journal of Experimental Social Psychology, 16*(2), 172–186. https://doi.org/10.1016/0022-1031(80)90007-4

Rusbult, C. E. (1987). Responses to dissatisfaction in close relationships: The exit-voice-loyalty-neglect model. In D. Perlman & S. Duck (Eds.), *Intimate relationships: Development, dynamics, and deterioration* (pp. 209–237). SAGE.

Saffrey, C., & Ehrenberg, M. (2007). When thinking hurts: Attachment, rumination, and post relationship adjustment. *Personal Relationships, 14*(3), 351–368. https://doi.org/10.1111/j.1475-6811.2007.00160.x

Sbarra, D. A. (2006). Predicting the onset of emotional recovery following non-marital relationship dissolution: Survival analyses of sadness and anger. *Personality and Social Psychology Bulletin, 32*(3), 298–312. https://doi.org/10.1177/0146167205280913

Sbarra, D. A., & Emery, R. E. (2005). The emotional sequelae of nonmarital relationship dissolution: Analysis of change and intraindividual variability over time. *Personal Relationships, 12*(2), 213–232. https://doi.org/10.1111/j.1350-4126.2005.00112.x

Schmitt, D. P., & Buss, D. M. (2001). Human mate poaching: Tactics and temptations for infiltrating existing mateships. *Journal of Personality and Social Psychology, 80*(6), 894–917. https://doi.org/10.1037/0022-3514.80.6.894

Schmitt, D. P., Shackelford, T. K., & Buss, D. M. (2001). Are men really more oriented toward short-term mating than women? A critical review of theory and research. *Psychology, Evolution, and Gender, 3*(3), 211–239. https://doi.org/10.1080/14616660110119331

Seto, M. C., Khattar, N. A., Lalumière, M. L., & Quinsey, V. L. (1997). Deception and sexual strategy in psychopathy. *Personality and Individual Differences, 22*(3), 301–307. https://doi.org/10.1016/S0191-8869(96)00212-7

Simpson, J. A. (1987). The dissolution of romantic relationships: Factors involved in relationship stability and emotional distress. *Journal of Personality and Social Psychology, 53*(4), 683–692. https://doi.org/10.1037/0022-3514.53.4.683

Slotter, E. B., Gardner, W. L., & Finkel, E. J. (2010). Who am I without you? The influence of romantic breakup on the self-concept. *Personality and Social Psychology Bulletin, 36*(2), 147–160. https://doi.org/10.1177/0146167209352250

Sorenson, K. A., Russell, S. M., Harkness, D. J., & Harvey, J. H. (1993). Account-making, confiding, and coping with the ending of a close relationship. *Journal of Social Behavior and Personality, 8*(1), 73–86.

Spielmann, S. S., Joel, S., & Impett, E. A. (2019). Pursuing sex with an ex: Does it hinder breakup recovery? *Archives of Sexual Behavior, 48*(3), 691–702. https://doi.org/10.1007/s10508-018-1268-6

Spielmann, S. S., Joel, S., MacDonald, G., & Kogan, A. (2012). Ex appeal: Current relationship quality and emotional attachment to ex-partners. *Social Psychological and Personality Science, 4*(2), 175–180. https://doi.org/10.1177/1948550612448198

Spielmann, S. S., MacDonald, G., & Wilson, A. E. (2009). On the rebound: Focusing on someone new helps anxiously attached individuals let go of ex-partners. *Personality and Social Psychology Bulletin, 35*(10), 1382–1394. https://doi.org/10.1177/0146167209341580

Spielmann, S. S., Maxwell, J. A., MacDonald, G., Peragine, D., & Impett, E. A. (2019). The predictive effects of fear of being single on physical attractiveness and less selective partner selection strategies. *Journal of Social and Personal Relationships, 37*(1), 100–123. https://doi.org/10.1177/0265407519856701

Spitzberg, B. H., & Cupach, W. R. (2014). *The dark side of relationship pursuit: From attraction to obsession and stalking* (2nd ed.). Routledge.

Sprecher, S. (1994). Two sides to the breakup of dating relationships. *Personal Relationships, 1*(3), 199–222. https://doi.org/10.1111/j.1475-6811.1994.tb00062.x

Sprecher, S., Felmlee, D., Metts, S., Fehr, B., & Vanni, D. (1998). Factors associated with distress following romantic relationship dissolution. *Personal Relationships, 15*(6), 791–809. https://doi.org/10.1177/0265407598156005

Sprecher, S., Felmlee, D., Schmeekle, M., & Shu, X. (2006). No breakup occurs on an island: Social networks and relationship dissolution. In M. A. Fine & J. H. Harvey (Eds.), *Handbook of divorce and relationship dissolution* (pp. 457–478). Erlbaum.

Sprecher, S., Sullivan, Q., & Hatfield, E. (1994). Mate selection preferences: Sex differences examined in a national sample. *Journal of Personality and Social Psychology, 66*(6), 1074–1080. https://doi.org/10.1037/0022-3514.66.6.1074

Stanley, S. M., Rhoades, G. K., & Markman, H. J. (2006). Sliding versus deciding: Inertia and the premarital cohabitation effect. Family Relations: An Interdisciplinary Journal *of Applied Family Studies, 55*(4), 499–509. https://doi.org/10.1111/j.1741-3729.2006.00418.x

Stephen, T. (1987). Attribution and adjustment to relationship termination. *Journal of Social and Personal Relationships, 4*(1), 47–61. https://doi.org/10.1177/0265407587041004

Tan, K., Agnew, C. R., VanderDrift, L. E., & Harvey, S. M. (2015). Committed to us: Predicting relationship closeness following nonmarital romantic relationship breakup. *Journal of Social and Personal Relationships, 32*(4), 456–471. https://doi.org/10.1177/0265407514536293

Tashiro, T., & Frazier, P. (2003). "I'll never be in a relationship like that again": Personal growth following romantic relationship breakups. *Personal Relationships, 10*(1), 113–128. https://doi.org/10.1111/1475-6811.00039

Thibaut, J. W., & Kelley, H. H. (1959). *The social psychology of groups*. John Wiley & Sons.

Tokunaga, R. (2011). Social networking site or social surveillance site? Understanding the use of interpersonal electronic surveillance in romantic relationships. *Computers in Human Behavior, 27*(2), 705–713. https://doi.org/10.1016/j.chb.2010.08.014

Tokunaga, R. (2015). Interpersonal surveillance over social network sites: Applying a theory of negative relational maintenance and the investment model. *Journal of Social and Personal Relationships, 33*(2), 171–190. https://doi.org/10.1177/0265407514568749

Tong, S. T., & Walther, J. B. (2010). Just say "no thanks": Romantic rejection in computer-mediated communication. *Journal of Social and Personal Relationships, 28*(4), 488–506. https://doi.org/10.1177/0265407510384895

Trivers, R. (1972). Parental involvement and sexual selection. In B. Campbell (Ed.), *Sexual selection and the descent of man, 1871–1971* (pp. 136–179). Aldine.

Vangelisti, A. L. (2006). Hurtful interactions and the dissolution of intimacy. In M. A. Fine & J. H. Harvey (Eds.), *Handbook of divorce and relationship dissolution* (pp. 133–152). Erlbaum.

Weiss, R. S. (1975). *Marital separation.* Basic Books.

Wilmot, W. W., Carbaugh, D. A., & Baxter, L. A. (1985). Communicative strategies used to terminate romantic relationships. *Western Journal of Speech Communication, 49*(3), 204–216. https://doi.org/10.1080/10570318509374195

Yıldırım, F. B., & Demir, A. (2015). Breakup adjustment in young adulthood. *Journal of Counseling & Development, 93*(1), 38–44. https://doi.org/10.1002/j.1556-6676.2015.00179.x

Zhang, J. W., & Chen, S. (2017). Self-compassion promotes positive adjustment for people who attribute responsibility of a romantic breakup to themselves. *Self and Identity, 16*(6), 732–759. http://doi.org/10.1080/15298868.2017.1305985

CHAPTER

27 Post-Relationship Romance

Michael R. Langlais *and* He Xiao

Abstract

The end of marriage does not mean the end of romantic relationships. In fact, many individuals form serious relationships within two years of filing for divorce. How people form relationships after divorce tends to vary, however, as some date multiple partners, some date only one partner, and some do not date at all. Evolutionary theory provides a theoretical foundation to explain the differences among individuals in terms of approaches, timing, and the number of co-occurring relationships surrounding the formation of romantic relationships again after divorce. The goal of this chapter is to discuss post-divorce relationship formation processes, variables that influence the maintenance of these relationships, and the consequences of forming post-divorce relationships from an evolutionary perspective. Additionally, we discuss the implications of post-divorce romance and provide some guidance for future studies to better understand how and why individuals form relationships after divorce, as well as the consequences of post-divorce relationships for all individuals involved.

Key Words: repartnering, post-divorce dating, evolutionary theory, divorce, family transition, relationship quality

Divorce is a difficult, often stressful experiences for both coupled partners. A common approach to resolving this stress is to form new romantic relationships, which is usually associated with mental health benefits, such as fewer depressive symptoms and increased life satisfaction (Bzostek et al., 2012; Langlais et al., 2016a; Symoens et al., 2014). There are differences in attitudes toward post-divorce romance and in how individuals form romantic relationships after divorce, as some choose not to date, some date only one person after divorce, and others date multiple partners either simultaneously (i.e., dating multiple people over a period of time) or serially (dating multiple people but no relationships overlap) (Langlais et al., 2015). There are similarities and variations in the characteristics and consequences of each of these approaches to forming relationships after divorce. Which approach is used has implications for post-divorce adjustment for everyone involved in the divorce.

The romantic relationship behaviors following divorce and the impact of these romantic relationships for interpersonal and relational well-being can be informed by evolutionary theory, particularly the theory of parental investment and sexual selection (Trivers, 1972). Evolutionary theory affords a framework to illustrate which strategies individuals adopt when navigating post-divorce romance and how men and women form relationships after divorce in discrepant ways. The goal of this chapter is to discuss post-divorce relationship formation processes, variables that influence these processes, and the consequences of forming post-divorce relationships from an evolutionary perspective. We focus on repartnering after divorce, as opposed to stepfamily formation, which involves a variety of different family-level factors that are beyond the scope of the current chapter. Repartnering can be defined as the formation of a romantic relationship after divorce, which includes dating after divorce, cohabiting after divorce, and remarrying (Amato, 2010; Anderson & Greene, 2005; Langlais et al., 2016b). To achieve the goals of this chapter, we first review evolutionary theory, followed by explanations of the different approaches to forming relationships after divorce, variables associated with post-divorce relationship maintenance, and consequences of post-divorce relationship formation.

Evolutionary Theory and Marital Relationships

The central premise of evolutionary theory is that evolved psychological mechanisms and their corresponding behaviors are enacted to tackle adaptive problems and promote survival and reproduction (Buss, 1995). Animals and humans have evolved over time, with certain behaviors increasing the chances of survival. As humans have evolved, certain relationship behaviors and characteristics of romantic partners were well-suited to facilitate survival and reproduction (Buss, 1995). For example, romantic relationships meet individuals' need to belong (Baumeister & Leary, 1995). For individuals to access resources, have optimal health, and have higher chances of survival and reproduction, they seek connection with others and fulfill their needs of belongingness (Hasan & Clark, 2017), particularly in romantic relationships. This need for connection is echoed by many other theories, including Erikson's (1985) psychosocial theory of development, which emphasizes that young adults seek to have their intimacy needs met, and the theory of emerging adulthood (Arnett, 2000), which specifies the importance of romantic relationship experiences for interpersonal and relational development.

Achieving a sense of belonging by forming and maintaining relationships constitutes one of the most fundamental human motives as it is closely associated with well-being and mental health (Morrison et al., 2012). Being able to form romantic relationships, regardless of the time in which it happens—whether early in life, later in life, or after divorce or widowhood—helps promote survival through the benefits provided by meeting belongingness needs. In other words, belonging with another person provides security, reproductive opportunities, and emotional and material support, which are behaviors that promote survival. In contrast, a compromised sense of belonging is linked to negative outcomes such as internalizing symptoms, anxiety, and counterproductive behaviors, such as eliciting behaviors in others to reflect one's own negative expectations about that relationship (Cacioppo & Hawkley, 2009; Twenge et al., 2002; Williams, 2007). For a majority of people, divorce is a taxing and emotionally draining experience to undergo as it is not a single event, but a process (Amato, 2000). Throughout the marriage dissolution, adults are faced with a wide range of issues to deal with such as distribution of property, competition for the guardianship of children, if any, emotional separation, relocation, parenting, and more. Without sufficient support and assistance, these crucial matters in various domains can become emerging stressors and intertwine with one another to encumber family adjustment (Wang & Amato, 2000). Even with the presence of resources, successfully addressing each of these issues is chronically challenging to a person's cognitive and mental capacity.

In the context of romantic relationships following divorce, dating and romantic relationship initiation can be social adaptive issues with implications for survival and reproduction. Within these issues lie a series of lower-level issues such as mate selection and attraction and the establishment and maintenance of a reciprocal dyadic coalition (Buss, 1995). As humans have evolved, the diversity and complexity of psychological mechanisms employed to respond to adaptive problems have developed as well. Beyond mechanisms that promote survival (e.g., fear of snakes and spiders and favoring food rich in fat and sugar), psychological mechanisms are becoming more domain specific (Buss, 1995). In this sense, the capacity to effectively manage and respond to post-divorce romance relies on the repertoire of psychological mechanisms pertinent to navigating the recurrent adaptive problems of romance and family administration. Evolutionary theory also provides evidence for why nearly half of divorced individuals remarry, even if they were not planning to do so (Livingston, 2014; Miller, 2017). Anderson and Greene (2004) showed that approximately 80% of individuals form new romantic relationships within two years of filing for divorce. Essentially, new romantic relationship formation after divorce is not unusual to the extent that people are motivated to establish romantic partnerships and a sense of belonging.

Gender Differences With Post-Divorce Dating

Evolutionary theory also explains differences in how men and women form relationships after divorce. According to the theory of parental investment and sexual selection (Buss, 1995), men and women take different approaches when forming romantic relationships. One of the pronounced sex differences is how much men and women invest in a sexual (romantic or sexually romantic) relationship; women typically invest more in these relationships than men, including bearing a child for approximately nine months, going through childbirth, and commonly assuming the bulk of parenting effort. Men on the other hand are only required to invest a tablespoon of semen (Bjorklund & Kipp, 1996). These variations partially contribute to the distinguishable approaches men and women take toward practicing romantic behaviors. Trivers (1972) suggested that women, compared to men, have evolved to be more selective and meticulous when choosing a mate due to exceedingly more effort, time, and energy invested in childrearing compared to men. The cost associated with finding an unsuitable partner is much higher for women than for men. In light of the unequal ratio of loss and gains in dating and mating, women tend to focus more on the quality of romantic partners to promote their survival, whereas men tend to focus more on the quantity of romantic partners to promote survival.

This gendered nature of the theory of parental investment is obvious in how men and women form romantic relationships after divorce. First, divorced men form post-divorce relationships faster than women given their focus on quantity of partners (Beaujouan, 2012; Bzostek et al., 2012; Kalmijn, 2015), whereas divorced women are slower to date as they are more likely to solely focus on the well-being of their children compared to men, and are more concerned with the quality of their partner rather than the quantity of dating partners (Hetherington & Kelly, 2003; Symoens et al., 2014; Tavares & Aassve, 2013; Wu & Schimmele, 2005). Additionally, divorced women are more apt to choose dating partners who can provide for them and their children (Langlais et al., 2018). In other words, women and men commonly resort to somewhat dissimilar methods to go about forming post-divorce dating relationships after divorce to promote their own survival, and in the case of married couples with children, the well-being of children. It is important to note that the presence of children often restricts when divorced individuals can start forming romantic relationships after divorce, often delaying repartnering. Age is also associated with delayed entrance into romantic relationships after divorce, although this is more common for divorced women than men (Hughes, 2000; Skew et al., 2009). The availability of potential dating partners also contributes to entrance into romantic relationships after divorce, as the increased presence of potential partners boosts the likelihood of forming a post-divorce romantic relationship (i.e., de Graaf, & Kalmijn, 2003). Generally, there are similarities and differences based on gender as it pertains to post-divorce romantic relationships.

The Development of Post-Divorce Romantic Relationships

Research has illustrated that individuals hold different orientations toward dating after divorce. Some choose to date immediately; some may take a break and wait to date again until they processed the dissolution of the previous relationship; and certain people possible would not enter a romantic relationship anymore. One commonly dates one partner at a time while dating multiple partners concurrently does happen in some cases. We review those possibilities and their pathways in which post-divorce relationships form.

The Decision Not to Date After Divorce

Although the majority of individuals form romantic relationships after divorce, a handful of people do not, either because they cannot find a partner or because they choose not to date. How do we account for these individuals from the lens of evolutionary theory? There is evidence of a threat of selection, meaning that some individuals are "selected" out of marriage due to maladaptive characteristics (Amato, 2000), which could explain why not all individuals form romantic relationships after divorce. Some divorced individuals may remain single because they possess undesired traits that make it difficult to form and maintain a romantic relationship, such as having high levels of neuroticism, narcissism, and attachment-avoidance (Amato, 2000; Wang & Amato, 2000). Possessing these traits may impact reproduction, meaning that there are fewer opportunities to engage in sexual behaviors and romantic relationships that would meet individuals' belongingness needs. Without being able to engage in romantic behaviors, individuals may not only be less apt to form romantic relationships after divorce, but potentially to survive, as there is some evidence for the association between divorce and shorter lifespan compared to those who are married (Zhang & Hayward, 2006).

However, there are a number of other factors to consider when it comes to forming post-divorce romantic relationships. Some individuals may not form post-divorce romantic relationships, at least not immediately after divorce, to instead focus on one's children's post-divorce adjustment. In other words, the prioritized adaptive problem for some divorced individuals is to restore family stability and functioning to assist children's adjustment. Hadfield and Nixon (2017) interviewed a group of single mothers to understand their perceptions of barriers to forming a romantic relationship. Many participants reported that a main hindrance to their romantic relationship was reduced time dedicated to parenting and the potential repercussion of this on their children's well-being. There is evidence that divorced individuals vary in their focus on the parent–child relationship after divorce. Anderson and Greene (2011) described two groups of parents who differ in the level of investment in their child, but they accurately note that all parents had some level of investment in the parent–child relationship. Individuals who focus more on romantic relationships after divorce are usually referred to as "adult-focused," whereas those that focus on their children's post-divorce adjustment are referred to as "child-focused" (Anderson & Greene, 2011). When children's adjustment to post-divorce stress takes precedence over forming romantic relationships, parents help children feel continuously loved, treasured, and supported, which is likely to reduce children's emotional and behavioral problems and retain optimal well-being (Hetherington & Kelly, 2003; Wang & Amato, 2000). Yet, evolutionary scholars have identified that parental and mating investment are not entirely separate processes; in some cases, investing in a mating relationship can also provide parental support, meaning that forming a romantic relationship may also reflect a parental investment (Stiver & Alonzo, 2009). It should be noted that these explanations are relative to divorced couples with children. However, childless, divorced individuals almost unanimously form romantic relationships after divorce (Miller, 2017).

Table 27.1 Descriptive Characteristics of Different Approaches to Dating After Divorce.

	No dating ($n = 49$)		Dating one partner ($n = 145$)		dating serially ($n = 65$)		Dating simultaneously ($n = 60$)	
	Mean	SD	Mean	SD	Mean	SD	Mean	SD
Length of marriage[a]	132.00	72.94	111.70	63.53	129.01	61.74	132.52	63.99
Length of separation[a]	$14.33_{a,b}$	22.34	20.13_{a}	24.70	9.78_{b}	12.88	6.47_{b}	7.01
Mother's age	39.14_{a}	7.06	35.71_{b}	6.42	$36.88_{a,b}$	6.48	$37.37_{a,b}$	6.27
Percent non-White	.39	.49	.41	.49	.37	.49	.22	.42
Education[b]	8.16	2.74	7.63	2.81	8.58	2.41	8.28	2.46
Income[c]	$11.02_{a,b}$	5.42	9.37_{a}	5.41	11.88_{b}	4.96	12.63_{b}	5.18
Number of children	2.00	.82	2.16	.96	1.94	.88	2.05	.79
Age of Oldest Child	10.39	3.85	10.07	3.81	9.74	4.11	9.58	4.18
Begin cohabitation[d]	$.02_{a}$	.14	$.47_{b}$	.50	$.29_{b}$	.46	$.35_{b}$	.48
Remarriage[d]	.02	.14	.13	.34	.03	.17	.08	.28
Pregnancy[d]	.00	.00	.06	.24	.09	.29	.02	.13

Note. Table adapted from Langlais et al. (2015). Means with no subscript in common differ at $p < 0.05$ using Bonferroni post hoc comparisons.

[a] Measured in months. [b] Measured on a scale of 1 (*8th grade or less*) to 13 (*advanced college degree, doctoral*). [c] Measured on a scale of 1 (*Less than $5,000 per year*) to 17 (*$80,000 or more*). [d] Percentage of mothers reporting this transition during the study period.

* $p < 0.05$; ** $p < 0.01$; *** $p < 0.001$.

Dating One Partner After Divorce

Although some parents are not able to or choose not to date after divorce, a majority of individuals do form post-divorce romantic relationships (Amato, 2010; Langlais et al., 2016b). However, the ways that individuals form post-divorce relationships vary (see table 27.1). One approach to post-divorce romance is to date a single partner after divorce, which usually results in cohabitation and/or remarriage (Miller, 2017). One of the psychological mechanisms humans have developed is preference (Buss, 1995), and such a tendency toward one option over another directs individuals to look for those who are rich in resources instrumental for survival and reproduction (Orians & Heerwagen, 1992). Applying this principle to the context of post-divorce romance, it is understandable that a romantic partner possessing the necessary assets to boost another person's survival and life quality is more likely to be popular and favored in the dating market. For divorced mothers, a romantic partner who offers emotional, parental, and financial support is not only considered a high-quality partner but also holds great potential to ease mothers' post-divorce stress (Langlais et al., 2016a, 2016b). Mothers may be more apt to remain in these high-quality relationships after divorce rather than test the dating market. Although men are less likely to date only one partner after divorce (Anderson et al., 2004; Noel-Miller, 2013), divorced men with children are more likely to shift their attention to their new relationship (Kalmijn, 2013).

Studies have also illustrated the importance of romantic stability for individuals involved with the divorce, including children. Divorce is a period of transition and change that produces disequilibrium, resulting in increased stress. The formation of a romantic relationship after divorce can provide constancy that alleviates post-divorce stress, whereas constant changes in romantic relationship status may maintain or induce further stress (Beck et al., 2010; Hetherington & Kelly, 2003). These changes impact multiple family members. For example, changing relationship status for divorced individuals means that they have to cope with breakup and changes in self-perceived interdependence (Slotter et al., 2009). These cognitive alterations are difficult and associated with declining self-esteem and increased depressive symptoms (i.e., Keller et al., 2007).

A relationship that can persist for a long period of time represents a widely endorsed solution for humans to resolve problems surrounding survival and reproduction (Buss, 1995). This reasoning explains the presence and importance of both educational programs and psychotherapies that focus on helping people foster psychological and cognitive functioning. Applying therapeutic tools, such as perspective-taking, emotional attunement, and conflict management, dating individuals enhances relational stability and sense of security (Nelson et al., 2017), which provides a foundation for a lasting relationship. Essentially, there is theoretical, empirical, and applied research that explains why some divorced individuals choose to pursue a single, high-quality relationship after divorce compared to multiple partners.

Dating Multiple People After Divorce

Although there is support that providing a steady relationship is beneficial to divorced couples, it doesn't mean that individuals should quickly enter a post-divorce romantic relationship after divorce, as they risk entering a low-quality romantic relationship. Studies have illustrated that many divorced individuals, particularly men, date multiple individuals, either serially or simultaneously (Kalmijn, 2015; Noel-Miller, 2013; Wu & Schimmele, 2005). Dating serially means that individuals will date one partner, experience a breakup of that relationship, and eventually enter another dating relationship. In other words, post-divorce romantic relationships do not overlap. On the other hand, some parents date multiple individuals simultaneously after divorce, where relationships overlap. Dating simultaneously means that a divorced individual will go on dates with different people over a similar period of time (i.e., a month). While one may assume that dating simultaneously is associated with casual dating, there is some evidence that this may not be the case. For instance, Langlais et al. (2015) found that mothers who engaged in simultaneous dating were motivated to form a steady romantic relationship. Although these mothers engaged in more alcohol consumption and unprotected sex compared to mothers who were not simultaneously dating, they were just as satisfied as mothers who were not dating or were dating one partner over a period of time. Regarding fathers, there is evidence that divorced men repartner more frequently than divorced mothers (it is unclear if this repartnering approach is serial or simultaneous), although the rates appear to be more similar when accounting for shared custody of children (i.e., Beaujouan, 2012).

In examining the concurrent attachment relationship with multiple partners, Moors et al. (2019) found supporting evidence for the perspective that attachment orientation toward one relationship was similar to that in another relationship, and individuals in the midst of multiple relationships tended to manage each relationship as distinct and independent units, which suggests the provision of distinguishable and specific benefits by each relational bond. Thus, one possible cause for those engaging in more than one romantic relationship concurrently after divorce attributes to the desire to maximize their financial, emotional, psychological, and sexual fulfillment within a relatively small amount of time. During this time, they have gleaned adequate information concerning each partner, which could enable them to make more informed decisions on which relationship deserves continued investment and commitment and which relationship(s) need to be ceased due to its poor potential for long-term advantages for survival and reproduction.

Even though some divorced individuals date simultaneously, it is more common for divorced individuals to date serially, meaning that they will date a romantic partner, a relationship will end, and a new relationship will form in the future. This process occurs most commonly when a divorced individual enters a low-quality relationship (Langlais et al., 2016b). Individuals—divorced or not—are likely to end relationships with romantic partners who do not contribute to the relationship, who are less invested in the relationship, or who exhibit low levels of commitment to the relationship. When a romantic partner does not provide resources to assist individual well-being, that relationship is no longer beneficial. Thus, it is not unusual for individuals to experience the end of post-divorce romantic relationships, particularly when the relationships are low quality. There is some evidence that the end of mothers' post-divorce dating relationships, compared to the end of cohabitation after divorce or remarriage, is not as consequential for individual well-being because dating relationships are not as serious and investments are commonly lower (Langlais et al., 2016b; Langlais, DeAnda et al., 2018). Despite this information, how and why some fathers date multiple partners after divorce and the implications of this approach to their interpersonal and relational well-being are unclear.

There is some evidence that dating serially is easier than dating simultaneously. For humans, the average capacity of the social network is 150 (Dunbar, 2008), encompassing families, friends, and acquaintances (Tamarit et al., 2018). Dunbar (2008) suggests that there is an approximate number of people with whom we are capable of developing and keeping a relatively close relationship. As the number of social relationships increase, maintaining these relationships becomes more cognitively demanding. Because dating, particularly when it is serious, calls for time, attention, and thinking, all of which are subsumed under cognitive capital, limiting a romantic partner to one at a time appears to be a sensible and adaptive decision in terms of allocation of cognitive resources. In comparison, being involved in multiple romantic relationships would likely place extra burden on the cognitive capacity, which could hinder psychological health.

Maintenance of Post-Divorce Romantic Relationships

Although the formation of post-divorce relationships is important to consider, it is equally important to examine relationship maintenance for post-divorce romantic relationships. For example, why do some couples stay together and why do others end? The context of divorce plays an important role in determining whether certain post-divorce romantic relationships will ultimately be successful (i.e., remain together as opposed to breakup) whereas others may struggle. Next, we discuss variables, specifically those associated with the romantic partner and those associated with the family, which impact the maintenance of post-divorce dating relationships.

Romantic Partner-Specific Variables

First, in accordance with information already reviewed, the quality of romantic relationships is important to consider, as this variable typically predicts whether post-divorce romance will be beneficial for divorced individuals or not. For many, the formation of high-quality relationships, meaning relationships in which both individuals are satisfied, conflict is low, and individuals find the relationship rewarding (Langlais et al., 2016b), is better for individual well-being and relationships across the family. For instance, Symoens et al. (2014) found that lower levels of conflict in post-divorce romantic relationships were associated with stronger mental health for mothers. Langlais et al. (2016a) found that mothers in higher-quality post-divorce dating relationships reported fewer depressive symptoms and higher life satisfaction. In the same study, the end of low-quality relationships was also associated with boosts in maternal well-being. Essentially, entering high-quality relationships after divorce is beneficial for interpersonal well-being. Murray and Holmes (1999) found that individuals who ascribed importance and values to the virtues of either the individual or the dyad were more likely to have a stable and committed relationship. The study revealed that deriving redeeming features of either one's own or partner's weaknesses predicted a greater relational solidarity.

It is also important to consider the traits of romantic partners. Romantic partners who provide resources to their partners benefit not only the divorced individual but also their children. There is empirical support that illustrates the benefits and drawbacks of certain traits of romantic partners. First, alcohol or drug use after divorce can be damaging for post-divorce relationships, individual well-being, and relationships with family members. More precisely, dating partners who have substance use issues are likely to hurt interpersonal and relational well-being (Hughes, 2000; Langlais et al., 2016b). On the other hand, romantic partners who provide support in a variety of ways, are likely to bring benefits to the relationship and the family. Empirical evidence has shown benefits for individuals when they have a romantic partner who provides financial assistance (Bzostek et al., 2012; Hughes, 2000; Jansen et al., 2009). For example, Jansen et al. (2009) found that romantic partners who provided monetary support to their partners after divorce decreased post-divorce stress and indirectly promoted adjustment to divorce. Additionally, the provision of parental support by romantic partners has also decreased post-divorce stress for mothers and fathers (Hetherington & Kelly, 2003; Zemp & Bodenmann, 2018). Most consistently in the literature are the benefits of emotional support provided by romantic partners. Being emotionally supportive not only helps alleviate post-divorce stress but also decreases feelings of loneliness and depression for divorced individuals (Langlais et al., 2016b).

Family-Specific Variables

Coincidentally, whether or not children are aware of their parents' dating relationships also contributes to the potential success of that relationship. Some studies have illustrated that, in the presence of children, some divorced individuals do not tell their child(ren) that they are dating (Anderson & Greene, 2005, 2011). Once a parent is in a dating relationship, a common concern that starts lingering is deciding whether and when the child should be informed of this relationship. Under the context of divorce, many children are negotiating this family transition and trying to cope with this circumstance. For some children, knowing that their parents are dating and are likely to have less time for them could evoke a sense of loss that agitates their sense of emotional security and further impedes their ability to cope (Davies & Cummings, 1994). Some children and adolescents are able to understand parents' romantic practices as they understand parents have relational needs to be met. Apparently, whether children's awareness impacts their own or parents' well-being hinges on numerous factors. Because of the heterogeneity of children's lived experiences, there is no uniform answer for parents regarding whether and when they will let children know of their dating status. The key might lie in parents' knowledge about their children. Children's developmental stage, their ability to accept the reduced time and attention from parents as a result of the dating, and the child–parent relationship are a few examples of child-related variables parents must take into consideration when making these decisions.

The literature suggests that as long as the child–parent relationship remains healthy and parenting remains consistent, the negativity of parents' romantic practices following divorce can be reduced considerably. From the evolutionary perspective, the secure attachment between child and parent serves an adaptive purpose as it can shield children from stressful events (see Simpson & Belsky, 2008). When the parent has an unpleasant experience with the romantic partner, the supportive child–parent relationship can provide comfort and strength for the parent and the children. For example, Nielsen (2017) and Montgomery et al. (1992) provided empirical and theoretical evidence of the importance of the child–parent relationship for parental adjustment after divorce, including during times of repartnering. Likewise, strong child–parent rapport could be reassuring for children that the parent is still available on demand and diminished time with parents because of their dating will be compensated by parents in the future. For example, Xiao et al. (2022) found that during certain romantic relationship transitions, the stronger child–parent relationship helped promote children's adjustment (see fig. 27.1). In these instances, children reported more prosocial behaviors and less externalizing behaviors during specific romantic relationship transitions when they had stronger relationships with their mothers.

There are other aspects of the parent–child relationship to consider for post-divorce relationship maintenance. After divorce, children will typically spend 50% or more of their time with one parent, commonly referred to as the residential parent (i.e., Amato, 2010; Anderson & Greene, 2005). Consequently, the involvement with the nonresidential parent usually declines after the divorce (Kalmijn, 2013, 2015). The absence of a parental figure could leave a void in children's socioemotional network. If children maintain a secure attachment with the residential parent, this emotional bond, in some ways, could partially fill the void and attenuate the negativity of the disconnection with another parent. However, a healthy child–parent relationship does not apply to every divorced family. When residential parents are unable to fulfill children's unmet needs that were satisfied by the previous partner or spouse, children's emotional security and adaptive responses are likely to be at stake (Davies & Cummings, 1994). So, it could be a time for the residential parent to gauge the fitness of the dating partner, if any, and consider introducing the partner to children.

The introduction of the dating partner to the family can result in changes in the family dynamic to some extent. First, family structure shifts by adding additional dyads encompassing the dating partner. The power differential, which is relatively stable when there is only one adult in the household, might be loosened in a direction that favors children. When the dating partner manages to establish a nurturing relationship with children, it not only promotes children's adjustment but also bodes well for the quality of the romantic relationship. Langlais et al. (2018) found that children reported less problem behaviors after divorce when they established rapport with a dating partner. In light of the potential benefits as well as disruptions brought about by the dating partner, residential parents ought to carefully evaluate whether the dating partner possesses accommodating traits as well as the degree of compatibility between children and the partner. When understanding the family through evolutionary theory, the survival is not limited to individuals; it

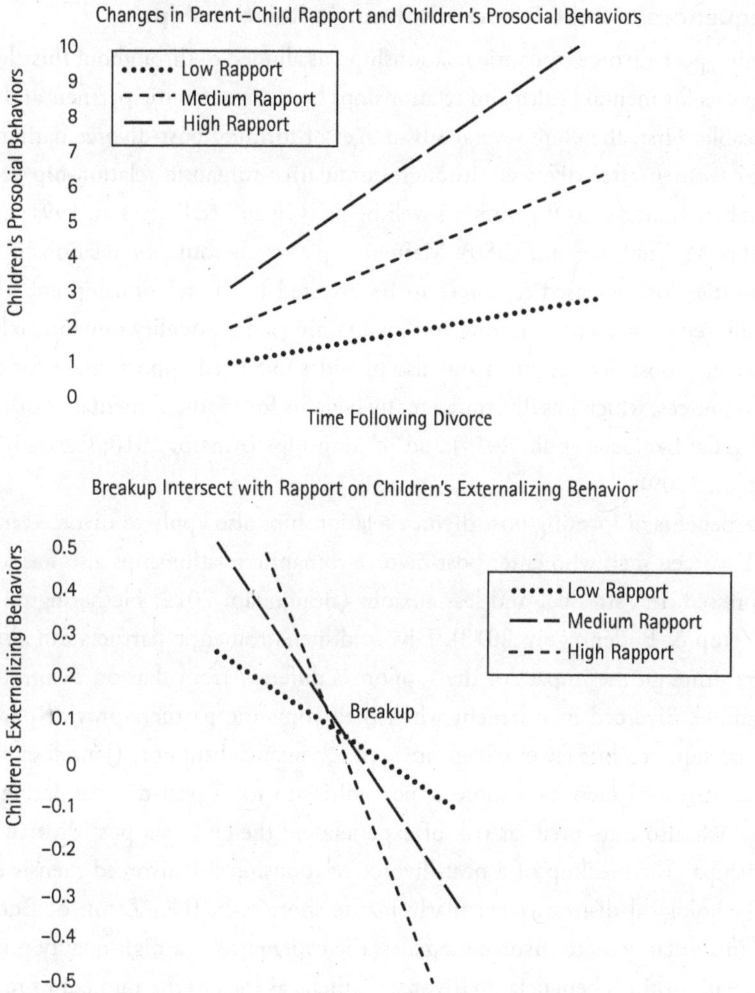

Figure 27.1 The top panel represents the interaction of parent-child rapport with time in a romantic relationship for children's prosocial (helpful, friendly) behaviors. The longer than a parent is in a romantic relationships, and the stronger parent-child rapport, the more prosocial behaviors a child is likely to exhibit. The bottom panel illustrates how the event of breakup interacts with the parent-child relationship to predict children's externalizing behaviors. In instances when parent-child rapport is high, after a post-divorce dating breakup, children exhibit fewer externalizing behaviors compared to instances when rapport is low.

From "Xiao, H., Langlais, M. B., Anderson, E., and Greene, S. (2022). Is it OK if Mommy dates? The influence of motherow. reakup, children exhibit fewerlofor Childrene Behaviors *Journal of Child and Family Studies, 31*, 1582-1595. https://doi.org/1007/s10826-021-02111-1. Reprinted by permission from Springer Nature. Copyright *Journal of Child and Family Studies*, "Is it OK if Mommy dates? The influence of mother's post-divorce dating transitions for children's behaviors," He Xiao et al., © 2021.

should be extended to the family unit. Having assets exclusively useful for mating and reproduction appear to be insufficient for single parents seeking a new romantic relationship; equally significant are characteristics that enable the partner to build a persistent connection that is in the best interest of children's survival and development.

Consequences of Post-Divorce Romantic Relationships

Forming post-divorce romantic relationships, as alluded to throughout this chapter, has implications for mental health and relationships between romantic partners and children, if applicable. First, there are several advantages of forming post-divorce dating relationships for women after divorce, although cumulative romantic relationship experiences may not be advantageous for women's well-being (Capaldi & Patterson, 1991; Langlais et al., 2016b; McCubbin et al., 1980). Maintaining a steady romantic relationship provides opportunities for increased resources to be invested in the relationship and the family when children are present. Entering and maintaining a high-quality romantic relationship helps decrease post-divorce stress and also provides increased opportunities for the provision of resources, which has illustrated many benefits for mothers' mental health (Langlais et al., 2016a; Symoens et al., 2014) and relationships (Amato, 2010; Cartwright, 2010; Skew et al., 2009).

Some benefits of forming post-divorce relationships also apply to divorced men's well-being. Divorced men who enter post-divorce romantic relationships also feel less lonely, less depressed, less stressed, and less anxious (Beaujouan, 2012; Hetherington & Kelly, 2003; Zemp & Bodenmann, 2018). Divorced men's romantic partners can also provide support, although the impact of the support is different from that on divorced women. For example, divorced men benefit when their romantic partners provide parental and emotional support, but fewer effects are seen for financial support (Jansen et al., 2009). However, divorced men have more opportunities to form post-divorce dating relationships, which also puts them at risk of experiencing the end of a post-divorce romantic relationships. The breakup of a post-divorce relationship for divorced men is correlated with psychological distress, particularly in the short term (i.e., Zemp & Bodenmann, 2018). In similar ways to divorced females, the experience of a high-quality post-divorce dating relationship is beneficial to divorced fathers, as long as the number of relationship transitions remains low.

Overall, forming post-divorce romantic relationships can impact family adjustment (Amato, 2000, 2010; Wang & Amato, 2010). Although the formation and maintenance of post-divorce relationships can benefit divorced individuals and children, particularly when these relationships are high quality, the impact on family post-divorce adjustment is mixed. For example, forming a post-divorce romantic relationship has implications for co-parenting, defined as the ability for two divorcing individuals to establish consistency with parenting behaviors and discipline for children after divorce. The introduction of another parental figure, meaning a new romantic partner, may alter how divorced families co-parent. In what ways will the new romantic partner be able to co-parent and how, if at all, should a romantic partner be involved with discipline? Research has evidenced that the formation of a new family structure (i.e., a family structure that encompasses a parent's romantic partner) increases stress for families (Capaldi & Patterson, 1991; Wang & Amato, 2000). Families have to establish new relationships, roles, and boundaries with the new and old family system. Although establishing equilibrium with the new family structure is associated with benefits for the family, the process of establishing equilibrium is difficult and stressful; this process does appear to be easier when children of the divorced couple are adults and reside outside the household (Nakonezny et al., 2003).

Future Directions for Post-Divorce Romantic Relationships

Although there is a fair amount of information available regarding how individuals form post-divorce relationships and the consequences of these relationships, there are still many questions that have yet to be answered. First, it is unclear how the seriousness of post-divorce relationships impacts individual well-being. Are there differences between forming casual and serious dating relationships? There are possible evolutionary benefits to both approaches, but much less is known regarding casual dating after divorce. Another common post-divorce relationship trend involves cohabiting and not marrying. Presumably, couples can save money by not getting married, but they risk low or declining levels of commitment without marrying. What are the consequences of divorced individuals who cohabit without getting remarried? Another area that has received limited attention is the end of same-sex marriages and the formation of same-sex romantic relationships after divorce. What are the variables that impact same-sex divorce and repartnering, and what are the consequences of forming these relationships after a same-sex divorce?

The current chapter specifically discussed post-divorce romantic relationships that precede remarriage. Not all post-divorce romantic relationships lead to remarriage, and yet, these relationships still possess some benefits for divorced individuals. Divorced individuals vary regarding how they form post-divorce romantic relationships, but a majority still get remarried. Not covered in this chapter is the motivation and impact of remarriage for individuals and families. The formation and maintenance of stepfamily relationships, although similar to repartnering processes, is uniquely different and includes a variety of other variables, including stepchildren, stepparents, co-parenting, and stepparenting. Because stepfamily processes are beyond the scope of this chapter, it is worth noting that these relationships may also provide unique affordances that could benefit individuals from an evolutionary perspective.

Another promising line of future research is to study how the previous marriage influences one's response to post-divorce romance. Divorce occurs for various reasons; some of them are financial strain, conflictual parenting, incompatible sex life, and oppressive relationships (Lowenstein, 2005). Varied experiences in a prior marriage, for better or worse, shape divorced individuals' motives, expectations, and beliefs regarding their next romantic relationship. For instance, women's pursuit of independence, particularly in career development, is a contributor to divorce (Lowenstein, 2005). For these women, they may care about whether a dating partner is supportive of their career ambitions. If the divorce occurs because of the negligence of parental duty of one parent, people may prioritize the extent to which a partner is willing to embrace the stepparent role and how capable they are of helping raise a child. For those who found their way out of an abusive and violent marriage, it is naturally understandable that they could be reluctant to dive into the dating market. A study by Godbout et al. (2009) revealed that those who were exposed to adult intimate partner violence or marital discord during childhood struggled to develop a secure attachment and exhibited anxiety in close relationship, which was linked a tendency to avoid intimacy. For some, a failed marriage could result in a heightened sensitivity and reluctance toward forming a new relationship. Their confidence in forming a new relationship may be worn out due to the past unpleasant experience. In contrast, some people are not discouraged by their marital history and remain driven to find a new partner who is capable of providing what they missed out in the marriage. How a dissolved marriage impacts emergent coping strategies—ways of thinking and behaving—pertaining to subsequent romantic matters remains uncertain. More evolutionary-focused research is needed to explicate these strategies and how they may have been shaped by recurrent adaptive challenges.

Although we explain different approaches that divorced people take to form new romantic relationships, empirical studies are needed to further substantiate these propositions. Dating after divorce is an essential step toward cohabitation and remarriage, two forms of romantic and family relationships that are expected to produce more enduring and critical advantages for survival and reproduction. However, some people choose to remain single and resist engaging in romantic behaviors despite possessing desired personal traits, financial resources, and availability in time. They prioritize something else, such as self-actualization, over mating and reproduction. There is a chance that survival and reproduction take on a different meaning for those who have been through a divorce. The decision to restrict one's romantic practice following divorce needs to be understood through an integrative lens encompassing one's individual, contextual, historical, and cultural circumstances. A major task for future studies is to disentangle these contributors to post-relationship romance and examine the evolutionary logic that guides how individuals choose to date and remate.

Conclusion

Post-divorce romantic relationships have implications for divorced women and men. The research shared in this chapter describes some similarities and differences when it comes to post-divorce romantic relationships, and how these commonalities and nuances are consistent with the theory of parental investment. The ways in which individuals form romantic relationships also vary, from not dating to dating one person after divorce to dating multiple people, either serially or simultaneously. Each of these approaches can be explained by the central tenets of evolutionary theory, which can also explain some of the beneficial consequences of post-divorce romantic relationships. Post-divorce romance is both an individual and social issue with depth and complexity, and it has profound meaning and implications for the divorced population as well as families involved. In this chapter, we have taken an evolutionary perspective to portray and understand some of the post-divorce romantic issues. As society is endlessly evolving, the values, beliefs, psychological mechanisms, and adaptive responses related to post-divorce romance are also concurrently evolving. As researchers, educators, and practitioners, we must follow the trend and keep evolving our professional and sociocultural identities, research methodologies, and practical tools to better understand and serve the divorced population.

References

Amato, P. R. (2000). The consequences of divorce for adults and children. *Journal of Marriage and the Family, 62*, 1269–1287. https://doi.org/10.1111/j.1741-3737.2000.01269.x

Amato, P. R. (2010). Research on divorce: Continuing trends and new developments. *Journal of Marriage and the Family, 72,* 650–666. https://doi.org/10.1111/j.1741-3737.2010.00723.x

Anderson, E. R., & Greene, S. M. (2005). Transitions in parental repartnering after divorce. *Journal of Divorce & Remarriage, 43*, 47–62. https://doi.org/10.1300/J087v43n03_03

Anderson, E. R., & Greene, S. M. (2011). "My child and I are a package deal": Balancing adult and child concerns in repartnering after divorce. *Journal of Family Psychology, 25*, 741–750. https://doi.org/10.1037/a0024620

Anderson, E. R., Greene, S. M., Walker, L., Malerba, C., Forgatch, M. S., & DeGarmo, D. S. (2004). Ready to take a chance again: Transitions into dating among divorced parents. *Journal of Divorce & Remarriage, 40*, 61–75. https://doi.org/10.1300/J087v40n03_04

Arnett, J. J. (2000). Emerging adulthood: A theory of development from the late teens through the twenties. *American Psychologist, 55*, 469–480. https://doi.org/10.1037/0003-066X.55.5.469

Baumeister, R. F., & Leary, M. R. (1995). The need to belong: Desire for interpersonal attachments as a fundamental human motivation. *Psychological Bulletin, 117*, 497–529. https://doi.org/10.1037/0033-2909.117.3.497

Beaujouan, E. (2012). Repartnering in France: The role of gender, age, and past fertility. *Advances in Life Course Research, 17*, 69–80. https://doi.org/10.1016/j.alcr.2012.03.001

Beck, A. N., Cooper, C. E., McLanahan, S., & Brooks-Gunn, J. (2010). Partnership transitions and maternal parenting. *Journal of Marriage and the Family, 72*, 219–233. https://doi.org/10.1111/j.1741-3737.2010.00695.x

Bjorklund, D. F., & Kipp, K. (1996). Parental investment theory and gender differences in the evolution of inhibition mechanisms. *Psychological Bulletin, 120*, 163–188. https://doi.org/10.1037/0033-2909.120.2.163

Buss, D. M. (1995). Evolutionary psychology: A new paradigm for psychological science. *Psychological Inquiry, 6*, 1–30. https://doi.org/10.1207/s15327965pli0601_1

Bzostek, S. H., McLanahan, S. S., & Carlson, M. J. (2012). Mothers' repartnering after a non-marital birth. *Social Forces, 90*, 817–841. https://doi.org/10.1093/sf/sos005

Cacioppo, J. T., & Hawkley, L. C. (2009). Perceived social isolation and cognition. *Trends in Cognitive Sciences, 13*(10), 447–454.

Capaldi, D. M., & Patterson, G. R. (1991). Relation of parental transitions to boys' adjustment problems: I. A linear hypothesis: II. Mothers at risk for transitions and unskilled parenting. *Developmental Psychology, 27*, 489–504. https://doi.org/10.1037/0012-1649.27.3.489

Cartwright, C. (2010). Preparing to repartner and live in a stepfamily: An exploratory investigation. *Journal of Family Studies, 16*, 237–250. https://doi.org/10.5172/jfs.16.3.237

Davies, P. T., & Cummings, E. M. (1994). Marital conflict and child adjustment: An emotional security hypothesis. *Psychological Bulletin, 116*, 387–411. https://doi.org/10.1037/0033-2909.116.3.387

de Graaf, P. M., & Kalmijn, M. (2003). Alternative routes in the remarriage market: Competing risk analyses of union formation after divorce. *Social Forces, 81*, 1459–1498.

Dunbar, R. I. (2008). Cognitive constraints on the structure and dynamics of social networks. *Group Dynamics: Theory, Research, and Practice, 12*(1), 7.

Erikson, E. H. (1985). *The life cycle completed: A review*. W. W. Norton.

Godbout, N., Dutton, D. G., Lussier, Y., & Sabourin, S. (2009). Early exposure to violence, domestic violence, attachment representations, and marital adjustment. *Personal Relationships, 16*(3), 365–384.

Hadfield, K., & Nixon, E. (2017). Benefits of and barriers to romantic relationships among mothers in Ireland. *Family Relations, 66*, 383–398. https://doi.org/10.1111/fare.12261

Hasan, M., & Clark, E. M. (2017). I get so lonely, baby: The effects of loneliness and social isolation on romantic dependency. *The Journal of Social Psychology, 157*(4), 429–444.

Hetherington, E., & Kelly, J. (2003). *For better or for worse: Divorce reconsidered*. W. W. Norton.

Hughes, J. (2000). Repartnering after divorce: Marginal mates and unwedded women. *Family Matters, 55*, 16–21.

Jansen, M., Mortelmans, D., & Snoeckx, L. (2009). Repartnering and (re)employment: Strategies to cope with the economic consequences of partnership dissolution. *Journal of Marriage and the Family, 71*, 1271–1293. https://doi.org/10.1111/j.1741-3737.2009.00668.x

Kalmijn, M. (2013). Long-term effects of divorce on parent-child relationships: Within-family comparisons of fathers and mothers. *European Sociological Review, 29*, 888–898. https://doi.org/10.1093/esr/jcs066

Kalmijn, M. (2015). Relationships between fathers and adult children: The cumulative effects of divorce and repartnering. *Journal of Family Issues, 36*, 737–759. https://doi.org/10.1177/0192513X13495398

Keller, M. C., Neale, M. C., & Kendler, K. S. (2007). Association of different adverse life events with distinct patterns of depressive symptoms. *The American Journal of Psychiatry, 164*, 1521–1529. https://doi.org/10.1176/appi.ajp.2007.06091564

Langlais, M. R., Anderson, E. R., & Greene, S. M. (2015). Characteristics of mother's dating after divorce. *Journal of Divorce and Remarriage, 56*, 180–198. https://doi.org/10.1080/10502556.2015.1012701

Langlais, M. R., Anderson, E. R., & Greene, S. M. (2016a). Consequences of repartnering for post-divorce maternal well-being. *Journal of Marriage and the Family, 78*, 1032–1046. https://doi.org/10.1111/jomf.12319

Langlais, M. R., Anderson, E. R., & Greene, S. M. (2016b). Mothers' dating after divorce. *Contemporary Perspectives in Family Research, 10*, 69–100.

Langlais, M. R., DeAnda, J. S., Anderson, E. R., & Greene, S. M. (2018). The impact of mothers' post-divorce breakups on children's problem behaviors. *Journal of Child and Family Studies, 27*, 2643–2655. https://doi.org/10.1007/s10826-018-1095-3

Livingston, G. (2014, November). Trends in remarriage in the U.S. *Pew Research Center*. Retrieved fromhttps://www.pewsocialtrends.org/2014/11/14/chapter-1-trends-in-remarriage-in-the-u-s/.

Lowenstein, L. F. (2005). Causes and associated features of divorce as seen by recent research. *Journal of Divorce & Remarriage, 42*, 153–171.

McCubbin, H. I., Joy, C. B., Cauble, A. E., Comeau, J. K., Patterson, J. M., & Needle, R. H. (1980). Family stress and coping: A decade review. *Journal of Marriage and the Family, 42*, 855–871. https://doi.org/rosi.unk.edu/10.2307/351829

Miller, R. S. (2017). *Intimate relationships* (8th ed.). McGraw Hill.

Montgomery, M. J., Anderson, E. R., Hetherington, E., & Clingempeel, W. (1992). Patterns of courtship for remarriage: Implications for child adjustment and parent–child relationships. *Journal of Marriage and the Family, 54*, 686–698.

Moors, A. C., Ryan, W., & Chopik, W. J. (2019). Multiple lovers: The effects of attachment with multiple concurrent romantic partners on relational functioning. *Personality and Individual Differences, 147*, 102–110.

Morrison, M., Epstude, K., & Roese, N. J. (2012). Life regrets and the need to belong. *Social Psychological and Personality Science, 3*, 675–681.

Murray, S. L., & Holmes, J. G. (1999). The (mental) ties that bind: Cognitive structures that predict relationship resilience. *Journal of Personality and Social Psychology, 77*, 1228–1244. https://doi.org/10.1037/0022-3514.77.6.1228

Nakonezny, P. A., Rodgers, J. L., & Nussbaum, J. F. (2003). The effect of later life parental divorce on adult-child/older-parent solidarity: A test of the buffering hypothesis. *Journal of Applied Social Psychology, 33*, 1153–1178. https://doi.org/10.1111/j.1559-1816.2003.tb01943.x

Nelson, B. W., Laurent, S. M., Bernstein, R., & Laurent, H. K. (2017). Perspective-taking influences autonomic attunement between partners during discussion of conflict. *Journal of Social and Personal Relationships, 34*, 139–165. https://doi.org/10.1177/0265407515626595

Nielsen, L. (2017). Re-examining the research on parental conflict, coparenting, and custody arrangements. *Psychology, Public Policy, and Law, 23*, 211–231. https://doi.org/10.1037/law0000109

Noël, M. C. M. (2013). Repartnering following divorce: Implications for older fathers' relations with their adult children. *Journal of Marriage and the Family, 75*(3), 697–712. https://doi.org/10.1111/jomf.12034

Orians, G. H., & Heerwagen, J. H. (1992). Evolved responses to landscapes. In J. H. Barkow, L. Cosmides, & J. Tooby (Eds.), *The adapted mind: Evolutionary psychology and the generation of culture* (pp. 555–579). Oxford University Press.

Simpson, J. A., & Belsky, J. (2008). Attachment theory within a modern evolutionary framework. In J. Cassidy & P. R. Shaver (Eds.), *Handbook of attachment: Theory, research, and clinical applications* (pp. 131–157). Guilford Press.

Skew, A., Evans, A., & Gray, E. (2009). Repartnering in the United Kingdom and Australia. *Journal of Comparative Family Studies, 40*, 563–585.

Slotter, E. B., Gardner, W. L., & Finkel, E. J. (2009). Who am I without you? The influence of romantic breakup on the self-concept. *Personality and Social Psychology Bulletin, 36*, 147–160. https://doi.org/10.1177/0146167209352250

Stiver, K. A., & Alonzo, S. H. (2009). Parent and mating effort: Is there necessarily a trade-off? *Ethology: International Journal of Behavioural Biology, 115*, 1101–1126. https://doi.org/10.1111/j.1439-0310.2009.01707.x

Symoens, S., Colman, E., & Bracke, P. (2014). Divorce, conflict, and mental health: How the quality of intimate relationships is linked to post-divorce well-being. *Journal of Applied Social Psychology, 44*, 220–233. https://doi.org/10.1111/jasp.12215

Tamarit, I., Cuesta, J. A., Dunbar, R. I., & Sánchez, A. (2018). Cognitive resource allocation determines the organization of personal networks. *Proceedings of the National Academy of Sciences, 115*, 8316–8321.

Tavares, L., & Aassve, A. (2013). Psychological distress of marital and cohabitation breakups. *Social Science Research, 42*, 1599–1611. https://doi.org/10.1016/j.ssresearch.2013.07.008

Trivers, R. (1972). Parental investment and sexual selection. In B. Campbell (Ed.), *Sexual selection and the descent of man: 1871–1971* (pp. 136–179). Aldine.

Twenge, J. M., Catanese, K. R., & Baumeister, R. F. (2002). Social exclusion causes self-defeating behavior. *Journal of Personality and Social Psychology, 83*, 606–615. https://doi.org/10.1037/0022-3514.83.3.606

Wang, H., & Amato, P. R. (2000). Predictors of divorce adjustment: Stressors, resources, and definitions. *Journal of Marriage and Family, 62*(3), 655–668. https://doi.org/10.1111/j.1741-3737.2000.00655.x

Williams, K. D. (2007). Ostracism. *Annual Review of Psychology, 58*, 425–452.

Wu, Z., & Schimmele, C. M. (2005). Repartnering after first union disruption. *Journal of Marriage and the Family, 67*, 27–36. https://doi.org/10.1111/j.0022-2445.2005.00003.x

Xiao, H., Langlais, M. R., Anderson, E., & Greene, S. (2022). Is it OK if mommy dates? The influence of mother's post-divorce dating transitions for children's behaviors. *Journal of Child and Family Study, 31*, 1582–1595. https://doi.org/10.1007/s10826-021-02111-1

Zemp, M., & Bodenmann, G. (2018). Family structure and the nature of couple relationships: Relationship distress, separation, divorce, and repartnering. In M. R. Sanders & A. Morawska (Eds.), Handbook of *parenting and child development across the lifespan* (pp. 415–440). Springer. https://doi.org/10.1007/978-3-319-94598-9_18

Zhang, Z., & Hayward, M. D. (2006). Gender, the marital life course, and cardiovascular disease in late midlife. *Journal of Marriage and the Family, 68*, 639–657. https://doi.org/10.1111/j.1741-3737.2006.00280.x

CHAPTER

28 Evolutionary Perspectives on Post-Separation Parenting

Lawrence J. Moloney *and* Bruce M. Smyth

Abstract

Can evolutionary theory, particularly as applied to human emotions, cast light on some of the apparently intractable problems in post-separation parenting disputes? We argue that (a) the adaptation and survival of many animals, especially primates, is closely linked to how they manage their emotions; (b) our own emotional lives are uncannily similar to those of chimpanzees, our closest living relative; (c) emotions play a central role in human thinking, decision-making, and the management of conflict; (d) in Western democracies, "no-fault" divorce legislation has inadvertently sidelined the pivotal role played by emotions in understanding and responding to the breakdown of parental relationships and its consequences for children; and (e) in problematic post-separation parenting disputes, emotions need to be fearlessly, accurately, and empathically acknowledged within legislative and decision-making processes and by those involved in mediation and relationship support services.

Key Words: conflict, emotions, evolutionary perspectives, relationship dissolution, no-fault divorce, separation-related violence

This chapter examines how evolutionary theory, particularly as applied to human emotions, can cast light on some of the apparently intractable problems in post-separation parenting disputes. It comprises seven main sections. The first section briefly describes divorce-related trends in English-speaking democracies. The second section examines recent data on post-separation co-parental relationships, including manifestations of entrenched interparental hatred and intimate partner violence. In the third section, we explore ways in which human evolved psychology might be related to post-relationship behavior. We then consider the importance of emotions in animal behavior and survival, and the evidence pointing to the critical role of these inherited emotions in human negotiations and human decision-making (fourth section). Next, we examine key unanticipated consequences of "no-fault" divorce (fifth section). In the sixth section, we briefly consider how professionals might better acknowledge and work with the emotional part of our evolutionary history, especially in separations characterized by entrenched conflict or dysfunctional and dangerous behaviors. Finally, in the last section, we offer ideas for future research.

Divorce: Key Issues in English-Speaking Democracies

About one in two marriages end in divorce in the United States compared with approximately one in three in Australia, and two in five in Canada and the UK (Apostolou et al., 2019; McCrindle, 2016).[1] Cohabiting, nonmarried unions have even higher rates of dissolution (Lamidi et al., 2019; Lichter et al., 2006; Wilson & Daly, 2016). Divorce rates are highest in the early years of marriage. In Australia, for example, one third of marriages break down in the first five years (Australian Bureau of Statistics, 2018), with young children disproportionately represented among children affected by parental separation.

Divorce is known to occur in all cultures (Betzig, 1989). In Western democracies, where its impact has been extensively studied, divorce has been perceived as responsible for a plethora of social ills for children—from poor academic achievement to youth suicide (see, e.g., Blankenhorn, 1995; Horn & Sylvester, 2002). But there is compelling evidence that it is not divorce per se but a constellation of mutually reinforcing factors pre- and post-separation (e.g., poverty, family violence and abuse, parental mental health and substance use, reduced parenting capacity, and separation-related conflict) that drive many of the negative consequences of relationship breakdown for children (Pryor & Rodgers, 2001).

Though post-separation conflicts over material resources can be difficult, emotionally driven, and potentially destructive, the division of matrimonial assets is largely guided by rules and heuristics. As a consequence, even when emotionally charged, the dispute resolution process is usually brief and reasonably straightforward: assets can be counted, divided, and apportioned. Resolution of conflicts focused on the continued parenting of children, however, are less amenable to the application of rules and less constrained by time.

Broadly speaking, conflicts over children reflect the fact that unlike most primates, human fathers, as well as mothers, invest heavily in their young.[2] While mothers and fathers remain together, this investment plays out in largely cooperative behaviors. Separation, however, presents former couples with three basic parenting choices: cooperate, live and let live (i.e., "parallel parenting" in which separated parents have minimal interaction and thus report relatively low levels of conflict), or fight.

---

[1] Unless otherwise specified, we use the term "marriage" in the remainder of this chapter to describe an intimate and committed relationship between two individuals. Our primary focus is on parents. Whether legally married or not, our assumption is that the issues discussed in the chapter continue to apply.

[2] Buss (2003) suggested that one reason for this is that unlike their nonhuman primate ancestors, human fathers can often (though not always) be sure of their paternity. Fathers play a central role in a range of other animals (see, e.g., Masson, 2000), but this issue is beyond the scope of the present chapter.

As long as parental relationships remain stable, fathers' investments in their children have many advantages. However, a failed relationship can bring into sharp focus those parental care and financial support arrangements that may not have been formally discussed or articulated while the couple were together.

In Western jurisdictions, post-separation parenting issues were initially considered against a backdrop of assumptions about the disposition of matrimonial property. Broadly speaking, during much of the 19th century, few married women had any rights in this regard. The fact that, like their children, most wives were the legal chattels of their husbands was reflected in the majority of court judgments, which awarded custody of children to fathers (Friedman, 1995; Mason, 1994).

The late part of that century, however, saw a developing appreciation of the child's need for emotional nurturance. In virtually all Western jurisdictions, this resulted in a reversal in the legal approach to post-separation parenting disputes. To put it simply, when disputes arose, the default starting point was to regard mothers as the preferred custodians (Maidment, 1984; Stiles, 1984).

During both the "father preference" and "mother preference" periods, however, allocation of blame for the breakup could also impact the outcome of a parenting dispute. Custody of a child could in these circumstances be awarded to the "innocent" parent, notwithstanding their gender (Friedman, 1995; Maidment, 1994).

The 1960s and 1970s saw the introduction of "no-fault" divorce.[3] This generally meant that applicants merely had to establish that they had been separated for a defined period of time; courts were no longer concerned with allocating blame. Set beside evolving challenges to the maternal preference assumption (e.g., Rutter, 1972) and an emerging human rights argument that children were entitled to an ongoing meaningful relationship with both parents,[4] the earlier gender- and blame-based decision-making principles gave way to an era of legal indeterminacy. First articulated by Mnookin (1975), this situation has persisted to the present day. Put simply, since the emergence of no fault divorce, the law has struggled to articulate a set of principles beyond that of the "best interests of the child" to guide decision-making in post-separation parenting disputes. (Bartlett & Scott, 2014). When indeterminacy meets adversarial dispute management processes, the stage is set for lengthy battles over the care of children.

---

[3] This is the popular term for the revolution that took place in divorce law. The thinking behind the change was that intimate relationships involve multiple negotiated reciprocal rights and responsibilities that are personally negotiated. It should not be the business of courts therefore, to determine which actions fell sufficiently short of expectations to support an application for divorce. Most jurisdictions now have a single ground for divorce, linked simply to an established length of separation. In Australia, for example, either party can expect to be granted a dissolution if they can establish that they have been separated for at least 12 months.

[4] See *Declaration of the Rights of the Child* (1959) and, more specifically, Article 9 *Convention on the Rights of the Child.*

The adverse impacts of enduring interparental conflicts on children's well-being are now well documented (e.g., Emery, 2012; Stallman & Ohan, 2016; van Dijk et al., 2020). Children and young people fare badly when they are caught in the middle of frequent, intense, unresolved interparental conflict and worse when their parents actively draw them into these conflicts (Johnston, 1994; Ricci, 1997). Disputes accompanied by family violence and other dangerous behaviors, as well as the witnessing of these behaviors, put children at even greater risk (Kerig, 2001).

Divorce has also been shown to have major physical, psychological, and financial impacts on mothers and fathers, though these vary considerably across relationships, individuals, and cultures (Kołodziej-Zaleska & Przybyła-Basista, 2020; Perilloux & Buss, 2008; Sprecher et al., 1998). Separated parents frequently report a range of complex, strong, and often contradictory emotional responses. These include distress, hurt, anger, jealousy, sadness, love/longing, as well as relief (e.g., Arditti & Allen, 1993; Metts et al., 2009; Morris, 2015; Sbarra & Emery, 2005; Sbarra & Ferrer, 2006; Willén, 2015). Three distinct yet interrelated emotions—anger, sadness, and love/longing—are known to frequently vacillate after relationship breakdown. Within this emotional rollercoaster, sadness and anger often co-occur; love is often accompanied by sadness; over time, anger typically diminishes faster than sadness; and sadness usually diminishes faster than love (Sbarra & Emery, 2005; Sbarra & Ferrer, 2006). For separated parents, a history of shared intimacies, resources, and children render the separation more emotionally and logistically complex than the ending of short-term casual or childless couple relationships in which a "clean break" is far more possible (Perilloux & Buss, 2008).

Hurt

In spite of being a commonly experienced emotion, hurt has attracted far less attention—within psychology more broadly, and evolutionary psychology, more specifically—than have the so-called primary emotions of joy, fear, anger, sadness, and disgust (Leary, 2015). For Leary (2015), "hurt feelings" captured a mixed bag of emotions that arise when individuals believe their relational value to others is low or may be in jeopardy. Hurt is a feeling of harm or injury felt "in response to actions or messages from others that are perceived to devalue one's character, importance, or worth" (Metts et al., 2009, p. 357). It includes the emotions of jealousy, guilt, shame, and embarrassment. However, other emotions, such as anger and sadness, often accompany rejection-related emotions: sadness typically arises from a perceived loss of important social relationships (Leary, 2015).

Nonresident fathers, for example, commonly experience an overwhelming sense of grief arising from the loss of a partner, everyday family life, and frequent or regular contact with their children (Stewart & Schwebel, 1986). By contrast, anger arises from the perception that a provocation is undeserved (Metts et al., 2009). Single mothers, for example, often harbor anger toward their former partner if thrust into poverty after separation. Relationship breakdown is fertile ground for nurturing hurt feelings.

Such feelings are frequently amplified by the fact that parental separation is often not a joint decision, with initiator status (leaver vs. left) being a well-known predictor of distress. In the United States, for instance, just over two thirds (69%) of women in heterosexual marriages initiate the separation (Rosenfeld, 2018; in Australia, see Hewitt, 2008; Wolcott & Hughes, 1999). The attribution of who initiated the separation and who was "left"—especially in the context of spousal infidelity (see below)—has been linked with important differences in emotional adjustment after separation. In particular, initiators report less post-separation distress than noninitiators (Fine & Sacher, 1997; Kołodziej-Zaleska & Przybyła-Basista, 2020; Morris, 2015), though this is not to say that initiators get off "scot free" (Morris et al., 2015). Nonmutuality typically affords an initiator a psychological and practical edge over the noninitiator (Buchanan et al., 2006; Vaughan, 1986), who is more likely to adopt a range of partner retention strategies ranging from being very loving and caring ("positive inducements") to being hypervigilant ("direct guarding") to resorting to violence ("negative inducements") (Buss, 1988, p. 297).

Post-Separation Relationships

Disagreements and disputes in emotionally bonded relationships, though sometimes challenging, also add to the richness and diversity of the relationship and contribute to its growth and survival. (Bell, 2013; Ellis, 2000; Mayer, 2009). At the same time, relationship conflict that continues to escalate or remains unresolved can be corrosive, highly destructive, and sometimes dangerous (Bell, 2013; Ellis, 2000; Mayer, 2009).

The focal points of post-separation interparental conflict are typically played out in disputes over money and resources (mainly child support, alimony, and the division of any matrimonial property) as well as in the details of parenting arrangements. But the key drivers of these conflicts are emotional.

Whether by agreement or court order, most children in Western countries have some ongoing time with both separated parents. However, around 10–30% have little or no contact with one parent, usually the father, a situation that has changed little over many years (see, e.g., Amato et al., 2009; Australian Bureau of Statistics, 2015; Juby et al., 2004). There is evidence that many fathers disengage from their children due to the belief that ongoing interparental conflict is not good for their children or for themselves (Smyth, 2004). For many, walking away can also be a way of dealing with grief, loss, role ambiguity (am I a *real* parent?), perceived injustice by "the system" and/or a former partner, and the pain of seeing children for slices of time in a superficial and artificial context (Smyth, 2004).

The Post-Separation Relationship Spectrum

Although interparental conflict is common prior to, during, and 12–24 months after relationship breakdown, it typically diminishes over time (Willén, 2015). Estimates of "high conflict" (variously defined) at discrete points in time after separation typically range from 10–25% in English-speaking countries, with 5–15% the most common range (e.g., Smyth & Moloney, 2017). Recent work in Australia found reports of *enduring* parenting disputes to be far from the norm. A four-year Australian longitudinal study of 10,000 separated parents in tandem with related cross-sectional studies found that 58–63% reported *friendly* or *cooperative* relationships over the past year, 19–27% reported that their relationship was *distant*, 11–14% reported *lots of conflict* (so-called *high-conflict*), while 4–5% described their relationship with their former partner as *fearful* (De Maio et al., 2013; Kaspiew et al., 2009; Kaspiew et al., 2015; Qu & Weston, 2010; Qu et al., 2014).

Separated mothers were twice as likely as separated fathers to report being *fearful* of their former partner (6% vs. 3%), the only dimension on which a significant gender difference was recorded. In addition, 40% of separated parents' relationships remained positive (*friendly* or *cooperative*) across all three waves of this four-year study, while 5% continued to be *distant*, and only 4% remained negative (*lots of conflict* or *fearful*).

When Love Turns to Hate

At the vanguard of work on post-relationship interparental conflict is the identification of subtypes of high conflict (Birnbaum & Bala, 2010). An emerging hypothesis is that the term "high conflict" oversimplifies the nature of destructive family dynamics, especially with respect to the small but resource-intensive group of separated parents who remain deeply enmeshed in legal battles and parental acrimony (Demby, 2009, 2017; see also Koppejan-Luitze et al., 2020). Smyth and Moloney (2017) have suggested that *entrenched interparental hatred* may be a key relationship dynamic driving the behavior of some in this group. They posit that such hatred is characterized by

> a relentless and unforgiving negativity involving: (a) a global assessment of the former partner as bad or evil and deserving of no respect as a person or a parent; (b) persistent bitter feelings, mistrust, accusatory thought, and destructive impulses; (c) a steadfast inability to self-reflect, see other perspectives or change, coupled with re-directing ("projecting") internal conflicts away from self and onto another; and (d) a willingness to incur harm to oneself and one's children in the service of harming or even destroying the other parent. (p. 408)

A "rational" approach to hatred might be to banish the hated object from one's life. Like love however, hatred tends to have an obsessive element that makes letting go difficult. Obsessive love sees only the good in someone (Fisher, 2000); hatred sees only the "bad." For Demby (2009, p. 477), "pathological hatred" can be seen as "an effort to destroy, while at the same time desperately needing"—the co-existence of desire and destructive urges. In a similar vein, Emery (2012, p. 31) has proposed that anger driven by hatred, like anger driven by love, can be understood as "reunion behavior," and that "[l]ove and hate (angry protest) both serve the same function, namely that of promoting proximity."

Outward expressions of entrenched interparental hatred can take numerous forms such as child–parent alignment (whereby a child is encouraged by a parent to reject the other parent), relocation disputes (in which a parent seeks to move interstate or overseas with the children to remove the child from the orbit of the other parent), child abduction (i.e., *child theft*), stalking, and harassment (online and offline). It can also at times be associated with violence and abuse, which at the extremes can take the form of murder or murder–suicide.

Family Violence and Abuse

Separation is an especially dangerous time for some parents (mainly women) and for some children, especially within the first few months after parental separation (Wilson, 2005; Wilson & Daly, 1993). Too often it would appear that family courts fail to protect parents and children and continue to endorse potentially dangerous post-separation parenting arrangements even in the face of allegations of serious violence (in Australia, see, e.g., Moloney et al., 2007). Moreover, opportunities to use parenting arrangements as a means of continuing acts of terror and abuse have tended to increase in the digital age and in the context of the COVID-19 forced isolation regimes (Humphreys et al., 2020; Mazza et al., 2020; Smyth et al., 2020).

Intimate partner violence refers to "a pattern of physical, sexual, and/or emotional abuse by a current or former intimate partner in the context of coercive control" (Hardesty & Chung, 2006, p. 200). It is primarily a gendered phenomenon that is complex and destructive in nature. Though frequently linked to a belief in the need to control a partner's life choices, intimate partner violence has no single cause or explanation (Wilson, 2005; Wilson & Daly, 2016). Some evolutionary theorists (e.g., Daly & Wilson 2000, p. 101; Wilson & Daly, 2016, p. 3) appear to treat spousal violence and homicide as "conflict 'assays' " (i.e., at the extreme end of the couple conflict spectrum). Similarly, conflict scholars (e.g., Johnston, 1994) have noted that violence is sometimes used as a means to resolve conflict. We, like many others (e.g., Archer-Kuhn, 2018; Johnson, 1995), suggest that, at its heart, intimate partner violence is not about conflict but rather is a collection of strategies to enforce partner control through coercion. Johnson (2006, p.1003) has suggested that intimate partner violence presents itself in several forms: *situational couple violence*; *intimate terrorism*; *violent resistance*; and *mutual violent control.*

In the case of Johnson's *intimate terrorism*, intimate partner violence is typically a one-sided phenomenon enacted almost universally by men, using tactics of coercion, control, domination, fear, manipulation, isolation, and degradation toward a partner. This pattern can be frequent and severe. At its most succinct, family violence is about domination whereas conflict is about disagreements—real or perceived.

Human Bonding and Dissolution: Evolutionary Insights

One line of thinking with respect to the evolutionary basis of relationship dissolution is predicated on the idea that marriage or marriage-like unions involve females conferring some exclusivity of sexual and reproductive rights to a male in exchange for his commitment to invest in and protect her and their offspring (Daly & Wilson, 2000). However, should either not fulfill their end of the bargain (e.g., either party is unfaithful, "freeloads," or becomes undependable), the relationship may dissolve. From this perspective, human mating and relationship dissolution are inherently strategic and constantly evolving to solve specific adaptive problems related to reproductive success (Buss & Schmitt, 1993).

The dissolution of human pair-bonds is typically accompanied by one of the three "D"s: divorce, desertion, or death[5] (Kushnick, 2016). Excluding cases of spousal homicide, death is out of a partner's control. From an evolutionary perspective, desertion or divorce could be predicted to be more likely to occur when one or both partners seek(s) to increase their fitness by leaving a partnership to seek out or be with a better mate—colloquially termed "trading-up" (Freese, 2000, p. 293) or "mate switching" (Buss et al., 2017). The behavior may not necessarily be a conscious act (R. M. Nesse, 1990a). Nor is it always clear that the behavior is adaptive (R. M. Nesse, 2017). In addition, as noted below, what is in the best interests of individual fitness may not always be in the best interests of a family or small group or species—and vice versa.[6]

Several lines of inquiry from evolutionary psychology offer intriguing insights into the ways in which human evolved psychology might be related to post-relationship behavior. Below, we focus on five particular issues: (a) repartnering; (b) spousal infidelity; (c)

---

[5] From a legal perspective, the granting of a divorce presumes that a de jure marriage (i.e., a marriage recognized as legitimate in the country granting the divorce) has occurred at some time in the past. Our use of the term, however, includes the dissolution of cohabiting relationships (or de facto marriages), which are now common in Western countries. As noted, de facto marriages dissolve more frequently than de jure marriages. Our interest from an evolutionary perspective is in the transition from a committed relationship that has produced children to the breakup of that relationship. We see no reason to assume that evolutionary insights would not apply equally to the dissolution of these de jure or de facto marriages. The same argument would apply to the term, "desertion," which was more commonly used in the days when fathers were sole breadwinners and mothers had no other means of financial support if a marriage was terminated. Though supporting parents and other social security benefits have softened this experience, it is still possible (even if technically illegal) for one parent to escape financial obligations and in that sense desert his or her partner.

[6] This raises the question of evidence of cooperation (see, e.g., Dugatkin, 1997) and altruism among many species (e.g., Ricard, 2013) versus individualism and selfishness (e.g., Dawkins, 1990). In our view, the evidence for cooperation among a large range of species is overwhelming. The concept of altruism assumes the possibility of consciousness and emotion. Though the evidence on altrusism does not apply (at least as yet) to as many species, there can now be no doubt that those species with which we share a large proportion of our genes show evidence of both consciousness and altruistic behavior (see, e.g., de Waal, 2019; Goodall, 1990; Wilson, 2012).

romantic rejection-related emotions; (d) entrenched interparental hatred; and (e) intimate partner violence.

Repartnering

Humans improve their reproductive success not simply by procreating but by contributing to the health and welfare of the children who carry their genes. But compared to most other animals, human children require an extensive period of nurturing, which in turn requires a considerable expenditure of parental and/or community resources. In Western democracies, in which women have sought equality of employment opportunities and in which sex is no longer exclusively linked to procreation, the way in which these tasks are distributed raises difficult issues of distributive fairness that are frequently seen as issues of gender equality. Many "intact" families manage these dilemmas through a combination of practical necessity, ongoing negotiations between parents and family members, and "muddling through". Parental separation, however, brings these issues into sharp focus.

That the need to manage these issues usually occurs at a time of increased relationship tension and distress increases the chances that parents will make poor choices. Poor choices include remaining in conflict, resorting to violence, or walking away from parenting responsibilities altogether (Weiss & Willis, 1985). All these responses are linked to a reduction in children's emotional and sometimes physical well-being. When poor responses are of a time-limited nature, children are likely to recover. But sometimes they can be of sufficient intensity and duration to be associated with problems that reach well into future generations. These then become bread-and-butter issues for an army of psychotherapists and mental health professionals who have proliferated in Western democracies.

There is also evidence that ruptures in intimate relationships between parents lead to a shift in reproductive strategies among men—from a focus on parenting to a refocus on mating. Sexual conflict theory posits that males and females have divergent interests in reproduction that are associated with anatomical differences and thereby distinctly different roles. Traits favored by one sex (e.g., multiple mating by males) are sometimes costly to members of the other sex who have traditionally had primary responsibility for prolonged periods of offspring dependency) (Chapman et al., 2003, p. 41).

A good example of this reproductive conflict is evident in "developed" countries. Men are significantly more likely than women to repartner after separation, even in later life (Brown et al., 2019; Raley & Sweeney, 2020). And when they do, they typically repartner with women who are younger than their former partners and are more likely to have children with that new partner. Women not only repartner less often but are less likely to have further children.

From the narrow perspective of the success of a single-family unit, such behaviors seem difficult to reconcile with theories of evolutionary adaptation. From a broader perspective of survival of the species, however, it could be argued that the more important outcome lies in the chances of "superior" mate selection the second time around and "superior" offspring. We are aware of no studies that have empirically examined the superiority of second marriages from this perspective. As researchers and practitioners in the field, however, our instinctive response would be that second marriages are, on average, unlikely to be superior.

Spousal Infidelity

In an extensive cross-cultural study, Betzig (1989) concluded that infidelity ranked with infertility as one of the two most common causes of dissolution of marriages. Public acts of infidelity between parents elicit varying levels of social and moral disapproval. There are substantial cross-cultural variations with respect to tolerance of "mitigating circumstances" (see, e.g., Barrett et al., 2016). But the level of difficulty in obtaining a divorce in many English-speaking countries has in the past been seen to be one method of placing a limit on such activities (Maidment, 1984).

Spousal infidelity (explicit or perceived: sexual, emotional, or both) has been found to be responded to differently by men and women—with (a) men more sensitive to sexual betrayals, (b) women more sensitive to extradyadic emotional involvement (Edmonson, 2011; Mogilski et al., 2019; Shackelford, 1998; Shackelford et al., 2002); and (c) men and women displaying different emotional and behavioral reactions to a partner's infidelity (anger and violent tendencies vs. sadness and the need to affiliate, respectively) (Miller & Maner, 2008). However, drawing on cross-national data from a two-part survey administered to 11 populations (3 urban, 8 small-scale societies), Scelza et al. (2019) suggest that the standard evolutionary psychology perspective of highly charged emotional responses to female infidelity by males might be somewhat simplistic—that it may not be as widespread or invariant as has been previously suggested.

Specifically, these researchers found that when sex and culture were considered in tandem, men *and* women in most of the focal populations were more upset by sexual infidelity. By contrast, in a small number of other populations, both sexes were more distressed by emotional infidelity. The key insight provided by Scelza et al (2019) is that sociocultural factors (e.g., paternal investment and norms for extramarital sex) are potent "contributors to cross-cultural variation in jealous response" (p. 23). Specifically, the greater paternal investment and the lower frequency of extramarital sex, the more severe the jealous response. It is noteworthy that this recent work does indeed conform to the evolutionary prediction that the intensity of jealousy should depend on the male's level of investment.

As noted, unlike most primates, human fathers tend to be heavily invested in the success of their children (Buss 2003). But the degree to which strong feelings such as jealousy manifest themselves may be mediated by norms related to how much involvement the father has in caring directly for his children. Direct father involvement varies widely across human societies (Scelza et al., 2019)[7] and has been shown by Lamb (2013) to be more

---

[7] We are again indebted to Geoff Kushnick for this insight.

influenced by cultural factors than by biology. But irrespective of its form and degree, infidelity frequently acts as a wedge in relationships because, from an evolutionary point of view, it can signal the reallocation of valuable reproductive resources, a lack of commitment to the relationship, and perceived unfairness in a relationship (Shackelford, 1998).

At a more fundamental level, the question as to whether humans evolved to be "faithful" partners or "serial monogamists" has been the subject of much debate among biologists and evolutionary scientists for over a century (Lukas & Clutton-Brock, 2013). For Short (1976), serial monogamy is thought to represent a compromise between our inherited inclination toward polygamy and the need for parental pair-bonding for the benefit of offspring. According to Schacht and Kramer (2019):

> On the one hand, sex differences in reproductive investment, and resultant differing potential reproductive rates, are argued to favor elevated mating effort behavior in males (i.e., a short-term, multiple mate seeking orientation . . .) and polygyny. However, on the other hand, an evolved sexual division of labor, with offspring dependence on paternal care, is argued to generate overlapping interests in long-term, monogamous relationships for both men and women. (p. 1)

Drawing on extensive studies of animal behavior, with particular emphasis on the observation of animal emotions, de Waal (2019) has noted that the well-known ethologist, Konrad Lorenz,

> idealized the life-long pair bonds of his geese. When one of his students pointed out that she'd noticed a few infidelities, she softened the blow by adding that this made geese, "only human". Monogamy or pair bonding is more typical of birds than mammals. In fact, very few primates are monogamous and whether humans truly are is debatable. (p. 41)

Lorenz's student implicitly raises the question of whether "infidelity" might be considered *normal* behavior during the course of cohabitation or marriage. The consensus is that the answer is in the affirmative.[8]

Fisher (1992) has pointed to a body of data, which suggests that humans have evolved a dual reproductive strategy and defined this strategy as lifelong and/or serial monogamy in conjunction with "clandestine adultery."[9] Fisher's (2012) data, moreover, suggest that de Waal's speculation is likely to be substantially correct. Although many humans do form pair-bonds, it is likely that our widespread willingness to couple with individuals other than our partners when opportunities present themselves probably falls somewhere

---

[8] For an interesting discussion on the evolution of social monogamy (where there is pair-bonding but not necessarily fidelity) in mammals in general, see Lukas and Clutton-Brock (2013).

[9] But see Freese's (2000) critique of Fisher's work.

between the more promiscuous behavior of most nonhuman primates and the imperfect faithfulness observed in Lorenz's geese.

That unfaithful behavior is ubiquitous among humans does not mean that when discovered or revealed it is without emotional consequences. Sex between humans is often charged with emotion. Clandestine sexual encounters are often accompanied by additional levels of excitement, simultaneously associated with the riskiness of the encounter. Even among more promiscuous primates, sex at the "wrong" time or in the "wrong" location can be emotionally complex. de Waal (2019, p. 148), for example, has observed that chimpanzees will contrive to have sex away from public view "when a male and female worry about the jealousy of rivals."

The excitement of sex can obscure its reproductive purpose. Infant chimps are raised mainly by their mothers, with fathers having no input into day-to-day nurturing. For the infant to thrive, parental pair-bonding after impregnation is not required. On the other hand, human couples who produce offspring usually have a strong vested interest in safeguarding the bond they have created—a bond strengthened by the sexual activity responsible for the child's existence.

Romantic Rejection-Related Emotions

Perilloux and Buss (2008, p. 166) hypothesized that males are more likely than females to engage in direct "unwanted pursuit behaviors" (e.g., turning up unannounced at an ex-partner's house, stalking online and/or offline, and constant texts and emails) if left by a partner, whereas females are more likely than males to engage in more equivocal methods of pursuit (e.g., leaving phone messages or texts). Higher testosterone levels in males have been hypothesized, in part, to underpin these apparent behavioral differences (DeLeece & Weisfeld, 2016).

Rantala et al. (2018) have suggested that several fitness-enhancing benefits underpinned the adaptive problem of intrusive thoughts about a lost mate. They note that getting locked into endless cycles of maladaptive cognitive-emotional rumination can eventually be a catalyst for insight, reassessment, personal growth, and improving overall relationship and mating intelligence (e.g., avoiding similar mistakes in future relationships and partner choices) (Rantala et al., 2018; see also Morris, 2015; Nesse, 1998). Rumination can also help to better align future mate choices with reassessed self-perceived mate value or desirability, as well as to send a clear message to the leaver that they are loved and wanted—creating the potential to win back the "lost love" (Rantala et al., 2018, p. 608).

Fisher (2004) termed this proclivity for a rejected partner to love the initiator harder after a relationship dissolution "frustration attraction." She pondered the question: "Why did our ancestors evolve brain links to cause us to hate the one we love?" (p. 43). Building on the work of neuroscientist colleagues, she argued that *love hatred*—or *loving hate*, as originally conceptualized by Bollas (1984, p. 43)—is an evolutionary adaptation grounded in the brain's biochemistry and neural circuits, designed ultimately "to enable jilted lovers to extricate themselves and start again." Whereas stress-induced rises in dopamine and norepinephrine accompanied by the suppression of serotonin explain in part the biology of frustration attraction (and the activation of approach-motivation systems), diminishing levels of the former neurotransmitters and rises in the latter lead to feelings of resignation, despair, and depression. Depression, like other emotions, communicates information to others and motivates action by others as well as by those in despair. In the case of depression, withdrawal permits overall functioning to continue, thereby increasing an individual's chances of survival (Plutchik, 2001).

From this perspective, depression can be adaptive in the sense of being something that has evolved because of its positive effects on fitness. It causes an individual to cease investing time and energy into fitness-detrimental behavior and other investments of energy. The "withdrawal" behaviors associated with depression may thus function as a survival-enhancing mechanism (R. M. Nesse, 2000).

Interparental Hatred

Smyth and Moloney (2017) recently made the distinction between two types of hatred found between separated parents: one that arises from responses to separation-related stresses (*reactive hatred*); the other (*entrenched hatred)* indicative of more embedded, dysfunctional, interpersonal dynamics and/or personality structures. They noted that although reactive hatred can interfere with the quality of parenting and parenting negotiations, its time-limited nature makes it amenable to a range of intervention strategies. By contrast, entrenched hatred is more likely to feed continually high levels of entrenched conflict over parenting.

From an evolutionary perspective, reactive hatred occurs for good reasons (as an evolved defensive pattern—as an appropriate and adaptive response to a threat or challenge in the environment[10]) whereas entrenched interparental hatred can be conceptualized as a darker form of mate retention (i.e., a negative attachment).

From within the emerging field of hate studies, Waller (2004) has argued that evolved psychological mechanisms underpin humans' deep capacity for caring, cooperative, compassionate, nonviolent relationships with others. But Waller is also quick to point out that against this "instinctive cooperativeness," "[a]cts of hatred are not beyond, or outside ordinary humanness . . . [and] while an impulse to hate may not be *the* defining characteristics of human nature, such an impulse certainly qualifies—at the very least—as a human capacity" (Waller, 2004, p. 131) (emphasis in original).

For Waller (2004, p. 128), "love, friendship, cooperativeness, nurturance, communication, a sense of fairness, and, even, self-sacrifice"—the things that instill social

[10] See Nesse (1990b, p. 281) for the foundations of the idea of "bad feelings for good reasons."

cohesion—enhanced the adaptive fitness of individuals within a group. But the evolved psychological adaptations of humans also include darker motives (e.g., defining in- and outgroups for the purpose of competing with others for power and control—i.e., "us" or "them"). Recent insights from brain science suggest that humans' universal reasoning circuits are innately hard-wired toward prejudice and ingroup favoritism (Masuda & Fu, 2015). The need to protect the young and females from harm by outgroup members, and to control scarce or valued resources (e.g., water, food, shelter, and land) have an obvious evolutionary basis given that "primate intergroup relations" (including those of our hunter–gatherer ancestors) are typically tense and often hostile (Fishbein, 2004, p. 113). Ingroup favoritism favors survival and reproduction.

Depending on the individuals, the relationship, and cultural context, the ending of an intimate relationship into a new business-like parenting relationship due to divorce can lead to a disorder of perception by one or both partners in which the love object becomes the hated object—that is, from ingroup to outgroup: from all-good to all-bad. In the extreme, an individual's willingness to incur personal costs in the harming of a former partner and their children appears to make little evolutionary sense. That is, even when the perceived costs of a particular course of action outweigh the perceived benefits, individuals consumed by hate may proceed with actions aimed at humiliation or destruction of the other, even to their own detriment. This perhaps explains why some individuals are prepared to bankrupt themselves over the legal costs associated with endless applications over children—or take even more serious or destructive actions.

Evolution and the Problem of Family Violence

For some time now, evolutionary theorists (e.g., Barbaro, 2017; Belsky, 2016; Shackelford et al., 2005; Wilson, 2005) have asked, "What could be the evolved function of, or reason for perpetrating violence against a romantic partner?" Buss (2003), for example, has examined multiple cross-cultural studies of mating behavior, of what keeps intimate partners together, of the nature of intimate partner conflict, and of the conditions that lead to breakup. Drawing on these studies, Buss has posited that male sexual jealousy is a universal phenomenon that spans all these behaviors. Jealousy, he suggests, has evolved as a psychological strategy to protect men's certainty of paternity. At its best, vigilance associated with a degree of "reactive" jealousy (which is typically related to a direct threat to a relationship) can enhance an intimate relationship by signaling to a romantic partner that their partner values the relationship enough to protect it (Buss, 2000)—unlike "anxious" jealousy (which generally occurs in the absence of a direct threat, and is typically negatively related to relationship quality) (Barelds & Barelds-Dijkstra, 2007, p. 176).[11]

[11] The *Oxford Dictionary* defines *vigilance* as "The action or state of keeping careful watch for possible danger or difficulties." We would argue that while excessive vigilance can be destructive of relationships, an absence of vigilance is akin to indifference, a response that is incompatible with the preservation of intimacy.

At its worst, however, when jealousy is associated with unwarranted possessiveness and a sense of entitlement to women's sexuality and reproductive capacity, it can culminate in the perpetration of violence and abuse as a dysfunctional method of retaining possession of a partner (Daly & Wilson, 1988, 2000; Fisher, 2000; Shackelford et al., 2005).

This apparent evolutionary predisposition by males to seek to "control the sexual resources of 'his' female" to ensure his certainty in paternity has also been found among nonhuman primates (Wilson, 2005, p. 296). Specifically, Wilson and Daly (1993) have argued that

> the particular cues and circumstances which inspire men to use violence against their partners reflect a domain-specific masculine psychology which evolved in a social milieu in which assaults and threats of violence functioned to deter wives from pursuing alternative reproductive opportunities, which would have represented consequential threats to husbands' fitness. (p. 290)

More broadly, Wilson and Daly (1993) summarized this line of thinking as follows: "[s]exual competition and cuckoldry risks are potent selection pressures affecting the evolution of psychological mechanisms and processes" (p. 276). They go on to suggest that whether it be through infidelity or desertion, the loss of control of female reproductive capacity and concomitant loss of ground in the reproductive competition between men can act as a powerful force in the threat or use of male violence.

There are clear legal and moral problems in justifying this pattern of jealousy and control just because it is naturally "common". Reflecting on this potential problem, Buss (2003) suggested that

> because there is an evolutionary origin for male sexual jealousy does not mean that we must condone or perpetuate it. Judgments of what *should* exist rest with people's value systems, not with science or with what currently exists. (p. 17 (emphasis added))

Consistent with this, a fundamental insight of human behavioral ecology is that biological factors in tandem with a given ecological context and cultural norms shape human behavior in the pursuit of optimizing inclusive fitness.[12] To put it succinctly, neither our genes nor our evolutionary history dictates human destiny. As Harari (2015) suggests, we are animals with imagination. The glue that holds human families, tribes, and nation-states together is in part at least a product of this imaginary capacity. So too are our values, as well as the laws that both guide our behavior and act as a brake on our tendency to harm those whom we see as threats.

---

[12] We are grateful, Geoff Kushnick for pointing this out.

Instincts, Emotions, and Reason

In this section, we point to key studies that demonstrate the importance of emotions in animal behavior and survival, focusing mainly on chimpanzees, our nearest living relatives. Having noted the close similarity of human emotions to those of chimpanzees, we consider evidence pointing to the critical role of these inherited emotions in human negotiations and human decision-making.

Animal Studies

According to Coates (1998), Pythagoreans believed that animals experience the same range of emotions as humans. This would probably not surprise the majority of dog owners or those who continue to live in societies in close daily contact with animals. The early 20th century, however, saw a surge in research into animal behavior in the stimulus–response tradition of Pavlov and parallel studies into human behavior in the tradition of B. F. Skinner. These reductionist approaches to understanding behavior leave little or no room for the consideration of internally driven motivations or inner states. The core argument made by the behaviorist school has been: what cannot be objectively measured is unworthy of scientific inquiry.

Since the latter part of the 20th century, however, we have witnessed an explosion of research into animal behaviors, in which internal states and motivations are inferred from persistent and long-term observations. During this period, ethologists in general and primatologists in particular increasingly recognized the value of what de Waal (2019, p. 2) termed "holistic observation" or "pattern recognition" research into animal behaviors. This form of analysis has moved far beyond stimulus–response models of learning. It assumes that each species has its own ways of processing and acting on information. Importantly, it also assumes that behaviors exhibited have meanings that are comprehended by those of the same species, and quite possibly by other species.

The holistic and pattern recognition research referred to by de Waal also recognizes the limitations of observations of individual behaviors and the need to consider how behaviors are understood and responded to within a social group. This approach has parallels to the systemic models of intervention in the mental health field that were pioneered by family therapists such as Salvador Minuchin in the 1960s. Systemic models are focused on relationships and relationship patterns and the reciprocal nature of interactions between individuals in families and other social groups. Systemic approaches also assume that the therapist or researcher is part of the system being observed and as such will have an influence on that system.

Looking back over roughly half a century, it is sometimes difficult to appreciate the profound limitations that strictly behaviorist approaches brought to the study of both animal and human behavior. Goodall, for example, reports being criticized for "contaminating" her data by giving names to the animals she was studying and by inserting *herself* inside the research. The dominant research model at the time reflected a Cartesian presumption of a mind–body split. As noted below, this has led to much misunderstanding about how humans process information and make decisions. It was also consistent with a common belief that animals could not "think"—that they were essentially automatons, whose behaviors reflected basic instincts that were largely immutable.

Though Darwin had demonstrated that all animals, including humans, were linked through evolutionary processes, there has been widespread visceral resistance to the idea that human beings are different only in degree. Until presented with formal evidence from pioneer ethologists, it has remained easier for many to believe that even animals with whom we shared the vast majority of our genes were qualitatively different to humans in the way they responded to the world around them and to each other.

The work of ethologists, such as de Waal, has provided increasingly convincing evidence of the sophistication of chimpanzee politics (de Waal, 1982), negotiating skills (de Waal, 1989), and capacity to empathize (de Waal, 2009). Following these analyses, de Waal (2016) has gone on to ask the provocative (if rhetorical) question: *Are we smart enough to know how smart animals are*? Recent work (de Waal, 2019) goes further by exploring what animal emotions can teach us about ourselves. Via observations that are repeated, persistent and holistic, de Waal provides multiple examples of animal behaviors, some in unstructured situations and some in carefully controlled experiments. He leaves us in no doubt that many animals lead richly nuanced emotional lives.

The conclusion reached by de Waal (2019, p. 277) is that though it can be argued that there is as yet no formal framework allowing for the formal study of animal emotions, it is clear that emotions are "how we operate and how most animals operate." "For me," he notes, "the question has never been whether animals have emotions but how science could have overlooked them for so long" (de Waal, 2019, p. 277).

In a key summary statement of his overarching approach, de Waal (2019) suggested:

> The possibility that animals experience emotions the way we do makes many hard-nosed scientists feel queasy, partly because animals never report any feelings, and partly because the existence of feelings presupposes a level of consciousness that these scientists are unwilling to grant to animals. But considering how much animals act like us, share our physiological reactions, have the same facial expressions, and possess the same sorts of brains, wouldn't it be strange indeed if their internal experiences were radically different? (p. 277)

Human Feeling, Thinking, and Decision-Making

From an evolutionary perspective, Randall Nesse (1998) asked a key question that speaks to an issue at the heart of negotiation and decision-making when separated parents are in dispute about the care of their children. "Wouldn't separating parents be better off," he asked, "if they were simply more rational?" The tongue-in-cheek question appears to be designed to elicit a negative or at the least a qualified response. But why?

After reviewing key empirical studies of child focused decision-making, Schaffer (1998) concluded:

> When one examines individual incidents of decision making [about children] and attempts to unravel the factors responsible for the course of action adopted, it soon becomes evident that we are confronted with a highly complex, frequently obscure and far from rational process. (p. 2)

A little earlier, Damasio (1994) recognized the profoundly significant implications of "Descartes' Error" (as he named it), the dualist assumption that called for the separation of mind and body, or more practically speaking, the elevation of rationality over emotion. As part of his evidence, Damasio cited the now well-known case of "Elliot," who was suffering from a problem with chronic indecision. Elliot had had a tumor removed from the cortex near the frontal lobe of his brain. Although his IQ remained the same following the operation, Elliot found himself endlessly deliberating over the most trivial of details. For Elliot, the simple act of choosing a meal in a restaurant had become a practical impossibility. His inability to make up his mind led to the termination of his employment. He made numerous attempts to start new businesses, all of which were unsuccessful. Eventually Elliot's wife divorced him.

Puzzled by these events, Damasio, a neurobiologist, conducted a series of tests from which he concluded that regardless of the stimulus presented to him, Elliot showed no physical reaction. He could feel nothing. At the time, the conventional wisdom was that superior decision-making relied on the exercise of reason and that the sound exercise of reason required that emotions be ignored or kept firmly in check. The classic behavioral image promoted by many philosophers, scientists, and psychotherapists had been that of the charioteer working to keep a tight rein on his potentially errant horses. Damasio's conclusion, however, was that the relationship between these metaphorical horses and drivers was more complex. Emotions were a critical part of our decision-making processes. A brain without feeling was incapable of making up its mind.

The critical role of emotions was also explored by Kahneman and Tversky, who demonstrated that contrary to the dominant economic theories at the time, the choices made in this domain are far from rational. In 2002, Kahneman won a Nobel Prize[13] for demonstrating that, as Voss and Raz (2016, p. 11) put it, "Feeling is a form of thinking." He was later to describe the intuitive, emotionally informed "fast thinking" as part of our evolutionary legacy, a part that was essential for our survival (Kahneman, 2011).

A little earliert, Lehrer (2009), a neurobiologist, had drawn together much of the evidence pointing to the mechanisms governing what he called "The decisive moment."

---

[13] Tversky died in 1996.

Lehrer too pointed to the critical role of feelings in human thinking processes. He concluded (Lehrer 2009 p. 131) that by failing to acknowledge the role of emotions, we find ourselves "choking on thought." In the highly challenging world of hostage negotiations, Voss and Raz (2016) came to a similar conclusion. When the stakes were almost unimaginably high, Voss and Raz (2016, p. 50) came to adopt a mantra that "Emotions are not the obstacles; they are the means."

In a series of experiments, Lieberman et al. (2007) found that looking at faces that were expressing strong emotions prompted activity in the amygdala—the part of our brain known to generate fear. But *naming* the emotion prompted activity in parts of the brain associated with rational thinking, making space for responses that are more reflective and more capable of modification.

In this section, we have done no more than scratch the surface of studies in animal and human behavior that point to the critical role of emotions in human decision-making. Our central argument, developed in the next section, is that legal processes, which increasingly come into play at the more seriously conflicted end of the spectrum of parenting disputes, struggle with acknowledging emotions or ignore them altogether.

The neurological evidence, however, suggests that far from making things worse—a common fear among many practitioners in the field of family law—the act of gently but firmly and empathically identifying strong emotions can modify their intensity and simultaneously open up possibilities for self-reflection and positive change. We next address how we might make use of this knowledge in a no-fault family law environment in which parents find themselves in high conflict over their children.

Reason, Emotions, and No-Fault Divorce

For more than a century, the key objective of divorce laws in Western democracies had been the preservation of social stability via the preservation of marriage and the control of sexuality (Star, 1996). No-fault divorce in Western jurisdictions was a response to major social developments such as growing employment opportunities for women and changing sexual mores, which were in turn propelled by the increasing availability of reliable contraception (Moloney et al., 2013). The 1960s ushered in the overt privileging of personal relationships and personal desire. The underpinning philosophy was captured by Swain's (2012) commentary on the growing social mores of the time, "If you want to be free, be free" (p. 1).

Over a period of less than two decades no-fault divorce laws were enacted in most Western democracies amidst fierce political debates. On one side of the political fence were those who argued that fault-focused divorce proceedings were damaging the institution of marriage and were the *cause* of ongoing vindictiveness, indignity, and hatred. On the other side were commentators who were convinced that no-fault divorce would lead to the unraveling of necessary societal constraints. In the Australian Parliament, for example, one senior politician suggested that "no fault" divorce would lead to an inevitable descent into "barnyard morality" (Finlay, 1970, p. 4).

Moloney (2014) has argued that in the 1960s and 1970s, the belief that divorce could—and should—be simplified became confused with a belief that the resolution of issues over money and children could be similarly streamlined. This was in turn accompanied by much unrealistically optimistic thinking about how these matters would be dealt with. The optimism was well captured in a press release, which accompanied the opening of the Family Court of Australia in 1976. The statement spoke of "sweeping away the laws and procedures of the past and providing a new era of calmness and rationality, presided over by specialist judges assisted by experts and which would introduce speedy, less expensive and less formal procedures" (cited in Fogarty, 2006, p. 4).

Of course, calmness and rationality are typically in short supply in the early stages of the breakdown of an intimate, emotionally bonded partnership. Indeed, an intimate relationship breakdown devoid of emotions would generally be thought of as highly unusual. We have already noted the evidence pointing to the fact that a year or so after separating, most Australian parents report that they are managing their post-separation relationships reasonably well. But the longitudinal data would suggest that at any given point in time, about one in five separated parents are in high conflict with each other and/or are attempting to resolve matters through the continued exercise of coercive control.

Emotions tend to be poorly managed by highly conflicted parents, many of whom continue to use up an inordinate proportion of court resources and services (Neff & Cooper, 2004; Smyth & Moloney, 2017). One result is that courts dealing with separation and divorce in most Western jurisdictions suffer from chronic delays, especially with respect to the resolution of disputes over children. In Australia, for example, unsatisfactory delays in hearing disputes over children have been a part of the Family Law Courts' experience for most of its 45 years. This has been the case despite numerous attempts at reform and despite—or perhaps because of—the increasing complexity and size of the legislation.

In our view, the reason most parenting disputes remain unresolved is only loosely linked to the pragmatics and endless debates about parenting time and living arrangements, the issues that mainly occupy family lawyers and courts. In our view, entrenched disputes are mainly driven by the reluctance of parents and their advisors to engage constructively (and nonadversarially) with the dispute's emotional drivers. We suggest that this reluctance springs partly from an overly naïve optimism that informed the philosophy underpinning no-fault divorce in the first place. As Ingleby (1989, p. 13) put it, "[e]motions are not contingent on legal rules for their existence." At a more fundamental level, we suggest that the mainstream approach to no-fault divorce exposes a misunderstanding about both the neurological importance of human emotions and their association with our evolutionary origins.

Our evidence for this lies in our familiarity with countless affidavits and related legal documents over many years. These reveal that although the language in parents' documents are frequently emotive, the emotions themselves are typically dismissed as irrelevant or, when referred to, are used in adversarial debate as weapons against "the other side." As Griffith (1986, p. 155) neatly put it: "[l]awyers and clients are in effect largely occupied with two different divorces: lawyers with a legal divorce, clients with a social and emotional divorce." Lawyers would appear to have few effective tools for dealing with this discrepancy. Perhaps this is why after considering the unanticipated consequences of no-fault divorce, Ingleby (1989) came to the following conclusion:

> The solicitor's function might be seen as *controlling* the feelings of anger held by one or both of the parties until such emotions have been mollified by the passage of time, the nature of the dispute being thereby changed. (p. 9 (emphasis added))

Taking adequate account of emotions is also largely absent from the process or arriving at court-based judgments about post separation parenting arrangemens. Instead, we almost invariably find a tortuous sequencing of "rational" arguments in children's cases, behind which are what Herring (1999) described as "strained judicial reasoning." As one Australian judicial officer (Reithmuller, 2015) wryly remarked, making a decision in a parenting dispute is merely a matter of engaging with "42 easy steps." More colorfully, O'Brien (2010), another judicial officer, likened the process to that of trying to follow the wiring diagram for the F-111, Australia's extremely complex and notoriously unreliable "swing wing" fighter bomber. Our point here is that decision-making about children requires a level of contextually based, tacit knowledge that transcends the detached rationality of current legal processes.

Valuing and responding appropriately to emotions are unfortunately also absent from many of the approaches to mediation, "alternative dispute resolution," and other facilitative practices that have been increasingly employed by family law systems to assist in managing or resolving parenting disputes. Though experienced mediators such as Parkinson (2011) in the UK, and Bowling and Hoffman (2003) in the United States, have spoken of mediation being both a left-brain (logical and sequential) and right-brain (connecting, holistic intuitive) activity, the reality for many *family* mediators is that they operate in an environment in which resources are scarce and in which they feel pressure to achieve "results" in a short space of time. In this pressured environment, many mediators feel safer and less potentially "out of control" by advising clients to leave their emotions at the door.

Back to Basics: Acknowledging Emotions in Separation and Divorce

Whereas human relationship formation and mating behavior have featured strongly in the evolutionary psychology literature, relationship dissolution appears to reside in the margins. This contrasts with studying "unfaithful" behavior or bond severance in a range of other pair-bonding species (Morris et al., 2015). In this chapter, we have suggested that in a culture that privileges personal relationships over the collective good, understanding and responding to the emotional responses we have inherited as a species is an important aspect of working constructively with the dynamics of parental separation – both for the sake of the parents themselves and for the sake of the children.

In this penultimate section, we briefly address the question of how those aiming to assist separating families might better acknowledge and work *with* this critical part of our evolutionary history rather than attempt to ignore or suppress it. We begin by considering the place of emotions in those cases in which parental conflict is not accompanied by threats of violence. We then ask whether there is a legitimate or useful place to work with emotions in cases of violence and abuse.

Our proposition is that an important but underrecognized legacy of no-fault divorce has been a general wariness to acknowledge or work with the emotional component of relationship breakdown and post-separation disputes. We have pointed to neurological evidence, which postdates no-fault divorce, that decision-making without access to our emotions is impossible. Having worked in the field for many years, we understand the volatile nature of many parental separations. Much is at stake. We appreciate that the fear expressed by many separated parents and by those who set out to help them is that expression of emotions will quickly lead to matters spinning out of control.

Our argument, however, stems from the paradoxical truth—implicitly or formally understood by generations of experienced therapists (e.g., Greenberg et al., 1993; Rogers, 1942), and mediators (e.g., Folger & Bush, 1994; Hoffman, 2003), as well as a more recent generation of negotiators (e.g., Voss & Raz, 2016) and neurobiologists (e.g., Lehrer, 2009; Lieberman et al 2007)—that by labeling negative emotions, we help to diffuse them. We are suggesting that in divorce proceedings, empathic assistance to name an emotion can elicit a sense of relief and create a greater capacity for self-reflection as well as recognition and perhaps even forgiveness of the other. This in turn can increase the chances that conflict can be managed or resolved.

The skills of empathic reflection (or what Voss and Raz, 2016, has referred to as "mirroring") need of course to be learned and practiced. For example, the outward emotional expression might be one of anger whereas the underlying feeling might be sadness, frustration, or fear. In making decisions and managing conflict, the human species' extensive vocabulary acts as both an advantage and a limitation when we compare ourselves with our chimpanzee relatives. With more limited linguistic abilities, we suspect that chimpanzees (and perhaps many other animals) are more naturally skillful at instantly recognizing and responding "intuitively" to a broad range of emotions.

Turning to the question of violence and abuse, it is important to recognize that during the period when no-fault divorce was being legislated for in Western democracies, these issues were being given very little attention. It was as if the excesses of fault-focused divorce regimes (and there had been many) needed first to be purged from the system. In addition, however, data on family violence and abuse were limited at that time. There were "voices in the wilderness" drawing attention to violence and abuse within families (e.g., Helfer & Kempe, 1976; Pizzey, 1973; Scutt, 1983; Walker, 1979). But these had little impact in the family law space until roughly the turn of the century. It was "news" for many, for example, that when drawing on a nationwide Australian sample of 650 individuals, 80% of whom were parents, Wolcott and Hughes (1999) found that 24% of women (though only 4% of men) reported abusive behaviors as the main reason for seeking a divorce. Shortly afterward, when reflecting on their own empirical work, Brown et al. (2001) declared that family violence had become "core business" in Australia's family courts. From roughly the mid-1990s onward, similar data and conclusions were being reported across all Western democracies.

In the years that have followed, a broad consensus has emerged with respect to issues such as structural imbalances, gender norms and stereotypes, social and economic exclusion, financial pressures, misuse of substances, mental health difficulties, and a range of personal experiences that contribute to family violence and abuse in complex interlocking ways. When expressed as a form of intimate terrorism, however, an especially dangerous form of violence (see Johnson, 2006), there is wide consensus that this is a primarily gendered phenomenon in which the male partner is largely motivated by the need to exercise coercive control.

Such expressions of violence and abuse are typically accompanied by extreme expressions of our inherited emotions—jealousy-fueled anger being perhaps the most common motivator. Though this and its evolutionary origins can add to our understanding of the behavior, such understanding cannot be a substitute for the exercise of moral behavior. Regardless of its root cause, coercive violence must first be stopped. To do this in a timely and effective manner, legal processes can be critical. Although there may be "mitigating circumstances" along the lines noted above, the role of law is clearly to offer protection as its priority and consider the possibility of appropriate penalties. Engagement with the perpetrator might then occur within the context of these interventions.

An example of this process was provided by Johnston et al. (2009), who cited part of a statement delivered by a judicial officer in the U.S. context:

> Mr R, what you have done to your wife is a criminal act under the laws of this state . . . and there are consequences that the Court is bound to impose. . . . Living in a violent home is bad for children. Mr R, I hear you when you say that you love your wife and children, that you are sorry for what you did and that you have promised not to do that again. The Court is going to help you keep that promise . . . first, by providing your family with protection until it can be sure that you are no longer a danger, and that you can show you are no longer a danger; secondly by providing you an opportunity to manage your anger better and to resolve conflict in a non-violent way; and third, by providing you and your children a safe place to visit together, where they will not be afraid, and you will be given an opportunity to show that you have a loving relationship with your son and daughter. (p. 27)

In this statement, the judicial officer has rightly focused primarily on structural arrangements designed to ensure that a mother and her children remain safe. But somewhat unusually, he has also made reference to an emotion that in his view is driving the father's unacceptable behavior. The important issue here is not whether the judicial officer is accurate in suggesting that the driving emotion is anger. Rather, the important issue is that the court is offering this father an opportunity to meaningfully reengage with his children by working with a practitioner who will assist him to accurately label the emotion and consider its meaning and consequences.

A good practitioner will be familiar with the range of emotions that men can experience during a separation. The practitioner's role is not to collude with the view that such intense emotions must inevitably lead to violence. "She made me do it" is not an acceptable response. But the practitioner *can* label the emotion - fearlessly, accurately, and empathically. In the context of forming an accepting relationship with the practitioner, there is every chance that this father will own his emotions, find a better way of expressing them, and come to better understand what they are telling him. Perhaps it is not too fanciful to suggest that such a father might also be encouraged to consider the work of a primatologist like de Waal (2009, 2019) who illuminated some of the origins of these emotions and demonstrated how they generally serve rather than sabotage the interests of our close primate cousins.

Future Directions

Evolutionary perspectives appear germane in several emerging areas of post-separation parenting research. For example, the idea that entrenched interparental hatred after relationship breakdown may be a darker form of mate retention warrants empirical investigation. Like love, hate is an intense, complex emotion comprising an amalgam of many other more easily defined and well-recognized emotions such as fear, shame, envy, humiliation, anger, rage, sadness, disgust, and contempt (Ben-Ze'ev, 2001). Its all-consuming nature after separation can overwhelm parents' ability to act in their children's best interests. On first blush, the inclusive fitness of interparental hatred is not obvious. But the capacity of such base emotions to invoke a potent negative attachment is likely to have evolutionary origins, which thus far remain unexplored.

Another important area to be explored is that of the intersection of mental health issues—particularly personality disorders and relationship breakdown. In a landmark longitudinal study of high-conflict families conducted in California through the 1980s, Johnston and Campbell (1988, p. 15) found that a "large proportion" of the families in their study "had indicators of personality disorder according to the DSM–III" classification system. Personality disorders can have substantial social consequences for individuals, especially with regard to relationship discord. For instance, compared to individuals who have not been diagnosed with a personality disorder, those with such a diagnosis have been shown to be less likely to marry, more likely to marry early, and more likely to experience divorce (Whisman et al., 2007).

Kelly (2003) has noted that mental health issues in the context of family law parenting disputes can be a dangerous combination, giving troubled individuals new opportunities to engage in adversarial and other conflictual actions. While some research on personality disorders from an evolutionary perspective has been conducted (e.g., Millon & Davis, 1996; Rushton et al., 2008), more detailed work is needed in the context of post-separation parenting.[14]

The "digital divorce" is another important line of inquiry worthy of investigation. Separated parents, like their still-together counterparts, are increasingly making use of digital technologies (e.g., smartphones, tablets, and computers) to manage co-parenting (see, e.g., Dworkin et al., 2016). These technologies are rapidly transforming communication within families and creating new ways for family members to connect with—and disconnect from—each other (Caughlin et al., 2016; Neustaedter et al., 2013). On the darker side of post-separation parenting, technologically mediated communication can be yet another tool for one parent to harass, humiliate, and punish the other parent after separation. New modes of criminality (e.g., cyberabuse, cyberbullying, and cyberstalking) are thus emerging in the context of technology-facilitated abuse (Smyth et al., 2020)—making it urgent to explain and predict both positive and negative forms of digital communication between separated parents.

To sum up: post-separation family life offers a rich context for understanding how our evolved human psychology both leads to and impacts on parental separation. In a rapidly changing world, the increasingly complex and fluid nature of post-separation family life presents many new challenges. We therefore think those in the business of supporting separating parents to find more positive and less destructive family transitions can learn much by reflecting on the evolutionary forces that drive both coupling and uncoupling.

In particular, our inherited neurobiology, which is at the heart of decision-making in our species, points to the importance of accepting and responding appropriately to the emotional drivers of moving toward and moving away from close and intimate relationships. Probably more than ever before, separation and divorce have become untethered from social expectations and from clear social rules about how we should act. The freedom this bestows is in part liberating and in part illusory. This is because despite too many acts of barbarity toward each other over the millennia, we, like many other species, have mainly survived by remaining social animals who do best when caring for and caring about each other.

---

[14] See also the work on "spousal personality attributes that signal trouble for a marriage" reported by Shackelford and Buss (1997, p. 12).

References

Amato, P. R., Meyers, C. E., & Emery, R. E. (2009). Changes in nonresident father-child contact from 1976 to 2002. *Family Relations, 58*(1), 41–53.

Apostolou, M., Constantinou, C., & Anagnostopoulos, S. (2019). Reasons that could lead people to divorce in an evolutionary perspective: Evidence from Cyprus. *Journal of Divorce & Remarriage, 60*, 27–46.

Archer-Kuhn, B. (2018). Domestic violence and high conflict are not the same: A gendered analysis. *Journal of Social Welfare and Family Law, 40*(2), 216–233.

Arditti, J. A., & Allen, K. R. (1993). Understanding distressed fathers' perceptions of legal and relational inequities postdivorce. *Family and Conciliation Courts Review, 31*(4), 461–476.

Australian Bureau of Statistics. (2015). *Family characteristics and transitions, 2012–13* (Catalogue No. 4442.0). ABS.

Australian Bureau of Statistics. (2018). *Marriages and divorces, Australia, 2018* (Catalogue No. 3310.0). ABS.

Barbaro, N. (2017, September 21). How can evolutionary psychology help explain intimate partner violence? *Behavioral Scientist.* https://behavioralscientist.org/can-evolutionary-psychology-help-explain-intimate-partner-violence/

Barelds, D. P. H., & Barelds-Dijkstra, P. (2007). Relations between different types of jealousy and self and partner perceptions of relationships quality. *Clinical Psychology and Psychotherapy, 14*, 176–188.

Barrett, H. C., Bolyanatz, A., Crittenden, A. N., Fessler, D. M. T., Fitzpatrick, S., Gurven, M., Henrich, J., Kanovsky, M., Kushnick, G., Pisor, A., Scelza, B., Stich, S., von Rueden, C., Zhao, W., & Laurence, S. (2016). Small-scale societies exhibit fundamental variation in the role of intentions in moral judgment. *Proceedings of the National Academy of Sciences, USA, 113*(7), 4688–4693.

Bartlett, K., & Scott, E. (2014). Child custody decision making. *Law and Contemporary Problems, 77*(1), i–vii.

Bell, M. (2013). *Hard feelings: The moral psychology of contempt.* Oxford University Press.

Belsky, J. (2016). Marital violence in evolutionary perspective. In A. Booth, A. C. Crouter, M. L. Clements, & T. Boone-Holladay (Eds.), *Couples in conflict* (Classic ed., pp. 27–55). Routledge.

Ben-Ze'ev, A. (2001). *The subtlety of emotions.* MIT Press.

Betzig, L. (1989). Causes of conjugal dissolution: A cross-cultural study. *Current Anthropology, 30*(5), 654–676.

Birnbaum, R., & Bala, N. (2010). Toward the differentiation of high-conflict families: An analysis of social science research and Canadian case law. *Family Court Review, 48*, 403–416.

Blankenhorn, D. (1995). *Fatherless America.* Basic Books.

Bollas, C. (1984). Loving hate. *Annual of Psychoanalysis, 12/13*, 221–237.

Bowling, D., & Hoffman, D. (Eds.). (2003). *Bringing peace into the room: How the personal qualities of the mediator impact the process of conflict resolution.* John Wiley & Sons.

Brown, S. L., Lin, I., Hammersmith, A. M., & Wright, M. R. (2019). Repartnering following gray divorce: The roles of resources and constraints for women and men. *Demography, 56*, 503–523.

Brown, T., Frederico, M., Hewitt, L., & Sheehan, R. (2001). The child abuse and divorce myth. *Child Abuse Review, 10*(2), 113–124.

Buchanan, M. C., O'Hair, H. D., & Becker, J. A. (2006). Strategic communication during marital relationship dissolution: Disengagement resistance strategies. *Communication Research Reports, 23*(3), 139–147.

Buss, D. M. (1988). From vigilance to violence: Tactics of mate retention in American undergraduates. *Ethology and Sociobiology, 9*(5), 291–317.

Buss, D. M. (2000). *The dangerous passion: Why jealousy is as necessary as love and sex.* Free Press.

Buss, D. M. (2003). *The evolution of desire. Strategies of human mating.* Basic Books.

Buss, D. M., Goetz, C., Duntley, J. D., Asao, K., & Conroy-Beam, D. (2017). The mate switching hypothesis. *Personality and Individual Differences, 104*, 143–149.

Buss, D. M., & Schmitt, D. P. (1993). Sexual strategies theory: An evolutionary perspective on human mating. *Psychological Review, 100*(2), 204–232.

Caughlin, J. P., Basinger, E. D., & Sharabi, L. L. (2016). The connections between communication technologies and relational conflict: A multiple goals and communication interdependence perspective. In J. Samp (Ed.), *Communicating interpersonal conflict in close relationships: Contexts, challenges, and opportunities* (pp. 73–88). Routledge.

Chapman, T., Arnqvist, G., Bangham, J., & Rowe, L. (2003). Sexual conflict. *Trends in Ecology & Evolution, 18*(1), 41–47.

Coates, P. (1998). *Nature: Western attitudes since ancient times.* University of California Press.

Daly, M., & Wilson, M. (1988). Evolutionary social psychology and family homicide. *Science, 242*(4878), 519–524.

Daly, M., & Wilson, M. (2000). The evolutionary psychology of marriage and divorce. In L. J. Waite & C. Bachrach (Eds.), *The ties that bind: Perspectives on marriage and cohabitation* (pp. 91–110). Aldine de Gruyter.

Damasio, A. (1994). *Descartes' error: Emotion, reason, and the human brain.* G. P. Putnam's Sons.

Dawkins, R. (1990). *The selfish gene* (2nd ed.). Oxford University Press.

De Maio, J., Kaspiew, R., Smart, D., Dunstan, J., & Moore, J. (2013). *Survey of Recently Separated Parents: A study of parents who separated prior to the implementation of the Family Law Amendment (Family Violence and Other Matters) Act 2011.* Attorney-General's Department, Canberra.

de Waal, F. (1982). *Chimpanzee politics.* Jonathan Cape.

de Waal, F. (1989). *Peacemaking among primates.* Harvard University Press.

de Waal, F. (2009). *The age of empathy. Nature's lessons for a kinder society.* Harmony Books.

de Waal, F. (2016). *Are we smart enough to know how smart animals are?* W. W. Norton.

de Waal, F. (2019). *Mamma's last hug: Animal emotions and what they teach us about ourselves.* W. W. Norton.

DeLecce, T., & Weisfeld, G. (2016). An evolutionary explanation for sex differences in nonmarital breakup experiences. *Adaptive Human Behavior and Physiology, 2*(3), 234–251.

Demby, S. (2009). Interparental hatred and its impact on parenting: Assessment in forensic custody evaluations. *Psychoanalytic Inquiry, 29*, 477–490.

Demby, S. (2017). Commentary on entrenched postseparation parenting disputes: The role of interparental hatred. *Family Court Review: An Interdisciplinary Journal, 55*, 417–423.

Dugatkin, L. A. (1997). *Cooperation among animals.* Oxford University Press.

Dworkin, J., McCann, E., & McGuire, J. K. (2016). Coparenting in the digital era: Exploring divorced parents' use of technology. In G. Gianesini & S. L. Blair (Eds.), *Divorce, separation, and remarriage: Vol. 10. The transformation of family* (Contemporary Perspectives in Family Research) (pp. 279–298). Emerald Group.

Edmonson, K. L. (2011). *An evolutionary psychology perspective on responsibility attributions for infidelity and relationship dissolution* [Master's theses digitization project. 3318]. California State University, San Bernardino. https://scholarworks.lib.csusb.edu/etd-project/3318

Ellis, E. M. (2000). *Divorce wars: Interventions with families in conflict.* American Psychiatric Association Press.

Emery, R. E. (2012). *Renegotiating family relationships: Divorce, child custody, and mediation* (2nd ed.). Guilford Press.

Fine, M. A., & Sacher, J. A. (1997). Predictors of distress following relationship termination among dating couples. *Journal of Social and Clinical Psychology, 16*(4), 381–388.

Finlay, H. A. (1970). Divorce law reform: The Australian approach. *Journal of Family Law, 10*, 1–14.

Fishbein, H. D. (2004). The genetic/evolutionary basis of prejudice and hatred. *Journal of Hate Studies, 3*(1), 113–119.

Fisher, H. E. (1992). *Anatomy of love: The natural history of monogamy, adultery, and divorce.* Simon & Schuster.

Fisher, H. E. (2000). Lust, attraction, attachment: Biology and evolution of the three primary emotion systems for mating, reproduction, and parenting. *Journal of Sex Education and Therapy, 25*(1), 96–104.

Fisher, H. E. (2004). Dumped! *New Scientist, 181*(2434), 40–43.

Fisher, H. E. (2012). Serial monogamy and clandestine adultery: Evolution and consequences of the dual human reproductive strategy. In S. C. Roberts (Ed.), *Applied evolutionary psychology* (pp. 93–111). Oxford University Press.

Fogarty, J. (2006). Thirty years of change. *Australian Family Lawyer, 18*(4), 4–15.

Folger, J., & Bush, R. B. (1994). *The promise of mediation. Responding to conflict through empowerment and recognition.* Jossey-Bass.

Freese, J. (2000). *What should sociology do about Darwin? Evaluating some potential contributions of sociobiology and evolutionary psychology to sociology* [Unpublished doctoral dissertation]. Indiana University.

Friedman, D. (1995). *Towards a structure of indifference. The social origins of maternal custody.* Aldine de Gruyter.

Goodall, J. (1990). *Through a window: My thirty years with the chimpanzees of Gombe.* Houghton Mifflin.

Greenberg, L. S., Rice, L. N., & Elliot, R. (1993). *Facilitating emotional change: The moment-by-moment process.* Guilford Press.

Griffiths, J. (1986). What do Dutch lawyers actually do in divorce cases? *Law and Society Review, 20*, 135–175.

Harari, Y. (2015). *Sapiens: A brief history of humankind.* Vintage Books.

Hardesty, J. L., & Chung, G. H. (2006). Intimate partner violence, parental divorce, and child custody: Directions for intervention and future research. *Family Relations, 55*(2), 200–210.

Helfer, R. E., & Kempe, C. H. (Eds.). (1976). *Child abuse and neglect: The family and the community.* Ballinger.

Herring, J. (1999). The welfare principle and the rights of parents. In A. Bainham, S. D. Sclater, & M. Richards (Eds.), *What is a parent? A socio-legal analysis* (pp. 89–106). Hart.

Hewitt, B. (2008). *Marriage breakdown in Australia: Social correlates, gender and initiator status* (FaHCSIA Social Policy Research Paper No. 35). Australian Bureau of Statistics, Department of Families, Housing, Community Services and Indigenous Affairs.

Hoffman, D. (2003). Paradoxes of mediation. In D. Bowling & D. Hoffman (Eds.), *Bringing peace into the room: How the personal qualities of the mediator impact the process of conflict resolution* (pp.167–182). Jossey-Bass.

Horn, W. F., & Sylvester, T. (2002). *Father facts* (4th ed.). National Fatherhood Initiative, USA.

Humphreys, K. L., Myint, M. T., & Zeanah, C. H. (2020). Increased risk for family violence during the COVID-19 pandemic. *Pediatrics, 145*(4), Article e20200982.

Ingleby, R. (1989). Matrimonial breakdown and the legal process: The limitations of no-fault divorce. *Law and Policy, 11*(1) 1–16.

Johnson, M. P. (1995). Patriarchal terrorism and common couple violence: Two forms of violence against women. *Journal of Marriage and the Family, 57,* 283–294.

Johnson, M. P. (2006). Conflict and control: Gender symmetry and asymmetry in domestic violence. *Violence Against Women, 12*(11), 1003–1018.

Johnston, J. R. (1994). High-conflict divorce. *Future of Children: Children and Divorce, 4*(1), 165–182.

Johnston, J. R., & Campbell, L. E. G. (1988). *Impasses of divorce: The dynamics and resolution of family conflict.* Free Press.

Johnston, J. R., Roseby, V., & Kuehnle, K. (2009). *In the name of the child. A developmental approach to understanding and helping children of conflicted and violent divorce.* Springer.

Juby, H., Le Bourdais, C., & Marcil-Gratton, N. (2004). *When parents separate: Further findings from the National Longitudinal Survey of Children and Youth.* Department of Justice.

Kahneman, D. (2011). *Thinking, fast and slow.* Macmillan.

Kaspiew, R., Carson, R., Qu, L., Horsfall, B., Tayton, S., Moore, S., Coulson, M., & Dunstan, J. (2015). *Court Outcomes Project: Evaluation of the 2012 Family Violence Amendments.* Australian Institute of Family Studies.

Kaspiew, R., Gray, M., Weston, R., Moloney, L., Hand, K., Qu, L., & the Family Law Evaluation Team. (2009). *Evaluation of the 2006 family law reforms.* Australian Institute of Family Studies.

Kelly, J. B. (2003). Parents with enduring child disputes: Multiple pathways to enduring disputes. *Journal of Family Studies, 9*(1), 37–50.

Kerig, P. K. (2001). Children's coping with interparental conflict. In J. H. Grych & F. D. Fincham (Eds.), *Interparental conflict and child development: Theory, research and applications* (pp. 213–248). Cambridge University Press.

Kołodziej-Zaleska, A., & Przybyła-Basista, H. (2020). The role of ego-resiliency in maintaining post-divorce well-being in initiators and non-initiators of divorce. *Journal of Divorce & Remarriage, 61*(5), 366–383.

Koppejan-Luitze, H. S., van der Wal, R. C., Kluwer, E. S., Visser, M. M., & Finkenauer, C. (2020). Are intense negative emotions a risk for complex divorces? An examination of the role of emotions in divorced parents and co-parenting concerns. *Journal of Social and Personal Relationships.* Advance online publication.

Kushnick, G. (2016). Ecology of pair-bond stability. In T. Shackelford & V. Weekes-Shackelford (Eds.), *Encyclopedia of evolutionary psychological science* (pp.1–7). Springer.

Lamb, M. E. (Ed.). (2013). *The father's role: Cross cultural perspectives.* Routledge.

Lamidi, E. O., Manning, W. D., & Brown, S. L. (2019). Change in the stability of first premarital cohabitation among women in the United States, 1983–2013. *Demography, 56*(2), 427–450.

Leary, M. R. (2015). Emotional responses to interpersonal rejection. *Dialogues in Clinical Neuroscience, 17*(4), 435–441.

Lehrer, J. (2009). *The decisive moment: How the brain makes up its mind.* Text Publishing.

Lichter, D. T., Qian, Z., & Mellott, L. M. (2006). Marriage or dissolution? Union transition among poor cohabiting women. *Demography, 43*(2), 223–240.

Lieberman, M. D., Eisenberger, N. I., Crockett, M. J., Tom, S. M., Pfeifer, J. H., & Way, B. M. (2007). Putting feelings into words: Affect labelling disrupts amygdala activity in response to affect stimuli. *Psychological Science, 18*(5), 421–428.

Lukas, D., & Clutton-Brock, T. H. (2013). The evolution of social monogamy in mammals. *Science, 341*(6145), 526–530.

Maidment, S. (1984). *Child custody and divorce. The law in social context.* Crook Helm.

Mason, M. (1995). *From fathers' property to children's rights.* Columbia University Press.

Masson, J. (2000). *Emperor's embrace: Reflections on animal families and fatherhood.* Penguin.

Masuda, N., & Fu, F. (2015). Evolutionary models of in-group favoritism. *F1000 Prime Reports, 7,* 27.

Mayer, B. S. (2009). *Staying with conflict: A strategic approach to ongoing disputes.* Jossey-Bass.

Mazza, M., Marano, G., Lai, C., Janiri, L., & Sani, G. (2020). Danger in danger: Interpersonal violence during COVID-19 quarantine. *Psychiatry Research, 289,* 113046.

McCrindle, M. (2016, July 15). Half of all marriages end in divorce; and other things you thought were true. *Huffington Post.* https://www.huffingtonpost.com.au/mark-mccrindle/is-australia-really-the-l_b_9129164.html

Metts, S., Braithwaite, D. O., & Fine, M. A. (2009). *Hurt in postdivorce relationships.* In A. L. Vangelisti (Ed.), *Advances in personal relationships. Feeling hurt in close relationships* (pp. 336–355). Cambridge University Press.

Miller, S. L., & Maner, J. K. (2008). Coping with romantic betrayal: Sex differences in responses to partner infidelity. *Evolutionary Psychology, 6*(3), 413–426.

Millon, T., & Davis, R. D. (1996). An evolutionary theory of personality disorders. In J. F. Clarkin & M. F. Lenzenweger (Eds.), *Major theories of personality disorder* (pp. 221–346). Guilford Press.

Mnookin, R. (1975). Child custody adjudication: Judicial functions in the face of indeterminacy. *Law and Contemporary Problems, 39,* 266–293.

Mogilski, J. K., Reeve, S. D., Nicolas, S. C., Donaldson, S. H., Mitchell, V. E., & Welling, L. L. (2019). Jealousy, consent, and compersion within monogamous and consensually non-monogamous romantic relationships. *Archives of Sexual Behavior, 48*(6), 1811–1828.

Moloney, L. (2014). Of dreams and data. Lionel Murphy and the dignified divorce. In A. Hayes & D. Higgins (Eds.), *Families, policy and the law: Selected essays on contemporary issues for Australia* (pp. 247–259). Australian Institute of Family Studies.

Moloney, L., Smyth, B., Weston, R., Richardson, N., Qu, L., & Gray, M. (2007). *Allegations of family violence and child abuse in child-related disputes in family law proceedings* (Research Report No. 15). Australian Institute of Family Studies.

Moloney, L., Weston, R., & Hayes, A. (2013). Key social issues in the development of Australian family law. Research and its impact on policy and practice. *Journal of Family Studies, 19*(2), 110–138.

Morris, C. E. (2015). *The Breakup Project: Using evolutionary theory to predict and interpret responses to romantic relationship dissolution* [Unpublished doctoral dissertation]. Binghamton University. https://orb.binghamton.edu/dissertation_and_theses/2

Morris, C. E., Reiber, C., & Roman, E. (2015). Quantitative sex differences in response to the dissolution of a romantic relationship. *Evolutionary Behavioral Sciences, 9*(4), 270–282.

Neff, R., & Cooper, K. (2004). Parental conflict resolution: Six-, twelve-, and fifteen-month follow-ups of a high-conflict program. *Family Court Review, 42,* 99–114.

Nesse, R. (1998). Emotional disorders in evolutionary perspective. *British Journal of Medical Psychology, 71*(4), 397–415.

Nesse, R. M. (1990a). The evolutionary functions of repression and the ego defenses. *Journal of the American Academy of Psychoanalysis, 18*(2), 260–285.

Nesse, R. M. (1990b). Evolutionary explanations of emotions. *Human Nature, 1*(3), 261–289.

Nesse, R. M. (2000). Is depression an adaptation? *Archives of General Psychiatry, 57,* 14–20.

Nesse, R. M. (2017). Evolutionary foundations for psychiatric research and practice. In B. J. Sadock, V. A. Sadock, & P. Ruiz (Eds.), *Kaplan & Sadock's comprehensive textbook of psychiatry* (10th ed., pp. 769–780). Wolters Kluwer.

Neustaedter, C., Harrison, S., & Sellen, A. (2013). Connecting families: An introduction. In C. Neustaedter, S. Harrison, & A. Sellen (Eds.), *Connecting families: The impact of new communication technologies on domestic life* (pp. 1–12). Springer.

O'Brien, R. (2010). Practice and innovation: Simplifying the system: Family law challenges–Can the system ever be simple? *Journal of Family Studies, 16*(3), 264–270.

Parkinson, L. (2011). *Family mediation: Appropriate dispute resolution in a new family justice system.* Jordan.

Perilloux, C., & Buss, D. M. (2008). Breaking up romantic relationships: Costs experienced and coping strategies deployed. *Evolutionary Psychology, 6*(1), 164–181.

Pizzey, E. (1973). *Scream quietly or the neighbours will hear.* Enslow.

Plutchik, R. (2001). The nature of emotions. *American Scientist, 89*(4), 344–350.

Pryor, J., & Rodgers, B. (2001). *Children in changing families: Life after parental separation.* Blackwell.

Qu, L., & Weston, R. (2010). *Parenting dynamics after separation: A follow-up study of parents who separated after the 2006 Family Law Reforms.* Australian Institute of Family Studies.

Qu, L., Weston, R., Moloney, L., Kaspiew, R., & Dunstan, J. (2014). *Post-separation parenting, property and relationship dynamics after five years.* Australian Institute of Family Studies.

Raley, R. K., & Sweeney, M. M. (2020). Divorce, repartnering, and stepfamilies: A decade in review. *Journal of Marriage and Family, 82*(1), 81–99.

Rantala, M. J., Luoto, S., Krams, I., & Karlsson, H. (2018). Depression subtyping based on evolutionary psychiatry: Proximate mechanisms and ultimate functions. *Brain, Behavior, and Immunity, 69*, 603–617.

Reithmuller, G. (2015). Deciding parenting cases under Part VII—42 easy steps. *Australian Family Lawyer, 24*(3), 1–8.

Ricard, M. (2013). *Altruism: The science and psychology of kindness.* Atlantic Books.

Ricci, I. (1997). *Mom's house, dad's house: Making two homes for your child.* Simon & Schuster.

Rogers, C. (1942). *Counseling and psychotherapy.* Riverside Press.

Rosenfeld, M. J. (2018). Who wants the breakup? Gender and breakup in heterosexual couples. In D. F. Alwin, D. Felmlee, & D. Kreager (Eds.), *Social networks and the life course: Integrating the development of human lives and social relational networks* (pp. 221–243). Springer.

Rushton, J. P., Bons, T. A., & Hur, Y. M. (2008). The genetics and evolution of the general factor of personality. *Journal of Research in Personality, 42*(5), 1173–1185.

Rutter, M. (1972). *Maternal deprivation re-assessed.* Penguin.

Sbarra, D. A., & Emery, R. E. (2005). The emotional sequelae of nonmarital relationship dissolution: Analysis of change and intraindividual variability over time. *Personal Relationships, 12*(2), 213–232.

Sbarra, D. A., & Ferrer, E. (2006). The structure and process of emotional experience following nonmarital relationship dissolution: Dynamic factor analyses of love, anger, and sadness. *Emotion, 6*(2), 224–238.

Scelza, B. A., Prall, S., Blumenfeld, T., Crittenden, A., Gurven, M., Kline, M., Koster, J., Kushnick, G., Mattison, S. M., Pillsworth, E., Shenk, M., Starkweather, K., Stieglitz, J., Sum, C.-Y., Yamaguchi, K., & McElreath, R. (2019). Patterns of paternal investment explain cross-cultural variance in jealous response. *Nature Human Behaviour, 4*, 20–26.

Schacht, R., & Kramer, K. L. (2019). Are we monogamous? A review of the evolution of pair-bonding in humans and its contemporary variation cross-culturally. *Frontiers in Ecology and Evolution, 7*, 230.

Schaffer, H. R. (1998). *Making decisions about children: Psychological questions and answers.* Blackwell.

Scutt, J. (1983). *Even in the best of homes: Violence in the family.* Penguin.

Shackelford, T. K. (1998). Divorce as a consequence of spousal infidelity. In V. C. de Munck (Ed.), *Romantic love and sexual behavior: Perspectives from the social sciences* (pp. 135–153). Praeger.

Shackelford, T. K., Buss, D. M., & Bennett, K. (2002). Forgiveness or breakup: Sex differences in responses to a partner's infidelity. *Cognition & Emotion, 16*(2), 299–307.

Shackelford, T. K., Goetz, A. T., Buss, D. M., Euler, H. A., & Hoier, S. (2005). When we hurt the ones we love: Predicting violence against women from men's mate retention. *Personal Relationships, 12*(4), 447–463.

Short, R. V. (1976). Definition of the problem: The evolution of human reproduction. *Proceedings of the Royal Society of London. Series B. Biological Sciences, 195*(1118), 3–24.

Smyth, B. M. (Ed.). (2004). *Parent–child contact and post-separation parenting arrangements* (Research Report No. 9). Australian Institute of Family Studies.

Smyth, B. M., Ainscough, G., & Payne, J. L. (2020). Modes of communication between high-conflict separated parents: Exploring the role of media multiplexity and modality switching. *Journal of Family Communication, 20*(3), 189–205.

Smyth, B. M., & Moloney L. J. (2017). Entrenched postseparation parenting disputes: The role of interparental hatred. *Family Court Review: An Interdisciplinary Journal, 55*, 404–416.

Smyth, B. M., Moloney, L. J., Brady, J. M., Harman, J., & Esler, M. (2020). COVID-19 in Australia: Impacts on separated families, family law professionals, and family courts. *Family Court Review, 58*(4), 1022–1039.

Sprecher, S., Felmlee, D., Metts, S., Fehr, B., & Vanni, D. (1998). Factors associated with distress following the breakup of a close relationship. *Journal of Social and Personal Relationships, 15*(6), 791–809.

Stallman, H. M., & Ohan, J. L. (2016). Parenting style, parental adjustment, and co-parental conflict: Differential predictors of child psychosocial adjustment following divorce. *Behaviour Change, 33*(2), 112–126.

Star, L. (1996). *Counsel of perfection: The Family Court of Australia.* Oxford University Press.

Stewart, J. R., & Schwebel, A. I. (1986). The impact of custodial arrangement on the adjustment of recently divorced fathers. *Journal of Divorce, 9*(3), 55–65.

Stiles, J. (1984). Nineteenth century child custody reform: Maternal authority and the development of the "best interests of the child" standard. *Probate Law Journal, 6*(5), 5–32.

Swain, S. (2012). *Born in hope. The first ten years of the Family Court of Australia.* University of New South Wales Press.

van Dijk, R., van der Valk, I. E., Deković, M., & Branje, S. J. (2020). A meta-analysis on interparental conflict, parenting, and child adjustment in divorced families: Examining mediation using meta-analytic structural equation models. *Clinical Psychology Review, 79*, 101861.

Vaughan, D. (1986). *Uncoupling: Turning points in intimate relationships.* Oxford University Press.

Voss, C., & Raz, T. (2016). *Never split the difference: Negotiating as if your life depended on it.* Harper Collins.

Walker, L. E. (1979). *The battered woman.* Harper & Row.

Waller, J. E. (2004). Our ancestral shadow: Hate and human nature in evolutionary psychology. *Journal of Hate Studies, 3*, 121–132.

Weiss, Y., & Willis, R. J. (1985). Children as collective goods and divorce settlements. *Journal of Labor Economics, 3*(3), 268–292.

Whisman, M. A., Tolejko, N., & Chatav, Y. (2007). Social consequences of personality disorders: Probability and timing of marriage and probability of marital disruption. *Journal of Personality Disorders, 21*(6), 690–695.

Willén, H. (2015). Challenges for divorced parents: Regulating negative emotions in post-divorce relationships. *Australian and New Zealand Journal of Family Therapy, 36*(3), 356–370.

Wilson, E. O. (2012). *The social conquest of earth.* Liveright.

Wilson, M. (2005). An evolutionary perspective on male domestic violence: Practical and policy implications. *American Journal of Criminal Law, 32*(3), 291–324.

Wilson, M., & Daly, M. (1993). An evolutionary psychological perspective on male sexual proprietariness and violence against wives. *Violence and Victims, 8*(3), 271–294.

Wilson, M., & Daly, M. (2016). The evolutionary psychology of couple conflict in registered versus de facto marital unions. In A. Booth, A. C. Crouter, M. L. Clements, & T. Boone-Holladay (Eds.), *Couples in conflict* (Classic ed., pp. 3–26). Routledge.

Wolcott, I., & Hughes, J. (1999). *Towards understanding the reasons for divorce.* Australian Institute of Family Studies.

CHAPTER

29

Dissolution of LGBTQ+ Relationships

Madeleine Redlick Holland *and* Pamela J. Lannutti

Abstract

In considering the nature of romantic relationship dissolution, it is important to recognize the unique experience that LGBTQ+ couples may have in the modern world. Specifically, as argued by Lannutti (2014), dynamic sociocultural contextual factors related to these relationships, such as discrimination and changes in legal recognition, may meaningfully affect the relational lives of non-heterosexual people. This assertion, that sociocultural context plays a meaningful role in the dissolution of romantic relationships, is echoed by evolutionary scholars. Thus, in this chapter, we seek to highlight research that recognizes the unique experience of LGBTQ+ relationship dissolution. Although the corpus of knowledge regarding LGBTQ+ relationship dissolution remains sparse, we will provide an overview of what knowledge has been generated up to this point. To begin, we will engage the somewhat thorny topic of how LGBTQ+ relationships have been incorporated into evolutionary theorizing and research. Following this discussion, we articulate some dissolution-relevant relationship features that make the experience of being in a LGBTQ+ relationship different from that of a mixed-sex relationship. Next, we discuss how the actual process of dissolution might differ in LGBTQ+ relationships. Where possible, we draw out insights that evolutionary perspectives may offer in interpreting some of the findings we review. Finally, we offer areas in which we feel that research on LGBTQ+ relationship dissolution can grow moving forward.

Key Words: dissolution, LGBTQ+, stress, marriage, divorce, consensual nonmonogamy

Opening Thoughts on LGBTQ+ Individuals and Evolutionary Psychology

When considering the intersection of evolutionary psychology and the dissolution of lesbian, gay, bisexual, transgender, queer, and other sexual identity minority (LGBTQ+) romantic relationships, it is important to first acknowledge the concerns that have been raised by the scholarly community about the validity of this theoretical perspective, especially as it relates to implications that the theory may have for the queer community. In doing so, we wish to give a description of the conversation surrounding evolutionary psychology's application to LGBTQ+ relationships, not to argue for the validity of one viewpoint over another.

Concerns

The crux of these concerns rests on the argument that evolutionary psychology's explanatory scope is limited to heterosexual individuals and their behavior, and relatedly, that it supports heteronormative discourses (e.g., the assumption that heterosexuality is the norm from which other sexualities deviate and an evaluative judgment that such a deviation is negative in character; Gannon, 2002; Jackson, 2006; Jonason & Schmitt, 2016). Critics of the theory have offered that if evolutionary psychology seeks to position itself as a unifying metatheory, then it should be able to explain much, if not all, human behavior. Proponents of this argument suggest that because there is no reasonable way of denying that queer people are humans, the inability to fully account for their existence represents a major concern with the true generalizability of the theory. A point of support for this argument comes from the well-documented lack of empirical evidence to support one of the most widespread evolutionary explanations for same-sex attraction (Playa et al., 2017; VanderLaan et al., 2016): the kin selection hypothesis (Wilson, 1975). The second concern that had plagued evolutionary psychology in the past is that, in positioning itself as a theory which points to the evolved or "natural" causes of human behaviors, this implies that behaviors not predicted or accounted for are unnatural (Gannon, 2002). As such, those who used to lodge such arguments argued that the theory becomes inherently homophobic when behaviors not aimed at procreation, including sexual attraction and activity between same-sex individuals, are cast as "deleterious heritable traits" (Jeffrey et al., 2019 p. 7) or resulting from some form of maladaptive dysfunction (Monk et al., 2019). This claim has been largely dismissed, however, in that more recent perspectives on evolutionary psychology point out a frequently observed behavior, such as sexual activity or attraction between individuals of different sexes, is not equivalent to a normal behavior, and further that a normal behavior is not necessarily a moral one (Floyd & Afifi, 2011; Monk et al., 2019).

Clarifications

Floyd and Afifi (2011) noted that critics have accused evolutionary perspectives of contributing to perceptions of determinism, immutability, and naturalism. However, in an effective defense of the theory, Floyd and Afifi engaged each of these criticisms in turn. They noted that in the view of many researchers, biology and behavior are *correlated* and not causally determined, undermining claims of biological determinism. Second, they raised the important distinction that while biology creates potentialities for a behavior, it does not dictate them or remove human agency in behaviors, such as dissolving relationships. Finally, Floyd and Afifi broke down the claims that findings from biologically oriented theories, such as evolutionary psychology, promote a discourse of naturalism. Floyd and Afifi (2011) were not the only researchers to address the previously noted concerns, and in fact, almost no evolutionary psychologists currently endorse the versions of the theory that are most problematic (Gowaty, 2001; Mogilski, 2016; van Anders,

2014). To encourage both critics and proponents of evolutionary psychology to engage in productive discussions, it should be pointed out that while the academic community has progressed in its understanding of evolutionary psychology, lay audiences and the media have not, and concerns that findings from the theory may be misappropriated to justify dysfunctional behavior or systems that perpetuate inequality persist (J. R. Garcia & Heywood, 2016; Jonason & Schmitt, 2016; Mogilski, 2016).

A Path Forward

There is room for almost every theoretical perspective to grow in terms of its inclusiveness of the queer community (e.g., discussions of transgender and gender nonbinary individuals; Manning & Joyner, 2019; Petruzella et al., 2019), and evolutionary psychology is no exception. Still, if one can incorporate the moderating statements offered above when interpreting work that draws on evolutionary theory, it is possible to extend some of its tenets to understanding relational dissolution in LGBTQ+ relationships. Indeed, recent theorizing on evolved sex differences has sought not to sideline the role of biology but rather to integrate it on equal footing with social determinants of behavior (e.g., Eagly & Wood, 2013; J. R. Garcia & Heywood, 2016; van Anders, 2014).

Language Matters

Before proceeding any further, a note on language in this chapter should also be made. To avoid contributing to a discourse of "difference as deficiency" or "deficit-comparison" models (Manning & Joyner, 2019, p. 43), we refrain from referring to same-sex relationships as "non-heterosexual." Rather, we refer to individuals as either being engaged in LGBTQ+ relationships or mixed-sex (meaning assumed to be heterosexual) relationships. We use the term "same-sex relationships," "lesbian relationships," and so on, when the research being discussed is specifically about these types of individuals or couples. In doing so, we position both heterosexual and LGBTQ+ people and their respective relationships as equal and recognize the fluid nature of human sexuality (Diamond, 2005; Kitzinger, 2001; Mock & Eibach, 2012). Further, we turn away from the tendency to hold heterosexual, monogamous relationships as the "gold standard" (Lavner, 2017, p. 7) or norm against which all other relationship types are judged and instead recognize the equal validity of various types of relationships.

As research on individuals in LGBTQ+ relationships has developed, the field has come to consensus that LGBTQ+ and mixed-sex relationships are more similar than different. For example, the emotional correlates of relational dissolution are not significantly different when comparing same- and mixed-sex relationships (Gottman et al., 2003) and further, Manning et al. (2016) found no significant difference in stability among cohabitating LGBTQ+ and mixed-sex couples. Indeed, acknowledging and validating the shared humanity of individuals in both LGBTQ+ and mixed-sex couples seems an important place from which to ground any discussion of the particularities of either type of relationship.

However, a focus on similarity can be taken too far, and treating such diverse types of relationships as identical can lead to a masking of the variation that exists *within* these relationship types (van Eeden-Moorefield et al., 2011). For example, women who are in cohabitating same-sex relationships experience more frequent dissolution than their male same-sex counterparts (Manning & Joyner, 2019). Additionally, men in same-sex relationships seem to be somewhat inured to the destabilizing force of extradyadic sexual activity in a way that women in same-sex relationships are not (van Eeden-Moorfield et al., 2011). Thus, to fully describe the unique experience of being in a LGBTQ+ relationship, it is important to investigate which factors distinct to LGBTQ+ relationships may create points of difference (though again, not deficiency or deviance) at any point in the life cycle of a relationship, including the process of ending a relationship. For example, both Ketcham and Bennett (2019) and Manning and Joyner (2019) found that formalized same-sex relationships involving two women are significantly more likely to be terminated than those involving two men or mixed-sex relationships. Additionally, two lines of research suggest that relationship variables such as commitment, investment, perceived quality of alternatives, and the ways that an LGBTQ+ couple responds to stress may function quite differently in same-sex versus mixed-sex relationships (cf. Doyle & Molix, 2014a, 2014b, 2014c, 2015; Lehmiller & Agnew, 2006, 2007). For example, Lehmiller and Agnew (2006) found that in a sample of individuals in marginalized relationships (including those in LGBTQ+ relationships), these individuals tended to invest significantly less in their relationships. To compensate for these decreased levels of investment, individuals in marginalized relationships tended to psychologically adjust their perceived availability of alternative mates, thereby making their current mate seem more attractive. It seems that this response is somewhat effective, in that this same study further found that individuals in marginalized relationships reported significantly higher levels of commitment to their relationships.

The remainder of this chapter is thus focused on discussing the limited knowledge that has been produced on the dissolution of LGBTQ+ relationships. To do so, we first articulate some dissolution-relevant relationship features that make the experience of being in a LGBTQ+ relationship different from that of a mixed-sex relationship. Next, we discuss how the actual process of dissolution might differ in LGBTQ+ relationships. Where possible, we seek to draw out insights that evolutionary perspectives may offer in interpreting some of the findings that we review. We close our remarks by identifying some key areas for growth in this field, including moving beyond simple correlational analyses, a consideration of more than sex-composition when classifying relationship types, an increased attention to the experiences of bisexual and transgender individuals, and finally a call for a deeper incorporation of intersectional approaches.

Features of LGBTQ+ Relationships

To better understand the dissolution of LGBTQ+ relationships, it is important to consider unique factors in the structures and experiences of these relationships which may impact relational quality and dissolution. First, it is important to consider two factors which may place LGBTQ+ relationships at greater or less risk for dissolution: division of labor and consensual nonmonogamy. Second, we consider the experiences of minority stress for those in LGBTQ+ relationships and the impact that this stress has on relational functions and dissolution.

Risk Factors: Division of Labor and Consensual Nonmonogamy

One question that has been investigated by many researchers is whether there is a significant difference in levels of relational quality and satisfaction in LGBTQ+ versus mixed-sex relationships. Some research suggests that individuals in same-sex relationships enjoy greater satisfaction (Balsam et al., 2017; M. A. Garcia & Umberson, 2019). However, research has also indicated that in spite of this elevated level of satisfaction, certain same-sex relationships (specifically those involving two women) are more likely to end (Balsam et al., 2017). Some have speculated that the increased levels of relational satisfaction may be attributable to a more equitable division of labor related to both emotional work and household tasks (Carlson et al., 2016; Cooke, 2006; Umberson et al., 2015). However, women in same-sex relationships may find that in spite of a more equitable division of labor in the household, they are not treated equally when it comes to being rewarded for their labor outside the household. Indeed, research suggests that women in same-sex relationships may experience greater levels of stress related to financial insecurity given that both individuals in the relationship are likely affected by gender-based disparities in earning power (Goldberg et al., 2015). This financial strain may introduce additional stress into the relationship, and place it at an elevated risk of dissolution (K. R. Allen & Goldberg, 2020). Indeed, research on heterosexual populations has clearly established that socioeconomic status and relationship satisfaction and stability are tightly linked (for a review, cf. Conger et al., 2010), and more specifically, research has also shown that lower levels of socioeconomic status are related to relationship instability (Amato et al., 2007).

Another factor which may or may not place same-sex couples at an increased risk of dissolution is the presence of an arrangement regarding consensual nonmonogamy. Although some researchers (Conley et al., 2012) have argued that there is little evidence to support the notion that maintaining monogamy is more beneficial to relationships than engaging in nonmonogamous relational models, monogamy has long been upheld as the heteronormative model for romantic relationships (also see Day, 2013; Day et al., 2011). However, social devaluation, discrimination, and prejudice against those who identify as LGBTQ+ has often led those individuals to reject adopting these heterosexual norms in their romantic relationships (Grov et al., 2014; Whitton et al., 2015). For many LGBTQ+ couples, especially male–male couples, the rejection of heterosexual relational norms extends to forming consensually nonmonogamous romantic relationships. Although there is no way to know the exact prevalence of consensual nonmonogamy among LGBTQ+ couples, previous studies have reported that such arrangements are common among male–male couples for at least part of the length of their relationship (Grov et al., 2014, Haupert et al., 2017; Parsons et al., 2012), and people who practice consensual nonmonogamy are more likely to report being bisexual compared to those in monogamous relationships (Balzarini et al., 2019; Levine et al., 2018; Mogilski et al., 2017; Mogilski et al., 2020; Mogilski et al., 2019).

Same-sex couples who engage in consensual nonmonogamy commonly establish rules and boundaries, known as consensual nonmonogamy agreements, to clarify what types of sexual behaviors and encounters are acceptable to the primary partners (Eeden-Moorefield et al., 2016; Grov et al., 2014; Perry et al., 2015; Wosick-Correa, 2010). Grov et al., (2014) pointed out that consensual nonmonogamy agreements may be complex and varied among couples, and may include rules about whether partners may engage in extradyadic sexual behavior alone or only as a couple, whether condoms must be used, if specific permission must be sought from the primary partner before extradyadic sexual activity, what types of sexual behavior are acceptable, and whether a partner may spend the night with an extradyadic sexual partner.

Thus, even though a relationship may involve consensual nonmonogamy, there still commonly exists the possibility of relational betrayal, resulting from deviating from the established consensual nonmonogamy agreement. Such betrayal could lead to relational dissatisfaction and by extension, dissolution (Perry et al., 2016). However, the majority of research on relational types among male–male couples finds either that there is no significant difference between monogamous and consensually nonmonogamous couples on relational quality factors such as relational satisfaction or that consensually nonmonogamous couples may have higher levels of relational quality factors, such as communication quality, than monogamous couples (Bonello, 2009; Parsons et al., 2012; Stults, 2019; Whitton et al., 2015). Thus, it can be expected that consensually nonmonogamous male–male couples' relationships are unlikely to be negatively affected by extradyadic sexual behavior, but that relational quality may decrease and dissolution may be more likely to occur if consensual nonmonogamy agreements are not followed.

Although most of the literature on consensual nonmonogamy among LGBTQ+ people focuses on gay men, there is some research involving other members of the LGBTQ+ community. Female–female couples are less likely to engage in consensual nonmonogamy than male–male couples (Haupert et al., 2017), though this same research found that women who have sex with women were more likely to engage in consensually nonmonogamous relationships than people who identify as heterosexual. In particular, bisexual people may engage more frequently in consensually nonmonogamous or polyamorous relationships than people who identify as heterosexual (Barker & Langdridge, 2010; McLean, 2004). However, caution should be taken when considering bisexuality and consensual nonmonogamy, to avoid conflating this relational approach with stereotypes that bisexual people are incapable of monogamy as a result of their sexual orientation (Klesse, 2005). Relational dynamics of those who identify as bisexual are generally understudied, and the consensually nonmonogamous relationships of those who identify as bisexual even more so (Haupert et al., 2017). Therefore, when considering consensual nonmonogamy and LGBTQ+ people other than gay men, researchers should be careful to recognize that little is known about how consensual nonmonogamy affects the relationship quality and possible dissolution of these relationships.

Minority Stress

In addition to alternative relational models, there are other factors that may uniquely contribute to LGBTQ+ relationship dissolution, including minority stress (Meyer, 2003). Specifically, minority stress theory articulates that individuals in LGBTQ+ relationships are placed at risk of experiencing increased levels of stress that come as a result of their current sexual orientation. Specifically, the theory articulates that individuals in same-sex relationships may experience (a) objectively stressful external events, (b) expectations that these aforementioned events may occur, and a vigilance toward detecting them, and (c) internalized homophobia, which is the personal endorsement of negative attitudes toward LGBTQ+ people by a member of that population (Meyer, 2003). The theory arranges these stressors on a continuum of distal to proximal. Distal stressors, sometimes called structural stigma, may include "societal level conditions, cultural norms, and institutional policies that constrain the opportunities, resources and well-being" (Hatzenbuehler, 2016, p. 742). Some examples of distal stressors might be anti-gay discourses or legislation, inability to access sexual health resources, or the (threat of) anti-gay violence. Proximal-level stressors, by contrast, are those that exist more closely around and within individuals. As mentioned previously, these stressors may manifest themselves as efforts to conceal sexual orientation to avoid stigmatization or in the endorsement of certain homophobic or anti-gay sentiments.

The distinction between distal and proximal stressors is important to tease out, given that the different types of stressors appear to be associated with different relationship-relevant variables (Petruzzella et al., 2019). For example, in a study considering the relationship quality of women in same-sex relationships, Lavner (2017) found that physical or verbal assaults based on sexual orientation (a distal stressor) were not as impactful on relationship quality as more chronic and proximal stressors, such as concealing sexual orientation or same-sex partners from family-of-origin members, or anticipating negative reactions to sexual orientation from those same family members. Additionally, in a meta-analysis of minority stress research, Cao et al. (2017) found that internalized homophobia was significantly and negatively related to relationship well-being among individuals in same-sex relationships, whereas experiences of discrimination or concealing one's sexual identity were not.

More recent work with minority theory stress has identified an additional domain of stress that individuals in LGBTQ+ relationships may face. This additional domain of stressors, referred to as couple-level stressors, are things that individuals in same-sex couples face, rather than stressors that individuals who identify as sexual minorities face on their own (Frost et al., 2017). One prominent example of a couple-level minority stressor is the long-standing unequal recognition of same-sex marriages. Previous research found that individuals in legally recognized relationships (i.e., marriages and civil unions) evinced better mental health than individuals in relationships that were not legally recognized (LeBlanc et al., 2018; Liu & Wilkinson, 2017).

However, same-sex marriage was only legally recognized at the federal level in the United States starting in 2015, following the *Obergefell v. Hodges* Supreme Court ruling. Research conducted among same-sex couples prior to this decision indicated that state-level bans on same-sex marriage were associated with decreased mental health (Fingerhut et al., 2011; Frost & Fingerhut, 2016; Maisel & Fingerhut, 2011). It is possible that uncertainty around the availability of legal marriages in the time before *Obergefell v. Hodges* may have contributed to this relationship. Indeed, it has been speculated that the absence of legal recognition may create unique challenges for same-sex couples (Goldberg & Allen, 2013). In spite of the 2015 ruling, the aforementioned uncertainty and its attendant negative sequelae may persist given that new Supreme Court appointments may give rise to questions about the continued availability or permanency of federal recognition of same-sex marriages.

Similarly to individual-level minority stressors, couple-level minority stressors can also be conceived of as ranging from distal to proximal. The previous example represents a more distal stressor, whereas a more proximal example may be found in the research of Balsam et al. (2017. When conducting interviews with women dissolving their same-sex relationships, these researchers found that many women reported an internalized pressure to be a perfect or model couple to prove to others that LGBTQ+ relationships could be just as successful as other types of relationships. This pressure may represent a particularly insidious form of minority stress, in that it is not as visible or acute as outright discrimination or prejudice, and thus it is harder for individuals to mobilize support that might help them cope with this stress (Lavner, 2017). Experiencing minority stress does not guarantee that a same-sex relationship will dissolve, however. Indeed, same-sex couples use a variety of strategies to cope with these experiences, such as disregarding prejudiced comments or experiences, actively attempting to endorse positive self-views of being in a same-sex relationship, reframing stigmatizing episodes as empowering, or denigrating those who attempt to marginalize them (Rostosky et al., 2007). Still, the experience of minority stress, specifically in the form of internalized homophobia and perceived discrimination, does contribute to lower perceptions of relationship quality (Otis et al., 2006) which may place these relationships at greater risk for dissolution.

Increased stress is likely just one of a constellation of factors that plays into the decision to dissolve a relationship. Most research suggests that rates of dissolution are relatively equal across same-sex and mixed-sex partnerships (Gates et al., 2008; Manning et al., 2016). However, if a dissolution does occur, there is some evidence to suggest that there may be significant differences in the frequency of termination across LGBTQ+ couple types. Specifically, some research suggests that same-sex relationships comprised of two women more likely to terminate than those comprised of two men (Manning & Joyner, 2019; Petruzzella et al., 2019). To add nuance to this finding, it is important to note that there is another factor that must be considered in predicting dissolution: cohabitation. Cohabitating couples are less stable than married ones, but more stable than noncohabitating couples (LeBlanc et al., 2018; Manning & Joyner, 2019). When considering noncohabitating couples, there is some evidence that men, not women as suggested by DeLeece and Wiessfiel (2016), are more likely to terminate their relationships than women (Joyner et al., 2017).

Evolutionary psychological metatheory provides a cogent explanation for this pattern. Given that women are choosier about their partners, they may have a lower threshold for exiting a relationship than men, and indeed, research by DeLeece and Weissfiel (2016) did find that women in mixed-sex relationships were more likely to be dissolution initiators than men. In support of this theorizing, Ketcham and Bennett (2019) did find that women in formalized same-sex relationships were more likely to dissolve their relationships than men in same-sex relationships or individuals in mixed-sex relationships.

Dissolution of LGBTQ+ Relationships

The previous section has considered the predictors of LGBTQ+ relationship dissolution. The question that logically follows is how these breakups might occur. Much theorizing on relational dissolution comes in the form of stage models, which specify the order in which individuals are presumed to move through certain phases of a breakup. However useful these models are as a general heuristic, they do not answer the question of how individuals move through each of these steps (Rollie & Duck, 2006). Some clarity on the question of how breakups occur may be answered by turning to the idea of scripts, or cultural rules for how certain interactions are expected to unfold (Simon & Gagnon, 1986). Indeed, script theory has been successfully extended to both the formation and the dissolution of mixed-sex relationships (e.g., Battaglia et al., 1998; Larmont, 2017), but no research has explicitly taken up the question of whether these scripts can be extended to same-sex relationships, or if a different one applies. In fact, there is some evidence to suggest that individuals in LGBTQ+ relationships intentionally deviate from heteronormative scripts (Larmont, 2017), and thus there is good reason to investigate if there are scripts that are specific to same-sex relationships.

One script that may exist for dissolving LGBTQ+ relationships is the idea that individuals must continue to be friends with their ex-partners following dissolution, turning their social circles into an "army of ex-lovers" (Hoffman, 2007, in K. R. Allen & Goldberg, 2020). Ex-partners are frequently identified as members of LGBTQ+ people's "chosen family," a group that are not biologically or legally related but serve as a family group, often functioning in place of biological and legal relations who are not supportive of the LGBTQ+ person's sexual and/or gender minority identity (Blair & Pukall, 2014 Duran & Perez, 2019; Lannutti & Cameron, 2002; Weston, 1991). Harkless and Fowers (2005) found that lesbians and gay men were significantly more likely to maintain a close relationship with an ex-partner than were heterosexual men and women, yet they point out that the specific behaviors that maintain these relationships may be different for lesbians and gay men. Again, an evolutionary perspective can be profitably applied here. Given that individuals want to retain access to social networks that provide resources or potential future mates, it is advantageous to maintain friendly relations with an ex-partner to avoid being ostracized from their social networks (Mogilski & Welling, 2017). One might speculate that maintaining friendly relations is particularly important to individuals who are dissolving LGBTQ+ relationships, as their pool of potential future mates is smaller, relative to individuals who engage in mixed-sex relationships, and thus losing access to a group of potential mates as a result of being shunned from a certain social network would represent a threat to finding a new mate. However, Lannutti and Cameron (2002) found that personal variables, such as liking for the ex-partner had a stronger influence on the quality of the same-sex post-dissolutional relationship than did structural variables, such as social network norms. Further, research suggests that when women perceived lower levels of available social support, they actually engaged in more negative relationship behaviors toward their partners, rather than positive ones, which might increase the likelihood of continued access to the social network of their partner should the relationship be terminated (Lewis et al., 2014).

It is possible that this script is one that is both an artifact of individuals' age and fading over time. Given the increasing levels of public support for LGBTQ+ relationships that have been documented over the past few decades (Gallup, 2019), individuals may no longer feel that they need to retain access to their ex-partners' social networks in order to obtain desired resources or find a new mate. Indeed, there has been a proliferation of technology that has stepped in to assist individuals in finding a same-sex mate (e.g., Fem, Grindr, Growlr, Her, Scruff).

Breaking up vs. Divorce

Legally recognized same-sex marriage has existed in at least some parts of the United States since 2004 and longer in many countries around the world, yet there is relatively little research investigating divorce among legally married same-sex couples. Oswald and Clausell (2005) discussed that institutionalization of same-sex relationships involves both legalization and ritualization (ceremonies, family traditions, rings, etc.), and that the level of institutionalization for a given relationship may vary. Interestingly, Gate et al. (2008)

noted that females in same-sex relationships are significantly more likely to seek legal recognition than their male counterparts. Evolutionary theory may provide some insight into this pattern. Given that women are generally inclined to look for a long-term partner who will provide them with steady access to resources, marriage offers a way to fulfill both of those needs. Men, by contrast, are given to seek shorter-term partnerships, and may thus step away from formalizing relationships to more easily exit them if they so desire. Indeed, individuals in same-sex relationships report that navigating evolving and shifting laws regarding dissolving a civil union constitute a "legal nightmare" (Balsam et al., 2016, p. 12).

Yet, even when legally married, a same-sex couple may not be completely institutionalized. This is likely a result of the fact that marriage does not automatically equate to the support and acceptance needed for many forms of ritualization, but also because the legalization aspect of marriage may not include important rights such as parental protections (Oswald & Clausell, 2005; Lannutti, 2014). Still, legal marriage may be an important factor when considering the dissolution of same-sex relationships. It is clear that the availability of legal marriage has changed not only how same-sex people may gain legal and civil recognition and protection for their relationships but also the way that LGBTQ+ people perceive their own relationships, their relational goals, and their perceived status in society (Lannutti, 2014). If legal marriage has not only changed the legal status of same-sex relationships but made many same-sex couples feel more accepted, supported, and protected (Lannutti, 2014), how might divorce differ from the nonmarital dissolution of same-sex partnerships?

Hoy (2018) interviewed a small sample of LGBTQ+ individuals who divorced after being legally married to a same-sex partner and found that the experience of same-sex divorce was not widely recognized or understood by others. Given the extensive media and social focus on same-sex marriage, those who divorced a same-sex partner felt there was a lack of awareness of same-sex divorce within the LGBTQ+ community and beyond (Hoy, 2018). This lack of awareness translated to divorced individuals feeling unsupported because the seriousness of divorce was not widely understood and recognized (Balsam et al., 2016; Hoy, 2018). Those experiencing same-sex divorce often had to explain and justify their divorce to others during uncomfortable interactions, which led to divorced individuals withdrawing from social interaction (Hoy, 2018). Women in particular reported experiencing shame and guilt after a same-sex divorce, connected to the idea that they had to overcome many challenges to get married in the first place and now were voluntarily exiting their relationships (Balsam et al., 2016).

Hoy (2019) further examined the explanations, or accounts, that LGBTQ+ people who divorced from a same-sex partner offered when discussing their divorce. Hoy (2019) found that LGBTQ+ divorced individuals used two kinds of accounts. First, relationship-focused accounts explained how the relationship failed. Second, self-focused accounts explained that the marriage had a negative effect on the divorced person. Hoy (2019) argued that LGBTQ+ individuals' conceptualizations of the meaning of marriage are reflected in their accounts for their divorce. Therefore by using both relationship-focused and self-focused accounts of divorce, LGBTQ+ divorced individuals showed that they endorsed two common ways of framing marriage: the individualized model of marriage (associated with self-focused accounts) and the companionate model of marriage (associated with relationship-focused accounts). This study showed not only that LGBTQ+ divorced individuals understood marriage and its dissolution in ways consistent with existing models of the meaning of marriage, but that the understanding of a marriage, and subsequently a divorce, may significantly differ from the understanding of a nonmarital relationship and its dissolution.

Another important aspect to the experience of same-sex divorce might be the role of children and co-parenting. There is conflicting data on whether or not same-sex couples with children are more likely to dissolve their relationships than those without children (D. Allen & Price, 2020; Farr & Goldberg, 2019; Wiik et al., 2014). Hull and Ortyl (2019) suggested that as LGBTQ+ people adopt more traditional family forms through legal marriage and increased parenting, they may increase an emphasis on legal and biological relationships when they consider their family form and decrease emphasis on "chosen" family ties. This shift in the LGBTQ+ understanding of family may make maintaining relationships with ex-partners less important. However, as LGBTQ+ parenting increased, co-parenting relationships may have to be renegotiated and maintained post-relational dissolution. Negotiating co-parenting relationships post same-sex divorce may be complicated by the type of parenting arrangement that the couple had predivorce. For example, a nonbiological lesbian mother may not have legal protection for her relationship with her child unless she legally adopted her wife's biological child. Gartrell et al. (2011) found that divorced lesbians were more likely to continue to co-parent their children if the nonbiological mother had legally adopted the child than if she had not. Although there are very few studies examining the post-divorce relationships of same-sex couples with children, the little research that does exists suggests that the negotiation of ex-partners' relationships and co-parenting arrangements are complex.

Future Directions

To review, we began this chapter by raising some of the important concerns that the LGBTQ+ community has raised with evolutionary perspectives on romantic relationships. After engaging recent scholarship on this topic, and ways that the theoretical perspective might grow to become more inclusive, we reviewed the major findings of the somewhat limited body of research that exists with regards to the dissolution of LGBTQ+ relationships. We noted some specific unique features of LGBTQ+ relationships (i.e., division of labor and consensual nonmonogamy agreements) as well as unique pressures that individuals in LGBTQ+ relationships face, invoking the theory of minority stress (Meyer, 2003). Finally, we turned to the notion of scripts for dissolving relationships, and investigated how they may be apparent in LGBTQ+ relationships, with special attention to the question of how individuals in these relationships navigate the experience of breaking up as distinct from the experience of divorce.

Researchers interested in the convergence of LGBTQ+ relationships, dissolution, and evolutionary psychology find themselves in an exciting position. Although the current corpus of empirical work is relatively limited, there is much room for growth in many directions. As of the time of this writing, most of the work done on LGBTQ+ relationship dissolution has been grounded in correlational analysis. Questions of whether certain factors, such as cohabitating status, relationship length, and degree of formalization are related to the likelihood of dissolution have all been raised. However, it is time for the field to move past these simple relationships and begin investigating whether the relationships between these variables and dissolution are potentially more nuanced than they may appear. In line with this thinking, it is time for researchers to begin considering and testing for the presence of mediated and/or moderated relationships (Lavner, 2017), to more fully understand both the likelihood and the process of dissolution in LGBTQ+ relationships. Additionally, socioeconomic status may be an important variable to begin to incorporate more fully, especially as access to resources may make interventions targeted at increasing relationship stigma more or less effective (Hatzenbuehler, 2016). Other research that has begun to take up this task has considered more cognitively oriented variables, such as psychological closeness (Totenhagen et al., 2012).

Researchers should also consider taking a more granular approach to their outcome variables. Most of the research reviewed in this chapter has focused on global appraisals of relationship quality and satisfaction and has considered dissolution of relationships as a binary decision. Doyle and Molix (2015) pointed out that certain aspects related to relationship quality may be differentially affected by minority stress and thus should be investigated separately, rather than in the aggregate. Specifically, Doyle and Molix (2015) argued for and found evidence to support the idea that the affective components of relationships (i.e., emotions) are more greatly impacted by stress associated with being in an LGBTQ+ relationship than cognitive components (i.e., assessments of the relationship) .The consideration of becoming more granular can also be extended to our understanding of the term "dissolution." The decision to end a relationship is one that is not always binary. Rather, individuals may go through periods of deescalation, or engage in cyclical relationship patterns, involving multiple dissolutions and reconciliations, sometimes called "on-again, off-again" relationships (e.g., Dailey et al., 2012; Dailey, Pfeister, et al., 2009; Dailey, Rosetto, et al., 2009). A fruitful area for future research may exist in learning more about these processes in same-sex relationships.

Additionally, it is time to add more richness to some of the variables that are being used in analyses. Almost all research conducted on LGBTQ+ relationship dissolution has categorized participants' relationships using sex composition of the couple as the operationalizing criterion (Manning & Joyner, 2019). However, this is somewhat of a reductive view of LGBTQ+ relationships. Future research should seek to consider both the sex composition of the couple as well as the current sexual orientation of each individual. In doing so, researchers will be able to consider the fluid nature of human sexuality (Patterson, 2000) more fully. Additionally, special care should be taken to investigate subpopulations within the queer community that often find their experiences sidelined, silenced, or ignored. In accordance with this thinking, researchers have an important task ahead of them in incorporating bisexual, transgender, and gender nonbinary participants into their future explorations (Petruzzella et al., 2019), and hopefully additional strides can be made toward this goal as the field continues to progress.

Finally, however complicated it may be, researchers must strive to more fully incorporate an intersectional approach in both their theorizing and empirical work. Research outside the context of relational dissolution suggests that multiple demographic variables interact in ways that meaningfully affect relational outcomes (e.g., Doyle & Molix, 2015; Langenderfer-Magruder et al., 2016). Thus, it is important to consider individuals' experiences from a lens that recognizes that they cannot be defined solely by their sexual orientation. Rather, we must account for the richness of their experiences by recognizing the multiple factors that meaningfully influence their experiences across the relationship life cycle.

References

Allen, D., & Price, J. (2020). Stability rates of same-sex couples: With and without children. *Marriage and Family Review*, *56*, 51–71. https://doi.org/10.1080/01494929.2019.1630048

Allen, K. R., & Goldberg, A. E. (2020). Lesbian women disrupting gendered, heteronormative discourses of motherhood, marriage, and divorce. *Journal of Lesbian Studies*, *24*, 12–24.

Amato, P. R., Booth, A., Johnson, D. R., & Rogers, S. J. (2007). *Alone together: How marriage in America is changing*. Harvard University Press.

Balsam, K. F., Rostosky, S. S., & Riggle, E. D. (2017). Breaking up is hard to do: Women's experience of dissolving their same-sex relationship. *Journal of Lesbian Studies*, *21*, 30–46.

Balzarini, R. N., Dharma, C., Kohut, T., Campbell, L., Lehmiller, J. J., Harman, J. J., & Holmes, B. M. (2019). Comparing relationship quality across different types of romantic partners in polyamorous and monogamous relationships. *Archives of Sexual Behavior*, *48*, 1749–1767.

Battaglia, D. M., Richard, F. D., Datteri, D. L., & Lord, C. G. (1998). Breaking up is (relatively) easy to do: A script for the dissolution of close relationships. *Journal of Social and Personal Relationships*, *15*, 829–845.

Barker, M., & Langdridge, D. (2010). Whatever happened to non-monogamies? Critical reflections on recent research and theory. *Sexualities*, *13*, 748–772. DOI: 10.1177/1363460710384645

Blair, K. L., & Pukall, C. F. (2014). Family matters, but sometimes chosen family matters more: Perceived social network influence in the dating decisions of same- and mixed-sex couples. *The Canadian Journal of Human Sexuality*, *24*, 257–270. https://doi.org/10.3138/cjhs.243-A3

Bonello, K. (2009). Gay monogamy and extra-dyadic sex: A critical review of the theoretical and empirical literature. *Counselling Psychology Review*, *24*, 51–65.

Cao, H., Zhou, N., Fine, M., Liang, Y., Li, J., & Mills-Koonce, W. R. (2017). Sexual minority stress and same-sex relationship well-being: A meta-analysis of research prior to the US nationwide legalization of same-sex marriage. *Journal of Marriage and the Family*, *79*, 1258–1277.

Carlson, D. L., Miller, A. J., Sassler, S., & Hanson, S. (2016). The gendered division of housework and couples' sexual relationships: A reexamination. *Journal of Marriage and the Family*, *78*, 975–995.

Conger, R. D., Conger, K. J., & Martin, M. J. (2010). Socioeconomic status, family processes, and individual development. *Journal of Marriage and the Family*, *72*, 685–704.

Conley, T. D., Ziegler, A., Moors, A. C., Matsick, J. L., & Valentine, B. (2012). A critical examination of popular assumptions about the benefits and outcomes of monogamous relationships. *Personality and Social Psychology Review, 17*, 124–141. https://doi.org/10.1177/1088868312467087

Cooke, L. P. (2006). "Doing" gender in context: Household bargaining and risk of divorce in Germany and the United States. *American Journal of Sociology, 112*, 442–472.

Dailey, R. M., Middleton, A. V., & Green, E. W. (2012). Perceived relational stability in on-again/off-again relationships. *Journal of Social and Personal Relationships, 29*, 52–76.

Dailey, R. M., Pfiester, A., Jin, B., Beck, G., & Clark, G. (2009). On-again/off-again dating relationships: How are they different from other dating relationships? *Personal Relationships, 16*, 23–47.

Dailey, R. M., Rossetto, K. R., Pfiester, A., & Surra, C. A. (2009). A qualitative analysis of on-again/off-again romantic relationships: "It's up and down, all around." *Journal of Social and Personal Relationships, 26*, 443–466.

Day, M. V. (2013). Stigma, halo effects, and threats to ideology: Comment on the fewer the merrier? *Analyses of Social Issues and Public Policy, 13*, 49–51.

Day, M. V., Kay, A. C., Holmes, J. G., & Napier, J. L. (2011). System justification and the defense of committed relationship ideology. *Journal of Personality and Social Psychology, 101*, 291–306.

DeLecce, T., & Weisfeld, G. (2016). An evolutionary explanation for sex differences in nonmarital breakup experiences. *Adaptive Human Behavior and Physiology, 2*(3), 234-251.

Diamond, L. M. (2005). A new view of lesbian subtypes: Stable versus fluid lesbian identity trajectories over an 8-year period. *Psychology of Women Quarterly, 29*, 119–128.

Doyle, D. M., & Molix, L. (2014a). How does stigma spoil relationships? Evidence that perceived discrimination harms romantic relationship quality through impaired self-image. *Journal of Applied Social Psychology, 44*, 600–610.

Doyle, D. M., & Molix, L. (2014b). Perceived discrimination as a stressor for close relationships: Identifying psychological and physiological pathways. *Journal of Behavioral Medicine, 37*, 1134–1144.

Doyle, D. M., & Molix, L. (2014c). Perceived discrimination and well-being in gay men: The protective role of behavioural identification. *Psychology & Sexuality, 5*, 117–130.

Doyle, D. M., & Molix, L. (2015). Perceived discrimination and social relationship functioning among sexual minorities: Structural stigma as a moderating factor. *Analyses of Social Issues and Public Policy, 15*, 357–381.

Duran, A., & Perez, D. (2019). The multiple roles of chosen familia: Exploring the interconnections of queer Latino men's community cultural wealth. *International Journal of Qualitative Studies in Education, 32*, 67–84. https://doi.org/10.1080/09518398.2018.1523484

Eagly, A. H., & Wood, W. (2013). The nature–nurture debates: 25 years of challenges in understanding the psychology of gender. *Perspectives on Psychological Science, 8*, 340–357.

Farr, R. H., & Goldberg, A. E. (2019). LGBTQ divorce and relationship dissolution: Psychological and legal perspectives and implications for practice. In A. E. Goldberg & A. P. Romero (Eds.), LGBTQ divorce and relationship dissolution: Psychological and legal perspectives and implications for practice (pp. 151–172). Oxford University Press.

Fingerhut, A. W., Riggle, E. D., & Rostosky, S. S. (2011). Same-sex marriage: The social and psychological implications of policy and debates. *Journal of Social Issues, 67*, 225–241.

Floyd, K., & Afifi, T. D. (2011). Biological and physiological perspectives on interpersonal communication. In M. L. Knapp & J. A. Daly (Eds.), *Handbook of interpersonal communication* (pp. 87–130). SAGE.

Frost, D. M., & Fingerhut, A. W. (2016). Daily exposure to negative campaign messages decreases same-sex couples' psychological and relational well-being. *Group Processes & Intergroup Relations, 19*, 477–492.

Frost, D. M., LeBlanc, A. J., de Vries, B., Alston-Stepnitz, E., Stephenson, R., & Woodyatt, C. (2017). Couple-level minority stress: An examination of same-sex couples' unique experiences. *Journal of Health and Social Behavior, 58*, 455–472.

Gallup. (2019). *Gay and lesbian rights*. Gallup. Retrieved from https://news.gallup.com/poll/1651/gay-lesbian-rights.aspx

Gannon, L. (2002). A critique of evolutionary psychology. *Psychology, Evolution & Gender, 4*, 173–218.

Garcia, J. R., & Heywood, L. L. (2016). VII. Moving toward integrative feminist evolutionary behavioral sciences. *Feminism & Psychology, 26*, 327–334.

Garcia, M. A., & Umberson, D. (2019). Marital strain and psychological distress in same-sex and different-sex couples. *Journal of Marriage and the Family, 81*, 1253–1268.

Gartrell, N., Bos, H., Peyser, H., Deck, A., & Rodas, C. (2011). Family characteristics, custody arrangements and adolescent psychological well-being after lesbian mothers break-up. *Family Relations, 60*, 572–585. https://doi.org/10.1111/j.1741-3729.2011.00667.x

Gates, G. J., Badgett, M., & Ho, D. (2008). *Marriage, registration and dissolution by same-sex couples in the US.* The Williams Institute, UCLA. https://escholarship.org/uc/item/5tg8147x

Goldberg, A. E., & Allen, K. R. (2013). Same-sex relationship dissolution and LGB stepfamily formation: Perspectives of young adults with LGB parents. *Family Relations, 62*, 529–544.

Goldberg, A. E., Moyer, A. M., Black, K., & Henry, A. (2015). Lesbian and heterosexual adoptive mothers' experiences of relationship dissolution. *Sex Roles, 73*, 141–156.

Gottman, J. M., Levenson, R. W., Gross, J., Frederickson, B. L., McCoy, K., Rosenthal, L., Ruef, A., & Yoshimoto, D. (2003). Correlates of gay and lesbian couples' relationship satisfaction and relationship dissolution. *Journal of Homosexuality, 45*(1), 23–43.

Gowaty, P. A. (2001). Women, psychology, and evolution. In R. K. Unger (Ed.), *Handbook of the psychology of women and gender* (pp. 53–65). John Wiley & Sons.

Grov, C., Starks, T. J., Rendina, H. J., & Parsons, J. (2014). Rules about casual sex partners, relationship satisfaction, and HIV risk in partnered gay and bisexual men. *Journal of Sex and Marital Therapy, 40*, 105–122. https://doi.org/10.1080/0092623X.2012.691948

Harkless, L. E., & Fower, B. J. (2005). Similarities and differences in relational boundaries among heterosexuals, gay men, and lesbians. *Psychology of Women Quarterly, 29*, 167–176.

Hatzenbuehler, M. L. (2016). Structural stigma: Research evidence and implications for psychological science. *American Psychologist, 71*, 742–751.

Haupert, M. L., Gesselman, A. N., Moors, A. C., Fisher, H. E., & Garcia, J. R. (2017). Prevalence of experiences with consensual nonmonogamous relationships: Findings from two national samples of single Americans. *Journal of Sex & Marital Therapy, 43*, 424–440. https://doi.org/10.1080/0092623X.2016.1178675

Hoffman, A. (2007). *An army of ex-lovers: My life at the* Gay Community News. University of Massachusetts Press.

Hoy, A. (2018). Invisibility, illegibility, and stigma: The citizenship experiences of divorced gays and lesbians. *Journal of Divorce & Remarriage, 59*, 69–91. https://doi.org/10.1080/10502556.2017.1375332

Hoy, A. (2019). Accounting for same-sex divorce: Relationship- vs. self-focused divorce accounts and the meanings of marriage among gays and lesbians. *Journal of Divorce & Remarriage, 61*(5), 1–24. https://doi.org/10.1080/10502556.2019.1619384

Hull, K. E., & Ortyl, T. A. (2019). Conventional and cutting-edge: Definitions of family in LGBT communities. *Sexuality Research and Social Policy, 16*, 31–43. https://doi.org/10.1007/s13178-018-0324-2

Jackson, S. (2006). Gender, sexuality and heterosexuality: The complexity (and limits) of heteronormativity. *Feminist Theory, 7*, 105–121.

Jonason, P. K., & Schmitt, D. P. (2016). Quantifying common criticisms of evolutionary psychology. *Evolutionary Psychological Science, 2*, 177–188.

Joyner, K., Manning, W., & Bogle, R. (2017). Gender and the stability of same-sex and different-sex relationships among young adults. *Demography, 54*, 2351–2374. doi.org/10.1007/s13524-017-0633-8

Ketcham, E., & Bennett, N. G. (2019). Comparative couple stability: Same-sex and male-female unions in the United States. *Socius, 5*, 1–15.

Kitzinger, C. (2001). Sexualities. In R. K. Unger (Ed.), *Handbook of the psychology of women and gender* (pp. 272–285). John Wiley & Sons.

Klesse, C. (2005). Bisexual women, non-monogamy and differentialist anti-promiscuity. *Sexualities, 8*, 445–464. https://doi.org/10.1177/1363460705056620

Lamont, E. (2017). "We can write the scripts ourselves": Queer challenges to heteronormative courtship practices. *Gender & Society, 31*, 624–646.

Langenderfer-Magruder, L., Whitfield, D. L., Walls, N. E., Kattari, S. K., & Ramos, D. (2016). Experiences of intimate partner violence and subsequent police reporting among lesbian, gay, bisexual, transgender, and queer adults in Colorado: Comparing rates of cisgender and transgender victimization. *Journal of Interpersonal Violence, 31*, 855–871.

Lannutti, P. J. (2014). *Experiencing same-sex marriage: Individuals, couples, and social networks.* Peter Lang.

Lannutti, P. J., & Cameron, K. A. (2002). Beyond the breakup: Heterosexual and homosexual post-dissolutional relationships. *Communication Quarterly, 50*, 153–170.

Lavner, J. A. (2017). Relationship satisfaction in lesbian couples: Review, methodological critique, and research agenda. *Journal of Lesbian Studies, 21*, 7–29.

LeBlanc, A. J., Frost, D. M., & Bowen, K. (2018). Legal marriage, unequal recognition, and mental health among same-sex couples. *Journal of Marriage and Family, 80*, 397–408. doi.org/10.1111/jomf.12460

Lehmiller, J. J., & Agnew, C. R. (2006). Marginalized relationships: The impact of social disapproval on romantic relationship commitment. *Personality and Social Psychology Bulletin, 32*, 40–51.

Lehmiller, J. J., & Agnew, C. R. (2007). Perceived marginalization and the prediction of romantic relationship stability. *Journal of Marriage and the Family, 69*, 1036–1049.

Levine, E. C., Herbenick, D., Martinez, O., Fu, T. C., & Dodge, B. (2018). Open relationships, nonconsensual nonmonogamy, and monogamy among US adults: Findings from the 2012 National Survey of Sexual Health and Behavior. *Archives of Sexual Behavior, 47*, 1439–1450.

Lewis, R. J., Milletich, R. J., Derlega, V. J., & Padilla, M. A. (2014). Sexual minority stressors and psychological aggression in lesbian women's intimate relationships: The mediating roles of rumination and relationship satisfaction. *Psychology of Women Quarterly, 38*, 535–550.

Liu, H., & Wilkinson, L. (2017). Marital status and perceived discrimination among transgender people. *Journal of Marriage and the Family, 79*, 1295–1313.

Maisel, N. C., & Fingerhut, A. W. (2011). California's ban on same-sex marriage: The campaign and its effects on gay, lesbian, and bisexual individuals. *Journal of Social Issues, 67*, 242–263.

Manning, W. D., Brown, S. L., & Stykes, J. B. (2016). Same-sex and different-sex cohabiting couple relationship stability. *Demography, 53*, 937–953.

Manning, W. D., & Joyner, K. (2019). Demographic approaches to same-sex relationship dissolution and divorce: Research findings, data challenges, and implications for further research. In A. E. Goldberg & A. P. Romero (Eds.), LGBTQ divorce and relationship dissolution: Psychological and legal perspectives and implications for practice (pp. 35–48). Oxford University Press.

McLean, K. (2004). Negotiating (non) monogamy: Bisexuality and intimate relationships. *Journal of Bisexuality, 4*, 83–97. doi=10.1300/J159v04n01_07

Meyer, I. H. (2003). Prejudice, social stress, and mental health in lesbian, gay, and bisexual populations: Conceptual issues and research evidence. *Psychological Bulletin, 129*, 674–697.

Mock, S. E., & Eibach, R. P. (2012). Stability and change in sexual orientation identity over a 10-year period in adulthood. *Archives of Sexual Behavior, 41*, 641–648.

Mogilski, J. K. (2016). Social Darwinism. In T. K. Shackelford & V. A. Weekes-Shackelford (Eds.), *Encyclopedia of evolutionary psychological science* (pp. 1–3). Springer International. https://doi.org/10.1007/978-3-319-16999-6_448-1.

Mogilski, J. K., Memering, S. L., Welling, L. L., & Shackelford, T. K. (2017). Monogamy versus consensual non-monogamy: Alternative approaches to pursuing a strategically pluralistic mating strategy. *Archives of Sexual Behavior, 46*, 407–417.

Mogilski, J. K., Mitchell, V. E., Reeve, S. D., Donaldson, S. H., Nicolas, S. C., & Welling, L. L. (2020). Life history and multi-partner mating: A novel explanation for moral stigma against consensual non-monogamy. *Frontiers in Psychology, 10*, Article 3033.

Mogilski, J. K., Reeve, S. D., Nicolas, S. C., Donaldson, S. H., Mitchell, V. E., & Welling, L. L. (2019). Jealousy, consent, and compersion within monogamous and consensually non-monogamous romantic relationships. *Archives of Sexual Behavior, 48*, 1811–1828.

Mogilski, J. K., & Welling, L. L. (2017). Staying friends with an ex: Sex and dark personality traits predict motivations for post-relationship friendship. *Personality and Individual Differences, 115*, 114–119.

Monk, J. D., Giglio, E., Kamath, A., Lambert, M. R., & McDonough, C. E. (2019). An alternative hypothesis for the evolution of same-sex sexual behaviour in animals. *Nature Ecology & Evolution, 3*(12), 1622–1631.

Obergefell v. Hodges, 135 S. Ct. 2071 (2015). https://www.supremecourt.gov/opinions/14pdf/14-556_3204. pdf

Oswald, R. F., & Clausell, E. (2005). Same-sex relationships and their dissolution. In M. A. Fine & J. H. Harvey (Eds.), *Handbook of divorce and relationship dissolution* (pp. 499–513). Routledge.

Otis, M. D., Rostosky, S. S., Riggle, E. D., & Hamrin, R. (2006). Stress and relationship quality in same-sex couples. *Journal of Social and Personal Relationships, 23*, 81–99.

Parsons, J. T., Starks, T. J., Gamarel, K. E., & Grov, C. (2012). Non-monogamy and sexual relationships quality among same-sex male couples. *Journal of Family Psychology, 26*, 669–677. https://doi.org/10.1037/a0029561

Patterson, C. J. (2000). Family relationships of lesbians and gay men. *Journal of Marriage and the Family, 62*, 1052–1069.

Perry, N. S., Huebner, D. M., Baucom, B. R., & Hoff, C. C. (2015). Relationship power, sociodemographics, and their relative influence on sexual agreements among gay male couples. *AIDS Behavior, 20*, 1302–1314. https://doi.org/10.1007/s10461-015-1196-6

Petruzzella, A., Feinstein, B. A., & Lavner, J. A. (2019). Sexual orientation-related stigma and relationship functioning among female same-sex couples. *Journal of Lesbian Studies, 23*, 439–450.

Playà, E., Vinicius, L., & Vasey, P. L. (2017). Need for alloparental care and attitudes toward homosexuals in 58 countries: Implications for the kin selection hypothesis. *Evolutionary Psychological Science, 3*, 345–352.

Rollie, S. S., & Duck, S. W. (2006). Stage theories of marital breakdown. In M. A. Fine & J. H. Harvey (Eds.), *Handbook of divorce and dissolution of romantic relationships* (pp. 176–193). Routledge.

Rostosky, S. S., Riggle, E. D., Gray, B. E., & Hatton, R. L. (2007). Minority stress experiences in committed same-sex couple relationships. *Professional Psychology: Research and Practice, 38*, 392–400.

Simon, W., & Gagnon, J. H. (1986). Sexual scripts: Permanence and change. *Archives of Sexual Behavior, 15*, 97–120.

Stults, C. B. (2019). Relationship quality among young gay and bisexual men in consensual nonmonogamous relationships. *Journal of Social and Personal Relationships, 36*, 3037–3056. https://doi.org/10.1177/0265407518809530

Totenhagen, C. J., Butler, E. A., & Ridley, C. A. (2012). Daily stress, closeness, and satisfaction in gay and lesbian couples. *Personal Relationships, 19*, 219–233. https://doi.org/10.1111/j.1475-6811.2011.01349.x

Umberson, D., Thomeer, M. B., & Lodge, A. C. (2015). Intimacy and emotion work in lesbian, gay, and heterosexual relationships. *Journal of Marriage and Family, 77*, 542–556.

van Anders, S. M. (2014). Comment: The social neuroendocrinology example: Incorporating culture resolves biobehavioral evolutionary paradoxes. *Emotion Review, 6*, 256–257.

Van Eeden-Moorefield, B., Malloy, K., & Benson, K. (2016). Gay men's (non)monogamy ideal and lived experiences. *Sex Roles, 75*, 43–55. https://doi.org/10.1007/s11199-015-0566-x

Van Eeden-Moorefield, B., Martell, C. R., Williams, M., & Preston, M. (2011). Same-sex relationships and dissolution: The connection between heteronormativity and homonormativity. *Family Relations, 60*, 562–571.

VanderLaan, D. P., Petterson, L. J., & Vasey, P. L. (2016. Elevated kin-directed altruism emerges in childhood and is linked to feminine gender expression in Samoan fa'afafine: A retrospective study. *Archives of Sexual Behavior, 46*, 95–108.

Weston, K. (1991). *Families we choose: Lesbians, gays, kinship*. Columbia University Press.

Whitton, S. A., Weitbrecht, E. M., & Kuryluk, A. D. (2015). Monogamy agreements in male same-sex couples: Associations with relationship quality and individual well-being. *Journal of Couple & Relationship Therapy, 14*, 39–63. https://doi.org/10.1080/15332691.2014.953649

Wiik, K. A., Seierstad, A., & Noack, T. (2014). Divorce in Norwegian same-sex marriages and registered partnerships: The role of children. *Journal of Marriage and the Family, 76*, 919–929. https://doi.org/10.1111/jomf.12132

Wilson, E. O. (1975). *Sociobiology: The new synthesis*. Harvard University Press.

Wosick-Correa, K. (2010). Agreements, rules and agentic fidelity in polyamorous relationships. *Psychology & Sexuality, 1*, 44–61.

CHAPTER

30 Relationship Dissolution Among Adults

Dimitri Mortelmans

Abstract

The end of a marriage or cohabitation is an intrusive life course event witnessed within a substantial number of romantic relationships. The uncoupling of relationships has transformed the family lives of both adults and children in most Western countries for the past half-century. This chapter first looks into the phenomenon from a legal perspective delineating when a breakup is witnessed and registered. Next, we examine both the causes and the consequences of breakups. For antecedents of divorce, we focus on intergenerational inheritance of breakups, educational attainment, economic risk factors, personality, and health. We also touch upon protective factors in a relationship that decreases the risk of ending a relationship. When taking consequences into account, the chapter is limited to adults. The chapter describes the financial consequences of divorce, their health, networks and lone parenthood, and poverty after divorce. The chapter concludes with a prospect of the future of this field.

Key Words: divorce, life course, divorce rate, divorce risks, risk factors of divorce, consequences of divorce, family dynamics

The rise of divorce in modern society

The study of relationship dissolution (whether married or cohabiting) originated in the 1970s. Explaining the relatively late development of this field of inquiry is straightforward: only from the late 1960s and early 1970s did divorce rates begin to climb notably (Bennett, 2017; Stevenson & Wolfers, 2007). The late origin of this field gives the impression that divorce is a relative new phenomenon. From a Christian perspective, it marks the end of the period in which Western societies were governed by the motto that "what God has joined together, let no one separate," or the assumption that marriage will last "till death do us part." The recency of divorce is a myth, however, as uncoupling has existed throughout human history, and is much older than the current Western tradition of marrying and divorcing. For example, the Babylonian Code of Hammurabi (1772 BCE) contained legal regulations governing marriage and divorce (Trevino, 2013). But the magnitude with which relationships have been dissolving since the late 1960s is unprecedented in history. In modern Western history, we have not seen relationships become so unstable and, as we will discuss, increasingly intertwined with social inequality. The aim of this chapter is to give an overview of the state of the art of the field of relationship dissolution. I cover risk factors and consequences of divorce for adult (ex-)partners. But first, I address definitions for divorce and separation and the major statistical trends behind these phenomena. Where possible, I introduce the reader to comparative studies that place divorce in an international perspective.

Defining Divorce and Separation

Divorce is the *legal dissolution of a marriage* (Emery, 2013; Halley, 2010; Mortelmans, 2020a). Based on this definition, official statistics around the world provide divorce rates that can be compared across time and countries. Despite the clear nature of the definition, it considers divorce a dichotomous event. But divorce can also be seen as a process during which the quality of a marriage deteriorates, as conflicts between the partners arise, and they become increasingly estranged. And even when one considers the breakup a dichotomous "before–after" event, there still is a difference between the moment of a legal divorce in which a marriage is officially dissolved and the empirical reality where researchers consider the end of living together as the time point of the divorce. But the end of a long-term relationship does not occur at a single moment in time or is difficult to pinpoint at a moment in time.

The dichotomous moment is also legally recognized as an official event after which the former partners receive the legal status of "no longer married." But also in family law, prior to the divorce, most countries have developed steps in the legal divorcing process. Most (Western European) family law recognizes two (potential) phases that couples go through. In the first phase, partners decide to end their relationship. Often, one partner moves out of the marital home, which means that the two ex-partners are, from a legal perspective, *spatially separated* but still married. In the next phase, the partners are *legally separated* (sometimes also known as "divorce from table and bed"). In some countries, the partners can ask the court to take preliminary measures that apply until the divorce is finalized. In this period, the partners remain married while a judge decides the rights and duties of the respective partners, such as their rights to property (e.g., who lives where), their obligations to pay alimony and child maintenance, and their rights to child visitation. In some countries (e.g., Italy and Germany), this period of legal separation represents an *obligatory legal separation*. The idea behind this obligatory separation is that the partners should have a "waiting period" (or probationary period) before their divorce is finalized. If the partners may be ending their marriage prematurely, they might benefit from a cooling-down period before they take the final step of dissolving their marriage. In practice, however, few legally separated couples reconcile. As a consequence, most countries have abolished this obligatory separation period.

The divorce itself is the second step in the legal path to uncoupling. Here, the former couple officially requests the judge to dissolve their marriage and award them the administrative status of "divorced" (or in some cases "unmarried"). In most countries, divorces are granted by a court decision but can also be finalized through an administrative procedure by a municipal officer or a notary. As divorce laws differ across countries, both the procedures used and the length of the divorce process can vary considerably, but the historical trends in most countries show a shortening of the legal trajectories.

A legal approach to divorce hides the reality that uncoupling takes many forms. The initial focus of the developing field of family dynamics was dissolution among married heterosexual couples. But as countries were opening up marriage to same-sex couples, divorce among them started to appear (and increase), enlarging the scope of the field. Furthermore, divorce researchers have expanded their focus as rates of marriage have declined and cohabitation and union dissolution have become more common. As a consequence, we still use the term "divorce" in academia (and outside), but increasingly it refers to a broader reality than the uncoupling of heterosexual spouses. Rather, it has become an umbrella term for all uncoupling processes, irrespective of the gender composition or the legal bond of the couple.

So far in this chapter, our definitional journey has concentrated on the question of *who* is experiencing a breakup. But we also need to consider a life course perspective on coupling and uncoupling. Focusing on the definition of divorce as the legal dissolution of marriage could give the impression that most people have one marriage or cohabiting relationship that might dissolve during the life course. In reality, life—but also the heart—goes on after divorce. When a new partner enters the life of an individual, they open themselves up not only to a new love but to new potential conflicts that could result in another breakup (and, hence, in new partnerships). When we consider divorce a singular event that a person experiences only once, all subsequent processes of bonding and relationship dissolution are not well understood. Most studies do not take the rank of the relationship (first, second, etc.) into account even though the process of finding a partner and then dissolving the relationship could occur many times over a person's life (Amato, 2010).

The Historical Development of Divorce Laws

Taking a legal perspective on the "dissolution of marriage" starts by considering the concept of marriage. Historically, marriage was a patriarchal institution. Both in Europe and the United States, a wife was the property of her husband. Exemplary in this light is the work of Thorstein Veblen (1965), who showed in his classic study on the "leisure class" how wealthy men used their spouses as signifiers of their wealth by adorning them with jewelry and expensive clothes. For centuries, men were given control over women's property, earnings, and sexuality. Moreover, in choosing a marital partner, whether the union enhanced the political power or property of the respective families was considered more important than the love and intimacy between partners (Coontz, 2006).[1] Rooted

[1] See, for example, the Head and Master laws in the United States and Europe (Coontz, 2006).

in diverse religious traditions, many nation-states either prohibited divorce or allowed divorce only under strict conditions. And when the possibility was granted, filing for divorce was expensive. So only the wealthy (men) had access to divorce, while poor people often split up without officially divorcing. The shift from arranged marriage to modern marriage, in which the main focus is on personal fulfilment and emotional attachment, also instigated a shift in thinking about marriage dissolution. The modernization of the "love match" (Coontz, 2007) not only revolutionized marriage but also set in motion a trend toward more divorces, as the focus on individual fulfilment and mutual love in marriage implied that loveless relationships should be ended. Another consequence of the prohibition of divorce was "underground relationships" as ex-spouses could not publicly transition to a new relationship or a new marriage. As the meaning of marriage shifted, family law was changed and increasingly made divorce accessible to all relationships.

It was only from the late 1950s and 1960s that divorce in Europe and the United States became more widely legalized. Until then, the dissolution of a marriage was only allowed in well-specified cases. The only grounds for leaving a marriage were adultery, violence, or (large) debts. A first step in the loosening of divorce laws was the introduction of *mutual consent regimes and fault divorces*. In such cases, divorce was allowed only when both partners consented (unless the aforementioned grounds for divorce were present) or when a guilty party could be identified. As in criminal law, the family judge who dissolved a marriage named a guilty party and an innocent party. The division of the marital property and the custody of the children often depended on which partner won or lost the divorce case. Two major changes occurred in divorce law from the 1970s onward (although these changes did not occur in every state and country, and the pace and the degree of these changes varied). First, the *no-fault divorce* was introduced, in which the end of a marriage was no longer legally attributed to the "fault" of one partner (Leeson & Pierson, 2015). The no-fault divorce occurred in two forms. A first implementation combined the classic divorce grounds with a no-fault possibility that was only offered as an alternative to seeking a divorce based on wrongdoing. The second approach was the abolishment of all grounds of divorce and the replacement with the no-fault principle as the only ground for divorce. In that case, proof of guilt was abandoned as a legal principle. Parallel to the introduction of no-fault divorce, *unilateral divorce* became a legal option (Bracke & Mulier, 2015). Under traditional divorce law, couples need to provide mutual consent to divorce. If one partner wanted to stay married, divorce was not possible (or had serious consequences in terms of property rights and child custody). The unilateral divorce option gave one partner the right to file for divorce even though the other spouse did not consent. The major reforms usually were accompanied with a streamlining and shortening of legal procedures. In most countries, probation periods were abolished. An overview of legalization of divorce and the shift toward no-fault and unilateral divorce can be found in González and Viitanen (2009).

The development of divorce laws and its effects on family life have been subject to several empirical studies. The central question in these studies is whether these "easier" legal options for obtaining a divorce have influenced overall divorce rates. The results show that legal changes usually caused sudden spikes in the overall trend in divorce rates that dissipated over time. Wolfers (2006) for the United States and González and Viitanen (2009) for Europe found that the shift to no-fault and unilateral divorce legal regimes has caused divorce rates to increase by between 0.2 to 0.4 divorces per 1,000 people per year. While the option of unilateral divorce contributed to this trend, it was the introduction of the no-fault divorce option that had a significant (albeit limited) surplus impact on the divorce rate.

Not only have improved access to divorce and expansion of legal options for obtaining a divorce affected trends in marriage dissolution. Equally important are, for example, child custody arrangements in divorce settlements. At first, divorce laws mostly focused on the material well-being and living arrangements of the children. As it was assumed that the welfare of children was best served by living with their mother (except in cases of abuse or neglect), mothers were automatically granted child custody, while fathers were automatically required to pay child maintenance. Although laws regarding financial obligations following divorce differ between countries, the general principle is that financial compensation is given to the financially weaker party, and to the party more involved in raising the children (Claessens & Mortelmans, 2018). But alongside the shifting meaning of marriage, societal views on parenting, and on fathering, in particular, have also shifted. The most visible exponent thereof is the rise in joint legal custody arrangements followed by joint physical custody (Bernardi & Mortelmans, 2021; Nielsen, 2018; Steinbach, 2019). Even if leaving a partnership has become easier, societies give parents the message that they have lifelong parenting responsibilities. In the Netherlands, for example, couples are obliged to draw up a "Parenting Plan," which is a binding agreement that outlines how the parents plan to provide care and support for their child, and how they intend to communicate and inform each other about the child's well-being (de Bruijn et al., 2018).

Divorce Trends

Even though the emphasis in this chapter is on the United States and Europe, divorce rates have been rising around the globe (until very recently) (Emery, 2013). In this section, we consider the official statistics produced by governments. In order to monitor the stability of marriages, statistical offices have produced a wide range of indicators. Without exception, these indicators have shown that rates of relationship dissolution have been rising. The most simple indicator that can be used to track divorce trends is the *absolute number of divorcees.* For a given population, we can count the number of people who are currently divorced (and not remarried), and can follow that number over time. The advantage of basing an analysis on the absolute number is that it reflects the current size of the group of divorcees. The disadvantage of doing so is that the proportion of divorcees could stay stable when the population itself is growing. Therefore, the *crude divorce rate* is used more frequently in time series. This measure is defined as "the ratio of the number of divorces during the year to the average population in that year. The value is expressed per 1000 inhabitants"(EuroStat, 2019). Table 30.1 gives an overview of the crude divorce rate for selected countries since 1960.

The disadvantage of relying on the crude divorce rate is that it does not take into account the composition of the population. For example, if the birth rate is decreasing, the divorce rate will rise automatically (even when the number of divorces stays stable). The divorce rate also increases when the age at marriage decreases, as couples have a higher risk of divorce at younger ages. Therefore, the *refined divorce rate* can be used to calculate the number of divorces in a given year relative to the number of married women in a certain age bracket.

For decades, scholars have been debating trends in divorce, particularly in the United States. These analyses have taken two different effects into account: period and (marriage) cohort effects. *Period effects* occur when all marriages are influenced by a phenomenon at the same time. An example of a period effect is a change in divorce law. *Cohort effects* (we are referring here to marriage cohorts, and not to birth cohorts, as is often done in demography) occur when couples marrying in a specific year do so under different conditions than cohorts marrying in another year. An example of a cohort effect is a change in attitudes or values that affects a certain marriage cohort. If members of a younger marriage cohort no longer see marriage as a lifelong commitment but as a contract that could be broken, this cohort might have different divorce risks than older cohorts. Most of these studies conclude that period effects in divorce are somewhat larger than cohort effects (Teachman, 2002).

Though it is widely known that divorce rates have been rising for decades, explaining these trends is more challenging. To explain why divorce rates have been increasing in the industrialized world, both economic and cultural theories have been developed. The economic theory of the family views specialization and mutual dependence in couples as protective factors in relationships. The sex-specific specialization in the male-breadwinner model led to the development of a family system that was supposed to optimize marital

Table 30.1 Crude Divorce Rate (1960–2010) in Five Selected Countries

	1960	1980	2000	2010
France			1.9	2.1
Germany	1.0	1.8	2.4	2.3
Sweden	1.2	2.4	2.4	2.5
UK		2.6	2.6	2.1
USA	2.2	3.5	4.0	3.6

Source: National Center for Health Statistics (2019); EuroStat (2019).

resources and human capital (Becker, 1981). The theory points to the sharp increase in women entering the labor market since the 1970s that disturbed the specialization of families, leading to more breakups. Even though this theory "blames" women for the increase in divorces, empirical evidence of a correlation between female employment and divorce trends has been found in many countries (Kalmijn, 2007). In opposition to the economic explanation, the cultural theory known as the second demographic transition framework (Lesthaeghe, 2010) points to societal developments such as individualization, secularization, and a rise in postmaterialist values. These changes have led to a deinstitutionalization of marriage (a weakening of the power of social norms to dictate the partners' behavior) and, in turn, a lowering of the threshold for leaving a marriage (Cherlin, 2004). An empirical test of this theory is more difficult, because validated and continuous measurements of values are often lacking in longitudinal household surveys (and are absent in administrative data). Kaufman (2000), however, showed that men with more egalitarian attitudes have a lower risk at divorce. None of these theories have succeeded in explaining all the trends in divorce as a mixture of both the economic and the cultural change is responsible for the period (and to a lesser degree the cohort) effects in divorce (Lesthaeghe, 2010; Teachman, 2002).

More recently, divorce trends have started to level off or even decline. First observed in the United States (Cohen, 2018; Smock & Schwartz, 2020), the reversal of the divorce trends has now become visible in several countries (Esping-Andersen, 2016). As theories had tried to explain the rise in divorce, a new question came up regarding macrolevel developments: "Have marriages become more stable?" As a decrease in divorce rates suggests that fewer people are divorcing, it may be assumed that marriages indeed have become more stable. However, a second, related question then arises: "Given that unmarried cohabitation is becoming increasingly common, is it possible that the plateauing of divorce rates is attributable to the rise in unmarried cohabitation?" After all, these couples do not enter marital or divorce statistics (Boertien, 2019). An advanced statistical analysis of U.S. divorce rates taking into account the population age structure and the marital order initially showed that there was no real decrease in divorce rates (Goldstein, 1999). More recent analyses produced a more nuanced picture: U.S. divorce rates did decrease between 1980 and 2000. The estimated annual divorce probability showed that more recent marriage cohorts are more stable, as the divorce risk has fallen among younger couples (Cohen, 2018). Referring to the second question, those who choose to marry during a period of time in which unmarried cohabitation is becoming the norm may be more likely to enter more stable marriages. Unmarried cohabitation is less stable than marriage (Guzzo, 2014), perhaps because those who enter unmarried cohabiting relationships are less selective (Dush et al., 2003; Perelli-Harris et al., 2017; Rosenfeld & Roesler, 2019). A cultural explanation is that value patterns of cohabiting couples are more individualized, resulting in relationships that are less stable. This individual effect is further reinforced on the macrolevel as the prevalence of cohabitation reinforces the instability effect found at the individual level (Liefbroer & Dourleijn, 2006). The explanation of decreasing divorce rates in terms of stability or selectivity as not been settled. The reversal of these trends is often too recent to be thoroughly examined.

These analyses are performed at the macrolevel. Observing and explaining aggregated trends is necessary though not sufficient for studying the uncoupling processes in society. Therefore, the macrolevel analyses are supplemented with individual-level studies to reveal the individual risk factors that predict divorce or cohabitation breakup. In the next section, we present an overview of these studies on divorce risk (after which we also look at the consequences for individuals). But first we present the main theoretical perspectives that have been developed to understand the process of uncoupling at the individual level.

Theoretical Perspectives on Divorce

No "grand theory" (Mills, 1959) has been proposed to explain the multiple individual pathways to divorce. Nevertheless, some scholars have developed theoretical frameworks that aim to produce a broad perspective on why partners decide to end their relationship. After, we consider how each theory predicts unique risk factors of divorce.

Levinger's Social Exchange Theory

A first, widely discussed theory of divorce is the social exchange theory of Levinger (1965, 1976). The theory starts from the observation that the marital bond can be explained by the cohesiveness of a social group. Understanding the reasons why spouses stay together therefore requires insight into the reasons why members remain in their social group. Partners are bound in a marriage by three forces: (a) the attractiveness of the marriage, (b) the costs of breaking up, and (c) the inverse relation between the attractiveness of the marriage and cost of the alternative (being single or entering another relationship). The first component of the theory (attractiveness) contains affectionate (love, charm), material (income, assets), and symbolic (status) rewards. The costs of leaving the marriage are also affectional (risk of loneliness), material (risk of becoming poor), and symbolic (risk of stigma as a divorcee). The last component refers to a continuous evaluative balance. Partners exchange benefits and costs and evaluate whether their balance is (still) greater than potential alternatives. This subjective cost-benefit ratio is referred to as "marital quality" and is measured using indicators of marital satisfaction. Levinger's framework has inspired divorce research on the macro- (e.g., Wagner, 2019) and micro-level (e.g., Boertien & Härkönen, 2018). The risk factors of divorce can be classified as benefits, costs, or alternative attractions.

Attachment Theory

Attachment theory was developed by Bowlby (1977), who defined attachment theory as "a way of conceptualizing the propensity of human beings to make strong affectional bonds to particular others" (Bowlby, 1977, p. 201). Initially, the theory addressed the relationship between an infant and its primary caretaker. As the field expanded, attachment theory encompassed adult attachment, explaining how adults function in their personal relationships (Hazan & Shaver, 1987). It is clear that a romantic relationship is different from the infant–caregiver one, and yet adults in a relationship tend to be attached to each other in similar ways. Hazan and Shaver (1987) defined three attachment styles in adults: secure, anxious, and anxious-ambivalent. Later, the three-styles model inspired a four-types model: secure, dismissing-avoidant, preoccupied, and fearful-avoidant (Bartholomew & Horowitz, 1991). Attachment theory has since been applied as a framework in divorce research to guide investigation of divorce risks and remarriage rates. Ceglian and Gardner (1999), for example, showed how nonsecure attachment styles in adulthood predict proneness to divorce.

Divorce Process Theories

As we have touched upon earlier, divorce is often treated as a dichotomous event for the sake of statistics, but in reality spouses go through a process of decoupling. Two main theoretical frameworks have been advanced to sketch the stages that spouses go through when ending a marriage. The first theory presents a six-stage process that individuals go through (Bohannon, 1973). The first step is *emotional divorce* in which one or both spouses start withdrawing from the relationship. Exit strategies are planned and lead to the second phase of *legal divorce*. Third, the *economic divorce* involves taking all practical steps to split up the household (e.g., finding a new place to live or starting to work). The *co-parental divorce* only applies to parents as they need to forge an agreement about post-divorce parenting and custody arrangement. The fifth step is the *community divorce* which refers to the shared networks of the ex-spouses that also will split as each might demand that their friends pick sides. The last stage is *psychic divorce* and involves the psychological process of regaining autonomy and emotional independence from the previous spouse.

Bohannon's last phase (psychic divorce) was further developed into a separate process theory by Wiseman (1975) who used the classic theory by Kubler-Ross (1969) on mourning. In the *denial* phase, the marriage is not (yet) in crisis, but spouses are doing what they can to keep the relationship up and running. Sometimes the common resources of the household or the well-being of the children keep the couple in this phase for a substantial period of their lives. The end of the denial period is caused by internal or external stress and the spouses enter the stage of *loss and depression*. The next phase is termed "anger and ambivalence" where it becomes clear to both partners that the marriage is going to end. In this phase, anger is characterized by a drifting away of both partners beyond a point of no return. The phase of *reorientation of lifestyle and identity* moves ex-partners beyond the marriage as they seek their way into their new life. Coping mechanisms (financial and psychological) are developed to deal with life after marriage. Often this phase sees individuals experimenting with sexual contacts, rediscovering new identities, or, on the contrary, avoiding social contact. Isolation and loneliness are imminent dangers at this point. The process is closed with finding a new equilibrium in *acceptance and a new level of functioning*. Other variations have been developed throughout time (e.g., Kaslow, 2008; Kessler, 1975; Van Gasse & Mortelmans, 2020), each showing variations on these two basic theories and each with specific family therapy implications.

The Divorce-Stress-Adjustment Perspective

The divorce-stress-adjustment perspective is a process model of divorce that explains how the (negative) consequences of divorce are produced (Amato, 2000). The core of the theory considers divorce a process that triggers stressful events. These stressful mediators determine how well ex-spouses will adapt to the divorce. The model identifies both stressors for adults and for children. Adults may be confronted with stress about the post-divorce parental role (lone parenthood or loss of custody), the loss of emotional support (loneliness), or continuous conflict with the ex-partner. For children, Amato (2000) identified factors like a decline in parental support, loss of contact with a parent, continuing parental conflict, and economic decline of the post-divorce household. The presence of these mediators determines the way adults and children experience the divorce. The model also takes into account that the process of ending a relationship and the mourning do not take place at the same moment for every member of the family (e.g., spouses or children) (Emery, 1994).

Outcomes of divorce might be influenced by moderating factors that worsen the outcomes or serve as buffers (protective factors). Amato (2000) identified three possible moderators. First, personal factors play a role, including self-efficacy, coping skills, and social skills (Muhlbauer et al., 2020) or health condition (Lam et al., 2020). Second, interpersonal factors such as one's social networks may intervene in limiting negative consequences (de Bel et al., 2018; Potter, 2020). And finally, structural or societal factors such as employment, community services, and family policies can help to reduce negative consequences of divorce (Ooms, 2019; Thielemans & Mortelmans, 2018). Demographic factors like gender, age, race, ethnicity, and culture can also play a role in the divorce process and determine the outcomes (Kaplan et al., 2020; Ryabov & Zhang, 2019; Van Damme, 2020).

An interesting component of this theory is the embeddedness of two outcome routes. The *crisis perspective* sees divorce as a stressful event people go through but that eventually results in an adjustment to a new life phase without substantial long-lasting issues. The *chronic strain perspective* implies that people will experience long-term negative consequences (strains) from their divorce. Amato (2000) did not problematize these two perspective in this singular framework as researchers can find evidence for both the crisis and the chronic strain perspective, depending on the outcome they are studying or the context they are looking at.

Divorce Risks

Gaining insight into the legal process of divorce does not explain why couples decide to split up and go through a process of leaving their marriage. When we focus on the divorce, the field of divorce studies is divided into three domains: the causes, processes, and consequences of divorce. Insights into the process of divorce are least developed. In fact, such little attention has been paid to the procedural questions of splitting up that I have decided to leave them out of this chapter (for more information, see: Poladian & Holtzworth-Munroe, 2019; van Dijk et al., 2020; Wall & Lynn, 2016). In this chapter, I give more attention to the antecedents of divorce, the risk factors. In the next paragraphs, I give an overview of the risk factors that increase the possibility of a breakup and the consequences experienced by adults after they have divorced.

The title of this section is "Divorce Risks." Although we often refer to the causes or antecedents of divorce, it is important to keep in mind that relationship instability can never be perfectly predicted. Although research has shown that certain couples have an elevated risk of divorce, such results do not tell us whether their relationships will actually end. Moreover, the phenomenon of divorce is so multifaceted that not a single marriage would survive if divorce risks were deterministic. As mentioned, I give an overview of the most important risk factors, but several other excellent in-depth reviews are also available (see: Bradbury et al., 2000; Lyngstad & Jalovaara, 2010).

Time-Related Risk Factors

Time-related factors can be considered from two angles. First, we can take historical time and look at the development of divorce through time. This is what we did earlier when we considered the different changes of divorce laws. Starting from a taboo and a legal prohibition on divorce, a transition can be observed to a life event that even though unpleasant, is accepted as part of (adult) life. A second angle, however, considers the personal time of individuals and more specifically their life course. A well-documented phenomenon is the *intergenerational transmission of divorce*. Having divorced parents increases the risk of divorce; thus, children of divorced parents are more likely to divorce themselves. The mechanisms behind this transmission are threefold. First, children of divorced parents might lack relationship skills, as they are less likely to learn these skills while being socialized. Second, children in broken families may "learn" from their parental home that a marriage is something that can be broken (Amato & DeBoer, 2001). Third, the stress of the divorce and a decline in financial resources may lead children of divorced parents to leave the parental home early, and to enter a partnership at a younger age than their peers. As this can result in a less optimal partner match, their risk of divorce increases. This last explanation is also used in a more general way to account for the effect of *age at marriage*: the younger a person is when they marry, the higher their divorce risk is (South, 1995).

Educational Attainment

A debate in the literature concerns the question whether having higher *educational attainment* increases or decreases the risk of divorce. The focus in this debate lies on the effect of female education as classic economic theories of the family state that women with higher education (i.e., more human capital) have more opportunities to leave the marriage, which destabilizes the relationship and thus increases the risk of divorce (Becker, 1981). A counterargument against this view is that women with higher educational levels tend to have higher levels of economic security, which can reduce the financial stress in a relationship and help to stabilize the marriage (Oppenheimer, 1997). The competing results in the debate are partially due to the reversal of the educational gradient over time (Matysiak et al., 2014; Van Damme, 2019): where women in the 1970s were more often higher educated when leaving a marriage (due to elevated resources), nowadays lower-educated women see their marriage dissolve more often. Cross-country analyses (Härkönen & Dronkers, 2006) uncovered evidence not only of a change in the gradient but of huge international differences in the effect.

Economic Risk Factors: Female Labor Participation

A second field in the gender debate on divorce is the influence of *female income and labor force participation*. I have already mentioned the Beckerian theory, which proposes that gender specialization in a marriage is disrupted by female employment leading to more pressure on the relationship and more divorces. And even though some evidence has been found for the specialization hypothesis (e.g., Jalovaara, 2001), it has been widely criticized, and countered with the argument that a marriage tends to be more stable when both spouses contribute to the income of the household (Oppenheimer, 1997). Also this question could not be solved independently from country contexts. There is evidence that the effect of female employment on a couple's divorce risk differs depending on whether the partners are living in a country with social policies that support (gender) equality and that encourage a more equitable division of unpaid household labor (Cooke et al., 2013). A renewed interest in the debate arose after the 2008 global economic crisis. As there is a negative relationship between the unemployment rate and the divorce rate (at the country level) due to the postponement of divorce (Amato & Beattie, 2011), the question was asked whether this would also be true at the individual level. The answer was surprisingly negative as men in particular showed that their unemployment had a negative impact on relationship stability (Charles & Stephens, 2001; Solaz et al., 2020).

Marriage Rank and Cohabitation

Another life course-related risk factor is the rank of the marriage. Even though a popular sentiment suggests that people learn from their mistakes, empirical research shows that higher-order marriages are less stable than first marriages. The evidence goes in the opposite direction, as having undergone a divorce lowers the threshold for separating a second or a third time (which can also be seen as a sort of learning effect) (Coleman et al., 2000).

Next to rank, the formal relationship type also matters. As most research on divorce started in the early 1970s, when marriage was the dominant relationship type, insights into cohabitation only started in the 1990s. These studies found that cohabitating relationships are less stable than marriages (Guzzo, 2014; Wu, 1995). A selection (or weeding-out) effect may be at play as the strongest cohabitations often develop into marriages, which, in turn, increases the dissolution risk of cohabitations as a whole. A second mechanism at play is that cohabitation might be considered a trial marriage (cohabiters are less certain of their partner choice, and may conclude that a match is not suitable), and that people who cohabit have different value patterns than people who marry (Liefbroer & Dourleijn, 2006). This value pattern is a third explanation as bearing more individualized *values* and being less *religious* tend to increase the risk of divorce (Lehrer & Chiswick, 1993).

Personality as a Risk Factor

Personality is defined as a set of relatively stable psychological traits and mechanisms within the individual potentially steering behavior (Larsen & Buss, 2008). It has been shown to influence the stability of a relationship, with some personality traits outperforming socioeconomic risk factors in predicting divorce (Roberts et al., 2007; Yu et al., 2020). We can expect personality to become an even more important risk factor in the future as the erosion of traditional family norms progresses (and external barriers to divorce weaken). Personality is often studied with the aid of the "big five" model, which refers to five traits that make up an individual's personality, and that influence their relationship stability to varying degrees (John et al., 2008; John & Srivastava, 1999). Neuroticism, extroversion, and openness are linked to an increased risk of relationship dissolution, whereas conscientiousness and agreeableness are associated with a reduced risk of relationship dissolution (e.g., Lundberg, 2012). People with high levels of agreeableness and conscientiousness tend to have stable marriages (e.g., Boertien & Mortelmans, 2017), while people who are highly neurotic (difficult to live with) or highly extroverted (constantly open to new alternatives) are more likely to divorce (Spikic, 2020).

Physical and Mental Health

A large amount of studies have documented the health consequences of divorce and separation (Booth & Johnson, 1994; Lam et al., 2020; Rabin, 2019). But both physical and mental health are also risk factors for relationships (Muhlbauer et al., 2020). A caveat to these results is the so-called health selection in marriage whereby studies have showed that healthier people are more likely to marry but also that marriage "causes" more healthy behavior (Guner et al., 2018; Joung et al., 1998). This leads to a subpopulation that diverges from the general population in health and health behavior.

Notwithstanding this health-selection-into-marriage process, health issues in themselves are found by some to lead to more divorces (Booth & Johnson, 1994; Yorgason et al., 2008) while others have found no effect (Konstam et al., 1998). Alcohol and drug use on the other hand are consistently found as a risk factor. Both in men and in women, increased substance use puts pressure on romantic relationships, facilitating their demise (Amato & Previti, 2003; Tran et al., 2016).

Individual psychopathology is also related to an increased risk in marital breakdown. In a large-scale study, Kessler et al. (1998) identified increased divorce risks in a wide range of psychiatric disorders like mood disorders, anxiety disorders (except for simple and social phobia), substance use disorders, and conduct disorders. Also the combination of multiple disorders further increased the risk.

Genetics and Divorce

Furthermore, genetic research has identified genetic components of the intergenerational transmission of divorce (D'Onofrio et al., 2007). Most research has been done on twin studies identifying the genetic contribution of spouses to the risk of divorce or separation (Jockin et al., 1996). McGue and Lykken (1992) found that more than one third of the variance in the overall heritability of divorce risk was attributable to genetic factors. More recently, most empirical work has addressed the role of genes in the link between marital status change and alcohol consumption (Dinescu et al., 2016; Prescott & Kendler, 2001; Smith & Gibson, 2020).

Protective Factors

When we discussed relationship type as a risk factor, we already showed how marrying is more protective to a breakup than cohabiting with a partner. More importantly, however, are children as a protective factor (both for the married and the cohabiting couples) (Steele et al., 2006). Children are a "marriage-specific capital" (Becker et al., 1977, p. 1154), which means that the "costs" of dissolving the marriage are higher, both emotionally and economically, when children are involved. Worth noting here is that the ages of the children also matter: that is, the protective effect of children diminishes as they grow older (Waite & Lillard, 1991).

Gray Divorce

A recent domain in divorce risk research is the study of the so-called gray divorce. This is defined as a divorce where at least one of the partners is age 50 or older. Estimations have shown that in the United States, one of four divorces is a gray divorce (Brown & Lin, 2012). The rise in divorce among older couples was not unexpected. In fact, already in the 1980s, Uhlenberg and Myers (1981) predicted the current trend and attributed it to four developments. First, as divorce becomes more common, remarriage is also increasing. As we argued before, remarriage is less stable leading to more new divorces at higher ages.

Second, the taboo on divorce has disappeared which lowers the threshold for older people as well to leave an unhappy marriage. Third, the increase in labor participation of women across all cohorts also makes leaving a marriage a real possibility for older women. And fourth, the sheer aging of populations makes that more people grow old and more people are at risk of divorce until higher ages.

The research on antecedents of gray divorce are very often based on qualitative or small-scale surveys (Canham et al., 2014; Crowley, 2019a). Nevertheless, reasons for divorce at an older age have recurred across several studies. First, divorcees express a lack of love as the reason for ending their relationship. Falling out of love after a long-term relationship is one of the main causes reported for gray divorce (Montenegro, 2004). Second, a lack of ability to achieve an expressive individualistic marriage or sometimes defined as "growing apart" is given as a cause to split up. This involves different lifestyles and values of both spouses (Crowley, 2019b). A third group of reasons are more commitment-based and include infidelity or adultery. For women, more often alcohol and drug abuse were mentioned as causes of the breakup (Taylor, 2009).

A surprising conclusion of this research is that the factors identified earlier in this section on divorce risks are less applicable to gray divorce. As marriages last longer, more ideational factors seem to play a role in ending these relationships. For example, we discussed how parental divorce can have intergenerational "learning effects" on their offspring, but as these children grow old and have a long relationship, these effects wade off. Nevertheless, some structural factors in the life course have also been identified as risk factors. First, the empty nest (i.e., when all children have left the household) leads to an increase in divorce. Because children are a protective factor in relationships, the departure of children also signals the end of the childrearing period in which this protective power clearly wanes. Second, retirement has a comparable effect because the end of the labor career implies that partners are spending more time at home, leading to potentially increased conflict (Canham et al., 2014). Though, it must be noted that healthy couples may strengthen their relationship through retirement instead of observing its demise (Wickrama et al., 2013). Third, health as a risk factor in divorce (see above) might play a significant role in relationships at older age. As spouses are each other's primary caretakers, health deterioration in one of the partners can also lead to more stress and lower marital quality (Booth & Johnson, 1994; Karraker & Latham, 2015; Pinquart & Sorensen, 2011).

Consequences of Divorce for Adults

We now turn from the antecedents of divorce to the consequences for adults. In their 1991 meta-analysis, Amato and Keith (1991) identified eight domains of the consequences of divorce for children, which were additionally mediated by several sociodemographic background characteristics. For adults, the consequences of divorce have been studied in the domains of psychological adjustment (well-being), health (physical and mental), social adjustment (social networks and loneliness), economics (income and poverty), behavioral adjustment (drinking, drug use, violence), and parenthood (both from the child's and the parent's perspective). These consequences have been studied in both the short and the long run (e.g., Amato & Cheadle, 2005; Bernardi & Radl, 2014; Fabricius & Luecken, 2007; Kalmijn, 2012a). Crucial when taking consequences into account is the selection-causation question. If studies find effects of divorce, it should always be taken into account that these factors might have been already present during the marriage. Thus, these consequences may have played a role in the deterioration of marital quality that eventually led to the breakup. As we discuss in more detail below, the ex-partners might suffer financially after a divorce. Moreover, as we pointed out above, financial stress and economic hardship can lead to marital problems and, eventually, to the dissolution of a marriage. Therefore, when evaluating studies on the consequences of divorce, we need to consider both the time since the divorce (as some consequences wane after a period of time) and selection issues (as these factors might significantly reduce the severity of the consequences).

Financial Consequences of Divorce

We start with the financial consequences of divorce as there is only one finding in this field so robust that in financial terms, women suffer more from a breakup than men (Mortelmans, 2020b). DiPrete and McManus (2000) reported for the United States that, on average, men lost 15% of their adjusted household income, while women lost 26% of their income following a divorce. This finding is surprisingly constant over time. In 2016, Hauser et al. (2016) showed that U.S. women experienced a decline in income of 25%, whereas de Vaus et al. (2017) found a decrease in income of 30% for U.S. women. Similar findings are reported for different European countries, with women losing more financially and men showing a more diverse pattern of gains and losses. Cross-country differences have been attributed to cross-country differences in labor market conditions, child care infrastructure, and family policies (e.g., marital taxation systems or financial subsidies for parental child care) (Andreß et al., 2006; Bayaz-Ozturk et al., 2018).

With regard to the dissolution of cohabiting unions, financial losses were more modest. First, compared to married couples, cohabiters tend to have a more equal division of paid work (Snoeckx et al., 2008). Thus, married women are more likely than cohabitating women to be financially dependent on their partner. Second, cohabiters are less likely to have children, and they tend to be younger when ending a relationship (Batalova & Cohen, 2002; Brines & Joyner, 1999; Hamplova, 2002; Rindfuss & Vandenheuvel, 1990). Although most studies consider previously married partners, far fewer results on post-dissolution income trajectories are available for previously cohabiting partners. The oldest study on the economic consequences of the dissolution of cohabitating relationships was conducted in the United States by Avellar and Smock (2005). They found that previously married men gained in equalized household income (+11%), while formerly cohabitating men lost a small percentage of their income (-1%).

The losses of previously cohabiting women were shown to be more limited (-24%) than those of previously married women (-48%). For the Netherlands, Manting and Bouman (2006) found that the post-relationship decline in economic well-being was greater for divorced women (-23%) than for formerly cohabitating women (-14%). The economic consequences of relationship dissolution were shown to be more severe for formerly cohabitating men (-4%) than for divorced men (+7%). Using Belgian register data, de Regt et al. (2012) also found a more substantial drop in income for divorced women (-33%) than for cohabiting women (-22%). Over time, there have been few studies on this issue that allow us to compare and observe trends. However, for the United States, Tach and Eads (2015) observed a diminishing gap in income losses between divorced and formerly cohabiting ex-partners. They argued that for U.S. women, the consequences of divorce have become more positive, but the consequences of the breakup of a cohabiting relationship have become more negative. They explained this surprising finding by pointing to the changing composition of both married and cohabiting couples in terms of economic background. In the United States, married households have become economically stronger and are more likely to have two earners, while cohabiting households tend to be situated at the lower end of the income distribution. Furthermore, the repartnering market has changed significantly, with more disadvantaged divorcees tending to cohabit instead of remarry.

In addition to estimating the changes in income, researchers have looked at the strategies ex-partners develop to cope with their financial losses. When considering financial behavior after a divorce, the literature tends to focus on two main coping mechanisms: finding a new partner and changing one's labor market behavior. Some studies have taken into account a third strategy: namely, returning to the parental home, which has also been called the "boomerang effect" (Albertini et al., 2018; Mortelmans et al., 2020). Studies that take *repartnering* into account as a coping strategy have observed different effects based on gender, with men, on average, repartnering more quickly and more frequently than women (Coleman et al., 2000; South, 1991). One explanation for this pattern is that having (young) children will intensify a divorcee's economic needs, at the same time lowering their chances of repartnering due to their decreased meeting opportunities and level of attractiveness. A second explanation looks at a divorcee's job, observing that having a good job tends to increase a person's attractiveness, while also increasing the individual's repartnering opportunities through intensified contacts and an enlarged network. From a Beckerian point of view, this latter explanation only applies to men. For women, being employed will reduce their repartnering needs (financially speaking) and make them less attractive, as they are less available to take on the female role in a specialized household with a single earner. Furthermore, socioeconomic factors influence the repartnering of both men and women, albeit in opposite directions. For women, a nonsignificant or a negative educational gradient has often been found. This has been characterized as an independence effect among higher-educated women (Ozawo & Yoon, 2002). For men, their chances of repartnering has been shown to increase as their educational level rises. The second strategy for coping with financial losses after divorce is to increase one's *labor market participation*. Increasing employment activities as a response to the breakdown of a relationship can improve a divorcee's income position, and lowers their risk of poverty (Dewilde, 2006). Not surprisingly, women find it more difficult than men to increase their labor market participation, as their care burden often hinders or prevents them from working more. Moreover, preseparation role patterns—with women tending to care for children at the expense of their careers—can influence a potential return to the labor market later on. These two strategies of repartnering and increasing one's labor market participation are related. Research has shown that when these strategies are combined, seeking or remaining in full-time employment outweighs the benefits of repartnering for women (Jansen et al., 2009).

Health After Divorce

Next to the effect of children, the research on the health consequences of divorce and relationship breakup is probably one of the most extensive. Reviewing this whole domain here would be impossible as there are already several review articles summarizing these hundreds of studies (Amato, 2000; Ross et al., 1990; Sbarra, 2015; Sbarra et al., 2011). However, there is quite some consistency in the findings and across time: health in divorced spouses tends to be worse than in married families. Mortality rates are higher and specifically among men (up to 250% higher for divorced men) (Gove, 1973; Rogers, 1995). The list of worse health outcomes go from simple colds (Cohen et al., 1997) to cardiovascular diseases (Manfredini et al., 2017), cancer treatments (Goodwin et al., 1987), and frailty (Kojima et al., 2020). It is also not helpful that physical activity decreases after being divorced (Engberg et al., 2012; Gropper et al., 2020).

With regard to mental health problems and psychological adjustment, the same story unfolds: divorced individuals have more negative outcomes like depression (Booth & Amato, 1991; Goldfarb & Trudel, 2019; Mandemakers & Kalmijn, 2018), negative self-esteem (Chung et al., 2002), and anxiety (Bramlett & Mosher, 2002; Hetherington & Kelly, 2002). Other studies show a higher suicide rate among the divorced (Evans et al., 2016; Kyung-Sook et al., 2018) and an increase in loneliness (Leopold, 2018). And comparable to the physical exercise, studies find a lower intention for divorced individuals to turn to professional help when confronted with mental health issues (Bracke et al., 2010).

Finding health differences appears also more straightforward than explaining them (Sbarra & Coan, 2017). Often general stress and coping theory (Pearlin, 1989) or the aforementioned stress-divorce-adjustment perspective (Amato, 2000) is used to explain these patterns of deteriorating health after life events. Also, the decrease in resources (especially financial resources) explains why both physical and mental health are worse after divorce. Important to mention in this respect is the potential self-selection of health issues into marriage that also partly explains the outcomes (see earlier).

Networks and Social Adjustment After Divorce

Social networks can be considered a form of marital capital. According to the dynamic withdrawal hypothesis (Milardo, 1982), networks of married individuals become smaller and more overlapping (Kalmijn, 2003). Following a divorce, a reduction of social networks is observed as both family and friend networks split (Aeby & van Hooff, 2019). This is called the *isolation hypothesis* which is contradicted by the *liberation hypothesis* that expects an increase in the social network of divorcees after an initial drop (Kalmijn, 2012b; Kalmijn & Van Groenou, 2005). New networks are sought after divorce to support divorcees in their post-divorce adjustment (Kramrei et al., 2007; McKenry & Price, 1991). New networks are built while moving to new neighborhoods (Spanier & Thompson, 1984) and while dating in search of a new partner (Wu & Schimmele, 2005), and shared physical custody also allows parents to meet new people and expand their social network (Botterman et al., 2015).

Lone Parenthood and Poverty After Divorce

As this chapter focuses on adult life, we do not go into the consequences of divorce for children. But having children implies different consequences in a number of domains. As we have explained, a woman's economic well-being after a relationship fails may be negatively affected if she has primary responsibility for her children (and is thus in a classic mother-centered custodial arrangement) (Poortman, 2000). First, the presence of children increases the economic needs of the family (as measured in equivalence scales in statistical models). Second, having children affects a woman's labor market options (Drobnic, 2000; Raeymaeckers et al., 2008; Thielemans & Mortelmans, 2018) and her attractiveness in the remarriage market (Buckle et al., 1996; Coleman et al., 2000). Therefore, the risk of poverty for the partner who takes care of the couple's children after the breakup (in most cases, the mother) is considerably higher for lone mothers (Hogendoorn et al., 2019; McKeever & Wolfinger, 2006, 2012). The highest at-risk-of-poverty rates among lone mothers were reported in U.S. studies: that is, 63% (without transfer payments) and 51% (with transfer payments) (Casey & Maldonado, 2012). Conversely, in European studies, the at-risk-of-poverty rates of lone mothers have generally been found to be lower, ranging from 7% in Poland to 37% in Latvia. Low at-risk-of-poverty rates for lone parents have also been reported for Sweden (15%), Norway (16%), and the Netherlands (16%). The highest at-risk-of-poverty rates in the European context have been reported for Eastern European countries like Lithuania (32%) and Hungary (31%) and for Ireland (29%), Spain (27%), and Italy (27%) (Hübgen, 2018, 2020; Organisation for Economic Co-operation and Development, 2011).

Divorce as a keystone of the family kaleidoscope

This chapter has shown that the field of divorce studies is extensive. We started the chapter by defining divorce—or, rather, uncoupling, as cohabitations also dissolve, and tend to do so at a faster pace than marriages. Next, we looked at family law and the changes in divorce procedures over time. The availability of unilateral and no-fault divorce has now spread to all industrialized countries. However, the main driver of the spectacular increase in divorce is not the law but rather a combination of economic and cultural factors that have significantly influenced family life over the past 50 years. In the second part of the chapter, we discussed the extensive research on the causes and consequences of divorce. The many studies on this topic that have been published over the decades clearly indicate that divorce is a multifaceted phenomenon. A wide range of risk factors endanger marital stability, with between one half and two thirds of marriages ending in a divorce. Many of the same factors appear to affect the consequences of divorce. There is evidence that divorce has negative effects on the relationship stability of both adults and children, and that some of these effects can be measured across generations.

What will the future bring? As Cherlin (2004) showed more than a decade ago, predicting trends in family life has become a complex endeavor. One trend seems to prevail: marriage is no longer a universal "till-death-do-us-part" arrangement. The life courses of most people living today will be characterized by multiple waves of coupling and uncoupling. Complexities in the family kaleidoscope (Mortelmans et al., 2016) are increasing and call for the development of new theoretical perspectives (Sigle, 2016). While families and stratification processes are becoming ever more intertwined, we do not yet fully understand the impact these family complexities are having on the life course. As divorce researchers, we are not (yet) equipped to deal with this hypercomplexity. Some initial progress has been made in studies on union dissolution among same-sex couples (Andersson et al., 2006), trans people (Dierckx et al., 2018), or living apart together (LAT) relationships (Connidis et al., 2017). Nevertheless, even though we have access to large-scale survey infrastructure and administrative data, most of these data are on traditional family forms like marriages and cohabitations. In order to develop new theoretical insights into the causes and consequences of divorce, mixed-method studies that provide timely insights into new and complex family processes are needed. One specific blind spot that demands attention is the role of technology. As Tinder and other dating platforms become increasingly widespread, family sociologists know little about whether the use of this technology represents a risk factor for relationships or a helpful tool in dealing with complex families by reducing stress and poor relationship quality. At this moment, we have no clue whether we should swipe left or swipe right.

References

Aeby, G., & van Hooff, J. (2019). Who gets custody of the friends? Online narratives of changes in friendship networks following relationship breakdown. *Families, Relationships and Societies*, *8*(3), 411–426. https://doi.org/10.1332/204674318x15271464535444

Albertini, M., Gähler, M., & Härkönen, J. (2018). Moving back to "mamma"? Divorce, intergenerational coresidence, and latent family solidarity in Sweden. *Population, Space and Place*, *24*(6), 1–12. https://doi.org/10.1002/psp.2142

Amato, P. R. (2000). The consequences of divorce for adults and children. *Journal of Marriage and the Family, 62*(4), 1269–1287. https://doi.org/10.1111/j.1741-3737.2000.01269.x

Amato, P. R. (2010). Research on divorce: Continuing trends and new developments. *Journal of Marriage and the Family, 72*(3), 650–666. https://doi.org/10.1111/j.1741-3737.2010.00723.x

Amato, P. R., & Beattie, B. (2011). Does the unemployment rate affect the divorce rate? An analysis of state data 1960–2005. *Social Science Research, 40*(3), 705–715. https://doi.org/https://doi.org/10.1016/j.ssresearch.2010.12.012

Amato, P. R., & Cheadle, J. (2005). The long reach of divorce: Divorce and child well-being across three generations. *Journal of Marriage and the Family, 67*(1), 191–206. https://doi.org/10.1111/j.0022-2445.2005.00014.x

Amato, P. R., & DeBoer, D. D. (2001). The transmission of marital instability across generations: Relationship skills or commitment to marriage? *Journal of Marriage and the Family, 63*(4), 1038–1051. https://doi.org/10.1111/j.1741-3737.2001.01038.x

Amato, P. R., & Previti, D. (2003). People's reasons for divorcing: Gender, social class, the life course, and adjustment. *Journal of Family Issues, 24*(5), 602–626. https://doi.org/10.1177/0192513x03254507

Andersson, G., Noack, T., Seierstad, A., & Weedon-Fekjær, H. (2006). The demographics of same-sex marriages in Norway and Sweden. *Demography, 43*(1), 79–98. https://doi.org/10.1353/dem.2006.0001

Andreß, H.-J., Borgloh, B., Bröckel, M., Giesselmann, M., & Hummelsheim, D. (2006). The economic consequences of partnership dissolution—A comparative analysis of panel studies from Belgium, Germany, Great Britain, Italy, and Sweden. *European Sociological Review, 22*(5), 533–560. https://doi.org/10.1093/esr/jcl012

Avellar, S., & Smock, P. J. (2005). The economic consequences of the dissolution of cohabiting unions. *Journal of Marriage and the Family, 67*(2), 315–327. https://doi.org/10.1111/j.0022-2445.2005.00118.x

Bartholomew, K., & Horowitz, L. M. (1991). Attachment styles among young adults: A test of a four-category model. *Journal of Personality and Social Psychology, 61*(2), 226–244. https://doi.org/10.1037/0022-3514.61.2.226

Batalova, J. A., & Cohen, P. N. (2002). Premarital cohabitation and housework: Couples in cross-national perspective. *Journal of Marriage and the Family, 64*(3), 743–755. https://doi.org/10.1111/j.1741-3737.2002.00743.x

Bayaz-Ozturk, G., Burkhauser, R. V., Couch, K. A., & Hauser, R. (2018). The effects of union dissolution on the economic resources of men and women: A comparative analysis of Germany and the United States, 1985–2013. *The Annals of the American Academy of Political and Social Science, 680*(1), 235–258. https://doi.org/10.1177/0002716218793608

Becker, G. S. (1981). *A treatise on the family*. Harvard University Press.

Becker, G. S., Landes, E. M., & Michael, R. T. (1977). An economic analysis of marital instability. *Journal of Political Economy, 85*(6), 1141–1187. https://doi.org/10.1086/260631

Bennett, N. G. (2017). A reflection on the changing dynamics of union formation and dissolution. *Demographic Research, 36*, 371–390. https://doi.org/10.4054/DemRes.2017.36.12

Bernardi, F., & Radl, J. (2014). The long-term consequences of parental divorce for children's educational attainment. *Demographic Research, 30*(61), 1653–1680. https://doi.org/10.4054/DemRes.2014.30.61

Bernardi, L., & Mortelmans, D. (Eds.). (2021). *Shared physical custody*. Springer.

Boertien, D. (2020). The conceptual and empirical challenges of estimating trends in union stability: Have unions become more stable in Britain? In D. Mortelmans (Ed.), *Divorce in Europe. New insights in trends, causes and consequences of relation break-ups* (pp. 17–36). Springer International. https://doi.org/10.1007/978-3-030-25838-2_2

Boertien, D., & Härkönen, J. (2018). Why does women's education stabilize marriages? The role of marital attraction and barriers to divorce. *Demographic Research, 38*, 1241–1276. https://doi.org/10.4054/DemRes.2018.38.41

Bohannon, P. (1973). The six stations of divorce. In M. E. Lawswell & T. E. Lasswell (Eds.), *Love, marriage, and family: A developmental approach* (pp. 475–489). Scott, Foresman.

Booth, A., & Amato, P. (1991). Divorce and psychological stress. *Journal of Health and Social Behavior, 32*(4), 396–407. https://doi.org/10.2307/2137106

Booth, A., & Johnson, D. R. (1994). Declining health and marital quality. *Journal of Marriage and the Family, 56*(1), 218–223. https://doi.org/10.2307/352716

Botterman, S., Sodermans, A. K., & Matthijs, K. (2015). The social life of divorced parents. Do custody arrangements make a difference in divorced parents' social participation and contacts? *Leisure Studies, 34*(4), 487–500. https://doi.org/10.1080/02614367.2014.938768

Bowlby, J. (1977). The making and breaking of affectional bonds: I. Aetiology and psychopathology in the light of attachment theory. *British Journal of Psychiatry, 130*, 201–210. https://doi.org/10.1192/bjp.130.3.201

Bracke, P., Colman, E., Symoens, S., & Van Praag, L. (2010). Divorce, divorce rates, and professional care seeking for mental health problems in Europe: A cross-sectional population-based study. *BMC Public Health, 10*(1), Article 224. https://doi.org/10.1186/1471-2458-10-224

Bracke, S., & Mulier, K. (2015). Making divorce easier: The role of no-fault and unilateral revisited. *European Journal of Law and Economics, 43*(2), 239–254. https://doi.org/10.1007/s10657-015-9485-0

Bradbury, T. N., Fincham, F. D., & Beach, S. R. H. (2000). Research on the nature and determinants of marital satisfaction: A decade in review. *Journal of Marriage and the Family, 62*(4), 964–980. https://doi.org/10.1111/j.1741-3737.2000.00964.x

Bramlett, M. D., & Mosher, W. D. (2002). Cohabitation, marriage, divorce, and remarriage in the United States. *Vital Health Stat 23*(22), 1–93. https://www.ncbi.nlm.nih.gov/pubmed/12183886

Brines, J., & Joyner, K. (1999). The ties that bind: Principles of cohesion in cohabitation and marriage. *American Sociological Review, 64*(3), 333–355. https://doi.org/10.2307/2657490

Brown, S. L., & Lin, I. F. (2012). The gray divorce revolution: Rising divorce among middle-aged and older adults, 1990–2010. *Journals of Gerontology Series B: Psychological Sciences and Social Sciences, 67*(6), 731–741. https://doi.org/10.1093/geronb/gbs089

Buckle, L., Gallup, G. G., & Rodd, Z. A. (1996). Marriage as a reproductive contract: Patterns of marriage, divorce, and remarriage. *Ethology and Sociobiology, 17*, 363–377. https://doi.org/10.1016/S0162-3095(96)00075-1

Canham, S. L., Mahmood, A., Stott, S., Sixsmith, J., & O'Rourke, N. (2014). 'Til divorce do us part: Marriage dissolution in later life. *Journal of Divorce & Remarriage, 55*(8), 591–612. https://doi.org/10.1080/10502556.2014.959097

Casey, T., & Maldonado, L. C. (2012). *Worst off: Single-parent families in the United States. A cross-national comparison of single parenthood in the US and sixteen other high-income countries*. Legal Momentum.

Ceglian, C. P., & Gardner, S. (1999). Attachment style: A risk for multiple marriages? *Journal of Divorce & Remarriage, 31*(1–2), 125–139. https://doi.org/10.1300/J087v31n01_07

Charles, K. K., & Stephens, M. (2001). Job displacement, disability, and divorce. *Journal of Labor Economics, 22*(2), 489–522. https://doi.org/10.3386/w8578

Cherlin, A. J. (2004). The deinstitutionalization of American marriage. *Journal of Marriage and the Family, 66*(4), 848–861. https://doi.org/10.1111/j.0022-2445.2004.00058.x

Chung, M. C., Farmer, S., Grant, K., Newton, R., Payne, S., Perry, M., Saunders, J., Smith, C., & Stone, N. (2002). Self-esteem, personality and post-traumatic stress symptoms following the dissolution of a dating relationship. *Stress and Health, 18*(2), 83–90. https://doi.org/10.1002/smi.929

Claessens, E., & Mortelmans, D. (2018). Challenges for child support schemes: Accounting for shared care and complex families. *Journal of European Social Policy, 28*(3), 211–223. https://doi.org/10.1177/0958928717753592

Cohen, P. N. (2018). The coming divorce decline. *Socius: Sociological Research for a Dynamic World, 5*, 1–6. https://doi.org/10.31235/osf.io/h2sk6

Cohen, S., Doyle, W. J., Skoner, D. P., Rabin, B. S., & Gwaltney, J. M., Jr. (1997). Social ties and susceptibility to the common cold. *JAMA, 277*(24), 1940–1944. https://doi.org/10.1001/jama.1997.03540480040036

Coleman, M., Ganong, L., & Fine, M. A. (2000). Reinvestigating remarriage: Another decade of progress. *Journal of Marriage and the Family, 62*(4), 1288–1307. https://doi.org/10.1111/j.1741-3737.2000.01288.x

Connidis, I. A., Borell, K., & Karlsson, S. G. (2017). Ambivalence and living apart together in later life: A critical research proposal. *Journal of Marriage and the Family, 79*(5), 1404–1418. https://doi.org/10.1111/jomf.12417

Cooke, L. P., Erola, J., Evertsson, M., Gahler, M., Harkonen, J., Hewitt, B., Jalovaara, M., Kan, M. Y., Lyngstad, T. H., Mencarini, L., Mignot, J. F., Mortelmans, D., Poortman, A.-R., Schmitt, C., & Trappe, H. (2013). Labor and love: Wives' employment and divorce risk in its socio-political context. *Social Politics: International Studies in Gender, State & Society, 20*(4), 482–509. https://doi.org/10.1093/sp/jxt016

Coontz, S. (2006). *Marriage, a history: How love conquered marriage*. Penguin.

Coontz, S. (2007). The origins of modern divorce. *Family Process, 46*(1), 7–16. https://doi.org/10.1111/j.1545-5300.2006.00188.x

Crowley, J. E. (2019a). Does everything fall apart? Life assessments following a gray divorce. *Journal of Family Issues, 40*(11), 1438–1461. https://doi.org/10.1177/0192513x19839735

Crowley, J. E. (2019b). Gray divorce: Explaining midlife marital splits. *Journal of Women & Aging, 31*(1), 49–72. https://doi.org/10.1080/08952841.2017.1409918

de Bel, V., Van Gasse, D., & Mortelmans, D. (2020). Knotting the safety net. A theoretical framework in studying interdependencies in post-divorce family networks. In D. Mortelmans (Ed.), *Divorce in Europe: New insights in trends, causes and consequences of relation break-ups* (pp. 237–252). Springer.

de Bruijn, S., Poortman, A.-R., & van der Lippe, T. (2018). Do parenting plans work? The effect of parenting plans on procedural, family and child outcomes. *International Journal of Law, Policy and the Family, 32*(3), 394–411. https://doi.org/10.1093/lawfam/eby012

de Regt, S., Mortelmans, D., & Marynissen, T. (2012). Financial consequences of relationship dissolution: A longitudinal comparison of formerly married and unmarried cohabiting men and women. *Sociology: The Journal of the British Sociological Association, 47*(1), 90–108. https://doi.org/10.1177/0038038512453793

de Vaus, D. A., Gray, M., Qu, L., & Stanton, D. (2017). The economic consequences of divorce in six OECD countries. *Australian Journal of Social Issues, 52*(2), 180–199. https://doi.org/10.1002/ajs4.13

Dewilde, C. (2006). Becoming poor in Belgium and Britain: The impact of demographic and labour market events. *Sociological Research Online, 11*(1), 87–103.

Dierckx, M., Mortelmans, D., & Motmans, J. (2018). Role ambiguity and role conflict among partners of trans people. *Journal of Family Issues, 40*(1), 85–110. https://doi.org/10.1177/0192513x18800362

Dinescu, D., Turkheimer, E., Beam, C. R., Horn, E. E., Duncan, G., & Emery, R. E. (2016). Is marriage a buzzkill? A twin study of marital status and alcohol consumption. *Journal of Family Psychology, 30*(6), 698–707. https://doi.org/10.1037/fam0000221

DiPrete, T. A., & McManus, P. A. (2000). Family change, employment transitions, and the welfare state: Household income dynamics in the United States and Germany. *American Sociological Review, 65*(3), 343–370.

Drobnic, S. (2000). The effects of children on married and lone mothers' employment in the United States and (West) Germany. *European Sociological Review, 16*(2), 137–157. https://doi.org/10.1093/esr/16.2.137

Dush, C. M. K., Cohan, C. L., & Amato, P. R. (2003). The relationship between cohabitation and marital quality and stability: Change across cohorts? *Journal of Marriage and the Family, 65*(3), 539–549. https://doi.org/10.1111/j.1741-3737.2003.00539.x

Emery, R. E. (1994). *Renegotiating family relationships: Divorce, child custody, and mediation.* Guilford Press.

Emery, R. E. (Ed.). (2013). *Cultural sociology of divorce: An encyclopedia.* SAGE.

Engberg, E., Alen, M., Kukkonen-Harjula, K., Peltonen, J. E., Tikkanen, H. O., & Pekkarinen, H. (2012). Life events and change in leisure time physical activity: A systematic review. *Sports Medicine, 42*(5), 433–447. https://doi.org/10.2165/11597610-000000000-00000

Esping-Andersen, G. (2016). *Families in the 21st century.* SNS förlag.

EuroStat. (2019). *Marriages and divorces (demo_nup).* Retrieved July 18, 2019, from https://ec.europa.eu/eurostat/cache/metadata/en/demo_nup_esms.htm

Evans, R., Scourfield, J., & Moore, G. (2016). Gender, relationship breakdown, and suicide risk: A review of research in Western countries. *Journal of Family Issues, 37*(16), 2239–2264. https://doi.org/0.1177/0192513X14562608

Fabricius, W. V., & Luecken, L. J. (2007). Postdivorce living arrangements, parent conflict, and long-term physical health correlates for children of divorce. *Journal of Family Psychology, 21*(2), 195–205. https://doi.org/10.1037/0893-3200.21.2.195

Goldfarb, M. R., & Trudel, G. (2019). Marital quality and depression: A review. *Marriage and Family Review, 55*(8), 737–763. https://doi.org/10.1080/01494929.2019.1610136

Goldstein, J. R. (1999). The leveling of divorce in the United States. *Demography, 36*(3), 409–414. https://doi.org/10.2307/2648063

González, L., & Viitanen, T. K. (2009). The effect of divorce laws on divorce rates in Europe. *European Economic Review, 53*(2), 127–138. https://doi.org/10.1016/j.euroecorev.2008.05.005

Goodwin, J. S., Hunt, W. C., Key, C. R., & Samet, J. M. (1987). The effect of marital status on stage, treatment, and survival of cancer patients. *JAMA, 258*(21), 3125–3130. https://doi.org/10.1001/jama.1987.03400210067027

Gove, W. R. (1973). Sex, marital status, and mortality. *American Journal of Sociology, 79*(1), 45–67. https://doi.org/10.1086/225505

Gropper, H., John, J. M., Sudeck, G., & Thiel, A. (2020). The impact of life events and transitions on physical activity: A scoping review. *PLoS ONE, 15*(6), Article e0234794. https://doi.org/10.1371/journal.pone.0234794

Guner, N., Kulikova, Y., & Llull, J. (2018). Marriage and health: Selection, protection, and assortative mating. *European Economic Review, 104*, 138–166. https://doi.org/10.1016/j.euroecorev.2018.02.005

Guzzo, K. B. (2014). Trends in cohabitation outcomes: Compositional changes and engagement among never-married young adults. *Journal of Marriage and the Family, 76*(4), 826–842. https://doi.org/10.1111/jomf.12123

Halley, J. E. (2010). Behind the law of marriage (I): From status/contract to the marriage system. *Unbound, 6*(1), 1–58.

Hamplova, D. (2002). Marriage and cohabitation: Qualitative differences in partnership arrangements. *Czech Sociological Review, 38*(6), 771–788.

Härkönen, J., & Dronkers, J. (2006). Stability and change in the educational gradient of divorce. A comparison of seventeen countries. *European Sociological Review, 22*(5), 501–517. https://doi.org/10.1093/esr/jcl011

Hauser, R., Burkhauser, R. V., Couch, K. A., & Bayaz-Ozturk, G. (2016). *Wife or frau, women still do worse: A comparison of men and women in the United States and Germany after union dissolutions in the 1990s and 2000s* (Working Paper No. 2016–39). University of Connecticut, Department of Economics Working Paper Series.

Hazan, C., & Shaver, P. (1987). Romantic love conceptualized as an attachment process. *Journal of Personality and Social Psychology, 52*(3), 511. https://doi.org/10.1037/0022-3514.52.3.511

Hetherington, E. M., & Kelly, J. (2002). *For better or for worse: Divorce reconsidered.* W. W. Norton.

Hogendoorn, B., Leopold, T., & Bol, T. (2019). Divorce and diverging poverty rates: A risk-and-vulnerability approach. *Journal of Marriage and the Family, 82*(3), 1089–1109. https://doi.org/10.1111/jomf.12629

Hübgen, S. (2018). 'Only a husband away from poverty'? Lone mothers' poverty risks in a European comparison. In L. Bernardi & D. Mortelmans (Eds.), *Lone parenthood in a life course perspective* (pp. 167–190). Springer.

Hübgen, S. (2020). Understanding lone mothers' high poverty in Germany: Disentangling composition effects and effects of lone motherhood. *Advances in Life Course Research, 44*, Article 100327. https://doi.org/10.1016/j.alcr.2020.100327

Jalovaara, M. (2001). Socio-economic status and divorce in first marriages in Finland 1991–93. *Population Studies, 55*(2), 119–133. https://doi.org/10.1080/00324720127685

Jansen, M., Mortelmans, D., & Snoeckx, L. (2009). Repartnering and (re)employment: Strategies to cope with the economic consequences of partnership dissolution. *Journal of Marriage and the Family, 71*(5), 1271–1293. https://doi.org/10.1111/j.1741-3737.2009.00668.x

Jockin, V., McGue, M., & Lykken, D. T. (1996). Personality and divorce: A genetic analysis. *Journal of Personality and Social Psychology, 71*(2), 288–299. https://doi.org/10.1037/0022-3514.71.2.288

John, O. P., Naumann, L., & Soto, C. (2008). Paradigm shift to the integrative Big Five trait taxonomy. In O. P. John, R. W. Robins, & L. A. Pervin (Eds.), *Handbook of personality. Theory and research* (3rd ed., pp. 114–158). Guilford Press.

John, O. P., & Srivastava, S. (1999). The Big Five trait taxonomy: History, measurement, and theoretical perspectives. In L. A. Pervin & O. P. John (Eds.), *Handbook of personality: Theory and research* (2nd ed., pp. 102–138). Guilford Press.

Joung, I. M. A., van de Mheen, H. D., Stronks, K., van Poppel, F. W. A., & Mackenbach, J. P. (1998). A longitudinal study of health selection in marital transitions. *Social Science & Medicine, 46*(3), 425–435. https://doi.org/10.1016/s0277-9536(97)00186-x

Kalmijn, M. (2003). Friendship networks over the life course: A test of the dyadic withdrawal hypothesis using survey data on couples. *Social Networks, 25*(3), 231–249.

Kalmijn, M. (2007). Explaining cross-national differences in marriage, cohabitation, and divorce in Europe, 1990–2000. *Population Studies: A Journal of Demography, 61*(3), 243–263. https://doi.org/10.1080/00324720701571806

Kalmijn, M. (2012a). Long-term effects of divorce on parent-child relationships: Within-family comparisons of fathers and mothers. *European Sociological Review, 29*(5), 888–898. https://doi.org/10.1093/esr/jcs066

Kalmijn, M. (2012b). Longitudinal analyses of the effects of age, marriage, and parenthood on social contacts and support. *Advances in Life Course Research, 17*(4), 177–190. https://doi.org/10.1016/j.alcr.2012.08.002

Kalmijn, M., & Van Groenou, M. B. (2005). Differential effects of divorce on social integration. *Journal of Social and Personal Relationships, 22*(4), 455–476. https://doi.org/10.1177/0265407505054516

Kaplan, A., Miri, E., & Herbst-Debby, A. (2020). The more the merrier? The effect of children on divorce in a pronatalist society. In D. Mortelmans (Ed.), *Divorce in Europe. New insights in trends, causes and consequences of relation break-ups* (pp. 123–146). Springer International. https://doi.org/10.1007/978-3-030-25838-2_6

Karraker, A., & Latham, K. (2015). In sickness and in health? Physical illness as a risk factor for marital dissolution in later life. *Journal of Health and Social Behavior, 56*(3), 420–435. https://doi.org/10.1177/0022146515596354

Kaslow, F. W. (2008). Divorce. *Journal of Divorce, 7*(3), 21–39. https://doi.org/10.1300/J279v07n03_02

Kaufman, G. (2000). Do gender role attitudes matter? Family formation and dissolution among traditional and egalitarian men and women. *Journal of Family Issues, 21*(1), 128–144. https://doi.org/10.1177/019251300021001006

Kessler, R. C., Walters, E. E., & Forthofer, M. S. (1998). The social consequences of psychiatric disorders, III: Probability of marital stability. *American Journal of Psychiatry, 155*(8), 1092–1096. https://doi.org/10.1176/ajp.155.8.1092

Kessler, S. (1975). *The American way of divorce: Prescriptions for change*. Nelson-Hall.

Kojima, G., Walters, K., Iliffe, S., Taniguchi, Y., & Tamiya, N. (2020). Marital status and risk of physical frailty: A systematic review and meta-analysis. *Journal of the American Medical Directors Association, 21*(3), 322–330. https://doi.org/10.1016/j.jamda.2019.09.017

Konstam, V., Surman, O., Hizzazi, K. H., Fierstein, J., Konstam, M., Turbett, A., Dec, G. W., Keck, S., Mudge, G., Flavell, C., McCormack, M., & Hurley, L. (1998). Marital adjustment in heart transplantation patients and their spouses: A longitudinal perspective. *The American Journal of Family Therapy, 26*(2), 147–158. https://doi.org/10.1080/01926189808251094

Kramrei, E., Coit, C., Martin, S., Fogo, W., & Mahoney, A. (2007). Post-divorce adjustment and social relationships. *Journal of Divorce & Remarriage, 46*(3–4), 145–166. https://doi.org/10.1300/j087v46n03_09

Kubler-Ross, E. (1969). *On death and dying*. Macmillan.

Kyung-Sook, W., SangSoo, S., Sangjin, S., & Young-Jeon, S. (2018). Marital status integration and suicide: A meta-analysis and meta-regression. *Social Science and Medicine, 197*, 116–126. https://doi.org/10.1016/j.socscimed.2017.11.053

Lam, J., Vidal, S., & Baxter, J. (2020). Chronic conditions, couple-level factors and union dissolution. *Advances in Life Course Research, 45*, 100340. https://doi.org/10.1016/j.alcr.2020.100340

Larsen, R. J., & Buss, D. M. (2008). *Personality psychology. Domains of knowledge about human nature* (3rd ed.). McGraw Hill.

Leeson, P. T., & Pierson, J. (2015). Economic origins of the no-fault divorce revolution. *European Journal of Law and Economics, 43*(3), 419–439. https://doi.org/10.1007/s10657-015-9501-4

Lehrer, E. L., & Chiswick, C. U. (1993). Religion as a determinant of marital stability. *Demography, 30*(3), 385–404. https://doi.org/10.2307/2061647

Leopold, T. (2018). Gender differences in the consequences of divorce: A study of multiple outcomes. *Demography, 55*(3), 769–797. https://doi.org/10.1007/s13524-018-0667-6

Lesthaeghe, R. (2010). The unfolding story of the second demographic transition. *Population and Development Review, 36*(2), 211–251. https://doi.org/10.1111/j.1728-4457.2010.00328.x

Levinger, G. (1965). Marital cohesiveness and dissolution—An integrative review. *Journal of Marriage and the Family, 27*(1), 19–28. https://doi.org/10.2307/349801

Levinger, G. (1976). A social psychological perspective on marital dissolution. *Journal of Social Issues, 32*(1), 21–47. https://doi.org/10.1111/j.1540-4560.1976.tb02478.x

Liefbroer, A., & Dourleijn, E. (2006). Unmarried cohabitation and union stability: Testing the role of diffusion using data from 16 European countries. *Demography, 43*(2), 203–221. https://doi.org/10.1353/dem.2006.0018

Lyngstad, T., & Jalovaara, M. (2010). A review of the antecedents of union dissolution. *Demographic Research, 23*(10), 257–292. https://doi.org/10.4054/DemRes.2010.23.10

Mandemakers, J., & Kalmijn, M. (2018). From bad to worse? Effects of multiple adverse life course transitions on mental health. *Longitudinal and Life Course Studies, 9*(3), 299–311. https://doi.org/10.14301/llcs.v9i3.484

Manfredini, R., De Giorgi, A., Tiseo, R., Boari, B., Cappadona, R., Salmi, R., Gallerani, M., Signani, F., Manfredini, F., Mikhailidis, D. P., & Fabbian, F. (2017). Marital status, cardiovascular diseases, and cardiovascular risk factors: A review of the evidence. *Journal of Women's Health, 26*(6), 624–632. https://doi.org/10.1089/jwh.2016.6103

Manting, D., & Bouman, A. M. (2006). Short- and long-term economic consequences of the dissolution of marital and consensual unions. The example of the Netherlands. *European Sociological Review, 22*(4), 413–429. https://doi.org/10.1093/esr/jcl005

Matysiak, A., Styrc, M., & Vignoli, D. (2014). The educational gradient in marital disruption: A meta-analysis of European research findings. *Population Studies, 68*(2), 197–215. https://doi.org/10.1080/00324728.2013.856459

McGue, M., & Lykken, D. T. (1992). Genetic influence on risk of divorce. *Psychological Science, 3*(6), 368–373. https://doi.org/10.1111/j.1467-9280.1992.tb00049.x

McKeever, M., & Wolfinger, N. H. (2006). Shifting fortunes in a changing economy. In L. Kowaleski-Jones & N. H. Wolfinger (Eds.), *Fragile families and the marriage agenda* (pp. 127–157). Springer. https://doi.org/10.1007/0-387-26025-0_6

McKeever, M., & Wolfinger, N. H. (2012). Over the long haul: The persistent economic consequences of single motherhood. In S. L. Blair (Ed.), *Economic stress and the family* (pp. 1–39). Emerald Group.

McKenry, P. C., & Price, S. J. (1991). Alternatives for support. *Journal of Divorce & Remarriage, 15*(3–4), 1–19. https://doi.org/10.1300/j087v15n03_01

Milardo, R. M. (1982). Friendship networks in developing relationships: Converging and diverging social environments. *Social Psychology Quarterly, 45*(3), 162–172. https://doi.org/10.2307/3033649

Mills, C. W. (1959). *The sociological imagination.* Oxford University Press.

Montenegro, X. P. (2004). The divorce experience—A study of divorce at midlife and beyond. *AARP The Magazine.* https://assets.aarp.org/rgcenter/general/divorce.pdf

Mortelmans, D. (Ed.). (2020a). *Divorce in Europe. New insights in trends, causes and consequences of relation break-ups.* Springer International. https://doi.org/10.1007/978-3-030-25838-2.

Mortelmans, D. (2020b). Economic consequences of divorce: A review. In M. Kreyenfeld & H. Trappe (Eds.), *Parental life courses after separation and divorce in Europe* (pp. 23–42). Springer. https://doi.org/10.1007/978-3-030-44575-1

Mortelmans, D., Matthijs, K., Alofs, E., & Segaert, B. (Eds.). (2016). *Changing family dynamics and demographic evolution: The family kaleidoscope.* Edward Elgar. https://doi.org/10.4337/9781785364983.

Mortelmans, D., Thielemans, G., & Van den Berg, L. (2020). Parents returning to parents: Does migration background have an influence on the "boomerang effect" among parents after divorce? In M. Kreyenfeld & H. Trappe (Eds.), *Parental life courses after separation and divorce in Europe* (pp. 83–104). Springer. https://doi.org/10.1007/978-3-030-44575-1

Muhlbauer, J. E., Ferrao, Y. A., Eppingstall, J., Albertella, L., do Rosario, M. C., Miguel, E. C., & Fontenelle, L. F. (2020). Predicting marriage and divorce in obsessive-compulsive disorder. *Journal of Sex & Marital Therapy, 47*(1), 90–98. https://doi.org/10.1080/0092623X.2020.1804021

National Center for Health Statistics. (2019). *Vital Statistics of the United States.* Retrieved July 18, 2019, from https://www.cdc.gov/nchs/products/vsus.htm

Nielsen, L. (2018). Joint versus sole physical custody: Outcomes for children independent of family income or parental conflict. *Journal of Child Custody, 15*(1), 35–54. https://doi.org/10.1080/15379418.2017.1422414

Organization for Economic Co-operation and Development. (2011). *Doing better for families.* Author. https://doi.org/10.1787/9789264098732-en

Ooms, T. (2019). The evolution of family policy: Lessons learned, challenges, and hopes for the future. *Journal of Family Theory & Review, 11*(1), 18–38. https://doi.org/10.1111/jftr.12316

Oppenheimer, V. K. (1997). Women's employment and the gain to marriage: The specialization and trading model. *Annual Review of Sociology, 23*, 431–453.

Ozawo, M., & Yoon, H. (2002). The economic benefit of remarriage: Gender and income class. *Journal of Divorce and Remarriage, 36*, 21–39. https://doi.org/10.1300/J087v36n03_02

Pearlin, L. I. (1989). The sociological study of stress. *Journal of Health and Social Behavior, 30*(3), 241–256. https://doi.org/10.2307/2136956

Perelli-Harris, B., Berrington, A., Sanchez Gassen, N., Galezewska, P., & Holland, J. A. (2017). The rise in divorce and cohabitation: Is there a link? *Population and Development Review*, *43*(2), 303–329. https://doi.org/10.1111/padr.12063

Pinquart, M., & Sorensen, S. (2011). Spouses, adult children, and children-in-law as caregivers of older adults: A meta-analytic comparison. *Psychology and Aging*, *26*(1), 1–14. https://doi.org/10.1037/a0021863

Poladian, A. R., & Holtzworth-Munroe, A. (2019). Families and the legal system: Approaches to parental divorce and separation. In B. H. Fiese, M. Celano, K. Deater-Deckard, E. N. Jouriles, & M. A. Whisman (Eds.), *APA handbooks in psychology®. APA handbook of contemporary family psychology: Applications and broad impact of family psychology* (pp. 281–296). American Psychological Association Press. https://doi.org/10.1037/0000100-018

Poortman, A.-R. (2000). Sex differences in the economic consequences of separation. A panel study of the Netherlands. *European Sociological Review*, *16*(4), 367–383. https://doi.org/10.1093/esr/16.4.367

Potter, M. H. (2020). Social support and divorce among American couples. *Journal of Family Issues*, *42*(1), 88–109. https://doi.org/10.1177/0192513x20916830

Prescott, C. A., & Kendler, K. S. (2001). Associations between marital status and alcohol consumption in a longitudinal study of female twins. *Journal of Studies on Alcohol*, *62*(5), 589–604. https://doi.org/10.15288/jsa.2001.62.589

Rabin, C. (2019). Impact of cancer on romantic relationships among young adults: A systematic review. *Journal of Clinical Psychology in Medical Settings*, *26*(1), 1–12. https://doi.org/10.1007/s10880-018-9566-7

Raeymaeckers, P., Dewilde, C., Snoeckx, L., & Mortelmans, D. (2008). Childcare strategies of divorced mothers in Europe: A comparative analysis. *European Sociological Review*, *24*(1), 115–131. https://doi.org/10.1093/esr/jcm04

Rindfuss, R. R., & Vandenheuvel, A. (1990). Cohabitation: Precursor to marriage or an alternative to being single? *Population and Development Review*, *16*(4), 703–726. https://doi.org/10.2307/1972963

Roberts, B. W., Kuncel, N. R., Shiner, R., Caspi, A., & Goldberg, L. R. (2007). The power of personality: The comparative validity of personality traits, socioeconomic status, and cognitive ability for predicting important life outcomes. *Perspectives on Psychological Science*, *2*(4), 313–345. https://doi.org/10.1111/j.1745-6916.2007.00047.x

Rogers, R. G. (1995). Marriage, sex, and mortality. *Journal of Marriage and the Family*, *57*(2), 515–526. https://doi.org/10.2307/353703

Rosenfeld, M. J., & Roesler, K. (2019). Cohabitation experience and cohabitation's association with marital dissolution. *Journal of Marriage and the Family*, *81*(1), 42–58. https://doi.org/10.1111/jomf.12530

Ross, C. E., Mirowsky, J., & Goldsteen, K. (1990). The impact of the family on health: The decade in review. *Journal of Marriage and the Family*, *52*(4), 1059–1078. https://doi.org/10.2307/353319

Ryabov, I., & Zhang, Y. (2019). Entry and stability of cross-national marriages in the United States. *Journal of Family Issues*, *40*(18), 2687–2706. https://doi.org/10.1177/0192513x19860186

Sbarra, D. A. (2015). Divorce and health: Current trends and future directions. *Psychosomatic Medicine*, *77*(3), 227–236. https://doi.org/10.1097/psy.0000000000000168

Sbarra, D. A., & Coan, J. A. (2017). Divorce and health: Good data in need of better theory. *Current Opinion in Psychology*, *13*, 91–95. https://doi.org/10.1016/j.copsyc.2016.05.014

Sbarra, D. A., Law, R. W., & Portley, R. M. (2011). Divorce and death. *Perspectives on Psychological Science*, *6*(5), 454–474. https://doi.org/10.1177/1745691611414724

Sigle, W. (2016). Why demography needs (new) theories. In D. Mortelmans, K. Matthijs, E. Alofs, & B. Segaert (Eds.), *Changing family dynamics and demographic evolution: The family kaleidoscope* (pp. 271–233). Edward Elgar. https://doi.org/10.4337/9781785364983

Smith, T. B., & Gibson, C. L. (2020). Marital strain, support, and alcohol use: Results from a twin design statistically controlling for genetic confounding. *Substance Use & Misuse*, *55*(3), 429–440. https://doi.org/10.1080/10826084.2019.1683202

Smock, P. J., & Schwartz, C. R. (2020). The demography of families: A review of patterns and change. *Journal of Marriage and the Family*, *82*(1), 9–34. https://doi.org/10.1111/jomf.12612

Snoeckx, L., Dehertogh, B., & Mortelmans, D. (2008). The distribution of household tasks in first-marriage families and stepfamilies across Europe. In J. Pryor (Ed.), *The international handbook of stepfamilies: Policy and practice in legal, research, and clinical environments* (pp. 277–298). John Wiley & Sons.

Solaz, A., Jalovaara, M., Kreyenfeld, M., Meggiolaro, S., Mortelmans, D., & Pasteels, I. (2020). Unemployment and separation: Evidence from five European countries *Journal of Family Research, 32*(1), 145–176. https://doi.org/10.20377/jfr-368

South, S. J. (1991). Sociodemographic differentials in mate selection preferences. *Journal of Marriage and the Family, 53*(4), 928–940. https://doi.org/10.2307/352998

South, S. J. (1995). Do you need to shop around? *Journal of Family Issues, 16*(4), 432–449. https://doi.org/10.1177/019251395016004002

Spanier, G. B., & Thompson, L. (1984). *Parting: The aftermath of separation and divorce.* SAGE.

Spikic, S. (2020). *Personality and divorce: Examining the association between the Big Five personality traits and marital separation* [Unpublished doctoral dissertation]. University of Antwerp.

Steele, F., Joshi, H., Kallis, C., & Goldstein, H. (2006). Changing compatibility of cohabitation and childbearing between young British women born in 1958 and 1970. *Population Studies, 60*(2), 137–152. https://doi.org/10.1080/00324720600598009

Steinbach, A. (2019). Children's and parents' well-being in joint physical custody: A literature review. *Family Process, 58*(2), 353–369. https://doi.org/10.1111/famp.12372

Stevenson, B., & Wolfers, J. (2007). Marriage and divorce: Changes and their driving forces. *Journal of Economic Perspectives, 21*(2), 27–52. https://doi.org/10.1257/jep.21.2.27

Tach, L. M., & Eads, A. (2015). Trends in the economic consequences of marital and cohabitation dissolution in the United States. *Demography, 52*(2), 401–432. https://doi.org/10.1007/s13524-015-0374-5

Taylor, L. W. (2009). The transition to mid-life divorce. *Review of Economics of the Household, 9*(2), 251–271. https://doi.org/10.1007/s11150-009-9063-8

Teachman, J. D. (2002). Stability across cohorts in divorce risk factors. *Demography, 39*(2), 331–351. http://www.ncbi.nlm.nih.gov/pubmed/12048955

Thielemans, G., & Mortelmans, D. (2018). Female labour force participation after divorce: How employment histories matter. *Journal of Family and Economic Issues, 40*(2), 180–193. https://doi.org/10.1007/s10834-018-9600-9

Tran, N. T., Clavarino, A., Williams, G., & Najman, J. M. (2016). Life course outcomes for women with different alcohol consumption trajectories: A population-based longitudinal study. *Drug and Alcohol Review, 35*(6), 763–771. https://doi.org/10.1111/dar.12428

Trevino, M. B. (2013). Origins of divorce. In R. E. Emery (Ed.), *Cultural sociology of divorce: An encyclopedia* (pp. 918–921). SAGE.

Uhlenberg, P., & Myers, M. A. (1981). Divorce and the elderly. *Gerontologist, 21*(3), 276–282. https://doi.org/10.1093/geront/21.3.276

Van Damme, M. (2020). The negative female educational gradient of union dissolution: Towards an explanation in six European countries. In D. Mortelmans (Ed.), *Divorce in Europe. New insights in trends, causes and consequences of relation break-ups* (pp. 93–122). Springer International. https://doi.org/10.1007/978-3-030-25838-2_5

van Dijk, R., van der Valk, I. E., Dekovic, M., & Branje, S. (2020). A meta-analysis on interparental conflict, parenting, and child adjustment in divorced families: Examining mediation using meta-analytic structural equation models. *Clinical Psychology Review, 79*, Article 101861. https://doi.org/10.1016/j.cpr.2020.101861

Van Gasse, D., & Mortelmans, D. (2020). Reorganizing the single-parent family system: Exploring the process perspective on divorce. *Family Relations, 69*(5), 1100–1112. https://doi.org/10.1111/fare.12432

Veblen, T. (1965). *The theory of the leisure class.* Sentry Press.

Wagner, M. (2020). On increasing divorce risks. In D. Mortelmans (Ed.), *Divorce in Europe. New insights in trends, causes and consequences of relation break-ups* (pp. 37–61). Springer International. https://doi.org/10.1007/978-3-030-25838-2

Waite, L. J., & Lillard, L. A. (1991). Children and marital disruption. *American Journal of Sociology, 96*(4), 930–953. https://doi.org/10.1086/229613

Wall, J. A., & Lynn, A. (2016). Mediation: A current review. *Journal of Conflict Resolution, 37*(1), 160–194. https://doi.org/10.1177/0022002793037001007

Wickrama, K. A. S., O'Neal, C. W., & Lorenz, F. O. (2013). Marital functioning from middle to later years: A life course-stress process framework. *Journal of Family Theory & Review, 5*(1), 15–34. https://doi.org/10.1111/jftr.12000

Wiseman, R. S. (1975). Crisis theory and the process of divorce. *Social Casework, 56*(4), 205–212. https://doi.org/10.1177/104438947505600402

Wolfers, J. (2006). Did unilateral divorce laws raise divorce rates? A reconciliation and new results. *The American Economic Review, 96*(5), 1802–1820.

Wu, Z. (1995). The stability of cohabitation relationships: The role of children. *Journal of Marriage and the Family, 57*(1), 231–236. https://doi.org/10.2307/353831

Wu, Z., & Schimmele, C. M. (2005). Repartnering after first union disruption. *Journal of Marriage and the Family, 67*(1), 27–36.

Yorgason, J. B., Booth, A., & Johnson, D. (2008). Health, disability, and marital quality: Is the association different for younger versus older cohorts? *Research on Aging, 30*(6), 623–648. https://doi.org/10.1177/0164027508322570

Yu, Y., Wu, D., Wang, J.-M., & Wang, Y.-C. (2020). Dark personality, marital quality, and marital instability of Chinese couples: An actor-partner interdependence mediation model. *Personality and Individual Differences, 154,* 109689. https://doi.org/10.1016/j.paid.2019.109689

Limitations and Future Directions in the Evolutionary Study of Romantic Relationships

Justin K. Mogilski *and* Todd K. Shackelford

Abstract

The evolutionary study of intimate relationships is a robust and generative science. Its premises and predictions have been, and continue to be, productive for relationship and social scientists. However, like every paradigm, it has limitations. There is yet need to improve sample representativeness (Pollett & Saxton, 2019) and interdisciplinary collaboration (Hahnel-Peeters, 2021; Zeder, 2018). Researchers yet discuss significant premises and findings, such as modularity of the mind (see Pietraszewski & Wertz, 2022), menstrual cycle effects (see Havlíček & Roberts, this volume), and causation of life history variation (Stearns & Rodrigues, 2020; Zietsch & Sidari, 20120. Evolutionary psychology has been thoroughly critiqued and defended elsewhere (Buss & Von Hippel, 2018; Confer et al., 2010; Davis, 2021). However, the editors have compiled several areas of current (or not-yet-recognized) inquiry that could improve the evolutionary study of intimate relationships.

Key Words: limitations, future directions, sex and gender, infidelity, alliances

Going Beyond Sex and Gender

Sex differences are interesting because they reveal how sexual selection may have shaped the ever-changing, culture-contingent milieu of phenotypes that males and females of a species employ to resolve the adaptive challenges of sexual conflict. A more fundamental distinction may be predator and prey, or that may be more broadly conceptualized as zero-sum competitive encounters (i.e., win–lose social exchanges; Różycka-Tran et al., 2015). The risks of succumbing to predation, such as physical injury, theft, coerced compliance, or death may be a more ancient set of adaptive problems than those crafted after the evolution of anisogamy—though coevolution would have undoubtedly occurred (e.g., Rankin et al., 2011). Studying adaptations to predation may help disentangle the considerable overlap in men's and women's relationship motives, desires, and preferences, such as interest in partner honesty and fidelity (Mogilski et al., 2019; Mogilski et al., 2014). Doing so may reveal adapted strategies in both men and women for establishing trust, negotiating interdependence, and avoiding interpersonal manipulation. Likewise, research on dark personality (i.e., individual differences in the willingness to exploit others for personal gain) (see Marcus et al., 2018) could reveal the motivational computation underlying intimate predation (see Zeigler-Hill & Jonason, 2018), such as sexual assault (Koscielska et al., 2020), intimate partner violence (Plouffe et al., 2020), and stalking (March et al., 2020).

Defining Infidelity

In consensual nonmonogamy (CNM), partners distinguish extra-pair interactions from infidelity. In these relationships, infidelity may more broadly be understood as lying or withholding information about extra-pair interactions that a partner would deem relevant to the in-pair relationship (Mogilski et al., this volume) or whether a partner violates an agreed-upon relationship boundary (see Andersson, 2022).

Distinguishing infidelity and extra-pair interaction in this way could help make sense of researching showing that CNM and monogamy report similar relationship quality and satisfaction (Rubel & Bogaert, 2015) and that people who open an existing relationship report more sexual satisfaction than those who do not (Murphy et al., 2021). People who take precaution to communicate with a partner about their extra-pair attractions, regulate their jealousy, or otherwise mitigate the harms of extra-pair relationships may successfully avoid the recurrent adaptive problems of multipartner mating. Relationship science and social policy (Stein, 2020) could benefit from accounting for recent or understudied intimate relationship practices (see Brady & Baker, 2021).

Relationships as Alliances

Relationships may be better viewed as alliances for achieving shared goals (Conroy-Beam et al., 2015; Orehek et al., 2018). Sex and intimacy are defining features of romance, but intimate partners routinely collaborate to produce and/or raise offspring, mutually advance their social status, provide physical and emotional caregiving to each other, share resources, create or preserve social networks (e.g., union of families), or otherwise coordinate to pursue shared goals. Studying romantic relationships as alliances could help to reveal how individuals manage third-party conflicts (Aoki, 1984) and coalitional rivalries (Gimeno, 2004), build and maintain a reputation with their partners (Ebbers & Wijnberg, 2010), negotiate social hierarchy (Gavrilets et al., 2008), or deal with commitment uncertainty (Thomas & Trevino, 1993).

Concluding Remarks

This volume reviews the historic and contemporary developments in evolutionary social sciences that have transformed how researchers study the intimate relationship process. Understanding the functional mechanisms that guide human mating has revealed previously unknown features of relationship initiation, maintenance, and dissolution.

Just as a mechanic might use architectural knowledge of a car to troubleshoot its performance, relationship scientists who consider evolutionary design features equip themselves with technical knowledge of how environment-gene interactions, domain specificity, and adaptationism (see Nettle & Scott-Phillips, 2021) have shaped the relationship processes observed in humans. We anticipate that this approach will continue to inspire novel research for generations to come.

References

Andersson, C. (2022). Drawing the line at infidelity: Negotiating relationship morality in a Swedish context of consensual non-monogamy. *Journal of Social and Personal Relationships*. Advance online publication. https://doi.org/10.1177/02654075211070556

Aoki, K. (1984). Evolution of alliance in primates: A population genetic model. *Journal of Ethology*, *2*(1), 55–61.

Brady, A., & Baker, L. R. (2021). The changing tides of attractive alternatives in romantic relationships: Recent societal changes compel new directions for future research. *Social and Personality Psychology Compass*, *16*(1), Article e12650.

Buss, D. M., & Von Hippel, W. (2018). Psychological barriers to evolutionary psychology: Ideological bias and coalitional adaptations. *Archives of Scientific Psychology*, *6*(1), 148.

Confer, J. C., Easton, J. A., Fleischman, D. S., Goetz, C. D., Lewis, D. M., Perilloux, C., & Buss, D. M. (2010). Evolutionary psychology: Controversies, questions, prospects, and limitations. *American Psychologist*, *65*(2), 110.

Conroy-Beam, D., Goetz, C. D., & Buss, D. M. (2015). Why do humans form long-term mateships? An evolutionary game-theoretic model. In M. P. Zanna (Ed.), *Advances in experimental social psychology* (Vol. 51, pp. 1–39). Academic Press.

Davis, A. C. (2021). Resolving the tension between feminism and evolutionary psychology: An epistemological critique. *Evolutionary Behavioral Sciences*, *15*(4), 368.

Ebbers, J. J., & Wijnberg, N. M. (2010). Disentangling the effects of reputation and network position on the evolution of alliance networks. *Strategic Organization*, *8*(3), 255–275.

Gavrilets, S., Duenez-Guzman, E. A., & Vose, M. D. (2008). Dynamics of alliance formation and the egalitarian revolution. *PLoS ONE*, *3*(10), Article e3293.

Gimeno, J. (2004). Competition within and between networks: The contingent effect of competitive embeddedness on alliance formation. *Academy of Management Journal*, *47*(6), 820–842.

Hahnel-Peeters, R. K. (2021). Potential for collaboration: Differences between evolutionary anthropology and evolutionary psychology as scientific disciplines. *PsyArXiv*. https://doi.org/10.31234/osf.io/kp4rc

Jonason, P. K., & Zeigler-Hill, V. (2018). The fundamental social motives that characterize dark personality traits. *Personality and Individual Differences*, *132*, 98–107.

Koscielska, R. W., Flowe, H. D., & Egan, V. (2020). The dark tetrad and mating effort's influence on sexual coaxing and coercion across relationship types. *Journal of Sexual Aggression*, *26*(3), 394–404.

March, E., Litten, V., Sullivan, D. H., & Ward, L. (2020). Somebody that I (used to) know: Gender and dimensions of dark personality traits as predictors of intimate partner cyberstalking. *Personality and Individual Differences*, *163*, Article 110084.

Marcus, D. K., Preszler, J., & Zeigler-Hill, V. (2018). A network of dark personality traits: What lies at the heart of darkness?. *Journal of Research in Personality*, *73*, 56–62.

Mogilski, J. K., Vrabel, J., Mitchell, V. E., & Welling, L. L. (2019). The primacy of trust within romantic relationships: Evidence from conjoint analysis of HEXACO-derived personality profiles. *Evolution and Human Behavior*, *40*(4), 365–374.

Mogilski, J. K., Wade, T. J., & Welling, L. L. (2014). Prioritization of potential mates' history of sexual fidelity during a conjoint ranking task. *Personality and Social Psychology Bulletin*, *40*(7), 884–897.

Murphy, A. P., Joel, S., & Muise, A. (2021). A prospective investigation of the decision to open up a romantic relationship. *Social Psychological and Personality Science*, *12*(2), 194–201.

Nettle, D., & Scott-Phillips, T. (2021). Is a non-evolutionary psychology possible? https://doi.org/10.31234/osf.io/wky9h

Orehek, E., Forest, A. L., & Barbaro, N. (2018). A people-as-means approach to interpersonal relationships. *Perspectives on Psychological Science, 13*(3), 373–389.
Pietraszewski, D., & A. E., Wertz (2022). Why evolutionary psychology should abandon modularity. *Perspectives on Psychological Science, 17*(2):465–490. https://doi.org/10.1177/1745691621997113
Plouffe, R. A., Wilson, C. A., & Saklofske, D. H. (2020). The role of dark personality traits in intimate partner violence: A multi-study investigation. *Current Psychology, 41,* 3481-3500. https://doi.org/10.1007/s12144-020-00871-5.
Pollet, T. V., & Saxton, T. K. (2019). How diverse are the samples used in the journals "evolution & human behavior" and "evolutionary psychology"? *Evolutionary Psychological Science, 5*(3), 357–368.
Rankin, D. J., Dieckmann, U., & Kokko, H. (2011). Sexual conflict and the tragedy of the commons. *American Naturalist, 177*(6), 780–791.
Różycka-Tran, J., Boski, P., & Wojciszke, B. (2015). Belief in a zero-sum game as a social axiom: A 37-nation study. *Journal of Cross-Cultural Psychology, 46*(4), 525–548.
Rubel, A. N., & Bogaert, A. F. (2015). Consensual nonmonogamy: Psychological well-being and relationship quality correlates. *The Journal of Sex Research, 52*(9), 961–982.
Stearns, S. C., & Rodrigues, A. M. (2020). On the use of "life history theory" in evolutionary psychology. *Evolution and Human Behavior, 41*(6), 474–485.
Stein, E. (2020). Adultery, infidelity, and consensual non-monogamy. *Wake Forest Law Review, 55,* 147.
Thomas, J. B., & Trevino, L. K. (1993). Information processing in strategic alliance building: A multiple-case approach. *Journal of Management Studies, 30*(5), 779–814.
Zeder, M. A. (2018). Why evolutionary biology needs anthropology: Evaluating core assumptions of the extended evolutionary synthesis. *Evolutionary Anthropology: Issues, News, and Reviews, 27*(6), 267–284.
Jonason, P. K., & Zeigler-Hill, V. (2018). The fundamental social motives that characterize dark personality traits. *Personality and Individual Differences, 132,* 98–107.
Zietsch, B. P., & Sidari, M. J. (2020). A critique of life history approaches to human trait covariation. *Evolution and Human Behavior, 41*(6), 527–535.

INDEX

For the benefit of digital users, indexed terms that span two pages (e.g., 52–53) may, on occasion, appear on only one of those pages.

Note: Tables and figures are indicated by *t* and *f* following the page number

D

E

H

I

J

N

R

T

U